Sixth Edition

Management

Richard L. Daft
Vanderbilt University

THOMSON

——✳——™

SOUTH-WESTERN

Australia · Canada · Mexico · Singapore · Spain · United Kingdom · United States

THOMSON

SOUTH-WESTERN

WEST

Management, Sixth Edition
Richard L. Daft

Vice President/Team Director:
Mike Roche

Acquisitions Editor:
Joe Sabatino

Developmental Editor:
Emma Guttler

Marketing Manager:
Rob Bloom

Production Editor:
Kelly Keeler

Manufacturing Coordinator:
Diane Lohman

Production House/Compositor:
DPS Associates, Inc.
SettingPace

Sr. Design Project Manager
Michelle Kunkler

Cover and Internal Designer:
Liz Harasymczuk Design

Cover Image:
© J.A. Kraulis/Masterfile

Photo Researcher:
Elm St. Productions

Media Technology Editor:
Vicky True

Media Developmental Editor:
Kristen Meere

Media Production Editor:
Karen Schaffer

Printer:
R.R. Donnelley and Sons

Library of Congress Cataloging-in-
Publication Data
Daft, Richard L.
Management / Richard L. Daft
p.cm.
Includes index.
ISBN: 0-03-035138-3
1. Industrial management. I. Title.

HD31 .D134 2002
658—dc21   200217917

Preface

The world of work is changing rapidly. And, in response, the field of management is undergoing a revolution. The result is "The New Workplace"—the theme of this edition of *Management*. Demands on today's managers go well beyond the techniques and ideas traditionally taught in management courses. The traditional world of work assumed the purpose of management was to control and limit people, enforce rules and regulations, seek stability and efficiency, design a top-down hierarchy to direct people, and achieve bottom-line results. The new workplace and emerging management paradigm recognizes that today's managers need different skills to engage workers' hearts and minds as well as take advantage of their physical labor. The new workplace asks that managers focus on leading change, on harnessing people's creativity and enthusiasm, on finding shared vision and values, and on sharing information and power. Teamwork, collaboration, participation and learning are guiding principles that help managers and employees maneuver the difficult terrain of today's complex business environment. Managers focus on developing, not controlling, people to adapt to new technologies and extraordinary environmental shifts, and thus achieve total corporate effectiveness.

Both the new workplace and the traditional paradigm are guiding management actions in the world today. My vision for the sixth edition of *Management* is to explore the new management ideas in a way that is interesting and valuable to students, while retaining the best of traditional management thinking. To achieve this vision, I have included the most recent management concepts and research as well as the contemporary application of management ideas in organizations. The combination of established scholarship, new ideas, and real-life applications gives students a taste of the energy, challenge, and adventure inherent in the dynamic field of management. The South-Western staff and I have worked together to provide a textbook better than any other at capturing the excitement of organizational management.

I revised *Management* to provide a book of utmost quality that will create in students both respect for the changing field of management and confidence that they can understand and master it. The textual portion of this book has been enhanced through the engaging, easy-to-understand writing style and the many in-text examples and boxed items that make the concepts come alive for students. The graphic component has been enhanced with several new exhibits and a new set of photo essays that illustrate specific management concepts. The well-chosen photographs provide vivid illustrations and intimate glimpses of management scenes, events, and people. The photos are combined with brief essays that explain how a specific management concept looks and feels. Both the textual and graphic portions of the textbook help students grasp the often abstract and distant world of management.

Focus on the Future

The sixth edition of *Management* is especially focused on the future of management education by identifying and describing emerging elements and examples of the new workplace and the changing management paradigm. New materials in the book include the following:

- Chapter 1 introduces the new workplace and defines the changing management paradigm. The chapter explores the growing importance of leadership and new management competencies needed to thrive in today's business world. It also discusses the forces affecting today's organizations and managers, including a segment on managing during crises and unexpected events, both of which are important skills in today's volatile workplace.

- Chapter 2 has a significantly expanded discussion of the behavioral sciences approach. This chapter also contains a new section on managing the technology-driven workplace, introducing the concepts of e-business (B2B, B2C, and C2C), intranets and extranets, enterprise resource planning, and knowledge management. There is continued coverage of the historical development of management and organizations.

- Chapter 3 has been revised to contain a discussion of interorganizational partnerships as a way to adapt to the corporate environment. Within the section on culture, the four types of culture (adaptability culture, achievement culture, bureaucratic culture, and clan culture) are explored in terms of their relationship to the external environment. A complete section of this chapter is devoted to trends such as virtual teams and telecommuting that put demands on managers trying to create strong adaptive cultures.

- Chapter 4 includes an updated and enlarged discussion of GATT and WTO.

- Chapter 5 presents an updated and expanded exploration of environmental responsibility and how today's organizations are meeting their responsibilities in this area. This chapter also includes a new section on ethical leadership, including a new discussion of ethical issues associated with information technology.

- Chapter 6 contains a new section on Internet start-ups and how they differ from traditional small businesses.

- Chapter 7 incorporates a new section on crisis management planning.

- Chapter 8 considers the impact of the Internet and e-business on strategy.

- Chapter 9 includes a discussion of new decision approaches for the new workplace, encompassing the more active involvement required of everyone in the organization as a result.

- Chapter 10 has an expanded and updated discussion of the network organization, and includes a new section on virtual organizations.

- Chapter 11 includes careful consideration of how digital technology affects structure. This chapter contains expanded coverage of innovations such as network and virtual organizations, comparing and contrasting the characteristics of traditional organizations with those of the emerging new workplace.

- Chapter 12 has been thoroughly revised and updated to reflect the various aspects of change and development as exhibited in the new workplace.

- Chapter 13 looks at how human resource management is changing due to globalization, information technology, and the need to build human capital. It also explores new information on trends such as telecommuting and flexible hours, virtual workers, e-recruiting, corporate universities, and new performance evaluation methods.

- Chapter 14 includes a new section on multicultural teams and employee network groups as ways to build and support a diverse workforce, leveraging the power of diversity for the benefit of the organization. The chapter places emphasis on the challenges faced by minorities and also includes a discussion of the potential benefits and difficulties of emotional connections in the workplace.

- Chapter 15 presents a new section on emotional intelligence and a discussion of both employees' and organizations' responses to stress management in today's organizations.

- Chapter 16 includes a new discussion about leadership for the new workplace, including Level 5 leadership, male versus female methods of leading, virtual leadership, and servant leadership. It also has a brief new discussion of visionary leadership.

- Chapter 17 contains an added discussion of the Q12—a Gallup Organization survey of the factors that influence employee motivation.

- Chapter 18 has a new section on feedback and learning as important components of the communication process.

- Chapter 19 considers global and virtual teams.

- Chapter 20 presents a new section on basic financial statements and the use of the balanced scorecard as a basis for control of the organization. This chapter also includes new information on six sigma quality control measurements and market value-added financial control measurements.

- Chapter 21 has a new section on the Internet and e-business, including e-business strategies, discussion of e-marketplaces, using ERP and CRM to improve business operations, and knowledge management. It also explores recent trends in information technology, such as the wireless Internet and instant messaging, and how they affect organizations and managers.

- Chapter 22 includes a new discussion of the Integrated Enterprise and how organizations are using the Internet and e-business linkages—intranets and extranets—to integrate and streamline the supply chain. New sections on procurement and distribution management have also been added.

In recognition of the role of technology in today's world, each chapter of the text integrates coverage of the Internet and emerging technology into the various topics covered in the chapter. In addition, most chapters contain a *Leading Online* box that features a technologically savvy company or highlights a trend that is impacting today's organizations. The book's technology emphasis is also reflected in the *Surf the Net* exercises at the end of each chapter.

In addition, South-Western has brought together a team of experts to create and coordinate color photographs, video cases, beautiful artwork, and supplemental materials for the best management textbook and package on the market.

Organization

The chapter sequence in *Management* is organized around the management functions of planning, organizing, leading, and controlling. These four functions effectively encompass both management research and characteristics of the manager's job.

Part One introduces the world of management, including the nature of management, issues surrounding the new workplace, the learning organization, and historical perspectives on management.

Part Two examines the environments of management and organizations. This section includes material on the business environment and corporate culture, the global environment, ethics and social responsibility, the natural environment, and the environment of entrepreneurship and small business management.

Part Three presents three chapters on planning, including organizational goal setting and planning, strategy formulation and implementation, and the decision-making process.

Part Four focuses on organizing processes. These chapters describe dimensions of structural design, the design alternatives managers can use to achieve strategic objectives, structural designs for promoting innovation and change, the design and use of the human resource function, and the ways managing diverse employees are significant to the organizing function.

Part Five is devoted to leadership. This section begins with a chapter on organizational behavior, providing a grounding in understanding people in organizations. The foundation paves the way for subsequent discussion of leadership, motivating employees, communication, and team management.

Part Six describes the controlling function of management, including basic principles of total quality management, the design of control systems, information technology, and techniques for control of operations management.

Special Features

One major goal of this book is to offer better ways of using the textbook medium to convey management knowledge to the reader. To this end, the book includes several special features.

Chapter Outline and Objectives. Each chapter begins with a clear statement of its learning objectives and an outline of its contents. These devices provide an overview of what is to come and can also be used by students to guide their study and test their understanding and retention of important points.

Management Problem and Solution. The text portion of each chapter begins with a real-life problem faced by an organization manager. The problem pertains to the topic of the chapter and will heighten students' interest in chapter concepts. The questions posed in the Management Problem are resolved in the Chapter Summary at the end of the chapter, where chapter concepts guiding the management's actions are highlighted.

Photo Essays. A key feature of the book is the use of photographs accompanied by detailed captions that describe management events and how they relate to chapter material. While the photos are beautiful to look at, they also convey the vividness, immediacy, and concreteness of management events in today's business world.

Contemporary Examples. Every chapter of the text contains a large number of written examples of management incidents. They are placed at strategic points in the chapter and are designed to demonstrate the application of concepts to specific companies. These in-text examples—indicated by an icon in the margin—include well-known companies such as Dell Computer, Toys 'R' Us, and Lockheed Martin, as well as less-well-known companies and not-for-profit organizations such as Juniper Networks, Tom's of Maine, Rhinotek Computer Products, and Bob's Big Boy. These examples put students in touch with the real world of organizations so that they can appreciate the value of management concepts.

Putting People First and Leading Online Boxes. Focusing on real companies, these features reflect the dual emphasis of the new workplace: the technology side and the human capital side. These boxes provide students with an in-depth analysis of the various issues facing today's organizations and managers.

Manager's Shoptalk Boxes. These features address topics straight from the field of management that are of special interest to students. They may describe a contemporary topic or problem that is relevant to chapter content or they may contain a diagnostic questionnaire or a special example of how managers handle a problem. These boxes will heighten student interest in the subject matter and provide an auxiliary view of management issues not typically available in textbooks.

Video Cases. The six parts of the text conclude with video cases, one per chapter, that illustrate the concepts presented in that part. The 22 videos enhance class discussion because students can see the direct application of the management theories they have learned. Each video case explores the issues covered in the video, allowing students to synthesize the material they've just viewed. The video cases culminate with several questions that can be used to launch classroom discussion or as homework. Suggested answers are provided in the Instructor's Manual.

Exhibits. Many aspects of management are research based, and some concepts tend to be abstract and theoretical. To enhance students' awareness and understanding of these concepts, many exhibits have been included throughout the book. These exhibits consolidate key points, indicate relationships among variables, and visually illustrate concepts. They also make effective use of color to enhance their imagery and appeal.

Glossaries. Learning the management vocabulary is essential to understanding contemporary management. This process is facilitated in three ways. First, key concepts are boldfaced and completely defined where they first appear in the text. Second, brief definitions are set out in the margins for easy review and follow-up. Third, a glossary summarizing all key terms and definitions appears at the end of the book for handy reference.

Chapter Summary and Discussion Questions. Each chapter closes with a summary of key points that students should retain. The discussion questions are a complementary learning tool that will enable students to check their understanding of key issues, to think beyond basic concepts, and to determine areas that require further study. The summary and discussion questions help students discriminate between main and supporting points and provide mechanisms for self-teaching.

Management in Practice Exercises. End-of-chapter exercises, called "Management in Practice: Experiential Exercise" and "Management in Practice: Ethical Dilemma," provide a self-test for students and an opportunity to experience management issues in a personal way. These exercises take the form of questionnaires, scenarios, and activities, and many also provide an opportunity for students to work in teams.

Surf the Net. Each chapter contains three Internet exercises to involve students in the high-tech world of cyberspace. Students are asked to explore the Web for research into topics related to each chapter. This hands-on experience helps them develop Internet, research, and management skills.

Cases for Critical Analysis. Also appearing at the end of each chapter is a brief but substantive case that provides an opportunity for student analysis and class discussion. Many of these cases are about companies whose names students will recognize; others are based on real management events with the identities of companies and managers disguised. These cases allow students to sharpen their diagnostic skills for management problem solving.

Continuing Case. Located at the end of each part, the Continuing Case is a running discussion of management topics as experienced by one company as they relate to the material discussed in that part. Focusing on one company, Ford Motor Co., allows students to follow the managers' and the organization's problems and solutions in a long-term way.

Supplementary Materials—Leading by Example

The sixth edition's ancillary package, another market innovation from Daft, is loaded with powerful resources for students and instructor alike.

Combining the latest technology with proven teaching tools, the package enables students to put chapter concepts into action and gain valuable insights into real-world practices. In addition, an expansive collection of supplemental teaching materials offers support to instructors—from the novice to the most seasoned professor.

Completely integrated with the text, this comprehensive package continues to lead the market with its innovative and real-world management application. Many new cutting-edge features have been added to create an unrivaled support system.

Instructor Resources include:

- **Instructor's Manual** (0-324-17086-6) Designed to provide support for instructors new to the course, as well as innovative materials for experienced professors, the Instructor's Manual includes Chapter Outlines, annotated learning objectives, Lecture Notes and sample Lecture Outlines. Additionally, the Instructor's Manual includes answers and teaching notes to end-of-chapter materials, including the video cases and continuing case.

- **Instructor's Resource CD-ROM** (0-324-17087-4) Key instructor ancillaries (Instructor's Manual, Test Bank, and PowerPoint slides) are provided on CD-ROM, giving instructors the ultimate tool for customizing lectures and presentations.

- **Test Bank** (0-324-17088-2) Scrutinized for accuracy, the Test Bank includes more than 2,000 true/false, multiple choice, short answer, and essay questions. Each question has been rated for level of difficulty and is designated either as factual or application so that instructors can provide a balanced set of questions for student exams.

- **ExamView** (0-324-17090-4) Available on the Instructor's Resource CD-ROM, ExamView contains all of the questions in the printed Test Bank. This program is an easy-to-use test creation software compatible with Microsoft Windows. Instructors can add or edit questions, instructions, and answers, and select questions (randomly or numerically) by previewing them on the screen. Instructors can also create and administer quizzes online, whether over the Internet, a local area network (LAN), or a wide area network (WAN).

- **PowerPoint Lecture Presentation** Available on the Instructor's Resource CD-ROM and the Web site, the PowerPoint Lecture Presentation enables instructors to customize their own multimedia classroom presentation. Containing approximately 350 slides, the package includes figures and tables from the text, as well as outside materials to supplement chapter concepts. Approximately one Web site URL is included per chapter, allowing instructors to simply click on links to move from the PowerPoints to pertinent Web sites. Material is organized by chapter, and can be modified or expanded for individual classroom use. PowerPoints are also easily printed to create customized transparency masters.

- **Overhead Transparency Acetates** (0-324-17091-2) Created from artwork in the text, as well as outside materials, the full color acetates are available with this text. These transparencies can supplement lectures by displaying the key concepts from the text.

- **WebTutor**™ (0-324-17080-7 on WebCT, or 0-324-17081-5 on BlackBoard) WebTutor is an interactive, web-based, student supplement on WebCT and/or BlackBoard that harnesses the power of the Internet to deliver innovative learning aids that actively engage students. The instructor can incorporate Web Tutor as an integral part of the course, or the students can use it on their own as a study guide. Benefits to students include automatic and immediate feedback from quizzes and exams; interactive, multimedia rich explanation of concepts; online exercises that reinforce what they've learned; flashcards that include audio support; and greater interaction and involvement through online discussion forums.

- **Management Videos** (0-324-17708-9) Videos created specifically to accompany *Management*, 6th Edition, utilize real-world companies to illustrate management concepts as outlined in the text. Focusing on both small and large business, the videos give students an inside perspective on the situations and issues that corporations face. Video cases at the end of every text part, one per chapter, reinforce what the student has just seen, and provide an opportunity for critical analysis and discussion.

- **Turner Learning/ CNN, Management and Organizations Video** (0-324-13495-9) Bring the news gathering and programming power of CNN into your classroom with this VHS cassette of high-interest clips from the world's leading 24-hour global news network. Short segments—perfect for introducing key concepts—cover a range of issues, from online anonymity to workplace privacy, affirmative action, compulsory overtime, biotechnology, and more.

- **Web Site** (*http://daft.swcollege.com*) The Daft Web site is a comprehensive, resource-rich location for both instructors and students to find pertinent information. It includes a complete listing of URLs from the text, case links, interactive quizzes, InfoTrac exercises, PowerPoint Lecture Presentations, and Search the Web features with links to additional sources. The Instructor Resources section contains an IM download, Test Bank sample chapter download, PowerPoint download, case material, and PDF files of two chapters. The Interactive Study Center includes Interactive Quizzes, complete text glossary and key end-of-chapter materials for online reference.

Student Resources include:

- **Study Guide** (0-324-17089-0) Packed with real-world examples and additional applications for helping students master management concepts, this learning supplement is an excellent resource. For each chapter of the text, the Study Guide includes a summary and completion exercise; a review with multiple-choice, true/false and short answer questions; a mini case with multiple-choice questions; management applications; and an experiential exercise that can be assigned as homework or used in class.

- **Xtra!** (0-324-17085-8) Xtra! is packaged with every new copy of *Management* and includes additional interactive quizzes, digitized versions of the Management videos (*Experiencing Management* by Dennis Middlemist), and additional activities. Xtra! is also available for purchase with used textbooks.

- **InfoTrac** Free with the purchase of each textbook, this online database of articles gives students access to full-text articles from hundreds of scholarly and popular periodicals such as *Newsweek*, *Time*, and *USA Today*. Updated daily, this tool allows students to research topics pertinent to classroom discussion and to keep up with current events.

Acknowledgments

A gratifying experience for me was working with the team of dedicated professionals at South-Western who were committed to the vision of producing the best management text ever. I am grateful to Joe Sabatino, Acquisitions Editor, whose enthusiasm, creative ideas, assistance, and vision kept this book's spirit alive. Rob Bloom, Senior Marketing Strategist, provided keen market knowledge and innovative ideas for instructional support. Emma Guttler, Developmental Editor, provided superb project coordination and offered excellent ideas and suggestions to help the team meet a demanding and sometimes arduous schedule. Molly Flynn, Editorial Assistant, and Emily Streutker, Marketing Assistant, skillfully pitched in to help keep the project on track. Kelly Keeler, Production Editor, cheerfully and expertly guided me through the production process. I am also indebted to the team at Elm Street Publishing Services for their production expertise and commitment to producing a quality book. Karen Hill provided extensive assistance on many aspects of this project. Jennifer Frazier coordinated the photo selection and permission process. A special thank you goes out to the entire team at Elm Street. Their careful attention to the various details and to the photo essays contributed greatly to the quality of the final book.

Here at Vanderbilt I want to extend special appreciation to my assistant, May Woods. May provided excellent support and assistance on a variety of projects that gave me time to write. I also want to acknowledge an intellectual debt to my colleagues, Bruce Barry, Ray Friedman, Barry Gerhart, Tom Mahoney, Neta Moye, Rich Oliver, David Owens, and Bart Victor. Thanks also to Dean Bill Christie, who has supported my writing projects and maintained a positive scholarly atmosphere in the school.

Another group of people who made a major contribution to this textbook are the management experts who provided advice, reviews, answers to questions, and suggestions for changes, insertions, and clarifications. I want to thank each of these colleagues for their valuable feedback and suggestions:

David C. Adams
Manhattanville College

Erin M. Alexander
University of Houston, Clear Lake

Hal Babson
Columbus State Community College

Reuel Barksdale
Columbus State Community College

Gloria Bemben
Finger Lakes Community College

Art Bethke
Northeast Louisiana University

Thomas Butte
Humboldt State University

Peter Bycio
Xavier University, Ohio

Diane Caggiano
Fitchburg State College

Douglas E. Cathon
St. Augustine's College

Jim Ciminskie
Bay de Noc Community College

Dan Connaughton
University of Florida

Bruce Conwers
Kaskaskia College

Byron L. David
The City College of New York

Richard De Luca
William Paterson University

Robert DeDominic
Montana Tech

Linn Van Dyne
Michigan State University

John C. Edwards
East Carolina University

Mary Ann Edwards
College of Mount St. Joseph

Janice M. Feldbauer
Austin Community College

Daryl Fortin
Upper Iowa University

Michael P. Gagnon
New Hampshire Community Technical College

Richard H. Gayor
Antelope Valley College

Dan Geeding
Xavier University, Ohio

James Genseal
Joliet Junior College

Peter Gibson
Becker College

Carol R. Graham
Western Kentucky University

Gary Greene
Manatee Community College

Paul Hayes
Coastal Carolina Community College

Dennis Heaton
Maharishi University of Management, Iowa

Jeffrey D. Hines
Davenport College

Bob Hoerber
Westminster College

James N. Holly
University of Wisconsin–Green Bay

Genelle Jacobson
Ridgewater College

C. Joy Jones
Ohio Valley College

Sheryl Kae
Lynchburg College

Jordan J. Kaplan
Long Island University

J. Michael Keenan
Western Michigan University

Paula C. Kougl
Western Oregon University

Cynthia Krom
Mount St. Mary College

William B. Lamb
Millsaps College

Robert E. Ledman
Morehouse College

George Lehma
Bluffton College

Janet C. Luke
Georgia Baptist College of Nursing

Jenna Lundburg
Ithaca College

Walter J. Mac Minhaw
Oral Roberts University

Myrna P. Mandell
California State University, Northridge

Daniel B. Marin
Louisiana State University

James C. McElroy
Iowa State University

Dennis W. Meyers
Texas State Technical College

Alan N. Miller
University of Nevada, Las Vegas

Irene A. Miller
Southern Illinois University

Micah Mukabi
Essex County College

I would like to extend a personal word of thanks to the many dedicated authors who contributed to the extensive supplement package for the sixth edition. Amit Shah has written a wonderful Test Bank. Tom Lloyd has made the Instructor's Manual a valuable teaching tool with innovative new features. Stephen Hiatt has worked hard to ensure that the Study Guide reflects the chapter material in the textbook. Nick Kaufman, Michelle Morgan, and Dena Wetzel produced the video package. Thanks to Stephen Peters for his work on creating the PowerPoint Lecture Presentation.

I'd like to pay special tribute to my editorial associate, Pat Lane. This revision is our fifth project together, and she has spoiled me to the point that I can't imagine how I ever got along on my own. Pat provided truly outstanding help throughout every step of the revision of this text. She skillfully added in drafted materials for a variety of cases and topics, researched topics when new sources were lacking, and did an absolutely superb job with the copyedited manuscript and page proofs. Her commitment to this text enabled us to achieve our dream for its excellence.

permission process. A special thank you goes out to the entire team at Elm Street. Their careful attention to the various details and to the photo essays contributed greatly to the quality of the final book.

Here at Vanderbilt I want to extend special appreciation to my assistant, May Woods. May provided excellent support and assistance on a variety of projects that gave me time to write. I also want to acknowledge an intellectual debt to my colleagues, Bruce Barry, Ray Friedman, Barry Gerhart, Tom Mahoney, Neta Moye, Rich Oliver, David Owens, and Bart Victor. Thanks also to Dean Bill Christie, who has supported my writing projects and maintained a positive scholarly atmosphere in the school.

Another group of people who made a major contribution to this textbook are the management experts who provided advice, reviews, answers to questions, and suggestions for changes, insertions, and clarifications. I want to thank each of these colleagues for their valuable feedback and suggestions:

David C. Adams
Manhattanville College

Erin M. Alexander
University of Houston, Clear Lake

Hal Babson
Columbus State Community College

Reuel Barksdale
Columbus State Community College

Gloria Bemben
Finger Lakes Community College

Art Bethke
Northeast Louisiana University

Thomas Butte
Humboldt State University

Peter Bycio
Xavier University, Ohio

Diane Caggiano
Fitchburg State College

Douglas E. Cathon
St. Augustine's College

Jim Ciminskie
Bay de Noc Community College

Dan Connaughton
University of Florida

Bruce Conwers
Kaskaskia College

Byron L. David
The City College of New York

Richard De Luca
William Paterson University

Robert DeDominic
Montana Tech

Linn Van Dyne
Michigan State University

John C. Edwards
East Carolina University

Mary Ann Edwards
College of Mount St. Joseph

Janice M. Feldbauer
Austin Community College

Daryl Fortin
Upper Iowa University

Michael P. Gagnon
New Hampshire Community Technical College

Richard H. Gayor
Antelope Valley College

Dan Geeding
Xavier University, Ohio

James Genseal
Joliet Junior College

Peter Gibson
Becker College

Carol R. Graham
Western Kentucky University

Gary Greene
Manatee Community College

Paul Hayes
Coastal Carolina Community College

Dennis Heaton
Maharishi University of Management, Iowa

Jeffrey D. Hines
Davenport College

Bob Hoerber
Westminster College

James N. Holly
University of Wisconsin–Green Bay

Genelle Jacobson
Ridgewater College

C. Joy Jones
Ohio Valley College

Sheryl Kae
Lynchburg College

Jordan J. Kaplan
Long Island University

J. Michael Keenan
Western Michigan University

Paula C. Kougl
Western Oregon University

Cynthia Krom
Mount St. Mary College

William B. Lamb
Millsaps College

Robert E. Ledman
Morehouse College

George Lehma
Bluffton College

Janet C. Luke
Georgia Baptist College of Nursing

Jenna Lundburg
Ithaca College

Walter J. Mac Minhaw
Oral Roberts University

Myrna P. Mandell
California State University, Northridge

Daniel B. Marin
Louisiana State University

James C. McElroy
Iowa State University

Dennis W. Meyers
Texas State Technical College

Alan N. Miller
University of Nevada, Las Vegas

Irene A. Miller
Southern Illinois University

Micah Mukabi
Essex County College

David W. Murphy
Madisonville Community College

James L. Moseley
Wayne State University

Nora Nurre
Upper Iowa University

Nelson Ocf
Pacific University

Tomas J. Ogazon
St. Thomas University

Allen Oghenejbo
Mills College

Linda Overstreet
Hillsborough Community College

Ken Peterson
Metropolitan State University

Clifton D. Petty
Drury College

James I. Phillips
Northeastern State University

Linda Putchinski
University of Central Florida

Kenneth Radig
Medaille College

Gerald D. Ramsey
Indiana University Southeast

Barbara Redmond
Briar Cliff College

William Reisel
St. John's University, New York

Walter F. Rohrs
Wagner College

Marcy Satterwhite
Lake Land College

Don Schreiber
Baylor University

Kilmon Shin
Ferris State University

Daniel G. Spencer
University of Kansas

Gary Spokes
Pace University

M. Sprencz
David N. Meyers College

Shanths Srinivas
California State Polytechnic University, Pomona

Jeffrey Stauffer
Ventura College

William A. Stower
Seton Hall University

Mary Studer
Southwestern Michigan College

James Swenson
Moorhead State University, Minnesota

Irwin Talbot
St. Peter's College

Andrew Timothy
Lourdes College

Frank G. Titlow
St. Petersburg Junior College

John Todd
University of Arkansas

Dennis L. Varin
Southern Oregon University

Gina Vega
Merrimack College

George S. Vozikis
University of Tulsa

Bruce C. Walker
Northeast Louisiana University

Mark Weber
University of Minnesota

Emilia S. Westney
Texas Tech University

Stan Williamson
Northeast Louisiana University

Alla L. Wilson
University of Wisconsin–Green Bay

Ignatius Yacomb
Loma Linda University

Imad Jim Zbib
Ramapo College of New Jersey

Vic Zimmerman
Pima Community College

I would like to extend a personal word of thanks to the many dedicated authors who contributed to the extensive supplement package for the sixth edition. Amit Shah has written a wonderful Test Bank. Tom Lloyd has made the Instructor's Manual a valuable teaching tool with innovative new features. Stephen Hiatt has worked hard to ensure that the Study Guide reflects the chapter material in the textbook. Nick Kaufman, Michelle Morgan, and Dena Wetzel produced the video package. Thanks to Stephen Peters for his work on creating the PowerPoint Lecture Presentation.

I'd like to pay special tribute to my editorial associate, Pat Lane. This revision is our fifth project together, and she has spoiled me to the point that I can't imagine how I ever got along on my own. Pat provided truly outstanding help throughout every step of the revision of this text. She skillfully added in drafted materials for a variety of cases and topics, researched topics when new sources were lacking, and did an absolutely superb job with the copyedited manuscript and page proofs. Her commitment to this text enabled us to achieve our dream for its excellence.

Finally, I want to acknowledge the love and contributions of my wife, Dorothy Marcic. Dorothy has been very supportive during this revision as we grew in our lives together. I also want to acknowledge my love and support for my five daughters, who make my life special during our precious time together. Thanks also to B. J. and Kaitlyn, and Kaci and Matthew for their warmth, silliness and smiles that brighten my life, especially during our skiing days together and on the beach.

Richard L. Daft
Nashville, Tennessee
May 2002

About the Author

Richard L. Daft, Ph.D., is Associate Dean for Academic Programs and the Brownlee O. Currey, Jr. Professor in Management in the Owen Graduate School of Management at Vanderbilt University. Professor Daft specializes in the study of organization theory and leadership, and enjoys applying these ideas in his role as Associate Dean. Dr. Daft is a Fellow of the Academy of Management and has served on the editorial boards of *Academy of Management Journal*, *Administrative Science Quarterly*, and *Journal of Management Education*. He was the Associate Editor-in-Chief of *Organization Science* and served for three years as associate editor of *Administrative Science Quarterly*.

Professor Daft has authored or co-authored 12 books, including *Organization Theory and Design* (South-Western College Publishing, 2002), *The Leadership Experience* (South-Western College Publishing, 2001) and *What to Study: Generating and Developing Research Questions* (Sage, 1982). He recently published *Fusion Leadership: Unlocking the Subtle Forces That Change People and Organizations* (Berrett-Koehler, 2000, with Robert Lengel). He has also authored dozens of scholarly articles, papers, and chapters. His work has been published in *Administrative Science Quarterly, Academy of Management Journal, Academy of Management Review, Strategic Management Journal, Journal of Management, Accounting Organizations and Society, Management Science, MIS Quarterly, California Management Review,* and *Organizational Behavior Teaching Review*. Professor Daft has been awarded several government research grants to pursue studies of organization design, organizational innovation and change, strategy implementation, and organizational information processing.

Dr. Daft also is an active teacher and consultant. He has taught management, leadership, organizational change, organizational behavior, organizational theory, and organizational behavior. He has been involved in management development and consulting for many companies and government organizations, including the American Banking Association, Bell Canada, National Transportation Research Board, NL Baroid, Nortel, TVA, Pratt & Whitney, State Farm Insurance, Tenneco, the United States Air Force, the U.S. Army, J. C. Bradford & Co., Central Parking System, Entergy Sales and Service, Bristol-Myers Squibb, First American National Bank, and the Vanderbilt University Medical Center.

Brief Contents

■ **PART 1**   INTRODUCTION TO MANAGEMENT   1

    1   Managing the New Workplace   2
    2   Historical Foundations of Management   36

■ **PART 2**   THE ENVIRONMENT OF MANAGEMENT   71

    3   The Environment and Corporate Culture   72
    4   Managing in a Global Environment   104
    5   Managerial Ethics and Corporate Social Responsibility   136
    6   Small Business and Internet Start-Ups   168

■ **PART 3**   PLANNING   207

    7   Organizational Planning and Goal Setting   208
    8   Strategy Formulation and Implementation   236
    9   Managerial Decision Making   270

■ **PART 4**   ORGANIZING   309

    10   Fundamentals of Organizing   310
    11   Using Structural Design to Achieve Strategic Goals   342
    12   Change and Development   372
    13   Human Resource Management   404
    14   Managing Diverse Employees   436

■ **PART 5**   LEADING   477

    15   Foundations of Behavior in Organizations   478
    16   Leadership in Organizations   512
    17   Motivation in Organizations   544
    18   Communicating in Organizations   578
    19   Teamwork in Organizations   612

■ **PART 6**   CONTROLLING   650

    20   The Importance of Control   652
    21   Information Technology and E-Business   680
    22   Operations and Service Management   708
       Glossary   745
       Name Index   758
       Company Index   771
       Subject Index   776

Contents

■ **PART 1**   INTRODUCTION TO MANAGEMENT   1

Chapter 1   **Managing the New Workplace   2**

The Definition of Management   5
The Four Management Functions   6
Planning 6 • Organizing 7 • Leading 7 •
Controlling 7
Organizational Performance   9
Management Skills   10
Conceptual Skills 11 • Human Skills 11 • Technical
Skills 12
Management Types   12
Vertical Differences 12 • Horizontal Differences 14
What Is It Like to Be a Manager?   15
Manager Activities 15 • Manager Roles 16
**Managing in Small Businesses and Not-For-Profit
Organizations   20**
Management and the New Workplace   22
Forces on Organizations 24 • New Management
Competencies 25 • Application: Managing Crises and
Unexpected Events 26
Summary and Management Solution 28
Discussion Questions 29
Management in Practice: Experiential Exercise 29
Management in Practice: Ethical Dilemma 31
Surf the Net 31
Case for Critical Analysis 32

Putting People First, 8
How Joe Torre Brings Out the Best in
His Players
Manager's Shoptalk, 18
Do You Really Want to Be a Manager?
Leading Online, 23
Click Here for Lower Taxes

Chapter 2   **Historical Foundations of Management   36**

Management and Organization   38
Classical Perspective   40
Scientific Management 41 • Bureaucratic
Organizations 43 • Administrative Principles 44
Humanistic Perspective   45
The Human Relations Movement 46 • The Human
Resources Perspective 47 • The Behavioral Sciences
Approach 49
Management Science Perspective   50
Recent Historical Trends   52
Systems Theory 52 • Contingency View 53 • Total
Quality Management 54
Current Directions in Management Thinking   55
The Learning Organization 55
Managing the Technology-Driven Workplace   56
Summary and Management Solution 60
Discussion Questions 60
Management in Practice: Experiential Exercise 61
Management in Practice: Ethical Dilemma 62
Surf the Net 62
Case for Critical Analysis 62

Leading Online, 41
Of Railroads and Web Sites
Putting People First, 49
Watson Opens the Door at IBM—and
Finds Happier Employees
Manager's Shoptalk, 51
Ebbs and Flows of Management
Innovations, 1950–2000

VIDEO CASES

Chapter 1: LeMeridien Managers Manage by Walking
Around 66 • Chapter 2: In the Beginning: A Bite Taken
from the Apple 67

CONTINUING CASE

Part One: Ford Motor Company Makes History 68

■ PART 2   THE ENVIRONMENT OF MANAGEMENT 71

Chapter 3   **The Environment and Corporate Culture 72**

The External Environment 74
General Environment 76 • Task Environment 80
The Organization-Environment Relationship 84
Environmental Uncertainty 84 • Adapting to the
Environment 84
The Internal Environment: Corporate Culture 88
Symbols 89 • Stories 89 • Heroes 90 • Slogans 90 •
Ceremonies 90
Environment and Culture 91
Adaptive Cultures 91 • Types of Cultures 91
Shaping Corporate Culture for the New Workplace 94
New Demands for Managing Corporate Culture 94 •
Cultural Leadership 96
Summary and Management Solution 97
Discussion Questions 98
Management in Practice: Experiential Exercise 98
Management in Practice: Ethical Dilemma 99
Surf the Net 100
Case for Critical Analysis 100

Leading Online, 81
Connecting to the Customer
Manager's Shoptalk, 87
The New Golden Rule: Cooperate!
Putting People First, 95
Athene's Culture Nurtures Loyalty and
Excellence

Chapter 4   **Managing in a Global Environment 104**

A Borderless World 107
The International Business Environment 109
The Economic Environment 110
The Legal-Political Environment 113
GATT and the World Trade Organization 114 • European
Union 115 • North American Free Trade Agreement
(NAFTA) 117 • Trade Alliances: Promise or Pitfall? 118
The Sociocultural Environment 118
Getting Started Internationally 122
Outsourcing 122 • Exporting 123 • Licensing 123 •
Direct Investing 124
Multinational Corporations 125
Managing in a Global Environment 126
Personal Challenges for Global Managers 126 •
Managing Cross-Culturally 126 • Global Learning 128
Summary and Management Solution 129
Discussion Questions 129
Management in Practice: Experiential Exercise 130
Management in Practice: Ethical Dilemma 130
Surf the Net 131
Case for Critical Analysis 132

Leading Online, 111
Virtual Reality: Negotiating the Cross-
Cultural Web
Manager's Shoptalk, 117
Globalization: A Catch 22?
Putting People First, 128
AES Corp.: Power to the People

Chapter 5   **Managerial Ethics and Corporate Social Responsibility   136**

What Is Managerial Ethics?   138
Criteria for Ethical Decision Making   140
Utilitarian Approach 141 • Individualism Approach 141 • Moral-Rights Approach 142 • Justice Approach 142
Factors Affecting Ethical Choices   143
The Manager 143 • The Organization 145
What Is Social Responsibility?   146
Organizational Stakeholders   147
The Natural Environment   149
Evaluating Corporate Social Performance   152
Economic Responsibilities 152 • Legal Responsibilities 152 • Ethical Responsibilities 153 • Discretionary Responsibilities 154
Managing Company Ethics and Social Responsibility   154
Ethical Individuals 155 • Ethical Leadership 155 • Organizational Structures and Systems 156
Ethics and the New Workplace   159
Summary and Management Solution 161
Discussion Questions 161
Management in Practice: Experiential Exercise 162
Management in Practice: Ethical Dilemma 163
Surf the Net 164
Case for Critical Analysis 164

Manager's Shoptalk, 147
Guidelines for Ethical Decision Making

Leading Online, 149
Using the Web to Promote Social Responsibility

Putting People First, 154
Reebok Scores with Workers in Indonesia

Chapter 6   **Small Business and Internet Start-Ups   168**

What Is Entrepreneurship?   170
Entrepreneurship and the Environment   172
Entrepreneurship Today 172 • Definition of Small Business 174 • Impact of Entrepreneurial Companies 174
Who Are Entrepreneurs?   176
Personality Traits 176 • Demographic Factors 178
Starting an Entrepreneurial Firm   179
New-Business Idea 179 • The Business Plan 179 • Legal Form 181 • Financial Resources 183 • Tactics 183
Internet Start-Ups   186
Launching an Internet Business 187
Managing A Growing Business   191
Stages of Growth 191 • Planning 192 • Organizing 192 • Leading 193 • Controlling 194
Summary and Management Solution 194
Discussion Questions 195
Management in Practice: Experiential Exercise 195
Management in Practice: Ethical Dilemma 196
Surf the Net 196
Case for Critical Analysis 197

VIDEO CASES

Chapter 3: Fallon Worldwide: Can Its Corporate Culture Be a Soul Survivor? 200 • Chapter 4: Fallon Worldwide—Its Name Spells Global 201 • Chapter 5: Timberland Walks the Walk of Social Responsibility 202 • Chapter 6: The Geek Squad: Providing Service that Makes You Smile 203

Putting People First, 180
The Soft Touch Leads to Success at Ipswitch Software

Manager's Shoptalk, 182
Helpful Hints for Writing the Business Plan

Leading Online, 190
Getting Google Right

CONTINUING CASE
Part Two: Ford Operates in a Complex Environment 204

■ **PART 3**   PLANNING   207

Chapter 7   **Organizational Planning and Goal Setting   208**

Overview of Goals and Plans 210
Purposes of Goals and Plans 211
Goals in Organizations 213
Organizational Mission 213 • Goals and Plans 214 •
Hierarchy of Goals 216
Criteria for Effective Goals 216
Planning Types and Performance 218
Management by Objectives 219 • Single-Use and
Standing Plans 221 • Contingency Plans 222 • Crisis
Management Planning 223
Planning in the New Workplace 226
Traditional Approaches to Planning 227 • New
Workplace Approaches to Planning 227
Summary and Management Solution 230
Discussion Questions 230
Management in Practice: Experiential Exercise 231
Management in Practice: Ethical Dilemma 231
Surf the Net 232
Case for Critical Analysis 233

Leading Online, 215
Start-Up E.piphany Plans to "Grow Up"
Fast

Manager's Shoptalk, 223
Regulating E-mail in the Workplace

Putting People First, 229
SRC Holdings Corporation: Changing
Lives by Changing Business

Chapter 8   **Strategy Formulation and Implementation   236**

Thinking Strategically 238
What Is Strategic Management? 239 • Grand Strategy
239 • Global Strategy 241 • Purpose of Strategy 243 •
Levels of Strategy 245
The Strategic Management Process 247
Strategy Formulation Versus Implementation 247 •
Situation Analysis 248
Formulating Corporate-Level Strategy 250
Portfolio Strategy 250 • The BCG Matrix 251
Formulating Business-Level Strategy 252
Porter's Competitive Forces and Strategies 253 •
Partnership Strategies 257
Formulating Functional-Level Strategy 259
Strategy Implementation and Control 259
Leadership 259 • Structural Design 260 • Information
and Control Systems 261 • Human Resources 261 •
Implementing Global Strategies 262
Summary and Management Solution 262
Discussion Questions 263
Management in Practice: Experiential Exercise 264
Management in Practice: Ethical Dilemma 264
Surf the Net 265
Case for Critical Analysis 265

Leading Online, 240
Ebay: Building on Success

Putting People First, 256
Happy Employees Want to Stay at the
Harleysville Group

Chapter 9   **Managerial Decision Making   270**

Types of Decisions and Problems 272
Programmed and Nonprogrammed Decisions 273 •
Certainty, Risk, Uncertainty, and Ambiguity 273

Leading Online, 274
Starbucks Makes a New Connection

Manager's Shoptalk, 285
Decision Biases to Avoid

Putting People First, 294
At Brady: "From No to Yo"

Decision-Making Models 276
Classical Model 276 • Administrative Model 278 •
Political Model 280
Decision-Making Steps 281
Recognition of Decision Requirement 282 • Diagnosis
and Analysis of Causes 282 • Development of
Alternatives 283 • Selection of Desired Alternative 283 •
Implementation of Chosen Alternative 284 • Evaluation
and Feedback 285
Personal Decision Framework 287
Increasing Participation in Decision Making 288
The Vroom-Jago Model 288 • New Decision Approaches
for the New Workplace 292
Summary and Management Solution 295
Discussion Questions 296
Management in Practice: Experiential Exercise 296
Management in Practice: Ethical Dilemma 297
Surf the Net 298
Case for Critical Analysis 298

VIDEO CASES

Chapter 7: Caribou Coffee Has a Mission 302 • Chapter 8:
Caribou Coffee's Strategy: Worth More than Beans 303 •
Chapter 9: Machado and Silvetti: A Business Based on
Decisions 304

CONTINUING CASE

Part Three: A Tale of Two Strategies 305

■ **PART 4**   ORGANIZING   309

Chapter 10   **Fundamentals of Organizing   310**

Organizing the Vertical Structure 313
Work Specialization 314 •   Chain of Command 314 •
Span of Management 317 • Centralization and
Decentralization 318 • Formalization 319
Departmentalization 320
Vertical Functional Approach 322 • Divisional
Approach 324 • Matrix Approach 327 • Team
Approach 330 • Network Approach 332 • The
Virtual Organization Approach 335
Summary and Management Solution 337
Discussion Questions 337
Management in Practice: Experiential Exercise 338
Management in Practice: Ethical Dilemma 338
Surf the Net 339
Case for Critical Analysis 339

Chapter 11   **Using Structural Design to Achieve Strategic
Goals   342**

The Horizontal Organization 344
The Need for Coordination 344 • Task Forces, Teams,
and Project Management 346 • Reengineering 348
Traditional Organizations Versus the New Workplace 349
Horizontal Structure 351 • Open Information 351 •

Manager's Shoptalk, 316
How to Delegate

Leading Online, 320
Tightening the Reins at Oracle

Putting People First, 332
Imagination Ltd.

Leading Online, 352
Intuit Spins a Wide Web

Putting People First, 354
Norsk Hydro: Working Better by
Working Less

Decentralized Decision Making and Participative
Strategy 352 • Empowered Employees and Shared
Responsibility 353 • Strong, Adaptive Culture 354
Factors Shaping Structure 356
Structure Follows Strategy 357 • Structure Reflects the
Environment 358 • Structure Fits the Technology 360 •
Structure Follows the Workflow 364
Summary and Management Solution 365
Discussion Questions 366
Management in Practice: Experiential Exercise 367
Management in Practice: Ethical Dilemma 368
Surf the Net 368
Case for Critical Analysis 369

Chapter 12   **Change and Development 372**
Change and the New Workplace 374
Model of Planned Organizational Change 375
Forces for Change 376 • Need for Change 376
Initiating Change 377
Search 378 • Creativity 378 • Idea Champions and
New-Venture Teams 379
Implementing Change 381
Resistance to Change 381 • Force-Field Analysis 383 •
Implementation Tactics 384
Types of Planned Change 387
Technology Changes 387 • New Product Changes 388 •
Structural Changes 390
Culture/People Changes 392
Training and Development 392 • Organizational
Development 393
Summary and Management Solution 397
Discussion Questions 398
Management in Practice: Experiential Exercise 399
Management in Practice: Ethical Dilemma 399
Surf the Net 400
Case for Critical Analysis 400

Chapter 13   **Human Resource Management 404**
The Strategic Role of Human Resource Management 406
Environmental Influences on HRM 407
Competitive Strategy 408 • Federal Legislation 409
The Changing Nature of Careers 411
The Changing Social Contract 411 • The New
Workplace 412
Attracting an Effective Workforce 413
Human Resource Planning 414 • Recruiting 415 •
Selecting 418
Developing an Effective Workforce 422
Training and Development 422 • Performance
Appraisal 423
Maintaining an Effective Workforce 426
Compensation 426 • Benefits 428 • Termination 429
Summary and Management Solution 430
Discussion Questions 430
Management in Practice: Experiential Exercise 431
Management in Practice: Ethical Dilemma 431
Surf the Net 432
Case for Critical Analysis 432

Manager's Shoptalk, 382
Making Change Stick

Leading Online, 391
Nestlé: Making "E-business the Way
We Do Business"

Putting People First, 397
Alberto-Culver Gets a Cultural
Makeover

Leading Online, 419
Vignette Corp. Hires Great People Fast

Manager's Shoptalk, 420
The Right Way to Interview a Job
Applicant

Chapter 14 **Managing Diverse Employees 436**

Valuing Diversity 438
Dimensions of Diversity 439 • Attitudes toward Diversity 441

The Changing Workplace 442
Challenges Minorities Face 443 • Management Challenges 445

Affirmative Action 446
Current Debates about Affirmative Action 447 • The Glass Ceiling 448

Current Responses to Diversity 449
Changing the Corporate Culture 450 • Changing Structure and Policies 451 • Diversity Awareness Training 454

Defining New Relationships in Organizations 456
Emotional Intimacy 456 • Sexual Harassment 457

Global Diversity 458
Selection and Training 458 • Communication Differences 459

Diversity in the New Workplace 459
Multicultural Teams 460 • Employee Network Groups 460
Summary and Management Solution 461
Discussion Questions 462
Management in Practice: Experiential Exercise 463
Management in Practice: Ethical Dilemma 464
Surf the Net 465
Case for Critical Analysis 465

VIDEO CASES

Chapter 10: Student Advantage Helps College Students Stay Organized 469 • Chapter 11: Machado and Silvetti: Building the Business of Building 470 • Chapter 12: Peter Pan Offers a Safe Ride 471 • Chapter 13: Fannie Mae: A Superstar to American Home Buyers and Workers 472 • Chapter 14: Fannie Mae Promotes a Diverse Workforce 473

CONTINUING CASE

Part Four: Managing Organizational Changes at Ford 474

Manager's Shoptalk, 442
Shifting Attitudes

Leading Online, 444
BETting on the Internet: BET.com

Putting People First, 452
Pitney Bowes Knows How to Play the Diversity Game

■ **PART 5** LEADING **477**

Chapter 15 **Foundations of Behavior in Organizations 478**

Organizational Behavior 480
Attitudes 481
Components of Attitudes 481 • Work-Related Attitudes 483 • Conflicts among Attitudes 485
Perception 485
Perceptual Selectivity 486 • Perceptual Distortions 487 • Attributions 488
Personality and Behavior 490
Personality Traits 490 • Emotional Intelligence 492 • Attitudes and Behaviors Influenced by Personality 493 • Person-Job Fit 496
Learning 498
The Learning Process 498 • Learning Styles 499 •

Putting People First, 486
The Rokenbok Magic

Leading Online, 492
At Aramark, B2B Still Needs the Human Touch

Manager's Shoptalk, 494
What's Your Crisis EQ?

Continuous Learning 499
Stress and Stress Management 501
Type A and Type B Behavior 501 • Causes of Work
Stress 502 • Stress Management 504
Summary and Management Solution 506
Discussion Questions 507
Management in Practice: Experiential Exercise 507
Management in Practice: Ethical Dilemma 508
Surf the Net 508
Case for Critical Analysis 509

Chapter 16   **Leadership in Organizations   512**
The Nature of Leadership 514
Leadership Versus Management 514
Position Power 516 • Personal Power 516 •
Empowerment 517
Leadership Traits 518
Autocratic Versus Democratic Leaders 518
Behavioral Approaches 520
Ohio State Studies 521 • Michigan Studies 521 • The
Leadership Grid 521
Contingency Approaches 523
Fiedler's Contingency Theory 523 • Hersey and
Blanchard's Situational Theory 526 • Path-Goal
Theory 527 • Substitutes for Leadership 531
Change Leadership 532
Charismatic and Visionary Leadership 532 •
Transformational Leaders 533 • Leading the New
Workplace 534
Summary and Management Solution 537
Discussion Questions 538
Management in Practice: Experiential Exercise 538
Management in Practice: Ethical Dilemma 539
Surf the Net 540
Case for Critical Analysis 540

Chapter 17   **Motivation in Organizations   544**
The Concept of Motivation 546
Foundations of Motivation 548
Traditional Approach 548 • Human Relations
Approach 548 • Human Resource Approach 548 •
Contemporary Approach 548
Content Perspectives on Motivation 549
Hierarchy of Needs Theory 549 • ERG Theory 551 •
Two-Factor Theory 551 • Acquired Needs Theory 553
Process Perspectives on Motivation 554
Equity Theory 554 • Expectancy Theory 556
Reinforcement Perspective on Motivation 558
Reinforcement Tools 558 • Schedules of
Reinforcement 560
Job Design for Motivation 562
Job Simplification 562 • Job Rotation 564 • Job
Enlargement 564 • Job Enrichment 564 • Job
Characteristics Model 565
Motivating in the New Workplace 567
Empowerment 567 • Giving Meaning to Work 569

Leading Online, 519
An E-Commerce Revolution at General
Motors

Manager's Shoptalk, 534
Are You a Charismatic Leader?

Putting People First, 536
Andy Pearson Transforms Himself as a
Leader

Leading Online, 549
At ATX Forms, Idea Labs Pay Off

Putting People First, 552
Software Technology Group's 'Healthy'
Culture

Manager's Shoptalk, 563
The Carrot-and-Stick Controversy

Summary and Management Solution 571
Discussion Questions 572
Management in Practice: Experiential Exercise 572
Management in Practice: Ethical Dilemma 573
Surf the Net 573
Case for Critical Analysis 574

Chapter 18   Communicating in Organizations   578

Communication and the Manager's Job 580
What Is Communication? 581 • The Communication
Process 582
Communicating among People 583
Communication Channels 583 • Persuasion and
Influence 586 • Nonverbal Communication 587 •
Listening 588
Organizational Communication 589
Formal Communication Channels 589 • Team
Communication Channels 594 • Informal Communication
Channels 596
Communicating in the New Workplace 598
Open Communication 599 • Dialogue 599 • Feedback
and Learning 600
Managing Organizational Communication 602
Barriers to Communication 602 • Overcoming
Communication Barriers 604
Summary and Management Solution 605
Discussion Questions 606
Management in Practice: Experiential Exercise 606
Management in Practice: Ethical Dilemma 607
Surf the Net 608
Case for Critical Analysis 608

Manager's Shoptalk, 584
How to Be a Master Communicator

Leading Online, 593
Amazon.com Keeps Track of
Employees' "Pulse Rate"

Putting People First, 600
Great Harvest Bread Company

Chapter 19   Teamwork in Organizations   612

Teams at Work 614
What Is a Team? 614 • Model of Work Team
Effectiveness 616
Types of Teams 617
Formal Teams 617 • Self-Directed Teams 619 • Teams
in the New Workplace 621
Team Characteristics 623
Size 623 • Member Roles 623
Team Processes 625
Stages of Team Development 625 • Team Cohesiveness 628
• Team Norms 629
Managing Team Conflict 631
Causes of Conflict 631 • Styles to Handle Conflict 632
Benefits and Costs of Teams 634
Potential Benefits of Teams 635 • Potential Costs of
Teams 635
Summary and Management Solution 636
Discussion Questions 638
Management in Practice: Experiential Exercise 639
Management in Practice: Ethical Dilemma 639
Surf the Net 640
Case for Critical Analysis 640

Putting People First, 616
A High-Tech Executive Learns about
Teamwork

Leading Online, 622
VeriFone's Virtual World

Manager's Shoptalk, 637
How to Run a Great Meeting

VIDEO CASES

Chapter 15: CVS Stands for Consumer Value Store 644 •
Chapter 16: Donna Fernandes: She's the Leader of the
Pack 645 • Chapter 17: Motivation Is a Wild Experience
at the Buffalo Zoo 646 • Chapter 18: Communication Is
Paramount at Le Meridien 647 • Chapter 19:
Cannondale Teams Perform in the Race for the Perfect
Bicycle 648

CONTINUING CASE

Part Five: Ford Enters a New Era of Leadership 649

■ PART 6   CONTROLLING   651

Chapter 20   **The Importance of Control   652**

The Meaning of Control 654
Organizational Control Focus 655
Feedforward Control 656 • Concurrent Control 656 •
Feedback Control 657
Feedback Control Model 657
Steps of Feedback Control 657 • Application to
Budgeting 660
Financial Control 662
Financial Statements 662 • Financial Analysis:
Interpreting the Numbers 663
The Changing Philosophy of Control 666
Total Quality Management 667
TQM Techniques 668 • TQM Success Factors 670
Trends in Quality and Financial Control 671
International Quality Standards 671 • New Financial
Control Systems 671
Control in the New Workplace 672
Open-Book Management 672 • The Balanced Scorecard 673
Summary and Management Solution 675
Discussion Questions 676
Management in Practice: Experiential Exercise 676
Management in Practice: Ethical Dilemma 676
Surf the Net 677
Case for Critical Analysis 677

Manager's Shoptalk, 655
E-Commerce Metrics

Leading Online, 665
Tesco.com

Putting People First, 673
Semco's Open Book Policy

Chapter 21   **Information Technology and E-Business   680**

Information Technology 682
Data versus Information 682 • Characteristics of Useful
Information 683
Types of Information Systems 683
Operations Information Systems 684 • Management
Information Systems 686 •
The Internet and E-Business 687
E-Business Strategies 689 • E-Marketplaces 691 •
Enterprise Resource Planning Systems 692 •
Customer Relationship Management 694 • Knowledge
Management 695

Putting People First, 692
Grant J. Hunt Co. Likes the Personal
Touch

Leading Online, 700
BMW's Ultimate Web Experience

Management Implications of Information Technology 697
Improved Employee Effectiveness 697 • Increased
Efficiency 698 • Empowered Employees 698 •
Information Overload 699 • Enhanced Collaboration 699
• Organizational Learning 700
IT Trends in the New Workplace 700
Instant Messaging 701 • Wireless Internet 701 • Peer-
to-Peer File Sharing 701
Summary and Management Solution 702
Discussion Questions 703
Management in Practice: Experiential Exercise 703
Management in Practice: Ethical Dilemma 704
Surf the Net 705
Case for Critical Analysis 705

Chapter 22   **Operations and Service Management   708**
Organizations as Production Systems 710
Manufacturing and Service Operations 711 • Operations
Strategy 712 • The Integrated Enterprise 715
Designing Operations Management Systems 716
Product and Service Design 716 • Procurement 718 •
Facilities Layout 719 • Technology Automation 721 •
Facility Location 723 • Capacity Planning 724
Inventory Management 725
The Importance of Inventory 725 • Economic Order
Quantity 727 • Material Requirements Planning 728 •
Just-in-Time Inventory 729 • Logistics and Distribution
Management 730
Managing Productivity 731
Measuring Productivity 731 • Improving Productivity 733
Summary and Management Solution 735
Discussion Questions 735
Management in Practice: Experiential Exercise 736
Management in Practice: Ethical Dilemma 736
Surf the Net 737
Case for Critical Analysis 738

VIDEO CASES

Chapter 20: Cannondale Has Finely Tuned Control
Processes 740 • Chapter 21: Cannondale's Information
Technology: From Office to Factory Floor—and Beyond 741
• Chapter 22: Cannondale's Consuming Passion for
Perfection 742

CONTINUING CASE

Part Six: At Ford, Quality Is Job 1—Again 743

Glossary 745
Name Index 758
Company Index 771
Subject Index 776

Putting People First, 714
Cosmi Corp. Likes the Old-School
Management Approach
Manager's Shoptalk, 722
A German Factory Shows How to Be
Fast and Flexible
Leading Online, 732
Nistevo's Online Distribution Network

Introduction to Management

Regardless of where you live, as the earth rotates around the sun each year, the seasons change. Whether you live where the signs are obvious—the varying colors of leaves, a blowing snowstorm, tiny buds on branches, a blistering heat wave—or where the signs are more subtle, such as a cool breeze in the evening or increased rain, nature is signaling change all the same. We come to expect these alterations as part of the natural order of life. Today's managers must expect change as well, as different influences both outside and within organizations force constant shifts and transformations that affect the way managers carry out their jobs. Blizzards of information, blossoming market opportunities, a multi-hued workforce, and hot competition all combine to challenge organizations to adapt in order to thrive and grow.

But some management principles remain constant, like evergreens that retain their color year round, through every season. Managers still need to be able to understand and communicate information to others, maintain good relationships with customers and members of the organization, and make clear, rational decisions. A manager makes plans for her department or company, organizes and leads staff, and monitors activities to keep the department or company on target toward its goals. Ultimately, managers who can read the signs that remain constant—the sun always rises in the east and sets in the west—while anticipating coming changes, like spotting the first spring crocus or robin on the lawn, will make the greatest contributions to their organizations.

Managing the New Workplace

CHAPTER OUTLINE

The Definition of Management

The Four Management Functions

Planning

Organizing

Leading

Controlling

Organizational Performance

Management Skills

Conceptual Skills

Human Skills

Technical Skills

Management Types

Vertical Differences

Horizontal Differences

What Is It Like to Be a Manager?

Manager Activities

Manager Roles

Managing in Small Businesses
and Not-for-Profit Organizations

Management and the New
Workplace

Forces on Organizations

New Management Competencies

*Application: Managing Crises
and Unexpected Events*

LEARNING OBJECTIVES

After studying this chapter, you should be able to

1 Describe the four management functions and the type of management activity associated with each.

2 Explain the difference between efficiency and effectiveness and their importance for organizational performance.

3 Describe management types and the horizontal and vertical differences between them.

4 Describe conceptual, human, and technical skills and their relevance for managers and nonmanagers.

5 Define ten roles that managers perform in organizations.

6 Discuss the transition to a new workplace and the management competencies needed to deal with issues such as diversity, globalization, and rapid change.

7 Explain the leadership skills needed for effective crisis management.

Management Challenge

Kenneth Chenault had just gotten his dream job as chairman and CEO of American Express Co., becoming one of the few African Americans ever to head a major U.S. corporation. He knew he would face challenges, but he never imagined anything like this in his worst nightmares. While he was on a business trip to Salt Lake City, talking with a colleague back in New York, terrorists crashed planes into the twin towers of the World Trade Center, just across the street from American Express headquarters. Chenault immediately telephoned security, and he instructed that they begin evacuation procedures immediately. Over the next two days, stuck in Salt Lake City, Chenault set up a command center and held hourly conference calls with top executives to keep tabs on what was happening and to deal with immediate problems. He learned that the attacks had left eleven American Express employees dead or missing.

American Express was already going through some difficult times before the September 11, 2001, terrorist attacks. In his first year on the job, Chenault twice had to report disappointing financial results and had announced layoffs of almost 7,000 jobs. Now, as the Number 1 issuer of credit cards and the Number 1 travel agency, he knew American Express would be at the center of an economic storm. As he returned to New York, Kenneth Chenault's heart was heavy and his mind was whirling. He knew that everyone–from the lowest-ranking employee of the company to the biggest shareholder–would be looking to him for leadership.[1]

If you were in Ken Chenault's position, how would you handle this situation? What approach would you take to deal with employees, shareholders, the media, and others?

Ken Chenault is being challenged in a way few American managers could have imagined until recently. The attacks on New York and Washington brought a new element to the manager's job in America—that of coping with crisis and extreme uncertainty and the human emotions that accompany it. For the past decade or so, managers have been talking about how their organizations struggle to keep pace in an uncertain world that changes faster than ever. The events of September 11, 2001 brought the uncertainty and turbulence of today's world clearly to the forefront of *everyone's* mind.

Managers are constantly dealing with uncertainty and unexpected events, whether it be something as small as the sudden loss of a major customer or something as large and dramatic as what happened on September 11. Solid management skills and actions are the key to helping any organization weather a crisis and remain healthy, inspired, and productive. Today's organizations are coping with diverse and far-reaching challenges. They must keep pace with ever-advancing technology, find ways to incorporate the Internet and e-business into their strategies and business models, and strive to remain competitive in the face of increasingly tough global competition, uncertain environments, cutbacks in personnel and resources, and massive worldwide economic, political, and social shifts. The growing diversity of the workforce creates other dynamics: How does the company maintain a strong corporate culture while supporting diversity; balancing work and family concerns; and coping with conflicting demands of all employees for a fair shot at power and responsibility. Workers are asking that managers share rather than hoard power. Organizational structures are becoming flatter, with power and information pushed down and out among fewer layers and with teams of front-line workers playing new roles as decision makers. New ways of working, such as virtual teams and telecommuting, put additional demands on managers.

Because of these changes, a revolution is taking place in the field of management. A new kind of leader is needed who can guide businesses through this turbulence—a strong leader who recognizes the complexity of today's world and realizes there are no perfect answers.[2] The revolution asks managers to do more with less, to engage whole employees, to see change rather than stability as the nature of things, and to create vision and cultural values that allow people to create a truly collaborative workplace. This new management approach is very different from a traditional mindset that emphasizes tight top-down control, employee separation and specialization, and management by impersonal measurements and analysis. In a situation such as the one Ken Chenault is facing at American Express, an impersonal, highly analytical approach could destroy the company.

Making a difference as a manager today and tomorrow requires integrating solid, tried-and-true management skills with new approaches that emphasize the human touch, enhance flexibility, and involve employees' hearts and minds as well as their bodies. Successful departments and organizations don't just happen—they are managed to be that way. Managers in every organization today face major challenges and have the opportunity to make a difference. For example, Lorraine Monroe made a difference at Harlem's Frederick Douglass Academy when she transformed it from one of the worst to one of the best schools in New York City. Stephen Quesnelle, head of quality programs at Mitel Corp. in Ottawa, Canada, made a difference when he organized "sacred cow hunts" to encourage employees to track down and do away with outdated policies and procedures that were holding the company back. Today, signs of energy, change, and renewal are everywhere at Mitel.[3]

©Mark Peterson, Corbis SABA

Managers like Bill Gates make a difference for their organizations by guiding them through the uncertainty of today's turbulent environment. Gates and his Microsoft marketing team had to decide whether, after over a year of preparation for the $500 million launch of Windows XP, it was appropriate or wise to launch the new PC operating system only six weeks after the September 11, 2001 terrorist attacks on America. On October 25, Gates introduced the new system in Manhattan following a gospel choir's stirring rendition of "America the Beautiful."

These managers are not unusual. Every day, managers solve difficult problems, turn organizations around, and achieve astonishing performances. To be successful, every organization needs skilled managers.

This textbook introduces and explains the process of management and the changing ways of thinking about and perceiving the world that are becoming increasingly critical for managers of today and tomorrow. By reviewing the actions of some successful and not-so-successful managers, you will learn the fundamentals of management. By the end of this chapter, you will already recognize some of the skills that managers use to keep organizations on track. By the end of this book, you will understand fundamental management skills for planning, organizing, leading, and controlling a department or an entire organization. In the remainder of this chapter, we will define management and look at the ways in which roles and activities are changing for today's managers. The final section of the chapter talks about a new kind of workplace that has evolved as a result of changes in technology, globalization, and other forces, and examines how managers can meet the challenges of this new environment and manage unexpected events.

The Definition of Management

What do managers such as Kenneth Chenault, Stephen Quesnelle, and Lorraine Monroe have in common? They get things done through their organizations. Managers create the conditions and environment that enable organizations to survive and thrive beyond the tenure of any specific supervisor or manager. For example, members of the Grateful Dead rock band created and managed a successful business, Grateful Dead Productions, that continues to thrive even though band member Jerry Garcia has been dead for more than five years and the band no longer regularly performs together. Grateful Dead Productions remains active in merchandise sales, CD releases, and Internet projects, bringing in about $70 million annually. The band members, who shared top management duties and responsibilities, created an organization with a powerful culture, a strong vision, and the motivation and human energy that set great organizations apart and help them survive over the long haul.[4]

A key aspect of managing is recognizing the role and importance of others. Good managers know that the only way they can accomplish anything at all is through the people of the organization. Early twentieth-century management scholar Mary Parker Follett defined management as "the art of getting things done through people."[5] More recently, noted management theorist Peter Drucker stated that the job of managers is to give direction to their organizations, provide leadership, and decide how to use organizational resources to accomplish goals.[6] Getting things done through people and other resources and providing leadership and direction are what managers do. These activities apply not only to top executives such as Kenneth Chenault, but also to the leader of a security team, a supervisor of an accounting department, or a director of marketing. Moreover, management often is considered universal because it uses organizational resources to accomplish goals and attain high performance in all types of profit and not-for-profit organizations. Thus, our definition of management is as follows:

> **Management** is the attainment of organizational goals in an effective and efficient manner through planning, organizing, leading, and controlling organizational resources.

management
The attainment of organizational goals in an effective and efficient manner through planning, organizing, leading, and controlling organizational resources.

There are two important ideas in this definition: (1) the four functions of planning, organizing, leading, and controlling and (2) the attainment of organizational goals in an effective and efficient manner. Managers use a multitude of skills to perform these functions. Management's conceptual, human, and technical skills are discussed later in the chapter. Exhibit 1.1 illustrates the process of how managers use resources to attain organizational goals. Although some management theorists identify additional management functions, such as staffing, communicating, or decision making, those additional functions will be discussed as subsets of the four primary functions in Exhibit 1.1. Chapters of this book are devoted to the multiple activities and skills associated with each function, as well as to the environment, global competitiveness, and ethics, which influence how managers perform these functions. The next section begins with a brief overview of the four functions.

The Four Management Functions

Planning

planning
The management function concerned with defining goals for future organizational performance and deciding on the tasks and resource use needed to attain them.

Planning defines where the organization wants to be in the future and how to get there. **Planning** means defining goals for future organizational performance and deciding on the tasks and use of resources needed to attain them. At Wells Fargo & Co., CEO Richard Kovacevich has set an ambitious goal of doubling the number of products sold per customer (such as checking accounts, credit cards, home equity loans, and certificates of deposit) from 4 to 8.[7] To meet the goal, managers will invest significant resources for training and incentives to motivate employees.

A lack of planning—or poor planning—can hurt an organization's performance. For example, clothing retailer Merry-Go-Round, a once-ubiquitous presence in malls across America, slid into bankruptcy and ultimately disappeared as a result of poor planning. Top managers' lack of vision in perceiving market direction and demographic trends, weak planning efforts regarding acquisitions and growth, and the failure to prepare for management succession helped to kill a 1,500-store, $1-billion nationwide chain.[8]

Exhibit *1.1*

The Process of Management

Management Functions

Resources
- Human
- Financial
- Raw materials
- Technological
- Information

Planning
Select goals and ways to attain them

Controlling
Monitor activities and make corrections

Organizing
Assign responsibility for task accomplishment

Leading
Use influence to motivate employees

Performance
- Attain goals
- Products
- Services
- Efficiency
- Effectiveness

Organizing

Organizing typically follows planning and reflects how the organization tries to accomplish the plan. **Organizing** involves the assignment of tasks, the grouping of tasks into departments, and the assignment of authority and allocation of resources across the organization. Hewlett-Packard, Sears, Xerox, and Microsoft have all undergone structural reorganizations to accommodate their changing plans. Wells Fargo, the nation's fourth largest banking company, is a highly decentralized organization that pushes decision-making authority down to banks at the local level. Kovacevich believes the decentralized structure enables the huge company to provide whiz-bang products and services while being as responsive to customers as a small community bank.[9]

organizing
The management function concerned with assigning tasks, grouping tasks into departments, and allocating resources to departments.

Leading

Providing leadership is becoming an increasingly important management function. **Leading** is the use of influence to motivate employees to achieve organizational goals. Leading means creating a shared culture and values, communicating goals to employees throughout the organization, and infusing employees with the desire to perform at a high level. Leading involves motivating entire departments and divisions as well as those individuals working immediately with the manager. In an era of uncertainty, international competition, and a growing diversity of the workforce, the ability to shape culture, communicate goals, and motivate employees is critical to business success.

leading
The management function that involves the use of influence to motivate employees to achieve the organization's goals.

Some top managers, such as Herb Kelleher, recently retired CEO of Southwest Airlines, and Michael Dell of Dell Computer, are known as exceptional leaders. They are able to communicate their vision throughout the organization and energize employees into action. Kelleher's leadership, for example, helped to make Southwest workers the most production in the airline industry. However, at Southwest, leadership filters down throughout the company, and everyone is encouraged to assume leadership responsibility, solve problems, and help motivate others. Providing leadership means helping other people be and do their best for the organization. The Putting People First box describes the leadership approach of Joe Torre, head coach of the New York Yankees.

Jean Kvasnica began her career at Hewlett-Packard as a secretary. She is currently head of a multifunctional sales team that competes for sales of computers, meters, and other equipment worth hundreds of millions of dollars. Kvasnica succeeds at leading partly because she tries to emulate the qualities she responds to in a leader: ". . . rooted in the ground . . . not defensive, not egotistical. . . . They can take a volatile situation and stay focused."

One doesn't have to be a well-known top manager to be an exceptional leader. There are many managers working quietly who also provide strong leadership within departments, teams, not-for-profit organizations, and small businesses. Valeria Maltoni is a marketing specialist for Destiny WebSolutions, where she leads teams that help clients solve their online business problems. Maltoni's philosophy of leadership is that leaders open themselves up to the ideas and opinions of others. "It's okay to ask for help," she says. "In any situation, whenever I think that I have more to give than I have to get, I'm wrong."[10]

©Kristine Larsen

Controlling

controlling
The management function concerned with monitoring employees' activities, keeping the organization on track toward its goals, and making corrections as needed.

Controlling is the fourth function in the management process. **Controlling** means monitoring employees' activities, determining whether the organization

Putting People First

How Joe Torre Brings Out the Best in His Players

Joe Torre was fired three times in a 15-year management career before signing on as manager of the New York Yankees. But since then, everything he's touched has seemed to turn to gold. The Yankees haven't missed the playoffs since Torre took over, and during his tenure they've won four out of five World Series. Although Torre himself is the first to point out that the team's success depends on a combination of factors, it is clear that his management approach plays a big role.

Torre believes his years of dedication, learning, and growing as a manager finally paid off. One of the biggest lessons he learned is that success and winning aren't the same thing. Success, says Torre, is "playing—or working—to the best of your ability." His philosophy is that people should strive every day to fulfill their potential as individuals and as members of a team, and to help them do so requires a management approach that puts the needs and feelings of people first. Torre's approach is based on knowing his team members as individuals and treating everyone with fairness, respect, and trust, the three elements he considers essential for productive work relationships. Torre doesn't give a lot of big motivational speeches. Instead, he relies on one-to-one communication. He watches, listens, and tries to understand the needs, motivations, and problems of each person, recognizing that what's going on in players' lives off the field affects their performance.

When Torre needs to sort out a problem with a player, he does it in private. He never uses fear, manipulation, or public humiliation to motivate or control players.

In addition, Torre understands that every player sometimes hits a slump, and he doesn't treat players differently just because they're not playing well. "I've worked for organizations in the past that are real quick to jump off the bandwagon when things aren't going well . . . ." says pitcher Mike Stanton. "With Joe, you don't really have to look over your shoulder, because you'll lose confidence in yourself a long time before Joe loses confidence in you." Torre sticks by his players, and he absorbs the flak from upper management without passing it on to the team. He also doesn't burden players with a lot of strict rules, preferring to treat them as responsible adults who are all working toward a shared goal.

Torre's emphasis on people and relationships has created a high-performance workplace where mistakes and failure are routinely accepted. It's the kind of workplace most organizations need in today's volatile environment. They can achieve it, Torre says, by handling their jobs based on the values of "respect, trust, integrity, and commitment to our work and the people we work with."

SOURCES: Joe Torre with Henry Dreher, *Joe Torre's Ground Rules for Winners: 12 Keys to Managing Team Players, Tough Bosses, Setbacks, and Success* (New York: Hyperion, 1999); Jerry Useem, "A Manager for All Seasons," *Fortune* (April 30, 2001), 66–72; and Malcolm Moran, "Conflict Resolution, the Joe Torre Way," *The New York Times* (July 14, 1997), C5.

is on target toward its goals, and making corrections as necessary. Managers must ensure that the organization is moving toward its goals. New trends toward empowerment and trust of employees have led many companies to place less emphasis on top-down control and more emphasis on training employees to monitor and correct themselves.

New information technology is also helping managers provide needed organizational control without strict top-down constraints. By using the Internet and other information technology to coordinate and monitor virtually every aspect of operations, managers at Cisco Systems can keep tabs on employee and company performance without maintaining daily authoritarian control over workers. Cisco employees have amazing freedom to make decisions and take action—for example, any employee can fly anywhere on earth without prior approval—but they also know that top managers keep a close eye on what's going on throughout the company with just a few mouse clicks.[11]

Companies may also use information technology to put *more* constraints on employees if managers believe the situation demands it. Managers at C. R. England, a long-haul refrigerated trucking company, implemented a strict computerized control system when the company was on the verge of bankruptcy.

The system monitors about 500 procedures, and managers grade employees weekly based on the computerized data. Although employees don't necessarily like such close monitoring, it helped to save the company.[12] Organization failure can result when managers are not serious about control or lack control information.

Organizational Performance

The other part of our definition of management is the attainment of organizational goals in an efficient and effective manner. Management is so important because organizations are so important. In an industrialized society where complex technologies dominate, organizations bring together knowledge, people, and raw materials to perform tasks no individual could do alone. Without organizations, how could technology be provided that enables us to share information around the world in an instant, electricity be produced from huge dams and nuclear power plants, and thousands of videos and DVDs be made available for our entertainment? Organizations pervade our society. Most college students will work in an organization—perhaps Sun Microsystems, Cinergy, or Hollywood Video. College students already are members of several organizations, such as a university, junior college, YMCA, church, fraternity, or sorority. College students also deal with organizations every day: to renew a driver's license, be treated in a hospital emergency room, buy food from a supermarket, eat in a restaurant, or buy new clothes. Managers are responsible for these organizations and for seeing that resources are used wisely to attain organizational goals.

Our formal definition of an **organization** is a social entity that is goal directed and deliberately structured. *Social entity* means being made up of two or more people. *Goal directed* means designed to achieve some outcome, such as make a profit (J. Crew, Microsoft), win pay increases for members (AFL-CIO), meet spiritual needs (Methodist church), or provide social satisfaction (college sorority). *Deliberately structured* means that tasks are divided and responsibility for their performance is assigned to organization members. This definition applies to all organizations, including both profit and not-for-profit. Vickery Stoughton runs Toronto General Hospital and manages a $200 million budget. He endures intense public scrutiny, heavy government regulation, and daily crises of life and death. Bob Stein founded Night Kitchen to provide authors with e-publishing tools for creating e-books and multimedia texts. Eleanor Josaitis worked with her parish priest, the late Father William Cunningham, to establish an organization in Detroit called Focus: Hope, which feeds 48,000 hungry people a day, runs a training program in precision machining and metalworking, sponsors a day-care center, and runs several for-profit manufacturing companies, whose plants and equipment are worth more than $100 million.[13] Small, offbeat, and not-for-profit organizations are more numerous than large, visible corporations—and just as important to society.

Based on our definition of management, the manager's responsibility is to coordinate resources in an effective and efficient manner to accomplish the organization's goals. Organizational **effectiveness** is the degree to which the organization achieves a stated goal. It means that the organization succeeds in accomplishing what it tries to do. Organizational effectiveness means providing a product or service that customers value. Organizational **efficiency** refers to the amount of resources used to achieve an organizational goal. It is based

organization
A social entity that is goal directed and deliberately structured.

effectiveness
The degree to which the organization achieves a stated goal.

efficiency
The use of minimal resources—raw materials, money, and people—to produce a desired volume of output.

©Josef Astor

Leonard Riggio, chief executive of Barnes & Noble Inc., whose book sales total $2.8 billion, is positioning his organization to achieve high performance. Riggio has set a goal to become the largest retailer for online book sales. Although Barnesandnoble.com got a late start in the world of online book sales, Riggio's goal is to outsell Amazon, the world's largest online bookseller.

performance
The organization's ability to attain its goals by using resources in an efficient and effective manner.

on how much raw materials, money, and people are necessary for producing a given volume of output. Efficiency can be calculated as the amount of resources used to produce a product or service.

Efficiency and effectiveness can both be high in the same organization. For example, by using new technology to produce full-color simulations of carpet samples that look almost like the real thing, Lees Carpets in Virginia doesn't have to interrupt machines to produce small batches of woven samples. Thus, Lees can make much more carpet with the same number of machines and employees. Effectiveness also is improved because the accelerated design system has won more customers, reduced the turnaround time for custom business, and improved product quality and customer satisfaction.[14] Managers in service firms are using new technology to improve efficiency and effectiveness, too. Freddie Mac, one of the largest mortgage underwriters in the United States, uses a system that can automatically—and almost instantly—calculate whether to underwrite a home loan. Since the Loan Prospector system was launched, Freddie Mac's transaction volume has increased 200 percent, without the addition of more staff.[15]

Sometimes, however, managers' efforts to improve efficiency can hurt organizational effectiveness. This is especially true in relation to severe cost cutting. At Delta Airlines, former CEO Robert W. Allen dramatically increased cost efficiency by cutting spending on personnel, food, cleaning, and maintenance. Allen believed the moves were needed to rescue the company from a financial tailspin, but Delta fell to last place among major carriers in on-time performance, the morale of employees sank, and customer complaints about dirty planes and long lines at ticket counters increased by more than 75 percent.[16] Current CEO Leo Mullin is striving to maintain the efficiencies instituted by Allen, but also improve organizational effectiveness.

The ultimate responsibility of managers is to achieve high **performance**, which is the attainment of organizational goals by using resources in an efficient and effective manner.

Management Skills

A manager's job is complex and multidimensional and, as we shall see throughout this book, requires a range of skills. Although some management theorists propose a long list of skills, the necessary skills for managing a department or an organization can be summarized in three categories: conceptual, human, and technical.[17] As illustrated in Exhibit 1.2, the application of these skills changes as managers move up in the organization. Though the degree of each skill necessary at different levels of an organization may vary, all managers must possess skills in each of these important areas to perform effectively.

Exhibit *1.2*

Relationship of Conceptual, Human, and Technical Skills to Management Level

Management Level
Top Managers

Middle Managers

First-Line Managers

Nonmanagers (Individual Contributors)

Conceptual Skills

Conceptual skill is the cognitive ability to see the organization as a whole and the relationship among its parts. Conceptual skill involves the manager's thinking, information processing, and planning abilities. It involves knowing where one's department fits into the total organization and how the organization fits into the industry, the community, and the broader business and social environment. It means the ability to *think strategically*—to take the broad, long-term view.

Conceptual skills are needed by all managers but are especially important for managers at the top. They must perceive significant elements in a situation and broad, conceptual patterns. For example, Microsoft, the giant software company, reflects the conceptual skills of its founder and chairman, Bill Gates. Overall business goals are clearly stated and effectively communicated throughout the company, contributing to Microsoft's leadership reputation and billion-dollar revenues. As one Microsoft manager pointed out, "Each part of the company has a life of its own now, but Bill is the glue that holds it all together."[18]

As managers move up the hierarchy, they must develop conceptual skills or their promotability will be limited. A senior engineering manager who is mired in technical matters rather than thinking strategically will not perform well at the top of the organization. Many of the responsibilities of top managers, such as decision making, resource allocation, and innovation, require a broad view.

Human Skills

Human skill is the manager's ability to work with and through other people and to work effectively as a group member. This skill is demonstrated in the way a manager relates to other people, including the ability to motivate, facilitate, coordinate, lead, communicate, and resolve conflicts. A manager with human skills allows subordinates to express themselves without fear of ridicule and encourages participation. A manager with human skills likes other people and is liked by them. Scott McNealy, CEO of Sun Microsystems, uses humor and hoopla to motivate employees and help them cope with the stress of their demanding jobs. Impromptu high jinks such as an intramural squirt gun war, at which McNealy played general, help bind together and energize employees.[19]

As globalization, workforce diversity, uncertainty, and competition for highly skilled knowledge workers increase, human skills become even more crucial. Today's managers need to be genuinely concerned with the emotional needs of their employees, not just the physical needs related to their job tasks. Young J. Shin, chief technology officer at Embark.com, an education Web site, notes that knowledge workers "don't want to be managed as serfs." These employees want guidance, respect, and a chance to contribute fully to the organization.[20] Meg Whitman, CEO of eBay, believes her most important contribution to the organization is creating a work ethic and culture that is "fun, open, and trusting." The attention Whitman

conceptual skill
The cognitive ability to see the organization as a whole and the relationship among its parts.

human skill
The ability to work with and through other people and to work effectively as a group member.

New York City Mayor Rudolph Giuliani displayed outstanding human skills *as he guided employees, volunteers, and the public following the destruction of the World Trade Center buildings on September 11, 2001. On the front lines, the mayor took charge with a mixture of compassion and command. "It's going to be OK," he told a distraught woman. "Shhhhhhhh," he admonished a rowdy crowd. During what the mayor called "the most difficult week in the history of New York," Giuliani's ability to motivate, facilitate, coordinate, lead, communicate, and resolve conflicts marked him as a true leader.*

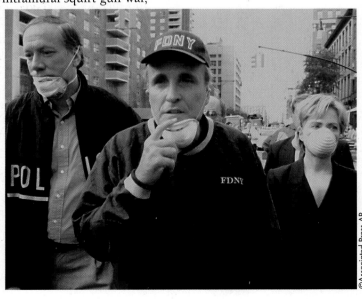

©Associated Press AP

and other eBay managers pay to human skills seems to be paying off. Motivated employees helped the organization expand its franchise in the face of stiff competition from larger rivals, and, unlike many Internet companies, eBay has been turning a healthy profit.[21] Human skills are becoming increasingly important for managers at all levels, and particularly for those who work with employees directly on a daily basis. Organizations frequently lose good employees because of front-line bosses who fail to show respect and concern for workers.[22]

Technical Skills

technical skill
The understanding of and proficiency in the performance of specific tasks.

Technical skill is the understanding of and proficiency in the performance of specific tasks. Technical skill includes mastery of the methods, techniques, and equipment involved in specific functions such as engineering, manufacturing, or finance. Technical skill also includes specialized knowledge, analytical ability, and the competent use of tools and techniques to solve problems in that specific discipline. Technical skills are particularly important at lower organizational levels. Many managers get promoted to their first management job by having excellent technical skills. However, technical skills become less important than human and conceptual skills as managers move up the hierarchy. For example, in his seven years as a manufacturing engineer at Boeing, Bruce Moravec developed superb technical skills in his area of operation. But when he was asked to lead the team designing a new fuselage for the Boeing 757, Moravec found that he needed to rely heavily on human skills in order to gain the respect and confidence of people who worked in areas he knew little about.[23]

Management Types

Managers use conceptual, human, and technical skills to perform the four management functions of planning, organizing, leading, and controlling in all organizations—large and small, manufacturing and service, profit and not-for-profit, traditional and Internet-based. But not all managers' jobs are the same. Managers are responsible for different departments, work at different levels in the hierarchy, and meet different requirements for achieving high performance. Kevin Kurtz is a middle manager at Lucasfilm, where he works with employees to develop marketing campaigns for some of the entertainment company's hottest properties, including the next *Star Wars* episode.[24] Domenic Antonellis is CEO of the New England Confectionary Co. (Necco), the company that makes those tiny pastel candy hearts stamped with phrases such as "Be Mine" and "Kiss Me."[25] Both are managers, and both must contribute to planning, organizing, leading, and controlling their organizations—but in different amounts and ways.

Vertical Differences

top manager
A manager who is at the top of the organizational hierarchy and is responsible for the entire organization.

An important determinant of the manager's job is hierarchical level. Three levels in the hierarchy are illustrated in Exhibit 1.3. **Top managers** are at the top of the hierarchy and are responsible for the entire organization. They have such titles as president, chairperson, executive director, chief executive officer (CEO), and executive vice-president. Top managers are responsible for setting organizational goals, defining strategies for achieving them, monitoring and

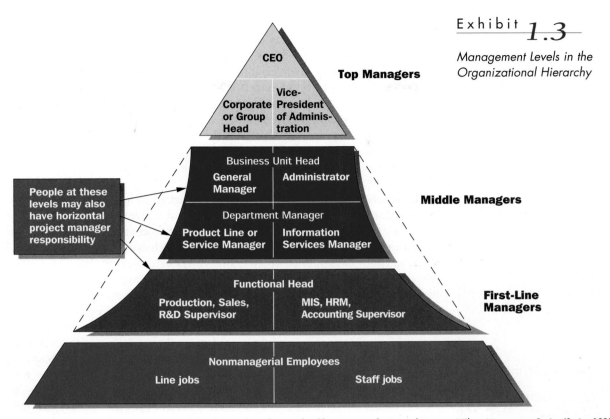

Management Levels in the Organizational Hierarchy

SOURCE: Adapted from Thomas V. Bonoma and Joseph C. Lawler, "Chutes and Ladders: Growing the General Manager," *Sloan Management Review* (Spring 1989), 27–37.

interpreting the external environment, and making decisions that affect the entire organization. They look to the long-term future and concern themselves with general environmental trends and the organization's overall success. Among the most important responsibilities for top managers are communicating a shared vision for the organization, shaping corporate culture, and nurturing an entrepreneurial spirit that can help the company keep pace with rapid change. Today more than ever before, top managers must engage the unique knowledge, skills, and capabilities of each employee.[26]

Middle managers work at middle levels of the organization and are responsible for business units and major departments. Examples of middle managers are department head, division head, manager of quality control, and director of the research lab. Middle managers typically have two or more management levels beneath them. They are responsible for implementing the overall strategies and policies defined by top managers. Middle managers generally are concerned with the near future and are expected to establish good relationships with peers around the organization, encourage teamwork, and resolve conflicts.

The middle manager's job has changed dramatically over the past two decades. During the 1980s and early 1990s, many organizations became lean and efficient by laying off middle managers and slashing middle management levels. Traditional pyramidal organization charts were flattened to allow information to flow quickly from top to bottom and decisions to be made with greater speed. The shrinking middle management is illustrated in Exhibit 1.3.

middle manager
A manager who works at the middle levels of the organization and is responsible for major departments.

project manager
A manager responsible for a temporary work project that involves the participation of other people from various functions and levels of the organization.

first-line manager
A manager who is at the first or second management level and is directly responsible for the production of goods and services.

As a general manager of Conoco's Rocky Mountain region, Carin Knickel created a climate of inspiration that cascaded down through the organization. She devised a system whereby her ten subordinate managers coached each other, then coached the people who reported to them, and so on down the line. Results of this team effort included a 12 percent growth in Conoco's share of a large metro retail gasoline market. The success also won Knickel a promotion to vice-president in charge of the company's new carbon-based group, making her Conoco's highest-ranking woman.

functional manager
A manager who is responsible for a department that performs a single functional task and has employees with similar training and skills.

However, although middle management levels have been reduced, the middle manager's job in many organizations has become much more important. As more and more work is organized around teams and projects, middle managers become involved in a wider range of organizational problems and issues. Strong project managers are in white-hot demand throughout the corporate world. A **project manager** is responsible for a temporary work project that involves the participation of people from various functions and levels of the organization, and perhaps from outside the company as well. Today's middle manager might work with a variety of projects and teams at the same time, some of which cross geographical and cultural as well as functional boundaries.

Rather than managing the flow of information up and down the hierarchy, they are responsible for creating horizontal networks to help the organization quickly respond to shifting demands from the environment. At Lend Lease, a leading real estate and financial services company in Australia, the organizational structure is based on project management. With each new project, managers and employees are plucked from one area of expertise and moved to another very quickly. The team for the Bluewater shopping complex in Kent, England, for example, included a revolving collection of architects, engineers, managers, manufacturers, community advocates, planning authorities, construction experts, retail-delivery specialists, financial analysts, and potential customers, all coordinated by a project manager.[27] Project management makes the middle manager's job much more challenging and exciting. In this new environment, middle managers need new skills: the ability to inspire and motivate a diverse group of people; negotiating skills; a willingness to listen and ability to communicate clearly; conscientiousness and integrity; and most of all, the ability to manage change and conflict.[28]

First-line managers are directly responsible for the production of goods and services. They are the first or second level of management and have such titles as supervisor, line manager, section chief, and office manager. They are responsible for groups of nonmanagement employees. Their primary concern is the application of rules and procedures to achieve efficient production, provide technical assistance, and motivate subordinates. The time horizon at this level is short, with the emphasis on accomplishing day-to-day goals. For example, Stephanie Carver, the kitchen manager at a Bennigan's Grill and Tavern restaurant, monitors and supervises kitchen employees to make sure food is prepared in a safe and efficient manner. She is responsible for motivating and guiding young, often inexperienced workers, providing assistance as needed, limiting waste, and ensuring adherence to health and safety rules.

Horizontal Differences

The other major difference in management jobs occurs horizontally across the organization. **Functional managers** are responsible for departments that perform a single functional task and have employees with similar training and skills. Functional departments include advertising, sales, finance, human resources, manufacturing, and accounting. Line managers are responsible for the manufacturing and marketing departments that make or sell the product or service. Staff managers are in charge of departments such as finance and human resources that support line departments.

General managers are responsible for several departments that perform different functions. A general manager is responsible for a self-contained division, such as a Dillard's department store, and for all of the functional departments within it. Project managers also have general management responsibility, because they coordinate people across several departments to accomplish a specific project.

Project management is a vital role in today's flatter, delayered organizations and enables middle managers to contribute significantly to corporate success.[29] As executive vice-president William Kelvie, chief information officer for Fannie-Mae, said, "Automation and empowerment take away the need to have managers oversee the day-to-day work. Everything has become projects. This is the way Fannie-Mae does business today."[30]

general manager
A manager who is responsible for several departments that perform different functions.

What Is It Like to Be a Manager?

So far we have described how managers at various levels perform four basic functions that help ensure that organizational resources are used to attain high levels of performance. These tasks require conceptual, human, and technical skills. Unless someone has actually performed managerial work, it is hard to understand exactly what managers do on an hour-by-hour, day-to-day basis. The manager's job is so diverse that a number of studies have been undertaken in an attempt to describe exactly what happens. The question of what managers actually do to plan, organize, lead, and control was answered by Henry Mintzberg, who followed managers around and recorded all their activities.[31] He developed a description of managerial work that included three general characteristics and ten roles. These characteristics and roles have been supported in subsequent research.[32]

Manager Activities

One of the most interesting findings about managerial activities is how busy managers are and how hectic the average workday can be. Bruce Nelson, CEO of Office Depot, works 14-hour days and is constantly tracking operations at 947 stores in eight time zones. A typical week for Nelson found him answering e-mails on his laptop while flying to stores in three different states, checking the competition by posing as a customer at an OfficeMax store, dining with the board of a major customer to give them a briefing about the office products industry, meeting with managers throughout headquarters in 15-minute back-to-back sessions to get updates and offer advice, talking with media representatives to outline his plan for reviving the troubled company, and accepting an award recognizing Office Depot's information technology performance.[33]

Managerial Activity Is Characterized by Variety, Fragmentation, and Brevity.[34] The manager's involvements are so widespread and voluminous that there is little time for quiet reflection. The average time spent on any one activity is less than nine minutes. Managers shift gears quickly. Significant crises are interspersed with trivial events in no predictable sequence. One example of just two typical hours for general manager, Janet Howard, follows. Note the frequent interruptions and the brevity and variety of tasks.

7:30 AM	Janet arrives at work and begins to plan her day.
7:37 AM	A subordinate, Morgan Cook, stops in Janet's office to discuss a dinner party the previous night and to review the cost-benefit analysis for a proposed microcomputer.
7:45 AM	Janet's secretary, Pat, motions for Janet to pick up the telephone. "Janet, they had serious water damage at the downtown office last night. A pipe broke, causing about $50,000 damage. Everything will be back in shape in three days. Thought you should know."
8:00 AM	Pat brings in the mail. She also asks instructions for typing a report Janet gave her yesterday.
8:14 AM	Janet gets a phone call from the accounting manager, who is returning a call from the day before. They talk about an accounting report.
8:25 AM	A Mr. Nance is ushered in. Mr. Nance complains that a sales manager mistreats his employees and something must be done. Janet rearranges her schedule to investigate this claim.
9:00 AM	Janet returns to the mail. One letter is from an irate customer. Janet dictates a helpful, restrained reply. Pat brings in phone messages.
9:15 AM	Janet receives an urgent phone call from Larry Baldwin. They discuss lost business, unhappy subordinates, and a potential promotion.[35]

The Manager Performs a Great Deal of Work at an Unrelenting Pace.[36] Managers' work is fast paced and requires great energy. The managers observed by Mintzberg processed 36 pieces of mail each day, attended eight meetings, and took a tour through the building or plant. As soon as a manager's daily calendar is set, unexpected disturbances erupt. New meetings are required. During time away from the office, executives catch up on work-related reading, paperwork, and e-mail.

At O'Hare International Airport, an unofficial count one Friday found operations manager Hugh Murphy interacting with about 45 airport employees. In addition, he listened to complaints from local residents about airport noise, met with disgruntled executives of a French firm who built the airport's new $128 million people-mover system, attempted to soothe a Hispanic city alderman who complained that Mexicana Airlines passengers were being singled out by overzealous tow-truck operators, toured the airport's new fire station, and visited the construction site for the new $20 million tower—and that was *before* the events of September 11, 2001, changed airport operations, making them even more complex. Hugh Murphy's unrelenting pace is typical for managers.[37] Management can be rewarding, but it can also be frustrating and stressful, as discussed in the Manager's Shoptalk box on page 18.

Manager Roles

Mintzberg's observations and subsequent research indicate that diverse manager activities can be organized into ten roles.[38] A **role** is a set of expectations for a manager's behavior. Exhibit 1.4 provides examples of each of the ten roles. These roles are divided into three conceptual categories: informational (managing by information); interpersonal (managing through people); and

role
A set of expectations for one's behavior.

Category	Role	Activity
Informational	**Monitor**	Seek and receive information, scan periodicals and reports, maintain personal contacts.
	Disseminator	Forward information to other organization members; send memos and reports, make phone calls.
	Spokesperson	Transmit information to outsiders through speeches, reports, memos.
Interpersonal	**Figurehead**	Perform ceremonial and symbolic duties such as greeting visitors, signing legal documents.
	Leader	Direct and motivate subordinates; train, counsel, and communicate with subordinates.
	Liaison	Maintain information links both inside and outside organization; use mail, phone calls, meetings.
Decisional	**Entrepreneur**	Initiate improvement projects; identify new ideas, delegate idea responsibility to others.
	Disturbance handler	Take corrective action during disputes or crises; resolve conflicts among subordinates; adapt to environmental crises.
	Resource allocator	Decide who gets resources; schedule, budget, set priorities.
	Negotiator	Represent department during negotiation of union contracts, sales, purchases, budgets; represent departmental interests.

SOURCES: Adapted from Henry Mintzberg, *The Nature of Managerial Work* (New York: Harper & Row, 1973), 92–93; and Henry Mintzberg, "Managerial Work: Analysis from Observation," *Management Science* 18 (1971), B97–B110.

decisional (managing through action). Each role represents activities that managers undertake to ultimately accomplish the functions of planning, organizing, leading, and controlling. Although it is necessary to separate the components of the manager's job to understand the different roles and activities of a manager, it is important to remember that the real job of management cannot be practiced as a set of independent parts; all the roles interact in the real world of management. As Mintzberg says, "The manager who only communicates or only conceives never gets anything done, while the manager who only 'does' ends up doing it all alone."[39]

Informational Roles. Informational roles describe the activities used to maintain and develop an information network. General managers spend about 75 percent of their time talking to other people. The *monitor* role involves seeking current information from many sources. The manager acquires information from others and scans written materials to stay well informed. John Chambers, CEO of Cisco Systems, spends about 50 percent of his time working directly with customers, asking what the company is doing right and what it could be doing better.[40] The *disseminator* and *spokesperson* roles are just the opposite: The manager transmits current information to others, both inside and outside the organization, who can use it. With the trend toward empowerment of lower-level employees, many managers are sharing as much information as possible. A recent example of the spokesperson role is Donald Carty, CEO of American Airlines, who tried to

THE NEW WORKPLACE   Manager's Shoptalk

Do You Really Want to Be a Manager?

The first training course aspiring managers at FedEx take is called "Is Management for Me?" Becoming a manager is considered by most people to be a positive, forward-looking career move. Indeed, there are lots of appealing aspects to life as a manager. However, there are also many challenges, and not every person will be happy and fulfilled in a management position. Here are some of the issues would-be managers in the new workplace should consider before deciding they want to pursue a management career:

The increased workload. It isn't unusual for managers to work 70–80 hour weeks, and some work even longer hours. A manager's job always starts before a shift and ends hours after the shift is over. Matt Scott, a software engineer promoted to management at Fore Systems, Inc., found himself frustrated by the increasing paperwork and crowded meeting schedule.

The unrelenting sense of obligation. A manager's work is never done. Nancy Carreon, an associate partner for an architectural firm, sometimes wakes up in the middle of the night thinking about something she needs to do—so she gets up and does it. George Pollard, a senior human resources official at FedEx, says, "Managers are always on the clock. We're representatives of [the company] even when we're not at work."

The headache of responsibility for other people. A lot of people get into management because they like the idea of having power, but the reality is that many managers feel overwhelmed by the responsibility of supervising and disciplining others. Laura Kelso, who today thrives on the fast pace and responsibility of being a manager, says that the first time she had to fire someone, she agonized for weeks over how to do it. New managers are often astonished at the amount of time it takes to handle "people problems." Kelly Cannell, who quit her job as a manager, puts it this way: "What's the big deal [about managing people]? The big deal is that people are human....To be a good manager, you have to mentor them, listen to their problems, counsel them, and at the end of the day you still have your own work on your plate....Don't take the responsibility lightly, because no matter what you think, managing people is not easy."

Being caught in the middle. For many people, this is the most difficult aspect of management. Except for those in the top echelons, managers find themselves acting as a backstop, caught between upper management and the workforce. A computer software designer explains why she wanted out of management: "I didn't feel comfortable touting the company line in organizational policies and technical decisions I disagreed with. It was very hard asking folks to do things I wouldn't like to do myself, like put in gobs of overtime or travel at the drop of a hat." Even when managers disagree with the decisions of top executives, they are responsible for implementing them.

For some people, the frustrations of management aren't worth it. For others, management is a fulfilling and satisfying career choice and the emotional rewards can be great. One key to being happy as a manager may be carefully evaluating whether you can answer yes to the question, "Do I really want to be a manager?"

SOURCES: Heath Row, "Is Management for Me? *That* is the Question," *Fast Company* (February–March 1998), 50–52; Timothy D. Schellhardt, "Want to Be a Manager? Many People Say No, Calling Job Miserable," *The Wall Street Journal* (April 4, 1997), A1, A4; Matt Murray, "A Software Engineer Becomes a Manager, with Many Regrets," *The Wall Street Journal,* May 14, 1997, A1, A14; Hal Lancaster, "Managing Your Career: Nancy Carreon Works Long, Hard Weeks. Does She Need To?" *The Wall Street Journal* (May 13, 1997), B1; and Matt Murray, "Managing Your Career—The Midcareer Crisis: Am I in This Business to Become a Manager?" *The Wall Street Journal* (July 25, 2000), B1.

keep family members and the public informed as new information was received following the crash of American flight 587 in New York two months after planes had been used in terrorist attacks in the city.

Interpersonal Roles. Interpersonal roles pertain to relationships with others and are related to the human skills described earlier. The *figurehead* role involves handling ceremonial and symbolic activities for the department or organization. The manager represents the organization in his or her formal managerial capacity as the head of the unit. The presentation of employee awards by a division manager at Taco Bell is an example of the figurehead role. The *leader* role encompasses relationships with subordinates, including motivation, communication, and influence. The *liaison* role pertains to the development of information sources both inside and outside the organization. The head of Coca-Cola Co., Douglas Daft, has placed new emphasis on the liaison role because of new challenges from the environment. A health scare in Belgium that turned into a public relations nightmare, combined with a failed attempt to take over Cadbury Schwepps without European Union clearance, left Coca-Cola's relationships with European customers, officials, and organizations in tatters. Daft went on a goodwill tour from Brussels to Rome, meeting and talking with governments, investors, and employees to find out what went wrong and how to fix it.[41]

Decisional Roles. Decisional roles pertain to those events about which the manager must make a choice and take action. These roles often require conceptual as well as human skills. The *entrepreneur* role involves the initiation of change. Managers are constantly thinking about the future and how to get there.[42] Managers become aware of problems and search for improvement projects that will correct them. The *disturbance handler* role involves resolving conflicts among subordinates or between the manager's department and other departments. For example, the division manager for a large furniture manufacturer got involved in a personal dispute between two section heads. One section head was let go because he did not fit the team. The *resource allocator* role pertains to decisions about how to allocate people, time, equipment, budget, and other resources to attain desired outcomes. The manager must decide which projects receive budget allocations, which of several customer complaints receive priority, and even how to spend his or her own time. The *negotiator* role involves formal negotiations and bargaining to attain outcomes for the manager's unit of responsibility. For example, the manager meets and formally negotiates with others—a supplier about a late delivery, the controller about the need for additional budget resources, or the union about a worker grievance.

The relative emphasis a manager puts on these ten roles depends on a number of factors, such as the manager's position in the hierarchy, natural skills and abilities, type of organization, or departmental goals to be achieved. For example, Exhibit 1.5 illustrates the varying importance of the leader and liaison roles as reported in a survey of top-, middle-, and lower-level managers. Note that the importance of the leader role typically declines while the importance of the liaison role increases as a manager moves up the organizational hierarchy.

Other factors, such as changing environmental conditions, may also determine which roles are more important for a manager at any given time. For example, a top manager may regularly put more emphasis on the roles of spokesperson, figurehead, and negotiator. However, the emergence of new competitors may require more attention to the monitor role, or a severe decline in employee morale and direction may mean that the CEO has to put more emphasis on the leader role. A marketing manager may focus on interpersonal roles because of the importance of personal contacts in the marketing process, whereas a financial manager may be more likely to emphasize decisional roles such as resource allocator and negotiator. Despite these differences, all managers carry out informational, interpersonal, and decisional roles to meet the needs of the organization. Managers stay alert to needs both within and outside the organization to determine what roles are most critical at various times.

Exhibit *1.5*

Hierarchical Levels and Importance of Leader and Liaison Roles

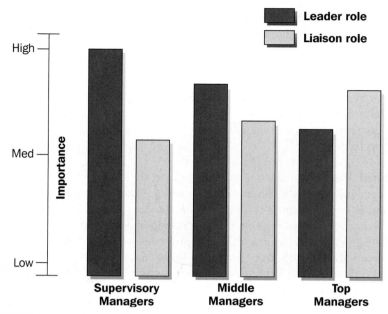

SOURCE: Based on information from A.I. Kraut, P.R. Pedigo, D.D. McKenna, and M.D. Dunnette, "The Role of the Manager: What's Really Important in Different Management Jobs," *Academy of Management Executive* 3 (1989), 286–293.

Managing in Small Businesses and Not-For-Profit Organizations

Small businesses are growing in importance. Hundreds of small businesses are opened every month by people who have found themselves squeezed out of the corporation due to downsizing or who voluntarily leave the corporate world to seek a slower pace and a healthier balance between work and family life. Many small businesses are opened by women or minorities who found limited opportunities for advancement in large corporations. In addition, the Internet has opened new avenues for small business formation. The huge wave of dot-com start-ups in the late 1990s was driven not just by dreams of wealth, but also by the desire of people to get out of big corporations and start something new and exciting.

The environment for small business has become increasingly complicated due to technology, globalization, government regulation, and increasing customer demands. Solid management is critical to success, but small companies sometimes have difficulty developing the managerial dexterity needed to survive in a complex environment. One survey on trends and future developments in small business found that nearly half of respondents saw inadequate management skills as a threat to their companies, as compared to less than 25 percent in larger organizations.[43] Managing in small businesses and entrepreneurial start-ups will be discussed in detail in Chapter 6.

One interesting finding is that managers in small businesses tend to emphasize roles different from those of managers in large corporations. Managers in small companies often see their most important role as spokesperson, because they must promote the small, growing company to the outside world. The entrepreneur role is also very important in small businesses, because managers must be creative and help their organizations develop new ideas to be competitive. Small-business managers tend to rate

©Gerry Gropp

John T. Chambers is the leader of Cisco Systems Inc., a San Jose, California-based company with annual revenues of more than $20 billion. Cisco is the global leader in networking for the Internet. In his inter-personal role as a leader, Chambers says that his vision is simple: "We can change the way people live and work, play and learn." This idealistic vision inspires and motivates Cisco's 35,000-plus employees worldwide. In the photo, Chambers attends a company picnic, demonstrating his emphasis on the value of employees.

lower on the leader role and on information-processing roles compared with counterparts in large corporations.

Not-for-profit organizations also represent a major application of management talent. The Red Cross, the Girl Scouts, universities, city governments, hospitals, public schools, symphonies, and art museums all require excellent management. The functions of planning, organizing, leading, and controlling apply to not-for-profits just as they do to business organizations, and managers in not-for-profits use similar skills and perform similar activities. The primary difference is that managers in businesses direct their activities toward earning money for the company, while managers in not-for-profits direct their efforts toward generating some kind of social impact. The unique characteristics and needs of not-for-profit organizations created by this distinction present unique challenges for managers.[44]

Financial resources for not-for-profits typically come from government appropriations, grants, and donations rather than from the sale of products or services to customers. In businesses, managers focus on improving the organization's products and services to increase sales revenues. In not-for-profits, however, services are typically provided to nonpaying clients, and a major problem for many organizations is securing a steady stream of funds to continue operating. Not-for-profit managers, committed to serving clients with limited resources, must focus on keeping organizational costs as low as possible.[45] Donors generally want their money to go directly to helping clients rather than for overhead costs. If not-for-profit managers can't demonstrate a highly efficient use of resources, they might have a hard time securing additional donations or government appropriations.

In addition, since not-for profit organizations do not have a conventional *bottom line*, managers may struggle with the question of what constitutes results and effectiveness. Whereas it is easy to measure dollars and cents, not-for-profits have to measure intangibles such as "improve public health" or "make a difference in the lives of the disenfranchised." It is more difficult to gauge the performance of employees and managers when the goal is providing a public service rather than increasing sales and profits. Managers in not-for-profits must market their services to attract not only clients but also the volunteers and donors on whom they depend. However, these volunteers cannot be supervised and controlled in the same way a business manager deals with employees.

The roles defined by Mintzberg also apply to not-for-profit managers, but these may differ somewhat. We might expect managers in not-for-profits to place more emphasis on the roles of spokesperson (to "sell" the organization to donors and the public), leader (to build a mission driven community of employees and volunteers), and resource allocator (to distribute government resources or grant funds that are often assigned top-down).

Managers in all organizations—large corporations, small businesses, and not-for-profit organizations—carefully integrate and adjust the management functions and roles to meet new challenges within their own circumstances and keep their organizations healthy. One way in which many organizations are meeting new challenges is through increased use of the Internet. Some government agencies are using the Web to cut bureaucracy, improve efficiency, and save money, as described in this chapter's Leading Online box.

Management and the New Workplace

The world of organizations and management is changing. Rapid environmental shifts are causing fundamental transformations that have a dramatic impact on the manager's job. These transformations are reflected in the transition to a new workplace, as illustrated in Exhibit 1.6. The primary characteristic of the new workplace is that it is centered around bits rather than atoms—*information* and ideas rather than machines and physical assets. The shift from an industrial age to an information age has altered the nature of work, employees, and the workplace itself.[46] The old workplace was characterized by routine, specialized tasks and standardized control procedures.

Exhibit *1.6*

The Transition to a New Workplace

	The Old Workplace	The New Workplace
Characteristics		
Resources	Atoms—physical assets	Bits—information
Work	Structured, localized	Flexible, virtual
Workers	Dependable employees	Empowered employees, free agents
Forces on Organizations		
Technology	Mechanical	Digital, e-business
Markets	Local, domestic	Global, including Internet
Workforce	Homogenous	Diverse
Values	Stability, efficiency	Change, speed
Events	Calm, predictable	Turbulent, more frequent crises
Management Competencies		
Leadership	Autocratic	Dispersed, empowering
Focus	Profits	Connection to customers, employees
Doing Work	By individuals	By teams
Relationships	Conflict, competition	Collaboration
Design	Efficient performance	Experimentation, learning organization

Leading Online

Click Here for Lower Taxes

Government agencies are often thought of as plodding, inefficient bureaucracies that waste the public's time as well as money. But new ideas are changing that perception, as some government agencies apply Internet technology to save taxpayers money and make their lives easier.

The Internal Revenue Service *(http://www.irs.gov)* provides one of the best examples in the government or corporate world of a Web site that is central to the organization's mission. Distributing tax forms has always been an expensive logistical nightmare for the IRS. Hordes of form pullers, envelope stuffers, label-addressers, and so forth are needed to process the millions of mail-in requests for various tax publications and forms. The cost of handling a single request is around three dollars. The IRS recognized the problem and made the distribution of tax forms a major focus when it opened its Web site five years ago. Today, more than 100 million tax forms are downloaded directly from the site, with each request costing the IRS (and thus the taxpayers) only a fraction of a penny. Many of the workers at the distribution facility have been retrained for other assignments because business is down so sharply.

State governments are also tapping into the power of the Web. In the state of Washington, the Access Washington Web site *(http://www.access.wa.gov)* offers more than 200 electronic resources and services. People can file for unemployment benefits, apply for various permits, transact workers' compensation claims, pay quarterly business taxes, reserve a state park campsite, find a nursing home, or even check a potential nanny for a possible criminal record. Managed by the state's Department of Information Services (DIS), Access Washington is recognized as the most advanced state site in the nation. By automating routine transactions and requests for information, Access Washington not only eases the burden on agency personnel but also saves people long hours of standing in line or waiting on the phone. Another interesting point for taxpayers is that DIS is completely self-supporting. The department supports itself by selling computers and electronic equipment to schools, nonprofits, and government agencies, and by providing a range of technology services, including Web hosting. One recent year, $7.9 million in profits were plowed back into developing the Web site and other new services. DIS director Steve Kolodney believes technology is a tool that can make people's lives easier and better. He's striving to shatter the image of government workers as paper-shufflers and replace it with one of real people providing real and valuable services to the public.

SOURCES: Les Gomes, "Fix It and They Will Come; E-commerce Isn't Dead, Just Broken," *The Wall Street Journal* (February 12, 2001), R4, and Missy Sullivan, "Red Tape Buster," *Forbes* (Best of the Web), (May 21, 2001), 42.

Employees typically perform their jobs in one specific company facility, such as an automobile factory located in Detroit or an insurance agency located in Des Moines. The organization is coordinated and controlled through the vertical hierarchy, with decision-making authority residing with upper-level managers.

In the new workplace, by contrast, work is free-flowing and *flexible*. The shift is most obvious in e-commerce and Internet-based organizations, which have to respond to changing markets and competition at a second's notice. However, all organizations are facing the need for greater speed and flexibility. *Empowered employees* are expected to seize opportunities and solve problems as they emerge. The workplace is organized around networks rather than rigid hierarchies, and work is often *virtual*. Thanks to modern information and communications technology, employees can often perform their jobs from home or another remote location, at any time of the day or night. Flexible hours, telecommuting, and virtual teams are increasingly popular ways of working that require new skills from managers. There are an estimated 9 million telecommuters in the United States, for example, and the number is expected to increase over the next few years. AT&T has 7,500 fully mobile workers.[47]

Teams in today's organizations may also include outside contractors, suppliers, customers, competitors, and *free agents* who are not affiliated with a specific organization but work on a project-by-project basis. The valued worker is one who learns quickly, shares knowledge, and is comfortable with risk, change, and ambiguity.

Forces on Organizations

The most striking change now affecting organizations and management is *technology*. In 1995, there were about 238 million computers in use and 39 million Internet users on a global basis. Five years later, the numbers had expanded to an estimated 530 million computers and more than 316 million Internet users.[48] There's a global technology explosion, and its impact on organizations and management is astonishing. Organizations are increasingly using *digital networking* technologies to tie together employees and company partners in far-flung operations. The growing use of *wireless technology* is expanding options even further, truly enabling people to work from practically anywhere, not just from a computer hooked to a company network. Wireless remote access to the Internet, for example, already enables salespeople to send and receive instant messages on hand-held devices from any location, helping them quickly close deals.[49]

One of the biggest technological advances is the *Internet*, which is transforming the way business is done. Only a few years ago, the Internet was still little more than a curiosity to many managers, but how things have changed. In January 1999, Jack Welch urged managers at General Electric to "destroyyourbusiness.com," and since then GE has been using the Web to cut layers of management, promote teamwork, improve customer service, and save money.[50] Companies develop *intranets* and *extranets*, communication systems that use Internet technology and tie employees, managers, free agents, customers, suppliers, partners, subcontractors, and shareholders together in a seamless information flow. Organizations are turning to *e-business* ideas and models to increase speed, cut costs, improve quality, and better serve customers.

The Internet and other new technologies are also tied closely to *globalization*, another force that is significantly affecting organizations. People around the world are connected in the flow of information, money, ideas, and products, and interdependencies are increasing. The French tire manufacturer Michelin gets 35 percent of its revenues in the United States, while U.S.-based Johnson & Johnson does 43 percent of its business abroad.[51] Schering AG, the German pharmaceuticals company, employees 56 percent of its 22,000 workers outside its home country.[52] Customers today operate globally and they expect organizations to provide worldwide service.

Managers have to understand cross-cultural patterns, and they often work with virtual team members from many different countries. *Diversity* of the population and the workforce has become a fact of life for all organizations. Talented, educated knowledge workers seek opportunities all over the world, just as organizations search the world for the best minds to help them compete in a global economy. The general population of the United States, and thus of the workforce, is also growing more ethnically and racially diverse. Generational diversity is another powerful force in today's workplace, with employees of all ages working together on teams and projects in a way rarely seen in the past. Although the workforce in general is growing older with the aging of the baby boomers and there is a trend toward staying in the workforce longer, Generation X employees, now in their late 20s and 30s, are having a profound impact on the workplace. And members of the next generation, Generation Y, which rivals the baby boomers in size, are beginning to enter the workforce.

In the face of these transformations, organizations are learning to value *change* and *speed* over stability and efficiency. The fundamental paradigm during much of the twentieth century was a belief that things can be stable. In contrast, the new paradigm recognizes change and chaos as the natural order of things.[53] Events in today's world are *turbulent* and *unpredictable*, with both small and large crises occurring on a more frequent basis.

In the face of these transitions, managers must rethink their approach to organizing, directing, and motivating workers. According to one consultant, many managers who have grown accustomed to the old workplace complain that employees no longer play by the rules. The consultant's response: "Why should they play by the rules? The rules are dead."[54]

New Management Competencies

As discussed earlier in the chapter, not all managers' jobs are the same. Managers rely on varied skills and perform different activities, depending on hierarchical level and job responsibilities. For all managers, however, human skills are becoming increasingly important.[55] In a survey of managers on their views of how the Internet has affected management, for example, the majority considered communicating effectively, retaining talented employees, and motivating workers to be essential management skills for the Internet world.[56] Although these abilities have always been important to managers, they take on added significance today, particularly when employees are dispersed and working in a virtual environment.

Today's best managers give up their command-and-control mindset to embrace ambiguity and create organizations that are fast, flexible, adaptable, and relationship-oriented. *Leadership* is dispersed throughout the organization, and managers empower others to gain the benefit of their ideas and creativity. The model of managers controlling workers no longer applies in a workplace where employee brainpower is more important than physical assets.[57] Moreover, managers often supervise employees who are scattered in various locations, requiring a new approach to leadership that focuses more on mentoring and providing direction and support than on giving orders and ensuring that they are followed.

Rather than a single-minded focus on profits, today's managers must recognize the critical importance of staying *connected to employees and customers*. The Internet has given increased knowledge and power to customers, so organizations have to remain flexible and adaptable to respond quickly to changing demands or competition. In some e-commerce organizations, managers have almost totally ignored profits in favor of building customer relationships. Although all organizations have to be concerned with profits sooner or later, as managers of numerous failed dot-coms learned, the emphasis these companies put on developing customers and relationships is a reflection of trends affecting all organizations.

Team-building skills are crucial for today's managers. Teams of front-line employees who work directly with customers have become the basic building block of organizations. Instead of managing a department of employees, many managers act as team leaders of ever-shifting, temporary projects. At SEI Investments, all work is distributed among 140 teams. Some are permanent, such as those that serve major customers or focus on specific markets, but many are designed to work on short-term projects or problems. Computer linkups, called *pythons*, drop from the ceiling. As people change assignments, they just unplug their pythons, move their desks and chairs to a new location, plug into a new python, and get to work on the next project.[58]

Success in the new workplace depends on the strength and quality of collaborative *relationships*. Partnerships, both within the organization and with outside customers, suppliers, and even competitors, are recognized as the key to a winning organization. New ways of working emphasize collaboration across functions and hierarchical levels as well as with other companies. E-business models that digitally link customers, suppliers, partners, and other stakeholders require managers to assess and manage relationships far beyond the confines of the traditional organization.

An important management challenge in the new workplace is to build a *learning organization* by creating an organizational climate that values experimentation and risk taking, applies current technology, tolerates mistakes and failure, and rewards nontraditional thinking and the sharing of knowledge. Everyone in the organization participates in identifying and solving problems, enabling the organization to continuously experiment, improve, and increase its capability. The role of managers is not to make decisions, but to create learning capability, where everyone is free to experiment and learn what works best.

Application: Managing Crises and Unexpected Events

Many managers may dream of working in an organization and a world where life seems relatively calm, orderly, and predictable. Today's world, though, is marked by increasing turbulence and disorder. Organizations face various levels of crisis every day—everything from the loss of computer data, to charges of racial discrimination, to a factory fire, to a flu epidemic. However, these organizational crises have been compounded by crises on a more global level. Consider a few of the major events that have affected U.S. companies within the last few years: an energy crisis in California that led to a virtual state takeover of the energy market; the massacre at Columbine High School, which prompted schools all over the country to form crisis teams to deal with school violence; the grounding of Concorde jets for 14 months after the fiery crash of an Air France Concorde in Paris. And then the U.S. was hit with the most devastating and far-reaching event of the twenty-first century to date: the September 11, 2001, terrorist attacks in New York and Washington that destroyed the World Trade Center, seriously damaged the Pentagon, killed thousands of people, and interrupted business around the world. The subsequent bombings in Afghanistan, continuing uncertainty over terrorist activities, and a deepening recession continue to affect companies worldwide. Anthrax scares altered companies' advertising and marketing plans as they weighed the public's perceptions of the U.S. mail. Organizations scrambled to implement videoconferencing as airport security checks stretched travel time beyond the point where business flights made economic sense.

Dealing with the unexpected has always been part of the manager's job, but our world has become so fast, interconnected, and complex that unexpected events happen more frequently and often with greater and more painful consequences. All of the new management skills and competencies we have discussed are important to managers in such an environment. In addition, crisis management is an emerging need that places further demands on today's managers. As California Governor Gray Davis put it, "Extraordinary times . . . require extraordinary leadership."[59] Some of the most recent thinking on crisis management suggests the importance of five leadership skills.[60]

1. Stay calm.

2. Be visible.

3. Put people before business.

4. Tell the truth.

5. Know when to get back to business.

Stay Calm. A leader's emotions are contagious, so leaders have to stay calm, focused, and optimistic about the future. Perhaps the most important part of a manager's job in a crisis situation is to absorb people's fears and uncertainties. Leaders have to suppress their own fears, doubts, and pain to comfort others. Although they acknowledge the danger and difficulties, they remain rock-steady and hopeful, which gives comfort, inspiration, and hope to others.

Be Visible. When people's worlds have become ambiguous and uncertain, they need to feel that someone is in control. George W. Bush got off to a shaky start as a crisis leader following the September 11 terrorist attacks because people didn't know where he was. As soon as he became visible, practically the entire country rallied behind him.

Put People Before Business. The companies that weather a crisis best, whether the crisis is large or small, are those in which managers make people and human feelings their top priority. Top managers of Thomson Financial, which had about 200 employees in the World Trade Center and 1,800 elsewhere in downtown Manhattan, spent basically no time at all on business issues for the first few days after September 11, concentrating instead on the physical and emotional needs of employees and helping the families of the eleven Thomson workers lost in the attacks.[61]

Tell the Truth. Managers should get as much information from as many diverse sources as they can, do their best to determine the facts, and then be open and straightforward about what's going on. Following the 2001 collapse of Enron Corp. and charges of unethical and possibly illegal activities, top managers at Enron compounded the crisis by destroying documents, refusing to be straightforward with employees and the media, and stonewalling investigators by pleading the fifth amendment. Managers at Arthur Andersen, Enron's accounting firm, also reportedly handled the crisis by destroying documents and pleading the fifth.

Know When to Get Back to Business. Although managers should first deal with the physical and emotional needs of people, they also need to get back to business as soon as possible. The company has to keep going, and most people want to be a part of the rebuilding process, to feel that they have a home with the company and something to look forward to. The rejuvenation of the business is a sign of hope and an inspiration to employees.

Moments of crisis also present excellent opportunities for looking forward and using the emotional energy that has emerged to build a better company.

Crisis management is an important aspect of any manager's job, particularly in today's turbulent times. This is a challenging time to be entering the field of management. Throughout this book, you will learn much more about the new workplace, about the new and dynamic roles managers are playing in the twenty-first century, and about how you can be an effective manager in a complex, ever-changing world.

■ Summary and Management Solution

This chapter introduced a number of important concepts and described the changing nature of management. High performance requires the efficient and effective use of organizational resources through the four management functions of planning, organizing, leading, and controlling. To perform the four functions, managers need three skills—conceptual, human, and technical. Conceptual skills are more important at the top of the hierarchy; human skills are important at all levels; and technical skills are most important for first-line managers.

Two characteristics of managerial work also were explained in the chapter: (1) Managerial activities involve variety, fragmentation, and brevity and (2) Managers perform a great deal of work at an unrelenting pace. Managers are expected to perform activities associated with ten roles: the informational roles of monitor, disseminator, and spokesperson; the interpersonal roles of figurehead, leader, and liaison; and the decisional roles of entrepreneur, disturbance handler, resource allocator, and negotiator.

These management characteristics apply to small businesses, entrepreneurial start-ups, and not-for-profit organizations just as they do in large corporations. In addition, they are being applied in a new workplace and a rapidly changing world. In the new workplace, work is free-flowing and flexible to encourage speed and adaptation, and empowered employees are expected to seize opportunities and solve problems. The workplace is organized around networks rather than vertical hierarchies, and work is often virtual. These changing characteristics have resulted from forces such as advances in technology and e-business, globalization, increased diversity, and a growing emphasis on change and speed over stability and efficiency. Managers need new skills and competencies in this new environment. Leadership is dispersed and empowering. Customer relationships are

critical, and most work is done by teams that work directly with customers. In the new workplace, managers focus on building relationships, which may include customers, partners, and suppliers. In addition, they strive to build learning capability throughout the organization. An emerging need is for leadership during crises and unexpected events. Managers in crisis situations should stay calm, be visible, put people before business, tell the truth, and know when to get back to business.

An excellent example of a leader during a crisis is Kenneth Chenault, described at the beginning of the chapter. Even though he was stuck in Salt Lake City, Chenault took control, gathering information, talking with managers back at headquarters hourly, and taking steps to ensure the safety of employees. "He was there, and he was in the middle of it," said one manager. From the moment the crisis began, Chenault remained calm, steady, and focused, dealing with personal losses, refusing to complain about his company's problems, listening to employees and sharing their grief, taking care of customers, doing favors for other companies, and getting the company back to business as quickly as possible. Every decision he made was guided by concerns for employees and customer service. After ordering the evacuation, his next move was to have the call center track down each and every employee. Then he turned to customers, helping 560,000 stranded American Express cardholders get home, waiving delinquent fees on late payments, and increasing credit limits if customers needed it. When he returned to New York, Chenault gathered his employees together at the Paramount Theater, where he expressed his own despair, anger, and sadness and gave employees a chance to do the same. At the end, he told them, "I represent the best company and the best people in the world. In fact, you are my strength, and I love you." Thus began the long healing process. Chenault continued to be a highly visible leader. In his visits to the various temporary offices, he exchanged hugs and handshakes, tears and laughter. When President Bush visited New York, Chenault was there, stressing the need for greater airport security, joining with New York Mayor Rudolph Giuliani and Governor George Pataki to ask for more aid, and meeting with other business leaders to support the president's plan for economic recovery. During all this time, Chenault was also studying his company's financial problems and how to help the organization survive this extremely difficult period in its history. "If you're the leader, you've got to feel you're the person where the decisions rest," he says. "This is no time for excuses."[62]

■ Discussion Questions

1. Assume you are a research scientist at a biotechnology company, collaborating with a marketing manager on a major product modification. You notice that every memo you receive from her has been copied to senior management. At every company function, she spends time talking to the big shots. You are also aware that sometimes when you are slaving away over the project, she is playing golf with senior managers. What is your evaluation of her behavior?

2. How do you feel about having a manager's responsibility in today's world characterized by uncertainty, ambiguity, and sudden changes or threats from the environment? Describe some skills and qualities that are important to managers under these conditions.

3. What similarities do you see among the four management functions of planning, organizing, leading, and controlling? Do you think these functions are related—that is, is a manager who performs well in one function likely to perform well in the others?

4. Why do some organizations seem to have a new CEO every year or two, whereas others have top leaders who stay with the company for many years (e.g., Jack Welch's 20 years as CEO at General Electric)? What factors about the manager or about the company might account for this difference?

5. What is the difference between efficiency and effectiveness? Which is more important for performance? Can an organization succeed in both simultaneously?

6. What changes in management functions and skills might occur as one is promoted up the management hierarchy? How can managers acquire the new skills?

7. If managerial work is characterized by variety, fragmentation, and brevity, how do managers perform basic management functions such as planning, which would seem to require reflection and analysis?

8. A college professor told her students, "The purpose of a management course is to teach students *about* management, not to teach them to be managers." Do you agree or disagree with this statement? Discuss.

9. Describe the characteristics of the new workplace. How do these characteristics compare to those of an organization in which you have worked?

10. How could the teaching of management change to prepare future managers to deal with workforce diversity? With empowerment? Do you think diversity and empowerment will have a substantial impact on organizations in the future? Explain.

■ Management in Practice: Experiential Exercise

Management Aptitude Questionnaire
Rate each of the following questions according to the following scale:

	1 I never am like this.	2 I rarely am like this.	3 I some- times am like this.	4 I often am like this.	5 I always am like this.
1. When I have a number of tasks or homework to do, I set priorities and organize the work around deadlines.	1	2	3	4	5
2. Most people would describe me as a good listener.	1	2	3	4	5

	1	2	3	4	5
3. When I am deciding on a particular course of action for myself (such as hobbies to pursue, languages to study, which job to take, special projects to be involved in), I typically consider the long-term (three years or more) implications of what I would choose to do.	1	2	3	4	5
4. I prefer technical or quantitative courses rather than those involving literature, psychology, or sociology.	1	2	3	4	5
5. When I have a serious disagreement with someone, I hang in there and talk it out until it is completely resolved.	1	2	3	4	5
6. When I have a project or assignment, I really get into the details rather than the "big picture" issues.*	5	4	3	2	1
7. I would rather sit in front of my computer than spend a lot of time with people.	1	2	3	4	5
8. I try to include others in activities or when there are discussions.	1	2	3	4	5
9. When I take a course, I relate what I am learning to other courses I have taken or concepts I have learned elsewhere.	1	2	3	4	5
10. When somebody makes a mistake, I want to correct the person and let her or him know the proper answer or approach.	5	4	3	2	1
11. I think it is better to be efficient with my time when talking with someone, rather than worry about the other person's needs, so that I can get on with my real work.	1	2	3	4	5
12. I know my long-term vision of career, family, and other activities and have thought it over carefully.	1	2	3	4	5
13. When solving problems, I would much rather analyze some data or statistics than meet with a group of people.	1	2	3	4	5
14. When I am working on a group project and someone doesn't pull a fair share of the load, I am more likely to complain to my friends rather than confront the slacker.*	5	4	3	2	1
15. Talking about ideas or concepts can get me really enthused or excited.	1	2	3	4	5
16. The type of management course for which this book is used is really a waste of time.	1	2	3	4	5
17. I think it is better to be polite and not to hurt people's feelings.*	5	4	3	2	1
18. Data or things interest me more than people.	1	2	3	4	5

Scoring key

Add the total points for the following sections. Note that starred * items are reverse scored, as such:

1 I always am like this.
2 I often am like this.
3 I sometimes am like this.
4 I rarely am like this.
5 I never am like this.

1, 3, 6, 9, 12, 15	**C**onceptual skills total score _____
2, 5, 8, 10, 14, 17	**H**uman skills total score _____
4, 7, 11, 13, 16, 18	**T**echnical skills total score _____

These skills are three abilities needed to be a good manager. Ideally, a manager should be strong (though not necessarily equal) in all three. Anyone noticeably weaker in any of the skills should take courses and read to build up that skill. For further background on the three skills, please refer to the model in pages 10–12.

*reverse scoring item

Note: This exercise was contributed by Dorothy Marcic.

Management in Practice: Ethical Dilemma

Can Management Afford to Look the Other Way?

Harry Rull had been with Shellington Pharmaceuticals for 30 years. After a tour of duty in the various plants and 7 years overseas, Harry was back at headquarters, looking forward to his new role as vice president of U.S. Marketing.

Two weeks into his new job, Harry received some unsettling news about one of the managers under his supervision. Over casual lunch conversation, the director of human resources mentioned that Harry should expect a phone call about Roger Jacobs, Manager of New Product Development. Jacobs had a history of being "pretty horrible" to his subordinates, she said, and one disgruntled employee had asked to speak to someone in senior management. After lunch, Harry did some follow-up work. Jacobs's performance reviews had been stellar, but his personnel file also contained a large number of notes documenting charges of Jacobs's mistreatment of subordinates. The complaints ranged from "inappropriate and derogatory remarks" to subsequently dropped charges of sexual harassment. What was more disturbing was that the amount as well as the severity of complaints had increased with each of Jacobs's ten years with Shellington.

When Harry questioned the company president about the issue, he was told, "Yeah, he's had some problems, but you can't just replace someone with an eye for new products. You're a bottom-line guy; you understand why we let these things slide." Not sure how to handle the situation, Harry met briefly with Jacobs and reminded him to "keep the team's morale up." Just after the meeting, Sally Barton from HR called to let him know the problem she'd mentioned over lunch had been worked out. However, she warned, another employee had now come forward demanding that her complaints be addressed by senior management.

What Do You Do?

1. Ignore the problem. Jacobs's contributions to new product development are too valuable to risk losing him, and the problems over the past ten years have always worked themselves out anyway. No sense starting something that could make you look bad.

2. Launch a full-scale investigation of employee complaints about Jacobs, and make Jacobs aware that the documented history over the past ten years has put him on thin ice.

3. Meet with Jacobs and the employee to try to resolve the current issue, then start working with Sally Barton and other senior managers to develop stronger policies regarding sexual harassment and treatment of employees, including clear-cut procedures for handling complaints.

SOURCE: Based on Doug Wallace, "A Talent for Mismanagement," *What Would You Do? Business Ethics*, Vol II (November–December 1992), 3–4.

Surf the Net

1. **Web Research.** You will be asked in many of the "Surf the Net" exercises throughout the text to locate information on the Web. This exercise is designed to help you improve your Web research skills. After spending some time at one of the Web Tutorial links listed below, outline three new ideas you discovered that would help you to find what you are looking for on the Web.
   UC Berkeley's Teaching Library Internet Workshops:
   http://www.lib.berkeley.edu/TeachingLib/Guides/Internet/FindInfo.html
   University of South Carolina's Basic Tutorial on Searching the Web:
   http://www.sc.edu/beaufort/library/bones.html

2. **Management Occupations.** The U.S. Department of Labor's Bureau of Labor Statistics uses the Standard Occupational Classification (SOC) system to classify workers into one of more than 820 occupations according to their occupational definition. To facilitate classification, occupations requiring similar job duties, skills, education, or experience are combined to form 23 major groups. Go to *http://stats.bls.gov/soc/soc_majo.htm* to see the 23 major groups; choose the link for "Management Occupations." Select one management occupation of interest to you under each of the four minor groups

(11-1000 Top Executives; 11-2000 Advertising, Marketing, Promotions, Public Relations, and Sales Managers; 11-3000 Operations Specialties Managers; and 11-9000 Other Management Occupations). List the SOC number, occupation title, and description for the four occupations you selected.

3. **Ten Manager Roles.** Find and read a feature story on a current leader of an organization. Look for examples of the leader performing activities from those listed in Exhibit 1.4, "Ten Manager Roles." On your sheet of paper, identify the source of your article, the leader featured, and the roles you identified the individual fulfilling, along with a brief description of the activity the individual performed. Use any of the links below to access current issues of business periodicals that often include feature stories on organizational leaders.
   http://www.business2.com
   http://www.businessweek.com
   http://www.fastcompany.com
   http://www.forbes.com
   http://www.fortune.com
   http://www.inc.com
   http://www.herring.com

■ Case for Critical Analysis

Electra-Quik

Barbara Russell, a manufacturing vice president, walked into the monthly companywide meeting with a light step and a hopefulness she hadn't felt in a long time. The company's new, dynamic CEO was going to announce a new era of empowerment at Electra-Quik, an 80-year-old, publicly held company that had once been a leading manufacturer and retailer of electrical products and supplies. In recent years, the company experienced a host of problems: market share was declining in the face of increased foreign and domestic competition; new product ideas were few and far between; departments such as manufacturing and sales barely spoke to one another; morale was at an all-time low, and many employees were actively seeking other jobs. Everyone needed a dose of hope.

Martin Griffin, who had been hired to revive the failing company, briskly opened the meeting with a challenge: "As we face increasing competition, we need new ideas, new energy, new spirit to make this company great. And the source for this change is you—each one of you." He then went on to explain that under the new empowerment campaign, employees would be getting more information about how the company was run and would be able to work with their fellow employees in new and creative ways. Martin proclaimed a new era of trust and cooperation at Electra-Quik. Barbara felt the excitement stirring within her; but as she looked around the room, she saw many of the other employees, including her friend Harry, rolling their eyes. "Just another pile of corporate crap," Harry said later. "One minute they try downsizing, the next reengineering. Then they dabble in restructuring. Now Martin wants to push empowerment. Garbage like empowerment isn't a substitute for hard work and a little faith in the people who have been with this company for years. We made it great once, and we can do it again. Just get out of our way." Harry had been a manufacturing engineer with Electra-Quik for more than 20 years. Barbara knew he was extremely loyal to the company, but he—and a lot of others like him—were going to be an obstacle to the empowerment efforts.

Top management assigned selected managers to several problem-solving teams to come up with ideas for implementing the empowerment campaign. Barbara loved her assignment as team leader of the manufacturing team, working on ideas to improve how retail stores got the merchandise they needed when they needed it. The team thrived, and trust blossomed among the members. They even spent nights and weekends working to complete their report. They were proud of their ideas, which they believed were innovative but easily achievable: permit a manager to follow a product from design through sales to customers; allow salespeople to refund up to $500 worth of merchandise on the spot; make information available to salespeople about future products; and swap sales and manufacturing personnel for short periods to let them get to know one another's jobs.

When the team presented its report to department heads, Martin Griffin was enthusiastic. But shortly into the meeting he had to excuse himself because of a late-breaking deal with a major hardware store chain. With Martin absent, the department heads rapidly formed a wall of resistance. The director of human resources complained that the ideas for personnel changes would destroy the carefully crafted job categories that had just been completed. The finance department argued that allowing salespeople to make $500 refunds would create a gold mine for unethical customers and salespeople. The legal department warned that providing information to salespeople about future products would invite industrial spying.

The team members were stunned. As Barbara mulled over the latest turn of events, she considered her options: keep her mouth shut; take a chance and confront Martin about her sincerity in making empowerment work; push slowly for reform and work for gradual support from the other teams; or look for another job and leave a company she really cared about. Barbara realized there would be no easy choices and no easy answers.

Questions

1. How might top management have done a better job changing Electra-Quik into a new kind of organization? What might they do now to get the empowerment process back on track?

2. Can you think of ways Barbara could have avoided the problems her team faced in the meeting with department heads?

3. If you were Barbara Russell, what would you do now? Why?

SOURCE: Based on Lawrence R. Rothstein, "The Empowerment Effort That Came Undone," *Harvard Business Review* (January–February 1995), 20–31.

■ Endnotes

1. John A. Byrne and Heather Timmons, "Tough Times for a New CEO," *BusinessWeek*, (October 29, 2001), 64–70; and Patrick McGeehan, "Sailing into a Sea of Troubles," *The New York Times* (October 5, 2001), C1, C4.

2. Nicholas Imparato and Oren Harari, *Jumping the Curve: Innovation and Strategic Choice in an Age of Transition* (San Francisco: Jossey-Bass Publishers, 1994); Tom Broersma, "In Search of the Future," *Training and Development*

(January 1995), 38–43; Rahul Jacob, "The Struggle to Create an Organization for the Twenty-First Century," *Fortune* (April 3, 1995) 90–99; and Charles Handy, *The Age of Paradox* (Boston: Harvard Business School Press, 1994).

3. Keith H. Hammonds, "The Monroe Doctrine," *Fast Company*, (October 1999), 230–236; and David Beardsley, "This Company Doesn't Brake for (Sacred) Cows," *Fast Company* (August 1998), 66–68.

4. John Jurgensen, "After Garcia's Death, Dead's Legacy Thrives," Associated Press story in *Johnson City Press* (August 9, 2000), 16; David E. Bowen and Caren Siehl, "Sweet Music: Grateful Employees, Grateful Customers, 'Grate' Profits," *Journal of Management Inquiry* (June 1992), 154–156; and Leslie Brokaw, "The Dead Have Customers, Too," *Inc.* (September 1994), 90–92.

5. James A. F. Stoner and R. Edward Freeman, *Management*, 4th ed. (Englewood Cliffs, N.J.: Prentice-Hall, 1989).

6. Peter F. Drucker, *Management Tasks, Responsibilities, Practices* (New York: Harper & Row, 1974).

7. John R. Engen, "Cross-Sell Campaign," *Banking Strategies* (November–December 2001), 34.

8. Justin Martin, "The Man Who Boogied Away a Billion," *Fortune* (December 23, 1996), 89–100.

9. C.J. Prince, "Cool Hand Kovacevich," *Chief Executive* (May 2001), 22–28.

10. Heath Row, "Fearless in Philly" (Company of Friends column), *Fast Company* (June 2001), 36.

11. Eryn Brown, "Nine Ways to Win on the Web," *Fortune* (May 24, 1999), 112–125.

12. Jaclyn Fierman, "Winning Ideas from Maverick Managers," *Fortune* (February 6, 1995), 66–80.

13. Kathleen Collins, "E-Publishing Through the Ages," *Working Woman* (Special Internet Issue, 2000), 22; Curtis Sittenfeld, "Hope Is a Weapon," *Fast Company* (February–March 1999), 179–184.

14. Anna Bernasek, "Pattern for Prosperity," *Fortune* (October 2, 2000), 100–108.

15. Ibid.

16. Martha Brannigan and Eleena De Lisser, "Cost Cutting at Delta Raises the Stock Price But Lowers the Service," *The Wall Street Journal* (June 20, 1996), A1.

17. Robert L. Katz, "Skills of an Effective Administrator," *Harvard Business Review* 52 (September–October 1974), 90–102.

18. Brenton Schlender, "How Bill Gates Keeps the Magic Going," *Fortune* (June 18, 1990), 82–89.

19. Robert D. Hof with Kathy Rebello and Peter Burrows, "Scott McNealy's Rising Sun," *BusinessWeek* (January 22, 1996), 66–73.

20. Diane Brady, "Wanted: Eclectic Visionary with a Sense of Humor," *BusinessWeek* (August 28, 2000), 143–144.

21. Mark Gimein, "CEOs Who Manage Too Much," *Fortune* (September 4, 2000), 235–242.

22. Sue Shellenbarger, "From Our Readers: The Bosses That Drove Me to Quit My Job", *The Wall Street Journal* (February 7, 2000), B1.

23. Eric Matson, "Congratulations, You're Promoted. (Now What?)," *Fast Company* (June–July 1997), 116–130.

24. Heath Row, "Force Play" (Company of Friends column), *Fast Company* (March 2001), 46.

25. Charles Fishman, "Sweet Company," *Fast Company* (February 2001), 136–145.

26. Christopher A. Bartlett and Sumantra Ghoshal, "Changing the Role of Top Management: Beyond Systems to People," *Harvard Business Review* (May–June 1995), 132–142; and Sumantra Ghoshal and Christopher A. Bartlett, "Changing the Role of Top Management: Beyond Structure to Processes," *Harvard Business Review* (January–February 1995), 86–96.

27. Polly LaBarre, "The Company Without Limits," *Fast Company* (September 1999), 160–186.

28. Jenny C. McCune, "Management's Brave New World," *Management Review* (October 1997), 10–14; "Middle Managers Are Back—But Now They're 'High-Impact Players,'" *The Wall Street Journal* (April 14, 1998), B1; and Geoffrey Colvin, "Revenge of the Nerds," *Fortune* (March 2, 1998), 223–224.

29. Steven W. Floyd and Bill Wooldridge, "Dinosaurs or Dynamos? Recognizing Middle Management's Strategic Role," *Academy of Management Executive* 8, no. 4 (1994), 47–57.

30. Thomas A. Stewart, "The Corporate Jungle Spawns a New Species: The Project Manager," *Fortune* (July 10, 1995), 179–180.

31. Henry Mintzberg, *The Nature of Managerial Work* (New York: Harper & Row, 1973); and Mintzberg, "Rounding Out the Manager's Job," *Sloan Management Review* (Fall 1994), 11–26.

32. Robert E. Kaplan, "Trade Routes: The Manager's Network of Relationships," *Organizational Dynamics* (Spring 1984), 37–52; Rosemary Stewart, "The Nature of Management: A Problem for Management Education," *Journal of Management Studies* 21 (1984), 323–330; John P. Kotter, "What Effective General Managers Really Do," *Harvard Business Review* (November–December 1982), 156–167; and Morgan W. McCall, Jr., Ann M. Morrison, and Robert L. Hannan, "Studies of Managerial Work: Results and Methods" (Technical Report No. 9, Center for Creative Leadership, Greensboro, N.C., 1978).

33. Jennifer Couzin, "Tick, Tick, Tick," *The Industry Standard* (April 16, 2001), 62–67.

34. Henry Mintzberg, "Managerial Work: Analysis from Observation," *Management Science* 18 (1971), B97–B110.

35. Based on Carol Saunders and Jack William Jones, "Temporal Sequences in Information Acquisition for Decision Making: A Focus on Source and Medium," *Academy of Management Review* 15 (1990), 29–46; Kotter, "What Effective General Managers Really Do"; and Mintzberg, "Managerial Work."

36. Mintzberg, "Managerial Work."

37. Anita Lienert, "A Day in the Life: Airport Manager Extraordinaire," *Management Review* (January 1995), 57–61.

38. Lance B. Kurke and Howard E. Aldrich, "Mintzberg Was Right!: A Replication and Extension of *The Nature of Managerial Work*," *Management Science* 29 (1983), 975–984; Cynthia M. Pavett and Alan W. Lau, "Managerial Work: The Influence of Hierarchical Level and Functional Specialty," *Academy of Management Journal* 26 (1983), 170–177; and Colin P. Hales, "What Do Managers Do? A Critical Review of the Evidence," *Journal of Management Studies* 23 (1986), 88–115.

39. Mintzberg, "Rounding out the Manager's Job."

40. John A. Byrne, "The Corporation of the Future," *BusinessWeek* (August 31, 1998), 102–106; and "And the Winner Is . . . Cisco Systems," in "In Depth: Business 2.0 100," compiled by Walid Mougayar, project head; Michael Mattis, Kate McKinley, and Nissa Crawford, *Business 2.0* (May 1999), 58–94.

41. Betsy McKay, "To Fix Coca-Cola, Daft Sets Out to Get Relationships Right," *The Wall Street Journal* (June 23, 2000), A1, A12.

42. Harry S. Jonas III, Ronald E. Fry, and Suresh Srivastva, "The Office of the CEO: Understanding the Executive Experience," *Academy of Management Executive* 4 (August 1990), 36–48.

43. Edward O. Welles, "There Are No Simple Businesses Anymore," *The State of Small Business* (1995), 66–79.

44. This section is based largely on Peter F. Drucker, *Managing the Non-Profit Organization: Principles and Practices* (New York: HarperBusiness, 1992); and Thomas Wolf, *Managing a Nonprofit Organization* (New York: Fireside/Simon & Schuster, 1990).

45. Christine W. Letts, William P. Ryan, and Allen Grossman, *High Performance Nonprofit Organizations* (New York: John Wiley & Sons, 1999), 30–35.

46. Toby J. Tetenbaum, "Shifting Paradigms: From Newton to Chaos," *Organizational Dynamics* (Spring 1998), 21–32. The following section is based on Tetenbaum, "Shifting Paradigms," John A. Byrne, "Management By Web," *BusinessWeek* (August 28, 2000), 84–96, and Mark Gimein, "CEOs Who Manage Too Much," *Fortune* (September 4, 2000), 235–242.

47. Nancy B. Kurland and Diane E. Bailey, "Telework: The Advantages and Challenges of Working Here, There, Anywhere, Anytime," *Organizational Dynamics* (Autumn 1999), 53–67; and Thomas H. Davenport and Keri Pearlson, "Two Cheers for the Virtual Office," *Sloan Management Review* (Summer 1998), 51–65.

48. American Electronics Association, 2000, reported in "The Great Migration (in Numbers), compiled and edited by Jill Kirschenbaum, *Fast Company* (July 2000), 199–206.

49. Randy Myers, "E-commerce, Unplugged," *eCFO* (Summer 2001), 53–57.

50. Faith Keenan, General Electric profile in "Giants Can Be Nimble" *BusinessWeek E.Biz* (September 18, 2000), EB98–EB104.

51. Gail Edmondson, with Kerry Capell, Pamela L. Moore, and Peter Burrows, "See the World, Erase Its Borders," *BusinessWeek* (August 28, 2000), 113–114.

52. G. Pascal Zachary, "Mighty Is the Mongrel," *Fast Company* (July 2000), 270–284.

53. Tetenbaum, "Shifting Paradigms: From Newton to Chaos."

54. Ibid.

55. Christopher A. Bartlett and Sumantra Ghoshal, "The Myth of the Generic Manager: New Personal Competencies for New Management Roles," *California Management Review* 40, No. 1 (Fall 1997), 92–116.

56. Tom Pohlmann with Bobby Cameron, Emily Jastrzembski, and Mary Lynn Pulley, "Building e-Business Leadership," (Forrester Research 2001), from the *Wharton Leadership Digest*, Wharton Center for Leadership and Change Management, *http://leadership.wharton.upenn.edu/digest/index.shtml*.

57. Byrne, "Management By Web."

58. Scott Kirsner, "Every Day, It's a New Place," *Fast Company* (April–May 1998), 130–134; Peter Coy, "The Creative Economy," *BusinessWeek* (August 28, 2000), 76–82; and Jeremy Main, "The Shape of the New Corporation," *Working Woman* (October 1998), 60–63.

59. Quoted in James Sterngold, "Power Crisis Abates, But It Hounds Gov. Davis," *The New York Times* (October 5, 2001), A16.

60. This section is based on Leslie Wayne and Leslie Kaufman, "Leadership, Put to a New Test," *The New York Times* (September 16, 2001), Section 3, 1, 4; Jerry Useem, "What It Takes," *Fortune* (November 12, 2001), 126–132; and Andy Bowen, "Crisis Procedures that Stand the Test of Time," *Public Relations Tactics* (August 2001), 16.

61. Susan Orenstein, "'Our Focus Had to Be on People,'" *Business 2.0* (November 2001), 30–31.

62. Byrne, "Tough Times for a New CEO," and McGeehan, "Sailing Into a Sea of Troubles."

Historical Foundations of Management

CHAPTER OUTLINE

Management and Organization

Classical Perspective

Scientific Management

Bureaucratic Organizations

Administrative Principles

Humanistic Perspective

The Human Relations Movement

The Human Resources Perspective

The Behavioral Sciences Approach

Management Science Perspective

Recent Historical Trends

Systems Theory

Contingency View

Total Quality Management

Current Directions in Management Thinking

The Learning Organization

Managing the Technology-Driven Workplace

LEARNING OBJECTIVES

After studying this chapter, you should be able to

1 Understand how historical forces influence the practice of management.

2 Identify and explain major developments in the history of management thought.

3 Describe the major components of the classical and humanistic management perspectives.

4 Discuss the management science perspective and its current use in organizations.

5 Explain the major concepts of systems theory, the contingency view, and total quality management.

6 Describe the learning organization and the changes in structure, empowerment, and information sharing managers make to support it.

7 Discuss the technology-driven workplace and the role of enterprise resource planning and knowledge management systems.

Management Challenge

Cementos Mexicanos (Cemex), based in Monterrey, Mexico, has been making and delivering concrete for nearly a century. The company specializes in delivering concrete in developing areas of the world, places where anything can, and usually does, go wrong. Even in Monterrey, for example, Cemex copes with unpredictable weather and traffic conditions, spontaneous labor disruptions, building permit snafus, and arbitrary government inspections of construction sites. In addition, more than half of all orders are changed or canceled by customers, usually at the last minute. Considering that a load of concrete is never more than 90 minutes from spoiling, those chaotic conditions mean high costs, complex scheduling, and frustration for employees, managers, and customers. As competition in the industry increased, Cemex managers began looking for ways to stand out from the crowd. One idea was a guaranteed delivery time, but despite the efforts of employees, the best Cemex could do was promise delivery within a three-hour window. To make matters worse, the construction business itself was becoming increasingly complex and competitive, leading to even more disruptions and cancellations. Builders were sometimes lucky to get their orders delivered on the right day, let along at the right hour. Cemex managers began to consider that the company needed a whole new approach to doing business—one that accepted rather than resisted the natural chaos of the marketplace. That would mean massive changes in operations, as well as finding ways to get dispatchers and drivers (who had an average of six years of formal education) to think like entrepreneurs.[1]

If you were a manager at Cemex, what changes would you implement to help the organization thrive in the face of constant chaos? What advice would you give managers concerning their management approach and the kind of company they might create?

Cemex is faced with a situation similar to many companies. The methods and patterns that kept the organization successful in the past no longer seem enough to keep it thriving in today's complex environment. Unexpected market forces or other changes in the environment can devastate a company. Another organization in Mexico, Producer and Importer of Paper S.A. (PIPSA), lost half its business overnight when the government abolished its monopoly in newsprint and privatized the company.[2] Managers at the U.S. company Barnes & Noble had to think fast and move fast when online bookseller Amazon.com created a new, unexpected form of competition. Confronted by these shifting conditions, managers may have to create a new kind of company, one with which they have little experience or skill.

As we discussed in Chapter 1, we are currently experiencing a shift to a new kind of workplace and a new approach to management. Managers today face the ultimate paradox: (1) Keep everything running efficiently and profitably, while, at the same time, (2) change everything.[3] It is no longer enough just to learn how to measure and control things. Success accrues to those who learn how to be leaders, to initiate change, and to participate in and even create organizations with fewer managers and less hierarchy that can change quickly.

Management philosophies and organizational forms change over time to meet new needs. The workplace of today is very different from what it was 50 years ago—indeed, from what it was even 10 years ago. Yet there are ideas and practices from the past that are still highly relevant and applicable to management today. Many students wonder why history matters to managers. A historical perspective provides a broader way of thinking, a way of searching for patterns and determining whether they recur across time periods. For example, certain management techniques that seem modern, such as employee stock-ownership programs, have repeatedly gained and lost popularity since the early 20th century because of historical forces.[4] William Cooper Procter, grandson of the co-founder of Procter & Gamble, introduced a profit-sharing plan in 1887, and expanded it by tying it to stock ownership a few years later. Sam Walton opened Wal-Mart's financial records, including salaries, to all employees in the 1960s, long before business magazines were touting the value of *open-book management*.[5]

A study of the past contributes to understanding both the present and the future. It is a way of learning from others' mistakes so as not to repeat them; learning from others' successes so as to repeat them in the appropriate situation; and most of all, learning to understand why things happen to improve our organizations in the future. This chapter provides an overview of the ideas, theories, and management philosophies that have contributed to making the workplace what it is today. We will examine several management approaches that have been popular and successful throughout the twentieth century. The final section of the chapter will look at recent trends and current approaches that build on this foundation of management understanding. This foundation illustrates that the value of studying management lies not in learning current facts and research but in developing a perspective that will facilitate the broad, long-term view needed for management success.

Management and Organization

A historical perspective on management provides a context or environment in which to interpret current opportunities and problems. However, studying history does not mean merely arranging events in chronological order; it means developing an understanding of the impact of societal forces on organizations. Studying history is a way to achieve strategic thinking, see the big picture, and improve conceptual skills. We will start by examining how social, political, and economic forces have influenced organizations and the practice of management.[6]

Social forces refer to those aspects of a culture that guide and influence relationships among people. What do people value? What do people need? What are the standards of behavior among people? These forces shape what is known as the *social contract*, which refers to the unwritten, common rules and perceptions about relationships among people and between employees and management.

A significant social force today is the changing attitudes, ideas, and values of Generation X and Generation Y employees. Generation X workers, those now in their late 20s and 30s, have had a profound impact on the workplace over the past decade or so, and Generation Y promises to have an even greater one.[7] People born between the years of 1980 and 1995 make up a whopping 26 percent of the population, and the older members are entering the workforce now. These young workers, the most educated generation in the history of the United States, grew up technologically adept and globally conscious. Some trends sparked by Generation X and Y workers are completely reshaping the social contract. Career life cycles are getting shorter, with workers typically changing jobs every few years and changing careers several times during their lifetime.[8] Young workers also expect to have access to cutting-edge technology, opportunities to learn and further their career and personal goals, and the power to make substantive decisions and changes in the workplace. Finally, there is a growing focus on work/life balance, reflected in trends such as telecommuting, flextime, shared jobs, and organization-sponsored sabbaticals.

Political forces refer to the influence of political and legal institutions on people and organizations. Political forces include basic assumptions underlying the political system, such as the desirability of self-government, property rights, contract rights, the definition of justice, and the determination of innocence or guilt of a crime. The spread of capitalism throughout the world has dramatically altered the business landscape. The dominance of the free-market system and growing interdependencies among the world's countries require organizations to operate differently and managers to think in new ways. At the same time, growing anti-American sentiments in many parts of the world create challenges for U.S. companies and managers. Another strong political force is the empowerment of citizens throughout the world. Power is being diffused both within and among countries as never before.[9] People are demanding empowerment, participation, and responsibility in all areas of their lives, including their work.

Economic forces pertain to the availability, production, and distribution of resources in a society. Governments, military agencies, churches, schools, and business organizations in every society require resources to achieve their goals, and economic forces influence the allocation of scarce resources. The economy of the United States and other developed countries is shifting dramatically, with the sources of wealth, the fundamentals of distribution, and the nature of economic decision making undergoing significant changes.[10] The emerging new economy is based largely on ideas, information, and knowledge rather than material resources. Supply chains and distribution of resources have been revolutionized by digital technology. Inventories, which once could

social forces
The aspects of a culture that guide and influence relationships among people—their values, needs, and standards of behavior.

political forces
The influence of political and legal institutions on people and organizations.

economic forces
Forces that affect the availability, production, and distribution of a society's resources among competing users.

trigger recessions, are declining or completely disappearing. Another economic trend is the booming importance of small and mid-sized businesses, including start-ups, which early in the twenty-first century grew at three times the rate of the national economy. "I call it 'the invisible economy,' yet it is *the* economy, " says David Birch of Cognetics Inc., a Cambridge, Massachusetts, firm that tracks business formation.[11] A massive shift in the economy is not without its upheavals, of course, as discussed in this chapter's Leading Online box. Years of seemingly endless growth ground to a halt as stock prices fell, particularly for dot-com and technology companies. Numerous Internet-based companies went out of business, and organizations throughout the U.S. and Canada began laying off hundreds of thousands of workers. However, this economic downturn may also be a stimulus for even greater technological innovation and small business vitality.

Management practices and perspectives vary in response to these social, political, and economic forces in the larger society. Exhibit 2.1 illustrates the evolution of significant management perspectives over time, each of which will be examined in the remainder of this chapter.

Classical Perspective

The practice of management can be traced to 3000 B.C. to the first government organizations developed by the Sumerians and Egyptians, but the formal study of management is relatively recent.[12] The early study of management as we know it today began with what is now called the *classical perspective*.

The **classical perspective** on management emerged during the nineteenth and early twentieth centuries. The factory system that began to appear in the 1800s posed challenges that earlier organizations had not encountered. Problems arose in tooling the plants, organizing managerial structure, training employees (many of them non-English-speaking immigrants), scheduling complex manufacturing operations, and dealing with increased labor dissatisfaction and resulting strikes.

These myriad new problems and the development of large, complex organizations demanded a new approach to coordination and control, and a "new subspecies of economic man—the salaried manager"[13]—was born. Between

classical perspective
A management perspective that emerged during the nineteenth and early twentieth centuries that emphasized a rational, scientific approach to the study of management and sought to make organizations efficient operating machines.

Exhibit **2.1**

Management Perspectives over Time

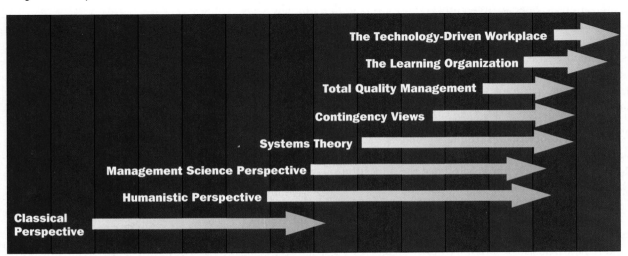

1870   1880   1890   1900   1910   1920   1930   1940   1950   1960   1970   1980   1990   2000   2010

Leading Online

Of Railroads and Web Sites

About 150 years ago, the railroad revolution transformed the economy. Today, the Internet revolution is doing the same thing. We all know that history doesn't really "repeat itself," but there are historical patterns that help us make sense of the present and predict what the future might be like.

The railroads and the Internet serve the same basic economic function: connecting buyers and sellers. And while few seem to know how to make the Internet economically profitable, the same thing could have been said about the railroad in its infancy. Yet the railroad's ability to move freight quickly and cheaply changed the world, and the Internet's ability to move information quickly and cheaply promises to do the same thing today. And whereas the railroads created the first national market, the Internet is creating the first truly global one. The railroad made it possible for companies such as Sears Roebuck, Montgomery Ward, and Woolworth to lower their prices and expand their operations nationally through catalog retailing, forcing small local retailers to compete in new ways. Similarly, Internet retailers such as Amazon.com are challenging bricks-and-mortar companies to rethink how they interact with suppliers and customers.

But nobody said changing the world was easy, and the recent turbulence in the technology sector is clearly an indication. Stock prices have taken a sharp plunge, many of the thousands of entrepreneurs who rushed in with dreams of getting rich on the Internet have fallen by the wayside, and many dot-com companies have gone out of business. Over a two-year period (1999–2000), the number of Internet IPOs (initial public offerings) grew at amazing speed, and crashed just as quickly. At the same time, though, the most popular Web sites continued to increase their visitor numbers. If the history of the railroad is any indication, this is merely the shake-out to be expected from such a major economic transformation, and new leaders will step in to revise, strengthen, and perfect the new business models. In the nineteenth century, railroad stocks soared and plunged as practical realities warred with potential profits and the hopes of investors fought with their fears. The railroad vastly overbuilt in the decades after the Civil War, and in the 1880s and 1890s, more than two-thirds of the railroad tracks in the United States passed through receivership and were reorganized by the big Wall Street banks. Savvy entrepreneurs who had stood on the sidelines took advantage of the shake-out in the railroad industry to build stronger companies and make themselves rich. For example, Cornelius (Commodore) Vanderbilt never built a railroad, but rather, bought badly run small, local railway lines, merged them into efficient operations, and managed them expertly, thereby creating the largest fortune of the railroad era. Similarly, the world of Internet commerce may be undergoing consolidation and focusing as today's best e-commerce leaders step in and make changes that will lead to a stronger, more stable future for the companies that survive.

SOURCES: John Steele Gordon, "The Golden Spike," *Forbes ASAP* (February 21, 2000), 118–122; and Lee Gomes, "Fix It and They Will Come: E-commerce Isn't Dead. Just Broken," *The Wall Street Journal* (February 12, 2001), R4.

1880 and 1920, the number of professional managers in the United States grew from 161,000 to more than a million.[14] These professional managers began developing and testing solutions to the mounting challenges of organizing, coordinating, and controlling large numbers of people and increasing worker productivity. Thus began the evolution of modern management with the classical perspective.

This perspective contains three subfields, each with a slightly different emphasis: scientific management, bureaucratic organizations, and administrative principles.[15]

Scientific Management

Organizations' somewhat limited success in achieving improvements in labor productivity led a young engineer to suggest that the problem lay more in poor management practices than in labor. Frederick Winslow Taylor (1856–1915) insisted that management itself would have to change and, further, that the manner of change could be determined only by scientific study; hence, the label **scientific management** emerged. Taylor suggested that decisions based

scientific management
A subfield of the classical management perspective that emphasized scientifically determined changes in management practices as the solution to improving labor productivity.

Frederick Winslow Taylor (1856–1915) Taylor's theory that labor productivity could be improved by scientifically determined management practices earned him the status of "father of scientific management."

Frederick Taylor's scientific management techniques were expanded by automaker Henry Ford, who replaced workers with machines for heavy lifting and moving. One of the first applications of the moving assembly line was the Magneto assembly operation at Ford's Highland Park plant in 1913. Magnetos moved from one worker to the next, reducing production time by one half. The same principle was applied to total-car assembly, improving efficiency and reducing worker-hours required to produce a Model-T Ford to less than two. Under this system, a Ford rolled off the assembly line every ten seconds.

on rules of thumb and tradition be replaced with precise procedures developed after careful study of individual situations.[16]

Taylor's philosophy is encapsulated in his statement, "In the past the man has been first. In the future, the system must be first."[17] The scientific management approach is illustrated by the unloading of iron from rail cars and reloading finished steel for the Bethlehem Steel plant in 1898. Taylor calculated that with correct movements, tools, and sequencing, each man was capable of loading 47.5 tons per day instead of the typical 12.5 tons. He also worked out an incentive system that paid each man $1.85 a day for meeting the new standard, an increase from the previous rate of $1.15. Productivity at Bethlehem Steel shot up overnight.

Although known as the "father of scientific management," Taylor was not alone in this area. Henry Gantt, an associate of Taylor's, developed the *Gantt Chart*—a bar graph that measures planned and completed work along each stage of production by time elapsed. Two other important pioneers in this area were the husband-and-wife team of Frank B. and Lillian M. Gilbreth. Frank B. Gilbreth (1868–1924) pioneered *time and motion study* and arrived at many of his management techniques independently of Taylor. He stressed efficiency and was known for his quest for the "one best way" to do work. Although Gilbreth is known for his early work with bricklayers, his work had great impact on medical surgery by drastically reducing the time patients spent on the operating table. Surgeons were able to save countless lives through the application of time and motion study. Lillian M. Gilbreth (1878–1972) was more interested in the human aspect of work. When her husband died at the age of 56, she had 12 children ages 2 to 19. The undaunted "first lady of management" went right on with her work. She presented a paper in place of her late husband, continued their seminars and consulting, lectured, and eventually became a professor at Purdue University.[18] She pioneered in the field of industrial psychology and made substantial contributions to human resource management.

The basic ideas of scientific management are shown in Exhibit 2.2. To use this approach, managers should develop standard methods for doing each job, select workers with the appropriate abilities, train workers in the standard methods, support workers and eliminate interruptions, and provide wage incentives.

The ideas of scientific management that began with Taylor dramatically increased productivity across all industries, and they are still important today. Indeed, the concept of arranging work based on careful analysis of tasks for maximum productivity is deeply embedded in our organizations.[19] However, because scientific management ignored the social context and workers' needs, it led to increased conflict and sometimes violent clashes between managers and employees. Under this system, workers often felt exploited. This was in sharp contrast to the harmony and cooperation that Taylor and his followers had envisioned.

General Approach
- Developed standard method for performing each job.
- Selected workers with appropriate abilities for each job.
- Trained workers in standard methods.
- Supported workers by planning their work and eliminating interruptions.
- Provided wage incentives to workers for increased output.

Contributions
- Demonstrated the importance of compensation for performance.
- Initiated the careful study of tasks and jobs.
- Demonstrated the importance of personnel selection and training.

Criticisms
- Did not appreciate the social context of work and higher needs of workers.
- Did not acknowledge variance among individuals.
- Tended to regard workers as uninformed and ignored their ideas and suggestions.

Exhibit **2.2**

Characteristics of Scientific Management

Bureaucratic Organizations

A systematic approach developed in Europe that looked at the organization as a whole is the **bureaucratic organizations** approach, a subfield within the classical perspective. Max Weber (1864–1920), a German theorist, introduced most of the concepts on bureaucratic organizations.[20]

During the late 1800s, many European organizations were managed on a personal, familylike basis. Employees were loyal to a single individual rather than to the organization or its mission. The dysfunctional consequence of this management practice was that resources were used to realize individual desires rather than organizational goals. Employees in effect owned the organization and used resources for their own gain rather than to serve customers. Weber envisioned organizations that would be managed on an impersonal, rational basis. This form of organization was called a *bureaucracy*. Exhibit 2.3 summarizes the six characteristics of bureaucracy as specified by Weber.

Weber believed that an organization based on rational authority would be more efficient and adaptable to change because continuity is related to formal structure and positions rather than to a particular person, who may leave or die. To Weber, rationality in organizations meant employee selection and advancement based on competence rather than on "whom you know." The organization relies on rules and written records for continuity. The manager depends not on his or her personality for successfully giving orders but on the legal power invested in the managerial position.

bureaucratic organizations
A subfield of the classical management perspective that emphasized management on an impersonal, rational basis through such elements as clearly defined authority and responsibility, formal recordkeeping, and separation of management and ownership.

©Corbis-Bettman

Lillian M. Gilbreth (1878–1972)
Frank B. Gilbreth (1868–1924)
Shown here using a "motion study" device, this husband-and-wife team contributed to the principles of scientific management. His development of time and motion studies and her work in industrial psychology pioneered many of today's management and human resource techniques.

Elements of Bureaucracy
1. Labor is divided with clear definitions of authority and responsibility that are legitimized as official duties.
2. Positions are organized in a hierarchy of authority, with each position under the authority of a higher one.
3. All personnel are selected and promoted based on technical qualifications, which are assessed by examination or according to training and experience.
4. Administrative acts and decisions are recorded in writing. Recordkeeping provides organizational memory and continuity over time.
5. Management is separate from the ownership of the organization.
6. Managers are subject to rules and procedures that will ensure reliable, predictable behavior. Rules are impersonal and uniformly applied to all employees.

Exhibit **2.3**

Characteristics of Weberian Bureaucracy

SOURCE: Adapted from Max Weber, *The Theory of Social and Economic Organizations*, ed. and trans. A.M. Henderson and Talcott Parsons (New York: Free Press, 1947), 328–337.

The term *bureaucracy* has taken on a negative meaning in today's organizations and is associated with endless rules and red tape. We have all been frustrated by waiting in long lines or following seemingly silly procedures. On the other hand, rules and other bureaucratic procedures provide a standard way of dealing with employees. Everyone gets equal treatment, and everyone knows what the rules are. This has enabled many organizations to become extremely efficient. Consider United Parcel Service (UPS), also called the "Brown Giant."

UNITED PARCEL SERVICE
http://www.ups.com

> United Parcel Service took on the U.S. Postal Service at its own game—and won. UPS specializes in the delivery of small packages. Why has the Brown Giant been so successful? One important reason is the concept of bureaucracy. UPS is bound up in rules and regulations. There are safety rules for drivers, loaders, clerks, and managers. Strict dress codes are enforced—no beards; hair cannot touch the collar; mustaches must be trimmed evenly; and no sideburns. Rules specify cleanliness standards for buildings and other properties. No eating or drinking is permitted at employee desks. Every manager is given bound copies of policy books and expected to use them regularly.
>
> UPS also has a well-defined division of labor. Each plant consists of specialized drivers, loaders, clerks, washers, sorters, and maintenance personnel. UPS thrives on written records. Daily worksheets specify performance goals and work output. Daily employee quotas and achievements are reported on a weekly and monthly basis.
>
> Technical qualification is the criterion for hiring and promotion. The UPS policy book says the leader is expected to have the knowledge and capacity to justify the position of leadership. Favoritism is forbidden. The bureaucratic model works just fine at UPS, "the tightest ship in the shipping business."[21] ❖

administrative principles
A subfield of the classical management perspective that focused on the total organization rather than the individual worker, delineating the management functions of planning, organizing, commanding, coordinating, and controlling.

Courtesy of German Information Center

Max Weber (1864–1920)
The German theorist's concepts on bureaucratic organizations have contributed to the efficiency of many of today's corporations.

Administrative Principles

Another major subfield within the classical perspective is known as the **administrative principles** approach. Whereas scientific management focused on the productivity of the individual worker, the administrative principles approach focused on the total organization. The contributors to this approach included Henri Fayol, Mary Parker Follett, and Chester I. Barnard.

Henri Fayol (1841–1925) was a French mining engineer who worked his way up to become head of a major mining group known as Comambault. Comambault survives today as part of Le Creusot-Loire, the largest mining and metallurgical group in central France. In his later years, Fayol wrote down his concepts on administration, based largely on his own management experiences.[22]

In his most significant work, *General and Industrial Management*, Fayol discussed 14 general principles of management, several of which are part of management philosophy today. For example:

- *Unity of command.* Each subordinate receives orders from one—and only one—superior.

- *Division of work.* Managerial and technical work are amenable to specialization to produce more and better work with the same amount of effort.

- *Unity of direction.* Similar activities in an organization should be grouped together under one manager.

- *Scalar chain.* A chain of authority extends from the top to the bottom of the organization and should include every employee.

Fayol felt that these principles could be applied in any organizational setting. He also identified five basic functions or elements of management: planning, organizing, commanding, coordinating, and controlling. These functions underlie much of the general approach to today's management theory.

Mary Parker Follett (1868–1933) was trained in philosophy and political science at what today is Radcliffe College. She applied herself in many fields, including social psychology and management. She wrote of the importance of common superordinate goals for reducing conflict in organizations.[23] Her work was popular with businesspeople of her day but was often overlooked by management scholars.[24] Follett's ideas served as a contrast to scientific management and are reemerging as applicable for modern managers dealing with rapid changes in today's global environment. Her approach to leadership stressed the importance of people rather than engineering techniques. She offered the pithy admonition, "Don't hug your blueprints," and analyzed the dynamics of management-organization interactions. Follett addressed issues that are timely today, such as ethics, power, and how to lead in a way that encourages employees to give their best. The concepts of empowerment, facilitating rather than controlling employees, and allowing employees to act depending on the authority of the situation opened new areas for theoretical study by Chester Barnard and others.[25]

Chester I. Barnard (1886–1961) studied economics at Harvard but failed to receive a degree because he lacked a course in laboratory science. He went to work in the statistical department of AT&T and in 1927 became president of New Jersey Bell. One of Barnard's significant contributions was the concept of the informal organization. The *informal organization* occurs in all formal organizations and includes cliques and naturally occurring social groupings. Barnard argued that organizations are not machines and informal relationships are powerful forces that can help the organization if properly managed. Another significant contribution was the *acceptance theory of authority*, which states that people have free will and can choose whether to follow management orders. People typically follow orders because they perceive positive benefit to themselves, but they do have a choice. Managers should treat employees properly because their acceptance of authority may be critical to organization success in important situations.[26]

The overall classical perspective as an approach to management was very powerful and gave companies fundamental new skills for establishing high productivity and effective treatment of employees. Indeed, America surged ahead of the world in management techniques, and other countries, especially Japan, borrowed heavily from American ideas.

Courtesy of Ronald G. Greenwood

Mary Parker Follett (1868–1933)
Follett was a major contributor to the administrative principles approach to management. Her emphasis on worker participation and shared goals among managers was embraced by many businesspeople of the day and has been recently "rediscovered" by corporate America.

Humanistic Perspective

Mary Parker Follett and Chester Barnard were early advocates of a more **humanistic perspective** on management that emphasized the importance of understanding human behaviors, needs, and attitudes in the workplace as well as social interactions and group processes.[27] We will discuss three subfields based on the humanistic perspective: the human relations movement, the human resources perspective, and the behavioral sciences approach.

humanistic perspective
A management perspective that emerged around the late nineteenth century that emphasized understanding human behavior, needs, and attitudes in the workplace.

This 1914 photograph shows the initiation of a new arrival at a Nebraska planting camp. This initiation was not part of the formal rules and illustrates the significance of the informal organization described by Barnard. Social values and behaviors were powerful forces that could help or hurt the planting organization depending on how they were managed.

Hawthorne studies
A series of experiments on worker productivity begun in 1924 at the Hawthorne plant of Western Electric Company in Illinois; attributed employees' increased output to managers' better treatment of them during the study.

This is the Relay Room of the Western Electric Hawthorne, Illinois, plant in 1927. Six women worked in this relay assembly test room during the controversial experiments on employee productivity. Professors Mayo and Roethlisberger evaluated conditions such as rest breaks and workday length, physical health, amount of sleep, and diet. Experimental changes were fully discussed with the women and were abandoned if they disapproved. Gradually the researchers began to realize they had created a change in supervisory style and human relations, which they believed was the true cause of the increased productivity.

The Human Relations Movement

America has always espoused the spirit of human equality. However, this spirit has not always been translated into practice when it comes to power sharing between managers and workers. The human relations school of thought considers that truly effective control comes from within the individual worker rather than from strict, authoritarian control.[28] This school of thought recognized and directly responded to social pressures for enlightened treatment of employees. The early work on industrial psychology and personnel selection received little attention because of the prominence of scientific management. Then a series of studies at a Chicago electric company, which came to be known as the **Hawthorne studies**, changed all that.

Beginning about 1895, a struggle developed between manufacturers of gas and electric lighting fixtures for control of the residential and industrial market.[29] By 1909 electric lighting had begun to win, but the increasingly efficient electric fixtures used less total power. The electric companies began a campaign to convince industrial users that they needed more light to get more productivity. When advertising did not work, the industry began using experimental tests to demonstrate their argument. Managers were skeptical about the results, so the Committee on Industrial Lighting (CIL) was set up to run the tests. To further add to the tests' credibility, Thomas Edison was made honorary chairman of the CIL. In one test location—the Hawthorne plant of the Western Electric Company—some interesting events occurred.

The major part of this work involved four experimental and three control groups. In all, five different "tests" were conducted. These pointed to the importance of factors *other* than illumination in affecting productivity. To more carefully examine these factors, numerous other experiments were conducted.[30] The results of the most famous study, the first Relay Assembly Test Room (RATR) experiment, were extremely controversial. Under the guidance of two Harvard professors, Elton Mayo and Fritz Roethlisberger, the RATR studies lasted nearly six years (May 10, 1927, to May 4, 1933) and involved 24 separate experimental periods. So many factors were changed and so many unforeseen factors uncontrolled that scholars disagree on the factors that truly contributed to the general increase in performance over that period. Most early interpretations, however, agreed on one thing: Money was not the cause of the increased output.[31] It was believed that the factor that best explained increased output was "human relations." Employees performed better when managers treated them in a positive manner. However, recent reanalyses of the experiments have revealed that a number of factors were different for the workers involved, and some suggest that money may well have been the single most important factor.[32] An interview with one of the original participants revealed that just getting into the experimental group had meant a huge increase in income.[33]

These new data clearly show that money mattered a great deal at Hawthorne. In addition, worker productivity increased partly as a result of the increased feelings of importance and group pride employees felt by virtue of being selected for this important project.[34] One unintended contribution of the experiments was a rethinking of field research practices. Researchers and scholars realized that the researcher can influence the outcome of an experiment by being too closely involved with research subjects. This has come to be known as the *Hawthorne effect* in research methodology. Subjects behaved differently because of the active participation of researchers in the Hawthorne experiments.[35]

From a historical perspective, whether the studies were academically sound is of less importance than the fact that they stimulated an increased interest in looking at employees as more than extensions of production machinery. The interpretation that employees' output increased when managers treated them in a positive manner started a revolution in worker treatment for improving organizational productivity. Despite flawed methodology or inaccurate conclusions, the findings provided the impetus for the **human relations movement.** IBM was one of the earliest proponents of a human relations approach, as described in the Putting People First box. This approach shaped management theory and practice for well over a quarter-century, and the belief that human relations is the best approach for increasing productivity persists today.

human relations movement
A movement in management thinking and practice that emphasized satisfaction of employees' basic needs as the key to increased worker productivity.

The Human Resources Perspective

The human relations movement initially espoused a "dairy farm" view of management—contented cows give more milk, so satisfied workers will give more work. Gradually, views with deeper content began to emerge. The human resources perspective maintained an interest in worker participation and considerate leadership but shifted the emphasis to consider the daily tasks that people perform. The **human resources perspective** combines prescriptions for design of job tasks with theories of motivation.[36] In the human resources view, jobs should be designed so that tasks are not perceived as dehumanizing or demeaning but instead allow workers to use their full potential. Two of the best-known contributors to the human resources perspective were Abraham Maslow and Douglas McGregor.

human resources perspective
A management perspective that suggests jobs should be designed to meet higher-level needs by allowing workers to use their full potential.

Abraham Maslow (1908–1970), a practicing psychologist, observed that his patients' problems usually stemmed from an inability to satisfy their needs. Thus, he generalized his work and suggested a hierarchy of needs. Maslow's hierarchy started with physiological needs and progressed to safety, belongingness, esteem, and, finally, self-actualization needs. Chapter 17 discusses his ideas in more detail.

Douglas McGregor (1906–1964) had become frustrated with the early simplistic human relations notions while president of Antioch College in Ohio. He challenged both the classical perspective and the early human relations assumptions about human behavior. Based on his experiences as a manager and consultant, his training as a psychologist, and the work of Maslow, McGregor formulated his Theory X and Theory Y, which are explained in Exhibit 2.4.[37] McGregor believed that the classical perspective was based on Theory X assumptions about workers. He also felt that a slightly modified version of Theory X fit early human relations ideas. In other words, human relations ideas did not go far enough. McGregor proposed Theory Y as a more realistic view of workers for guiding management thinking.

The point of Theory Y is that organizations can take advantage of the imagination and intellect of all their employees. Employees will exercise self-control and will contribute to organizational goals when given the opportunity. A few

Assumptions of Theory X

- The average human being has an inherent dislike of work and will avoid it if possible....
- Because of the human characteristic of dislike for work, most people must be coerced, controlled, directed, or threatened with punishment to get them to put forth adequate effort toward the achievement of organizational objectives....
- The average human being prefers to be directed, wishes to avoid responsibility, has relatively little ambition, wants security above all.

Assumptions of Theory Y

- The expenditure of physical and mental effort in work is as natural as play or rest. The average human being does not inherently dislike work....
- External control and the threat of punishment are not the only means for bringing about effort toward organizational objectives. A person will exercise self-direction and self-control in the service of objectives to which he or she is committed....
- The average human being learns, under proper conditions, not only to accept but to seek responsibility....
- The capacity to exercise a relatively high degree of imagination, ingenuity, and creativity in the solution of organizational problems is widely, not narrowly, distributed in the population.
- Under the conditions of modern industrial life, the intellectual potentialities of the average human being are only partially utilized.

SOURCE: Douglas McGregor, *The Human Side of Enterprise* (New York: McGraw-Hill, 1960), 33–48.

companies today still use Theory X management, but many are trying Theory Y techniques. One organization that taps into the full potential of every worker by operating from Theory Y assumptions is Finland's SOL Cleaning Service.

SOL CLEANING SERVICE
http://www.sol.fi

They work in one of the world's least glamorous industries, but employees at SOL love their jobs. The industrial cleaning business is characterized by back-breaking labor, low wages, high turnover, and lousy service. SOL, however, presents a different picture—that of a fast-paced, high-energy, knowledge-driven company with happy employees and superior customer service. Each SOL supervisor leads a team of up to 50 cleaners who cheerfully fan out across Finland each morning wearing bright red-and-yellow jumpsuits. The company headquarters in Helsinki explodes with color and creativity. Employees wander the halls talking on bright-yellow cordless phones and meet in rooms that look more like playgrounds than offices. In Finland, and increasingly across Europe, SOL is known as an icon of what it takes to win in today's tough business environment.

Part of SOL's success is its management approach based on Theory Y assumptions. There are no job titles, executive perks, or assigned parking spaces and other status symbols at SOL. Everyone is considered equal, and each employee's contribution is valued. In addition, SOL has no individual offices and no set working hours. All work is performed by self-directed teams that create their own budgets, do their own hiring, set their own performance goals, and negotiate their own arrangements with customers. Employees actively and enthusiastically strive toward meeting goals and solving customer problems. If a team builds up enough business, it can set up its own satellite office and run it like a minibusiness. SOL also has a training program that would be the envy of any high-tech corporation, providing training in topics such as time management, budgeting, relationship skills, and customer service.

Putting People First

Watson Opens the Door at IBM—and Finds Happier Employees

During the early 1900s, managers in most manufacturing companies were focused on reducing jobs to repetitive, standardized tasks, following the scientific management approach advocated by Frederick Taylor and others. However, the ideals that Thomas Watson Sr. planted at IBM were based on a different approach, and they eventually helped transform the company into a corporate giant.

In 1914, Watson joined a failing conglomerate that primarily made scales, coffee grinders, cheese slicers, and time clocks. The *Computing-Tabulating-Recording* component of the conglomerate grew quickly and soon overtook the other businesses, even though the name wasn't changed to International Business Machines until 1924. Rather than putting the production system first, as Taylor advised, Watson vowed to make people the cornerstone of his corporate culture. He abolished piecework, spruced up factories, paid above-average wages, and borrowed money to fund in-house education programs. Foremost among his innovations was an open-door policy that encouraged any employee to take a complaint directly to Watson himself. He virtually guaranteed lifetime employment (even during the Depression) so workers would feel free to speak their minds. In the early years of Watson's tenure with IBM, when the company didn't have funds for generous benefit plans, Watson sponsored company picnics, complete with bands, to build spirit and keep workers motivated. As the company prospered, he passed the good times on. A group life insurance plan was launched in 1934, with survivor benefits and paid vacations added soon afterward.

The human relations approach to management was continued by Thomas Watson, Jr., who took over as CEO in 1956 and first pushed the company into computers. Leading IBM through one of the longest and most spectacular periods of growth in business history, the younger Watson was known as a hard-charger and a tough boss. However, he maintained his father's emphasis on treating employees fairly. IBM became famous for putting all employees on salary and for its extremely generous compensation and benefit plans, as well as the continued guarantee of lifetime employment. Watson liberally distributed stock options to his executives, but stopped taking them himself as early as 1957, saying, "We didn't want to look like pigs." There are many factors involved in IBM's successful history. However, the early emphasis on treating employees well helped put the company on the map. Watson's belief that a focus on people and meeting the needs of employees was the real key to increased productivity and performance was ahead of its time.

SOURCES: "IBM: The Open Door," vignette in Matthew Boyle, "How the Workplace Was Won," *Fortune* (January 22, 2001), 139; and Thomas A. Stewart, Alex Taylor III, Peter Petre, and Brent Schlender, "The Businessman of the Century," *Fortune* (November 22, 1999), 108–128.

By operating from Theory Y principles, SOL has turned cleaners into entrepreneurs and changed the perception of the industrial cleaning industry in Finland. Few people grow up dreaming of becoming an industrial cleaner, but at SOL employees are motivated and fulfilled, committed to doing their best for the team, the company, and the customer.[38]❖

The Behavioral Sciences Approach

The **behavioral sciences approach** develops theories about human behavior based on scientific methods and study. Behavioral science draws from sociology, psychology, anthropology, economics, and other disciplines to understand employee behavior and interaction in an organizational setting. The approach can be seen in practically every organization. When General Electric conducts research to determine the best set of tests, interviews, and employee profiles to use when selecting new employees, it is employing behavioral science techniques. When Gap clothing stores train new managers in the techniques of employee motivation, most of the theories and findings are rooted in behavioral science research.

One specific set of management techniques based in the behavioral sciences approach is *organization development* (OD). In the 1970s, organization

behavioral sciences approach
A subfield of the humanistic management perspective that applies social science in an organizational context, drawing from economics, psychology, sociology, and other disciplines.

development evolved as a separate field that applied the behavioral sciences to improve the organization's health and effectiveness through its ability to cope with change, improve internal relationships, and increase problem-solving capabilities.[39] The techniques and concepts of organization development have since been broadened and expanded to cope with the increasing complexity of organizations and the environment, and OD is still a vital approach for managers. OD will be discussed in detail in Chapter 12. Other concepts that grew out of the behavioral sciences approach include matrix organizations, self-managed teams, ideas about corporate culture, and management by wandering around. Indeed, the behavioral sciences approach has influenced the majority of tools, techniques, and approaches managers have applied to organizations since the 1970s. In recent years, behavioral sciences and OD techniques have been applied to help managers build learning organizations.

All of the remaining chapters of this book contain research findings and management applications that can be attributed to the behavioral sciences approach. This chapter's Shoptalk box illustrates a number of management innovations that have become popular over the past 50 years. Note the trend of new management concepts from the behavioral sciences, increasing about 1970 and then again from 1980 to the present. The rapid pace of change and the increased pressure of global competition have spurred even greater interest in improved behavioral approaches to management.

Management Science Perspective

management science perspective
A management perspective that emerged after World War II and applied mathematics, statistics, and other quantitative techniques to managerial problems.

World War II caused many management changes. The massive and complicated problems associated with modern global warfare presented managerial decision makers with the need for more sophisticated tools than ever before. The **management science perspective** emerged to address those problems. This view is distinguished for its application of mathematics, statistics, and other quantitative techniques to management decision making and problem solving. During World War II, groups of mathematicians, physicists, and other scientists were formed to solve military problems. Because those problems frequently involved moving massive amounts of materials and large numbers of people quickly and efficiently, the techniques had obvious applications to large-scale business firms.[40]

Operations research grew directly out of the World War II groups (called *operational research teams* in Great Britain and *operations research teams* in the United States).[41] It consists of mathematical model building and other applications of quantitative techniques to managerial problems.

Operations management refers to the field of management that specializes in the physical production of goods or services. Operations management specialists use quantitative techniques to solve manufacturing problems. Some of the commonly used methods are forecasting, inventory modeling, linear and nonlinear programming, queuing theory, scheduling, simulation, and break-even analysis.

Information technology (IT) is the most recent subfield of the management science perspective, which is often reflected in management information systems. These systems are designed to provide relevant information to managers in a timely and cost-efficient manner. More recently, information technology within organizations has evolved to include intranets and extranets, as well as various software programs that help managers estimate costs, plan and track

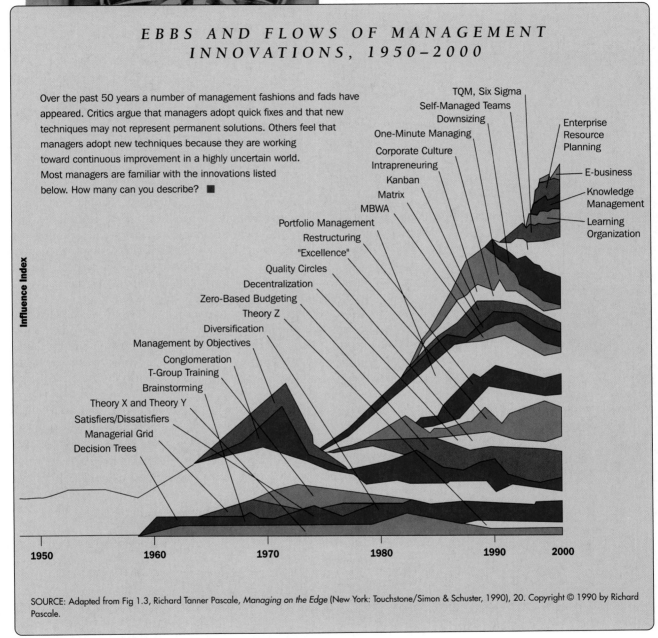

THE NEW WORKPLACE — Manager's Shoptalk

EBBS AND FLOWS OF MANAGEMENT INNOVATIONS, 1950–2000

Over the past 50 years a number of management fashions and fads have appeared. Critics argue that managers adopt quick fixes and that new techniques may not represent permanent solutions. Others feel that managers adopt new techniques because they are working toward continuous improvement in a highly uncertain world. Most managers are familiar with the innovations listed below. How many can you describe? ■

Influence Index

TQM, Six Sigma
Self-Managed Teams
Downsizing
One-Minute Managing
Corporate Culture
Intrapreneuring
Kanban
Matrix
MBWA
Portfolio Management
Restructuring
"Excellence"
Quality Circles
Decentralization
Zero-Based Budgeting
Theory Z
Diversification
Management by Objectives
Conglomeration
T-Group Training
Brainstorming
Theory X and Theory Y
Satisfiers/Dissatisfiers
Managerial Grid
Decision Trees

Enterprise Resource Planning
E-business
Knowledge Management
Learning Organization

1950   1960   1970   1980   1990   2000

SOURCE: Adapted from Fig 1.3, Richard Tanner Pascale, *Managing on the Edge* (New York: Touchstone/Simon & Schuster, 1990), 20. Copyright © 1990 by Richard Pascale.

production, manage projects, allocate resources, or schedule employees. When Weyerhaeuser Company's door factory implemented an intranet combined with software to track inventory, calculate estimates, schedule production, and automate order-taking, it was applying information technology to cut both manufacturing costs and production time.[42]

Most of today's organizations have departments of information technology specialists to help them apply management science techniques to complex organizational problems. IT specialists helped Turner Industries, a large-scale construction company, develop a system that combines project estimating and control systems with planning and scheduling software that can automatically calculate the cost of a project down to the last nail and then track costs and construction progress on a daily basis.[43]

Recent Historical Trends

Management is by nature complex and dynamic. Elements of each of the perspectives we have discussed are still in use today. The most prevalent is the humanistic perspective, but even it has been undergoing change in recent years. Three recent trends that grew out of the humanistic perspective are systems theory, the contingency view, and total quality management.

Systems Theory

system
A set of interrelated parts that function as a whole to achieve a common purpose.

systems theory
An extension of the humanistic perspective that describes organizations as open systems that are characterized by entropy, synergy, and subsystem interdependence.

open system
A system that interacts with the external environment.

closed system
A system that does not interact with the external environment.

A **system** is a set of interrelated parts that function as a whole to achieve a common purpose.[44] A system functions by acquiring inputs from the external environment, transforming them in some way, and discharging outputs back to the environment. Exhibit 2.5 shows the basic **systems theory** of organizations. Here there are five components: inputs, a transformation process, outputs, feedback, and the environment. *Inputs* are the material, human, financial, or information resources used to produce goods or services. The *transformation process* is management's use of production technology to change the inputs into outputs. *Outputs* include the organization's products and services. *Feedback* is knowledge of the results that influence the selection of inputs during the next cycle of the process. The *environment* surrounding the organization includes the social, political, and economic forces noted earlier in this chapter.

Some ideas in systems theory have had substantial impact on management thinking. These include open and closed systems, entropy, synergy, and subsystem interdependencies.[45]

Open systems must interact with the environment to survive; **closed systems** need not. In the classical and management science perspectives,

Exhibit *2.5*

The Systems View of Organizations

organizations were frequently thought of as closed systems. In the management science perspective, closed system assumptions—the absence of external disturbances—are sometimes used to simplify problems for quantitative analysis. In reality, however, all organizations are open systems, and the cost of ignoring the environment may be failure.

Entropy is a universal property of systems and refers to their tendency to run down and die. If a system does not receive fresh inputs and energy from its environment, it will eventually cease to exist. Organizations must monitor their environments, adjust to changes, and continuously bring in new inputs in order to survive and prosper. Managers try to design the organization/environment interfaces to reduce entropy.

entropy
The tendency for a system to run down and die.

Synergy means that the whole is greater than the sum of its parts. When an organization is formed, something new comes into the world. Management, coordination, and production that did not exist before are now present. Organizational units working together can accomplish more than those same units working alone. The sales department depends on production, and vice versa.

synergy
The concept that the whole is greater than the sum of its parts.

Subsystems are parts of a system that depend on one another. Changes in one part of the organization affect other parts. The organization must be managed as a coordinated whole. Managers who understand subsystem interdependence are reluctant to make changes that do not recognize subsystem impact on the organization as a whole. For example, Buckman Laboratories International introduced a knowledge-sharing network, called K'Netix, to keep its international workforce connected and to bring all of the organization's brain power to bear in serving each customer.[46] However, the success of the knowledge-sharing network required changes in organizational structure, job design, work processes, and cultural values. The vertical hierarchy at Buckman was shattered and replaced by coordinated teams. Cultural values had to be shifted to emphasize sharing rather than hoarding information. A change of this nature might take quite some time because of the interconnection of the organization's subsystems.

subsystems
Parts of a system that depend on one another for their functioning.

Contingency View

A second contemporary extension to management thinking is the contingency view. The classical perspective assumed a *universalist* view. Management concepts were thought to be universal; that is, whatever worked—leader style, bureaucratic structure—in one organization would work in another. In business education, however, an alternative view exists. This is the *case* view, in which each situation is believed to be unique. There are no universal principles to be found, and one learns about management by experiencing a large number of case problem situations. Managers face the task of determining what methods will work in every new situation.

To integrate these views the **contingency view** has emerged, as illustrated in Exhibit 2.6.[47] Here neither of the other views is seen as entirely correct. Instead, certain contingencies, or variables, exist for helping management identify and understand situations. The contingency view means that a manager's response depends on identifying key contingencies in an organizational situation. For example, a consultant might mistakenly recommend the same *management-by-objectives* (MBO) system for a manufacturing firm that was successful in a school system. The contingency view tells us that what works in one setting might not work in another. Management's job is to search for

contingency view
An extension of the humanistic perspective in which the successful resolution of organizational problems is thought to depend on managers' identification of key variations in the situation at hand.

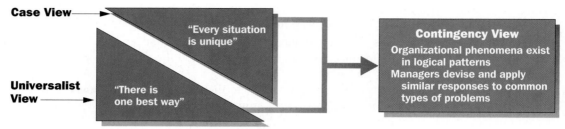

Case View → "Every situation is unique"

Universalist View → "There is one best way"

Contingency View
Organizational phenomena exist in logical patterns
Managers devise and apply similar responses to common types of problems

Exhibit *2.6*

Contingency View of Management

total quality management (TQM)
A concept that focuses on managing the total organization to deliver quality to customers. Four significant elements of TQM are employee involvement, focus on the customer, benchmarking, and continuous improvement.

important contingencies. When managers learn to identify important patterns and characteristics of their organizations, they can then fit solutions to those characteristics.

Important contingencies that managers must understand include industry, technology, the environment, and international cultures. Management practice in a rapidly changing industry, for example, will be very different from that in a stable one.

Total Quality Management

The quality movement in Japan emerged partly as a result of American influence after World War II. The ideas of W. Edwards Deming, known as the "father of the quality movement," were initially scoffed at in America, but the Japanese embraced his theories and modified them to help rebuild their industries into world powers.[48] Japanese companies achieved a significant departure from the American model by gradually shifting from an inspection-oriented approach to quality control toward an approach emphasizing employee involvement in the prevention of quality problems.[49]

During the 1980s and into the 1990s, **total quality management (TQM)**, which focuses on managing the total organization to deliver quality to customers, was at the forefront in helping managers deal with global competition. The approach infuses quality values throughout every activity within a company, with front-line workers intimately involved in the process. Four significant elements of quality management are employee involvement, focus on the customer, benchmarking, and continuous improvement.

Employee involvement means that TQM requires companywide participation in quality control. All employees are *focused on the customer*; TQM companies find out what customers want and try to meet their needs and expectations. *Benchmarking* refers to a process whereby companies find out how others do something better than they do and then try to imitate or improve on it. *Continuous improvement* is the implementation of small, incremental improvements in all areas of the organization on an ongoing basis. TQM is not a quick fix, but companies such as Motorola, Procter & Gamble, and DuPont have achieved astonishing results in efficiency, quality, and customer satisfaction through total quality management.[50] TQM is still an important part of today's organizations, and many companies pursue challenging quality goals to demonstrate their commitment to improving quality. For example, *Six Sigma* is a highly ambitious quality standard popularized by Motorola that specifies a goal of no more than 3.4 defects per million parts. Numerous companies, including DuPont, Texas Instruments, General Electric, and Nokia, pursue Six Sigma quality standards. Quality goals and initiatives will be discussed in detail in Chapter 20.

Current Directions in Management Thinking

All of the ideas and approaches discussed so far in this chapter go into the mix that makes up current management. However, the world has changed dramatically over the past decade or so, and organizations are experimenting with new ways of managing that more adequately respond to the demands of today's environment and customers. Two current directions in management thinking are the shift to a learning organization and managing the technology-driven workplace.

The Learning Organization

Managers began thinking about the concept of the learning organization after the publication of Peter Senge's book, *The Fifth Discipline: The Art and Practice of Learning Organizations.*[51] Senge described the kind of changes managers needed to undergo to help their organizations adapt to an increasingly chaotic world. These ideas gradually evolved to describe characteristics of the organization itself. There is no single view of what the learning organization looks like. The learning organization is an attitude or philosophy about what an organization can become.

The **learning organization** can be defined as one in which everyone is engaged in identifying and solving problems, enabling the organization to continuously experiment, change, and improve, thus increasing its capacity to grow, learn, and achieve its purpose. The essential idea is problem solving, in contrast to the traditional organization designed for efficiency. In the learning organization all employees look for problems, such as understanding special customer needs. Employees also solve problems, which means putting things together in unique ways to meet a customer's needs.

To develop a learning organization, managers make changes in all the subsystems of the organization. Three important adjustments to promote continuous learning are shifting to a team-based structure, empowering employees, and sharing information. These three characteristics are illustrated in Exhibit 2.7 and each is described here.

Team-Based Structure. An important value in a learning organization is collaboration and communication across departmental and hierarchical boundaries. Self-directed teams are the basic building block of the structure.

learning organization
An organization in which everyone is engaged in identifying and solving problems, enabling the organization to continuously experiment, improve, and increase its capability.

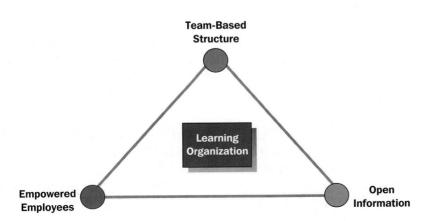

Team-Based Structure

Learning Organization

Empowered Employees

Open Information

Exhibit 2.7

Elements of a Learning Organization

These teams are made up of employees with different skills who share or rotate jobs to produce an entire product or service. Traditional management tasks are pushed down to lower levels of the organization, with teams often taking responsibility for training, safety, scheduling, and decisions about work methods, pay and reward systems, and coordination with other teams. Although team leadership is critical, in learning organizations the traditional boss is practically eliminated. People on the team are given the skills, information, tools, motivation, and authority to make decisions central to the team's performance and to respond creatively and flexibly to new challenges or opportunities that arise.

Employee Empowerment.   *Empowerment* means unleashing the power and creativity of employees by giving them the freedom, resources, information, and skills to make decisions and perform effectively. Traditional management tries to limit employees, while empowerment expands their behavior. Empowerment may be reflected in self-directed work teams, quality circles, job enrichment, and employee participation groups as well as through decision-making authority, training, and information so that people can perform jobs without close supervision.

In learning organizations, people are a manager's primary source of strength, not a cost to be minimized. Companies that adopt this perspective believe in treating employees well by providing competitive wages, good working conditions, and opportunities for personal and professional development. In addition, they often provide a sense of employee ownership by sharing gains in productivity and profits.[52]

Open Information.   A learning organization is flooded with information. To identify needs and solve problems, people have to be aware of what's going on. They must understand the whole organization as well as their part in it. Formal data about budgets, profits, and departmental expenses are available to everyone. At Solectron Corp., the world's largest and fastest-growing contract manufacturer, managers widely share information to carry out the company's guiding principles: superior customer service and respect for individual workers. "If you really want to respect individuals," says Winston Chen, "you've got to let them know how they're doing—and let them know soon enough so they can do something about it."[53] Open information becomes extraordinarily important in organizations that deal with ideas rather than material goods. Managers know that providing too much information is better than providing too little. In addition, managers encourage people throughout the organization to share information. At Viant Inc., which helps companies build and maintain Web-based businesses, people are rewarded for their willingness to absorb and share knowledge. Rather than encouraging consultants to hoard specialized knowledge, CEO Bob Gett says, "We value you more for how much information you've given to the guy next to you."[54]

Managing the Technology-Driven Workplace

The shift to the learning organization goes hand-in-hand with the current transition to a technology-driven workplace. Today's organizations can't be managed and controlled in the same way organizations were managed 100 years ago—or perhaps even 20 years ago.

The physical world that Frederick Taylor and other proponents of scientific management measured determines less and less of what is valued in organizations and society. Our lives and organizations have been engulfed by information technology. Ideas, information, and relationships are becoming more important than production machinery, physical products, and structured jobs.[55] Many employees perform much of their work on computers and may work in virtual teams, connected electronically to colleagues around the world. Even in factories that produce physical goods, machines have taken over much of the routine and uniform work, freeing workers to use more of their minds and abilities. Managers and employees in today's companies focus on opportunities rather than efficiencies, which requires that they be flexible, creative, and unconstrained by rigid rules and structured tasks.

In addition to employees being connected electronically, organizations are becoming enmeshed in electronic networks. The world of e-business is booming as more and more business takes place by digital processes over a computer network rather than in physical space. **E-business** refers to the work an organization does by using electronic linkages (including the Internet) with customers, partners, suppliers, employees, or other key constituents. For example, organizations that use the Internet or other electronic linkages to communicate with employees or customers are engaged in e-business. A company might set up an **intranet**, an internal communications system that uses the technology and standards of the Internet but is accessible only to people within the company. The intranet looks and acts like a Web site, but it is cordoned off from the public with the use of software programs known as *firewalls*.[56] Some companies extend the communication system's function with an **extranet**, which gives access to key suppliers, partners, customers, or others outside the organization.

E-commerce is a narrower term referring specifically to business exchanges or transactions that occur electronically. E-commerce replaces or enhances the exchange of money and products with the exchange of data and information from one computer to another. Three types of e-commerce—business-to-consumer, business-to-business, and consumer-to-consumer—are illustrated in Exhibit 2.8. Today, most e-commerce takes place on the Internet. Companies such as Gateway, Amazon.com, 800-Flowers, Expedia.com, and Progressive are engaged in what is referred to as *business-to-consumer e-commerce (B2C)*, because they sell products and services to consumers over the Internet. Consumers can log onto Internet Web sites and purchase computers, books, CDs, flowers and gifts, airline tickets, insurance policies, or practically anything else they desire. In addition, they can pay bills online, chat with consultants about business opportunities or doctors about medical problems, shop for the lowest-priced refrigerator directly from the manufacturer, or check the history of a used car.

Although this is probably the most visible expression of e-commerce to the public, the fastest growing area of e-commerce is *business-to-business e-commerce (B2B)*, which refers to electronic transactions between organizations. Many companies handle B2B commerce over private *electronic data interchange (EDI)* networks. For example, Wal-Mart has used a private network to transmit sales data to suppliers such as Procter & Gamble, where the network can automatically trigger a shipment of new products as they're needed to restock Wal-Mart's shelves.

More and more companies are using Web-based technology because the Internet systems are easier to use than EDI and are accessible to a larger number of suppliers and vendors.[57] Large organizations such as General Electric,

e-business
Work an organization does by using electronic linkages.

intranet
An internal communications system that uses the technology and standards of the Internet but is accessible only within the company.

extranet
A company communications system that gives access to suppliers, partners, and others outside the company.

e-commerce
Business exchanges or transactions that occur electronically.

©Gail Albert Halaban/Corbis SABA

As president and chief operating officer at oil company Unocal, Tim Ling is among the young executives who are eschewing the oil industry's traditional closed, old-economy methods to embrace open information and communication. Ling prodded Unocal employees, from drillers to managers, to share information and become financially sophisticated. To extend the benefits of this open information culture, Ling also wants to get expert analysis from outside the company by feeding seismic data via broadband to geologists around the world.

Exhibit *2.8*

Three Types of E-commerce

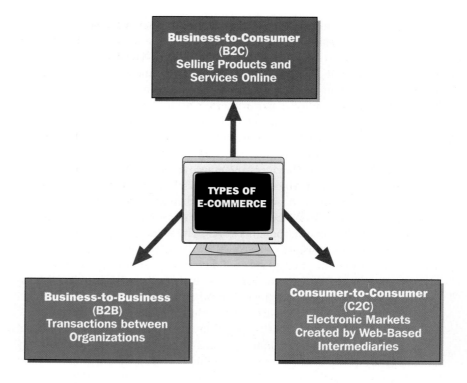

Carrier Corp., and Ford Motor Company purchase billions of dollars worth of goods and services a year electronically via Internet or private computer linkages to supplier companies.[58] GE is focused on "digitizing" every function it possibly can, from buying airline tickets to paying suppliers. For example, GE used to process more than 3 million paper invoices a year. Now, most of GE's purchasing and payments are handled digitally. GE managers predict that automating transactions with suppliers will save the company well over a billion dollars a year.[59] Ford Motor Company purchases a large portion of the steel it uses to build cars through e-Steel. Rather than Ford managers having to go through a maze of processes and paperwork before steel ends up on the assembly line, e-Steel software automatically tracks steel movements on an Internet-based system.[60]

Some companies have taken e-commerce to very high levels to achieve amazing performance. Dell Computer pioneered the use of end-to-end digital supply-chain networks to keep in touch with customers, take orders, buy components from suppliers, coordinate with manufacturing partners, and ship customized products directly to consumers. This trend is affecting every industry, prompting a group of consultants at a Harvard University conference to conclude that businesses today must either "Dell or be Delled."[61] These advances mean managers not only need to be technologically savvy, but they become responsible for managing a web of relationships that reaches far beyond the boundaries of the physical organization, building flexible e-links between a company and its employees, suppliers, partners, and customers.[62]

The third area of e-commerce, *consumer-to-consumer (C2C)*, is made possible when an Internet-based business acts as an intermediary between and among consumers. One of the best-known examples of C2C e-commerce is Web-based auctions such as those made possible by eBay or QXL. Internet auctions have created a large electronic marketplace where consumers can buy and sell directly with one another, often handling practically the entire transaction via the Web. Another popular area of C2C commerce is peer-to-peer file-sharing networks. Companies such as Napster, BearShare, and Morpheus provide the technology for swapping music files, video clips, software, and other files. This area of e-commerce will likely grow in coming years.

In an increasingly digital world, many organizations and employees deal almost entirely with intangibles such as ideas and information. Consider Frederick Taylor's comment about the kind of worker needed in the iron business a century ago: "Now one of the first requirements for a man who is fit to handle pig iron as a regular occupation is that he shall be so stupid and so phlegmatic that he more nearly resembles in his mental makeup the ox than any other type."[63] The philosophy of scientific management was that managers structured and controlled jobs so carefully that thinking on the part of employees wasn't required—indeed, it was usually discouraged. How different things are today! Companies such as Microsoft or Ipswitch that develop software and Internet applications depend on employees' minds more than their physical bodies. In companies where the power of an idea determines success, managers' primary goal is to tap into the creativity and knowledge of every employee.

New electronic technologies also shape the organization itself and how it is managed. Technology provides the architecture that supports and reinforces the new workplace. For example, one approach to information management is **enterprise resource planning (ERP)** systems, which unite all of a company's major business functions, such as order processing, product design, purchasing, inventory, manufacturing, distribution, human resources, receipt of payments, and forecasting of future demand. Because ERP weaves together all of the company's systems, managers anywhere in the organization can see the big picture and act quickly, based on up-to-the-minute information.[64] ERP prompts a new approach to management—a companywide management system in which everyone, from the CEO down to a machine operator on the factory floor, has instant access to critical information. Thus, ERP also supports management attempts to harness and leverage organizational *knowledge*.

Peter Drucker coined the term *knowledge work* more than 40 years ago,[65] but it is only in recent years that managers have genuinely recognized knowledge as an important organizational resource that should be managed just as they manage cash flow or raw materials. **Knowledge management** refers to the efforts to systematically find, organize, and make available a company's intellectual capital and to foster a culture of continuous learning and knowledge sharing so that a company's activities build on what is already known.[66] Information technology plays an important role by enabling the storage and dissemination of data and information across the organization, but technology is only one part of a larger management system.[67] A complete knowledge management system includes not only the technology for capturing and storing knowledge for easy access, but also new management values that support risk-taking, learning, and collaboration. Rather than seeing employees as factors of production and looking for ways to use human and material resources for greatest efficiency, today's most successful managers cherish people for their ability to think, create, share knowledge, and build relationships.

enterprise resource planning (ERP)
Systems that unite a company's major business functions—order processing, product design, purchasing, inventory, etc.

knowledge management
The efforts to systematically find, organize, and make available a company's intellectual capital and to foster a culture of continuous learning and knowledge sharing.

■ Summary and Management Solution

This chapter has examined the historical background leading up to new approaches to managing learning organizations and the digital workplace. An understanding of the evolution of management helps current and future managers understand where we are now and continue to progress toward better management.

The three major perspectives on management that have evolved since the late 1800s are the classical perspective, the humanistic perspective, and the management science perspective. Each perspective has several specialized subfields. Recent extensions of management perspectives include systems theory, the contingency view, and total quality management. The most recent thinking about organizations has been brought about by the shift to a new workplace described in Chapter 1. Many managers are redesigning their companies toward the learning organization, which fully engages all employees in identifying and solving problems. The learning organization is characterized by a team-based structure, empowered employees, and open information. The learning organization represents a substantial departure from the traditional management hierarchy.

The shift to a learning organization goes hand-in-hand with today's transition to a technology-driven workplace. Ideas, information, and relationships are becoming more important than production machinery and physical assets, which requires new approaches to management. E-commerce is burgeoning as more economic activity takes place over digital computer networks rather than in physical space. Two specific management tools that support the digital workplace are enterprise resource planning and knowledge management. Both require managers to think in new ways about the role of employees in the organization. Managers value employees for their ability to think, build relationships, and share knowledge, which is quite different from the scientific management perspective of a century ago.

One almost century-old organization that is thriving as a technology-driven workplace is Cementos Mexicanos (Cemex), described at the beginning of the chapter. To help the organization compete in a rapidly changing, complex environment, managers looked for both technological and management innovations. A core element of the new approach is the company's complex information technology infrastructure, which includes a global positioning satellite system and onboard computers in all delivery trucks that are continuously fed with streams of day-to-day data on customer orders, production schedules, traffic problems, weather conditions, and so forth. Even more important are changes in how managers and employees think about and do their work. All drivers and dispatchers attended weekly secondary education classes for two years. Regular training in quality, customer service, and computer skills continues, with Cemex devoting at least 8 percent of total work time to employee training and development. Strict and demanding work rules have been abolished so that workers have more discretion and responsibility for identifying and solving problems.

As a result, Cemex trucks now operate as self-organizing business units, run by well-trained employees who think like businesspeople. The three-hour delivery window has been reduced to 20 minutes, and managers believe a goal of 10 minutes is within reach. According to Francisco Perez, operations manager at Cemex in Guadalajara, "They used to think of themselves as drivers. But anyone can deliver concrete. Now our people know that they're delivering a service that the competition cannot deliver." Cemex has transformed the industry by combining extensive networking technology with a new management approach that taps into the mindpower of everyone in the company. People at Cemex are constantly learning—on the job, in training classes, and through visits to other organizations. As a result, the company has a startling capacity to anticipate customer needs, solve problems, and innovate quickly.[68]

■ Discussion Questions

1. Why is it important to understand the different perspectives and approaches to management theory that have evolved throughout the history of organizations?

2. How do societal forces influence the practice and theory of management? Do you think management techniques are a response to these forces?

3. Based on your experience at work or school, describe some ways in which the principles of scientific management and bureaucracy are still used in organizations. Do you believe these characteristics will ever cease to be a part of organizational life? Discuss.

4. A management professor once said that for successful management, studying the present was most important, studying the past was next, and studying the future was least important. Do you agree? Why?
5. Which of the three characteristics of learning organizations do you find most appealing? Which would be hardest for you to adopt?
6. As organizations become more technology-driven, which do you think will become more important—the management of the human element of the organization or the management of technology? Discuss.
7. What is the behavioral sciences approach? How does it differ from earlier approaches to management?
8. Explain the basic idea underlying the contingency view and provide an example.
9. Why can an event such as the Hawthorne studies be a major turning point in the history of management even if the idea is later shown to be in error? Discuss.
10. Identify the major components of systems theory. Is this perspective primarily internal or external? Explain.
11. Do you think management theory will ever be as precise as theories in the fields of physics, chemistry, or experimental psychology? Why or why not?
12. Many e-commerce companies have gone out of business and others are struggling. Would you consider a career in e-commerce at this time? Why or why not?

■ Management in Practice: Experiential Exercise

Theory X and Theory Y Scale

The following are various types of behavior that a manager may engage in when relating to subordinates. Read each statement carefully and rate each one in terms of the extent to which you would use that behavior, according to the following scale. *Note that Items 4 and 10 are reverse scored.*

Make a Great Effort to Do This	Tend to Do This	Tend to Avoid Doing This	Make a Great Effort to Avoid This
1	2	3	4

1. Closely supervise my subordinates in order to get better work from them.

1	2	3	4

2. Set the goals and objectives for my subordinates and sell them on the merits of my plans.

1	2	3	4

3. Set up controls to assure that my subordinates are getting the job done.

1	2	3	4

4. Encourage my subordinates to set their own goals and objectives.

4	3	2	1

5. Make sure that my subordinates' work is planned out for them.

1	2	3	4

6. Check with my subordinates daily to see if they need any help.

1	2	3	4

7. Step in as soon as reports indicate that the job is slipping.

1	2	3	4

8. Push my people to meet schedules if necessary.

1	2	3	4

9. Have frequent meetings to keep in touch with what is going on.

1	2	3	4

10. Allow subordinates to make important decisions.

4	3	2	1

Scoring:

Add the total points and mark your score on the scale below. Refer back to Exhibit 2.4 and review the assumptions related to Theory X and Theory Y. A person who fully subscribes to the assumptions of Theory X would have a score of 10, whereas a person who fully subscribes to the assumptions of Theory Y would have a score of 40. Strong Theory X assumptions are typically considered inappropriate for today's workplace. Where do you fit on the X–Y scale? Does your score reflect your perception of yourself as a current or future manager?

Theory X ├————————————————┼————————————————┼————————————————┤ Theory Y
10   20   30   40

SOURCE: J. William Pfeiffer and John E. Jones, eds., "Supervisory Attitudes: The X–Y Scale," *The 1972 Annual Handbook for Group Facilitators*, 65–68. This material is used by permission of John Wiley & Sons, Inc. The X–Y scale was adapted from an instrument developed by Robert N. Ford of AT & T for in-house manager training.

■ Management in Practice: Ethical Dilemma

The Supervisor

Karen Lowry, manager of a social service agency in a mid-sized city in Illinois, loved to see her employees learn and grow to their full potential. When a rare opening for a supervising clerk occurred, Karen quickly decided to give Charlotte Hines a shot at the job. Charlotte had been with the agency for 17 years and had shown herself to be a true leader. Charlotte worked hard at being a good supervisor, just as she had always worked hard at being a top-notch clerk. She paid attention to the human aspects of employee problems and introduced modern management techniques that strengthened the entire agency.

However, the Civil Service Board decided that a promotional exam should be given to find a permanent placement for the supervising clerk position. For the sake of fairness, the exam was an open competition—anyone, even a new employee, could sign up and take it. The board wanted the candidate with the highest score to get the job but allowed Karen, as manager of the agency, to have the final say-so.

Since she had accepted the provisional opening and proven herself on the job, Charlotte was upset that the entire clerical force was deemed qualified to take the test. When the results came back, she was devastated. Charlotte placed twelfth in the field of candidates, while one of her newly hired clerks placed first. The Civil Service Board, impressed by the new clerk's high score, is urging Karen to give her the permanent supervisory job. Karen wonders if it's fair to base her decision only on the test results.

What Do You Do?

1. Ignore the test. Charlotte has proven herself and deserves the job.
2. Give the job to the candidate with the highest score. You don't need to make enemies on the Civil Service Board, and, after all, it is an objective way to select a permanent placement.
3. Devise a more comprehensive set of selection criteria—including test results as well as supervisory experience, ability to motivate employees, and knowledge of agency procedures—that can be explained and justified to the board and to employees.

SOURCE: Based on Betty Harrigan, "Career Advice," *Working Woman* (July 1986), 22–24.

■ Surf the Net

1. **Generation Y.** Generation Y, the newest generation to enter the workforce, gets lots of press attention. Use a Web browser such as *http://www.google.com* and type in the search phrase "Managing Generation Y." Choose, read, and summarize an article by writing a two- to three-paragraph description of general characteristics used to describe this new generation of workers.
2. **The Learning Organization.** Locate information about a recent Malcolm Baldrige National Quality Award (MBNQA) winner available at *http://www.quality.nist.gov*. Using the three elements of a learning organization presented in Exhibit 2.7, list examples of any or all of the three elements that the MBNQA company illustrates.
3. **B2B e-commerce.** Go to *http://www.thomasregister.com* to try out one of the world's leading resources for B2B

e-commerce. The Thomas Register database contains information from 173,000 American and Canadian companies; 152,000 brand names; and 8,000 online supplier catalogs and Web links. Complete these steps to get an idea of what you would do if you were getting information about a product to buy for the company you were working for: (a) click the option that will let you try ThomasRegister.com before you register, (b) in the search options, select the one that says you're looking for a product or service, (c) key in a product such as "printer cartridges" and follow the links through to see the information and options available for you to order the product.

■ Case for Critical Analysis

SuperJuice

Luisa de la Cruz sat in her new office thinking about her company's future. After working her way up the corporate ladder for 15 years, she has just been appointed CEO of SuperJuice, a Florida-based company that makes juice and juice drinks that are marketed to high schools and restaurants throughout the Southeast. For nearly two decades, SuperJuice has been the most successful juice drink maker in the region. However, profits haven't risen for four straight years, and several new competitors continue to steal market share. In fact, one of the new companies was started by two former SuperJuice employees who left the company after top management continually rejected their ideas for new exotic drink mixes or new approaches to marketing. It made Luisa cringe to realize that the hottest selling drink flavors in Florida and several other states had been invented in SuperJuice's own labs but were now being made and sold by a competitor. Competitors were setting up drink carts at outdoor festivals and advertising with jingles and slogans that caught the imaginations of the region's youth. Even Luisa's own 17-year-old son often purchased her competitors' products, saying that "SuperJuice is for kids. This stuff is hot."

SuperJuice management has always prided itself on the company's efficient set of systems, both in the factory and at headquarters. Managers concentrated on making a high-quality product as inexpensively as possible. "SuperJuice is like a well-oiled machine," Luisa told herself with some pride. Most of the company's 200 employees had joined SuperJuice right out of high school or college and liked the way the company operated. They showed up for work on time, performed their jobs efficiently, and rarely complained. The long-standing rules and procedures, combined with an organizational culture that reflected the traditional, family-oriented background of SuperJuice's Cuban-born founder, contributed to a level of politeness and civility in the company that sometimes seemed like a throwback to the 1950s. "SuperJuice is a calm and civilized place to work in the midst of a rapidly changing, chaotic world," Luisa reflected with pleasure.

But her pleasure evaporated as she realized that the company could collapse beneath her if it didn't somehow respond to the changes in the environment. She remembered the scandal that had erupted several years ago when two new employees started "breaking the rules" and pushing for changes in the company. The two worked odd hours, played rock music, and decorated their offices with brightly colored posters, unique photographs, and fanciful "dream catchers" hung from the ceiling. Occasionally, one would tape a note to his door that read, "Gone to the movies to get my creative juices flowing!" Although both workers were highly productive, top management quickly took action to try to bring the two back in line. They worried that this kind of attitude would have a negative impact on the productivity of other employees, who were accustomed to coming to work and putting in their solid eight hours. The previous CEO really blew his stack when the two presented four new drink flavors they had concocted on the sly. He was so angry about the unauthorized use of lab time that he nearly fired both employees on the spot. Luisa remembered finding one of the employees in the lab dejectedly pouring the prototypes down the drain. "You know you can't do anything new in this company," Luisa told her at that time. "It's just not the SuperJuice way." Since that time, SuperJuice has lost a few other young, ambitious employees who have chafed under the tight management control.

Luisa knew she was promoted because she had always followed the rules. But she also realized that continuing to follow the rules could take this company she loved right into bankruptcy. She knows the company has a lot of potential, starting with its loyal, committed workforce. But where should she begin? Can SuperJuice really change itself into a forward-thinking, creative company?

Questions

1. What are some of the social, political, and economic forces affecting SuperJuice and calling for a new approach to management?
2. What do you believe Luisa needs to do first to begin a transformation at SuperJuice?
3. How would you suggest she turn SuperJuice into a learning organization? Think about specific changes she can make to get all employees thinking of new and exciting ways to revitalize the product line and way of doing business.

SOURCE: Based on Suzy Wetlaufer, "What's Stifling the Creativity at CoolBurst?" *Harvard Business Review* (September–October 1997), 36–40.

■ Endnotes

1. Thomas Petzinger, Jr., *The New Pioneers: The Men and Women Who Are Transforming the Workplace and Marketplace* (New York: Simon & Schuster, 1999) 91–93, and "In Search of the New World of Work," *Fast Company* (April 1999), 214–220+; and Peter Katel, "Bordering on Chaos," *Wired* (July 1997), 98–107.
2. Eric Matson, "You Can Teach This Old Company New Tricks," *Fast Company* (October/November, 1997), 44–46.
3. John Huey, "Managing in the Midst of Chaos," *Fortune* (April 5, 1993), 38–48; and Toby J. Tetenbaum, "Shifting Paradigms: From Newton to Chaos," *Organizational Dynamics* (Spring 1998), 21–32.
4. Eric Abrahamson, "Management Fashion," *Academy of Management Review* 21, no. 1 (January 1996), 254–285. Also see "75 Years of Management Ideas and Practice," a supplement to the *Harvard Business Review* (September–October 1997), for a broad overview of historical trends in management thinking.
5. "Of Water Coolers and Coffee Breaks," timeline in Matthew Boyle, "How the Workplace Was Won," *Fortune* (January 22, 2001), 139+.
6. Daniel A. Wren, *The Evolution of Management Thought*, 2d ed. (New York: Wiley, 1979), 6–8. Much of the discussion of these forces comes from Arthur M. Schlesinger, *Political and Social History of the United States, 1829–1925* (New York: Macmillan, 1925); and Homer C. Hockett, *Political and Social History of the United States, 1492–1828* (New York: Macmillan, 1925).

7. Alison Wellner, "Get Ready for Generation Next," *Training* (February 1999), 42+; Roger Herman, "Gen X Won't Like What Their Parents Did," *American Drycleaner* (February 2001), 184; and Julie Wallace, "After X Comes Y," *HRMagazine* (April 2001), 192.

8. The discussion of trends is based on Marnie E. Green, "Beware and Prepare: The Government Workforce of the Future," *Public Personnel Management* (Winter 2000), 435+.

9. Robin Wright and Doyle McManus, *Flashpoints: Promise and Peril in a New World* (New York: Alfred A. Knopf, 1991).

10. This section is based heavily on Thomas Petzinger, Jr., "So Long Supply and Demand," *The Wall Street Journal* (January 1, 2000), R31.

11. Petzinger, "So Long Supply and Demand."

12. Daniel A. Wren, "Management History: Issues and Ideas for Teaching and Research," *Journal of Management* 13 (1987), 339–350.

13. Business historian Alfred D. Chandler, Jr., quoted in Jerry Useem, "Entrepreneur of the Century," *Inc.* (20th Anniversary Issue, 1999), 159–174.

14. Useem, "Entrepreneur of the Century."

15. The following is based on Wren, *Evolution of Management Thought*, Chapters 4, 5; and Claude S. George, Jr., *The History of Management Thought* (Englewood Cliffs, N.J.: Prentice-Hall, 1968), Chapter 4.

16. Charles D. Wrege and Ann Marie Stoka, "Cooke Creates a Classic: The Story behind F. W. Taylor's Principles of Scientific Management," *Academy of Management Review* (October 1978), 736–749; Robert Kanigel, *The One Best Way: Frederick Winslow Taylor and the Enigma of Efficiency* (New York: Viking, 1997); and Alan Farnham, "The Man Who Changed Work Forever," *Fortune* (July 21, 1997), 114.

17. Quoted in Ann Harrington, "The Big Ideas," *Fortune* (November 22, 1999), 152–154.

18. Wren, *Evolution of Management Thought*, 171; and George, *History of Management Thought*, 103–104.

19. Geoffrey Colvin, "Managing in the Info Era," *Fortune* (March 6, 2000), F-5–F-9.

20. Max Weber, *General Economic History*, trans. Frank H. Knight (London: Allen & Unwin, 1927); Max Weber, *The Protestant Ethic and the Spirit of Capitalism*, trans. Talcott Parsons (New York: Scribner, 1930); and Max Weber, *The Theory of Social and Economic Organizations*, ed. and trans. A. M. Henderson and Talcott Parsons (New York: Free Press, 1947).

21. "UPS," *The Atlanta Journal and Constitution* (April 26, 1992), H1; Richard L. Daft, *Organization Theory and Design*, 3d ed. (St. Paul, Minn.: West, 1989), 181–182; and Kathy Goode, Betty Hahn, and Cindy Seibert, "United Parcel Service: The Brown Giant" (unpublished manuscript, Texas A&M University, 1981).

22. Henri Fayol, *Industrial and General Administration*, trans. J. A. Coubrough (Geneva: International Management Institute, 1930); Henri Fayol, *General and Industrial Management*, trans. Constance Storrs (London: Pitman and Sons, 1949); and W. J. Arnold and the editors of *Business Week, Milestones in Management* (New York: McGraw-Hill, vol. I, 1965; vol. II, 1966).

23. Mary Parker Follett, *The New State: Group Organization: The Solution of Popular Government* (London: Longmans, Green, 1918); and Mary Parker Follett, *Creative Experience* (London: Longmans, Green, 1924).

24. Henry C. Metcalf and Lyndall Urwick, eds., *Dynamic Administration: The Collected Papers of Mary Parker Follett* (New York: Harper & Row, 1940); Arnold, *Milestones in Management*.

25. Follett, *The New State*; Metcalf and Urwick, *Dynamic Administration* (London: Sir Isaac Pitman, 1941).

26. William B. Wolf, *How to Understand Management: An Introduction to Chester I. Barnard* (Los Angeles: Lucas Brothers, 1968); and David D. Van Fleet, "The Need-Hierarchy and Theories of Authority," *Human Relations* 9 (Spring 1982), 111–118.

27. Gregory M. Bounds, Gregory H. Dobbins, and Oscar S. Fowler, *Management: A Total Quality Perspective* (Cincinnati, Ohio: South-Western Publishing, 1995), 52–53.

28. Curt Tausky, *Work Organizations: Major Theoretical Perspectives* (Itasca, Ill.: F. E. Peacock, 1978), 42.

29. Charles D. Wrege, "Solving Mayo's Mystery: The First Complete Account of the Origin of the Hawthorne Studies—The Forgotten Contributions of Charles E. Snow and Homer Hibarger" (paper presented to the Management History Division of the Academy of Management, August 1976).

30. Ronald G. Greenwood, Alfred A. Bolton, and Regina A. Greenwood, "Hawthorne a Half Century Later: Relay Assembly Participants Remember," *Journal of Management* 9 (Fall/Winter 1983), 217–231.

31. F. J. Roethlisberger, W. J. Dickson, and H. A. Wright, *Management and the Worker* (Cambridge, Mass.: Harvard University Press, 1939).

32. H. M. Parson, "What Happened at Hawthorne?" *Science* 183 (1974), 922–932; John G. Adair, "The Hawthorne Effect: A Reconsideration of the Methodological Artifact," *Journal of Applied Psychology* 69, no. 2 (1984), 334–345; and Gordon Diaper, "The Hawthorne Effect: A Fresh Examination," *Educational Studies* 16, no. 3 (1990), 261–268.

33. Greenwood, Bolton, and Greenwood, "Hawthorne a Half Century Later," 219–221.

34. F. J. Roethlisberger and W. J. Dickson, *Management and the Worker*.

35. Ramon J. Aldag and Timothy M. Stearns, *Management*, 2nd ed. (Cincinnati, Ohio: South-Western Publishing, 1991), 47–48.

36. Tausky, *Work Organizations: Major Theoretical Perspectives*, 55.

37. Douglas McGregor, *The Human Side of Enterprise* (New York: McGraw-Hill, 1960), 16–18.

38. Gina Imperato, "Dirty Business, Bright Ideas," *Fast Company* (February–March 1997), 89–93.

39. Wendell L. French and Cecil H. Bell Jr., "A History of Organizational Development," in Wendell L. French, Cecil H. Bell Jr., and Robert A. Zawacki, *Organization Development and Transformation: Managing Effective Change* (Burr Ridge, Illinois: Irwin McGraw-Hill, 2000), 20–42.

40. Mansel G. Blackford and K. Austin Kerr, *Business Enterprise in American History* (Boston: Houghton Mifflin, 1986),

Chapters 10, 11; and Alex Groner and the editors of *American Heritage and BusinessWeek, The American Heritage History of American Business and Industry* (New York: American Heritage Publishing, 1972), Chapter 9.

41. Larry M. Austin and James R. Burns, *Management Science* (New York: Macmillan, 1985).

42. Marcia Stepanek, "How an Intranet Opened Up the Door to Profits," *BusinessWeek E.Biz* (July 26, 1999), EB32–EB38.

43. Matt Vilano, "A Lead-Pipe Cinch," *CIO*, Section 1 (March 15, 1999), 51–59.

44. Ludwig von Bertalanffy, Carl G. Hempel, Robert E. Bass, and Hans Jonas, "General Systems Theory: A New Approach to Unity of Science," *Human Biology* 23 (December 1951), 302–361; and Kenneth E. Boulding, "General Systems Theory—The Skeleton of Science," *Management Science* 2 (April 1956), 197–208.

45. Fremont E. Kast and James E. Rosenzweig, "General Systems Theory: Applications for Organization and Management," *Academy of Management Journal* (December 1972), 447–465.

46. "CIO Panel: Knowledge-Sharing Roundtable," Information Week Online, News in Review (April 26, 1999), *Information Week* Web site, downloaded on April 30, 1999; and Glenn Rifkin, "Nothing But 'Net,'" *Fast Company* (June–July 1996), 118–127.

47. Fred Luthans, "The Contingency Theory of Management: A Path Out of the Jungle," *Business Horizons* 16 (June 1973), 62–72; and Fremont E. Kast and James E. Rosenzweig, *Contingency Views of Organization and Management* (Chicago: Science Research Associates, 1973).

48. Samuel Greengard, "25 Visionaries Who Shaped Today's Workplace," *Workforce* (January 1997), 50–59; and Harrington, "The Big Ideas."

49. Mauro F. Guillen, "The Age of Eclecticism: Current Organizational Trends and the Evolution of Managerial Models," *Sloan Management Review* (Fall 1994), 75–86.

50. Jeremy Main, "How to Steal the Best Ideas Around," *Fortune* (October 19, 1992), 102–106.

51. Peter Senge, *The Fifth Discipline: The Art and Practice of Learning Organizations* (New York: Doubleday/Currency, 1990).

52. Jeffrey Pfeffer, "Producing Sustainable Competitive Advantage through the Effective Management of People," *Academy of Management Executive* 9, no. 1 (1995), 55–69.

53. Alex Markels, "The Wisdom of Chairman Ko," *Fast Company* (November 1999), 258–276.

54. Edward O. Welles, "Mind Gains," *Inc.* (December 1999), 112–124.

55. Kevin Kelly, *New Rules for the New Economy: 10 Radical Strategies for a Connected World* (New York: Viking Penguin, 1998).

56. Wayne Kawamoto, "Click Here for Efficiency," *BusinessWeek Enterprise* (December 7, 1998), 12–14.

57. Nick Wingfield, "In the Beginning...," *The Wall Street Journal* (May 21, 2001), R18.

58. Andy Reinhardt,"From Gearhead to Grand High Pooh-Bah," *BusinessWeek* (August 28, 2000), 129–130.

59. Matt Murray and Jathon Sapsford, "GE Reshuffles Its Dot-Com Strategy to Focus on Internal 'Digitizing'," *The Wall Street Journal* (May 4, 2001) B1, B4; Daniel Lyons, "Lion in Winter," *Forbes* (April 30, 2001), 68–70.

60. William J. Holstein and Edward Robinson, "The Re-Education of Jacques Nasser," *Business2.Com* (May 29, 2001), 60–73.

61. Bernard Wysocki, Jr., "Corporate Caveat: Dell or Be Delled," *The Wall Street Journal* (May 10, 1999), A1.

62. Andy Reinhardt, "From Gearhead to Grand High Pooh-Bah," *BusinessWeek* (August 28, 2000), 129–130.

63. Quoted in Colvin, "Managing in the Info Era."

64. Jeffrey Zygmont, "The Ties That Bind," *Inc. Tech* no. 3, (1998), 70–84; and Nancy Ferris, "ERP: Sizzling or Stumbling?" *Government Executive* (July 1999), 99–102.

65. Harrington, "The Big Ideas." Also see Peter Drucker, *Post-Capitalist Society*, (Oxford: Butterworth Heinemann, 1993), 5.

66. Based on Andrew Mayo, "Memory Bankers," *People Management* (January 22, 1998), 34–38; William Miller, "Building the Ultimate Resource," *Management Review* (January 1999), 42–45; and Todd Datz, "How to Speak Geek," *CIO Enterprise*, Section 2 (April 15, 1999), 46–52.

67. Louisa Wah, "Behind the Buzz," *Management Review* (April 1999), 17–26.

68. Petzinger, *The New Pioneers: The Men and Women Who Are Transforming the Workplace and Marketplace*, and "In Search of the New World of Work,"; Katel, "Bordering on Chaos"; and Oren Harari, "The Concrete Intangibles," *Management Review* (May 1999), 30–33.

Chapter 1: LeMeridien Managers Manage by Walking Around

LEMERIDIEN IS A CHAIN OF 125 LUXURY HOTELS IN 55 countries around the globe. You can find Le Meridien hotels in the United States, throughout Europe, in Africa, Australia, India, Egypt, and other locations. Premium customer service is key to the success of a hotel chain, and a manager's skills can make or break a hotel. At Le Meridien Hotel in Boston, a manager's work is never done. Take the typical day of Bob van den Oord, assistant general manager of the hotel, which is part of a luxury chain owned by Great Eagle in Hong Kong and managed by Le Meridien in London. He arrives at the hotel before 8:00 A.M. and does a walk-through of the entire hotel, inspecting empty rooms, the kitchen, dining rooms, reservations desk, front lobby, and even the laundry, to be certain that everything is running smoothly. He may meet with other managers, such as the Dutch-born manager, Michiel Lugt, who runs room service and stewarding (restaurant and catering services) for the hotel, or the housekeeping or security managers if they have a specific issue to discuss. By 9:30, all managers—including Bob—are assembled for the daily operational meeting, in which everyone reports briefly on the hotel's activities for the past 24 hours. Managers for the information technology department, reservations, housekeeping, and human resource departments give thumbnail reports on problems currently needing solutions or ones that have already been dealt with—such as a brief lack of hot water in some of the building's guest rooms. By 9:45 the meeting is over and all managers return to their posts.

Bob van den Oord fulfills all the four management functions every day he's on the job. As assistant general manager, he meets with the general manager to "set the overall goals for the hotel, so I take a more strategic role and provide the tools and resources to the other managers" so they can do their jobs. He functions in an organizational role, assigning responsibility to other managers—such as the head of security—to accomplish particular tasks or assignments, such as evaluating and updating security at the hotel. He leads and motivates workers by constantly keeping in touch with them—he manages by walking around. "It's a good tool to see what's going on," he says, from the kitchen to the plants out front of the building. "Ninety-percent of problems are because of management screw-ups," he notes candidly. "I like [walking around], the staff likes it, and guests like to see management around as well." Van den Oord admits that he asks a lot of his managers, but he devotes a lot of himself to the job as well. "The hotel is a 24-hour operation," he explains. "We have to be here when other people are having fun." Finally, he fulfills the control function by monitoring activities and making necessary corrections. His daily walk-through is a prime example of this function. "Management is about constant feedback," Van den Oord comments. "It allows people to improve their performance."

Michiel Lugt, the functional manager who runs room service—which is open 24 hours a day, 7 days a week—fully agrees with his boss's philosophy of management. He likes to lead by example and is always ready to help out when necessary, even if it means serving coffee to guests in one of the dining rooms. He believes that people skills are vitally important in the hotel industry, not only in dealing with staff but in dealing with guests as well. He remarks that, as a young manager, "Sometimes you have to manage people who are older than you are; that's a massive challenge. People should realize that experience is important." He makes a special effort to learn whatever he can from staff members who have been in the business longer than he has. "I try to be one of the gang, basically," he says of his relationship with his staff. "We have to run, and business and things have to be done, but that doesn't mean you have to be a tyrant." He encourages staff members to approach him with questions and concerns whenever possible.

Le Meridien—a single hotel in a huge organization—is a complex organization itself, hosting more than 100,000 visitors each year. On any given day, Bob van den Oord and his staff may welcome honeymooners, international tourists, business travelers, groups for conventions or conferences, and college reunions. "It's hard work, but it's fun," notes Van den Oord. Of his staff he says, "We're all in it together." That, in a nutshell, is the new paradigm of management at Le Meridien Hotel.

Questions

1. In addition to human skills, a hotel manager needs technical skills and conceptual skills. Identify what you think some of those technical skills and conceptual skills might be, either for a general manager or for a functional manager at a hotel.
2. Would you call Le Meridien Hotel in Boston a learning organization? Why or why not?
3. Describe at least one social force, political force, and economic force that may influence Le Meridien and its management practices.

SOURCE: Company Web site, *http://www.lemeridien-hotels.com*, accessed January 4, 2002.

Chapter 2: In the Beginning: A Bite Taken from the Apple

ON APRIL FOOL'S DAY 1976, APPLE COMPUTER WAS FOUNDED by two guys who had been friends in high school, who liked to tinker with electronics, and who had dropped out of college to pursue jobs in the new computer industry in what would later be called the Silicon Valley of California. Apple was no April Fool's joke, although not many people took it seriously at first. Consumers hadn't yet grasped the idea that they could use computers for anything themselves. They saw large mainframes in secluded, air-conditioned rooms at work. But personal computers were still unheard of. Even businesses were reluctant to invest in computers for their employees; after all, they had typewriters, and calculators were available for number crunching. But Steve Jobs and Steve Wozniak had a product they thought they could sell: first the Apple I computer, and shortly thereafter the Apple II. They had created the first personal computer in Steve Jobs's garage. The face of business, and daily life, has never been the same.

The Apple computer did sell—in fact, the Apple II sold like crazy, once it gained momentum. Within three years, the Apple II had earned $139 million, representing a 700 percent growth. Consumers were snapping up Apple IIs for writing and calculating as quickly as the company could produce them. With success came further company growth, and the necessity for management. Through the first few years of Apple's existence, Steve Jobs controlled the business side of the company, taking on all of the management functions: planning, organizing, leading, and controlling. He hired a succession of presidents, financial officers, public relations people, and marketing people to handle the company's expanding business. Then there were the product design teams, midlevel managers, and ultimately, more and more investors. Although the atmosphere during the early days was radical—both employees and management liked to foster the counterculture image—as new investors began to take their seats on the board of directors, things changed. These older, more conservative directors insisted that the company be managed in a more traditional fashion. Meanwhile, only five years into the venture, Steve Wozniak was injured in a plane crash and forced to take a leave of absence. Steve Jobs became chairman of Apple at only 26 years old.

As a young manager, Jobs certainly had technical skills. After all, the Apple computer was his brainchild. Although some critics might disagree, he also had conceptual skills: he understood where his organization was and had a vision of where he wanted it to go. But Jobs has never been known for his human skills. Driven toward perfection himself, he expected perfection from his managers and employees. One former employee recalls that Jobs rejected anyone's work the first time he saw it, just on principle. He earned himself a notorious reputation as a manager, one that has followed him to this day.

In 1981, a competitor of goliath proportions emerged: IBM—the powerhouse of mainframe computing—introduced its first personal computer to the marketplace. Jobs, who was essentially an engineer, recognized that he did not have the business or management skills necessary to take his company to the next level. So, he began to pursue John Sculley, who was then president of Pepsi-Cola. He lured Sculley to Apple with the language of a visionary: "If you stay at Pepsi, five years from now all you'll have accomplished is selling a lot more sugar water to kids . . . If you come to Apple you can change the world." Sculley accepted the challenge.

As the company went public and began to compete with larger organizations like IBM, the people who had originally gone to work for Apple found themselves in a changing environment. Despite Jobs's iron grip, they viewed themselves as a young, hip, innovative group who did things their own way. Even though both Apple founders had dropped out of college, Apple workers were highly educated, creative, and technically skilled. They valued their independence, and most likely chafed under the new "business" orientation. On a larger scale, Apple was charged with changing the way the general public viewed—and ultimately valued—computers. Apple was lauded for its product innovations and creativity, and its users became devoted followers.

The economic environment, both inside and outside Apple, was ripe for success. The economic boom of the 1980s meant that people had money to spend. But it also meant that competition followed closely on Apple's heels. By the early 1980s, Apple management, including new CEO John Sculley (who was a sharp businessman, but who didn't know much about computers), made some costly mistakes. For instance, the Lisa, which was the first mouse-controlled personal computer, was priced at $10,000, far above what the public would accept. No one bought it. And the Apple III was so filled with design flaws that the first 14,000 computers had to be recalled. That computer's image never recovered. Still, many more ups and downs lay ahead for the company as Apple continued to grow and change as an organization.

Questions

1. From the overview presented in this case, what features of Apple's culture are similar to learning organizations? To bureaucratic organizations? What steps might Apple managers take toward creating—or strengthening—a learning organization?

2. Of the four management functions, which do you think Jobs excelled at? Which was his weakest? Why?

3. What types of roles does a person in Jobs's position at Apple need to perform? List as many informational, interpersonal, and decisional roles that you think apply and explain why you think so.

SOURCES: Apple Computer Inc. Web site, "Business Summary," "History," and "Steve Paul Jobs" accessed March 23, 1999, at http://www.apple.com; Brent Schlender and Michael Martin, "Paradise Lost," Fortune (February 19, 1996), accessed at http://www.pathfinder.com. iMac.

Part One: Ford Motor Company Makes History

THE HISTORY OF FORD MOTOR COMPANY EMBODIES THE history of American management itself. When Henry Ford began a manufacturing revolution with his company's mass production of automobiles, much of the country was still bouncing along in horse-drawn carriages. A hundred years later, despite many ups and downs, Ford Motor Company is firmly established as the world's largest pickup truck manufacturer and the number-two maker of cars (behind General Motors). Ford has progressed from an offering of one color—black—to a wide range of makes, models, and hues from which consumers may choose, depending on their budget, lifestyle, and mood. In addition to the autos it produces under its own name, Ford's brands now include Jaguar, Lincoln, Mercury, and Volvo, a 33 percent stake in Mazda, BMW's Land Rover SUV, along with the Hertz rental agency. Ford has had hugely successful models, such as the Taurus, as well as duds that it would rather forget, such as the Pinto. In recent years, the company has been mired in a public relations disaster surrounding its popular SUV, the Explorer, and the vehicle's standard tires, which were manufactured by Firestone/Bridgestone. Still, the company has managed to survive by making changes in leadership, improving efficiency and effectiveness of its management and manufacturing operations, and embracing new management competencies. As you study your course of management this semester, you'll follow the rises, dips, and turns of one of America's most well-known and enduring organizations.

Fast-forward from that original assembly line spewing out those black Model Ts and Model As to the end of the twentieth century, when a whirlwind known as Jacques Nasser took over as CEO of Ford Motor Company and immediately began to change management practices that previously had included a complex bureaucracy bogged down by centralized decision making and an unwillingness to budge from the status quo.

Although Nasser didn't explicitly use the term learning organization, he set out to turn his company into one. He hired a group of skilled managers from different automakers around the world (including Volkswagen and BMW), lured a number of marketers and salespeople from consumer-goods manufacturers, and pushed the entire Ford workforce to get as close to customers as possible to find out what people really wanted in their automobiles. He encouraged information sharing with such initiatives as a venture with MSN's CarPoint Web site that would provide data from online purchases. Ford marketers and designers would learn which models, colors, and features certain buyers preferred. And he let managers know in no uncertain terms that Ford Motor Company was now on the move—with their help as empowered workers who were accountable for their own (and their employees') performance. "You've got to earn [a promotion,]" Nasser supposedly thundered in one meeting. "The days of entitlement at Ford Motor Company are gone forever." To that end, he instituted a forced-ranking system, under which a certain number of employees would be considered underperformers and laid off each year. The system, which worked something like a grading curve, drew much criticism and was eventually abandoned.

On a grand scale, Nasser announced an organizational shakeup that meant decentralizing authority and decision-making powers, and transferring them to semiautonomous business units around the world. "Jac learned to make decisions without a lot of bureaucratic oversight from [Ford headquarters at] Dearborn," recalled Robert Lutz, Nasser's former boss. Now Nasser was promoting this kind of independent decision making throughout a new generation of Ford managers.

All of these actions were part of Nasser's strategy to transform a century-old industrial giant into a nimble, flexible company that could rapidly meet consumers' wants and needs. Designers, engineers, and marketers were required to attend seminars at a Consumer Insight Center to learn how to listen to customers and engage them in conversations designed to reveal what products and features they would most likely buy. Then they were sent in small teams out into the field for eight weeks of "customer immersion." Nasser wasn't kidding. He wanted all managers at all levels to understand their customers, inside and out.

Nasser made some radical changes at Ford Motor Company, an organization that has long been a symbol of American business and ingenuity. The company has been around so long that it has passed through several historical phases of management, from scientific management to today's learning organization. In 1913, one of the first moving assembly lines was installed in the company's Highland Park plant, reducing production time by 50 percent. With this new system, a Ford Model T came off the assembly line every ten seconds. Today, Ford managers rely on teams, empowerment, the Internet, and high-speed technology to produce thousands of cars a day. Ford's ability to change when the environment demands it may be the single most important factor in its long-term survival.

Questions

1. How have the necessary skills for a successful manager changed at Ford over the decades?
2. Why was it important for Ford to become a learning organization?
3. Do you think that Jacques Nasser was an effective manager? Why or why not?

SOURCES: "Ford Motor Company," Hoover's Capsule, Hoover's Online (November 16, 2001), http://www.hoovers.com; "Profile—Ford Motor Company," Yahoo! Finance, http://www.biz.yahoo.com; Julie Cantwell, "Exec Changes Help Ford with Basics," Automotive News (November 12, 2001), http://www.autonews.com; Geoffrey Colvin, "We Can't All Be Above Average," Fortune, August 13, 2001, www.fortune.com; Kathleen Kerwin and Keith Naughton, "Remaking Ford," BusinessWeek Online (October 11, 1999), http://www.businessweek.com.

The Environment of Management

Perhaps no element of nature evokes greater images of power than wind. Hurricanes, blizzards, and tornadoes all pack the full force of nature in their pounding winds. Languages and cultures the world over have different names for wind and windstorms: gust, gale, cyclone, twister, Nor'easter, typhoon, and monsoon, to name a few. All of these natural phenomena can inflict considerable damage to their environments. They can literally huff and puff and blow houses down. By the same token, their gentle counterparts—breezes and zephyrs—can be cool oases in the midst of searing heat. Wind may blow in like the March lion or simply exhale like the March lamb. In either case, harnessing the power of wind may give the inhabitants of its surrounding environment an advantage.

Managers strive to harness the various forces in their environment that have an impact on their organizations. The general environment—the gale of a booming economy, political hurricanes, the cyclone of rapidly changing technology—affects the organization indirectly. The task environment—a gust of customers or suppliers—affects the way a manager plans, organizes, and implements or delegates tasks. Managers who work for large corporations with offices in many countries may have to deal with a variety of languages and cultures. Other managers may look for ways to harness environmental factors in a socially responsible way. Entrepreneurs who start small, innovative businesses may sometimes feel that they are in a vortex, always spinning, always changing in the need to juggle environmental factors.

Regardless of the type of organization a manager works within, the environment of management is a powerful force—not to take shelter from, but to harness for a competitive edge.

The Environment and Corporate Culture

CHAPTER OUTLINE

The External Environment

General Environment

Task Environment

The Organization–Environment Relationship

Environmental Uncertainty

Adapting to the Environment

The Internal Environment: Corporate Culture

Symbols

Stories

Heroes

Slogans

Ceremonies

Environment and Culture

Adaptive Cultures

Types of Cultures

Shaping Corporate Culture for the New Workplace

New Demands for Managing Corporate Culture

Cultural Leadership

LEARNING OBJECTIVES

After studying this chapter, you should be able to

1 Describe the general and task environments and the dimensions of each.

2 Explain the strategies managers use to help organizations adapt to an uncertain environment.

3 Define corporate culture and give organizational examples.

4 Explain organizational symbols, stories, heroes, slogans, and ceremonies and their relationship to corporate culture.

5 Describe how corporate culture relates to the environment.

6 Define a cultural leader and explain the tools a cultural leader uses to change corporate culture.

Management Challenge

"It's lunch time. Do you know where your baby's food comes from?" For many parents, the comforting answer is that it comes from Gerber, a trusted name in the industry for decades. The Gerber baby-food company produces more than 5 million jars of baby food a day in the United States and has U.S. sales of $700 million annually, plus $300 million abroad. But Gerber's reputation was threatened when the activist group Greenpeace held a news conference accusing Gerber of using genetically altered corn that produces dangerous toxins.

Gerber didn't dispute the basic fact that some of its products contain ingredients from genetically modified crops. But managers at Gerber and its parent company, Novartis AG of Switzerland, angrily countered the notion that these ingredients produce dangerous toxins. The U.S. Food and Drug Administration agrees, calling foods produced with genetically altered foods "as safe as other foods in the grocery store." Nevertheless, there is growing concern around the world about the long-term effects of genetically engineered crops on humans and the natural environment. Buoyed by their success getting baby food and other products yanked from store shelves in Europe, Greenpeace and other activists have turned their attention to the U.S. The growing movement has companies in the food industry scrambling for an appropriate response. More than half the nation's soybean crop and a third of its corn crop contain transplanted genes, and these crops turn up in products ranging from hamburger buns to corn chips to cake mixes. Although the FDA continues to report that there is no health risk, activists have homed in on the emotional issue of baby-food safety to provoke wider public interest in their cause.[1]

If you were a manager at Gerber, how would you address this threat from the external environment? How might managers gauge public feelings and anticipate future problems?

73

Even in a seemingly simple, low-tech industry such as manufacturing baby food, challenges from the environment can wreak havoc on an organization's reputation, sales, and profits. In high-tech industries, environmental conditions are even more volatile. Xerox, one of the original high-tech companies emerging after World War II, once owned the copier market but has suffered huge losses in recent years, partly because managers misread cues from the environment and changes in technology needs.

Dialog Corp., the pioneer of the data-retrieval industry, founded by Lockheed in 1963, is now fighting for its life after managers missed an opportunity to be a leader of the Internet revolution. "Dialog had a chance at the inception of the Web to index it, in essence to be a Yahoo," says Jeffrey Gault, former head of the business. "But we passed on it because we couldn't see how we could make money on it."[2] The environment surprises many companies. Bookstores such as Barnes & Noble and Borders were caught napping when a new approach to bookselling emerged. Amazon.com was ringing up sales on the Internet for a year before Barnes & Noble managers even began thinking about selling online, and the company had a whopping three-year head start over Borders' online site.[3]

Government actions and red tape can also affect an organization's environment and foment a crisis. Deregulation of the electric utilities industry is forcing a massive restructuring of power companies in states such as California, Texas, and Massachusetts, and will eventually impact companies all across the United States. Changes in Medicaid are hurting hospitals such as La Rabida, on Chicago's South Side, which is dedicated to serving the poor.[4]

The study of management traditionally has focused on factors within the organization—a closed systems view—such as leading, motivating, and controlling employees. The classical, behavioral, and management science schools described in Chapter 2 focused on internal aspects of organizations over which managers have direct control. These views are accurate but incomplete. Globalization and the trend toward a borderless world affect companies in new ways. Even for those companies that try to operate solely on the domestic stage, events that have greatest impact typically originate in the external environment. To be effective, managers must monitor and respond to the environment—an open systems view.

This chapter explores in detail components of the external environment and how they affect the organization. We will also examine a major part of the organization's internal environment—corporate culture. Corporate culture is shaped by the external environment and is an important part of the context within which managers do their jobs.

The External Environment

The world as we know it is undergoing tremendous and far-reaching changes. These changes can be understood by defining and examining components of the external environment.

organizational environment
All elements existing outside the organization's boundaries that have the potential to affect the organization.

The external **organizational environment** includes all elements existing outside the boundary of the organization that have the potential to affect the organization.[5] The environment includes competitors, resources, technology, and economic conditions that influence the organization. It does not include those events so far removed from the organization that their impact is not perceived.

The organization's external environment can be further conceptualized as having two layers: general and task environments, as illustrated in Exhibit 3.1.[6]

The **general environment** is the outer layer that is widely dispersed and affects organizations indirectly. It includes social, demographic, and economic factors that influence all organizations about equally. Increases in the inflation rate or the percentage of dual-career couples in the workforce are part of the organization's general environment. These events do not directly change day-to-day operations, but they do affect all organizations eventually. The **task environment** is closer to the organization and includes the sectors that conduct day-to-day transactions with the organization and directly influence its basic operations and performance. It is generally considered to include competitors, suppliers, and customers.

The organization also has an **internal environment**, which includes the elements within the organization's boundaries. The internal environment is composed of current employees, management, and especially corporate culture, which defines employee behavior in the internal environment and how well the organization will adapt to the external environment.

Exhibit 3.1 illustrates the relationship among the general, task, and internal environments. As an open system, the organization draws resources from the external environment and releases goods and services back to it. We will now discuss the two layers of the external environment in more detail. Then we will discuss corporate culture, the key element in the internal environment. Other aspects of the internal environment, such as structure and technology, will be covered in Parts Four and Five of this book.

general environment
The layer of the external environment that affects the organization indirectly.

task environment
The layer of the external environment that directly influences the organization's operations and performance.

internal environment
The environment within the organization's boundaries.

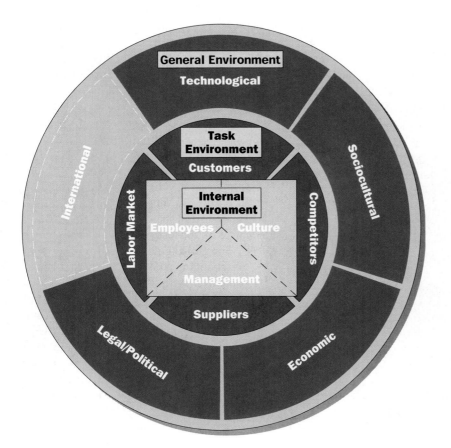

Exhibit 3.1

Location of the Organization's General, Task, and Internal Environments

General Environment

The general environment represents the outer layer of the environment. These dimensions influence the organization over time but often are not involved in day-to-day transactions with it. The dimensions of the general environment include international, technological, sociocultural, economic, and legal–political.

international dimension
Portion of the external environment that represents events originating in foreign countries as well as opportunities for American companies in other countries.

International.   The **international dimension** of the external environment represents events originating in foreign countries as well as opportunities for American companies in other countries. Note in Exhibit 3.1 that the international dimension represents a context that influences all other aspects of the external environment. The international environment provides new competitors, customers, and suppliers and shapes social, technological, and economic trends, as well.

Today, every company has to compete on a global basis. Dixon Ticonderoga Co., which makes pencils, is in trouble because of increased foreign competition, especially from low-cost pencil companies in China. Today, about 50 percent of the pencils bought in the United States come from overseas, compared to 16 percent a decade ago.[7] High-quality, low-priced automobiles from Japan and Korea have permanently changed the American automobile industry. With the development of the Internet as a place for doing business, even the smallest companies can look at the whole world as their market. When operating globally, managers have to consider legal, political, sociocultural, and economic factors not only in their home country but in various other countries as well. For example, a drop in the U.S. dollar's foreign exchange rate lowers the price of U.S. products overseas, increasing export competitiveness.

Many companies have had to cut prices to remain competitive in the new global economy. Economic problems in other parts of the world now have a tremendous impact on U.S. companies. Companies such as Coca-Cola, which get a large percentage of sales from Asia, are feeling the pinch of the Asian economic crisis. Russia's economic woes also are affecting U.S. companies. For example, a small distributor of vitamins and sports supplements near Nashville, Tennessee, gets 20 percent of its sales from Russia. The economic turmoil in that country, however, has left U.S.A. Laboratories struggling to get paid and make up for lost orders.[8]

The global environment represents an everchanging and uneven playing field compared with the domestic environment. Changes in the international domain can abruptly turn the domestic environment upside down. The mad-cow epidemic in Europe affected U.S. companies in numerous ways because of concerns about the spread of the disease to the United States. The Red Cross adopted a rule against blood donations from persons who have spent six months

China's membership in the World Trade Organization will dramatically change the international dimension of the external environment. With 1.3 billion people, China is already an attractive market, but WTO membership will spur economic growth even more. For U.S. construction companies such as Caterpillar, and sales representative Anny Wong, pictured here, China is a dream market, with highways, dams, and buildings springing up everywhere. However, doing business in this new market also presents many challenges, such as setting up distribution chains, service centers, and dealer networks.

©Fritz Hoffmann/Network

or more in mad-cow countries, even though there's no evidence the human form of the disease is transmitted this way. The ruling has decreased the already declining supply of blood, affecting hospitals, insurance companies, and consumers, who must cope with higher health care costs.

Managers who are used to thinking only about the domestic environment must learn new rules to cope with goods, services, and ideas circulating around the globe. Chapter 4 describes how today's businesses are operating in an increasingly borderless world and examines in detail how managing in a global environment differs from the management of domestic operations. Perhaps the hardest lesson for managers in the United States to learn is that they do not always know best. U.S. decision makers know little about issues and competition in foreign countries. U.S. arrogance is a shortcut to failure. To counter this, Pall Corporation keeps a team of Ph.D.s traveling around the world gathering current information on markets and issues.[9]

Technological. The **technological dimension** includes scientific and technological advancements in a specific industry as well as in society at large. In recent years, this dimension has created massive and far-reaching changes for organizations in all industries. Fifteen years ago, many organizations didn't even use desktop computers. Today, computer networks, Internet access, videoconferencing capabilities, cell phones, fax machines, pagers, and laptops are practically taken for granted as the minimum tools for doing business. Technological advancements that make the Internet accessible to nearly everyone have changed the nature of competition and of organizations' relationships to customers. Many companies are adopting technologically sophisticated e-business methods that use private networks or the Internet to handle practically all their operations. Wireless technology and new software applications are making the Internet easily accessible from a cell phone or other hand-held devices. Communications and computing devices are getting smaller, more powerful, and more affordable. A technology research firm reports that more than half of all U.S. households have a cell phone, and in

technological dimension
The dimension of the general environment that includes scientific and technological advancements in the industry and society at large.

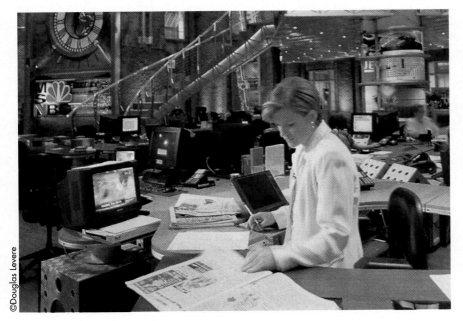

©Douglas Levere

MSNBC, the cable and online television news network, was begun by Microsoft Corp. and General Electric Co.'s NBC unit in recognition of the technological dimension of the companys' general environment. MSNBC positions NBC for a high-tech future where TV and the Internet are combined. With high-tech appeal beamed out of a converted warehouse in hues of metallic orange-tinted blue, MSNBC draws the affluent 25–54 age group, viewers that advertisers covet.

©Meredith Heuer

American consumers' growing taste for international foods reflects a change in the sociocultural dimension of the environment. Interest in Italian cuisine, for example, has been growing rapidly. Gourmet pasta maker Monterey Pasta was recently ranked Number 26 on Fortune magazine's list of the 100 fastest-growing companies, based partly on an annual earnings-per-share growth rate of 147 percent.

sociocultural dimension
The dimension of the general environment representing the demographic characteristics, norms, customs, and values of the population within which the organization operates.

eight European countries, including Finland, Portugal, and Italy, the number of cell phones now outweighs the number of fixed-line telephones.[10]

Other technological advances will also affect organizations and managers. The recent decoding of the human genome could lead to revolutionary medical advances. Cloning technology and stem cell research are raising both scientific and ethical concerns. Scientists interpreting the secrets of matter at the level of the atom have been able to create amazing new materials, such as "smart gels" that mold to human needs on cue. Shoes made with smart gels in the soles conform to the wearer's feet to achieve a perfect fit. High-tech composites, embedded with sensors that enable them to think for themselves, are being used to earthquake-proof bridges and highways as well as build better airplanes and railcars.[11]

Sociocultural.   The **sociocultural dimension** of the general environment represents the demographic characteristics as well as the norms, customs, and values of the general population. Important sociocultural characteristics are geographical distribution and population density, age, and education levels. Today's demographic profiles are the foundation of tomorrow's workforce and consumers. Forecasters see increased globalization of both consumer markets and the labor supply, with increasing diversity both within organizations and consumer markets.[12] Consider the following key demographic trends in the United States:

1. By 2050, non-Hispanic whites will make up only about half of the population, down from 74 percent in 1995. Hispanics are expected to make up nearly a quarter of the U.S. population.[13]
2. The huge post-World War II baby-boom generation is aging and losing its interest in high-cost goods. Meanwhile, their sons and daughters, sometimes called Generation Y, rival the baby boomers in size and will soon rival them in buying power.
3. The fastest-growing type of living arrangement is single-father households, which rose 62 percent in 10 years, even though two-parent and single-mother households are still much more numerous.[14]
4. The U.S. will continue to receive a flood of immigrants, largely from Asia and Mexico.

The sociocultural dimension also includes societal norms and values. A groundswell of interest in spirituality in the U.S. since the mid-1990s is beginning to affect organizations. In 1999, 78 percent of Americans reported feeling a need to experience spiritual growth, compared to only 20 percent five years earlier. Sales of books and other materials related to religion and spirituality are booming, and some companies are openly bringing spiritual values and ideas into the workplace.[15] Other sociocultural trends also affect organizations. Handgun manufacturers struggled as public acceptance and support of guns in the home fell in the wake of tragic school shootings, and then witnessed a surge in buying following the September 11, 2001, terrorist attacks. The anti-cholesterol and low-fat fervor of a few years back has cooled, hurting the profit margins of companies manufacturing healthy food products.

economic dimension
The dimension of the general environment representing the overall economic health of the country or region in which the organization functions.

Economic.   The **economic dimension** represents the general economic health of the country or region in which the organization operates. Consumer purchasing power, the unemployment rate, and interest rates are part of an organization's economic environment. Because organizations today are operating in a global environment, the economic dimension has become exceedingly complex and creates even more uncertainty for managers. The economies of countries are more closely tied together now. For example, an economic recession and the decline of consumer confidence in the U.S. following the September 11 terrorist attacks affected economies and organizations around the world. Similarly, economic problems in Asia and Europe have had a tremendous impact on companies and the stock market in the United States.

One significant recent trend in the economic environment is the frequency of mergers and acquisitions. Citibank and Travelers merged to form Citigroup, Glaxo Wellcome bought out SmithKline Beecham, and Wal-Mart purchased Britain's ASDA Group. In the toy industry, the three largest toy makers—Hasbro, Mattel, and Tyco—gobbled up at least a dozen smaller competitors within a few years. At the same time, however, there is a tremendous vitality in the small business sector of the economy. Entrepreneurial start-ups are a significant aspect of today's U.S. economy and will be discussed in Chapter 6.

Legal–Political. The **legal–political dimension** includes government regulations at the local, state, and federal levels as well as political activities designed to influence company behavior. The U.S. political system encourages capitalism, and the government tries not to overregulate business. However, government laws do specify rules of the game. The federal government influences organizations through the Occupational Safety and Health Administration (OSHA), Environmental Protection Agency (EPA), fair trade practices, libel statutes allowing lawsuits against business, consumer protection legislation, product safety requirements, import and export restrictions, and information and labeling requirements. Litigation and regulation can create big problems for companies. Microsoft Corporation has been involved in a long, expensive, and exhausting antitrust battle with the U.S. Department of Justice. Microsoft managers have learned the huge impact this environmental sector can have on an organization. Many organizations also have to contend with government and legal issues in other countries. Coca-Cola came under government regulatory surveillance in parts of Europe because of alleged unsanitary conditions in some of its bottling plants. General Electric's attempted $41 billion purchase of Honeywell International won regulatory approval in the U.S., but was squashed by European Union (EU) regulators on the grounds that it would severely reduce competition and raise prices for consumers.

Managers must recognize a variety of **pressure groups** that work within the legal–political framework to influence companies to behave in socially responsible ways. Automobile manufacturers, toy makers, and airlines have been targeted by Ralph Nader's Center for Responsive Law. Tobacco companies today are certainly feeling the far-reaching power of antismoking groups. Middle-aged activists who once protested the Vietnam War have gone to battle to keep Wal-Mart from "destroying the quality of small-town life." Some groups have also attacked the giant retailer on environmental issues, which likely will be one of the strongest pressure points in the coming years.[16] Two of the hottest current issues for pressure groups that are also related to environmental concerns are biotechnology, as illustrated by this chapter's opening case, and world trade. Environmental and human rights protesters have disrupted World Trade Organization meetings and meetings of the World Bank and the International Monetary Fund to protest a system of worldwide integration that has food,

legal–political dimension
The dimension of the general environment that includes federal, state, and local government regulations and political activities designed to influence company behavior.

pressure group
An interest group that works within the legal–political framework to influence companies to behave in socially responsible ways.

goods, people, and capital freely moving across borders. This current international issue will be discussed in more detail in Chapter 4.

Task Environment

As described earlier, the task environment includes those sectors that have a direct working relationship with the organization, among them customers, competitors, suppliers, and the labor market.

customers
People and organizations in the environment who acquire goods or services from the organization.

Customers.   Those people and organizations in the environment who acquire goods or services from the organization are **customers**. As recipients of the organization's output, customers are important because they determine the organization's success. Patients are the customers of hospitals, students the customers of schools, and travelers the customers of airlines. Clothing companies have to stay constantly in touch with shifting customer tastes. Levi Strauss's fortunes have faded faster than a pair of new jeans in recent years because of the company's failure to respond quickly to fashion trends such as flared legs, cargo pockets, and baggy pants. Young, fashion-conscious consumers think of Levi's as "for the older generation, like middle-aged people."[17] Abercrombie & Fitch picked up on the trends, making its clothes the hottest fashion among college-age students a few years back, but now the company is also having trouble coming up with fresh, new styles to boost sagging sales. Marketers are hoping the controversial magazine-style catalog, featuring racy photographs of teenagers, will revive Abercrombie's image among youth, but parents are rebelling against what many consider pornographic displays of children.

One concern for managers today is that the Internet has given increased power to customers and enabled them to directly impact the organization. For example, gripe sites such as walmart-sucks.com, where customers and sales associates cyber-vent about the nation's largest retailer, and untied.com, where United Airlines employees and disgruntled fliers rail against the air carrier, can quickly damage a company's reputation and sales. "In this new information environment," says Kyle Shannon, CEO of e-commerce consultancy Agency.com, "you've got to assume everyone knows everything."[18] However, smart managers and companies are also tapping into the power of the Internet to learn all they can about customers as well, as described in this chapter's Leading Online box.

competitors
Other organizations in the same industry or type of business that provide goods or services to the same set of customers.

Competitors.   Other organizations in the same industry or type of business that provide goods or services to the same set of customers are referred to as **competitors**. Each industry is characterized by specific competitive issues. The recording industry differs from the steel industry and the pharmaceutical industry.

Competitive wars are being waged worldwide in all industries. Coke and Pepsi continue to battle it out for the soft drink market. UPS and FedEx are fighting the overnight delivery wars. In the home improvement market, competition between Home Depot and Lowe's is getting sharper than a buzz saw. Home Depot revolutionized the home improvement retail industry with its immense orange warehouse stores and well-trained sales force. But in recent years, the industry's Number 2 retailer, Lowe's, has been building even larger stores on Home Depot's turf and slowly stealing market share. To fight back, Home Depot recently announced that it will begin selling appliances to compete with Lowe's appliance business.[19]

Leading Online

Connecting to the Customer

Managers in companies all over the world are discovering how the Internet keeps customers informed and interconnected. Some are also learning to use the power of the Internet to learn everything they can about customers, as well. Managers in many companies regularly monitor gripe sites to see what is being said about them so they can make changes and respond to problems. Keeping tabs on gripe sites provides a kind of free focus group for companies.

Now, a new market research company, Look-Look, headquartered in Hollywood, is taking a further step toward helping companies use the Web to tap into the needs and interests of the coveted youth market. Look-Look uses the Web to monitor rapidly changing youth market trends and provides the information to apparel companies, beverage firms, cosmetics companies , and movie studios. However, the most innovative aspect of Look-Look is its global corps of teen correspondents, who are paid to e-mail information about their styles, trends,

opinions, and ideas. Look-Look's clients pay an annual fee of about $20,000 to instantly reach a virtual, worldwide focus group, 24-7 (twenty four hours a day, seven days a week). The company's founders, DeeDee Gordon and Sharon Lee, read and study everything their correspondents tell them to, from J.K. Rowling's Harry Potter series of books to Web sites such as *Ain't It Cool*, to spot trends, make connections, and give their clients predictions about what will sell and what won't.

"We want to be as close as possible to what's going on with kids," says Gordon, "so we get it from the kids themselves." Look-Look's online approach enables their company to deliver up-to-the-minute market research with the speed and accuracy that companies need. With youth spending estimated at $140 billion a year and growing, companies that target the youth market are logging on fast.

SOURCES: Sarah Moore, "On Your Markets," *Working Woman* (February 2001), 26; and John Simons, "Stop Moaning about Gripe Sites and Log On," *Fortune* (April 2, 2001), 181–182.

Suppliers. The raw materials the organization uses to produce its output are provided by **suppliers**. A steel mill requires iron ore, machines, and financial resources. A small, private university may utilize hundreds of suppliers for paper, pencils, cafeteria food, computers, trucks, fuel, electricity, and textbooks. Large companies such as General Motors, Westinghouse, and Exxon depend on as many as 5,000 suppliers. However, many companies are now using fewer suppliers and trying to build good relationships with them so that they will receive high-quality parts at low prices. The relationship between manufacturers and suppliers has traditionally been an adversarial one, but many companies are finding that cooperation is the key to saving money, maintaining quality, and speeding products to market.

suppliers
People and organizations who provide the raw materials the organization uses to produce its output.

Labor Market. The **labor market** represents people in the environment who can be hired to work for the organization. Every organization needs a supply of trained, qualified personnel. Unions, employee associations, and the availability of certain classes of employees can influence the organization's labor market. Labor market forces affecting organizations right now include (1) the growing need for computer-literate information technology workers; (2) the necessity for continuous investment in human resources through recruitment, education, and training to meet the competitive demands of the borderless world; and (3) the effects of international trading blocs, automation, and shifting plant location upon labor dislocations, creating unused labor pools in some areas and labor shortages in others.

labor market
The people available for hire by the organization.

Changes in these various sectors of the environment can create tremendous challenges, especially for organizations operating in complex, rapidly changing industries. Nortel Networks, a Canadian company with multiple U.S. offices, is an example of an organization operating in a highly complex environment.

The external environment for Nortel Networks (formerly Northern Telecom) is illustrated in Exhibit 3.2. The Canadian-based company began in 1895 as a manufacturer of telephones and has reinvented itself many times to keep up with changes in the environment. Since the late 1990s, the company has been undergoing another re-invention, transforming itself into a major player in providing equipment for connecting businesses and individuals to the Internet. When John Roth took over as CEO in 1997, the company was about to be run over by rivals such as Cisco Systems that were focused on Internet gear. Roth knew he needed to do something bold to respond to changes in the technological environment. A name change to Nortel Networks symbolized and reinforced the company's new goal of providing unified network solutions to customers worldwide.

Roth's major response to the competitive environment was to spend billions to acquire data and voice networking companies, including Bay Networks (which makes Internet and data equipment), Cambrian Systems (a hot maker of optical technology), Periphonics (maker of voice-response systems), and Clarify (customer management software). These companies brought Nortel top-notch technology to help the company, as Roth put it, "move at Net speed." Nortel began snatching customers away from rivals Cisco and Lucent Technologies.

Internationally, Nortel has made impressive inroads in Taiwan, China, Mexico, Colombia, Japan, and Sweden, among other countries. It has also won customers by recognizing the continuing need for traditional equipment and offering hybrid gear that combines old telephone technology with new Internet features, allowing companies to transition from the old to the new. Bold new technologies Nortel is pursuing include optical systems that move voice and data at the speed of light and third-generation wireless networks (3G), which zap data and video from phone to phone. Nortel is also venturing into software and services and recently established partnerships with IBM and with Sun Microsystems to provide integrated packages of hardware and software for e-business.

However, companies moving in a Net speed environment risk a very hard landing. The dot-com crash and the recent upheaval in the technology sector of the economic environment have devastated Nortel. The hot Internet-based and start-up market has disappeared. In addition, because of a weakening economy, Nortel's most important customers, the telephone companies, are cutting back their spending on telecommunications gear. Major corporations, forced to cut costs, are also slashing technology spending. The environment has gone from one where everything seems possible to one in which managers have to make tough decisions about where to focus their time, energy, and money. Nortel has a dominant share of the fast-growing market for optical systems, but that hasn't been enough. The company posted an operating *loss* of $385 million during the first quarter of 2001, compared to its operating earnings of $347 million in the same quarter a year earlier. The stock price has tumbled from a high of $124.50 per share to less than $23. More than 20,000 of Nortel's 80,000 worldwide employees have already lost their jobs.[20] ❖

Exhibit 3.2

The External Environment
of Nortel Networks

Economic
- Dot-com crash
- Weakening U.S. and Canadian economy
- Worldwide economic slowdown

Legal/Political
- Canadian ownership
- Breakup of AT&T in 1984
- Tough EU regulations
- NAFTA
- New tax laws
- Protectionist legislation abroad

Competitors
- Lucent and Cisco, U.S.
- Siemens, Germany
- Alcatel, France
- Ericson, Sweden
- NEC, Japan

Customers
- Telephone companies, major corporations for e-business
- Businesses and not-for-profit organizations
- New demand for optical and wireless equipment
- Targeting start-ups with Web products

Technological
- New optical fiber networks
- Expanding wireless technologies (3G)
- Continued need for traditional equipment
- Data and voice networking

Nortel Networks

Sociocultural
- Web surfers
- Opening of new markets worldwide
- Wireless lifestyles

Suppliers
- Components from subcontractors
- Banks, bondholders provide capital
- Obtain quality parts from suppliers worldwide

Labor Market
- U.S.: Texas, North Carolina, Tennessee, and California
- Treat employees well
- Hire computer-literate college graduates

International
- Headquarters in Brampton, Ontario
- Competes in more than 100 countries
- New opportunities in China, Sweden, Australia, Russia, and Taiwan
- Growing market for telecommunications gear in Japan
- Joint ventures in Spain, Poland, and Israel
- Alliance with Alcatel and Lagardere Group of France
- Forty percent of business outside North America

SOURCES: William C. Symonds, J.B. Levine, N. Gross, and P. Coy, "High-Tech Star: Northern Telecom Is Challenging Even AT&T," *BusinessWeek*, July 27, 1992, 54–58; Ian Austen, "Hooked on the Net," *Canadian Business*, June 26–July 10, 1998, 95–103; Joseph Weber with Andy Reinhardt and Peter Burrows, "Racing Ahead at Nortel," *BusinessWeek*, November 8, 1999, 93–99; "Commentary: Nortel-Optimism or Hubris?" *BusinessWeek*, March 12, 2001, 86+; and "Nortel's Waffling Continues: First Job Cuts, Then Product Lines, and Now the CEO," *Telephony*, May 21, 2001, 12.

The Organization–Environment Relationship

Why do organizations care so much about factors in the external environment? The reason is that the environment creates uncertainty for organization managers, and they must respond by designing the organization to adapt to the environment.

Environmental Uncertainty

Organizations must manage environmental uncertainty to be effective. *Uncertainty* means that managers do not have sufficient information about environmental factors to understand and predict environmental needs and changes.[21] As indicated in Exhibit 3.3, environmental characteristics that influence uncertainty are the number of factors that affect the organization and the extent to which those factors change. A large multinational like Nortel Networks has thousands of factors in the external environment creating uncertainty for managers. When external factors change rapidly, the organization experiences very high uncertainty; examples are telecommunications and aerospace firms, computer and electronics companies, and e-commerce organizations that sell products and services over the Internet. Companies have to make an effort to adapt to the rapid changes in the environment. When an organization deals with only a few external factors and these factors are relatively stable, such as for soft-drink bottlers or food processors, managers experience low uncertainty and can devote less attention to external issues.

Adapting to the Environment

If an organization faces increased uncertainty with respect to competition, customers, suppliers, or government regulation, managers can use several strategies to adapt to these changes, including boundary-spanning roles, interorganizational partnerships, and mergers or joint ventures.

Exhibit 3.3

The External Environment and Uncertainty

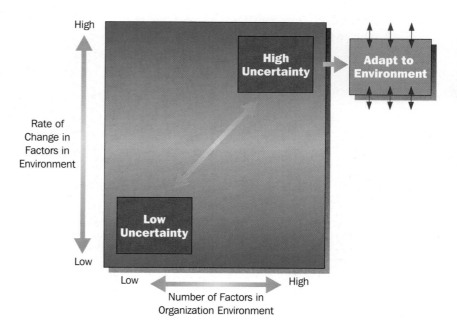

Boundary-Spanning Roles.   Departments and **boundary-spanning roles** link and coordinate the organization with key elements in the external environment. Boundary spanners serve two purposes for the organization: They detect and process information about changes in the environment, and they represent the organization's interest to the environment.[22] People in departments such as marketing and purchasing span the boundary to work with customers and suppliers, both face-to-face and through market research. The Leading Online box earlier in this chapter describes how some organizations are staying in touch with customers through the Internet, for example. Employees in engineering or research and development scan for new technological developments, innovations, and raw materials.

A growing area in boundary spanning is *competitive intelligence* (CI). Membership in the Society of Competitive Intelligence Professionals more than doubled between 1997 and 2001, and at least one U.S. college has introduced a master's degree program in competitive intelligence.[23] Today's managers need to know more about their competitors and customers than ever before to help them make good decisions. United Technologies Corp., a huge, diversified, global firm, set up a special CI unit to monitor the global environment. According to group leader Dottie Moon, the unit looks "at megatrends that can affect all the business units: the Asian flu, the euro, a new chancellor in Germany, unease in Russia, the emergence of a technology such as the Internet."[24]

A growing number of software applications aid in competitive intelligence searches on the Internet, and company intranets help get the information to the people who need it. In addition, commercial services that monitor the Internet are increasingly providing competitive intelligence to organizations.[25] Competitive intelligence specialists use Web sites, commercial databases, financial reports, market activity, news clippings, trade publications, personal contacts, and numerous other sources to scan an organization's environment and spot potential threats or opportunities. Most CI work is strictly legal and many companies provide ethical guidelines that CI specialists must follow.[26]

Interorganizational Partnerships.   An increasingly popular strategy for adapting to the environment is by reducing boundaries and increasing collaboration with other organizations. North American companies have typically worked alone, competing with one another, but an uncertain, interconnected, global environment has changed all that. Companies are joining together to become more effective and to share scarce resources. Texas Instruments and Hitachi joined their semiconductor businesses to share the best engineering talents of both companies.[27] Large computer and software companies such as Microsoft and IBM have joined forces with small e-commerce start-ups to get access to innovative new technologies and markets. Head-to-head competition among independent firms is giving way to competition among networks of alliances. For example, the aerospace industry is controlled by two networks—those of Boeing and Airbus, each of which is made up of more than 100 partner organizations.[28]

As described in Chapter 1, many companies are engaged in e-business relationships with suppliers and partners, aided by digital network connections and the Internet. Managers have shifted from an adversarial orientation to a partnership orientation, as summarized in Exhibit 3.4. The new paradigm is based on trust and the ability of partners to work out equitable solutions to

boundary-spanning roles
Roles assumed by people and/or departments that link and coordinate the organization with key elements in the external environment.

©Courtesy of Campbell Soup

A consumer focus group in Mexico evaluates Campbell's soups, reviewing qualities such as packaging, preparation, appearance, and taste. The passage of NAFTA broadened market opportunities in Mexico, where nearly 9 billion servings of soup are consumed each year. Marketing executives act as boundary spanners to test reactions and assess whether products meet local needs. Boundary spanning provided competitive intelligence that Mexican consumers like convenient dry-soup varieties as well as condensed and ready-to-serve soups.

Exhibit *3.4*

The Shift to a Partnership Paradigm

From Adversarial Orientation ➡	To Partnership Orientation
• Suspicion, competition, arm's length	• Trust, value added to both sides
• Price, efficiency, own profits	• Equity, fair dealing, everyone profits
• Information and feedback limited	• E-business links to share information and conduct digital transactions
• Lawsuits to resolve conflict	• Close coordination; virtual teams and people on site
• Minimal involvement and up-front investment	• Involvement in partner's product design and production
• Short-term contracts	• Long-term contracts
• Contracts limit the relationship	• Business assistance goes beyond the contract

©Serge Cohen

To better compete in the global market, French media mogul Jean-Marie Messier joined his company, Vivendi, with British telecommunications leader Vodafone in a joint venture to create Vizzavi. The new company is Messier's distribution arm in Europe, beaming content over wireless Web to Vivendi's 8 million and Vodafone's 14 million subscribers. Through joint ventures and mergers, Messier has transformed Vivendi from a 147-year-old water treatment company into a fast-moving media player that owns Universal Studios and Universal Music, online music service MP3.com, and educational publisher Houghton Mifflin.

merger
The combining of two or more organizations into one.

joint venture
A strategic alliance or program by two or more organizations.

conflicts so that everyone profits from the relationship. Managers work to reduce costs and add value to both sides, rather than trying to get all the benefits for their own company. The new model is also characterized by a high level of information sharing, including e-business linkages for automatic ordering, payments, and other transactions. In addition, there is a lot of person-to-person interaction to provide corrective feedback and solve problems. People from other companies may be onsite or participate in virtual teams to enable close coordination. Partners are frequently involved in one another's product design and production, and they are committed for the long term. It is not unusual for business partners to help one another, even outside of what is specified in the contract.[29] The Manager's Shoptalk further examines the new partnership orientation and offers some guidelines for building successful partnerships.

Mergers and Joint Ventures.   A step beyond strategic partnerships is for companies to become involved in mergers or joint ventures to reduce environmental uncertainty. A frenzy of merger and acquisition activity both in the United States and internationally in recent years is an attempt by organizations to cope with the tremendous volatility of today's environment.[30] A **merger** occurs when two or more organizations combine to become one. For example, to cope with uncertainty in the communications industry, the leading provider of online services, America Online (AOL), merged with Time-Warner, the world's largest media company, in an astonishing $165 billion deal. Managers at the two companies believed combining the two giants was the best way to win in the era of the Internet.[31]

A **joint venture** involves a strategic alliance or program by two or more organizations. This typically occurs when a project is too complex, expensive, or uncertain for one firm to handle alone. For example, a joint venture led by Sprint, Deutsche Telecom, and France Telecom, and involving several smaller firms, serves 65 countries, functioning as one company to meet the telecommunications needs of global corporations.[32] Joint ventures are on the rise as companies strive to keep pace with rapid technological change and compete in the global economy. Barnes & Noble formed a joint venture with Germany's Bertelsmann AG to establish Barnesandnoble.com and compete with

THE NEW WORKPLACE — Manager's Shoptalk

The New Golden Rule: Cooperate!

News flash: Companies all over the world are sleeping with the enemy. A decade ago, many managers would have considered it heresy to collaborate with competitors, but today they are finding that collaboration is necessary to compete in a rapidly changing environment. Worldwide, research and development budgets are shrinking even as technological complexity grows by leaps and bounds. Collaboration in product development is sweeping every field from autos to aircraft to biotechnology. Archrivals GE Aircraft Engines and Pratt & Whitney teamed up to share the $1 billion cost of developing a new jet engine. Bayer, Germany's $28-billion-a-year drug company, partnered with CuraGen, a tiny U.S. genomics company, to search for new obesity and diabetes drugs. What's remarkable about the partnership is that the unequal partners will split profits from any products they develop 50–50.

Suppliers are also a part of this new collaborative business model. Speed is essential in today's economy, which requires a seamless integration between a company and its suppliers. Volkswagen, Europe's biggest automaker, has stretched the supplier relationship to new limits at its revolutionary plant in Brazil. Twelve international suppliers work directly in Volkswagen's factory, making their own components and then fastening them together into finished trucks and buses. Although few have stretched the supplier relationship as far as VW, other auto companies, including Ford, DaimlerChrysler, and General Motors, are also experimenting with this *modular approach*, in which suppliers provide premade chunks of a vehicle that can be quickly assembled into a finished car or truck by a handful of workers. Manufacturers win with lower costs, while suppliers gain in higher volume, and transaction costs go down for everyone. In the quest for speed and efficiency, collaboration is a trend that is likely to go even further in coming years.

Experts have looked at the key elements that help make collaborative relationships successful and offer the following tips:

- *Enter the relationship with a spirit of true partnership.* An arm's length, semi-adversarial, no-trust, "dump-them-tomorrow-if-we-get-a-better-deal" mindset guarantees failure. Successful partnerships are based on openness, trust, and long-term commitment.
- *Outline what each partner is expected to bring to the relationship from the beginning to the end of the collaborative project.* This enables managers to determine where there are gaps and how to fill them. It also establishes what the partners expect from one another to help maintain good relationships throughout the life of the partnership.
- *Clarify the responsibilities of all partnership members.* This includes defining those who will lead the project, how decisions will be made, review and oversight responsibilities, and who has final authority regarding any negotiations, contract approvals, and so forth.
- *Determine how the risks and profits will be shared.* Include the stake expected from each member and how profits will be divided.
- *Put it in writing.* An open, trusting relationship does not mean there should not be a legal contract and clear, written guidelines for how the partnership will conduct business. A legal contract prevents misunderstandings and provides continuity through changes in personnel and management.

SOURCES: Based on information in Lee Berton, "Shall We Dance?" *CFO* (January 1998), 28–35; Brian O'Reilly, "There's Still Gold in Them Thar Pills," *Fortune* (July 23, 2001), 58–70; David Woodruff with Ian Katz and Keith Naughton, "VW's Factory of the Future," *BusinessWeek* (October 7, 1996), 52–56; Diana Jean Schemo, "Is VW's New Plant Lean, or Just Mean? *New York Times* (November 19, 1996), D1; Philip Siekman, "Building 'Em Better in Brazil," *Fortune* (September 6, 1999), 246(c)–246(v); Oren Harari, "The Logistics of Success," *Management Review* (June 1999), 24–26; and Gail Dutton, "The New Consortiums," *Management Review* (January 1999), 46–50.

Amazon.[33] Many small businesses are turning to joint ventures with large firms or with international partners. A larger partner can provide sales staff, distribution channels, financial resources, or a research staff. Small businesses seldom have the expertise to deal internationally, so a company such as Nypro, Inc., a plastic injection-molding manufacturer in Clinton, Massachusetts, joins with overseas experts who are familiar with the local rules. Nypro now does business in four countries.[34]

The Internal Environment: Corporate Culture

The internal environment within which managers work includes corporate culture, production technology, organization structure, and physical facilities. Of these, corporate culture has surfaced as extremely important to competitive advantage. The internal culture must fit the needs of the external environment and company strategy. When this fit occurs, highly committed employees create a high-performance organization that is tough to beat.[35]

culture
The set of key values, beliefs, understandings, and norms that members of an organization share.

Culture can be defined as the set of key values, beliefs, understandings, and norms shared by members of an organization.[36] The concept of culture helps managers understand the hidden, complex aspects of organizational life. Culture is a pattern of shared values and assumptions about how things are done within the organization. This pattern is learned by members as they cope with external and internal problems and taught to new members as the correct way to perceive, think, and feel. Culture can be analyzed at three levels, as illustrated in Exhibit 3.5, with each level becoming less obvious.[37] At the surface level are visible artifacts, which include such things as manner of dress, patterns of behavior, physical symbols, organizational ceremonies, and office layout. Visible artifacts are all the things one can see, hear, and observe by watching members of the organization. At a deeper level are the expressed values and beliefs, which are not observable but can be discerned from how people explain and justify what they do. These are values that members of the organization hold at a conscious level. They can be interpreted from the stories, language, and symbols organization members use to represent them. Some values become so deeply embedded in a culture that members are no longer consciously aware of them. These basic, underlying assumptions and beliefs are the essence of culture and subconsciously guide behavior and decisions. In some organizations, a basic assumption might be that people are essentially lazy and will shirk their duties whenever possible; thus, employees are closely supervised and given little freedom, and colleagues are frequently suspicious of one another. More enlightened organizations operate on the basic assumption that people want to do a good job; in these organizations, employees are given more freedom and responsibility, and colleagues trust one another and work cooperatively. Basic assumptions in an organization's culture often begin with strongly held values espoused by a founder or early leader.

E x h i b i t **3.5**

Levels of Corporate Culture

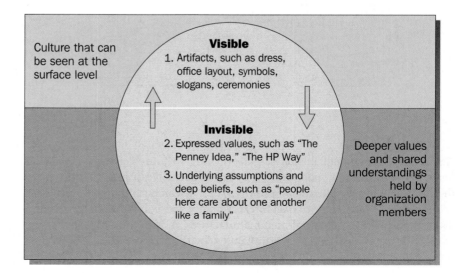

One of the most important things leaders do is create and influence organizational culture because it has a significant impact on performance. In comparing 18 companies that have experienced long-term success with 18 similar companies that have not done so well, James C. Collins and Jerry I. Porras found the key determining factor in successful companies to be a culture in which employees share such a strong vision that they know in their hearts what is right for the company. Their book, *Built to Last: Successful Habits of Visionary Companies*, describes how companies such as Disney and Procter & Gamble have successfully adapted to a changing world without losing sight of the core values that guide the organization.[38] Some companies put values in writing so they can be passed on to new generations of employees. PSS World Medical, a specialty marketer and distributor of medical products, gives every employee a booklet titled *The Blue Ribbon Scorecard—A Foundation for PSS Culture*.[39] Companies known for their strong, distinctive cultures, such as Southwest Airlines, the Container Store, and SAS Institute, regularly show up on *Fortune* magazine's list of the best companies to work for in America.

The fundamental values that characterize cultures at these and other companies can be understood through the visible manifestations of symbols, stories, heroes, slogans, and ceremonies. Any company's culture can be interpreted by observing these factors.

Symbols

A **symbol** is an object, act, or event that conveys meaning to others. Symbols associated with corporate culture convey the organization's important values. For example, managers at WorldNow, a New York–based start-up that provides Internet solutions to local television broadcasters, wanted a way to symbolize the company's unofficial mantra of "drilling down to solve problems." They bought a dented old drill for $2 and dubbed it The Team Drill. Each month, the drill is presented to a different employee in recognition of exceptional work, and the employee personalizes the drill in some way before passing it on to the next winner.[40]

At Siebel Systems in San Mateo, California, employees are surrounded by symbolic reminders that the customer always comes first. Every conference room is named after a major Siebel customer. All the artwork on office walls comes from customer ads or annual reports. "The cornerstone of our corporate culture," says CEO Tom Siebel, "is that we are committed to do whatever it takes to make sure that each and every one of our customers succeeds."[41]

Stories

A **story** is a narrative based on true events that is repeated frequently and shared among organizational employees. Stories are told to new employees to keep the organization's primary values alive. One of Nordstrom's primary means of emphasizing the importance of customer service is through corporate storytelling. An example is the story about men's clothing salesman Van Mensah, who received a letter explaining that a customer had mistakenly washed his 12 new shirts in hot water, causing the shirts to shrink. The customer wanted to know whether Mensah had any suggestions to help him out of his predicament. Mensah immediately called the customer in Sweden and informed him that a dozen new shirts—in the same size, style, and colors—

Tom Loutzenheiser, technology president of software company Apexx Technology, appreciates the many positive attributes of the company's Boise, Idaho location, including affordable housing, short commutes, and the opportunity to kayak on the Boise River just minutes away. Employees at Apexx also appreciate the company's corporate culture, which values the individual and believes in giving employees freedom, privacy, and responsibility. Apexx Technology's office layout reflects its cultural values by offering employees more personal space, offices with real windows, and solid walls that rise all the way to the ceiling. "It's not a cube farm," says employee Jennifer Bedford, reflecting her approval.

©Robbie McClaren/SABA

symbol
An object, act, or event that conveys meaning to others.

story
A narrative based on true events that is repeated frequently and shared by organizational employees.

were being mailed out that day, compliments of the company.[42] A frequently-told story at UPS concerns an employee who, without authorization, ordered an extra Boeing 737 to ensure timely delivery of a load of Christmas packages that had been left behind in the holiday rush. As the story goes, rather than punishing the worker, UPS rewarded his initiative. By telling this story, UPS workers communicate that the company stands behind its commitment to worker autonomy and customer service.[43]

Heroes

hero
A figure who exemplifies the deeds, character, and attributes of a strong corporate culture.

A **hero** is a figure who exemplifies the deeds, character, and attributes of a strong culture. Heroes are role models for employees to follow. Sometimes heroes are real, such as Lee Iacocca, who proved the courage of his convictions by working for $1 a year when he first went to Chrysler. Other times they are symbolic, such as the mythical sales representative at Robinson Jewelers who delivered a wedding ring directly to the church because the ring had been ordered late. The deeds of heroes are out of the ordinary, but not so far out as to be unattainable by other employees. Heroes show how to do the right thing in the organization. Companies with strong cultures take advantage of achievements to define heroes who uphold key values.

At Minnesota Mining and Manufacturing (3M), top managers keep alive the heroes who developed projects that were killed by top management. One hero was a vice president who was fired earlier in his career for persisting with a new product even after his boss had told him, "That's a stupid idea. Stop!" After the worker was fired, he would not leave. He stayed in an unused office, working without a salary on the new product idea. Eventually he was rehired, the idea succeeded, and he was promoted to vice president. The lesson of this hero as a major element in 3M's culture is to persist at what you believe in.[44]

Slogans

slogan
A phrase or sentence that succinctly expresses a key corporate value.

A **slogan** is a phrase or sentence that succinctly expresses a key corporate value. Many companies use a slogan or saying to convey special meaning to employees. H. Ross Perot of Electronic Data Systems established the philosophy of hiring the best people he could find and noted how difficult it was to find them. His motto was, "Eagles don't flock. You gather them one at a time." At Sequins International, where 80 percent of the employees are Hispanic, words from W. Edwards Deming, "You don't have to please the boss; you have to please the customer," are embroidered in Spanish on the pockets of workers' jackets.[45] Cultural values can also be discerned in written public statements, such as corporate mission statements or other formal statements that express the core values of the organization. The mission statement for Hallmark Cards, for example, emphasizes values of excellence, ethical and moral conduct in all relationships, business innovation, and corporate social responsibility.[46]

Ceremonies

ceremony
A planned activity that makes up a special event and is conducted for the benefit of an audience.

A **ceremony** is a planned activity that makes up a special event and is conducted for the benefit of an audience. Managers hold ceremonies to provide dramatic examples of company values. Ceremonies are special occasions that reinforce valued accomplishments, create a bond among people by allowing them to share an important event, and anoint and celebrate heroes.[47]

The value of a ceremony can be illustrated by the presentation of a major award. Mary Kay Cosmetics Company holds elaborate awards ceremonies, presenting gold and diamond pins, furs, and luxury cars to high-achieving sales consultants. The setting is typically an auditorium, in front of a large, cheering audience, and everyone dresses in glamorous evening clothes. The most successful consultants are introduced by film clips, like the kind used to present award nominees in the entertainment industry. These ceremonies recognize and celebrate high-performing employees and emphasize the rewards for performance.[48] An award can also be bestowed secretly by mailing it to the employee's home or, if a check, by depositing it in a bank. But such procedures would not make the bestowal of rewards a significant organizational event and would be less meaningful to the employee.

In summary, organizational culture represents the values, norms, understandings, and basic assumptions that employees share, and these values are signified by symbols, stories, heroes, slogans, and ceremonies. Managers help define important symbols, stories, and heroes to shape the culture.

Environment and Culture

A big influence on internal corporate culture is the external environment. Cultures can vary widely across organizations; however, organizations within the same industry may often reveal similar cultural characteristics because they are operating in similar environments.[49] The internal culture should embody what it takes to succeed in the environment. If the external environment requires extraordinary customer service, the culture should encourage good service; if it calls for careful technical decision making, cultural values should reinforce managerial decision making.

Adaptive Cultures

Research at Harvard on 207 U.S. firms illustrated the critical relationship between corporate culture and the external environment. The study found that a strong corporate culture alone did not ensure business success unless the culture encouraged healthy adaptation to the external environment. As illustrated in Exhibit 3.6, adaptive corporate cultures have different values and behavior from unadaptive corporate cultures. In adaptive cultures, managers are concerned about customers and those internal people and processes that bring about useful change. In the unadaptive corporate cultures, managers are concerned about themselves, and their values tend to discourage risk taking and change. Thus a strong culture alone is not enough, because an unhealthy culture may encourage the organization to march resolutely in the wrong direction. Healthy cultures help companies adapt to the environment.[50]

Types of Cultures

In considering what cultural values are important for the organization, managers consider the external environment as well as the company's strategy and goals. Studies have suggested that the right fit between culture, strategy, and the environment is associated with four categories or types of culture, as illustrated in Exhibit 3.7. These categories are based on two dimensions: (1) the extent to which the external environment requires flexibility or stability; and

Exhibit *3.6*

Environmentally Adaptive versus Unadaptive Corporate Cultures

	Adaptive Corporate Cultures	Unadaptive Corporate Cultures
Visible Behavior	Managers pay close attention to all their constituencies, especially customers, and initiate change when needed to serve their legitimate interests, even if it entails taking some risks.	Managers tend to behave somewhat insularly, politically, and bureaucratically. As a result, they do not change their strategies quickly to adjust to or take advantage of changes in their business environments.
Expressed Values	Managers care deeply about customers, stockholders, and employees. They also strongly value people and processes that can create useful change (e.g., leadership initiatives up and down the management hierarchy).	Managers care mainly about themselves, their immediate work group, or some product (or technology) associated with that work group. They value the orderly and risk-reducing management process much more highly than leadership initiatives.

SOURCE: John P. Kotter and James L. Heskett, *Corporate Culture and Performance* (New York: The Free Press, 1992), 51.

(2) the extent to which a company's strategic focus is internal or external. The four categories associated with these differences are adaptability, achievement, clan, and bureaucratic.[51]

The *adaptability culture* emerges in an environment that requires fast response and high-risk decision making. Managers encourage values that support the company's ability to rapidly detect, interpret, and translate signals from the environment into new behavior responses. Employees have autonomy to make decisions and act freely to meet new needs, and responsiveness to customers is highly valued. Managers also actively create change by encouraging and rewarding creativity, experimentation, and risk taking. One good example of an adaptability culture is 3M, the maker of Post-it notes, Scotch-

Exhibit *3.7*

Four Types of Corporate Cultures

SOURCES: Based on Daniel R. Denison and Aneil K. Mishra, "Toward a Theory of Organizational Culture and Effectiveness," *Organization Science* 6, no. 2 (March–April 1995): 204–223; Robert Hooijberg and Frank Petrock, "On Cultural Change: Using the Competing Values Framework to Help Leaders Execute a Transformational Strategy," *Human Resource Management* 32, no.1 (1993): 29–50; and R.E. Quinn, *Beyond Rational Management: Mastering the Paradoxes and Competing Demands of High Performance* (San Francisco: Jossey-Bass, 1988).

Brite scrubbing pads, and hundreds of other innovative products. All employees attend a class on risk taking and are encouraged to use 15 percent of their time working on projects of their own choosing, without management approval. Most e-commerce companies, as well as companies in the electronics, cosmetics, and fashion industries, use this type of culture because they must move quickly to respond to changes in the environment.

The *achievement culture* is suited to organizations that are concerned with serving specific customers in the external environment but without the intense need for flexibility and rapid change. This is a results-oriented culture that values competitiveness, aggressiveness, personal initiative, and willingness to work long and hard to achieve results. An emphasis on winning and achieving specific ambitious goals is the glue that holds the organization together.[52] Siebel Systems, which sells complex software systems, has thrived on an achievement culture. Employees who succeed at Siebel are intense, competitive, and driven to win. Those who perform and meet stringent goals are handsomely rewarded; those who don't are fired. Nearly every employee at Siebel is given a ranking within each department, and every six months the bottom 5 percent are axed. Employees who thrive on the competitive culture helped Siebel's revenues grow rapidly.[53]

The *clan culture* has an internal focus on the involvement and participation of employees to rapidly meet changing needs from the environment. This culture places high value on meeting the needs of employees, and the organization may be characterized by a caring, family-like atmosphere. Managers emphasize values such as cooperation, consideration of both employees and customers, and avoiding status differences. One company that achieves success with a clan culture is SAS Institute, based in Cary, North Carolina.

SAS INSTITUTE
http://www.sas.com

SAS, which stands for statistical analysis software, writes software that makes it possible to gather and understand data, producing products that set the industry standard in the world of knowledge management. It is a competitive field with high stakes, but the atmosphere at SAS headquarters in Cary, North Carolina, is relaxed, almost serene. Jim Goodnight, co-founder of SAS, created a caring corporate culture where employees are respected and given the freedom and information they need to perform at the top of their abilities.

The most important value is taking care of employees and making sure they have whatever they need to be satisfied and productive. Employees are encouraged to lead a balanced life rather than to work long hours and express a hard-charging, competitive spirit. The company even adopted a seven-hour workday to give employees more personal time. SAS also offers amazing benefits, including two Montessori day-care centers, a 36,000 square foot fitness center, unlimited sick days, an on-site health clinic, elder care advice and referrals, and live music in the cafeteria, where employees may eat with their families. Other key values at SAS are equality, fairness, and cooperation.

SAS's culture places a high value on people and human relationships. Managers at the company trust employees to do their jobs to the best of their ability—and then they expect them to go home and enjoy their friends and families. As one employee put it, "Because you're treated well, you treat the company well."[54]

Thanks to SAS's clan culture, employees care about one another and about the company, a focus that has helped SAS adapt to stiff competition and changing markets. ❖

The final category of culture, the *bureaucratic culture,* has an internal focus and a consistency orientation for a stable environment. Following the rules and being thrifty are valued, and the culture supports and rewards a methodical, rational, orderly way of doing things. In today's fast-changing world, few companies operate in a stable environment, and most managers are shifting away from bureaucratic cultures because of a need for greater flexibility. However, one thriving new company, Pacific Edge Software, has successfully implemented some elements of a bureaucratic culture, ensuring that all their projects are on time and on budget. The husband-and-wife team of Lisa Hjorten and Scott Fuller implanted a culture of order, discipline, and control from the moment they founded the company. The emphasis on order and focus means employees can generally go home by 6:00 P.M. rather than working all night to finish an important project. Hjorten insists that the company's culture isn't rigid or uptight, just *careful.* Although sometimes being careful means being slow, so far Pacific Edge has managed to keep pace with the demands of the external environment.[55]

Each of these four categories of culture can be successful. The relative emphasis on various cultural values depends on the needs of the environment and the organization's focus. Managers are responsible for instilling the cultural values the organization needs to be successful in its environment.

Shaping Corporate Culture for the New Workplace

Research conducted over the last decade by a Stanford University professor indicates that the one factor that increases a company's value the most is people and how they are treated.[56] In addition, a recent *Fortune* magazine survey found that CEOs cite organizational culture as their most important mechanism for attracting, motivating, and retaining talented employees, a capability they consider the single best predictor of overall organizational excellence.[57] At Athene Software, managers created a strong, people-oriented culture to keep talented engineers happy and productive, as described in the Putting People First box. However, managers face new challenges in shaping and maintaining strong, adaptive corporate cultures because of changes in the nature of work and the workplace.

New Demands for Managing Corporate Culture

In today's increasingly global and virtual organizations, shared cultural values are what holds far-flung people and operations together. Culture can provide the glue that gives people a sense of belonging, serves as a compass for employee behavior, and enables dispersed employees to work in concert toward shared goals that meet changing needs from the environment.[58] But how do managers create and maintain a strong culture in a workplace where some employees may never even see one another? Trends such as virtual teams, networks, flexible hours, and telecommuting, in addition to global dispersion, mean that the traditional mechanisms for transmitting culture may be lost. Employees have little opportunity to learn about the values of the organization from observing others and sharing in activities such as stories and cultural symbolism on a regular basis.

One way managers are addressing this issue is by putting increased emphasis on *selection and socialization* of new employees. Dale Pratt, director of

Putting People First

Athene's Culture Nurtures Loyalty and Excellence

At Athene Software, a Boulder, Colorado-based developer of software for communications service providers, ISPs, and other e-businesses, managers deliberately created an "engineer-friendly" culture that has helped the small company keep good employees and compete in a tough, changing industry.

They began with the basic assumption that creating great software is all about people joyfully working together. To make that happen meant treating people with care and respect. Athene's culture depends first and foremost on hiring the right people. The hiring process begins with phone interviews with the company's technical advisors and background checks to screen candidates for technical qualifications. These are followed by a series of interviews with key managers and potential colleagues. Finally, candidates are required to "audition" before a voluntary group of company employees by demonstrating something about themselves that shows how they will fit in at Athene. The audition process serves an added function of helping to retain current employees because they have a chance to help select top-quality people who strive for excellence and want to be part of building a great company.

After people are hired, Athene makes sure they have whatever they need to perform. Managers have built an environment that adapts to people's needs rather than expecting the opposite. "A big part of our culture is balance," says CEO Eric Johnson. "Everyone has a hierarchy of things that are important to them. . . . We want to support [the employee] as a whole person." Whenever employees have to work extra hours, their contribution is recognized with monetary bonuses, public thank-yous, and extra time off that they are required to take. Athene also ensures that its people get to work on leading-edge technology, have the tools and equipment they need, and have opportunities for training and career development. The company gives all engineers private offices, spends around $10,000 on each for hardware and software, and offers in-house training classes once a week. That commitment leads directly to higher job satisfaction and higher retention rates. "A technology business is all about people," says Johnson. "It is suicide not to treat people with compassion and integrity."

SOURCE: Mark Gordon, "Corporate Culture Manifesto," *CIO* (March 15, 2001), 62–66.

---

human resources for Nortel Networks, described earlier in the chapter, manages a virtual team with colleagues as far away as Europe and China.[59] She and other managers emphasize that success in the new workplace begins with selecting the right people. For example, at Microsoft, the interview process is designed to find employees who "fit" the company's culture and already share many of the values the organization promotes. The interview consists of a grueling ritual in which job candidates are grilled by their prospective colleagues with questions such as, "Why are manhole covers round?" and, "Given a gold bar that can be cut exactly twice and a contractor who must be paid one-seventh of a gold bar a day for seven days, what do you do?" The correct answers aren't as important as how candidates handle the pressure and think on their feet. Microsoft wants employees who are smart, passionate, and unconventional. Those who make it through the process feel like members of a special club. The mystique of the entrance exam is only one element that reinforces Microsoft's esprit de corps.[60] But it is an important one because it ensures that people who join the company are likely to fit the company's distinctive corporate culture.

Other companies also have strenuous interviewing and hiring practices. PSS World Medical doesn't call candidates back for follow-up interviews. Requiring the candidate to take the initiative through every step of the hiring process, which takes six to eight weeks, ensures that PSS hires people with the right values and attitudes to fit its culture.[61]

After employees are hired, socializing them into the culture is also important. Putting the company's values in writing and distributing them in various forms—through newsletters and magazines, videos, intranets, in training classes—is important when people are working in far-flung locations, but people generally need more than that to begin to internalize the values. Many companies that have global and virtual employees bring people together with long-time employees early in their employment so they can learn the culture. Nokia, the mobile phone supplier, has all new employees take a cultural awareness class, where they learn how the Swedish company's culture and management style is different from many American companies. Costco, a discount warehouse operator, brings new overseas managers to the United States for up to 10 weeks to work side-by-side with long-time employees so they can learn about the company's values.[62]

Few organizations have yet adequately addressed the problem of transmitting culture to virtual workers. In the late 1990s, Hewlett-Packard created a training and development program for managers called "Managing Remotely." The forums addressed such issues as work/life balance, communication processes, and how to orient virtual employees to HP's culture.[63] However, most companies do not have anything so extensive. Many companies that use virtual workers require that people work on-site for a period of time in the beginning to allow the culture to sink in. Some also require periodic office visits or occasional face-to-face forums where the culture is reinforced.[64] As the number of virtual teams and telecommuters grows, managers will face the growing challenge of building and maintaining a unifying culture. Managers can learn to create a sense of connectedness that binds virtual employees together and brings them into the cultural fold.[65] One key aspect of shaping culture in all organizations is cultural leadership.

Cultural Leadership

One way managers change norms and values toward what is adaptive to the external environment or for smooth internal integration is through *cultural leadership*. Managers must *overcommunicate* to ensure that employees understand the new culture values, and they signal these values in actions as well as words.

cultural leader
A manager who uses signals and symbols to influence corporate culture.

A **cultural leader** defines and uses signals and symbols to influence corporate culture. Cultural leaders influence culture in two key areas:

1. *The cultural leader articulates a vision for the organizational culture that employees can believe in and that generates excitement.* This means the leader defines and communicates central values that employees believe in and will rally around.
2. *The cultural leader heeds the day-to-day activities that reinforce the cultural vision.* The leader makes sure that work procedures and reward systems match and reinforce the values. Actions speak louder than words, so cultural leaders "walk their talk."[66]

One way leaders create a culture that everyone can believe in is by directly involving employees in determining what the company's values should be. Managers at United Stationers built a new, adaptive culture from the ground up by asking all 6,000 globally dispersed employees to help define the values that would be the building blocks of the culture.[67]

Managers also widely communicate the cultural values through words and actions. At Starbucks, CEO Howard Schultz welcomes all new employees by video, where he tells about the company's history and culture and shares some stories of his own personal experiences. Each employee also receives 24 hours of initial training, during which they talk with managers and other employees about Starbucks' mission and values.[68] Starbucks managers use these mechanisms as a way to maintain the culture as the company expands internationally. At MTW Corp., managers work with every new employee to create an "expectations agreement," an ever-evolving document that ensures that actions and work procedures that reinforce the company's cultural values will be adhered to by both managers and workers.[69] Top executives at Weirton Steel act as cultural leaders by participating in every team training session to symbolize their commitment to a team-based culture—a significant commitment in an 8,000-employee organization.[70]

Some companies also directly tie compensation to how well people live the values. Gillette Co., based in Boston, Massachusetts, and Germany's Siemens both consider managers' and employees' commitment to the cultural values as part of their overall performance during salary reviews, a powerful reminder that culture is important.[71] Creating and maintaining a strong, adaptive culture is not easy in today's changing workplace, but through their words—and particularly their actions—cultural leaders let everyone in the organization know what really counts.

■ Summary and Management Solution

This chapter discussed several important ideas about internal and external organizational environments. Events in the external environment are considered important influences on organizational behavior and performance. The external environment consists of two layers: the task environment and the general environment. The task environment includes customers, competitors, suppliers, and the labor market. The general environment includes technological, sociocultural, economic, legal-political, and international dimensions. Management techniques for helping the organization adapt to the environment include boundary-spanning roles, interorganizational partnerships, and mergers and joint ventures.

Even companies in relatively simple, stable industries may face significant challenges from the external environment, as illustrated by the opening story of the Gerber baby-food company. Managers at Gerber and its parent company, Norvartis AG, responded quickly to activists' allegation that Gerber baby food contained ingredients that could be harmful. While maintaining their stand that genetically altered products are not dangerous, Gerber is dropping some of its existing corn and soybean suppliers in favor of ones that pro-

duce crops that are not genetically altered. Plans for labeling changes to indicate if some products may contain minuscule amounts of genetically altered ingredients are being discussed. Gerber's rapid response was made at considerable cost and inconvenience, but managers knew the repercussions of ignoring this threat from the environment could be much more expensive in the long run. "I have got to listen to my customers," says Al Piergallini, president and CEO of Novartis's U.S. consumer health operations. "If there is an issue, or even an inkling of an issue, I am going to make amends." To keep in touch with this growing environmental issue, Gerber is consulting with various non-Greenpeace-affiliated environmentalists and consumer groups. Managers want to anticipate future problems from the external environment and be ready with a rapid response. [72]

One internal organizational factor that enabled Gerber to respond so quickly is the company's adaptive culture. Corporate culture is a major element of the internal organizational environment and includes the key values, beliefs, understandings, and norms that organization members share. Organizational activities that illustrate corporate culture include symbols, stories, heroes, slogans, and ceremonies. For the organization to be effective, corporate culture should be aligned with the needs of the external environment.

Four types of culture are adaptability, achievement, clan, and bureaucratic. Strong cultures are effective when they enable an organization to adapt to changes in the external environment. Shared cultural values are important for binding people together in today's changing workplace where employees may be dispersed. Managers are putting greater emphasis on selection and socialization of employees so that employees fit the cultural values of the organization. In addition, cultural leaders strengthen or change corporate culture by (1) communicating a compelling vision to employees and (2) reinforcing the vision through day-to-day activities, work procedures, and reward systems.

■ Discussion Questions

1. Some scientists predict major changes in the earth's climate, including a temperature rise of 8°F over the next 60 years. Should any companies be paying attention to this possible long-range environmental trend? Explain.
2. Would the task environment for a bank contain the same elements as that for a government welfare agency? Discuss.
3. What do you think are the most important forces in the external environment creating uncertainty for organizations today? Do the forces you identified typically arise in the task environment or the general environment?
4. Contemporary best-selling management books often argue that customers are the most important element in the external environment. Do you agree? Are there company situations for which this may not be true?
5. American Airlines was thriving until the September 11, 2001, terrorist attacks against the United States, when fear of flying, general uncertainty, and a worldwide recession stunned the airline. Discuss the type of response American Airlines managers might make to this change in the environment.
6. Why are interorganizational partnerships becoming so important for today's companies? Do you think the terrorist attacks against the United States will likely contribute to an increase or decrease in interorganizational collaboration? Why?
7. Define corporate culture and explain its importance for managers.
8. Why are symbols important to a corporate culture? Do stories, heroes, slogans, and ceremonies also have symbolic value? Discuss.
9. Describe the cultural values of a company for which you have worked. Did those values fit the needs of the external environment? Of employees?
10. What type of environmental situation is associated with an adaptability culture? How does this culture differ from the clan culture?
11. Do you think a corporate culture with strong values is better for organizational effectiveness than a culture with weak values? Are there times when a strong culture might reduce effectiveness? Discuss.

■ Management in Practice: Experiential Exercise

What is a Strong Corporate Culture?

Think about an organization with which you are familiar, such as your school or a company for which you have worked.

Answer the questions below based on whether you agree that they describe the organization.

	Disagree Strongly				Agree Strongly
1. Virtually all managers and most employees can describe the company's values, purpose, and customer importance.	1	2	3	4	5
2. There is clarity among organization members about how their jobs contribute to organizational goals.	1	2	3	4	5
3. It is very seldom that a manager will act in a way contrary to the company's espoused values.	1	2	3	4	5

	Disagree Strongly				Agree Strongly
4. Warmth and support of other employees is a valued norm, even across departments.	1	2	3	4	5
5. The company and its managers value what's best for the company over the long term more than short-term results.	1	2	3	4	5
6. Leaders make it a point to develop and mentor others.	1	2	3	4	5
7. Recruiting is taken very seriously, with multiple interviews in an effort to find traits that fit the culture.	1	2	3	4	5
8. Recruits are given negative as well as positive information about the company so they can freely choose whether to join.	1	2	3	4	5
9. Employees are expected to acquire real knowledge and mastery—not political alliances—before they can be promoted.	1	2	3	4	5
10. Company values emphasize what the company must do well to succeed in a changing environment.	1	2	3	4	5
11. Conformity to company mission and values is more important than conformity to procedures and dress.	1	2	3	4	5
12. You have heard stories about the company's leaders or "heroes" who helped make the company great.	1	2	3	4	5
13. Ceremonies and special events are used to recognize and reward individuals who contribute to the company in significant ways.	1	2	3	4	5

Total Score _____

Compute your score. If your total score is 52 or above, your organization has a strong culture, similar to a Procter & Gamble or IBM. A score from 26 to 51 suggests a culture of medium strength, which is positive for the organization, such as for American Airlines, Coca-Cola, and Citigroup. A score of 25 or below indicates a weak culture, which is probably not helping the company adapt to the external environment or meet the needs of organization members. Discuss the pros and cons of a strong culture. Does a strong culture mean everyone has to be alike?

SOURCES: Adapted from Richard Pascale, "The Paradox of 'Corporate Culture': Reconciling Ourselves to Socialization," *California Management Review* 27, no. 2 (1985); and David A. Kolb, Joyce S. Osland, and Irwin M. Rubin, *Organizational Behavior: An Experiential Approach*, 6th ed. (Englewood Cliffs, N.J.: Prentice-Hall, 1995), 346–347.

■ Management in Practice: Ethical Dilemma

Competitive Intelligence Predicament

Miquel Vasquez was proud of his job as a new product manager for a biotechnology start-up, and he loved the high stakes and tough decisions that went along with the job. But as he sat in his den after a long day, he was troubled, struggling over what had happened earlier that day and the information he now possessed.

Just before lunch, Miquel's boss had handed him a stack of private strategic documents from their closest competitor. It was a competitive intelligence gold mine—product plans, pricing strategies, partnership agreements, and other documents, most clearly marked "proprietary and confidential." When Miquel asked where the documents came from, his boss told him with a touch of pride that he had taken them right off the competing firm's server. "I got into a private section of their intranet and downloaded everything that looked interesting," he said. Later, realizing Miquel was suspicious, the boss would say only that he had obtained "electronic access" via a colleague and had not personally broken any passwords. Maybe not, Miquel thought to himself, but this wouldn't pass the *60 Minutes* test. If this ever got out to the press, the company's reputation would be ruined.

Miquel didn't feel good about using these materials. He spent the afternoon searching for answers to his dilemma, but found no clear company policies or regulations that offered any guidance. His sense of fair play told him this was unethical, if not downright illegal. What bothered him even more was the knowledge that this kind of thing might happen again. Using this confidential information would certainly give him and his company a competitive advantage, but Miquel wasn't sure he wanted to work for a firm that would stoop to such tactics.

What Would You Do?

1. Go ahead and use the documents to the company's benefit, but make clear to your boss that you don't want him passing confidential information to you in the future. If he threatens to fire you, threaten to leak the news to the press.

2. Confront your boss privately and let him know you're uncomfortable with how the documents were obtained and what this says about the company's culture. In addition to the question of the legality of using the information, point out that it is a public relations nightmare waiting to happen.

3. Talk to the company's legal counsel and contact the Society of Competitive Intelligence Professionals for guidance. Then, with their opinions and facts to back you up, go to your boss.

SOURCE: Adapted from Kent Weber, "Gold Mine or Fool's Gold?" *BusinessEthics* (January–February 2001), 18.

Surf the Net

1. **Monitor the Environment.** A comprehensive informational Web site designed especially for executives is at *http://www.ceoexpress.com*. After familiarizing yourself with this site, send an e-mail message to your instructor. Your instructor will play the role of your boss, who is currently unaware that CEOExpress® exists. In your e-mail, present evidence to convince your "boss" that the information at this site would help him or her monitor the environment and, therefore, is a site worthy of bookmarking and visiting regularly.

2. **Mergers and Acquisitions.** To learn more about merger and acquisition activity that affects the economic environment, locate and record the merger and acquisition announcements made in the past two weeks. Use a search engine to locate this information that can be found at such sites as *http://www.theonlineinvestor.com/*.

3. **Corporate Culture.** Select two sites from the list below. Print out the information the organization presents about its corporate culture. On your printouts, try to identify one aspect of the organization's culture at each of the three levels described in Exhibit 3.5. Be prepared to present your findings in a class discussion on corporate culture.

AES Corporation: *http://www.aesc.com/culture/*
Galileo International: *http://www.galileo.com/careers/carcorpc.htm*
Gore: *http://www.gore.com/corp/about/index.html*
J.D. Edwards: *http://www.jdedwards.com/*; click on Company, then on Careers
LMI: *http://www.lmi.org/Careers.htm*
Motorola: *http://www.motorolacareers.com/ufsd2/corporate.cfm*
Mutual of Omaha: *http://www.careerlink.org/emp/mut/corp.htm*
Pella: *http://www.pellacareers.com/culture/ceo.asp*
Sony: *http://sel.newjobs.com/Corporate.html*

Case for Critical Analysis

Society of Equals

Ted Shelby doesn't make very many mistakes, but . . .

"Hey Stanley," says Ted Shelby, leaning in through the door, "you got a minute? I've just restructured my office. Come on and take a look. I've been implementing some great new concepts!"

Stanley is always interested in Ted Shelby's new ideas, for if there is anyone Stanley wants to do as well as, it is Edward W. Shelby IV. Stanley follows Ted back to his office and stops, nonplussed.

Restructured is right! Gone are Ted's size B (Junior Exec.) walnut veneer desk and furniture, and his telephone table. In fact, the room is practically empty save for a large, round, stark white cafeteria table and the half-dozen padded vinyl swivel chairs that surround it.

"Isn't it a beauty! As far as I know, I'm the first executive in the plant to innovate this. The shape is the crucial factor here—no front or rear, no status problems. We can all sit there and communicate more effectively."

We? Communicate? Effectively? Well, it seems that Ted has been attending a series of Executive Development Seminars given by Dr. Faust. The theme of the seminars was—you guessed it—*participative management.* Edward W. Shelby IV has always liked to think of himself as a truly democratic person.

"You see, Stanley," says Ted, managing his best sincere/intense attitude, "the main thing wrong with our culture is that most of the communication is top-down. We in the executive suite send our messages down the line, but we never ask for ideas and suggestions from the rest of the company.

Just because we have more status and responsibility doesn't mean that we are necessarily (Stanley duly noted the word *necessarily*) better than the people below us. In fact, with our customers' needs changing so fast these days, we need all the ideas we can get. We've got to shift to a culture of participation and employee involvement if we want to keep up with today's fast pace of business."

"So that's what the cafeteria table is for?" Stanley asks.

"Yes!" says Ted. "We need better two-way communication—up the line as well as down the line. We managers don't have all the answers, and I don't know why I never realized it before that seminar. Why, for example, the folks who run those machines out there. I'll bet any one of them knows a thing or two about how to speed up our manufacturing process that I've never thought of. So I've transformed my office into a full-feedback communication net."

"That certainly is an innovation around here," says Stanley.

A few days later Stanley passed by Ted Shelby's office and was surprised that Ted's desk, furniture, and telephone table were back where they used to be.

Stanley, curious about the unrestructuring, went to Bonnie for enlightenment. "What," he asked, "happened to Shelby's round table?"

"That table we were supposed to sit around and input things?" she said. "All I know is, about two days after he had it put in, Mr. Drake came walking through here. He looked in that

office, and then he sort of stopped and went back—and he looked in there for a long time. Then he came over to me, and you know how his face sort of gets red when he's really mad? Well, this time he was so mad that his face was absolutely white. And when he talked to me, I don't think he actually opened his mouth; and I could barely hear him, he was talking so low. And he said, 'Have that removed. Now. Have Mr. Shelby's furniture put back in his office. Have Mr. Shelby see me.'"

My, my. You would think Ted would have known better, wouldn't you? But then, by now you should have a pretty firm idea of just why it is those offices are set up as they are.

Questions

1. How would you characterize the culture in this company? What are the dominant values?

2. Why did Ted Shelby's change experiment fail? To what extent did Ted use the appropriate change tools to increase employee communication and participation?

3. What would you recommend Ted do to change his relationship with subordinates? Is it possible for a manager to change cultural values if the rest of the organization, especially top management, does not agree?

SOURCE: R. Richard Ritti and G. Ray Funkhouser, *The Ropes to Skip & The Ropes to Know*, 3d. ed. (New York: Wiley, 1987), 176–177. This material is used by permission of John Wiley & Sons, Inc.

■ Endnotes

1. Lucette Lagnado, "Strained Peace: Gerber Baby Food, Grilled by Greenpeace, Plans Swift Overhaul," *The Wall Street Journal* (July 30, 1999), A1, A6, and "Group Sows Seeds of Revolt Against Genetically Altered Foods in U.S.," *The Wall Street Journal* (October 12, 1999), B1, B4.

2. Seth Lubove, "Dial-a-Mess," *Forbes* (January 24, 2000), 68–70.

3. Warren St. John, "Barnes & Noble's Epiphany," *Wired* (June 1999), 132–144; Patrick M. Reilly, "In the Age of the Web, a Book Chain Flounders," *The Wall Street Journal* (February 22, 1999), B1, B4.

4. Chuck Hutchcraft, "Fiscal Worries Pain La Rabida in Its 100th Year," *Chicago Tribune* (March 17, 1996), Sec. 5, 1, 6.

5. Richard L. Daft, *Organization Theory and Design*, 5th ed. (St. Paul, Minn.: West, 1995).

6. L.J. Bourgeois, "Strategy and Environment: A Conceptual Integration," *Academy of Management Review* 5 (1980), 25–39.

7. Ann Carrns, "Point Taken: Hit Hard by Imports, American Pencil Icon Tries to Get a Grip," *The Wall Street Journal* (November 24, 1999), A1, A6.

8. Lawrence Chimerine, "The New Economic Realities in Business," *Management Review* (January 1997), 12–17; Ram Charan, "The Rules Have Changed," *Fortune* (March 16, 1998), 159–162; and Lisa Benavides, "Handful of Tennessee Companies Feel a Pinch," *The Tennessean* (September 5, 1998), 1E, 2E.

9. Richard I. Kirkland, Jr., "Entering a New Age of Boundless Competition," *Fortune* (March 14, 1988), 40–48; and Kenichi Ohmae, "Managing in a Borderless World," *Harvard Business Review* (May–June 1989), 152–161.

10. Darlene Superville, "Gadget-Giddy Americans Love Communicating," AP story, *The Johnson City Press* (July 7, 2001), 7; Janet Guyon, "The World is Your Office," *Fortune* (June 12, 2000), 227–234.

11. Gene Bylinsky, "Mutant Materials," *Fortune* (October 13, 1997), 140–147;

12. William B. Johnston, "Global Work Force 2000: The New World Labor Market," *Harvard Business Review* (March–April 1991), 115–127.

13. Statistics reported in Peter Coy, "The Creative Economy," *BusinessWeek* (August 28, 2000), 76–82.

14. U.S. Census, *http://www.census.gov/*

15. Marc Gunter, "God & Business," *Fortune* (July 9, 2001), 58–80.

16. Linda Himelstein and Laura Zinn, with Maria Mallory, John Carey, Richard S. Dunham, and Joan O'C. Hamilton, "Tobacco: Does It Have a Future?" *BusinessWeek* (July 4, 1994), 24–29; Bob Ortega, "Aging Activists Turn, Turn, Turn Attention to Wal-Mart Protests," *The Wall Street Journal* (October 11, 1994), A1, A8;

17. Louise Lee, "Can Levi's Be Cool Again?" *BusinessWeek* (March 13, 2000), 144, 148.

18. John Simons, "Stop Moaning About Gripe Sites and Log On," *Fortune* (April 2, 2001), 181–182.

19. Rick Brooks, "Home Depot Turns Copycat in Its Efforts to Stoke New Growth," *The Wall Street Journal* (November 21, 2000), A1; Dan Sewell, "Home Depot, Lowe's Building Up Competition," *Lexington Herald-Leader*, Business Profile supplement (December 8, 1997), 3.

20. Joseph Weber with Andy Reinhardt and Peter Burrows, "Racing Ahead at Nortel," *BusinessWeek* (November 8, 1999), 93–99; "Commentary: Nortel: Optimism or Hubris?" *BusinessWeek* (March 12, 2001), 86; John Rendleman, "IBM and Nortel Integrate Products for Service Providers," *InformationWeek* (June 11, 2001), 107; "Sun, Nortel Partner" *Internet Week* (June 25, 2001), 7; "Nortel Networks Slashes 5,000 More," *United Press International* (April 20, 2001), http://www.comtexnews.com; "Nortel Crashes Again," *Maclean's* (June 25, 2001), 14; "Nortel's Waffling Continues; First Job Cuts, Then Product Lines, and Now the CEO. What's Next?" *Telephony* (May 21, 2001), 12.

21. Robert B. Duncan, "Characteristics of Organizational Environment and Perceived Environmental Uncertainty," *Administrative Science Quarterly* 17 (1972), 313–327; and Daft, *Organization Theory and Design*.

22. David B. Jemison, "The Importance of Boundary Spanning Roles in Strategic Decision-Making," *Journal of Management Studies* 21 (1984), 131–152; and Marc J. Dollinger, "Environmental Boundary Spanning and Information Processing Effects on Organizational Performance," *Academy of Management Journal* 27 (1984), 351–368.

23. Pia Nordlinger, "Know Your Enemy," *Working Woman* (May 2001), 16.

24. Gary Abramson, "All Along the Watchtower," *CIO Enterprise* (Section 2, July 15, 1999), 24–34.

25. Ibid.; and Mike France with Joann Muller, "A Site for Soreheds," *BusinessWeek* (April 12, 1999), 86–90.

26. Abramson, "All Along the Watchtower."

27. Lee Berton, "Shall We Dance?" *CFO* (January 1998), 28–35.

28. Cyrus F. Freidheim, Jr. *The Trillion-Dollar Enterprise: How the Alliance Revolution Will Transform Global Business* (New York: Perseus Books, 1998).

29. Peter Smith Ring and Andrew H. Van de Ven, "Developmental Processes of Corporate Interorganizational Relationships," *Academy of Management Review* 19 (1994): 90–118; Myron Magnet, "The New Golden Rule of Business," *Fortune* (February 21, 1994), 60–64; and Peter Grittner, "Four Elements of Successful Sourcing Strategies," *Management Review* (October 1996), 41–45.

30. Richard L. Daft, "After the Deal: The Art of Fusing Diverse Corporate Cultures Into One," paper presented at the Conference on International Corporate Restructuring, Institute of Business Research and Education, Korea University, Seoul, Korea (June 16, 1998).

31. Joseph Nocera, "The Men Who Would Be King," *Fortune* (February 7, 2000), 66–69; and Marc Gunther, "These Guys Want It All," *Fortune* (February 7, 2000), 71–78.

32. Freidheim, *The Trillion-Dollar Enterprise*.

33. Warren St. John, "Barnes & Noble's Epiphany," *Wired* (June 1999), 132–144.

34. James E. Svatko, "Joint Ventures," *Small Business Reports* (December 1988), 65–70; and Joshua Hyatt, "The Partnership Route," *Inc.* (December 1988), 145–148.

35. Yoash Wiener, "Forms of Value Systems: A Focus on Organizational Effectiveness and Culture Change and Maintenance," *Academy of Management Review* 13 (1988), 534–545; V. Lynne Meek, "Organizational Culture: Origins and Weaknesses," *Organization Studies* 9 (1988), 453–473; John J. Sherwood, "Creating Work Cultures with Competitive Advantage," *Organizational Dynamics* (Winter 1988), 5–27; and Andrew D. Brown and Ken Starkey, "The Effect of Organizational Culture on Communication and Information," *Journal of Management Studies* 31, no. 6 (November 1994), 807–828.

36. Ralph H. Kilmann, Mary J. Saxton, and Roy Serpa, "Issues in Understanding and Changing Culture," *California Management Review* 28 (Winter 1986), 87–94; and Linda Smircich, "Concepts of Culture and Organizational Analysis," *Administrative Science Quarterly* 28 (1983), 339–358.

37. Based on Edgar H. Schein, *Organizational Culture and Leadership*, 2d ed. (San Francisco: Jossey-Bass, 1992), 3–27.

38. James C. Collins, "Change is Good—But First Know What Should Never Change," *Fortune* (May 29, 1995), 141.

39. Charles A. O'Reilly III and Jeffrey Pfeffer, "Star Makers," *CIO* (September 15, 2000), 225–246.

40. Christine Canabou, "Here's the Drill," *Fast Company* (February 2001), 58.

41. Melanie Warner, "Confessions of a Control Freak," *Fortune* (September 4, 2000), 130–140.

42. Elizabeth Weil, "Every Leader Tells a Story," *Fast Company* (June–July 1998), 38–39; and Robert Specter, "The Nordstom Way," *Corporate University Review* (May–June 1997), 24–25, 60.

43. Robert E. Quinn and Gretchen M. Spreitzer, "The Road to Empowerment: Seven Questions Every Leader Should Consider," *Organizational Dynamics* (Autumn 1997), 37–49.

44. Terrence E. Deal and Allan A. Kennedy, *Corporate Cultures: The Rites and Rituals of Corporate Life* (Reading, Mass.: Addison-Wesley, 1982).

45. Barbara Ettorre, "Retooling People and Processes," *Management Review*, (June 1995), 19–23.

46. Patricia Jones and Larry Kahaner, *Say It and Live It: 50 Corporate Mission Statements That Hit the Mark* (New York: Currency Doubleday, 1995).

47. Harrison M. Trice and Janice M. Beyer, "Studying Organizational Cultures through Rites and Ceremonials," *Academy of Management Review* 9 (1984), 653–669.

48. Alan Farnham, "Mary Kay's Lessons in Leadership," *Fortune* (September 20, 1993), 68–77.

49. Jennifer A. Chatman and Karen A. Jehn, "Assessing the Relationship Between Industry Characteristics and Organizational Culture: How Different Can You Be?" *Academy of Management Journal* 37, no. 3 (1994), 522–553.

50. John P. Kotter and James L. Heskett, *Corporate Culture and Performance* (New York: The Free Press, 1992).

51. This discussion is based on Paul McDonald and Jeffrey Gandz, "Getting Value from Shared Values," *Organizational Dynamics* 21, no. 3 (Winter 1992), 64–76; Daniel R. Denison and Aneil

K. Mishra, "Toward a Theory of Organizational Culture and Effectiveness," *Organization Science* 6, no. 2 (March–April 1995), 204–223; and Richard L. Daft, *The Leadership Experience* (Fort Worth: Dryden, 2002), 524–528.

52. Robert Hooijberg and Frank Petrock, "On Cultural Change: Using the Competing Values Framework to Help Leaders Execute a Transformational Strategy," *Human Resource Management* 32, no. 1 (1993), 29–50.

53. Warner, "Confessions of a Control Freak."

54. Charles Fishman, "Sanity Inc.," *Fast Company* (January 1999), 85–96; and Sharon Overton, "And to All a Goodnight," *Sky* (October 1996), 37–40.

55. Rekha Balu, "Pacific Edge Projects Itself," *Fast Company* (October 2000), 371–381.

56. Jeffrey Pfeffer, *The Human Equation: Building Profits by Putting People First* (Boston, Mass.: Harvard Business School Press, 1998).

57. Jeremy Kahn, "What Makes a Company Great?" *Fortune* (October 26, 1998), 218; James C. Collins and Jerry I. Porras, *Built to Last: Successful Habits of Visionary Companies* (New York: HarperCollins, 1994); and James C. Collins, "Change is Good—But First Know What Should Never Change," *Fortune* (May 29, 1995), 141.

58. Jenny C. McCune, "Exporting Corporate Culture," *Management Review* (December 1999), 52–56.

59. Charlene Marmer Solomon, "Managing Virtual Teams," *Workforce* (June 2001), 60.

60. Mark Gimein, "Smart Is Not Enough," *Fortune* (January 8, 2001), 124–136.

61. Charles A. O'Reilly III and Jeffrey Pfeffer, "Star Makers."

62. Jenny C. McCune, "Exporting Corporate Culture," *Management Review* (December 1999), 52–56.

63. Thomas H. Davenport, "Two Cheers for the Virtual Office," *Sloan Management Review* (Summer 1998), 51–65.

64. Nancy B. Kurland and Diane E. Bailey, "Telework: The Advantages and Challenges of Working Here, There, Anywhere, Anytime," *Organizational Dynamics* (Autumn 1999), 53–68.

65. Solomon, "Managing Virtual Teams."

66. Thomas J. Peters and Robert H. Waterman, Jr., *In Search of Excellence* (New York: Warner, 1988).

67. McCune, "Exporting Corporate Culture."

68. Stephanie Gruner, "Lasting Impressions," *Inc.* (July 1998), 126.

69. Jill Rosenfeld, "MTW Puts People First," *Fast Company* (December 1999), 86–88.

70. Excerpt from Peter B. Grazier, "Before It's Too Late: Employee Involvement . . . An Idea Whose Time Has Come," *Pete's Corner* by Peter B. Grazier, http://www.teambuilding.com.

71. McCune, "Exporting Corporate Culture."

72. Lagnado, "Strained Peace."

Managing in a Global Environment

CHAPTER OUTLINE

A Borderless World

The International Business Environment

The Economic Environment

The Legal-Political Environment

GATT and the World Trade Organization

European Union

North American Free Trade Agreement

Trade Alliances: Promise or Pitfall?

The Sociocultural Environment

Social Values

Other Cultural Characteristics

Getting Started Internationally

Outsourcing

Exporting

Licensing

Direct Investing

Multinational Corporations

Managing in a Global Environment

Personal Challenges for Global Managers

Managing Cross-Culturally

Global Learning

LEARNING OBJECTIVES

After studying this chapter, you should be able to

1 Describe the emerging borderless world.

2 Define international management and explain how it differs from the management of domestic business operations.

3 Indicate how dissimilarities in the economic, sociocultural, and legal-political environments throughout the world can affect business operations.

4 Describe market entry strategies that businesses use to develop foreign markets.

5 Describe the characteristics of a multinational corporation.

6 Explain the challenges of managing in a global environment.

Management Challenge

Wal-Mart's first blunder was stocking its shelves with footballs in a country where soccer rules. In the suburbs of São Paulo, Brazil, the highly successful U.S. company discovered that its merchandise, tactics, and attitudes don't always translate well internationally. With opportunities for growth dwindling at home, Wal-Mart has embarked on a crusade to bring "everyday low prices" to the emerging markets of Brazil, Argentina, China, and Indonesia. But doing business internationally is a learning—and sometimes a losing—process. In its first two years in South America, Wal-Mart lost an estimated $48 million. Part of the difficulty is due to stiff competition from companies such as Brazil's Grupo Pao de Acucar SA and France's Carrefour SA, which have much stronger footholds in the region. However, analysts also blame Wal-Mart. By failing to do its homework, Wal-Mart made mistakes such as stocking footballs instead of soccer balls, live trout instead of sushi, and leaf blowers that are useless in the concrete world of São Paulo. It brought in stock-handling equipment that didn't work with standardized local pallets and installed a computerized bookkeeping system that didn't take Brazil's complicated tax system into account. Perhaps most damaging, the company's insistence on doing things "the Wal-Mart way" has alienated some local suppliers and employees.[1]

Why do you think Wal-Mart has had such difficulty duplicating its U.S. success overseas? What recommendations would you have for Wal-Mart managers as they continue their quest in emerging markets?

Wal-Mart is a well-established company facing enormous challenges in developing a successful international business. Other large, successful U.S. companies, including Federal Express and Nike, also have found that "the rest of the world is not the United States of America," as one FedEx competitor put it. However, all of these companies recognize that international expansion is necessary, despite the risks. Companies such as McDonald's, IBM, Coca-Cola, Kellogg, Texas Instruments, and Gillette all rely on international business for a substantial portion of sales and profits. Internet-based companies headquartered in the United States, such as Amazon, Yahoo, and America Online, are also rapidly expanding internationally and finding that, even on the Web, going global is fraught with difficulties. These and other online companies have encountered problems ranging from cultural blunders to violations of foreign laws. All organizations face special problems in trying to tailor their products and business management to the unique needs of foreign countries—but if they succeed, the whole world is their marketplace.

How important is international business to the study of management? *If you are not thinking international, you are not thinking business management.* It's that serious. As you read this page, ideas, takeover plans, capital investments, business strategies, products, and services are traveling around the planet by telephone, computer, fax, and overnight mail. The events of September 11, 2001, when terrorists attacked New York and Washington, underscored the point that isolation is impossible. The future of our businesses and our societies will be determined by global rather than local relationships. The warning Andrew Grove, chairman of Intel, issued to business leaders in a 1995 *Fortune* magazine article has struck home with full force: "[There is] no choice but to operate in a world shaped by globalization."[2]

Rapid advances in technology and communications have made the international dimension an important part of the external environment that is discussed in Chapter 3. Companies can locate different parts of the organization wherever it makes the most business sense—top leadership in one place, technical brainpower and production in other locales. Virtual connections enable close, rapid coordination and communication among people working in different parts of the world, so it is no longer necessary to keep all operations in one place. Samsung, the Korean electronics giant, moved its semiconductor-making facilities to the Silicon Valley to be closer to the best scientific brains in the industry. Canada's Nortel Networks selected a location in the southwest of England as its world manufacturing center for a new fixed-access radio product. Siemens of Germany has moved its electronic ultrasound division to the United States, while the U.S. company DuPont shifted its electronic operations headquarters to Japan.[3]

If you think you are isolated from global influence, think again.

Contract manufacturers such as Taiwan's Quanta Computer Inc., the world's No. 1 maker of notebook PCs, operate in a global environment. Taiwan makes about 60 percent of the world's notebook PCs, and one out of every seven notebooks comes from Quanta, whose U.S. customers include Dell, Gateway, Hewlett-Packard, Apple, and Compaq. A recent international management challenge for Quanta occurred when the U.S. halted air traffic for three days after the September 11 terrorist attacks. Finished computers began to pile up in Quanta's cavernous warehouse in Linkou. So managers improvised, loading thousands of notebooks on a plane leased by Dell, which flew them to Texas.

©David Hartung/Liaison Agency

Even if you do not budge from your hometown, your company may be purchased tomorrow by the English, Japanese, or Germans. People working for Ben & Jerry's Ice Cream, Dr. Pepper, Pillsbury, Carnation, Shell Oil, and Burger King already work for foreign bosses.

All this means that the environment for companies is becoming extremely complex and extremely competitive. Less-developed countries are challenging mature countries in a number of industries. India has become a major player in software development, and electronics manufacture is rapidly leaving Japan for other countries in Asia.

This chapter introduces basic concepts about the global environment and international management. First, we consider the difficulty managers have operating in an increasingly borderless world. We will address challenges—economic, legal-political, and sociocultural—facing companies within the global business environment. Then we will discuss multinational corporations and touch upon the various types of strategies and techniques needed for entering and succeeding in foreign markets.

A Borderless World

Why do companies such as Wal-Mart, Federal Express, and America Online want to pursue a global strategy, despite failures and losses? They recognize that business is becoming a unified global field as trade barriers fall, communication becomes faster and cheaper, and consumer tastes in everything from clothing to cellular phones converge. Thomas Middelhoff of Germany's Bertelsmann AG, which purchased U.S. publisher Random House, put it this way: "There are no German and American companies. There are only successful and unsuccessful companies."[4]

Companies that think globally have a competitive edge. Consider Hong Kong's Johnson Electric Holdings Ltd., a large producer of micromotors that power hair dryers, blenders, and automobile power windows and door locks. With factories in South China and a research and development lab in Hong Kong, Johnson is thousands of miles away from a leading automaker. Yet the company has cornered the market for electric gizmos in U.S. automobiles by using new information technology. Via videoconferencing, Johnson design teams meet "face-to-face" for two hours each morning with their customers in the United States and Europe. The company's processes and procedures are so streamlined that Johnson can take a concept and deliver a prototype to the United States in six weeks.[5]

In addition, domestic markets are saturated for many companies. The only potential for significant growth lies overseas. Kimberly-Clark and Procter & Gamble, which spent years slugging it out in the flat U.S. diaper market, are targeting new markets such as

Today's companies compete in a borderless world. Procter & Gamble sales in Southeast Asia are only 3 percent of its worldwide sales, but those numbers are increasing. These shoppers are purchasing P&G's diaper products, Pampers, in Malaysia.

©Munshi Ahmed

China, India, Israel, Russia, and Brazil. The demand for steel in China, India, and Brazil together is expected to grow 10 percent annually in the coming years—three times the U.S. rate, providing opportunities for companies such as Nucor and North Star Steel.[6] For online companies, too, going global is a key to growth. Predictions are that within a few years two-thirds of the world's Internet users will be outside the United States, and Western Europe and Japan together will account for almost half of the world's e-commerce revenue.[7]

The reality of today's borderless companies also means consumers can no longer tell from which country they're buying. Your Mercury Marauder may have come from Ontario, while a neighbor's Nissan may have been built in Tennessee. A Gap polo shirt may be made from cloth cut in the United States but sewn in Honduras. Eat an all-American Whopper and you've just purchased from a British company.

Corporations can participate in the international arena on a variety of levels, and the process of globalization typically passes through four distinct stages as illustrated in Exhibit 4.1.

1. In the *domestic stage*, market potential is limited to the home country, with all production and marketing facilities located at home. Managers may be aware of the global environment and may want to consider foreign involvement.
2. In the *international stage*, exports increase, and the company usually adopts a *multidomestic* approach, probably using an international division to deal with the marketing of products in several countries individually.
3. In the *multinational stage*, the company has marketing and production facilities located in many countries, with more than one-third of its sales outside the home country. Companies typically have a single home country, although they might opt for a *binational* approach, whereby two parent companies in separate countries maintain ownership and control. Examples are Unilever and the Royal Dutch/Shell Group, both of which are based in the United Kingdom and the Netherlands.
4. Finally, the *global (or stateless) stage* of corporate international development transcends any single home country. These corporations operate in true global fashion, making sales and acquiring resources in whatever country offers the best opportunities and lowest cost. At this stage, ownership, control, and top management tend to be dispersed among several nationalities.[8]

Exhibit *4.1*

Four Stages of Globalization

	1. Domestic	2. International	3. Multinational	4. Global
Strategic Orientation	Domestically oriented	Export-oriented, multidomestic	Multinational	Global
Stage of Development	Initial foreign involvement	Competitive positioning	Explosion of international operations	Global
Cultural Sensitivity	Of little importance	Very important	Somewhat important	Critically important
Manager Assumptions	"One best way"	"Many good ways"	"The least-cost way"	"Many good ways"

SOURCE: Based on Nancy J. Adler, *International Dimensions of Organizational Behavior*, 4th ed. (Cincinnati, Ohio: South-Western, 2002), 8–9.

As the number of stateless corporations increases, so too the awareness of national borders decreases, as reflected by the frequency of foreign participation at the management level. Rising managers are expected to know a second or third language and to have international experience. The need for global managers is intense. Corporations around the world want the brightest and best candidates for global management, and young managers who want their careers to move forward recognize the importance of global experience. According to Harvard Business School professor Christopher Bartlett, author of *Managing Across Borders*, people should try to get global exposure when they are young in order to start building skills and networks that will grow throughout their careers.[9] Consider the makeup of today's global companies. Nestlé (Switzerland) personifies the stateless corporation with 98 percent of sales and 96 percent of employees outside the home country. Nestlé's CEO is Austrian-born Peter Brabeck-Letmathe, and half of the company's general managers are non-Swiss. The CEO puts strong faith in regional managers who are native to the region and know the local culture. The combination of strong brands and autonomous regional managers has made Nestlé the largest branded food company in Mexico, Brazil, Chile, and Thailand, and the company is on its way to becoming the leader in Vietnam and China as well. U.S. firms also show a growing international flavor. The Coca-Cola Company's critical European operations (which account for 28 percent of profits) used to be dominated by American managers, but CEO Doug Daft is changing that. Non-Americans now run 9 of Coke's 10 European groups, and Daft is giving them new autonomy to create and market products as they see fit, based on their understanding of the local environment.[10] At British firm ICI, 40 percent of the top 170 executives are non-British. Meanwhile, German companies such as Hoechst and BASF rely on local managers to run foreign operations.[11]

Both Ford Motor Company and IBM are globalizing their management structures. To aid its efforts, IBM has studied power equipment giant Asea Brown Boveri Ltd. (ABB), a major player in the global game. ABB generates more than $25 billion in revenues and employs 240,000 in Europe, North and South America, Asia, and India. ABB has no geographical center. With a Swedish CEO, a Zurich headquarters, a multinational board, and financial results posted in American dollars, ABB is "a company with many homes."[12]

The International Business Environment

International management is the management of business operations conducted in more than one country. The fundamental tasks of business management, including the financing, production, and distribution of products and services, do not change in any substantive way when a firm is transacting business across international borders. The basic management functions of planning, organizing, leading, and controlling are the same whether a company operates domestically or internationally. However, managers will experience greater difficulties and risks when performing these management functions on an international scale. For example:

- When Coors Beer tried to translate a slogan with the phrase "Turn It Loose" into Spanish, it came out as "Drink Coors and Get Diarrhea." Budweiser goofed when its Spanish ad promoted Bud Light as "Filling, less delicious."[13]

international management
The management of business operations conducted in more than one country.

- It took McDonald's more than a year to figure out that Hindus in India do not eat beef. The company's sales took off only after McDonald's started making burgers sold in India out of lamb.[14]
- In Africa, the labels on bottles show pictures of what is inside so illiterate shoppers can know what they're buying. When a baby-food company showed a picture of an infant on its label, the product didn't sell very well.[15]
- United Airlines discovered that even colors can doom a product. The airline handed out white carnations when it started flying from Hong Kong, only to discover that to many Asians such flowers represent death and bad luck.[16]

Some of these examples might seem humorous, but there's nothing funny about them to managers trying to operate in a competitive global environment. Companies seeking to expand their international presence on the Internet also can run into cross-cultural problems, as discussed in the Leading Online box. What should managers of emerging global companies look for to avoid obvious international mistakes? When they are comparing one country with another, the economic, legal-political, and sociocultural sectors present the greatest difficulties. Key factors to understand in the international environment are summarized in Exhibit 4.2.

The Economic Environment

The economic environment represents the economic conditions in the country where the international organization operates. This part of the environment includes such factors as economic development; infrastructure; resource

Exhibit 4.2

Key Factors in the International Environment

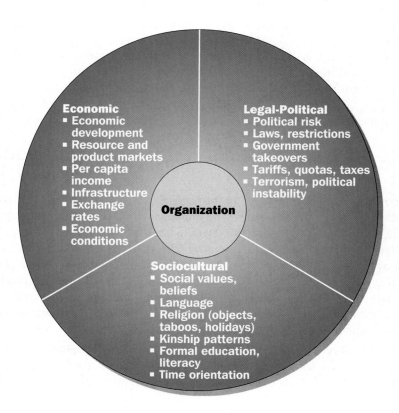

Economic
- Economic development
- Resource and product markets
- Per capita income
- Infrastructure
- Exchange rates
- Economic conditions

Legal-Political
- Political risk
- Laws, restrictions
- Government takeovers
- Tariffs, quotas, taxes
- Terrorism, political instability

Organization

Sociocultural
- Social values, beliefs
- Language
- Religion (objects, taboos, holidays)
- Kinship patterns
- Formal education, literacy
- Time orientation

Leading Online

Virtual Reality: Negotiating the Cross-Cultural Web

With worldwide acceptance of the Internet ballooning, going global has the green light. But technological and cultural issues are so tightly interwoven, that there are a multitude of new ways to offend or alienate customers in other nations. For instance, certain gestures, colors, and phrases don't translate well or are considered offensive. A thumb's up sign means approval or encouragement to Americans and many Europeans, but the gesture is considered an obscenity in Greece. Purple is a sign of royalty in some parts of the world, but in others it is associated with death. Credit cards are the backbone of e-commerce in the United States, but they are still a rarity in many countries, causing all sorts of payment problems. And consumers in Germany view credit as a crutch for people who cannot control their finances.

Managers should also consider that many online shoppers want to buy from sites that cater to their native language—for example, research has found that Japanese managers are much more likely to conduct an online transaction when addressed in Japanese. Unfortunately, although just 6 percent of the world's people speak English as a first language, 96 percent of all e-commerce sites are written in English. In fact, less than half of U.S. companies have even attempted to pattern their Web sites to the culture or language of foreign users. This complacent attitude adds up to lost opportunities and negative attitudes toward U.S. Internet companies.

Some companies are leading the way in overcoming global challenges on the Internet. Autobytel.com, an online car buying and information site, relies on partnerships. These regional partners help navigate through a myriad of social laws and European online privacy laws. As Autobytel pushes into Japan, it has teamed with six Japan-based corporations, hoping to tap into their expertise. Josh McCarter, vice president of international development, says, "You have to understand how cars are built and sold" in any market you enter. For example, in the U.S., most vehicles have only a few option packages available. By contrast, in Japan and most of Europe, it is usual for customers to spec out a vehicle. Local partners can help companies surmount these differences by developing a Web site that can offer numerous configurations.

QXL.com, based in London, is battling to become the dominant online auctioneer in Europe. QXL's home-field advantage makes it easier to go international, but leaders also credit their European mindset that readily accepts cultural and linguistic differences. This openness to other cultures and ways of doing things has given American managers at eBay a run for their money. Another Internet auction site, Baazee.com, based in Bombay, India, has also found innovative ways to adapt to local cultures. Baazee's managers have found that most Indians associate auctions with bankruptcy liquidations. In addition, they don't place trust in buying without seeing the merchandise up close and personal. To solve this problem, managers set up "exchange centers" in different cities, where the seller and winning bidder can complete their business in person after the buyer is satisfied with the item.

The Internet might someday build its own global Web culture, but so far, the "virtual reality" for managers is a need to shape their Web sites to reach local communities.

SOURCES: Steve Ulfelder, "All the Web's a Stage," *CIO* (October 1, 2000), 133–142; Daniel Pearl, "Lost in the Translation," *The Wall Street Journal* (February 12, 2001), R12, R14; and Adam Lincoln, "Lost in Translation," *eCFO* (Spring, 2001), 38–43.

and product markets; exchange rates; and inflation, interest rates, and economic growth.

Economic Development. Economic development differs widely among the countries and regions of the world. Countries can be categorized as either *developing* or *developed*. Developing countries are referred to as *less-developed countries (LDCs)*. The criterion traditionally used to classify countries as developed or developing is *per capita income*, which is the income generated by the nation's production of goods and services divided by total population. The developing countries have low per capita incomes. LDCs generally are located in Asia, Africa, and South America. Developed countries are generally located in North America, Europe, and Japan. Today, developing countries in Southeast Asia, Latin America, and Eastern Europe are driving global growth.[17]

A solid infrastructure, including decent highways, a Pacific port, and nonstop air service to the U.S., helps make Guadalajara a favorite factory town for U.S. companies such as IBM, Hewlett-Packard, and Siemens. Guadalajara and surrounding areas in the Mexican state of Jalisco boast the world's largest concentration of electronic contract manufacturers. Factories are bright, shining, and sophisticated, and the annual worker turnover rate is less than 5 percent. Single-use Kodaks, like the one being manufactured in the photo, are made with film coated in Rochester, New York, but assembled and packaged in Mexico.

©Keith Dannemiller/Corbis SABA

Most international business firms are headquartered in the wealthier, economically advanced countries. However, smart companies are investing heavily in Asia, Eastern Europe, and Latin America. For example, the number of Internet users in Latin America is expected to grow to 19 million by 2003, up from only 4.8 million in 1998, and e-commerce sales are expected to zoom to $8 billion.[18] Both Compaq and Dell have launched online stores for Latin American customers to buy computers over the Internet. America Online sees Latin America as crucial to expanding its global presence, even though Universo Online International (UOL), based in Brazil, got a tremendous head start over AOL.[19] These companies face risks and challenges today, but they stand to reap huge benefits in the future.

infrastructure
A country's physical facilities that support economic activities.

Infrastructure.   A country's physical facilities that support economic activities make up its **infrastructure**, which includes transportation facilities such as airports, highways, and railroads; energy-producing facilities such as utilities and power plants; and communication facilities such as telephone lines and radio stations. Companies operating in LDCs must contend with lower levels of technology and perplexing logistical, distribution, and communication problems. Undeveloped infrastructures represent opportunities for some firms, such as United Technologies Corporation, based in Hartford, Connecticut, whose businesses include jet engines, air conditioning and heating systems, and elevators. As countries such as China, Russia, and Vietnam open their markets, new buildings need elevators and air and heat systems; opening remote regions for commerce requires more jet engines and helicopters.[20]

Resource and Product Markets.   When operating in another country, company managers must evaluate the market demand for their products. If market demand is high, managers may choose to export products to that country. To develop plants, however, resource markets for providing needed raw materials and labor must also be available. For example, the greatest challenge for McDonald's, which now sells Big Macs on every continent except

Antarctica, is to obtain supplies of everything from potatoes to hamburger buns to plastic straws. At McDonald's in Cracow, the burgers come from a Polish plant, partly owned by Chicago-based OSI Industries; the onions come from Fresno, California; the buns come from a production and distribution center near Moscow; and the potatoes come from a plant in Aldrup, Germany. McDonald's tries to contract with local suppliers when possible. In Thailand, McDonald's actually helped farmers cultivate Idaho russet potatoes of sufficient quality to produce their golden french fries.[21]

Exchange Rates. *Exchange rate* is the rate at which one country's currency is exchanged for another country's. Changes in the exchange rate can have major implications for the profitability of international operations that exchange millions of dollars into other currencies every day.[22] For example, assume that the U.S. dollar is exchanged for 0.8 euros. If the dollar increases in value to 0.9 euros, U.S. goods will be more expensive in France because it will take more euros to buy a dollar's worth of U.S. goods. It will be more difficult to export U.S. goods to France, and profits will be slim. If the dollar drops to a value of 0.7 euros, on the other hand, U.S. goods will be cheaper in France and can be exported at a profit.

The Legal–Political Environment

Businesses must deal with unfamiliar political systems when they go international, as well as with more government supervision and regulation. Government officials and the general public often view foreign companies as outsiders or even intruders and are suspicious of their impact on economic independence and political sovereignty. Some of the major legal–political concerns affecting international business are political risk, political instability, and laws and regulations.

Political Risk and Instability. A company's **political risk** is defined as its risk of loss of assets, earning power, or managerial control due to politically based events or actions by host governments.[23] Political risk includes government takeovers of property and acts of violence directed against a firm's properties or employees. Because such acts are not uncommon, companies must formulate special plans and programs to guard against unexpected losses. For example, Hercules, Inc., a large chemical company, increased the number of security guards at several of its European plants. Some companies buy political risk insurance, especially as they move into high-risk areas such as Eastern Europe, China, and Brazil. Political risk analysis has emerged as a critical component of environmental assessment for multinational organizations.[24]

Another frequently cited problem for international companies is **political instability**, which includes riots, revolutions, civil disorders, and frequent changes in government. Political instability increases uncertainty. Civil wars and large-scale violence have occurred in Indonesia, Malaysia, Thailand, Sri Lanka (Ceylon), and Myanmar (Burma) in recent decades. Companies moving into former Soviet republics face continued instability because of changing government personnel and political philosophies.

Although most companies would prefer to do business in stable countries, some of the greatest growth opportunities lie in areas characterized by instability. The greatest threat of violence is in countries experiencing political,

political risk
A company's risk of loss of assets, earning power, or managerial control due to politically based events or actions by host governments.

political instability
Events such as riots, revolutions, or government upheavals that affect the operations of an international company.

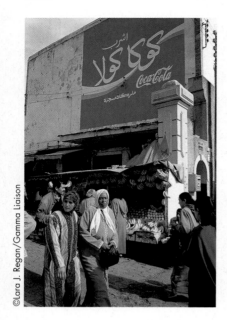

Despite the political risk, political instability, and the local laws and regulations of countries such as Morocco, The Coca-Cola Company earns about 80 percent of its profits from markets outside North America. The soft-drink company recently suffered in global markets after complaints of tainted products from Belgium bottling plants. Managers are busily trying to rebuild relationships because of the importance of international sales.

most favored nation
A term describing a GATT clause that calls for member countries to grant other member countries the most favorable treatment they accord any country concerning imports and exports.

ethnic, or religious upheaval. In China, for example, political winds have shifted rapidly, and often dangerously. Yet it is the largest potential market in the world for the goods and services of developed countries, and Xerox, AT&T, Motorola, and Kodak are busy making deals there.

U.S. firms or companies linked to the United States often are subject to major threats in countries characterized by political instability. For example, when barricades and tear gas blocked thousands of protesters in Pakistan from storming the U.S. consulate in Karachi on the first Muslim holy day after the U.S. began bombings in Afghanistan, the demonstrators turned instead to KFC, where they set fire to the restaurant as a symbol of America.[25]

Laws and Regulations.   Government laws and regulations differ from country to country and make doing business a true challenge for international firms. Host governments have myriad laws concerning libel statutes, consumer protection, information and labeling, employment and safety, and wages. International companies must learn these rules and regulations and abide by them. For example, Wal-Mart offers stock options to U.S. employees to build company spirit and loyalty, but when it entered Germany in 1997, managers learned that this form of compensation violates German laws. Managers had to look for other ways to reward German employees.[26] The Internet has increased the impact of foreign laws on U.S. companies because it expands the potential for doing business on a global basis. Land's End, the Dodgeville, Wisconsin, mail-order retailer, ran afoul of Germany's laws banning lifetime guarantees, rebates, and other forms of sales promotion.[27] First Net Card, started in 1999 to provide credit for online transactions to anyone in the world, found the complication of dealing with international credit and banking laws mind-boggling. After two years and a mountain of legal research, the company was licensed to provide credit only in the U.S., Canada, and Britain.[28] When Yahoo's Web site hosted an auction of Nazi paraphernalia, a French court ruled that the company must block access to French users because selling such items violates French law.[29]

The most visible changes in legal-political factors grow out of international trade agreements and the emerging international trade alliance system. Consider, for example, the impact of the General Agreement on Tariffs and Trade (GATT), the European Union (EU), and the North American Free Trade Agreement (NAFTA).

GATT and the World Trade Organization

The General Agreement on Tariffs and Trade (GATT), signed by 23 nations in 1947, started as a set of rules to ensure nondiscrimination, clear procedures, the negotiation of disputes, and the participation of lesser developed countries in international trade. GATT and its successor, the World Trade Organization (WTO), primarily use tariff concessions as a tool to increase trade. Member countries agree to limit the level of tariffs they will impose on imports from other members, and the **most favored nation** clause, which calls for each member country to grant to every other member country the most favorable treatment it accords to any country with respect to imports and exports.[30]

GATT sponsored eight rounds of international trade negotiations aimed at reducing trade restrictions. The 1986 to 1994 Uruguay Round (the first to be named for a developing country) involved 125 countries and cut more tariffs than ever before. The Round's multilateral trade agreement, which took effect January 1, 1995, was the most comprehensive pact since the original 1947 agreement. It boldly moved the world closer to global free trade by calling for the establishment of the WTO. The WTO represents the maturation of GATT into a permanent global institution that can monitor international trade and has legal authority to arbitrate disputes on some 400 trade issues.[31] Currently, 144 countries are members of the WTO.

The goal of the WTO is to guide—and sometime urge—the nations of the world toward free trade and open markets.[32] The WTO encompasses the GATT and all its agreements, as well as various other agreements related to trade in services and intellectual property issues in world trade. As a permanent membership organization, the WTO is bringing greater trade liberalization in goods, information, technological developments, and services; stronger enforcement of rules and regulations; and greater power to resolve disputes. However, the power of the WTO is partly responsible for a growing backlash against global trade. An increasing number of individuals and public interest groups are protesting that global trade locks poor people into poverty and harms wages, jobs, and the environment, as described in the Manager's Shoptalk box.

European Union

Formed in 1958 to improve economic and social conditions among its members, the European Economic Community, now called the European Union (EU), has expanded to a 15-nation alliance illustrated in Exhibit 4.3. Poland, Hungary, the Czech Republic, Cyprus, Slovenia, and Estonia are in negotiations to join the EU, and at least seven other countries are considering opening membership negotiations.

In the early 1980s, Europeans initiated steps to create a powerful single market system called *Europe '92*. The initiative called for creation of open markets for Europe's 340 million consumers. Europe '92 consisted of 282 directives proposing dramatic reform and deregulation in such areas as banking, insurance, health, safety standards, airlines, telecommunications, auto sales, social policy, and monetary union.

Initially opposed and later embraced by European industry, the increased competition and economies of scale within Europe will enable companies to grow large and efficient, becoming more competitive in U.S. and other world markets. Some observers fear that the EU will become a trade barrier, creating a "fortress Europe" that will be difficult to penetrate by companies in other nations. Indeed, a recent EU directive adopting strict privacy protection laws has some U.S. officials worried about the alliance's power over U.S. companies wanting to do international business over the Internet. One member of Congress asserts that "the EU privacy directive could be the imposition of one of the largest trade barriers ever seen and a direct reversal of the efforts we have made in various free trade agreements." U.S. legal negotiators have developed a "safe harbor" initiative that allows U.S. companies to swear allegiance to EU privacy principles and subject themselves to enforcement by U.S. government agencies. Large companies such as Microsoft have agreed to sign on, but many U.S. officials as well as businesses are vigorously fighting the EU directive.[33]

Another aspect of significance to countries operating globally is the EU's monetary revolution and the introduction of the euro. In January 2002, the

Exhibit *4.3*

The Fifteen Nations within the EU

euro

A single European currency that replaced the currencies of 11 European nations.

euro, a single European currency, replaced 11 national currencies and unified a huge marketplace, creating a competitive economy second only to the United States.[34] Germany, France, Spain, Italy, Ireland, the Netherlands, Austria, Belgium, Finland, Portugal, and Luxembourg traded their deutschemarks, francs, lira and other currencies to adopt the euro, a currency with a single exchange rate. The United Kingdom has thus far refused to accept the euro, in part because of a sense of nationalism, but many believe that the United Kingdom will eventually adopt the currency. The implications of a single European currency are enormous within as well as outside Europe. As it replaces up to 15 European domestic currencies, the euro will affect legal contracts, financial management, sales and marketing tactics, manufacturing, distribution, payroll, pensions, training, taxes, and information management systems. Every corporation that does business in or with EU countries will feel the impact.[35] In addition, economic union is likely to speed deregulation, which has already reordered Europe's corporate and competitive landscape.

Although building alliances among countries is difficult, the benefits of doing so are overcoming divisions and disagreements. Canada, Mexico, and the United States have established what is expected to be an equally powerful alliance.

Manager's Shoptalk

Globalization: A Catch 22?

A young protester is shot and killed. Hundreds of police and demonstrators are injured. Thousands more respond to the shooting by taking to the streets, hurling bottles, bricks, or anything else within reach and shouting, "Assassins! Assassins!" It is not a flashback to 1970s Vietnam War demonstrations on America's college campuses. It is the 2001 G8 summit meeting in Genoa, Italy, and the latest episode in an increasingly-intense series of protests against globalization.

Most of the protests have centered on what activists are calling "The Iron Triangle" of globalization: The World Trade Organization (WTO), the International Monetary Fund (IMF), and the World Bank. Perhaps the first highly visible antiglobalization protest occurred at the meeting of the WTO in Seattle, Washington, in the fall of 1999, where business and political leaders were caught off guard by the strong sentiments. Since then, protesters have converged on both the IMF and the World Bank.

In the spring of 2001, the G8—leaders from the world's seven wealthiest nations plus Russia—were discussing ways to fight global economic woes, the AIDS crisis, and world poverty, while protesters outside miles of fences and concrete barriers were charging that the global policies of wealthy nations and corporations lock poor people into a web of poverty, suffering, and premature death. Globalization triggers concerns ranging from the export of jobs to countries with lower wages on the one hand to concerns about environmental destruction on the other hand.

Leaders have battled to assure the public of the advantages of globalization and free trade, with President George Bush recently admonishing those who oppose globalization as "no friends to the poor." Yet it is clear that the antiglobalization fervor is just getting hotter—and not going away anytime soon. The Public Citizen's Global Trade Watch, a U.S.-based activist organization, is growing in power, challenging the policies of government and big business. Director Lori Wallach, a Harvard-trained lawyer, is known as a fierce debater and a skillful organizer for the movement. "We are not a campaign," Wallach says. "We are not a fluke. We are a mainstream public-interest movement and we are not going to go away."

With protests growing stronger and opposition more widespread, managers who once saw antiglobalists as a fringe group are starting to sit up and pay attention. In the end, it is not whether globalization is good or bad, but how business and government can work together to ensure that the advantages of a global world are fully and fairly shared.

SOURCES: Jerry Useem, "There's Something Happening Here," *Fortune* (May 15, 2000); Paul Magnusson, "Meet Free Traders' Worst Nightmare," *BusinessWeek* (March 20, 2000), 113–118; Elisabeth Malkin, "Backlash," *BusinessWeek* (April 24, 2000), 38–44; and Ron Fournier, AP White House correspondent, "Protests Overshadow Summit," *The Johnson City Press* (July 21, 2001), 1.

North American Free Trade Agreement (NAFTA)

The North American Free Trade Agreement, which went into effect on January 1, 1994, merged the United States, Canada, and Mexico into a megamarket with more than 360 million consumers. The agreement breaks down tariffs and trade restrictions on most agricultural and manufactured products over a 15-year period. The treaty builds on the 1989 U.S.–Canada agreement and is expected to spur growth and investment, increase exports, and expand jobs in all three nations.[36]

The negotiations resulted in agreements in a number of key areas.

- *Agriculture.* Immediate removal of tariffs on half of U.S. farm exports to Mexico with phasing out of remaining tariffs over 15 years.
- *Autos.* Immediate 50 percent cut of Mexican tariffs on autos, reaching zero in 10 years. Mandatory 62.5 percent North American content on cars and trucks to qualify for duty-free status.
- *Transport.* U.S. trucking of international cargo allowed in Mexican border area by mid-1990s and throughout Mexico by the end of the decade.

- *Intellectual property.* Mexico's protection for pharmaceutical patents boosted to international standards and North American copyrights safeguarded.

Between 1994, when NAFTA went into effect, and 1998, U.S. trade with Mexico increased a whopping 113 percent to $173.4 billion, while trade with Canada rose 63 percent, to $329.9 billion.[37] NAFTA has also spurred the entry of small businesses into the global arena. Jeff Victor, general manager of Treatment Products, Ltd., which makes car cleaners and waxes, credits NAFTA for his surging export volume. Prior to the pact, Mexican tariffs as high as 20 percent made it impossible for the Chicago-based company to expand its presence south of the border. Similarly, StoneHeart, Inc., of Cheney, Washington, began selling its scooters for people with leg or foot injuries to a distributor in Canada.[38] Although many groups in the United States opposed the agreement, warning of job loss and the potential for industrial ghost towns, results so far have been positive. Criticism of NAFTA continues, but experts stress that NAFTA will enable companies in all three countries to compete more effectively with rival Asian and European companies.[39]

Trade Alliances: Promise or Pitfall?

The creation of trading blocs is an increasingly popular part of international business. The Association of Southeast Asian Nations (ASEAN) is a trading alliance of 10 Southeast Asian nations, including Cambodia, Vietnam, Singapore, Malaysia, and the Philippines. This region will likely be one of the fastest-growing economic regions of the world, and the ASEAN could eventually be as powerful as NAFTA and the EU. A free trade block known as Mercosur encompasses Argentina, Brazil, Bolivia, Chile, Paraguay, and Uruguay. And more than 30 countries in Central and South America and the Caribbean region are negotiating to establish a Free Trade Area of the Americas (FTAA).[40] These agreements entail a new future for international companies and pose a range of new questions for international managers.

- Will the creation of multiple trade blocs lead to economic warfare among them?
- Will trade blocs gradually evolve into three powerful trading blocs composed of the American hemisphere, Europe (from Ireland across the former Soviet Union), and the "yen bloc" encompassing the Pacific Rim?
- Will the expansion of global, stateless corporations bypass trading zones and provide economic balance among them?[41]

Only the future will provide answers to these questions. International managers and global corporations will both shape and be shaped by these important trends.

The Sociocultural Environment

culture
The shared knowledge, beliefs, values, behaviors and ways of thinking among members of a society.

A nation's **culture** includes the shared knowledge, beliefs, and values, as well as the common modes of behavior and ways of thinking, among members of a society. Cultural factors are more perplexing than political and economic factors in foreign countries. Culture is intangible, pervasive, and difficult to learn. It is absolutely imperative that international businesses and managers comprehend the significance of local cultures and deal with them effectively.

Social Values

Research done by Geert Hofstede on 116,000 IBM employees in 40 countries identified four dimensions of national value systems that influence organizational and employee working relationships.[42] Examples of how countries rate on the four dimensions are shown in Exhibit 4.4.

1. *Power distance.* High **power distance** means that people accept inequality in power among institutions, organizations, and people. Low power distance means that people expect equality in power. Countries that value high power distance are Malaysia, the Philippines, and Panama. Countries that value low power distance are Denmark, Austria, and Israel.

2. *Uncertainty avoidance.* High **uncertainty avoidance** means that members of a society feel uncomfortable with uncertainty and ambiguity and thus support beliefs that promise certainty and conformity. Low uncertainty avoidance means that people have high tolerance for the unstructured, the unclear, and the unpredictable. High uncertainty avoidance countries include Greece, Portugal, and Uruguay. Countries with low uncertainty avoidance values are Singapore and Jamaica.

3. *Individualism and collectivism.* **Individualism** reflects a value for a loosely knit social framework in which individuals are expected to take care of themselves. **Collectivism** means a preference for a tightly knit social framework in which individuals look after one another and organizations protect their members' interests. Countries with individualist values include the United States, Canada, Great Britain, and Australia. Countries with collectivist values are Guatemala, Ecuador, and China.

4. *Masculinity/femininity.* **Masculinity** stands for preference for achievement, heroism, assertiveness, work centrality (with resultant high stress), and material success. **Femininity** reflects the values of relationships, cooperation, group decision making, and quality of life. Societies with strong masculine values are Japan, Austria, Mexico, and Germany. Countries with feminine values are Sweden, Norway, Denmark, and France. Both men and women subscribe to the dominant value in masculine and feminine cultures.

power distance
The degree to which people accept inequality in power among institutions, organizations, and people.

uncertainty avoidance
A value characterized by people's intolerance for uncertainty and ambiguity and resulting support for beliefs that promise certainty and conformity.

individualism
A preference for a loosely knit social framework in which individuals are expected to take care of themselves.

collectivism
A preference for a tightly knit social framework in which individuals look after one another and organizations protect their members' interests.

masculinity
A cultural preference for achievement, heroism, assertiveness, work centrality, and material success.

femininity
A cultural preference for cooperation, group decision making, and quality of life.

Country	Power Distance[a]	Uncertainty Avoidance[b]	Individualism[c]	Masculinity[d]
Australia	7	7	2	5
Costa Rica	8 (tie)	2 (tie)	10	9
France	3	2 (tie)	4	7
West Germany	8 (tie)	5	5	3
India	2	9	6	6
Japan	5	1	7	1
Mexico	1	4	8	2
Sweden	10	10	3	10
Thailand	4	6	9	8
United States	6	8	1	4

[a] 1=highest power distance
10=lowest power distance
[b] 1=highest uncertainty avoidance
10=lowest uncertainty avoidance
[c] 1=highest individualism
10=highest collectivisim
[d] 1=highest masculinity
10=highest femininity

Exhibit 4.4

Rank Orderings of Ten Countries along Four Dimensions of National Value Systems

SOURCE: From Dorothy Marcic, *Organizational Behavior and Cases*, 4th ed. (St. Paul, Minn.: West, 1995). Based on Geert Hofstede, *Culture's Consequences* (London: Sage Publications, 1984); and *Cultures and Organizations: Software of the Mind* (New York: McGraw-Hill, 1991).

long-term orientation
A greater concern for the future and high value on thrift and perseverence.

short-term orientation
A concern with the past and present and a high value on meeting social obligations.

Hofstede and his colleagues later identified a fifth dimension, **long-term orientation** versus **short-term orientation**. The long-term orientation, found in China and other Asian countries, includes a greater concern for the future and highly values thrift and perseverance. A short-term orientation, found in Russia and West Africa, is more concerned with the past and the present and places a high value on tradition and meeting social obligations.[43]

Social values influence organizational functioning and management styles. For example, managers attempting to implement self-directed work teams in Mexico have run into problems because Mexico is characterized by very high power distance and a relatively low tolerance for uncertainty. These characteristics often conflict with the American concept of teamwork, which emphasizes shared power and authority, with team members working on a variety of problems without formal guidelines, rules, and structure. Many workers in Mexico, as well as France and Mediterranean countries, expect organizations to be hierarchical. Germany and other central European countries have organizations that strive to be impersonal, well-oiled machines. In India, Asia, and Africa, organizations are viewed as large families. Effective management styles differ in each country, depending on cultural characteristics.[44]

Other Cultural Characteristics

Other cultural characteristics that influence international organizations are language, religion, attitudes, social organization, and education. Some countries, such as India, are characterized by *linguistic pluralism*, meaning that several languages exist there. Other countries rely heavily on spoken versus written language. Religion includes sacred objects, philosophical attitudes toward life, taboos, and rituals. Attitudes toward achievement, work, and time can all affect organizational productivity. An attitude called **ethnocentrism** means that people have a tendency to regard their own culture as superior and to downgrade other cultures. Ethnocentrism within a country makes it difficult for foreign firms to operate there. Social organization includes status systems, kinship and families, social institutions, and opportunities for social mobility. Education influences the literacy level, the availability of qualified employees, and the predominance of primary or secondary degrees.

ethnocentrism
A cultural attitude marked by the tendency to regard one's own culture as superior to others.

American managers are regularly accused of an ethnocentric attitude that assumes the American way is the best way. At an executive training seminar at IMD, a business school in Lausanne, Switzerland, managers from Europe expressed a mixture of admiration and disdain for U.S. managers. "They admire the financial results," says J. Peter Killing, an IMD professor, "but when they meet managers from the U.S. they see that even these educated, affluent Americans don't speak any language besides English, don't know how or when to eat and drink properly, and don't know anything about European history, let alone geography."[45] As business grows increasingly global, U.S. managers are learning that cultural differences cannot be ignored if international operations are to succeed. For example, Coke withdrew its two-liter bottle from the Spanish market after discovering that compartments of Spanish refrigerators were too small for it.[46] McDonald's hasn't even tried to market Egg McMuffins in Brazil because of the deeply ingrained tradition of eating breakfast at home. On the other hand, Kellogg introduced breakfast cereal into Brazil through carefully chosen advertising. Although the traditional breakfast is coffee and a roll, many Brazilians have been won over to the American breakfast and now start their day with Kellogg's Sucrilhos (Frosted Flakes) and Crokinhos (Cocoa Krispies).[47]

Organizations that recognize and manage cultural differences report major successes. Consider the cultural challenges managers of Bob's Big Boy face in Thailand.

BOB'S BIG BOY
http://www.bigboy.com

McDonald's and Burger King have taken American fast food worldwide, and now a host of smaller companies, including A&W, Shakey's, and Dairy Queen, are heading overseas to serve customers who are hungry for more. But one adventurous franchiser who opened a Big Boy restaurant in Thailand learned quickly that there are plenty of barriers to overcome.

Peter Smythe first began scouting for a franchise on behalf of a Thailand arms dealer who wanted to start a business for his daughters to run. When he met the owners of Big Boy, Elias Brothers of Warren, Michigan, Smythe knew he'd found a match. Big Boy, with 600 restaurants worldwide, seemed a natural for further global expansion. Its 1950s-roadside decor, diverse menu, and famous Big Boy icon all added up to a great American brand. "All you have to do is open the door and they will come," the 78-year-old Louis Elias told Smythe. But when Smythe opened the door in Thailand, no one came (not even the arms dealer and his daughters, who showed no interest in running the business).

Smythe was left on his own to save Big Boy in Thailand, so he began talking to people about why they were not coming to the restaurant. The reasons were many and varied, ranging from feelings that the restaurant had bad "room energy" to the cost of the food. Many people told Smythe they'd rather get a noodle bowl or sweet satay from a street vendor for one-fifth what they'd have to pay for a greasy American burger. And one of the biggest reasons was that Thai customers found the pudgy, grinning Big Boy statue just a little creepy. They couldn't figure out what it meant or what they were supposed to do with it. A few eventually decided it was a religious icon and began laying bowls of rice and incense at his feet. Smythe realized the attempt to transport a 65-year-old brand and food to a 3,500-year-old culture without making any adjustments wasn't going to fly. He began adding a few inexpensive Thai dishes to the menu, and customers began trickling in. He added sugar and chile powder to the burger recipe to better match Thai taste buds. The Big Boy statue stayed, but by educating employees, who pass what they learn on to friends and family, Thailand customers aren't as spooked by him as they once were. Smythe took the comments about room energy seriously too, even though he hasn't totally solved the problem.

And he still has plenty of other problems to contend with, as well. All the bakers he contacted told him the buns he wanted were "too complicated," so Smythe had to make his own bun molds. When small suppliers go out of business, he has to scramble to find replacements. And one of the biggest problems he's encountered is that at the peak of lunch hour the entire staff disappears into the back to eat their lunch of noodles and soup. "I asked them to take turns eating," Smythe says. "They say, 'No, we all have to eat at the same time.'" Smythe just has to do the best he can to work around the problem. His five-year adventure in Thailand has not been easy, but by listening to the local people and making adjustments to meet cultural differences, Smythe has now opened three additional—and highly profitable—Big Boy franchises in the country.[48] ❖

Getting Started Internationally

Small and medium-sized companies have a couple of ways to become involved internationally. One is to seek cheaper sources of supply offshore, which is called *outsourcing*. Another is to develop markets for finished products outside their home country, which may include exporting, licensing, and direct investing. These are called **market entry strategies** because they represent alternative ways to sell products and services in foreign markets. Most firms begin with exporting and work up to direct investment. Exhibit 4.5 shows the strategies companies can use to enter foreign markets.

market entry strategy
An organizational strategy for entering a foreign market.

Outsourcing

global outsourcing
Engaging in the international division of labor so as to obtain the cheapest sources of labor and supplies regardless of country; also called *global sourcing*.

Global outsourcing, sometimes called *global sourcing*, means engaging in the international division of labor so that manufacturing can be done in countries with the cheapest sources of labor and supplies. A company may take away a contract from a domestic supplier and place it with a company in the Far East, 8,000 miles away. Manufacturers in Asia and Latin America are rapidly getting wired into the Internet to help them compete in an e-business world. Large companies outsource to companies all over Asia, and they like the convenience, speed, and efficiency of handling business by electronic transactions. Singapore-based Advanced Manufacturing Online uses a system that enables both suppliers and clients to send orders and solicit price quotes over the Web.[49]

A unique variation of global outsourcing is the *Maquiladora* industry along the Texas–Mexico border. In the beginning, twin plants were set up, with the U.S. plant manufacturing components with sophisticated machinery and the Mexican plant assembling components using cheap labor. With increasing sophistication in Mexico, new factories with sophisticated equipment are being built farther south of the border, with assembled products imported into the United States at highly competitive prices. General Electric, for example, employs more than 30,000 people in appliance factories in Mexico, and is now

E x h i b i t **4.5**

Strategies for Entering International Markets

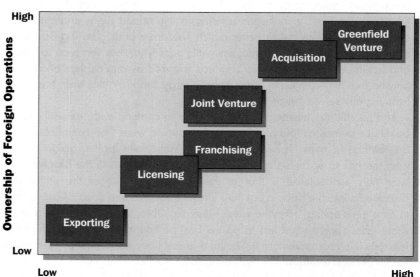

Cost to Enter Foreign Operations

shifting some of its engineering work to that country as well as to India, Brazil, and Turkey. And service companies are taking advantage of the *maquiladora* concept as well. U.S. data-processing companies use high-speed data lines to ship document images to Mexico and India, where 45,000 workers do everything from processing airline tickets to screening U.S. credit-card applications.[50]

Exporting

With **exporting**, the corporation maintains its production facilities within the home nation and transfers its products for sale in foreign countries.[51] Exporting enables a country to market its products in other countries at modest resource cost and with limited risk. Exporting does entail numerous problems based on physical distances, government regulations, foreign currencies, and cultural differences, but it is less expensive than committing the firm's own capital to building plants in host countries. For example, a high-tech equipment supplier called Gerber Scientific Inc. prefers not to get involved directly in foreign country operations. Because machinery and machine tools are hot areas of export, executives are happy to ship overseas. U.S. exports are on the rise, and small to mid-size companies are benefiting. Multiplex Co., a St. Louis manufacturer of beverage-dispensing equipment for fast-food service, exports about 40 percent of its products. National Graphics, a specialty coater of papers and films, ships 60 percent of its products overseas, and National's CEO believes exports helped to save the company.[52]

A form of exporting to less-developed countries is called **countertrade**, which is the barter of products for products rather than the sale of products for currency. Many less-developed countries have products to exchange but have no foreign currency. An estimated 20 percent of world trade is countertrade.

Licensing

The next stage in pursuing international markets is licensing and franchising, which are similar approaches. With **licensing**, a corporation (the licensor) in one country makes certain resources available to companies in another country (the licensee). These resources include technology, managerial skills, and/or patent and trademark rights. They enable the licensee to produce and market a product similar to what the licensor has been producing. This arrangement gives the licensor an opportunity to participate in the production and sale of products outside its home country at relatively low cost. Hasbro has licensing agreements with companies in several Latin American countries and Japan. Hasbro builds brand identity and consumer awareness by contracting with toy companies in other countries to manufacture products locally. Heineken, which has been called the world's first truly global brand of beer, usually begins by exporting to help boost familiarity with its product; if the market looks enticing enough, Heineken then licenses its brands to a local brewer.

©Chris Brown/SABA

Daewoo Campus Advisers at U.S. universities? Through exporting, Korea's Daewoo Motor Co. sold 30,000 vehicles in its first year in the U.S. market. The Campus Advisers, a group of 2,000 college students at some 200 campuses, run Daewoo events and direct potential buyers to the nearest Daewoo sales showroom. The advisers receive $300 to $500 per car sold and an all-expense-paid seven-day trip to Korea, plus free use of a car for 3 months and the option to buy it at a discount.

exporting
An entry strategy in which the organization maintains its production facilities within its home country and transfers its products for sale in foreign countries.

countertrade
The barter of products for other products rather than their sale for currency.

licensing
An entry strategy in which an organization in one country makes certain resources available to companies in another in order to participate in the production and sale of its products abroad.

franchising
A form of licensing in which an organization provides its foreign franchisees with a complete package of materials and services.

Franchising is a special form of licensing that occurs when the franchisee buys a complete package of materials and services, including equipment, products, product ingredients, trademark and trade name rights, managerial advice, and a standardized operating system. Whereas with licensing, a licensee generally keeps its own company name and operating systems, a franchise takes the name and systems of the franchisor. For example, Anheuser-Busch licenses the right to brew and distribute Budweiser beer to several breweries, including Labatt in Canada and Kirin in Japan, but these breweries retain their own company names, identities, and autonomy. On the other hand, a Burger King franchise anywhere in the world is a Burger King, and managers use standard procedures designed by the franchisor. The fast-food chains are some of the best-known franchisors. KFC, Burger King, Wendy's, and McDonald's outlets are found in almost every large city in the world. The story is often told of the Japanese child visiting Los Angeles who excitedly pointed out to his parents, "They have McDonald's in America."

Licensing and franchising offer a business firm relatively easy access to international markets at low cost, but they limit its participation in and control over the development of those markets.

Direct Investing

A higher level of involvement in international trade is direct investment in manufacturing facilities in a foreign country. **Direct investing** means that the company is involved in managing the productive assets, which distinguishes it from other entry strategies that permit less managerial control.

direct investing
An entry strategy in which the organization is involved in managing its production facilities in a foreign country.

Currently, the most popular type of direct investment is to engage in strategic alliances and partnerships. In a **joint venture**, a company shares costs and risks with another firm, typically in the host country, to develop new products, build a manufacturing facility, or set up a sales and distribution network.[53] A partnership is often the fastest, cheapest, and least risky way to get into the global game. Entrepreneurial companies such as Molex, a manufacturer of connectors, and Nypro, a maker of industrial components, have used partnerships to gain overseas access to several countries. Heineken Breweries has entered into a joint venture with Singapore's Asia Pacific Breweries, makers of Tiger Beer, and Ci-Co S.A. Auburn Farms, a Sacramento, California, manufacturer of all-natural snack foods, recently entered into a joint venture with South Africa's Beacon Sweets & Chocolates.[54] Internet companies have also used joint ventures as a way to expand. AOL created a joint venture with Venezuela's Cisneros Group to smooth its entry into Latin America.[55]

joint venture
A variation of direct involvement in which an organization shares costs and risks with another firm to build a manufacturing facility, develop new products, or set up a sales and distribution network.

wholly owned foreign affiliate
A foreign subsidiary over which an organization has complete control.

The other choice is to have a **wholly owned foreign affiliate**, over which the company has complete control. Direct *acquisition* of an affiliate may provide cost savings over exporting by shortening distribution channels and reducing storage and transportation costs. Local managers also have heightened awareness of economic, cultural, and political conditions. For example, General Electric purchased Hungarian bulbmaker Tungsram in 1990, and quality was so good that GE eventually shifted all European light-bulb production there.[56]

greenfield venture
The most risky type of direct investment, whereby a company builds a subsidiary from scratch in a foreign country.

The most costly and risky direct investment is called a **greenfield venture**, which means a company builds a subsidiary from scratch in a foreign country. The advantage is that the subsidiary is exactly what the company wants and has the potential to be highly profitable. The disadvantage is that the company has to acquire all market knowledge, materials, people, and know-how in a different culture, and mistakes are possible. An example of a greenfield venture is the Mercedes-Benz plant in Vance, Alabama. This was the first time the company had built a plant outside Germany. The venture was high risk because the new plant was building a new product (sport-utility vehicle) with a new workforce, to be sold in a foreign country.[57]

Multinational Corporations

The size and volume of international business are so large that they are hard to comprehend. The revenue of General Motors is comparable to the gross domestic product (GDP) of Finland, that of General Electric is comparable in size to Israel's GDP, Toyota revenues to Hong Kong's GDP, and those of the Royal Dutch/Shell Group to the GDP of Norway.[58]

As discussed earlier in this chapter, a large volume of international business is being carried out in a seemingly borderless world by very large international businesses that can be thought of as *global corporations*, *stateless corporations*, or *transnational corporations*. In the business world, these large international firms typically are called *multinational corporations (MNCs)*, which have been the subject of enormous attention. MNCs can move a wealth of assets from country to country and influence national economies, politics, and cultures.

Although there is no precise definition, a **multinational corporation (MNC)** typically receives more than 25 percent of its total sales revenues from operations outside the parent's home country. MNCs also have the following distinctive managerial characteristics:

1. An MNC is managed as an integrated worldwide business system. This means that foreign affiliates act in close alliance and cooperation with one another. Capital, technology, and people are transferred among country affiliates. The MNC can acquire materials and manufacture parts wherever in the world it is most advantageous to do so.
2. An MNC is ultimately controlled by a single management authority that makes key strategic decisions relating to the parent and all affiliates. Although some headquarters are binational, such as the Royal Dutch/Shell Group, some centralization of management is required to maintain worldwide integration and profit maximization for the enterprise as a whole.
3. MNC top managers are presumed to exercise a global perspective. They regard the entire world as one market for strategic decisions, resource acquisition, location of production, advertising, and marketing efficiency.

In a few cases, the MNC management philosophy may differ from that just described. For example, some researchers have distinguished among *ethnocentric companies*, which place emphasis on their home countries,

multinational corporation (MNC)
An organization that receives more than 25 percent of its total sales revenues from operations outside the parent company's home country; also called *global corporation* or *transnational corporation*.

Wal-Mart, the world's largest retailer, has built a solid international presence by using a market entry strategy of direct investment, including joint ventures, acquisitions, and building new operations. Although Wal-Mart's international record is full of merchandising missteps and management upheaval, the company is gradually becoming a more savvy global player. It is now the biggest retailer in Canada and Mexico, and in 2000 its $32 billion international business equaled 17 percent of its $191 billion in sales. The company has more than 1,100 stores in nine countries, including the German store in the photo, which Wal-Mart bought as part of Germany's Wertkauf hypermarket chain.

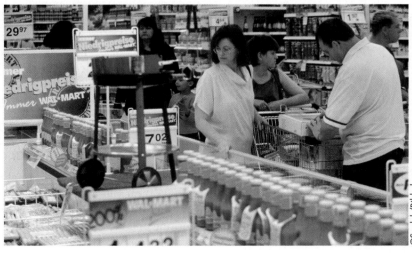
©Spalek/Bilderberg

polycentric companies, which are oriented toward the markets of individual foreign host countries, and *geocentric companies*, which are truly world oriented and favor no specific country.[59] The truly global companies that transcend national boundaries are growing in number. These companies no longer see themselves as American, Chinese, or German; they are totally globally operating and serve a global market.

Managing in a Global Environment

Managing in a foreign country is particularly challenging. Before undertaking a foreign assignment, managers must understand that they will face great personal challenges. Managers working in foreign countries must be sensitive to cultural subtleties and understand that the ways to provide proper leadership, decision making, motivation, and control vary in different cultures. When companies operate internationally, the need for personal learning and growth is critical.

Personal Challenges for Global Managers

Managers will be most successful in foreign assignments if they are culturally flexible and easily adapt to new situations and ways of doing things. A tendency to be ethnocentric—to believe that your own country's cultural values and ways of doing things are superior—is a natural human condition. Managers can learn to break down those prejudices and appreciate another culture. As one Swedish executive of a large multinational corporation put it, "We Swedes are so content with . . . the Swedish way, that we forget that 99 percent of the rest of the world isn't Swedish."[60] Managers working in foreign countries may never come to understand the local culture like a native; the key is to be sensitive to cultural differences and understand that other ways of thinking and doing are also valid.

Most managers in foreign assignments face a period of homesickness, loneliness, and culture shock from being suddenly immersed in a culture with completely different languages, foods, values, beliefs, and ways of doing things. **Culture shock** refers to the frustration and anxiety that result from constantly being subjected to strange and unfamiliar cues about what to do and how to do it. Even simple, daily events can become sources of stress.[61]

Preparing managers to work in foreign cultures is essential. Some companies try to give future managers exposure to foreign cultures early in their careers. American Express Company's Travel-Related Services unit gives American business-school students summer jobs in which they work outside the United States for up to 10 weeks. Colgate-Palmolive selects 15 recent graduates each year and then provides up to 24 months of training prior to multiple overseas job stints.[62]

culture shock
Feelings of confusion, disorientation, and anxiety that result from being immersed in a foreign culture.

Managing Cross-Culturally

To be effective on an international level, managers can first understand their own cultural values and assumptions, as discussed in Chapter 3; then they can interpret the culture of the country and organization in which they are working and develop the sensitivity required to avoid making costly cultural blunders.[63]

In the United States, cross-cultural training is a popular way of helping managers prepare for overseas assignments. Sixty-three percent of global companies now offer managers at least one full day of cultural training about the foreign country where they have been assigned. "Americans tend to think everyone's the same, " says Steven Jones of East–West Business Strategies in San Francisco. "It's a dangerous assumption."[64] One way managers prepare for foreign assignments is to understand how the country differs in terms of Hofstede's social values (power distance, individualism, uncertainty avoidance, masculinity, and orientation) as discussed earlier in this chapter. These values greatly influence how a manager should interact with subordinates and colleagues in the new assignment. For example, the United States scores extremely high on individualism, and a U.S. manager working in a country such as Japan, which scores very high on collectivism, will have to modify his or her approach to leading and controlling in order to be successful. The following examples illustrate how cultural differences can be significant for expatriate managers.

Leading. In relationship-oriented societies which rank high on collectivism, such as those in Asia, the Arab world, and Latin America, leaders should use a warm, personalized approach with employees. One of the greatest difficulties U.S. leaders have had doing business in China, for example, is failing to recognize that to the Chinese any relationship is a personal relationship.[65] Managers are expected to have periodic social visits with workers, inquiring about morale and health. Leaders should be especially careful about criticizing others. To Asians, Africans, Arabs, and Latin Americans, the loss of self-respect brings dishonor to themselves and their families. One researcher tells of a Dutch doctor managing a company clinic who had what he considered a "frank discussion" with a Chinese subordinate. The subordinate, who perceived the doctor as a father figure, took the criticism as a "savage indictment" and committed suicide.[66] Though this is an extreme example, the principle of *saving face* is highly important in some cultures.

Decision Making. In the United States, mid-level managers may discuss a problem and give the boss a recommendation. German managers, on the other hand, expect the boss to issue specific instructions. In Mexico, employees often don't understand participatory decision making. Mexico ranks extremely high on power distance, and many workers expect managers to exercise their power in making decisions and issuing orders. American managers working in Mexico have been advised to rarely explain a decision, lest workers perceive this as a sign of weakness.[67] In contrast, managers in Arab and African nations are expected to use consultative decision making in the extreme.

Motivating. Motivation must fit the incentives within the culture. In Japan, employees are motivated to satisfy the company. A financial bonus for star performance would be humiliating to employees from Japan, China, or Ecuador. An American executive in Japan offered a holiday trip to the top salesperson, but employees were not interested. After he realized that Japanese are motivated in groups, he changed the reward to a trip for everyone if together they achieved the sales target. They did. Managers in Latin America, Africa, and the Middle East must show respect for employees as individuals with needs and interests outside of work.[68]

Putting People First

AES Corp.: Power to the People

Managers at AES Corporation, the world's largest independent power company, with headquarters in Arlington, Virginia, believe the best way to show people they're valued and appreciated is to give them the power and freedom to think, learn, grow, and achieve. Lots of companies talk about pushing power and responsibility to lower levels, but few have pushed as far as AES. With nearly 60,000 employees around the world, AES has never established departments for human resources, operations, purchasing, or legal affairs. All functions—even finance—are handled by decentralized teams that include coal handlers and maintenance workers. For example, two control-room operators led the team that raised $350 million to finance a joint venture in Northern Ireland. Teams seek advice from managers or anyone else who may have helpful ideas, but they make their own decisions.

According to co-founder and CEO Dennis Bakke, "If all information about finance goes to the finance department and all information about legal matters goes to the legal department, it's impossible to get well-rounded people who can think about the whole world." AES needs people to think about the whole world as it continues its rapid expansion internationally. The company opened its first plant in 1986. Today, it owns or has an interest in 182 power plants in the United States, Argentina, China, Brazil, Hungary, and other countries. The company has revenues of about $6,691 million and profits of $665 million. AES also believes in being a good corporate citizen in the countries in which it operates. It has planted 52 million trees in Guatemala, funded medical care in Kazakhstan, organized food banks in Argentina, and built schools in China.

Bakke and co-founder and chairman Roger Sant believe AES has been able to expand so rapidly because giving people on the front lines the power to make decisions has made AES faster and nimbler than competitors. Oscar Prieto, a chemical engineer picked to lead AES's expansion into Brazil, agrees. He'd worked at AES only two years when he was given the challenging assignment, but he'd experienced the power of empowerment and believed it could work crossculturally. He chose Carlos Baldi, a 34-year-old engineer, to manage the plant in Santa Branca, a small facility near São Paolo that had previously been run as a top-heavy bureaucracy. After agreeing on shared goals and expectations, Prieto turned the plant over to Baldi and told him to run it as he saw fit. Now Baldi operates the same way with his people—he gives advice, not approval.

"Power to the people" doesn't always translate so well to other countries, however. For example, managers in Northern Ireland are having a hard time giving up control and operating the AES way. Yet, Bakke and Sant are committed to expanding AES's bottom-up system around the world.

SOURCES: Alex Markels, "Power to the People," *Fast Company* (February–March 1998), 155–165; and http://www.aesc.com.

Controlling.   When things go wrong, managers in foreign countries often are unable to get rid of employees who do not work out. In Europe, Mexico, and Indonesia, to hire and fire based on performance seems unnaturally brutal. Workers are protected by strong labor laws and union rules.

In foreign cultures, managers also should not control the wrong things. A Sears manager in Hong Kong insisted that employees come to work on time instead of 15 minutes late. The employees did exactly as they were told, but they also left on time instead of working into the evening as they had previously. A lot of work was left unfinished. The manager eventually told the employees to go back to their old ways. His attempt at control had a negative effect.

Global Learning

Managing across borders calls for organizations to learn across borders. One reason Japanese companies have been so successful internationally is that their culture encourages learning and adaptability. In Asia generally, teaching and learning are highly regarded, and the role of managers is seen as one of teaching or facilitating—of helping those around them to learn.[69] It is partly this emphasis on continuous learning that has helped Matsushita Electric master markets and diverse cultures in 38 countries, from Malaysia to Brazil, from Austria to China, from Iran to Tanzania. One of Matsushita's top lessons for going global is to be a good corporate citizen in every country, respecting cultures, customs, and languages. In countries with Muslim religious practices, for example, Matsushita provides special prayer rooms and allows two prayer sessions per shift.[70] AES Corporation, an American corporation that encourages continuous learning by giving freedom and power to front-line workers, is now trying to expand its business model internationally, as described in the Putting People First box.

■ Summary and Management Solution

This chapter has emphasized the growing importance of an international perspective on management. Successful companies are expanding their business overseas and successfully competing with foreign companies on their home turf. Business in the global arena involves special risks and difficulties because of complicated economic, legal-political, and sociocultural forces. Moreover, the global environment changes rapidly, as illustrated by the emergence of the European Union, the North American Free Trade Agreement, and the shift in Eastern Europe to democratic forms of government. Major alternatives for serving foreign markets are exporting, licensing, franchising, and direct investing through joint ventures or wholly owned subsidiaries.

International markets provide many opportunities but are also fraught with difficulty, as Wal-Mart, described at the beginning of this chapter, discovered. The company has revised its merchandising and changed some of its tactics to better suit local cultures in Brazil and China. In Brazil, for example, it has scaled back the size of stores and moved to midsize cities where competition is less fierce. Wal-Mart is trying to work with local partners who can help the company translate its business cross-culturally. Despite problems, the company is opening more stores in both Brazil and Argentina. Bob Martin, Wal-Mart's head of international operations, believes the international market is worth the risks. "The market is ripe and wide open for us."[71]

Much of the growth in international business has been carried out by large businesses called *MNCs*. These large companies exist in an almost borderless world, encouraging the free flow of ideas, products, manufacturing, and marketing among countries to achieve the greatest efficiencies. Managers in *MNCs* as well as those in much smaller companies doing business internationally face many challenges. Managers often experience culture shock when transferred to foreign countries. They must learn to be sensitive to cultural differences and tailor their management style to the culture. For managers and organizations in an increasingly borderless world, learning across borders is critical.

■ Discussion Questions

1. Why do you think international businesses traditionally prefer to operate in industrialized countries? Discuss.

2. What might be some long-term ramifications of the war on terrorism for U.S. managers and companies operating internationally?

3. What policies or actions would you recommend to an e-commerce company wanting to do business internationally?

4. What steps could a company take to avoid making product design and marketing mistakes when introducing new products into a foreign country?

5. Compare the advantages associated with the foreign-market entry strategies of exporting, licensing, and wholly owned subsidiaries.

6. Should a multinational corporation operate as an integrated, worldwide business system, or would it be more effective to let each national subsidiary operate autonomously?

7. What does it mean to say that the world is becoming "borderless"? That large companies are "stateless"?

8. What might managers do to avoid making mistakes concerning control and decision making when operating in a foreign culture?

9. What is meant by the cultural values of individualism and power distance? How might these values affect organization design and management processes?

10. How do you think trade alliances such as NAFTA and the EU may affect you as a future manager?

■ Management in Practice: Experiential Exercise

Rate Your Global Management Potential

A global environment requires that managers learn to deal effectively with people and ideas from a variety of cultures. How well prepared are you to be a global manager? Read the following statements and circle the number on the response scale that most closely reflects how well the statement describes you.

	Good Description							Poor Description		
1. I reach out to people from different cultures.	10	9	8	7	6	5	4	3	2	1
2. I frequently attend seminars and lectures about other cultures or international topics.	10	9	8	7	6	5	4	3	2	1
3. I believe female expatriates can be equally as effective as male expatriates.	10	9	8	7	6	5	4	3	2	1
4. I have a basic knowledge about several countries in addition to my native country.	10	9	8	7	6	5	4	3	2	1
5. I have good listening and empathy skills.	10	9	8	7	6	5	4	3	2	1
6. I have spent more than two weeks traveling or working in another country.	10	9	8	7	6	5	4	3	2	1
7. I easily adapt to the different work ethics of students from other cultures when we are involved in a team project.	10	9	8	7	6	5	4	3	2	1
8. I can speak a foreign language.	10	9	8	7	6	5	4	3	2	1
9. I know which countries tend to cluster into similar sociocultural and economic groupings.	10	9	8	7	6	5	4	3	2	1
10. I feel capable of assessing different cultures on the basis of power distance, uncertainty avoidance, individualism, and masculinity.	10	9	8	7	6	5	4	3	2	1

Total Score _____

Scoring: Add up the total points for the 10 questions. If you scored between 81–100 points, you have a great capacity for developing good global management skills. A score of 61–80 points indicates that you have potential but may lack skills in certain areas, such as language or foreign experience. A score of 60 or less means you need to do some serious work to improve your potential for global management. Regardless of your total score, go back over each item and make a plan of action to increase scores of less than 5 on any question.

Source: Based in part on "How Well Do You Exhibit Good Intercultural Management Skills?" in John W. Newstrom and Keith Davis, *Organizational Behavior: Human Behavior at Work* (Boston, Mass: McGraw-Hill Irwin, 2002), 415–416.

■ Management in Practice: Ethical Dilemma

The Problem in Asia

Cindy Wilkinson should have been smiling as she stared out the window of the plane headed toward Illinois. She had just successfully completed three challenging years in Asia for Axcor Inc. and was now headed home to a plum assignment at headquarters and a chance to have Thanksgiving dinner with her family again.

But Cindy's thoughts kept turning to what she had come to think of as The Problem. She knew she'd be debriefed upon her return to headquarters, and she was either going to have to hide an ugly matter or reveal a serious problem in the Asian operations, a move that could threaten her career with Axcor. The ugliness centered on Wang Zing, who had been Axcor's director of Asian operations for the past five years. It hadn't taken Cindy long to realize that Zing consistently undermined people's confidence and caused them to suffer undeserved shame. He seemed to have an uncanny ability to spot people's weaknesses and use them to manipulate staff members. One of his favorite activities was humiliating employees in public. Cindy had learned in her cross-cultural training prior to her assignment that obedience was highly valued in Asian cultures, along with the concept of saving face. Zing abused those cultural values, his position, and the staff, resulting in an inefficient operation that wasn't meeting its potential. Yet, because top managers had never clearly defined goals for the Asian operation, evaluating Zing was tricky. Whenever the corporate comptroller made his annual visit, Zing would lavish him with hospitality and the executive would leave thinking everything in Asia was going just grand.

Cindy knew the comptroller liked Zing and influenced the views of other top executives, but she felt that she needed to describe the degradation of employees that she had witnessed. Even if she simply identified some basic changes that could increase productivity, it would end up pointing the finger at Zing. Possible retribution could sidetrack or even destroy her career.

What Do You Do?

1. Keep your mouth shut. This is the comptroller's responsibility. You've just gotten the job you wanted at headquarters, and to rock the boat now could do more harm to your career that it would do good for the company.
2. Tell top executives straight out that Zing is mistreating employees and creating an environment that is detrimental to productivity and performance.
3. Frame your remarks in terms of the inefficiencies you witnessed in the Asian operation, with specific details to back you up. Recommend that clear, high standards be established for the Asian business and suggest some elements of those standards, including treatment of employees.

SOURCE: Adapted from Doug Wallace, "When Being Right Isn't Enough," *BusinessEthics* (March–April 1999), 18.

Surf the Net

1. **Largest Companies in the World.** *Fortune* magazine, in its annual listing called the "Global 500," ranks the world's largest companies based on sales revenue. Go to *http://www.fortune.com* and locate the Global 500. Fill in the chart below:

Global 500 Ranking for _____ (Year)

Ranking	Company	Headquarters (Country)
1		
2		
3		
4		
5		
6		
7		
8		
9		
10		

2. **World Trade Organization.** Visit the WTO at *http://www.wto.org* and answer the following questions:
   - Where is the WTO located?
   - When was it established?
   - How many countries are members?
   - What are the WTO's main functions?
3. **The World Fact Book.** You will find fascinating information is available at *http://www.odci.gov/cia/publications/factbook/index.html*. Access the "Field Listing" option for "GDP—per capita." On a separate sheet of paper list how much the per capita GDP is for the United States and countries with a higher per capita GDP than the United States. Next, identify two or three countries with per capita GDP closest to that of the United States. Finally, indicate the country with the lowest per capita GDP, including the amount.

■ Case for Critical Analysis

Unocal Corporation

Unocal Corporation seemed an unlikely candidate for a high-risk global rampage. Consumers everywhere recognized the ubiquitous 76 logo of this quintessential California oil company. They knew it as a large petroleum retailer, with a prestigious downtown headquarters and important role as a Los Angeles civic booster. Casting aside its reputation as a conservative company with tightly defined domestic markets and focused petroleum interests in California, Unocal spent the 1990s transforming itself into an international company with major investments in some of the world's least-developed economies.

In 1995, immediately after becoming chairman of Unocal, Roger Beach began to sell off domestic retail assets and eliminate exploration and refining activities in the United States. Resources shifted to unlikely places where few other major oil producers had risked operations—places such as Myanmar (formerly known as Burma), Turkmenistan, Uzbekistan, and the strife-ridden Balkans. Beach turned up the heat on company investments in Indonesian oil fields, launched full-service energy subsidiaries through government alliances in Thailand, broadened holdings in Malaysia, and began negotiations for an integrated refining/retailing enterprise in Pakistan. Nearly 40 percent of Unocal's exploration and extraction budget was thrown into these emerging markets, much of it pinpointed for very-high-risk locations in the former Soviet republics and the Persian subcontinent.

Why take these risks? Beach answers that Unocal, unable to compete head-to-head with the oil industry giants for capital markets, decided to create an extremely attractive strategic package of full-service energy production in countries grasping to develop infrastructure. "What every government likes about Unocal's strategy is one-stop shopping; one group able to take the whole project from development to the marketing end," Beach said. "We have become partners in their development and as important to them as they are to us." The Unocal strategy defies normal industry trends based on distributing huge capital investments to tie up oil reserves and mineral rights, then cutting deals for operations. Instead, Unocal comes in the front door with packaged energy services ranging from turning the first spade of dirt on exploration to delivering power to the end user, and that proposal includes oil, gas, or electric power generation.

Beach sees far less risk than industry analysts perceive in the emerging markets. The dangers of war, political upheaval, and currency fluctuations are clear and present, yet the company says it has hedged against these threats by diversifying investments. However, according to Beach, success will depend on creating a globally managed company capable of understanding and participating in foreign market environments. Consequently, in 1996, he initiated a major transformation in Unocal's management systems, beginning by relocating its headquarters from its stately downtown offices

to a small, highly efficient suite near the Los Angeles International Airport. Mid-level managers were either repositioned in regional offices, such as Singapore, Istanbul, or Jakarta, or they left the company. The executive core, which had been distinctly Los Angeleno in character, gained a multicultural character, representing Eastern European and Asian group alliances. Subsidiaries in Jakarta, Thailand and Burma took on local names and corporate identities, shedding their American profiles, and Unocal's many foreign alliances have made it part of the communities in which it operates.

In Thailand, Unocal worked on the country's privatization plan to convert its Petroleum Authority of Thailand (PTT) operations into privately owned and operated international oil services. Unocal and the PTT have begun to build pipelines in the Gulf of Thailand linking Unocal's hydrocarbon fields in the nation's rugged peninsula, and a joint venture in Malaysia has begun to open regional energy markets from Myanmar to the Phillipines. Surface evaluations have hailed this consortium as a master stroke of strategy; however, related activities have exposed Unocal to strong criticism. Unocal became the largest single U.S. investor in Myanmar as part of the expansion, but Myanmar's military government has languished in political and economic isolation as a result of U.S legislation aimed at boycotting the country for its unacceptable human-rights practices. Political activists in more than a dozen U.S. states have won passage of legislation barring imports from Myanmar and outlawing private investments there by U.S. firms. Municipal governments in five states have passed boycott laws, as well, and Unocal, together with PepsiCo and several other American companies operating in Myanmar, have become major targets for international pressure groups. PepsiCo bowed to the pressure and moved out of Myanmar, but Unocal has flatly refused to budge.

The company's insistence on remaining in Myanmar, however, is not a vote in support of the country's human-rights record. Indeed, Unocal would find it difficult to withdraw, because it has formed an equity agreement with the giant French petrochemical company Total, which also has substantial pipeline investments with Unocal in the Persian Gulf and southern Asia. Unocal's contracts with Total make it a *de facto* partner of the French government. Moreover, Unocal has invested in public and private interests in Myanmar that spread to five other major Southeast Asian states. But a Unocal representative cites the importance of the company's role in helping the nation's development. "To withdraw and isolate [Myanmar] would have no effect. Questionable human-rights leadership and political practices would continue and perhaps proliferate," she said. "On the other hand, our strength and the fact that we can provide meaningful jobs and ethical international business, encourages changes for the good. Even if every American firm vacated, firms from other nations would welcome the chance to develop [Myanmar] without American competition."

That position doesn't relieve the political or financial risk to Unocal. Ethics and U.S. policies aside, Myanmar lacks a strong track record for keeping its promises. As a closed military state, self-isolated for ideological reasons since the end of World War II, it has few friends anywhere in the world. For years, it was linked to the Soviet Union for aid and military support, and it backed insurgent forces in several neighboring civil conflicts. These situations did not endear the government to potential regional economic allies. However, the country is strategically positioned within the Southeast Asian theater, and it has attracted consideration, with much controversy, for membership in ASEAN.

Unocal holds a rather exposed position in the country, as it does in Uzbekistan, Turkmenistan, and the Balkans. An American company without the legal or political support of its home government can expect little help should the host government decide to freeze its assets, bar currency repatriation, or resort to outright expropriation. Meanwhile, Unocal has tied up several billion dollars in the region while maintaining no safety net at home. Indeed, it faces potentially costly threats from home, and if the company is pushed to the wall by legislation, the chairman says, he will take Unocal out of U.S. control.

Questions

1. What market entry strategies has Unocal used, based on the activities described in the case? Would you classify Unocal as a multinational corporation (MNC)? Why or why not?

2. Identify and discuss the various types of risks faced by Unocal in emerging markets (consider the economic, legal-political, and sociocultural environment). Which risks seem most threatening to the company?

3. What do you think of the Unocal representative's statement that "to withdraw and isolate Myanmar would have no effect" regarding that country's poor human-rights record? Do you believe U.S. companies should stay in such countries in the hope of improving the ethical climate? Discuss.

SOURCE: "Unocal Corporation," from *International Management: Text and Cases*, 143–145, David H. Holt, Copyright © 1998 by Harcourt, Inc. Revised and reprinted by permission of the publisher.

■ Endnotes

1. Jonathan Friedland and Louise Lee, "The Wal-Mart Way Sometimes Gets Lost in Translation Overseas," *The Wall Street Journal* (October 8, 1997), A1, A12.

2. David Kirkpatrick, "One World—For Better or Worse," *Fortune* (November 26, 2001), 74–75; Andy Grove quoted in Brian O'Keefe, "Global Brands," *Fortune* (November 26, 2001), 102–110.

3. Nilly Ostro-Landau and Hugh D. Menzies, "The New World Economic Order," in *International Business 97/98, Annual Editions*, Fred Maidment, ed., (Guilford, Conn.: Dushkin Publishing Group, 1997), 24–30; and Murray Weidenbaum, "American Isolationism Versus the Global Economy," in *International Business 97/98, Annual Editions*, Fred Maidment, ed., (Guilford Conn.: Dushkin Publishing Group, 1997), 12–15.

4. Joseph B. White, "There Are No German or U.S. Companies, Only Successful Ones," *The Wall Street Journal* (May 7, 1998), A1.

5. Pete Engardio, with Robert D. Hof, Elisabeth Malkin, Neil Gross, and Karen Lowry Miller, "High-Tech Jobs All Over the Map," *BusinessWeek/21st Century Capitalism* (November 18, 1994), 112–117.

6. Raju Narisetti and Jonathan Friedland, "Diaper Wars of P&G and Kimberly-Clark Now Heat Up in Brazil," *The Wall Street Journal* (June 4, 1997), and Stephen Baker, "The Bridges Steel is Building," *BusinessWeek* (June 2, 1997), 39.

7. Figures provided by CXO Media, reported in Steve Ulfelder, "All the Web's a Stage," *CIO* (October 1, 2000), 133–142.

8. Nancy J. Adler, *International Dimensions of Organizational Behavior*, 4th ed. (Cincinnati, Ohio: South-Western Publishing, 2002), 8–9; William Holstein, Stanley Reed, Jonathan Kapstein, Todd Vogel, and Joseph Weber, "The Stateless Corporation," *BusinessWeek* (May 14, 1990), 98–105; and Richard Daft, *Organization Theory and Design* (St. Paul, Minn.: West, 1992).

9. Eric Matson, "How to Globalize Yourself," *Fast Company* (April–May 1997), 133–139; and Gunnar Beeth, "Multicultural Managers Wanted," *Management Review* (May 1997), 17–21.

10. William Echikson and Dean Foust, "For Coke, Local Is It," *BusinessWeek* (July 3, 2000), 122.

11. Holstein et al., "The Stateless Corporation"; Carla Rapoport, "Nestlé's Brand Building Machine," *Fortune* (September 19, 1994), 147–156; and Mark Landler, with Joyce Barnathan, Geri Smith, and Gail Edmondson, "Think Globally, Program Locally," *BusinessWeek/21st Century Capitalism* (November 18, 1994), 186–189.

12. Holstein et al., "The Stateless Corporation"; and John A. Byrne and Kathleen Kerwin, with Amy Cortese and Paula Dwyer, "Borderless Management," *BusinessWeek* (May 23, 1994), 24–26.

13. "Slogans Often Lose Something in Translation," *The New Mexican* (July 3, 1994), F1, F2.

14. Jim Holt, "Gone Global?" *Management Review* (March 2000), 13.

15. Ibid.

16. "Slogans Often Lose Something in Translation."

17. Louis S. Richman, "Global Growth is on a Tear," in *International Business 97/98, Annual Editions*, Fred Maidment, ed., (Guilford, Conn.: Dushkin Publishing Group, 1997), 6–11.

18. International Data Corporation, reported in Ian Katz and Elisabeth Malkin, "Battle for the Latin American Net," *BusinessWeek* (November 1, 1999), 194–200.

19. Katz and Malkin, "Battle for the Latin American Net"; Pamela Drukerman and Nick Wingfield, "Lost in Translation: AOL's Big Assault on Latin America Hits Snags in Brazil," *The Wall Street Journal*, (July 11, 2000), A1.

20. Amal Kumar Jaj, "United Technologies Looks Far from Home for Growth," *The Wall Street Journal* (May 26, 1994), B4.

21. Kathleen Deveny, "McWorld?" *BusinessWeek* (October 13, 1986), 78–86; and Andrew E. Serwer, "McDonald's Conquers the World," *Fortune* (October 17, 1994), 103–116.

22. Bruce Kogut, "Designing Global Strategies: Profiting from Operational Flexibility," *Sloan Management Review* 27 (Fall 1985), 27–38.

23. Mark Fitzpatrick, "The Definition and Assessment of Political Risk in International Business: A Review of the Literature," *Academy of Management Review* 8 (1983), 249–254.

24. "Multinational Firms Act to Protect Overseas Workers from Terrorism," *The Wall Street Journal* (April 29, 1986), 31; Robert J. Bowman, "Are You Covered?" *World Trade* (March 1995), 100–104; and Frederick Stapenhurst, "Political Risk Analysis in North American Multinationals: An Empirical Review and Assessment," *The International Executive* (March–April, 1995), 127–145.

25. O'Keefe, "Global Brands."

26. Jenny C. McCune, "Exporting Corporate Culture," *Management Review* (December 1999), 52–56.

27. Brandon Mitchener, "Border Crossings," *The Wall Street Journal* (November 22, 1999), R41.

28. Barbara Whitaker, "The Web Makes Going Global Easy, Until You Try to Do It," *The New York Times* (September 2000), 20

29. Alan Charles Raul, "World to America: Zip It!" *eCompany Now* (July 2001), 26–29.

30. Michael R. Czinkota, Ilkka A. Ronkainen, Michael H. Moffett, and Eugene O. Moynihan, *Global Business* (Fort Worth, Texas: The Dryden Press, 1995) 151; and Robert D. Gatewood, Robert R. Taylor, and O. C. Ferrell, *Management* (Burr Ridge, Ill.: Irwin, 1995), 131–132.

31. "For Richer, for Poorer," *The Economist* (December 1993), 66; Richard Harmsen, "The Uruguay Round: A Boon for the World Economy," *Finance & Development* (March 1995), 24–26; Salil S. Pitroda, "From GATT to WTO: The Institutionalization of World Trade," *Harvard International Review* (Spring 1995), 46–47 and 66–67; and David H. Holt, *International Management: Text and Cases* (Fort Worth: Dryden, 1998).

32. This discussion of WTO is based on William J. Kehoe, "GATT and WTO Facilitating Global Trade," *Journal of Global Business* (Spring 1998), 67–76.

33. Raul, "World to America: Zip It!"

34. Justin Fox, "Introducing the Euro," *Fortune*, (December 19, 2001), 229–236.

35. Lynda Radosevich, "New Money," *CIO Enterprise*, Section 2 (April 15, 1998), 54–58.

36. Barbara Rudolph, "Megamarket," *Time* (August 10, 1992), 43–44.

37. J. S. McClenahan, "NAFTA Works," *IW* (January 10, 2000), 5–6.

38. Amy Barrett, "It's a Small (Business) World," *BusinessWeek* (April 17, 1995), 96–101.

39. Amy Borrus, "A Free-Trade Milestone, with Many More Miles to Go," *BusinessWeek* (August 24, 1992), 30–31.

40. C. Sims, "Chile Will Enter a Big South American Free-Trade Bloc," *The New York Times* (June 26, 1996), C2; "NAFTA: Five-Year Anniversary," *Latin Trade* (January 1999), 44–45; and Stephen P. Robbins and Mary Coulter, *Management*, 7th ed. (Upper Saddle River, NJ: Prentice-Hall, 2002), 92.

41. Keith Bradsher, "As Global Talks Stall, Regional Trade Pacts Multiply," *The New York Times* (August 23, 1992), F5.

42. Geert Hofstede, "The Interaction between National and Organizational Value Systems," *Journal of Management Studies* 22 (1985), 347–357; and Geert Hofstede, "The Cultural Relativity of the Quality of Life Concept," *Academy of Management Review* 9 (1984), 389–398.

43. Geert Hofstede, "Cultural Constraints in Management Theory," *Academy of Management Executive* 7 (1993): 81–94; and G. Hofstede and M. H. Bond, "The Confucian Connection: From Cultural Roots to Economic Growth," *Organizational Dynamics* 16 (1988): 4–21.

44. Chantell E. Nicholls, Henry W. Lane, and Mauricio Brehm Brechu, "Taking Self-Managed Teams to Mexico," *Academy of Management Executive* 13, No. 2 (1999), 15–27; Ellen F. Jackofsky, John W. Slocum, Jr., and Sara J. McQuaid, "Cultural Values and the CEO: Alluring Companions?" *Academy of Management Executive* 2 (1988), 39–49.

45. Carol Hymowitz, "Companies Go Global, But Many Managers Just Don't Travel Well," (In the Lead column) *The Wall Street Journal* (August 15, 2000), B1.

46. Orla Sheehan, "Managing a Multinational Corporation: Tomorrow's Decision Makers Speak Out," *Fortune* (August 24, 1992), 233.

47. Richard Gibson and Matt Moffett, "Why You Won't Find Any Egg McMuffins for Breakfast in Brazil," *The Wall Street Journal*, (October 23, 1997), A1, A8; and Kenneth Labich, "America's International Winners," *Fortune* (April 14, 1986), 34–46.

48. Robert Frank, "Big Boy's Adventures in Thailand," *The Wall Street Journal* (April 12, 2000), B1, B4.

49. Jonathan Moore with Bruce Einhorn, "A Business-to-Business E-Boom," *BusinessWeek* (October 25, 1999), 62.

50. Elisabeth Malkin, "Backlash," *BusinessWeek* (April 24, 2000), 38–44.

51. Jean Kerr, "Export Strategies," *Small Business Reports* (May 1989), 20–25.

52. Robert S. Greenberger, "As U.S. Exports Rise, More Workers Benefit," *The Wall Street Journal* (September 10, 1997), A1.

53. Kathryn Rudie Harrigan, "Managing Joint Ventures," *Management Review* (February 1987), 24–41; and Therese R. Revesz and Mimi Cauley de Da La Sierra, "Competitive Alliances: Forging Ties Abroad," *Management Review* (March 1987), 57–59.

54. Julia Flynn with Richard A. Melcher, "Heineken's Battle to Stay Top Bottle," *BusinessWeek* (August 1, 1994), 60–62; and "Importing Can Help a Firm Expand and Diversify," *Nation's Business* (January 1995), 11.

55. Katz and Malkin, "Battle for the Latin American Net."

56. Karen Lowry Miller, with Bill Javetski, Peggy Simpson, and Tim Smart, "Europe: The Push East," *BusinessWeek* (November 7, 1994), 48–49.

57. David Woodruff, with Karen Lowry Miller, "Mercedes' Maverick in Alabama," *BusinessWeek* (September 11, 1995), 64–65; and Michael A. Hitt, R. Duane Ireland, and Robert E. Hoskisson, *Strategic Management: Competitiveness and Globalization* (St. Paul, Minn.: West, 1995).

58. "How Revenues of the Top Ten Global Companies Compare with Some National Economies," *Fortune* (July 27, 1992), 16.

59. Howard V. Perlmutter, "The Tortuous Evolution of the Multinational Corporation," *Columbia Journal of World Business* (January–February 1969), 9–18; and Youram Wind, Susan P. Douglas, and Howard V. Perlmutter, "Guidelines for Developing International Marketing Strategies," *Journal of Marketing* (April 1973), 14–23.

60. Robert T. Moran and John R. Riesenberger, *The Global Challenge* (London: McGraw-Hill, 1994), 260.

61. James L. Gibson, John M. Ivancevich, and James H. Donnelly, Jr., *Organizations*, 8th ed. (Burr Ridge, Ill.: Irwin, 1994), 83.

62. Joann S. Lublin, "Younger Managers Learn Global Skills," *The Wall Street Journal* (March 31, 1992), B1.

63. Moran and Riesenberger, *The Global Challenge*, 251–262.

64. Patricia M. Carey, "Culture Club," *Working Woman* (July/August 1999), 71–72.

65. Valerie Frazee, "Keeping Up on Chinese Culture," *Global Workforce* (October 1996), 16–17; and Jack Scarborough, "Comparing Chinese and Western Cultural Roots: Why 'East is East and . . .'" *Business Horizons* (November/December 1998), 15–24.

66. Fons Trompenaars, *Riding the Waves of Culture: Understanding Diversity in Global Business* (Burr Ridge, Ill.: Irwin, 1994).

67. Randall S. Schuler, Susan E. Jackson, Ellen Jackofsky, and John W. Slocum, Jr., "Managing Human Resources in Mexico: A Cultural Understanding," *Business Horizons* (May–June 1996), 55–61.

68. Shari Caudron, "Lessons from HR Overseas," *Personnel Journal* (February 1995), 88.

69. Moran and Riesenberger, *The Global Challenge*, 255; and Caudron, "Lessons from HR Overseas."

70. Brenton R. Schlender, "Matsushita Shows How to Go Global," *Fortune* (July 11, 1994), 159–166.

71. Friedland and Lee, "The Wal-Mart Way Sometimes Gets Lost in Translation Overseas."

Managerial Ethics and Corporate Social Responsibility

CHAPTER OUTLINE

What Is Managerial Ethics?

Criteria for Ethical Decision Making

Utilitarian Approach

Individualism Approach

Moral-Rights Approach

Justice Approach

Factors Affecting Ethical Choices

The Manager

The Organization

What Is Social Responsibility?

Organizational Stakeholders

The Natural Environment

Evaluating Corporate Social Performance

Economic Responsibilities

Legal Responsibilities

Ethical Responsibilities

Discretionary Responsibilities

Managing Company Ethics and Social Responsibility

Ethical Individuals

Ethical Leadership

Organizational Structures and Systems

Ethics and the New Workplace

LEARNING OBJECTIVES

After studying this chapter, you should be able to

1 Define ethics and explain how ethical behavior relates to behavior governed by law and free choice.

2 Explain the utilitarian, individualism, moral-rights, and justice approaches for evaluating ethical behavior.

3 Describe how both individual and organizational factors shape ethical decision making.

4 Define corporate social responsibility and how to evaluate it along economic, legal, ethical, and discretionary criteria.

5 Describe four organizational approaches to environmental responsibility.

6 Explain the concept of stakeholder and identify important stakeholders for organizations.

7 Discuss how ethical organizations are created through ethical leadership and organizational structures and systems.

Management Challenge

The global AIDS crisis has trapped large U.S. drug companies in an ethical quandary. They want to be seen as helping to fight this global tragedy, but international activists portray the drug companies as arrogant and greedy. They charge that the companies are putting their own profits above the value of human lives by keeping patented life-saving medicines beyond the reach of the world's poor. A lawsuit filed by 40 drug makers against the South African government reinforced the Scrooge-like image. When Nelson Mandela was president of South Africa, he signed a law allowing the country to import cheap generic versions of patented medicines without getting permission from the patent owners. Concerned with the spread of AIDS, the U.S. government agreed to "look the other way" if poor nations make and import generic drugs. However, the pharmaceutical companies framed the issue as a fight over intellectual property rights, attempting to avoid the question of how it might affect the treatment and spread of AIDS. A widening circle of activist organizations, including Doctors Without Borders and Oxfam, have attacked the patents of U.S. drug companies as a direct threat to the health and well-being of the world's poor. Some activist groups have gone so far as to accuse the companies of genocide.[1]

Do you believe it is unethical for U.S. drug companies to file suit against poor nations that cannot afford name-brand drugs? Where should managers draw the line between protecting their organization's intellectual property and bending the rules to alleviate human suffering?

This situation illustrates how difficult ethical issues can be and symbolizes the growing importance of discussing ethics and social responsibility. Corporations are rushing to adopt codes of ethics and develop socially responsible policies: Ethics consultants are doing a land-office business. Unfortunately, the trend is necessary. In recent years, numerous companies, including Sears, Archer-Daniels-Midland, and Tyson Foods, have been charged with major breaches of ethical or legal standards. Bridgestone/Firestone and the Ford Motor Company spent months blaming each other for a series of deadly tire failures. And Enron, America's seventh-largest corporation in mid-2000, was essentially destroyed by a combination of deceit, arrogance, shady financial dealings, and inappropriate accounting practices that inflated earnings and hid debt. The world of cyberspace is opening new avenues for potential ethical lapses. Alibris, an online bookseller specializing in rare books, pled guilty to a charge of intercepting e-mail messages sent by Amazon.com to customers. Former iVillage executives have accused that company of cheating employees out of promised stock options.[2]

On the other hand, there also is positive news to report. The toy maker Mattel conducts social audits of its policies and practices to make sure its factories are adhering to ethical and socially responsible guidelines. Managers at American Electric Power Company are spending $5.5 million on a reforestation program in Bolivia in an effort to offset the carbon dioxide the company releases into the environment.[3] Internet start-ups such as eBay and Infoseek have made significant donations to charitable causes.[4] And Eastman Kodak Company took an unprecedented step several years ago by tying a percentage of managers' pay to factors such as how well they treat their employees.[5]

This chapter expands on the ideas about environment, corporate culture, and the international environment discussed in Chapters 3 and 4. We will first focus on specific ethical values that build on the idea of corporate culture. Then we will examine corporate relationships to the external environment as reflected in social responsibility. Ethics and social responsibility are hot topics in corporate America. This chapter discusses fundamental approaches that help managers think through ethical issues. Understanding ethical approaches helps managers build a solid foundation on which to base future decision making.

What Is Managerial Ethics?

ethics
The code of moral principles and values that govern the behaviors of a person or group with respect to what is right or wrong.

Ethics is difficult to define in a precise way. In a general sense, **ethics** is the code of moral principles and values that govern the behaviors of a person or group with respect to what is right or wrong. Ethics sets standards as to what is good or bad in conduct and decision making.[6] Ethics deals with internal values that are a part of corporate culture and shapes decisions concerning social responsibility with respect to the external environment. An ethical issue is present in a situation when the actions of a person or organization may harm or benefit others.[7]

Ethics can be more clearly understood when compared with behaviors governed by laws and by free choice. Exhibit 5.1 illustrates that human behavior falls into three categories. The first is codified law, in which values and standards are written into the legal system and enforceable in the courts. In this area, lawmakers have ruled that people and corporations must behave in a certain way, such as obtaining licenses for cars or paying corporate taxes. The

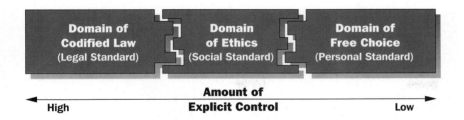

Exhibit *5.1*

Three Domains of Human Action

Internet revolution has raised new legal issues, such as how copyrights are interpreted in cyberspace. For example, the courts ruled that Napster, the file-swapping service that enabled people to download music for free, was guilty of music piracy and must stop letting users exchange copyrighted material.[8] The domain of free choice is at the opposite end of the scale and pertains to behavior about which law has no say and for which an individual or organization enjoys complete freedom. An individual's choice of religion or a music company's choice of the number of artists to sign or CDs to release are examples of free choice.

Between these domains lies the area of ethics. This domain has no specific laws, yet it does have standards of conduct based on shared principles and values about moral conduct that guide an individual or company. In the domain of free choice, obedience is strictly to oneself. In the domain of codified law, obedience is to laws prescribed by the legal system. In the domain of ethical behavior, obedience is to unenforceable norms and standards about which the individual or company is aware. An ethically acceptable decision is both legally and morally acceptable to the larger community.

Many companies and individuals get into trouble with the simplified view that choices are governed by either law or free choice. It leads people to mistakenly assume that "If it's not illegal, it must be ethical," as if there were no third domain.[9] A better option is to recognize the domain of ethics and accept moral values as a powerful force for good that can regulate behaviors both inside and outside corporations. As principles of ethics and social responsibility are more widely recognized, companies can use codes of ethics and their corporate cultures to govern behavior, thereby eliminating the need for additional laws and avoiding the problems of unfettered choice.

Because ethical standards are not codified, disagreements and dilemmas about proper behavior often occur. An **ethical dilemma** arises in a situation when each alternative choice or behavior is undesirable because of potentially harmful consequences. Right or wrong cannot be clearly identified.

The individual who must make an ethical choice in an organization is the *moral agent.*[10] Consider the dilemmas facing a moral agent in the following situations:

- A top employee at your small company tells you he needs some time off because he has AIDS. You know the employee needs the job as well as the health insurance benefits. Providing health insurance has already stretched the company's budget, and this will send premiums through the roof. You recently read of a case in which federal courts upheld the right of an employer to modify health plans by putting a cap on AIDS benefits. Should you investigate whether this is a legal possibility for your company?
- As a sales manager for a major pharmaceuticals company, you've been asked to promote a new drug that costs $2,500 per dose. You've read the reports saying the drug is only 1 percent more effective than an alternate drug that

ethical dilemma
A situation that arises when all alternative choices or behaviors have been deemed undesirable because of potentially negative consequence, making it difficult to distinguish right from wrong.

Discovered in 1998, human embryonic stem cells have the potential to revolutionize medical practice and improve the quality and length of life, but they present an ethical dilemma for many people. Embryonic stem cells come from in vitro fertilization clinics, and human fetal stem cells are drawn from aborted fetuses, putting researchers in the middle of America's reproductive rights debate. Federal funding for human fetal-cell research was banned from 1987 to 1993, and a five-year ban on federal funding of human embryonic-cell research was lifted only recently. Because his son was diagnosed with a brain tumor, Richard Garr, CEO of NeuralStem Biopharmaceuticals, is diligent with his company's research. He hopes that stem cells will be able to replace neurons lost to otherwise incurable brain disorders.

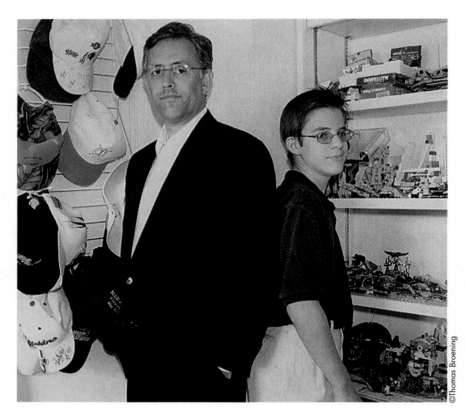

©Thomas Broening

costs less than one-fourth as much. Can you in good conscience aggressively promote the $2,500-per-dose drug? If you don't, could lives be lost that might have been saved with that 1 percent increase in effectiveness?

- Your company has been asked to pay a gratuity in India to speed the processing of an import permit. This is standard procedure, and your company will suffer if you do not pay the gratuity. Is this different from tipping a maître d' in a nice restaurant?

- You are the accounting manager of a division that is $15,000 below profit targets. Approximately $20,000 of office supplies were delivered on December 21. The accounting rule is to pay expenses when incurred. The division general manager asks you not to record the invoice until February.

- Your boss says he cannot give you a raise this year because of budget constraints, but he will look the other way if your expense accounts come in a little high because of your good work this past year.

These are the kinds of dilemmas and issues with which managers must deal that fall squarely in the domain of ethics. Now let's turn to approaches to ethical decision making that provide criteria for understanding and resolving these difficult issues.

Criteria for Ethical Decision Making

Most ethical dilemmas involve a conflict between the needs of the part and the whole—the individual versus the organization or the organization versus society as a whole. For example, should a company install mandatory alcohol and drug testing for employees, which might benefit the organization as a whole but reduce the individual freedom of employees? Or should products that fail to meet tough FDA standards be exported to other countries where government standards are lower, benefiting the company but being potentially harmful to world citizens? Sometimes ethical decisions entail a conflict between two groups. For example, should the potential for local health problems resulting from a company's effluents take precedence over the jobs it creates as the town's leading employer?

Managers faced with these kinds of tough ethical choices often benefit from a normative approach—one based on norms and values—to guide their decision making. Normative ethics uses several approaches to describe values for guiding ethical decision making. Four of these that are relevant to managers are the utilitarian approach, individualism approach, moral-rights approach, and justice approach.[11]

Utilitarian Approach

The **utilitarian approach,** espoused by the nineteenth-century philosophers Jeremy Bentham and John Stuart Mill, holds that moral behavior produces the greatest good for the greatest number. Under this approach, a decision maker is expected to consider the effect of each decision alternative on all parties and select the one that optimizes the satisfaction for the greatest number of people. Because actual computations can be very complex, simplifying them is considered appropriate. For example, a simple economic frame of reference could be used by calculating dollar costs and dollar benefits. Also, a decision could be made that considers only the people who are directly affected by the decision, not those who are indirectly affected. The utilitarian ethic is cited as the basis for the recent trend among companies to police employee personal habits such as alcohol and tobacco consumption on the job, and in some cases after hours as well, because such behavior affects the entire workplace. Similarly, many companies argue that monitoring how employees spend their time on the Internet is necessary to maintain the company's ethical climate and workplace productivity. If employees are viewing pornographic sites, visiting racist chat rooms, or spending hours shopping or day-trading online, the entire organization ultimately suffers.[12]

The utilitarian ethic was the basis for the state of Oregon's decision to extend Medicaid to 400,000 previously ineligible recipients by refusing to pay for high-cost, high-risk procedures such as liver transplants and bone-marrow transplants. Although a few people needing these procedures have died because the state would not pay, many people have benefited from medical services they would otherwise have had to go without.[13] Critics claim that the Oregon decision does not fully take into account the concept of justice toward the unfortunate victims of life-threatening diseases.[14] The justice approach will be discussed later in this chapter.

Individualism Approach

The **individualism approach** contends that acts are moral when they promote the individual's best long-term interests. Individual self-direction is paramount, and external forces that restrict self-direction should be severely limited.[15] Individuals calculate the best long-term advantage to themselves as a measure of a decision's goodness. The action that is intended to produce a greater ratio of good to bad for the individual compared with other alternatives is the right

utilitarian approach
The ethical concept that moral behaviors produce the greatest good for the greatest number.

individualism approach
The ethical concept that acts are moral when they promote the individual's best long-term interests, which ultimately leads to the greater good.

one to perform. In theory, with everyone pursuing self-direction, the greater good is ultimately served because people learn to accommodate each other in their own long-term interest. Individualism is believed to lead to honesty and integrity because that works best in the long run. Lying and cheating for immediate self-interest just causes business associates to lie and cheat in return. Thus, individualism ultimately leads to behavior toward others that fits standards of behavior people want toward themselves.[16] One value of understanding this approach is to recognize short-term variations if they are proposed. People might argue for short-term self-interest based on individualism, but that misses the point. Because individualism is easily misinterpreted to support immediate self-gain, it is not popular in the highly organized and group-oriented society of today. Individualism is closest to the domain of free choice described in Exhibit 5.1.

Moral-Rights Approach

moral-rights approach
The ethical concept that moral decisions are those that best maintain the rights of those people affected by them.

The **moral-rights approach** asserts that human beings have fundamental rights and liberties that cannot be taken away by an individual's decision. Thus, an ethically correct decision is one that best maintains the rights of those people affected by it.

Six moral rights should be considered during decision making:

1. *The right of free consent.* Individuals are to be treated only as they knowingly and freely consent to be treated.
2. *The right to privacy.* Individuals can choose to do as they please away from work and have control of information about their private life.
3. *The right of freedom of conscience.* Individuals may refrain from carrying out any order that violates their moral or religious norms.
4. *The right of free speech.* Individuals may criticize truthfully the ethics or legality of actions of others.
5. *The right to due process.* Individuals have a right to an impartial hearing and fair treatment.
6. *The right to life and safety.* Individuals have a right to live without endangerment or violation of their health and safety.

To make ethical decisions, managers need to avoid interfering with the fundamental rights of others. For example, a decision to eavesdrop on employees violates the right to privacy. Sexual harassment is unethical because it violates the right to freedom of conscience. The right of free speech would support whistle-blowers who call attention to illegal or inappropriate action within a company.

Justice Approach

justice approach
The ethical concept that moral decisions must be based on standards of equity, fairness, and impartiality.

distributive justice
The concept that different treatment of people should not be based on arbitrary characteristics. In the case of substantive differences, people should be treated differently in proportion to the differences among them.

The **justice approach** holds that moral decisions must be based on standards of equity, fairness, and impartiality. Three types of justice are of concern to managers. **Distributive justice** requires that different treatment of people not be based on arbitrary characteristics. Individuals who are similar in respects relevant to a decision should be treated similarly. Thus, men and women should not receive different salaries if they are performing the same job. However, people who differ in a substantive way, such as job skills or job responsibility, can be treated differently in proportion to the differences in skills or responsibility among them. This difference should have a clear relationship to organizational goals and tasks.

Procedural justice requires that rules be administered fairly. Rules should be clearly stated and be consistently and impartially enforced. **Compensatory justice** argues that individuals should be compensated for the cost of their injuries by the party responsible. Moreover, individuals should not be held responsible for matters over which they have no control.

The justice approach is closest to the thinking underlying the domain of law in Exhibit 5.1, because it assumes that justice is applied through rules and regulations. This theory does not require complex calculations such as those demanded by a utilitarian approach, nor does it justify self-interest as the individualism approach does. Managers are expected to define attributes on which different treatment of employees is acceptable. Questions such as how minority workers should be compensated for past discrimination are extremely difficult. However, this approach does justify as ethical behavior efforts to correct past wrongs, playing fair under the rules, and insisting on job-relevant differences as the basis for different levels of pay or promotion opportunities. Most of the laws guiding human resource management (Chapter 13) are based on the justice approach.

These various approaches offer general principles that managers can recognize as useful in making ethical decisions. However, understanding the approaches is only a first step; managers still have to consider how to apply them.

procedural justice
The concept that rules should be clearly stated and consistently and impartially enforced.

compensatory justice
The concept that individuals should be compensated for the cost of their injuries by the party responsible and also that individuals should not be held responsible for matters over which they have no control.

Factors Affecting Ethical Choices

When managers are accused of lying, cheating, or stealing, the blame is usually placed on the individual or on the company situation. Most people believe that individuals make ethical choices because of individual integrity, which is true, but it is not the whole story. Ethical or unethical business practices usually reflect the values, attitudes, beliefs, and behavior patterns of the organizational culture; thus, ethics is as much an organizational as a personal issue.[17] Let's examine how both the manager and the organization shape ethical decision making.[18]

The Manager

Managers bring specific personality and behavioral traits to the job. Personal needs, family influence, and religious background all shape a manager's value system. Specific personality characteristics, such as ego strength, self-confidence, and a strong sense of independence may enable managers to make ethical decisions.

One important personal trait is the stage of moral development.[19] A simplified version of one model of personal moral development is shown in Exhibit 5.2. At the *preconventional level*, individuals are concerned with external rewards and punishments and obey authority to avoid detrimental personal consequences. In an organizational context, this level may be associated with managers who use an autocratic or coercive leadership style, with employees oriented toward dependable accomplishment of specific tasks. At level two, called the *conventional level*, people learn to conform to the expectations of good behavior as defined by colleagues, family, friends, and society. Meeting social and interpersonal obligations is important. Work group collaboration is the preferred manner for accomplishment of organizational goals, and managers use a leadership style that encourages interpersonal relationships and

Exhibit **5.2**

Three Levels of Personal Moral Development

Level 3: Postconventional

Follows self-chosen principles of justice and right. Aware that people hold different values and seeks creative solutions to ethical dilemmas. Balances concern for individual with concern for common good.

Level 2: Conventional

Lives up to expectations of others. Fulfills duties and obligations of social system. Upholds laws.

Level 1: Preconventional

Follows rules to avoid punishment. Acts in own interest. Obedience for its own sake.

Leadership Style:	Autocratic/coercive	Guiding/encouraging, team oriented	Transforming, or servant leadership
Employee Behavior:	Task accomplishment	Work group collaboration	Empowered employees, full participation

SOURCES: Based on L. Kohlberg, "Moral Stages and Moralization: The Cognitive-Developmental Approach," in *Moral Development and Behavior: Theory, Research, and Social Issues*, ed. T. Lickona (New York: Holt, Rinehart, and Winston, 1976), 31–53; and Jill W. Graham, "Leadership, Moral Development and Citizenship Behavior," *Business Ethics Quarterly* 5, no. 1 (January 1995), 43–54.

cooperation. At the *postconventional*, or *principled* level, individuals are guided by an internal set of values and standards and will even disobey rules or laws that violate these principles. Internal values become more important than the expectations of significant others. For example, when the *USS Indianapolis* sank after being torpedoed during World War II, one Navy pilot disobeyed orders and risked his life to save men who were being picked off by sharks. The pilot was operating from the highest level of moral development in attempting the rescue despite a direct order from superiors. When managers operate from this highest level of development, they use transformative or servant leadership, focusing on the needs of followers and encouraging others to think for themselves and to engage in higher levels of moral reasoning. Employees are empowered and given opportunities for constructive participation in governance of the organization.

The great majority of managers operate at level two. A few have not advanced beyond level one. Only about 20 percent of American adults reach the level-three stage of moral development. People at level three are able to act in an independent, ethical manner regardless of expectations from others inside or outside the organization. Managers at level three of moral development will make ethical decisions whatever the organizational consequences for them.

One interesting study indicates that most researchers have failed to account for the different ways in which women view social reality and develop psychologically and have thus consistently classified women as being stuck at lower levels of development. Researcher Carol Gilligan has suggested that the moral domain be enlarged to include responsibility and care in relationships. Women may, in general, perceive moral complexities more astutely than men and make moral decisions based not on a set of absolute rights and wrongs but on principles of not causing harm to others.[20]

One reason higher levels of ethical conduct are increasingly important is the impact of globalization on organizational ethics and corporate culture. Globalization has made ethical issues even more complicated for today's managers.[21] American managers working in foreign countries need sensitivity and an openness to other systems, as well as mature ethical judgment to work out differences. For example, although tolerance for bribery is waning, it is still an accepted way of doing business in many countries. Foreign managers sometimes resent Americans' "holier-than-thou" attitudes and the stereotypical belief that all foreign managers are corrupt.[22] It is not always easy to resolve international issues. There are, however, increasing calls for the development of global standards for ethical business conduct, which may help managers negotiate the difficult terrain of international ethics. In 1999, the United Nations completed a nine-point Global Compact that outlines global ethical principles in the areas of human rights, labor standards, and the environment. So far, 44 major corporations have made a commitment to incorporate the guidelines into their business practices.[23] This chapter's Manager's Shoptalk lists some general guidelines that can help managers make ethical decisions whether in their home country or abroad.

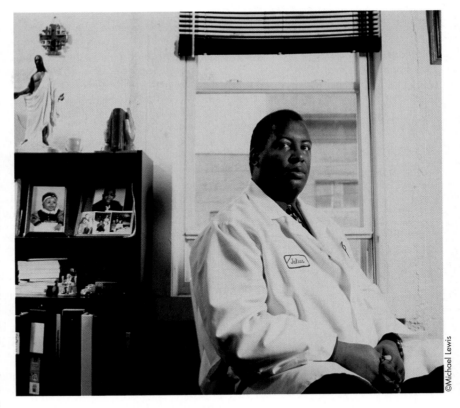

Julius Walls, Jr., chief executive of Greyston Bakery, demonstrates the postconventional level of moral development. Greyston makes gourmet brownies, cakes, and tarts. Walls hires employees off the street, first come, first served, because he thinks everyone deserves a chance at a job. He also helps workers with problems whether or not they're job related. Greyston serves the poor by feeding the rich. Much of its $4 million in annual sales are generated by selling bits of brownies to Ben & Jerry's for its chocolate fudge brownie ice cream and frozen yogurt, and the company donates all profits to the needy.

The Organization

The values adopted within the organization are important, especially when we understand that most people are at the level-two stage of moral development, which means they believe their duty is to fulfill obligations and expectations of others. All ethical decisions are made within the context of our interactions with other people, and the social networks within an organization play an important role in guiding people's actions. For example, for most of us, doing something we know is wrong becomes easier when "everyone else is doing it." In organizations, an important influence on ethical behavior is the norms and values of the team, department, or organization as a whole. Research has shown that these values strongly influence employee actions and decision making.[24] In particular, corporate culture serves to let employees know what beliefs and behaviors the company supports and those it will not tolerate. If unethical behavior is tolerated or even encouraged, it will become routine. For example, an investigation of thefts and kickbacks in the oil business found that the cause was the historical acceptance of thefts and kickbacks. Employees were socialized into those values and adopted them as appropriate. In most companies, employees believe that if they do not go along with the ethical values expressed, their jobs will be in jeopardy or they will not fit in.[25]

Culture can be examined to see the kinds of ethical signals given to employees. Exhibit 5.3 indicates questions to ask to understand the cultural system. High ethical standards can be affirmed and communicated through public

Exhibit 5.3

*Questions for Analyzing
a Company's Cultural
Impact on Ethics*

SOURCE: Linda Klebe Treviño, "A Cultural Perspective on Changing and Developing Organizational Ethics," in *Research in Organizational Change and Development*, ed. R. Woodman and W. Pasmore (Greenwich, Conn.: JAI Press, 1990), 4.

1. Identify the organization's heroes. What values do they represent? Given an ambiguous ethical dilemma, what decision would they make and why?
2. What are some important organizational rituals? How do they encourage or discourage ethical behavior? Who gets the awards, people of integrity or individuals who use unethical methods to attain success?
3. What are the ethical messages sent to new entrants into the organization—must they obey authority at all costs, or is questioning authority acceptable or even desirable?
4. Does analysis of organizational stories and myths reveal individuals who stand up for what's right, or is conformity the valued characteristic? Do people get fired or promoted in these stories?
5. Does language exist for discussing ethical concerns? Is this language routinely incorporated and encouraged in business decision making?
6. What informal socialization processes exist, and what norms for ethical/unethical behavior do they promote?

awards and ceremonies. Heroes provide role models that can either support or refute ethical decision making. For example, Wendy's founder, Dave Thomas, stood for integrity and was a highly effective salesman for the company. People viewed Wendy's food favorably in part because they liked Dave's down-to-earth, honest, and friendly manner. When he died in January 2002, Wendy's signs across the country bid farewell to "our founder and friend."

Culture is not the only aspect of an organization that influences ethics, but it is a major force because it defines company values. Other aspects of the organization, such as explicit rules and policies, the reward system, the extent to which the company cares for its people, the selection system, emphasis on legal and professional standards, and leadership and decision processes, can also have an impact on ethical values and manager decision making.[26] At Levi Strauss, for example, the selection system is aimed at promoting diversity of background and thought among workers, a set of "corporate aspirations" written by top management is to guide all major decisions, and one-third of a manager's raise can depend on how well he or she toes the values line.[27]

What Is Social Responsibility?

social responsibility
The obligation of organization management to make decisions and take actions that will enhance the welfare and interests of society as well as the organization.

Now let's turn to the issue of social responsibility. In one sense, the concept of corporate social responsibility, like ethics, is easy to understand: It means distinguishing right from wrong and doing right. It means being a good corporate citizen. The formal definition of **social responsibility** is management's obligation to make choices and take actions that will contribute to the welfare and interests of society as well as the organization.[28]

As straightforward as this definition seems, social responsibility can be a difficult concept to grasp, because different people have different beliefs as to which actions improve society's welfare.[29] To make matters worse, social responsibility covers a range of issues, many of which are ambiguous with respect to right or wrong. For example, if a bank deposits the money from a trust fund into a low-interest account for 90 days, from which it makes a substantial profit, has it been unethical? How about two companies' engaging in intense competition, such as that between Microsoft and Netscape? Is it socially responsible for the stronger corporation to drive the weaker one into bankruptcy or a forced merger? Or consider companies such as Chiquita, Kmart, or Global Crossing, all

THE NEW WORKPLACE

Manager's Shoptalk

Guidelines for Ethical Decision Making

If a "60 Minutes" crew were waiting on your doorstep one morning, would you feel comfortable justifying your actions to the camera? One young manager, when confronted with ethical dilemmas, gives them the "60 Minutes" test. Others say they use such criteria as whether they would be proud to tell their parents or grandparents about their decision, or whether they could sleep well at night and face themselves in the mirror in the morning. Managers often rely on their own personal integrity in making ethical decisions. But knowing what to do is not always easy. As a future manager, you will almost surely face ethical dilemmas one day. The following guidelines will not tell you exactly what to do, but, taken in the context of the text discussion, they will help you evaluate the situation more clearly by examining your own values and those of your organization. The answers to these questions will force you to think hard about the social and ethical consequences of your behavior.

1. Is the problem/dilemma really what it appears to be? If you are not sure, *find out*.
2. Is the action you are considering legal? Ethical? If you are not sure, *find out*.
3. Do you understand the position of those who oppose the action you are considering? Is it reasonable?

4. Whom does the action benefit? Harm? How much? How long?
5. Would you be willing to allow everyone to do what you are considering doing?
6. Have you sought the opinion of others who are knowledgeable on the subject and who would be objective?
7. Would your action be embarrassing to you if it were made known to your family, friends, coworkers, or superiors?
8. Even if you are sure the decision is reasonable and that you could defend it to others, does your gut instinct tell you it is the right thing to do?

There are no correct answers to these questions in an absolute sense. Yet, if you determine that an action is potentially harmful to someone or would be embarrassing to you, or if you do not know the ethical or legal consequences, these guidelines will help you clarify whether the action is socially responsible.

SOURCES: Anthony M. Pagano and Jo Ann Verdin, *The External Environment of Business* (New York: Wiley, 1988), Chapter 5; Joseph L. Badaracco, Jr., and Allen P. Webb, "Business Ethics: A View from the Trenches," *California Management Review* 37, no. 2 (Winter 1995), 8–28; and Sherry Baker, "Ethical Judgment," *Executive Excellence* (March 1992), 7–8.

---

of which declared bankruptcy—which is perfectly legal—to avoid mounting financial obligations to suppliers, labor unions, or competitors. These examples contain moral, legal, and economic considerations that make socially responsible behavior hard to define. A company's environmental impact must also be taken into consideration.

Organizational Stakeholders

One reason for the difficulty understanding social responsibility is that managers must confront the question "responsibility to whom?" Recall from Chapter 3 that the organization's environment consists of several sectors in both the task and general environment. From a social responsibility perspective, enlightened organizations view the internal and external environment as a variety of stakeholders.

A **stakeholder** is any group within or outside the organization that has a stake in the organization's performance. Each stakeholder has a different criterion of responsiveness, because it has a different interest in the organization.[30] For example, Wal-Mart uses aggressive bargaining tactics with suppliers so that it is able to provide low prices for customers. Some stakeholders see this as socially responsible behavior because it benefits customers

stakeholder

Any group within or outside the organization that has a stake in the organization's performance.

and forces suppliers to be more efficient. Others, however, argue that the aggressive tactics are an abuse of power and may prevent suppliers from even paying their own employees a decent wage.[31]

Exhibit 5.4 illustrates important stakeholders for a software company. Investors and shareholders, employees, customers, and suppliers are considered primary stakeholders, without whom the organization cannot survive. Investors, shareholders, and suppliers' interests are served by managerial efficiency—that is, use of resources to achieve profits. Employees expect work satisfaction, pay, and good supervision. Customers are concerned with decisions about the quality, safety, and availability of goods and services. When any primary stakeholder group becomes seriously dissatisfied, the organization's viability is threatened.[32]

Other important stakeholders are the government and the community. Most corporations exist only under the proper charter and licenses and operate within the limits of safety laws, environmental protection requirements, antitrust regulations, and other laws and regulations in the government sector. The community includes local government, the natural and physical environments, and the quality of life provided for residents. Special-interest groups, still another stakeholder, may include trade associations, political action committees, professional associations, and consumerists. Social activists have discovered the power of the Internet for organizing stakeholders and pressuring corporations to honor their ethical, human rights, and environmental responsibilities. For example, the As You Sow foundation uses the Internet to mobilize investors and shareholders to push for social reforms, as described in this chapter's Leading Online box.

Exhibit *5.4*

Stakeholders Relevant to a Software Company

Leading Online

Using the Web to Promote Social Responsibility

The Internet has become a crucial weapon in the fight to make corporations more socially responsible. For example, social activists have long used shareholder pressure as an important means of promoting their goals. Now, with the ability to rapidly spread information on the Web, nonprofit organizations such as the As You Sow Foundation can quickly rally shareholders and mount campaigns against corporate practices they consider irresponsible.

As You Sow (AYS) is a not-for-profit organization with a specific mission to promote corporate responsibility and "hold corporations accountable for complying with consumer, workplace, and environmental laws." It does so primarily by organizing shareholder campaigns related to specific social or environmental issues, working closely with other activist organizations such as the Interfaith Center on Corporate Responsibility (ICCR), a group of Protestant, Catholic, and Jewish institutional investors that pioneered shareholder activism in the 1970s, and the Shareholder Action Network, an information, networking, and resource center that AYS

helped to found. One campaign resulted in Home Depot agreeing to phase out the sale of old-growth timber. Another is aimed at eradicating labor and human rights abuses in contract supplier plants that make products for companies such as Nike and Wal-Mart. A recent campaign against genetically altered foods, targeting companies such as DuPont, Hershey, Kellogg, and Sysco, has become the fastest-growing shareholder movement in history. AYS is working with the Shareholder Action Network on the massive campaign. Its Web site urges visitors, even if they are not shareholders, to talk with managers in stores and restaurants or send e-mail directly to CEOs to protest the growing use of genetically modified crops. Project director Tracey Rembert explains the value of using the Internet for social activism: "It used to be you'd call 20 people you know on the telephone and ask them to write a letter. . . . Now you can bring together many more people with just one e-mail. You can accomplish in one year what it might have taken 10 years of pickets and protests in the streets to accomplish."

SOURCE: Mark Schapiro, "All Over the Board," *grok* (February–March 2001), 110–112; and http://www.asyousow.org accessed on September 5, 2001.

Socially responsible organizations consider the effects of their actions on all stakeholder groups and may invest in a number of philanthropic causes that benefit stakeholders. For example, Engage Media, an online marketing company, participates in blood drives and clothing drives for the needy, and employees recently joined a breast cancer walk in San Francisco. The company gives employees one day off per quarter for volunteer activities.[33] The Body Shop weaves social responsibility and environmental protection into every facet of company operations. For example, the Body Shop buys cocoa butter directly from farmers in poor countries rather than purchasing it on the commodities market. Then the company sets up a social fund in the communities where it conducts trade so that needed schools or health clinics can be built.[34] These companies are acting in a socially responsible way by helping stakeholders.

Today, special-interest groups continue to be one of the largest stakeholder concerns that companies face. Environmental responsibility has become a primary issue as both business and the public acknowledge the damage that has been done to our natural environment.

The Natural Environment

When the first Earth Day celebration was held in 1970, most managers considered environmentalists to be an extremist fringe group and felt little need to respond to environmental concerns.[35] Today environmental issues have become a hot topic among business leaders, and managers and organizations

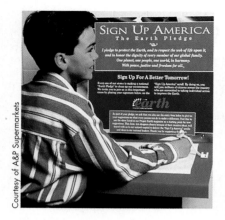

As part of its "Project Earth" program, A&P Stores urges customers to take an Earth Pledge and get involved in efforts to improve the natural environment. Environmental responsibility has become a primary issue for business. A&P adopted the turtle and frog, which are disappearing all over the world, as the company's mascots to roll out a new program aimed at building environmental awareness. One way A&P contributes directly to conservation efforts is its Energy Conservation System, which monitors and adjusts operating equipment to ensure maximum energy efficiency.

in all industries are jumping on the environmental bandwagon by "going green." Environmentalism has become an integral part of organizational strategy for many companies. The relationship between corporations and environmental activist groups has shifted from one of adversity to one of collaboration. Forty-eight companies, including Ford Motor Company, Bristol-Myers Squibb, Procter & Gamble, General Motors, and Royal Dutch/Shell, volunteered to respond to guidelines set up by the Coalition for Environmentally Responsible Economies.[36]

Huge corporations are joining the fight against global warming by counting greenhouse gases and changing business policies to cut emissions. Pratt & Whitney, a division of United Technologies Corp., now uses computers to simulate some tests of its jet engines instead of running the turbines. And at BP Amoco PLC, managers are now evaluated not just on their division's financial results but also on how well they cut emissions in their unit.[37]

Ford Motor Company has pledged to improve the average fuel economy of its sport-utility vehicles by 25 percent over five years. Managers voluntarily reported that Ford's plants and vehicles alone emit the equivalent of 1.7 percent of the world's carbon dioxide emissions, and they promised that the company's response to environmental problems will be a top criterion for evaluating corporate performance over the next decade.[38] In addition, in January 2002 the federal government announced a partnership with U.S. automakers to develop a car that runs on hydrogen fuel cells. GM President and CEO Rick Wagoner said, "If this works, this is the holy grail, this is the breakthrough."[39]

One model uses the phrase *shades of green* to evaluate a company's commitment to environmental responsibility.[40] The various shades, which represent a company's approach to addressing environmental concerns, are illustrated in Exhibit 5.5. Under the *legal approach*, an organization does just what is necessary to satisfy legal requirements. In general, managers and the company show little concern for environmental issues. For example, Willamette Industries of Portland, Oregon, agreed to install $7.4 million worth of pollution control equipment in its 13 factories to comply with Environmental Protection Agency requirements. The move came only after Willamette was fined a whopping $11.2 million for violating emissions standards.[41] The next shade, the *market approach*, represents a growing awareness of and sensitivity to environmental concerns, primarily to satisfy customers. A company might provide environmentally friendly products because customers want them, for instance, not necessarily because of strong management commitment to the environment.

A further step is to respond to multiple demands from the environment. The *stakeholder approach* means that companies attempt to answer the environmental concerns of various stakeholder groups, such as customers, the local community, business partners, and special interest groups. Ontario Power Generation, DuPont, Shell, and Alcan Aluminum are among the large companies that are partnering with Environmental Defense to reduce greenhouse gases.[42] The move comes in response to growing concerns among customers, communities where the companies operate, and environmental groups, as well as a recognition that emissions are likely to be regulated by government actions.

Finally, at the highest level of green, organizations take an *activist approach* to environmental issues by actively searching for ways to conserve the Earth's resources. Interface, a leader in the floor covering industry, provides an excellent illustration of a manager and a company taking an activist approach.

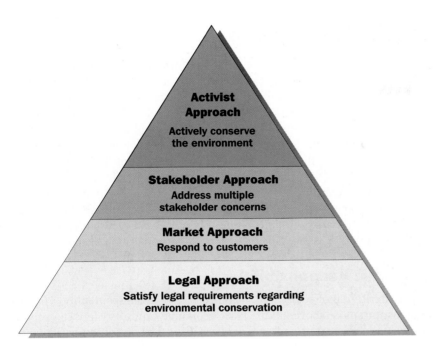

SOURCE: Based on R.E. Freeman, J. Pierce, and R. Dodd, *Shades of Green: Ethics and the Environment* (New York: Oxford University Press, 1995).

Exhibit 5.5

The Shades of Corporate Green

INTERFACE INC.
http://www.interfaceinc.com

Ray Anderson spent most of his life as an environmental glutton. His company, Interface, Inc., an Atlanta-based business with 7,300 employees, turns petrochemicals into textiles. The petroleum the company uses took millions of years to make and is irreplaceable; the carpets that come from it last forever—and most of them end up in landfills after only a decade of use.

But Ray Anderson had a revelation when he came across a book called *The Ecology of Commerce*, by Paul Hawken. As he read about the breadth of toxins accumulating in humans from one generation to the next and the speed at which natural resources were being depleted, the captain of industrial capitalism thought of his grandchildren and wept. Today, Ray Anderson is becoming a radical environmentalist who makes the folks from Greenpeace look timid. He has embraced the concept of sustainability, which calls for mimicking nature—everything's waste is something else's food. Anderson's goal for Interface: Create zero waste and consume zero oil while making a healthy profit. It took Anderson a year to convince the rest of his company (the largest maker of commercial carpeting and upholstery for office cubicles) that Interface could save the earth and still make money. Today, however, from the factory floor to the R&D lab, sustainability has become as important a consideration in every business decision as profitability.

Interface's performance shatters the idea that social responsibility and profits can't go hand in hand. Over a one-year period, sales grew from $800 million to one billion. During that time, the amount of raw materials used by the company dropped almost 20 percent per dollar of sales. That means, Anderson points out, "$200 million of sustainable business." The company's latest innovation is an "Evergreen Lease," with building owners renting rather than buying carpet. Interface installs, maintains, replaces, carries away, and recycles carpet tiles as they wear out. The old tiles become new carpet. Interface also hopes to soon offer commercial hemp carpet, which can be composted completely when its use is over.

Ray Anderson is not timid about explaining why he is instituting all these changes. He wants to save the world—and make sure his grandchildren will still have one.[43] ❖

Evaluating Corporate Social Performance

A model for evaluating corporate social performance is presented in Exhibit 5.6. The model indicates that total corporate social responsibility can be subdivided into four criteria—economic, legal, ethical, and discretionary responsibilities.[44] Managers and organizations are typically involved in several issues at the same time, and a company's ethical and discretionary responsibilities are increasingly considered as important as economic and legal issues. These four criteria fit together to form the whole of a company's social responsiveness.

Note the similarity between the categories in Exhibit 5.6 and those in Exhibit 5.1. In both cases, ethical issues are located between the areas of legal and freely discretionary responsibilities. Exhibit 5.6 also has an economic category, because profits are a major reason for corporations' existence.

Economic Responsibilities

The first criterion of social responsibility is *economic responsibility*. The business institution is, above all, the basic economic unit of society. Its responsibility is to produce the goods and services that society wants and to maximize profits for its owners and shareholders. Economic responsibility, carried to the extreme, is called the *profit-maximizing* view, advocated by Nobel economist Milton Friedman. This view argues that the corporation should be operated on a profit-oriented basis, with its sole mission to increase its profits so long as it stays within the rules of the game.[45]

The purely profit-maximizing view is no longer considered an adequate criterion of performance in Canada, the United States, and Europe. This approach means that economic gain is the only social responsibility and can lead companies into trouble.

Legal Responsibilities

All modern societies lay down ground rules, laws, and regulations that businesses are expected to follow. *Legal responsibility* defines what society deems as important with respect to appropriate corporate behavior.[46] Businesses are expected to fulfill their economic goals within the legal framework. Legal requirements are imposed by local town councils, state legislators, and federal regulatory agencies.

Organizations that knowingly break the law are poor performers in this category. Intentionally manufacturing defective goods or billing a client for work

E x h i b i t *5.6*

Criteria of Corporate Social Performance

SOURCES: Based on Archie B. Carroll, "A Three-Dimensional Conceptual Model of Corporate Performance," *Academy of Management Review* 4 (1979), 499; and "The Pyramid of Corporate Social Responsibility: Toward the Moral Management of Corporate Stakeholders," *Business Horizons* 34 (July–August 1991), 42.

not done is illegal. Organizations ultimately pay for ignoring their legal responsibilities. An example of the punishment given to one company that broke the law is described in the press release shown in Exhibit 5.7.

Ethical Responsibilities

Ethical responsibility includes behaviors that are not necessarily codified into law and may not serve the corporation's direct economic interests. As described earlier in this chapter, to be *ethical*, organization decision makers should act with equity, fairness, and impartiality, respect the rights of individuals, and provide different treatment of individuals only when relevant to the organization's goals and tasks.[47] *Unethical* behavior occurs when decisions enable an individual or company to gain at the expense of other people or society as a whole. For example, investigation of the Enron scandal revealed that some managers forged business deals that were not always in the best interest of the company in order to earn sizable brokering commissions. In addition, top Enron executives profited by selling their stock when they realized the company was sliding toward bankruptcy, while unsuspecting employees and other investors lost billions. Reebok provides an example of ethical action by making a firm commitment to human rights in its overseas factories, as described in the Putting People First box.

For businesses, the first criterion of corporate social responsibility is economic responsibility. Recently, companies such as Enron, Lucent, and Nortel have failed to carry out their economic responsibility, especially when the value of the company stock plummeted. Not only have Enron employees such as those in the photo lost their jobs, but some lost most of their 401(k) retirement plans. One 61-year-old administrative assistant, who had dutifully placed 15 percent of her salary into a 401(k) plan, invested the entire amount in the company's rapidly climbing stock. She amassed close to $500,000, only to be forced out of work with a 401(k) worth only $22,000 when Enron collapsed.

≋EPA United States
Environmental Protection Agency

Headquarters Press Release
Washington, DC

Date   07/12/2001
Published:
Title: WASHINGTON STATE/ALASKA COMPANY SENTENCED
                  IN ASBESTOS CASE

FOR RELEASE: THURSDAY, JULY 12, 2001
**WASHINGTON STATE/ALASKA COMPANY SENTENCED IN
ASBESTOS CASE**

Luke C. Hester 202-564-7818 / hester.luke@epa.gov

On June 27, Great Pacific Seafood, a Washington State corporation operating in Alaska, and its General Manager, Roger D. Stiles, were sentenced for violations of the Clean Air Act. Great Pacific Seafood was sentenced to serve five years probation, pay a $75,000 fine, pay $7,000 in restitution, publish a public apology statement in the local newspaper and adopt an environmental management program. Stiles was sentenced to pay a $5,000 fine, perform 120 hours of community service, and serve two to three years probation. Great Pacific Seafood and Stiles pleaded guilty to having five of its employees directly or indirectly exposed to asbestos fibers without the proper training, equipment or protective clothing. The hazardous nature of abatement was never disclosed to two of the employees. Failure to follow asbestos work practices can expose workers to the inhalation of airborne asbestos fibers which can cause lung cancer, a lung disease known as "asbestosis" and mesothelioma, a cancer of the chest and abdominal cavities. This case was investigated by the EPA Criminal Investigation Division, the FBI and the Alaska State Occupational Safety and Health Administration. Technical assistance was provided by the EPA Office of Air Quality. The case was prosecuted by the U.S. Attorney's Office in Anchorage.

R-105 ###

Exhibit **5.7**

*One Company's Punishment
for Breaking the Law*

Putting People First

Reebok Scores with Workers in Indonesia

During 1998 and 1999, the Indonesian consulting firm Insan Hitawasana Sejahtera (IHS) spent 1,400 hours studying labor conditions and interviewing factory workers at two contract factories in Indonesia that manufacture 75 percent of the footwear sold by U.S.-based Reebok. The final report, "Peduli Hak" ("Caring for Rights" in Indonesian) outlined some disturbing facts, including problems with health and safety procedures and worker–manager communication.

Disturbing conditions in overseas factories is nothing new. What was new about this study was that Reebok asked for it and then candidly discussed the negative findings in the press. Reebok wanted an independent evaluation of working conditions so managers could make improvements and meet their ethical responsibilities toward Indonesian factory workers. One project that came out of the report was a pilot project conducted by an arm of the AFL-CIO to strengthen the union's role as an advocate for workers in five Indonesian factories. Although unions were already in place in the factories, they had little power compared to unions in the United States.

A corporation training its employees in how to make their union stronger might seem hard to believe, but Reebok considered it an ethical duty. Because most factory workers in Indonesia are functionally illiterate and often cannot understand or defend their rights, the union must be powerful enough to be an advocate for them. Reebok also has an innovative worker communication system that provides a secure way for employees to report their concerns. Drop boxes are placed not only in factories and dormitories, but also in places where privacy is assured, such as public bathrooms and mosques. Each location has forms in the local language, with Reebok's human rights standards printed on the back.

Doug Cahn, Reebok's vice president of human rights programs, recently visited Indonesian factories to see if the efforts had made a difference. "I saw specially designed chairs for pregnant women. I saw job rotation systems, and signs posted in Indonesian encouraging workers to take water breaks as frequently as they wished," he said. "I saw seminars on how to use fire safety equipment, saw scrubbers on smokestacks, saw procedures for [safe] chemical handling. It was a sea change in what I'd seen beginning to take place a year ago."

SOURCE: Doug Cahn, "Reebok Takes the Sweat out of Sweatshops," *Business Ethics* (January–February 2000), 9.

Discretionary Responsibilities

discretionary responsibility
Organizational responsibility that is voluntary and guided by the organization's desire to make social contributions not mandated by economics, law, or ethics.

Discretionary responsibility is purely voluntary and is guided by a company's desire to make social contributions not mandated by economics, law, or ethics. Discretionary activities include generous philanthropic contributions that offer no payback to the company and are not expected. An example of discretionary behavior occurred when Pittsburgh Brewing Company helped laid-off steelworkers by establishing and contributing to food banks in the Pittsburgh area. Discretionary responsibility is the highest criterion of social responsibility, because it goes beyond societal expectations to contribute to the community's welfare.

Managing Company Ethics and Social Responsibility

Many managers are concerned with improving the ethical climate and social responsiveness of their companies. As one expert on the topic of ethics said, "Management is responsible for creating and sustaining conditions in which people are likely to behave themselves."[48] Managers must take active steps to ensure that the company stays on an ethical footing. As we discussed earlier in this chapter, ethical business practices depend on both individual managers and the organization's values, policies, and practices. Exhibit 5.8 illustrates the three pillars that support an ethical organization.[49]

The Ethical Organization

Ethical Individuals	Ethical Leadership	Organizations Structures and Systems
• Integrity • Honesty • Inspire Trust • Treat People Right • Play Fair • High Level of Moral Development	• Role Modeling • Uphold Ethical Values in Organization • Communicate About Ethics and Values • Reward Ethical Behavior • Swift Discipline of Unethical Behavior	• Corporate Culture • Code of Ethics • Ethics Committee • Chief Ethics Officer • Ethics Training • Whistle-Blowing Mechanisms

SOURCE: Adapted from Linda Klebe Treviño, Laura Pincus Hartman, and Michael Brown, "Moral Person and Moral Manager," *California Management Review* 42, No. 4 (Summer 2000), 128–142.

Exhibit **5.8**

The Three Pillars of an Ethical Organization

Ethical Individuals

Managers who are essentially ethical individuals make up the first pillar. These individuals possess honesty and integrity, which is reflected in their behavior and decisions. People inside and outside the organization trust them because they can be relied upon to follow the standards of fairness, treat people right, and be ethical in their dealings with others. Ethical individuals strive for a high level of moral development, as discussed earlier in the chapter.

However, being a moral person and making ethical decisions is not enough. Managers must also create a strong ethical climate for others. They find ways to focus the entire organization's attention on ethical values and create an organizational environment that encourages, guides, and supports the ethical behavior of all employees. Two additional pillars are needed to provide a strong foundation for an ethical organization: ethical leadership and organizational structures and systems.

Ethical Leadership

In a study of ethics policy and practice in successful, ethical companies such as Boeing, Chemical Bank, General Mills, GTE, Xerox, and Johnson & Johnson, no point emerged more clearly than the crucial role of leadership.[50] For example, a survey of readers of *The Secretary* magazine found that employees are acutely aware of their bosses' ethical lapses.[51] The company grapevine quickly communicates situations in which top managers choose an

©Todd France

Beatrice E. Rangel, senior vice-president for corporate strategies at Venezuela's largest private conglomerate, the $3.6 billion Cisneros Group, reflects her company's commitment to discretionary responsibility. Rangel is a vocal advocate for Latin America's investment in its people through higher corporate spending on education. Rangel reports that Cisneros spends 8 percent of its corporate budget on training and that via unused channels of Galaxy Latin America, a Cisneros satellite TV venture with Hughes Electronics, the company is launching a broadcast that will reach seven countries to train teachers.

code of ethics
A formal statement of the organization's values regarding ethics and social issues.

expedient action over an ethical one.[52] The primary way in which leaders set the tone for an organization's ethics is through their own actions. In addition, leaders make a commitment to ethical values and help others throughout the organization embody and reflect those values.[53]

If people don't hear about values from top leadership, they get the idea that ethical values are not important in the organization. Peter Holt, CEO of the Holt Companies, sees himself as the company's chief ethics officer. Ethical values are woven into the organizational culture, and Holt continually works to renew the values and signal his total commitment to them. Most importantly, he visits each of the firm's locations twice a year to meet with employees, answer questions, and talk about the importance of each employee upholding Holt's core values every day in every action. Holt's evaluation and reward systems are also tied to how well managers and employees live the values in their everyday actions.[54] Using performance reviews and rewards effectively is a powerful way for managers to signal that ethics counts. Consistently rewarding ethical behavior and disciplining unethical conduct at all levels of the company is a critical component of providing ethical leadership.[55]

Organizational Structures and Systems

The third pillar of ethical organizations is the set of tools that managers use to shape values and promote ethical behavior throughout the organization. Three of these tools are codes of ethics, ethical structures, and supporting whistle-blowers.

Code of Ethics.   A **code of ethics** is a formal statement of the company's values concerning ethics and social issues; it communicates to employees what the company stands for. Codes of ethics tend to exist in two types: principle-based statements and policy-based statements. *Principle-based statements* are designed to affect corporate culture; they define fundamental values and contain general language about company responsibilities, quality of products, and treatment of employees. General statements of principle are often called *corporate credos.* Examples are GTE's "Vision and Values" and Johnson & Johnson's "The Credo." [56]

Policy-based statements generally outline the procedures to be used in specific ethical situations. These situations include marketing practice, conflicts of interest, observance of laws, proprietary information, political gifts, and equal opportunities. Examples of policy-based statements are Boeing's "Business Conduct Guidelines," Chemical Bank's "Code of Ethics," GTE's "Code of Business Ethics" and "Anti-Trust and Conflict of Interest Guidelines," and Norton's "Norton Policy on Business Ethics."[57]

Codes of ethics state the values or behaviors that are expected and those that will not be tolerated, backed up by management's action. A recent survey of *Fortune* 1,000 companies found that 98 percent address issues of ethics and business conduct in formal corporate documents, and 78 percent of those have separate codes of ethics that are widely distributed.[58] When top management supports and enforces these codes, including rewards for compliance and discipline for violation, ethics codes can uplift a company's ethical climate.[59] The code of ethics at Lockheed Martin reflects the theme "Setting the Standard."

Lockheed Martin's board of directors adopted a booklet called *Setting the Standard* as the company's complete code of ethics and business conduct. The directors emphasize that ethical conduct requires more than complying with laws and regulations. An abbreviated version of the ethics code is included in the letter that accompanies the booklet sent to all employees:

> "While maintaining sensitivity to the diverse social and cultural settings in which we conduct our business, Lockheed Martin aims to *set the standard* for ethical conduct at all of our localities throughout the world. We will achieve this through behavior in accordance with six virtues: Honesty, Integrity, Respect, Trust, Responsibility, and Citizenship.
>
> - **Honesty:** to be truthful in all our endeavors; to be honest and forthright with one another and with our customers, communities, suppliers, and shareholders.
> - **Integrity:** to say what we mean, to deliver what we promise, and to stand for what is right.
> - **Respect:** to treat one another with dignity and fairness, appreciating the diversity of our workforce and the uniqueness of each employee.
> - **Trust:** to build confidence through teamwork and open, candid communication.
> - **Responsibility:** to speak up—without fear of retribution—and report concerns in the workplace, including violations of laws, regulations, and company policies, and seek clarification and guidance whenever there is doubt.
> - **Citizenship:** to obey all the laws of the countries in which we do business and to do our part to make the communities in which we live and work better.
>
> There are numerous resources available to assist you in meeting the challenge of performing your duties and responsibilities. . . .
>
> We are proud of our employees and the leadership role we play in making the world a better place to live. Thank you for doing your part to create and maintain an ethical work environment . . . and for *Setting the Standard.*"[60] ❖

LOCKHEED MARTIN
http://www.lockheedmartin.com

An area of growing concern for companies doing business internationally is developing ethics codes that focus on the issue of human rights. Responding to the public outcry against sweatshops in the garment industry, a New York nonprofit organization and a number of influential companies have proposed a set of global labor standards to deal with issues such as child labor, low wages, and unsafe working environments. The group has come up with a scheme called Social Accountability 8000, or SA 8000, which is designed to work like the ISO 9000 quality-auditing system of the International Standards Organization. The SA 8000 is the first auditable social standard in the world. Fashion designer and retailer Eileen Fisher has taken steps to ensure that every factory supplying her $100 million business is in compliance with SA 8000. Fisher has set a standard for corporate social responsibility by training suppliers to prepare for certification and even footing the bill for their audits. Other companies, including Avon and Toys 'R' Us, are also certifying their factories and requiring their suppliers to do likewise.[61]

ethics committee
A group of executives assigned to oversee the organization's ethics by ruling on questionable issues and disciplining violators.

Ethical Structures.   Ethical structures represent the various systems, positions, and programs a company can undertake to implement ethical behavior. An **ethics committee** is a group of executives appointed to oversee company ethics. The committee provides rulings on questionable ethical issues. The ethics committee assumes responsibility for disciplining wrongdoers, which is essential if the organization is to directly influence employee behavior. For example, Motorola has an Ethics Compliance Committee that is charged with interpreting, clarifying, and communicating the company's code of ethics and with adjudicating suspected code violations. Many companies, such as Sears, Northup Grumman, and Columbia/HCA Healthcare, have set up ethics offices with full-time staff to ensure that ethical standards are an integral part of company operations. These offices are headed by a **chief ethics officer**, a company executive who oversees all aspects of ethics and legal compliance, including establishing and broadly communicating standards, ethics training, dealing with exceptions or problems, and advising senior managers in the ethical and compliance aspects of decisions.[62] The title of *chief ethics officer* was almost unheard of a decade ago, but there is a growing demand for these ethics specialists because of highly publicized ethical and legal problems faced by companies in recent years. The Ethics Officer Association, a trade group, reports that membership has soared to more than 700 companies, up from only 12 in 1992.[63] Most ethics offices also work as counseling centers to help employees resolve difficult ethical issues. A toll-free confidential hotline allows employees to report questionable behavior as well as seek guidance concerning ethical dilemmas.

chief ethics officer
A company executive who oversees ethics and legal compliance.

ethics training
Training programs to help employees deal with ethical questions and values.

Ethics training programs also help employees deal with ethical questions and translate the values stated in a code of ethics into everyday behavior.[64] Training programs are an important supplement to a written code of ethics. The Boeing Corporation requires all employees to go through at least one hour of ethical training a year; senior managers have to participate in at least five hours. At McMurray Publishing Company in Phoenix, all employees attend a *weekly* meeting on workplace ethics, where they discuss how to handle ethical dilemmas and how to resolve conflicting values.[65]

A strong ethics program is important, but it is no guarantee against lapses. Dow Corning, whose faulty silicone breast implants shocked the business community, pioneered an ethics program that was looked upon as a model. Established in the mid-1970s, Dow's ambitious ethics program included the Business Conduct committee, training programs, regular reviews and audits to monitor compliance, and reports to the Audit and Social Responsibility committee. What went wrong? The ethics program dealt with the overall environment, but specific programs such as product safety were handled through normal channels—in this case the Medical Device Business Board, which slowed further safety studies.[66] Dow Corning's problems sent a warning to other industries. It is not enough to *have* an impressive ethics program. The ethics program must be merged with day-to-day operations, encouraging ethical decisions to be made throughout the company.

whistle-blowing
The disclosure by an employee of illegal, immoral, or illegitimate practices by the organization.

Whistle-Blowing.   Employee disclosure of illegal, immoral, or illegitimate practices on the employer's part is called **whistle-blowing**.[67] No organization can rely exclusively on codes of conduct and ethical structures to prevent all unethical behavior. Holding organizations accountable depends to some degree on individuals who are willing to blow the whistle if they detect illegal, dangerous, or unethical activities. Whistle-blowers often report wrongdoing to outsiders, such as regulatory agencies, senators, or newspaper reporters. Some firms have instituted innovative programs and confidential hotlines to encourage and support internal whistle-blowing. For this to be an effective ethical safeguard, however, companies must view whistle-blowing as a benefit to the company and make dedicated efforts to protect whistle-blowers.[68]

When there are no effective protective measures, whistle-blowers suffer. Although whistle-blowing has become widespread in recent years, it is still risky for employees, who can lose their jobs, be ostracized by coworkers, or be transferred to lower-level positions. For example, when Judith Neal blew the whistle at Honeywell's munitions plant in Joliet, Illinois, she ended up feeling as if she were the one being punished. Neal discovered that plant managers were falsifying test data to meet production goals, allowing substandard and potentially dangerous ammunition that Air Force and Army pilots and soldiers staked their lives on to pass inspection. Honeywell eventually settled with the federal government and two of the wrongdoers were punished, but Neal herself may have suffered the most. She heard rumors that a high-level manager was referring to her as "dead meat." She reported the rumors to Honeywell officials, but no action was taken. Eventually, the manager was promoted to a job at another plant, while Neal was asked to stay home for a month "for her own protection." When she returned, Neal found that most of her job responsibilities had been transferred to other employees, and she eventually quit in frustration. She filed suit years later and was awarded a financial settlement, but Neal emphasizes that money can never compensate for "the loss of privacy, the humiliation of having your personal life dredged up. Or for the nightmares, the anxiety of wondering if something is going to happen to you because you've spoken out."[69]

Managers can be trained to view whistle-blowing as a benefit rather than a threat, and systems can be set up to effectively protect employees who report illegal or unethical activities.

Ethics and the New Workplace

Many of today's best companies realize that success can be measured in many ways, not all of which show up on the financial statement. However, the relationship of a corporation's ethics and social responsibility to its financial performance concerns both managers and management scholars and has generated a lively debate.[70] One concern of managers is whether good citizenship will hurt performance—after all, ethics programs cost money. A number of studies have been undertaken to determine whether heightened ethical and social responsiveness increases or decreases financial performance. Studies have provided varying results but generally have found that there is a small positive relationship between social responsibility and financial performance.[71] For example, the Domini Social Index, created in 1989 to track the stock performance of socially responsible companies, indicates that they perform as well as or better than companies that are not socially responsible.[72] A recent study by Walker Research found that when price and quality are equal, two-thirds of customers say they would switch brands to do business with a company that is ethical and socially responsible.[73] Although results from these studies are not proof, they do provide an indication that use of resources for ethics and social responsibility does not hurt companies.[74] Enlightened companies realize that integrity and trust are essential

With funding by the Davenport Works division of Alcoa, the world's largest producer of aluminum, college student and commercial fisherman Chad Pregracke is leading a group of volunteers in an attempt to rid the Mississippi River banks of trash and debris in the Quad cities area. Pregracke, who was named the Illinois Wildlife Federation's Environmental Citizen of the Year, has cleared the shores of 30,000 pounds of debris, including 92 metal barrels, 153 tires, 3 refrigerators, a stove, and a television. By funding such a program, Alcoa enhances its reputation as a socially responsible company.

elements in sustaining successful and profitable business relationships with an increasingly connected web of employees, customers, suppliers, and partners. Although doing the right thing might not always be profitable in the short run, it develops a level of trust that money cannot buy and that will ultimately benefit the company.

In the world of fast-moving Internet companies, ethics sometimes takes a back seat as managers and employees do whatever it takes to get the most business in the least amount of time. However, smart managers are finding that old-fashioned integrity pays off. Managers at one Silicon Valley start-up, CenterBeam Inc., have made integrity the guiding principle of their corporate culture, and employees routinely tell stories that signify the "make-or-break" importance the company puts on keeping its promises. One, for example, concerns an employee who was offered a job just before a résumé from a positively dazzling candidate arrived. At many fast-moving start-ups, the job offer to the first candidate would have been rescinded, but CenterBeam had made a commitment and stuck to it. Another story concerns a similar situation with a supplier, when CenterBeam managers honored their promise even though it cost the company thousands of dollars. Both decisions ultimately served the company well because they built trust among employees, suppliers, and partners, as well as customers.[75] The importance of credibility in Internet start-ups will be discussed in more detail in the next chapter.

Changes in the workplace have brought other new ethical issues for managers. Options such as telecommuting, virtual work, and flexible hours open the door to employee abuse of the flexibility offered by the organization, but the success of these new ways of working depends on mutual trust. New information technology provides tools for managers to keep an even tighter rein on workers. Managers can choose to closely monitor when employees are logged on to the network and what they are doing, as well as where they are spending their time on the Internet. The American Management Association's survey of electronic monitoring and surveillance of employees found that nearly 74 percent of large U.S. businesses record and review employees' communications and activities on the job, a figure that nearly doubled between 1997 and 2000.[76] Although most companies have a policy that lets employees know they're subject to being watched, some do not. In addition, some ethical managers believe such close monitoring not only wastes time and money but is just downright wrong because it invades employees' privacy.

Companies need effective ways to investigate sexual harassment or other illegal and inappropriate workplace activities. However, snooping for snooping's sake is ethically questionable. Showing distrust of virtual workers and telecommuters can also backfire by weakening the employee's trust and commitment. "If you hire great people and you engage them in the business and they really have that passion and they know that you care, you shouldn't be sitting around babysitting or monitoring them," said one manager.[77] Another issue of growing concern in the new workplace is the privacy of customers on the Internet. Companies are compiling vast portfolios of personal information on their Web site visitors. This information is marketing gold for organizations, but critics argue that it is a serious violation of the individual's right to privacy.[78] A recent survey found that 71 percent of Americans polled are either very concerned or somewhat concerned about threats to their personal privacy over the Web. To head off the passage of new privacy laws now being debated in Washington, many companies are developing their own ways to protect individual privacy on the Internet.[79]

These are complicated ethical issues, and they become even more complicated because of the increasing globalization of business. However, companies that make an unwavering commitment to maintaining high standards of ethics and social responsibility will lead the way toward a brighter future for both business and society.

◼ Summary and Management Solution

Ethics and social responsibility are hot topics for today's managers. The ethical domain of behavior pertains to values of right and wrong. Ethical decisions and behavior are typically guided by a value system. Four value-based approaches that serve as criteria for ethical decision making are utilitarian, individualism, moral-rights, and justice. For an individual manager, the ability to make correct ethical choices will depend on both individual and organizational characteristics. An important individual characteristic is level of moral development. Corporate culture is an organizational characteristic that influences ethical behavior.

Corporate social responsibility concerns a company's values toward society. How can organizations be good corporate citizens? The model for evaluating social performance uses four criteria: economic, legal, ethical, and discretionary. Evaluating corporate social behavior often requires assessing its impact on organizational stakeholders. One issue of growing concern is environmental responsibility. Organizations may take a legal, market, stakeholder, or activist approach to addressing environmental concerns.

Ethical organizations are supported by three pillars: ethical individuals, ethical leadership, and organizational structures and systems, including codes of ethics, ethics committees, chief ethics officers, training programs, and mechanisms to protect whistle-blowers. Companies that are ethical and socially responsible perform as well as— and often better than—those that are not socially responsible. However, changes in the workplace are raising new ethical issues for managers and organizations, such as ethical use of technology for monitoring employees,

trust among business partners, and the privacy of individuals on the Internet.

Returning to our management challenge at the beginning of the chapter, there are no easy right-or-wrong answers to the drug companies' dilemma. Protecting intellectual property rights (drug patents) is a legitimate right of organizations, and the drug companies would argue that it is also a responsibility to their employees and shareholders, as well as customers. Managers who take a utilitarian approach to ethics, for example, might argue that protecting their patents ultimately provides the most good for the most people, since patents are the foundation of research and development of new drugs. However, those who take a justice approach might argue that this decision doesn't take into account the concept of justice toward the unfortunate victims of AIDS in poor countries. In response to bad publicity and public outcry over the South Africa dispute, companies are taking some action, going beyond purely economic and legal responsibilities to take ethical issues into consideration. One response to social demands is to reduce the prices of AIDS drugs to Africa and other developing areas of the world. Merck, for example, says it will make no profit from the AIDS drugs it sells in developing countries. Officials with Doctors Without Borders welcomed the announcement, but warned that it might still leave drugs out of the reach of many poor AIDS sufferers in the developing world.[80] Most activists would like to see the drug companies take a further step toward *discretionary responsibility* by ensuring that anyone who needs HIV and AIDS medicines has access to them.

◼ Discussion Questions

1. Dr. Martin Luther King, Jr., said, "As long as there is poverty in the world, I can never be rich. . . . As long as diseases are rampant, I can never be healthy. . . . I can never be what I ought to be until you are what you ought to be." Discuss this quote with respect to the material in this chapter. Would this be true for corporations, too?

2. Environmentalists are trying to pass laws for oil spills that would remove all liability limits for the oil companies. This would punish corporations financially. Is this the best way to influence companies to be socially responsible?

3. Compare and contrast the utilitarian approach with the moral-rights approach to ethical decision

making. Which do you believe is the best for managers to follow? Why?

4. Imagine yourself in a situation of being encouraged to inflate your expense account. Do you think your choice would be more affected by your individual moral development or by the cultural values of the company for which you worked? Explain.

5. Is it socially responsible for organizations to undertake political activity or join with others in a trade association to influence the government? Discuss.

6. The criteria of corporate social responsibility suggest that economic responsibilities are of the greatest magnitude, followed by legal, ethical, and discretionary responsibilities. Do you agree? Discuss.

7. What are some current ethical issues in the business news? Identify one company that seems to be handling an issue in an ethical and socially responsible manner and one that appears to be unethical or socially irresponsible.

8. Do you believe it is ethical for companies to compile portfolios of personal information on their Web site visitors without informing them? How about for organizations to monitor their employees' use of the Web? Discuss.

9. Which do you think would be more effective for shaping long-term ethical behavior in an organization: a written code of ethics combined with ethics training or strong ethical leadership? Why?

10. Lincoln Electric considers customers and employees to be more important stakeholders than shareholders. Is it appropriate for management to define some stakeholders as more important than others? Should all stakeholders be considered equal?

■ Management in Practice: Experiential Exercise

Ethical Work Climates

Answer the following questions by circling the number that best describes an organization for which you have worked.

	Disagree				Agree
1. What is the best for everyone in the company is the major consideration here.	1	2	3	4	5
2. Our major concern is always what is best for the other person.	1	2	3	4	5
3. People are expected to comply with the law and professional standards over and above other considerations.	1	2	3	4	5
4. In this company, the first consideration is whether a decision violates any law	1	2	3	4	5
5. It is very important to follow the company's rules and procedures here.	1	2	3	4	5
6. People in this company strictly obey the company policies.	1	2	3	4	5
7. In this company, people are mostly out for themselves.	1	2	3	4	5
8. People are expected to do anything to further the company's interests, regardless of the consequences.	1	2	3	4	5
9. In this company, people are guided by their own personal ethics.	1	2	3	4	5
10. Each person in this company decides for himself or herself what is right and wrong.	1	2	3	4	5

Add up your score: _____. These questions measure the dimensions of an organization's ethical climate. Questions 1 and 2 measure caring for people, questions 3 and 4 measure lawfulness, questions 5 and 6 measure rules adherence, questions 7 and 8 measure emphasis on financial and company performance, and questions 9 and 10 measure individual independence. *Questions 7 and 8 are reverse scored* (1 = 5, 2 = 4, 3 = 3, 4 = 2, 5 = 1). A total score above 40 indicates a very positive ethical climate. A score from 30 to 40 indicates above-average ethical climate. A score from 20 to 30 indicates a below-average ethical climate, and a score below 20 indicates a very poor ethical climate.

Go back over the questions and think about changes that you could have made to improve the ethical climate in the organization. Discuss with other students what you could do as a manager to improve ethics in future companies you work for.

SOURCE: Based on Bart Victor and John B. Cullen, "The Organizational Bases of Ethical Work Climates," *Administrative Science Quarterly* 33 (1988), 101–125.

■ Management in Practice: Ethical Dilemma

What is Right?

It is often hard for a manager to determine what is "right" and even more difficult to put ethical behavior into practice. A manager's ethical orientation often brings him or her into conflict with people, policies, customers, or bosses. Consider the following dilemmas. How would you handle them?

1. A well-liked member of your staff with an excellent record confides to you that he has Acquired Immune Deficiency Syndrome (AIDS). Although his illness has not affected his performance, you're concerned about his future health and about the reactions of his coworkers. You
   a. tell him to keep you informed about his health and say nothing to his coworkers.
   b. arrange for him to transfer to an area of the organization where he can work alone.
   c. hold a staff meeting to inform his coworkers and ask them how they feel about his continued presence on your team.
   d. consult your human resources officer on how to proceed.

2. During a reorganization, you're told to reduce staff in the department you manage. After analyzing staffing requirements, you realize the job would be a lot easier if two professionals, who both are over age 60, would retire. You
   a. say nothing and determine layoffs based purely on performance and length of service.
   b. schedule a meeting with both employees and ask if they'd consider early retirement.
   c. schedule a meeting with all staff and ask if anyone is interested in severance or early retirement.
   d. lay off the older workers.

3. One of your colleagues has recently experienced two personal tragedies—her husband filed for divorce and her mother died. Although you feel genuine sympathy for her, her work is suffering. A report you completed, based on inaccurate data she provided, has been criticized by management. Your manager asks you for an explanation. You
   a. apologize for the inaccuracies and correct the data.
   b. tell your manager that the data supplied by your colleague was the source of the problem.
   c. say your colleague has a problem and needs support.
   d. tell your manager that because of your work load, you didn't have time to check the figures in the report.

4. Your firm recently hired a new manager who is at the same level you are. You do not like the man personally and consider him a rival professionally. You run into a friend who knows your rival well. You discover this man did not attend Harvard as he stated on his résumé and, in fact, has not graduated from any college. You know his supposed Harvard background was instrumental in getting him hired. You
   a. expose the lie to your superiors.
   b. without naming names, consult your human resources officer on how to proceed.
   c. say nothing. The company obviously failed to check him out, and the lie probably will surface on its own.
   d. confront the man with the information and let him decide what to do.

5. During a changeover in the accounting department, you discover your company has been routinely overcharging members of the public for services provided to them. Your superiors say repayment of charges would wreak havoc on company profits. Your company is federally regulated, and the oversight commission has not noticed the mistake. Your bosses say the problem will never come to light and they will take steps to correct the problem so it never happens again. You
   a. contact the oversight commission.
   b. take the matter public, anonymously or otherwise.
   c. say nothing. It is now in the hands of the bosses.
   d. work with the bosses on a plan to recognize the company's error and set up a schedule of rebates that would not unduly penalize the company.

Questions

1. Use the guidelines described in the Shoptalk: "Guidelines for Ethical Decision Making" to determine the appropriate behavior in these cases. Do you have all the information you need to make an ethical decision? How would family or friends react to each alternative if you were in these situations?

2. Which approach to ethical decision making—utilitarian, individualism, justice, or moral-rights—seems most appropriate for handling each situation?

SOURCES: Game developed by Katherine Nelson, "Board Games," *Owen Manager* (Spring 1990), 14–16; Craig Dreilinger and Dan Rice, "Office Ethics," *Working Woman* (December 1991), 35–39, and Kevin Kelly and Joseph Weber, "When a Rival's Trade Secret Crosses Your Desk . . .," *BusinessWeek* (May 20, 1991), 18.

Surf the Net

1. **Ethics Quiz.** The Internet contains many interactive sites where you can learn more about ethical decision making. Visit one of the sites below or find one of your own that will allow you to gain further insight about ethical issues.
   http://www.nevada.edu/~pernellj/quiz.html
   http://confessonline.com/quiz.asp
   http://library.humboldt.edu/infoservices/OWLS/OWL8Test.htm
   http://www.ethicsandbusiness.org/stylequiz.htm
   http://www.ai.org/ethics/pubs/newsarticles/Quiz.html

2. **The Global Compact.** To learn more about the Nine Principles of the Global Compact Network, find answers to the following questions at *http://www.unglobalcompact.org/un/gc/unweb.nsf/content/whatitis.htm*

   a. What are the Nine Principles?
   b. How does a company participate in the Global Compact?

3. **Internet Legal Issues.** An Internet law library that provides extensive summaries of court decisions shaping the law of the Web can be found at *http://www.phillipsnizer.com/internetlib.htm*
   Topics addressed include copyright, trademark, dilution and other intellectual property issues, jurisdiction, linking, framing, meta tags, clip-art, defamation, domain name, e-mail, encryption, gambling, click-wrap agreements, shrink-wrap licenses, spamming, and many other subjects (50+ topics are linked from the home page at this site). Select a topic of interest, print out the summary, and bring it to class.

Case for Critical Analysis

Massengill's Department Store

Massengill's Department Store had been a fixture in small and mid-sized cities across the Southeast for 75 years. But for the past couple of decades, the Atlanta-based chain had been slowly going downhill. Once a cutting-edge retailer, Massengill's had come to be known primarily for its dilapidated stores and dowdy-looking clothes. Everyone knew the chain was on the verge of bankruptcy. But that was before Marv Heimler. Heimler had been lured away from his job running a nationwide chain based in Dallas–Fort Worth to rescue Massengill's. And rescue it he had. Massengill's was now the talk of the retail industry, thanks to its soaring sales and accompanying surge in stock price.

Heimler had been offered a generous compensation package that was tied to his performance in leading Massengill's through a rapid turnaround. And, indeed, Heimler realized he had no time to lose if Massengill's was to survive. He came in with an aggressive plan for change that included remodeling shabby stores, cutting overhead costs, and offering modern, trendy merchandise sold by sophisticated, knowledgeable sales associates. "Link selling," in which shoppers enter the store looking for one item but end up leaving with three or four, was an important part of the new strategy. Unfortunately, the new strategy also meant layoffs were inevitable. Massengill's had long been run by old-fashioned, patriarchal managers who had held fast to their no-layoffs policy. However, to save the company meant aggressively slashing costs and investing the savings in remodeling, new merchandise, and training programs. Closing the in-store snack bars and consolidating distribution centers were the first steps, which eliminated about 500 jobs. In addition, many of the long-time salespeople had neither the abilities required for link-selling nor a feel for the chic, sophisticated

clothing Massengill's was now offering. Heimler knew he had to cut out the "deadwood" (a term he was careful to never use in public) to make room for a new breed of modern, energized sales associates.

Layoff notices went out to more than 500 floor supervisors and long-time salespeople on Friday before lunch. That would give people time to clean out their desks and say goodbye to their colleagues before the end of the day. And most of the survivors would have a weekend to process what had happened before returning to work.

Heimler had expected people to be upset about the layoffs, but the severity of the reaction surprised him. Even the new employees he had brought in seemed to be upset. An article in a recent industry magazine had speculated that Massengill's success would be short-lived if morale continued to decline. "There's no trust at Massengill's," the article had said. "People feel like senior management isn't honest with its people. They just want to fix up the company fast and mop up the damage later."

Claire Sparkes, his head of human resources, confirmed that the article was on target. "People are really angry," she told him. "They think you should have held meetings to explain what was happening with the company and give people some warning."

"Everybody knew Massengill's was on the verge of financial collapse," Heimler snapped back. "When a new CEO is brought in to turn things around, everybody knows layoffs are coming. Why rub their noses in it? And if I hadn't moved quickly, nobody here would have a job! The whole chain would have gone down the tubes, and instead of 1,000 or so jobs being lost there would have been 5,000 people out of work! How would people have liked that?"

When Claire left his office, Heimler evaluated his situation. Massengill's was clearly soaring again. Customers were flocking in, sales and profits were going up, and Heimler was a hero on Wall Street. His compensation package is already worth more than $1 million, and his contract has just been renewed for two more years, with an increased salary and more stock options. He knows he has transformed Massengill's from an outdated chain that catered to older women to a hip, fun place for affluent young customers. Heimler reviewed last quarter's results and saw that sales and profits are still going up. So why does everyone keep telling him morale is going down?

Questions

1. What approach to ethical decision making (utilitarian, individualism, moral rights, or justice) seems to best describe Marv Heimler's turnaround strategy at Massengill's?
2. At what level of moral development would you place Heimler? Why?
3. How could Heimler have handled the layoffs to avoid the problems he's now facing? If you were in his position, what would you do now?

SOURCE: Based on Suzy Wetlaufer, "After the Layoffs, What Next?" *Harvard Business Review* (September–October 1998), 24–42.

■ Endnotes

1. Helene Cooper, Rachel Zimmerman, and Laurie McGinley, "Patents Pending: AIDS Epidemic Traps Drug Firms in a Vise: Treatment vs. Profits," *The Wall Street Journal* (March 2, 2001), A1, A6.
2. Bethany McLean, "Why Enron Went Bust," *Fortune* (December 24, 2001), 58–68; Jeffrey L. Seglin, "Dot.com," *Forbes ASAP* (February 21, 2000), 135; Jerry Useem, "New Ethics . . . or No Ethics?" *Fortune* (March 20, 2000), 82–86; and Jeremy Kahn, "Presto Chango! Sales Are Huge!" *Fortune* (March 20, 2000), 90–96.
3. Amy Zipkin, "Getting Religion on Corporate Ethics," *The New York Times* (October 18, 2000), C1, C10; Steve Liesman, "Inside the Race to Profit from Global Warming," *The Wall Street Journal*, (October 19, 1999), B1, B4.
4. "The Socially Correct Corporate Business," segment in Leslie Holstrom and Simon Brady, "The Changing Face of Global Business," special advertising section, *Fortune* (July 24, 2000), S1–S38.
5. Dale Kurschner, "Tying Executive Pay to Social Responsibility," *Business Ethics* (September–October 1995), 47.
6. Gordon F. Shea, *Practical Ethics* (New York: American Management Association, 1988); and Linda K. Treviño, "Ethical Decision Making in Organizations; A Person-Situation Interactionist Model," *Academy of Management Review* 11 (1986), 601–617.
7. Thomas M. Jones, "Ethical Decision Making by Individuals in Organizations: An Issue-Contingent Model," *Academy of Management Review* 16 (1991), 366–395.
8. Dan Goodin, "Can Napster Change Its Tune?" *The Industry Standard* (February 26, 2001), 39–42.
9. Rushworth M. Kidder, "The Three Great Domains of Human Action," *Christian Science Monitor* (January 30, 1990).
10. Jones, "Ethical Decision Making."
11. This discussion is based on Gerald F. Cavanagh, Dennis J. Moberg, and Manuel Velasquez, "The Ethics of Organizational Politics," *Academy of Management Review* 6 (1981), 363–374; Justin G. Longenecker, Joseph A. McKinney, and Carlos W. Moore, "Egoism and Independence: Entrepreneurial Ethics," *Organizational Dynamics* (Winter 1988), 64–72; Carolyn Wiley, "The ABCs of Business Ethics: Definitions, Philosophies, and Implementation," *IM* (February 1995), 22–27; and Mark Mallinger, "Decisive Decision Making: An Exercise Using Ethical Frameworks," *Journal of Management Education* (August 1997), 411–417.
12. Michael J. McCarthy, "Now the Boss Knows Where You're Clicking," and "Virtual Morality: A New Workplace Quandary," *The Wall Street Journal* (October 21, 1999), B1, B4; and Jeffrey L. Seglin, "Who's Snooping on You?" *Business 2.0* (August 8, 2000), 202–203.
13. Ron Winslow, "Rationing Care," *The Wall Street Journal* (November 13, 1989), R24.
14. Alan Wong and Eugene Beckman, "An Applied Ethical Analysis System in Business," *Journal of Business Ethics* 11 (1992), 173–178.
15. John Kekes, "Self-Direction: The Core of Ethical Individualism," *Organizations and Ethical Individualism*, ed. Konstanian Kolenda (New York: Praeger, 1988), 1–18.
16. Tad Tulega, *Beyond the Bottom Line* (New York: Penguin Books, 1987).
17. Lynn Sharp Paine, "Managing for Organizational Integrity," *Harvard Business Review* (March–April 1994), 106–117.
18. This discussion is based on Treviño, "Ethical Decision Making in Organizations."
19. L. Kohlberg, "Moral Stages and Moralization: The Cognitive-Developmental Approach," in *Moral Development and Behavior: Theory, Research, and Social Issues*, ed. T. Lickona (New York: Holt, Rinehart & Winston, 1976) 31–83; L. Kohlberg, "Stage and Sequence: The Cognitive-Developmental Approach to Socialization," in *Handbook of Socialization Theory and Research*, ed. D. A. Goslin (Chicago: Rand McNally, 1969); and Jill W. Graham, "Leadership, Moral Development, and Citizenship Behavior," *Business Ethics Quarterly* 5, no. 1 (January 1995), 43–54.
20. Carol Gilligan, *In a Different Voice: Psychological Theory and Women's Development* (Cambridge, Mass.: Harvard University Press, 1982).
21. See Thomas Donaldson and Thomas W. Dunfee, "When Ethics Travel: The Promise and Peril of Global Business Ethics," *California Management Review* 41, No. 4 (Summer 1999), 45–63.

22. Andrew W. Singer, "Ethics: Are Standards Lower Overseas?" *Across the Board* (September 1991), 31–34; and David Vogel, "Is U.S. Business Obsessed with Ethics?" *Across the Board* (November–December 1993), 31–33.

23. The Global Compact Web site *http://www.unglobalcompact.org*, accessed on July 18, 2001; and Zipkin, "Getting Religion on Corporate Ethics."

24. Duane M. Covrig, "The Organizational Context of Moral Dilemmas: The Role of Moral Leadership in Administration in Making and Breaking Dilemmas," *The Journal of Leadership Studies* 7, no. 1 (2000), 40–59; and James Weber, "Influences Upon Organizational Ethical Subclimates: A Multi-Departmental Analysis of a Single Firm," *Organizational Science* 6, no. 5 (September–October 1995), 509–523.

25. This discussion is based on Linda Klebe Treviño, "A Cultural Perspective on Changing and Developing Organizational Ethics," in *Research and Organizational Change and Development*, ed. R. Woodman and W. Pasmore (Greenwich, Conn.: JAI Press, 1990), 4.

26. Ibid; John B. Cullen, Bart Victor, and Carroll Stephens, "An Ethical Weather Report: Assessing the Organization's Ethical Climate," *Organizational Dynamics* (Autumn 1989), 50–62; and Bart Victor and John B. Cullen, "The Organizational Bases of Ethical Work Climates," *Administrative Science Quarterly* 33 (1988), 101–125.

27. Russell Mitchell with Michael Oneal, "Managing by Values," *BusinessWeek* (August 1, 1994), 46–52; and Alan Farnham, "State Your Values, Hold the Hot Air," *Fortune* (April 19, 1993), 117–124.

28. Eugene W. Szwajkowski, "The Myths and Realities of Research on Organizational Misconduct," in *Research in Corporate Social Performance and Policy*, ed. James E. Post (Greenwich, Conn.: JAI Press, 1986), 9:103–122; and Keith Davis, William C. Frederick, and Robert L. Blostrom, *Business and Society: Concepts and Policy Issues* (New York: McGraw-Hill, 1979).

29. Douglas S. Sherwin, "The Ethical Roots of the Business System," *Harvard Business Review* 61 (November–December 1983), 183–192.

30. Nancy C. Roberts and Paula J. King, "The Stakeholder Audit Goes Public," *Organizational Dynamics* (Winter 1989), 63–79; and Thomas Donaldson and Lee E. Preston, "The Stakeholder Theory of the Corporation: Concepts, Evidence, and Implications," *Academy of Management Review* 20, no. 1 (1995), 65–91.

31. Jeffrey S. Harrison and Caron H. St. John, "Managing and Partnering with External Stakeholders," *Academy of Management Executive* 10, no. 2 (1996), 46–60.

32. Max B. E. Clarkson, "A Stakeholder Framework for Analyzing and Evaluating Corporate Social Performance," *Academy of Management Review* 20, no. 1 (1995), 92–117.

33. Erika Rasmusson, "Doing Well, Doing Good: Inspiring Ways to Share the Wealth," *Working Woman* (December/January 2001), 42, 44.

34. Elizabeth Roberts, "From Soap to Soapbox," *Working Woman* (December–January 2001), 22–25.

35. Mark A. Cohen, "Management and the Environment," *The Owen Manager* 15, no. 1 (1993), 2–6.

36. Zipkin, "Getting Religion on Corporate Ethics."

37. Liesman, "Inside the Race to Profit from Global Warming."

38. Jeffrey Ball, "Warming Trend: Auto Makers Juggle Substance and Style in New Green Policies," *The Wall Street Journal* (May 15, 2001), A1, A6.

39. Ed Garsten, "GM Calls Fuel Cells 'Holy Grail,'" Associated Press (January 18, 2002), accessed at *http://www.yahoo.com*.

40. R. E. Freeman, J. Pierce, and R. Dodd, *Shades of Green: Business Ethics and the Environment* (New York: Oxford University Press, 1995).

41. Greg Toppo, "Company Agrees to Pay Record Pollution Fine," Associated Press, *Johnson City Press* (July 21, 2000), 9.

42. Andrew C. Revkin, "7 Companies Agree to Cut Gas Emissions," *The New York Times* (October 18, 2000), C1, C6.

43. Gwen Kinkead, "In the Future, People Like Me Will Go to Jail," *Fortune* (May 24, 1999), 190–200; Charles Fishman, "I Want to Pioneer the Company of the Next Industrial Revolution," *Fast Company* (April–May 1998), 136–142; Thomas Petzinger, Jr., "Business Achieves Greatest Efficiency When at Its Greenest," *The Wall Street Journal* (July 11, 1997), B1; and Catherine Arnst, "When Green Begets Green," *BusinessWeek* (November 10, 1997), 98–106.

44. Archie B. Carroll, "A Three-Dimensional Conceptual Model of Corporate Performance," *Academy of Management Review* 4 (1979), 497–505. For a discussion of various models for evaluating corporate social performance, also see Diane L. Swanson, "Addressing a Theoretical Problem by Reorienting the Corporate Social Performance Model," *Academy of Management Review* 20, no. 1 (1995), 43–64.

45. Milton Friedman, *Capitalism and Freedom* (Chicago: University of Chicago Press, 1962), 133; and Milton Friedman and Rose Friedman, *Free to Choose* (New York: Harcourt Brace Jovanovich, 1979).

46. Eugene W. Szwajkowski, "Organizational Illegality: Theoretical Integration and Illustrative Application," *Academy of Management Review* 10 (1985), 558–567.

47. David J. Fritzsche and Helmut Becker, "Linking Management Behavior to Ethical Philosophy—An Empirical Investigation," *Academy of Management Journal* 27 (1984), 165–175.

48. Saul W. Gellerman, "Managing Ethics from the Top Down," *Sloan Management Review* (Winter 1989), 73–79.

49. This discussion is based on Linda Klebe Treviño, Laura Pincus Hartman, and Michael Brown, "Moral Person and Moral Manager: How Executives Develop a Reputation for Ethical Leadership," *California Management Review* 42, no. 4 (Summer 2000), 128–142.

50. "Corporate Ethics: A Prime Business Asset," *The Business Roundtable*, 200 Park Avenue, Suite 2222, New York, New York, 10166, February 1988.

51. Michael Barrier, "Doing the Right Thing," *Nation's Business* (March 1998), 33–38.

52. Joseph L. Badaracco, Jr., and Allen P. Webb, "Business Ethics: A View from the Trenches, *California Management Review* 37, no. 2 (Winter 1995), 8–28.

53. Linda Klebe Treviño, Gary R. Weaver, David G. Gibson, and Barbara Ley Toffler, "Managing Ethics and Legal Compliance: What Works and What Hurts?" *California Management Review* 41, no. 2 (Winter 1999), 131–151.

54. Linda Klebe Treviño and Katherine A. Nelson, *Managing Business Ethics: Straight Talk About How to Do It Right*, 2nd ed. (New York: John Wiley & Sons, 1999), 274–283.

55. Treviño, Hartman, and Brown, "Moral Person and Moral Manager."

56. "Corporate Ethics."

57. Ibid.

58. Treviño et al., "Managing Ethics and Legal Compliance."

59. Carolyn Wiley, "The ABC's of Business Ethics: Definitions, Philosophies, and Implementation," *IM* (January–February 1995), 22–27; Badaracco and Webb, "Business Ethics: a View from the Trenches"; and Ronald B. Morgan, "Self- and Co-Worker Perceptions of Ethics and Their Relationships to Leadership and Salary," *Academy of Management Journal* 36, no. 1 (February 1993), 200–214.

60. "Setting the Standard," *http://www.lockheedmartin.com/exeth/html/code/code.html*, accessed on August 7, 2001.

61. Cassandra Kegler, "Holding Herself Accountable," *Working Woman* (May 2001), 13; and Louisa Wah, "Treading the Sacred Ground," *Management Review* (July–August, 1998), 18–22.

62. Alan Yuspeh, "Do the Right Thing," *CIO* (August 1, 2000), 56–58.

63. Zipkin, "Getting Religion on Corporate Ethics."

64. Beverly Geber, "The Right and Wrong of Ethics Offices," *Training* (October 1995), 102–118.

65. Zipkin, "Getting Religion on Corporate Ethics."

66. John A. Byrne, "The Best Laid Ethics Programs . . .," *BusinessWeek* (March 9, 1992), 67–69.

67. Marcia Parmarlee Miceli and Janet P. Near, "The Relationship among Beliefs, Organizational Positions, and Whistle-Blowing Status: A Discriminant Analysis," *Academy of Management Journal* 27 (1984), 687–705.

68. Eugene Garaventa, "*An Enemy of the People* by Henrik Ibsen: The Politics of Whistle-Blowing," *Journal of Management Inquiry* 3, no. 4 (December 1994), 369–374; Marcia P. Miceli and Janet P. Near, "Whistleblowing: Reaping the Benefits," *Academy of Management Executive* 8, no. 3 (1994), 65–74.

69. Patricia Kiger, "Truth and Consequences," *Working Woman* (May 2001), 56–61.

70. Philip L. Cochran and Robert A. Wood, "Corporate Social Responsibility and Financial Performance," *Academy of Management Journal* 27 (1984), 42–56.

71. Dale Kurschner, "5 Ways Ethical Business Creates Fatter Profits," *Business Ethics* (March–April 1996), 20–23.

72. Mark Schapiro, "All Over the Board," *grok* (February–March 2001), 110–112.

73. Reported in "The Socially Correct Corporate Business."

74. Jean B. McGuire, Alison Sundgren, and Thomas Schneeweis, "Corporate Social Responsibility and Firm Financial Performance," *Academy of Management Journal* 31 (1988), 854–872; and Louisa Wah, "Treading the Sacred Ground," *Management Review* (July–August 1998), 18–22.

75. George Anders, "Honesty is the Best Policy," *Fast Company* (August 2000), 262–266.

76. This discussion is based on Seglin, "Who's Snooping on You?"

77. Ibid.

78. Jeffery L. Seglin, "Dot.Con", *Forbes ASAP* (February 21, 2000), 135; and Edward C. Baig, Marcia Stepanek, and Neil Gross, "Privacy," *BusinessWeek* (April 5, 1999), 84–90.

79. Glenn R. Simpson, "The Battle Over Web Privacy," *The Wall Street Journal* (March 21, 2001), B1, B4; and Jason Sykes and Glenn R. Simpson, "Some Big Sites Back P3P Plan; Others Wait," *The Wall Street Journal* (March 21, 2001), B1, B4.

80. Lori Hinnant, "Company Lowers HIV-Drug Prices for Africa, Others," Associated Press, *Johnson City Press* (March 8, 2001), 16.

CHAPTER

6

Small Business and Internet Start-Ups

CHAPTER OUTLINE

What Is Entrepreneurship?

Entrepreneurship and the Environment

Entrepreneurship Today

Definition of Small Business

Impact of Entrepreneurial Companies

Who Are Entrepreneurs?

Personality Traits

Demographic Factors

Starting an Entrepreneurial Firm

New Business Idea

The Business Plan

Legal Form

Financial Resources

Tactics

Internet Start-Ups

Launching an Internet Business

Managing a Growing Business

Stages of Growth

Planning

Organizing

Leading

Controlling

LEARNING OBJECTIVES

After studying this chapter, you should be able to

1 Describe the importance of entrepreneurship to the U.S. economy.

2 Define personality characteristics of a typical entrepreneur.

3 Describe the planning necessary to undertake a new business venture.

4 Explain the steps involved in launching an Internet start-up.

5 Describe the five stages of growth for an entrepreneurial company.

6 Explain how the management functions of planning, organizing, leading, and controlling apply to a growing entrepreneurial company.

Management Challenge

The year was 1994, and Jeff Rix had caught the Internet bug. Fresh out of college and working for his father's successful safety-equipment business, Rix was determined to take Pro-Am Safety Inc. into cyberspace. But after two years of trying, including building a solid, technologically sophisticated e-commerce site, the orders for gas masks and fire extinguishers were not pouring in. Jeff's father pulled the plug and sent his son to do outside sales. However, a chance discussion with John-Michael D'Arcangelo, the key programmer at Pro-Am, gave Jeff a different idea—he and D'Arcangelo would start their own separate Internet company to sell a different product—one they considered perfect for online sales. D'Arcangelo had just purchased a DVD player and had trouble finding DVD titles locally. He found a wider selection on the Internet, but he also found the technology of the sites he visited far inferior to what he and Rix had developed for Pro-Am Safety. At the time, there were only a couple hundred DVD titles in circulation, but Rix was sure the new technology would eventually replace VHS as surely as CDs had replaced vinyl LPs. So, in the fall of 1997, using the technology they had developed at Pro-Am and $6,000 of personal and family funds, Rix and D'Arcangelo launched DVD Empire. The site took off like a rocket, and DVD Empire took in $250,000 in its first four months. Since then, sales have zoomed to $16 million. What is even more amazing in the world of e-commerce is that Rix and D'Arcangelo's business has been profitable since day one. Now, however, the two entrepreneurs are facing some difficult decisions. So far, they have refused to seek outside funding, but they wonder how long they can continue to compete against giants such as Amazon.com without investment money.[1]

If you were Jeff Rix or John-Michael D'Arcangelo, would you search for venture capital to grow the business faster? Do you believe it is even possible for DVD Empire to compete with big Internet companies?

Despite the dot-com crash of late 2000 and early 2001, when many shooting stars quickly fizzled and burned out, there are still numerous small companies quietly doing business on the Internet. Many people dream of starting their own business, and the Internet has opened a new avenue for small business formation. Interest in entrepreneurship and small business is at an all-time high. At college campuses across the United States, ambitious courses, programs, and centers teach the fundamentals of starting a small business. Entrepreneurs have access to business incubators, support networks, and online training courses. The enormous growth of franchising gives beginners an escorted route into a new business. For the past three decades, the number of businesses in the U.S. economy has been growing faster than the labor force, and the annual number of business launches continues to increase.[2]

Running a small business—in physical space or cyberspace—is difficult and risky. The Small Business Administration reports that the survival rate of small businesses is barely 40 percent after six years.[3] Those that survive continue to face tremendous challenges, yet despite the risks, Americans are entering the world of entrepreneurship at an unprecedented rate.

entrepreneurship
The process of initiating a business venture, organizing the necessary resources, and assuming the associated risks and rewards.

entrepreneur
Someone who recognizes a viable idea for a business product or service and carries it out.

What Is Entrepreneurship?

©Austin MacRae

Carol Weinstock, a true entrepreneur, recognized a market for multicultural greeting cards and launched EthnoGraphics, creating cards for the African-American, American Indian, Latino, Chinese-American, and Jewish consumer. Weinstock hired artists from the various cultures to create cards that would be true to the lives and feelings of ethnic customers. By filling a niche the major companies left behind, Weinstock found a ready market and is reaping the rewards of entrepreneurship, with EthnoGraphics' revenues tripling each year for three years running.

Entrepreneurship is the process of initiating a business venture, organizing the necessary resources, and assuming the associated risks and rewards.[4] An **entrepreneur** is someone who engages in entrepreneurship. An entrepreneur recognizes a viable idea for a business product or service and carries it out. This means finding and assembling necessary resources—money, people, machinery, location—to undertake the business venture. Entrepreneurs also assume the risks and reap the rewards of the business. They assume the financial and legal risks of ownership and receive the business's profits.

For example, Vivian Jimenez, Lorraine Brennan O'Neil, and Karen Janson started a business called 10 Minute Manicure, which they hope to open in airports across the country.[5] Responding to the exploding number of female business travelers and the limited services available to women in airports, they thought of setting up inexpensive two-chair kiosks and offering travelers a luxury manicure while they wait for their boarding call. The three women have invested their own savings, cut back their hours or quit their jobs to devote time to building the business, and are lining up investors and selling the idea to airport officials. Jimenez, O'Neil and Janson spotted an opportunity and are willing to assume the risks of making it happen.

Successful entrepreneurs have many different motivations, and they measure rewards in different ways. A recent study classified small business owners in five different categories, as illustrated in Exhibit 6.1. Some people are *idealists*, who like the idea of working on something that is new, creative, or personally meaningful. *Optimizers* are rewarded by the personal satisfaction of being a business owner. Entrepreneurs in the *sustainer* category like the chance to balance work and personal life and often don't want the business to grow too large, while *hard workers* enjoy putting in the long hours and dedication to build a larger, more profitable business. The *juggler* category includes entrepreneurs who like the chance a small business gives them to handle everything themselves. These are high-energy people who thrive on the pressure of paying bills, meeting deadlines, and making payroll.[6]

Rewarded by chance to work on something new and creative

Thrive on the challenge of building a larger, more profitable business

Enjoy chance to balance work and personal life

Idealists	Optimizers	Hard Workers	Jugglers	Sustainers
24%	21%	20%	20%	15%

Get personal satisfaction from being a business owner

High energy people who enjoy handling every detail of their own business

Exhibit *6.1*

Five Types of Small Business Owners

SOURCE: Study conducted by Yankelovich Partners, reported in Mark Henricks, "Type-Cast," *Entrepreneur* (March 2000), 14–16.

For decades, half the working population has been confiding secretly to pals and pollsters the desire to leave corporate America and go it alone or with a few partners, but until recently, such dreams were often squashed in their infancy by worried parents, friends, and spouses. Clearly, times have changed. After growing steadily since the 1950s, America's largest companies began cutting their payrolls during the economic downturn of the late 1980s. Downsizing throughout the corporate world forced many employees to consider other options. Bob Kuenzig started a small business that makes while-you-wait hearing aids after he lost his job at one of the nation's largest home builders in 1990.[7] With the recent round of major layoffs, today's latent entrepreneurs also may get just the push they need to strike out on their own. "I don't think I would have had the nerve to have left on my own," said Robin Gorman Newman, who lost her job as vice president of a public relations firm due to a restructuring. Now Newman runs her own PR business, RGN Communications, and has also fashioned a whole new career as the "Love Coach," a separate business that offers counseling to singles.[8] Many experts actually believe an economic downturn is the best time to start a small business because it forces entrepreneurs to keep costs in line, enables them to hire good people, and gives them the time needed to build something of lasting value rather than struggle to keep pace with rapid growth.[9]

Many people also regard entrepreneurship as a better use of their time, talent, and energy. Women and minorities, who have sometimes found their opportunities limited in the corporate world, are often seeing entrepreneurship as the only way to go. The National Federation of Women Business Owners (NFWBO) reports that women owned 38 percent of all U.S. businesses in 1999, with about 13 percent of those companies owned by minority women.[10] Many of these are small businesses started by women and minority entrepreneurs who found limited opportunities in established firms. For instance, NFWBO reports that Hispanic women are starting companies at four times the national growth rate. "The [corporate] work environment is not friendly to Latinas," says Alma Morales Fiojas, CEO of Mana, a National Latina Organization. "Sometimes the best avenue . . . is to go into your own business, where there is more flexibility and you can accomplish more."[11] The National Urban League's 2001 annual review of black America also found that black-owned businesses have steadily increased and, significantly, more than two-thirds of those surveyed said they have entrepreneurial dreams for the future.[12]

Entrepreneurship and the Environment

Not so long ago, scholars and policy makers were worrying about the potential of small business to survive. The recent turbulence in the Internet economy and the demise of many dot-com start-ups again has some questioning whether small companies can compete with big business. However, entrepreneurship and small business are vital, dynamic, and increasingly important parts of the U.S. economy. There are an estimated 15 to 17 million small businesses in the United States, which account for a tremendous portion of the goods and services provided.[13] Another interesting finding is that there are approximately 10 million Americans who make their living as *solo professionals*, often working out of their homes providing services to other companies. Some popular businesses for solo professionals are insurance agencies and brokerages, real estate, legal or medical services, translation and interpretation, and technical, scientific, and professional services. Overall, about half of all small businesses or solo professionals are in the service sector, (including finance, insurance, and real estate).[14]

Entrepreneurship Today

There are a number of reasons small business is such a dynamic part of today's economy, including economic changes, globalization and increased competition, advancing technology, and new market niches.[15]

Economic Changes.   Today's economy is fertile soil for entrepreneurs. The economy changes constantly, providing opportunities for new businesses. For example, the demand for services is booming, and 97 percent of service firms are small, with fewer than 100 employees. Since government deregulation removed restrictions that inhibited small business formation in the trucking industry, thousands of small trucking companies have been started. In addition, long-distance freight trucking has become the biggest industry for one-person businesses, accounting for about $12.5 billion.[16]

Globalization and Increased Competition.   Even the largest of companies can no longer dominate their industry in a fast-changing global marketplace. Globalization demands entrepreneurial behavior—companies have to find ways to do things faster, better, and less expensively. Large companies are cutting costs by outsourcing work to smaller businesses or freelancers and selling off extraneous operations. Globalization and increased competition also give an advantage to the flexibility and fast response small business can offer rather than to huge companies with economies of scale.

Technology.   Rapid advances and dropping prices in computer technology have spawned whole new industries, as well as entirely new methods of producing goods and delivering services. Unlike technological advances of the past, these are within the reach of companies of all sizes. The explosive growth of the Internet has created tremendous opportunities for entrepreneurs. For every story of a failed dot-com business, there are any number of small companies using the Web to sell products and services, to improve productivity, communications, and customer service, or to obtain information and market their services. Singer–songwriter Peter Breinholt recently started selling CDs, song books, and T-shirts on his Web site, and he reports that his

©Robert Gallagher

Technological advances *provide new opportunities for entrepreneurs like Kevin Nakao, founder of MusicBlitz Inc. (http:// www.musicblitz.com). Nakao was formerly general manager for music content company Launch.com and developed its first Web strategy. Nakao learned from his experience at Launch.com and founded MusicBlitz with goals of keeping employee turnover to a minimum, grounding financial expectations in reality, and blending online and offline operations. The obstacles of running a dot-com still exist, but the company meets them by keeping staff small and minimizing operating costs.*

sales have nearly doubled. Thos. Moser Cabinetmakers, a Maine-based business that makes and sells handcrafted furniture, uses the Web as an onsite catalog to build offsite sales. Visitors can take a virtual tour of how the furniture gets made and view contextual pictures of the furniture in a home. The Web site has enabled the small company to reach people it could never reach before the advent of the Internet—and that's led to lots of new buyers.[17] Of the 27 percent of companies with 50 or fewer employees that have a Web site, more than half report that the site has broken even or paid for itself in increased business.[18]

Other technological advances also provide opportunities for small business. Biotechnology, aided by recent work in genomics, is a growing field for small businesses. Research into microelectromechanical systems (MEMS), tiny machines used in numerous applications from biotechnology and telecommunications to the auto industry, is being conducted primarily by small companies. By keeping up with new technological developments, entrepreneur Pradeep Sindhu was able to grab a share of the fast-growing market for routers and other Internet gear.

In 1998, Cisco Systems had more than 90 percent market share in the rapidly growing and highly profitable core router market. But when Pradeep Sindhu looked at the systems provided by Cisco and other leading vendors, he was unimpressed. They were using, he noted, technology that was "three or four generations behind state-of-the-art." Sindhu spotted an entrepreneurial opportunity and left his job to start Juniper Networks. Sindhu's start-up has been gradually stealing market share from the giants, and Cisco CEO John Chambers admits that his own company was slow to respond to changing router networking requirements.

Big companies like Cisco are often tied to doing things a certain way and have a hard time moving swiftly. "Cisco encountered the problem that comes from operating a multibillion-dollar business: Corporate bureaucracy slowed down delivery of new technology," said Rick Malone of Vertical Systems Group, a market research firm. Juniper, on the other hand, without an initial user base, was free to rethink router design and exploit the latest technological advancements. Sindhu hired top-quality engineers to ensure that product quality and reliability was top-notch. He worked with large carriers to understand their needs and often let customers sample the products before they were released. An analyst for J.P. Morgan Chase says Juniper "has done everything right" since its inception. Cisco still sells twice as many routers as Juniper, but Sindhu is branching into new areas to sustain growth, and he is betting that his smaller, nimbler company can continue to give the giants a run for their money.[19]❖

JUNIPER NETWORKS
http://www.juniper.net

New Opportunities and Market Niches. Today's entrepreneurs are taking advantage of the opportunity to meet changing needs in the marketplace. Sisters Dana Schulz and Jessica Taylor of Garland, Texas, started FunPhones to create interchangeable cell phone covers, ranging from stars and stripes to sporty bouncing balls to wild animal prints. Since cell phones have become almost as ubiquitous a part of a woman's outfit as her purse, the two spotted an opportunity to make them a fashion accessory. The demand for their designs catapulted FunPhones to around a million in sales in only its second year of operation.[20] Recognizing the need for a magazine to serve the

©Marc Longwood

Entrepreneurs Chet and Terrie Van Scyoc spotted an opportunity to profit from "shoppertainment," a new trend in today's retailing environment that blends entertainment with tried and true merchandising techniques. Shoppertainment helped the Scyocs build their Sacramento, California hobby store, R/C Country Hobbies, to revenues of approximately $1.2 million. R/C Country Hobbies sells remote-control planes and cars, model-building kits, and other toys to customers who can test a collector train on display or ask an employee to build a model so they can see and feel it. They can even fly a model airplane using a computer program that simulates the event. "This is something our biggest competitors, mail-order catalogs, can't give them," says Terrie.

United States' estimated 3 million educated, affluent Latina professionals, Anna Maria Arias founded *Latina Style*, a spicy mix of Hispanic cultural, business, and entertainment news.[21]

Definition of Small Business

The full definition of "small business" used by the Small Business Administration (SBA) is detailed and complex, taking up 37 pages of SBA regulations. Most people think of a business as small if it has fewer than 500 employees. This general definition works fine, but the SBA further defines it by industry. Exhibit 6.2 gives a few examples of how the SBA defines small business for a sample of industries. It also illustrates the types of businesses most entrepreneurs start—retail, manufacturing, and service. Additional types of new small businesses are construction, agriculture, and wholesaling.

Impact of Entrepreneurial Companies

The impact of entrepreneurial companies on our economy is astonishing. According to the Internal Revenue Service, only about 16,000 businesses in the United States employ more than 500 people, and the majority employ fewer than 100. In addition, the 5.7 million U.S. businesses that have fewer than 100 employees generate 40 percent of the nation's output.[22] Small business formation is also at an all-time high. The U.S. Small Business Administration reports that 2.9 million companies were started between the years of 1989 and 1995.[23] Approximately 600,000 new businesses are started in the United States each year, and the status of the SBA administrator was recently elevated to a cabinet-level position in recognition of the importance of small business in the U.S. economy.[24] Many recent converts to entrepreneurship are corporate refugees (often middle management victims of corporate layoffs and downsizing) and corporate dropouts (those who prefer the uncertainty of self-employment to the corporate bureaucracy). In addition, growing numbers of executives are voluntarily leaving their big-company pay and perks at companies such as AT&T, IBM, and American Express to work for small start-up companies, citing the opportunity to do something new, creative, and exciting.[25]

Traditionally, new entrepreneurs most frequently start businesses in the areas of business services and restaurants. Today, inspired by the growth of companies such as Amazon.com, entrepreneurs are still flocking to the Internet to start new businesses. Demographic and lifestyle trends have created new opportunities in areas such as environmental services, children's markets, fitness, and home health care. Entrepreneurship and small business in the United States is an engine for job creation, innovation, and diversity.

Job Creation.   Researchers disagree over what percentage of new jobs is created by small business. Research has found that the *age* of a company, more than its size, determines the number of jobs it creates. That is, virtually *all* of the net new jobs in recent years have come from new companies, which includes not only small companies but also new branches of huge, multinational organizations. However, small companies still are thought to create a large percentage of new jobs. According to the U.S. Small Business Administration, small companies created 76.5 percent of net new jobs from 1990 to 1995 and 75.8 percent from 1996 to 1997.[26] Jobs created by small businesses give the United States an economic vitality no other country can claim.

Manufacturing	
Computer terminals and peripheral equipment	Number of employees does not exceed 1,000
Motor vehicle parts and accessories	Number of employees does not exceed 750
Apparel and footwear	Number of employees does not exceed 500
Retail	
Department stores	Average annual receipts do not exceed 20.0 million
Computer and software stores	Average annual receipts do not exceed 6.5 million
Sporting goods stores and bicycle shops	Average annual receipts do not exceed 5.0 million
Services	
Business consulting services	Average annual receipts do not exceed 5.0 million
Architectural services	Average annual receipts do not exceed 2.5 million
Building cleaning and maintenance	Average annual receipts do not exceed 12.0 million
Miscellaneous	
Book, magazine, or newspaper publishing	Number of employees does not exceed 1,000
Banks and credit unions	Has no more than $100 million in assets

Exhibit 6.2

Examples of SBA Definitions of Small Business

Innovation.   According to Cognetics, Inc., a research firm run by David Birch that traces the employment and sales records of some 9 million companies, new and smaller firms have been responsible for 55 percent of the innovations in 362 different industries and 95 percent of all radical innovations. In addition, fast-growing businesses, which Birch calls "gazelles," produce twice as many product innovations per employee as do larger firms. Among the notable products for which small businesses can be credited are cellophane, the jet engine, and the ballpoint pen. Virtually every new business represents an innovation of some sort, whether a new product or service, how the product is delivered, or how it is made.[27] Entrepreneurial innovation often spurs larger companies to try new things. Lamaur, Inc., created a new shampoo for permanent-waved hair. Soon three giant competitors launched similar products. Small-business innovation keeps U.S. companies competitive, which is especially important in today's global marketplace.

Diversity.   Entrepreneurship offers opportunities for individuals who may feel blocked in established corporations. Women-owned and minority-owned businesses may be the emerging growth companies of the next decade. There are approximately 9.1 million women-owned businesses that employ almost 30 million people and contribute $3.6 trillion to the U.S. economy.[28] Statistics for minorities are also impressive. Between 1987 and 1997, the number of Asian-owned companies in the United States increased a whopping 157 percent; Hispanic-owned businesses increased 144 percent. The number of black-owned businesses grew much slower, but still increased 27 percent over the 10 year period.[29] Exhibit 6.3 illustrates the growth of minority-owned businesses in the United States. Michael and Barbara Turney started Mama Turney's Pie Company in Nashville in the mid-1990s. Mama Turney's is an example of a successful black-owned business that builds on family traditions. Using recipes handed down from Michael Turney's mother has led to tremendous success for the company, which sells pies to numerous restaurants as well as through Kroger stores and in vending machines.[30]

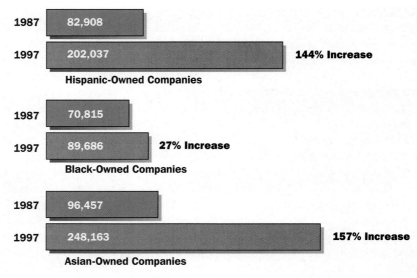

Exhibit 6.3

Growth of Minority-Owned Businesses in the United States, 1987–1997

SOURCES: U.S. Small Business Administration, Office of Advocacy, *Minorities in Business* (Washington, D.C.: U.S. Government Printing Office, 1999); SBA, Office of Advocacy, *The Facts about Small Business 1999*, reported in "Tomorrow's Self-Employed American," *Inc.* (State of Small Business 2001), 46–48.

NOTE: Includes only businesses that have employees.

Who Are Entrepreneurs?

The heroes of American business—Fred Smith, Spike Lee, Henry Ford, Sam Walton, Mary Kay Ash, Bill Gates, Michael Dell—are almost always entrepreneurs. Entrepreneurs start with a vision. Often they are unhappy with their current jobs and see an opportunity to bring together the resources needed for a new venture. However, the image of entrepreneurs as bold pioneers probably is overly romantic. A survey of the CEOs of the nation's fastest-growing small firms found that these entrepreneurs could be best characterized as hardworking and practical, with great familiarity with their market and industry.[31] For example, Bobby Frost worked 22 years in the mirror-manufacturing industry before leaving his employer. He started a mirror and glass fabrication business to use technology that his former employer refused to try and that Frost believed would work. It did. Eight years after its founding, Consolidated Glass & Mirror Corp. had 600 employees and $36 million in sales.

Personality Traits

A number of studies have investigated the personality characteristics of entrepreneurs and how they differ from successful managers in established organizations. Some suggest that entrepreneurs in general want something different from life than do traditional managers. Entrepreneurs seem to place high importance on being free to achieve and maximize their potential. Some 40 traits have been identified as associated with entrepreneurship, but 6 have special importance.[32] These characteristics are illustrated in Exhibit 6.4.

internal locus of control
The belief by individuals that their future is within their control and that external forces will have little influence.

Internal Locus of Control.   The task of starting and running a new business requires the belief that you can make things come out the way you want. The entrepreneur not only has a vision but also must be able to plan to achieve that vision and believe it will happen. An **internal locus of control** is the belief by individuals that their future is within their control and that external forces will have little influence. For entrepreneurs, reaching the future is seen as being

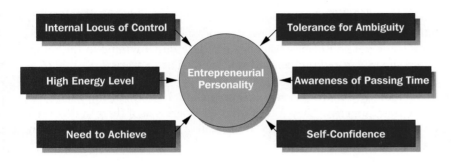

E x h i b i t **6.4**

Characteristics of Entrepreneurs

SOURCE: Adapted from Charles R. Kuehl and Peggy A. Lambing, *Small Business: Planning and Management* (Ft. Worth: The Dryden Press, 1994), 45.

in the hands of the individual. Many people, however, feel that the world is highly uncertain and that they are unable to make things come out the way they want. An **external locus of control** is the belief by individuals that their future is not within their control but rather is influenced by external forces. Entrepreneurs are individuals who are convinced they can make the difference between success and failure; hence they are motivated to take the steps needed to achieve the goal of setting up and running a new business.

external locus of control
The belief by individuals that their future is not within their control but rather is influenced by external forces.

High Energy Level. A business start-up requires great effort. Most entrepreneurs report struggle and hardship. They persist and work incredibly hard despite traumas and obstacles. A survey of business owners reported that half worked 60 hours or more per week. Another reported that entrepreneurs worked long hours, but that beyond 70 hours little benefit was gained. The data in Exhibit 6.5 show findings from a survey conducted by the National Federation of Independent Business. New business owners work long hours, with only 23 percent working fewer than 50 hours, which is close to a normal workweek for managers in established businesses.

Need to Achieve. Another human quality closely linked to entrepreneurship is the **need to achieve**, which means that people are motivated to excel and pick situations in which success is likely.[33] People who have high achievement needs like to set their own goals, which are moderately difficult. Easy goals present no challenge; unrealistically difficult goals cannot be achieved. Intermediate goals are challenging and provide great satisfaction when achieved. High achievers also like to pursue goals for which they can obtain feedback about their success.

need to achieve
A human quality linked to entrepreneurship in which people are motivated to excel and pick situations in which success is likely.

Self-Confidence. People who start and run a business must act decisively. They need confidence about their ability to master the day-to-day tasks of the

E x h i b i t **6.5**

Reported Hours per Week Worked by Owners of New Businesses

SOURCE: National Federation of Independent Business. Reported in Mark Robichaux, "Business First, Family Second," *The Wall Street Journal* (May 12, 1989), B1.

business. They must feel sure about their ability to win customers, handle the technical details, and keep the business moving. Entrepreneurs also have a general feeling of confidence that they can deal with anything in the future; complex, unanticipated problems can be handled as they arise.

Awareness of Passing Time.   Entrepreneurs tend to be impatient; they feel a sense of urgency. They want things to progress as if there is no tomorrow. They want things moving immediately and seldom procrastinate. Entrepreneurs "seize the moment."

Tolerance for Ambiguity.   Many people need work situations characterized by clear structure, specific instructions, and complete information. **Tolerance for ambiguity** is the psychological characteristic that allows a person to be untroubled by disorder and uncertainty. This is an important trait, because few situations present more uncertainty than starting a new business. Decisions are made without clear understanding of options or certainty about which option will succeed.

tolerance for ambiguity
The psychological characteristic that allows a person to be untroubled by disorder and uncertainty.

Demographic Factors

In addition to the six personality traits described so far, entrepreneurs often have background and demographic characteristics that distinguish them from other people. Entrepreneurs are more likely to be the first born within their families, and their parents are more likely to have been entrepreneurs. Children of immigrants also are more likely to be entrepreneurs, as are children for whom the father was absent for at least part of the childhood.[34]

Some research suggests that there are particular times during a person's career life cycle when the opportunities for entrepreneurship are particularly favorable. The two most obvious "windows of opportunity" are when a young person is just beginning a career and when a person is retiring from a career. Other windows present themselves along a continuum as a person grows in experience, industry knowledge, understanding of the marketplace, or financial ability. In addition, unplanned events such as the loss of a job, inheritance, or divorce may create opportunities for entrepreneurship. The important point is that entrepreneurship should be viewed as a career-long process, not something that has to be done at a certain time or age.[35]

In the past, most entrepreneurs launched their businesses between the ages of 25 and 40. Today, however, early retirement programs and corporate downsizing have created a whole new class of older entrepreneurs with high-level skills and years of experience. Many of these former managers have decided their chances are better in becoming entrepreneurs than in trying to reenter an overcrowded job market.[36] Today's successful entrepreneurs come in all ages and may have a combination of personality traits. No one should be discouraged from starting a business because he or she doesn't fit a specific profile. Michael Napoliello, Jr. and Jason Moskowitz launched their first business as college sophomores. While making summer plans at the Jersey Shore, they noticed that no newspaper catered to the numerous socially active young people. The two friends launched *The Wave*, a summer arts and entertainment publication that proved to be a huge hit. R.E. Coleberd, on the other hand, started his first business, Pacific West Oil Data, at the age of 51. Rumors of restructuring, downsizing, and potential layoffs, combined with his uncertainty about finding another job, convinced Coleberd to take the plunge. Now, he says he would pick cotton in Georgia before going back to work for a large corporation. "I have felt like a kid with a new red wagon ever since I started my business."[37]

Starting an Entrepreneurial Firm

The first step in pursuing an entrepreneurial dream is to start with a viable idea and plan like crazy. Once you have a new idea in mind, a business plan must be drawn and decisions must be made about legal structure, financing, and basic tactics, such as whether to start the business from scratch and whether to pursue international opportunities from the start.

New-Business Idea

To some people, the idea for a new business is the easy part. They do not even consider entrepreneurship until they are inspired by an exciting idea. Other people decide they want to run their own business and set about looking for an idea or opportunity. Exhibit 6.6 shows the most important reasons people start a new business and the source of new-business ideas. Note that 37 percent of business founders got their idea from an in-depth understanding of the industry, primarily because of past job experience. Interestingly, almost as many—36 percent—spotted a market niche that wasn't being filled.[38]

The trick for entrepreneurs is to blend their own skills and experience with a need in the marketplace. Acting strictly on one's own skills may produce something no one wants to buy. On the other hand, finding a market niche that you do not have the ability to fill does not work either. Both personal skill and market need typically must be present. Entrepreneur Roger Greene found a way to blend his skills and interests with a need in the marketplace to create a new kind of software company, as described in this chapter's Putting People First box.

The Business Plan

Once an entrepreneur is inspired by a new-business idea, careful planning is crucial. A **business plan** is a document specifying the business details prepared by an entrepreneur prior to opening a new business. Planning forces the entrepreneur to carefully think through all of the issues and problems associated with starting and developing the business. Most entrepreneurs

business plan
A document specifying the business details prepared by an entrepreneur prior to opening a new business.

E x h i b i t **6.6**

Sources of Entrepreneurial Motivation and New-Business Ideas

Reasons for Starting a Business

41%	Joined Family Business
36%	To Control My Future
27%	To Be My Own Boss
25%	To Fulfill a Dream
5%	Downsized/Laid Off

Source of New-Business Ideas

37%	In-depth Understanding of Industry/Profession
36%	Market Niche Spotted
7%	Brainstorming
4%	Copying Someone Else
4%	Hobby
11%	Other

SOURCES: "The Rewards," *Inc.* State of Small Business, 2001 (May 29, 2001), 50–51; and Leslie Brokaw, "How to Start an *Inc.* 500 Company," *Inc. 500* (1994), 51–65.

Putting People First

The Soft Touch Leads to Success at Ipswitch Software

In 1991, Roger Greene set out to use his skills and experience in software and the Internet to build a different kind of software company—one where he and his employees could live happy, balanced lives while producing innovative, low-cost products that would appeal to a broad market. Ipswitch, based in Lexington, Massachusetts, specializes in Windows-based software that makes the Internet and intranets accessible and manageable. In addition, the company is well known among programmers for its WS_FTP software that can move huge amounts of data across different computer platforms. Ipswitch has amassed a treasure trove of praise in the form of positive product reviews and awards, including *PC Magazine* Editors' Choice, *Internet Week* Approved, *Network Computing* Editors' Choice, and *VARBusiness* Editors' Choice.

In most software companies, employees work long hours under intense pressure to beat the competition. But Greene provides the foundation for high performance at Ipswitch by maintaining an easy-does-it attitude and a philosophy that puts employees ahead of profits. He is constantly encouraging people to take more personal days and vacation time. "A lot of people work really hard for 30 or 40 years and then they retire and try to do all the things they didn't do before," Greene says. "I'd much rather live life as it goes along and do neat things while you're working and enjoy every year of your life." To be sure employees have the time to "do neat things,"

Greene recently bumped up the three weeks' vacation time to five weeks—and he pushes people to take every minute of it. At Ipswitch, the idea of being a workaholic is downgraded, and no one ever gets rewarded for burning the midnight oil.

Ipswitch's worker-friendly environment is also reflected in other aspects of the workplace. For example, when an employee's boyfriend died, Greene hired a bereavement counselor to help her through the crisis. He believes people should be allowed to embrace the whole of human experience at work as well as in their personal lives. Greene's emphasis on treating people as whole human beings contributes directly to a low 9 percent turnover rate, roughly half the technology-company average. In addition, Greene and other managers have made a conscious decision to keep the organization small so people get to know one another on a more personal level. Betty Lang-Holmes, vice president of human resources, says, "I don't ever want to see a face here I don't know." The decision to stay small also means Ipswitch has been able to develop slowly and steadily rather than burning out because of the pressures of rapid growth.

Greene's formula of applying his skills to a market he understood, using a soft touch with employees, and plotting a slow and steady course for the future has led to success for Ipswitch and to better lives for many employees.

SOURCES: Based on Eleena DeLisser, "A Software Startup Attracts Staff with Ban on Midnight Oil," *The Wall Street Journal* (August 23, 2000), A1; and http://www.ipswitch.com, accessed on August 8, 2001.

have to borrow money, and a business plan is absolutely critical to persuading lenders and investors to participate in the business. Studies have shown that small businesses with a carefully thought out, written business plan are much more likely to succeed than those without one.[39]

The details of a business plan may vary, but successful business plans generally share several characteristics:[40]

- Demonstrate a clear, compelling vision that creates an air of excitement.
- Provide clear and realistic financial projections.
- Give detailed information about the target market.
- Include detailed information about the industry and competitors.
- Provide evidence of an effective entrepreneurial management team.
- Pay attention to good formatting and clear writing.
- Keep the plan short—no more than 50 pages long.
- Highlight critical risks that may threaten business success.
- Spell out the sources and uses of start-up funds and operating funds.
- Capture the reader's interest with a killer summary.

The business plan should indicate where the product or service fits into the overall industry and should draw on concepts that will be discussed throughout this book. For example, Chapter 8 will describe competitive strategies that entrepreneurs can use. Detailed suggestions for writing a business plan are provided in the Manager's Shoptalk box.

Legal Form

Before entrepreneurs have founded a business, and perhaps again as it expands, they must choose an appropriate legal structure for the company. The three basic choices are proprietorship, partnership, or corporation.

Sole Proprietorship.   A **sole proprietorship** is defined as an unincorporated business owned by an individual for profit. Proprietorships make up 70 percent of all businesses in the United States. This form is popular because it is easy to start and has few legal requirements. A proprietor has total ownership and control of the company and can make all decisions without consulting anyone. However, this type of organization also has drawbacks. The owner has unlimited liability for the business, meaning that if someone sues, the owner's personal as well as business assets are at risk. Also, financing can be harder to obtain because business success rests on one person's shoulders.

Partnership.   A **partnership** is an unincorporated business owned by two or more people. Partnerships, like proprietorships, are relatively easy to start. Two friends may reach an agreement to start a pet store. To avoid misunderstandings and to make sure the business is well planned, it is wise to draw up and sign a formal partnership agreement with the help of an attorney. The agreement specifies how partners are to share responsibility and resources and how they will contribute their expertise. The disadvantages of partnerships are the unlimited liability of the partners and the disagreements that almost always occur among strong-minded people. A poll by *Inc.* magazine illustrated the volatility of partnerships. Fifty-nine percent of respondents considered partnerships a bad business move, citing reasons such as partner problems and conflicts. Partnerships often dissolve within 5 years. Respondents who liked partnerships pointed to the equality of partners (sharing of workload and emotional and financial burdens) as the key to a successful partnership.[41]

Corporation.   A **corporation** is an artificial entity created by the state and existing apart from its owners. As a separate legal entity, the corporation is liable for its actions and must pay taxes on its income. Unlike other forms of ownership, the corporation has a legal life of its own; it continues to exist regardless of whether the owners live or die. And the corporation, not the owners, is sued in the case of liability. Thus, continuity and limits on owners' liability are two principal advantages of forming a corporation. For example, a physician can form a corporation so that liability for malpractice will not affect his or her personal assets. The major disadvantage of the corporation is that it is expensive and complex to do the paperwork required to incorporate the business and to keep the records required by law. When proprietorships and partnerships are successful and grow large, they often incorporate to limit liability and to raise funds through the sale of stock to investors.

sole proprietorship
An unincorporated business owned by an individual for profit.

partnership
An unincorporated business owned by two or more people.

corporation
An artificial entity created by the state and existing apart from its owners.

For Mark Begelman, millionaire and former president of Office Depot, financing his new business, MARS music product stores, involved raising $65 million. However, each of his 11 stores features a stage for impromptu performances, a fully functional recording studio, and music clinics on everything from drums to recording equipment, which raises the cost of opening a store to an estimated $1.2 million. Begelman envisions obtaining the financial resources to have 70 MARS outlets with revenues of more than $500 million by 2003.

©1999 Brian Smith

THE NEW WORKPLACE

Manager's Shoptalk

Helpful Hints for Writing the Business Plan

The Summary

- Make it no more than three pages.
- This is the most crucial part of your plan because it must capture the reader's interest.
- What, how, why, where, etc., must be summarized.
- Complete this part *after* the finished business plan has been written.

The Business Description Segment

- Name of the business.
- A background of the industry with history of the company (if any) should be covered here.
- The potential of the new venture should be described clearly.
- Any unique or distinctive features of the venture should be spelled out.

The Marketing Segment

- Convince investors that sales projections and competition can be met.
- Market studies should be used and disclosed.
- Identify target market, market position, and market share.
- Evaluate *all* competition and specifically cover why and how you will be better than the competitors.
- Identify all market sources and assistance used for this segment.
- Demonstrate pricing strategy, since your price must penetrate and maintain a market share to *produce profits*. Thus the lowest price is *not* necessarily the "best" price.
- Identify your advertising plans with cost estimates to validate the proposed strategy.

The Research, Design, and Development Segment

- Cover the *extent of* and *costs involved* in needed research, testing, or development.
- Explain carefully what has been accomplished *already* (prototype, lab testing, early development).
- Mention any research or technical assistance provided for you.

The Manufacturing Segment

- Provide the advantages of your location (zoning, tax laws, wage rates).
- List the production needs in terms of facilities (plant, storage, office space) and equipment (machinery, furnishings, supplies).
- Describe the access to transportation (for shipping and receiving).
- Explain proximity to your suppliers.
- Mention the availability of labor in your location.
- Provide estimates of manufacturing costs—be careful; too many entrepreneurs underestimate their costs.

The Management Segment

- Provide résumés of all key people in the management of the venture.
- Carefully describe the legal structure of the venture (sole proprietorship, partnership, or corporation).
- Cover the added assistance (if any) of advisers, consultants, and directors.
- Provide information on how everyone is to be compensated (how much, also).

The Critical-Risks Segment

- Discuss potential risks *before* investors point them out. Some examples follow:
  - Price cutting by competitors
  - Potentially unfavorable industry-wide trends
  - Design or manufacturing costs in excess of estimates
  - Sales projections not achieved
  - Product development schedule not met
  - Difficulties or long lead times encountered in the procurement of parts or raw materials
  - Larger-than-expected innovation and development costs to stay competitive
- Name alternative courses of action.

The Financial Segment

- Provide statements.
- Describe the needed sources for your funds and the uses you intend for the money.
- Provide a budget.
- Create stages of financing for the purpose of allowing evaluation by investors at various points.

The Milestone Schedule Segment

- Provide a timetable or chart to demonstrate when each phase of the venture is to be completed. This shows the relationship of events and provides a deadline for accomplishment.

SOURCE: Donald F. Kuratko, Ray V. Montagno, and Frank J. Sabatine, *The Entrepreneurial Decision* (Muncie, IN: The Midwest Entrepreneurial Education Center, Ball State University, 1997), 45–46. Reprinted with permission.

Financial Resources

A crucial concern for entrepreneurs is the financing of the business. An investment usually is required to acquire labor and raw materials and perhaps a building and equipment. The financing decision initially involves two options—whether to obtain loans that must be repaid (debt financing) or whether to share ownership (equity financing). A survey of successful growth businesses asked, "How much money was needed to launch the company?" Approximately one-third were started on less than $10,000, one-third needed from $10,000 to $50,000, and one-third needed more than $50,000. The primary source of this money was the entrepreneurs' own resources, but they often had to mortgage their homes, depend on credit cards, borrow money from the bank, or give part of the business to a venture capitalist.[42]

A major concern for entrepreneurs is securing funds through debt financing or equity financing. For example, to grow HeartWise, her healthy-fast-food business, into a nationwide chain, Rosemary Deahl must first obtain significant funding from bank loans and venture capitalists. Angel investors and noted Chicago restaurant consultants liked her concept of a restaurant serving high-quality, healthy fast food, but they questioned its national appeal. Finding money can be tough going, and venture capitalists could take more than 51 percent ownership, leading to a loss of control for the entrepreneur.

Debt Financing. Borrowing money that has to be repaid at a later date in order to start a business is **debt financing**. One common source of debt financing for a start-up is to borrow from family and friends. Another common source is a bank loan. Banks provide some 25 percent of all financing for small business. Sometimes entrepreneurs can obtain money from a finance company, wealthy individuals, or potential customers.

Another form of loan financing is provided by the Small Business Administration (SBA). The SBA supplies direct loans to some entrepreneurs who are unable to get bank financing because they are considered high risk. The SBA is especially helpful for people without substantial assets, providing an opportunity for single parents, minority group members, and others with a good idea. For example, in recent years the SBA has tripled the number of loans to women entrepreneurs.[43]

Equity Financing. Any money invested by owners or by those who purchase stock in a corporation is considered equity funds. **Equity financing** consists of funds that are invested in exchange for ownership in the company.

A **venture capital firm** is a group of companies or individuals that invests money in new or expanding businesses for ownership and potential profits. This is a potential form of capital for businesses with high earning and growth possibilities. For example, during 2000, venture capitalists invested $103 billion in 5,380 new companies. About 40 percent of those businesses were Internet-specific, but venture capitalists also invested heavily in communications, software, and services.[44] Venture capital firms want new businesses that have the potential for an extremely high rate of return. This is reflected in the amount of financing provided to Internet ventures over the past few years. Investment slowed dramatically during the latter part of 2000 when Internet companies by the scores began going out of business. Venture capitalists also usually provide assistance, advice, and information to help the entrepreneur prosper.

debt financing
Borrowing money that has to be repaid at a later date in order to start a business.

equity financing
Financing that consists of funds that are invested in exchange for ownership in the company.

venture capital firm
A group of companies or individuals that invests money in new or expanding businesses for ownership and potential profits.

Tactics

There are several ways an aspiring entrepreneur can become a business owner. These include starting a new business from scratch, buying an existing business, or starting a franchise. Another popular entrepreneurial tactic is to participate in a business incubator.

Start a New Business.   One of the most common ways to become an entrepreneur is to start a new business from scratch. This is exciting because the entrepreneur sees a need for a product or service that has not been filled before and then sees the idea or dream become a reality. Jennifer and Brian Maxwell, both long-distance runners, founded PowerBar Inc. to give athletes a snack bar that would provide quick energy but be easy to digest. Jennifer, who studied nutrition and food science at the University of California, hit on the idea after Brian told her of losing the London Marathon largely because of a case of stomach cramps.[45] The advantage of starting a business is the ability to develop and design the business in the entrepreneur's own way. The entrepreneur is solely responsible for its success. A potential disadvantage is the long time it can take to get the business off the ground and make it profitable. The uphill battle is caused by the lack of established clientele and the many mistakes made by someone new to the business. Moreover, no matter how much planning is done, a start-up is risky; there is no guarantee that the new idea will work.

Buy an Existing Business.   Because of the long start-up time and the inevitable mistakes, some entrepreneurs prefer to reduce risk by purchasing an existing business. This offers the advantage of a shorter time to get started and an existing track record. The entrepreneur may get a bargain price if the owner wishes to retire or has other family considerations. Moreover, a new business may overwhelm an entrepreneur with the amount of work to be done and procedures to be determined. An established business already has filing systems, a payroll tax system, and other operating procedures. Potential disadvantages are the need to pay for goodwill that the owner believes exists and the possible existence of ill will toward the business. In addition, the company may have bad habits and procedures or outdated technology, which may be why the business is for sale.

Buy a Franchise.   Franchising is perhaps the most rapidly growing path to entrepreneurship. The International Franchise Association reports that about 1,500 franchises do business through 320,000 franchise outlets in the United States. Franchises account for an estimated one-third of the nation's annual retail sales.[46] According to some estimates, franchises account for 1 out of every 12 businesses in the United States, and a franchise opens every eight minutes of every business day.[47] **Franchising** is an arrangement by which the owner of a product or service allows others to purchase the right to distribute the product or service with help from the owner. The franchisee invests his or her money and owns the business but does not have to develop a new product, create a new company, or test the market. The franchisee typically pays a flat fee plus a percentage of gross sales. Franchises exist for weight-loss clinics, pet-sitting services, sports photography, bakeries, janitorial services, auto repair shops, real estate offices, and numerous other types of businesses. Exhibit 6.7 lists the top 10 franchises in a recent year, based on financial strength and stability, growth rate, and size of the franchise system. The exhibit also shows the up-front fee required by each franchise. Fees typically range from $10,000 to $25,000, and that doesn't count the other start-up costs the entrepreneur will have to cover. A study by an economics professor found that the typical franchise costs $94,886 to open. For a company such as McDonald's, the cost is much higher, from about $400,000 to $500,000, depending on the restaurant location.[48]

franchising
An arrangement by which the owner of a product or service allows others to purchase the right to distribute the product or service with help from the owner.

Franchise	Number of Outlets	Year Founded	Up-Front Fee
1. Yogen Fruz Worldwide	4,722	1986	$25,000
2. McDonald's	16,319	1955	$45,000
3. Subway	13,395	1965	$10,000
4. Wendy's	4,032	1969	$25,000
5. Jackson Hewitt Tax Service	1,836	1960	$25,000
6. KFC	6,635	1930	$25,000
7. Mail Boxes, Etc.	3,655	1980	$29,950
8. TCBY Treats	2,913	1981	$5,000–$20,000
9. Taco Bell Corp.	2,927	1962	$45,000
10. Jani-King	7,038	1969	$6,500–$33,000

Exhibit **6.7**

Top Ten Franchises Based on Financial Strength, Growth Rate, and Size

SOURCE: *Entrepreneur* magazine, 1998, reported in Lisa Benavides, "Linking Up with a Chain," *The Tennessean* (April 6, 1999), 1E.

The powerful advantage of a franchise is that management help is provided by the owner. For example, Burger King does not want a franchisee to fail and will provide the studies necessary to find a good location. The franchisor also provides an established name and national advertising to stimulate demand for the product or service. Potential disadvantages are the lack of control that occurs when franchisors want every business managed in exactly the same way. In some cases, franchisors require that franchise owners use certain contractors or suppliers which may cost more than others would. In addition, franchises can be very expensive, and the high start-up costs are followed with monthly payments to the franchisor that can run from 2 percent to 15 percent of sales.

Entrepreneurs who are considering buying a franchise should investigate the company thoroughly. The prospective franchisee is legally entitled to a copy of franchisor disclosure statements, which include information on 20 topics, including litigation and bankruptcy history, identities of the directors and executive officers, financial information, identification of any products the franchisee is required to buy, and from whom those purchases must be made.[49] The entrepreneur also should talk with as many franchise owners as possible, since they are among the best sources of information about how the company really operates. Wild Birds Unlimited lists 26 questions on its Web site (*http://www.wbu.com*) that it recommends interested franchise applicants ask current franchisees. The Internet has become franchising's hottest marketing tool, but entrepreneurs should be aware that there are few rules about what the company must disclose over the Web. Not all companies are as above-board as Wild Birds Unlimited about exploring the potential downside of the franchise.[50] Exhibit 6.8 lists some specific questions entrepreneurs should ask about themselves and the company when considering buying a franchise. Answering such questions may improve the chances for a successful career as a franchisee.

Participate in a Business Incubator. An attractive innovation for entrepreneurs who want to start a business from scratch is to join a business incubator. The **business incubator** provides shared office space, management support services, and management advice to entrepreneurs. By sharing office space with other entrepreneurs, managers share information about local business, financial aid, and market opportunities.

business incubator
An innovation that provides shared office space, management support services, and management advice to entrepreneurs.

Questions about the Entrepreneur	Questions about the Franchisor	Before Signing on the Dotted Line
1. Will I enjoy the day-to-day work of this business?	1. What assistance does the company provide in terms of selection of location, set-up costs, and securing credit; day-to-day technical assistance; marketing; and ongoing training and development?	1. Do I understand the risks associated with this business, and am I willing to assume them?
2. Do my background, experience, and goals make this a good choice for me?	2. How long does it take the typical franchise owner to start making a profit?	2. Have I had an advisor review the disclosure documents and franchise agreement?
3. Am I willing to work within the rules and guidelines established by the franchisor?	3. How many franchises changed ownership within the past year, and why?	3. Do I understand all the terms of the contract?

E x h i b i t **6.8**

Sample Questions for Choosing a Franchise

SOURCES: Based on Thomas Love, "The Perfect Franchisee," *Nation's Business* (April 1998), 59–65; and Roberta Maynard, "Choosing a Franchise," *Nation's Business* (October 1996), 56–63.

This innovation arose two decades ago to nurture start-up companies. Business incubators have become a significant segment of the small business economy: the number of incubators nationwide jumped from 385 in 1990 to about 1,000 today.[51] Many of these are operated as not-for-profit organizations, including government agencies and universities, to boost the viability of small business and spur job creation. The big growth in more recent years, however, is in for-profit incubators in the United States, which jumped from only 24 in early 1999 to 213 by May 2000.[52] Spurred by dreams of dot-com riches and glory, ambitious entrepreneurs set up incubators to help other ambitious entrepreneurs start Internet-based companies. These high-profile incubators dominated headlines during the dramatic rise—and the even more dramatic fall—of the Internet market, and many of them are now going out of business. The incubators that are thriving are primarily not-for-profits and those that cater to niches or focus on helping women or minority entrepreneurs. The value of an incubator is the expertise of an in-house mentor, who serves as adviser, role model, and cheerleader. Incubators also give budding entrepreneurs a chance to network and learn from one another.[53]

Internet Start-Ups

As this textbook is being written, thousands of dot-com companies have crashed and technology stocks have taken a steep dive. Yet the Internet is still a growing part of our lives and businesses, and new companies are springing up every day. A well-known pet site, Pets.com, bombed but the SitStay GoOut Store (*http://www.sitstay.com*), a small company that sells upscale dog toys and supplies on the Web, is still pulling in profits.[54] Garden.com bit the dust, but Etera (*http://www.etera.com*), an online plant seller based in Mount Vernon, Washington, is thriving, selling $30 million worth of plants a year.[55] A study by *The Industry Standard* found that at least half of all business-to-consumer dot-com companies survived the e-commerce bloodbath of late 2000 and early 2001.[56] Just as with other small companies, many of the Internet companies being started now will fail, but many others will go on to become highly successful businesses. Small business formation is the primary process by which an economy recreates and reinvents itself,[57] and the huge bubble of Internet start-ups—and the turbulence they face—is evidence of a shifting but thriving U.S. economy.

Launching an Internet Business

Internet start-ups face many of the same challenges as other small businesses. However, they may also face some unique issues and problems. People starting traditional small businesses, such as a hair salon, day-care center, or local delicatessen, might be able to get started using their own savings, borrowing money from family and friends, and relying on credit cards. They might build their businesses slowly, starting with only a few clients and gradually building a larger clientele. If there are problems with products or services, they are solved as the entrepreneurs learn from experience. Entrepreneurs starting Internet companies, on the other hand, often need big money up front to build a technology infrastructure before they can even begin doing business. In addition, because the Internet world moves so swiftly, dot-com entrepreneurs might not have the luxury of building slowly and learning from experience. If the Web site crashes too often, for example, a company may be doomed—there are too many other options on the Web for visitors to give the company a second chance. There's little time for trial and error. All the kinks must be ironed out before the company puts its offering before the customer. In this section, we will examine what's involved in launching an Internet start-up, based on what is known about these companies so far.

Starting with the Idea. As with any small company, an entrepreneur has to have a viable idea for the business, and one that is appropriate to the fast-changing world of the Internet. Cache Flow Inc. started because the founders had an idea for a way to help customers access frequently used Web pages more quickly by providing local storage, or *caching*, of frequently used Internet data.[58] Research has found that the chances are only six in one million that an idea for a high-tech business eventually turns into a successful public company.[59] A good idea for an Internet company has to be one that can grow in scale and adapt quickly. Start-ups have the advantage of being nimble, but the idea itself must be one that is flexible enough to allow rapid adaptation as the environment changes. In addition, there should be innovative Web-based marketing techniques to promote the idea. For example, HotMail grew rapidly because every customer became a way to advertise the product to friends and colleagues.[60]

Writing the Business Plan. With the lightning-fast pace of the Internet, a traditional business plan is usually obsolete by the time it is written. Internet entrepreneurs have to create a compelling story about why their idea is the seed of the next big Internet success. The entrepreneur has to convince venture capitalists and potential employees to join in a risky adventure that has huge potential but few guarantees. The plan should cover eight basic points:

1. A description of the business and why it is unique

2. A profile of potential customers and market needs

3. The key ingredient of the business that will attract millions of customers

4. Why customers will come to this site rather than competitors

5. What the company has accomplished so far, including partnerships or early customer relationships

6. The entrepreneur's background and role in the company

7. Specific data about where the company is located, key management people, and contact information

8. Essential information about funding received so far, funding and staffing needs, and expectations for growth of the business over the next year.[61]

Note that many of these topics are also covered by a traditional business plan as described in the Shoptalk box earlier in this chapter. The key for the Internet start-up is to condense the essential information into a vivid, compelling story that can be told quickly and adapted quickly as the Internet world changes.

Getting Initial Financing.   A vivid story, told with passion and enthusiasm, is crucial to obtaining needed up-front financing. As with other small business start-ups, the entrepreneur relies on numerous sources, including family, friends, personal savings, and credit. However, Internet start-ups often need a large amount of funding just to get started. Forrester Research estimates that the cost to get a business up and running on the Web typically ranges from $2 million to $40 million.[62] One typical source of first funds is through **angel financing**. Angels are wealthy individuals, typically with business experience and contacts, who believe in the idea for the start-up and are willing to invest their personal funds to help the business get started. This first round of financing is extremely important. It can enable the entrepreneur to quit another job to devote time to building a foundation for the new company, filing for necessary permits or patents, hiring technical consultants, marketing the new product or service, and so forth. Significantly, angels also provide advice and assistance as the entrepreneur is developing the company. The entrepreneur wants angels who can make business contacts, help find talented employees, and serve as all-around advisors.

angel financing
Financing provided by a wealthy individual who believes in the idea for a start-up and provides personal funds and advice to help the business get started.

Building and Testing the Product or Service.   Once an entrepreneur has up-front financing, it is time to build and test the product. This stage may include hiring employees and consultants, buying or building the technological infrastructure, and perhaps securing office space or other needed facilities. Start-ups should also begin securing top-flight legal and financial assistance. The time to begin working with lawyers and bankers is early in the process, not after the company runs into trouble, needs specific legal or financial advice, or is ready to go public. Most experts agree, however, that the most critical hire in the early phases of the company is the system architect who can bring the entrepreneur's dream to life by putting together the hardware and software. Expert software engineers, Web site developers, product developers, and network administrators are also important to build the product or service and get it out to the public.[63] An indispensable part of this stage is making sure the idea and the basic technology to support it actually work.

Reliability is crucial in the world of e-business. For example, a string of crashes at eBay's Web site almost destroyed the company.[64] At one point, the site went down for more than 20 hours, leaving collectors as well as investors furious. EBay eventually hired a troubleshooter to make sure the problems never happened again, offering him a salary package that outstripped that of the CEO. Managers knew that having the technology right is a matter of life and death for an Internet-based company. Google's founders went through alpha and beta tests of their Web site before launching the official site, as described in this chapter's Leading Online box.

Launching the Company.   The launch phase is when the company's products and services are officially made available to the public over the Internet. Marketing is the most important focus at this stage of development. Internet start-ups cannot afford to take years to build a brand; they have to make a name for themselves virtually overnight.[65] A catchy logo and a visually appealing Web site are important in creating the "look" of the company. The name, if not yet selected, should be chosen with care or modified to give the company a distinctive personality that sticks in the mind of customers. For example, Ask.com, a Web site devoted to answering questions on just about anything, revised its brand name to Ask Jeeves, which proved to be a stroke of marketing genius.[66]

Hiring a competent public relations firm at this stage can help to create a buzz about the new company in the business community, which helps attract future investors as well as get the word out to customers. Just as important is creating buzz by building an interactive *community of customers* so that word about the new business spreads from person to person. Today's most popular Internet sites are those that give users a chance to share information about their common interests.[67]

Amazon.com encourages buyers or browsers to write online reviews of books for other customers and vote on how useful they find others' reviews. EBay members rate the quality of their buying and selling experiences with other members, and those ratings are aggregated into a symbol for each member that others can immediately recognize. Many members strive to develop a high status in the community by securing good ratings.[68] Other online features including chat rooms, message boards, and a customer newsletter have made eBay a round-the clock forum for people to share their passion for trading or for their various hobbies.[69] These community-building mechanisms work because people enjoy the chance to provide feedback and interact with others who share their interests.

Securing Additional Financing.   Almost every Internet start-up eventually has to secure further funding to support growth and expansion. The entrepreneur has to make sure salaries are paid, infrastructure is maintained, and marketing efforts are continued. In addition, as the company grows, it might need to add more staff, expand office space, or purchase new hardware and software to support growth. The most obvious source of funding at this stage is *venture capital*. As described earlier, venture capitalist firms are groups of companies or individuals that invest money in exchange for a stake in the company. For example, the top source of funding for Internet start-ups in 1999 was Softbank Venture Capital.[70] Another source of venture capital is large corporations that want to play an active role in the emerging Internet economy. Companies such as Microsoft, Cisco Systems, and Intel have invested huge sums in exchange for a stake in Internet start-ups. Many start-ups form a board of directors to lend a sense of stability and permanence to the new company and to help the business move to the next level. A board of directors can help the company stay focused on the core issues that will lead to success.[71]

Leading Online

Getting Google Right

Larry Page and Sergey Brin met in 1995 while they were doctoral candidates at Stanford University, where they decided to collaborate on a search engine initially called BackRub. After polishing their technology, in the summer of 1998 the two put their academic careers on hold to bet everything on the Internet search engine they renamed Google (*http://www.google.com*).

In the early days, Page and Brin worked out of a friend's garage, conducting hi-tech meetings around a ping-pong table. They knew the perfect way to improve their product would be through various *alpha* testing stages, with continuous testing, feedback, and refining. The Stanford University community proved to be the perfect testing ground in which Google could evolve. Through this testing, testing, and re-testing, Page and Brin were assured that the basic technology was solid enough to put before a wider public. However, they also wanted to do a further *beta* testing phase with the public before launching the official site. This beta phase gave much needed elbow room because it warned visitors that Google's technology was a work in progress. The company had to make sure its users knew the developers were "making things better not worse," as Page put it. Putting the search engine

before the public forced Google to grow with the Web and meet the needs of actual users. An added benefit was that it earned the company a loyal following among users who appreciated the chance to act as testers and shape how the site would work. Google has relied almost entirely on word-of-mouth advertising. People who used the site had such a good experience that they told others, helping Google's traffic grow from the thousands to the millions by the time the official site was launched in September of 1999.

Simplicity of design is a key to Google's success. For example, Google uses only text-based advertising, which makes for a less-cluttered look and faster loading. The goal is to get the user to an answer as quickly, simply, and accurately as possible. Although the company is working on the next generation of technologies that will broaden search capabilities and present information in fresh ways across multiple platforms, the founders emphasize that "Google's charge will forever be to ensure that every search is a find."

SOURCES: Larry Page and Sergey Brin, "Merits of a Beta Launch," *Business 2.0* (March 2000), 180; "When Larry Met Sergey," *http://www.up-mag.com/themag/feature1htm*, accessed on July 31, 2001; *http://www.google.com/press/overview.html*, accessed on July 31, 2001; and *http://www.google.com/press/milestones.html*, accessed on July 31, 2001.

Developing Partnerships.   Another role the board often plays is to help a start-up create alliances with other companies, which are critical to helping the business grow. Partnerships for Internet start-ups are generally of two types.[72] A start-up that primarily needs exposure and marketing assistance will partner with a larger, well-established company that can help the smaller firm gain rapid market awareness. The second type involves partnering with a company that assists in actual operations such as customer service, logistics, or warehousing and shipping, and involves electronic linkages between the partners. The company might outsource some functions to focus on core strategic issues. Shoebuy.com established strategic alliances with several established Internet shopping sites and e-tailers to keep its marketing costs low. In addition, the entire Shoebuy concept is based on close partnerships with shoe manufacturers who will drop-ship shoes directly to Shoebuy customers from their own warehouses.[73]

Going Public.   The final step in the start-up process is often the initial public offering (IPO), in which stock in the new company is sold to the public. The dream for many Internet entrepreneurs is to grow fast, go public, and get rich if the stock price increases. Although the "get rich quick" dreams have faded, the goal of most Internet entrepreneurs is to eventually take the company public and become a corporation rather than remain a sole proprietorship or partnership, as described earlier in this chapter. During this stage, the entrepreneur begins interviewing bankers who are interested in leading the IPO and puts together a team of bankers, lawyers, and other advisors who can steer the company through the process. The money generated from public investors can help grow the business further and help it become firmly established in its market.

Managing a Growing Business

Once an entrepreneurial business is up and running, how does the owner manage it? Often the traits of self-confidence, creativity, and internal locus of control lead to financial and personal grief as the enterprise grows. A hands-on entrepreneur who gave birth to the organization loves perfecting every detail. But after the start-up, continued growth requires a shift in management style. Those who fail to adjust to a growing business can be the cause of the problems rather than the solution.[74] In this section, we will look at the stages through which entrepreneurial companies move and then consider how managers should carry out their planning, organizing, leading, and controlling.

Stages of Growth

Entrepreneurial businesses go through distinct stages of growth, with each stage requiring different management skills. The five stages are illustrated in Exhibit 6.9.

1. *Start-up.* In this stage, the main problems are producing the product or service and obtaining customers. Key issues facing managers are: Can we get enough customers? Will we survive? Do we have enough money? Many Internet companies are still in the start-up stage, although a few, such as Amazon.com and Yahoo!, have progressed to survival and are moving toward the success stage of growth.

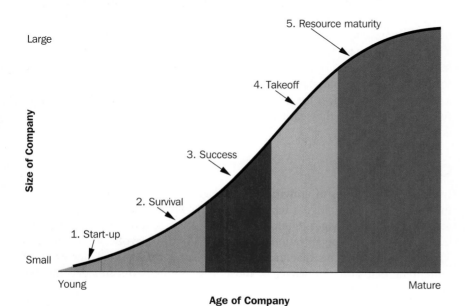

Exhibit 6.9

Five Stages of Growth for an Entrepreneurial Company

SOURCE: Based on Neil C. Churchill and Virginia L. Lewis, "The Five Stages of Small Business Growth," *Harvard Business Review* (May–June 1993), 30–50.

2. *Survival.* At this stage, the business has demonstrated that it is a workable business entity. It is producing a product or service and has sufficient customers. Concerns here have to do with finances—generating sufficient cash flow to run the business and making sure revenues exceed expenses. The organization will grow in size and profitability during this period.

3. *Success.* At this point, the company is solidly based and profitable. Systems and procedures are in place to allow the owner to slow down if desired. The owner can stay involved or consider turning the business over to professional managers.

4. *Takeoff.* Here the key problem is how to grow rapidly and finance that growth. The owner must learn to delegate, and the company must find sufficient capital to invest in major growth. This is a pivotal period in an entrepreneurial company's life. Properly managed, the company can become a big business. However, another problem for companies at this stage is how to maintain the advantages of "smallness" as the company grows.

5. *Resource maturity.* At this stage, the company has made substantial financial gains, but it may start to lose the advantages of small size, including flexibility and the entrepreneurial spirit. A company in this stage has the staff and financial resources to begin acting like a mature company with detailed planning and control systems.

Planning

In the early start-up stage, formal planning tends to be nonexistent except for the business plan described earlier in this chapter. The primary goal is simply to remain alive. As the organization grows, formal planning usually is not instituted until around the success stage. Recall from Chapter 1 that planning means defining goals and deciding on the tasks and use of resources needed to attain them. Chapters 7, 8, and 9 will describe how entrepreneurs can define goals and implement strategies and plans to meet them. It is important that entrepreneurs view their original business plan as a living document that evolves as the company grows or the market changes. Johann Verheem started a business called Application Technologies, which develops and licenses proprietary technology for packaging consumer products, based on a business plan he wrote as a student at San Diego State University. The professor gave the plan a B–, but he loved the concept and encouraged Verheem to take the plunge and start the business. Verheem and his student partner, now marketing manager for Application Technologies, kept shifting and fine-tuning their plans as they gathered input from venture capitalists, professors, and other experts.[75]

Organizing

In the first two stages of growth, the organization's structure is typically very informal with all employees reporting to the owner. At about stage 3—success—functional managers often are hired to take over duties performed by the owner. A functional organization structure will begin to evolve with managers in charge of finance, manufacturing, and marketing. During the latter stages of entrepreneurial growth, managers must learn to delegate and decentralize authority. If the business has multiple product lines, the owner may consider creating teams or divisions responsible for each line. The organization must hire competent managers and have sufficient management talent to handle fast growth and eliminate problems caused by increasing size. As an organization grows, it might also be characterized by greater use of rules, procedures, and written job descriptions. For example, Tara Cronbaugh started a small coffeehouse in a college town, but its success quickly led to the opening of three additional houses. With the rapid growth, Cronbaugh found that she needed a way to ensure consistency across operations. She decided to put together an operations manual with detailed rules, procedures, and job descriptions so managers and employees at each coffeehouse would be following the same pattern.[76] Chapters 10 through 14 will discuss organizing in detail.

©Linda Ford

Workplace Interiors LLC, a full-service office furniture dealership founded by husband-and-wife team Robert and Brooke Jones-Blomstrom (shown here with Robert's sister, Sally, in the middle), has grabbed the 11th spot on Entrepreneur *magazine's Hot 100 listing. Founded in 1999, Workplace Interiors has grown from first-year sales of $3.7 million to sales of $21 million. Although the business is successful, Workplace Interiors is still in the survival stage of growth. The owners know they still face significant challenges. They attribute their early success to effective leadership that gives employees recognition and support. "Our organization is the people," says Sally.*

Leading

The driving force in the early stages of development is the leader's vision. This vision, combined with the leader's personality, shapes corporate culture. The leader can signal cultural values of service, efficiency, quality, or ethics. Often entrepreneurs do not have good people skills but do have excellent task skills in either manufacturing or marketing. By the success stage of growth, the owner must either learn to motivate employees or bring in managers who can. Rapid takeoff is not likely to happen without employee cooperation.

Stepping from the self-absorption of the early days of a company to the more active communication necessary for growth can be tricky for entrepreneurs. Charles Barnard, the owner of Foot Traffic, a chain of specialty sock stores based in Kansas City, Missouri, believes leaders should focus on communication as a company grows. "A lot of the time," Barnard says, "you get to running real fast, and you don't think about the people around you. But you can never get anywhere if you're pulling your staff around behind you all the time."[77] The president of Foreign Candy Company of Hull, Iowa, saw his company grow rapidly when he concentrated more on employee needs and less on financial growth. He made an effort to communicate with employees, conducted surveys to learn how they were feeling about the company, and found ways to involve them in decision making. His leadership style allowed the company to enter the takeoff stage with the right corporate culture and employee attitudes to sustain rapid growth.

Leadership also is important because many small firms have a hard time hiring qualified employees. Labor shortages often hurt small firms that grow rapidly. A healthy corporate culture can help attract and retain good people.[78] You will learn more about leadership in Chapters 15 through 19.

Controlling

Financial control is important in each stage of the entrepreneurial firm's growth. In the initial stages, control is exercised by simple accounting records and by personal supervision. By stage 3—success—operational budgets are in place, and the owner should start implementing more structured control systems. During the takeoff stage, the company will need to make greater use of budgets and standard cost systems and use computer systems to provide statistical reports. These control techniques will become more sophisticated during the resource maturity stage.

As Amazon.com has grown and expanded internationally, entrepreneur and CEO Jeff Bezos has found a need for increasingly sophisticated control mechanisms. For example, as the company struggled to standardize procedures and achieve profitability, Bezos hired a computer systems expert to develop a system to track and control all of the company's operations.[79] Control will be discussed further in Chapters 20 through 22.

■ Summary and Management Solution

This chapter explored entrepreneurship and small-business management. Entrepreneurs start new businesses, and entrepreneurship plays an important role in the economy by stimulating job creation, innovation, and opportunities for minorities and women. An entrepreneurial personality includes the traits of internal locus of control, high energy level, need to achieve, tolerance for ambiguity, awareness of passing time, and self-confidence.

Starting an entrepreneurial firm requires a new-business idea. At that point a comprehensive business plan should be developed and decisions made about legal structure and financing. Tactical decisions for the new venture include whether to start, buy, or franchise, and whether to participate in a business incubator.

A new kind of small business is the Internet start-up. These companies face the same challenges as other small businesses, but Internet entrepreneurs also encounter some unique issues. Based on what is known about Internet start-ups, entrepreneurs typically follow eight steps: 1) formulating the idea and concept for the company; 2) developing a business plan and a "story" to sell the idea; 3) securing up-front financing; 4) building and testing the product and service; 5) officially launching the Web site; 6) obtaining additional financing; 7) developing partnerships with other organizations; and 8) perhaps taking the company public through an initial public offering.

After a business is started, it generally proceeds through five stages of growth—start-up, survival, success, takeoff, and resource maturity. The management functions of planning, organizing, leading, and controlling should be tailored to each stage of growth.

Most Internet companies, including DVD Empire, described at the beginning of the chapter, are still in the start-up stage. In addition, DVD Empire might be considered to be at the "launch" step of Internet start-ups. The two founders, Jeff Rix and John-Michael D'Arcangelo, had a good idea and were able to use a solid technology infrastructure that had been built and tested within a successful, well-established company (Rix's father's business, Pro-Am Safety). Thus, they were able to start their business using only personal and family funds. The two also benefited from the elder Rix's business experience. He advised caution about the "get-big-fast" Internet mindset. The entrepreneurs have chosen to build slowly and steadily, continuing to invest in infrastructure to ensure that the site and their operations are reliable so customers will keep coming back. Now they are at step 5—securing additional financing to support growth. Although the founders have no current plans to court venture capital funding, it is likely they will have to do so as they seek to expand their product offerings and customer base. They might also find a need to develop partnerships with other companies to keep the business growing and thriving. Will DVD Empire continue to grow and succeed, or will it be another small-business casualty? Time will tell. So far, Rix and D'Arcangelo are off to a good start.

Discussion Questions

1. Dan McKinnon started an airline with one airplane. To do so required filing more than 10,000 pages of manuals, ordering 50,000 luggage tags, buying more than $500 million in insurance, and spending more than $300,000 to train employees. A single inspection test cost $18,000. Evaluate whether you think this is a good entrepreneurial opportunity, and discuss why you think Dan McKinnon undertook it.

2. What do you think are the most important contributions of small business to our economy?

3. Why would small-business ownership have great appeal to immigrants, women, and minorities?

4. Consider the six personality characteristics of entrepreneurs. Which two traits do you think are most like those of managers in large companies? Which two are least like those of managers in large companies?

5. Why is purchasing an existing business or franchise less risky than starting a new business?

6. If you were to start a new business, would you have to search for an idea, or do you already have an idea to try? Explain.

7. Many entrepreneurs say they did little planning, perhaps scratching notes on a legal pad. How is it possible for them to succeed?

8. What is the difference between debt financing and equity financing? What are common sources of each type?

9. How does an entrepreneurial firm in the start-up stage differ from one in the success stage?

10. How does starting an online business differ from starting a small business such as a local auto repair shop or delicatessen? What is the role of alliances and partnerships in online versus traditional small businesses?

11. How might the management functions of planning and controlling differ for an online business as compared to a traditional business?

Management in Practice: Experiential Exercise

What's Your Entrepreneurial IQ?

Rate yourself on the following 15 behaviors and characteristics, according to the following scale.

1 = Strongly disagree   2 = Disagree   3 = Agree   4 = Strongly agree

_____ 1. I am able to translate ideas into concrete tasks and outcomes.

_____ 2. When I am interested in a project, I tend to need less sleep.

_____ 3. I am willing to make sacrifices to gain long-term rewards.

_____ 4. Growing up, I was more of a risk-taker than a cautious child.

_____ 5. I often see trends, connections, and patterns that are not obvious to others.

_____ 6. I have always enjoyed spending much of my time alone.

_____ 7. I have a reputation for being stubborn.

_____ 8. I prefer working with a difficult but highly competent person to working with someone who is congenial but less competent.

_____ 9. As a child, I had a paper route, lemonade stand, or other small enterprise.

_____ 10. I usually keep New Year's resolutions.

_____ 11. I'm not easily discouraged, and I persist when faced with major obstacles.

_____ 12. I recover quickly from emotional setbacks.

_____ 13. I would be willing to dip deeply into my "nest egg"—and possibly lose all I had saved—to go it alone.

_____ 14. I get tired of the same routine day in and day out.

_____ 15. When there is something I want, I keep the goal clearly in mind.

Scoring: Total your score for the 15 items. If you tallied 50–60 points, you have a very strong entrepreneurial IQ. A score of 30–50 indicates good entrepreneurial possibilities. Your chances of starting a successful entrepreneurial business are good if you have the desire and motivation. If you scored below 30, you probably do not have much entrepreneurial potential.

Go back over each question, thinking about changes you might make to become more or less entrepreneurial, depending on your career interests.

■ Management in Practice: Ethical Dilemma

As the new, heavily recruited CEO of an Internet start-up backed by several of Silicon Valley's leading venture capitalists, Chuck Campbell is flying high—great job, good salary, stock options, and a chance to be in on the ground floor and build one of the truly great e-commerce organizations. Just a few days into the job, Chuck helped make a presentation to a new group of potential investors for funding that could help the company expand marketing, improve its services, and invest in growth. By the end of the meeting, the investors had verbally committed $15 million in funding.

But things turned sour pretty fast. As Chuck was leaving around 9 P.M., the corporate controller, Betty Mars, who has just returned from an extended leave, cornered him. He was surprised to find her working so late, but before he could even open his mouth, Betty blurted out her problem: The numbers Chuck had presented to the venture capitalists were flawed. "The assumptions behind the revenue growth plan are absolutely untenable," she said. "Not a chance of ever happening." Chuck was stunned. He told Betty to get on home and he'd stay and take a look at the figures.

At 11 P.M., Chuck was still sitting in his office wondering what to do. His research showed that the numbers were indeed grossly exaggerated, but most of them were at least statistically possible (however remote that possibility was!). However, what really troubled him was that the renewal income figure was just flat-out false—and it was clear that one member of the management team who participated in the presentation knew this all along. To make matters worse, it was the renewal income figure that ultimately made the investment so attractive to the venture capital firm. Chuck knew what was at stake—no less that the life or death of the company itself. If he told the truth about the deceptive numbers, the company's valuation would almost certainly be slashed and the $15 million possibly canceled.

What Do You Do?

1. Say nothing about the false numbers. Of course, the company will miss the projections and have to come up with a good explanation, but, after all, isn't that par for the course among fledgling e-businesses? Chances are the whole thing will blow over without a problem.

2. Go ahead and close the deal, but come clean later. Explain that the controller had been on an extended leave of absence and, because you had been on the job only a few days you had not had time to personally do an analysis of the numbers.

3. Take swift action to notify the venture capitalists of the truth of the situation—and start cleaning house to get rid of people who would knowingly lie to close a deal.

SOURCE: Adapted from Kent Weber, "The Truth Could Cost You $16 Million," *Business Ethics* (March–April 2001), 18.

■ Surf the Net

1. **Do You Have What It Takes?** Have you ever thought about starting your own business where you could be your own boss? Although there are many appealing aspects to starting your own business, you need to consider all aspects of being an entrepreneur carefully. The following sites will give you a balanced perspective of what it will take for you to be successful in starting your own business. After completing the self-assessment at one of these sites, be prepared to explain why the results suggest you either are or are not suited to fill the role of an entrepreneur.
   http://www.liraz.com/webquiz.htm;
   http://www.bondbusiness.co.za/Entrepreneurship%20 Checklist.htm
   http://www.beina.com/quiz.html

2. **SBA.** The U.S. Small Business Administration is "America's Small Business Resource." Visit the SBA's home page at *http://www.sba.gov*, list three links from the home page that you believe provided the most helpful or interesting information, and briefly explain what you found at each of the three links.

3. **Business Incubators.** The National Business Incubation Association, the world's leading organization advancing business incubation and entrepreneurship, provides a wealth of information about business incubation. Learn more by going to the NBIA Web site at *http:// www.nbia.org*.

   Find out where the incubators are located in your state or another state assigned by your instructor. Print out the page describing the state's incubators and bring it to class.

■ Case for Critical Analysis

Radiata Software

The founders of one of the hottest young software companies of the decade were meeting in Rob Larson's den to decide what to do. Radiata Software, founded by the three friends right after they graduated from college, makes financial software targeted to small professional service firms. Radiata had been an instant hit among solo professionals such as accountants and financial planners, as well as among small businesses that did not have the resources and equipment to run big, complex software programs. With a solid customer base, Radiata has been able to expand its product line and add a Web site providing customers with an all-in-one site for small business accounting and finance. One of the most popular features of the site is the electronic bulletin boards where solo professionals trade comments, seek advice, and share their stories of what it's like to be a free agent.

But Radiata's success had also come with some problems. Rapid growth left the founders struggling to keep pace with managing staff, handling development of new products and services, marketing, negotiating contracts, and so forth. Rob, who had come up with the idea for the company, served as CEO, and the other founders each had specific titles and duties, but all three were involved in essentially every aspect of the business. Whenever a major decision had to be made, they made it together, often after hours or days talking with one another to reach an agreement. Eventually, Susan Boyd, a representative from the venture capital firm that was Radiata's biggest source of funds, suggested they needed to bring in professional managers to help run the place. "You'll still have plenty of say in running the business," she said. "But after six years, Radiata is getting too big to manage as an entrepreneurial start-up. You need some professional help to take things to the next level." The founders agreed she was right, and Susan quickly recruited a chief operating officer, a chief information officer, and a chief financial officer to help Radiata through its growing pains. The three brought a tremendous wealth of knowledge and experience to the young company, and everyone seemed sure Radiata would grow even faster and be even more successful with a solid management team behind it.

"So, what went wrong?" Rob asks his co-founders now, after six months of working with the new management team. From the beginning, the three founders and the three new managers had seemed to segregate into two separate camps. The founders had been friends since their freshman year in college, had lived together until the last couple of years, and still partied together on the weekends. It came naturally for them to get together separately from the three newcomers and talk about the business, how the new managers were doing, and so forth. Feeling left out, the three seasoned managers gradually began turning to one another more and more, ignoring the younger trio. Although in the beginning the team of six had vowed to have regular Monday morning meetings, the meetings often got canceled for one reason or another. In addition, over time it became clear to the new managers that the three founders had already met and discussed issues prior to the formal meeting, so the three new managers began doing the same. By now, there were clearly two separate teams trying to run Radiata. Tomorrow, the group will be discussing whether to merge with a larger software company. "They'll swallow us," said Jessie. "Our dream of running our own business will be dead."

"Ha!" barked Thai. "You think it's not already dead? I expect our "dream team" of senior managers are holed up somewhere right now discussing their strategy. They want this deal to go through, and you know they've got Susan in their back pocket. Who do you think is in charge of this company these days?"

"Look," said Rob. "We have to accept that a lot of this is our fault. It's always been us against them. We never made any effort to really make them a part of the company and share our ideas and vision with them. Almost every day, we find some way to meet without them and make some decision behind their backs—like when we signed that partnership agreement with an accounting services firm without even talking to them about it. It was an innocent mistake, but it clearly didn't sit well. Now they're meeting without us and maybe wanting to take the company in a direction we don't want to go. Also, I heard from our venture capital rep that our CIO is thinking of jumping ship. She's frustrated and miserable here, feels like she's spinning her wheels and wasting her time. If that happens, I don't think Susan and the venture capital team are going to be very happy. If we lose them, we're in serious trouble. Is there any way to get out of this mess?"

Questions

1. What is the underlying cause of the problems at Radiata? Can you think of ways to bring the two sides together and get the company back on the right track?
2. What management functions seem to be needed most at this point—planning, organizing, leading, or controlling? Discuss.
3. What do you think the founders need to do in this situation? What do you think the three new managers should do?

SOURCE: Based on Regina Fazio Maruca, "Entrepreneurs versus Executives at Socaba.com," *Harvard Business Review* (July–August 2000), 30–38.

■ Endnotes

1. Christopher Caggiano, "Net Flix," *Inc. Tech*, No. 1 (2001), 38–41.

2. John Case, "Where We Are Now," *Inc.,* State of Small Business 2001 (May 29, 2001), 18–19.

3. Reported in Christina Le Beau, "Kick in the Pants," *The Wall Street Journal* (May 14, 2001), R8.

4. Donald F. Kuratko and Richard M. Hodgetts, *Entrepreneurship: A Contemporary Approach*, 4th ed. (Fort Worth: The Dryden Press, 1998), 30.

5. Karen Dillon, "Three Women and a Kiosk," *Inc.* (January 2000), 60–62.

6. Study conducted by Yankelovich Partners, reported in Mark Henricks, "Type-Cast," *Entrepreneur* (March 2000), 14–16.

7. Christina Le Beau, "Kick in the Pants," *The Wall Street Journal* (May 14, 2001), R8.

8. Ibid.

9. Hilary Stout, "Start Low," *The Wall Street Journal* (May 14, 2001), R8.

10. Statistics from the Small Business Administration and the National Foundation for Women Business Owners, reported in "Tomorrow's Self-Employed American," *Inc.,* State of Small Business 2001 (May 29, 2001), 46–48.

11. Kathleen Collins, "¡La Vida Próspera! Latin-Owned Businesses Explode," *Working Woman* (October 2000), 13.

12. National Urban League, *http://www.nul.org.* Statistics also reported in Gina Holland, "Black America," Associated Press story, *The Johnson City Press* (July 22, 2001), 6.

13. Reported in John Case, "Counting Companies," *Inc.,* State of Small Business 2001 (May 29, 2001), 21–23.

14. Based on information in "Market Share," *Inc.* State of Small Business 2001 (May 29, 2001), 25–26; and "The Soloists," *Inc.,* State of Small Business 2001 (May 29, 2001), 37–39.

15. This section is based on John Case, "The Wonderland Economy," *The State of Small Business* (1995), 14–29; and Richard L. Daft, *Management*, 3d ed. (Fort Worth, Texas: The Dryden Press, 1992).

16. U. S. Census Bureau, 1997 Economic Census: Nonemployer Statistics, reported in "The Soloists," *Inc.* State of Small Business 2001 (May 29, 2001), 37–39.

17. George Mannes, "Don't Give Up on the Web," Fortune Small Business section, *Fortune* (March 5, 2001), 184[B]–184[L].

18. Ibid.

19. Paul Korzeniowski, "Jumpin' Juniper," *Business2.Com* (May 15, 2001), 24–25.

20. Jane Shealy, "Designing Women," *Success* (July/August 2000), 52–53.

21. Marc Ballon, "Start-up Mambos to Beat of Booming Market," *Inc.,* September 1997, 23; and Collins, "¡La Vida Próspera!"

22. Bill Meyers, "Worker Shortage Forces Small Businesses into Creative Hiring," *USA Today* (October 30, 1998), 1B, 2B.

23. Reported in Gene Koretz, "Cycles of Death and Rebirth," *BusinessWeek* (November 16, 1998), 26.

24. Barbara Benham, "Big Government, Small Business," *Working Woman* (February 2001), 24.

25. Jerry Useem, "The New Entrepreneurial Elite," *Inc.* (December 1997), 50–68.

26. Research and statistics reported in "The Job Factory," *Inc.* State of Small Business 2001 (May 29, 2001), 40–43.

27. Kuratko and Hodgetts, *Entrepreneurship: A Contemporary Approach*, 4th ed., 11; and "100 Ideas for New Businesses," *Venture* (November 1988), 35–74.

28. Benham, "Big Government, Small Business."

29. Reported in "Tomorrow's Self-Employed American," *Inc.,* State of Small Business 2001 (May 29, 2001), 46–48.

30. Lisa Benavides, "Success Easy as Pie," *The Tennessean* (November 2, 1997), 3E.

31. John Case, "The Origins of Entrepreneurship," *Inc.* (June 1989), 51–63.

32. This discussion is based on Charles R. Kuehl and Peggy A. Lambing, *Small Business: Planning and Management*, 3d ed. (Ft. Worth: The Dryden Press, 1994).

33. David C. McClelland, *The Achieving Society* (New York: Van Nostrand, 1961).

34. Robert D. Hisrich, "Entrepreneurship-Intrapreneurship," *American Psychologist* (February 1990), 209–222.

35. Michael Harvey and Rodney Evans, "Strategic Windows in the Entrepreneurial Process," *Journal of Business Venturing* 10 (1995), 331–347.

36. "Downsized Chickens Come Home to Roost," *Managing Office Technology*, January 1994, 68.

37. Ron MacLean, "Big Manager on Campus," *Inc. 500* (1999), 62–66; R. E. Coleberd, "The Business Economist at Work: The Economist as Entrepreneur," *Business Economics* (October, 1994), 54–57.

38. Leslie Brokaw, "How to Start an *Inc.* 500 Company," *Inc. 500* 1994, 51–65.

39. Paul Reynolds, "The Truth about Start-ups," *Inc.* (February 1995), 23; Brian O'Reilly, "The New Face of Small Business," *Fortune* (May 2, 1994) 82–88.

40. Based on Linda Elkins, "Tips for Preparing a Business Plan," *Nation's Business* (June 1996), 60R–61R; Carolyn M. Brown, "The Do's and Don'ts of Writing a Winning Business Plan," *Black Enterprise* (April 1996), 114–116; and Kuratko and Hodgetts, *Entrepreneurship*, 4th ed., 295–297. For a clear, thorough step-by-step guide to writing an effective business plan, see Linda Pinson and Jerry Jinnett, *Anatomy of a Business Plan*, 5th ed. (Virginia Beach, Va: Dearborn, 2001).

41. The INC. FAXPOLL, *Inc.* (February 1992), 24.

42. "Venture Capitalists' Criteria," *Management Review* (November 1985), 7–8.

43. Benham, "Big Government, Small Business."

44. Statistics from Venture Economics and Venture Capital Association, reported in "Cash Flow," *Inc.* State of Small Business 2001, 76–77.

45. Jennifer Maxwell profile in Betsy Wiesendanger, "Labors of Love," *Working Woman* (May 1999), 43–56.

46. Small Business Administration statistics, reported in Henry Weil, "Business in a Box," *Working Woman* (September 1999), 59–64.

47. Echo Montgomery Garrett, "The Twenty-First-Century Franchise," *Inc.* (January 1995), 79–88; Lisa Benavides, "Linking Up with a Chain," *The Tennessean* (April 6, 1999), 1E.

48. Weil, "Business in a Box."

49. Roberta Maynard, "Choosing a Franchise," *Nation's Business* (October 1996), 56–63.

50. Richard Gibson, "Richard Gibson on Franchising: Make Sure to Read Between the Web Lines," *The Wall Street Journal* (May 14, 2001), R12.

51. Dale Buss, "Bringing New Firms Out of Their Shell," *Nation's Business* (March 1997), 48–50; and Amy Oringel, "Sowing Success," *Working Woman* (May 2001), 72.

52. Harvard Business School statistics, reported in Kimberly Weisul, "Incubators Lay an Egg," *BusinessWeek Frontier* (October 9, 2000), F14.

53. Oringel, "Sowing Success."

54. Jill Hecht Maxwell, "Sit! Stay! Make Money! Good Company!," *Inc. Tech* No. 1 (2001), 43–44.

55. Miguel Helft, "Dot-Com Survivors," *The Industry Standard* (July 9–16, 2001), 30–39.

56. Ibid.

57. John Case, "Who's Looking at Start-Ups?" *Inc.*, State of Small Business 2001 (May 29, 2001), 60.

58. Suzanne McGee, "CacheFlow: The Life Cycle of a Venture-Capital Deal," *The Wall Street Journal* (February 22, 2000), C1.

59. Reported in "Did You Know?" sidebar in J. Neil Weintraut, "Told Any Good Stories Lately?" *Business 2.0* (March 2000), 139–140.

60. Steve Jurvetson and Andreas Stavropoulos, "Does Your Idea Make Sense?" *Business 2.0* (March 2000), 138–139.

61. J. Neil Weintraut, "Told Any Good Stories Lately?" *Business 2.0* (March 2000), 139–140.

62. Reported in H. M. Dietel, P. J. Dietel, and K. Steinbuhler, *e-Business and e-Commerce for Managers* (Upper Saddle River, NJ: Prentice Hall, 2001), 58.

63. Jeff Green, "Employees by the Round," *Business 2.0* (March 2000), 168–169.

64. Julie Pitta, "Webb Master," *Forbes* (December 13, 1999), 322–324.

65. This section is based on Glen Rifkin and Ken Lambert, "Marketing Your Startup," *Business 2.0* (March 2000), 181–184.

66. Clay Timon, "10 Tips for Naming," *Business 2.0* (March 2000), 151–152.

67. Queena Sook Kim, "People Like Us," *The Wall Street Journal* (February 12, 2001), R34.

68. Katherine Mieszkowski, "Community Standards," *Fast Company* (September 2000), 368+.

69. Rosabeth Moss Kanter, "A More Perfect Union," *Inc.* (February 2001), 92–98.

70. Bob Kagle, "The VC Meeting," *Fast Company* (March 2000), 147–148.

71. Bruce Golden, "Forming a Board," *Fast Company* (March 2000), 171.

72. Wendy Lea, "Dancing with a Partner," *Fast Company* (March 2000), 159–161.

73. Christopher Caggiano, "E-tailing by the Numbers," *Inc. Tech* No. 1, (2001), 46–49.

74. Carrie Dolan, "Entrepreneurs Often Fail as Managers," *The Wall Street Journal* (May 15, 1989), B1.

75. Michael Warshaw, "Plan B-minus," *Inc.* (January 2000), 56–58.

76. Amanda Walmac, "Full of Beans," *Working Woman* (February 1999), 38–40.

77. Michael Barrier, "The Changing Face of Leadership," *Nation's Business* (January 1995), 41–42.

78. Udayan Gupta and Jeffrey A. Tannenbaum, "Labor Shortages Force Changes at Small Firms," *The Wall Street Journal* (May 22, 1989), B1, B2; "Harnessing Employee Productivity," *Small Business Report* (November 1987), 46–49; and Molly Klimas, "How to Recruit a Smart Team," *Nation's Business* (May 1995), 26–27.

79. Saul Hansell, "Listen Up! It's Time for a Profit: A Front Row Seat as Amazon Gets Serious," *The New York Times* (May 20, 2001), Section 3, 1.

Chapter 3: Fallon Worldwide: Can Its Corporate Culture Be a Soul Survivor?

WHEN A CORPORATE GIANT TAKES OVER A SMALLER FIRM, the question everyone asks is, What will happen to the culture of the small company? Will the quirks, the flexibility, and the creativity of the small fish be swallowed by the larger fish? When Paris-based Publicis Group SA announced its acquisition of Minneapolis-based advertising agency Fallon Worldwide, the worry was on every manager's, staffer's, and client's mind. "One of my greatest fears was that our people would think we sold out," recalls Pat Fallon, founder and chairman of the company. "People were worried that we would become more corporate and less like the home they knew. And if people feel as if a bond has been broken, then everything is up for grabs." Fallon Worldwide had always been known for its high-energy, creative culture. People who worked there loved the atmosphere. Clients enjoyed Fallon's cozy, quirky, sometimes outrageous spirit. "It was a time of uncertainty," says Anne Bologna, planning director of Fallon's Minneapolis office. "There was this sense that we no longer had the freedom to be entrepreneurs." So Bologna made a call to action throughout the agency for new ideas. What began as hallway chatfests turned into a full-scale company initiative bent on preserving Fallon's culture.

"People wanted proof that the soul of the company wasn't going to change," recalls Rob White, co-president of Fallon. "We had to show them that the acquisition [by Publicis] was a strategic move to help us achieve very ambitious goals that we probably couldn't achieve on our own." That was the catch: Fallon founders had to find a way to mesh the driving force of their company—its high level of energy, its creative spirit—with an external environment that included a sluggish economy, fierce competitors, and a new boss. "Staying energized is the only way to survive," insists Anne Bologna. "In a down economy, creativity as currency is needed more than ever." So, if Fallon could enhance its already-existing culture, the company might not just survive but actually thrive under the umbrella of Publicis. During the year after Bologna's initial call for new ideas, the agency launched Fallonet, an intranet that allows the free-flow of ideas, humor, and challenges. Fallon also established an interactive consulting group as a full-fledged company division.

One employee who took Anne Bologna's directive seriously was John King, a young media planner. He proposed a new program called Dream Catchers, in which Fallon would assist employees in funding their own "impossible" dreams, thus fueling their creativity. Employees who wanted to participate simply decided how much they wanted to deduct from their paychecks on a regular basis to set aside for their "dream" sabbatical. Fallon then matched their deductions up to $2,500. Once an employee had been with the company three years, he or she could take a two-week, paid sabbatical—in addition to vacation time—to pursue a dream. One staffer used the sabbatical to visit the Van Gogh Museum in Amsterdam while another ran with the bulls in Pamplona. "Dream Catchers gives you license to be selfish if you want to be," says program designer King. "So many people get caught up in day-to-day living and put their dreams on hold indefinitely. The program is supposed to be a kick in the [butt]." A company whose internal culture promotes creativity in a variety of ways is likely to see the impact in its products and services. Since Fallon instituted its new initiatives, the agency has won new clients as well as several prestigious advertising awards for its work.

Today, despite a tight labor market and a slow economy, Fallon has billings of more than $800 million per year and a client list that reads like a Who's Who of corporate giants: BMW of North America, Citibank, EDS, Holiday Inn, Nikon, Nordstrom, Nuveen Investments, PBS, Ralston Purina, Starbucks Coffee Company, Timex, and United Airlines, to name a few. In selecting Fallon, United's director of Worldwide Marketing Communications, Jerry Dow, indicated the importance of Fallon's innovative culture to the decision. "In the end, Fallon showed United that the agency best understood the airline's brand vision, and had the tools to develop and deliver a hard-hitting, integrated global message and global brand platform."

There's no doubt that Fallon faces some tough challenges as it continues to try to integrate with Publicis without losing its own identity, trudges through an economic downturn, and looks for ways to keep employees energized, happy, and productive. But company founder Pat Fallon remains optimistic. "It comes down to one thing," he says. "Do you or don't you live by your values? Even in this tough economic climate, we can never invest enough in our people if we want them to do the best work of their lives." Pat Fallon intends his agency to be a soul survivor.

Questions

1. Imagine that you are a member of Fallon's staff. Write a brief paragraph proposing your own idea for sparking creativity at Fallon.
2. Why is maintaining Fallon's corporate culture so important?
3. How is Fallon's corporate culture linked to its external environment?

SOURCES: "Forecasters Predict Drop in Ad Spending," *The New York Times*, December 3, 2001, *http://college3nytimes.com*; Christine Canabou, "Free to Innovate," *Fast Company*, November 2001, *http://www.fastcompany.com*; "United Selects Fallon Worldwide to Manage Its North American and International Advertising," *United Airlines press release*, January 22, 2001, *http://www.ual.com*.

Chapter 4: Fallon Worldwide—Its Name Spells Global

EVEN BEFORE THE MINNEAPOLIS-BASED ADVERTISING agency Fallon Worldwide was acquired by France's Publicis, Pat Fallon was on the hunt for alliances he could make with other companies around the world. Managing the global environment is more important than ever for companies as technology expands boundaries or eliminates them altogether. In early 1999, Pat Fallon met Robert Senior in London for a cup of tea. Fallon was searching for his first foreign partners in Britain. Fallon Worldwide (then called Fallon McElligott) had already established its reputation for passion and independence. Senior and his colleagues were quick to jump on board. In less than a year, the Fallon London office had a dozen top clients and billings of $40 million. What made the international alliance work? Shared values, reported Britain's Senior. "Passion for great advertising is part of Pat Fallon's DNA," he enthused. "Part of exporting the Fallon brand is to find folks who share that ambition. You need those people who are going to get out there and push harder. You can try to dress up people in a set of beliefs and values, but it's much more potent if it is fueled from within."

Julie Thompson, Fallon's director of communications said at the time, "It all comes down to relationships. We searched for two years to find our partners in London. We are very, very careful to find people of like mind. It has been a longtime goal of the partners to expand globally, but it will be a measured, well-planned expansion."

One aspect of global expansion is overcoming cultural and language barriers. As Fallon began to make plans for alliances farther afield, Julie Thompson explained how the agency would address this issue. "We suspect the models will vary in every city. Our values do seem to translate across the continents, but we'll ward off [language and other barriers to understanding] by partnering with local talent who can help us crack that code." Industry expert David Tree, who helped Young and Rubicam, Inc. open branches in Paris, Oslo, Tokyo, and Hong Kong, agreed with Fallon's approach. "There are certain cultural givens, certain global truths," he noted. "Every kid around the world wants a Coke. But there are cultural nuances that you would never understand like a national. The creative expertise you must leave up to the locals."

About a year after the London deal took place, Publicis acquired Fallon and the global focus intensified. Clients had been pressing the advertising industry in general to service them on a global basis; the only way Fallon could do that, reasoned its founders, was to partner with a larger organization. From the start, Publicis and Fallon intended to expand to up to a dozen other locations outside the United States. The company also faced the issue of e-commerce, which was mushrooming around the world. "It will take a new kind of branding communications company to succeed in the emerging worldwide digital economy, and with Publicis' support, we intend to be that company," said Pat Fallon of the merger and expansion plans. A year after the Publicis deal was finalized, Fallon Worldwide's expansion was well under way. The company announced the formation of three new "creativity centers" located on two continents, with six internationally known partners. Fallon would open agencies in Sao Paulo, Singapore, and Hong Kong. This strategy was formulated not only to overcome cultural, economic, and legal-political barriers in each region but also to maintain the flexible, innovative reputation that Fallon had built its business on. "The traditional agency network model is about distribution, which is fine for certain marketers," explained Pat Fallon. "But we believe there are clients who will get excited by the idea of a lean, agile network built around the power of creativity, not mass."

Fallon Worldwide chose the locations for the creativity centers carefully so that they would cover certain economic regions, giving multinational clients access to these markets without simply blanketing the globe with tiny agency outposts. Selecting partners to manage the centers would be crucial to the success of the entire endeavor. "Our philosophy is to find the best people in the world and give them a once-in-a-lifetime opportunity under a great brand name with collaborative support and resources from the other partners," remarked John Gerzema, Fallon's managing partner for international expansion. "Our network will be highly intimate—with people who know each other, respect each other, and share a passion for work that drives business results." These international partners share both risks and rewards based on an agreement that includes shared ownership and accountability.

Each of Fallon's top managers around the world has a global perspective on culture and on business. For instance, Calvin Soh, a creative partner for Fallon Singapore and Fallon Hong Kong, has worked in both New York and Singapore in the past. "As Asians, we found that Fallon's Midwestern values of humility, hard work, respect, and integrity weren't very different from ours. Particularly enlightening was Fallon's belief that to excel in Asia, you need to develop local talent and expose them to the world. For us, Fallon felt right." Fallon hopes to find such partners—and clients—the world over.

Questions

1. Do you think Fallon's approach to global expansion by establishing regional creativity centers will be an effective one? Why or why not?
2. How might ASEAN affect Fallon's business in Asia?
3. What are some of the personal challenges that Fallon's global managers might face?

SOURCES: Sandy Hunter, "Fallon Worldwide Expands," *Boards Magazine*, November 1, 2001, http://www.boardsmag.com; "Fallon Expands Global Network," *Business Wire*, October 9, 2001, http://hoovnews.hoovers.com; Jennifer Franklin, "Fallon's British Invasion," *City Business*, July 30, 1999, http://twincities.bcentral.com; Christine Whitehouse, "The New Ad Ventures," *Time Europe*, April 3, 2000, http://www.time.com; "Publicis Scoops Up Fallon McElligott to Forge New Global Branding Network," *Media*, March 3, 2000, www.media.com; "Publicis Boosts Midwest Clout with Fallon Buy," *Chicago Tribune*, February 3, 2000, http://cgi.chicago.tribune.com.

Chapter 5: Timberland Walks the Walk of Social Responsibility

THE TIMBERLAND COMPANY DESIGNS, MANUFACTURES, AND sells premium boots, casual shoes, hiking boots, and boat shoes, as well as high-performance outdoor clothing and accessories. The New Hampshire based company builds its products to last—"to withstand the elements of nature," as the company's Web site states. But Timberland is striving to build something more permanent than just high-quality footwear and clothing. It's trying to make the world a better, safer place to live and work—one person and one community at a time.

Along with the customers who buy its high-quality products, Timberland considers its other stakeholders in its business dealings. First, it recognizes its responsibility to be profitable for investors and employees. With yearly revenues of nearly $1.1 billion, the company recently reported 20 consecutive quarters of record revenue and improved earnings. Even in the face of an economic downturn, which hit retail establishments hard, CEO Jeffrey Schwartz said, "Timberland delivered record revenues for 2001 in a difficult environment" that included higher leather costs, increased competition, and softer U.S. sales. But he is not deterred from his goal of making Timberland a leading global lifestyle brand.

Timberland also considers its employee stakeholders as critical to its success. The company was again listed in *Fortune* magazine's list of best companies to work for, ranked at number 65. The company is committed to diversity in its workforce, with 29 percent of its employees being minorities and nearly half women. The company provides 22 hours of professional training per year to employees to improve their skills. Timberland is also concerned about its global manufacturing workforce. With repeated news reports about exploitation of foreign workers at other companies, Timberland instituted a year-long audit of all its manufacturing facilities and some of its licensee's facilities, including tanneries and other major suppliers. It hired Verit, a nonprofit nongovernmental organization, to check working conditions such as health and safety, air quality, noise, and lighting. The company also monitors its Asian factories every eight to twelve weeks to ensure that workers are paid decent wages, provided periodic work breaks, and not required to work excessive overtime. It considers its commitment an ongoing process, requiring continual checks and improvements.

Companies often profess their belief in good corporate citizenship to their communities, but Timberland is an organization that literally considers what it is like to walk in someone else's shoes. From the CEO to office workers to sales associates on the floor, Timberland encourages all its employees to become involved in their communities. Through its long-standing Path of Service program, the company gives full-time employees 40 hours of paid time off for community volunteer service during regular working hours. The company also recently instituted a paid sabbatical program, allowing four employees each year to contribute their professional skills to nonprofit organizations for up to six months. And, it has long been involved in City Year, a national youth service organization for young people aged 17 to 24 years who serve different communities for a full year. The company serves as a City Year National Leadership Sponsor, and CEO Schwartz chairs the City Year board. In addition to these efforts, the company partners with many other service organizations, working on activities as wide ranging as prevention of child hunger, skills training, eliminating exploitative working conditions, and closing the technology gap between organizations. The company's Web site also provides a link to SERVnet, an online news and events site listing needed community service projects.

Finally, Timberland considers the impact on the environment that its activities may have. It created an Environmental Affairs department to reduce the harmful effects of its production on the environment. The company is committed to recycling leather scraps and minimizing its use of toxic compounds and nonrenewable resources, as well as reducing carbon dioxide emissions to help curb global warming. Using innovative methods to reduce its energy consumption and conserve other resources, Timberland includes skylights at its sites to reduce power consumption and constructs some of its retail stores with furnishings and fixtures made from recycled materials such as salvaged wood and bricks. Its shoe boxes are made entirely from recycled products and printed with environmentally friendly vegetable dyes.

Through its daily efforts to improve its operations while offering products with proven workmanship, Timberland certainly walks the walk when it comes to ethical and socially responsible behavior. Perhaps one incident can best capture Timberland's commitment to its communities: On September 11, 2001, CEO Schwartz and more than 100 other employees were volunteering at a school in the Bronx, New York City. After the World Trade Center's collapse of the towers was reported, the Timberland employees were advised to evacuate the city. Instead, they chose to stay and finish their job of repairing windows, painting hallways, and doing various cleaning and repair jobs. No wonder *Fortune* magazine says of Timberland, "No one takes social responsibility more seriously."

Questions

1. Consider the three stages of ethical development. If Timberland were an individual, what level of moral development do you think the company has attained? Explain.
2. How much does Timberland's organizational culture influence its employees' socially responsible behavior?
3. Name some ways that Timberland demonstrates a high level of discretionary responsibility in its social performance. Would you like to work at Timberland?

SOURCES: Timberland company Web site, *http://www.timberland.com*, accessed March 29, 2002; "Best Companies to Work for," *Fortune*, *http://www.fortune.com*, accessed March 26, 2002; Marjorie Kelly, "Capitalism Has Its Shining Side," the *Corporate Social Responsibility Newswire*, *http://www.csrwire.com*, accessed March 26, 2002.

Chapter 6: The Geek Squad: Providing Service that Makes You Smile

COMPUTERS AND TECHNOLOGY SEEM TO BE EVERYWHERE these days. From the office desktop to home Internet surfing to e-mail on cell phones, the computer chip has invaded our lives. But the simple fact is that most of us don't have a clue how any of that technology actually works—or even worse, why it *doesn't* work. Enter the Geek Squad, a computer-repair, technical assistance, and maintenance service based in Minneapolis, Los Angeles, Chicago, and San Francisco. The Geek Squad offers computer service—with a twist.

Founded by twenty-something Robert Stephens in the mid-1990s, the company has "special agents" who wear white shirts, clip-on ties, too-short pants, and pocket protectors. They drive to their on-site repairs, or "crime scenes," in Geekmobiles—black and white VW Beetles, renovated ice cream trucks, and even an old police squad car emblazoned with the Geek Squad logo. Stephens, who calls himself the Chief Inspector, got the idea for his company when he overheard two people in a grocery store checkout line discussing whether they were going to upgrade the RAM on their computer hard drives at home. At that time, the Internet was just beginning to take off. Stephens says of his vision, "That's a fundamental social shift that occurred—that you have normal people talking computers. I thought, 'This is going to blow big.'" So Stephens saw his window of opportunity, quit his computer programming job at the University of Minnesota, and started his company with $200 and a good dose of humor.

From its humble beginnings, the Geek Squad grew under Stephens's guidance (the company motto is "Creativity in the Absence of Capital") and through his personal connections. A lucky break came when a movie was being filmed in Minneapolis, and the crew's computers crashed. The Geek Squad repaired the damage. Soon, the company was known as "computer people for the movie industry in the Twin Cities," recalls Stephens. The company repaired computers for *Grumpy Old Men* and a *Mighty Ducks* hockey movie. The company also began to help rock bands with their computers. Over the years, they've helped U2, the Rolling Stones, Ice Cube, and Jonny Lang, among others. "You wouldn't think rock stars use computers," says Stephens. "But rock stars use laptops on the road, so actually they're the most finicky, demanding people. They're great practice for us." An added bonus for employees is getting great seats at concerts.

With customers' increasing dissatisfaction with the computer support provided by large hardware and software companies, the Geek Squad has found its niche by offering personalized carry-in, on-site, and emergency service 24 hours a day, seven days a week. The company prices its services by the job, not the hour, so customers know up front what the cost of the service will be. And the company will quote the cost of the service over the phone. Geek Squad employees maintain and repair everything from IBM-compatible and Macintosh hardware and software, to networks, printers, and even cell phones and personal digital assistants. They also give their customers set time frames for when a problem will be fixed.

Once a sole proprietorship owned by Stephens, the Geek Squad has now become a corporation with several million dollars in annual sales. The Geek Squad qualifies as a small business, currently employing fewer than 100 employees. Throughout the company's growth, Stephens has managed to maintain the fun work atmosphere for his employees, and he relies on their imaginations to play the role of computer nerd for sometimes tense customers. The company dubs its carry-in service "counter intelligence." Flashing their badges before they begin work, employees quickly calm the fears and gain the trust of anxious customers, and the invoices they present carry the words, "Pay up, sucka!" All of this humor helps create not only fun for employees but goodwill for the company and referrals for future business.

Stephens has received offers to buy the company, but he says he isn't interested in selling. He takes those offers as evidence that he has created something unique and useful. In fact, Stephens has even extended his business by writing a book with coauthor Dale Burg called *The Geek Squad Guide to Solving Any Computer Glitch*, published by Simon & Schuster. The book is a compilation of useful tips, written in normal language that any nontechie can understand. Of his business, Stephens says, "I'm just having a lot of fun. I'm energized by that. For me, the Geek Squad is an artistic experiment."

Questions

1. Review the six types of business owners in Exhibit 6.1. Which type do you think Robert Stephens is?
2. How did Stephens come up with his business idea for the Geek Squad? What qualities have helped make the company a success?
3. At what stage of growth do you think the Geek Squad is currently? Explain.

SOURCES: The Geek Squad company Web site, *http://www.geeksquad.com*, accessed March 28, 2002; Bob Weinstein, "Company Builds on 'Geek' Image," *Chicago Sun-Times*, April 30, 2000, *http://www.suntimes.com*; "Geek Squad's Robert Stephens—No Geek at Marketing," *Minnesota Entrepreneurs' Inc. Newsletter*, February 2000, *http://www.mn-entrepreneurs.org*; Jamie Allen, "'Geek Squad Guide' Offers Unique Computer Help," CNN, September 3, 1999, *http://www.cnn.com*.

Part Two: Ford Operates in a Complex Environment

HENRY FORD WAS AN ENTREPRENEUR WHOSE COMPANY became an American icon over the course of a century. He never could have guessed that by late 2001, CEO Jac Nasser, the aggressive, embattled Australian businessman who had been in Ford's driver's seat for only three years, would be standing by the side of the road, briefcase in hand. Nasser had shaken up Ford's stodgy, bureaucratic corporate culture and attempted to lead the organization through the worst crisis of its history—the Firestone tire debacle—but the company had suffered too many blows during his reign. During this period, Ford and its managers faced enormous challenges involving ethics, social responsibility, a change in culture, and a competitive, constantly changing environment both in the United States and abroad. Ultimately, Nasser was asked to step aside.

In August 2000, Ford's world blew apart as it became apparent that some of its standard tires, those manufactured by Bridgestone/Firestone and installed on Ford's top-selling Explorer SUV, were doing exactly that: the treads were separating from the tire's core, leading to injurious and fatal crashes. Although Nasser chose to endure public scrutiny and Bridgestone/Firestone's Japanese leaders remained in relative seclusion, neither company immediately took responsibility. Instead, they engaged in finger pointing, damaging a relationship that had gone back as far as Henry Ford and Harvey Firestone. Firestone recalled the six million tires it believed were faulty but meanwhile accused Ford of poor automobile design. Ford announced that it would replace all 13 million of the Wilderness AT tires that were on its Explorers, even those that were presumed safe. Then Firestone severed its relationship with Ford. The recall program took so long that consumers and dealers became frustrated and fearful of the consequences—and increasingly distrustful of both companies. Ford and Firestone officials were called to testify before Congress. Meanwhile, as more accidents were investigated and analyzed, the death toll associated with the faulty tires rose to more than two hundred. Who was right, Ford or Firestone? Did Ford handle the situation ethically? Much has been written about the debacle, and the answers most likely will not come for many years.

Meanwhile, Ford's general and task environments were continually changing. General Motors revamped its truck lineup, and Toyota opened up the throttle on its SUVs with its new Highlander and Sequoia models. Ford's quality was suffering, increasing the cost of its warranties and decreasing consumers' confidence in its products. Also, Ford had purchased several European brands, including Volvo and BMW Land Rover, and the economic downturn in Europe was of concern. Ford, along with other car manufacturers, tried to attract new buyers with innovative features and design. "It is a reflection of the market softening generally," explained Ford Europe's chairman and chief executive, David Thursfield. "We have to bring out more new innovative products to give the market a boost. That is what we are certainly doing at Ford." And the slowdown of the American economy, along with the $3 billion price tag attached to the tire recall, forced Ford to offer early retirement packages to nearly 5,000 managers in order to cut costs. Finally, relationships with dealers and suppliers, who continued to struggle with the tire recall, needed to be repaired. In this midst of all the turmoil, Ford's board of directors announced that Jac Nasser would be leaving the company and that Bill Ford, Jr. would be taking over. Ford, in his mid-forties, is the first Ford family member to be CEO of the company since Henry Ford II resigned in 1979.

Bill Ford, known for his commitment to environmental issues, immediately pledged to make Ford Motor Company a leader in environmental protection as part of a company turnaround plan. A visit to the company's Web site reveals a whole host of environmentally friendly initiatives—not all introduced by Bill Ford, but indicative of the company's push toward social responsibility. For instance, Ford has teamed up with Environmental Defense to "provide automotive shoppers with comprehensive information about the environmental impact of automobiles sold in North America." Environmental Defense is a group that sponsors "For My World," a Web site that allows visitors to learn about the "Green Score" of particular vehicles. In addition, Ford is experimenting with water-based paints for its vehicles and working on ways to tackle pollution-producing manufacturing processes as well as traffic congestion.

Of course, these measures deal with only one facet of the overall environment in which Ford conducts its business. Bill Ford and his team of managers need to deal with quality issues, resolve the Firestone tire situation, and get new, more exciting autos into the pipeline. As he took the wheel of his family's company, Ford was closemouthed about his strategy for guiding the company into the future. "Everything is up for review—every asset, every piece of geography," he said. "We continue to review our mix of businesses." In November 2001, Ford announced that its Australian subsidiary would begin designing and manufacturing a new vehicle for the local Australian market, creating as many as 10,000 jobs there. Code-named Raptor, the new model would be poised to take on new cars introduced in Australia by General Motors. Despite the many roadblocks, Ford was showing signs of rolling forward again.

Part Two: Ford Operates in a Complex Environment

Questions

1. Add to your knowledge of the Firestone tire debacle by researching it on the Internet or at the library. Then prepare for a class discussion or written summary on whether or not you believe Ford acted ethically throughout the crisis and why.
2. Visit the Ford Web site and click on several of the company's pages dealing with socially responsible initiatives—the environment, education, and so forth. Then discuss the role you think these initiatives play in Ford's overall corporate culture.
3. Ford Motor Company was founded by an entrepreneur and was once a small business. Name three ways in which you think Ford has contributed to the American economy and culture over the last century.

SOURCES: Ford Motor Company Web site, *http://www.ford.com*, accessed January 8, 2002; Tim Burt, "Thursfield Champions Ford of Europe," *Financial Times*, November 28, 2001, *http://news.ft.com*; Virginia Marsh, "Ford Launch Could Create 10,000 Jobs in Australia," *Financial Times*, November 15, 2001, *http://news.ft.com*; Kathleen Kerwin and Joann Muller, "Bill Ford Takes the Wheel," *BusinessWeek Online*, November 1, 2001, *http://www.businesseek.com*; Charles Child and Mary Connelly, "Nasser Out; Bill Ford Takes Over," *Automotive News*, October 29, 2001, *http://www.autonews.com*; "Ford Concern on Europe Downturn," *BBC News*, September 10, 2001, *http://news.bbc.co.uk*; Jamie Butters, "Job Cuts at Ford Likely to Increase," *Auto.com*, August 10, 2001, *http://www.auto.com*; "Tire Trouble: The Ford-Firestone Blowout," *Forbes*, June 20, 2001, *http://www.forbes.com*.

Planning

Beavers have a reputation for working hard. They are also shy. If you surprise one during a hike along a riverbank, you might hear a soft plop as it slides stealthily into the water. Beavers are constantly busy building complex living quarters, called lodges, or dams. And believe it or not, those random twigs and logs have a pattern or order to them: they have a plan.

Even though beavers build their dams according to natural instinct, these structures are strategically located and constructed. The beaver has to determine the best location for its family lodge, the best size to accommodate a group, and the best available materials for construction. All of these decisions are part of an overall strategy designed to protect the group so that it can survive and grow, just like a corporation. Without realizing it, the beaver—like the manager— recognizes a problem, chooses among alternatives, and decides where to build. If the location, size, and construction turn out to be faulty (for instance, if spring rains overwhelm a small dam), the beaver has made the wrong decision and must start over. Likewise, if a product doesn't sell, a manufacturing process is too slow, or employees remain unmotivated, a manager knows that a decision must be reevaluated, a strategy reconsidered, and a plan reconstructed.

Managers—just like beavers—do much of their work behind the scenes. They make decisions, formulate strategies, and determine plans for action. People inside and outside the organization experience the results of the manager's work. If all the pieces are put together well, the organization will hold its own against an uncertain environment and predatory competitors.

Organizational Planning and Goal Setting

CHAPTER OUTLINE

Overview of Goals and Plans
Purposes of Goals and Plans
Goals in Organizations
Organizational Mission
Goals and Plans
Hierarchy of Goals
Criteria for Effective Goals
Planning Types and Performance
Management by Objectives
Single-Use and Standing Plans
Contingency Plans
Crisis Management Planning
Planning in the New Workplace
Traditional Approaches
to Planning
New Workplace Approaches
to Planning

LEARNING OBJECTIVES

After studying this chapter, you should be able to

1 Define goals and plans and explain the relationship between them.

2 Explain the concept of organizational mission and how it influences goal setting and planning.

3 Describe the types of goals an organization should have and why they resemble a hierarchy.

4 Define the characteristics of effective goals.

5 Describe the four essential steps in the MBO process.

6 Explain the difference between single-use plans and standing plans.

7 Describe and explain the importance of the three stages of crisis management planning.

8 Discuss how planning in the new workplace differs from traditional approaches to planning.

When the 12-story Europa Hotel first opened on Belfast's Grand Victoria Street in 1971, it was a symbol of hope and glamour for a town sorely in need of both. The Europa was the first hotel in Northern Ireland to offer bathrooms en suite and a popular top-floor nightclub. But within a month, the Europa had been bombed by the Irish Republican Army, who saw their act as a powerful strike against British capitalism. Twenty more explosions followed over the next four years, leading hotel management to erect security walls around the entrance and institute policies requiring that all guests be frisked and their luggage searched. The tourist trade disappeared, leaving only business customers and journalists who came to cover the Northern Ireland conflict from the perfect vantage point. Business gradually increased over the years, but the Europa remained a high-profile terrorist target. By 2001, the hotel had been bombed at least 30 times, making it second only to the Holiday Inn in Sarajevo for the enviable title of "world's most bombed hotel." And yet, the Europa has survived and remains an important Belfast landmark. In fact, John Toner, Europa's current general manager of the four-star hotel, believes the Europa has become a stronger, more robust business because of the adversity its managers have faced. During each crisis, hotel managers followed carefully thought-out plans for ensuring the safety of guests and employees, securing the building, and getting back to business as quickly as possible. By now, says Toner, "security is in the bones of the people who work here."[1]

How do you think the Europa Hotel survived and even thrived, in spite of 30 years of bombings that have disrupted business and wrecked managers' plans? Can managers do anything to prepare their organizations to cope with unexpected problems and crises?

One of the primary responsibilities of managers is to decide where the organization should go in the future and how to get it there. But how do managers plan for the future in an uncertain and constantly changing environment? As we discussed in Chapter 1 of this textbook, most organizations are facing growing uncertainty. The September 11, 2001, terrorist attacks in the United States and subsequent events have left many managers wondering how to cope and have sparked a renewed interest in organizational planning, particularly planning for unexpected problems and events.

In some organizations, typically small ones, planning is informal. In others, managers follow a well-defined planning framework. The company establishes a basic mission and develops formal goals and strategic plans for carrying it out. Companies such as Royal Dutch/Shell, IBM, Mazda, and United Way undertake a strategic planning exercise each year—reviewing their missions, goals, and plans to meet environmental changes or the expectations of important stakeholders such as the community, owners, or stockholders. Many of these companies also develop *contingency plans* for unexpected circumstances and disaster recovery plans for what the organization would do in the event of a major disaster such as a hurricane, earthquake, or other crisis.

Of the four management functions—planning, organizing, leading, and controlling—described in Chapter 1, planning is considered the most fundamental. Everything else stems from planning. Yet planning also is the most controversial management function. Planning cannot read an uncertain future. Planning cannot tame a turbulent environment. A statement by General Colin Powell, now U.S. Secretary of State, offers a warning for managers: "No battle plan survives contact with the enemy."[2]

In this chapter, we will explore the process of planning and consider how managers develop effective plans that can grow and change to meet new conditions. Special attention is given to goal setting, for that is where planning starts. Then, the various types of plans that managers use to help the organization achieve those goals are discussed, with special attention paid to crisis management planning. Finally, we will examine new approaches to planning that emphasize the involvement of employees, customers, partners, and other stakeholders in strategic thinking and execution. Chapter 8 will look at strategic planning in depth and examine a number of strategic options managers can use in a competitive environment. In Chapter 9, we look at management decision making. Proper decision-making techniques are crucial to selecting the organization's goals, plans, and strategic options.

Overview of Goals and Plans

goal
A desired future state that the organization attempts to realize.

plan
A blueprint specifying the resource allocations, schedules, and other actions necessary for attaining goals.

planning
The act of determining the organization's goals and the means for achieving them.

Goals and plans have become general concepts in our society. A **goal** is a desired future state that the organization attempts to realize.[3] Goals are important because organizations exist for a purpose, and goals define and state that purpose. A **plan** is a blueprint for goal achievement and specifies the necessary resource allocations, schedules, tasks, and other actions. Goals specify future ends; plans specify today's means. The word **planning** usually incorporates both ideas; it means determining the organization's goals and defining the means for achieving them.[4]

Exhibit 7.1 illustrates the levels of goals and plans in an organization. The planning process starts with a formal mission that defines the basic

Exhibit *7.1*

Levels of Goals/Plans and Their Importance

purpose of the organization, especially for external audiences. The mission is the basis for the strategic (company) level of goals and plans, which in turn shapes the tactical (divisional) level and the operational (departmental) level.[5] Top managers are typically responsible for establishing *strategic* goals and plans that reflect a commitment to both organizational efficiency and effectiveness, as described in Chapter 1. *Tactical* goals and plans are the responsibility of middle managers, such as the heads of major divisions or functional units. A division manager will formulate tactical plans that focus on the major actions the division must take to fulfill its part in the strategic plan set by top management. *Operational* plans identify the specific procedures or processes needed at lower levels of the organization, such as individual departments and employees. Front-line managers and supervisors develop operational plans that focus on specific tasks and processes and that help to meet tactical and strategic goals. Planning at each level supports the other levels.

Purposes of Goals and Plans

The complexity of today's environment and uncertainty about the future overwhelm many managers and lead them to focus on operational issues and short-term results rather than long-term goals and plans. However, planning generally positively affects a company's performance.[6] In addition to improving financial and operational performance, developing explicit goals and plans at each level illustrated in Exhibit 7.1 is important because of the external and internal messages they send. These messages go to both external and internal audiences and provide important benefits for the organization:[7]

Courtesy of the Valspar Corporation

A company's mission *describes what the organization stands for and its reason for existence. Valspar Corporation, a manufacturer of industrial coatings, relies on its employees to meet customer needs. It states its mission broadly for internal and external audiences: "to be the recognized leader in the coatings industry—by meeting customer requirements, current and future; by believing in our employees and empowering them to maximize productivity; and by creating exceptional value for our shareholders." Recently, the company recorded its 26th straight year of record sales and earnings.*

- *Legitimacy.* An organization's mission describes what the organization stands for and its reason for existence. It symbolizes legitimacy to external audiences such as investors, customers, and suppliers. The mission helps them and the local community look on the company in a favorable light and, hence, accept its existence. A strong mission also has an impact on employees, enabling them to become committed to the organization because they can identify with its overall purpose and reason for existence. One of the traits often cited by employees in *Fortune* magazine's list of the "100 Best Companies to Work For in America" is a sense of purpose and meaning. For example, at Medtronic, a medical products company, employees are inspired by the mission to "alleviate pain, restore health, and extend life."[8]

- *Source of Motivation and Commitment.* Goals and plans facilitate employees' identification with the organization and help motivate them by reducing uncertainty and clarifying what they should accomplish. Lack of a clear goal can damage employee motivation and commitment. When Main Street Muffins lost sight of its goal and began branching into new lines of business, morale sank so low that bakers were calling in sick at 3 A.M. or walking off the job with no notice. The company took a nosedive toward bankruptcy before the owners developed a statement to remind everyone that the primary goal of Main Street Muffins was "to profitably improve an organization that overwhelms the food industry with its devotion to high-quality products and services." With the new goal statement as a guide, employee commitment and motivation gradually improved, and the company became profitable again within three months.[9] Whereas a goal provides the "why" of an organization or subunit's existence, a plan tells the "how." A plan lets employees know what actions to undertake to achieve the goal.

- *Guides to Action.* Goals and plans provide a sense of direction. They focus attention on specific targets and direct employee efforts toward important outcomes. Hartford Technology Services Co., for example, set goals to establish a customer profile database, survey customer satisfaction, and secure service agreements with ten new customers.[10]

- *Rationale for Decisions.* Through goal setting and planning, managers learn what the organization is trying to accomplish. They can make decisions to ensure that internal policies, roles, performance, structure, products, and expenditures will be made in accordance with desired outcomes. Decisions throughout the organization will be in alignment with the plan.

- *Standard of Performance.* Because goals define desired outcomes for the organization, they also serve as performance criteria. They provide a standard of assessment. If an organization wishes to grow by 15 percent, and actual growth is 17 percent, managers will have exceeded their prescribed standard. Top managers at Procter & Gamble have set a goal to double consumer products sales to $70 billion by 2006.[11]

The overall planning process prevents managers from thinking merely in terms of day-to-day activities. When organizations drift away from goals and plans, they typically get into trouble. This occurred at Amex Life Assurance, a former American Express subsidiary. A new president implemented a strong planning system that illustrates the power of planning to improve organizational performance.

Sarah Nolan knew that the chairman of American Express was a self-professed maniac on quality. But when Nolan arrived as the new president of Amex Life Assurance, she found a paperwork assembly line that served customers at a snail's pace. A simple change of address took 2 days; sending out a new insurance policy took at least 10 days. Nolan's primary goal was to get everyone at Amex working together while keeping the focus on the customer. She sent five managers representing different specialties to an empty office park and told them to imagine they were setting up an entirely new business. Nolan gave the group only three rules to follow in their task of planning a new operation:

1. Put the customer first.
2. Don't copy anything we do here.
3. Be ready to process applications yourselves in six months.

When the planning group returned, 10 layers of personnel had been collapsed into 3, each of which would deal directly with the public. Fewer employees were needed, so more than one-third were transferred to other divisions. Expenses were cut in half and profitability increased sixfold. Nolan used planning to help managers break out of their focus on day-to-day activities and reorient the company toward its strategic goal of customer satisfaction.[12] ❖

AMEX LIFE ASSURANCE

Goals in Organizations

Setting goals starts with top managers. The overall planning process begins with a mission statement and strategic goals for the organization as a whole.

Organizational Mission

At the top of the goal hierarchy is the **mission**—the organization's reason for existence. The mission describes the organization's values, aspirations, and reason for being. A well-defined mission is the basis for development of all subsequent goals and plans. Without a clear mission, goals and plans may be developed haphazardly and not take the organization in the direction it needs to go.

The formal **mission statement** is a broadly stated definition of basic business scope and operations that distinguishes the organization from others of a similar type.[13] The content of a mission statement often focuses on the market and customers and identifies desired fields of endeavor. Some mission statements describe company characteristics such as corporate values, product quality, location of facilities, and attitude toward employees. Mission statements often reveal the company's philosophy as well as purpose. One example is the mission statement for the franchise, Mail Boxes Etc., presented in Exhibit 7.2. Mail Boxes Etc. devised its concise mission statement to express its commitment to ethical considerations as well as good business practices. Such short, straightforward mission statements describe basic business activities and purposes, as well as the values that guide the company. Another example of this type of mission statement is that of Bertucci's, a chain of full-service pizza restaurants with headquarters in Wakefield, Massachusetts:

> Bertucci's is committed to serving our customers as guests in an atmosphere that reflects the traditional welcome, warmth, and abundance of an Italian Home.

mission
The organization's reason for existence.

mission statement
A broadly stated definition of the organization's basic business scope and operations that distinguishes it from similar types of organizations.

Exhibit 7.2

Mission Statement for Mail Boxes Etc.

SOURCE: Mail Boxes Etc. Web site, *http://www.mbe.com,* accessed on August 29, 2001.

Mission Statement for Mail Boxes Etc.

Our Mission
Making Business Easier Worldwide
Through Our Service and Distribution Network,
Delivering Personalized and Convenient Business Solutions
With World-Class Customer Service.

Our Core Values

Caring	Honesty	Fairness
Integrity	Trust	Respect
	Commitment	Accountability

Boeing's strategic goal is to remain an aerospace industry giant despite a drop in air travel and resulting decrease in demand for airplanes. To meet this challenge, the strategic plan includes cutting production in its airplane manufacturing division and reassigning financial resources. Boeing is slicing its commercial aircraft business by 15 percent, cutting 10,000 to 15,000 manufacturing jobs. The change meant closing one of the three assembly lines for 737 jets at the company's Renton, Washington, plant shown here.

To this we add value, quality, and service as the restaurant cornerstones upon which we have built and will continue to build our futures.

We are dedicated to provide the best experience for our guests so that our entire family of team members, stockholders, suppliers, and, in addition, our communities benefit.[14]

Because of mission statements such as those of Mail Boxes Etc. and Bertucci's, employees as well as customers, suppliers, and stockholders know the company's stated purpose and values.

Goals and Plans

Broad statements describing where the organization wants to be in the future are called **strategic goals**. They pertain to the organization as a whole rather than to specific divisions or departments. Strategic goals are often called *official goals*, because they are the stated intentions of what the organization wants to achieve. For example, five years after he started Physician Sales and Service, Pat Kelly set a strategic goal for PSS to become the first national physician supply chain, a goal he soon reached. Now, Kelly wants the company to become a world distributor of medical products.[15] E.piphany has a strategic goal to become the No. 2 provider of customer relationship management software, as described in this chapter's Leading Online box.

Strategic plans define the action steps by which the company intends to attain strategic goals. The strategic plan is the blueprint that defines the organizational activities and resource allocations—in the form of cash, personnel, space, and facilities—required for meeting these targets. Strategic planning tends to be long term and may define organizational action steps from two to five years in the future. The purpose of strategic plans is to turn organizational goals into realities within that time period.

As an example, a small company wanted to improve its market share from 15 percent to 20 percent over the next three years. This strategic goal was pursued through the following strategic plans: (1) allocate resources for the development of new, competitive products with high growth potential; (2) improve production methods to

Leading Online

Start-Up E.piphany Plans to "Grow Up" Fast

CEO Roger Siboni proudly proclaims that E.piphany is not a start-up anymore. "We're a grown-up," he says. He may be stretching things a bit, but few competitors doubt that Siboni's company is becoming a force to be reckoned with. E.piphany has made a name for itself by pulling ahead of scores of companies vying for a share of the $9 billion market for customer relationship management (CRM) software that works with the Internet. The young company still has a long way to go to meet Siboni's strategic goal of becoming No. 2 (after Siebel Systems) in CRM, but many observers think Siboni is right on track.

The first focus of Siboni's plan is on turning a profit, and he has salespeople busily courting new customers while making sure everyone throughout the company keeps costs in line. E.piphany relies on industry buzz and customer recommendations to help attract new customers, rather than spending millions on marketing blitzes. For example, the company spent just $400,000 on targeted advertising in 1999, while other companies burned through millions. He urges his staff to watch their pennies and let the dollars take care of themselves. Every decision in the company is made with a consideration of the bottom line. Even with this careful approach, E.piphany has been able to attract some major clients, including about 20 percent of the top 100 U.S. companies and some of the leading technology and dot-com businesses.

Another aspect of Siboni's plan is to nurture relationships with people and organizations that can help E.piphany reach its goals. As a former deputy chairman at KPMG, Siboni has established many key relationships, and today nearly every KPMG customer, executive, and partner is somehow linked to E.piphany. Even when relationships have turned from collegial to competitive, such as Siboni's relationship with Tom Siebel of rival Siebel Systems, he still tends to them with care and respect. "It's the power of the Rolodex," says Karen Richardson, who left her job to join E.piphany. "I wouldn't have come if I hadn't known who the CEO was," she adds.

Siboni's careful attention to costs, customers, and relationships has E.piphany on target to meet his short-term goal of increasing revenue by 100 percent and becoming profitable by the end of 2002. And as for the long-term plan? Oracle's CEO Larry Ellison has seen the upstart gaining ground, and he doesn't like it. As for Siebel Systems, the giant is so far ahead in market share that managers barely acknowledge E.piphany as a competitor. They might regret that. Taking a four-year-old company into battle against Oracle and Siebel will not be easy, but Siboni is determined to take his enemies head on to reach his strategic goals.

SOURCES: Kim Cross, "Captain Connected," *Business 2.0* (April 17, 2001), 31–33; and Joy. D. Russell, "E.piphany Aims at Siebel's Market—Company Says Its New Generation of CRM Software Will Give Siebel a Run for Its Money." *VARbusiness* (January 7, 2002), 26.

---

achieve higher output at lower costs; and (3) conduct research to develop alternative uses for current products and services.[16]

The results that major divisions and departments within the organization intend to achieve are defined as **tactical goals**. These goals apply to middle management and describe what major subunits must do in order for the organization to achieve its overall goals.

Tactical plans are designed to help execute major strategic plans and to accomplish a specific part of the company's strategy.[17] Tactical plans typically have a shorter time horizon than strategic plans—over the next year or so. The word *tactical* originally comes from the military. In a business organization, tactical plans define what major departments and organizational subunits will do to implement the organization's strategic plan. For example, the overall strategic plan of a florist such as 1-800-Flowers might involve becoming a leading telephone and Internet-based purveyor of flowers, which requires high-volume sales during peak seasons such as Valentine's Day and Mother's Day. Human resource managers at 1-800-Flowers developed tactical plans to ensure that the company has the dedicated order takers and customer service representatives it needs during this critical period. Tactical plans include cross-training employees so they can switch to different jobs as departmental needs change, allowing order takers to transfer to jobs at

strategic goals
Broad statements of where the organization wants to be in the future; pertain to the organization as a whole rather than to specific divisions or departments.

strategic plans
The action steps by which an organization intends to attain strategic goals.

tactical goals
Goals that define the outcomes that major divisions and departments must achieve in order for the organization to reach its overall goals.

tactical plans
Plans designed to help execute major strategic plans and to accomplish a specific part of the company's strategy.

headquarters during off-peak times to prevent burnout, and using regular order takers to train and supervise temporary workers during peak seasons.[18] These actions help top managers implement their overall strategic plan. Normally, it is the middle manager's job to take the broad strategic plan and identify specific tactical plans.

operational goals

Specific, measurable results expected from departments, work groups, and individuals within the organization.

The specific results expected from departments, work groups, and individuals are the **operational goals**. They are precise and measurable. "Process 150 sales applications each week," "achieve 90 percent of deliveries on time," "reduce overtime by 10 percent next month," and "develop two new elective courses in accounting" are examples of operational goals.

operational plans

Plans developed at the organization's lower levels that specify action steps toward achieving operational goals and that support tactical planning activities.

Operational plans are developed at the lower levels of the organization to specify action steps toward achieving operational goals and to support tactical plans. The operational plan is the department manager's tool for daily and weekly operations. Goals are stated in quantitative terms, and the department plan describes how goals will be achieved. Operational planning specifies plans for supervisors, department managers, and individual employees.

Schedules are an important component of operational planning. Schedules define precise time frames for the completion of each operational goal required for the organization's tactical and strategic goals. Operational planning also must be coordinated with the budget, because resources must be allocated for desired activities. For example, Apogee Enterprises, a window and glass fabricator with 150 small divisions, is fanatical about operational planning and budgeting. Committees are set up that require inter- as well as intradivisional review and challenge of budgets, profit plans, and proposed capital expenditures. Assigning the dollars makes the operational plan work for everything from hiring new salespeople to increasing travel expenses.

Hierarchy of Goals

Effectively designed organizational goals fit into a hierarchy; that is, the achievement of goals at low levels permits the attainment of high-level goals. This is called a *means-ends chain* because low-level goals lead to accomplishment of high-level goals. Operational goals lead to the achievement of tactical goals, which in turn lead to the attainment of strategic goals. Strategic goals are traditionally considered the responsibility of top management, tactical goals that of middle management, and operational goals that of first-line supervisors and workers. However, the shrinking of middle management combined with a new emphasis on employee empowerment have led to a greater involvement of all employees in goal setting and planning at each level.

An example of a goal hierarchy is illustrated in Exhibit 7.3. Note how the strategic goal of "excellent service to customers" translates into "Open one new sales office" and "Respond to customer inquiries within two hours" at lower management levels.

Criteria for Effective Goals

To ensure goal-setting benefits for the organization, certain characteristics and guidelines should be adopted. The characteristics of both goals and the goal-setting process are listed in Exhibit 7.4. These characteristics pertain to organizational goals at the strategic, tactical, and operational levels:

Exhibit 7.3

Hierarchy of Goals for a Manufacturing Organization

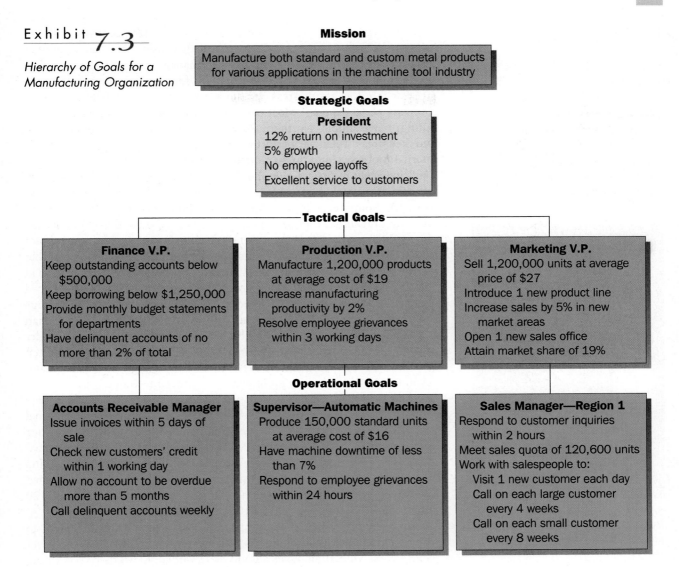

Mission

Manufacture both standard and custom metal products for various applications in the machine tool industry

Strategic Goals

President
12% return on investment
5% growth
No employee layoffs
Excellent service to customers

Tactical Goals

Finance V.P.
Keep outstanding accounts below $500,000
Keep borrowing below $1,250,000
Provide monthly budget statements for departments
Have delinquent accounts of no more than 2% of total

Production V.P.
Manufacture 1,200,000 products at average cost of $19
Increase manufacturing productivity by 2%
Resolve employee grievances within 3 working days

Marketing V.P.
Sell 1,200,000 units at average price of $27
Introduce 1 new product line
Increase sales by 5% in new market areas
Open 1 new sales office
Attain market share of 19%

Operational Goals

Accounts Receivable Manager
Issue invoices within 5 days of sale
Check new customers' credit within 1 working day
Allow no account to be overdue more than 5 months
Call delinquent accounts weekly

Supervisor—Automatic Machines
Produce 150,000 standard units at average cost of $16
Have machine downtime of less than 7%
Respond to employee grievances within 24 hours

Sales Manager—Region 1
Respond to customer inquiries within 2 hours
Meet sales quota of 120,600 units
Work with salespeople to:
  Visit 1 new customer each day
  Call on each large customer every 4 weeks
  Call on each small customer every 8 weeks

- *Specific and measurable.* When possible, goals should be expressed in quantitative terms, such as increasing profits by 2 percent, decreasing scrap by 1 percent, or increasing average teacher effectiveness ratings from 3.5 to 3.7. A team at Sealed Air Corporation, a manufacturer of packaging materials, was motivated by a goal to reduce by two hours the average time needed to change machine settings.[19] Not all goals can be expressed in numerical terms, but vague goals have little motivating power for employees. By necessity, goals are qualitative as well as quantitative, especially at the top of the organization. The important point is that the goals be precisely defined and allow for measurable progress. For example, Liisa Joronen, chairman of SOL Cleaning Service, believes in giving teams the right to set their own performance goals; however, she's a stickler for accountability. "The more we free our people from rules," she says, "the more we need good measurements." Every time SOL lands a contract, the salesperson works at the new customer's site along with the SOL team that will do the future cleaning. Together they establish performance goals. Every month, customers rate the team's performance based on the goals.[20]

Exhibit 7.4

Characteristics of Effective Goal Setting

Goal Characteristics
- Specific and measurable
- Cover key result areas
- Challenging but realistic
- Defined time period
- Linked to rewards

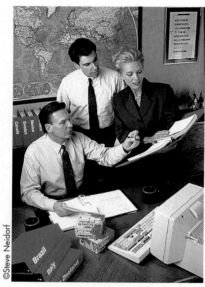

3M marketers carefully planned the global launch of Scotch-Brite Never Rust soap pads to maximize sales of the new product. Innovation is the cornerstone of 3M's culture, and the company's challenging but realistic goals have 3M employees turning new ideas into new products faster than ever before. The new goal of achieving 30 percent of sales from products introduced in the past four years was quickly met, thanks to the successful launch of new products such as the soap pads.

©Steve Neidorf

- *Cover key result areas.* Goals cannot be set for every aspect of employee behavior or organizational performance; if they were, their sheer number would render them meaningless. Instead, managers should identify a few key result areas—perhaps up to four or five for any organizational department or job. Key result areas are those activities that contribute most to company performance.[21] Most companies use a balanced approach to goal setting. For example, Northern States Power Co. tracks measurements in four key areas: financial performance, customer service and satisfaction, internal processes, and innovation and learning.[22]

- *Challenging but realistic.* Goals should be challenging but not unreasonably difficult. One newly hired manager discovered that his staff would have to work 100-hour weeks to accomplish everything expected of them. When goals are unrealistic, they set employees up for failure and lead to decreasing employee morale.[23] However, if goals are too easy, employees may not feel motivated. *Stretch goals* are extremely ambitious but realistic goals that challenge employees to meet high standards. For example, top managers at 3M set a goal that 30 percent of sales must come from products introduced in the past four years; the old standard was 25 percent. Setting ambitious goals helps to keep 3M churning out innovative new products—more than 500 in one recent year alone—and has entrenched the company as a leader in some of today's most dynamic markets.[24] The key to effective stretch goals is ensuring that goals are set within the existing resource base, not beyond departments' time, equipment, or financial resources.

- *Defined time period.* Goals should specify the time period over which they will be achieved. A time period is a deadline stating the date on which goal attainment will be measured. A goal of launching a company intranet, for example, might have a deadline such as June 30, 2003. If a strategic goal involves a two-to-three-year time horizon, specific dates for achieving parts of it can be set up. For example, strategic sales goals could be established on a three-year time horizon, with a $100 million target in year one, a $129 million target in year two, and a $165 million target in year three.

- *Linked to rewards.* The ultimate impact of goals depends on the extent to which salary increases, promotions, and awards are based on goal achievement. People who attain goals should be rewarded. Rewards give meaning and significance to goals and help commit employees to achieving goals. Failure to attain goals often is due to factors outside employees' control. For example, failure to achieve a financial goal may be associated with a drop in market demand due to industry recession; thus, an employee could not be expected to reach it. Nevertheless, a reward may be appropriate if the employee partially achieved goals under difficult circumstances.[25]

Planning Types and Performance

The purpose of planning and goal setting is to help the organization achieve high performance. Managers use strategic, tactical, and operational goals to direct employees and resources toward achieving specific outcomes that enable the organization to perform efficiently and effectively. Overall organizational performance depends on achieving outcomes identified by the planning process. Managers use a number of planning approaches to focus the organization toward high performance. Among the most popular are management by objectives, single-use plans, standing plans, and contingency (or scenario) plans.

Management by Objectives

Management by objectives (MBO) is a method whereby managers and employees define goals for every department, project, and person and use them to monitor subsequent performance.[26] A model of the essential steps of the MBO process is presented in Exhibit 7.5. Four major activities must occur in order for MBO to be successful:[27]

1. *Set goals.* This is the most difficult step in MBO. Setting goals involves employees at all levels and looks beyond day-to-day activities to answer the question "What are we trying to accomplish?" A good goal should be concrete and realistic, provide a specific target and time frame, and assign responsibility. Goals may be quantitative or qualitative, depending on whether outcomes are measurable. Quantitative goals are described in numerical terms, such as "Salesperson Jones will obtain 16 new accounts in December." Qualitative goals use statements such as "Marketing will reduce complaints by improving customer service next year." Goals should be jointly derived. Mutual agreement between employee and supervisor creates the strongest commitment to achieving goals. In the case of teams, all team members may participate in setting goals.
2. *Develop action plans.* An *action plan* defines the course of action needed to achieve the stated goals. Action plans are made for both individuals and departments.
3. *Review progress.* A periodic progress review is important to ensure that action plans are working. These reviews can occur informally between managers and subordinates, where the organization may wish to conduct three-, six-, or nine-month reviews during the year. This periodic checkup allows managers and employees to see whether they are on target or whether corrective action is necessary. Managers and employees should not be locked into predefined behavior and must be willing to take whatever steps are necessary to produce meaningful results. The point of MBO is to achieve goals. The action plan can be changed whenever goals are not being met.
4. *Appraise overall performance.* The final step in MBO is to carefully evaluate whether annual goals have been achieved for both individuals and

management by objectives
A method of management whereby managers and employees define goals for every department, project, and person and use them to monitor subsequent performance.

Appraising performance of a Web site can be tricky, much like finding your way through a dense forest. But Roger Greene, president of Ipswitch Inc., a software vendor based in Lexington, Massachusetts, needed to evaluate costs to see if the site was contributing to his company's bottom line. He was pleasantly surprised. Even though the site cost $1.3 million to operate plus another $150,000 in related costs in a recent year, it accounted for $13 million in both direct and indirect sales—more than 60 percent of the company's total revenues.

Exhibit **7.5**

Model of the MBO Process

departments. Success or failure to achieve goals can become part of the performance appraisal system and the designation of salary increases and other rewards. The appraisal of departmental and overall corporate performance shapes goals for the next year. The MBO cycle repeats itself on an annual basis.

The specific application of MBO must fit the needs of each company. For example, Siemens used MBO to improve its overall financial performance.

SIEMENS
http://www.siemens.com

Siemens of Germany, which makes everything from mobile phones to gas-turbine generators to light bulbs, has always had great engineers bent on producing products of the highest quality. But in recent years, managers have learned that competing with the likes of U.S.-based General Electric and Sweden's Nokia takes more than quality—it also requires speed to market, relentless innovation, and ruthless attention to costs. Between 1996 and 1998, profits sank by two-thirds and company shares fell even faster. CEO Heinrich von Pierer developed a plan for getting Siemens back on track, with a specific goal (MBO Step 1) of strengthening the overall business to be in financial shape for listing on a U.S. stock exchange within three years.

Managers developed an action plan (MBO Step 2) that included: (1) cutting the time it takes to develop and produce new products; (2) selling or closing poor-performing units and strengthening remaining businesses through acquisitions to achieve world leadership; (3) setting tough profit targets for managers and tying pay to performance; and (4) converting accounting practices to report results according to U.S. accounting standards. Managers of the various business divisions then developed action plans for employees in their own units. Progress was reviewed (MBO Step 3) at quarterly meetings where managers from the 14 business units reported on their advancements directly to von Pierer.

Managers were required to explain if benchmarks weren't met and how shortcomings would be corrected. At the end of each year of the turnaround plan, an overall performance appraisal was held for each business and the corporation as a whole (MBO Step 4). Managers who met goals were rewarded; those who had consistently failed to meet them were let go, with the poorest performers going first.

Since the plan was implemented, Siemens has dramatically improved its speed and overall financial performance. For example, mobile phones that once took a painstaking 13 hours each to produce are now sliding off the assembly line in five minutes. Many of Siemens' businesses have been transformed from money losers to profit drivers, and the stock performance has taken a sharp upturn. Siemens is on track to begin reporting results according to U.S. principles and listing on the U. S. stock exchange. The MBO system helped to energize manager and employee actions companywide toward goals deemed critical by top management. [28] ❖

Many companies, such as Intel, Tenneco, Black & Decker, and DuPont, have adopted MBO, and most managers believe that MBO is an effective management tool.[29] Managers believe they are better oriented toward goal achievement when MBO is used. Like any system, MBO achieves benefits when used properly but results in problems when used improperly. Benefits and problems are summarized in Exhibit 7.6.

Benefits of MBO	Problems with MBO
1. Manager and employee efforts are focused on activities that will lead to goal attainment.	1. Constant change prevents MBO from taking hold.
2. Performance can be improved at all company levels.	2. An environment of poor employer–employee relations reduces MBO effectiveness.
3. Employees are motivated.	3. Strategic goals may be displaced by operational goals.
4. Departmental and individual goals are aligned with company goals.	4. Mechanistic organizations and values that discourage participation can harm the MBO process.
	5. Too much paperwork saps MBO energy.

Exhibit **7.6**

MBO Benefits and Problems

The benefits of the MBO process can be many. Corporate goals are more likely to be achieved when they focus manager and employee efforts. Performance is improved because employees are committed to attaining the goal, are motivated because they help decide what is expected, and are free to be resourceful. Goals at lower levels are aligned with and enable the attainment of goals at top management levels.

Problems with MBO occur when the company faces rapid change. The environment and internal activities must have some stability for performance to be measured and compared against goals. When new goals must be set every few months, there is no time for action plans and appraisal to take effect. Also, poor employer-employee relations reduce effectiveness because there is an element of distrust between managers and workers. Sometimes goal "displacement" occurs if employees focus exclusively on their operational goals to the detriment of other teams or departments. Overemphasis on operational goals can harm the attainment of overall goals. Another problem arises in mechanistic organizations characterized by rigidly defined tasks and rules that may not be compatible with MBO's emphasis on mutual determination of goals by employee and supervisor. In addition, when participation is discouraged, employees will lack the training and values to jointly set goals with employers. Finally, if MBO becomes a process of filling out annual paperwork rather than energizing employees to achieve goals, it becomes an empty exercise. Once the paperwork is completed, employees forget about the goals, perhaps even resenting the paperwork in the first place.

Single-Use and Standing Plans

Single-use plans are developed to achieve a set of goals that are not likely to be repeated in the future. **Standing plans** are ongoing plans that are used to provide guidance for tasks performed repeatedly within the organization. Exhibit 7.7 outlines the major types of single-use and standing plans. Single-use plans typically include both programs and projects. The primary standing plans are organizational policies, rules, and procedures. Standing plans generally pertain to such matters as employee illness, absences, smoking, discipline, hiring, and dismissal. Many companies are discovering a need to develop standing plans regarding the use of e-mail, as discussed in the Manager's Shoptalk box.

single-use plans
Plans that are developed to achieve a set of goals that are unlikely to be repeated in the future.

standing plans
Ongoing plans that are used to provide guidance for tasks performed repeatedly within the organization.

Exhibit 7.7

Major Types of Single-Use and Standing Plans

Single-Use Plans	Standing Plans
Program • Plans for attaining a one-time organizational goal • Major undertaking that may take several years to complete • Large in scope; may be associated with several projects **Examples:** Building a new headquarters Converting all paper files to digital	**Policy** • Broad in scope—a general guide to action • Based on organization's overall goals/strategic plan • Defines boundaries within which to make decisions **Examples:** Drug-free workplace policies Sexual harassment policies
Project • Also a set of plans for attaining a one-time goal • Smaller in scope and complexity than a program; shorter time horizon • Often one part of a larger program **Examples:** Renovating the office Setting up a company intranet	**Rule** • Narrow in scope • Describes how a specific action is to be performed • May apply to specific setting **Example:** No-smoking rule in areas of plant where hazardous materials are stored **Procedure** • Sometimes called a standard operating procedure • Defines a precise series of steps to attain certain goals **Examples:** Procedures for issuing refunds Procedures for handling employee grievances

Contingency Plans

contingency plans

Plans that define company responses to specific situations, such as emergencies, setbacks, or unexpected conditions.

When organizations are operating in a highly uncertain environment or dealing with long time horizons, sometimes planning can seem like a waste of time. In fact, strict plans may even hinder rather than help an organization's performance in the face of rapid technological, social, economic, or other environmental change. In these cases, managers can develop multiple future scenarios to help them form more flexible plans. **Contingency plans**, sometimes referred to as *scenarios*, define company responses to be taken in the case of emergencies, setbacks, or unexpected conditions. To develop contingency plans, managers identify uncontrollable factors, such as recession, inflation, technological developments or safety accidents. To minimize the impact of these potential factors, managers can forecast the worst-case scenarios. For example, if sales fall 20 percent and prices drop 8 percent, what will the company do? Managers can develop contingency plans that might include layoffs, emergency budgets, or new sales efforts.[30] As another example, top managers at Duke Energy Corp., which has invested heavily in building new power plants to meet increasing demand, developed contingency plans for what the company would do if U.S. economic growth slowed to 1 percent a year, leaving the company with too much capacity amid weakening prices.[31]

Manager's Shoptalk

Regulating E-mail in the Workplace

Top executives around the globe are discovering that casual e-mail messages can come back to haunt them—in court. Messages dashed off years ago by Bill Gates became digital "smoking guns" in the Justice Department's antitrust case against Microsoft. Chevron Corp. had to pay female employees $2.2 million to settle a sexual harassment lawsuit arising from inappropriate e-mail circulated by male co-workers.

As with any powerful tool, e-mail has the potential to be hazardous, backfiring not only on the employee but on the organization as well. One study found that "potentially dangerous or nonproductive" messages account for fully 31 percent of all company e-mail. Experts say a formal written policy is the best way for companies to protect themselves, and they offer some tips for managers on developing effective policies governing the use of e-mail.

- *Make clear that all e-mail and its contents are the property of the company.* Many experts recommend warning employees that the company reserves the right to read any messages transmitted over its system. "Employees need to understand that a company can access employees' e-mail at any time without advance notice or consent," says lawyer Pam Reeves. This helps to discourage frivolous e-mails or those that might be considered crude and offensive.
- *Tie the policy to the company's sexual harassment policy or other policies governing employee behavior on the job.*

In almost all sexual harassment cases, judges have ruled that the use of e-mail was considered part of the workplace environment.

- *Establish clear guidelines on matters such as the use of e-mail for jokes and other non-work related communications, the sending of confidential messages, and how to handle junk e-mail.* At Prudential Insurance, for example, employees are prohibited from using company e-mail to share jokes, photographs, or any kind of nonbusiness information.
- *Set a time limit for how long messages will be saved before they are automatically deleted by network managers.* Retention periods of 30 to 90 days are typical. Most organizations also set up a centralized archive for retaining essential e-mail messages.
- *Require that all employees read updates from the company's network and security managers.*

A solid e-mail policy is no guarantee that e-mail won't someday be used against the company in a lawsuit. For example, even deleted e-mails can usually be tracked down by a computer-forensics expert. However, an effective policy is the best step companies can take to manage the potential risks of e-mail abuse.

SOURCES: Marcia Stepanek with Steve Hamm, "When the Devil Is in the E-mails," *BusinessWeek* (June 8, 1998), 72–74; and Joseph McCafferty, "The Phantom Menace," *CFO* (June 1999), 89–91.

Crisis Management Planning

A special type of contingency planning is crisis management planning. Sometimes, events are so sudden and devastating that they require immediate response. Consider events such as the November 12, 2001, crash of American Airlines Flight 587 in a New York neighborhood already devastated by terrorist attacks, the 1982 Tylenol crisis, when four people died after taking cyanide-laced capsules, the 1993 deaths due to e-coli bacteria from Jack-in-the-Box hamburgers, or the 1986 Challenger space shuttle explosion. Companies also face many smaller crises that call for rapid response, such as allegations of tainted Coca-Cola in Belgium or charges of child labor abuse against Kathy Lee Gifford's clothing company. Crises have become integral features of our organizations.[32] For managers to respond appropriately, they need carefully thought-out and coordinated plans. Although crises may vary, a good crisis management plan can be used to respond to any disaster at any time of the day or night.

Exhibit 7.8 outlines the three essential stages of crisis management.[33] The prevention stage involves activities managers undertake to try to prevent

Exhibit **7.8**

Three Stages of Crisis Management

Prevention
- Build relationships.
- Detect signals from environment.

Preparation
- Designate crisis management team and spokesperson.
- Create detailed crisis management plan.
- Set up effective communications system.

Containment
- Rapid response: Activate the crisis management plan.
- Get the awful truth out.
- Meet safety and emotional needs.
- Return to business.

SOURCE: Based on information in W. Timothy Coombs, *Ongoing Crisis Communication: Planning, Managing, and Responding* (Thousand Oaks, Calif.: Sage Publications, 1999).

crises from occurring and to detect warning signs of potential crises. The preparation stage includes all the detailed planning to handle a crises when it occurs. Containment focuses on the organization's response to an actual crisis and any follow-up concerns.

Prevention   Although unexpected events and disasters will happen, managers should do everything they can to prevent crises. One critical part of the prevention stage is building relationships with key stakeholders such as employees, customers, suppliers, governments, unions, and the community. By developing favorable relationships, managers can often prevent crises from happening. Similarly, organizations that build a reputation as a solid, reputable company are able to avert many crises and respond more effectively to those that cannot be avoided.

Open communication with employees, customers, and all stakeholders enables the organization and stakeholder groups to better understand one another and develop mutual respect. For example, organizations that have open, trusting relationships with employees and unions may avoid crippling labor strikes. Open communication also helps managers identify problems early so they do not turn into major issues. For example, Nike had early warning from distributors in the Middle East that its flame logo on a basketball shoe looked like the word *Allah* in Arabic script and would be considered offensive to Muslims. Although the company made some minor changes, managers failed to take the warning seriously. Eventually, Nike had to recall nearly 40,000 pairs of the shoes and issue an apology to Muslims.[34] Similarly, Coca-Cola suffered a major crisis in Europe because it failed to respond quickly to reports of "foul-smelling" Coke in Belgium. CEO Douglas Daft recently observed that every problem the company has faced in recent years "can be traced to a singular cause: We neglected our relationships."[35]

Preparation   Three steps in the preparation stage are: designating a crisis management team and spokesperson, creating a detailed crisis management plan, and setting up an effective communications system. The crisis management team is a cross-functional group of people who are designated to swing into action if a crisis occurs. They are closely involved in creating the crisis management plan, and they'll be called upon to implement the plan if a disaster hits. The U.S. Office of Personnel Management in Washington, D.C., has nearly 200 people assigned and trained to take immediate action if a disaster occurs, including 8 employees assigned to each of 10 floors to handle an evacuation.[36]

The organization should also designate a spokesperson who will be the voice of the company during the crisis. The spokesperson in many cases is the top leader of the organization. After the terrorist attacks on the World Trade Center, Mayor Rudolph Guilliani was the spokesperson for the city of New York. Donald Carty, CEO of American Airlines, was the spokesperson following the crash of Flight 587. However, organizations typically assign more than one spokesperson so that someone else will be prepared if the top leader is not available.

The crisis management plan (CMP) should be a detailed, written plan that specifies the steps to be taken, and by whom, if a crisis occurs. The CMP should list complete contact information for members of the crisis management team, as well as for outside agencies such as emergency personnel, insurance companies, and so forth. It should include plans for ensuring the safety of employees and customers, procedures for back-up and recovery of computer systems and protecting proprietary information, details on where people should go if they need to be evacuated, plans for alternative work sites if needed, and guidelines for handling media and other outside communications. Some firms hand out wallet-sized cards that inform employees about evacuation procedures and what to do following an evacuation.[37] Morgan Stanley Dean Witter, the World Trade Center's largest tenant with 3,700 employees, adopted a crisis management plan after bomb threats during the Persian Gulf War in 1991. Top managers credit its detailed evacuation procedures for saving the lives of all but six employees during the September 11 attack. "Everybody knew about the . . . plan," said a spokesman. "We met constantly to talk about it."[38] A key point is that a crisis management plan should be a living, changing document that is regularly reviewed, practiced, and updated as needed.

A major part of the CMP is a communications plan that designates a crisis command center and sets up a complete communications and messaging system. The command center serves as a place for the crisis management team to meet, gather data and monitor incoming information, and disseminate information to the media and the public. The plan should designate alternate communication centers in case the main center is disrupted and should include plans for varied communication methods, such as toll-free call centers, Internet and intranet communications, and plans for rerouting data traffic if necessary. All employees should have multiple ways to get in touch with the organization and report their whereabouts and status after a disaster. The organization should also have varied ways to contact employees and notify them of changing circumstances and plans.

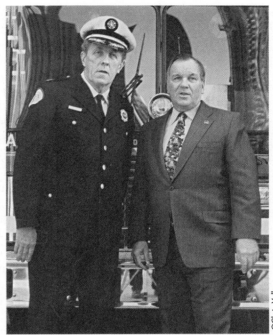

©Chris Volk

Ever since the great Chicago fire of 1871, the city of Chicago has emphasized crisis management planning to prepare for fires, floods, chemical spills, or other disasters. Following the events of September 11, 2001, and the subsequent anthrax attacks in the U.S., officials such as Fire Chief James Joyce and Mayor Richard Daley, pictured here, adapted crisis plans to deal with the threat of bioterrorism. The city's crisis management team spent four days and nights at the Emergency Communications Center, smoothly deploying police and paramedics to investigate sightings of suspicious powder and updating the press twice daily. "We calmed people because we spoke with one voice," said Police Superintendent Terry Hillard.

Containment Some crises are inevitable no matter how well prepared an organization is. When a crisis hits, a rapid response is crucial. The team should be able to immediately implement the crisis management plan, so training and practice are important. In addition, the organization should "get the awful truth out" to employees and the public as soon as possible.[39] This is the stage where it becomes critical for the organization to speak with one voice so that employees, customers, and the public do not get conflicting stories about what happened and what the organization is doing about it. The crisis team gathers as much information as possible and the designated spokesperson presents the facts as they are known. Failing to get the truth out quickly lowers an organization's chances of recovering from the crisis. After the Exxon Valdez oil spill in Prince William Sound, it took CEO Lawrence Rawls more than a week to comment on the disaster, which left employees and the public bitter and angry.[40] When he did speak out, Rawls tried to minimize the disaster by implying that the death of 30,000 birds in the oil spill was not very significant. His inability to understand and respond to people's emotions damaged his and the company's reputation.

Likewise, when anthrax-laced letters contaminated the Hart Senate office building in 2001, Capitol Hill staffers were tested and placed on antibiotics, but the U.S. Postal Service (USPS) was not as quick to respond. Two postal workers died and several others were infected by the deadly spores, and the American Postal Workers Union was vocal in its anger. The USPS, relying on bad information about anthrax and not wanting to bring mail service to a halt, downplayed the dangers to the mail handlers and to the public. The crisis ended with no further postal worker deaths, but the slow reaction of the USPS to protect its employees left a bitter taste in the mouths of postal workers.[41]

After ensuring the physical safety of people (and in some cases, animal life) the next focus should be on responding to the emotional needs of employees, customers, and the public. Giving facts and statistics to try to downplay the disaster always backfires because it does not meet people's emotional need to feel that someone cares about them and what the disaster has meant to their lives. After a crisis as devastating as the World Trade Center attacks or the Columbine school shootings, companies may provide counseling and other services to help people cope.

Organizations also strive to give people a sense of security and belonging. Getting back to business quickly is essential because it helps people believe that things can return to normal. Companies that cannot get up and running within 10 days after any major crisis are not likely to stay in business.[42] People want to feel that they are going to have a job and be able to take care of their families. Taking steps to protect people from danger during future disasters is important at this stage also. In this sense, crisis management planning comes full circle, because managers use the crisis to strengthen their prevention abilities and be better prepared in the future. A crisis is an important time for companies to strengthen their stakeholder relationships. By being open and honest about the crisis and putting people first, organizations build stronger bonds with employees, customers and other stakeholders, and gain a reputation as a trustworthy company. Although layoffs might be necessary in some situations, experts on crisis management suggest they should be a last resort following a major crisis because they damage trust, morale, and the company's reputation.

Planning in the New Workplace

The process of planning is changing. Traditionally, strategy and planning have been the domain of top managers. However, in today's workplace, top managers no longer control the planning process; everyone becomes involved. In some companies, planning is being taken out of the executive boardroom and central planning department to become a part of everyday work throughout the organization. We will first discuss traditional, top-down approaches to planning and then examine some of the newer approaches that emphasize bottom-up planning and the involvement of stakeholders in the planning process.

Traditional Approaches to Planning

Traditionally, corporate planning has been done entirely by top executives, by consulting firms, or, most commonly, by central planning departments. **Central planning departments** are groups of planning specialists who report directly to the CEO or president. This approach was popular during the 1970s. Planning specialists were hired to gather data and develop detailed strategic plans for the corporation as a whole. This planning approach was top down because goals and plans were assigned to major divisions and departments from the planning department after approval by the president. This approach worked well in many applications.

central planning department
A group of planning specialists who develop plans for the organization as a whole and its major divisions and departments and typically report directly to the president or CEO.

   Although traditional approaches to planning still are popular with some companies, formal planning increasingly is being criticized as inappropriate for today's fast-paced environment. Central planning departments may be out of touch with the constantly changing realities faced by front-line employees, which may leave employees struggling to follow a plan that no longer fits the environment and customer needs. In addition, formal plans dictated by top managers and central planning departments inhibit creativity and learning because employees have less incentive to think for themselves and come up with new ideas. In the new workplace, managers take a different approach to planning.

New Workplace Approaches to Planning

A new approach to planning is to involve everyone in the organization, and sometimes outside stakeholders as well, in the planning process. The evolution to a new approach began with a shift to **decentralized planning**, which means that planning experts work with managers in major divisions or departments

decentralized planning
Managers work with planning experts to develop their own goals and plans.

Courtesy of AMETEK, Inc.

This Corporate Financial Process Team is composed of a blend of AMETEK colleagues from the corporate office and several operating locations. The team developed an integrated financial forecasting program to help automate inventory reporting at AMETEK, a leading manufacturer of electric motors and electronic instruments in North America, Europe, and Asia. For its efforts, this planning task force was awarded the company's annual Dr. John H. Lux Total Quality Accomplishment Award.

to develop their own goals and plans. This enabled managers throughout the company to come up with their own creative solutions to problems and become more committed to following through on the plans. As the environment became even more volatile, top executives saw the benefits of pushing decentralized planning even further, by having planning experts work directly with line managers and front-line workers to develop dynamic plans that meet fast-changing needs.

In a complex and competitive business environment, traditional planning done by a select few no longer works. Strategic thinking and execution become the expectation of every employee.[43] For an example of a company that is finding hidden sources of ideas and innovation by involving all its workers in planning, consider Springfield Remanufacturing, described in the Putting People First box.

Planning comes alive when employees are involved in setting goals and determining the means to reach them. Here are some guidelines for planning in the new workplace.

Start with a Strong Mission.

Planning in the new workplace requires flexibility to meet ever-changing demands from the environment. Employees may have to constantly adapt plans to meet new needs. E-commerce organizations, for example, operate second-to-second rather than year-to-year, so traditional plans can serve only as a general guideline. In such an environment, a powerful sense of purpose and direction becomes even more important. Without a strong mission to guide employee thinking and behavior, the resources of a fast-moving company such as an e-commerce business can quickly become uncoordinated, with employees pursuing radically different plans and activities. A compelling mission can also serve to increase employee commitment and motivation, which are critical to helping organizations compete in a fast-shifting environment.[44]

Set Stretch Goals.

Stretch goals are highly ambitious goals that are so clear, compelling, and imaginative that they fire up employees and fuel progress. As we discussed earlier in the chapter, an important criterion for effective goals is that they be challenging yet realistic. In today's workplace, stretch goals are extremely important because things are moving so fast. A company that focuses on gradual, incremental improvements in products, processes, or systems will get left behind. Managers can use stretch goals to compel employees to think in new ways that can lead to bold, innovative breakthroughs. Motorola used stretch goals to achieve *six sigma* quality, as described in Chapter 2, which has now become the standard for numerous companies. Managers first set a goal of a tenfold increase in quality over a two-year period. After this goal was met, they set a new stretch goal of a hundred-fold improvement over a four-year period.[45]

Create a Culture that Encourages Learning.

In the new workplace, managers create a culture that celebrates diversity, supports risk-taking, and encourages constant experimentation and learning. An important value is questioning the status quo. Tomorrow's opportunities might come from very different directions than the basis of today's success. For example, soft-drink makers missed out on huge opportunities for new drinks such as chilled teas, sports drinks, and New Age beverages because they were focused on continuing the status quo rather than experimenting with new products.[46] Managers

Putting People First

SRC Holdings Corporation: Changing Lives by Changing Business

Jack Stack and twelve other former International Harvester managers started Springfield Remanufacturing Corporation on a shoestring in 1983. The company still exists, but today it is part of SRC Holdings Corporation, a group of 22 semiautonomous companies located in the Springfield, Missouri area. Stack, CEO of SRC Holdings, has built this amazingly successful corporation by tapping into people's universal desire to win. Stack's philosophy is that "the best, most efficient, most profitable way to operate a business is to give everybody a voice in how the company is run and a stake in the financial outcome, good or bad."

SRC involves everyone in the planning process and uses a bonus system based on hitting the plan's targets. Top managers meet with middle managers, supervisors, and front-line employees throughout their divisions to develop and sell their long-range plans. If a manager's plan is beyond the plant's capacity, the workers feel free to suggest workable alternatives. By the time managers present their plans to the top brass, everyone in the various divisions has had a say and has thus developed a sense of ownership in the plan.

All SRC businesses make their operating and financial performance numbers freely available so employees can compare performance to the plan. People "huddle" at least weekly around mural-sized charts in the employee cafeteria to talk about the numbers and what needs to be done to meet the targets. Employees take the company's success personally because they all own shares in the company through employee stock ownership plans (ESOPs). SRC has invested heavily in financial education for all workers so that everyone understands what is at stake and what is to be gained. "What we're doing . . ." Stack says, "is showing people how to get through life without fear. Once people understand what it takes to be a businessperson, not just a cog in the system but someone on the brighter side of capitalism, then their lives can change forever."

SOURCES: Jay Finegan, "Everything According to Plan," *Inc.* (March 1995), 78–85; and Art Kleiner, "Jack Stack's Story is an Open Book," *Strategy & Business* (Third Quarter 2001), 76–85.

---

in the new workplace might have to change plans at the drop of a hat, which requires a mindset that embraces ambiguity, risk taking, making mistakes, and learning.

Design New Roles for Planning Staff. Companies transform the conventional planner's job.[47] Planning specialists serve as facilitators and supporters; they do not decide on the substance of goals and plans. Planning experts can be very helpful in gathering data, performing statistical analyses, and doing other specialized tasks. The key difference is that, rather than looking for the *right answers*, they supply information in order to broaden the consideration of issues and support strategic thinking.

Use Temporary Task Forces. A **planning task force** is a temporary group of managers and employees who take responsibility for developing a strategic plan. Many of today's companies use interdepartmental task forces to help establish goals and make plans for achieving them. In the new workplace, the task force often includes outside stakeholders as well, such as customers, suppliers, strategic partners, investors, or even members of the general community. Today's companies are highly focused on satisfying the needs and interests of all stakeholder groups, so they bring these stakeholders into the planning and goal-setting process.[48] LendLease, an Australian real estate and financial services company, for example, involves numerous stakeholders, including community advocates and potential customers, in the planning process for every new project it undertakes.[49]

planning task force
A group of managers and employees who develop a strategic plan.

Planning Still Starts and Stops at the Top. Top managers create a mission that is worthy of employees' best efforts and provide a framework for planning and goal setting. Even though planning is decentralized, top managers must show support and commitment to the planning process. Top managers also accept responsibility when planning and goal setting are ineffective, rather than blaming the failure on lower-level managers or workers.

Summary and Management Solution

This chapter focused on organizational planning. Organizational planning involves defining goals and developing a plan with which to achieve them. An organization exists for a single, overriding purpose known as its *mission*—the basis for strategic goals and plans. Goals within the organization are defined in a hierarchical fashion, beginning with strategic goals followed by tactical and operational goals. Plans are defined similarly, with strategic, tactical, and operational plans used to achieve the goals. Other goal concepts include characteristics of effective goals and goal-setting behavior.

Several types of plans were described, including strategic, tactical, operational, single-use, standing, and contingency plans, as well as management by objectives. A special type of contingency planning is crisis management planning, which involves the stages of prevention, preparation, and containment. The Europa Hotel, described at the beginning of the chapter, provides an example of crisis management planning. The Europa, like most major hotels, has long had clear procedures for evacuation and dealing with disasters, and the hotel has a good record of getting people out fast. Amazingly, no one has ever been killed by a bomb at the Europa. Because the Europa has had so much experience dealing with crises, managers and employees have become ever alert to even the smallest signals that something is amiss, so they have been able to take quick action and prevent even greater damage or loss of life. The Europa is highly skilled at handling the containment stage of

crisis. After one bomb that ripped a huge hole in the side of the hotel and injured 13 people, everyone was back to work as usual by lunchtime. Hotel manager John Toner uses every crisis as a way to learn more, be better prepared, and make the company better and stronger. He believes the tendency to immediately look for ways to cut costs and lay people off following a crisis is dangerous. "I don't look for cost savings. I don't look at the bottom line—it'll look after itself," he says. Instead, Toner focuses on taking care of employees and guests and finding ways to make the business better. Because of that attention, hotel staff and guests have remained resolutely loyal to the Europa.

In the past, planning was almost always done entirely by top managers, by consultants, or by central planning departments. In the new workplace, planning is decentralized and people throughout the organization are involved in establishing dynamic plans that can meet fast-changing needs from the environment. Some guidelines for planning in the new workplace include starting with a powerful mission, setting stretch goals, creating a culture that encourages learning, designing new roles for planning staff, and using temporary task forces that may include outside stakeholders. In the new workplace, employees on the front lines may constantly be adapting plans to meet new needs. However, top managers are still responsible for providing a guiding mission and a solid framework for planning and goal setting.

Discussion Questions

1. To what extent would planning have helped the U.S. Postal Service respond more quickly and effectively to the crisis of anthrax-tainted letters being sent through the mail? What types of planning would be appropriate for unexpected events?

2. Write a brief mission statement for a local business with which you are familiar. How might having a

clear, written mission statement benefit a small organization?

3. What strategic plans could the college or university at which you are taking this management course adopt to compete for students in the marketplace? Would these plans depend on the school's goals?

4. If you were a top manager of a medium-sized real estate sales agency, would you use MBO? If so, give examples of goals you might set for managers and sales agents.

5. A new business venture has to develop a comprehensive business plan to borrow money to get started. Companies such as Federal Express, Nike, and Rolm Corporation say they did not follow the original plan very closely. Does that mean that developing the plan was a waste of time for these eventually successful companies?

6. What are the characteristics of effective goals? Would it be better to have no goals at all than to have goals that do not meet these criteria?

7. How is planning changing in the new workplace? Do you think planning becomes more important or less important in a world where everything is changing fast and crises have become a regular part of organizational life? Why?

8. Assume Southern University decides to (1) raise its admission standards and (2) initiate a business fair to which local townspeople will be invited. What types of plans would it use to carry out these two activities?

■ Management in Practice: Experiential Exercise

Company Crime Wave

Senior managers in your organization are concerned about internal theft. Your department has been assigned the task of writing an ethics policy that defines employee theft and prescribes penalties. Stealing goods is easily classified as theft, but other activities are more ambiguous. Before writing the policy, go through the following list and decide which behaviors should be defined as stealing and whether penalties should apply. Discuss the items with your department members until agreement is reached. Classify each item as an example of (1) theft, (2) acceptable behavior, or (3) in between with respect to written policy. Is it theft when an employee

- Gets paid for overtime not worked?
- Takes a longer lunch or coffee break than authorized?
- Punches a time card for another?
- Comes in late or leaves early?

- Fakes injury to receive workers' compensation?
- Takes care of personal business on company time?
- Occasionally uses company copying machines or makes long-distance telephone calls for personal purposes?
- Takes a few stamps, pens, or other supplies for personal use?
- Takes money from the petty cash drawer?
- Uses company vehicles or tools for own purposes but returns them?
- Damages merchandise so a cohort can purchase it at a discount?
- Accepts a gift from a supplier?

Now consider those items rated "in between." Do these items represent ethical issues as defined in Chapter 5? How should these items be handled in the company's written policy?

■ Management in Practice: Ethical Dilemma

Completing Project WebFirst

After two years with HealthFirst, Mary Palmer was handed her first big assignment, Project WebFirst. HealthFirst, a marketer of health products and services, was pushing hard to reposition itself on the Internet, and she was going to play a major role. Mary remembered with pride the rush she felt when the senior vice president of operations had explained that she'd been chosen to lead the project because of her reputation for getting results. "Put together a team that can do the job fast," he had said.

Mary had never been one to let any grass grow under her feet. She quickly put together a skeleton team and got down to business. Mary worked with the others to carefully develop goals and plans for every step of the project and set a clear timeline for meeting them. As the project progressed, more people were added to the team and things moved along nicely. But, unexpectedly, HealthFirst announced to senior managers a major acquisition that would mean at least a 20 percent reduction in the workforce. Mary was informed that the employees working on Project WebFirst would be affected, and that the workforce reduction timetable was aggressive. "You've done a great job managing the project so far," the senior VP of operations told her. "We know you'll manage this aspect just as well. We've got to keep things moving and get the Web strategy up and rolling."

Mary knew what that meant—she couldn't afford to lose the commitment and motivation of even one team member, or the carefully laid plans would fall to pieces. As word about the acquisition and possible layoffs spread through the company, team members began asking if they would be affected. Mary knows her employees want the truth, but she fears that telling them some of them will lose their jobs will delay the project. The company wants results *now*, and Mary wants the successful completion of Project WebFirst on her résumé.

What Do You Do?

1. Level with the Project WebFirst team members that some of them will probably be let go. Emphasize, however, that the success of the project will benefit each one of them, whether they stay with HealthFirst or need to find another job, so they need to stay focused.

2. Tell the team members that their jobs are not in jeopardy. Keeping the project moving to a successful completion is your first priority.

3. Get as much specific information as you can from top management about the merger and impending job reductions. Put together a group to develop an action plan, including a severance package that can help cushion the loss of jobs. Then, meet with your team and be as honest as you can about what is going on with the company.

SOURCE: Based on Doug Wallace, "Ripping Away a Curtain of Denial," *BusinessEthics* (Millennium-End Double Issue, 1999), 26.

Surf the Net

1. **Mission Statement.** Select a company you are interested in, or choose one from the Company Index at the back of this text. Using a search engine such as *http://www.alltheweb.com*, locate the company's Web site. Because not all companies include their mission statement at their Web site, be prepared to look at more than one company's Web site until you find a site that does publish the company's mission statement. Complete this exercise by submitting to your instructor a printout similar to the following for the company you selected:

Example Chapter 7, Surf the Net Exercise 1. I went to Dell Computer's Web site at *http://www.dell.com* and selected the following links to locate the mission statement: "About Dell," "Dell Vision," and "Mission Statement." Printed below is Dell's mission statement:

Mission Statement

Dell's mission is to be the most successful computer company in the world at delivering the best customer experience in markets we serve. In doing so, Dell will meet customer expectations of:
1. Highest quality
2. Leading technology
3. Competitive pricing
4. Individual and company accountability
5. Best-in-class service and support
6. Flexible customization capability
7. Superior corporate citizenship
8. Financial stability

---

2. **Goal Setting.** You've learned in this chapter about organizational goal setting. Many similarities exist between organizational and personal goal setting. The goal-setting skills you develop in setting personal goals will easily transfer to an organizational setting. Therefore, this exercise allows you to practice personal goal setting. Use one of the following sites or locate one of your own that will help you write a personal goal statement. Your goal statement should reflect specific ideas you learned about goal statements from the Web site.

http://www.topachievement.com/goalsetting.html
http://www.about-goal-setting.com
http://www.bodyresults.com/E2SMARTgoals.htm

3. **Contingency Plans.** The Federal Emergency Management Agency (FEMA), founded in 1979, is an independent agency of the federal government that reports to the president. Its mission is "to reduce loss of life and property and protect our nation's critical infrastructure from all types of hazards, through a comprehensive, risk-based emergency management program of mitigation, preparedness, response, and recovery." In this exercise you will focus on FEMA's preparedness information located at *http://www.fema.gov/pte/prep.htm*.

FEMA encourages the use of contingency plans by stating at this link: "Disasters take many forms. They're caused by gale force winds, sudden floods, releases of deadly chemicals, fire, ice, even upheavals of the earth itself. When disaster strikes, the best protection is knowing what to do." Select a natural or technological disaster, read the preparedness information provided, and write a brief outline of a contingency plan for what an organization should do before, during, and after the disaster.

■ Case for Critical Analysis

H.I.D.

Dave Collins, president of H.I.D., sat down at the conference table with his management team members, Karen Setz, Tony Briggs, Dave King, and Art Johnson. H.I.D. owns ten Holiday Inns in Georgia, eight hotels of different types in Canada, and one property in the Caribbean. It also owns two Quality Inns in Georgia. Dave Collins and his managers got together to define their mission and goals and to set strategic plans. As they began their strategic planning session, the consultant they had hired suggested that each describe what he or she wanted for the company's domestic operations in the next 10 years—how many hotels it should own, where to locate them, and who the target market was. Another question he asked them to consider was what the driving force of the company should be—that is, the single characteristic that would separate H.I.D. from other companies.

The team members wrote their answers on flip charts, and the consultant summarized the results. Dave Collins's goal included 50 hotels in 10 years, with the number increasing to 26 or 27 in 5 years. All the other members saw no more than 20 hotels in 10 years and a maximum of 15 or 16 within 5 years. Clearly there was disagreement among the top managers about long-term goals and the desirable growth rate.

With the consultant's direction, the team members began to critique their growth targets. Dave King, director of operations and development, observed, "We just can't build that many hotels in that time period, certainly not given our current staffing, or any reasonable staffing we could afford. I don't see how we could achieve that goal." Art Johnson, the accountant, agreed. Karen Setz then asked, "Could we build them all in Georgia? You know we've centered on the medium-priced hotel in smaller towns. Do we need to move to bigger towns now, such as Jacksonville, or add another to the one we have in Atlanta?" Dave Collins responded, "We have an opportunity out in California, we may have one in New Jersey, and we are looking at the possibility of going to Jacksonville."

The consultant attempted to refocus the discussion: "Well, how does this all fit with your mission? Where are you willing to locate geographically? Most of your operation is in Georgia. Can you adequately support a national building effort?"

Tony Briggs responded, "Well, you know we have always looked at the smaller-town hotels as being our niche, although we deviated from that for the hotel in Atlanta. But we generally stay in smaller towns where we don't have much competition. Now we are talking about an expensive hotel in California."

Dave Collins suggested, "Maybe it's time we changed our target market, changed our pricing strategy, and went for larger hotels in urban areas across the whole country. Maybe we need to change a lot of factors about our company."

Questions

1. What is H.I.D.'s mission at present? How may this mission change?
2. What do you think H.I.D.'s mission, strategic goals, and strategic plans are likely to be at the end of this planning session? Why?
3. What goal-setting behavior is being used here to reach agreement among H.I.D.'s managers? Do managers typically disagree about the direction of their organization?

SOURCE: This case was provided by James Higgins.

■ Endnotes

1. Ian Wylie, "He's Belfast's Security Blanket," *Fast Company* (December 2001), 54–58.
2. Oren Harari, "Good/Bad News about Strategy," *Management Review* (July 1995), 29–31.
3. Amitai Etzioni, *Modern Organizations* (Englewood Cliffs, N.J.: Prentice-Hall, 1984), 6.
4. Ibid.
5. Max D. Richards, *Setting Strategic Goals and Objectives*, 2d ed. (St. Paul, Minn.: West, 1986).
6. C. Chet Miller and Laura B. Cardinal, "Strategic Planning and Firm Performance: A Synthesis of More than Two Decades of Research," *Academy of Management Journal* 37, no. 6 (1994), 1649–1685.
7. This discussion is based on Richard L. Daft and Richard M. Steers, *Organizations: A Micro/Macro Approach* (Glenview, Ill.: Scott, Foresman, 1986), 319–321; Herbert A. Simon,

"On the Concept of Organizational Goals," *Administrative Science Quarterly* 9 (1964), 1–22; and Charles B. Saunders and Francis D. Tuggel, "Corporate Goals," *Journal of General Management* 5 (1980), 3–13.
8. David Whitford, "A Human Place to Work," *Fortune* (January 8, 2001), 108–121.
9. Steven L. Marks, "Say When," *Inc.* (February 1995), 19–20.
10. David Pearson, "Breaking Away," *CIO*, Section 1 (May 1, 1998), 34–46.
11. Peter Galuszka and Ellen Neuborne with Wendy Zellner, "P&G's Hottest New Product: P&G," *BusinessWeek* (October 5, 1998), 92, 96.
12. Frank Rose, "Now Quality Means Service Too," *Fortune* (April 22, 1991), 99–108.
13. Mary Klemm, Stuart Sanderson, and George Luffman, "Mission Statements: Selling Corporate Values to

Employees," *Long-Range Planning* 24, no. 3 (1991), 73–78; John A. Pearce II and Fred David, "Corporate Mission Statements: The Bottom Line," *Academy of Management Executive* (1987), 109–116; Jerome H. Want, "Corporate Mission: The Intangible Contributor to Performance," *Management Review* (August 1986), 46–50; and Alan Farnham, "Brushing Up Your Vision Thing," *Fortune* (May 1, 1995), 129.

14. Paul Haschak, *Corporate Statements: The Official Missions, Goals, Principles, and Philosophies of Over 900 Companies* (Jefferson, NC: McFarland & Company, 1998), 63.

15. Charles A. O'Reilly III and Jeffrey Pfeffer, "Star Makers," (book excerpt from *From Hidden Value: How Great Companies Achieve Extraordinary Results with Ordinary People* (Boston, Mass.: Harvard University Press, 2000), in *CIO* (September 15, 2000), 226–246.

16. "Strategic Planning: Part 2," *Small Business Report* (March 1983), 28–32.

17. Paul Meising and Joseph Wolfe, "The Art and Science of Planning at the Business Unit Level," *Management Science* 31 (1985), 773–781.

18. Jenny C. McCune, "On the Train Gang," *Management Review* (October 1994), 57–60.

19. Mark Fischetti, "Team Doctors, Report to ER!" *Fast Company* (February/March 1998), 170–177.

20. Gina Imperato, "Dirty Business, Bright Ideas," *Fast Company* (February/March, 1997), 89–93.

21. John O. Alexander, "Toward Real Performance: The Circuit-Breaker Technique," *Supervisory Management* (April 1989), 5–12.

22. Mark J. Fritsch, "Balanced Scorecard Helps Northern States Power's Quality Academy Achieve Extraordinary Performance," *Corporate University Review* (September–October 1997), 22.

23. Joy Riggs, "Empowering Workers by Setting Goals," *Nation's Business* (January 1995), 6.

24. Joel Hoekstra, "3M's Global Grip," *WorldTraveler* (May 2000), 31–34; and Thomas A. Stewart, "3M Fights Back," *Fortune* (February 5, 1996), 94–99.

25. Edwin A. Locke, Garp P. Latham, and Miriam Erez, "The Determinants of Goal Commitment," *Academy of Management Review* 13 (1988), 23–39.

26. George S. Odiorne, "MBO: A Backward Glance," *Business Horizons* 21 (October 1978), 14–24.

27. Jan P. Muczyk and Bernard C. Reimann, "MBO as a Complement to Effective Leadership," *The Academy of Management Executive* 3 (1989), 131–138; and W. Giegold, *Objective Setting and the MBO Process*, vol. 2 (New York: McGraw-Hill, 1978).

28. Jack Ewing, "Siemens Climbs Back," *BusinessWeek* (June 5, 2000), 79–82.

29. John Ivancevich, J. Timothy McMahon, J. William Streidl, and Andrew D. Szilagyi, "Goal Setting: The Tenneco Approach to Personnel Development and Management Effectiveness," *Organizational Dynamics* (Winter 1978), 48–80.

30. "Corporate Planning: Drafting a Blueprint for Success," *Small Business Report* (August 1987), 40–44.

31. Bernard Wysocki Jr., "Soft Landing or Hard? Firm Tests Strategy on 3 Views of Future," *The Wall Street Journal* (July 7, 2000), A1, A6.

32. Ian Mitroff with Gus Anagnos, *Managing Crises Before They Happen* (New York: AMACOM, 2001).

33. This discussion is based largely on W. Timothy Coombs, *Ongoing Crisis Communication: Planning, Managing, and Responding* (Thousand Oaks, California: Sage Publications, 1999).

34. Coombs, *Ongoing Crisis Communication*, 28–29.

35. Ian I. Mitroff, "Crisis Leadership," *Executive Excellence* (August 2001), 19; Andy Bowen, "Crisis Procedures That Stand the Test of Time," *Public Relations Tactics* (August 2001), 16.

36. Kirstin Downey Grimsley, "Many Firms Lack Plans for Disaster," *The Washington Post* (October 3, 2001), E1.

37. "Disaster Planning," *Ioma's Report on Controlling Law Firm Costs* (October 2001), 9.

38. Grimsley, "Many Firms Lack Plans for Disaster"; "Girding Against New Risks: Global Executives Are Working to Better Protect Their Employees and Businesses from Calamity," *Time* (October 8, 2001), B8+.

39. Mitroff, "Crisis Leadership."

40. Ian I. Mitroff, Christine M. Pearson, and L. Katharine Harrington, *The Essential Guide to Managing Corporate Crises: A Step-by-Step Handbook for Surviving Major Catastrophes* (New York: Oxford University Press, 1996),13–17.

41. "Delayed Anthrax Treatments? Postal Workers Angered, Health Officials Admit Surprise," (October 23, 2001), accessed at *http://abcnews.go.com/sections/us/DailyNews/anthrax_postal.html* on January 29, 2002.

42. "Girding Against New Risks."

43. Harari, "Good News/Bad News about Strategy."

44. Gerald E. Ledford, Jr., Jon R. Wendenhof, and James T. Strahley, "Realizing a Corporate Philosophy," *Organizational Dynamics* (Winter 1995), 5–18; James C. Collins, "Building Companies to Last," *The State of Small Business* (1995), 83–86; James C. Collins and Jerry I. Porras, "Building a Visionary Company," *California Management Review* 37, no. 2 (Winter 1995), 80–100; and James C. Collins and Jerry I. Porras, "The Ultimate Vision," *Across the Board* (January 1995), 19–23.

45. See Kenneth R. Thompson, Wayne A. Hockwarter, and Nicholas J. Mathys, "Stretch Targets: What Makes Them Effective?" *Academy of Management Executive* 11, no. 3 (August 1997), 48.

46. Gary Hamel, "Avoiding the Guillotine," *Fortune* (April 2, 2001), 139–144.

47. Henry Mintzberg, "The Fall and Rise of Strategic Planning," *Harvard Business Review* (January–February, 1994), 107–114.

48. Jeffrey A. Schmidt, "Corporate Excellence in the New Millennium," *Journal of Business Strategy* (November–December 1999), 39–43.

49. Polly LaBarre, "The Company Without Limits," *Fast Company* (September 1999), 160–186.

Strategy Formulation and Implementation

CHAPTER OUTLINE

Thinking Strategically

What Is Strategic Management?

Grand Strategy

Global Strategy

Purpose of Strategy

Levels of Strategy

The Strategic Management Process

Strategy Formulation Versus Implementation

Situation Analysis

Formulating Corporate-Level Strategy

Portfolio Strategy

The BCG Matrix

Formulating Business-Level Strategy

Porter's Competitive Forces and Strategies

Partnership Strategies

Formulating Functional-Level Strategy

Strategy Implementation and Control

Leadership

Structural Design

Information and Control Systems

Human Resources

Implementing Global Strategies

LEARNING OBJECTIVES

After studying this chapter, you should be able to

1 Define the components of strategic management.

2 Describe the strategic planning process and SWOT analysis.

3 Understand Grand Strategies for domestic and international operations

4 Define corporate-level strategies and explain the portfolio approach.

5 Describe business-level strategies, including Porter's competitive forces and strategies and partnership strategies.

6 Explain the major considerations in formulating functional strategies.

7 Enumerate the organizational dimensions used for implementing strategy.

Management Challenge

Coke might be the world's most powerful brand, but that has not helped much lately. When Douglas Daft took over as CEO of the Coca-Cola Company, he inherited a host of troubles. Soda sales had slumped in the important U.S. market and to a lesser extent around the world, and Coke had failed to match rival Pepsi's aggressive moves into nonsoda businesses. A high-profile racial discrimination suit in the United States and a soda-contamination scare overseas had damaged the company's reputation and its relationships with customers, governments, and bottlers. Under the previous CEO, M. Douglas Ivester, there was no real sense of crisis at Coke's headquarters, where managers pretty much continued business as usual. The Australian-born Daft knew that needed to change if Coca-Cola was to remain one of the world's most admired and respected companies. During his first year on the job, Daft began dismantling the stale old regime at headquarters and brought in new top managers willing to make the tough changes to turn the company around. He also spent much of his time repairing relationships with government regulators in Europe and handling the backlash from financially strapped bottlers who charged that Coke had been trying to eke out profits at the bottlers' expense. Despite these early moves, Coke's sales and profits have stayed flat and the stock has continued to decline. The CEO knows he needs to come up with a powerful strategic plan to reignite the company in a hurry.[1]

If you were the CEO of Coca-Cola, what strategies might you adopt to regain the competitive edge? How would you go about formulating and implementing a new strategic plan?

The story of Coca-Cola illustrates the importance of strategic planning. Coke had been stumbling along for years, ever since the departure of beloved Chairman and CEO Roberto Goizueta. The late Goizueta had been a master at providing vision and strategic direction for the company, but his hand-picked successor, Douglas Ivester, proved incapable of keeping Coke on the path of success. Now, employees, board members, and investors are hoping Douglas Daft can formulate and implement strategies that can ignite growth and revive the troubled company.

Every company is concerned with strategy. Japan's Fuji Photo Film Company developed a strategy of being a low-cost provider to compete with Kodak. Fuji's relentless internal cost-cutting enabled the company to offer customers lower prices and gradually gain market share over the giant U.S. firm.[2] Hershey devised a new strategy of being a fierce product innovator to compete with Mars in the candy wars.[3] Hershey scored big with the introduction of such products as Twizzlers twisted licorice sticks, Jolly Rancher lollipops, and Bites, bite-sized pieces of favorite candy bars. Strategic blunders can hurt a company. Mattel suffered in recent years by losing sight of its core business and trying to compete as a maker of computer games. New CEO Robert A. Eckert has implemented a "back to basics" strategy that he hopes will get the toymaker back on track.[4]

Managers at Mattel, Hershey, Fuji, and Coca-Cola are all involved in strategic management. They are finding ways to respond to competitors, cope with difficult environmental changes, meet changing customer needs, and effectively use available resources. Research has shown that strategic thinking and planning positively affects a firm's performance and financial success.[5] Strategic planning has taken on new importance in today's world of globalization, deregulation, advancing technology, and changing demographics and lifestyles. Managers are responsible for positioning their organizations for success in a world that is constantly changing. Today's top companies thrive by changing the rules of an industry to their advantage or by creating entirely new industries.[6] For example, Champion Enterprises was going broke selling inexpensive, factory-built houses. CEO Walter Young Jr. says, "People thought we were in the trailer park business. It was a real perception problem." Young wanted to redraw the rules of the manufactured housing industry. Today, Champion is thriving by building full-size houses in its factories and offering customers such options as porches, skylights, and whirlpool baths.[7]

In this chapter, we focus on the topic of strategic management. First we define components of strategic management and then discuss a model of the strategic management process. Next we examine several models of strategy formulation. Finally, we discuss the tools managers use to implement their strategic plans.

Thinking Strategically

Chapter 7 provided an overview of the types of goals and plans that organizations use. In this chapter, we will explore strategic management, which is considered one specific type of planning. Strategic planning in for-profit business organizations typically pertains to competitive actions in the marketplace. In not-for-profit organizations such as the Red Cross, strategic planning pertains to events in the external environment. The final responsibility for strategy rests with top managers and the chief executive. For an organization to succeed, the CEO must be actively involved in making the tough choices and trade-offs that define and support strategy.[8] However, senior executives at such companies as General Electric, 3M, and Johnson & Johnson want middle- and low-level managers to think strategically. Some companies also are finding ways to get front-line workers involved in strategic thinking and planning. Strategic thinking means to take the long-term view and to see the big picture, including the organization and the competitive environment, and to consider how they fit together. Understanding the strategy concept, the levels of strategy, and strategy formulation versus implementation is an important start toward strategic thinking.

What Is Strategic Management?

Strategic management is the set of decisions and actions used to formulate and implement strategies that will provide a competitively superior fit between the organization and its environment so as to achieve organizational goals.[9] Managers ask questions such as, "What changes and trends are occurring in the competitive environment? Who are our customers? What products or services should we offer? How can we offer those products and services most efficiently?" Answers to these questions help managers make choices about how to position their organization in the environment with respect to rival companies.[10] Superior organizational performance is not a matter of luck. It is determined by the choices that managers make. Top executives use strategic management to define an overall direction for the organization, which is the firm's grand strategy.

Grand Strategy

Grand strategy is the general plan of major action by which a firm intends to achieve its long-term goals.[11] Grand strategies fall into three general categories: growth, stability, and retrenchment. A separate grand strategy can also be defined for global operations.

Growth. *Growth* can be promoted internally by investing in expansion or externally by acquiring additional business divisions. Internal growth can include development of new or changed products, such as Starbucks' introduction of Frappuccino, a bottled coffee drink, or expansion of current products into new markets, such as Avon's attempt to begin selling products in major retail stores. External growth typically involves *diversification*, which means the acquisition of businesses that are related to current product lines or that take the corporation into new areas. The number of companies choosing to grow through mergers and acquisitions is astounding, as organizations strive to acquire the size and resources to compete on a global scale, to invest in new technology, and to control distribution channels and guarantee access to markets. WorldCom, once an obscure long-distance carrier, has acquired more than 40 companies in the past decade and expanded into local phone services, data transmission, and Internet traffic. Another strategy for international growth is the formation of a joint venture, such as WorldCom's venture with Spanish telecom giant Telefónica, which extended WorldCom's reach into South America.[12] This chapter's Leading Online box describes how eBay is pursuing a growth strategy.

Stability. *Stability*, sometimes called a *pause strategy*, means that the organization wants to remain the same size or grow slowly and in a controlled fashion.

strategic management
The set of decisions and actions used to formulate and implement strategies that will provide a competitively superior fit between the organization and its environment so as to achieve organizational goals.

grand strategy
The general plan of major action by which an organization intends to achieve its long-term goals.

©Chuck Eaton

Kingsley Management LLC is pursuing a growth strategy with its high-tech car washes trademarked "Swash." So far, the Boston-based company has single-bay car washes in only three markets—Rochester, New York, Greenville, North Carolina, and Jacksonville, Florida—but founders Matthew Lieb (standing) and Chris Jones (in the driver's seat) are aiming for growth by forming partnerships to add their state-of-the-art car washes to gas stations and hypermarkets and developing plans for multi-bay units in high-traffic areas. At Swash, a customer pulls up to an ATM-like machine, pays with cash, credit, or a prepaid card, watches video instructions, and gets a software-controlled brushless wash, all in less than five minutes.

Leading Online

EBay: Building on Success

At a time when almost every Internet and technology company is handing out pink slips, the scene is quite different within the walls of San Jose, California-based eBay. In fact, the online auction company is planning to add to its work force of 2,400. EBay, which began as a site for selling collectibles, is pursuing a growth strategy, successfully molding itself into a platform for selling everything from computers to clothes. Every 60 minutes on the site, 120 PCs, 10 diamond rings, and 1,200 articles of clothing are sold, and someone buys a Corvette every three hours.

EBay CEO Meg Whitman sees her biggest job as keeping the company nimble and maintaining community spirit as the organization grows. From day one, eBay has been profitable, and in the second quarter of 2001, the company reported profits of $24.6 million, more than triple those reported a year earlier. Part of the reason for the success is because top managers have kept their focus on the community of buyers and sellers even as they have invested steadily in the company's growth.

There are several elements to eBay's strategic plan for growth. First, to branch out from its auction format, the company purchased Half.com, a site where new and used items can be listed at a fixed price. In addition, the company added a new feature called "Buy It Now," which allows users to acquire an item immediately, omitting the time-consuming auction process altogether. About 35 percent of all items listed by sellers on eBay now offer that option, which speeds up the rate of trading on the site. Another approach has been to allow businesses such as JCPenney, IBM, and Sun Microsystems to set up virtual storefronts. Ebay expected to attract around 2,000 businesses, but nearly 10 times that number wanted a piece of the action, recognizing the inexpensive potential for reaching millions of consumers. On the global front, eBay has acquired iBazar, a European trading site, and invested in the growth of its German, Canadian, and U.K. operations.

Mark Goldstein, former CEO of BlueLight.com, the online unit of Kmart, says, "eBay is what all of us wanted our Internet businesses to be." Even as e-commerce stalls in today's declining economy, online shoppers-turned-bargain-hunters surf the value-priced aisles of eBay, finding anything and everything. In fact, eBay is rapidly becoming "the Wal-Mart of the Internet."

SOURCE: Miguel Helft, "What Makes eBay Unstoppable?" *The Industry Standard* (August 6–13, 2001), 32–37.

The corporation wants to stay in its current business, such as Allied Tire Stores, whose motto is, "We just sell tires." After organizations have undergone a turbulent period of rapid growth, executives often focus on a stability strategy to integrate strategic business units and ensure that the organization is working efficiently. Mattel is currently pursuing a stability strategy to recover from former CEO Jill Barad's years of big acquisitions and new businesses. The current top executive is seeking only modest new ventures to get Mattel on a slower-growth, more stable course.[13]

Retrenchment. *Retrenchment* means that the organization goes through a period of forced decline by either shrinking current business units or selling off or liquidating entire businesses. The organization may have experienced a precipitous drop in demand for its products or services, prompting managers to order across-the-board cuts in personnel and expenditures. For example, Nortel Networks, described in Chapter 3, laid off 20,000 employees and closed several business units to cope with reduced demand. Some mid-sized companies are scaling back or abandoning their Web-based businesses because of poor results and a declining economy. Gaylord Entertainment, a Nashville-based entertainment company that traces its roots to the Grand Ole Opry, had counted on digital entertainment as a growth business, but just two years later managers closed the Gaylord Digital subsidiary, cut jobs, and put the company's Web business up for sale. Top executives felt that a period of retrenchment was necessary to strengthen profitability across the company.

Liquidation means selling off a business unit for the cash value of the assets, thus terminating its existence. An example is the liquidation of Minnie Pearl Fried Chicken. *Divestiture* involves the selling off of businesses that no longer seem central to the corporation. Germany's Siemens recently sold businesses that make power cables, automatic teller machines, and diesel locomotives because these businesses no longer seemed central to the company, which is staking much of its future on telecommunications.[14] Studies show that between 33 percent and 50 percent of all acquisitions are later divested. When Figgies International Inc. sold 15 of its 22 business divisions, including crown jewel Rawlings Sporting Goods, and when Sears sold its financial services businesses, both corporations were going through periods of retrenchment, also called *downsizing*.[15]

Global Strategy

In addition to the three preceding alternatives—growth, stability, and retrenchment—companies may pursue a separate grand strategy as the focus of global business. In today's global corporations, senior executives try to formulate coherent strategies to provide synergy among worldwide operations for the purpose of fulfilling common goals. A systematic strategic planning process for deciding on the appropriate strategic alternative should be used. The grand strategy of growth is a major motivation for both small and large businesses going international. Each country or region represents a new market with the promise of increased sales and profits.

In the international arena, companies face a strategic dilemma between global integration and national responsiveness. Organizations must decide whether they want each global affiliate to act autonomously or whether activities should be standardized and centralized across countries. This choice leads managers to select a basic grand strategy alternative such as globalization versus multidomestic strategy. Some corporations may seek to achieve both global integration and national responsiveness by using a transnational strategy. The three global strategies are shown in Exhibit 8.1.

Globalization. When an organization chooses a strategy of **globalization**, it means that its product design and advertising strategies are standardized throughout the world.[16] This approach is based on the assumption that a single global market exists for many consumer and industrial products. The theory is that people everywhere want to buy the same products and live the same way. People everywhere want to drink Coca-Cola and eat McDonald's hamburgers.[17] A globalization strategy can help an organization reap efficiencies by standardizing product design and manufacturing, using common suppliers, introducing products around the world faster, coordinating prices, and eliminating overlapping facilities. Ford Motor Company's Ford 2000 initiative built a single global automotive operation. By sharing technology, design, suppliers, and manufacturing standards worldwide, Ford saved $5 billion during the first three years.[18] Similarly, Gillette Company, which makes grooming products such as the Mach3 for men and the Venus razor for women, has large production facilities that use common suppliers and processes to manufacture products whose technical specifications are standardized around the world.[19]

Globalization enables marketing departments alone to save millions of dollars. For example, Colgate-Palmolive Company sells Colgate toothpaste in more than 40 countries. For every country where the same commercial runs,

globalization
The standardization of product design and advertising strategies throughout the world.

Exhibit *8.1*

Global Corporate Strategies

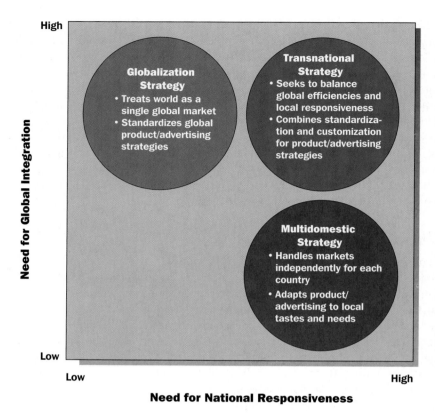

SOURCE: Based on Michael A. Hitt, R. Duane Ireland, and Robert E. Hoskisson, *Strategic Management: Competitiveness and Globalization* (St. Paul, Minn.: West, 1995), 239.

it saves $1 million to $2 million in production costs alone. More millions have been saved by standardizing the look and packaging of brands.[20]

multidomestic strategy
The modification of product design and advertising strategies to suit the specific needs of individual countries.

Multidomestic Strategy. When an organization chooses a **multidomestic strategy**, it means that competition in each country is handled independently of industry competition in other countries. Thus, a multinational company is present in many countries, but it encourages marketing, advertising, and product design to be modified and adapted to the specific needs of each country.[21] Many companies reject the idea of a single global market. They have found that the French do not drink orange juice for breakfast, that laundry detergent is used to wash dishes in parts of Mexico, and that people in the Middle East prefer toothpaste that tastes spicy. Procter & Gamble standardized diaper design across European markets, but discovered that Italian mothers preferred diapers that covered the baby's navel. This design feature was so important to the successful sale of diapers in Italy that the company eventually incorporated it specifically for the Italian market. Baskin-Robbins introduced a green-tea flavored ice cream in Japan, and Häagen-Dazs developed a new flavor called *dulce de leche* primarily for sale in Argentina.[22]

transnational strategy
A strategy that combines global coordination to attain efficiency with flexibility to meet specific needs in various countries.

Transnational Strategy. A **transnational strategy** seeks to achieve both global integration and national responsiveness.[23] A true transnational strategy is difficult to achieve, because one goal requires close global coordination while the other goal requires local flexibility. However, many industries are finding that, although increased competition means they must achieve global efficiency, growing pressure to meet local needs demands national responsiveness.[24] One company that effectively uses a transnational strategy is

These KitKat candy bars, being stocked by a salesperson in a Malaysian shop, are manufactured with locally grown beans—at a price 30 percent below imports. Nestlé, the world's biggest branded food company, rejects the idea of a single global market, opting for a multidomestic strategy that handles competition in each country independently. The Switzerland-based powerhouse is charging across the developing world by hiring people in the region, manipulating ingredients or technology for local conditions, and slapping on one of the company's 8,000 brand names. Of those 8,000 worldwide brands, only 750 are registered in more than one country.

Caterpillar, Inc., a heavy equipment manufacturer. Caterpillar achieves global efficiencies by designing its products to use many identical components and centralizing manufacturing of components in a few large-scale facilities. However, assembly plants located in each of Caterpillar's major markets add certain product features tailored to meet local needs.[25]

Although most multinational companies want to achieve some degree of global integration to hold costs down, even global products may require some customization to meet government regulations in various countries or some tailoring to fit consumer preferences. In addition, some products are better suited for standardization than others. Most large multinational corporations with diverse products will attempt to use a partial multidomestic strategy for some product lines and global strategies for others. Coordinating global integration with a responsiveness to the heterogeneity of international markets is a difficult balancing act for managers, but an increasingly important one in today's global business world.

Purpose of Strategy

Within the overall grand strategy of an organization, executives define an explicit **strategy**, which is the plan of action that describes resource allocation and activities for dealing with the environment and attaining the organization's goals. The essence of formulating strategy is choosing how the organization will be different.[26] Managers make decisions about whether the company will perform different activities or will execute similar activities differently than competitors do. Strategy necessarily changes over time to fit environmental conditions, but to remain competitive, companies develop strategies that focus on core competencies, develop synergy, and create value for customers.

strategy
The plan of action that prescribes resource allocation and other activities for dealing with the environment and helping the organization attain its goals.

Core Competence. A company's **core competence** is something the organization does especially well in comparison to its competitors. A core competence represents a competitive advantage because the company acquires expertise that competitors do not have. A core competence may be in the area

core competence
A business activity that an organization does particularly well in comparison to competitors.

of superior research and development, expert technological know-how, process efficiency, or exceptional customer service.[27] At Amgen, a pharmaceutical company, strategy focuses on the company's core competence of high-quality scientific research. Rather than starting with a specific disease and working backward, Amgen takes brilliant science and finds unique uses for it.[28] Boeing Corporation has a core competence in flexible design and assembly of aircraft.[29] And Home Depot thrives because of a strategy focused on superior customer service. Managers stress to all employees that listening to customers and helping them solve their do-it-yourself worries takes precedence over just making a sale.[30] In each case, leaders identified what their company does particularly well and built strategy around it. Dell Computer has succeeded with its core competencies of speed and cost efficiency.

DELL COMPUTER
http://www.dell.com

Dell Computer is constantly changing, adapting, and finding new ways to master its environment, but one thing hasn't changed from the days when Michael Dell first began building computers in his dorm room: the focus on speed and low cost. Most observers agree that a major factor in Dell's success is that it has retained a clear image of what it does best. The company spent years developing a core competence in speedy delivery by squeezing time lags and inefficiencies out of the manufacturing and assembly process, then extended the same brutal standards to the supply chain. Good relationships with a few key suppliers and precise coordination mean that Dell can sometimes receive parts in minutes rather than days.

The system is most evident at Dell's new OptiPlex factory in Austin, Texas, where Dell first introduced a new way of making PCs, called Metric 12, that combines just-in-time inventory delivery with a complicated, integrated computer system that practically hands a worker the right part—whether it be any of a dozen different microprocessors or a combination of software—at just the right time. The goal of the new system is not only to cut costs, but also to save time by decreasing the number of worker touches per machine. Rather than building computers in progressive, assembly-line fashion, small teams of workers at OptiPlex build a complete machine by following precise guidelines and using the components that arrive in carefully indicated racks in front of them. A small glassed-in office above the factory floor functions as a control tower, where employees take orders, alert suppliers, order parts, and arrange shipping, much of this handled over the Internet. By using sophisticated supply-chain software, Dell can keep a few hours' worth of parts on hand and replenish only what it needs throughout the day. Dell's just-in-time system works so smoothly that nearly 85 percent of orders are built, customized, and shipped within eight hours.

Dell's fixation with speed and thrift comes directly from the top. Michael Dell believes the core competencies that made Dell a star in PCs and servers can also make the company a winner as it moves into developing low-cost storage systems and Internet services. To anyone who doubts that Dell can compete in this new market, he says, "Bring them on. We're coming right at them."[31] ❖

synergy
The condition that exists when the organization's parts interact to produce a joint effect that is greater than the sum of the parts acting alone.

Synergy. When organizational parts interact to produce a joint effect that is greater than the sum of the parts acting alone, **synergy** occurs. The organization may attain a special advantage with respect to cost, market power, technology, or management skill. When properly managed, synergy can create additional value with existing resources, providing a big boost to the bottom line.[32] A good example is PepsiCo's new "Power of One" strategy, which is aimed at leveraging the synergies of its soft drink and snack-food divisions to achieve greater market power. PepsiCo CEO Roger Enrico has used the company's clout with supermarkets to move Pepsi drinks next to Frito-Lay snacks on store shelves, increasing the chance that when shoppers pick up chips and soda, the soda of choice will be a Pepsi product. Managers are betting that the strength of Frito-Lay, which enjoys near-total dominance of the snack-food market, will gain not only greater shelf space for Pepsi, but increased market share as well.[33]

Synergy can also be obtained by good relations with suppliers, as at Dell Computer, or by strong alliances among companies. Sweden's appliance giant Electrolux partnered with Ericsson, the Swedish telecommunications giant, in a joint venture called *e2 Home* to create a new way to make and sell appliances. Together, Electrolux and Ericsson are offering products such as the Screenfridge, a refrigerator with Internet connections that enables users to check traffic conditions, order take-out, or buy groceries, and an experimental *pay-per-use* washing machine. Neither company could have offered these revolutionary products on its own. "The technology was there, the appliances were there, but we needed a way to connect those two elements—to add value for consumers," said Per Grunewald, e2 Home's president.[34]

Value Creation. Delivering value to the customer should be at the heart of strategy. Value can be defined as the combination of benefits received and costs paid by the customer. Managers help their companies create value by devising strategies that exploit core competencies and attain synergy. Managers at California's Gallo Winery are finding new ways to use core competencies to create better value. Gallo, long-famous for its inexpensive wines, produces one of every four bottles of wine sold in the U.S. Today, the company is pouring $100 million into Gallo of Sonoma, a line of upscale wines with value prices. As the low-cost producer, Gallo is able to sell upscale wines for $1 to $30 less per bottle than comparable-quality competitors.[35] Likewise, McDonald's made a thorough study of how to use its core competencies to create better value for customers, resulting in the introduction of "Extra Value Meals" and the decision to open restaurants in different locations, such as inside Wal-Mart and Sears stores.[36]

Levels of Strategy

Another aspect of strategic management concerns the organizational level to which strategic issues apply. Strategic managers normally think in terms of three levels of strategy—corporate, business, and functional—as illustrated in Exhibit 8.2.[37]

Corporate-Level Strategy. The question, "*What business are we in?*" concerns **corporate-level strategy**. Corporate-level strategy pertains to the organization as a whole and the combination of business units and product lines that make up the corporate entity. Strategic actions at this level usually relate to the acquisition of new businesses; additions or divestments of business units, plants, or product lines; and joint ventures with other corporations in new areas. An example of corporate-level strategy is Cisco Systems, which bought 71 companies between the years of 1993 and 2000 to complement the company's core business of selling hardware and software for the Internet. Rather than pouring money into research, Cisco managers' strategy has been to buy companies that make products that will round out Cisco's existing product line and move the company into new markets. Now, many analysts

corporate-level strategy
The level of strategy concerned with the question, "What business are we in?" Pertains to the organization as a whole and the combination of business units and product lines that make it up.

Exhibit 8.2

Three Levels of Strategy in Organizations

Corporate-Level Strategy: What business are we in?

Business-Level Strategy: How do we compete?

Functional-Level Strategy: How do we support the business-level strategy?

think it is time for Cisco to take the opposite approach and begin shedding some businesses, such as the ATM and frame relay businesses, that no longer make sense as part of the company's overall business.[38]

business-level strategy
The level of strategy concerned with the question "How do we compete?" Pertains to each business unit or product line within the organization.

Business-Level Strategy. The question, *"How do we compete?"* concerns **business-level strategy**. Business-level strategy pertains to each business unit or product line. It focuses on how the business unit competes within its industry for customers. Strategic decisions at the business level concern amount of advertising, direction and extent of research and development, product changes, new-product development, equipment and facilities, and expansion or contraction of product lines. For example, top managers at Clorox sparked amazing new growth with simple product changes and advertising campaigns that make old brands seem new again. Making the household cleaner Pine-Sol smell like lemon and masking the odor of chlorine in Clorox bleach has made sales of these products take off. Similarly, Procter & Gamble is trying to stay competitive in the slow-growing consumer products industry by bringing out new versions of long-standing products, such as Tide Free, Tide WearCare, and Tide Kick, and by beefing up advertising budgets.[39]

Many companies are opening e-commerce units as a part of business-level strategy. For example, Hallmark's Web site is a marketing vehicle for the company's products and retail stores, as well as a place to sell gifts and flowers online.[40]

functional-level strategy
The level of strategy concerned with the question "How do we support the business-level strategy?" Pertains to all of the organization's major departments.

Functional-Level Strategy. The question, *"How do we support the business-level competitive strategy?"* concerns **functional-level strategy**. It pertains to the major functional departments within the business unit. Functional strategies involve all of the major functions, including finance, research and development, marketing, and manufacturing. The functional-level strategy for Procter & Gamble's research and development department, for example, is to invest heavily in developing new formulations of existing products, particularly its famous Tide laundry detergent. Another good example of functional-level strategy was when Sherwin-Williams' marketing department developed an advertising campaign several years ago aimed at specific markets for its paint. The Dutch Boy brand, touted as "the look that gets the looks," was advertised primarily to do-it-yourselfers who shopped the discount chains. The still-popular "Ask Sherwin-Williams" advertisements were targeted toward professionals. This marketing strategy helped the company increase sales at a time when total industry sales had fallen flat.[41]

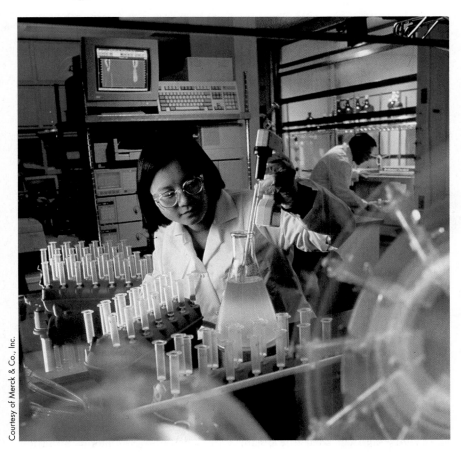

Courtesy of Merck & Co., Inc.

Merck has a business-level strategy of competing through product innovation. Merck researchers like Amy Cheung and Thomas Rano, using advanced technology, are producing more new compounds in less time than has ever been possible. Merck spends more than $2 billion on research and development and uses every means possible to reduce by months the drug discovery, development, and application processes. Merck maintains a competitive edge by having innovative products in many therapeutic categories for human and animal health.

The Strategic Management Process

The overall strategic management process is illustrated in Exhibit 8.3. It begins when executives evaluate their current position with respect to mission, goals, and strategies. They then scan the organization's internal and external environments and identify strategic factors that might require change. Internal or external events might indicate a need to redefine the mission or goals or to formulate a new strategy at either the corporate, business, or functional level. The final stage in the strategic management process is implementation of the new strategy.

Strategy Formulation Versus Implementation

Strategy formulation includes the planning and decision making that lead to the establishment of the firm's goals and the development of a specific strategic plan.[42] Strategy formulation may include assessing the external environment and internal problems and integrating the results into goals and strategy. This is in contrast to **strategy implementation**, which is the use of managerial and organizational tools to direct resources toward accomplishing strategic results.[43] Strategy implementation is the administration and execution of the strategic plan. Managers may use persuasion, new equipment, changes in organization structure, or a reward system to ensure that employees and resources are used to make formulated strategy a reality.

strategy formulation
The stage of strategic management that involves the planning and decision making that lead to the establishment of the organization's goals and of a specific strategic plan.

strategy implementation
The stage of strategic management that involves the use of managerial and organizational tools to direct resources toward achieving strategic outcomes.

Exhibit *8.3*

The Strategic Management Process

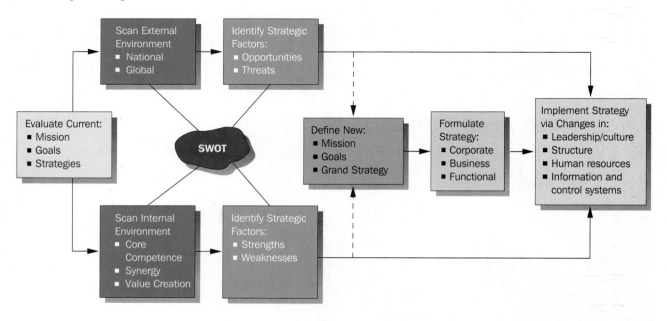

Situation Analysis

Formulating strategy often begins with an assessment of the internal and external factors that will affect the organization's competitive situation. **Situation analysis** typically includes a search for SWOT—strengths, weaknesses, opportunities, and threats that affect organizational performance. Situation analysis is important to all companies but is crucial to those considering globalization because of the diverse environments in which they will operate. External information about opportunities and threats may be obtained from a variety of sources, including customers, government reports, professional journals, suppliers, bankers, friends in other organizations, consultants, or association meetings. Many firms hire special scanning organizations to provide them with newspaper clippings, Internet research, and analyses of relevant domestic and global trends. Some firms use more subtle techniques to learn about competitors, such as asking potential recruits about their visits to other companies, hiring people away from competitors, debriefing former employees or customers of competitors, taking plant tours posing as "innocent" visitors, and even buying competitors' garbage.[44] In addition, many companies are hiring competitive intelligence professionals to scope out competitors, as we discussed in Chapter 3.

Executives acquire information about internal strengths and weaknesses from a variety of reports, including budgets, financial ratios, profit and loss statements, and surveys of employee attitudes and satisfaction. Managers spend 80 percent of their time giving and receiving information. Through frequent face-to-face discussions and meetings with people at all levels of the hierarchy, executives build an understanding of the company's internal strengths and weaknesses.

Internal Strengths and Weaknesses. *Strengths* are positive internal characteristics that the organization can exploit to achieve its strategic performance goals. *Weaknesses* are internal characteristics that might inhibit or restrict the organization's performance. Some examples of what executives evaluate to interpret strengths and weaknesses are given in Exhibit 8.4. The information sought typically pertains to specific functions such as marketing, finance, production, and R & D. Internal analysis also examines overall organization structure, management competence and quality, and human resource characteristics. Based on their understanding of these areas, managers can determine their strengths or weaknesses vis-à-vis other companies. For example, Citigroup has been able to grow rapidly because of its financial strength and reliable business processes. The company has developed sophisticated financial and product know-how in the United States and was able to leverage that knowledge to support its global strategy and provide more than 100 million customers worldwide with any financial service, in any currency, reliably and at a low cost.[45]

External Opportunities and Threats. *Threats* are characteristics of the external environment that may prevent the organization from achieving its strategic goals. *Opportunities* are characteristics of the external environment that have the potential to help the organization achieve or exceed its strategic goals. Executives evaluate the external environment with information about the nine sectors described in Chapter 3. The task environment sectors are the most relevant to strategic behavior and include the behavior of competitors, customers, suppliers, and the labor supply. The general environment contains those sectors that have an indirect influence on the organization but nevertheless must be understood and incorporated into strategic behavior. The general environment includes technological developments, the economy, legal-political and international events, and sociocultural changes. Additional areas that might reveal opportunities or threats include pressure groups, interest groups, creditors, natural resources, and potentially competitive industries.

An example of how external analysis can uncover a threat occurred in Kellogg Company's cereal business. Scanning the environment revealed that Kellogg's once-formidable share of the U.S. cold-cereal market had dropped nearly 10 percent. Information from the competitor and customer sectors

Bill Gross knows that the primary strengths of his company, idealab!, are creativity and rapid product development. Product innovation keeps idealab! at the forefront of the Net revolution with ventures such as cooking.com, tickets.com, and Wedding Channel.com. Since Gross recognized that he is better at starting companies than at running them, he turned control of the remaining business functions over to his brother, Larry, whom he credits with the company's survival.

Management and Organization	Marketing	Human Resources
Management quality	Distribution channels	Employee experience, education
Staff quality	Market share	Union status
Degree of centralization	Advertising efficiency	Turnover, absenteeism
Organization charts	Customer satisfaction	Work satisfaction
Planning, information, control systems	Product quality	Grievances
	Service reputation	
	Sales force turnover	

Finance	Production	Research and Development
Profit margin	Plant location	Basic applied research
Debt-equity ratio	Machinery obsolescence	Laboratory capabilities
Inventory ratio	Purchasing system	Research programs
Return on investment	Quality control	New-product innovations
Credit rating	Productivity/efficiency	Technology innovations

Exhibit 8.4

Checklist for Analyzing Organizational Strengths and Weaknesses

indicated that major rivals were stepping up new-product innovations and cutting prices. In addition, private-label versions of such standbys as corn-flakes were cutting into Kellogg's sales. Kellogg executives used knowledge of this threat as a basis for a strategic response.

The value of situation analysis in helping executives formulate the correct strategy is illustrated by Toys 'R' Us.

TOYS 'R' US
http://www.toysrus.com

Toys 'R' Us was started in a bicycle shop more than 50 years ago and grew to become the hottest toy store around during the 1980s. But by the mid-1990s, the once high-flying company was struggling just to stay aloft. John Eyler is the third CEO since 1994 to try to fix the company's massive problems. He has developed a new strategic direction for Toys 'R' Us that can be explained with SWOT analysis.

One of the company's greatest *strengths* is its reputation for carrying the widest selection of toys around. No other store carries the broad variety of toys and games found on Toys 'R' Us shelves. In addition, the company has tremendous market presence. With more than 700 U.S. stores, most people have a Toys 'R' Us store within easy reach—and many still think of Toys 'R' Us as *the* place to go if they are shopping specifically for toys. Unfortunately, the company's *weaknesses* far outweigh these strengths, including deplorable customer service, dirty and dilapidated stores, crowded aisles and poor product displays, and weak inventory management that puts too many slow-selling toys in stores and too few of the latest "must-have" products.

The biggest *threat* to the company is increased competition. A few years ago, Wal-Mart overtook Toys 'R' Us as the No. 1 U.S. toy seller. Other discount chains have also increased their toy selection and become more sophisticated toy retailers. In addition, online toy sellers hurt the company's sales during the late 1990s. However, Eyler and other managers also see a tremendous *opportunity* to become a unique kind of toy store.

To capitalize on the company's strengths and opportunities, Eyler has formulated a business-level strategy that attempts to provide the magic of upscale toy vendor FAO Schwarz at a reasonable Toys 'R' Us price. Rather than trying to compete with discount competitors on price, Toys 'R' Us will focus on superior customer service and creating a unique shopping environment. Eyler is remodeling and reorganizing stores, revamping inventory management, beefing up staffing and training, and increasing the percentage of private-label proprietary toys that will be sold exclusively at Toys 'R' Us. The new look of Toys 'R' Us does away with the warehouse-style aisles and replaces them with toys clustered by interest groups in cul-de-sacs and bright, interesting displays that are determined by factors such as age level and gender. Proprietary products, such as the Animal Planet line of animatronic wild animals and the new collection of licensed *E.T.* toys and gizmos, will be displayed in cubby holes close to the entrance to make them more visible and to give Toys 'R' Us a hit product that discount competitors cannot match.[46] ❖

Formulating Corporate-Level Strategy

Portfolio Strategy

Portfolio strategy pertains to the mix of business units and product lines that fit together in a logical way to provide synergy and competitive advantage for the corporation. For example, an individual might wish to diversify in an investment portfolio with some high-risk stocks, some low-risk stocks, some growth stocks, and perhaps a few income bonds. In much the same way, corporations like to have a balanced mix of business divisions called **strategic business units (SBUs)**. An SBU has a unique business mission, product line, competitors, and markets relative to other SBUs in the corporation.[47] Executives in charge of the entire corporation generally define the grand strategy and then bring together a portfolio of strategic business units to carry it out. One useful way to think about portfolio strategy is the BCG matrix.

The BCG Matrix

The BCG (for Boston Consulting Group) matrix is illustrated in Exhibit 8.5. The **BCG matrix** organizes businesses along two dimensions—business growth rate and market share.[48] *Business growth rate* pertains to how rapidly the entire industry is increasing. *Market share* defines whether a business unit has a larger or smaller share than competitors. The combinations of high and low market share and high and low business growth provide four categories for a corporate portfolio.

The *star* has a large market share in a rapidly growing industry. The star is important because it has additional growth potential, and profits should be plowed into this business as investment for future growth and profits. The star is visible and attractive and will generate profits and a positive cash flow even as the industry matures and market growth slows.

The *cash cow* exists in a mature, slow-growth industry but is a dominant business in the industry, with a large market share. Because heavy investments in advertising and plant expansion are no longer required, the corporation earns a positive cash flow. It can milk the cash cow to invest in other, riskier businesses.

portfolio strategy
A type of corporate-level strategy that pertains to the organization's mix of SBUs and product lines that fit together in such a way as to provide the corporation with synergy and competitive advantage.

strategic business unit (SBU)
A division of the organization that has a unique business mission, product line, competitors, and markets relative to other SBUs in the same corporation.

BCG matrix
A concept developed by the Boston Consulting Group that evaluates SBUs with respect to the dimension of business growth rate and market share.

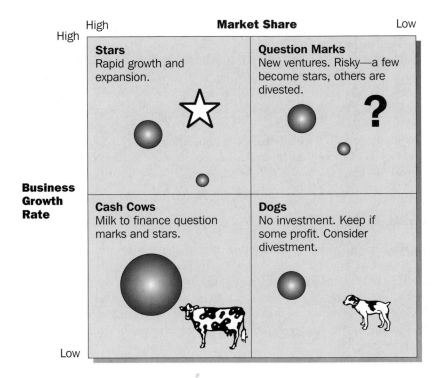

The BCG Matrix

The *question mark* exists in a new, rapidly growing industry but has only a small market share. The question mark business is risky: it could become a star, or it could fail. The corporation can invest the cash earned from cash cows in question marks with the goal of nurturing them into future stars.

The *dog* is a poor performer. It has only a small share of a slow-growth market. The dog provides little profit for the corporation and may be targeted for divestment or liquidation if turnaround is not possible.

The circles in Exhibit 8.5 represent the business portfolio for a hypothetical corporation. Circle size represents the relative size of each business in the company's portfolio. Most organizations, such as Gillette, have businesses in more than one quadrant, thereby representing different market shares and growth rates.

GILLETTE COMPANY
http://www.gillette.com

The most famous cash cow in Gillette's portfolio is the shaving division, which accounts for more than half of the company's profits and holds a large share of a stable market. Gillette's razors hold a commanding share of the U.S. market, and sales in other countries are also strong. The Oral-B division with its steady stream of new products has also been a cash cow, although sales have slowed in recent years.

The Braun subsidiary has star status, and managers are pumping money into research and development of new electric toothbrushes, personal diagnostic equipment, and other products. The Duracell division is a question mark. When Gillette purchased the division in 1996, it hoped Duracell would be a vehicle for rapid growth, becoming a star and eventually as big a cash cow as razors and blades. However, so far, the heavy investment in batteries is not paying off. Rivals Energizer and Rayovac have pummeled Duracell's new high-priced, long-lasting batteries with price cuts and special promotions. Rather than charging up Gillette's bottom line, Duracell has proven to be a serious drain on company profits. The toiletries division is also a question mark. A line of women's toiletries aimed at the European market failed, and products such as Right Guard and Soft & Dri deodorant have enjoyed only cyclical success. A new line of men's toiletries, including a gel-based deodorant, a gel shaving cream, and a new body wash, has had only limited success. Some critics believe the division is a dog, but Gillette is still trying to come up with some new products to save it from the fate of the Cricket disposable lighter several years ago. Bic dominated the disposable lighter line so completely that Gillette had to recognize Cricket as a dog and put it out of its misery through liquidation. Gillette is investing heavily in its question marks, particularly Duracell, to ensure that its portfolio will continue to include stars and cash cows in the future.[49] ❖

Formulating Business-Level Strategy

Now we turn to strategy formulation within the strategic business unit, in which the concern is how to compete. The same three generic strategies—growth, stability, and retrenchment—apply at the business level, but they are accomplished through competitive actions rather than the acquisition or divestment of business divisions. One model for formulating strategy is Porter's competitive strategies, which provides a framework for business unit competitive action.

Porter's Competitive Forces and Strategies

Michael E. Porter studied a number of business organizations and proposed that business-level strategies are the result of five competitive forces in the company's environment.[50] More recently, Porter has examined the impact of the Internet on business-level strategy.[51] New Web-based technology is influencing industries in both positive and negative ways, and understanding this impact is essential for managers to accurately analyze their competitive environments and design appropriate strategic actions.

Five Competitive Forces. Exhibit 8.6 illustrates the competitive forces that exist in a company's environment and indicates some ways Internet technology is affecting each area. These forces help determine a company's position vis-à-vis competitors in the industry environment.

1. *Potential new entrants.* Capital requirements and economies of scale are examples of two potential barriers to entry that can keep out new competitors. It is far more costly to enter the automobile industry, for example, than to start a specialized mail-order business. In general, Internet technology has made it much easier for new companies to enter an industry, for example, by curtailing the need for such organizational elements as an

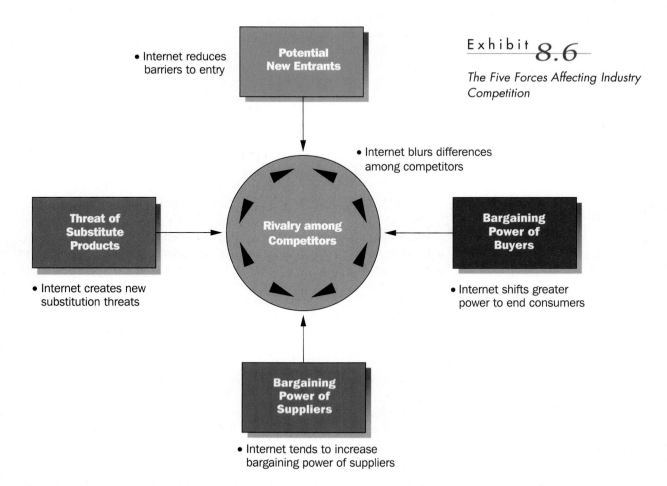

Exhibit 8.6

The Five Forces Affecting Industry Competition

- Internet reduces barriers to entry

Potential New Entrants

- Internet blurs differences among competitors

Threat of Substitute Products

Rivalry among Competitors

Bargaining Power of Buyers

- Internet creates new substitution threats

- Internet shifts greater power to end consumers

Bargaining Power of Suppliers

- Internet tends to increase bargaining power of suppliers

SOURCES: Based on Michael E. Porter, *Competitive Strategy: Techniques for Analyzing Industries and Competitors* (New York: Free Press, 1980); and Michael E. Porter, "Strategy and the Internet," *Harvard Business Review* (March, 2001), 63–78.

Talk about a differentiation strategy! By 2007, entrepreneurs at Space Island Group plan to offer tourists a trip to a privately-funded space station, complete with hotels, restaurants, and attractions. Founder and president Gene Meyers is enlisting the help of more than 150 high-level engineers, many of whom worked on the original NASA space shuttle program. Space Island plans on building a fleet of 50 commercial shuttles at a cost of $300 million each over the next ten years. The first should be up and running by 2005, with the first commercial station scheduled for full operations by 2007. Space Island will rely on superior technological know-how, employee creativity, and strong marketing abilities to make its unique project a success.

established sales force, physical assets such as buildings and machinery, or access to existing supplier and sales channels.

2. *Bargaining power of buyers.* Informed customers become empowered customers. The Internet provides easy access to a wide array of information about products, services, and competitors, thereby greatly increasing the bargaining power of end consumers. For example, a customer shopping for a car can gather extensive information about various options, such as wholesale prices for new cars or average value for used vehicles, detailed specifications, repair records, and even whether a used car has ever been involved in an accident

3. *Bargaining power of suppliers.* The concentration of suppliers and the availability of substitute suppliers are significant factors in determining supplier power. The sole supplier of engines to a manufacturer of small airplanes will have great power, for example. The impact of the Internet in this area can be both positive and negative. That is, procurement over the Web tends to give a company greater power over suppliers, but the Web also gives suppliers access to a greater number of customers, as well as the ability to reach end users. Overall, the Internet tends to raise the bargaining power of suppliers.

4. *Threat of substitute products.* The power of alternatives and substitutes for a company's product may be affected by cost changes or trends such as increased health consciousness that will deflect buyer loyalty to companies. Companies in the sugar industry suffered from the growth of sugar substitutes; manufacturers of aerosol spray cans lost business as environmentally conscious consumers chose other products. The Internet has created a greater threat of new substitutes by enabling new approaches to meeting customer needs. For example, traditional travel agencies have been hurt by the offering of low-cost airline tickets over the Internet.

5. *Rivalry among competitors.* As illustrated in Exhibit 8.6, rivalry among competitors is influenced by the preceding four forces, as well as by cost and product differentiation. With the leveling force of the Internet and information technology, it has become more difficult for many companies to find ways to distinguish themselves from their competitors, so rivalry has intensified.

Porter referred to the "advertising slugfest" when describing the scrambling and jockeying for position that often occurs among fierce rivals within an industry. Famous examples include the competitive rivalry between Pepsi and Coke and between UPS and FedEx. IBM and Oracle Corp. are currently involved in a fight for the No. 1 spot in the $50 billion corporate-software market. IBM recently rented a billboard near Oracle's headquarters proclaiming a "search for intelligent software." A few days later, Oracle fired the next shot with a competing billboard retorting, "Then you've come to the right place." [52]

Competitive Strategies. In finding its competitive edge within these five forces, Porter suggests that a company can adopt one of three strategies: differentiation, cost leadership, and focus. Companies can use the Internet to support and strengthen the strategic approach they choose. The organizational characteristics typically associated with each strategy are summarized in Exhibit 8.7.

1. *Differentiation.* The **differentiation** strategy involves an attempt to distinguish the firm's products or services from others in the industry. The organization may use advertising, distinctive product features, exceptional

differentiation
A type of competitive strategy with which the organization seeks to distinguish its products or services from competitors'.

Strategy	Organizational Characteristics
Differentiation	Acts in a flexible, loosely knit way, with strong coordination among departments
	Strong capability in basic research
	Creative flair, thinks "out of the box"
	Strong marketing abilities
	Rewards employee innovation
	Corporate reputation for quality or technological leadership
Cost Leadership	Strong central authority; tight cost controls
	Maintains standard operating procedures
	Easy-to-use manufacturing technologies
	Highly efficient procurement and distribution systems
	Close supervision; finite employee empowerment
	Frequent, detailed control reports
Focus	May use combination of above policies directed at particular strategic target
	Values and rewards flexibility and customer intimacy
	Measures cost of providing service and maintaining customer loyalty
	Pushes empowerment to employees with customer contact

SOURCES: Based on Michael E. Porter, *Competitive Strategy: Techniques for Analyzing Industries and Competitors* (New York: The Free Press, 1980); Michael Treacy and Fred Wiersema, "How Market Leaders Keep Their Edge," *Fortune*, February 6, 1995, 88–98; and Michael A. Hitt, R. Duane Ireland, and Robert E. Hoskisson, *Strategic Management* (St. Paul, Minn.: West, 1995), 100–113.

Exhibit 8.7

Organizational Characteristics of Porter's Competitive Strategies

service, or new technology to achieve a product perceived as unique. The differentiation strategy can be profitable because customers are loyal and will pay high prices for the product. Examples of products that have benefited from a differentiation strategy include Mercedes-Benz automobiles, Maytag appliances, and Tommy Hilfiger clothing, all of which are perceived as distinctive in their markets. Service companies, such as American Express and Hilton Hotels, can also use a differentiation strategy. The Harleysville Group uses its corporate culture to differentiate itself in the insurance industry, as described in this chapter's Putting People First box.

Companies that pursue a differentiation strategy typically need strong marketing abilities, a creative flair, and a reputation for leadership.[53] A differentiation strategy can reduce rivalry with competitors if buyers are loyal to a company's brand. Consider the example of online company eBay, described earlier in the chapter. Rather than cutting prices when Amazon.com and other rivals entered the online auction business, eBay continued to focus on building a distinctive community, offering customers services and experiences they could not get on other sites. Customers stayed loyal to eBay rather than switching to low-cost rivals. Successful differentiation can also reduce the bargaining power of large buyers because other products are less attractive, and this also helps the firm fight off threats of substitute products. In addition, differentiation erects entry barriers in the form of customer loyalty that a new entrant into the market would have difficulty overcoming.

2. *Cost Leadership.* With a **cost leadership** strategy, the organization aggressively seeks efficient facilities, pursues cost reductions, and uses tight cost controls to produce products more efficiently than competitors. A low-cost position means that the company can undercut competitors' prices and still offer comparable quality and earn a reasonable profit. Comfort Inn and

cost leadership
A type of competitive strategy with which the organization aggressively seeks efficient facilities, cuts costs, and employs tight cost controls to be more efficient than competitors.

Putting People First

Happy Employees Want to Stay at the Harleysville Group

The Harleysville Group is not your average, run-of-the-mill insurance company, and employees as well as customers know it. At Harleysville, managers strive to provide their employees with an appealing atmosphere and plenty of perks. The goal is to create a work environment that makes people want to stay. They must be doing things right, because the Harleysville Group boasts a 95 percent retention rate over the past several years. That translates into experienced, knowledgeable employees who can provide top-quality service. Customers who have grown tired of working with companies where the staff is constantly changing can appreciate the difference that comes from working with people who are happy and knowledgeable.

Harleysville does plenty to keep employees happy. Besides an impressive vacation plan, extensive medical benefits, a cafeteria that serves freshly made food, and snack carts that go about the building selling coffee and pastries, the company also provides onsite ATMs and a clothes-cleaning service that includes pick-up and delivery. A massage therapist comes in once a week, and employees pay 10 dollars for a 15-minute session, far below the market rate. The CEO pays for a 15-minute session each week and often gives it away to an employee as a way to say thanks for some extra effort. Two other, highly important perks are the company's project bonuses

and matching 401(k) investments. It is not unusual for the company to hand out checks for $1,500 or $2,000 to reward people for excellent work on a team project. For the 401(k) plan, Harleysville will match an employee's contribution anywhere from 25 percent to 100 percent, depending on company performance. In the last four years, the company has matched contributions one-to-one. For example, if an employee put in $5,000, the company would add that amount.

Other perks are aimed at increasing employees' knowledge and career skills. Tech-savvy workers are critical to the Harleysville Group, so the company spends more than $600,000 every year in technical training for the IS department alone. And that doesn't include the corporate funding for employees who are taking college courses and working toward higher degrees. To make it even easier, the company brings community college professors to the company campus so employees can take some courses without having to travel at the end of their work day.

Harleysville refuses to pay sky-high salaries, but the extensive benefits and the people-friendly work environment help the company stand out in the insurance industry. Inevitably, some employees do leave, but it usually isn't for a $5,000 raise, notes CEO Wayne Ratz. "It's more for an extravagant opportunity or for a lifestyle change."

SOURCE: Erik Sherman, "Happy in Harleysville," *CIO* (October 15, 2000), 84–86.

Motel 6 are low-priced alternatives to Holiday Inn and Ramada Inn. Dell Computer, described earlier in the chapter, has squeezed every cent possible out of the cost of building and selling PCs, making it the undisputed low-cost leader and the number-one maker of personal computers.

Being a low-cost producer provides a successful strategy to defend against the five competitive forces in Exhibit 8.6. For example, the most efficient, low-cost company is in the best position to succeed in a price war while still making a profit. For example, Dell declared a brutal price war in mid-2001, just as the PC industry entered its worst slump ever. The result? Dell racked up $361 million in profits while the rest of the industry reported losses of $1.1 billion. Likewise, the low-cost producer is protected from powerful customers and suppliers, because customers cannot find lower prices elsewhere, and other buyers would have less slack for price negotiation with suppliers. If substitute products or potential new entrants occur, the low-cost producer is better positioned than higher-cost rivals to prevent loss of market share. The low price acts as a barrier against new entrants and substitute products.[54]

focus
A type of competitive strategy that emphasizes concentration on a specific regional market or buyer group.

3. *Focus.* With a **focus** strategy, the organization concentrates on a specific regional market or buyer group. The company will use either a differentiation or low-cost approach, but only for a narrow target market.

Enterprise Rent-A-Car has made its mark by focusing on a market the major companies such as Hertz and Avis don't even play in—the low-budget insurance replacement market. Drivers whose cars have been wrecked or stolen have one less thing to worry about when Enterprise delivers a car right to their driveway. By using a focus strategy, Enterprise has been able to grow rapidly. [55]

Managers think carefully about which strategy will provide their company with its competitive advantage. Gibson Guitar Corp., famous in the music world for its innovative, high-quality products, found that switching to a low-cost strategy to compete against Japanese rivals such as Yamaha and Ibanez actually hurt the company. When managers realized people wanted Gibson products because of their reputation, not their price, they went back to a differentiation strategy and invested in new technology and marketing.[56] In his studies, Porter found that some businesses did not consciously adopt one of these three strategies and were stuck with no strategic advantage. Without a strategic advantage, businesses earned below-average profits compared with those that used differentiation, cost leadership, or focus strategies. In addition, because the Internet is having such a profound impact on the competitive environment in all industries, it is more important than ever that companies distinguish themselves through careful strategic positioning in the marketplace.[57]

Partnership Strategies

So far, we have been discussing strategies that are based on how to compete with other companies. An alternative approach to strategy emphasizes collaboration. In some situations, companies can achieve competitive advantages by cooperating with other firms rather than competing. Partnership strategies are becoming increasingly popular as firms in all industries join with other organizations to promote innovation, expand markets, and pursue joint goals. Partnering was once a strategy adopted primarily by small firms that needed greater marketing muscle or international access. Today, however, it has become a way of life for most companies, large and small. The question is no longer whether to collaborate, but rather where, how much, and with whom to collaborate.[58] Competition and cooperation often exist at the same time. In New York City, Time Warner (now AOL Time Warner) refused to carry Fox's 24-hour news channel on its New York City cable systems. The two companies engaged in all-out war that included court lawsuits and front-page headlines. This conflict, however, masked a simple fact: the two companies can't live without each other. Fox and Time Warner are wedded to one another in separate business deals around the world. They will never let the local competition in New York upset their larger cooperation on a global scale.[59]

The Internet is both driving and supporting the move toward partnership thinking. The ability to rapidly and smoothly conduct transactions, communicate information, exchange ideas, and collaborate on complex projects via the Internet means that companies such as Citigroup, Dow Chemical, and Herman Miller have been able to enter entirely new businesses by partnering in business areas that were previously unimaginable. IBM is collaborating with numerous partners around the world on the Internet, including competitors such as Dell and Hewlett-Packard, to develop, enhance, and market Linux-based software and services.[60]

Mutual dependencies and partnerships have become a fact of life, but the degree of collaboration varies. Organizations can choose to build cooperative relationships in many ways, such as through preferred suppliers, strategic business partnering, joint ventures, or mergers and acquisitions. Exhibit 8.8 illustrates these major types of strategic business relationships according to the degree of collaboration involved. With preferred supplier relationships, a company such as Wal-Mart, for example, develops a special relationship with a key supplier such as Procter & Gamble that eliminates middlemen by sharing complete information and reducing the costs of salespeople and distributors. Preferred supplier arrangements provide long-term security for both organizations, but the level of collaboration is relatively low. Strategic business partnering requires a higher level of collaboration. Toys 'R' Us and Amazon.com have negotiated a strategic partnership to sell toys online. Amazon agreed to provide warehousing, order fulfillment, and site design, and in return got warrants to purchase 5 percent of toysrus.com, plus up-front payments and a share of the site's sales.[61]

A still higher degree of collaboration is reflected in joint ventures, which are separate entities created with two or more active firms as sponsors. For example, MTV Networks was originally created as a joint venture of Warner Communications and American Express in the late 1970s. In a joint venture, organizations share the risks and costs associated with the new venture. It is estimated that the rate of joint venture formation between U.S. and international companies has been growing by 27 percent annually since 1985. Merck has put together major ventures with such competitors as Johnson & Johnson DuPont, and AstraZeneca.[62]

Mergers and acquisitions represent the ultimate step in collaborative relationships. U.S. business has been in the midst of a tremendous merger and acquisition boom. The U.S. pharmaceuticals company Upjohn merged with Sweden's Pharmacia. Boeing acquired McDonnell Douglas to form the industry's largest company, and Phillips Petroleum and Conoco recently merged to create the nation's third largest oil and gas company.

Today's companies simultaneously embrace both competition and cooperation. Few companies can go it alone under a constant onslaught of international competition, changing technology, and new regulations. In this new environment, businesses choose a combination of competitive and partnership strategies that add to their overall sustainable advantage.[63]

Exhibit 8.8

A Continuum of Partnership Strategies

SOURCE: Adapted from Roberta Maynard, "Striking the Right Match," *Nation's Business* (May 1996), 18–28.

Formulating Functional-Level Strategy

Functional-level strategies are the action plans adopted by major departments to support the execution of business-level strategy. Major organizational functions include marketing, production, finance, human resources, and research and development. Senior managers in these departments adopt strategies that are coordinated with the business-level strategy to achieve the organization's strategic goals.[64]

For example, consider a company that has adopted a differentiation strategy and is introducing new products that are expected to experience rapid growth. The human resources department should adopt a strategy appropriate for growth, which would mean recruiting additional personnel and training middle managers for movement into new positions. The marketing department should undertake test marketing, aggressive advertising campaigns, and consumer product trials. The finance department should adopt plans to borrow money, handle large cash investments, and authorize construction of new production facilities.

A company with mature products or a low-cost strategy will have different functional strategies. The human resources department should develop strategies for retaining and developing a stable work force, including transfers, advancements, and incentives for efficiency and safety. Marketing should stress brand loyalty and the development of established, reliable distribution channels. Production should maintain long production runs, routinization, and cost reduction. Finance should focus on net cash flows and positive cash balances.

Strategy Implementation and Control

The final step in the strategic management process is *implementation*—how strategy is put into action. Some people argue that strategy implementation is the most difficult and important part of strategic management.[65] No matter how creative the formulated strategy, the organization will not benefit if it is incorrectly implemented. In today's competitive environment, there is an increasing recognition of the need for more dynamic approaches to formulating as well as implementing strategies. Strategy is not a static, analytical process; it requires vision, intuition, and employee participation.[66] Many organizations are abandoning central planning departments, and strategy is becoming an everyday part of the job for workers at all levels. Strategy implementation involves using several tools—parts of the firm that can be adjusted to put strategy into action—as illustrated in Exhibit 8.9. Once a new strategy is selected, it is implemented through changes in leadership, structure, information and control systems, and human resources.[67] For strategy to be implemented successfully, all aspects of the organization need to be in congruence with the strategy. Implementation involves regularly making difficult decisions about doing things in a way that supports rather than undermines the organization's chosen strategy. Remaining chapters of this book examine in detail topics such as leadership, organizational structure, information and control systems, and human resource management.

Leadership

The primary key to successful strategy implementation is leadership. *Leadership* is the ability to influence people to adopt the new behaviors needed

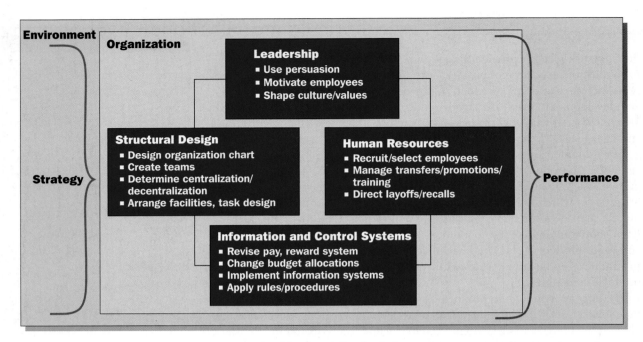

Environment

Organization

Leadership
- Use persuasion
- Motivate employees
- Shape culture/values

Strategy

Structural Design
- Design organization chart
- Create teams
- Determine centralization/ decentralization
- Arrange facilities, task design

Human Resources
- Recruit/select employees
- Manage transfers/promotions/ training
- Direct layoffs/recalls

Performance

Information and Control Systems
- Revise pay, reward system
- Change budget allocations
- Implement information systems
- Apply rules/procedures

Exhibit **8.9**

Tools for Putting Strategy into Action

SOURCE: Adapted from Jay R. Galbraith and Robert K. Kazanjian, *Strategy Implementation: Structure, Systems, and Process*, 2d ed. (St. Paul, Minn.: West, 1986), 115. Used with permission.

for strategy implementation. An important part of implementing strategy is building consensus. People throughout the organization have to believe in the new strategy and have a strong commitment to achieving the vision and goals. Leadership means using persuasion, motivating employees, and shaping culture and values to support the new strategy. Managers may make speeches to employees, build coalitions of people who support the new strategic direction, and persuade middle managers to go along with their vision for the company. Michael Dell of Dell Computer is a master of strategic leadership. Dell builds support for his vision and strategy at each year's employee meeting, where he has a chance to tell employees face-to-face exactly where he wants them to take the company in the year ahead. Dell's charisma and persuasive leadership keep employees fired up about his goals for the company.[68] With a clear sense of direction and a shared purpose, employees feel motivated, challenged, and empowered to pursue new strategic goals. Another way leaders build consensus and commitment is through broad participation. When people participate in strategy formulation, implementation is easier because managers and employees already understand the reasons for the new strategy and feel more committed to it.

Structural Design

Structural design typically begins with the organization chart. It pertains to managers' responsibilities, their degree of authority, and the consolidation of facilities, departments, and divisions. Structure also pertains to such matters as centralization versus decentralization, the design of job tasks, and the organization's production technology. Structure will be discussed in detail in Chapter 10.

In many cases, implementing a new strategy requires making changes in organizational structure, such as adding or changing positions, reorganizing to teams, redesigning jobs, or shifting managers' responsibility and accountability. For example, a cereal manufacturing company that wanted to reduce costs and improve efficiency to pursue a low-cost leadership strategy revised task design by combining several packing positions into one job and cross-training employees to operate all of the packing line's equipment. This reduced the number of workers needed during peak times and avoided leaving some workers idle during slow periods. The structural changes cut overall plant costs and manufacturing expenses while significantly increasing the factory's productivity and yield, thus helping to implement the new strategy.[69] At Limited Inc., a chain of specialty stores including Express and Victoria's Secret, founder and chairman Leslie Wexner decided to shift to a centralized organizational structure to implement a differentiation strategy. Limited was losing its fashion direction and customer insight, with many different stores pursuing their own goals and ideas. The new centralized structure, which includes a "corporate brain trust" of executives who oversee design, marketing, and distribution across the company's nearly 5,000 stores, has gotten the company refocused.[70]

Information and Control Systems

Information and control systems include reward systems, pay incentives, budgets for allocating resources, information technology systems, and the organization's rules, policies, and procedures. Changes in these systems represent major tools for putting strategy into action. For example, managers can reassign resources from research and development to marketing if a new strategy requires increased advertising but no product innovations. Managers and employees must also be rewarded for adhering to the new strategy and making it a success.[71]

At ConAgra, maker of Healthy Choice and Banquet brands, top executives instituted top-down cost controls in the corporation's operating units and developed new systems for pooling resources to reduce purchasing, warehousing, and transportation costs. To ensure that managers embraced the new strategy of cooperation and efficiency, leaders tied 25 percent of their bonuses directly to savings targets. Division heads saved $100 million in the first fiscal year. Top leaders also made changes in information systems by introducing a computerized network to track how much suppliers charge each ConAgra unit.[72]

Human Resources

The organization's *human resources* are its employees. The human resource function recruits, selects, trains, transfers, promotes, and lays off employees to achieve strategic goals. For example, training employees can help them understand the purpose and importance of a new strategy or help them develop the necessary specific skills and behaviors. Sometimes employees may have to be let go and replaced. One newspaper shifted its strategy from an evening to a morning paper to compete with a large newspaper from a nearby city. The new strategy fostered resentment and resistance among department heads. In order to implement it, 80 percent of the department heads had to be let go because they refused to cooperate. New people were recruited and placed in those positions, and the morning newspaper strategy was a resounding success.[73]

Mannie Jackson revived the Harlem Globetrotters, an organization on the brink of bankruptcy and irrelevancy, by recruiting new players who could recapture the glory the Globetrotters enjoyed in the 1960s and 1970s. Jackson rates potential players on their skill, charisma, punctuality, and attitude. He wants only top athletes who can promote the Globetrotter brand and are willing to be role models.[74]

Implementing Global Strategies

The difficulty of implementing strategy is greater when a company goes global. In the international arena, flexibility and superb communication emerge as mandatory leadership skills. Likewise, structural design must merge successfully with foreign cultures as well as link foreign operations to the home country. Managers must make decisions about how to structure the organization to achieve the desired level of global integration and local responsiveness, as described earlier. Information and control systems must fit the needs and incentives within local cultures. In a country such as Japan or China, financial bonuses for star performance would be humiliating to an individual, whereas group motivation and reward are acceptable. As in North America, control is typically created through timetables and budgets and by monitoring progress toward desired goals. Finally, the recruitment, training, transfer, promotion, and layoff of international human resources create an array of problems not confronted in North America. Labor laws, guaranteed jobs, and cultural traditions of keeping unproductive employees on the job provide special problems for strategy implementation.

In summary, strategy implementation is essential for effective strategic management. Managers implement strategy through the tools of leadership, structural design, information and control systems, and human resources. Without effective implementation, even the most creative strategy will fail.

■ Summary and Management Solution

This chapter described important concepts of strategic management. Strategic management begins with an evaluation of the organization's current mission, goals, and strategy. This evaluation is followed by situation analysis (called SWOT analysis), which examines opportunities and threats in the external environment as well as strengths and weaknesses within the organization. Situation analysis leads to the formulation of explicit strategic plans, which then must be implemented.

Strategy formulation takes place at three levels: corporate, business, and functional. Corporate grand strategies include growth, stability, retrenchment, and global. One framework for accomplishing them is the BCG matrix. An approach to business-level strategy is Porter's competitive forces and strategies. The Internet

is having a profound impact on the competitive environment, and managers should consider this when analyzing the five competitive forces and formulating business strategies. An alternative approach to strategic thought emphasizes cooperation rather than competition. Partnership strategies include preferred supplier arrangements, strategic business partnering, joint ventures, and mergers and acquisitions. Most of today's companies choose a mix of competitive and partnership strategies. Once business strategies have been formulated, functional strategies for supporting them can be developed.

Even the most creative strategies have no value if they cannot be translated into action. Managers implement strategy by aligning all parts of the organization to be in congruence with the new strategy. Four areas that managers focus on for strategy implementation are leadership, structural design, information and control systems, and human resources.

Returning to the opening problem at Coca-Cola, CEO Douglas Daft has made several strategic moves to try to get the company back on top. Although Coke continues to use primarily a globalization strategy, Daft recognizes the growing need to be more responsive to the heterogeneity of international markets. Therefore, he is gradually shifting toward a transnational strategy. Whereas the company once sought unity in its marketing and advertising strategies, for example, it is now giving bottlers both in the United States and abroad a free hand to tailor promotions to local events and activities. Daft is pushing global managers to think outside the conventional boundaries and come up with ideas for everything from new products to new ways to gather market research. New products include calcium-fortified waters, vitamin-enriched drinks, and new products for inter-

national markets such as an Asian tea and a coffee drink. Partnerships are an important part of Coke's new business-level strategy. Coke hopes to attain synergy through a 50–50 joint venture with Procter & Gamble, by marrying Coke's distribution muscle with P&G's successful juice and snack brands. A similar partnership with Nestlé will develop new coffee and tea drinks for the global market. A deal with Warner Bros. allows Coke to co-market with the film *Harry Potter and the Sorcerer's Stone* around the world. And plans are in the works to create an "incubator" project that will provide office space and seed money to start-ups with innovative ideas that could benefit the giant corporation. The partnership approach is new for Coke, which has long been seen as an insular company bent on doing it all. According to Marketing Director Stephen C. Jones, Daft realizes that "there are too many changes now for us to have all the answers."[75]

Discussion Questions

1. Assume you are the general manager of a large hotel and have formulated a strategy of renting banquet facilities to corporations for big events. At a monthly management meeting, your sales manager informed the head of food operations that a big reception in one week will require converting a large hall from a meeting room to a banquet facility in only 60 minutes—a difficult but doable operation that will require precise planning and extra help. The food operations manager is furious about not being informed earlier. What is wrong here?

2. Which is more important—strategy formulation or strategy implementation? Do they depend on each other? Is it possible for strategy implementation to occur first?

3. If an organization has hired strategic management professionals to help top managers, during which part of the strategic management process would they play the largest role?

4. Perform a situation (SWOT) analysis for the university you attend. Do you think university administrators consider these factors when devising their strategy?

5. What is meant by the core competence and synergy components of strategy? Give examples.

6. Using Porter's competitive strategies, how would you describe the strategies of Wal-Mart, Bloomingdale's, and Target? Do any of these companies also use partnership strategies? Discuss.

7. Walt Disney Company has four major strategic business units: movies (Touchstone), theme parks, consumer products, and television (primarily cable). Place each of these SBUs on the BCG matrix based on your knowledge of them.

8. As administrator for a medium-sized hospital, you and the board of directors have decided to change to a drug dependency hospital from a short-term, acute-care facility. Which organizational dimensions would you use to implement this strategy?

9. How would functional strategies in marketing, research and development, and production departments differ if a business changed from a differentiation to a low-cost strategy?

10. Describe how the Internet increases the bargaining power of consumers, one of Porter's five competitive forces. Have you felt increased power as a consumer because of the Internet? Explain.

■ Management in Practice: Experiential Exercise

Developing Strategy for a Small Business

Instructions: Your instructor may ask you to do this exercise individually or as part of a group. Select a local business with which you (or group members) are familiar. Complete the following activities.

Activity 1 Perform a SWOT analysis for the business.

Strengths: _____
_____
_____
_____
_____

Opportunities: _____
_____
_____
_____
_____

Weaknesses: _____
_____
_____
_____
_____

Threats: _____
_____
_____
_____
_____

Activity 2 Write a statement of the business's current strategy.

Activity 3 Decide on a goal you would like the business to achieve in two years, and write a statement of proposed strategy for achieving that goal.

Activity 4 Write a statement describing how the proposed strategy will be implemented.

Activity 5 What have you learned from this exercise?

■ Management in Practice: Ethical Dilemma

A Great Deal for Whom?

It seemed like a great deal for Kevin Haley, the retired president of a small accounting firm, when he took the job. To sit on the board of Keldine Technologies, all he had to do was listen to some general talk about the company at bimonthly meetings, vote on operations issues, and collect a nice fee. He didn't worry about his lack of expertise in the company's business of manufacturing transistors, because "nothing ever changed at Keldine."

That was two years ago. Now Keldine Technologies, with 250 employees and 10 years in business, is faced with a buyout offer from Graham Industries. Chairman of the Board at Keldine, Greg Bingham, called the deal a "no-brainer."

Graham Industries' offer of $65 a share was high, a great deal for shareholders. The problem for Haley was that he knew Graham Industries was close to bankruptcy, and that it was probably only buying Keldine to leverage some of its debt and hold off creditors. The odds were that both companies would be wiped out within a year if the sale went through. As news of a buyout offer spread, Keldine stock had changed hands rapidly, and speculators in the shareholder ranks were pressuring for a sale. Bingham asserted, "Our mission is to create as much value for shareholders as possible."

He also assured the board that the executives were protected by contingency compensation packages in the event of a "downturn for Keldine." But Haley was torn. The deal was a short-term moneymaker but an almost guaranteed disaster for the company's future and the majority of its employees. Haley's commitment to shareholders seemed compromised by the presence of speculators in their ranks. He questioned whether the interests of loyal, long-time employees weren't a higher priority than those of speculators.

What Do You Do?

1. Vote to accept the offer of Graham Industries and assure a short-term profit for the shareholders and executives. They are your first responsibility.

2. Reject the buyout bid. Providing Keldine a future, even if uncertain because of its resistance to change, is more important than accepting what may be the best offer ever received.

3. Pass, and hope a board majority prevails without your vote. You aren't qualified to make a decision on this anyway.

SOURCE: Based on Doug Wallace, "When the Sharks Are Circling," *What Would You Do? Business Ethics,* vol. I (September–October 1991), 42–44.

Surf the Net

1. **Globalization.** McDonald's was cited in the text as an example of the globalization strategy because it has standardized its product and advertising strategies throughout the world. Go to *http://www.mcdonalds.com* and find the number of countries in which McDonald's has restaurants. In addition, find information for locations in three different parts of the world and describe for each country such characteristics as current promotions, employment opportunities, specialty food products, or community projects.

2. **Corporate-Level Strategy.** Corporate Information is a great Web resource for company profiles and research reports for foreign, domestic, public, and private companies. The content is from Wright Investor's Service, where you can find 350,000 profiles available for free. Become familiar with the features available at *http://www.corporateinformation.com*

    Use the "Research Company" option to find the research report for the following companies (or your

instructor may assign other companies): Southwest Airlines, Walt Disney Company, and General Electric Company. Under the "Company Description" in each report, you will find information to help you determine each company's corporate-level strategy (What business(es) are we in?).

3. **Partnership Strategies.** As stated earlier in this chapter, IBM is collaborating with numerous partners around the world on the Internet. Go to IBM's Web site at *http://www.ibm.com* and locate the link to IBM's business partners. To understand the wealth of information contained at this site, you may want to download and view the "PartnerWorld Video" that will show you what you need to know to navigate the site. Check out the "Member Success Stories" under the "Membership Center," and write down two or three examples of partnership strategies.

Case for Critical Analysis

Starbucks Coffee

Beginning with 9 Seattle stores in 1987, Starbucks Chairman Howard Schultz has exported the company's chic cafes throughout the world. Service is anything but fast, and the price of a cup of coffee could make the Dunkin' Donuts crowd faint, but each week millions of people in cities from Atlanta to Tokyo hit Starbucks to sip cappuccinos and double lattes.

Starbucks has pursued rapid expansion both at home and abroad. Today, Starbucks boasts more than 4,600 outlets around the world, and Schultz has no plans to slow the growth. Starbucks has proven so popular in Japan, where sales per store are twice as high as in the United States, that the company recently opened its 300th store, with plans to add nearly 200 more over the next three years. The company

moved into China in 1999 and now has 35 stores, mainly in Beijing and Shanghai. A joint venture with Germany's largest department store company, KarstadtQuelle, is helping Starbucks push into Germany. The company's current six shops in Switzerland, as well as plans to open a store in Vienna in late 2001, are part of a long-term plan to open at least 650 outlets in continental Europe by the end of 2003. And in Canada, Starbucks has partnered with Interaction Restaurants, which hopes to be running 50 to 70 Starbucks in Quebec within five years. Starbucks' strategies have long been criticized as risky, but there's no arguing with success. Many analysts think the company has the flexibility and management strength to continue to grow and prosper.

Many of Starbucks' managers have years of experience from such companies as Burger King, Taco Bell, Wendy's, and Blockbuster. Schultz believes a top executive should "hire people smarter than you are and get out of their way." Equally crucial to Starbucks' success are the "baristas" who prepare coffee drinks. Starbucks recruits its workers from colleges and community groups and gives them 24 hours' training in coffeemaking and lore—a key to creating the company's hip image and quality service. When customers go to Starbucks, they are buying not just a great cup of coffee, but an experience. In a new store in Beijing, for instance, customers line up daily to have a barista dispense jolts of java from a "Mercury machine" strapped to his back. Starbucks also emphasizes listening to customers and giving them what they want. One reason the company agreed to a deal allowing Interaction to run storefront outlets in Quebec was to ensure that Starbucks adapts to local market needs, particularly in Montreal, which already has a strong coffee culture and vibrant local competitors.

A computer network links the expanding Starbucks empire, and Schultz hired a top information-technology specialist from McDonald's to design a point-of-sale system to enable managers to track sales. Every night, computers from stores around the world send information to headquarters in Seattle so that executives can spot buying trends.

Starbucks' same-store sales in mid-2001were already the lowest since 1998, and the declining economy following the September 11, 2001, terrorist attacks hurt sales even more. However, this does not worry Schultz and other top managers. To them, meeting such challenges is just part of the job.

Questions

1. What is Starbucks' grand strategy? Which of Porter's competitive strategies is the company using?
2. Discuss how Schultz is using leadership, structure, information and control systems, and human resources to implement strategy at Starbucks.
3. Starbucks has typically maintained a uniform look and feel to its outlets. The adaptations being made in Quebec are the first time the company has varied from this formula. What do you think this change might mean for Starbucks in terms of further international expansion?

SOURCES: Based on Dori Jones Yang, "The Starbucks Enterprise Shifts into Warp Speed," *BusinessWeek* (October 24, 1994), 76; Michael Treacy, "You Need a Value Discipline—But Which One?" *Fortune* (April 17, 1995), 195; Nelson D. Schwartz, "Still Perking After All These Years," *Fortune* (May 24, 1999); Ken Belson, "As Starbucks Grows, Japan, Too, Is Awash," *The New York Times* (October 21, 2001), C3; "Business: Coffee with Your Tea? Starbucks in China," *The Economist* (October 6, 2001), 62; "Starbucks in Joint Venture with German Retailer," *The New York Times* (October 5, 2001), C3; and Zena Olijnyk, "Latte, S'il Vous Plait?" *Canadian Business*, (September 3, 2001), 50–52.

■ Endnotes

1. Dean Foust with Gerry Khermouch, "Repairing the Coke Machine," *BusinessWeek* (March 19, 2001), 86–88.
2. Edward W. Desmond, "What's Ailing Kodak? Fuji," *Fortune* (October 27, 1997), 185–192.
3. Bill Saporito, "The Eclipse of Mars," *Fortune* (November 28, 1994), 82–92.
4. Christopher Palmeri, "Mattel: Up the Hill Minus Jill," *BusinessWeek* (April 9, 2001), 53–54.
5. Chet Miller and Laura B. Cardinal, "Strategic Planning and Firm Performance: A Synthesis of More than Two Decades of Research," *Academy of Management Journal* 37, no. 6 (1994), 1649–1665.
6. Gary Hamel, "Killer Strategies," *Fortune* (June 23, 1997), 70–84; and Costantinos Markides, "Strategic Innovation," *Sloan Management Review* (Spring 1997), 9–23.
7. Hamel, "Killer Strategies."
8. Keith H. Hammonds, "Michael Porter's Big Ideas," *Fast Company* (March 2001), 150–156.
9. John E. Prescott, "Environments as Moderators of the Relationship between Strategy and Performance," *Academy of Management Journal* 29 (1986), 329–346; John A. Pearce II and Richard B. Robinson, Jr., *Strategic Management: Strategy, Formulation, and Implementation*, 2d ed. (Homewood, Ill.: Irwin, 1985); and David J. Teece, "Economic Analysis and Strategic Management," *California Management Review* 26 (Spring 1984), 87–110.
10. Markides, "Strategic Innovation."
11. Kotha Suresh and Daniel Orna, "Generic Manufacturing Strategies: A Conceptual Synthesis," *Strategic Management Journal* 10 (1989), 211–231; and John A. Pearce II, "Selecting among Alternative Grand Strategies," *California Management Review* (Spring 1982), 23–31.
12. Andrew Kupfer, "MCI WorldCom: It's the Biggest Merger Ever. Can It Rule Telecom?" *Fortune* (April 27, 1998), 119–128.
13. Palmeri, "Mattel: Up the Hill Minus Jill."
14. Jack Ewing, "Siemens Climbs Back," *BusinessWeek* (June 5, 2000), 79–82.
15. Laura Landro, "Entertainment Giants Face Pressure to Cut Costs, Get in Focus." *The Wall Street Journal* (February 11, 1997), A1, A10; Terence P. Pare, "The New Merger Boom," *Fortune*, (November 28, 1994), 95–106; and Zachary Schiller, "Figgies Turns Over a New Leaf," *BusinessWeek* (February 27, 1995), 94–96.
16. Kenichi Ohmae, "Managing in a Borderless World," *Harvard Business Review* (May–June 1990), 152–161.
17. Theodore Levitt, "The Globalization of Markets," *Harvard Business Review* (May–June 1983), 92–102.
18. Cesare R. Mainardi, Martin Salva, and Muir Sanderson, "Label of Origin: Made on Earth," *Strategy & Business*, Issue 15 (Second Quarter, 1999), 42–53; Joann S. Lublin, "Place vs. Product: It's Tough to Choose a Management Model," *The Wall Street Journal* (June 27, 2001), A1, A4.

19. Mainardi, Salva, and Sanderson, "Label of Origin."

20. Joanne Lipman, "Marketers Turn Sour on Global Sales Pitch Harvard Guru Makes," *The Wall Street Journal* (May 12, 1988), 1, 8.

21. Michael E. Porter, "Changing Patterns of International Competition," *California Management Review* 28 (Winter 1986), 40.

22. Anil K. Gupta and Vijay Govindarajan, "Converting Global Presence into Global Competitive Advantage," *Academy of Management Executive* 15, no. 2 (2001), 45–56; David Leonhardt, "It was a Hit in Buenos Aires-So Why Not Boise?" *BusinessWeek* (September 7, 1998), 56–58.

23. Based on Michael A. Hitt, R. Duane Ireland, and Robert E. Hoskisson, *Strategic Management: Competitiveness and Globalization* (St. Paul, Minn.: West, 1995), 238.

24. Gupta and Govindarajan, "Converting Global Presence into Global Competitive Advantage."

25. Thomas S. Bateman and Carl P. Zeithaml, *Management: Function and Strategy*, 2d ed. (Homewood, Ill.: Irwin, 1993), 231.

26. Michael E. Porter, "What is Strategy?" *Harvard Business Review* (November–December 1996), 61–78.

27. Arthur A. Thompson, Jr., and A. J. Strickland III, *Strategic Management: Concepts and Cases*, 6th ed. (Homewood, Ill.: Irwin, 1992); and Briance Mascarenhas, Alok Baveja, and Mamnoon Jamil, "Dynamics of Core Competencies in Leading Multinational Companies," *California Management Review* 40, no. 4 (Summer 1998), 117–132.

28. Ronald B. Lieber, "Smart Science," *Fortune* (June 23, 1997), 73.

29. Mascarenhas, Baveja, and Jamil, "Dynamics of Core Competencies."

30. Paul Roberts, "Live! From Your Office! It's . . . " *Fast Company* (October 1999), 151–170.

31. Betsy Morris, "Can Michael Dell Escape The Box?" *Fortune* (October 16, 2000), 93–110; and Stewart Deck, "Fine Line," *CIO* (February 1, 2000), 88–92.

32. Michael Goold and Andrew Campbell, "Desperately Seeking Synergy," *Harvard Business Review* (September–October 1998), 131–143.

33. John A. Byrne, "PepsiCo's New Formula," *BusinessWeek* (April 10, 2000), 172–184.

34. Cathy Olofson, "No Place Like Home," *Fast Company* (July 2000), 328–329.

35. Bethany McLean, "Growing Up Gallo," *Fortune* (August 14, 2000), 211–220.

36. Hitt, Ireland, and Hoskisson, *Strategic Management*.

37. Milton Leontiades, *Strategies for Diversification and Change* (Boston: Little, Brown, 1980), 63; and Dan E. Schendel and Charles W. Hofer, eds., *Strategic Management: A New View of Business Policy and Planning* (Boston: Little, Brown, 1979), 11–14.

38. Kim Girard, "Cisco or Crisco?" *Business 2.0* (May 1, 2001), 74–77.

39. Joan O'C. Hamilton, "Brighter Days at Clorox," *BusinessWeek*, (June 16, 1997), 62, 65; and Katrina Brooker, "A Game of Inches," *Fortune* (February 5, 2001), 98–100.

40. Susan Orenstein, "Roses Are Red, Violets Are Blue, Hallmark's Online, But What Can It Do?" *The Industry Standard* (November 27–December 4, 2000).

41. Kathleen Madigan, Julia Flynn, and Joseph Walker, "Masters of the Game," *BusinessWeek* (October 12, 1992), 110, 118.

42. Milton Leontiades, "The Confusing Words of Business Policy," *Academy of Management Review* 7 (1982), 45–48.

43. Lawrence G. Hrebiniak and William F. Joyce, *Implementing Strategy* (New York: Macmillan, 1984).

44. James E. Svatko, "Analyzing the Competition," *Small Business Reports* (January 1989), 21–28; and Brian Dumaine, "Corporate Spies Snoop to Conquer," *Fortune* (November 7, 1988), 68–76.

45. Mascarenhas, Baveja, and Jamil, "Dynamics of Core Competencies."

46. Nanette Byrnes, "Old Stores, New Rivals, and Changing Trends Have Hammered Toys 'R' Us," *BusinessWeek* (December 4, 2000), 128–140.

47. Frederick W. Gluck, "A Fresh Look at Strategic Management," *Journal of Business Strategy* 6 (Fall 1985), 4–19.

48. Thompson and Strickland, *Strategic Management*; and William L. Shanklin and John K. Ryans, Jr., "Is the International Cash Cow Really a Prize Heifer?" *Business Horizons* 24 (1981), 10–16.

49. William C. Symonds, with Carol Matlack, "Gillette's Edge," *BusinessWeek* (January 19, 1998), 70–77; William C. Symonds, "Would You Spend $1.50 for a Razor Blade?" *BusinessWeek* (April 27, 1998), 46; Barbara Carton, "Gillette Looks Beyond Whiskers to Big Hair and Stretchy Floss," *The Wall Street Journal* (December 14, 1994), B1, B4; and William C. Symonds, "Can Gillette Regain Its Voltage?" *BusinessWeek* (October 16, 2000), 102–104.

50. Michael E. Porter, *Competitive Strategy* (New York: Free Press, 1980), 36–46; Danny Miller, "Relating Porter's Business Strategies to Environment and Structure: Analysis and Performance Implementations," *Academy of Management Journal* 31 (1988), 280–308; and Michael E. Porter, "From Competitive Advantage to Corporate Strategy," *Harvard Business Review* (May–June 1987), 43–59.

51. Michael E. Porter, "Strategy and the Internet," *Harvard Business Review* (March 2001), 63–78.

52. Jim Kerstetter and Spencer E. Ante, "IBM vs. Oracle: It Could Get Bloody," *BusinessWeek* (May 28, 2001), 65–66.

53. Thomas L. Wheelen and J. David Hunger, *Strategic Management and Business Policy* (Reading, Mass.: Addison-Wesley, 1989).

54. Andrew Park and Peter Burrows, "Dell, the Conqueror," *BusinessWeek* (September 24, 2001), 92–102; and Thompson and Strickland, *Strategic Management*.

55. Greg Burns, "It Only Hertz When Enterprise Laughs," *BusinessWeek* (December 12, 1994), 44.

56. Joshua Rosenbaum, "Guitar Maker Looks for a New Key," *The Wall Street Journal* (February 11, 1998), B1, B5.

57. Porter, "Strategy and the Internet"; and Hammonds, "Michael Porter's Big Ideas."

58. Based on John Burton, "Composite Strategy: The Combination of Collaboration and Competition," *Journal of General Management* 21, No. 1 (Autumn 1995), 1–23; and Roberta Maynard, "Striking the Right Match," *Nation's Business* (May 1996), 18–28.

59. Elizabeth Jensen and Eben Shapiro, "Time Warner's Fight with News Corp. Belies Mutual Dependence," *The Wall Street Journal* (October 28, 1996), A1, A6.

60. Don Tapscott, "Rethinking Strategy in a Networked World," *Strategy & Business*, Issue 24 (Third Quarter 2001), 34–41.

61. Byrnes, "Old Stores, New Rivals, and Changing Trends."

62. David Lei, "Strategies for Global Competition," *Long-Range Planning* 22 (1989) 102–109; and Russ Banham, "Judy C. Lewent" profile in "The Class of 2000," *CFO* (October 2000), 69–70.

63. Burton, "Composite Strategy: The Combination of Collaboration and Competition."

64. Harold W. Fox, "A Framework for Functional Coordination," *Atlanta Economic Review* (now *Business Magazine*) (November– December 1973).

65. L. J. Bourgeois III and David R. Brodwin, "Strategic Implementation: Five Approaches to an Elusive Phenomenon," *Strategic Management Journal* 5 (1984), 241–264; Anil K. Gupta and V. Govindarajan, "Business Unit Strategy, Managerial Characteristics, and Business Unit Effectiveness at Strategy Implementation," *Academy of Management Journal* (1984), 25–41; and Jeffrey G. Covin, Dennis P. Slevin, and Randall L. Schultz, "Implementing Strategic Missions: Effective Strategic, Structural, and Tactical Choices," *Journal of Management Studies* 31, no. 4 (1994), 481–505.

66. Rainer Feurer and Kazem Chaharbaghi, "Dynamic Strategy Formulation and Alignment," *Journal of General Management* 20, no. 3 (Spring 1995), 76–90; and Henry Mintzberg, *The Rise and Fall of Strategic Planning* (Toronto: Maxwell Macmillan Canada, 1994).

67. Jay R. Galbraith and Robert K. Kazanjian, *Strategy Implementation: Structure, Systems and Process*, 2d ed. (St. Paul, Minn.: West, 1986); and Paul C. Nutt, "Selecting Tactics to Implement Strategic Plans," *Strategic Management Journal* 10 (1989), 145–161.

68. Morris, "Can Michael Dell Escape the Box?"

69. Glenn L. Dalton, "The Collective Stretch," *Management Review* (December 1998), 54–59.

70. Rebecca Quick, "A Makeover That Began at the Top," *The Wall Street Journal* (May 25, 2000), B1.

71. Gupta and Govindarajan, "Business Unit Strategy"; and Bourgeois and Brodwin, "Strategic Implementation."

72. Greg Burns, "How a New Boss Got ConAgra Cooking Again," *BusinessWeek* (July 25, 1994), 72–73.

73. James E. Skivington and Richard L. Daft, "A Study of Organizational 'Framework' and 'Process' Modalities for the Implementation of Business-Level Strategies" (unpublished manuscript, Texas A&M University, 1987).

74. Roger Thurow, "A Sports Icon Regains Its Footing by Using the Moves of the Past," *The Wall Street Journal* (January 21, 1998), A1, A10.

75. Foust with Khermouch, "Repairing the Coke Machine."

Managerial Decision Making

CHAPTER OUTLINE

Types of Decisions and Problems

*Programmed and
Nonprogrammed Decisions*

*Certainty, Risk, Uncertainty, and
Ambiguity*

Decision-Making Models

Classical Model

Administrative Model

Political Model

Decision-Making Steps

*Recognition of Decision
Requirement*

*Diagnosis and Analysis
of Causes*

Development of Alternatives

Selection of Desired Alternative

*Implementation of Chosen
Alternative*

Evaluation and Feedback

Personal Decision Framework

Increasing Participation
in Decision Making

The Vroom-Jago Model

*New Decision Approaches for
the New Workplace*

LEARNING OBJECTIVES

After studying this chapter, you should be able to

1 Explain why decision making is an important component of good management.

2 Explain the difference between programmed and nonprogrammed decisions and the decision characteristics of risk, uncertainty, and ambiguity.

3 Describe the classical, administrative, and political models of decision making and their applications.

4 Identify the six steps used in managerial decision making.

5 Explain four personal decision styles used by managers.

6 Discuss the advantages and disadvantages of participative decision making.

7 Identify techniques for improving decision making in today's fast-moving and uncertain environment.

Management Challenge

For most of its 230-year history, the *Encyclopedia Britannica* has been viewed as an illustrious repository of cultural and historical knowledge—almost a national treasure. Generations of students and librarians relied on the *Britannica* to research everything from the Aleutian Islands to the history of zydeco—but that was before CD-ROMs and the Internet became the study tools of choice. Suddenly, the 32-volume collection of encyclopedias seemed destined to fade into history. Britannica was slow to move into electronic media and practically ceded the market to upstarts such as Microsoft's *Encarta*. Managers made a serious blunder when they sold the company's Compton unit, a CD-ROM pioneer now being used by millions of consumers. Even when Britannica finally introduced a CD-ROM, it was priced at a staggering $1,200, while Microsoft was offering cut-rate deals or giving *Encarta* away free with personal computers. When Jacob Safra and a Swiss investment group bought Britannica, new top executives immediately began installing managers who could lead the company into the digital age. Safra believed Britannica could once again be the quality leader. However, decisions had to be made about how to compete with rivals such as Compton's and Microsoft's *Encarta*, as well as the numerous free options available on the Internet.[1]

If you were a member of the management team at Britannica, what decisions would you make to successfully compete in today's world? What alternatives would you consider, and what course of action would you choose?

Top executives at Encyclopedia Britannica Holding SA made and implemented early decisions that kept Britannica alive and kicking. Now, the new managers, including a new senior vice president for product development, have to sharpen their skills to make important decisions that will affect the future of their business. Every organization grows, prospers, or fails as a result of decisions by its managers.

Managers often are referred to as *decision makers*. Although many of their important decisions are strategic, managers also make decisions about every other aspect of an organization, including structure, control systems, responses to the environment, and human resources. Managers scout for problems, make decisions for solving them, and monitor the consequences to see whether additional decisions are required. Good decision making is a vital part of good management, because decisions determine how the organization solves its problems, allocates resources, and accomplishes its goals.

Decision making is not easy. It must be done amid ever-changing factors, unclear information, and conflicting points of view. For example, launching a separate Internet company named Cozone that expanded CompUSA's product line and market seemed a good idea when managers made the decision in 1999, but the spinoff fell apart after only six months. Managers and board members had conflicting views about establishing an entirely new and distinct brand online. Other decisions, such as the confusing name, the failure to take advantage of cooperative marketing, and the refusal to allow merchandise bought online to be returned at CompUSA retail stores, helped to doom the new business.[2] Both Mattel and Hasbro, the top U.S. toymakers, passed on the Ninja Turtles idea in the late 1980s, and the action figures went on to sell billions. Coca-Cola pumped some $30 million into developing the Break-Mate, a miniature soda fountain, but the product flopped in the marketplace and Break-Mate fountains now sit gathering dust in storage sheds.[3]

The business world is also full of evidence of good decisions. Andy Grove, former CEO of Intel Corporation, decided to get out of the DRAM memory-chip business in the mid-1980s and focus relentlessly on microprocessors. The decision was a risky one, and many Intel executives opposed it, but it set Intel on course to become one of the richest and most powerful companies in the world.[4] Nokia became a $10 billion leader in the cellular phone industry because managers at the company decided to sell off unrelated businesses such as paper, tires, and aluminum and concentrate the company's resources on electronics.[5]

Chapters 7 and 8 described strategic planning. This chapter explores the decision process that underlies strategic planning. Plans and strategies are arrived at through decision making; the better the decision making, the better the strategic planning. First we will examine decision characteristics. Then we will look at decision-making models and the steps executives should take when making important decisions. We will also examine participative decision making and discuss techniques for improving decision making in today's organizations.

Types of Decisions and Problems

decision
A choice made from available alternatives.

A **decision** is a choice made from available alternatives. For example, an accounting manager's selection among Bill, Tasha, and Jennifer for the position of junior auditor is a decision. Many people assume that making a choice is the major part of decision making, but it is only a part.

Decision making is the process of identifying problems and opportunities and then resolving them.[6] Decision making involves effort both before and after the actual choice. Thus, the decision as to whether to select Bill, Tasha, or Jennifer requires the accounting manager to ascertain whether a new junior auditor is needed, determine the availability of potential job candidates, interview candidates to acquire necessary information, select one candidate, and follow up with the socialization of the new employee into the organization to ensure the decision's success.

Programmed and Nonprogrammed Decisions

Management decisions typically fall into one of two categories: programmed and nonprogrammed. **Programmed decisions** involve situations that have occurred often enough to enable decision rules to be developed and applied in the future.[7] Programmed decisions are made in response to recurring organizational problems. The decision to reorder paper and other office supplies when inventories drop to a certain level is a programmed decision. Other programmed decisions concern the types of skills required to fill certain jobs, the reorder point for manufacturing inventory, exception reporting for expenditures 10 percent or more over budget, and selection of freight routes for product deliveries. Once managers formulate decision rules, subordinates and others can make the decision, freeing managers for other tasks.

Nonprogrammed decisions are made in response to situations that are unique, are poorly defined and largely unstructured, and have important consequences for the organization. Many nonprogrammed decisions involve strategic planning, because uncertainty is great and decisions are complex. Decisions to build a new factory, develop a new product or service, enter a new geographical market, or relocate headquarters to another city are all nonprogrammed decisions. Starbucks' decision to incorporate the Internet as part of its growth strategy, described in the Leading Online box, is a good example of the complexity and uncertainty of nonprogrammed decisions. Another example of a nonprogrammed decision was when Ronald Zarella, president of General Motors North American operations, shelved plans to introduce a new design for the company's best-selling car, the Chevrolet Cavalier. He delayed building new factories and invested the millions of dollars saved in getting innovative new models of trucks and sport-utility vehicles on the market quickly. Zarella and his top executives had to analyze complex problems, evaluate alternatives, and make a decision about the best way to reverse GM's declining market share.[8]

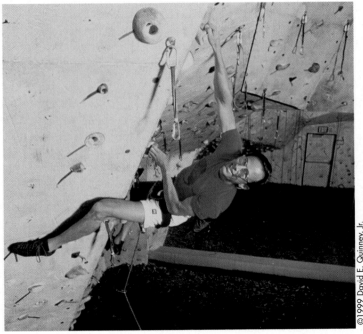

Peter Metcalf feels on top of the world since sales of his company's climbing equipment and backcountry skis have doubled to hit $20 million. As CEO of Salt Lake City, Utah-based Black Diamond Equipment, Ltd., Metcalf made a strategic **nonprogrammed decision** three years ago to relocate company headquarters from Ventura, California. Real estate prices in Ventura were sky-high, and Black Diamond faced strict regulations, high workers' compensation costs, and rapidly rising health insurance premiums. Yet, relocation would be costly, and there were no guarantees it would pull the company out of its slump. After evaluating alternatives, Metcalf made a decision that proved to be right on target.

Certainty, Risk, Uncertainty, and Ambiguity

One primary difference between programmed and nonprogrammed decisions relates to the degree of certainty or uncertainty managers deal with in making

Leading Online

Starbucks Makes a New Connection

Starbucks has made its presence known in the physical world for quite some time, but two years ago managers set out on a mission to connect with their customers in a different way: by means of the Internet. Top executives wanted to leverage the power of the Starbucks brand to build a presence in cyberspace, and they moved swiftly with plans to set up Starbucks X, a Web site where they dreamed of being involved in the online merchandising of everything from furniture to videocassettes.

But the decision to redefine the business in radical ways proved to be unwise, and the company stumbled badly in the online world. In addition, the complexity and uncertainty of the venture caused the company to lose its balance, and Starbucks' physical stores also began reporting disappointing sales and earnings. Starbucks' chairman Howard Schultz and other top executives pulled back to analyze the complex problem, evaluate alternatives, and make a choice about how to successfully make a connection between Starbucks' physical stores and the realm of the Internet. Eventually, they decided to tie their Web site closely to the company's central mission and goals. Combining an online store with the company's small catalog division, together known as Starbucks Direct, was a smart move; Starbucks Direct now brings in about $20

million a year—a welcome revenue stream. Rather than trying to expand its business into new areas, Starbucks now runs a simple, easy-to-use Web site that sells coffee beans, brewing machines, and mugs, and has online hosts that offer coffee history and lore to interested visitors.

However, with the Internet such a major part of people's lives, managers faced other decisions about connecting to the new technology. They did not want to create cybercafés, which tend to be dimly lit with people hunched over machines. In addition, they were concerned about cluttering up the cozy café atmosphere with cumbersome computer gear. With the proliferation of PDAs and affordable laptops, Starbucks' managers began to see a way to provide high-speed wireless Internet connections in stores without damaging the traditional café experience and scaring away customers. When asked about the risk of people coming in, using the Internet, and not buying anything, Darren Huston, senior vice president for new initiatives, said he was not worried about loitering. "The reality is exactly the opposite. Our most successful stores turn out to be the ones with the most loitering. We think it's great if people want to stay awhile. It creates a sense of community."

SOURCE: George Anders, "Starbucks Brews A New Strategy," *Fast Company* (August 2001), 145–146.

the decision. In a perfect world, managers would have all the information necessary for making decisions. In reality, however, some things are unknowable; thus, some decisions will fail to solve the problem or attain the desired outcome. Managers try to obtain information about decision alternatives that will reduce decision uncertainty. Every decision situation can be organized on a scale according to the availability of information and the possibility of failure. The four positions on the scale are certainty, risk, uncertainty, and ambiguity, as illustrated in Exhibit 9.1. Whereas programmed decisions can be made in situations involving certainty, many situations that managers deal with every day involve at least some degree of uncertainty and require nonprogrammed decision making.

certainty
All the information the decision maker needs is fully available.

Certainty. **Certainty** means that all the information the decision maker needs is fully available.[9] Managers have information on operating conditions, resource costs or constraints, and each course of action and possible outcome. For example, if a company considers a $10,000 investment in new equipment that it knows for certain will yield $4,000 in cost savings per year over the next five years, managers can calculate a before-tax rate of return of about 40 percent. If managers compare this investment with one that will yield only $3,000 per year in cost savings, they can confidently select the 40 percent return. However, few decisions are certain in the real world. Most contain risk or uncertainty.

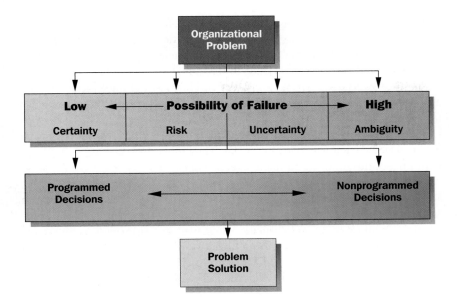

Exhibit **9.1**

Conditions That Affect the Possibility of Decision Failure

Risk. **Risk** means that a decision has clear-cut goals and that good information is available, but the future outcomes associated with each alternative are subject to chance. However, enough information is available to allow the probability of a successful outcome for each alternative to be estimated.[10] Statistical analysis might be used to calculate the probabilities of success or failure. The measure of risk captures the possibility that future events will render the alternative unsuccessful. Some oil companies use a quantitative simulation approach to estimate hydrocarbon reserves, enabling oil executives to evaluate the variation in risk at each stage of exploration and production and make better decisions. Saturn took a risk with the introduction of a mid-sized car to compete with the Toyota Camry and Honda's Accord. Managers had information that indicated the new L-series would sell well, based on the strength of the Saturn brand. However, they underestimated the extent to which people perceived Saturn as a "small-car" company and failed to put the emphasis they needed into marketing the new vehicle.[11]

risk
A decision has clear-cut goals and good information is available, but the future outcomes associated with each alternative are subject to chance.

Federal Express took a big risk when it decided to become an integral part of the movie Cast Away. *Product integration goes beyond displaying a product in the background of a movie scene—with integration, products actually become part of the script. FedEx had to weigh the downside of linking its services with an unrelated and volatile film industry against the positive exposure it could possibly gain by being associated with celebrity star Tom Hanks and a blockbuster movie.*

Uncertainty. **Uncertainty** means that managers know which goals they wish to achieve, but information about alternatives and future events is incomplete.[12] Managers do not have enough information to be clear about alternatives or to estimate their risk. Factors that may affect a decision, such as price, production costs, volume, or future interest rates, are difficult to analyze and predict. Managers may have to make assumptions from which to forge the decision even though it will be wrong if the assumptions are incorrect. Managers may have to come up with creative approaches to alternatives and use personal judgment to determine which alternative is best.

uncertainty
Managers know which goals they wish to achieve, but information about alternatives and future events is incomplete.

Mary Hadar, an assistant managing editor of the *Washington Post*, faces uncertainty every day as she has to make quick decisions about which stories will run in one of the world's most influential newspapers. Although she has a base of knowledge and experience to rely on, Hadar often has to make many assumptions and use personal judgment and intuition to make decisions such as whether to run a controversial story or when to cut back on coverage of certain issues.[13]

Many decisions made under uncertainty do not produce the desired results, but managers face uncertainty every day. They must find creative ways to cope with uncertainty in order to make effective decisions.

Ambiguity.　Ambiguity is by far the most difficult decision situation. **Ambiguity** means that the goals to be achieved or the problem to be solved is unclear, alternatives are difficult to define, and information about outcomes is unavailable.[14] Ambiguity is what students would feel if an instructor created student groups, told each group to complete a project, but gave the groups no topic, direction, or guidelines whatsoever. Ambiguity has been called a "wicked" decision problem. Managers have a difficult time coming to grips with the issues. Wicked problems are associated with manager conflicts over goals and decision alternatives, rapidly changing circumstances, fuzzy information, and unclear linkages among decision elements.[15] Sometimes managers will come up with a "solution" only to realize that they hadn't clearly defined the real problem to begin with.[16] A recent example of a wicked decision problem was when managers at Ford Motor Company and Firestone confronted the problem of tires used on the Ford Explorer coming apart on the road, causing deadly blow-outs and rollovers. Just defining the problem and whether the tire itself or the design of the Explorer was at fault was the first hurdle. Information was fuzzy and fast-changing, and managers were in conflict over how to handle the problem. Neither side has dealt with this ongoing decision situation very effectively, and the reputations of both companies have suffered as a result. Fortunately, most decisions are not characterized by ambiguity. But when they are, managers must conjure up goals and develop reasonable scenarios for decision alternatives in the absence of information.

ambiguity
The goals to be achieved or the problem to be solved is unclear, alternatives are difficult to define, and information about outcomes is unavailable.

Decision-Making Models

The approach managers use to make decisions usually falls into one of three types—the classical model, the administrative model, or the political model. The choice of model depends on the manager's personal preference, whether the decision is programmed or nonprogrammed, and the extent to which the decision is characterized by risk, uncertainty, or ambiguity.

Classical Model

classical model
A decision-making model based on the assumption that managers should make logical decisions that will be in the organization's best economic interests.

The **classical model** of decision making is based on economic assumptions. This model has arisen within the management literature because managers are expected to make decisions that are economically sensible and in the organization's best economic interests. The assumptions underlying this model are as follows:

1. The decision maker operates to accomplish goals that are known and agreed upon. Problems are precisely formulated and defined.
2. The decision maker strives for conditions of certainty, gathering complete information. All alternatives and the potential results of each are calculated.
3. Criteria for evaluating alternatives are known. The decision maker selects the alternative that will maximize the economic return to the organization.
4. The decision maker is rational and uses logic to assign values, order preferences, evaluate alternatives, and make the decision that will maximize the attainment of organizational goals.

The classical model of decision making is considered to be **normative**, which means it defines how a decision maker *should* make decisions. It does not describe how managers actually make decisions so much as it provides guidelines on how to reach an ideal outcome for the organization. The value of the classical model has been its ability to help decision makers be more rational. For example, many senior managers rely solely on intuition and personal preferences for making decisions.[17] In recent years, the classical approach has been given wider application because of the growth of quantitative decision techniques that use computers. Quantitative techniques include such things as decision trees, payoff matrices, break-even analysis, linear programming, forecasting, and operations research models. The use of computerized information systems and databases has increased the power of the classical approach.

In many respects, the classical model represents an "ideal" model of decision making that is often unattainable by real people in real organizations. It is most valuable when applied to programmed decisions and to decisions characterized by certainty or risk, because relevant information is available and probabilities can be calculated. For example, new analytical software programs for front-line decision making can automate many programmed decisions, such as freezing the account of a customer who has failed to make payments.[18] GE Capital Mortgage uses a decision software program called Loss Mitigation Optimizer to improve the decision making of loss management representatives. These employees have to decide whether the company can "cure" loans for customers who have stopped making payments or whether it will have to recommend foreclosure. By analyzing and measuring relevant variables, the program helped GE Capital Mortgage improve its cure rates from 30 percent of cases to more than 50 percent, while representatives were taking about 40 percent less time per deal.[19] Another organization that makes extensive use of the classical approach is the SABRE Group, which began as a system for keeping track of reservations for American Airlines.

Managers at Hudson Products Corporation, a manufacturer of heat-exchange equipment for the hydrocarbon processing industry, followed the classical model of decision making *to reach their long-term goal to maintain Hudsons's market share in air-cooled heat exchangers while generating income from new products. Hudson just completed one of its best years, with records for bookings, revenues and backlog, and continued high performance toward meeting schedules. Hudson managers have made the decision to participate in alliances with Shell, Dow Chemical, and Bechtel in order to maintain their strong market share. They also plan to generate income from new products including steam condensers, tank heaters, and a small-footprint gas-oil separator (in the photo) that is particularly suited for off-shore platforms.*

Originally developed as a system for tracking airline reservations, the SABRE Group is today made up of a number of companies that provide information technology solutions to a wide variety of businesses.

The power of SABRE is illustrated by its yield management system for American Airlines. American operates more than 4,000 flights a day, each one offering multiple fare classes, and begins taking reservations 330 days prior to each departure. The job of yield management is to forecast demand by inventory class and to optimize the decision of whether to sell at a lower price than the customer is willing to pay now or wait for higher-value, late-arriving demand.

THE SABRE GROUP
http://www.sabre.com

SABRE has estimated that the use of its computer-based system generates almost $1 billion in annual incremental revenue for American Airlines.

Another problem for airlines is scheduling. For a large carrier such as American, scheduling is an extremely complex problem with thousands of decision constraints and millions of variables. Some of those variables include where to fly, how often to serve a specific market, what time of day to fly, what type of aircraft to assign to each route, and what flights to designate as through-flights. SABRE designed a system that relies on sophisticated forecasting models and optimization models that make these complex decisions. The system added millions of dollars to American's bottom line each year and SABRE has now succeeded in selling it to such airlines as Delta, Lufthansa, Swissair, Northwest, Air France, US Air, and Air New Zealand.[20] ❖

Administrative Model

The **administrative model** of decision making describes how managers actually make decisions in difficult situations, such as those characterized by nonprogrammed decisions, uncertainty, and ambiguity. Many management decisions are not sufficiently programmable to lend themselves to any degree of quantification. Managers are unable to make economically rational decisions even if they want to.[21]

Bounded Rationality and Satisficing. The administrative model of decision making is based on the work of Herbert A. Simon. Simon proposed two concepts that were instrumental in shaping the administrative model: bounded rationality and satisficing. **Bounded rationality** means that people have limits, or boundaries, on how rational they can be. The organization is incredibly complex, and managers have the time and ability to process only a limited amount of information with which to make decisions.[22] Because managers do not have the time or cognitive ability to process complete information about complex decisions, they must satisfice. **Satisficing** means that decision makers choose the first solution alternative that satisfies minimal decision criteria. Rather than pursuing all alternatives to identify the single solution that will maximize economic returns, managers will opt for the first solution that appears to solve the problem, even if better solutions are presumed to exist. The decision maker cannot justify the time and expense of obtaining complete information.[23]

An example of both bounded rationality and satisficing occurs when a junior executive on a business trip spills coffee on her blouse just before an important meeting. She will run to a nearby clothing store and buy the first satisfactory replacement she finds. Having neither the time nor the opportunity to explore all the blouses in town, she satisfices by choosing a blouse that will solve the immediate problem. In a similar fashion, managers generate alternatives for complex problems only until they find one they believe will work. For example, several years ago then-Disney chairman Ray Watson and chief operating officer Ron Miller attempted to thwart takeover attempts, but they had limited options. They satisficed with a quick decision to acquire Arivda Realty and Gibson Court Company. The acquisition of these companies had the potential to solve the problem at hand; thus, they looked no further for possibly better alternatives.[24]

The administrative model relies on assumptions different from those of the classical model and focuses on organizational factors that influence individual

---

normative
An approach that defines how a decision maker should make decisions and provides guidelines for reaching an ideal outcome for the organization.

administrative model
A decision-making model that describes how managers actually make decisions in situations characterized by nonprogrammed decisions, uncertainty, and ambiguity.

bounded rationality
The concept that people have the time and cognitive ability to process only a limited amount of information on which to base decisions.

satisficing
To choose the first solution alternative that satisfies minimal decision criteria regardless of whether better solutions are presumed to exist.

decisions. It is more realistic than the classical model for complex, nonprogrammed decisions. According to the administrative model,

1. Decision goals often are vague, conflicting, and lack consensus among managers. Managers often are unaware of problems or opportunities that exist in the organization.
2. Rational procedures are not always used, and, when they are, they are confined to a simplistic view of the problem that does not capture the complexity of real organizational events.
3. Managers' search for alternatives is limited because of human, information, and resource constraints.
4. Most managers settle for a satisficing rather than a maximizing solution. This is partly because they have limited information and partly because they have only vague criteria for what constitutes a maximizing solution.

The administrative model is considered to be **descriptive**, meaning that it describes how managers actually make decisions in complex situations rather than dictating how they *should* make decisions according to a theoretical ideal. The administrative model recognizes the human and environmental limitations that affect the degree to which managers can pursue a rational decision-making process.

Intuition.   Another aspect of administrative decision making is intuition. **Intuition** represents a quick apprehension of a decision situation based on past experience but without conscious thought.[25] Intuitive decision making is not arbitrary or irrational, because it is based on years of practice and hands-on experience that enable managers to quickly identify solutions without going through painstaking computations. In today's fast-paced, uncertain business environment, intuition plays an increasingly important role in decision making. A study of 60 business professionals from a variety of industries, for example, found that nearly half said they relied on intuition often in making decisions in the workplace, while another 30 percent reported using intuition sometimes.[26]

Cognitive psychologist Gary Klein has studied how people make good decisions using their intuition under extreme time pressure and uncertainty.[27] Klein has found that intuition begins with *recognition*. When people build a depth of experience and knowledge in a particular area, the right decision often comes quickly and effortlessly as a recognition of information that has been largely forgotten by the conscious mind. For example, firefighters make decisions by recognizing what is typical or abnormal about a fire, based on their experience. Similarly, in the business world, managers are continuously perceiving and processing information that they may not consciously be aware of, and their base of knowledge and experience helps them make decisions that may be characterized by uncertainty and ambiguity.

The Dodge Viper, which became a smashing success for Chrysler (now DaimlerChrysler) in the 1990s, would never have been made if Bob Lutz, then the company's president, had not followed his intuition despite opposition and criticism. In explaining one of the most critical decisions of his career, Lutz says that ". . . it just felt right."[28] Another example comes from the Fox television network, where prime time ratings were dismal until Steven Chao came up with *America's Most Wanted* and *Cops*. Initially, everyone hated the idea for these raw, crime-oriented shows, but Chao and his boss Barry Diller stuck with their gut feelings and pushed the projects.[29]

descriptive
An approach that describes how managers actually make decisions rather than how they should.

intuition
The immediate comprehension of a decision situation based on past experience but without conscious thought.

"It's a major gut story," Bruce Goldsmith says about his decision to open a retail store right in the warehouse of his family's mail-order coffee business. Since Baronet Coffee, Inc.'s warehouse is in an industrial area with little foot traffic, most employees thought the idea was a little wacky, but Goldsmith's intuition told him it was the right thing to do. His years of experience observing customers and a few assumptions about human nature gave him a hunch that people would like the idea of picking up their coffee directly from the source. The hunch was right, and Baronet's retail sales quadrupled Goldsmith's original projections.

Political Model

The third model of decision making is useful for making nonprogrammed decisions when conditions are uncertain, information is limited, and there is disagreement among managers about what goals to pursue or what course of action to take. Most organizational decisions involve many managers who are pursuing different goals, and they have to talk with one another to share information and reach an agreement. Managers often engage in coalition building for making complex organizational decisions. A **coalition** is an informal alliance among managers who support a specific goal. *Coalition building* is the process of forming alliances among managers. In other words, a manager who supports a specific alternative, such as increasing the corporation's growth by acquiring another company, talks informally to other executives and tries to persuade them to support the decision. When the outcomes are not predictable, managers gain support through discussion, negotiation, and bargaining. Without a coalition, a powerful individual or group could derail the decision-making process. Coalition building gives several managers an opportunity to contribute to decision making, enhancing their commitment to the alternative that is ultimately adopted.[30]

The political model closely resembles the real environment in which most managers and decision makers operate. Decisions are complex and involve many people, information is often ambiguous, and disagreement and conflict over problems and solutions are normal. There are four basic assumptions of the political model:

1. Organizations are made up of groups with diverse interests, goals, and values. Managers disagree about problem priorities and may not understand or share the goals and interests of other managers.
2. Information is ambiguous and incomplete. The attempt to be rational is limited by the complexity of many problems as well as personal and organizational constraints.
3. Managers do not have the time, resources, or mental capacity to identify all dimensions of the problem and process all relevant information. Managers talk to each other and exchange viewpoints to gather information and reduce ambiguity.
4. Managers engage in the push and pull of debate to decide goals and discuss alternatives. Decisions are the result of bargaining and discussion among coalition members.

One of today's most visible coalition builders is President George W. Bush, who, following terrorist bombings in the United States, successfully built a coalition of world leaders to support a U.S.-led campaign against terrorism. The inability of leaders to build coalitions often makes it difficult or impossible for managers to see their decisions implemented. Hershell Ezrin resigned as CEO of Canada's Speedy Muffler King because he was unable to build a coalition of managers who supported his decisions for change at the troubled company. Many senior-level executives resented Ezrin's appointment and refused to go along with his ideas for reviving the company.[31]

The key dimensions of the classical, administrative, and political models are listed in Exhibit 9.2. Recent research into decision-making procedures has found rational, classical procedures to be associated with high performance for organizations in stable environments. However, administrative and

coalition
An informal alliance among managers who support a specific goal.

Classical Model	Administrative Model	Political Model
Clear-cut problem and goals	Vague problem and goals	Pluralistic; conflicting goals
Condition of certainty	Condition of uncertainty	Condition of uncertainty/ambiguity
Full information about alternatives and their outcomes	Limited information about alternatives and their outcomes	Inconsistent viewpoints; ambiguous information
Rational choice by individual for maximizing outcomes	Satisficing choice for resolving problem using intuition	Bargaining and discussion among coalition members

Exhibit **9.2**

Characteristics of Classical, Administrative, and Political Decision-Making Models

political decision-making procedures and intuition have been associated with high performance in unstable environments in which decisions must be made rapidly and under more difficult conditions.[32]

Decision-Making Steps

Whether a decision is programmed or nonprogrammed and regardless of managers' choice of the classical, administrative, or political model of decision making, six steps typically are associated with effective decision processes. These are summarized in Exhibit 9.3.

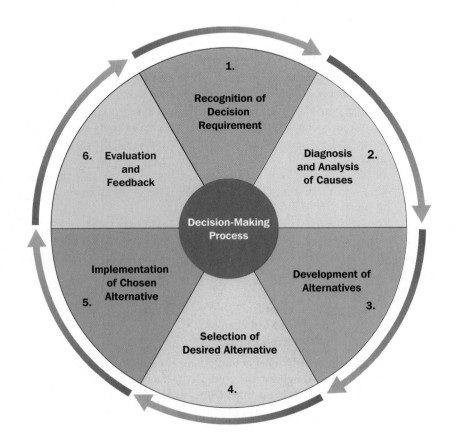

Exhibit **9.3**

Six Steps in the Managerial Decision-Making Process

Recognition of Decision Requirement

problem
A situation in which organizational accomplishments have failed to meet established goals.

opportunity
A situation in which managers see potential organizational accomplishments that exceed current goals.

Managers confront a decision requirement in the form of either a problem or an opportunity. A **problem** occurs when organizational accomplishment is less than established goals. Some aspect of performance is unsatisfactory. An **opportunity** exists when managers see potential accomplishment that exceeds specified current goals. Managers see the possibility of enhancing performance beyond current levels.

Awareness of a problem or opportunity is the first step in the decision sequence and requires surveillance of the internal and external environment for issues that merit executive attention.[33] This resembles the military concept of gathering intelligence. Managers scan the world around them to determine whether the organization is satisfactorily progressing toward its goals.

Some information comes from periodic financial reports, performance reports, and other sources that are designed to discover problems before they become too serious. For example, sharply declining sales figures in the Oldsmobile and Buick divisions of General Motors signaled a problem that needed to be addressed. Managers could see that Oldsmobile and Buick had been on a downhill slide for years as the loyal buyers of these brands were aging and the cars failed to appeal to younger buyers.[34] Recognition of the problem led managers to focus on decisions about the fate of these two divisions in their overall efforts to lead GM out of the downturn. Managers also take advantage of informal sources. They talk to other managers, gather opinions on how things are going, and seek advice on which problems should be tackled or which opportunities embraced.[35]

Recognizing decision requirements is difficult, because it often means integrating bits and pieces of information in novel ways.

Diagnosis and Analysis of Causes

diagnosis
The step in the decision-making process in which managers analyze underlying causal factors associated with the decision situation.

Once a problem or opportunity has come to a manager's attention, the understanding of the situation should be refined. **Diagnosis** is the step in the decision-making process in which managers analyze underlying causal factors associated with the decision situation. Managers make a mistake here if they jump right into generating alternatives without first exploring the cause of the problem more deeply.

Kepner and Tregoe, who have conducted extensive studies of manager decision making, recommend that managers ask a series of questions to specify underlying causes, including the following:

- What is the state of disequilibrium affecting us?
- When did it occur?
- Where did it occur?
- How did it occur?
- To whom did it occur?
- What is the urgency of the problem?
- What is the interconnectedness of events?
- What result came from which activity?[36]

More than 100 customers recently reported fraudulent charges to their credit cards immediately after placing an order with UltiMutt, a $300,000 Web-based business that designs and sells posters combining dogs and motivational quotes. Diagnosis of the problem for business owners Ron Johnson and Lori Scherping involved understanding how hackers gained access to their site. Further analysis led Johnson and Scherping to discover that international hackers had stolen UltiMutt's on-line customer database. Within hours, software engineers updated the site's shopping cart software and security was reinstated. "Whatever doesn't kill me makes me stronger," states Johnson, who is now working on a way to eliminate the need to store customer data on his server.

Such questions help specify what actually happened and why. Managers at Yahoo! are struggling to diagnose the underlying factors in the company's recent troubles. The problem is an urgent one, as the stock price has fallen dramatically, advertising sales have plunged, and numerous executives, including the heads of four international units, have resigned. As Yahoo!

scrambles to remain an important part of the Internet, managers are looking at the interconnectedness of issues such as the dot-com crash and declining economy, the failure of top executives to delegate responsibility as the company grew larger, aggressive and arrogant sales tactics that alienated "old economy" clients, the lack of effective control systems, and an insular culture that caused Yahoo! to lose experienced executives and miss out on some important opportunities.[37]

Development of Alternatives

Once the problem or opportunity has been recognized and analyzed, decision makers begin to consider taking action. The next stage is to generate possible alternative solutions that will respond to the needs of the situation and correct the underlying causes. One study found that limiting the search for alternatives is a primary cause of decision failure in organizations.[38]

For a programmed decision, feasible alternatives are easy to identify and in fact usually are already available within the organization's rules and procedures. Nonprogrammed decisions, however, require developing new courses of action that will meet the company's needs. For decisions made under conditions of high uncertainty, managers may develop only one or two custom solutions that will satisfice for handling the problem.

Decision alternatives can be thought of as the tools for reducing the difference between the organization's current and desired performance. At General Motors, executives considered alternatives such as attempting to revive the Oldsmobile and Buick divisions through increased marketing, closing down one or both divisions, or taking the risky step of authorizing one of the divisions to bring out a bold new vehicle model. Eventually, GM decided to pull the plug on its 103-year-old Oldsmobile line and bring out a different kind of Buick, a "crossover" vehicle that looks like a sport-utility vehicle, drives like a car, and is Buick's first departure from its line of stodgy sedans. Buick and GM managers hope the contemporary, thoughtful design of the Rendezvous will appeal to younger drivers, especially women, who represent a growing percentage of new car buyers.[39]

Courtesy of UPS

UPS knows many businesses have a low risk propensity when it come to matters affecting their cash flow, so it spotted a business opportunity. UPS is reducing its customers' risk of delayed payments through its UPS Capital division. With services such as Next Day Cash, UPS Capital advances clients funds for shipped products and deposits them directly into the clients' bank accounts within 24 hours, providing small or growing companies faster access to needed cash. Managers can decide whether to pay UPS a small fee to get advance funds or take a chance on slow-paying customers.

Selection of Desired Alternative

Once feasible alternatives have been developed, one must be selected. The decision choice is the selection of the most promising of several alternative courses of action. The best alternative is one in which the solution best fits the overall goals and values of the organization and achieves the desired results using the fewest resources.[40] The manager tries to select the choice with the least amount of risk and uncertainty. Because some risk is inherent for most nonprogrammed decisions, managers try to gauge prospects for success. Under conditions of uncertainty, they might have to rely on their intuition and experience to estimate whether a given course of action is likely to succeed. Basing choices on overall goals and values can also effectively guide selection of alternatives. For example, stockbroker Edward Jones was hit hard by the gloomy stock market and the declining economy following the September, 2001 terrorist attacks in the United States. To make decisions about how to

THE NEW WORKPLACE   # Manager's Shoptalk

Decision Biases to Avoid

At a time when decision making is so important, many corporate executives do not know how to make a good choice among alternatives. They may rely on computer analyses or personal intuition without realizing that their own cognitive biases affect their judgment. The complexities of modern corporate life make good judgment more critical than ever. Many errors in judgment originate in the human mind's limited capacity and in the natural biases most managers display during decision making. Awareness of the six biases below can help managers make more enlightened choices:

1. *Being influenced by initial impressions.* When considering decisions, the mind often gives disproportionate weight to the first information it receives. These initial impressions, statistics, or estimates act as an anchor to our subsequent thoughts and judgments. Anchors can be as simple as a random comment by a colleague or a statistic read in a newspaper. Past events and trends also act as anchors. For example, in business, managers frequently look at the previous year's sales when estimating sales for the coming year. However, in rapidly changing environments, giving too much weight to the past can lead to poor forecasts and misguided decisions.

2. *Justifying past decisions.* Many people fall into the trap of making choices that justify their past decisions, even if those decisions no longer seem valid. For example, managers may invest tremendous time and energy into improving the performance of a problem employee whom they now realize should never have been hired in the first place. Another example is when investors continue to pour money into failing businesses hoping to turn things around. People are often unwilling to admit they made a mistake, so they continue to make flawed decisions in an effort to correct the past.

3. *Seeing what you want to see.* People frequently look for information that supports their existing instinct or point of view and avoid information that contradicts it. This bias affects where managers look for information when considering decisions, as well as how they interpret the information they find. People tend to give too much weight to supporting information and too little to information that conflicts with their established viewpoints. It is important for managers to be honest with themselves about their motives and to examine all the evidence with equal rigor. Having a devil's advocate to argue against a decision can also help avoid this decision trap.

4. *Perpetuating the status quo.* Managers may base decisions on what has worked in the past and fail to explore new options, dig for additional information, or investigate new

technologies. For example, DuPont clung to its cash cow, nylon, despite growing evidence in the scientific community that a new product, polyester, was superior for tire cords. Celanese, a relatively small competitor, blew DuPont out of the water by exploiting this new evidence, quickly capturing 75 percent of the tire market.

5. *Being influenced by problem framing.* The decision response of a manager can be influenced by the mere wording of a problem. For example, consider a manager faced with a decision about salvaging the cargo of three barges that sank off the coast of Alaska. If managers are given the option of approving (A) a plan that has a 100 percent chance of saving the cargo of one of the three barges, worth $200,000 or (B) a plan that has a one-third chance of saving the cargo of all three barges, worth $600,000 and a two-thirds chance of saving nothing, most managers choose option A. The same problem with a negative frame would give managers a choice of selecting (C) a plan that has a 100 percent chance of losing two of the three cargoes, worth $400,000 or (D) a plan that has a two-thirds chance of losing all three cargoes but a one-third chance of losing no cargo. With this framing, most managers choose option D. Because both problems are identical, the decision choice depends strictly on how the problem is framed.

6. *Overconfidence.* One of the interesting research findings on decision-making biases is that most people overestimate their ability to predict uncertain outcomes. Before making a decision, managers have unrealistic expectations of their ability to understand the risk and make the right choice. Overconfidence is greatest when answering questions of moderate to extreme difficulty. For example, when people are asked to define quantities about which they have little direct knowledge ("What was Wal-Mart's 1999 revenue?" "What was the market value of Microsoft as of March 14, 2000?"), they overestimate their accuracy. Evidence of overconfidence is illustrated in cases in which subjects were so certain of an answer that they assigned odds of 1,000 to 1 of being correct but in fact were correct only about 85 percent of the time. These findings are especially important for strategic decision making, in which uncertainty is high because managers may unrealistically expect that they can successfully predict outcomes and hence select the wrong alternative.

SOURCES: Based on John Hammond, Ralph L. Keeney, and Howard Raiffa, "The Hidden Traps in Decision Making," *Harvard Business Review* (September–October 1998), 47–58; Oren Harari; "The Thomas Lawson Syndrome," *Management Review* (February 1994), 58–61; and Max H. Bazerman, *Judgment in Managerial Decision Making*, 5th ed. (New York: John Wiley & Sons, 2002).

cope, managers relied on the company's values and goals of treating employees right and building long-term relationships. Not a single employee was laid off, and although bonuses were reduced, the company issued them a week early to help employees hurt by the trading decline. Edward Jones' values-based decision making helped win the company the Number 1 spot on *Fortune* magazine's 2001 list of best companies to work for.[41]

Making choices depends on managers' personality factors and willingness to accept risk and uncertainty. For example, **risk propensity** is the willingness to undertake risk with the opportunity of gaining an increased payoff. The level of risk a manager is willing to accept will influence the analysis of cost and benefits to be derived from any decision. Consider the situations in Exhibit 9.4. In each situation, which alternative would you choose? A person with a low risk propensity would tend to take assured moderate returns by going for a tie score, building a domestic plant, or pursuing a career as a physician. A risk taker would go for the victory, build a plant in a foreign country, or embark on an acting career. The Manager's Shoptalk box describes biases to avoid when selecting the desired alternative.

risk propensity
The willingness to undertake risk with the opportunity of gaining an increased payoff.

Implementation of Chosen Alternative

The **implementation** stage involves the use of managerial, administrative, and persuasive abilities to ensure that the chosen alternative is carried out. This is similar to the idea of strategic implementation described in Chapter 8. The ultimate success of the chosen alternative depends on whether it can be translated into action. Sometimes an alternative never becomes reality because managers lack the resources or energy needed to make things happen. Implementation may require discussion with people affected by the decision. Communication, motivation, and leadership skills must be used to see that the decision is carried out.

At General Motors, Chief Executive Rick Wagoner has hired new top executives, including Bob Lutz, former product development chief at Chrysler, who share his vision and can help to implement his decisions for livening up GM's global product portfolio. Paul J. Liska, executive vice president and CFO at the St. Paul Cos., a commercial insurer, successfully implemented decisions that led to annual cost savings of about $500 million and kept the company competitive in the cut-throat insurance industry. For example, Liska revised incentive plans to persuade managers to go along with some of the cost-reduction decisions.[42] If managers lack the ability or desire to implement decisions, the chosen alternative cannot be carried out to benefit the organization.

implementation
The step in the decision-making process that involves using managerial, administrative, and persuasive abilities to translate the chosen alternative into action.

For each of the following decisions, which alternative would you choose?

1 In the final seconds of a game with the college's traditional rival, the coach of a college football team may choose a play that has a 95 percent change of producing a tie score or one with a 30 percent chance of leading to victory or to sure defeat if it fails.

2 The president of a Canadian company must decide whether to build a new plant within Canada that has a 90 percent chance of producing a modest return on investment or to build it in a foreign country with an unstable political history. The latter alternative has a 40 percent chance of failing, but the returns would be enormous if it succeeded.

3 A college senior with considerable acting talent must choose a career. She has the opportunity to go on to medical school and become a physician, a career in which she is 80 percent likely to succeed. She would rather be an actress but realizes that the opportunity for success is only 20 percent.

Exhibit *9.4*

Decision Alternatives with Different Levels of Risk

Evaluation and Feedback

In the evaluation stage of the decision process, decision makers gather information that tells them how well the decision was implemented and whether it was effective in achieving its goals. For example, Tandy executives evaluated their decision to open computer centers for businesses and feedback revealed poor sales performance. Feedback indicated that implementation was unsuccessful, and computer centers were closed so Tandy could focus on its successful Radio Shack retail stores.

Feedback is important because decision making is a continuous, never-ending process. Decision making is not completed when an executive or board of directors votes yes or no. Feedback provides decision makers with information that can precipitate a new decision cycle. The decision may fail, thus generating a new analysis of the problem, evaluation of alternatives, and selection of a new alternative. Many big problems are solved by trying several alternatives in sequence, each providing modest improvement. Feedback is the part of monitoring that assesses whether a new decision needs to be made.

An illustration of the overall decision-making process, including evaluation and feedback, was the decision to introduce a new deodorant at Tom's of Maine.

TOM'S OF MAINE
http://www.tomsofmaine.com

Tom's of Maine, known for its all-natural personal hygiene products, saw an opportunity to expand its line with a new natural deodorant. However, the opportunity quickly became a problem when the deodorant worked only half of the time with half of the customers who used it, and its all-recyclable plastic dials were prone to breakage.

The problem of the failed deodorant led founder Tom Chappell and other managers to analyze and diagnose what went wrong. They finally determined that the company's product development process had run amok. The same group of merry product developers was responsible from conception to launch of the product. They were so attached to the product that they failed to test it properly or consider potential problems, becoming instead "a mutual admiration society." Managers considered several alternatives for solving the problem. The decision to publicly admit the problem and recall the deodorant was an easy one for Chappell, who runs his company on principles of fairness and honesty. Not only did the company apologize to its customers but also listened to their complaints and suggestions. Chappell himself helped answer calls and letters. Even though the recall cost the company $400,000 and led to a stream of negative publicity, it ultimately helped the company improve relationships with customers.

Evaluation and feedback also led Tom's of Maine to set up "acorn groups," from which it hopes mighty oaks of successful products will grow. Acorn groups are cross-departmental teams that will shepherd new products from beginning to end. The cross-functional teams are a mechanism for catching problems—and new opportunities—that ordinarily would be missed. They pass on their ideas and findings to senior managers and the product-development team.

Tom's was able to turn a problem into an opportunity, thanks to evaluation and feedback. Not only did the disaster ultimately help the company solidify relationships with customers, but it also led to a formal mechanism for learning and sharing ideas—something the company did not have before.[43] ❖

Tom's of Maine's decision illustrates all the decision steps, and the process ultimately ended in success. Strategic decisions always contain some risk, but feedback and follow-up decisions can help get companies back on track. By learning from their decision mistakes, managers and companies can turn problems into opportunities.

Personal Decision Framework

Imagine you were a manager at Tom's of Maine, Yahoo!, a local movie theater, or the public library. How would you go about making important decisions that might shape the future of your department or company? So far we have discussed a number of factors that affect how managers make decisions. For example, decisions may be programmed or nonprogrammed, situations are characterized by various levels of uncertainty, and managers may use the classical, administrative, or political model of decision making. In addition, there are six recognized steps to take in the decision-making process.

However, not all managers go about making decisions in the same way. In fact, there are significant differences in the ways individual managers may approach problems and make decisions concerning them. These differences can be explained by the concept of personal decision styles. Exhibit 9.5 illustrates the role of personal style in the decision-making process. Personal **decision style** refers to differences among people with respect to how they perceive problems and make decisions. Research has identified four major decision styles: directive, analytical, conceptual, and behavioral.[44]

decision style
Differences among people with respect to how they perceive problems and make decisions.

1. The *directive style* is used by people who prefer simple, clear-cut solutions to problems. Managers who use this style often make decisions quickly because they do not like to deal with a lot of information and may consider only one or two alternatives. People who prefer the directive style generally are efficient and rational and prefer to rely on existing rules or procedures for making decisions.

2. Managers with an *analytical style* like to consider complex solutions based on as much data as they can gather. These individuals carefully consider alternatives and often base their decisions on objective, rational data from management control systems and other sources. They search for the best possible decision based on the information available.

3. People who tend toward a *conceptual style* also like to consider a broad amount of information. However, they are more socially oriented than those with an analytical style and like to talk to others about the problem and possible alternatives for solving it. Managers using a conceptual style consider many broad alternatives, rely on information from both people and systems, and like to solve problems creatively.

Exhibit **9.5**

Personal Decision Framework

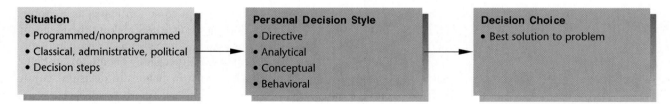

4. The *behavioral style* is often the style adopted by managers having a deep concern for others as individuals. Managers using this style like to talk to people one-on-one and understand their feelings about the problem and the effect of a given decision upon them. People with a behavioral style usually are concerned with the personal development of others and may make decisions that help others achieve their goals.

Most managers have a dominant decision style. For example, every Friday, Richard Scrushy, founder and CEO of HealthSouth, reviews a stack of computer printouts concerning every detail of the performance of each facility in his chain of outpatient orthopedic clinics.[45] Scrushy likes to have as much data as he can to help him make decisions regarding the $4 billion company. However, managers frequently use several different styles or a combination of styles in making the varied decisions they confront daily. For example, a manager might use a directive style for deciding on which printing company to use for new business cards, yet shift to a more conceptual style when handling an interdepartmental conflict. The most effective managers are able to shift among styles as needed to meet the situation. Being aware of one's dominant decision style can help a manager avoid making critical mistakes when his or her usual style may be inappropriate to the problem at hand.

Increasing Participation in Decision Making

Managers do make some decisions as individuals, but decision makers more often are part of a group. Indeed, major decisions in the business world rarely are made entirely by an individual. Effective decision making often depends on whether managers involve the right people in the right ways in helping them solve problems.[46] One model that provides guidance for practicing managers was originally developed by Victor Vroom and Arthur Jago.[47]

The Vroom-Jago Model

Vroom-Jago model
A model designed to help managers gauge the amount of subordinate participation in decision making.

The **Vroom-Jago** model helps a manager gauge the appropriate amount of participation by subordinates in making a specific decision. The model has three major components: leader participation styles, a set of diagnostic questions with which to analyze a decision situation, and a series of decision rules.

Leader Participation Styles.   The model employs five levels of subordinate participation in decision making ranging from highly autocratic (leader decides alone) to highly democratic (leader delegates to group), as illustrated in Exhibit 9.6.[48] The exhibit shows five decision styles, starting with the leader making the decision alone (Decide); presenting the problem to subordinates individually for their suggestions and then making the decision (Consult Individually); presenting the problem to subordinates as a group, collectively obtaining their ideas and suggestions, then making the decision (Consult Group); sharing the problem with subordinates as a group and acting as a facilitator to help the group arrive at a decision (Facilitate); or delegating the problem and permitting the group to make the decision within prescribed limits (Delegate).

Diagnostic Questions. How does a manager decide which of the five decision styles to use? The appropriate degree of decision participation depends on a number of situational factors, such as the required level of decision quality, the level of leader or subordinate expertise, and the importance of having subordinates commit to the decision. Leaders can analyze the appropriate degree of participation by answering seven diagnostic questions.

1. *Decision Significance: How significant is this decision for the project or organization?* If the quality of the decision is highly important to the success of the project or organization, the leader has to be actively involved.

2. *Importance of Commitment: How important is subordinate commitment to carrying out the decision?* If implementation requires a high level of commitment to the decision, leaders should involve subordinates in the decision process.

3. *Leader Expertise: What is the level of the leader's expertise in relation to the problem?* If the leader does not have a high amount of information, knowledge, or expertise, the leader should involve subordinates to obtain it.

4. *Likelihood of Commitment: If the leader were to make the decision alone, would subordinates have high or low commitment to the decision?* If subordinates typically go along with whatever the leader decides, their involvement in the decision-making process will be less important.

Exhibit **9.6**

Five Leader Participation Styles

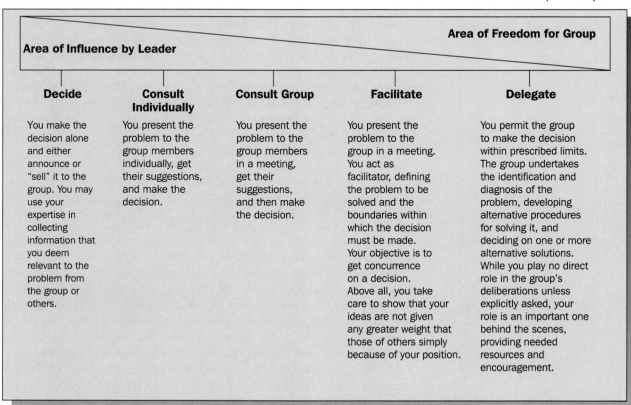

Area of Influence by Leader				**Area of Freedom for Group**
Decide	**Consult Individually**	**Consult Group**	**Facilitate**	**Delegate**
You make the decision alone and either announce or "sell" it to the group. You may use your expertise in collecting information that you deem relevant to the problem from the group or others.	You present the problem to the group members individually, get their suggestions, and make the decision.	You present the problem to the group members in a meeting, get their suggestions, and then make the decision.	You present the problem to the group in a meeting. You act as facilitator, defining the problem to be solved and the boundaries within which the decision must be made. Your objective is to get concurrence on a decision. Above all, you take care to show that your ideas are not given any greater weight that those of others simply because of your position.	You permit the group to make the decision within prescribed limits. The group undertakes the identification and diagnosis of the problem, developing alternative procedures for solving it, and deciding on one or more alternative solutions. While you play no direct role in the group's deliberations unless explicitly asked, your role is an important one behind the scenes, providing needed resources and encouragement.

SOURCE: Victor H. Vroom, "Leadership and the Decision Making Process," *Organizational Dynamics* 28, no. 4 (Spring 2000), 82–94. This is Vroom's adaptation of Tannenbaum and Schmidt's Taxonomy. Used with permission.

5. *Group Support for Goals: What is the degree of subordinate support for the team's or organization's objectives at stake in this decision?* If subordinates have low support for the goals of the organization, the leader should not allow the group to make the decision alone.

6. *Group Expertise: What is the level of group members' knowledge and expertise in relation to the problem?* If subordinates have a high level of expertise in relation to the problem, more responsibility for the decision can be delegated to them.

7. *Team Competence: How skilled and committed are group members to working together as a team to solve problems?* When subordinates have high skills and high desire to work together cooperatively to solve problems, more responsibility for decision making can be delegated to them.

These questions seem detailed, but considering these seven situational factors can quickly narrow the options and point to the appropriate level of group participation in decision making.

Selecting a Decision Style.   The decision matrix in Exhibit 9.7 allows a manager to adopt a participation style by answering the diagnostic questions in sequence. The manager enters the matrix at the left-hand side, at Problem Statement, and considers the seven situational questions in sequence from left to right, answering high (H) or low (L) to each one and avoiding crossing any horizontal lines. The first question would be: *How significant is this decision for the project or organization?* If the answer is High, the leader proceeds to importance of commitment: *How important is subordinate commitment to carrying out the decision?* An answer of High leads to a question about leader expertise: *What is the level of the leader's expertise in relation to the problem?* If the leader's knowledge and expertise is High, the leader next considers likelihood of commitment: *If the leader were to make the decision alone, how likely is it that subordinates would be committed to the decision?* If there is a high likelihood that subordinates would be committed, the decision matrix leads directly to the Decide style of decision making, in which the leader makes the decision alone and presents it to the group.

The Vroom-Jago model has been criticized as being less than perfect,[49] but it is useful to managers, and the body of supportive research is growing.[50] Managers can use the model to make timely, high-quality decisions. Consider the application of the model to the following hypothetical problem.

MADISON MANUFACTURING

When Madison Manufacturing won a coveted contract from a large auto manufacturer to produce an engine to power their flagship sports car, Dave Robbins was thrilled to be selected as project manager. This project has dramatically enhanced the reputation of Madison, and Robbins and his team of engineers have taken great pride in their work. However, their enthusiasm was dashed by a recent report of serious engine problems in cars delivered to customers. Taking quick action, the auto manufacturer suspended sales of the sports car, halted current production, and notified owners of the current model not to drive the car. Everyone involved knows this is a disaster. Unless the engine problem is solved quickly, Madison Manufacturing could be exposed to extended litigation. In addition, Madison's valued relationship with one of the world's largest auto manufacturers would likely be lost forever.

As the project manager, Robbins has spent two weeks in the field inspecting the seized engines and the auto plant where they were installed. Based

Instructions: The matrix operates like a funnel. You start at the left with a specific decision problem in mind. The column headings denote situational factors which may or may not be present in that problem. You progress by selecting High or Low (H or L) for each relevant situational factor. Proceed down the funnel, judging only those situational factors for which a judgement is called for, until you reach the recommended process.

Decision Significance?	Importance of Commitment?	Leader Expertise?	Likelihood of Commitment?	Group Support?	Group Expertise?	Team Competence?	Process
H	H	H	H	–	–	–	Decide
			L	H	H	H	Delegate
						L	
					L	–	Consult (Group)
				L	–	–	
	H	L	H	H	H	H	Facilitate
						L	
					L	–	Consult (Individually)
				L	–	–	
			L	H	H	H	Facilitate
						L	
					L	–	Consult (Group)
				L	–	–	
	L	H	–	–	–	–	Decide
		L	–	H	H	H	Facilitate
						L	
					L	–	Consult (Individually)
				L	–	–	
L	H	–	H	–	–	–	Decide
			L	–	–	H	Delegate
						L	Facilitate
	L	–	–	–	–	–	Decide

SOURCE: Victor H. Vroom "Leadership and the Decision-Making Process," *Organizational Dynamics* 28, no. 4 (Spring 2000), 82–94. Used with permission.

on this extensive research, Robbins has some pretty good ideas about what is causing the problem, but he knows there are members of his team who may have stronger expertise for solving it. In addition, while he has been in the field, other team members have been carefully evaluating the operations and practices in Madison's plant where the engine is manufactured. Therefore, Robbins chooses to get the team together and discuss the problem before making his final decision. The group meets for several hours, discussing the problem in detail and sharing their varied perspectives, including the information Robbins and team members have gathered. Following the group session, Robbins makes his decision, which will be presented at the team meeting the following morning, after which testing and correction of the engine problem will begin.[51] ❖

The Vroom-Jago model in Exhibit 9.7 shows that Robbins used the correct decision style. Moving from left to right in Exhibit 9.7, the questions and answers are as follows: *How significant is the decision?* Definitely high. The company's future might be at stake. *How important is subordinate commitment to the decision?* Also high. The team members must support and implement Robbins's solution. *What is the level of Robbins's information and expertise?* Probably low. Even though he has spent several weeks researching the seized engines, other team members have additional information and expertise that needs to be considered. *If Robbins makes the decision on his own, would team members have high or low commitment to it?* The answer to this question is probably also low. Even though team members respect Robbins, they take pride in their work as a team and know Robbins does not have complete information. This leads to the question, *What is the degree of subordinate support for the team's or organization's objectives at stake in this decision?* Definitely high. This leads to the question, *What is the level of group members' knowledge and expertise in relation to the problem?* The answer to this question is low, which leads to the Consult Group decision style, as described earlier in Exhibit 9.6. Thus, Robbins used the style that would be recommended by the Vroom-Jago model.

In many situations, several decision styles might be equally acceptable. However, in today's workplace, managers are encouraging greater employee participation in solving problems whenever possible. Broad participation often leads to better decisions. Involving others in decision making also contributes to individual and organizational learning, which is critical for rapid decision making in the new workplace.

New Decision Approaches for the New Workplace

The ability to make fast, widely supported, high-quality decisions on a frequent basis is a critical skill in today's fast-moving organizations.[52] In many industries, the rate of competitive and technological change is so extreme that opportunities are fleeting, clear and complete information is seldom available, and the cost of a slow decision means lost business or even company failure. Does this mean managers in today's workplace should make the majority of decisions on their own? No. The rapid pace of today's business environment calls for just the opposite—that is, for people throughout the organization to be involved in decision making and have the information, skills, and freedom they need to respond immediately to problems and questions. Managers—as well as employees throughout the organization—often have to act first and analyze later.[53] There is no time for top managers to evaluate options, conduct research, develop alternatives, and tell people what to do and how to do it. When speed matters, a slow decision may be as ineffective as the wrong decision, and companies can learn to make decisions fast. Effective decision making in today's fast-moving businesses relies on the following guidelines.

Learn, Don't Punish.   Decisions made under conditions of uncertainty and time pressure produce many errors, but managers in the new workplace are willing to take the risk in the spirit of trial and error. If a chosen decision alternative fails, the organization can learn from it and try another alternative that better fits the situation. Each failure provides new information and learning. People throughout the organization are encouraged to take risks and learn from their mistakes. Good managers know that every time a person makes a decision, whether it turns out to have positive or negative consequences, it helps the employee learn and be a better decision maker the next time around. By making mistakes, people go through the process of *decision learning*, which means that they gain valuable experience and knowledge to perform more effectively in the future.

When people are afraid to make mistakes, the company is stuck. For example, when Robert Crandall led American Airlines, he built a culture in which any problem that caused a flight delay was followed by finding someone to blame. People became so scared of making a mistake that whenever something went wrong, no one was willing to jump in and try to fix the problem. In contrast, Southwest Airlines uses what it calls *team delay*, which means a flight delay is everyone's problem. This puts the emphasis on fixing the problem rather than on finding an individual to blame.[54] In the new workplace, managers do not use mistakes and failure to create a climate of fear. Instead, they encourage people to take risks and move ahead with the decision process, despite the potential for errors. At the Brady Corporation, described in this chapter's Putting People First box, managers used humor to break down a culture of fear and mistrust.

Know When to Bail.   Even though the new workplace encourages risk taking and learning from mistakes, it also teaches people to know when to pull the plug on something that is not working. Research has found that organizations often continue to invest time and money in a solution despite strong evidence that it is not appropriate. This tendency is referred to as **escalating commitment**. Managers might block or distort negative information because they don't want to be responsible for a bad decision, or they might simply refuse to accept that their solution is wrong. In today's successful companies, people don't get so attached to their own ideas that they're unwilling to recognize when to move on. According to Stanford University professor Robert Sutton, the key to successful creative decision making is to "fail early, fail often, and pull the plug early."[55]

escalating commitment
Continuing to invest time and resources in a failing decision.

Practice the Five Whys.   One way to encourage good decision making under high uncertainty is to get people to think more broadly and deeply about problems rather than going with a superficial understanding and a first response. However, this doesn't mean people have to spend hours analyzing a problem and gathering research. One simple procedure adopted by a number of leading companies is known as the *five whys*.[56] For every problem, employees learn to ask "Why?"not just once, but five times. The first *why* generally produces a superficial explanation for the problem, and each subsequent *why* probes deeper into the causes of the problem and potential solutions. The point of the *five whys* is to improve how people think about problems and generate alternatives for solving them.

Build Collective Intuition.   Earlier in the chapter, we discussed the role of intuition in decision making. Managers in the new workplace encourage people to develop and use their intuition on an individual level as they make rapid decisions to serve customers. However, they also build what has been called *collective intuition* for making complex, uncertain organizational decisions.[57] Just as an individual develops his or her intuition based on knowledge

Putting People First

At Brady: "From No to Yo"

The Brady Corporation was founded in 1914 as a maker of advertising calendars and tin road signs. The founder, William H. Brady, Jr., who served as CEO for 30 years, instilled a patriarchal, conservative, and cautious culture that became entrenched in the organization. In fact, Brady Corp. took business so seriously that coffee was not even allowed at employees' desks until 1989. No wonder that, when Katherine M. Hudson came to Brady as president and CEO in 1994, employees seemed exceptionally uptight and guarded.

Hudson also discovered that the uptight culture had led to some serious problems at the company, which now had 3,200 employees, ran operations in 20 countries, and sold about 50,000 different products. For example, she found that local managers of two Canadian units had barely communicated with one another for 15 years due to old conflicts and mistrust. Then, the cautious side of the culture became apparent to Hudson on a trip to Asia, when a manager timidly asked if he could "hire another half person." The manager was shocked when Hudson told him he could hire five more people if he could give her a business justification for it.

Hudson began referring to the reluctance to collaborate and the fear of taking risks as a *culture of no*. She was determined to get people to say yes to information sharing, yes to cooperation, and yes to risk-taking and learning. To encourage an open, collaborative, reliable, can-do climate, Hudson coined an official corporate motto, "from no to yo." To give manufacturing workers more power and flexibility, she instituted flextime and began treating blue-collar employees like salaried workers. This approach empowered workers and gave them more authority and responsibility for making decisions, enabling them to get the job done without managers looking over their shoulders. Now, if an employee needs to juggle his schedule, he works it out with team members rather than going to a manager. The company also emphasizes honesty with employees, customers, and the community to build trust and encourage flexible behavior. Hudson wants employees to feel confident enough to take risks, acknowledge mistakes, and share their experience with co-workers.

Another way to get people to go from no to yo was to get everyone to loosen up and enjoy themselves. Hudson set out to make fun a fundamental part of Brady's new culture—and she had solid business reasons for doing so. The benefits of the new, more relaxed approach are many. Jealously guarded turf boundaries have broken down, and a company-wide *esprit de corps* has taken their place. Hudson also believes humor helps people make better decisions because it relieves stress, promotes creativity, opens people up to new ideas, and encourages people to take action. Fear limits decision making power, and a fun, friendly work environment overcomes fear. "Our performance is a sign that a company can be fun and friendly for its employees and fierce with its competitors," Hudson says. "In fact, the fun has made us fiercer, by making the organization more flexible and dynamic and our people more creative and enthusiastic." Needless to say, it has probably also made Brady a more enjoyable place to work.

SOURCE: Katherine M. Hudson, "One Laugh at a Time," *Harvard Business Review* (July–August, 2001), 45–54.

and experience, collective intuition comes from the combined knowledge, experience, and understanding of the group.

Managers may hold frequent "don't miss" meetings at which they discuss real-time information that helps them perceive problems and opportunities sooner and more completely. For example, top managers at one highly successful computer company are known for being able to respond to threats or opportunities at the drop of a hat. They do it by constantly tracking internal and external information and then discussing it in regular, intensive meetings. The broad sharing of information and interplay of diverse ideas at group meetings develop a deeper understanding of problems and ensure that people consider different sides of an issue before developing alternatives and reaching solutions. Research has shown that bringing people together to discuss problems and decision alternatives in a group leads to more effective decision making than having a manager consult with each member individually.[58] One reason for this is the collective intuition of the group.

Engage in Constructive Conflict.   A technique for better group decision making is to encourage constructive conflict. Managers in today's successful companies recognize that conflict based on divergent points of view can bring a problem into focus, stimulate creative thinking, create a broader under-standing of issues and alternatives, and improve decision quality.[59] Constructive conflict means that the conflict is related to the work and the issue or problem at hand, not to personal or political rivalries.

There are several ways to stimulate constructive conflict. One way is by ensuring that the group is diverse in terms of age and gender, functional area of expertise, hierarchical level, and experience with the business. Some groups assign a **devil's advocate**, who has the role of challenging the assumptions and assertions made by the group.[60] The devil's advocate may force the group to rethink its approach to the problem and avoid reaching premature conclu-sions. Another approach is to have group members develop as many alterna-tives as they can as quickly as they can.[61] This allows the team to work with multiple alternatives and encourages people to advocate ideas they might not prefer simply to encourage debate. Still another way to encourage constructive conflict is to use a technique called **point-counterpoint**, which breaks a deci-sion-making group into two subgroups and assigns them different, often com-peting responsibilities.[62] The groups then develop and exchange proposals and discuss and debate the various options until they arrive at a common set of understandings and recommendations.

Decision making in today's high-speed, complex environment is one of the most important—and most challenging—responsibilities for managers. By involving others, learning from mistakes rather than assigning blame, know-ing when to bail, practicing the *five whys*, building collective intuition, and engaging in constructive conflict, managers can improve the quality and effec-tiveness of decision making.

devil's advocate
A decision-making technique in which an individual is assigned the role of challenging the assumptions and assertions made by the group to prevent premature consensus.

point-counterpoint
A decision-making technique in which peo-ple are assigned to express competing points of view.

■ Summary and Management Solution

This chapter made several important points about the process of organizational decision making. The study of decision making is important because it describes how managers make successful strategic and operational decisions. Managers must confront many types of deci-sions, including programmed and nonprogrammed, and these decisions differ according to the amount of risk, uncertainty, and ambiguity in the environment.

Three decision-making approaches were described: the classical model, the administrative model, and the political model. The classical model explains how managers should make decisions so as to maximize economic efficiency. The administrative model describes how managers actually make nonpro-grammed, uncertain decisions with skills that include intuition. The political model relates to making non-programmed decisions when conditions are uncertain,

information is limited and ambiguous, and there is conflict among managers about what goals to pursue or what course of action to take. Managers have to engage in discussion and coalition building to reach agreement for decisions.

Decision making should involve six basic steps: problem recognition, diagnosis of causes, development of alternatives, choice of an alternative, implementa-tion of the alternative, and feedback and evaluation. Problem recognition at Encyclopaedia Britannica, Inc., described at the beginning of the chapter, was easy: the venerable old company was about to go under. In diag-nosing the causes, new owners determined that a major factor was an ossified management culture dominated by book salesmen, leading to years of squabbling over new product development and thus hindering the move into electronic media. One of the first decisions Jacob

Safra made was to bring in a new management team. The team then considered various alternatives for reviving the faltering company. The first decisions were to rush out a revamped, lower-cost CD-ROM package, targeted particularly to schools, and to launch the Britannica.com Web site, which allows users to call up encyclopedia entries online, as well as get a list of links to other Web sites related to the topic. Top executives also decided to create a separate digital media division to focus on new product development for the digital world. Managers in this new division quickly focused on the wireless Web as the route to the future. After evaluating alternatives for how to establish Britannica as the wireless Web's brand-name information source, they decided not to go it alone, but to create alliances with wireless carriers and license Britannica's content to other Web sites. Impressed with Britannica's content, companies have so far been glad to establish partnerships. These decisions have helped the company cross the bridge to the digital era, but so far the wireless Web has not proven to be much of a money maker. Managers are in the process of evaluation to determine what new decisions need to be made.

Another factor affecting decision making is the manager's personal decision style. The four major decision styles are directive, analytical, conceptual, and behavioral. The chapter also explained the Vroom-Jago model, which managers can use to determine when a decision calls for group participation. Involving others in decision making contributes to individual and organizational learning, which is critical in today's fast-paced environment. In the new workplace, decisions often have to be made quickly and with limited information. To improve the effectiveness of decision making in fast-moving organizations, managers use the following guidelines: learn, don't punish; know when to bail; practice the five whys; build collective intuition; and engage in constructive conflict.

◼ Discussion Questions

1. You are a busy partner in a legal firm, and an experienced secretary complains of continued headaches, drowsiness, dry throat, and occasional spells of fatigue and flu. She tells you she believes air quality in the building is bad and would like something done. How would you respond?
2. Why is decision making considered a fundamental part of management effectiveness?
3. Explain the difference between risk and ambiguity. How might decision making differ for each situation?
4. Analyze three decisions you made over the past six months. Which of these were programmed and which were nonprogrammed?
5. Why are many decisions made by groups rather than by individuals?
6. The Vroom-Jago model describes five decision styles. How should a manager go about choosing which style to use?

7. What are the major differences between the administrative and political models of decision making?
8. List some possible advantages and disadvantages to using computer technology for managerial decision making.
9. Do you think intuition is a valid approach to making decisions in an organization? Why or why not? How might intuition be combined with a rational decision approach?
10. Do you see a conflict between the new workplace emphasis on risk taking and decision learning and the six steps in Exhibit 9.3 that are associated with effective decision making? Discuss.
11. How might constructive conflict contribute to better decision making?

◼ Management in Practice: Experiential Exercise

What's Your Personal Decision Style?

Read each of the following questions and circle the answer that *best* describes you. Think about how you typically act in a work or school situation and mark the answer that first comes to mind. There are no right or wrong answers.

1. In performing my job or class work, I look for:
   a. practical results
   b. the best solution
   c. creative approaches or ideas
   d. good working conditions

2. I enjoy jobs that:
   a. are technical and well-defined
   b. have a lot of variety
   c. allow me to be independent and creative
   d. involve working closely with others
3. The people I most enjoy working with are:
   a. energetic and ambitious
   b. capable and organized
   c. open to new ideas
   d. agreeable and trusting
4. When I have a problem, I usually:
   a. rely on what has worked in the past
   b. apply careful analysis
   c. consider a variety of creative approaches
   d. seek consensus with others
5. I am especially good at:
   a. remembering dates and facts
   b. solving complex problems
   c. seeing many possible solutions
   d. getting along with others
6. When I don't have much time, I:
   a. make decisions and act quickly
   b. follow established plans or priorities
   c. take my time and refuse to be pressured
   d. ask others for guidance and support
7. In social situations, I generally:
   a. talk to others
   b. think about what's being discussed
   c. observe
   d. listen to the conversation

8. Other people consider me:
   a. aggressive
   b. disciplined
   c. creative
   d. supportive
9. What I dislike most is:
   a. not being in control
   b. doing boring work
   c. following rules
   d. being rejected by others
10. The decisions I make are usually:
   a. direct and practical
   b. systematic or abstract
   c. broad and flexible
   d. sensitive to others' needs

Scoring: These questions rate your personal decision style, as described in the text and listed in Exhibit 9.5.

Count the number of *a* answers. This is your *directive* score.
Count the number of *b* answers for your *analytical* score.
The number of *c* answers is your *conceptual* score.
The number of *d* answers is your *behavioral* score.

What is your dominant decision style? Are you surprised, or does this reflect the style you thought you used most often?

SOURCE: Adapted from Alan J. Rowe and Richard O. Mason, *Managing with Style: A Guide to Understanding, Assessing, and Improving Decision Making* (San Francisco: Jossey-Bass, 1987), 40–41.

■ Management in Practice: Ethical Dilemma

The No-Show Consultant

Jeffrey Moses was facing one of the toughest decisions of his short career as a manager with International Consulting. Andrew Carpenter, one of his best consultants, was clearly in trouble, and his problems were affecting his work. International Consulting designs, installs, and implements complex back-office software systems for companies all over the world. About half the consultants work out of the main office, while the rest, including Andrew, work primarily from home.

This Monday morning, Moses had gotten an irate call from a major New York client saying Andrew never showed up at the company's headquarters, where the client had been expecting his new computer system to go live for the first time. In calling around to other customers on the East Coast trying to locate the missing consultant, Moses heard other stories. Andrew had also missed a few other appointments—all on Monday mornings—but no one had felt the need to report it since he had called to reschedule. In addition, he had practically come to blows with an employee who challenged him about the capabilities of the new system, and he had inexplicably walked out of one customer's office in the middle of the day without a word to anyone. Another client

reported that the last time he saw Andrew he appeared to have a serious hangover. Most of the clients liked Andrew, but they were concerned that his behavior was increasingly erratic. One client suggested that she would prefer to work with someone else. As for the major New York customer, they preferred that Andrew rather than a new consultant finish the project, but they were also demanding that International eat half the $250,000 consultant's fee.

After Moses finally located Andrew by calling his next-door neighbor, Andrew confessed that he'd had a "lost weekend" and been too drunk to get on the plane. He then told Moses that his wife had left and taken their two-year-old son with her. He admitted that he had been drinking a little more than usual lately, but insisted that he was getting himself under control and promised there would be no more problems. "I'm really not an alcoholic or anything," he said. "I've just been upset about Brenda leaving, and I let it get out of hand this weekend." Moses told Andrew that if he would get to New York and complete the project, all would be forgiven.

Now, however, he wondered if he should really just let things slide. Moses talked to Andrew's team leader about the situation and was told that the leader was aware of Andrew's recent problems but thought everything would smooth itself over. "Consultants with his knowledge, level of skill, and willingness to travel are hard to find. He's well-liked among all the customers; he'll get his act together." However, when Moses discussed the problem with Carolyn Walter, vice president of operations, she argued that Andrew should be dismissed. "You're under no obligation to keep him just because you said you would," she pointed out. "This was a major screw-up, and it's perfectly legal to fire someone for absenteeism. Your calls to customers should make it clear that this was not a one-time thing. Get rid of him now before things get worse. If you think eating half that $250,000 fee hurts now, just think what could happen if this behavior continues."

What Do You Do?

1. Give him a month's notice and terminate. He's known as a good consultant, so he probably won't have any trouble finding a new job, and you'll avoid any further problems associated with his emotional difficulties and his possible alcohol problem.

2. Let it slide. Missing the New York appointment is Andrew's first big mistake. He says he is getting things under control and you believe he should be given a chance to get himself back on track.

3. Let Andrew know that you care about what he's going through, but insist that he take a short paid leave and get counseling to deal with his emotional difficulties and evaluate the seriousness of his problems with alcohol. If the alcohol abuse continues, require him to attend a treatment program or find another job.

SOURCES: Based on Jeffrey L. Seglin, "The Savior Complex," *Inc.* (February 1999), 67–69; and Nora Johnson, "'He's Been Beating Me,' She Confided," *Business Ethics* (Summer 2001), 21.

■ Surf the Net

1. **Brain Teasers.** Problem solving is part of the decision-making process. The purpose of many decisions is to determine the best alternative for solving a problem. Just for fun, visit one of the sites listed below, and try your hand at solving some of the brain teasers. Be prepared to share during class your favorite brain teaser and the way you solved the problem.
   http://www.billsgames.com/brain-teasers
   http://www.afunzone.com/brainteaserzone.html
   http://www.ed.uiuc.edu/courses/satex/sp97/projects/ PickYourBrain/BrainTeasers/

2. **Decision Making.** Use one of the sites listed or conduct your own Web search for information on management decision making. Identify the most informative site on the subject and submit to your instructor the Web address, along with a summary of the information you found that would prove helpful to anyone making management decisions.
   http://ubmail.ubalt.edu/~harsham/opre640/opre640.htm
   http://www.mapnp.org/library/prsn_prd/decision.htm
   http://horizon.unc.edu/courses/papers/ AnticipatoryManagement.asp
   http://www.myprimetime.com/work/entrepreneur_toolkit/ content/yahoo/top10_management/index.shtml

3. **Mindmapping.** Go to one of the sites listed, or locate your own site, to learn about mindmapping:
   http://www.thinksmart.com/mission/workout/ mindmapping_intro.html
   http://home.snafu.de/h.nauheimer/cp_03.htm

   Go to Exhibit 9.3 and suggest where in the managerial decision-making process mindmapping might be useful.

■ Case for Critical Analysis

The Merger

Peter Lundgren poured his fifth cup of coffee down the drain and checked his watch. More caffeine was just going to make matters worse at this point. He needed to be calm for the meeting with Ashton if they were going to reach any sort of agreement at all. Stanley Ashton and Peter Lundgren were trying something new by serving as co-CEOs of Arlington Inc., which resulted from a merger of Arlington Oil with Dunsford Petroleum Co.

The merger, announced as a marriage of equals, created a corporation with nearly $40 billion in assets better able to compete with huge corporations in the rough-and-tumble oil industry. It was expected that the merger would result in significant cost savings in refining, marketing, and transportation, as well as more capital to fund worldwide exploration and production. The media and stock market had both responded favorably, but the euphoria had faded and the hard work of integrating the two organizations had begun. The most difficult aspect was proving to be merging the two cultures and creating an effective human resource integration strategy. It had been widely reported in the press that cost savings would come from operating efficiencies rather than widespread job cuts, but that told only part of the story. The merger had left Arlington with two managers for almost every available position at upper and middle management levels. The very top levels had been selected prior to the merger, with Lundgren and Ashton negotiating so that each could keep his most trusted executives on board. Ashton has brought the director of HR, head of global marketing, and chief information officer from Dunsford. Lundgren kept his chief operating officer, chief financial officer, and head of R & D. Both Lundgren and Ashton knew they were facing some tough decisions concerning the other positions. Of course, the managers knew it too, and several of the best from both companies had already taken other jobs because of the uncertainty.

Peter has always preferred making personnel decisions based largely on gut instinct. He likes to talk to people face-to-face, look them in the eye, find out what they care about and what their personal and professional goals are, and decide if they would be a good fit with the organization. He is naturally biased toward some of his own executives because he knows them, but he is more than willing to negotiate just as he did with the top slots. In fact, there are several managers he would just as soon get rid of, and this presents a good opportunity. Ashton, on the other hand, except for the few high-level positions he's already argued for, doesn't seem to have much of a personal interest in whether Dunsford managers stay on. He wants to put all the executives through an outside evaluation

and appraisal process that includes personality testing, IQ and emotional intelligence testing, and all sorts of other tests, in addition to looking at their performance and business results. Peter realizes an objective process would take the bias and emotion out of the decision making, but he is concerned that Ashton's plan will take too long and that the best executives will leave the company rather than go through all the testing and evaluation. In addition, it has been his experience that the best managers are those who just "feel right" for the company, rather than those who look good on paper. He can feel a headache coming on as the time for meeting with Ashton nears.

Questions

1. Is the decision facing Lundgren and Ashton programmed or nonprogrammed? Why?

2. Based on the information in this case, what is Lundgren's dominant decision style according to the personal decision framework? What is Ashton's dominant style? Can the two executives effectively co-lead the company considering their different perspectives and approaches?

3. Which model of decision making–classical, administrative, or political–do you think would be most appropriate to make personnel decisions for the new company? Discuss.

SOURCE: Based on David A. Light, "Who Goes, Who Stays?" *Harvard Business Review* (January 2001), 35–44.

■ Endnotes

1. Richard A. Melcher, "Dusting Off the *Britannica*," *Business Week*, (October 21), 1997, 143, 146; and Pui-Wing Tam, "One for the History Books: The Tale of How Britannica is Trying to Leap from the Old Economy Into the New One," *The Wall Street Journal* (December 11, 2000), R32.

2. Kim Girard, "Cozone in the Ozone," *Business 2.0* (June 27, 2000), 90–95.

3. "Tickling a Child's Fancy," *The Tennessean* (February 6, 1997), 1E, 4E; and John R. Emshwiller and Michael J. McCarthy, "Coke's Soda Fountain for Offices Fizzles, Dashing High Hopes,"*The Wall Street Journal*, (June 14, 1993), A1, A6.

4. Dean Takahashi, "How the Competition Got Ahead of Intel in Making Cheap Chips,"*The Wall Street Journal*, (February 12, 1998), A1.

5. Linda Yates and Peter Skarzynski, "How Do Companies Get to the Future First?" *Management Review* (January 1999), 16-22.

6. Ronald A. Howard, "Decision Analysis: Practice and Promise," *Management Science* 34 (1988), 679–695.

7. Herbert A. Simon, *The New Science of Management Decision* (Englewood Cliffs, N.J.: Prentice-Hall, 1977), 47.

8. Gregory L. White, "Why GM Rewound Its Product Strategy, Delaying New Cavalier,"*The Wall Street Journal* (July 30, 1999), A1, A6.

9. Samuel Eilon, "Structuring Unstructured Decisions," *Omega* 13 (1985), 369–377; and Max H. Bazerman, *Judgment in Managerial Decision Making* (New York: Wiley, 1986).

10. James G. March and Zur Shapira, "Managerial Perspectives on Risk and Risk Taking," *Management Science* 33 (1987), 1404–1418; and Inga Skromme Baird and Howard Thomas, "Toward a Contingency Model of Strategic Risk Taking," *Academy of Management Review* 10 (1985), 230–243.

11. J. G. Higgins, "Planning for Risk and Uncertainty in Oil Exploration," *Long Range Planning* 26, no. 1 (February 1993), 111–122; Alex Taylor III, "Wrong Turn at Saturn," *Fortune* (July 24, 2000), 371-372.

12. Eilon, "Structuring Unstructured Decisions"; and Philip A. Roussel, "Cutting Down the Guesswork in R&D," *Harvard Business Review* 61 (September–October 1983), 154–160.

13. Russell Wild, "Think Fast!" *Working Woman* (September 2000), 89–90.

14. Michael Masuch and Perry LaPotin, "Beyond Garbage Cans: An AI Model of Organizational Choice," *Administrative Science Quarterly* 34 (1989), 38–67; and Richard L. Daft and Robert H. Lengel, "Organizational Information Requirements, Media Richness and Structural Design," *Management Science* 32 (1986), 554–571.

15. David M. Schweiger, William R. Sandberg, and James W. Ragan, "Group Approaches for Improving Strategic Decision

Making: A Comparative Analysis of Dialectical Inquiry, Devil's Advocacy, and Consensus," *Academy of Management Journal* 29 (1986), 51–71; and Richard O. Mason and Ian I. Mitroff, *Challenging Strategic Planning Assumptions* (New York: Wiley Interscience, 1981).

16. Michael Pacanowsky, "Team Tools for Wicked Problems," *Organizational Dynamics* 23, no. 3 (Winter 1995), 36–51.

17. Boris Blai, Jr., "Eight Steps to Successful Problem Solving," *Supervisory Management* (January 1986), 7–9; and Earnest R. Archer, "How to Make a Business Decision: An Analysis of Theory and Practice," *Management Review* 69 (February 1980), 54–61.

18. Stacie McCullough, "On the Front Lines," Section 1, *CIO*, (October 15, 1999), 78–81.

19. Anna Muoio, "Decisions, Decisions," (Unit of One column), *Fast Company* (October 1998), 93–101.

20. Thomas M. Cook, "SABRE Soars," *OR/MS Today* (June 1998), 26–35.

21. Herbert A. Simon, *The New Science of Management Decision* (New York: Harper & Row, 1960), 5–6; and Amitai Etzioni, "Humble Decision Making," *Harvard Business Review* (July–August 1989), 122–126.

22. James G. March and Herbert A. Simon, *Organizations* (New York: Wiley, 1958).

23. Herbert A. Simon, *Models of Man* (New York: Wiley, 1957), 196–205; and Herbert A. Simon, *Administrative Behavior*, 2d ed. (New York: Free Press, 1957).

24. John Taylor, "Project Fantasy: A Behind-the-Scenes Account of Disney's Desperate Battle against the Raiders," *Manhattan* (November 1984).

25. Weston H. Agor, "The Logic of Intuition: How Top Executives Make Important Decisions," *Organizational Dynamics* 14 (Winter 1986), 5–18; and Herbert A. Simon, "Making Management Decisions: The Role of Intuition and Emotion," *Academy of Management Executive* 1 (1987), 57–64.

26. Lisa A. Burke and Monica K. Miller, "Taking the Mystery Out of Intuitive Decision Making," *Academy of Management Executive* 13, no. 4 (1999), 91–99.

27. Bill Breen, "What's Your Intuition?" *Fast Company* (September 2000), 290–300.

28. Alden M. Hayashi, "When to Trust Your Gut," *Harvard Business Review* (February 2001), 59–65.

29. Chris Smith, "Chao, Baby," *New York* (October 18, 1993), 66–75; and "Chao in Charge," *Cablevision* (November 29, 1999), 24.

30. William B. Stevenson, Jon L. Pierce, and Lyman W. Porter, "The Concept of 'Coalition' in Organization Theory and Research," *Academy of Management Review* 10 (1985), 256–268.

31. Jonathan Harris, "Why Speedy Got Stuck in Reverse," *Canadian Business* (September 26, 1997), 87–88.

32. James W. Fredrickson, "Effects of Decision Motive and Organizational Performance Level on Strategic Decision Processes," *Academy of Management Journal* 28 (1985), 821–843; James W. Fredrickson, "The Comprehensiveness of Strategic Decision Processes: Extension, Observations, Future Directions," *Academy of Management Journal* 27 (1984), 445–466; James W. Dean, Jr., and Mark P. Sharfman, "Procedural Rationality in the Strategic Decision-Making Process," *Journal of Management Studies* 30, no. 4 (July 1993), 587–610; Nandini Rajagopalan, Abdul M. A. Rasheed, and Deepak K. Datta, "Strategic Decision Processes: Critical Review and Future Directions," *Journal of Management* 19, no. 2 (1993), 349–384; and Paul J. H. Schoemaker, "Strategic Decisions in Organizations: Rational and Behavioral Views," *Journal of Management Studies* 30, no. 1 (January 1993), 107–129.

33. Marjorie A. Lyles and Howard Thomas, "Strategic Problem Formulation: Biases and Assumptions Embedded in Alternative Decision-Making Models," *Journal of Management Studies* 25 (1988), 131–145; and Susan E. Jackson and Jane E. Dutton, "Discerning Threats and Opportunities," *Administrative Science Quarterly* 33 (1988), 370–387.

34. Anita Lienert, "Can Liz Wetzel's Baby Save Buick?" *Working Woman* (May 2001), 33–36, 78.

35. Richard L. Daft, Juhani Sormumen, and Don Parks, "Chief Executive Scanning, Environmental Characteristics, and Company Performance: An Empirical Study" (unpublished manuscript, Texas A&M University, 1988).

36. C. Kepner and B. Tregoe, *The Rational Manager* (New York: McGraw-Hill, 1965).

37. Mylene Mangalindan and Suein L. Hwang, "Gang of Six: Coterie of Early Hires Made Yahoo! A Hit But an Insular Place," *The Wall Street Journal* (March 9, 2001), A1, A6.

38. Paul C. Nutt, "Surprising But True: Half the Decisions in Organizations Fail," *Academy of Management Executive* 13, no. 4 (1999), 75–90.

39. Lienert, "Can Liz Wetzel's Baby Save Buick?"

40. Peter Mayer, "A Surprisingly Simple Way to Make Better Decisions," *Executive Female* (March–April 1995), 13–14; and Ralph L. Keeney, "Creativity in Decision-Making with Value-Focused Thinking," *Sloan Management Review* (Summer 1994), 33–41.

41. Robert Levering and Milton Moskowitz, "The 100 Best Companies to Work For: The Best in the Worst of Times," *Fortune* (February 4, 2002), 60

42. Gregory L. White and Joseph B. White, "GM Appoints An Industry Guru To Fix Its Lineup," *The Wall Street Journal* (August 3, 2001), B1, B6; Ian Springsteel, "Paul J. Liska" profile in "The Class of 2000," *CFO* (October 2000), 72–74.

43. Jenny C. McCune, "Making Lemonade," *Management Review*, (June 1997), 49–53, 51.

44. Based on A. J. Rowe, J. D. Boulgaides, and M. R. McGrath, *Managerial Decision Making* (Chicago: Science Research Associates, 1984); and Alan J. Rowe and Richard O. Mason, *Managing with Style: A Guide to Understanding, Assessing, and Improving Your Decision Making* (San Francisco: Jossey-Bass, 1987).

45. Peter Elkind, "Vulgarians at the Gate," *Fortune* (June 21, 1999), 133–145.

46. Victor H. Vroom, "A New Look at Managerial Decision Making," *Organizational Dynamics* (Spring 1972), 66–80.

47. V. H. Vroom and Arthur G. Jago, *The New Leadership: Managing Participation in Organizations* (Englewood Cliffs, N.J.: Prentice-Hall, 1988).

48. Victor H. Vroom, "Leadership and the Decision-Making Process," *Organizational Dynamics* 28, no. 4 (Spring 2000), 82–94.

49. R. H. G. Field, "A Test of the Vroom-Yetton Normative Model of Leadership," *Journal of Applied Psychology* (October 1982), 523–532; and R. H. G. Field, "A Critique of the Vroom-Yetton Contingency Model of Leadership Behavior," *Academy of Management Review* 4 (1979), 249–257.

50. Vroom, "Leadership and the Decision Making Process"; Jennifer T. Ettling and Arthur G. Jago, "Participation under Conditions of Conflict: More on the Validity of the Vroom-Yetton Model," *Journal of Management Studies* 25 (1988), 73–83; Madeline E. Heilman, Harvey A. Hornstein, Jack H. Cage, and Judith K. Herschlag, "Reactions to Prescribed Leader Behavior as a Function of Role Perspective: The Case of the Vroom-Yetton Model," *Journal of Applied Psychology* (February 1984), 50–60; and Arthur G. Jago and Victor H. Vroom, "Some Differences in the Incidence and Evaluation of Participative Leader Behavior," *Journal of Applied Psychology* (December 1982), 776–783.

51. Based on a decision problem presented in Victor H. Vroom, "Leadership and the Decision-Making Process," *Organizational Dynamics* 28, no. 4 (Spring, 2000): 82–94.

52. Kathleen M. Eisenhardt, "Strategy as Strategic Decision Making," *Sloan Management Review* (Spring, 1999), 65–72.

53. See Katharine Mieskowski, "Digital Competition," *Fast Company* (December 1999), 155–162; Thomas A. Stewart, "Three Rules for Managing in the Real-Time Economy," *Fortune* (May 1, 2000), 333–334; and Geoffrey Colvin, "How to Be a Great eCEO," *Fortune* (May 24, 1999), 104–110.

54. Michael V. Copeland, "Mistakes Happen," *Red Herring* (May 2000), 346–354.

55. Ibid.

56. Joshua Klayman, Richard P. Larrick, and Chip Heath, "Organizational Repairs," *Across the Board* (February 2000), 26-31.

57. The discussion of collective intuition is based on Eisenhardt, "Strategy as Strategic Decision Making."

58. Ettling and Jago, "Participation under Conditions of Conflict."

59. Eisenhardt, "Strategy as Strategic Decision Making"; and David A. Garvin and Michael A. Roberto, "What You Don't Know About Making Decisions," *Harvard Business Review* (September 2001), 108–116.

60. David M. Schweiger and William R. Sandberg, "The Utilization of Individual Capabilities in Group Approaches to Strategic Decision-Making," *Strategic Management Journal* 10 (1989), 31–43; and "The Devil's Advocate," *Small Business Report* (December 1987), 38–41.

61. Eisenhardt, "Strategy as Strategic Decision Making.

62. Garvin and Roberto, "What You Don't Know About Making Decisions."

Chapter 7: Caribou Coffee Has a Mission

JOHN AND KIM PUCKETT LOVE THE OUTDOORS. THEY ALSO love coffee. About a decade ago, they were hiking Sable Mountain in Alaska. When they reached the summit, they were inspired not only by the scenery surrounding them but also by the sight of a distant herd of caribou galloping through the valley below. No, the Pucketts didn't suddenly pull a coffeemaker out of a backpack and start brewing coffee on the mountaintop, but when they got home after their mountain trip, they wanted to find a way to re-create the sights and sounds of the Alaskan wilderness, preserving some of the feelings they had experienced. They wanted to establish a place where people could gather to share good and simple things: casual conversation with friends, time for the daily newspaper, a tasty cup of coffee, "an escape from the daily grind." They also wanted to start their own business. So they opened their first coffee shop in Minneapolis, in December of 1992.

Today, Caribou Coffee is the nation's second largest specialty coffee company, with 160 stores and 2,000 employees across eight states. The Pucketts have remained true to their original vision of bringing the wilderness home: each store is built and decorated to look like an Alaskan lodge, with knotty-pine cabinets, a rustic fireplace, and comfortable seating. "We still strive to make the Caribou experience adventurous, rewarding, and fun," says the company's Web site. "Our mission is to be the best neighborhood gathering place; fast and friendly service is at the heart of this goal."

A clear mission is the soul of an organization, but achievable goals and good planning are its heart and lungs. Caribou Coffee integrates all three, but its development and growth have not been without struggle. The Pucketts perfected the company's rustic image and style. With the help of Barry Judge, vice president of marketing, and the Carmichael Lynch advertising agency in Minneapolis, Caribou came up with buzzwords to capture the Caribou experience: "Outdoorsy. Leave smiling. Hand-made. Down to earth. Clever. Transformational."

People near Caribou shops immediately became loyal customers. They seemed to prefer Caribou's brew to that of its largest competitor, Starbucks. (In fact, Caribou debuted certain flavors and brewing methods that Starbucks followed later.) Quality, service, satisfied customers—all were goals that Caribou could achieve. But the company had problems with setting more specific goals and planning for growth. For one thing, Caribou lacked the funds for the kind of expansion that the Pucketts envisioned. For another, their expansion from Minneapolis to other locations was driven by the competition—they simply went where Starbucks *wasn't*, instead of establishing growth goals independently. By 1997, Caribou Coffee had 123 stores, with only Starbucks ahead of it. Caribou company president Jay Willoughby declared, "Our intent is to be a national player." But Starbucks had more than 2,000 stores, including nearly 190 overseas: Caribou wasn't even close. That doesn't mean being number two is necessarily bad. In fact, said Alan Hickok, an industry analyst, "In markets where [Caribou] competes head-to-head with Starbucks, they've done just fine . . . There's no consumer category, with the exception of Microsoft, where consumers have been satisfied with having just one choice. Absolutely, there's room for a No. 2."

Caribou still wanted to grow, but they were having trouble coming up with a clear plan and the money to back it. Enter Don Dempsey, former head of McDonald's China division. Dempsey joined Caribou as its new CEO in 1999. Why would he make the leap from a giant like McDonald's to the small beans of Caribou Coffee? "When you're running an international company for McDonald's, you really have a lot of autonomy," he explained. "I wanted to take what I had learned at a large company and apply it to a small one." When one newswriter asked Dempsey about his goal for the company, he answered that he wanted to "reliably and consistently grow profits." But he needed a plan, and he needed a way to raise the money to achieve his overall goal.

Dempsey recalls that when he needed more money to fund a project at McDonald's, he just called up the CEO and asked for it. Funding wasn't so easy for Caribou. Eventually, though, the Crescent Capital group of Atlanta agreed to purchase a percentage of the company, which would pump the needed growth dollars into the organization. Dempsey outlined a plan for expansion: stick with locations in which Caribou already had stores and strengthen the Caribou brand within those locations. Caribou's largest market is its hometown of Minneapolis-St. Paul, but other markets include Columbus and Cleveland, Ohio; Raleigh and Charlotte, North Carolina; Atlanta; Detroit; Chicago; and Washington, D.C. "We have to increase penetration and increase brand awareness in order to improve our economics," Dempsey said. Meanwhile, Caribou would continue to brew a good cup of coffee in a place where people can get away from the daily grind.

Questions

1. Write what you think would be an effective, updated mission statement for Caribou Coffee.
2. What is the relationship between Dempsey's goal and his plan for sticking with existing markets?
3. How important is the Pucketts' original vision to the company's identity today? Explain your answer.

SOURCES: Company Web site, *http://www.cariboucoffee.com*, accessed February 21, 2002; Jessica Griffith, "Caribou Coffee Brewing a Caffeine-Fueled Expansion," *Finance and Commerce*, December 26, 2001, *http://www.finance-commerce.com*; Eleni Chamis, "Sale Stalling Coffee Chain's Local Growth," *Washington Business Journal*, October 30, 2000, *http://washington.bizjournals.com*; Jim McCartney, "Caribou Coffee Taking on King of the Hill," *Shopping Centers Today*, May 1, 1999, *http://www.icsc.org*.

Chapter 8: Caribou Coffee's Strategy: Worth More than Beans

PICTURE DRINKING YOUR DAILY CUPPA JOE IN AN ALASKAN lodge. You have plenty of time to chat with friends, scan the daily paper, and imagine that when you step outside you'll have a sweeping view of Denali itself, with a few stray caribou grazing its foothills. That's what the folks at Caribou Coffee want you to feel, whether you're in Minneapolis, Atlanta, or Washington, D.C. The rustic image conveyed by Caribou's 160 coffee shops is a major part of the company's strategy, which is to create a comfortable, attractive, unique atmosphere in which customers can relax and enjoy their coffee.

But the company's *grand* strategy is growth. At first, founders John and Kim Puckett followed a strategy of placing Caribou shops wherever their major competitor, Starbucks, didn't have shops. But that growth strategy lacked cohesiveness and planning. The company also tried to grow too fast, a pitfall of many young firms. "There's a lot of instability with rapid growth," says Jay Willoughby, a restaurant executive whom the Pucketts hired to be president of their company in 1997, five years after they opened their first shop in Minneapolis. Willoughby determined that before Caribou grew any more, it had to become more stable financially, without sacrificing value to its customers. In other words, every cup of coffee served by Caribou staff, from Kenya AA to Fireside Blend, had to be fresh, hot, and full of flavor. It also had to come at a reasonable price. To offer value and still make a profit, Willoughby had to make sure that the company's warehouse and field operations were functioning efficiently and cost effectively so that all coffee goods moved through the system quickly, remaining fresh. Only then would a grand strategy of growth make sense.

In 1999, Don Dempsey joined Caribou as its new CEO. After 20 years with McDonald's, Dempsey was ready for a new challenge. Like Willoughby, he examined the company's previous expansion strategy. "Their strategy was to go where Starbucks wasn't, and that was a flawed strategy," noted Dempsey. "They had a half-dozen stores here and a half-dozen there, but no strong brand awareness in any one market. Then, they ran out of money." First Dempsey had to come up with more backing for the company, then create a strategy of controlled growth. He found the backing he needed in the form of Crescent Capital of Atlanta, which agreed to purchase a portion of the company for $80 million, giving Caribou the funding it needed for growth. Dempsey has so far resisted franchising as a source of income or expansion, however. All Caribou stores are company owned. "Our stores run pretty well, and I like getting all of the profit from the stores," he explains. Also, the recapitalization from Crescent has given the company enough money to carry through its growth

plans without franchising or making an offer of public stock. "I'd love to have a nice, big private company," Dempsey admits.

It was important to accomplish controlled growth while maintaining Caribou's woodsy, rustic, comfortable style. Everyone involved with Caribou—from its founders to its loyal customers—already knew that the Caribou shops performed well against Starbucks. In fact, claims Dempsey, "You can put us right next to a Starbucks. But our place cannot be less convenient or attractive than the Starbucks." Industry analyst Alan Hickok agrees with Dempsey. "Even in my little suburb, there are three Caribous within a couple of miles and a couple of Starbucks, and they are all doing quite well. Dempsey is a smart guy, and he knows exactly what he is doing." Minneapolis investor Jim Jundt concurs with Dempsey's strategic management. "He is using a strategy that has succeeded for him in the past," Jundt says.

Where can you go for a cup of Caribou? If you live in a few Midwestern states or Georgia, North Carolina, or Washington, D.C., you're in luck. If not, you can order coffee beans and other products through Caribou's catalog or online. If you visit the Web site, you can find out how much caffeine is in a cup of coffee, why you should use an oxygen-bleached filter, and why it's a bad idea to microwave a cooled cup of premium coffee. But you don't have to be a coffee aficionado to appreciate the aroma of success that seems to be wafting around Caribou Coffee. Don Dempsey had never sipped a cup of gourmet coffee before he came to Caribou. "I recently had some of the coffee I used to drink, and I was astounded at how bad it was," he recalls. "Once you've had good coffee . . . you can't go back."

Questions

1. Why was it important for Caribou to achieve stability before proceeding with further growth?
2. How would you define Caribou's core competence?
3. Identify two of Caribou's internal strengths and two internal weaknesses.

SOURCES: Company Web site, *http://www.cariboucoffee.com*, accessed February 21, 2002; Jessica Griffith, "Caribou Coffee Brewing a Caffeine-Fueled Expansion," *Finance and Commerce*, December 26, 2001, *http://www.finance-commerce.com*; Ashley Gibson, "The Uptown Coffee Buzz: More Starbucks, Caribous," *The Business Journal*, October 27, 2000, *http://charlotte.bizjournals.com*; Eleni Chamis, "Sale Stalling Coffee Chain's Local Growth," *Washington Business Journal*, October 27, 2000, *http://washington.bizjournals.com*; Jim McCartney, "Caribou Coffee Taking on King of the Hill," *Shopping Centers Today*, May 1, 1999, *http://www.icsc.org*.

Chapter 9: Machado and Silvetti: A Business Based on Decisions

WHEN WAS THE LAST TIME YOU DESIGNED A BUILDING? Maybe you cut a door in a large cardboard box when you were a child, painted on windows and crawled inside your new "house" with a couple of friends. Maybe you were one of those lucky kids who actually had a tree fort. Or perhaps an ambitious school teacher assigned you a project that involved planning and constructing an imaginary structure. Regardless of how simple or complex your building project was, it involved many decisions, from materials to dimensions. Harvard professors Rodolfo Machado and Jorge Silvetti, who also head up their own architectural firm, are examples of advanced design and architecture decision makers. In fact, almost everyone who works at Machado and Silvetti Associates makes decisions—whether programmed or nonprogrammed.

Machado and Silvetti Associates, based in Boston, specializes in creating housing and other structures for colleges and universities, as well as public buildings such as a branch of the Boston Public Library. The firm has an impressive roster of clients, including the J. Paul Getty Trust, the Utah Museum of Fine Arts, the Federal Reserve Bank of Boston, and the City of Vienna. Like most architectural firms, Machado and Silvetti is essentially organized around its projects, so that professionals such as associate Michael Yusem, a project manager, can focus on all the decisions related to a certain assignment. Since every project is different, many of these decisions are nonprogrammed, and much effort goes into reducing both uncertainty and risk. For instance, once initial design choices are made and a budget approved by a client, Yusem and his colleagues need to figure out how to deliver the design requirements within the budget, or risk losing money. Then come the building details, all of which must satisfy the customer while producing revenue for the firm. As the team develops a new graduate housing facility for a Boston-based university, they must consider the needs of future residents, the overall look or image of the complex, as well as the choice of quality materials including carpet, tiles, flooring, bathroom fixtures, and appliances. They need to determine the number and size of the rooms. They must be certain that the facility complies with local building and environmental codes. They must select and coordinate subcontractors for various phases of the project. And they must deliver the project on a schedule. All of this coordination is just for one of the firm's projects.

Across the country, another Machado and Silvetti team has undertaken the renovation of the Getty Villa, which is part of the J. Paul Getty Museum in southern California. The mission for the Getty Villa is entirely different from their graduate housing project—its residents are works of art from the museum's Antiquities Collection, which contains roughly 50,000 objects ranging from statues to ancient tools. In this case, the design team had to come up with a plan that incorporated the classical inspiration of the works themselves with the surrounding buildings of the museum. To achieve this, they chose pattern mosaic and terrazzo floors, coffered ceilings, and colorful plaster walls, with detailing in wood and bronze. The team also considered the modern needs of visitors and museum caretakers. In doing so, they added skylights and reopened some of the old windows to bring in natural light for better viewing, and added a variety of other modern amenities for comfort. Each of these decisions involved development of and selection among alternatives, along with feedback from the client. And all of the decisions had to contribute somehow to the mission of the project as a whole.

Machado and Silvetti enjoys a top-notch reputation around the world for its designs, both with clients and critics. "The new branch of the Boston Public Library in Allston is a delight: an airy, spacious place where the breeze seems to flow through uninterrupted. . . . This is the best new public building in Boston in years," writes architecture critic Robert Campbell of *The Boston Globe*. When the firm won the First Award in Architecture from the American Academy of Arts and Letters, the awards committee wrote, "In a series of boldly conceived and brilliantly executed urban projects completed over the past two decades Rodolfo Machado and Jorge Silvetti have pursued an extended and vigorous program of research through design. Their investigations . . . have been uncompromisingly dedicated to envisioning a meaningful architecture of the public realm." And it's all done one brick—and one decision—at a time.

Questions

1. How might project managers at Machado and Silvetti use the classical model of decision making to make a decision about what type of windows to install in a building?
2. What might be the consequences of using satisficing in a project like the Getty Villa or the graduate housing facility?
3. How might project managers at Machado and Silvetti use decision making to enhance performance beyond its current levels?

SOURCES: Company Web site, *http://www.machado-silvetti.com*, accessed February 5, 2002; Alex Ulam, "Harvard Inc.," *Metropolis Magazine*, February 2001, *http://www.metropolismag.com*; "The New Getty Villa," Getty Museum Web Site, 2000, *http://www.getty.edu*.

Part Three: A Tale of Two Strategies

THE STORY OF BILL FORD AND JAC NASSER IS NOT ONLY THE story of two leaders but also the story of two strategies marked by differing management styles, differing goals, and perhaps even differing views of the company's mission. When Jac Nasser came to the top position at Ford, he had already worked for the company for thirty years. No one would argue that his sometimes harsh, autocratic decision-making style made him less than popular among Ford workers, managers, and media members. But Nasser arrived at the top in the late 1990s with bold plans to turn an aging, stumbling company into a streamlined, flexible contender in the auto industry. Ford's ventures into the financial services and defense industries in the 1980s had turned out to be disastrous. Nasser pledged that his new mission for the company, "to be the world's leading consumer company for automotive services and products," would be backed by solid strategic planning. "It's a world going through tremendous change," said Nasser early in his reign, "not just through economic events, but largely through technology. We're trying not to be left behind." So Nasser set a goal of hiring 20 percent new managers while also developing leaders from within the company. He also emphasized team building. He began to acquire other brands, in the United States and abroad, including Land Rover, Jaguar, and a chain of British auto-service centers called Kwik-Fit. He vowed to turn Ford's less profitable car lines around (the company was much stronger in the truck and SUV business): "In the past, we tried to do too much in the car business and dispersed our resources. Now we're simplifying the product line. And we're separating the models that remain and giving them better brand identities." He planned to jump into e-business with all four wheels. "Technology and networks in particular determine the shape of everything else," Nasser remarked. He began with a joint venture with Microsoft's CarPoint, which allowed consumers to build cars to order online (the site also provided Ford with data about car buyers).

How did Nasser's planning work out? Within a couple of years, Wall Street named Ford the most profitable and best-managed automaker of the Big Three (the other two are General Motors and DaimlerChrysler). Then came the Firestone tire recall, quality problems that began to surface, a sluggish economy, and other woes. Nasser's grand Internet plans didn't work out as he had hoped—the information technology department simply wasn't ready. In the summer of 2001, Ford's board of directors voted to give company chairman Bill Ford "a greater strategic role" in the company. In other words, Ford and Nasser would share power and responsibilities that would "focus on policy, strategy, key issues affecting the future direction of the company and other major business issues." For several months, the two men remained diplomatic in public, but there was no mistaking their differing

management styles, visions for the company, or proposed strategies. Eventually, Nasser was voted out. Bill Ford had a huge task ahead of him.

First, Bill Ford created a triumvirate—a team of three top executives—to formulate a new vision and strategies for the company. He named Carl E. Reichardt vice-chairman and Nick Scheele chief operating officer. Scheele came from Ford's Jaguar division and Reichardt, former head of a bank, from the board of directors. "I expect the three of us will have an easygoing relationship," noted Ford. Scheele began his term with a "back to basics" slogan that indicated the company's new strategy would focus on its core business: making and selling cars and trucks. Then came the massive restructuring plan, whose goal was to cut $3 billion to $5 billion in costs. Most experts believe that Nasser would have favored downsizing in order to meet Ford's shrinking share in the marketplace, but Bill Ford would likely favor other strategies. Still, he warned in an early press release that the company would have to take "tough action" to reverse its losses. "It is not going to surprise anyone that there will be some pretty dramatic changes," noted Greg Melich of Morgan Stanley Dean Witter. "The one area where you can do more quickly is in the managerial and administrative areas, whereas restructuring the manufacturing side is much more difficult." However, it was clear that there was surplus manufacturing capacity in North America that needed to be addressed. And before Nasser's departure, the company was considering laying off as much as 20 percent of its U.S. white-collar staff, or more than 8,000 salaried workers, as part of a strategic overhaul. Also, the company proposed delaying the release of certain new auto models, including the Ford Ranger. Another part of the plan involved using more shared parts to cut manufacturing costs, even in Ford's premium car lines such as Volvo and Jaguar. A "strategy board" was developed specifically to formulate plans for the Premier Automotive Group (PAG), which would open the door for more than shared parts—perhaps shared engineering, sales, and purchasing teams—while maintaining the individual identities of the brands. "We have developed a structure which will allow us to more effectively support all our PAG brands," announced Wolfgang Reitzle, chairman of the PAG. "Individually, the companies do not have the critical mass to compete on equal terms."

Finally, Bill Ford began to push for a reconciliation between his company and Firestone/Bridgestone; after all, there are Fords and Firestones in both families. Mending the relationship might indicate a return to normalcy on the road "back to the basics." What are Ford's basics? "It's not the Internet, junkyards, or auto parts," quips David E. Cole, director of the Center for Automotive Research in Ann Arbor, Michigan. "It's building cars and trucks." Now there's a plan.

Part Three: A Tale of Two Strategies

Questions

1. Based on what you've read, formulate a brief mission statement for the "new" Ford Motor Company.

2. Imagine that you are part of Bill Ford's management team. Set a stretch goal either for the company as a whole or for the Premier group strategy board that you think would realistically help the company turn around. Explain why you chose this goal.

3. Describe the differences between Jac Nasser and Bill Ford as decision makers.

SOURCES: John Griffiths and Tim Burt, "Moving to Drive the Premier Growth Machine Faster," *Financial Times*, November 23, 2001, *http://news.ft.com*; Tim Burt and Nikki Tait, "Ford May Axe 20 percent of U.S. White Collar Staff," *Financial Times*, November 6, 2001, *http://news.ft.com*; Kathleen Kerwin and Joann Muller, "Bill Ford Takes the Wheel," *BusinessWeek Online,* November 1, 2001, *http://www.businessweek.com*; David Ibison, "New Ford Chief Edges Closer to Truce with Bridgestone," *Financial Times*, November 1, 2001, *http://news.ft.com*; Tim Burt, "Nasser Signals Further Cuts in Ford's U.S. Production," *Financial Times*, October 25, 2001, *http://news.ft.com*; Tim Burt, "Nasser Says Ford Has the Strategy to Confound Critics," *Financial Times*, September 13, 2001, *http://news.ft.com*; Jerry Flint, "Ford: A Distracted Driver," *Forbes.com*, September 6, 2001, *http://www.forbes.com*; Tim Burt and Nikki Tait, "Getting Ford Around the Corner," *Financial Times*, July 30, 2001, *http://news.ft.com*; Jeff Moad, "Ford Rebuilds IT Engine," ZDNet News, January 28, 2001, *http://www.zdnet.com*; Amey Stone and Kathleen Kerwin, "Can Nasser Get Ford's Stock onto a Smoother Road?" *BusinessWeek Online*, October 11, 1999, *http://www.businessweek.com*; "Jac Nasser: In the Past, We Tried to Do Too Much," *BusinessWeek Online*, October 11, 1999, *http://www.businessweek.com*.

Organizing

When we think of structured organizations in nature, none deserves more admiration than the beehive. A colony of bees is a huge organization, containing as many as 50,000 inhabitants. The hive itself is highly structured, as is the population of bees that lives within it. The structure varies according to bee type. Bumblebees work within a horizontal structure, in which the top manager—the queen—shares many of the tasks performed by her workers. The need for coordination among worker bees and the queen is vital. A honeybee colony illustrates a vertical structure; the queen bee does not share her workers' tasks. Instead, she spends most of her life laying eggs while the workers gather food, care for the young, and clean and protect the hive. A beehive is departmentalized just like a large corporation. Inside the hive, rows of wax combs store eggs, larvae, pollen, and honey. Each type of bee— worker, drone, and queen—performs a specific task designed to help the colony and hive thrive and grow.

As with any organization, the environment affects the structure of a beehive and the jobs its inhabitants perform. During warm months of the year, bees must find and store food to carry them through the winter, just as managers must find ways to strengthen the organization in a positive environment so it can be protected during an economic downturn or when it is threatened by competitors. When a honeybee finds a source of nectar or pollen, it does a little dance in a figure-eight pattern to show its co-workers where the food is in relation to the position of the sun. Managers may be glad they don't have to dance for their food; but they know how to coordinate efforts to nourish their organization.

Fundamentals of Organizing

CHAPTER OUTLINE

Organizing the Vertical Structure

Work Specialization

Chain of Command

Span of Management

Centralization and Decentralization

Formalization

Departmentalization

Vertical Functional Approach

Divisional Approach

Matrix Approach

Team Approach

Network Approach

The Virtual Organization Approach

LEARNING OBJECTIVES

After studying this chapter, you should be able to

1   Discuss the fundamental characteristics of organizing, including such concepts as work specialization, chain of command, line and staff, and span of management.

2   Explain when specific structural characteristics such as centralization and formalization should be used within organizations.

3   Describe the functional approach to structure.

4   Describe the divisional approach to structure.

5   Explain the matrix approach to structure and its application to both domestic and international organizations.

6   Explain the contemporary team and network structures and why they are being adopted by organizations.

7   Discuss the advantages and disadvantages of the new virtual approach to organizing.

Management Challenge

During the 1980s and early 1990s, sales at food giant ConAgra Inc. exploded from $570 million to more than $20 billion amid a string of high-profile acquisitions, including Butterball, Hunt-Wesson, and Swift Premium. The blockbuster line of Healthy Choice frozen dinners seemed to seal the company's financial strength. But by the time Bruce Rohde took over as chairman and CEO in 1997, ConAgra was facing a crisis. A surplus of beef, pork, poultry, and grains flooded commodity markets at the same time financial problems in Asia closed the door to export opportunities. ConAgra was unprepared to deal with the plunge in prices and profits.

Managers in the 80 or so business units were more concerned about protecting their own divisions' profits than about helping ConAgra as a whole. For example, sales reps who sold frozen french fries to restaurants never bothered to let other divisions know if the restaurants were looking to buy fresh beef. In addition, a big customer might have to deal with dozens of representatives, most of whom knew nothing about what was going on in the other divisions. And even ConAgra's own divisions often bought from competitors instead of their own sister companies. The managers of far-flung divisions had been accustomed to running their units as they saw fit, but the CEO knew that needed to change. "We weren't working together," Rohde said. "We were probably working at cross-purposes." Rohde needed to find a way to get everyone sharing information, knowledge, and products across company lines to better serve customers.[1]

What advice would you give Bruce Rohde about structural design? What structural changes might help ConAgra solve its problems with poor coordination across divisions?

The problem confronting ConAgra Foods is one of structural design. Bruce Rohde wants to change the company's structure to increase coordination across divisions and help ConAgra be more competitive during difficult economic times.

Every firm wrestles with the problem of how to organize. Reorganization often is necessary to reflect a new strategy, changing market conditions, or innovative technology. Today, many companies have found a need to make structural changes that are compatible with use of the Internet for e-business. For example, Brady Corporation, a Milwaukee-based manufacturer of identification and safety products, is reorganizing to increase cross-functional collaboration in connection with the rollout of a new system that links customers, distributors, and suppliers over the Internet.[2] Hewlett-Packard consolidated its 83 independently-run units into four major divisions to increase internal collaboration and enhance flexibility.[3] A growing number of companies operate as network organizations, limiting themselves to a few core activities and letting outside specialists handle the rest. Others function as virtual organizations, groups of people or companies that come together for a specific purpose or project and then disband when the project is complete.

Each of these organizations is using fundamental concepts of organizing. **Organizing** is the deployment of organizational resources to achieve strategic goals. The deployment of resources is reflected in the organization's division of labor into specific departments and jobs, formal lines of authority, and mechanisms for coordinating diverse organization tasks.

Organizing is important because it follows from strategy—the topic of Part 3. Strategy defines *what* to do; organizing defines *how* to do it. Organization structure is a tool that managers use to harness resources for getting things done. Part 4 explains the variety of organizing principles and concepts used by managers. This chapter covers fundamental concepts that apply to all organizations and departments. These ideas are extended in Chapter 11, where we look at how structural designs are tailored to the organization's situation. Chapter 12 discusses how organizations can be structured to facilitate innovation and change. Chapters 13 and 14 examine how to utilize human resources to the best advantage within the organization's structure.

organizing

The deployment of organizational resources to achieve strategic goals.

Organizing *helps Verizon Communications remain competitive in the volatile, worldwide telecommunications industry. Verizon, formed by the merger of Bell Atlantic and GTE, is the largest provider of wireline and wireless communications in the United States and the largest provider of print and online directory information in the world. The $67 billion company is structured into four main divisions: Domestic Telecom, Domestic Wireless, Verizon International, and Verizon Information Services. At this high-tech Network Operations Center in the Dallas area, employees continuously monitor the company's nationwide telephone network, which reaches one-third of U.S. households and more than one-third of Fortune 500 companies.*

Organizing the Vertical Structure

The organizing process leads to the creation of organization structure, which defines how tasks are divided and resources deployed. **Organization structure** is defined as (1) the set of formal tasks assigned to individuals and departments; (2) formal reporting relationships, including lines of authority, decision responsibility, number of hierarchical levels, and span of managers' control; and (3) the design of systems to ensure effective coordination of employees across departments.[4]

The set of formal tasks and formal reporting relationships provides a framework for vertical control of the organization. The characteristics of vertical structure are portrayed in the **organization chart**, which is the visual representation of an organization's structure.

A sample organization chart for a soda bottling plant is illustrated in Exhibit 10.1. The plant has four major departments—accounting, human resources, production, and marketing. The organization chart delineates the chain of command, indicates departmental tasks and how they fit together, and provides order and logic for the organization. Every employee has an appointed task, line of authority, and decision responsibility. The following sections discuss several important features of vertical structure in more detail.

organization structure
The framework in which the organization defines how tasks are divided, resources are deployed and departments are coordinated.

organization chart
The visual representation of an organization's structure.

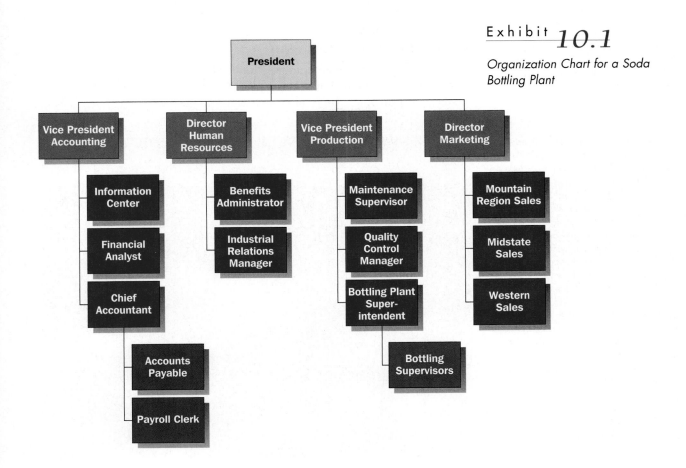

Exhibit **10.1**

Organization Chart for a Soda Bottling Plant

Work Specialization

Organizations perform a wide variety of tasks. A fundamental principle is that work can be performed more efficiently if employees are allowed to specialize.[5] **Work specialization**, sometimes called *division of labor*, is the degree to which organizational tasks are subdivided into separate jobs. Work specialization in Exhibit 10.1 is illustrated by the separation of production tasks into bottling, quality control, and maintenance. Employees within each department perform only the tasks relevant to their specialized function. When work specialization is extensive, employees specialize in a single task. Jobs tend to be small, but they can be performed efficiently. Work specialization is readily visible on an automobile assembly line where each employee performs the same task over and over again. It would not be efficient to have a single employee build the entire automobile or even perform a large number of unrelated jobs.

Despite the apparent advantages of specialization, many organizations are moving away from this principle. With too much specialization, employees are isolated and do only a single, boring job. Many companies are enlarging jobs to provide greater challenges or assigning teams to tasks so that employees can rotate among the several jobs performed by the team. For example, at BHP Copper Metals in San Manuel, Arizona, managers disbanded the traditional assembly line and cross-trained teams of workers to handle all the steps in the copper-refining process. After shifting to the team approach, production increased 20 percent and the unit's safety record improved dramatically.[6] The team approach to organization design will be discussed later in this chapter, and approaches to designing jobs to fit employee needs are described in Chapters 17 and 19.

Chain of Command

The **chain of command** is an unbroken line of authority that links all persons in an organization and shows who reports to whom. It is associated with two underlying principles. *Unity of command* means that each employee is held

work specialization
The degree to which organizational tasks are subdivided into individual jobs; also called division of labor.

chain of command
An unbroken line of authority that links all individuals in the organization and specifies who reports to whom.

Recently, Bill Gates, outspoken founder and CEO of Microsoft, redesigned the company's authority structure to include three CEOs: one to manage sales, customer support, finance, and other operations; another to focus on strategy, marketing, and public relations; and himself to concentrate on software development. Gates formed a new chain of command, with group managers assigned to report to one of the three CEOs. In the photo are managers who report to the head of the Productivity and Business Services Group. From left to right are Doug Burgum of Great Plains, a recent Microsoft acquisition and the leading maker of enterprise management and accounting software for small businesses, Microsoft strategist David Vaskevitch, Office Software boss Steven Sonofsky, and Kathleen Herbert, vice president in charge of bCentral, Microsoft's Web site and hosting service for small business.

©Alyson Aliano

accountable to only one supervisor. The *scalar principle* refers to a clearly defined line of authority in the organization that includes all employees. Authority and responsibility for different tasks should be distinct. All persons in the organization should know to whom they report as well as the successive management levels all the way to the top. In Exhibit 10.1, the payroll clerk reports to the chief accountant, who in turn reports to the vice president, who in turn reports to the company president.

Authority, Responsibility, and Delegation.

The chain of command illustrates the authority structure of the organization. **Authority** is the formal and legitimate right of a manager to make decisions, issue orders, and allocate resources to achieve organizationally desired outcomes. Authority is distinguished by three characteristics:[7]

1. *Authority is vested in organizational positions, not people.* Managers have authority because of the positions they hold, and other people in the same positions would have the same authority.
2. *Authority is accepted by subordinates.* Although authority flows top down through the organization's hierarchy, subordinates comply because they believe that managers have a legitimate right to issue orders. The *acceptance theory of authority* argues that a manager has authority only if subordinates choose to accept his or her commands. If subordinates refuse to obey because the order is outside their zone of acceptance, a manager's authority disappears.[8] For example, Richard Ferris, the former chairman of United Airlines, resigned because few people accepted his strategy of acquiring hotels, a car rental company, and other organizations to build a travel empire. When key people refused to accept his direction, his authority was lost, and he resigned.
3. *Authority flows down the vertical hierarchy.* Positions at the top of the hierarchy are vested with more formal authority than are positions at the bottom.

Responsibility is the flip side of the authority coin. **Responsibility** is the duty to perform the task or activity an employee has been assigned. Typically, managers are assigned authority commensurate with responsibility. When managers have responsibility for task outcomes but little authority, the job is possible but difficult. They rely on persuasion and luck. When managers have authority exceeding responsibility, they may become tyrants, using authority toward frivolous outcomes.[9]

Accountability is the mechanism through which authority and responsibility are brought into alignment. **Accountability** means that the people with authority and responsibility are subject to reporting and justifying task outcomes to those above them in the chain of command.[10] Subordinates must be aware that they are accountable for a task and accept the responsibility and authority for performing it. Accountability can be built into the organization structure. For example, at Whirlpool, incentive programs provide strict accountability. Performance of all managers is monitored, and bonus payments are tied to successful outcomes.

Another concept related to authority is delegation.[11] **Delegation** is the process managers use to transfer authority and responsibility to positions below them in the hierarchy. Most organizations today encourage managers to delegate authority to the lowest possible level to provide maximum flexibility to meet customer needs and adapt to the environment. Managers are encouraged to delegate authority, although they often find it difficult. Techniques for delegation are discussed in the Manager's Shoptalk box.

authority
The formal and legitimate right of a manager to make decisions, issue orders, and allocate resources to achieve organizationally desired outcomes.

responsibility
The duty to perform the task or activity an employee has been assigned.

accountability
The fact that the people with authority and responsibility are subject to reporting and justifying task outcomes to those above them in the chain of command.

delegation
The process managers use to transfer authority and responsibility to positions below them in the hierarchy.

Manager's Shoptalk

How to Delegate

The attempt by top management to decentralize decision making often gets bogged down because middle managers are unable to delegate. Managers may cling tightly to their decision-making and task responsibilities. Failure to delegate occurs for a number of reasons: Managers are most comfortable making familiar decisions; they feel they will lose personal status by delegating tasks; they believe they can do a better job themselves; or they have an aversion to risk—they will not take a chance on delegating because performance responsibility ultimately rests with them.

Yet decentralization offers an organization many advantages. Decisions are made at the right level, lower-level employees are motivated, and employees have the opportunity to develop decision-making skills. Overcoming barriers to delegation in order to gain these advantages is a major challenge. The following approach can help each manager delegate more effectively:

1. *Delegate the whole task.* A manager should delegate an entire task to one person rather than dividing it among several people. This gives the individual complete responsibility and increases his or her initiative while giving the manager some control over the results.
2. *Select the right person.* Not all employees have the same capabilities and degree of motivation. Managers must match talent to task if delegation is to be effective. They should identify subordinates who have made independent decisions in the past and have shown a desire for more responsibility.
3. *Ensure that authority equals responsibility.* Merely assigning a task is not effective delegation. Managers often load subordinates with increased responsibility but do not extend their decision-making range. In addition to having responsibility for completing a task, the worker must be given the authority to make decisions about how best to do the job.
4. *Give thorough instruction.* Successful delegation includes information on what, when, why, where, who, and how.

The subordinate must clearly understand the task and the expected results. It is a good idea to write down all provisions discussed, including required resources and when and how the results will be reported.

5. *Maintain feedback.* Feedback means keeping open lines of communication with the subordinate to answer questions and provide advice, but without exerting too much control. Open lines of communication make it easier to trust subordinates. Feedback keeps the subordinate on the right track.
6. *Evaluate and reward performance.* Once the task is completed, the manager should evaluate results, not methods. When results do not meet expectations, the manager must assess the consequences. When they do meet expectations, the manager should reward employees for a job well done with praise, financial rewards when appropriate, and delegation of future assignments.

Are You a Positive Delegator?

Positive delegation is the way an organization implements decentralization. Do you help or hinder the decentralization process? If you answer yes to more than three of the following questions, you may have a problem delegating:

- I tend to be a perfectionist.
- My boss expects me to know all the details of my job.
- I don't have the time to explain clearly and concisely how a task should be accomplished.
- I often end up doing tasks myself.
- My subordinates typically are not as committed as I am.
- I get upset when other people don't do the task right.
- I really enjoy doing the details of my job to the best of my ability.
- I like to be in control of task outcomes.

SOURCES: Thomas R. Horton "Delegation and Team Building: No Solo Acts Please," *Management Review* (September 1992), 58–61; Andrew E. Schwartz, "The Why, What, and to Whom of Delegation," *Management Solutions* (June 1987), 31–38; "Delegation," *Small Business Report* (June 1986), 38–43; and Russell Wild, "Clone Yourself," *Working Woman* (May 2000), 79–80.

Line and Staff Authority.   An important distinction in many organizations is between line authority and staff authority, reflecting whether managers work in line or staff departments in the organization's structure. *Line departments* perform tasks that reflect the organization's primary goal and mission. In a software company, line departments make and sell the product. In an Internet-based company, line departments would be those that develop and manage online offerings and sales. *Staff departments* include all those that provide specialized skills in support of line departments. Staff departments have an advisory relationship with line departments and typically include marketing, labor relations, research, accounting, and human resources.

Line authority means that people in management positions have formal authority to direct and control immediate subordinates. **Staff authority** is narrower and includes the right to advise, recommend, and counsel in the staff specialists' area of expertise. Staff authority is a communication relationship; staff specialists advise managers in technical areas. For example, the finance department of a manufacturing firm would have staff authority to coordinate with line departments about which accounting forms to use to facilitate equipment purchases and standardize payroll services.

Span of Management

The **span of management** is the number of employees reporting to a supervisor. Sometimes called the *span of control*, this characteristic of structure determines how closely a supervisor can monitor subordinates. Traditional views of organization design recommended a span of management of about seven subordinates per manager. However, many lean organizations today have spans of management as high as 30, 40, and even higher. For example, at Consolidated Diesel's team-based engine assembly plant, the span of management is 100.[12] Research on the Lockheed Missile and Space Company and other manufacturing companies has suggested that span of management can vary widely and that several factors influence the span.[13] Generally, when supervisors must be closely involved with subordinates, the span should be small, and when supervisors need little involvement with subordinates, it can be large. The following factors are associated with less supervisor involvement and thus larger spans of control:

1. Work performed by subordinates is stable and routine.
2. Subordinates perform similar work tasks.
3. Subordinates are concentrated in a single location.

line authority
A form of authority in which individuals in management positions have the formal power to direct and control immediate subordinates.

staff authority
A form of authority granted to staff specialists in their area of expertise.

span of management
The number of employees reporting to a supervisor; also called *span of control*.

©Dennis Kleiman

Ian Adamson is a businessman and adventure racer whose team won the Eco-Challenge in Borneo, which involves 320 miles of hiking, running, swimming, biking, canoeing, and rappelling. The flat structure of his sports team is highly efficient for meeting such challenges. It has no leader; instead, members gather on the course and make decisions collectively as quickly as possible or spontaneously defer to someone who has expert knowledge. Teammates pitch in to help one another. For a fee, Adamson's recently formed company, Colorado Adventure Training, shows managers from companies such as Starbucks how to benefit from this non-hierarchical approach.

4. Subordinates are highly trained and need little direction in performing tasks.
5. Rules and procedures defining task activities are available.
6. Support systems and personnel are available for the manager.
7. Little time is required in nonsupervisory activities such as coordination with other departments or planning.
8. Managers' personal preferences and styles favor a large span.

tall structure
A management structure characterized by an overall narrow span of management and a relatively large number of hierarchical levels.

flat structure
A management structure characterized by an overall broad span of control and relatively few hierarchical levels.

The average span of control used in an organization determines whether the structure is tall or flat. A **tall structure** has an overall narrow span and more hierarchical levels. A **flat structure** has a wide span, is horizontally dispersed, and has fewer hierarchical levels.

The trend in recent years has been toward wider spans of control as a way to facilitate delegation.[14] Exhibit 10.2 illustrates how an international metals company was reorganized. The multilevel set of managers shown in panel *a* was replaced with ten operating managers and nine staff specialists reporting directly to the CEO, as shown in panel *b*. The CEO welcomed this wide span of 19 management subordinates because it fit his style, his management team was top quality and needed little supervision, and they were all located on the same floor of an office building.

Centralization and Decentralization

centralization
The location of decision authority near top organizational levels.

decentralization
The location of decision authority near lower organizational levels.

Centralization and decentralization pertain to the hierarchical level at which decisions are made. **Centralization** means that decision authority is located near the top of the organization. With **decentralization**, decision authority is pushed downward to lower organization levels. Organizations may have to experiment to find the correct hierarchical level at which to make decisions.

In the United States and Canada, the trend over the past 30 years has been toward greater decentralization of organizations. Decentralization is believed to relieve the burden on top managers, make greater use of workers' skills and abilities, ensure that decisions are made close to the action by well-informed people, and permit more rapid response to external changes.

Exhibit *10.2*

Reorganization to Increase Span of Management for President of an International Metals Company

a. Old, Tall Structure

President

- Executive Vice President
  - Staff Specialists (6)
- Executive Vice President
  - Operating Managers (5)
  - Staff Specialists (3)
- Executive Vice President
  - Operating Managers (4)
  - Staff Specialists (5)
- Vice President
  - Operating Managers (10)
  - Staff Specialists (5)

b. New, Flat Structure

President

Operating Managers (10)   Staff Specialists (9)

However, this trend does not mean that every organization should decentralize all decisions. Managers should diagnose the organizational situation and select the decision-making level that will best meet the organization's needs. Factors that typically influence centralization versus decentralization are as follows:

1. Greater change and uncertainty in the environment are usually associated with decentralization. A good example of how decentralization can help cope with rapid change and uncertainty occurred following the September 11, 2001, attacks on the World Trade Center. UPS trucks, which carry 7 percent of the country's gross domestic product on any given day, were able to keep running on time, thanks largely to a decentralized management system that gives local managers authority to make key decisions. "I've learned to stay out of the way and let our folks run the system," says UPS Vice-Chairman Michael L. Eskew.[15] Today, most companies feel greater uncertainty because of intense global competition; hence, many have decentralized.

2. The amount of centralization or decentralization should fit the firm's strategy. For example, Johnson & Johnson gives almost complete authority to its 180 operating companies to develop and market their own products. Decentralization fits the corporate strategy of empowerment that gets each division close to customers so it can speedily adapt to their needs.[16] Taking the opposite approach, Larry Ellison at Oracle used the Internet to centralize operations in order to cut costs and focus everyone on the goal of providing global Internet systems for customers, as described in the Leading Online box.

3. In times of crisis or risk of company failure, authority may be centralized at the top. When Honda could not get agreement among divisions about new car models, President Nobuhiko Kawamoto made the decision himself.[17]

Formalization

Formalization is the written documentation used to direct and control employees. Written documentation includes rule books, policies, procedures, job descriptions, and regulations. These documents complement the organization chart by providing descriptions of tasks, responsibilities, and decision authority. The use of rules, regulations, and written records of decisions is part of the bureaucratic model of organizations described in Chapter 2. As proposed by Max Weber, the bureaucratic model defines the basic organizational characteristics that enable the organization to operate in a logical and rational manner.

Although written documentation is intended to be rational and helpful to the organization, it often creates "red tape" that causes more problems than it solves. Some U.S. government departments are notorious for bureaucratic inefficiency. MDP Construction, for example, found that winning a government contract meant the small company had to contend with loads of regulations and a mountain of paperwork. MDP managers use the Internet, project management software, and other information technology to manage these complex projects with limited administrative personnel.[18]

As a practical matter, many organizations are reducing formalization and bureaucracy. Narrowly defined job descriptions, for example, tend to limit the creativity, flexibility, and rapid response needed in today's knowledge-based organizations. One sales consultant told a story of approaching a customer with a media product guaranteed to increase the customer's sales. After finally determining the person who was "in charge" of this particular area, the consultant arranged a meeting at which the vice president expressed enthusiasm.

Courtesy of Synovus Financial Corp.

These employees at CB&T® bank, an affiliate of Synovus Financial Corp.®, have the power to honor the commitment of "Everything You Expect from a Bank. And More." Synovus, a multifinancial services company, has held fast to a philosophy of decentralization for more than a century. Each of its 32 affiliate banks retains its own name, management team, board of directors, and decision-making autonomy. Pushing decision authority as close to the customer as possible allows Synovus to take advantage of experienced local teams, making the company one of the highest performers in the financial services industry.

formalization
The written documentation used to direct and control employees.

Leading Online

Tightening the Reins at Oracle

Much has been written about the power of the Internet to give employees more information and greater freedom. But Larry Ellison, CEO of Oracle Corporation, knows the global network also offers a major opportunity for strengthening top management command and control. By requiring employees to do their work via the Internet, Ellison can carefully track, analyze, and control the behavior of each unit, manager, and employee on a global basis.

Oracle got into trouble some years ago because sales managers were cutting back-room deals or hammering out private, individualized compensation agreements with salespeople in different countries. Today all the terms, including sales contracts and commissions, are dictated from the top and spelled out in a global database. In addition, all deals must be reported into the database, where they can easily be tracked by Ellison back at headquarters. "I love running the business now," Ellison says. "I love getting involved in every detail. . . ." Clearly, Larry Ellison loves being in control, but he has solid business reasons for centralizing information and decision making. Several years ago, Oracle realized its future rested on building a complete suite of Internet applications that could work together on a global basis, and Ellison knew the first step would be to roll out the global system inside of Oracle itself, or as Ellison put it, to "eat our own dog food."

He first had to dismantle the separate fiefdoms that had developed inside Oracle. Each country manager had separate e-mail, human resources, and financial reporting systems, which were supported by more than 40 data centers scattered around the world. "Not only did we have 70 separate accounting systems in 70 different countries, but all of those countries hired IT departments to change them in different ways," Ellison marvels. Naturally, managers balked when the CEO decreed that there would now be only two data centers (one at headquarters and a backup center in Colorado Springs) and a single global database for each major function. To break down resistance, Ellison started by globalizing e-mail, allowing managers to see how much easier, more effective, and cheaper it was to do business. Then, he gradually rolled out other global Internet-based applications.

Some managers still aren't happy about the tighter grip Ellison has over global operations, but the CEO believes it is needed to effectively manage a sprawling, global company. "Executives. We sit up here . . . and think very hard on something, tell people to do something," Ellison says. "But as these orders go out through many layers of bureaucracy, they change and change and change." Ellison believes using the Internet to centralize control and manage more "scientifically" is the best way to take Oracle to the next level.

SOURCE: G. Christian Hill, "Dog Eats Dog Food. And Damn If It Ain't Tasty," *ECompany News* (November 2000), 168–178.

However, as the meeting came to a close, he said: "Even though this is exactly what we need, I can't buy it. My job description doesn't allow me to buy media aimed at the small-business market." After further questioning and research, the consultant determined that the extensive formalization meant no one at the company could authorize the purchase of a product that could dramatically improve the organization's performance.[19]

Departmentalization

departmentalization
The basis on which individuals are grouped into departments and departments into the total organization.

Another fundamental characteristic of organization structure is **departmentalization**, which is the basis for grouping positions into departments and departments into the total organization. Managers make choices about how to use the chain of command to group people together to perform their work. There are five approaches to structural design that reflect different uses of the chain of command in departmentalization. The functional, divisional, and matrix are traditional approaches that rely on the chain of command to define departmental groupings and reporting relationships along the hierarchy. Two contemporary approaches are the use of teams and networks. A brief illustration of the five structural alternatives is presented in Exhibit 10.3. In addition, some

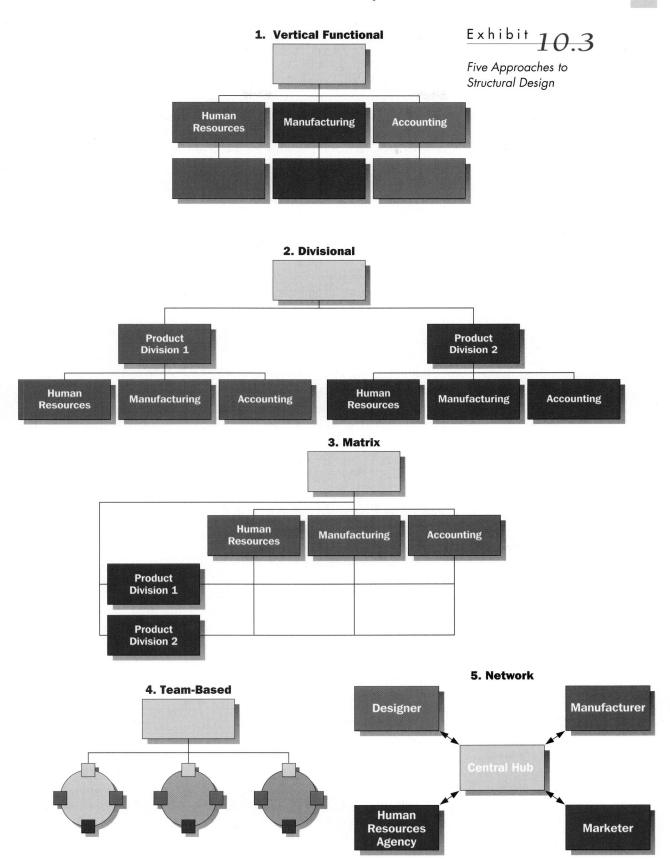

Exhibit *10.3*

Five Approaches to Structural Design

1. **Vertical Functional**

Human Resources

Manufacturing

Accounting

2. **Divisional**

Product Division 1

Product Division 2

Human Resources

Manufacturing

Accounting

Human Resources

Manufacturing

Accounting

3. **Matrix**

Human Resources

Manufacturing

Accounting

Product Division 1

Product Division 2

4. **Team-Based**

5. **Network**

Designer

Manufacturer

Central Hub

Human Resources Agency

Marketer

companies are using a *virtual* approach to organization, which we will describe at the end of this chapter. Newer approaches such as teams, networks, and virtual organizations have emerged to meet changing organizational needs in an increasingly global, knowledge-based business environment.

1. *Vertical functional approach.* People are grouped together in departments by common skills and work activities, such as in an engineering department and an accounting department.

2. *Divisional approach.* Departments are grouped together into separate, self-contained divisions based on a common product, program, or geographical region. Diverse skills rather than similar skills are the basis of departmentalization.

3. *Matrix approach.* Functional and divisional chains of command are implemented simultaneously and overlay one another in the same departments. Two chains of command exist, and some employees report to two bosses.

4. *Team-based approach.* The organization creates a series of teams to accomplish specific tasks and to coordinate major departments. Teams can exist from the office of the president all the way down to the shop floor.

5. *Network approach.* The organization becomes a small, central hub electronically connected to other organizations that perform vital functions. Departments are independent, contracting services to the central hub for a profit. Departments can be located anywhere in the world.

Each approach to structure serves a distinct purpose for the organization, and each has advantages and disadvantages. The basic difference among structures is the way in which employees are departmentalized and to whom they report. The differences in structure illustrated in Exhibit 10.3 have major consequences for employee goals and motivation. Let us now turn to each of the five structural designs and examine their implications for managers.[20]

Vertical Functional Approach

functional structure
The grouping of positions into departments based on similar skills, expertise, and resource use.

Functional structure is the grouping of positions into departments based on similar skills, expertise, and resource use. A functional structure can be thought of as departmentalization by organizational resources, because each type of functional activity—human resources, engineering, manufacturing—represents specific resources for performing the organization's task. People and facilities representing a common organizational resource are grouped into a single department.

How It Works.   An example of a functional structure for American Airlines is presented in Exhibit 10.4. The major departments under the chairman are groupings of similar expertise and resources, such as finance, safety and security, government affairs, information technology, and marketing. Each of the functional departments at American Airlines is concerned with the airline as a whole. The safety and security vice president is concerned with security issues for the entire airline, and the marketing department is responsible for all sales and marketing.

The functional structure is a strong vertical design. Information flows up and down the vertical hierarchy, and the chain of command converges at the top of the organization. In a functional structure, people within a department communicate primarily with others in the same department to coordinate

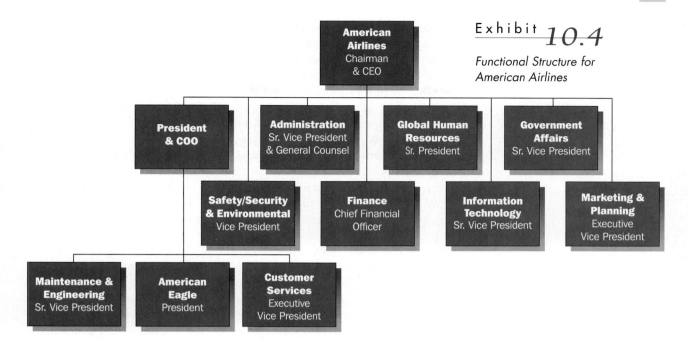

Exhibit 10.4

Functional Structure for American Airlines

work and accomplish tasks or implement decisions that are passed down the hierarchy from top managers. Managers and employees are compatible because of similar training and expertise. Typically, there are rules and procedures governing the duties and responsibilities of each employee, and employees at lower hierarchical levels accept the right of those higher in the hierarchy to make decisions and issue orders. Career progress is based on functional expertise, and people who develop their skills may be promoted up the hierarchy.

Advantages and Disadvantages. These characteristics of functional structure provide many advantages for an organization. Grouping employees by common task permits economies of scale and efficient resource use. At American Airlines, as illustrated in Exhibit 10.4, all information technology (IT) people work in the same, large department. They have the expertise and skills to handle almost any IT problem for the organization. Large, functionally based departments enhance the development of in-depth skills because people work on a variety of related problems and are associated with other experts within their own department. Employees are motivated to enhance their skills and move up the hierarchy.

Because the chain of command converges at the top, the functional structure also provides a way to centralize decision making and provide unified direction from top managers. Sometimes the functional structure is also associated with wider spans of control because of large departments and common expertise. Communication and coordination among employees within each department are excellent. Finally, the functional structure promotes high-quality technical problem solving. Having a pool of well-trained experts, especially those who work with sophisticated technology, motivated toward functional expertise gives the company an important resource.

The disadvantages of functional structure reflect the barriers that exist across departments and a slow response to environmental changes. Because

Senior research biochemist Robert Lobell, Ph.D., is a member of a functional team at Merck & Co., a global research-driven pharmaceutical company, that is using molecular and biochemical methods to develop compounds that inhibit the action of oncogenes (genes that cause abnormal growth). The research conducted by this team of experts is part of Merck's 15-year cancer research initiative that has yielded many new insights, as reflected by Lobell's statement, "My greatest satisfaction is being part of a team that may actually beat cancer."

people are separated into distinct departments, communication and coordination across functions are often poor. Poor coordination means a slow response to environmental changes, because innovation and change require involvement of several departments. Because the chains of command are separate beneath the top of the organization, decisions involving more than one department may pile up at the top of the organization and be delayed. The functional structure also stresses work specialization and division of labor, which may produce routine, nonmotivating employee tasks.

The functional structure also creates management problems, such as difficulty in pinpointing problems within departments. In the case of an insurance company, for example, each function works on all products and performs only a part of the task for any product line. Hence, if one life insurance product is not performing well, there is no specific department or group that bears responsibility. In addition, employees tend to focus on the attainment of departmental goals, often to the exclusion of organizational goals. They see only their respective tasks, not the big picture. Because of this narrow task specialization, employees are trained to become experts in their fields, not to manage and coordinate diverse departments. Thus, they fail to become groomed for top management and general management positions.

The advantages and disadvantages of functional structure are summarized in Exhibit 10.5.

Divisional Approach

divisional structure
An organization structure in which departments are grouped based on similar organizational outputs.

In contrast to the functional approach, in which people are grouped by common skills and resources, the **divisional structure** occurs when departments are grouped together based on organizational outputs.

The divisional structure is sometimes called a *product structure, program structure*, or *self-contained unit structure*. Each of these terms means essentially the same thing: Diverse departments are brought together to produce a single organizational output, whether it be a product, a program, or a service to a single customer.

In very large companies, a divisional structure is essential. Most large corporations have separate business divisions that perform different tasks, serve different clients, or use different technologies. When a huge organization produces products for different markets, the divisional structure works because each division is an autonomous business. For example, Microsoft has seven divisions focused on different product and customer areas: a

Exhibit *10.5*

Advantages and Disadvantages of Functional Structure

Advantages	Disadvantages
• Efficient use of resources, economies of scale	• Poor communication across functional departments
• In-depth skill specialization and development	• Slow response to external changes, lagging innovation
• Career progress within functional departments	• Decisions concentrated at top of hierarchy, creating delay
• Top manager direction and control	• Responsibility for problems is difficult to pinpoint
• Excellent coordination within functions	• Limited view of organizational goals by employees
• High-quality technical problem solving	• Limited general management training for employees

Business and Enterprise division, a Home and Retail Division, a Business Productivity Group, a Sales and Support Group, a Developer Group, a Consumer and Commerce Group, and a Consumer Windows division. In addition, a Microsoft Research division conducts basic research for use across the organization.[21] The managers of each division have authority to run their units as they see fit, as long as they meet certain goals.

How It Works. Functional and divisional structures are illustrated in Exhibit 10.6. In the divisional structure, divisions are created as self-contained units with separate functional departments for each division. For example, in Exhibit 10.6, each functional department resource needed to produce the product is assigned to each division. Whereas in a functional structure, all engineers are grouped together and work on all products, in a divisional structure separate engineering departments are created within each division. Each department is smaller and focuses on a single product line or customer segment. Departments are duplicated across product lines.

The primary difference between divisional and functional structures is that the chain of command from each function converges lower in the hierarchy. In a divisional structure, differences of opinion among research and development, marketing, manufacturing, and finance would be resolved at the divisional level rather than by the president. Thus, the divisional structure encourages decentralization. Decision making is pushed down at least one level in the hierarchy, freeing the president and other top managers for strategic planning.

Geographic-Based Divisions. An alternative for assigning divisional responsibility is to group company activities by geographic region, as illustrated in Exhibit 10.7. In this structure, all functions in a specific country or region report to the same division manager. This structure focuses company activities on local market conditions. For example, competitive advantage may come from the production or sale of a product adapted to a given country. At LSI Logic Corporation, management divided the world into three geographic

Exhibit **10.6**

Functional versus Divisional Structures

a. Functional Structure

President

R&D — Finance — Manufacturing — Marketing

b. Divisional Structure

President

Division 1 — Division 2 — Division 3

Division 1: R&D, Manufacturing, Finance, Marketing
Division 2: R&D, Manufacturing, Finance, Marketing
Division 3: R&D, Manufacturing, Finance, Marketing

Exhibit *10.7*

*Geographic-Based Global
Organization Structure*

markets—Japan, the United States, and Europe. Each division had all the resources to focus on the fierce competition in its part of the world. McDonald's has divided its U.S. operations into five geographic divisions, each with its own staff functions, such as human resources and legal, and its own president. McDonald's CEO Jack Greenberg believes this geographic structure will help speed up decision making, improve communication with franchisees, and enhance innovation.[22]

Advantages and Disadvantages. For medium-sized companies, the choice between functional and divisional structure is difficult because each represents different strengths and weaknesses. The advantages and disadvantages of the divisional structure are listed in Exhibit 10.8. By dividing employees and resources along divisional lines, the organization will be flexible and responsive to change because each unit is small and tuned in to its environment. By having employees working on a single product line, the concern for customers' needs is high. Coordination across functional departments is better because employees are grouped together in a single location and committed to one product line. Great coordination exists within divisions. The divisional structure also enables top management to pinpoint responsibility for performance problems in product lines. Because each division is a self-contained unit, poor performance can be assigned directly to the manager of that unit. Finally, employees' goals typically are directed toward product success rather than toward their own functional departments. Employees develop a broader goal orientation that can help them develop into general managers.

Exhibit *10.8*

*Advantages and Disadvantages of
Divisional Structure*

Advantages	Disadvantages
• Fast response, flexibility in an unstable environment	• Duplication of resources across divisions
• Fosters concern for customers' needs	• Less technical depth and specialization in divisions
• Excellent coordination across functional departments	• Poor coordination across divisions
• Easy pinpointing of responsibility for product problems	• Less top management control
• Emphasis on overall product and division goals	• Competition for corporate resources
• Development of general management skills	

The divisional structure also has well-defined disadvantages. The major disadvantage is duplication of resources and the high cost of running separate divisions. Instead of a single research department in which all research people use a single facility, there may be several. The organization loses efficiency and economies of scale. Because departments within each division are small, there is a lack of technical specialization, expertise, and training. The divisional structure fosters excellent coordination within divisions, but coordination across divisions often is poor. Hewlett-Packard prided itself on the divisional structure that gave autonomy to many small divisions. Problems occurred, however, when these divisions went in opposite directions. The software produced in one division did not fit the hardware produced in another. Thus, the divisional structure was realigned to establish adequate coordination across divisions. Moreover, divisions may feel themselves in competition with one another, especially for resources from corporate headquarters. This can lead to political behavior that is unhealthy for the company as a whole. Because top management control is somewhat weaker under the divisional structure, top managers must assert themselves in order to get divisions to work together.

Many companies must carefully decide whether the divisional or functional structure better suits their needs. It is not uncommon for a company to try one structure and then switch to another as its needs change.

Matrix Approach

The **matrix approach** combines aspects of both functional and divisional structures simultaneously in the same part of the organization.[23] The matrix structure evolved as a way to improve horizontal coordination and information sharing. One unique feature of the matrix is that it has dual lines of authority. In Exhibit 10.9, the functional hierarchy of authority runs vertically, and the divisional hierarchy of authority runs horizontally.

matrix approach
An organization structure that utilizes functional and divisional chains of command simultaneously in the same part of the organization.

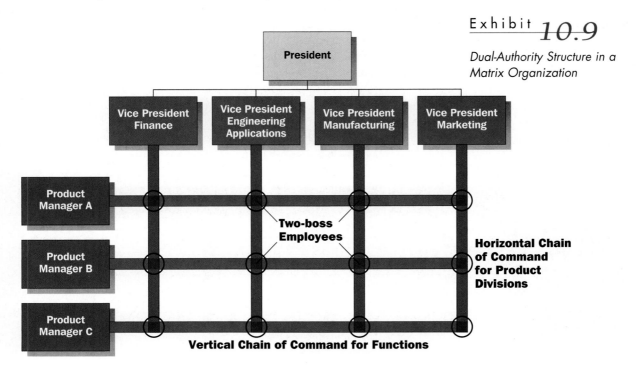

While the vertical structure provides traditional control within functional departments, the horizontal structure provides coordination across departments. The matrix structure therefore provides a formal chain of command for both functional (vertical) and divisional (horizontal) relationships. As a result of this dual structure, some employees actually report to two supervisors simultaneously.

The matrix structure often is used by global corporations such as Dow Corning or Asea Brown Boveri. The problem for global companies is to achieve simultaneous coordination of various products within each country or region and for each product line.

How It Works.   The dual lines of authority make the matrix unique. To see how the matrix works, consider the global matrix structure illustrated in Exhibit 10.10. The two lines of authority are geographic and product. The geographic boss in Germany coordinates all affiliates in Germany, and the plastics products boss coordinates the manufacturing and sale of plastics products around the world. Managers of local affiliate companies in Germany would report to two superiors, both the country boss and the product boss. The dual authority structure violates the unity-of-command concept described earlier in this chapter but is necessary to give equal emphasis to both functional and divisional lines of authority. Dual lines of authority can be confusing, but after managers learn to use this structure, the matrix provides excellent coordination simultaneously for each geographic region and each product line.

The success of the matrix structure depends on the abilities of people in key matrix roles. **Two-boss employees**, those who report to two supervisors simultaneously, must resolve conflicting demands from the matrix bosses. They must confront senior managers and reach joint decisions. They need excellent human relations skills with which to confront managers and resolve conflicts. The **matrix boss** is the product or functional boss, who is responsible for one side of the matrix. The top leader is responsible for the entire matrix. The **top leader** oversees both the product and functional chains of command. His or her responsibility is to maintain a power balance between the two sides of the matrix. If disputes arise between them, the problem will be kicked upstairs to the top leader.[24]

two-boss employees
Employees who report to two supervisors simultaneously.

matrix boss
The product or functional boss, responsible for one side of the matrix.

top leader
The overseer of both the product and functional chains of command, responsible for the entire matrix.

Exhibit *10.10*

Global Matrix Structure

Advantages and Disadvantages. The matrix structure is controversial because of the dual chain of command. However, it has been used successfully by companies such as IBM, Unilever, and Ford Motor Company, which have fine-tuned the matrix structure to suit their particular goals and cultures. The matrix can be highly effective in a complex, rapidly changing environment in which the organization needs to be flexible and adaptable.[25] The conflict and frequent meetings generated by the matrix allow new issues to be raised and resolved. The matrix structure makes efficient use of human resources because specialists can be transferred from one division to another. The matrix also provides training for both specialist and general management skills. People within a functional department or within a specific country in a global matrix have access to in-depth training and specialization. At the same time, they coordinate with other programs or divisions, which helps employees develop a general management perspective. Finally, the matrix structure engages the participation of employees in team meetings and in the achievement of divisional goals. Thus, it challenges and motivates employees, giving them a larger task than would be possible in a functional structure.

The matrix structure also has several disadvantages, however. The major problem is the confusion and frustration caused by the dual chain of command. Matrix bosses and two-boss employees have difficulty with the dual reporting relationships. The matrix structure also can generate high conflict because it pits divisional against functional goals in a domestic structure, or product line versus country goals in a global structure. This leads to the third disadvantage: time lost to meetings and discussions devoted to resolving this conflict. Often the matrix structure leads to more discussion than action because different goals and points of view are being addressed.[26] To survive and perform well in a matrix, employees need human relations training to learn to deal with two bosses, to get by with only "half" of each employee, and to confront and manage conflict. Finally, many organizations find it difficult to maintain the power balances essential for matrix success. The functional and divisional sides of the matrix must have equal power. If one side acquires greater formal authority, the advantages of the matrix structure are lost. The organization then operates like a functional structure with informal lateral relationships.

The advantages and disadvantages of the matrix structure are summarized in Exhibit 10.11.

At General Electric's Lighting division, John Opie created a matrix that helped the division cut costs and increase effectiveness.

Advantages	Disadvantages
• More efficient use of resources than single hierarchy	• Frustration and confusion from dual chain of command
• Flexibility, adaptability to changing environment	• High conflict between two sides of matrix
• Development of both general and specialist management skills	• Many meetings, more discussion than action
• Interdisciplinary cooperation, expertise available to all divisions	• Human relations training needed
• Enlarged tasks for employees	• Power dominance by one side of matrix

Exhibit 10.11

Advantages and Disadvantages of Matrix Structure

GENERAL ELECTRIC
http://www.ge.com

When Jack Welch, then-CEO of General Electric, hired John Opie to head GE's Lighting division, the business was in serious decline. Opie realized that Lighting needed to radically alter the way it operated to cut costs, simplify and speed decision making, and bring the business closer to its customers. He first organized the three plants into one large operation and then created a matrix structure. Employees are grouped according to functions, such as manufacturing, human resources, and finance. Linking the functions are product managers, each of whom is responsible for a particular product—for example, incandescent lamps. Employees from different functional areas work together in teams, with the product managers serving as team leaders. Lighting workers thus report to both the functional chief and the product manager.

Implementing the matrix structure met with some resistance, but the disruptions the new structure caused were more than compensated for by the efficiencies gained. Overall, the reorganization eliminated 700 white-collar positions and reduced seven layers of management to four. Opie's Lighting team continually looked for ways to simultaneously cut costs and increase effectiveness, and the methods worked. Within two years, GE's Lighting division was producing solid results as sales, profit, market share, and employee productivity dramatically increased.[27] ❖

Team Approach

Probably the most widespread trend in departmentalization has been the effort by companies to implement team concepts. The vertical chain of command is a powerful means of control, but passing all decisions up the hierarchy takes too long and keeps responsibility at the top. Today, companies are trying to find ways to delegate authority, push responsibility to low levels, and create participative teams that engage the commitment of workers. This approach enables organizations to be more flexible and responsive in the competitive global environment. Chapter 19 will discuss teams in detail.

How It Works.   There are two ways to think about using teams in organizations. **Cross-functional teams** consist of employees from various functional departments who are responsible to meet as a team and resolve mutual problems. Team members typically still report to their functional departments, but they also report to the team, one member of whom may be the leader. For example, Coca-Cola Fountain Manufacturing's Baltimore Syrup Operation used cross-functional teams to work on policies for vacation and compensation.[28]

Hallmark uses teams made up of artists, writers, lithographers, designers, and photographers to develop new greeting cards, with each team empowered to make decisions about cards for a particular holiday or season. The team approach cut in half the time it takes for Hallmark to get new cards to market.[29] With cross-functional teams, teams are used to provide needed horizontal coordination to complement an existing divisional or functional structure.

The second approach is to use **permanent teams**, groups of employees who are brought together similar to a formal department. Each team brings together employees from all functional areas focused on a specific task or project, such as parts supply and logistics for an automobile plant. Emphasis is on horizontal communication and information sharing because representatives from all functions are coordinating their work and skills to complete a

cross-functional teams
A group of employees from various functional departments that meet as a team to resolve mutual problems.

permanent teams
A group of participants from several functions who are permanently assigned to solve ongoing problems of common interest.

specific organizational task. Authority is pushed down to lower levels, and front-line employees are often given the freedom to make decisions and take action on their own. Team members may share or rotate team leadership. With a **team-based structure**, the entire organization is made up of teams that coordinate their work and work directly with customers to accomplish the organization's goals. Imagination Ltd., Britain's largest design firm, is based entirely on teamwork. Imagination puts together a diverse team at the beginning of each new project it undertakes, whether it be creating the lighting for Disney cruise ships or redesigning the packaging for Ericsson's cell-phone products. The team then works closely with the client throughout the project. "Teamwork is a harder way of doing the work," says Ralph Ardill, director of marketing and strategic planning. "But when it clicks, the result is a seamless experience."[30] Imagination Ltd. has managed to make it click every time by building a culture that supports teamwork, as described in this chapter's Putting People First box.

team-based structure
Structure in which the entire organization is made up of teams that coordinate their work and work directly with customers to accomplish the organization's goals.

Advantages and Disadvantages. Designing team relationships often helps overcome shortcomings in a functional, top-down approach to organizing. With cross-functional teams, the organization is able to retain some advantages of a functional structure, such as economies of scale and in-depth training, while gaining the benefits of team relationships. The team concept breaks down barriers across departments. Team members know one another's problems and compromise rather than blindly pursue their own goals. The team concept also allows the organization to more quickly adapt to customer requests and environmental changes and speeds decision making because decisions need not go to the top of the hierarchy for approval. Another big advantage is the morale boost. Employees are enthusiastic about their involvement in bigger projects rather than narrow departmental tasks. Jobs are enriched. The creation of teams also enables responsibility and authority to be pushed down the hierarchy, requiring fewer managers for supervision.

But the team approach has disadvantages as well. Employees may be enthusiastic about team participation, but they may also experience conflicts and dual loyalties. A cross-functional team may make different demands on members than do their department managers, and members who participate in more than one team must resolve these conflicts. A large amount of time is devoted to meetings, thus increasing coordination time. Unless the organization truly needs teams to coordinate complex projects and adapt to the environment, it will lose production efficiency with them. Finally, the team approach may cause too much decentralization. Senior department managers who traditionally made decisions might feel left out when a team moves ahead on its own. Team members often do not see the big picture of the corporation and may make decisions that are good for their group but bad for the organization as a whole. Top management can help keep the team in alignment with corporate goals.

These members of the Avery Hi-Liter® EverBold™ marker team, part of the North American consumer products division at Avery Dennison Corporation, collaborated as a cross-functional team to launch a new pen-style highlighter product. Avery Dennison is a company committed to using the team-based approach to maintain and grow their market leadership. The company empowers multi-functional teams of employees to develop and launch new consumer products.

Courtesy of Avery Dennison Corp.

Putting People First

Imagination Ltd.

The essence of teamwork is that people contribute selflessly, putting the good of the whole above their own individual interests. It doesn't always work that way, but Imagination Ltd. seems to have found the secret ingredient to seamless teamwork. According to Adrian Caddy, Imagination's creative director: "The culture at Imagination is this: You can articulate your ideas without fear."

Imagination Ltd. has put together a company made up of teams of designers, architects, lighting experts, writers, theater people, film directors, and artists, in addition to IT specialists, marketing experts, and other functional specialties. By having employees with a wide range of skills, the company is able to put together a diverse team to provide each client with a new approach to its design problems. Imagination is deliberately nonhierarchical; only four people have formal titles, and on most project teams, no one is really in charge. Teams meet weekly, and everyone participates in every meeting from the very beginning, so there is no perception that any particular talent is primary—or secondary. Information technology specialists, production people, and client-contact personnel

are just as much a part of the team as the creative types. In addition, each person is expected to come up with ideas outside his or her area of expertise. The philosophy is that people at Imagination must be willing to *make* all kinds of suggestions and also to *take* all kinds of suggestions. So many ideas get batted around, revised, and adapted at the weekly meetings that no one can ever really claim ownership of a particular element of the project. The team also works closely with the client as a source of ideas and inspiration.

Talent and respect help to make the system work. Imagination hires its employees carefully, based not only on the quality of their work but also on their open-mindedness and curiosity about the world beyond their functional area of expertise. Then, the company makes sure everyone's work is so closely integrated that people gain an understanding and respect for what others do. "The integrated approach breeds respect for one another," says writer Chris White. "When you work alone, or in isolation within your discipline, you can get an overblown sense of your own importance to a project."

SOURCE: Charles Fishman, "Total Teamwork: Imagination Ltd.," *Fast Company* (April 2000), 156–168.

The advantages and disadvantages of the team structure are summarized in Exhibit 10.12.

Network Approach

The most recent approach to departmentalization extends the idea of horizontal coordination and collaboration beyond the boundaries of the organization. The **network structure** means that the firm subcontracts many of its major functions to separate companies and coordinates their activities from a small headquarters organization.[31]

network structure
An organization structure that disaggregates major functions to separate companies that are brokered by a small headquarters organization.

How It Works.   The organization may be viewed as a central hub surrounded by a network of outside specialists, as illustrated in Exhibit 10.13.

Exhibit *10.12*

Advantages and Disadvantages of Team Structure

Advantages	Disadvantages
• Some advantages of functional structure	• Dual loyalties and conflict
• Reduced barriers among departments, increased compromise	• Time and resources spent on meetings
• Less response time, quicker decisions	• Unplanned decentralization
• Better morale, enthusiasm from employee involvement	
• Reduced administrative overhead	

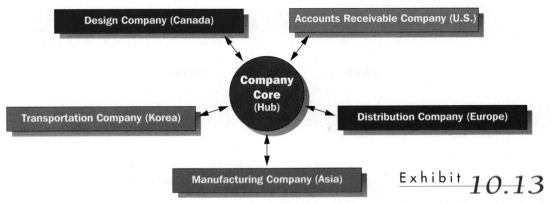

Exhibit **10.13**

Network Approach to Departmentalization

Rather than being housed under one roof, services such as accounting, design, manufacturing, and distribution are outsourced to separate organizations that are connected electronically to the central office.[32] Networked computer systems and the Internet enable organizations to exchange data and information so rapidly and smoothly that a loosely connected network of suppliers, manufacturers, assemblers, and distributors can look and act like one seamless company.

The idea behind networks is that a company can concentrate on what it does best and contract out other activities to companies with distinctive competence in those specific areas. This enables a company to do more with less.[33] For example, R & D Laboratories develops specialized vitamin and mineral supplements for dialysis patients, but the products are manufactured and packaged by subcontracted pharmaceutical companies and warehoused and distributed by 200 wholesalers. When R & D has a promising new product, it can ramp up production just by making a few phone calls to its network partners.[34] Three former Compaq Computer managers, Doug Johns, David Hocker, and Nicholas Forlenza, started a computer company that ran from 1995 to 2002 using the network approach.

When Doug Johns left Compaq Computer Corporation, he was managing 6 million square feet of warehouse and office space. He and his partners David Hocker and Nicholas Forlenza wanted to start a different kind of computer company, one that had only a few core employees and relied on partnerships to accomplish its goals. The three believed there were only two things that couldn't be outsourced: world-class management expertise and a knack for establishing the right partnerships.

Monorail was able to succeed and grow rapidly by using a network structure. The company, based in Marietta, Georgia, operated from a single leased floor of an office building. It had no factories, no warehouses, no credit departments, and no help desks or call centers. The company's 50 core employees focused on product design and marketing and outsourced everything else. Here's how the Monorail system worked: When a retailer such as CompUSA ordered a computer from Monorail, the order was transmitted electronically through FedEx Logistics Services to one of Monorail's many contract manufacturers, who assembled the PC and shipped it directly to the retailer. Meanwhile, FedEx wired an invoice to Sun Trust bank in Atlanta, whose factoring department handled billing and credit approvals. All other functions were also outsourced,

MONORAIL

http://www.monorail.com

which meant Johns, Hocker, and Forlenza spent much of their time managing relationships to maintain seamless integration with their network partners.

In January, 2002, facing a shrinking market for personal computers, the founders of Monorail decided to close its doors and pursue other opportunities. However, the partners remain convinced that the network model was a primary reason their company was able to succeed for as long as it did in the tough PC industry.[35] ❖

With a network structure, it is difficult to answer the question "Where is the organization?" in traditional terms. For example, a firm might contract for expensive services such as training, transportation, legal, and engineering, so these functions are no longer part of the organization. Or consider a piece of ice hockey equipment that is designed in Scandinavia, engineered in the United States, manufactured in Korea, and distributed in Canada by a Japanese sales organization. These pieces are drawn together contractually and coordinated electronically, creating a new form of organization. Much like building blocks, parts of the network can be added or taken away to meet changing needs.[36] The ability to arrange and rearrange resources gives the network organization greater flexibility and rapid response. However, relationships with subcontractors are the glue that holds the organization together, so these ties are not taken lightly.

modular approach
A manufacturing company uses outside suppliers to provide large components of the product, which are then assembled into a final product by a few workers.

A similar approach to networking is called the **modular approach**, in which a manufacturing company uses outside suppliers to provide entire chunks of a product, which are then assembled into a final product by a handful of workers. Computer companies such as Dell and Gateway purchase premade pieces of computers and handle only the final assembly. Automobile plants, including General Motors, Ford, Volkswagen, and DaimlerChrysler, are leaders in using the modular approach. GM has a modular factory in Brazil and plans to open several more to replace inefficient plants in the United States. The modular approach hands off responsibility for engineering and production of entire sections of an automobile, such as the chassis or interior, to outside suppliers. Suppliers design a module, making some of the parts themselves and subcontracting others. These modules are delivered right to the assembly line, where a handful of GM employees bolt them together into a finished vehicle.[37]

Advantages and Disadvantages. The biggest advantage to the network structure seems to be competitiveness on a global scale. Network organizations, even small ones, can be truly global. A network organization can draw on resources worldwide to achieve the best quality and price and can sell its products and services worldwide. A second advantage is workforce flexibility and challenge. Flexibility comes from the ability to hire whatever services are needed, such as engineering design or maintenance, and to change a few months later without constraints from owning plant, equipment, and facilities. The organization can continually redefine itself to fit new product and market opportunities. For those employees who are a permanent part of the organization, the challenge comes from greater job variety and job satisfaction from working within the lean structure. Finally, this structure is perhaps the leanest of all organization forms because little supervision is required. Large teams of staff specialists and administrators are not needed. A network organization may have only two or three levels of hierarchy, compared with ten or more in traditional organizations.[38] These advantages of a network structure, along with the disadvantages, are summarized in Exhibit 10.14.

One of the major disadvantages is lack of hands-on control.[39] Managers do not have all operations under one roof and must rely on contracts, coordination, negotiation, and electronic linkages to hold things together. A problem of equal importance is the possibility of losing an organizational part. If a subcontractor fails to deliver, goes out of business, or has a plant burn down, the headquarters organization can be put out of business. Uncertainty is higher because necessary services are not under one roof and under direct management control. Finally, in this type of organization, employee loyalty can weaken. Employees may feel they can be replaced by contract services. A cohesive corporate culture is less likely to develop, and turnover tends to be higher because emotional commitment between organization and employee is weak. With changing products and markets, the organization may need to reshuffle employees at any time to acquire the correct mix of skills.

The Virtual Organization Approach

As illustrated by the discussion of networks, ways of organizing are changing quite dramatically. In a variety of industries, vertically integrated hierarchical organizations are giving way to loosely interconnected groups of companies with permeable boundaries.[40] An extension of the network approach is the **virtual organization**, which brings together people temporarily to exploit specific opportunities, then disbands when objectives are met.[41]

How It Works. The virtual organization will have few full-time employees, choosing instead to temporarily hire outside specialists to complete a specific project, such as a major advertising campaign or a new software application. These people do not become a part of the organization, but join together as a separate entity for a specific purpose. Companies use a virtual approach to harness the talents and energies of the best people for a particular job, rather than trying to develop those capabilities in-house.[42] For example, Host Universal, an advertising agency, is based entirely on a virtual approach. Rather than running an agency full of employees, founders Robin Smith and Steven Hess contract work out to small ad hoc teams of creative professionals that offer the best combination of talent for each particular project. The "organization" itself consists only of Smith and Hess. Everyone else is a freelance professional hired on a project-by-project basis. Then, the team works directly for and is paid directly by the client. Host Universal takes a percentage off the top for finding clients and matching them with the right combination of talent for the project.[43]

When an organization uses a virtual approach, the virtual group typically has full authority to make decisions and take action within certain predefined

virtual organization
An organization that has few full-time employees and temporarily hires outside specialists to work on specific opportunities, then disband when objectives are met.

Advantages	Disadvantages
• Global competitiveness	• No hands-on control
• Workforce flexibility/challenge	• Can lose organizational part
• Reduced administrative overhead	• Employee loyalty weakened

E x h i b i t *10.14*

*Advantages and Disadvantages
of Network Structure*

boundaries and goals. In addition, the group itself monitors and controls performance and members' behavior.

Most virtual organizations use electronic connections for the sharing of data and information. Collaborative software enables virtual members such as those at Host Universal to work simultaneously on the same document in cyberspace, for example.[44] However, participants may also meet face to face to coordinate their work. Some organizations have redesigned offices to provide temporary space for virtual workers to meet or work on-site. Recent workplace design trends such as *hoteling*, which means multiple workers serially share a single space, and *free-address offices*, where employees choose a desk each day on a first-come, first-served basis, are in response to the growing use of virtual workers. Virtual workers use laptops and cell phones, which they set up on work tables at the client's office, and then pack everything up at night.

Advantages and Disadvantages.   The virtual approach enables a company to put together a collection of the most-skilled professionals for a particular project on an as-needed basis. As such, virtual organizations are incredibly responsive and flexible. Like network organizations, virtual organizations can be truly global and draw on resources and expertise worldwide. The virtual form also enables a company to take advantage of world-class talent on a temporary basis without having to hire these people as full-time employees. Many knowledge professionals value personal time and autonomy over a stable job and income, and the virtual form gives them opportunities to work on projects that are of particular interest to them.

One of the major disadvantages is the lack of control. The boundaries of a virtual organization are weak and ambiguous. Thus, top managers have to provide a strong definition of project goals to keep the group focused, but they then turn day-to-day decision making over to the people participating directly in the virtual project.[45] Virtual teams also place new demands on managers, who are constantly working with new people, new ideas, and new problems. Not only must managers be technologically adept, they also face enormous communication and motivation challenges. The potential for misunderstanding is tremendous when people are communicating primarily via phone and e-mail. In addition, people working in a virtual environment lose the motivation that comes from regular interaction with others and the development of close relationships in the workplace.[46] The advantages and disadvantages of the virtual approach are summarized in Exhibit 10.15.

Exhibit *10.15*

Advantages and Disadvantages of the Virtual Approach

Advantages	Disadvantages
• Can draw on expertise worldwide	• Lack of control, weak boundaries
• Highly flexible and responsive	• Greater demands on managers
• Reduced overhead costs	• Communication difficulties and potential for misunderstanding

Summary and Management Solution

This chapter introduced a number of important organizing concepts. Fundamental characteristics of organization structure include work specialization, chain of command, authority and responsibility, span of management, and centralization and decentralization. These dimensions of organization represent the vertical hierarchy and indicate how authority and responsibility are distributed along the hierarchy.

The other major concept is departmentalization, which describes how organization employees are grouped. Three traditional approaches are functional, divisional, and matrix; contemporary approaches are team and network structures. The most recent trend in organizing is the virtual approach. The functional approach groups employees by common skills and tasks. The opposite structure is divisional, which groups people by organizational output such that each division has a mix of functional skills and tasks. The matrix structure uses two chains of command simultaneously, and some employees have two bosses. The two chains of command in a domestic organization typically are functional and product division, and, for international firms, the two chains of command typically are product and geographic regions. The team approach uses permanent teams and cross-functional teams to achieve better coordination and employee commitment than is possible with a pure functional structure. The network approach means that a firm concentrates on what it does best and subcontracts other functions to separate organizations that are connected to the headquarters electronically. The virtual approach brings together a group of specialists to complete a specific project, and the group disbands when objectives are met. Each organization form has advantages and disadvantages and can be used by managers to meet the needs of the competitive situation. In addition, managers adjust elements of the vertical structure, such as the degree of centralization or decentralization, to meet changing needs.

At ConAgra Foods, described at the beginning of the chapter, a new CEO found that the highly decentralized divisional structure was causing problems. Although he is keeping a divisional structure, Bruce Rohde is revising it to increase the focus on the customer. His broad plan, named Operation Overdrive, calls for closing inefficient distribution centers and plants and reorganizing the dozens of separate units and product groups into three main divisions: food service (restaurants); retail (grocery stores); and agricultural products. By focusing the new structure on customers rather than product groups, Rohde hopes to get everyone working together to provide better service. Rohde has also centralized decision making. Managers of the separate companies will no longer have full authority to run their companies as they see fit. They now have specific goals directed from the top that include sharing customers, knowledge, and products across company lines. Rhode is requiring, for example, that ConAgra's companies buy materials from each other rather than outside suppliers. If managers find this isn't cost-effective, they are required to explain why directly to the top. In addition, Rohde has centralized computing and accounting systems rather than having the many separate companies using their own systems. He believes this stronger centralized control is needed to help the company through its current crisis. So far, ConAgra's restructuring seems to be having positive effects. The stock has bounced back from a five-year low and the company has been reporting higher sales and earnings since Rohde began the reorganization.[47]

Discussion Questions

1. Sandra Holt, manager of Electronics Assembly, asked Hector Cruz, her senior technician, to handle things in the department while Sandra worked on the budget. She needed peace and quiet for at least a week to complete her figures. After 10 days, Sandra discovered that Hector had hired a senior secretary, not realizing that Sandra had promised interviews to two other people. Evaluate Sandra's approach to delegation.

2. Many experts note that organizations have been making greater use of teams in recent years. What factors might account for this trend?

3. Contrast centralization with formalization. Would you expect these characteristics to affect each other in organizations? Why?

4. An organizational consultant was heard to say, "Some aspect of functional structure appears in every organization." Do you agree? Explain.

5. The divisional structure is often considered almost the opposite of a functional structure. Do you agree? Briefly explain the major differences in these two approaches to departmentalization.

6. Some people argue that the matrix structure should be adopted only as a last resort because the dual chains of command can create more problems than they solve. Do you agree or disagree? Why?

7. What is the network approach to structure? Is the use of authority and responsibility different compared with other forms of departmentalization? Explain.

8. How is a virtual organization different from a network organization? When might a company choose to use a virtual approach rather than a network structure?

9. A few of today's organizations pride themselves on the fact that they have no organization charts. What do you think this says about a company's structure?

10. An international matrix structure tends to be organized by product divisions and geographic regions. Why would these two chains of command be used rather than product and function as in domestic companies? Explain.

■ Management in Practice: Experiential Exercise

Family Business

You are the parent of 10 children and have just used your inheritance to acquire a medium-sized pharmaceutical company. Last year's sales were down 18 percent from the previous year. In fact, the last three years have been real losers. You want to clean house of current managers over the next 10 years and bring your children into the business. Being a loving parent, you agree to send your children to college to educate each of them in one functional specialty. The 10 children are actually five sets of twins exactly one year apart. The first set will begin college this fall, followed by the remaining sets the next four years. The big decision is which specialty each child should study. You want to have the most important functions taken over by your children as soon as possible, so you will ask the older children to study the most important areas.

Your task right now is to rank in order of priority the functions to which your children will be assigned and develop reasons for your ranking.

The ten functions follow:

____ Distribution

____ Manufacturing

____ Market Research

____ New-Product Development

____ Human Resources

____ Product Promotion

____ Quality Assurance

____ Sales

____ Legal and Governmental Affairs

____ Office of the Controller

Analyze your reasons for how functional priority relates to the company's environmental/strategic needs. Now rank the functions as part of a group. Discuss the problem until group members agree on a single ranking. How does the group's reasoning and ranking differ from your original thinking?

■ Management in Practice: Ethical Dilemma

Caught in the Middle

Tom Harrington loved his job as an assistant quality control officer for Rockingham Toys. After six months of unemployment, he was anxious to make a good impression on his boss, Frank Golopolus. One of the responsibilities of his boss was ensuring that new product lines met federal safety guidelines. Rockingham had made several manufacturing changes over the past year. Golopolus and the rest of the quality control team had been working 60-hour weeks to troubleshoot the new production process.

While sorting incoming mail during the past weeks, Harrington had become aware of numerous changes in product safety guidelines that he knew would impact the new Rockingham toys. Golopolus was taking no action to implement new guidelines, and he didn't seem to understand or care about them. Harrington, who avoided the questions he received from the floor to cover for his boss, was beginning to wonder if Rockingham would have time to make changes with the Christmas season rapidly approaching.

Harrington knew it was not his job to order the changes, and he didn't want to alienate Golopolus by interfering, but he was beginning to worry what might happen if he didn't act. Rockingham had a fine product safety reputation and was rarely challenged on matters of quality. He felt loyalty to Golopolus for giving him a job, but he worried Golopolus was in over his head.

What Do You Do?

1. Prepare a memo to Golopolus, summarizing the new safety guidelines that affect the Rockingham product line and recommending implementation.
2. Mind your own business. You do not have authority to monitor the federal regulations. Besides, you've been unemployed and need this job.
3. Send copies of the reports anonymously to the operations manager, who is Golopolus's boss.

SOURCE: Based on Doug Wallace, "The Man Who Knew Too Much," What Would You Do? *Business Ethics*, vol. II (March–April 1993), 7–8.

■ Surf the Net

1. **Organization Structure.** Using the search phrase "organization chart," locate an organization chart for a government agency, print it out, analyze it based on what you have learned in the chapter about the various organization structures, and be prepared to discuss your example during class.
2. **Team-based Approach.** Go to the "Career" section of any of the following companies' Web sites to locate how the company presents a discussion of the team-based emphasis the company uses.

   Merck: *http://www.merck.com/*
   Pizza Hut: *http://www.pizzahut.com/*
   Reliant Energy: *http://www.reliantenergy.com*

3. **Team Player Analysis.** Go to the following site, carefully read the exercise instructions, and then go to the exercise (where you will be asked to complete a free registration process to gain access to the exercise).

   http://www.managementlearning.com/inv/gegiwti/index.html

   After completing the exercise, print your results profile, along with the description of the eight team strengths (producer, diplomat, driver, inventor, judge, scout, supporter, and inspector). Bring your printouts to class and be prepared to discuss your results.

■ Case for Critical Analysis

Tucker Company

In 1993 the Tucker Company underwent an extensive reorganization that divided the company into three major divisions. These new divisions represented Tucker's three principal product lines. Mr. Harnett, Tucker's president, explained the basis for the new organization in a memo to the board of directors as follows:

> The diversity of our products requires that we reorganize along our major product lines. Toward this end I have established three new divisions: commercial jet engines, military jet engines, and utility turbines. Each division will be headed by a new vice president who will report directly to me. I believe that this new approach will enhance our performance through the commitment of individual managers. It should also help us to identify unprofitable areas where the special attention of management may be required.
>
> For the most part, each division will be able to operate independently. That is, each will have its own engineering, manufacturing, accounting departments, etc. In some cases, however, it will be necessary for a division to utilize the services of other divisions or departments. This is necessary because the complete servicing with individual divisional staffs would result in unjustifiable additional staffing and facilities.

The old companywide laboratory was one such service department. Functionally, it continued to support all of the major divisions. Administratively, however, the manager of the laboratory reported to the manager of manufacturing in the military jet engine division.

From the time the new organization was initiated until February 1999, when the laboratory manager Mr. Garfield retired, there was little evidence of interdepartmental or interdivisional conflict. His replacement, Ms. Hodge, unlike Mr. Garfield, was always eager to gain the attention of management. Many of Hodge's peers perceived her as an empire builder who was interested in her own advancement rather than the company's well-being. After about six months in the new position, Hodge became involved in several interdepartmental conflicts over work that was being conducted in her laboratory.

Historically, the engineering departments had used the laboratory as a testing facility to determine the properties of materials selected by the design engineers. Hodge felt that the laboratory should be more involved in the selection of these materials and in the design of experiments and subsequent evaluations of the experimental data. Hodge discussed this with Mr. Franklin of the engineering department of the utility turbine division. Franklin offered to consult with Hodge but stated that the final responsibility for the selection of materials was charged to his department.

In the months that followed, Hodge and Franklin had several disagreements over the implementation of the results. Franklin told Hodge that, because of her position at the testing lab, she was unable to appreciate the detailed design considerations that affected the final decision on materials selection. Hodge claimed that Franklin lacked the materials expertise that she, as a metallurgist, had.

Franklin also noted that the handling of his requests, which had been prompt under Garfield's management, was taking longer and longer under Hodge's management. Hodge explained that military jet engine divisional problems had to be assigned first priority because of the administrative reporting structure. She also said that if she were more involved in Franklin's problems, she could perhaps appreciate when a true sense of urgency existed and could revise priorities.

The tensions between Franklin and Hodge reached a peak when one of Franklin's critical projects failed to receive the scheduling that he considered necessary. Franklin phoned Hodge to discuss the need for a schedule change. Hodge suggested that they have a meeting to review the need for the work. Franklin then told Hodge that this was not a matter of her concern and that her function was merely to perform the

tests as requested. He further stated that he was not satisfied with the low-priority rating that his division's work received. Hodge reminded Franklin that when Hodge had suggested a means for resolving this problem, Franklin was not receptive. At this point, Franklin lost his temper and hung up on Hodge.

Questions

1. Sketch out a simple organization chart showing Tucker Company's three divisions, including the location of the laboratory. Why would the laboratory be located in the military jet engine division?
2. Analyze the conflict between Ms. Hodge and Mr. Franklin. Do you think the conflict is based on personalities or on the way in which the organization is structured?
3. Sketch out a new organization chart showing how you would restructure Tucker Company so that the laboratory would provide equal services to all divisions. What advantages and disadvantages do you see in the new structure compared to the previous one?

SOURCE: Reprinted with permission of Macmillan Publishing Company from "The Laboratory," *Organizational Behavior: Readings and Cases*, 2d ed., 385–387, by L. Katz, prepared under the supervision of Theodore T. Herbert. Copyright© 1981 by Theodore T. Herbert.

■ Endnotes

1. Joe Ruff, "ConAgra CEO Finds Strength in Unity," Associated Press story, *Johnson City Press* (May 5, 2000), 30, 32; Brandon Copple, "Synergy in Ketchup?" *Forbes* (February 7, 2000), 68; and Jack Neff, "The Biggest Nobody Really Knows," *Food Processing* (February 2001), 19.
2. Karen Chan, "From Top to Bottom," *The Wall Street Journal* (May 21, 2001), R12.
3. Peter Burrows, "The Radical," *BusinessWeek* (February 19, 2001), 70–80.
4. John Child, *Organization: A Guide to Problems and Practice*, 2d ed. (London: Harper & Row, 1984).
5. Adam Smith, *The Wealth of Nations* (New York: Modern Library, 1937).
6. Glenn L. Dalton, "The Collective Stretch," *Management Review* (December 1998), 54–59.
7. This discussion is based on Richard L. Daft, *Organization Theory and Design*, 4th ed. (St. Paul, Minn.: West, 1992), 387–388.
8. C. I. Barnard, *The Functions of the Executive* (Cambridge, Mass.: Harvard University Press, 1938).
9. Thomas A. Stewart, "CEOs See Clout Shifting," *Fortune* (November 6, 1989), 66.
10. Michael G. O'Loughlin, "What Is Bureaucratic Accountability and How Can We Measure It?" *Administration & Society* 22, no. 3 (November 1990), 275–302.
11. Carrie R. Leana, "Predictors and Consequences of Delegation," *Academy of Management Journal* 29 (1986), 754–774.
12. Curtis Sittenfeld, "Powered By the People," *Fast Company* (July-August 1999), 178–189.
13. Paul D. Collins and Frank Hull, "Technology and Span of Control: Woodward Revisited," *Journal of Management Studies* 23 (March 1986), 143–164; David D. Van Fleet and Arthur G. Bedeian, "A History of the Span of Management," *Academy of Management Review* 2 (1977), 356–372; and C. W. Barkdull, "Span of Control—A Method of Evaluation," *Michigan Business Review* 15 (May 1963), 25–32.
14. Brian Dumaine, "What the Leaders of Tomorrow See," *Fortune* (July 3, 1989), 48–62.
15. Charles Haddad, "How UPS Delivered Through the Disaster," *BusinessWeek* (October 1, 2001), 66.
16. Brian O'Reilly, "J&J Is on a Roll," *Fortune* (December 26, 1994), 178–191; and Joseph Weber, "A Big Company That Works," *Business Week* (May 4, 1992), 124–132.
17. Clay Chandler and Paul Ingrassia, "Just as U.S. Firms Try Japanese Management, Honda Is Centralizing," *The Wall Street Journal* (April 11, 1991), A1, A10.
18. Christopher Caggiano, "Thriving on Bureaucracy," *Inc. Technology* no. 1 (1997), 63–66.
19. Seth Godin, "Does Clinging to an Occupation Make You Better at Your Job?" *Fast Company* (April 2000), 324.
20. The following discussion of structural alternatives draws heavily on Jay R. Galbraith, *Designing Complex Organizations* (Reading, Mass.: Addison-Wesley, 1973); Jay R. Galbraith, *Organization Design* (Reading, Mass.: Addison-Wesley, 1977); Robert Duncan, "What Is the Right Organization

Structure?" *Organizational Dynamics* (Winter 1979), 59–80; and J. McCann and Jay R. Galbraith, "Interdepartmental Relations," in *Handbook of Organizational Design,* ed. P. Nystrom and W. Starbuck (New York: Oxford University Press, 1981), 60–84.

21. Michael Moeller with Steve Hamm and Timothy J. Mullaney, "Remaking Microsoft," *BusinessWeek* (May 17, 1999), 106–114.

22. Mike Tharp, "LSI Logic Corp. Does as the Japanese Do," *The Wall Street Journal* (April 17, 1986), 6; and Shelly Branch, "What's Eating McDonald's?" *Fortune* (October 13, 1997), 122–125.

23. Lawton R. Burns, "Matrix Management in Hospitals: Testing Theories of Matrix Structure and Development," *Administrative Science Quarterly* 34 (1989), 349–368.

24. Stanley M. Davis and Paul R. Lawrence, *Matrix* (Reading, Mass.: Addison-Wesley, 1977).

25. Robert C. Ford and W. Alan Randolph, "Cross-Functional Structures: A Review and Integration of Matrix Organization and Project Management," *Journal of Management* 18, no. 2 (1992), 267–294; and Paula Dwyer with Pete Engardio, Zachary Schiller, and Stanley Reed, "Tearing Up Today's Organization Chart," *BusinessWeek/Twenty-first Century Capitalism,* 80–90.

26. Dwyer et al., "Tearing Up Today's Organization Chart."

27. Noel M. Tichy and Stratford Sherman, *Control Your Destiny or Someone Else Will* (New York: Currency Doubleday, 1993), 176–178.

28. Sandra N. Phillips, "Team Training Puts Fizz in Coke Plant's Future," *Personnel Journal* (January 1996), 87–92.

29. John Hillkirk, "Challenging Status Quo Now in Vogue," *USA Today* (November 9, 1993); and Thomas A. Stewart, "The Search for the Organization of Tomorrow," *Fortune* (May 18, 1992), 92–98.

30. Charles Fishman, "Total Teamwork: Imagination Ltd.," *Fast Company* (April 2000), 156–168.

31. Raymond E. Miles and Charles C. Snow, "The New Network Firm: A Spherical Structure Built on a Human Investment Philosophy," *Organizational Dynamics* (Spring 1995), 5–18; and Raymond E. Miles, Charles C. Snow, John A. Matthews, Grant Miles, and Henry J. Coleman, Jr., "Organizing in the Knowledge Age: Anticipating the Cellular Form," *Academy of Management Executive* 11, no. 4 (1997), 7–24.

32. Raymond E. Miles and Charles C. Snow, "Organizations: New Concepts for New Forms," *California Management Review* 28 (Spring 1986), 62–73; and "Now, The Post-Industrial Corporation," *BusinessWeek* (March 3, 1986), 64–74.

33. N. Anand, "Modular, Virtual, and Hollow Forms of Organization Design," Working paper, London Business School, 2000; Don Tapscott, "Rethinking Strategy in a Networked World," *Strategy & Business,* Issue 24 (Third Quarter 2001), 34-41.

34. John Case, "The Age of the Specialist," *Inc.* (August 1995), 15-16.

35. Heath Row, "This 'Virtual' Company is for Real," *Fast Company* (December–January 1998), 48–50; Evan Ramstad, "A PC Maker's Low-Tech Formula: Start with the Box," *The Wall Street Journal* (December 29, 1997), B1, B8; and *http://www. monorail.com.company/company.htm* accessed on February 19, 2002.

36. Gregory G. Dess, Abdul M. A. Rasheed, Kevin J. McLaughlin, and Richard L. Priem, "The New Corporate Architecture," *Academy of Management Executive* 9, no. 3 (1995), 7–20.

37. Kathleen Kerwin, "GM: Modular Plants Won't Be a Snap," *BusinessWeek* (November 9, 1998), 168, 172.

38. Raymond E. Miles, "Adapting to Technology and Competition: A New Industrial Relations System for the Twenty-First Century," *California Management Review* (Winter 1989), 9–28 and Miles and Snow, "The New Network Firm."

39. Dess et al., "The New Corporate Architecture."

40. Melissa A. Schilling, "Industry Determinants of the Adoption of Modular Organizational Forms: An Empirical Test," *Academy of Management Journal,* forthcoming.

41. John Byrne, "The Virtual Corporation," *BusinessWeek* (February 8, 1993), 99–103; Dess et al., "The New Corporate Architecture," and Anand, "Modular, Virtual, and Hollow Forms."

42. M. Lynne Markus, Brook Manville, and Carole E. Agres, "What Makes a Virtual Organization Work?" *Sloan Management Review* (Fall 2000), 13–26.

43. Keith H. Hammonds, "This Virtual Agency Has Big Ideas," *Fast Company* (November 1999), 70–72.

44. Adam Lashinsky, "It Worked in Kindergarten," *Fortune* (April 2, 2001), 174.

45. N. Anand, "Modular, Virtual, and Hollow Forms," and Markus et. al., "What Makes a Virtual Organization Work?"

46. Thomas H. Davenport and Keri Pearlson, "Two Cheers for the Virtual Office," *Sloan Management Review* (Summer 1998), 51–65.

47. Ruff, "ConAgra CEO Finds Strength in Unity"; Neff, "The Biggest Nobody Really Knows"; Copple, "Synergy in Ketchup?"; and "ConAgra Attributes Acquisitions, Brands in Results," *Feedstuffs* (January 22, 2001), 6.

Using Structural Design to Achieve Strategic Goals

CHAPTER OUTLINE

The Horizontal Organization

The Need for Coordination

Task Forces, Teams, and Project Management

Reengineering

Traditional Organizations Versus the New Workplace

Horizontal Structure

Open Information

Decentralized Decision Making and Participative Strategy

Empowered Employees and Shared Responsibility

Strong Adaptive Culture

Factors Shaping Structure

Structure Follows Strategy

Structure Reflects the Environment

Structure Fits the Technology

Structure Follows the Workflow

LEARNING OBJECTIVES

After studying this chapter, you should be able to

1 Explain why organizations need coordination across departments and hierarchical levels.

2 Describe mechanisms for achieving coordination and when they may be applied.

3 Explain the major differences between traditional vertical organizations and the new workplace learning organization.

4 Describe how structure can be used to achieve an organization's strategic goals.

5 Describe how organization structure can be designed to fit environmental uncertainty.

6 Define production technology (manufacturing, service, and digital) and explain how it influences organization structure.

7 Explain the types of departmental interdependence and how structure can be used to accommodate them.

Management Challenge

Christopher B. Galvin was watching the company his grandfather had founded more than 70 years ago slowly fall apart. How had the mighty Motorola come to this? The company that had invented the cellular telephone industry was being hammered by rivals such as Finland's Nokia. Neglect of the Internet and failure to develop cutting-edge wireless network gear, combined with an arrogant sales approach, was hurting sales, profits, and the stock price. And, perhaps worst of all, rivals were ridiculing the company that once won the Malcolm Baldrige National Quality Award for its now-shoddy products. Employee morale was sinking with the company's fortunes. Galvin inherited this mess in 1997—and he knew he needed to do something fast or Motorola would fade into history. Galvin wanted to transform Motorola into a major Internet player, but intense internal competition and slow product development was hindering the company's efforts to compete in the fast-paced Internet world. For Motorola to once again be a world-class competitor, Galvin had to find ways to cut costs, increase innovation, build employee morale, and serve customers better and faster.[1]

If you were Christopher Galvin, how would you transform Motorola to speed up innovative product development for the Internet? What advice would you give him about using organization structure to achieve this goal?

Managers in companies like Motorola frequently must rethink structure and may reorganize to meet new competitive conditions in the environment. In Chapter 10, we examined the fundamentals of structure that apply to all organizations. In this chapter, we focus more precisely on structure as a tool, especially on how managers can use such concepts as departmentalization and chain of command to achieve specific goals. In recent years, many corporations, including American Express, Apple, IBM, Microsoft, and Ford Motor Co., have realigned departmental groupings, chains of command, and teams and task forces to attain new strategic goals. Structure is a powerful tool for reaching strategic goals, and a strategy's success often is determined by its fit with organization structure. The basic structural designs described in Chapter 10 are still valid, but a shift to a new kind of workplace and the increasing use of the Internet frequently mean an organization needs to use structural mechanisms to achieve stronger horizontal coordination.

The Horizontal Organization

Many companies are recognizing that traditional vertical organization structures are ineffective in today's fast-shifting environment, which is one reason for the growing use of teams, networks, and virtual approaches, as described in the previous chapter. Managers are looking for ways to transform their organizations into more flexible systems that emphasize rapid response and customer focus. Particularly for companies using the Internet to conduct business, a tight vertical approach such as a traditional functional structure does not work. In general, the trend is toward breaking down barriers between departments, and many companies are moving toward horizontal structures based on work processes rather than departmental functions.[2] Regardless of the type of structure, all organizations need mechanisms for horizontal coordination.

The Need for Coordination

As organizations grow and evolve, two things happen. First, new positions and departments are added to deal with factors in the external environment or with new strategic needs.[3] For example, many organizations have established Information Technology departments to cope with the proliferation of new information systems, or *chief knowledge officers* to find ways to leverage organizational knowledge in today's information-based economy. The executive search firm Russell Reynolds Associates created the position of *chief experience officer* to be in charge of the customer's total experience with the firm.[4] Many of today's organizations, particularly Internet and technology-based companies, are using unique job titles to reflect new needs. For example, Impact Online created a title of *chief imagination officer* for its Volunteer-Match Web site. The job reflects the need to imagine the possibilities for matching enthusiastic people with non-profit organizations that need volunteers.[5] As companies add positions and departments to meet changing needs, they grow more complex, with hundreds of positions and departments performing incredibly diverse activities.

Second, senior managers have to find a way to tie all of these departments together. The formal chain of command and the supervision it provides is effective, but it is not enough. The organization needs systems to process information and enable communication among people in different departments and at different levels. **Coordination** refers to the quality of collaboration across departments. Without coordination, a company's left hand will

coordination
The quality of collaboration across departments.

not act in concert with the right hand, causing problems and conflicts. Coordination is required regardless of whether the organization has a functional, divisional, or team structure. Employees identify with their immediate department or team, taking its interest to heart, and may not want to compromise with other units for the good of the organization as a whole.

Without a major effort at coordination, an organization may be like Chrysler Corporation in the 1980s when Lee Iacocca took over:

> What I found at Chrysler were 35 vice presidents, each with his own turf. . . . I couldn't believe, for example, that the guy running engineering departments wasn't in constant touch with his counterpart in manufacturing. But that's how it was. Everybody worked independently. I took one look at that system and I almost threw up. That's when I knew I was in really deep trouble.
>
> I'd call in a guy from engineering, and he'd stand there dumbfounded when I'd explain to him that we had a design problem or some other hitch in the engineering-manufacturing relationship. He might have the ability to invent a brilliant piece of engineering that would save us a lot of money. He might come up with a terrific new design. There was only one problem: he didn't know that the manufacturing people couldn't build it. Why? Because he had never talked to them about it. Nobody at Chrysler seemed to understand that interaction among the different functions in a company is absolutely critical. People in engineering and manufacturing almost have to be sleeping together. These guys weren't even flirting![6]

If one thing changed at Chrysler (now DaimlerChrysler) in the years before Iacocca retired, it was improved coordination. Cooperation among engineering, marketing, and manufacturing enabled the rapid design and production of the Chrysler PT Cruiser, for example.

In the international arena, coordination is especially important. How can managers ensure that needed coordination will take place in their company, both domestically and globally? Coordination is the outcome of information and cooperation. Managers can design systems and structures to promote horizontal coordination. Exhibit 11.1 illustrates the evolution of organizational structures, with a growing emphasis on horizontal coordination and communication. The vertical functional structure, discussed in the previous chapter, dates back nearly a century and was the first to be widely used by large organizations.[7] Although the structure is effective in stable environments, it does not provide the horizontal coordination needed in times of rapid change. Innovations such as teams, task forces, and project managers work within the vertical structure but provide a means to increase cross-functional

Source: Erica Freudenstein

Jo DeMars is president of DeMars & Associates Ltd., a company that manages warranty dispute arbitration programs for major automakers. DeMars had grown her business, now 13 years old, by meticulously managing every aspect of the company's operations. "I found myself getting so wrapped up in the day-to-day tasks that I couldn't be strategic," states DeMars. One day she went out to lunch and didn't come back to the office for four months. She spent the time setting up systems to improve horizontal coordination at DeMars. She hired an interim CEO and an operations manager, who helped DeMars improve communication and coordination among the company's 17 employees, 36 independent contractors, and 300 volunteer arbitrators.

E x h i b i t **11.1**

Evolution of Organization Structures

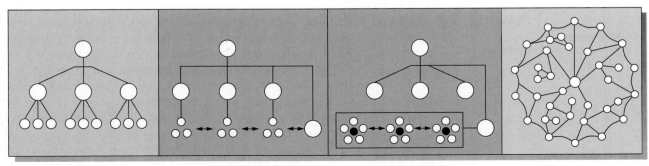

| Traditional Vertical Structure | Teams and Project Managers for Horizontal Coordination | Reengineering to Horizontal Processes | New Workplace Learning Organization |

communication and cooperation. The next stage involves reengineering to structure the organization around horizontal processes rather than vertical functions. The vertical hierarchy is flattened, with perhaps only a few senior executives in traditional support functions such as finance and human resources. Some organizations have taken a further step to the learning organization, doing away with all vestiges of an organizational hierarchy. The learning organization represents the ultimate in horizontal coordination. The following sections examine in more detail these methods for achieving horizontal coordination.

Task Forces, Teams, and Project Management

task force
A temporary team or committee formed to solve a specific short-term problem involving several departments.

A **task force** is a temporary team or committee designed to solve a short-term problem involving several departments.[8] Task force members represent their departments and share information that enables coordination.

For example, the Shawmut National Corporation created two task forces in human resources to consolidate all employment services into a single area. The task force looked at job banks, referral programs, employment procedures, and applicant tracking systems; found ways to perform these functions for all Shawmut's divisions in one human resource department; and then disbanded.[9] General Motors uses task forces to solve temporary problems in its manufacturing plants. When a shipment of car doors arrived from a fabricating plant with surface imperfections, the plant manager immediately created a task force to solve the problem. He got everybody together on the factory floor to examine the part that was causing the trouble, and the task force resolved the problem in about two hours.[10]

team
A group of participants from several departments who meet regularly to solve ongoing problems of common interest.

In addition to creating task forces, companies also set up teams. As used for coordination, a **team** is a group of participants from several departments who meet regularly to solve ongoing problems of common interest.[11] The permanent team is similar to a task force except that it works with continuing rather than temporary problems and might exist for several years. Teams used for coordination are like the cross-functional teams described in Chapter 10. For example, to improve coordination at Simplicity Pattern Company, CEO Louis Morris set up a Creative Committee, made up of the heads of the sales, finance, marketing, and creative departments. DaimlerChrysler sent managers and engineers to a three-day seminar held by Performance Learning Inc. to help them work better in teams. The seminar includes having team members participate in a relay race, driving high-speed race cars around a course of orange traffic cones. The exercise is designed to help team members think in terms of working together for the good of the whole rather than just for their own department.[12]

project manager
A person responsible for coordinating the activities of several departments on a full-time basis for the completion of a specific project.

Companies also use project managers to increase coordination between functional departments. A **project manager** is a person who is responsible for coordinating the activities of several departments for the completion of a specific project.[13] Project managers are critical today because many organizations are almost constantly reinventing themselves, creating flexible structures, and working on projects with an ever-changing assortment of people and organizations.[14] Project managers might work on several different projects at one time and might have to move in and out of new projects at a moment's notice.

The distinctive feature of the project manager position is that the person is not a member of one of the departments being coordinated. Project managers are located outside of the departments and have responsibility for coordinating several departments to achieve desired project outcomes. For example, General Mills, Procter & Gamble, and General Foods all use product managers to coordinate their product lines. A manager is assigned to each line, such as Cheerios, Bisquick, and Hamburger Helper. Product managers set budget goals, marketing targets, and strategies and obtain the cooperation from advertising, production, and sales personnel needed for implementing product strategy.

In some organizations, project managers are included on the organization chart, as illustrated in Exhibit 11.2. The project manager is drawn to one side of the chart to indicate authority over the project but not over the people assigned to it. Dashed lines to the project manager indicate responsibility for coordination and communication with assigned team members, but department managers retain line authority over functional employees.

Project managers might also have titles such as product manager, integrator, program manager, or process owner. Project managers need excellent people skills. They use expertise and persuasion to achieve coordination among various departments, and their jobs involve getting people together, listening, building trust, confronting problems, and resolving conflicts and disputes in the best interest of the project and the organization. Consider the role of Hugh Hoffman at American Standard Companies.

Hugh J. Hoffman began working at American Standard as a ceramic engineer in 1970. Today, he works as a full-time project manager in the company's chinaware business, which makes toilets and bidets. Hoffman, whose official title is *process owner, chinaware order fulfillment,* coordinates all the activities that ensure that American Standard's factories turn out the products customers order and deliver them on time. Hoffman's job requires that he think about everything that happens between the time an order comes in and the time it gets paid for, including design, manufacturing, painting, sales, shipping and receiving, and numerous other tasks. Project managers such as Hoffman have to act as if they are running their own business, setting goals and developing strategies for achieving them. It is not always easy because Hoffman works outside the boundaries and authority structure of traditional departments. His years of expertise and good people skills help him motivate others and coordinate the work of many departments and geographically dispersed factories. "I move behind the scenes," Hoffman says. "I understand the workings of the company and know how to get things done."[15] ❖

AMERICAN STANDARD COMPANIES
http://www.amstd-comfort.com

Using project managers has helped American Standard do things faster, better, and cheaper than competitors. Many organizations move to a stronger

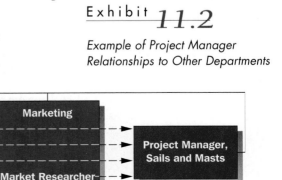

E x h i b i t *11.2*

Example of Project Manager Relationships to Other Departments

horizontal approach such as the use of permanent teams, project managers, or process owners after going through a redesign procedure called reengineering.

Reengineering

reengineering
The radical redesign of business processes to achieve dramatic improvements in cost, quality, service, and speed.

Reengineering, sometimes called *business process reengineering*, is the radical redesign of business processes to achieve dramatic improvements in cost, quality, service, and speed.[16] Because the focus of reengineering is on process rather than function, reengineering generally leads to a shift away from a strong vertical structure to one emphasizing stronger horizontal coordination and greater flexibility in responding to changes in the environment.

Reengineering changes the way managers think about how work is done in their organizations. Rather than focusing on narrow jobs structured into distinct, functional departments, they emphasize core processes that cut horizontally across the company and involve teams of employees working to provide value directly to customers.[17] A **process** is an organized group of related tasks and activities that work together to transform inputs into outputs and create value. Common examples of processes include new product development, order fulfillment, and customer service.[18]

process
An organized group of related tasks and activities that work together to transform inputs into outputs and create value.

Reengineering frequently involves a shift to a horizontal structure based on teams. For example, reengineering at Texas Instruments led to the formation of product development teams that became the fundamental organizational unit. Each team is made up of people drawn from engineering, marketing, and other departments and takes full responsibility for a product from conception through launch. Functional departments still exist, but their responsibility is no longer to do the work but to train people in the skills required to work in horizontal teams.[19]

Reengineering basically means starting over, throwing out all the notions of how work *was* done and deciding how it can best be done now. It requires identifying customer needs and then designing processes and aligning people to meet those needs. Several years ago, IBM went through business process reengineering in order to standardize its operations worldwide and better serve customers who were operating on a global basis. Today, the company is once again going through a rapid redesign of processes to make them compatible with e-business and the Internet.[20] Reengineering can also squeeze out the dead space and time lags in work flows, as illustrated by reengineering of the travel system at the U.S. Department of Defense.

U.S. DEPARTMENT OF DEFENSE
http://www.dod.gov

The Pentagon can act quickly to move thousands of tons of humanitarian aid material or hundreds of thousands of troops, but until recently, sending employees on routine travel has been a different story. Before Pentagon travelers could even board a bus, they had to secure numerous approvals and fill out reams of paperwork. Coming home wasn't any easier—the average traveler spent six hours preparing vouchers for reimbursement following a trip.

The Department of Defense set up a task force to reengineer the cumbersome travel system, aiming to make it cheaper, more efficient, and more customer friendly. The reengineered system reduces the steps in the pretravel process from an astounding 13 to only 4, as shown in Exhibit 11.3. Travel budgets and authority to approve travel requests and vouchers, which have traditionally rested in the budget channels of the various service commands, were transferred to local supervisors. Travelers make all their arrangements

Steps in the Pre-Travel Process—Old System

Steps in the Pre-Travel Process—Reengineered System

SOURCE: Richard Koonce, "Reengineering the Travel Game," *Government Executive*, (May 1995), 28–34, 69–70.

Exhibit **11.3**

Reengineering the Travel System— U.S. Department of Defense

through a commercial travel office, which prepares a "should-cost" estimate for each trip. This document is all a traveler needs before, during, and after a trip: With a supervisor's signature, it becomes a travel authorization; during travel, it serves as an itinerary; after amendments to reflect variations from plans, it becomes an expense report. Other travel expenses and needed cash or travelers' checks can be charged to a government-issued travel card, with payment made directly to the travel card company through electronic funds transfer.[21] ❖

As illustrated by this example, reengineering can lead to stunning results, but, like all business ideas, it has its drawbacks. Simply defining the organization's key business processes can be mind-boggling. AT&T's Network Systems division started with a list of 130 processes and then began working to pare them down to 13 core ones.[22] Organizations often have difficulty realigning power relationships and management processes to support work redesign, and thus do not reap the intended benefits of reengineering. According to some estimates, 70 percent of reengineering efforts fail to reach their intended goals.[23] Because reengineering is expensive, time consuming, and usually painful, it seems best suited to companies that are facing serious competitive threats.

Traditional Organizations Versus the New Workplace

Recall that the purpose of structure is to organize resources to accomplish organizational goals. Elements of structure such as chain of command, centralization/decentralization, formal authority, teams, and coordination devices fit together to form an overall structural approach. In some organizations, the formal, vertical hierarchy is emphasized as the way to achieve control and coordination. In other organizations, decision making is decentralized, cross-functional teams are implemented, and employees are given great freedom to pursue their tasks as they see fit.

The Engineering Division of Rohm and Haas Company used business process reengineering to achieve radical goals of building new plants faster and with dramatically lower costs. At one critical stage, existing processes were "mapped" using symbols so that inefficiencies could be identified and eliminated. Rohm and Haas, long recognized as an innovative leader in the specialty chemicals business, has committed itself to reanalyzing its work processes so the company can meet the higher expectations of today's customers, employees, and shareholders.

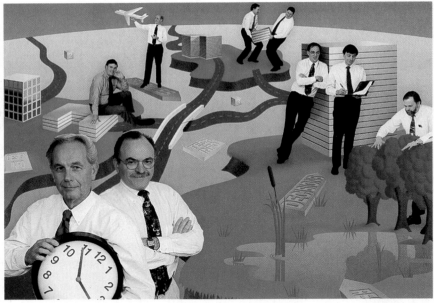

Courtesy Rohm and Haas Company

The increasing shift toward more horizontal versus vertical structures reflects the trend toward greater employee empowerment, broad information sharing, and decentralized decision making. At the apex of this movement is a type of organization called the *learning organization*. There is no single view of what the learning organization looks like. It is an attitude or philosophy about what an organization can become. Exhibit 11.4 compares characteristics of the new workplace learning organization with the traditional vertical organization.

In the traditional organization, the vertical structure predominates, with few task forces, teams, or project managers for horizontal coordination. Information is formally communicated up and down the organizational hierarchy and is not widely shared. In addition, jobs are broken down into narrow, specialized tasks, and employees generally have little say over how they do their work. The culture is rigid and does not encourage risk taking and

Exhibit *11.4*

Differences in Traditional versus Learning Organizations

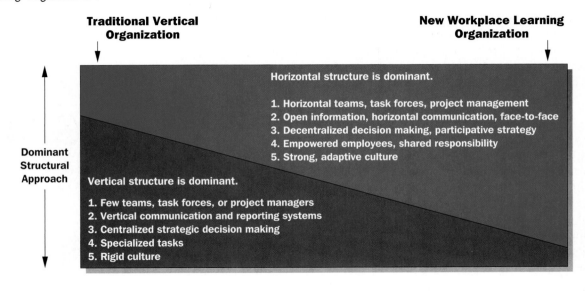

Traditional Vertical Organization

New Workplace Learning Organization

Dominant Structural Approach

Horizontal structure is dominant.

1. Horizontal teams, task forces, project management
2. Open information, horizontal communication, face-to-face
3. Decentralized decision making, participative strategy
4. Empowered employees, shared responsibility
5. Strong, adaptive culture

Vertical structure is dominant.

1. Few teams, task forces, or project managers
2. Vertical communication and reporting systems
3. Centralized strategic decision making
4. Specialized tasks
5. Rigid culture

change, and decision making is centralized. At the opposite end of the scale is the learning organization. The **learning organization** can be defined as one in which everyone is engaged in identifying and solving problems, enabling the organization to continuously experiment, change, and improve, thus increasing its capacity to grow, learn, and achieve its purpose. The learning organization is characterized by a horizontal team-based structure, open information, decentralized decision making, empowered employees, and a strong adaptive culture.

learning organization
An organization in which everyone is engaged in identifying and solving problems, enabling the organization to continuously experiment, improve, and increase its capability.

Horizontal Structure

In the new workplace learning organization, the vertical structure that created distance between the top and bottom of the organization is disbanded. Structure is created around workflows or core processes rather than departmental functions. All the people who work on a particular process, such as new product development or order fulfillment, have access to one another so they can easily communicate and coordinate their efforts, share knowledge, and provide value directly to customers.[24] Self-directed teams are the fundamental unit in a learning organization. Self-directed teams are made up of employees with different skills who rotate jobs to produce an entire product or service, and they deal directly with customers, making changes and improvements as they go along. Team members have the authority to make decisions about new ways of doing things, including taking responsibility for training, safety, scheduling vacations, and decisions about work methods, pay and reward systems, and coordination with other teams. Teams are discussed in detail in Chapter 19.

Learning organizations also strive to break down boundaries with other companies. New organizational forms such as the network organization, described in Chapter 10, are horizontal teams of companies rather than teams of individuals. Learning organizations may use a combination of self-directed teams, virtual teams, alliances and partnerships, virtual organizations, and other structural innovations to support collaboration within and between organizations. The Leading Online box describes how Intuit uses the Internet to support collaboration within the company as well as with outside organizations.

Open Information

In the new workplace learning organization, information is widely shared. To identify needs and solve problems, people have to be aware of what's going on. They must understand the whole organization as well as their part in it. Formal data about budgets, profits, and departmental expenses are available to everyone. This approach, which will be described in Chapter 20, is called *open-book management*. Every employee is free to look at the books and exchange information with anyone in the company. At Whole Foods Markets, for example, employees are trained to understand financial and operational information. Even sensitive data such as salaries and bonuses are available to any employee. Managers at Solectron Corp., the world's largest contract manufacturer, emphasize open sharing of information as a way to carry out the company's two primary values: superior customer service and respect for individual workers. "If you really want to respect individuals," says Solectron's Winston Chen, "you've got to let them know how they're doing—and let them know soon enough so they can do something about it."[25]

Leading Online

Intuit Spins a Wide Web

The financial services industry today is made up of numerous companies that are interlinked in multiple ways. But few companies have taken the partnership approach as far as Intuit, best known for its financial software.

Intuit was struggling in the mid-1990s, and managers began looking for a way to make the company central to customers' finance management in the networked marketplace. Realizing the company could not provide every financial service on its own, they began building alliances and partnership relationships. Today, Intuit has spun such a wide web that the line between competitors and partners is barely visible. More than 1,500 financial institutions connect to Intuit's array of products and services through the Internet. For example, Intuit's Web sites, Quicken.com and QuickBooks.com, provide links to dozens of finance resources. Small businesses log onto QuickBooks.com and have easy access to online payroll services, purchasing systems, and even Web site design tools. Other customers can use Quicken.com as an all-in-one site to manage their portfolios, pay bills, apply for loans, or access their bank account information, in addition to regular accounting and finance functions. The packaged versions of Quicken and Turbo Tax software also now come with embedded browsers that link them to a multitude of finance resources on the Web. One of Intuit's partners, Fidelity Investments, the

mutual fund and investing giant, licenses Turbo Tax and offers it free to customers as a value-added service. "It's a huge customer benefit," says Fidelity's Scott Gilmore, "so it's a win-win for everybody."

Intuit's internal operation is a reflection of its external one, with hundreds of product managers and teams of workers linked through an intranet to smoothly coordinate their work on a product-by-product basis. A business development team manages relationships that cut across multiple product lines. Top managers set goals and timelines, but day-to-day decision making and implementation is decentralized to the product managers and teams. "You don't want an executive making decisions on how a feature works," explains Steven Aldrich, Intuit's general manager of corporate partner development.

The smooth integration of internal and external operations has become a core strength for Intuit, and it becomes even more important as the financial services market grows ever-more turbulent. "It's impossible to imagine Intuit without alliances and links," says Aldrich. "We need the partners to be successful. The business is too complex."

SOURCE: Loren Fox, "Turn Your Company Outside In—Intuit: Spinning a Wide, Wide Web," in "Outsmart, Outgun, Outlast: Seven Winning Business Strategies for the Long Haul," edited by Jeffrey Davis, Loren Fox, and James Lardner, *Business2.Com* (March 20, 2001), 92–103.

Electronic communication is essential to information and knowledge sharing in a learning organization. Networks of computers, Internet technology, and the use of intranets and extranets change the locus of knowledge by getting information to the people who really need it and enabling employees to stay constantly in touch with one another. However, the learning organization also recognizes the importance of getting people communicating face-to-face, with the emphasis on listening. Some companies are using *dialogue*, which takes people away from work in groups of 30 or 40 to communicate deeply and honestly. Open communication and information sharing will be discussed in detail in Chapters 18 and 21.

Decentralized Decision Making and Participative Strategy

In traditional organizations, decisions are passed up the hierarchy for approval. In a learning organization, the people closest to the problem are given the authority and responsibility for decision making. Because people at all levels are intimately involved in making decisions, this allows strategy to emerge bottom up as well as top down. In traditional vertical organizations, top executives are responsible for strategy because only they have the big picture, knowledge, and expertise to direct the corporation. In the learning organization, leaders still influence overall vision and direction, but they do not control or direct strategy alone. Everyone helps. Information is gathered by employees who work directly with customers, suppliers, and other organizations. Perhaps thousands of people are in touch with the environment, providing data about external changes in technology and customer needs. They are the ones to identify needs and solutions, passing these ideas into the organization for discussion.[26]

Participative strategy relies on an experimental mindset. People are encouraged to try new things, and failure is accepted. Managers realize that problems and decisions present new learning opportunities, and they encourage employees to step outside their comfort zone and take risks. Strategy in learning organizations also may emerge from partnership linkages with suppliers, customers, and even competitors. Learning organizations have permeable boundaries and often are linked with other companies, giving each organization greater access to information about new strategic needs and directions.[27] Instead of looking at customers or suppliers at arm's length, the new workplace learning organization brings them into the company as partners working together to provide benefits for all. Onvia.com, for example, which sells to small businesses, asked its customers to help determine how the organization should stock its virtual shelves.[28]

Empowered Employees and Shared Responsibility

Learning organizations empower employees to an extraordinary degree, giving them the authority and responsibility to use their own discretion and ability to achieve an outcome. *Empowerment* means giving employees the power, freedom, knowledge, and skills to make decisions and perform effectively. Rather than dividing jobs into rigidly defined, specialized tasks, learning organizations allow people the freedom and opportunity to react quickly to changing conditions. There are few rules and procedures, and knowledge and control of tasks are located with workers rather than top managers. Individuals are encouraged to experiment, learn, and solve problems within the team. How do companies implement empowerment? It starts by promoting the decentralization of decision making and broader worker participation. For example, there are very few rules for teams at SEI Investments. Teams have as few as 2 members or as many as 30, and the various teams are structured differently. The teams themselves make the decisions about what roles each worker plays, how the team will operate, when it is time to disband, and so forth. The company's CEO calls it "fluid leadership."[29]

In learning organizations, people are considered a primary source of strength, not a cost to be minimized. This chapter's Putting People First box describes how Norsk Hydro, a Norway-based organization that operates in 70 countries and employs 39,000 people, has gone to extraordinary lengths to demonstrate its commitment to people as the key source of competitive advantage. Firms that adopt this perspective often employ the following practices: Treat employees well. Provide employment security and good wages. Provide a sense of employee ownership by sharing gains in productivity and profits. Commit to education for all members' growth and development. Help employees become world-renowned experts. Cross-train to help people acquire multiple skills. Promote from within.[30]

Larry Gaynor, founder, president, and CEO of The Nailco Group (TNG), a beauty salon products distribution company located in Farmington Hills, Michigan, attributes his company's success to its strong, adaptive culture. At TNG's annual meeting in 1994, Gaynor boldly invited his 65 employees to push sales from $18 million per year to $50 million—and they reached the goal in 5 years. TNG's culture includes "sales-enthusiastic [values], a learning friendly environment, and incredible customer service." Almost as soon as new employees arrive, they are introduced to TNG's winning team spirit. As Maureen Mann, vice president of sales for the Industry Source division, states, "You have to want to play on the team, and you have to want to win."

Putting People First

Norsk Hydro: Working Better by Working Less

Norwegians have always had a very different attitude than Americans about the meaning of work and its place in one's life. Their view is rooted in the notion of balance, and the idea that working less often means working better. As one of Norway's dominant institutions, Norsk Hydro has long been involved in innovative work approaches that enable employees to live a balanced life. Hydro is involved in numerous businesses, from salmon farming, to fertilizers, to oil and metal. But despite its diverse businesses, the core values of the company haven't changed in its 95 years of operation. "What is deep in the culture of Hydro is to think in the long term, to think more holistically—to think about the connections between employees, the company, and society," says Roald Nomme, a consultant and former Hydro manager.

Today, Hydro is expanding its thinking about those connections further than ever before in a project called Hydroflex, which offers employees varying combinations of flexible hours, teamwork, home offices, new technology, and redesigned office space. For example, Atle Tærum, chief agronomist at Norsk Hydro, spends two days a week at home, where he tends to his farm and cares for his children. With his cell phone constantly within reach, Tærum may be consulting with customers from Africa or the Middle East while he's plowing a field or chaperoning his son's kindergarten class. Before the flexible arrangement, Tærum says he was tired and unhappy most of the time. "Now I can manage my day and my life a bit better. I think I'm doing a better job for Hydro." Another employee, Unni Foss, who works as a graphic artist at Hydro Media, was able to work at home full time during the months before her father's death, to be with him and help her mother. The arrangement enabled her to keep a job and salary she needed and enabled Hydro to get good work from a talented worker. "We used to focus on how many hours people were in the office," says Ole Johan Sagafos, the head of Hydro Media. "Now we focus on results. It doesn't really matter to me what my colleagues are doing as long as they deliver the results on time."

Hydro sees its work–life balance initiatives as critical strategic elements for remaining competitive. Offering people flexibility in terms of how, where, and when they work attracts better workers and makes them more productive. In addition, the initiatives promote flexibility and diversity of thinking that is critical for success in today's fast-paced world. Ragnhild Sohlberg, vice president of external relations and special projects, uses the analogy of an experienced farmer who knows better than to plant, harvest, plow, and reseed the same field season after season—he knows that the soil needs a period of time to rest and rejuvenate. Modern corporations, though, think nothing of working their most talented people ceaselessly until they burn out and leave. "And all their experience goes with them," she says. "It's lost. That practice is not good business."

SOURCE: Charles Fishman, "The Way to Enough," *Fast Company* (July–August 1999), 160–174.

Strong, Adaptive Culture

Corporate culture is the set of key values, beliefs, understandings, and norms shared by members of the organization. The culture is the foundation of a learning organization. The culture of a learning organization is strong and typically includes strong values in the following three areas:

1. *The whole is more important than the part, and boundaries between parts are minimized.*[31] People in the new workplace learning organization are aware of the whole system and how parts fit together. The emphasis on the whole reduces boundaries. People no longer hoard information or ideas for themselves. The move toward a *boundaryless organization* means reducing barriers among departments, divisions, and external organizations. The free flow of people, ideas, and information allows coordinated action to occur in an uncertain and changing environment.

2. *The culture is egalitarian.* The culture of a learning organization creates a sense of community, compassion, and caring for one another. People count. Every person has value. The learning organization becomes a place for creating a web of relationships that nurtures and develops each person to his

or her maximum potential. Executive perks such as private dining rooms or reserved parking spots are eliminated. For example, the igus Inc. manufacturing company in Cologne, Germany, built a new plant to foster an open and egalitarian work environment. Walls separating the office area from the factory floor are transparent, to eliminate perceived barriers between employees and managers. There are no designated parking spaces for managers, and everyone comes in the same entrance, uses the same restrooms, and eats in the same cafeteria.[32] In learning organizations, everyone may share in stock options or performance bonuses, too. The orientation toward people provides safety for experimentation, frequent mistakes, and failures that enable learning. People are treated with respect and thereby contribute their best to the company.

3. *The culture values change, risk-taking, and improvement.* A basic value is to question the status quo, the current way of doing things. Can we do this any better? Why do we do this job that way? Constant questioning of assumptions and challenging the status quo open the gates to creativity and improvement. The organization learns to do things faster and to improve everything on an ongoing basis. An adaptive culture means that people care about important stakeholders, including employees, customers, and stockholders. Managers pay close attention to stakeholders and initiate change when needed. The culture also celebrates and rewards the creators of new ideas, products, and work processes.

In the learning organization, the culture encourages openness, boundarylessness, equality, continuous improvement, and change. The learning organization is always moving forward. Although no company represents a perfect example of a learning organization, one excellent example is Chaparral Steel, which has been called a learning laboratory.

The tenth-largest U.S. steel producer, Chaparral Steel has won international recognition for quality and productivity. Chaparral produces 1,100 tons of steel each year compared to the U.S. average of 350 tons. It has become an experimental laboratory for the latest techniques of learning organizations.

What makes Chaparral so effective? Managers articulate a clear vision—to lead the world in the low-cost, safe production of high-quality steel—along with the cultural values of egalitarianism and respect for the individual. Everyone participates. Everyone is empowered to solve problems. When a cooling hose burst, a group of operators—a welder, a foreman, and a buyer—all responded because they saw the problem. There is no assumption that other people are expected to do a job. Since employees know the vision and values, supervisors do not micromanage. Chaparral has few supervisors, and only two levels of hierarchy separate the CEO from operators in the rolling mill.

Employees are rewarded for learning new skills and for performance. Ideas are contributed by just about everyone. Employees are paid a salary rather than an hourly wage—hence, everyone acts like an owner and a manager. People are also rewarded with bonuses from company profits, which are shared with everyone, including janitors and secretaries.

All employees contribute to sharing information and knowledge. A steel plant is deliberately held to fewer than 1,000 employees so that people can communicate easily. An employee experimenting with new equipment will tell other people how it works. Employees who visit a competitor's plant will

CHAPARRAL STEEL
http://www.chaparralsteel.com

explain to others what they learned. There are no staff people and no boundaries among departments because there are few departments. Everyone is considered a salesperson and is free to communicate with customers and potential customers. There is no research and development department because employees on the line are responsible for innovation in new techniques and products. To reinforce continuous learning, employees are encouraged to attend school, and many are teachers of other employees in formal classes. The culture values ideas that benefit the whole company rather than individual ownership of ideas, so new knowledge is shared liberally.

Experimentation is rampant. The cultural value is: If you have an idea, try it. First-level managers can authorize thousands of dollars for employee experiments. Everyone is encouraged to push beyond current knowledge. This involves risk, which is another cultural value. Employees tolerate, even welcome, risk on a production line that is very expensive to shut down.

Strategy emerges from employee contacts outside the organization. Employees travel constantly, scanning for new ideas at trade shows and other companies. Teams of employees that include vice-presidents and shop people travel together to investigate a new technology.

Chaparral is so good at what it does that it welcomes competitors to visit the plant. A competitor can be shown everything Chaparral does and yet take away nothing, because a learning organization is created by leadership, culture, and empowered people. Most other steelmakers have been unable to achieve this, because they don't have the commitment or the vision.[33] ❖

Chaparral Steel is becoming a true learning organization. The leadership provides a flat, team-based design, a shared vision, and an attitude of serving employees. The culture stresses egalitarian values, providing support for risk taking. There are no boundaries separating departments. People are empowered to the point where no one has to take orders if he or she feels the order is wrong. The strategy emerges through the experiences of employees who work with customers and new technologies. Chaparral is flooded with information from experiments and travel, which is liberally shared.

Factors Shaping Structure

How do managers know whether to design a structure that emphasizes the formal, vertical hierarchy or one with an emphasis on horizontal communication and collaboration? The answer lies in the contingency factors that influence organization structure. Recall from Chapter 2 that *contingency* pertains to those factors on which structure depends. Research on organization structure shows that the emphasis given to a rigid or flexible structure depends on the contingency factors of strategy, environment, production technology, and departmental interdependence. The right structure is designed to "fit" the contingency factors as illustrated in Exhibit 11.5. Let us look at the relationship between each contingency factor and organization structure in more detail. The four contingency factors affect whether an organization should have a traditional vertical structure or a new workplace horizontal structure. These four areas are changing quite dramatically for most organizations, creating a need for stronger horizontal coordination.

Contingency Factors

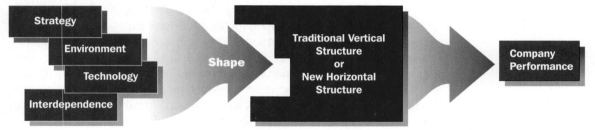

Contingency Factors

Exhibit **11.5**

Contingency Factors that Influence Organization Structure

Structure Follows Strategy

In Chapter 8, we discussed several strategies that business firms can adopt. Two strategies proposed by Porter are differentiation and cost leadership.[34] With a differentiation strategy, the organization attempts to develop innovative products unique to the market. With a cost leadership strategy, the organization strives for internal efficiency. The strategies of cost leadership versus differentiation typically require different structural approaches, so managers try to pick strategies and structures that are congruent.

Exhibit 11.6 shows a simplified continuum that illustrates how structural approaches are associated with strategic goals. The pure functional structure is appropriate for achieving internal efficiency goals. The vertical functional structure uses task specialization and a strict chain of command to gain efficient use of scarce resources, but it does not enable the organization to be flexible or innovative. In contrast, the learning organization is appropriate when the primary goal is innovation and flexibility. Each team is small, is able to be responsive, and has the people and resources necessary for performing its task. The flexible horizontal structure enables organizations to differentiate themselves and respond quickly to the demands of a shifting environment but at the expense of efficient resource use. Changing strategy and environmental conditions also shape structure in government organizations. For example, under financial pressure to cut costs and political pressure to keep customers happy, Departments of Motor Vehicles in some states are farming out DMV business whenever possible, by building strong partnerships with other companies. For example, in several states, including Illinois, Oregon, and Tennessee, auto dealers register new cars on site when they are sold.[35]

Exhibit **11.6**

Relationship of Strategic Goals to Structural Approach

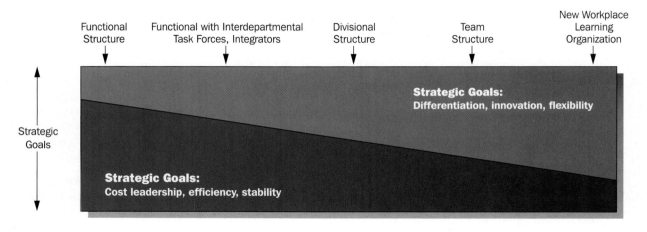

Exhibit 11.6 also illustrates how other forms of structure described in Chapter 10—decentralized with horizontal coordination, divisional, and team—represent intermediate steps on the organization's path to efficiency and/or innovation. The functional structure with horizontal teams and integrating managers provides greater coordination and flexibility than the pure functional structure. The divisional structure promotes differentiation because each division can focus on specific products and customers, although divisions tend to be larger and less flexible than small teams. Exhibit 11.6 does not include all possible structures, but it illustrates how structures can be used to facilitate the strategic goals of cost leadership or differentiation. For example, General Motors has changed the structure of the Saturn company to reflect a new strategy of cost efficiency.

SATURN
http://www.saturnbp.com

General Motors created Saturn in the mid-1980s as a different kind of car company to build a different kind of car. Saturn was set up as a separate autonomous division, with the president of Saturn overseeing the entire Saturn operation and reporting directly to GM's president. Teams of assembly-line workers collaborated closely with engineers and managers to hire new employees, choose suppliers, approve parts, select their own equipment, decide the best way to build the cars, and handle administrative matters. But as Saturn has struggled in recent years to remain competitive, GM executives are shifting back to a vertical, functional structure to reflect a new strategy of cost efficiency.

GM realized that it needed to find ways to cut costs and run Saturn more efficiently. "The only way we can make Saturn work economically is to leverage the rest of General Motors," says Ronald Zarella, GM's president for North American auto operations. That means Saturn will no longer be an autonomous division, and assembly-line workers will no longer have very much say in how Saturn cars are designed, built, or marketed. The white-collar staffs for design, production, and marketing have been moved back to the GM headquarters, where they report to various GM executives. The president of Saturn now serves primarily as a plant manager and reports to a GM vice president. All major decisions about Saturn are made by top executives at GM headquarters. Some workers are nostalgic for the old way Saturn operated, but GM executives believe the vertically integrated functional structure is needed to facilitate the new strategic emphasis on cost-efficiency. "A small company just cannot make it alone in the car industry [today]," says Richard G. LeFauve, who was Saturn's first president. "You need to have a big brother to help you with high fixed-cost resources like engineering, purchasing, financial, and the sales end of the business."[36] ❖

Structure Reflects the Environment

In Chapter 3, we discussed the nature of environmental uncertainty. Environmental uncertainty means that decision makers have difficulty acquiring good information and predicting external changes. Uncertainty occurs when the external environment is rapidly changing and complex. An uncertain environment causes three things to happen within an organization.

1. *Increased differences occur among departments.* In an uncertain environment, each major department—marketing, manufacturing, research and development—focuses on the task and environmental sectors for which it is

responsible and hence distinguishes itself from the others with respect to goals, task orientation, and time horizon.[37] Departments work autonomously. These factors create barriers among departments.

2. *The organization needs increased coordination to keep departments working together.* Additional differences require more emphasis on horizontal coordination to link departments and overcome differences in departmental goals and orientations.

3. *The organization must adapt to change.* The organization must maintain a flexible, responsive posture toward the environment. Changes in products and technology require cooperation among departments, which means additional emphasis on coordination through the use of teams, project managers, and horizontal information processing.[38]

The contingency relationship between environmental uncertainty and structural approach is illustrated in Exhibit 11.7. When the external environment is more stable, the organization can succeed with a traditional structure that emphasizes vertical control. There is little need for change, flexibility, or intense coordination. The structure can emphasize specialization, centralized decision making, and wide spans of control. When environmental uncertainty is high, a horizontal structure that emphasizes lateral relationships such as teams and horizontal projects is appropriate. Vertical structure characteristics such as specialization, centralization, and formalized procedures should be downplayed. In an uncertain environment, the organization figures things out as it goes along, departments must cooperate, and decisions should be decentralized to the teams and task forces working on specific problems. The flight deck of the *USS Dwight D. Eisenhower*, a nuclear-powered aircraft carrier, provides an excellent example of the relationship between structure and the environment.

©Fritz Hoffman—Network

Since China joined the World Trade Organization, companies such as Angang Iron and Steel have experienced greater environmental uncertainty that comes from participating in the global economy. Angang, one of the largest and most prestigious metal-bending companies in China, is restructuring to become more flexible with a trimmed, more efficient workforce. Angang has cut 30,000 people from its workforce of 165,000 at steel plants such as the one shown in the photo.

Exhibit **11.7**

Relationship between Environment and Structure

| | **STRUCTURE** | |
	Vertical	Horizontal
Uncertain (Unstable)	**Incorrect Fit:** Vertical structure in uncertain environment **Structure too tight**	**Correct Fit:** Horizontal structure in uncertain environment
Certain (Stable)	**Correct Fit:** Vertical structure in certain environment	**Incorrect Fit:** Horizontal structure in certain environment **Structure too loose**

ENVIRONMENT

THE USS *DWIGHT D. EISENHOWER*

On an aircraft carrier such as the USS *Dwight D. Eisenhower*, there are thousands of disastrous accidents just waiting to happen. Launching or landing a plane from the oil-slicked deck of a nuclear-powered carrier is a tricky, finely balanced procedure. A sudden wind shift, a mechanical breakdown, or the slightest of miscommunications could spell disaster. Yet, surprisingly, flight deck operations generally run as smooth as silk, and accidents are quite rare. The reason has a lot to do with organizational structure.

At first glance, a nuclear aircraft carrier is structured in a rigid, hierarchical way—the captain issues orders to commanders, who direct lieutenants, who pass orders on to ensigns, and on down the hierarchy. There is a strict chain of command, and people are expected to follow orders promptly and without question. Formalization is high, with manuals detailing standard operating procedures for everything. But an interesting thing happens in times of high demand, such as the launching and recovery of planes during real or simulated wartime. In this different environment, the hierarchy dissolves and a loosely organized, collaborative structure in which sailors and officers work together as colleagues takes its place. People discuss and negotiate the best procedure to use, and everyone typically follows the lead of whoever has the most experience and knowledge in a particular area, no matter the person's rank or job title. During this time, no one is thinking about job descriptions, authority, or chain of command; they are just thinking about getting the job done safely. With planes landing every 60 seconds, there is no time to send messages up the chain of command and wait for decisions to come down from the top. Anyone who notices a problem is expected to respond quickly, and each member of the crew has the power—and the obligation—to shut down flight operations immediately if the circumstances warrant it.[39] ❖

Researchers have studied this ability to glide smoothly from a rigid, hierarchical structure to a loosely structured, horizontal one, not only on aircraft carriers but in other organizations that have to be exceptionally responsive to environmental changes—for example, air-traffic controllers or nuclear power plants. The hierarchical side helps keep discipline and ensure adherence to rules that have been developed and tested over many years to cope with expected and well-understood problems and situations. However, during times of complexity and high uncertainty, the most effective structure is one that loosens the lines of command and enables people to work across departmental and hierarchical lines to anticipate and avoid problems.[40]

Not all organizations have to be as super-responsive to the environment as the USS *Dwight D. Eisenhower*, but using the correct structure for the environment is important for businesses as well. When managers use the wrong structure for the environment, reduced performance results. A rigid, vertical structure in an uncertain environment prevents the organization from adapting to change. Likewise, a loose, horizontal structure in a stable environment is inefficient. Too many resources are devoted to meetings and discussions when employees could be more productive focusing on specialized tasks.

Structure Fits the Technology

technology
The knowledge, tools, techniques, and activities used to transform organizational inputs into outputs.

Technology includes the knowledge, tools, techniques, and activities used to transform organizational inputs into outputs.[41] Technology includes machinery, employee skills, and work procedures. A useful way to think about technology is as production activities. The production activities may be to produce steel castings, television programs, or computer software.

Production technology is significant because it has direct influence on the organization structure. Structure must be designed to fit the technology as well as to accommodate the external environment. Technologies vary between manufacturing and service organizations. In addition, new digital technology has an impact on structure as well. In the following paragraphs, we discuss each characteristic of technology and the structure that best fits it.

Woodward's Manufacturing Technology. The most influential research into the relationship between manufacturing technology and organization structure was conducted by Joan Woodward, a British industrial sociologist.[42] She gathered data from 100 British firms to determine whether basic structural characteristics, such as administrative overhead, span of control, centralization, and formalization, were different across firms. She found that manufacturing firms could be categorized according to three basic types of production technology:

1. *Small-batch and unit production.* **Small-batch production** firms produce goods in batches of one or a few products designed to customer specification. Each customer orders a unique product. This technology also is used to make large, one-of-a-kind products, such as computer-controlled machines. Small-batch manufacturing is close to traditional skilled-craft work, because human beings are a large part of the process; they run machines to make the product. Examples of items produced through small-batch manufacturing include custom clothing, special-order machine tools, space capsules, satellites, and submarines.

2. *Large-batch and mass production.* **Mass production** technology is distinguished by standardized production runs. A large volume of products is produced, and all customers receive the same product. Standard products go into inventory for sale as customers need them. This technology makes greater use of machines than does small-batch production. Machines are designed to do most of the physical work, and employees complement the machinery. Examples of mass production are automobile assembly lines and the large-batch techniques used to produce computers, tobacco products, and textiles.

3. *Continuous process production.* In **continuous process production**, the entire work flow is mechanized. This is the most sophisticated and complex form of production technology. Because the process runs continuously, there is no starting and stopping. Human operators are not part of actual production because machinery does all of the work. Human operators simply read dials, fix machines that break down, and manage the production process. Examples of continuous process technologies are chemical plants, distilleries, petroleum refineries, and nuclear power plants.

The difference among the three manufacturing technologies is called technical complexity. **Technical complexity** means the degree to which machinery is involved in the production to the exclusion of people. With a complex technology, employees are hardly needed except to monitor the machines.

The structural characteristics associated with each type of manufacturing technology are illustrated in Exhibit 11.8. Note that formalization and centralization are high for mass production technology and low for continuous process. Unlike small-batch and continuous process, standardized mass production

small-batch production
A type of technology that involves the production of goods in batches of one or a few products designed to customer specification.

mass production
A type of technology characterized by the production of a large volume of products with the same specifications.

continuous process production
A type of technology involving mechanization of the entire work flow and nonstop production.

technical complexity
The degree to which complex machinery is involved in the production process to the exclusion of people.

Computer companies such as IBM, Compaq, and Hewlett-Packard are initiating new small-batch production *methods in order to compete with Dell Computer's low-cost strategy.* Unlike Dell, which builds PCs only after they have been ordered and sends them directly to customers, IBM, Compaq, and H-P have previously employed mass production *techniques—building, testing, inspecting, boxing, and storing large volumes before shipping products to resellers.* In the photo, Mike Rust unpacks the case of an IBM PC for Entex, a reseller that IBM has delegated to complete assembly of its computers in smaller batches as they are ordered.

machinery requires centralized decision making and well-defined rules and procedures. The administrative ratio and the percentage of indirect labor required also increase with technological complexity. Because the production process is nonroutine, closer supervision is needed. More indirect labor in the form of maintenance people is required because of the machinery's complexity; thus, the indirect/direct labor ratio is high. Span of control for first-line supervisors is greatest for mass production. On an assembly line, jobs are so routinized that a supervisor can handle an average of 48 employees. The number of employees per supervisor in small-batch and continuous process production is lower because closer supervision is needed. Overall, small-batch and continuous process firms have somewhat loose, flexible structures, and mass production firms have tight, vertical structures.

The important conclusion about manufacturing technology was described by Woodward as follows: "Different technologies impose different kinds of demands on individuals and organizations, and these demands have to be met through an appropriate structure."[43] Woodward found that the relationship between structure and technology was directly related to company performance. Low-performing firms tended to deviate from the preferred structural form, often adopting a structure appropriate for another type of technology. High-performing organizations had characteristics very similar to those listed in Exhibit 11.8.

Service Technology.   Service organizations are becoming increasingly important in North America. For the past two decades, more people have been employed in service organizations than in manufacturing organizations. Thus, research has been undertaken to understand the structural characteristics of service organizations. Examples of service organizations include consulting companies, law firms, brokerage houses, airlines, hotels, advertising firms, amusement parks, and educational organizations. In addition, service technology characterizes many departments in large corporations, even manufacturing firms. In a manufacturing company such as Ford Motor Company, the legal, human resources, finance, and market research departments all provide service. Thus, the structure and design of these departments reflect their own service technology rather than the manufacturing plant's technology. **Service technology** can be defined as follows:

service technology
Technology characterized by intangible outputs and direct contact between employees and customers.

E x h i b i t *11.8*

Relationship between Manufacturing Technology and Organization Structure

	Manufacturing Technology		
	Small Batch	**Mass Production**	**Continuous Process**
Technical Complexity of Production Technology	Low	Medium	High
Organization structure:			
Formalization	Low	High	Low
Centralization	Low	High	Low
Top administrator ratio	Low	Medium	High
Indirect/direct labor ratio	1/9	1/4	1/1
Supervisor span of control	23	48	15
Communication:			
Written (vertical)	Low	High	Low
Verbal (horizontal)	High	Low	High
Overall structure	Flexible	Rigid	Flexible

SOURCE: Based on Joan Woodward, *Industrial Organizations: Theory and Practice* (London: Oxford University Press, 1965).

1. *Intangible output.* The output of a service firm is intangible. Services are perishable and, unlike physical products, cannot be stored in inventory. The service is either consumed immediately or lost forever. Manufactured products are produced at one point in time and can be stored until sold at another time.

2. *Direct contact with customers.* Employees and customers interact directly to provide and purchase the service. Production and consumption are simultaneous. Service firm employees have direct contact with customers. In a manufacturing firm, technical employees are separated from customers, and hence no direct interactions occur.[44]

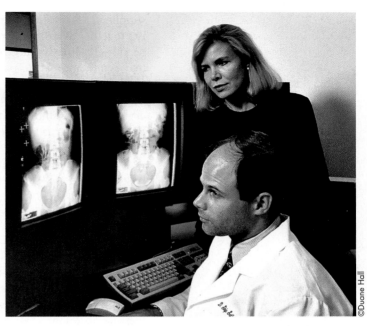

Skip Sallee and Susan Hinson of Team Radiology in Durham, North Carolina, use "telemedicine" to relieve hospitals of the costly administrative burdens associated with radiology. By connecting to Team Radiology over a computer network, small rural hospitals can offer radiology services previously not financially feasible. Advanced information technology has revolutionized service technology, allowing the creation of structures that couldn't have existed before. New computerized forms of communication and cooperation support the informal, flexible, and decentralized structure needed in many service organizations.

One distinct feature of service technology that directly influences structure is the need for employees to be close to the customer.[45] Structural characteristics are similar to those for continuous manufacturing technology, shown in Exhibit 11.8. Service firms tend to be flexible, informal, and decentralized. Horizontal communication is high because employees must share information and resources to serve customers and solve problems. Services also are dispersed; hence each unit is often small and located geographically close to customers. For example, banks, hotels, fast-food franchises, and doctors' offices disperse their facilities into regional and local offices to provide faster and better service to customers.

Some services can be broken down into explicit steps, so that employees can follow set rules and procedures. For example, McDonald's has standard procedures for serving customers and Marriott has standard procedures for cleaning hotel rooms. When services can be standardized, a tight centralized structure can be effective, but service firms in general tend to be more flexible and decentralized.

Digital Technology.

Digital technology is characterized by use of the Internet and other digital processes to conduct or support business online. E-commerce organizations such as Amazon.com, which sells books and other products to consumers over the Internet, eBay, an online auction site, Yahoo!, an Internet search engine, and Priceline.com, which allows consumers to name their own prices and then negotiates electronically with its partner organizations on behalf of the consumer, are all examples of firms based on digital technology. In addition, large companies such as General Electric, Dell Computer, and Ford Motor Company are involved in business-to-business commerce, using digital technology to conduct transactions with suppliers and partners.

Like service firms, organizations based on digital technology tend to be flexible and decentralized. The fast-paced digital world practically demands a focus on horizontal processes rather than departmental functions. Horizontal communication and collaboration are typically very high, and these companies may frequently be involved in network and virtual arrangements. Digital technology is driving the move toward horizontal forms that link customers,

digital technology
Technology characterized by use of the Internet and other digital processes to conduct or support business operations.

suppliers, and partners into the organizational network, with everyone working together as if they were one organization. People may use electronic connections to link themselves together into teams. For example, an employee may send an e-mail to people both within and outside the organization who can help with a particular customer problem and quickly form a virtual team to develop a solution.[46] In other words, digital technology encourages *boundarylessness*, where information and work activities flow freely among various organizational participants. Formalization and centralization are low, and employees are empowered to work in teams to meet fast-changing needs. Verbal and electronic communication is high, both up and down as well as across the organization because up-to-the minute information is essential. In the digital world, advantage comes from seeing first and moving fastest, which requires extraordinary openness and flexibility.[47]

Structure Follows the Workflow

The final characteristic of the organization's situation that influences structure is called *workflow interdependence*. **Interdependence** means the extent to which departments depend on each other for resources or materials to accomplish their tasks. A low level of workflow interdependence means that departments do their work independently and have little need for interaction, coordination, or exchange of materials. A high level of workflow interdependence means that departments must constantly exchange information and resources. Three types of interdependence that influence organization structure are illustrated in Exhibit 11.9.[48]

interdependence
The extent to which departments depend on each other for resources or materials to accomplish their tasks.

Pooled Interdependence.   *Pooled interdependence* means that each department is part of the organization and contributes to the common good, but each department is relatively independent because work does not flow between units. AmSouth branch banks or Wendy's restaurants are examples of pooled interdependence. They share financial resources from a common pool but do not interact with each other.

Sequential Interdependence.   *Sequential interdependence* means that parts or outputs of one department become inputs to another department in serial fashion. The first department must perform correctly so that the second department can perform correctly. An example is assembly line technology, such as in the automobile industry. This is greater interdependence than with the pooled type, because departments exchange resources and depend on others to perform well.

Reciprocal Interdependence.   The highest level is *reciprocal interdependence*, which means that the output of operation A is the input to operation B, and the output of operation B is the input back again to operation A. Departmental outputs influence other departments in reciprocal fashion. For example, hospitals must coordinate services to patients, such as when a patient moves back and forth among the surgery, physical therapy, and X-ray departments.

Structural Implications.   When interdependence among departments is pooled, coordination is relatively easy. Managers can develop standardized procedures, rules, and regulations that ensure similar performance in all

Form of Inter-dependence	Type of Coordination Required
1. Pooled (bank) Clients	■ Chain of command ■ Standardization of procedures ■ Rules and regulations
2. Sequential (assembly line) Client	■ Plans and schedules ■ Scheduled meetings ■ Liaison roles
3. Reciprocal (hospital) Client	■ Unscheduled meetings ■ Teams ■ Task forces ■ Project managers

Exhibit *11.9*

Types of Interdependence and Required Coordination

SOURCE: Based on John F. Rockart and James E. Short, "IT in the 1990s: Managing Organizational Interdependence," *Sloan Management Review* (Winter 1989), 7–17.

Exhibit *11.10*

Product Development, Product Delivery, and Customer Service Interdependencies

branches. For sequential interdependence, coordination is somewhat more difficult, requiring future planning and scheduling so that the flow of outputs and resources is coordinated to the benefit of all departments. Moreover, scheduled meetings and face-to-face discussions are used for day-to-day coordination among departments. Reciprocal interdependence is the most difficult. These departments should be located physically close together in the organization so that communication is facilitated. Structural mechanisms for coordination include teams, task forces, unscheduled meetings, and perhaps project managers to ensure that departments are working out workflow coordination problems on a daily basis.[49]

Within most organizations, interdependence will be high (reciprocal) for some departmental activities and low (pooled) for others. For example, Exhibit 11.10 illustrates how reciprocal interdependence among sets of departments exists for the tasks of product development, product delivery, and customer service. The design and purchasing departments can work independently on many tasks, but for product development, they must be coordinated, perhaps with a team or task force. Purchasing must be coordinated with distribution for the delivery of products. Suppliers and customers also are a part of the interdependence and in some organizations may be included as part of a team.

■ Summary and Management Solution

This chapter introduced a number of important organizing concepts. As organizations grow, they add new departments, functions, and hierarchical levels. A major problem confronting management is how to tie the whole organization together. Structural characteristics such as chain of command, work specialization, and departmentalization are valuable organization concepts but often are not sufficient to coordinate far-flung departments. Horizontal coordination mechanisms provide coordination across departments and include reengineering, task forces, teams, and project managers.

There is an increasing shift toward more horizontal versus vertical structures, which reflects the trend toward greater employee involvement and participation. At the apex of this movement is a type of organization called the learning organization. The learning organization is characterized by a horizontal structure, open information, decentralized decision making, empowered employees, and a strong, adaptive culture. Contingency factors of strategy, environment, production technology, and departmental interdependence influence the correct structural approach. When a firm's strategy is to differentiate the firm's product from competitors, a flexible structural approach using teams, decentralization, and empowered employees is appropriate. When environmental uncertainty is high, horizontal coordination is important, and the organization should have a looser, flexible structure, such as in a learning organization.

Other factors that influence structure are technology and interdependence. For manufacturing firms, small batch, continuous process, and flexible manufacturing technologies tend to be structured loosely, whereas a tighter vertical structure is appropriate for mass production. Service technologies are people oriented, and firms are located geographically close to dispersed customers. In general, services have more flexible, horizontal structures, with decentralized decision making. Similarly, organizations based on new digital technology are typically horizontally structured and highly decentralized. Digital connections enable and encourage the free flow of information and work activities among various organizational participants, which might include customers, partners, and other outsiders, as well as employees.

Finally, departmental interdependence also determines the form of structure. An organization with a low level of interdependence can be controlled mainly with the vertical chain of command and standardization of procedures, rules, and regulations. When interdependence is high, such as for new-product introductions, then horizontal coordination mechanisms such as unscheduled meetings, teams, and project managers are required, or the organization may place the interdependent groups into separate, self-contained units.

At Motorola, described at the beginning of the chapter, a lack of horizontal communication and collaboration was turning the company once admired around the world into a has-been. Galvin worked with other top managers to initiate a complete overhaul of the company and transform Motorola into a new kind of organization that could adapt to the rapid changes of the digital era. To increase horizontal communication and collaboration, they combined all of the 30 different units that make cell phone, wireless equipment, satellite, and cable modem products into one large communications division. Managers are paid based on their ability to work collaboratively to give customers easy-to-use ways to stay tapped into the Internet, whether it be via cell phone, pager, modem, or something no one has even invented yet. Furthermore, two horizontal coordination units were put in place: one charged with coordinating all the communication businesses to meet customer needs and the second charged with coordinating Internet strategies across all of Motorola's operations. Galvin's primary goal was to break down the intensely competitive culture that had developed within Motorola and replace it with one in which everyone puts the good of the whole above their individual business units.

After putting the new structure in place, managers began to work on external relationships. Motorola has developed strategic alliances with some of the most important players in the Internet world, including Cisco Systems, Yahoo!, America Online, and Amazon.com. In addition, the company is bringing major customers into the information network so they can also help shape the strategic direction Motorola will take. Motorola's shift to a more flexible, horizontal structure reflects its strategy of differentiating itself with innovative, Net-ready wireless products, the need to respond to rapid environmental changes, and the complexity and fast pace of digital technology. So far, the results of the shift have been dramatic. Motorola was able to bring out innovative phones embedded with Web browsers ahead of competitors, and customers are impressed with the quality and technological sophistication of the new equipment.[50] The increased horizontal communication and collaboration, both within the company and with outside organizations, have made Motorola mighty once again.

■ Discussion Questions

1. Carnival Cruise Lines provides pleasure cruises to the masses. Carnival has several ships and works on high volume/low price rather than offering luxury cruises. What would you predict about the organization structure of a Carnival Cruise ship?

2. Why is structure different depending on whether a firm's strategy is low cost or differentiation?

3. The chapter suggested that structure should be designed to fit strategy. Some theorists argue that strategy should be designed to fit the organization's

structure. With which theory do you agree? Explain.

4. Explain the three levels of departmental interdependence and give an example of each.

5. Some experts argue that interdependence within organizations is greater now than 15 years ago because of rapid changes in the global environment. If so, what does this mean for the current structure of organizations compared with that of 15 years ago?

6. What type of skills does a person need to be an effective project manager? Why do you think so many of today's companies are organizing around projects?

7. Discuss why an organization in an uncertain environment requires more horizontal relationships than one in a certain environment.

8. Why are empowered employees, open information, and cultural values of minimal boundaries and equality important in a new workplace learning organization as opposed to a traditional, vertical organization?

9. What is the difference between manufacturing and service technology? How would you classify a university, a local discount store, a nursery school? How would you expect the structure of a service organization to differ from that of a manufacturing organization?

10. What impact does the growing use of digital technology have on organizational structure? Would you expect the structure of an Internet-based organization such as eBay, which operates almost entirely online, to be different from a bricks-and-mortar company such as General Electric that uses the Internet for business-to-business transactions with vendors? Why or why not?

■ Management in Practice: Experiential Exercise

Loose versus Tight Organization Structure

Interview an employee at your university, such as a department head or secretary. Have the employee answer the following 13 questions about his or her job and organizational conditions.

	Disagree Strongly				Agree Strongly
1. Your work would be considered routine.	5	4	3	2	1
2. There is a clearly known way to do the major tasks you encounter.	5	4	3	2	1
3. Your work has high variety and frequent exceptions.	1	2	3	4	5
4. Communications from above consist of information and advice rather than instructions and directions.	1	2	3	4	5
5. You have the support of peers and supervisor to do your job well.	1	2	3	4	5
6. You seldom exchange ideas or information with people doing other kinds of jobs.	5	4	3	2	1
7. Decisions relevant to your work are made above you and passed down.	5	4	3	2	1
8. People at your level frequently have to figure out for themselves what their jobs are for the day.	1	2	3	4	5
9. Lines of authority are clear and precisely defined.	5	4	3	2	1
10. Leadership tends to be democratic rather than autocratic in style.	1	2	3	4	5
11. Job descriptions are written and up-to-date for each job.	5	4	3	2	1
12. People understand each other's jobs and often do different tasks.	1	2	3	4	5
13. A manual of policies and procedures is available to use when a problem arises.	5	4	3	2	1

Total Score _____

A score of 52 or above suggests that the employee is working in a "loosely structured" organization. The score reflects a flexible structure that is often associated with uncertain environments and small-batch technology. People working in this structure feel empowered. Many organizations today are moving in the direction of flexible structures and empowerment.

A score of 26 or below suggests a "tight structure." This structure utilizes traditional control and functional specialization, which often occurs in a certain environment, a stable organization, and routine or mass-production technology. People in this structure may feel controlled and constrained.

Discuss the pros and cons of loose versus tight structure. Does the structure of the employee you interviewed fit the nature of the organization's environment, strategic goals, and technology? How might you redesign the structure to make the work organization more effective?

■ Management in Practice: Ethical Dilemma

A Matter of Giving

Renee Washington was proud to have been recruited out of college to work at Standol Corporation. In addition to a spotless reputation in environmental responsibility, Standol was famous for its active part in supporting various civic and cultural organizations in the community. When the opportunity came to participate in the Helping Hands drive, Washington quickly volunteered. She soon had reason to regret her decision.

A memo was issued to the volunteer coordinator in each department, indicating the expected donation from each employee. It was Washington's job to collect a "pledge" to be withdrawn from each payroll check, or a lump-sum payment. The memo indicated Standol expected each volunteer coordinator to collect the suggested amount or make up the difference out of their own pockets. Washington found herself listening to countless hard-luck stories as she applied pressure to fellow employees for their contributions. As she enlisted the aid of managers in the coercion, Washington felt her pride and excitement in the project diminishing.

She began to question whether a sterling reputation in community charities was worth the embarrassment and resentment it caused Standol employees. She wondered if people might give more freely if they felt they weren't being ordered to give at levels set by top management. She wanted to make suggestions for changes, but feared doing so would threaten her future at Standol.

What Do You Do?

1. Comply with the traditional fund-raising approach, blaming the company for putting you in the position of the bad guy.
2. Collect only the funds that are genuinely donated, without making up the difference out of pocket. If you are criticized, expose the coercive practices to Helping Hands officials and the press.
3. Propose changes for coordinating fund-raising across departments that emphasize teamwork and come from within the organization, rather than from the top down.

SOURCE: Based on Doug Wallace, "A Twisted Arm," *What Would You Do? Business Ethics*, vol. II (January–February 1994), 17–18.

■ Surf the Net

1. **Project Management Software.** Go to *http://www. infogoal.com/pmc/pmcswr.htm* and answer the following questions about the project management software information available at this site: (a) Under what headings does this Web site organize the many project management software applications available today? (b) What are examples of three different types of projects these software applications manage? Next, go to *http://www. microsoft.com/office/project/evaluation/tour/default.htm* and take a tour of the features available in Microsoft Project 2000 (*Note:* If this link is no longer available, do a search at Microsoft's site for "Microsoft Project tour.")

2. **Reengineering.** @BRINT.com, the BizTech Network, is recommended by *The Wall Street Journal, Harvard Business Publishing, Fortune, Fast Company, Forbes, CIO, Computerworld,* and *InfoWorld.*

   Use this site, *http://www.brint.com/interest.html,* to gather information about reengineering and write a one- to two-page report in which you provide examples of organizations that have gone through this process.

3. **Production Technology.** The following Web sites provide virtual tours of production facilities. The sites that provide a 360° panoramic view require a plug-in that you will be able to download and install using the links or responding to the options provided at the sites that

require the plug-in. The first two links are for the same company. Visit all four sites and be prepared to share in class what you learned about production technology by going on these virtual plant tours.

http://breesepublishing.papadocs.com/breesepub_files/ vtour_balcony.htm

http://breesepublishing.papadocs.com/breesepub_files/ tour.html
http://www.jliebfoods.com/plant.htm
http://virtualtours.bp.com/floridariver/default.htm
http://www.apsoutsource.com/tour.html

■ Case for Critical Analysis

Malard Manufacturing Company

Malard Manufacturing Company produces control valves that regulate flows through natural gas pipelines. Malard has approximately 1,400 employees and has successfully produced a standard line of control valves that are price competitive in the industry. However, whenever the production of a new control valve is required, problems arise. Developments in electronics, metallurgy, and flow control theory require the introduction of new products every year or two. These new products have been associated with interdepartmental conflict and disagreement.

Consider the CV305, which is in process. As usual, the research and development group developed the basic design, and the engineering department converted it into a prototype control valve. Now the materials department must acquire parts for the prototype and make plans for obtaining parts needed for production runs. The production department is to manufacture and assemble the product, and marketing is responsible for sales.

Department managers believe that future work on the CV305 should be done simultaneously instead of sequentially. Top executives worked with the department heads to create a temporary task force, with one member from each department and coordinated by a project manager, to try to get the work done simultaneously. The idea was that, by working together on the task force, marketing could provide input to research and development so that the design will meet customer needs. Production could make sure the design will fit machine limitations and be cost-efficient to manufacture.

So far, however, the task force has led to more conflicts, controversies, and problems than before. The production task force member has been pushing to speed up development of the final plans so that the production department can acquire tooling and be ready for standard production. The engineering representative, on the other hand, says his department wants to slow down development to ensure that specifications are correct and have been thoroughly tested.

Department managers are frustrated and becoming uncommunicative. The research and development and engineering departments are keeping their developmental plans secret, causing frustration for the other departments, the task force, and the project manager. Moreover, several department managers are new and inexperienced in new-product development. Ms. Crandell, the executive vice president, likes to keep tight control over the organization. Department managers must check with her before making major decisions. However, with the CV305, she has been unable to keep things running smoothly. Crandell has no time to personally shepherd the CV305 through the system and expects the project manager to handle these problems through the task force.

On November 1, Crandell received a memo from the marketing department head. It said, in part,

> The CV305 must go to market immediately. This is urgent. It is needed now because it provides the precision control our competitors' products already have. Three of our salespeople reported that loyal customers are about to place orders with competitors. We can keep this business if we have the CV305 ready for production in 30 days.

Questions

1. What is the balance between vertical and horizontal structure in Malard Manufacturing? Is it appropriate that department managers always turn to the executive vice-president for help rather than to one another?
2. If you were Ms. Crandell, how would you resolve this problem? What could you do to facilitate production of the CV305 over the next 30 days?
3. What structural changes would you recommend to prevent these problems in future new-product developments?

■ Endnotes

1. Roger O. Crockett, "A New Company Called Motorola," *BusinessWeek* (April 17, 2000), 86.

2. Laurie P. O'Leary, "Curing the Monday Blues: A U.S. Navy Guide for Structuring Cross-Functional Teams," *National Productivity Review* (Spring 1996), 43–51; and Alan Hurwitz, "Organizational Structures for the 'New World Order,'" *Business Horizons* (May–June 1996), 5–14.

3. Richard L. Daft, *Organization Theory and Design*, 7th ed. (Cincinnati, Ohio: South-Western College Publishing, 2001).

4. Michelle Conlin, "Write Your Own Title," *BusinessWeek* (August 28, 2000), 148.

5. "Job Titles of the Future" column in *Fast Company* (December 1999), 92.

6. Lee Iacocca with William Novak, *Iacocca: An Autobiography* (New York: Phantom Books, 1984), 152–153.

7. Alan Webber, "The Best Organization is No Organization," *USA Today* (March 6, 1997), 13A.

8. William J. Altier, "Task Forces: An Effective Management Tool," *Management Review* (February 1987), 52–57.

9. "Task Forces Tackle Consolidation of Employment Services," *Shawmut News*, Shawmut National Corp. (May 3, 1989), 2.

10. Michael Brody, "Can GM Manage It All?" *Fortune* (July 8, 1985), 22–28.

11. Henry Mintzberg, *The Structure of Organizations* (Englewood Cliffs, N.J.: Prentice Hall, 1979).

12. Barbara Ettorre, "Simplicity Cuts a New Pattern," *Management Review* (December 1993), 25–29; and Jeffrey Ball, "A Car Veteran Explains Why IPC = (A + W + P – I) × S," *The Wall Street Journal* (June 8, 1999), B1, B20.

13. Paul R. Lawrence and Jay W. Lorsch, "New Managerial Job: The Integrator," *Harvard Business Review* (November–December 1967), 142–151.

14. Ronald N. Ashkenas and Suzanne C. Francis, "Integration Managers: Special Leaders for Special Times," *Harvard Business Review* (November–December 2000), 108–116.

15. Jeffrey A. Tannenbaum, "Why Are Companies Paying Close Attention to This Toilet Maker?" (The Front Lines column), *The Wall Street Journal* (August 20, 1999), B1.

16. This discussion is based on Michael Hammer and Steven Stanton, "How Process Enterprises *Really* Work," *Harvard Business Review* (November–December 1999), 108–118; Richard L. Daft, *Organization Theory and Design,* 5th ed. (Minneapolis, Minn.: West Publishing Company, 1995), 238; Raymond L. Manganelli and Mark M. Klein, "A Framework for Reengineering," *Management Review* (June 1994), 9–16; and Barbara Ettorre, "Reengineering Tales from the Front," *Management Review* (January 1995), 13–18.

17. Hammer and Stanton, "How Process Enterprises *Really* Work."

18. Michael Hammer, definition quoted in "The Process Starts Here," *CIO* (March 1, 2000), 144–156; and David A. Garvin, "The Processes of Organization and Management," *Sloan Management Review* (Summer 1998), 33-50.

19. Hammer and Stanton, "How Process Enterprises *Really* Work."

20. Ibid.

21. Richard Koonce, "Reengineering the Travel Game," *Government Executive* (May 1995), 28–34, 69–70.

22. John A. Byrne, "The Horizontal Corporation," *BusinessWeek* (December 20, 1993), 76–81.

23. Erik Brynjolfsson, Amy Austin Renshaw, and Marshall Van Alstyne, "The Matrix of Change," *Sloan Management Review* (Winter 1997), 37–54.

24. Frank Ostroff, *The Horizontal Organization: What the Organization of the Future Looks Like and How It Delivers Value to Customers* (New York: Oxford University Press, 1999).

25. Julie Carrick Dalton, "Between the Lines: The Hard Truth about Open Book Management," *CFO* (March 1999), 58–64; Alex Markels, "The Wisdom of Chairman Ko," *Fast Company* (November 1999), 258-276.

26. E. C. Nevis, A. J. DiBella, and J. M. Gould, "Understanding Organizations as Learning Systems," *Sloan Management Review* (Winter 1995), 73–85; and G. Hamel, "Strategy as Revolution," *Harvard Business Review* (July–August 1996), 69–82.

27. Marc S. Gerstein and Robert B. Shaw, "Organizational Architectures for the Twenty-First Century," in David A. Nadler, Marc S. Gerstein, Robert B. Shaw and Associates, eds., *Organizational Architecture: Designs for Changing Organizations* (San Francisco: Jossey-Bass, 1992), 263–274.

28. Thomas A. Stewart, "Three Rules for Managing in the Real-Time Economy," *Fortune* (May 1, 2000), 333–334.

29. Scott Kirsner, "Every Day, It's a New Place," *Fast Company* (April–May 1998), 130–134.

30. Jeffrey Pfeffer, "Producing Sustainable Competitive Advantage Through the Effective Management of People," *Academy of Management Executive* 9, no. 1 (1995), 55–69.

31. Mary Anne Devanna and Noel Tichy, "Creating the Competitive Organization of the Twenty-First Century: The Boundaryless Corporation," *Human Resource Management* 29 (Winter 1990), 455–471; and Fred Kofman and Peter M. Senge, "Communities of Commitment: The Heart of Learning Organizations," *Organizational Dynamics* (Autumn 1993), 4–23.

32. Chuck Salter, "This is One Fast Factory," *Fast Company* (August 2001), 32–33.

33. Dorothy Leonard-Barton, "The Factory as a Learning Laboratory," *Sloan Management Review* (Fall 1992), 23–38.

34. Michael E. Porter, *Competitive Strategy* (New York: Free Press, 1980), 36–46.

35. Pam Black, "Finally, Human Rights for Motorists," *BusinessWeek* (May 1, 1995), 45.

36. Keith Bradsher, "The Reality Behind the Slogan: Saturn Unit, Once a Maverick, Is Looking a Lot More Like GM," *The New York Times* (August 23, 2001), C1, C10.

37. Paul R. Lawrence and Jay W. Lorsch, *Organization and Environment* (Homewood, Ill.: Irwin, 1969).

38. Robert B. Duncan, "Characteristics of Organizational Environments and Perceived Environmental Uncertainty," *Administrative Science Quarterly* 17 (1972), 313–327; W. Alan

Randolph and Gregory G. Dess, "The Congruence Perspective of Organization Design: A Conceptual Model and Multivariate Research Approach," *Academy of Management Review* 9 (1984), 114–127; and Masoud Yasai-Ardekani, "Structural Adaptations to Environments," *Academy of Management Review* 11 (1986), 9–21.

39. Robert Pool, "In the Zero Luck Zone," *Forbes ASAP* (November 27, 2000), 85+.

40. Ibid.

41. Denise M. Rousseau and Robert A. Cooke, "Technology and Structure: The Concrete, Abstract, and Activity Systems of Organizations," *Journal of Management* 10 (1984), 345–361; Charles Perrow, "A Framework for the Comparative Analysis of Organizations," *American Sociological Review* 32 (1967), 194–208; and Denise M. Rousseau, "Assessment of Technology in Organizations: Closed versus Open Systems Approaches," *Academy of Management Review* 4 (1979), 531–542.

42. Joan Woodward, *Industrial Organizations: Theory and Practice* (London: Oxford University Press, 1965); and Joan Woodward, *Management and Technology* (London: Her Majesty's Stationery Office, 1958).

43. Woodward, *Industrial Organizations*, vi.

44. Peter K. Mills and Thomas Kurk, "A Preliminary Investigation into the Influence of Customer-Firm Interface on Information Processing and Task Activity in Service Organizations," *Journal of Management* 12 (1986), 91–104; Peter K. Mills and Dennis J. Moberg, "Perspectives on the Technology of Service Operations," *Academy of Management Review* 7 (1982), 467–478; and Roger W. Schmenner, "How Can Service Businesses Survive and Prosper?" *Sloan Management Review* 27 (Spring 1986), 21–32.

45. Richard B. Chase and David A. Tansik, "The Customer Contact Model for Organization Design," *Management Science* 29 (1983), 1037–1050; and Gregory B. Northcraft and Richard B. Chase, "Managing Service Demand at the Point of Delivery," *Academy of Management Review* 10 (1985), 66–75.

46. Michael Hammer in "The Process Starts Here"; and Emelie Rutherford, "End Game," (an interview with David Weinberger, coauthor of *The Cluetrain Manifesto*), *CIO* (April 1, 2000), 98–104.

47. Stewart, "Three Rules for Managing in the Real-Time Economy."

48. James Thompson, *Organizations in Action* (New York: McGraw-Hill, 1967).

49. Jack K. Ito and Richard B. Peterson, "Effects of Task Difficulty and Interdependence on Information Processing Systems," *Academy of Management Journal* 29 (1986), 139–149; and Andrew H. Van de Ven, Andre Delbecq, and Richard Koenig, "Determinants of Coordination Modes within Organizations," *American Sociological Review* 41 (1976), 322–338.

50. Crockett, "A New Company Called Motorola."

Change and Development

CHAPTER OUTLINE

Change and the New Workplace

Model of Planned
Organizational Change

Forces for Change

Need for Change

Initiating Change

Search

Creativity

Idea Champions and
New-Venture Teams

Implementing Change

Resistance to Change

Force Field Analysis

Implementation Tactics

Types of Planned Change

Technology Changes

New-Product Changes

Structural Changes

Culture/People Changes

Training and Development

Organizational Development

LEARNING OBJECTIVES

After studying this chapter, you should be able to

1   Define organizational change and explain the forces for change.

2   Describe the sequence of four change activities that must be performed in order for change to be successful.

3   Explain the techniques managers can use to facilitate the initiation of change in organizations, including idea champions, new-venture teams, and idea incubators.

4   Define sources of resistance to change.

5   Explain force field analysis and other implementation tactics that can be used to overcome resistance to change.

6   Explain the differences among technology, product, structure, and culture/people changes.

7   Explain the change process—bottom up, top down, horizontal—associated with each type of change.

8   Define organizational development and large-group interventions.

Management Challenge

Corning Inc. was started nearly 150 years ago and has long been on the cutting edge of technologies that changed the world. It is the company that invented the glass casing for Thomas Edison's light bulb, perfected the processes for mass-producing television tubes, gave us Pyrex baking dishes, and revolutionized the telecommunications industry with fiber optics. But by the mid-1990s, it looked as if the company would not make it to the twenty-first century. As half-owner of the Dow Corning joint venture, Corning lost 25 percent of its earnings practically overnight when the venture was forced into bankruptcy following litigation over silicone breast implants. The cookware division was hurting because of the growing power of retail giants such as Wal-Mart and Target, which demanded that the company cut prices by 5 percent a year. To boost sales, top executives were pushing for improved quality, but it was clear that things weren't improving very fast. When engineer Roger Ackerman, who had been with Corning since 1962, took over as top leader, he knew he needed to spur innovation and get some dazzling new products to market fast.[1]

If you were Roger Ackerman, what would you do to change Corning? How would you encourage employee innovation and make sure ideas get translated into new products for the marketplace?

Roger Ackerman and Corning Inc. are not alone. Every organization sometimes faces the need to change quickly and dramatically to survive in a
changing environment. Sometimes, changes are brought about by forces
outside the organization. Other times, managers within the company want
to initiate major changes but don't know how. Lack of innovation from
within is widely recognized as one of the critical problems facing business
today in the United States and Canada. To be successful, organizations must
embrace many types of change. Businesses must develop improved production
technologies, create new products desired in the marketplace, implement
new administrative systems, and upgrade employees' skills. Companies such
as Whirlpool, Black & Decker, and Merck implement all of these changes and
more.

How important is organizational change? Consider this: The parents of
today's college students grew up without digital cameras, e-mail, laptop computers, DVDs, Web-access cell phones, and online shopping. Companies that
produce the new products and services have prospered, but many companies
caught with outdated products and technologies have failed. Today's successful companies are constantly striving to come up with new products and services. For example, Kyocera Wireless Corp. developed a device that combines
a high-end mobile phone with a Palm OS digital assistant in a stylish package
barely bigger than a deck of playing cards. Even at a list price of $500, the
demand for the Smartphone was so great that Kyocera could barely keep up.[2]
Engineers at automakers such as DaimlerChrysler, General Motors, and
Toyota are perfecting fuel-cell power systems that could make today's internal
combustion engine as obsolete as the steam locomotive. Pharmaceutical companies and biotechnology firms around the world are searching for new drugs
and vaccines to fight diseases such as AIDS and cancer.[3] Organizations that
change successfully are both profitable and admired.

organizational change
The adoption of a new idea or behavior
by an organization.

Organizational change is defined as the adoption of a new idea or behavior by an organization.[4] In this chapter, we will look at how organizations can
be designed to respond to the environment through internal change and
development. First we will examine the basic forces for organizational change.
Then we will look closely at how managers facilitate two change requirements: initiation and implementation. Finally, we will discuss the four major
types of change—technology, new product, structure, and culture/people—
and how the organization can be designed to facilitate each.

Change and the New Workplace

Today's organizations need to continuously adapt to new situations if they are
to survive and prosper. As we discussed in Chapter 2, one of the most dramatic elements of change is the shift to a technology-driven workplace in
which ideas, information, and relationships are becoming critically important.
Many changes are being driven by advances in information technology and
the Internet. New trends such as e-business, enterprise resource planning, and
knowledge management require profound changes in the organization. These
shifts are frequently linked to development of the *learning organization*, which
is the epitome of continuous organizational learning and change.

As described in Chapter 11, the new workplace learning organization
involves everyone in problem solving and continuous improvement based on
the lessons of experience.[5] The various elements of the learning organization

discussed in Chapter 11 interact with one another in such a way that each element responds to and influences every other element toward changing the organization to keep pace with today's digital world. For example, a *horizontal structure* breaks down boundaries within the organization, as well as with other companies, to promote collaboration for learning and change, which requires changes in employee empowerment, information sharing, and culture. *Empowerment* liberates employees but also places upon them the added responsibilities of working collaboratively, initiating changes, and participating in strategy to benefit the entire company. Redefining *culture* demands the rethinking of roles, processes, and values, breaking down barriers that have separated departments so that everyone shares information and works together. *Information sharing* requires adjustments on the part of managers for the inclusion of employees, suppliers, and customers, often necessitating cultural and structural changes. *Strategy* is likewise linked to structure and culture as the organization changes its fundamental way of doing business and allows change initiatives to flow bottom up as well as top down and to emerge from linkages with customers and partner organizations.

The learning organization simultaneously embraces two types of planned change: *incremental change*, which refers to organizational efforts to gradually improve basic operational and work processes in different parts of the company, and *transformational change*, which involves redesigning and renewing the entire organization.[6] Change, particularly transformational change, does not happen easily. However, managers can learn to anticipate and facilitate change to help their organizations keep pace with the rapid changes in the external environment.

©Shelly Harrison

After years of wowing investors with stories of laboratory developments rather than predictable earnings, many biotechnology firms are undergoing transformational change to redesign and renew their entire organizations and show concrete evidence of growth. For example, Millennium Pharmaceuticals Inc., in the photo, is buying COR Therapeutics to get its experienced sales force and an established anticlotting drug. To compete with huge pharmaceutical companies such as Pfizer, biotech companies need to expand their product lines and make changes in systems, structures, and culture to promote growth.

Model of Planned Organizational Change

Change can be managed. By observing external trends, patterns, and needs, managers use planned change to help the organization adapt to external problems and opportunities.[7] When organizations are caught flat-footed, failing to anticipate or respond to new needs, management is at fault.

An overall model for planned change is presented in Exhibit 12.1. Four events make up the change sequence: (1) Internal and external forces for change exist; (2) organization managers monitor these forces and become aware of a need for change; and (3) the perceived need triggers the initiation of change, which (4) is then implemented. How each of these activities is handled depends on the organization and managers' styles.

We now turn to a brief discussion of the specific activities associated with the first two events—forces for change and the perceived need for the organization to respond.

Exhibit *12.1*

*Model of Change
Sequence of Events*

Forces for Change

Forces for organizational change exist both in the external environment and within the organization.

Environmental Forces.   As described in Chapters 3 and 4, external forces originate in all environmental sectors, including customers, competitors, technology, economic forces, and the international arena. For example, changes in customer needs caused automotive supplier Delphi Automotive Systems to completely change the way it makes catalytic converters. Managers discovered that the traditional assembly line at Delphi's Oak Creek, Wisconsin, factory was too slow and inflexible to meet the needs of auto manufacturers who wanted catalytic converters customized to their individual needs. The powered conveyor system has now been eliminated, and the factory floor is divided into work cells, each made up of a few workers who make an entire converter from start to finish. Teams are empowered to determine their own schedules, inspect for quality, and work directly with customers. The new system has cut costs, increased flexibility, and dramatically increased the speed of production. In addition, workers are constantly coming up with new ideas for improvement because they feel responsible for a complete, finished product rather than a narrow, disconnected task.[8]

Internal Forces.   Internal forces for change arise from internal activities and decisions. If top managers select a goal of rapid company growth, internal actions will have to be changed to meet that growth. New departments or technologies will be created. Demands by employees, labor unions, and production inefficiencies all can generate a force to which management must respond with change. At the New York law firm of Cadwalader, Wickersham, and Taft, for example, growing complaints from younger partners about the firm's outmoded ways of doing business led to changes such as ending money-losing practices, revising pay systems that generated rivalries among partners, and changing archaic and time-consuming procedures. The changes helped turn the declining organization into one of the hottest firms on Wall Street.[9]

Need for Change

As indicated in Exhibit 12.1, external or internal forces translate into a perceived need for change within the organization. Many people are not willing to change unless they perceive a problem or a crisis. For example, many U.S. companies have changed how they conduct business as a result of the terrorist attacks of September 11, 2001. Top managers at E Commerce Group, a company that processes payments by phone and online, had been trying to find ways to promote teamwork and collaboration, but they kept running into resistance. However, after the hijacked planes struck the World Trade Center, across the street from E Commerce's offices, employees immediately began pitching in to help one another any way they could, and the new spirit of collaboration and teamwork has continued. "This crisis broke down the barriers," said Marc Mehl, co-founder and chief operating officer.[10]

In many cases, there is no crisis that prompts change. Most problems are subtle, so managers have to recognize and then make others aware of the need for change.[11] One way managers sense a need for change is when there is a **performance gap**—a disparity between existing and desired performance levels. They then try to create a sense of urgency so that others in the organization will recognize and understand the need for change. For example, the chief component-purchasing manager at Nokia noticed that order numbers for some of the computer chips it purchased from Philips Electronics weren't adding up, and he discovered that a fire at Philips' Albuquerque, New Mexico, plant had delayed production. The manager moved quickly to alert top managers, engineers, and others throughout the company that Nokia could be caught short of chips unless it took action. Within weeks, a crisis team had redesigned chips, found new suppliers, and restored the chip supply line. In contrast, managers at Ericsson, a competitor that also purchased chips from Philips, had the same information but failed to recognize or create a sense of crisis for change, which left the company millions of chips short of what it needed to produce a key product.[12]

Recall from Chapter 8 the discussion of SWOT analysis. Managers are responsible for monitoring threats and opportunities in the external environment as well as strengths and weaknesses within the organization to determine whether a need for change exists.

Managers in every company must be alert to problems and opportunities, because the perceived need for change is what sets the stage for subsequent actions that create a new product or technology. Big problems are easy to spot. Sensitive monitoring systems are needed to detect gradual changes that can fool managers into thinking their company is doing fine. An organization may be in greater danger when the environment changes slowly, because managers may fail to trigger an organizational response. Failing to use planned change to meet small needs can place the organization in hot water, as illustrated in the following passage:

> When frogs are placed in a boiling pail of water, they jump out—they don't want to boil to death. However, when frogs are placed in a cold pail of water, and the pail is placed on a stove with the heat turned very low, over time the frogs will boil to death.[13]

Despite an impressive victory in Afghanistan, President George W. Bush finds a performance gap, a disparity between existing and desired performance levels, in the U.S. military. The president is creating a sense of urgency for change, emphasizing that although the U.S. military took a scant two months to help crush Afghanistan's Taliban regime, continued success fighting the wars of the 21st century will require more agile, quicker-responding forces. Bush believes the military needs "new concepts, new strategies, and new resolve" to respond to the new face of war. In the photo are Hornets, fighter jets aboard the USS Theodore Roosevelt, *which played a significant role in the war in Afghanistan.*

performance gap
A disparity between existing and desired performance levels.

Initiating Change

After the need for change has been perceived and communicated, change must be initiated. This is a critical phase of change management—the stage where the ideas that solve perceived needs are developed. Responses that an organization can make are to search for or create a change to adopt.

search
The process of learning about current developments inside or outside the organization that can be used to meet a perceived need for change.

Search

Search is the process of learning about current developments inside or outside the organization that can be used to meet the perceived need for change. Search typically uncovers existing knowledge that can be applied or adopted within the organization. Managers talk to friends and colleagues, read professional reports, or hire consultants to learn about ideas used elsewhere.

Many needs, however, cannot be resolved through existing knowledge but require that the organization develop a new response. Initiating a new response means that managers must design the organization so as to facilitate creativity of both individuals and departments, encourage innovative people to initiate new ideas, or create structural elements such as new venture departments, skunkworks, and idea incubators.

Creativity

creativity
The generation of novel ideas that may meet perceived needs or offer opportunities for the organization.

Creativity is the generation of novel ideas that may meet perceived needs or respond to opportunities for the organization. Creativity is the essential first step in innovation, which is vital to long-term organizational success.[14] People noted for their creativity include Edwin Land, who invented the Polaroid camera; Frederick Smith, who came up with the idea for Federal Express's overnight delivery service during an undergraduate class at Yale; and Swiss engineer George de Mestral, who created Velcro after noticing the tiny hooks on the burrs caught on his wool socks. Each of these people saw unique and creative opportunities in a familiar situation.

Each of us has the capacity to be creative. Characteristics of highly creative people are illustrated in the left-hand column of Exhibit 12.2. Creative people often are known for originality, open-mindedness, curiosity, a focused approach to problem solving, persistence, a relaxed and playful attitude, and receptivity to new ideas.[15]

E x h i b i t *12.2*

Characteristics of Creative People and Organizations

SOURCES: Based on Gary A. Steiner, ed., *The Creative Organization* (Chicago: University of Chicago Press, 1965), 16–18; Rosabeth Moss Kanter, "The Middle Manager as Innovator," *Harvard Business Review* (July–August 1982), 104–105; James Brian Quinn, "Managing Innovation: Controlled Chaos," *Harvard Business Review* (May–June 1985), 73–84; and Robert I. Sutton, "The Weird Rules of Creativity," *Harvard Business Review* (September 2001), 94–103.

The Creative Individual	The Creative Organization or Department
1. Conceptual fluency Open-mindedness	1. Open channels of communication Contact with outside sources Overlapping territories Suggestion systems, brainstorming, group techniques
2. Originality	2. Assigning nonspecialists to problems Eccentricity allowed Hiring people who make you uncomfortable
3. Less authority Independence Self-confidence	3. Decentralization, loosely defined positions, loose control Acceptance of mistakes People encouraged to defy their bosses
4. Playfulness Undisciplined exploration Curiosity	4. Freedom to choose and pursue problems Not a tight ship, playful culture, doing the impractical Freedom to discuss ideas, long time horizon
5. Persistence Commitment Focused approach	5. Resources allocated to creative personnel and projects without immediate payoff Reward system encourages innovation Absolution of peripheral responsibilities

Creativity can also be designed into organizations. Companies or departments within companies can be organized to be creative and initiate changes. Most companies want more highly creative employees and often seek to hire creative individuals. However, the individual is only part of the story, and everyone has some potential for creativity. Managers are responsible for creating a work environment that allows creativity to flourish.[16] The characteristics of creative organizations correspond to those of individuals, as illustrated in the right-hand column of Exhibit 12.2. Creative organizations are loosely structured. People find themselves in a situation of ambiguity, assignments are vague, territories overlap, tasks are poorly defined, and much work is done through teams.[17] Creative organizations have an internal culture of playfulness, freedom, challenge, and grass-roots participation.[18] They harness all potential sources of new ideas from within. Many participative management programs are born out of the desire to enhance creativity for initiating changes. People are not stuck in the rhythm of routine jobs.

To keep creativity alive at MaMaMedia.com, a New York-based company that provides Web-based "playful learning" for kids, top managers hold weekly meetings called *thought provoking sessions*.[19] Each week, a different team hosts the meeting and sets the format, but the guiding principle is to learn by having fun. One team, for example, had everyone make peanut butter and jelly sandwiches by following simple programming-like instructions. The goal was to show people how explicit programmers need to be when they are writing code, thus increasing cross-functional understanding and collaboration. These weekly meetings keep MaMaMedia's playful, creative culture alive even as employees deal with day-to-day deadlines and demands.

The most creative companies embrace risk and encourage employees to make mistakes. Jim Read, president of the Read Corporation, says, "When my employees make mistakes trying to improve something, I give them a round of applause. No mistakes mean no new products. If they ever become afraid to make one, my company is doomed."[20] Similarly, former Time Warner chairman Steve Ross believed people who didn't make enough mistakes should be fired.[21]

Idea Champions and New-Venture Teams

If creative conditions are successful, new ideas will be generated that must be carried forward for acceptance and implementation. This is where idea champions come in. The formal definition of an **idea champion** is a person who sees the need for and champions productive change within the organization. For example, Wendy Black of Best Western International championed the idea of coordinating the corporate mailings to the company's 2,800 hoteliers into a single packet every two weeks. Some hotels were receiving three special mailings a day from different departments. Her idea saved $600,000 a year in postage alone.[22]

Remember: Change does not occur by itself. Personal energy and effort are required to successfully promote a new idea. Often a new idea is rejected by management. Champions are passionately committed to a new product or idea despite rejection by others. At Kyocera Wireless, lead engineer Gary Koerper was a champion for the Smartphone. When he could not get his company's testing department to validate the new product, he had an outside firm do the testing for him—at a cost of about $30,000—without approval from Kyocera management.[23]

idea champion
A person who sees the need for and champions productive change within the organization.

Championing an idea successfully requires roles in organizations, as illustrated in Exhibit 12.3. Sometimes a single person may play two or more of these roles, but successful innovation in most companies involves an interplay of different people, each adopting one role. The *inventor* develops a new idea and understands its technical value but has neither the ability nor the interest to promote it for acceptance within the organization. The *champion* believes in the idea, confronts the organizational realities of costs and benefits, and gains the political and financial support needed to bring it to reality. The *sponsor* is a high-level manager who approves the idea, protects the idea, and removes major organizational barriers to acceptance. The *critic* counterbalances the zeal of the champion by challenging the concept and providing a reality test against hard-nosed criteria. The critic prevents people in the other roles from adopting a bad idea.[24]

Managers can directly influence whether champions will flourish. When Texas Instruments studied 50 of its new-product introductions, a surprising fact emerged: Without exception, every new product that had failed had lacked a zealous champion. In contrast, most of the new products that succeeded had a champion. Texas Instruments' managers made an immediate decision: No new product would be approved unless someone championed it. Researchers have also found that the new ideas that succeed are generally those that are backed by someone who believes in the idea wholeheartedly and is determined to convince others of its value.[25]

Another way to facilitate corporate innovation is through a new-venture team. A **new-venture team** is a unit separate from the rest of the organization that is responsible for developing and initiating a major innovation.[26] New-venture teams give free reign to members' creativity because their separate facilities and location free them from organizational rules and procedures. These teams typically are small, loosely structured, and flexible, reflecting the characteristics of creative organizations described in Exhibit 12.2. Peter Drucker advises organizations that wish to innovate to use a separate team or department:

> For the existing business to be capable of innovation, it has to create a structure that allows people to be entrepreneurial. . . . This means, first, that the entrepreneurial, the new, has to be organized separately from the old and the existing. Whenever we have tried to make an existing unit the carrier of the entrepreneurial project, we have failed.[27]

One variation of a new venture team is called a *skunkworks*.[28] A **skunkworks** is a separate small, informal, highly autonomous, and often secretive group that

new-venture team
A unit separate from the mainstream of the organization that is responsible for developing and initiating innovations.

skunkworks
A separate small, informal, highly autonomous, and often secretive group that focuses on breakthrough ideas for the business.

Exhibit *12.3*

Four Roles in Organizational Change

Inventor	Champion	Sponsor	Critic
Develops and understands technical aspects of idea	Believes in idea	High-level manager who removes organizational barriers	Provides reality test
Does not know how to win support for the idea or make a business of it	Visualizes benefits	Approves and protects idea within organization	Looks for shortcomings
	Confronts organizational realities of cost, benefits		Defines hard-nosed criteria that idea must pass
	Obtains financial and political support		
	Overcomes obstacles		

SOURCES: Based on Harold L. Angle and Andrew H. Van de Ven, "Suggestions for Managing the Innovation Journey," in *Research in the Management of Innovation: The Minnesota Studies*, ed. A. H. Van de Ven, H. L. Angle, and Marshall Scott Poole (Cambridge, Mass.: Ballinger/Harper & Row, 1989); and Jay R. Galbraith, "Designing the Innovating Organization," *Organizational Dynamics* (Winter 1982), 5–25.

focuses on breakthrough ideas for the business. The original skunkworks, which still exists, was created by Lockheed Martin more than 50 years ago. The essence of a skunkworks is that highly talented people are given the time and freedom to let creativity reign.[29] The laser printer was invented by a Xerox researcher who was transferred to the Xerox Palo Alto Research Center (PARC) after his ideas about using lasers were stifled within the company for being "too impractical and expensive."[30]

A related idea is the **new venture fund**, which provides resources from which individuals and groups can draw to develop new ideas, products, or businesses. Intel, for example, has been highly successful with new venture funds that provide resources to small companies to develop ideas that will benefit the larger organization.[31]

Another popular way to facilitate the development of new ideas in-house is the *idea incubator*. An **idea incubator** is run entirely in-house but provides a safe harbor where ideas from employees throughout the organization can be developed without interference from company bureaucracy or politics.[32] One value of an internal incubator is that an employee with a good idea has somewhere to go with it, rather than having to shop the idea all over the company and hope someone pays attention. Companies as diverse as Boeing, Adobe Systems, Ball Aerospace, United Parcel Service, and Ziff Davis are using incubators to quickly produce products and services related to the company's core business.[33]

new venture fund
A fund providing resources from which individuals and groups can draw to develop new ideas, products, or businesses.

idea incubator
An in-house program that provides a safe harbor where ideas from employees throughout the organization can be developed without interference from company bureaucracy or politics.

Implementing Change

Creative culture, idea champions, new-venture teams, and idea incubators are ways to facilitate the initiation and development of new ideas. The other step to be managed in the change process is implementation. A new, creative idea will not benefit the organization until it is in place and being fully utilized. One frustration for managers is that employees often seem to resist change for no apparent reason. To effectively manage the implementation process, managers should be aware of the reasons for employee resistance and be prepared to use techniques for obtaining employee cooperation. Major, corporate-wide changes can be particularly difficult, as discussed in the Shoptalk box.

Resistance to Change

Idea champions often discover that other employees are unenthusiastic about their new ideas. Members of a new-venture group may be surprised when managers in the regular organization do not support or approve their innovations. Managers and employees not involved in an innovation often seem to prefer the status quo. Employees appear to resist change for several reasons, and understanding them helps managers implement change more effectively.

Self-Interest.   Employees typically resist a change they believe will take away something of value. A proposed change in job design, structure, or technology may lead to a real or perceived loss of power, prestige, pay, or company benefits. The fear of personal loss is perhaps the biggest obstacle to organizational change.[34] When Federated Department Stores announced in 2002 that it was closing Fingerhut, a division it had acquired in 1999, Fingerhut employees were so outraged that they staged a demonstration outside Federated's Cincinnati, Ohio, headquarters. Employees at Fingerhut argued that the company had three prospective buyers, but that Federated was interested only in

Making Change Stick

Employees are not always receptive to change. A combination of factors can lead to rejection of, or even outright rebellion against, management's "new and better ideas."

Land's End, Inc., of Dodgeville, Wisconsin, began as a small mail-order business specializing in sailing gear. Employees enjoyed the family-like atmosphere and uncomplicated work environment. By the mid-1990s, the company had mushroomed into a $1 billion company with several overseas outlets and had passed giant L. L. Bean as number one in specialty catalog sales in the United States.

Such success encouraged founder and chairman Gary Comer to embark on a dramatic management experiment incorporating many of today's trends—teams, 401 (k) plans, peer reviews, and the elimination of guards and time clocks. Comer brought in top talent, including former L. L. Bean executive William T. End as CEO, to implement the changes.

But employees balked. Weekly production meetings became a nuisance. "We spent so much time in meetings that we were getting away from the basic stuff of taking care of business," says one employee. Even a much-ballyhooed new mission statement seemed "pushy." One long-time employee complained that "we don't need anything hanging over our heads telling us to do something we're already doing."

Confusion and frustration reigned at Land's End and was reflected in an earnings drop of 17 percent. Eventually, End left the company, and a new CEO initiated a return to the familiar "Land's End Way" of doing things. Teams were disbanded, and many of the once-promising initiatives were shelved as workers embraced what was familiar and uncomplicated.

The inability of people to adapt to change is not new. Neither is the failure of management to sufficiently lay the groundwork to prepare employees for change. Harvard professor John P. Kotter established an eight-step plan for implementing change that can provide a greater potential for successful transformation of a company:

1. Establish a sense of urgency through careful examination of the market and identification of opportunities and potential crises.
2. Form a powerful coalition of managers able to lead the change.
3. Create a vision to direct the change and the strategies for achieving that vision.
4. Communicate the vision throughout the organization.
5. Empower others to act on the vision by removing barriers, changing systems, and encouraging risk taking.
6. Plan for visible, short-term performance improvements and create those improvements.
7. Consolidate improvements, reassess changes, and make necessary adjustments in the new programs.
8. Articulate the relationship between new behaviors and organizational success.

Major change efforts can be messy and full of surprises, but following these guidelines can break down resistance and mean the difference between success and failure.

SOURCES: Gregory A. Patterson, "Land's End Kicks Out Modern New Managers, Rejecting a Makeover," *The Wall Street Journal* (April 3, 1995), A1, A6; and John P. Kotter, "Leading Changes: Why Transformation Efforts Fail," *Harvard Business Review* (March–April 1995), 59–67.

---

liquidating Fingerhut. In this case, the interests of Fingerhut's employees were definitely at odds with those of Federated's management.[35]

Lack of Understanding and Trust.   Employees often do not understand the intended purpose of a change or distrust the intentions behind it. If previous working relationships with an idea champion have been negative, resistance may occur. One manager had a habit of initiating a change in the financial reporting system about every 12 months and then losing interest and not following through. After the third time, employees no longer went along with the change because they did not trust the manager's intention to follow through to their benefit.

Uncertainty.   *Uncertainty* is the lack of information about future events. It represents a fear of the unknown. Uncertainty is especially threatening for employees who have a low tolerance for change and fear the novel and unusual. They do not know how a change will affect them and worry about whether they will be able to meet the demands of a new procedure or technology.[36] Union leaders at General Motors' Steering Gear Division in Saginaw, Michigan, resisted the introduction of employee participation programs. They were uncertain about how the program would affect their status and thus initially opposed it.

Different Assessments and Goals.   Another reason for resistance to change is that people who will be affected by innovation may assess the situation differently from an idea champion or new-venture group. Often critics voice legitimate disagreements over the proposed benefits of a change. Managers in each department pursue different goals, and an innovation may detract from performance and goal achievement for some departments. For example, if marketing gets the new product it wants for its customers, the cost of manufacturing may increase, and the manufacturing superintendent thus will resist. Resistance may call attention to problems with the innovation. At a consumer products company in Racine, Wisconsin, middle managers resisted the introduction of a new employee program that turned out to be a bad idea. The managers truly believed that the program would do more harm than good.[37]

These reasons for resistance are legitimate in the eyes of employees affected by the change. The best procedure for managers is not to ignore resistance but to diagnose the reasons and design strategies to gain acceptance by users.[38] Strategies for overcoming resistance to change typically involve two approaches: the analysis of resistance through the force-field technique and the use of selective implementation tactics to overcome resistance.

Force-Field Analysis

Force-field analysis grew from the work of Kurt Lewin, who proposed that change was a result of the competition between *driving* and *restraining forces*.[39] Driving forces can be thought of as problems or opportunities that provide motivation for change within the organization. Restraining forces are the various barriers to change, such as a lack of resources, resistance from middle managers, or inadequate employee skills. When a change is introduced, management should analyze both the forces that drive change (problems and opportunities) as well as the forces that resist it (barriers to change). By selectively removing forces that restrain change, the driving forces will be strong enough to enable implementation, as illustrated by the move from A to B in Exhibit 12.4. As barriers are reduced or removed, behavior will shift to incorporate the desired changes.

Just-in-time (JIT) inventory control systems schedule materials to arrive at a company just as they are needed on the production line. In an Ohio manufacturing company, management's analysis showed that the driving forces (opportunities) associated with the implementation of JIT were (1) the large cost savings from reduced inventories, (2) savings from needing fewer workers to handle the inventory, and (3) a quicker, more competitive market response for the company. Restraining forces (barriers) discovered by managers were (1) a freight system that was too slow to deliver inventory on time, (2) a facility layout that emphasized inventory maintenance over new deliveries, (3) worker skills inappropriate for handling rapid inventory deployment, and (4) union resistance to loss of jobs. The driving forces were not sufficient to overcome the restraining forces.

force-field analysis
The process of determining which forces drive and which resist a proposed change.

Exhibit *12.4*

Using Force-Field Analysis to Change from Traditional to Just-in-Time Inventory System

To shift the behavior to JIT, managers attacked the barriers. An analysis of the freight system showed that delivery by truck provided the flexibility and quickness needed to schedule inventory arrival at a specific time each day. The problem with facility layout was met by adding four new loading docks. Inappropriate worker skills were attacked with a training program to instruct workers in JIT methods and in assembling products with uninspected parts. Union resistance was overcome by agreeing to reassign workers no longer needed for maintaining inventory to jobs in another plant. With the restraining forces reduced, the driving forces were sufficient to allow the JIT system to be implemented.

Implementation Tactics

The other approach to managing implementation is to adopt specific tactics to overcome employee resistance. For example, resistance to change may be overcome by educating employees or inviting them to participate in implementing the change. Researchers have studied various methods for dealing with resistance to change. The following five tactics, summarized in Exhibit 12.5, have proven successful.[40]

Exhibit *12.5*

Tactics for Overcoming Resistance to Change

Approach	When to Use
Communication, education	• Change is technical. • Users need accurate information and analysis to understand change.
Participation	• Users need to feel involved. • Design requires information from others. • Users have power to resist.
Negotiation	• Group has power over implementation. • Group will lose out in the change.
Coercion	• A crisis exists. • Initiators clearly have power. • Other implementation techniques have failed.
Top management support	• Change involves multiple departments or reallocation of resources. • Users doubt legitimacy of change.

SOURCE: Based on J.P. Kotter and L.A. Schlesinger, "Choosing Strategies for Change," *Harvard Business Review 57* (March–April 1979), 106–114.

Communication and Education. *Communication* and *education* are used when solid information about the change is needed by users and others who may resist implementation. Education is especially important when the change involves new technical knowledge or users are unfamiliar with the idea. Canadian Airlines International spent a year and a half preparing and training employees before changing its entire reservations, airport, cargo, and financial systems as part of a new "Service Quality" strategy. Smooth implementation resulted from this intensive training and communications effort, which involved 50,000 tasks, 12,000 people, and 26 classrooms around the world.[41]

Participation. *Participation* involves users and potential resisters in designing the change. This approach is time-consuming, but it pays off because users understand and become committed to the change. Participation also helps managers determine potential problems and understand the differences in perceptions of change among employees.[42] When General Motors tried to implement a new management appraisal system for supervisors in its Adrian, Michigan, plant, it met with immediate resistance. Rebuffed by the lack of cooperation, top managers proceeded more slowly, involving supervisors in the design of the new appraisal system. Through participation in system design, managers understood what the new approach was all about and dropped their resistance to it.

Negotiation. Negotiation is a more formal means of achieving cooperation. *Negotiation* uses formal bargaining to win acceptance and approval of a desired change. For example, if the marketing department fears losing power if a new management structure is implemented, top managers may negotiate with marketing to reach a resolution. Companies that have strong unions frequently must formally negotiate change with the unions. The change may become part of the union contract reflecting the agreement of both parties. For example, when General Motors changed the way it runs Saturn, a part of implementation involved negotiating new labor rules with the United Auto Workers union local.

Coercion. *Coercion* means that managers use formal power to force employees to change. Resisters are told to accept the change or lose rewards or even their jobs. In most cases, this approach should not be used because employees feel like victims, are angry at change managers, and may even sabotage the changes. However, coercion may be necessary in crisis situations when a rapid response is urgent. For example, a number of top managers at Coca-Cola were reassigned or forced out after they refused to go along with new CEO Douglas Daft's changes for revitalizing the sluggish corporation.[43]

Top Management Support. The visible support of top management also helps overcome resistance to change. *Top management support* symbolizes to all employees that the change is important for the organization. Top management support is especially important when a change involves multiple departments or when resources are being reallocated among departments. Without top management support, these changes can get bogged down in squabbling among departments. Moreover, when top managers fail to support a project, they can inadvertently undercut it by issuing contradictory orders. This happened at Flying Tiger Lines before it was acquired by Federal Express. The airborne freight hauler came up with a plan to eliminate excessive paperwork by changing the

Herman Wright, PruCare of Austin's director of sales and marketing, shown here with his sales and service staff, knows that top management support *is essential to overcoming resistance to change. In PruCare's thrust toward customer satisfaction, Wright used the implementation tactics of communication and participation. He communicated his desire to build customer relationships based on trust and then pushed responsibility down to everyone in the organization: "We stopped telling people what to do and started listening."*

©1994 Bill Albrecht

layout of offices so that two agents rather than four could handle each shipment. No sooner had part of the change been implemented than top management ordered another system; thus, the office layout was changed again. The new layout was not as efficient, but it was the one that top management supported. Had middle managers informed top managers and obtained their support earlier, the initial change would not have been defeated by a new priority.[44]

The following example illustrates how smart implementation techniques can smooth the change process.

GENERAL STAIR CORPORATION
http://generalstair.com

General Stair Corp., a maker of prefabricated stairs and railings, was facing a desperate situation in the mid-1990s. Competition was increasing, and General Stair's profit and market share were declining. The company found itself dealing with a constant price war. To distinguish his company from the competition, founder Saby Behar decided General Stair should start offering a money-back delivery guarantee, something he knew his customers (who often worked on 30 or more buildings at a time) would appreciate. However, managers and other employees were aghast at the suggestion. Workers weren't sure they could meet the requirements for such a guarantee and were concerned that it might require more overtime. Managers worried about the cost of upgrading communications systems for field reps to stay in touch with headquarters as well as builders and contractors.

Implementation of the change involved several steps. To combat the initial resistance among his managers, Behar held several meetings explaining his reasons for making the change and answering managers' questions. This at least got people talking about whether and how such a guarantee could actually work. Next, managers brought in the rest of the employees to discuss the proposed change and how to put it into action. They knew they had to revamp communications, but discussions with employees led them to realize other systems, such as distribution and compensation, needed to change as well. In addition, rather than a complete money-back guarantee, the group eventually settled on a fine of $50 per day for late deliveries. Although the company already had a good on-time delivery record, employees were trained in new procedures that would help assure consistent performance.

Because top management involved employees from the early stages, the changes went smoothly. Labor costs were slashed by 30 percent, even though employees were earning up to 60 percent more money because of a new piece-rate system. Productivity was up 300 percent. And, within the first year, the company had to pay out only a few $50 vouchers for late deliveries. General Stair's market share and profits are once again looking healthy.[45] ❖

Types of Planned Change

Now that we have explored how the initiation and implementation of change can be carried out, let us look at the different types of change that occur in organizations. We will address two issues: what parts of the organization can be changed and how managers can apply the initiation and implementation ideas to each type of change.

The types of organizational change are strategy, technology, products, structure, and culture/people, as illustrated in Exhibit 12.6. Organizations may innovate in one or more areas, depending on internal and external forces for change. In the rapidly changing toy industry, a manufacturer has to introduce new products frequently. In a mature, competitive industry, production technology changes are adopted to improve efficiency. The arrows connecting the types of change in Exhibit 12.6 show that a change in one part may affect other parts of the organization: A new product may require changes in technology, and a new technology may require new people skills or a new structure. For example, when Shenandoah Life Insurance Company computerized processing and claims operations, the structure had to be decentralized, employees required intensive training, and a more participative culture was needed. Related changes were required for the new technology to increase efficiency.

Technology Changes

A **technology change** is related to the organization's production process—how the organization does its work. Technology changes are designed to make the production of a product or service more efficient. The adoption of automatic mail-sorting machines by the U.S. Postal Service is an example of a technology change, as is the adoption by supermarkets of laser scanning checkout systems linked to computers that provide instant inventory information. These are examples of technology change in service organizations. Manufacturing organizations also adopt many technology changes. For

technology change
A change that pertains to the organization's production process.

E x h i b i t *12.6*

Types of Organizational Change

SOURCE: Based on Harold J. Leavitt, "Applied Organizational Change in Industry: Structural, Technical, and Human Approaches," in *New Perspectives in Organization Research*, ed. W. W. Cooper, H. J. Leavitt, and M. W. Shelly II (New York: Wiley, 1964), 55–74.

The Boeing Company

Technology changes *in computers and aircraft design allow Boeing Company aircraft designers to skip the paper drawings and work in teams with input from the airlines, mechanics, and marketers. These Boeing designers working on the 777 wide-body, twin-jet program can use the new technology to reduce errors through digital design and preassembly. A three-dimensional digital mechanic can crawl through on-screen aircraft images to locate defects. This technology allows designers to test innovative ideas without the cost of building a full mock-up.*

product change
A change in the organization's product or service output.

example, at Dana Corporation's Elizabethtown, Kentucky, plant, a new system for automatically loading steel sheets into a forming press was a technology change that saved the auto parts manufacturer $250,000 a year.[46]

How can managers encourage technology change? The general rule is that technology change is bottom up.[47] The *bottom-up approach* means that ideas are initiated at lower organization levels and channeled upward for approval. Lower-level technical experts act as idea champions—they invent and champion technological changes. Employees at lower levels understand the technology and have the expertise needed to propose changes.

Managers can facilitate the bottom-up approach by designing creative departments as described earlier in this chapter. A loose, flexible, decentralized structure provides employees with the freedom and opportunity to initiate continuous improvements. A rigid, centralized, standardized structure stifles technology innovation. Anything managers can do to involve the grass roots of the organization—the people who are experts in their parts of the production process—will increase technology change. Great Harvest Bread Company encourages bottom-up change among its franchisees by giving them almost complete freedom to run their businesses as they see fit. This freedom inspires new and better ways of doing things that quickly spread to other stores by phone, fax, and e-mail.[48]

A *top-down approach* to technology change usually does not work.[49] Top managers are not close to the production process and lack expertise in technological developments. Mandating technology change from the top produces fewer rather than more technology innovations. The spark for a creative new idea comes from people close to the technology.

New-Product Changes

A **product change** is a change in the organization's product or service output. New-product innovations have major implications for an organization, because they often are an outcome of a new strategy and may define a new market.[50] In addition, product life cycles are getting shorter, so that companies need to continuously come up with innovative ideas for new products and services that meet needs in the marketplace. Product innovation is the primary way in which many organizations adapt to changes in markets, technologies, and competition.[51] Examples of new products include Mountain Dew Code Red, the Buick Rendezvous, and Gillette's Venus razor for women.

Introducing a new product is not easy, but hundreds of new products are introduced every day. Even though the cost of successfully launching a new product is $20 million to $50 million, approximately 25,000 new products appeared in one recent year, including 5,000 new toys. [52] Many of those products will fail in the marketplace. Estimates are that between 33 and 60 percent of all new products that reach the marketplace never generate an economic return.[53] Consider such flops as the Apple Newton, Procter & Gamble's Fit Produce wash, or Gerber's "Singles," a line of meals for adults. Product development is a risky, high-stakes game for organizations. Companies that successfully develop new products usually have the following characteristics:

1. People in marketing have a good understanding of customer needs.
2. Technical specialists are aware of recent technological developments and make effective use of new technology.

3. Members from key departments—research, manufacturing, marketing—cooperate in the development of the new product.[54]

These findings mean that the ideas for new products typically originate at the lower levels of the organization just as they do for technology changes. The difference is that new-product ideas flow horizontally among departments. Product innovation requires expertise from several departments simultaneously. A new-product failure is often the result of failed cooperation.[55]

One approach to successful new-product innovation is called the **horizontal linkage model**, which is illustrated in Exhibit 12.7.[56] The model shows that research, manufacturing, and marketing must simultaneously develop new products. People from these departments meet frequently in teams and task forces to share ideas and solve problems. Research people inform marketing of new technical developments to learn whether they will be useful to customers. Marketing people pass customer complaints to research to use in the design of new products. Manufacturing informs other departments whether a product idea can be manufactured within cost limits. When the horizontal linkage model is used, the decision to develop a new product is a joint one.

In addition, today's most successful companies are including customers, strategic partners, and suppliers in the product development process. For example, during Boeing's development of the 777, flight attendants, pilots, and engineers from major airlines worked closely with Boeing's engineers to make sure the new plane was designed for maximum functionality and comfort. Representatives from key suppliers such as General Electric were also included on the project team, so that the plane would be designed for compatibility with suppliers.[57] 3M, recognized as one of the most innovative companies in the world, goes to great lengths to understand the needs of potential customers. 3M's product development process involves cross-functional teams that develop close working relationships with leading-edge customers and other outsiders.[58] Consider 3M's Medical-Surgical Markets Division.

horizontal linkage model
An approach to product change that emphasizes shared development of innovations among several departments.

To identify new customer needs and develop radical new ways of looking for product ideas, 3M's Medical-Surgical Markets Division turned to something called the *lead-user process*. Many great products are first thought of by users to meet specific needs, rather than by manufacturers. 3M's innovation process brings together teams from various functional areas within the company, who then work with outside people and companies who have leading-edge expertise in areas related to a product.

Rita Shor, a senior product specialist, and her co-leader, Susan Hiestand, put together a team of people from R&D, marketing, and manufacturing to search for a better and less expensive way to prevent the spread of infection in hospitals. The team spent the first month conducting research and interviewing specialists inside and outside the company. Then, team members worked directly

3M MEDICAL-SURGICAL MARKETS DIVISION
http://www.3m.com/healthcare/

Organization

E x h i b i t **12.7**

Horizontal Linkage Model for New-Product Innovation

with doctors, especially in developing countries where infectious diseases are still major killers and traditional products have been financially out of reach. This led to searching out people who were on the cutting edge of inexpensive infection control. One surprising source of information was veterinary hospitals. As one of the country's foremost veterinary surgeons told the team, "Our patients are covered with hair, they don't bathe, and they don't have medical insurance, so the infection controls we use can't cost much." Another source of ideas was Hollywood, where makeup artists have developed tricks for using materials that adhere well to the skin, are not irritating, and can be removed easily.

The final step was to bring all these people together in a two-and-a-half-day workshop to help the team generate concepts for new products. Although 3M naturally does not want to disclose details about the product ideas that came out of this extraordinary process, managers believe the ideas will open up major new markets for 3M.[59] ❖

time-based competition

A strategy of competition based on the ability to deliver products and services faster than competitors.

structural changes

Any change in the way in which the organization is designed and managed.

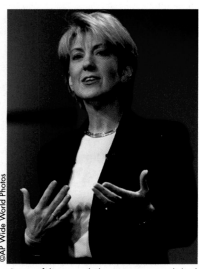

©AP Wide World Photos

Successful structural change is accomplished through a top-down approach. Hewlett-Packard Co. Chief Executive Carleton S. Fiorina is managing HP through the changes caused by her company's proposal to purchase Compaq Computer Corp. If the merger goes through, HP's congenial, egalitarian culture will careen headlong into Compaq's confrontational one. In addition, blending the two companies will require melding operations in 160 countries, trimming redundant product lines, cutting the workforce, and many other structural changes. Despite the difficulties, Fiorina remains bold and unflinching: "We started this because we think it's the right thing to do."

This approach to breakthrough thinking has now been used in several of 3M's 55 divisions, and many other leading companies are using similar approaches compatible with the horizontal linkage model to increase innovation.

Innovation is becoming a major strategic weapon in the global marketplace. One example of innovation is the use of **time-based competition**, which means delivering products and services faster than competitors, giving companies a significant strategic advantage. For example, by using the Internet to collaborate on new designs with suppliers, Moen teams take a new kitchen or bath faucet from drawing board to store shelf in only 16 months. The time savings means engineers can work on three times as many projects and introduce up to15 new designs a year for today's fashion-conscious consumers, helping Moen move from number three in market share to a tie for number one with rival Delta Faucet Co.[60] Dillard's department stores went to an automatic reorder system that replenishes stocks in 12 days rather than 30, providing retail goods to customers more quickly.[61] Sprinting to market with a new product requires a *parallel approach*, or *simultaneous linkage* among departments. This is similar to a rugby match wherein players run together, passing the ball back and forth as they move downfield. The teamwork required for the horizontal linkage model is a major component of using rapid innovation to beat the competition with speed.[62]

Structural Changes

Structural changes involve the hierarchy of authority, goals, structural characteristics, administrative procedures, and management systems.[63] Almost any change in how the organization is managed falls under the category of structural change. For example, to revitalize consumer-goods giant Procter & Gamble, managers reorganized into seven global business units based on product categories, spent billions on new information technology systems, and decentralized the IT staff so that IT employees now work in P&G's individual product, market, and business teams.[64]

Other examples of structural or administrative change include shifting to a team-based structure, implementing no-smoking policies, and centralizing information and accounting systems. At Nestlé USA, CEO Joe Weller has initiated a number of structural changes, as described in this chapter's Leading Online box.

Leading Online

Nestlé: Making "E-business the Way We Do Business"

Leaders at Nestlé USA are turning to the Internet to change everything about how the giant company operates, from buying raw materials to processing purchase orders, to marketing the company's 2,000 or so products, such as Nestlé Crunch bars, Toll House cookie dough, and Lean Cuisine frozen dinners. The size and past success of the company make some people reluctant to change (the "if it ain't broke, don't fix it" mindset), but top managers are determined to gradually implement administrative and structural changes to help reach Chairman and CEO Joe Weller's goal to "make e-business the way we do business."

Change at Nestlé USA, the largest subsidiary of the world's largest food company, began literally at the top—on the 21st floor of the company's glass-and-steel headquarters office building in Glendale, California. Top managers rolled up their Oriental rugs and moved their offices down several floors to work more closely with people in the trenches, turning the former executive suites into meeting rooms and temporary office space for telecommuters and virtual workers. Weller also implemented a number of top-down changes designed to make the company a leaner, faster organization. One was the "No meetings after 10 A.M.. on Friday" rule. Weller believed people were spending so much time in meetings that they did not have time to think about strategy and

long-term goals. Another was his "Blueprint for Success" document, a two-sided sheet of paper that serves as a mission statement as well as a guide for turning Nestlé into a fast-moving, entrepreneurial company.

But the biggest change is the Internet strategy itself. Instead of creating a separate e-business division, top leaders decided to make e-business an integral part of every division and department in the company. Each operating division was assigned an "e-business catalyst" who helps managers develop business-to-consumer (B2C) and business-to-business (B2B) functions. The company's overall B2C strategy is focused on creating sites that help and inform consumers rather than push Nestlé's brands. A VeryBestBaking.com site offers recipes and cooking tips; VeryBestPets.com gives advice on grooming, health care, and nutrition for dogs and cats. The goal is that the sites will increase the percentage of consumers who have a "bonded relationship" to Nestlé products. As for B2B, the company recently launched NestléEZOrder, which will eliminate many of the 100,000 phone and fax orders the company gets each year—and the high transaction costs that go along with them.

Nestlé's top managers still face challenges getting buy-in for all these structural changes from employees, but they believe with careful implementation the changes will take root and become the everyday way the company does business.

SOURCE: Bill Breen, "Change is Sweet," *Fast Company* (June 2001), 168–177.

Successful structural change is accomplished through a top-down approach, which is distinct from technology change (bottom up) and new products (horizontal).[65] Structural change is top down because the expertise for administrative improvements originates at the middle and upper levels of the organization. The champions for structural change are middle and top managers. Lower-level technical specialists have little interest or expertise in administrative procedures. If organization structure causes negative consequences for lower-level employees, complaints and dissatisfaction alert managers to a problem. Employee dissatisfaction is an internal force for change. The need for change is perceived by higher managers, who then take the initiative to propose and implement it.

The top-down process does not mean that coercion is the best implementation tactic. Implementation tactics include education, participation, and negotiation with employees. Unless there is an emergency, managers should not force structural change on employees. They may hit a resistance wall, and the change will fail. Andrea Jung, CEO of Avon, is keeping this in mind as she attempts to take the cosmetics company onto the Web and into retail stores, moves that could seriously threaten the sales and profits of the company's independent sales representatives. When the company first printed its Web site address on the catalog, many reps covered it up with their own stickers and complained so forcefully that the company quickly removed it. Now, Jung is trying to involve sales reps closely in every step the company takes toward a new way of doing business. The emphasis she puts on the importance of the independent sales force has more "Avon Ladies" signing up than ever before.[66]

Top-down change means that initiation of the idea occurs at upper levels and is implemented downward. It does not mean that lower-level employees are not educated about the change or allowed to participate in it.

Culture/People Changes

culture/people change
A change in employees' values, norms, attitudes, beliefs, and behavior.

A **culture/people change** refers to a change in employees' values, norms, attitudes, beliefs, and behavior. Changes in culture and people pertain to how employees think; these are changes in mindset rather than technology, structure, or products and services. *People change* pertains to just a few employees, such as when a handful of middle managers is sent to a training course to improve their leadership skills. *Culture change* pertains to the organization as a whole, such as when Union Pacific Railroad changed its basic mindset by becoming less bureaucratic and focusing employees on customer service and quality through teamwork and employee participation.[67] Two specific tools for changing people and culture are training and development programs and organizational development (OD).

Training and Development

Training is one of the most frequently used approaches to changing the organization's mindset. A company might offer training programs to large blocks of employees on subjects such as teamwork, diversity, emotional intelligence, quality circles, communication skills, or participative management. Training and development programs aimed at changing individual behavior and interpersonal skills have become a big business for consultants, universities, and training firms.

Some companies particularly emphasize training and development for managers, with the idea that the behavior and attitudes of managers will influence people throughout the organization and lead to culture change. A number of Silicon Valley companies, including Intel, Sun Microsystems, and Netscape, regularly send managers to the Growth and Leadership Center (GLC), where they learn to use emotional intelligence to build better relationships. Nick Kepler, director of technology development at Advanced Micro Devices Inc., was surprised to learn how his emotionless approach to work was intimidating people and destroying the rapport needed to shift to a culture based on collaborative teamwork.[68]

Leading companies also want to provide training and development opportunities for everyone. An excellent example of training is First Data Corp., which uses a multifaceted, team-based approach first initiated by CFO Kim Patmore to boost morale among finance personnel.[69] First Data's "Extreme Teams" bring together employees from all hierarchical levels to organize departmental training and development programs for each of First Data's six regional finance units. One team is charged with organizing a mentoring program that pairs less-experienced personnel with seasoned managers who support and encourage them to make changes needed to further their own and the organization's well-being. Another team focuses on a program called *Fast Tracks*, an annual two-day seminar that brings people from all areas and levels of the company together to learn skills such as communication or conflict resolution.

Organizational Development

Organizational development (OD) is a planned, systematic process of change that uses behavioral science knowledge and techniques to improve an organization's health and effectiveness through its ability to adapt to the environment, improve internal relationships, and increase learning and problem-solving capabilities.[70] OD focuses on the human and social aspects of the organization and works to change individual attitudes and relationships among employees.[71]

The following are three types of current problems that OD can help managers address.[72]

1. *Mergers/acquisitions.* The disappointing financial results of many mergers and acquisitions are caused by the failure of executives to determine whether the administrative style and corporate culture of the two companies fit. Executives may concentrate on potential synergies in technology, products, marketing, and control systems but fail to recognize that two firms may have widely different values, beliefs, and practices. These differences create stress and anxiety for employees, and these negative emotions affect future performance. Cultural differences should be evaluated during the acquisition process, and OD experts can be used to smooth the integration of two firms.

2. *Organizational decline/revitalization.* Organizations undergoing a period of decline and revitalization experience a variety of problems, including a low level of trust, lack of innovation, high turnover, and high levels of conflict and stress. The period of transition requires opposite behaviors, including confronting stress, creating open communication, and fostering creative innovation to emerge with high levels of productivity. OD techniques can contribute greatly to cultural revitalization by managing conflicts, fostering commitment, and facilitating communication.

3. *Conflict management.* Conflict can occur at any time and place within a healthy organization. For example, a product team for the introduction of a new software package was formed at a computer company. Made up of strong-willed individuals, the team made little progress because members could not agree on project goals. At a manufacturing firm, salespeople promised delivery dates to customers that were in conflict with shop supervisor priorities for assembling customer orders. In a publishing company, two managers disliked each other intensely. They argued at meetings, lobbied politically against each other, and hurt the achievement of both departments. Organizational development efforts can help solve these kinds of conflicts.

organizational development (OD)
The application of behavioral science techniques to improve an organization's health and effectiveness through its ability to cope with environmental changes, improve internal relationships, and increase learning and problem-solving capabilities.

Lincoln Electric in Cleveland, Ohio, has one of the oldest and most radical pay-for-performance incentive programs in the country. The Lincoln Electric system paid employees up to 100 percent of their wages in annual performance bonuses. However, due to recent global competition and an increase in institutional shareholders, workers' bonuses have decreased while revenues reached $1 billion. Many workers are concerned about future bonus reductions. As managers struggle to meet new competitive threats, they may use organizational development techniques to adapt to current conditions without sacrificing employee goodwill.

©Daniel Levin

Organizational development can be used to solve the types of problems just described and many others. However, to be truly valuable to companies and employees, organizational development practitioners go beyond looking at ways to solve specific problems. Instead, they become involved in broader issues that contribute to improving organizational life, such as encouraging a sense of community, pushing for an organizational climate of openness and trust, and making sure the company provides employees with opportunities for personal growth and development.[73] Specialized techniques have been developed to help meet OD goals.

OD Activities.   A number of OD activities have emerged in recent years. Three of the most popular and effective are as follows.

1. *Team-building activities.* **Team building** enhances the cohesiveness and success of organizational groups and teams. For example, a series of OD exercises can be used with members of cross-departmental teams to help them learn to act and function as a team. An OD expert can work with team members to increase their communication skills, facilitate their ability to confront one another, and accept common goals.

2. *Survey-feedback activities.* **Survey feedback** begins with a questionnaire distributed to employees on values, climate, participation, leadership, and group cohesion within their organization. After the survey is completed, an OD consultant meets with groups of employees to provide feedback about their responses and the problems identified. Employees are engaged in problem solving based on the data.

3. *Large-Group Interventions.* In recent years, there has been a growing interest in applications of OD techniques to large group settings, which are more attuned to bringing about fundamental organizational change in today's complex, fast-changing world.[74] The **large-group intervention** approach brings together participants from all parts of the organization— often including key stakeholders from outside the organization as well—to discuss problems or opportunities and plan for change. A large-group intervention might involve 50 to 500 people and last several days. The idea is to include everyone who has a stake in the change, gather perspectives from all parts of the system, and enable people to create a collective future through sustained, guided conversation and dialogue.

Large-group interventions reflect a significant shift in the approach to organizational change from earlier OD concepts and approaches. Exhibit 12.8 lists the primary differences between the traditional OD model and the large-scale intervention model of organizational change.[75] In the newer approach, the focus is on the entire system, which takes into account the organization's interaction with its environment. The source of information for discussion is expanded to include customers, suppliers, community members, even competitors, and this information is shared widely so that everyone has the same picture of the organization and its environment. The acceleration of change when the entire system is involved can be remarkable. In addition, learning occurs across all parts of the organization simultaneously, rather than in individuals, small groups, or business units. The end result is that the large-group approach offers greater possibilities for fundamental, radical transformation of the entire culture, whereas the traditional approach creates incremental change in a few individuals or small groups at a time. General Electric's Work Out Program provides an excellent example of the large-group intervention approach.

team building
A type of OD intervention that enhances the cohesiveness of departments by helping members learn to function as a team.

survey feedback
A type of OD intervention in which questionnaires on organizational climate and other factors are distributed among employees and their results reported back to them by a change agent.

large-group intervention
An approach that brings together participants from all parts of the organization (and may include key outside stakeholders as well) to discuss problems or opportunities and plan for major change.

	Traditional Organizational Development Model	**Large-Group Intervention Model**
Focus for action:	Specific problem or group	Entire system
Information		
Source:	Organization	Organization and environment
Distribution:	Limited	Widely shared
Time frame:	Gradual	Fast
Learning:	Individual, small group	Whole organization

Change process:	Incremental change	Rapid transformation

Exhibit 12.8

OD Approaches to Culture Change

SOURCE: Adapted from Barbara Benedict Bunker and Billie T. Alban, "Conclusion: What Makes Large Group Interventions Effective," *The Journal of Applied Behavioral Science* 28, no. 4 (December 1992), 579–591.

GE's Work Out began in large-scale off-site meetings facilitated by a combination of top leaders, outside consultants, and human resources specialists. In each business unit, the basic pattern was the same. Hourly and salaried workers came together from many different parts of the organization in an informal 3-day meeting to discuss and solve problems. Gradually, the Work Out events began to include external stakeholders such as suppliers and customers as well as employees. Today, Work Out is not an event, but a process of how work is done and problems are solved at GE.

The format for Work Out includes seven steps:

1. Choose a work process or problem for discussion.
2. Select an appropriate cross-functional team, to include external stakeholders.
3. Assign a "champion" to follow through on recommendations.
4. Meet for several days and come up with recommendations to improve processes or solve problems.
5. Meet with leaders, who are asked to respond to recommendations on the spot.
6. Hold additional meetings as needed to implement the recommendations.
7. Start the process all over again with a new process or problem.

GE's Work Out process not only solves problems and improves productivity for the company but also gives employees the experience of openly and honestly interacting with one another without regard to vertical or horizontal differences. By doing so, the process has helped to create a "culture of boundarylessness" that is critical for continuous learning and improvement.[76] ❖

GENERAL ELECTRIC
http://www.ge.com

Large-group interventions represent a significant shift in the way leaders think about change and reflect an increasing awareness of the importance of dealing with the entire system, including external stakeholders, in any significant change effort.

OD Steps. Consider the culture change at Rowe Furniture Corporation, which reduced the time for making and delivering custom-made pieces from six months to an amazing 10 days. A major aspect was a change in mindset of both managers and employees to give front-line employees more authority and responsibility, as well as open access to company information. Rather than waiting for supervisors to make decisions, every Rowe team now has instant access to up-to-date information about order flows, output, productivity, and quality and is empowered to make decisions and take action as needed to meet schedules and deadlines set by the teams themselves.[77]

Organizational development experts acknowledge that corporate culture and human behavior are relatively stable and that companywide changes, such as those at Rowe Furniture, require major effort. The theory underlying organizational development proposes three distinct stages for achieving behavioral and attitudinal change: (1) unfreezing, (2) changing, and (3) refreezing.[78] The Putting People First box describes how Alberto-Culver created a new employee-focused culture that helped turn the business around by following the stages of unfreezing, changing, and refreezing.

The first stage, **unfreezing**, means that people throughout the organization are made aware of problems and the need for change. This stage creates the motivation for people to change their attitudes and behaviors. Unfreezing may begin when managers present information that shows discrepancies between desired behaviors or performance and the current state of affairs. In addition, as we discussed earlier in the chapter, managers need to establish a sense of urgency to unfreeze people throughout the organization and create an openness and willingness to change. The unfreezing stage is often associated with *diagnosis*, which uses an outside expert called a *change agent*. The **change agent** is an OD specialist who performs a systematic diagnosis of the organization and identifies work-related problems. He or she gathers and analyzes data through personal interviews, questionnaires, and observations of meetings. The diagnosis helps determine the extent of organizational problems and helps unfreeze managers by making them aware of problems in their behavior.

The second stage, **changing**, occurs when individuals experiment with new behavior and learn new skills to be used in the workplace. This is sometimes known as *intervention*, during which the change agent implements a specific plan for training managers and employees. The changing stage might involve a number of specific steps.[79] Recall the eight steps for leading change from the Manager's Shoptalk box earlier in this chapter. For example, managers put together a coalition of people with the will and power to guide the change, create a vision for change that everyone can believe in, and widely communicate the vision and plans for change throughout the company. In addition, successful change involves empowering employees throughout the organization to act on the plan to accomplish the desired changes.

The third stage, **refreezing**, occurs when individuals acquire new attitudes or values and are rewarded for them by the organization. The impact of new behaviors is evaluated and reinforced. The change agent supplies new data that show positive changes in performance. Managers may provide updated data to employees that demonstrate positive changes in individual and organizational performance. Top executives celebrate successes and reward positive behavioral changes. This is the stage where changes are institutionalized in the organizational culture, so that employees begin to view the changes as a normal, integral part of how the organization operates. Employees may also participate in refresher courses to maintain and reinforce the new behaviors.

---

unfreezing
The stage of organizational development in which participants are made aware of problems in order to increase their willingness to change their behavior.

change agent
An OD specialist who contracts with an organization to facilitate change.

changing
The intervention stage of organizational development in which individuals experiment with new workplace behavior.

refreezing
The reinforcement stage of organizational development in which individuals acquire a desired new skill or attitude and are rewarded for it by the organization.

Putting People First

Alberto-Culver Gets a Cultural Makeover

"Do we make people happy and then the business gets better; or do we fix the business, which will make people happier?" That's the question top executives were asking Carol Lavin Bernick, president of Alberto-Culver North America. It became clear to Bernick that the company was facing a cultural crisis. For years, Alberto-Culver had suffered from general overall employee dissatisfaction, a turnover rate that was double the national average, deflated sales and slipping margins on their most popular brands, and an organization that was not equal to the challenge of an emerging competitive environment. Bernick wanted to make culture change a priority, but she had to find a way to get everyone throughout the organization committed to change.

She began the change process with a companywide meeting aimed at letting everyone know where the company stood and where it needed to go in the future (unfreezing). Before the meeting began, Bernick scattered pennies around the floor and observed employees as they entered the room—no one attempted to pick up a cent. "Can anyone name our best-selling product?" she asked. "VO5 shampoo!" came the resounding response. "Look around you on the floor, and if you see a penny, pick it up," Bernick continued. "That penny represents our total profit on a bottle of Alberto VO5 shampoo." Employees were already aware of many problems in the business, but this was an eye-opener. Thus began the process of creating a culture of honesty and shared ownership, where employees think like business people and act like team players.

The next stage (changing) involved creating a specific plan for change. One step was to develop a list of 10 cultural imperatives: honesty, ownership, trust, customer orientation, commitment, fun, innovation, risk taking, speed and urgency, and teamwork. Another was to create a specific role called the *growth development leader* (GDL). Each handpicked GDL mentors about a dozen people, helping to bring about culture change at the individual and small-group level. GDLs work to build team spirit and help people understand how their work fits into the big picture. One specific task is helping to spell out *Individual Economic Values*, or IEVs, short statements that describe how each individual contributes to the organization's productivity and profitability. With the IEVs, managers have given employees greater freedom and power to drive the success of the company. Growth development leaders also get intimately involved in people's lives and careers. For example, they help people set personal and professional goals that achieve the right balance for the individual, reinforcing the idea that Alberto-Culver is a company that respects and values its employees as individuals with lives outside of work.

Finally, Bernick needed to find ways to make the changes stick (refreezing). At every opportunity, managers reinforce the central cultural tenet that individuals can make a difference, and that companies don't succeed—people do. Managers regularly measure individual and organizational progress against the cultural goals. "I'm a firm believer that you change what you measure," says Bernick. "Once a year, we do an all-employee survey to assess our progress against cultural goals and to gather feedback." Managers also celebrate every success and reward people for exhibiting the attitudes and behaviors that fit the new culture, such as through stock options, Business Builder Awards, and People's Choice Awards. "If you want something to grow," claims Bernick, "pour champagne on it."

SOURCE: Carol Lavin Bernick, "When Your Culture Needs a Makeover," *Harvard Business Review* (June 2001), 53–61.

■ Summary and Management Solution

Change is inevitable in organizations. This chapter discussed the techniques available for managing the change process. One of the most dramatic elements of change for today's organizations is the shift to a technology-driven workplace and an emphasis on information and relationships. Current trends such as e-business require profound changes in the organization and may be associated with a shift to the learning organization, which embraces continuous learning and change. Managers should think of change as having four elements—the forces for change, the perceived need for change, the initiation of change, and the implementation of change. Forces for change can originate either within or outside the firm, and managers are responsible for monitoring events that may require a planned organizational response. Techniques for initiating changes include designing the organization for creativity, encouraging change agents, and establishing new-venture teams and idea incubators. The final step is implementation. Force field analysis is one technique for diagnosing barriers, which often can be removed. Managers also should draw on the implementation tactics of communication, participation, negotiation, coercion, or top management support.

This chapter also discussed specific types of change. Technology changes are accomplished through a bottom-up approach that utilizes experts close to the technology. Successful new-product introduction requires horizontal linkage among marketing, research and development, manufacturing, and perhaps other departments or customers, partners, and suppliers. Structural changes tend to be initiated in a top-down fashion, because upper managers are the administrative experts and champion these ideas for approval and implementation. Culture/people change pertains to the skills, behaviors, and attitudes of employees. Training and organizational development are important approaches to change people's mindset and corporate culture. The OD process entails three steps—unfreezing (diagnosis of the problem), the actual change (intervention), and refreezing (reinforcement of new attitudes and behaviors). Popular OD techniques include team building, survey feedback, and large-group interventions.

Corning Inc., described at the beginning of the chapter, has successfully transformed itself numerous times over its 150-year history. However, in recent years innovation has slowed and the company was making only small, incremental improvements in existing products. When Roger Ackerman took over, he wanted to spur the creation of radical new ideas and rapidly translate them into new products for the marketplace. Ackerman and his top executives made both cultural and structural changes to facilitate the creation and implementation of new ideas. They closed low-profit and low-growth businesses and used the money to finance growth in other parts of the company, such as the fast-growing area of fiber optics. In addition, they stripped out layers of management bureaucracy that separated technologists and engineers from top decision makers who controlled the distribution of resources and they took steps to create a culture that encouraged creativity and the sharing of information and ideas across functions. Corning doubled R & D spending and sent teams working on specific new ideas to a skunkworks so they could be separated from the bureaucracy and distractions of the larger company. The company began encouraging and supporting idea champions, giving people the time and space needed to work on "slightly crazy ideas." For example, a rule that researchers spend 10 percent of their time on "Friday afternoon experiments" means scientists can work on projects their bosses know nothing about—or even projects that superiors have already pulled the plug on. An entire genomics business is being built on an idea that was officially killed by the head of research but was pursued in Friday afternoon experiments. Corning's new emphasis on collaboration and innovation has led to several breakthrough products. An amazing 84 percent of products sold in 2000 were introduced within the past four years.[80]

■ Discussion Questions

1. The September 11, 2001, terrorist attack on the World Trade Center led many companies that had been bitter rivals to put their competitive spirit aside and focus on cooperation and courtesy. Do you believe this type of change will be a lasting one? Discuss.

2. A manager of an international chemical company said that very few new products in her company were successful. What would you advise the manager to do to help increase the company's success rate?

3. What are internal and external forces for change? Which force do you think is the major cause of organizational change in a university? In a pharmaceuticals firm?

4. Carefully planned change often is assumed to be effective. Do you think unplanned change can sometimes be beneficial to an organization? Discuss.

5. Why do organizations experience resistance to change? What techniques can managers use to overcome resistance?

6. Explain force field analysis. Analyze the driving and restraining forces for a change with which you have been associated.

7. Define the roles associated with an idea champion. Why do you think idea champions are so essential to the initiation of change?

8. To what extent would changes in technology affect new products, and vice versa? Compare the process for changing technology and that for product change.

9. Given that structural change is often made top down, should coercive implementation techniques be used? Discuss.

10. Do the underlying values of organizational development differ from assumptions associated with other types of change? Discuss.

11. How do large-group interventions differ from OD techniques such as team building and survey feedback?

■ Management in Practice: Experiential Exercise

Is Your Company Creative?

An effective way to assess the creative climate of an organization for which you have worked is to fill out the questionnaire below. Answer each question based on your work experience in that firm. Discuss the results with members of your group, and talk about whether changing the firm along the dimensions in the questions would make it more creative.

Instructions: Answer each of the following questions using the five-point scale (*Note: There is no rating of 4*): 0, we never do this; 1, we rarely do this; 2, we sometimes do this; 3, we frequently do this; and 5, we always do this.)

_____ We are encouraged to seek help anywhere inside or outside the organization with new ideas for our work unit.

_____ Assistance is provided to develop ideas into proposals for management review.

_____ Our performance reviews encourage risky, creative efforts, ideas, and actions.

_____ We are encouraged to fill our minds with new information by attending professional meetings and trade fairs, visiting customers, and so on.

_____ Our meetings are designed to allow people to freewheel, brainstorm, and generate ideas.

_____ All members contribute ideas during meetings.

_____ During meetings, there is much spontaneity and humor.

_____ We discuss how company structure and our actions help or spoil creativity within our work unit.

_____ During meetings, the chair is rotated among members.

_____ Everyone in the work unit receives training in creativity techniques and maintaining a creative climate.

To measure how effectively your organization fosters creativity, use the following scale:

Highly effective: 35–50
Moderately effective: 20–34
Moderately ineffective: 10–19
Ineffective: 0–9

SOURCE: Adapted from Edward Glassman, *Creativity Handbook: Idea Triggers and Sparks That Work* (Chapel Hill, N.C.: LCS Press, 1990). Used by permission. (919/967–2015)

■ Management in Practice: Ethical Dilemma

Research for Sale

Lucinda Jackson walked slowly back to R & D Laboratory 4 at Reed Pharmaceuticals. She was stunned. Top management was planning to sell her entire team project to Trichem Industries in an effort to raise the capital Reed needed to buy a small, competing drug company. Two years ago, when she was named project administrator for the cancer treatment program, Jackson was assured that the program was the highest priority at Reed. She was allowed to recruit the best and the brightest in the research center in their hunt for an effective drug to treat lung cancer. There had been press releases and personal appearances at stockholder meetings.

When she first approached a colleague, Len Rosen, to become head chemist on the project, he asked her whether Reed was in cancer research for the long haul or if they were just grabbing headlines. Based on what she had been told by the vice president in charge of R & D, Jackson assured him that their project was protected for as long as it took. Now, a short two years later, she learned that not only was Reed backing out but also that the project was being sold as a package to an out-of-state firm. There were no jobs at Reed being offered as alternatives for the team. They were only guaranteed jobs if they moved with the project to Trichem.

Jackson felt betrayed, but she knew it was nothing compared to what the other team members would feel. Rosen was a 10-year veteran at Reed, and his wife and family had deep roots in the local community. A move would be devastating to them. Jackson had a few friends in top management, but she didn't know if any would back her if she fought the planned sale.

What Do You Do?

1. Approach top management with the alternative of selling the project and sending the team temporarily to train staff at Trichem but allowing them to return to different projects at Reed after the transition. After all, they promised a commitment to the project.

2. Wait for the announcement of the sale of the project and then try to secure as much support as possible for the staff and families in their relocation: moving expense reimbursement, job placement for spouses, and so on.

3. Tell a few people, such as Rosen, and then combine forces with them and threaten to quit if the project is sold. Make attempts to scuttle the sale to Trichem before it happens, and perhaps even leak the news to the press. Perhaps the threat of negative publicity will cause top management to reconsider.

SOURCE: Adapted from Doug Wallace, "Promises Made, Promises Broken," *What Would You Do? Business Ethics* 1 (March–April 1990), 16–18. Reprinted with permission from *Business Ethics*, P.O. Box 8439, Minneapolis, MN 55408, (612) 879-0695.

◼ Surf the Net

1. **Technological Change.** Check out three well-known technology news sites and write a note or e-mail to your professor concerning the site you think would help you most to stay current on technology trends. After visiting the three sites listed, choose the site you prefer and give two reasons you selected this site over the other two.
   http://techupdate.zdnet.com
   http://www.techreview.com
   http://www.cnet.com

2. **Creativity.** Using information found at the sites listed or at another site with creativity information, prepare a 3- to 5-minute oral presentation on any aspect of creativity that interests you and that you could make interesting to your professor and classmates. Remember that both content and creative presentation format will contribute to your success on this assignment.
   http://www.jvdcreativity.com/info.htm
   http://members.ozemail.com.au/~caveman/Creative/Admin/crbigpic.htm
   http://www.creativityatwork.com/

3. **Negotiation.** Type in the search phrase "negotiation articles" in a search engine such as *http://www.wisenut.com*. Select one article, print it out, read and highlight relevant points, and be prepared to share a thought or two from your article during a class discussion on negotiation.

◼ Case for Critical Analysis

Southern Discomfort

Jim Malesckowski remembers the call of two weeks ago as if he just put down the telephone receiver. "I just read your analysis and I want you to get down to Mexico right away," Jack Ripon, his boss and chief executive officer, had blurted in his ear. "You know we can't make the plant in Oconomo work anymore—the costs are just too high. So go down there, check out what our operational costs would be if we move, and report back to me in a week."

At that moment, Jim felt as if a shiv had been stuck in his side, just below the rib cage. As president of the Wisconsin Specialty Products Division of Lamprey, Inc., he knew quite well the challenge of dealing with high-cost labor in a third-generation, unionized U.S. manufacturing plant. And although he had done the analysis that led to his boss's knee-jerk response, the call still stunned him. There were 520 people who made a living at Lamprey's Oconomo facility, and if it closed, most of them wouldn't have a journeyman's prayer of finding another job in the town of 9,000 people.

Instead of the $16-per-hour average wage paid at the Oconomo plant, the wages paid to the Mexican workers—who lived in a town without sanitation and with an unbelievably toxic effluent from industrial pollution—would amount to about $1.60 an hour on average. That's a savings of nearly $15 million a year for Lamprey, to be offset in part by increased costs for training, transportation, and other matters.

After two days of talking with Mexican government representatives and managers of other companies in the town, Jim had enough information to develop a set of comparative figures of production and shipping costs. On the way home, he started to outline the report, knowing full well that unless some miracle occurred, he would be ushering in a blizzard of pink slips for people he had come to appreciate.

The plant in Oconomo had been in operation since 1921, making special apparel for persons suffering injuries and other medical conditions. Jim had often talked with employees who would recount stories about their fathers or grandfathers working in the same Lamprey company plant—the last of the original manufacturing operations in town.

But friendship aside, competitors had already edged past Lamprey in terms of price and were dangerously close to overtaking it in product quality. Although both Jim and the plant manager had tried to convince the union to accept lower wages, union leaders resisted. In fact, on one occasion when Jim and the plant manager tried to discuss a cell manufacturing approach, which would cross-train employees to perform up to three different jobs, local union leaders could barely restrain their anger. Yet probing beyond the fray, Jim sensed the fear that lurked under the union reps' gruff exterior. He sensed their vulnerability, but could not break through the reactionary bark that protected it.

A week has passed and Jim just submitted his report to his boss. Although he didn't specifically bring up the point, it was apparent that Lamprey could put its investment dollars in a bank and receive a better return than what its Oconomo operation is currently producing.

Tomorrow, he'll discuss the report with the CEO. Jim doesn't want to be responsible for the plant's dismantling, an act he personally believes would be wrong as long as there's a chance its costs can be lowered. "But Ripon's right," he says to himself. "The costs are too high, the union's unwilling to cooperate, and the company needs to make a better return on its investment if it's to continue at all. It sounds right but feels wrong. What should I do?"

Questions

1. Assume you want to lead the change to save the Oconomo plant. Describe how you would proceed, using the four stages of the change process described in the chapter—forces, need, initiation, and implementation.

2. What is the primary type of change needed—technology, product, structure, or people/culture? To what extent will the primary change have secondary effects on other types of change at the Oconomo factory?

3. What techniques would you use to overcome union resistance and implement change?

SOURCE: Doug Wallace, "What Would You Do?" *Business Ethics* (March/April 1996), 52–53. Reprinted with permission.

■ Endnotes

1. William J. Holstein, "Dump the Cookware," *Business2.com* (May 1, 2001), 68+.

2. George Anders, "Hard Cell," *Fast Company* (May 2001), 108–122.

3. Stuart F. Brown, "The Automaker's Big-Time Bet on Fuel Cells," *Fortune* (March 30, 1998), 122(B)–122(D); and Geeta Anand, "Inventor Struggles to Breathe Life Into Cancer Vaccine," *The Wall Street Journal* (May 22, 2001), B1, B4.

4. Richard L. Daft, "Bureaucratic vs. Nonbureaucratic Structure in the Process of Innovation and Change," in *Perspectives in Organizational Sociology: Theory and Research*, ed. Samuel B. Bacharach (Greenwich, Conn.: JAI Press, 1982), 129–166.

5. This discussion is based on Richard L. Daft, *Organization Theory and Design,* 5th ed. (St. Paul, Minn.: West, 1995); and Don Hellriegel and John W. Slocum, Jr., *Management*, 7th ed. (Cincinnati, Ohio: South-Western, 1996).

6. Tom Broersma, "In Search of the Future," *Training and Development* (January 1995), 38–43.

7. Andre L. Delbecq and Peter K. Mills, "Managerial Practices That Enhance Innovation," *Organizational Dynamics* 14 (Summer 1985), 24–34.

8. David Dorsey, "Change Factory," *Fast Company* (June 2000), 210–224.

9. Paul M. Barrett, "A Once-Stodgy Firm Makes a Flashy Return, But at What Cost?" *The Wall Street Journal* (August 17, 1998), A1, A6.

10. Carol Hymowitz, "Managing in a Crisis Can Bring Better Ways to Conduct Business," (In the Lead column) *The Wall Street Journal* (October 23, 2001), B1.

11. John P. Kotter, *Leading Change* (Boston: Harvard University Press, 1996), 20–25; and "Leading Change: Why Transformation Efforts Fail," *Harvard Business Review* (March–April, 1995), 59–67.

12. Almar Latour, "Trial by Fire: A Blaze in Albuquerque Sets Off Major Crisis for Cell-Phone Giants," *The Wall Street Journal* (January 29, 2001), A1, A8.

13. Attributed to Gregory Bateson in Andrew H. Van de Ven, "Central Problems in the Management of Innovation," *Management Science* 32 (1986), 595.

14. Teresa M. Amabile, "Motivating Creativity in Organizations: On Doing What You Love and Loving What You Do," *California Management Review* 40, no. 1 (Fall 1997), 39–58; and Timothy A. Matherly and Ronald E. Goldsmith, "The Two Faces of Creativity," *Business Horizons* (September/October 1985), 8.

15. Gordon Vessels, "The Creative Process: An Open-Systems Conceptualization," *Journal of Creative Behavior* 16 (1982), 185–196.

16. Robert J. Sternberg, Linda A. O'Hara, and Todd I. Lubart, "Creativity as Investment," *California Management Review* 40, no. 1 (Fall 1997), 8–21; Teresa M. Amabile, "Motivating Creativity in Organizations"; and Ken Lizotte, "A Creative State of Mind," *Management Review* (May 1998), 15–17.

17. James Brian Quinn, "Managing Innovation: Controlled Chaos," *Harvard Business Review* 63 (May–June 1985), 73–84; Howard H. Stevenson and David E. Gumpert, "The Heart of Entrepreneurship," *Harvard Business Review* 63 (March–April 1985), 85–94; and Marsha Sinetar, "Entrepreneurs, Chaos, and Creativity—Can Creative People Really Survive Large Company Structure?" *Sloan Management Review* 6 (Winter 1985), 57–62.

18. Cynthia Browne, "Jest for Success," *Moonbeams* (August 1989), 3–5; and Rosabeth Moss Kanter, *The Change Masters* (New York: Simon and Schuster, 1983).

19. Cathy Olofson, "Play Hard, Think Big," *Fast Company* (January 2001), 64.

20. "Hands On: A Manager's Notebook," *Inc.* (January 1989), 106.

21. Robert I. Sutton, "The Weird Rules of Creativity," *Harvard Business Review* (September 2001), 94–103.

22. Katy Koontz, "How to Stand Out from the Crowd," *Working Woman* (January 1988), 74–76.

23. Anders, "Hard Cell."

24. Harold L. Angle and Andrew H. Van de Ven, "Suggestions for Managing the Innovation Journey," in *Research in the Management of Innovation: The Minnesota Studies*, ed. A. H. Van de Ven, H. L. Angle, and Marshall Scott Poole (Cambridge, Mass.: Ballinger/Harper & Row, 1989).

25. Sutton, "The Weird Rules of Creativity."

26. C. K. Bart, "New Venture Units: Use Them Wisely to Manage Innovation," *Sloan Management Review* (Summer 1988), 35–43; and Michael Tushman and David Nadler, "Organizing for Innovation," *California Management Review* 28 (Spring 1986), 74–92.

27. Peter F. Drucker, *Innovation and Entrepreneurship* (New York: Harper & Row, 1985).

28. Christopher Hoenig, "Skunk Works Secrets," *CIO* (July 1, 2000), 74–76; and Tom Peters and Nancy Austin, *A Passion for Excellence: The Leadership Difference* (New York: Random House, 1985).

29. Hoenig, "Skunk Works Secrets."

30. Sutton, "The Weird Rules of Creativity."

31. Sherri Eng, "Hatching Schemes," *The Industry Standard* (November 27–December 4, 2000), 174–175.

32. Eng, "Hatching Schemes."

33. Ibid.

34. J. P. Kotter and L. A. Schlesinger, "Choosing Strategies for Change," *Harvard Business Review* 57 (March–April 1979), 106–114.

35. James McNair, "Workers Take Case to Federated," *Cincinnati Enquirer* (February 9, 2002), B1.

36. G. Zaltman and Robert B. Duncan, *Strategies for Planned Change* (New York: Wiley Interscience, 1977).

37. Leonard M. Apcar, "Middle Managers and Supervisors Resist Moves to More Participatory Management," *The Wall Street Journal* (September 16, 1985), 25.

38. Dorothy Leonard-Barton and Isabelle Deschamps, "Managerial Influence in the Implementation of New Technology," *Management Science* 34 (1988), 1252–1265.

39. Kurt Lewin, *Field Theory in Social Science: Selected Theoretical Papers* (New York: Harper & Brothers, 1951).

40. Paul C. Nutt, "Tactics of Implementation," *Academy of Management Journal* 29 (1986), 230–261; Kotter and Schlesinger, "Choosing Strategies"; R. L. Daft and S. Becker, *Innovation in Organizations: Innovation Adoption in School Organizations* (New York: Elsevier, 1978); and R. Beckhard, *Organization Development: Strategies and Models* (Reading, Mass.: Addison-Wesley, 1969).

41. Rob Muller, "Training for Change," *Canadian Business Review* (Spring 1995), 16–19.

42. Taggart F. Frost, "Creating a Teamwork-Based Culture within a Manufacturing Setting," *IM* (May–June 1994), 17–20.

43. Dean Foust with Gerry Khermouch, "Repairing the Coke Machine," *Business Week* (March 19, 2001), 86-88.

44. Jeremy Main, "The Trouble with Managing Japanese-Style," *Fortune* (April 2, 1984), 50–56.

45. J. Hyatt, "Guaranteed Growth," *Inc.* (September 1995), 69–78.

46. Richard Teitelbaum, "How to Harness Gray Matter," *Fortune* (June 9, 1997), 168.

47. Daft, *Organization Theory and Design*; and Tom Burns and G. M. Stalker, *The Management of Innovation* (London: Tavistock Publications, 1961).

48. Thomas Petzinger, Jr., "The Front Lines: Bread Store Chain Tells Its Franchisees: Do Your Own Thing," *The Wall Street Journal* (November 21, 1997), B1.

49. Richard L. Daft, "A Dual-Core Model of Organizational Innovation," *Academy of Management Journal* 21 (1978), 193–210; and Kanter, *The Change Masters.*

50. Harold J. Leavitt, "Applied Organizational Change in Industry: Structural, Technical, and Human Approaches," in *New Perspectives in Organization Research*, ed. W. W. Cooper, H. J. Leavitt, and M. W. Shelly II (New York: Wiley, 1964), 55–74.

51. Glenn Rifkin, "Competing through Innovation: The Case of Broderbund," *Strategy & Business Issue* 11 (Second Quarter, 1998), 48–58; and Deborah Dougherty and Cynthia Hardy, "Sustained Product Innovation in Large, Mature Organizations: Overcoming Innovation-to-Organization Problems," *Academy of Management Journal* 39, no. 5 (1996), 1120–1153.

52. Robert McMath, *What Were They Thinking? Marketing Lessons I've Learned from Over 80,000 New Product Innovations and Idiocies* (New York: Times Business, 1998); Paul Lukas, "The Ghastliest Product Launches," *Fortune* (March 16, 1998), 44.

53. Melissa A. Schilling and Charles W. L. Hill, "Managing the New Product Development Process," *Academy of Management Executive* 12, no. 3 (1998), 67–81.

54. Andrew H. Van de Ven, "Central Problems in the Management of Innovation," *Management Science* 32 (1986), 590–607; Daft, *Organization Theory;* and Science Policy Research Unit, University of Sussex, *Success and Failure in Industrial Innovation* (London: Centre for the Study of Industrial Innovation, 1972).

55. William L. Shanklin and John K. Ryans, Jr., "Organizing for High-Tech Marketing," *Harvard Business Review* 62 (November–December 1984), 164–171; and Arnold O. Putnam, "A Redesign for Engineering," *Harvard Business Review* 63 (May–June 1985), 139–144.

56. Daft, *Organization Theory.*

57. Schilling and Hill, "Managing the New Product Development Process."

58. Eric von Hippel, Stefan Thomke, and Mary Sonnack, "Creating Breakthroughs at 3M," *Harvard Business Review* (September–October, 1999), 47–57.

59. Ibid.

60. Faith Keenan, "Opening the Spigot," *BusinessWeek E.biz* (June 4, 2001), EB17-EB20.

61. Susan Caminiti, "A Quiet Superstar Rises in Retailing," *Fortune* (October 23, 1989), 167–174.

62. Brian Dumaine, "How Managers Can Succeed through Speed," *Fortune* (February 13, 1989), 54–59; and George Stalk, Jr., "Time—The Next Source of Competitive Advantage," *Harvard Business Review* (July–August 1988), 41–51.

63. Fariborz Damanpour, "The Adoption of Technological, Administrative, and Ancillary Innovations: Impact of Organizational Factors," *Journal of Management* 13 (1987), 675–688.

64. Marianne Kolbasuk McGee, "Lessons From a Cultural Revolution," *informationweek.com* (October 25, 1999), 47–60.

65. Daft, "Bureaucratic vs. Nonbureaucratic Structure."

66. Nanette Byrnes, "Avon: The New Calling," *BusinessWeek* (September 18, 2000), 136-148; and Katrina Brooker, "It Took a Lady to Save Avon," *Fortune* (October 15, 2001), 203–208.

67. E. H. Schein, "Organizational Culture," *American Psychologist* 45 (February 1990), 109–119; and A. Kupfer, "An Outsider Fires Up a Railroad," *Fortune* (December 18, 1989), 133–146.

68. Michelle Conlin, "Tough Love for Techie Souls," *BusinessWeek* (November 29, 1999), 164–170.

69. Alix Nyberg, "Kim Patmore," profile in "The Class of 2000," *CFO* (October 2000), 81–82.

70. M. Sashkin and W. W. Burke,"Organizational Development in the 1980s," *General Management* 13 (1987), 393–417; and Richard Beckhard, "What Is Organization Development?" in *Organization Development and Transformation: Managing Effective Change*, Wendell L. French, Cecil H. Bell, Jr., and Robert A. Zawacki, eds., (Burr Ridge, Illinois: Irwin McGraw Hill, 2000), 16–19.

71. Wendell L. French and Cecil H. Bell, Jr., "A History of Organizational Development," in French, Bell, and Zawacki, *Organization Development and Transformation*, 20–42.

72. Paul F. Buller, "For Successful Strategic Change: Blend OD Practices with Strategic Management," *Organizational Dynamics* (Winter 1988), 42–55; and Robert M. Fulmer and Roderick Gilkey, "Blending Corporate Families: Management and Organization Development in a Postmerger Environment," *The Academy of Management Executive* 2 (1988), 275–283.

73. W. Warner Burke, "The New Agenda for Organizational Development," *Organizational Dynamics* (Summer 1997), 7–19.

74. This discussion is based on Kathleen D. Dannemiller and Robert W. Jacobs, "Changing the Way Organizations Change: A Revolution of Common Sense," *The Journal of Applied Behavioral Science* 28, no. 4 (December 1992), 480–498; and Barbara Benedict Bunker and Billie T. Alban, "Conclusion: What Makes Large Group Interventions Effective?" *The Journal of Applied Behavioral Science* 28, no. 4 (December 1992), 570–591.

75. Bunker and Alban, "What Makes Large Group Interventions Effective?"

76. J. Quinn, "What a Work-Out!" *Performance* (November 1994), 58–63; and B. B. Bunker and B. T. Alban, "Conclusion: What Makes Large Group Interventions Effective?" *The Journal of Applied Behavioral Science* 28, no. 4 (December 1992), 572–591.

77. Thomas Petzinger Jr., *The New Pioneers: The Men and Women Who Are Transforming the Workplace and the Marketplace* (New York: Simon & Schuster, 1999), 27–32.

78. Kurt Lewin, "Frontiers in Group Dynamics: Concepts, Method, and Reality in Social Science," *Human Relations* 1 (1947), 5–41; and E. F. Huse and T. G. Cummings, *Organization Development and Change,* 3rd ed. (St. Paul, Minn.: West, 1985).

79. Based on John Kotter's eight-step model of planned change, which is described in John Kotter, *Leading Change* (Boston: Harvard Business School Press, 1996), 20–25, and "Leading Change: Why Transformation Efforts Fail," *Harvard Business Review* (March–April, 1995), 59–67.

80. Holstein, "Dump the Cookware," and Sutton, "The Weird Rules of Creativity."

Human Resource Management

CHAPTER OUTLINE

The Strategic Role of Human Resource Management

Environmental Influences on HRM

Competitive Strategy

Federal Legislation

The Changing Nature of Careers

The Changing Social Contract

The New Workplace

Attracting an Effective Workforce

Human Resource Planning

Recruiting

Selecting

Developing an Effective Workforce

Training and Development

Performance Appraisal

Maintaining an Effective Workforce

Compensation

Benefits

Termination

LEARNING OBJECTIVES

After studying this chapter, you should be able to

1 Explain the role of human resource management in organizational strategic planning.

2 Describe federal legislation and societal trends that influence human resource management.

3 Explain what the changing social contract between organizations and employees means for workers and human resource managers.

4 Explain how organizations determine their future staffing needs through human resource planning.

5 Describe the tools managers use to recruit and select employees.

6 Describe how organizations develop an effective workforce through training and performance appraisal.

7 Explain how organizations maintain a workforce through the administration of wages and salaries, benefits, and terminations.

Management Challenge

As vice-president of human resources for Mirage Resorts Inc., Arte Nathan was facing the most daunting challenge of his career. Mirage was about to launch Bellagio, a lavish 3,000-room Las Vegas resort, and Nathan and his human resources team were charged with hiring 9,600 employees—in only 24 weeks. This meant recruiting and screening 84,000 applicants for jobs in more than 600 categories, everything from dealers, food servers, and maids to accountants and vice presidents. Then, the team would have to narrow the applicants down to a list of 27,000 finalists, carefully interview the finalists, conduct background checks and drug screens, and process the final hires. To top it off, complete personnel, benefits, and tax files would have to quickly be set up, and each employee would need to be trained. The enormity of the task was comparable to moving a complex military operation around the globe. Nathan knew the traditional approach to HR was not up to such a challenge. He and his team needed to come up with a new way to address the problem, one that separated HR staff from much of the direct work of interviewing and hiring and instead made them strategic partners with managers throughout the organization.[1]

If you were Arte Nathan, how would you address this enormous human resources challenge? How can human resources play a strategic role in keeping a company competitive?

Walgreens Co., the leader in the chain drugstore industry in both sales and profits, recognizes the strategic role of human resource management. In its Annual Report, the company states, "Well-trained pharmacy technicians like Celeste Burgess (photo) are pivotal to both patient service and the efficient operation of Walgreens Intercom Plus workflow system. Approximately 2,000 technicians passed a national certification exam, enhancing their pay and pharmacy knowledge."

human resource management (HRM)

Activities undertaken to attract, develop, and maintain an effective workforce within an organization.

The situation at Mirage Resorts' Bellagio Hotel (now owned by MGM Grand Inc.) provides a dramatic example of the challenges that human resource managers face every day. The people who make up an organization give that organization its primary source of competitive advantage, and human resource management plays a key role in finding and developing the organization's people as human resources that contribute to and directly affect company success. The term **human resource management (HRM)** refers to the design and application of formal systems in an organization to ensure the effective and efficient use of human talent to accomplish organizational goals.[2] This includes activities undertaken to attract, develop, and maintain an effective workforce.

Companies such as Southwest Airlines, Disney, and Dell Computer have become famous for their philosophy about human resource management, which is the foundation of their success. HRM is equally important for government and nonprofit organizations. For example, public schools in the United States are facing a severe teacher shortage, with HRM directors struggling with how to fill an estimated 2.2 million teacher vacancies over the next decade. Many are trying innovative programs such as recruiting in foreign countries, establishing relationships with leaders at top universities, and having their most motivated and enthusiastic teachers work with university students considering teaching careers.[3]

Over the past decade, human resource management has shed its old "personnel" image and gained recognition as a vital player in corporate strategy. Research has found that effective human resource management has a positive impact on organizational performance, including higher employee productivity and stronger financial performance.[4] Human resource personnel are considered key players on the management team. In addition, today's flatter organizations often require that managers throughout the organization play an active role in human resource management. Activities and tasks that were once handled by HRM professionals, such as recruiting and selecting the right personnel, developing effective training programs, or creating appropriate performance appraisal systems, may be pushed out to managers across the organization. Thus, all managers need to be skilled in the basics of human resource management.

The Strategic Role of Human Resource Management

The strategic approach to human resource management recognizes three key elements. First, as we just discussed, all managers are human resource managers. For example, at IBM every manager is expected to pay attention to the development and satisfaction of subordinates. Line managers use surveys, career planning, performance appraisal, and compensation to encourage commitment to IBM.[5] Second, employees are viewed as assets. Employees, not buildings and machinery, give a company a competitive advantage. How a company manages its workforce may be the single most important factor in sustained competitive success.[6] Third, human resource management is a matching process, integrating the organization's strategy and goals with the correct approach to managing the firm's human resources.[7] Some current strategic issues of particular concern to managers include becoming more competitive on a global basis; improving quality, productivity, and customer service; managing mergers and acquisitions; and applying new information technology for e-business. All of these strategic decisions determine a company's need for skills and employees.

This chapter examines the three primary goals of HRM as illustrated in Exhibit 13.1. HRM activities and goals do not take place inside a vacuum but within the context of issues and factors affecting the entire organization, such as increasing globalization, changing technology and the shift to knowledge work, rapid shifts in markets and the external environment, societal trends, government regulations, and changes in the organization's culture, structure, strategy, and goals.

The three broad HR activities outlined in Exhibit 13.1 are to attract an effective workforce to the organization, develop the workforce to its potential, and maintain the workforce over the long term.[8] Achieving these goals requires skills in planning, training, performance appraisal, wage and salary administration, benefit programs, and even termination. Each of the activities in Exhibit 13.1 will be discussed in this chapter.

Environmental Influences on HRM

"Our strength is the quality of our people."

"Our people are our most important resource."

These often-repeated statements by executives emphasize the importance of HRM. Human resource managers must find, recruit, train, nurture, and retain the best people.[9] Without the proper personnel, the brightest idea or

Exhibit 13.1

Strategic Human Resource Management

Company Strategy

Attract an Effective Workforce
HRM planning
Job analysis
Forecasting
Recruiting
Selecting

Maintain an Effective Workforce
Wage and salary
Benefits
Labor relations
Terminations

Develop an Effective Workforce
Training
Development
Appraisal

HRM Environment
Legislation
Trends in society
International events
Changing technology

management trend—whether virtual teams, e-business, telecommuting, or flexible compensation—is doomed to failure. In addition, when employees don't feel valued, usually they are not willing to give their best to the company and often leave to find a more supportive work environment. For these reasons, it is important that human resource executives be involved in competitive strategy. Human resource executives also interpret federal legislation and respond to the changing nature of careers and work relationships.

Competitive Strategy

HRM contributes directly to the bottom line through its appreciation that it is the organization's human assets—its people—that meet or fail to meet strategic goals. To keep companies competitive, HRM is changing in three primary ways: focusing on building human capital; developing global HR strategies; and using information technology.

human capital
The economic value of the knowledge, experience, skills, and capabilities of employees.

Even in a "cold" job market, successful companies recognize the need to build human capital *by hiring people with special knowledge, skills, or experience. For example, during a time when U.S. companies shed 415,000 jobs in one month, Bill Conner found work just one day after turning to an online job board. Conner, an executive in the telecom industry, lost his job overseeing the inspection of cell-tower parts and found a new position managing quality control for Boston's Solectria Corp., which makes parts for electric vehicles. Even as many companies have begun hiring freezes, firms such as Solectria see the economic value of snapping up highly experienced workers such as Bill Conner.*

Building Human Capital.   Today, more than ever, strategic decisions are related to human resource considerations. For example, in an information- and knowledge-based economy, success depends on an organization's ability to manage *human capital*.[10] **Human capital** refers to the economic value of the knowledge, experience, skills, and capabilities of employees.[11] To build human capital, HRM develops strategies for ensuring a workforce with superior knowledge and skills. This means recruiting to find the best talent, enhancing their skills and knowledge with training programs and opportunities for personal and professional development, and providing compensation and benefits that enhance the sharing of knowledge and appropriately reward people for their contributions to the organization. Human resource managers also help create an environment that gives highly talented people compelling reasons to stay with the company. Judy Lyles of DET Distributing Company in Nashville, Tennessee, sees the human resource department not just as the keeper of the rules, but as the "keeper of workers' hearts—the keeper of why they want to come to work every day."[12]

Globalization.   Another issue for today's organizations is competing on a global basis, which brings tremendous new challenges for human resource management.   Most companies are still in the early stages of developing effective HRM policies, structures, and services that respond to the current reality of globalization.[13] In a study of more than 200 global companies, including Eli Lilly, PPG Industries, and UPS, managers reported that the biggest challenge for HRM is leadership development and training for the international arena. Companies in all industries report a growing need for capable global leaders, people who not only have good leadership abilities but can also manage across geographical and cultural boundaries. HRM departments are busily developing policies and procedures for recruiting and training people for global leadership. In addition, HRM is responsible for recruitment, training, and performance management of

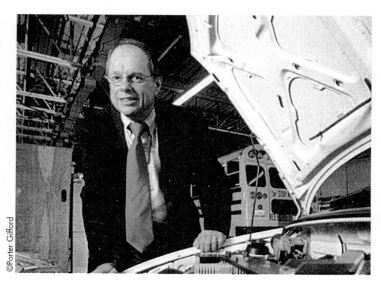

employees who might have to work across geographical, technical, and cultural boundaries to help the organization achieve its goals. The success of global business strategies is closely tied to the effectiveness of the organization's global HR strategies.[14]

Information Technology. Information technology is helping HRM meet these and other challenges. A **human resource information system** is an integrated computer system designed to provide data and information used in HR planning and decision making. The most basic use is the automation of payroll and benefits activities. However, new software programs and Web-based human resource service providers such as ManCom Team Inc. (www.mancom.com) allow companies to automate practically the entire human resources function, from recruiting and hiring, to orientation and training, to payroll and benefits administration. Some leading organizations are coming close to a paperless HR system, which saves time and money as well as frees HRM staff from mundane chores so they can focus on more strategic issues.[15] For example, by simplifying the task of analyzing vast amounts of data, human resource information systems can dramatically improve the effectiveness of long-term HR planning.

Federal Legislation

Over the past 40 years, several federal laws have been passed to ensure equal employment opportunity (EEO). Some of the most significant legislation and executive orders are summarized in Exhibit 13.2. The point of the laws is to stop discriminatory practices that are unfair to specific groups and to define enforcement agencies for these laws. EEO legislation attempts to balance the pay given to men and women; provide employment opportunities without regard to race, religion, national origin, and sex; ensure fair treatment for employees of all ages; and avoid discrimination against disabled individuals.

The Equal Employment Opportunity Commission (EEOC) created by the Civil Rights Act of 1964 initiates investigations in response to complaints concerning discrimination. The EEOC is the major agency involved with employment discrimination. **Discrimination** occurs when some applicants are hired or promoted based on criteria that are not job relevant. For example, refusing to hire a black applicant for a job he is qualified to fill or paying a woman a lower wage than a man for the same work are discriminatory acts. When discrimination is found, remedies include providing back pay and taking affirmative action. **Affirmative action** requires that an employer take positive steps to guarantee equal employment opportunities for people within protected groups. An affirmative action plan is a formal document that can be reviewed by employees and enforcement agencies. The goal of organizational affirmative action is to reduce or eliminate internal inequities among affected employee groups.

Failure to comply with equal employment opportunity legislation can result in substantial fines and penalties for employers. For example, Shoney's was accused of discrimination against black employees and job applicants. The class-action suit charged that company policy conspired to limit the number of black employees working in public areas of the restaurant. In 1992 the company agreed to pay $105 million to victims of its hiring, promotion, and firing policies, dating back to 1985.[16] Suits for discriminatory practices can cover a broad range of employee complaints. One issue of growing concern is

human resource information system
An integrated computer system designed to provide data and information used in HR planning and decision making.

discrimination
The hiring or promoting of applicants based on criteria that are not job relevant.

affirmative action
A policy requiring employers to take positive steps to guarantee equal employment opportunities for people within protected groups.

Federal Law	Year	Provisions
Equal Opportunity/Discrimination Laws		
Civil Rights Act	1991	Provides for possible compensatory and punitive damages plus traditional back pay for cases of intentional discrimination brought under Title VII of the 1964 Civil Rights Act. Shifts the burden of proof to the employer.
Americans with Disabilities Act	1990	Prohibits discrimination against qualified individuals by employers on the basis of disability and demands that "reasonable accommodations" be provided for the disabled to allow performance of duties.
Vocational Rehabilitation Act	1973	Prohibits discrimination based on physical or mental disability and requires that employees be informed about affirmative action plans.
Age Discrimination in Employment Act (ADEA)	1967 (amended 1978, 1986)	Prohibits age discrimination and restricts mandatory retirement.
Civil Rights Act, Title VII	1964	Prohibits discrimination in employment on the basis of race, religion, color, sex, or national origin.
Compensation/Benefits Laws		
Health Insurance Portability and Accountability Act (HIPPA)	1996	Allows employees to switch health insurance plans when changing jobs and get the new coverage regardless of preexisting health conditions; prohibits group plans from dropping a sick employee.
Family and Medical Leave Act	1993	Requires employers to provide up to 12 weeks unpaid leave for childbirth, adoption, or family emergencies.
Equal Pay Act	1963	Prohibits sex differences in pay for substantially equal work.
Health/Safety Laws		
Consolidated Omnibus Budget Reconciliation Act (COBRA)	1985	Requires continued health insurance coverage (paid by employee) following termination.
Occupational Safety and Health Act (OSHA)	1970	Establishes mandatory safety and health standards in organizations.

sexual harassment, which is also a violation of Title VII of the Civil Rights Act. The EEOC guidelines specify that behavior such as unwelcome advances, requests for sexual favors, and other verbal and physical conduct of a sexual nature becomes sexual harassment when submission to the conduct is tied to continued employment or advancement or when the behavior creates an intimidating, hostile, or offensive work environment.[17] Sexual harassment will be discussed in detail in Chapter 14.

Exhibit 13.2 also lists the major federal laws related to compensation and benefits and health and safety issues. The scope of human resource legislation is increasing at federal, state, and municipal levels. The working rights and conditions of women, minorities, older employees, and the disabled will probably receive increasing legislative attention in the future.

The Changing Nature of Careers

Another current issue is the changing nature of careers. HRM can benefit employees and organizations by responding to recent changes in the relationship between employers and employees and new ways of working, such as telecommuting, job sharing, and virtual organizations.

The Changing Social Contract

In the old social contract between organization and employee, the employee could contribute ability, education, loyalty, and commitment and expect in return the company would provide wages and benefits, work, advancement, and training throughout the employee's working life. But the volatile changes in the environment have disrupted this contract. Many organizations have been downsized, eliminating many employees. Employees who are left may feel little stability. In a fast-moving company, a person is hired and assigned to a project. The project changes over time, as do the person's tasks. Then the person is assigned to another project and then to still another. These new projects require working with different groups and leaders and schedules, and people may be working in a virtual environment, where they rarely see their colleagues face to face. Workers often have no place to call their own.[18] Careers no longer progress up a vertical hierarchy but move across jobs horizontally. People succeed only if the organization succeeds, and they might lose their jobs. Particularly in learning organizations, everyone is expected to be a self-motivated worker who has excellent interpersonal relationships and is continuously acquiring new skills.

Exhibit 13.3 lists some elements of the new social contract. The new contract is based on the concept of employability rather than lifetime employment. Individuals manage their own careers; the organization no longer takes care of them or guarantees employment. Companies agree to pay somewhat higher wages and invest in creative training and development opportunities so that people will be more employable when the company no longer needs their services. Employees take more responsibility and control in their jobs,

	New Contract	Old Contract
Employee	Employability, personal responsibility	Job security
	Partner in business improvement	A cog in the machine
	Learning	Knowing
Employer	Continuous learning, lateral career movement, incentive compensation	Traditional compensation package
	Creative development opportunities	Standard training programs
	Challenging assignments	Routine jobs
	Information and resources	Limited information

E x h i b i t *13.3*

The Changing Social Contract

SOURCES: Based on Louisa Wah, "The New Workplace Paradox," *Management Review* (January 1998), 7; and Douglas T. Hall and Jonathan E. Moss, "The New Protean Career Contract: Helping Organizations and Employees Adapt," *Organizational Dynamics* (Winter, 1998), 22–37.

becoming partners in business improvement rather than cogs in a machine. In return, the organization provides challenging work assignments as well as information and resources to enable workers to continuously learn new skills. The new contract can provide many opportunities for employees to be more involved and express new aspects of themselves.

However, many employees are not prepared for new levels of cooperation or responsibility on the job. Employment insecurity is stressful for most employees, and it is harder than it was in the past to gain an employee's full commitment and enthusiasm. In addition, one study found that while most workers today feel they are contributing to their companies' success, they are increasingly skeptical that their hard work is being fully recognized.[19] Some companies are finding it difficult to keep good workers because employee trust has been destroyed. To respond to these problems, HRM departments can help organizations develop a mix of training, career development opportunities, compensation packages, and rewards and incentives. They can provide career information and assessment, combined with career coaching, to help employees determine new career directions.[20]

The New Workplace

What company boasts of being America's largest employer in the opening years of the twenty-first century? It's not General Motors, McDonald's, or even the still-growing Wal-Mart, with more than a million employees.[21] The answer is that America's largest employer is a temporary agency, Manpower Inc.[22] Temporary employment agencies such as Manpower grew rapidly during the 1980s and 1990s, and by 2001, more than 3.3 million workers were in temporary firm placements. People in these temporary jobs do everything from data entry to becoming the interim CEO. Although in the past, most temporary workers were in clerical and manufacturing positions, in recent years, demand has grown for professionals, particularly financial analysts, information technology specialists, accountants, product managers, and operations experts.[23]

In addition to the growth of temporary placement agencies, other changes in the workplace and workforce are occurring on a massive, global scale.[24] Not since the advent of mass production and modern organizations has a redefinition of work and career been so profound. The emergence of the *virtual organization*, as described in Chapter 10, means that many or even most of a company's workforce is made up of people who are hired on a project-by-project basis. **Contingent workers** are people who work for an organization, but not on a permanent or full-time basis. This may include temporary placements, contracted professionals, leased employees, or part-time workers. One estimate is that contingent workers make up at least 25 percent of the U.S. workforce.[25] The use of contingent workers means reduced payroll and benefit costs, as well as increased flexibility for both employers and employees.

A related trend is telecommuting. **Telecommuting** means using computers and telecommunications equipment to do work without going to an office. TeleService Resources has more than 25 telephone agents who work entirely from home, using state-of-the-art call-center technology that provides seamless interaction with TSR's Dallas-Fort Worth call center.[26] In 2000, an estimated 24 million people in the United States telecommuted on a regular or occasional basis, and Europe reported an estimated 10 million telecommuters.[27] Wireless

contingent workers
People who work for an organization, but not on a permanent or full-time basis, including temporary placements, contracted professionals, or leased employees.

telecommuting
Using computers and telecommunications equipment to perform work from home or another remote location.

Internet devices, laptops, cell phones, and fax machines make it possible for people to work just about anywhere. There's a growth of what is called *extreme telecommuting*, which means that people live and work in countries far away from the organization's physical location. For example, Paolo Concini works from his home in Bali, Indonesia, even though his company's offices are located in China and Europe.[28] Virtual workers and managers can live and work anywhere they want, untethered to any office or specific location. *Flexible scheduling* for regular employees is also important in today's work-place. Approximately 27 percent of the workforce has flexible hours. When and where an employee does the job is becoming less important.[29]

The advent of *teams* and *project management* is another significant trend in the new workplace. People who used to work alone on the shop floor, in the advertising department, or in middle management are now thrown into teams and succeed as part of a group. Each member of the team acts like a manager, becoming responsible for quality standards, scheduling, and even hiring and firing other team members. With the emphasis on projects, the distinctions between job categories and descriptions are collapsing. Many of today's work-ers straddle functional and departmental boundaries and handle multiple tasks and responsibilities.[30]

These new ways of working bring many advantages, but they also present many challenges for organizations and human resource management, such as new ways of recruiting and compensation that address the interests and needs of contingent and virtual workers, or new training methods that help people work cross-functionally. All human resource managers, whether in traditional organizations or new virtual organizations, have to achieve the three primary goals described earlier: attracting, developing, and maintaining an effective workforce.

Attracting an Effective Workforce

The first goal of HRM is to attract individuals who show signs of becoming valued, productive, and satisfied employees. The first step in attracting an effective workforce involves human resource planning, in which managers or HRM professionals predict the need for new employees based on the types of vacancies that exist, as illustrated in Exhibit 13.4. The second step is to use recruiting procedures to communicate with potential applicants. The third step is to select from the applicants those persons believed to be the best potential contributors to the organization. Finally, the new employee is wel-comed into the organization.

Underlying the organization's effort to attract employees is a matching model. With the **matching model**, the organization and the individual attempt to match the needs, interests, and values that they offer each other.[31] HRM professionals attempt to identify a correct match. For example, a small software developer might require long hours from creative, technically skilled employees. In return, it can offer freedom from bureaucracy, tolerance of idio-syncrasies, and potentially high pay. A large manufacturer can offer employ-ment security and stability, but it might have more rules and regulations and require greater skills for "getting approval from the higher-ups." The individ-ual who would thrive working for the software developer might feel stymied and unhappy working for a large manufacturer. Both the company and the employee are interested in finding a good match. A new approach, called *job*

matching model
An employee selection approach in which the organization and the applicant attempt to match each other's needs, interests, and values.

Exhibit 13.4

Attracting an Effective Workforce

human resource planning
The forecasting of human resource needs and the projected matching of individuals with expected vacancies.

sculpting, attempts to match people to jobs that enable them to fulfill deeply embedded life interests.[32] This often requires that HR managers play detective to find out what really makes a person happy. The idea is that people can fulfill deep-seated needs and interests on the job, which will induce them to stay with the organization.

Human Resource Planning

Human resource planning is the forecasting of human resource needs and the projected matching of individuals with expected vacancies. Human resource planning begins with several questions:

- What new technologies are emerging, and how will these affect the work system?
- What is the volume of the business likely to be in the next five to ten years?
- What is the turnover rate, and how much, if any, is avoidable?

The responses to these questions are used to formulate specific questions pertaining to HR activities, such as the following:

- How many senior managers will we need during this time period?
- What types of engineers will we need, and how many?
- Are persons with adequate computer skills available for meeting our projected needs?
- How many administrative personnel—technicians, IT specialists—will we need to support the additional managers and engineers?
- Can we use temporary, contingent, or virtual workers to handle some tasks?[33]

Answers to these questions help define the direction for the organization's HRM strategy. For example, if forecasting suggests that there will be a strong need for more technically trained individuals, the organization can (1) define the jobs and skills needed in some detail, (2) hire and train recruiters to look for the specified skills, and (3) provide new training for existing employees. By anticipating future HRM needs, the organization can prepare itself to meet competitive challenges more effectively than organizations that react to problems only as they arise.

One of the most successful applications of human resource planning is the Tennessee Valley Authority's development of an eight-step system.

In the confusion and uncertainty following a period of reorganization and downsizing, a crucial role for HRM is balancing the need for future workforce planning with the creation of a climate of stability for the remaining workers. TVA created an eight-step plan that assesses future HR needs and formulates actions to meet those needs. The first step is laying the groundwork for later implementation of the program by creating planning and oversight teams within each business unit. Step two involves assessing processes and functions that can be benchmarked. Step three involves the projection of skills and employee numbers (demand data) necessary to reach goals within each business unit. Once these numbers are in place, step four involves projection of the current employee numbers (supply data) over the "planning horizon" without new hires and taking into consideration the normal attrition of staff through death, retirement, resignation, and so forth. Comparison of the difference between supply and demand (step five) gives the "future gap" or "surplus situation." This knowledge enables HR to develop strategies and operational plans (step six). Step seven involves communication of the action plan to employees. The final step is to periodically evaluate and update the plan as the organization's needs change.

Although, in a small organization, developing demand and supply data could be handled with a pad and a calculator, TVA uses a sophisticated automated system to update and revise the plan as needed to meet new competitive situations. Determining skills-gap and surplus information (step five) helped TVA develop a workforce plan to implement cross-organizational placement and retraining as alternatives to further employee cutbacks in the individual business units, thereby providing a greater sense of stability for workers. If needs change and TVA faces a demand for additional employees, this process will enable the company to recruit workers with the skills needed to help meet organizational goals.[34] ❖

TVA
http://www.tva.com

Recruiting

Recruiting is defined as "activities or practices that define the characteristics of applicants to whom selection procedures are ultimately applied."[35] Although we frequently think of campus recruiting as a typical recruiting activity, many organizations use *internal recruiting*, or "promote-from-within" policies, to fill their high-level positions.[36] At Mellon Bank, for example, current employees are given preference when a position opens. Internal recruiting has several advantages: It is less costly than an external search, and it generates higher employee commitment, development, and satisfaction because it offers opportunities for career advancement to employees rather than outsiders.

Frequently, however, *external recruiting*—recruiting newcomers from outside the organization—is advantageous. Applicants are provided by a variety of outside sources including advertising, state employment services, private employment agencies (*headhunters*), job fairs, and employee referrals.

recruiting
The activities or practices that define the desired characteristics of applicants for specific jobs.

Craig Johnson (standing, with some of his recruits) is the founder of Venture Law Group, a firm that redefined what a law firm can do by seizing a unique niche for itself. The firm helps launch successful start-up companies using services that include external recruiting. Joseph Grundfest, a Stanford University professor, called Johnson with the vaguest glimmer of a business idea. Johnson recognized the elements of a successful start-up and used his expertise to get the business off the ground. "What we needed was somebody who could act as a coach and a team builder, who could bring to the table the right mix of people early on," comments Grundfest, who compares Johnson's role in Silicon Valley to that of a talent agent in Hollywood.

©Robert Holmgren

job analysis
The systematic process of gathering and interpreting information about the essential duties, tasks, and responsibilities of a job.

job description
A concise summary of the specific tasks and responsibilities of a particular job.

job specification
An outline of the knowledge, skills, education, and physical abilities needed to adequately perform a job.

realistic job preview
A recruiting approach that gives applicants all pertinent and realistic information about the job and the organization.

Assessing Organizational Needs.   An important step in recruiting is to get a clear picture of what kinds of people the organization needs. Basic building blocks of human resource management include job analysis, job descriptions, and job specifications. **Job analysis** is a systematic process of gathering and interpreting information about the essential duties, tasks, and responsibilities of a job, as well as about the context within which the job is performed.[37] To perform job analysis, managers or specialists ask about work activities and work flow, the degree of supervision given and received in the job, knowledge and skills needed, performance standards, working conditions, and so forth. The manager then prepares a written **job description**, which is a clear and concise summary of the specific tasks, duties, and responsibilities, and **job specification**, which outlines the knowledge, skills, education, physical abilities, and other characteristics needed to adequately perform the job.

Job analysis helps organizations recruit the right kind of people and match them to appropriate jobs. For example, to enhance internal recruiting, Sara Lee Corporation identified six functional areas and 24 significant skills that it wants its finance executives to develop, as illustrated in Exhibit 13.5. Managers are tracked on their development and moved into other positions to help them acquire the needed skills.[38]

Realistic Job Previews.   Job analysis also helps enhance recruiting effectiveness by enabling the creation of realistic job previews. A **realistic job preview** gives applicants all pertinent and realistic information—positive and negative—about the job and the organization.[39] RJPs enhance employee satisfaction and reduce turnover, because they facilitate matching individuals, jobs, and organizations. Individuals have a better basis on which to determine their suitability to the organization and "self-select" into or out of positions based on full information.

Legal Considerations.   Organizations must ensure that their recruiting practices conform to the law. As discussed earlier in this chapter, equal employment opportunity (EEO) laws stipulate that recruiting and hiring decisions cannot discriminate on the basis of race, national origin, religion, or sex.

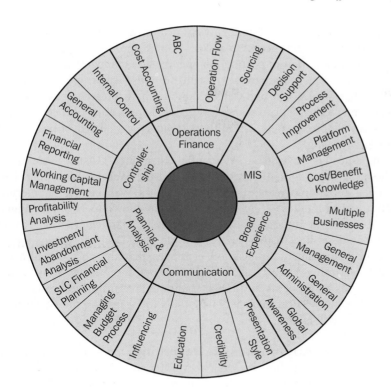

SOURCE: Victoria Griffith, "When Only Internal Expertise Will Do," *CFO* (October 1998), 95–96, 102.

Exhibit 13.5

Sara Lee's Required Skills for Finance Executives

The Americans with Disabilities Act underscored the need for well-written job descriptions and specifications that accurately reflect the mental and physical dimensions of jobs. *Affirmative action* refers to the use of goals, timetables, or other methods in recruiting to promote the hiring, development, and retention of *protected groups*—persons historically underrepresented in the workplace. For example, a city might establish a goal of recruiting one black firefighter for every white firefighter until the proportion of black firefighters is commensurate with the black population in the community.

Most large companies try to comply with affirmative action and EEO guidelines. Prudential Insurance Company's policy is presented in Exhibit 13.6. Prudential actively recruits employees and takes affirmative action steps to recruit individuals from all walks of life.

E-cruiting.   One of the fastest-growing approaches to recruiting today is use of the Internet, which dramatically extends an organization's recruiting reach.[40] Although traditional recruiting methods such as print advertisements

Exhibit 13.6

Prudential's Corporate Recruiting Policy

An Equal Opportunity Employer

Prudential recruits, hires, trains, promotes, and compensates individuals without regard to race, color, religion or creed, age, sex, marital status, national origin, ancestry, liability for service in the armed forces of the United States, status as a special disabled veteran or veteran of the Vietnam era, or physical or mental handicap.

This is official company policy because: • we believe it is right
• it makes good business sense
• it is the law

We are also committed to an ongoing program of affirmative action in which members of under-represented groups are actively sought out and employed for opportunities in all parts and at all levels of the company. In employing people from all walks of life, Prudential gains access to the full experience of our diverse society.

SOURCE: Prudential Insurance Company.

e-cruiting
Recruiting job applicants online.

and job fairs work quite well for many companies, **e-cruiting**, or recruiting job applicants online, offers access to a wider pool of applicants and can save time and money. In addition to posting job openings on company Web sites, many organizations use commercial recruiting sites such as Monster.com, CareerPath, HotJobs.com, and Career Mosaic, where job seekers can post their resumes and companies can search for qualified applicants. Forrester Research reports that approximately 2.5 million resumes are posted online, and the number is growing.[41]

Companies as diverse as Prudential Insurance, Cisco Systems, and Atkinsson Congregational Church have used the Web for recruiting. Cisco, which gets about 66 percent of new hires from the Web, claims that e-cruiting has cut the time it takes to fill a job from 113 days down to 45 days.[42] Vignette Corp. also uses the Internet as part of its recruiting strategy to hire great people fast, as described in the Leading Online box. Costs go down, too. The Employee Management Association estimates that the cost per hire using Internet recruiting is $377, versus $3,295 per hire using print media.[43] Organizations have not given up their traditional recruiting strategies, but the Internet has given HRM managers new tools for searching the world to find the best available talent.

Other Recent Approaches to Recruiting.   Organizations are also finding other ways to enhance their recruiting success. Most companies are putting renewed emphasis on referrals from current employees. A company's employees often know of someone who would be qualified for a position and fit in with the organization's culture. Many organizations offer cash awards to employees who submit names of people who subsequently accept employment, because referral by current employees is one of the cheapest and most reliable methods of external recruiting.[44] The professional service firm Deloitte & Touche has shelled out more than $3.5 million in cash awards to employees who refer candidates through the "Refer Potential Movers and Shakers" program, the firm's single best source of high-talent hires.[45]

In addition, some companies turn to nontraditional sources to find dedicated employees, particularly when there is a tight labor market. Manufacturer Dee Zee, which makes aluminum truck accessories in a factory in Des Moines, Iowa, found a source of loyal, hard-working employees among refugees from Bosnia, Vietnam, and Kosovo.[46] Since 1998, Bank of America has hired and trained more than 3,000 former welfare recipients in positions that offer the potential for promotions and long-term careers.[47] Days Inn has experimented with hiring the homeless, offering them wages plus a room for a small fee.[48] Recruiting on a global basis is on the rise, as well. Public schools are recruiting teachers from overseas. High-tech companies are looking for qualified workers in foreign countries because they cannot find people with the right skills in the United States.[49]

Selecting

selection
The process of determining the skills, abilities, and other attributes a person needs to perform a particular job.

The next step for managers is to select desired employees from the pool of recruited applicants. In the **selection** process, employers assess applicants' characteristics in an attempt to determine the "fit" between the job and applicant characteristics. Several selection devices are used for assessing applicant qualifications. The most frequently used are the application form, interview, employment test, and assessment center. Human resource professionals may

Leading Online

Vignette Corp. Hires Great People Fast

As soon as a job seeker posts a resume on Vignette's Web site, a notice pops up in a recruiter's e-mail inbox. Vignette doesn't want to give the competition time to strike first in the war for the best high-tech talent. Vignette's Web site gets around 100 resumes a day, and every qualified applicant gets a phone call the same day. Many people are hired within 48 hours.

Vignette, which makes software applications for online business, had to learn how to hire great people fast during the heady days when it grew from 100 to 2,300 worldwide employees in less than three years. But, despite the time pressure, Vignette also learned how to recruit and hire smart. One approach is leveraging the company's own flagship product—a business platform used by companies as an online channel for customer acquisition and retention—as a recruiting database. "We're looking for people who aren't looking for work," says recruiting director Stephanie Beard. "We want industry veterans . . . with the ability to get a product to market fast."

Another key is that the burden of recruiting does not all fall on the shoulders of HRM—at Vignette, all employees devote 10 percent of their time to recruiting. Greg Peters, chairman, CEO, and president, believes a company will quickly get left behind in the search for talent if the human resources department does it all. So, employees throughout the company search for qualified applicants and send online referral forms to recruiters via the company's intranet. More than 60 percent of all new hires come through employee referrals.

The final element in Vignette's effective hiring strategy is tag-team interviews, in which candidates are interviewed by as many as eight different staffers, each of whom focuses on a different area of the candidate's abilities. An internal recruiter wraps up the final interview, but people throughout the company have a chance to offer their varied perspectives and impressions.

Vignette's approach to online recruiting and rapid hiring is not as critical today, with growth slowing and more people looking for work. However, managers at Vignette know the war for high-tech talent is never over, and the company's recruiters, Web site, and employees are still actively recruiting to fill positions all over the world.

SOURCES: Debra Hunter, "How to Hire Great People at Web Speed," *Fast Company* (January 2001), 124–125; and *http://www.vignette.com*.

---

use a combination of these devices to obtain a valid prediction of employee job performance. **Validity** refers to the relationship between one's score on a selection device and one's future job performance. A valid selection procedure will provide high scores that correspond to subsequent high job performance.

Application Form.

The **application form** is used to collect information about the applicant's education, previous job experience, and other background characteristics. Research in the life insurance industry shows that biographical information inventories can validly predict future job success.[50]

One pitfall to be avoided is the inclusion of questions that are irrelevant to job success. In line with affirmative action, the application form should not ask questions that will create an adverse impact on protected groups unless the questions are clearly related to the job.[51] For example, employers should not ask whether the applicant rents or owns his or her own home because (1) an applicant's response might adversely affect his or her chances at the job, (2) minorities and women may be less likely to own a home, and (3) home ownership is probably unrelated to job performance. On the other hand, the CPA exam is relevant to job performance in a CPA firm; thus, it is appropriate to ask whether an applicant for employment has passed the CPA exam, even if only one-half of all female or minority applicants have done so versus nine-tenths of male applicants.

Interview.

The interview is used in the hiring process in almost every job category in virtually every organization. The *interview* serves as a two-way

validity
The relationship between an applicant's score on a selection device and his or her future job performance.

application form
A device for collecting information about an applicant's education, previous job experience, and other background characteristics.

THE NEW WORKPLACE   # Manager's Shoptalk

The Right Way to Interview a Job Applicant

A so-so interview usually nets a so-so employee. Many hiring mistakes can be prevented during the interview. The following techniques will ensure a successful interview:

1. *Know what you want.* Before the interview, prepare questions based on your knowledge of the job to be filled.
2. *Prepare a road map.* Develop questions that will reveal whether the candidate has the correct background and qualifications. The questions should focus on previous experiences that are relevant to the current job.
3. *Use open-ended questions in which the right answer is not obvious.* Ask the applicant to give specific examples of previous work experiences. For example, don't ask, "Are you a hard worker?" or "Tell me about yourself." Instead ask, "Can you give me examples from your previous work history that reflect your level of motivation?" or "How did you go about getting your current job?"
4. *Do not ask questions that are irrelevant to the job.* This is particularly important when the irrelevant questions might adversely affect minorities or women.
5. *Listen; don't talk.* You should spend most of the interview listening. If you talk too much, the focus will shift to you, and you might miss important cues. One expert actually recommends stating all your questions right at the beginning of the interview. This forces you to sit back and listen and also gives you a chance to watch a candidate's behavior and body language.
6. *Allow enough time so that the interview will not be rushed.* Leave time for the candidate to ask questions about the job. The types of questions the candidate asks can be an important clue to his or her interest in the job.

7. *Avoid reliance on your memory.* Request the applicant's permission to take notes; then do so unobtrusively during the interview or immediately after.

Even a well-planned interview may be disrupted by the unexpected. Robert Half asked vice presidents and human resource directors at 100 major American corporations to describe the most unusual thing that they were aware of ever happening during a job interview. Various applicants reportedly:

- "Wore a Walkman and said she could listen to me and the music at the same time."
- "Announced she hadn't had lunch and proceeded to eat a hamburger and french fries in the interviewer's office."
- "A balding candidate abruptly excused himself. He returned to the office a few minutes later wearing a hairpiece."
- "Not only did he ignore the 'No Smoking' sign in my office, he lit up the wrong end of several filter-tip cigarettes."
- "She chewed bubble gum and constantly blew bubbles."
- "Job applicant challenged the interviewer to arm wrestle."
- "He interrupted to telephone his therapist for advice on answering specific interview questions."
- "He dozed off and started snoring during the interview."

SOURCES: James M. Jenks and Brian L. P. Zevnik, "ABCs of Job Interviewing," *Harvard Business Review* (July–August 1989), 38–42; Dr. Pierre Mornell, "Zero Defect Hiring," *Inc,* (March 1998), 75–83; and Martha H. Peak, "What Color Is Your Bumbershoot?" Reprinted by permission of publisher from *Management Review* (October 1989), 63, ©1989. American Management Association, New York. All rights reserved.

communication channel that allows both the organization and the applicant to collect information that would otherwise be difficult to obtain.

This is another area where the organization can get into legal trouble if the interviewer asks questions that violate EEO guidelines. Exhibit 13.7 lists some examples of appropriate and inappropriate interview questions.

Although widely used, the interview is not generally a valid predictor of job performance. However, it has high *face validity*. That is, it seems valid to employers, and managers prefer to hire someone only after they have been through some form of interview, preferably face-to-face. This chapter's Manager's Shoptalk box offers some tips for effective interviewing. Today's organizations are trying different approaches to overcome the limitations of the interview. Some put candidates through a series of interviews, each one conducted by a different person and each one probing a different aspect of the candidate. Companies such as Virginia Power and Philip Morris USA use *panel interviews*, in which the candidate meets with several interviewers who take turns asking questions, to increase interview validity.[52]

Category	Okay to Ask	Inappropriate or Illegal to Ask
National origin	• The applicant's name • If applicant has ever worked under a different name	• The origin of applicant's name • Applicant's ancestry/ethnicity
Race	• Nothing	• Race or color of skin
Disabilities	• Whether applicant has any disabilities that might inhibit performance of job	• If applicant has any physical or mental defects • If applicant has ever filed workers' compensation claim
Age	• If applicant is over 18	• Applicant's age • When applicant graduated from high school
Religion	• Nothing	• Applicant's religious affiliation • What religious holidays applicant observes
Criminal record	• If applicant has ever been convicted of a crime	• If applicant has ever been arrested
Marital/family status	• Nothing	• Marital status, number of children or planned children • Child care arrangements
Education and Experience	• Where applicant went to school • Prior work experience	• When applicant graduated • Hobbies
Citizenship	• If applicant has a legal right to work in the United States	• If applicant is a citizen of another country

SOURCES: Based on "Appropriate and Inappropriate Interview Questions," in George Bohlander, Scott Snell, and Arthur Sherman, *Managing Human Resources*, 12th ed. (Cincinnati, Ohio: South-Western College Publishing, 2001), 207; and "Guidelines to Lawful and Unlawful Preemployment Inquiries," Appendix E, in Robert L. Mathis and John H. Jackson, *Human Resource Management*, 2nd ed., (Cincinnati, Ohio: South-Western, 2002), 189–190.

Exhibit 13.7

Employment Applications and Interviews: What Can You Ask?

Some organizations are also using *computer-based interviews* to complement traditional interviewing information. These typically require a candidate to answer a series of multiple-choice questions tailored to the specific job. The answers are compared to an ideal profile or to a profile developed on the basis of other candidates. Companies such as Pinkerton Security, Coopers & Lybrand, and Pic n' Pay Shoe Stores have found computer-based interviews to be valuable for searching out information regarding the applicant's honesty, work attitude, drug history, candor, dependability, and self-motivation.[53]

Employment Test. **Employment tests** may include intelligence tests, aptitude and ability tests, and personality inventories, particularly those shown to be valid predictors. Many companies today are particularly interested in personality inventories that measure such characteristics as openness to learning, initiative, responsibility, creativity, and emotional stability.

employment test
A written or computer-based test designed to measure a particular attribute such as intelligence or aptitude.

Assessment Center. First developed by psychologists at AT&T, assessment centers are used to select individuals with high potential for managerial careers by such organizations as IBM, General Electric, and JCPenney.[54] **Assessment centers** present a series of managerial situations to groups of applicants over, say, a two- or three-day period. One technique is the *in-basket simulation*, which requires the applicant to play the role of a manager who must decide how to respond to 10 memos in his or her in-basket within a two-hour

assessment center
A technique for selecting individuals with high managerial potential based on their performance on a series of simulated managerial tasks.

period. Panels of two or three trained judges observe the applicant's decisions and assess the extent to which they reflect interpersonal, communication, and problem-solving skills.

Assessment centers have proven to be valid predictors of managerial success, and some organizations now use them for hiring front-line workers as well. Mercury Communications in England uses an assessment center to select telecommunications customer assistants. Applicants participate in simulated exercises with customers and in various other exercises designed to assess their listening skills, customer sensitivity, and ability to cope under pressure.[55]

Developing an Effective Workforce

on-the-job training (OJT)
A type of training in which an experienced employee "adopts" a new employee to teach him or her how to perform job duties.

The mentoring program at General Electric pairs seasoned GE professionals with new employees. Mentoring serves as a training program for the new employee, but it also helps introduce the experienced employee to new techniques and ideas. Pairing industrious women and minorities with professionals for guidance and support is an important goal of the GE program. As this advertisement states, "When Paula Burris came to GE, she was given an office, a laptop and a Vice President."

Following selection, the next goal of HRM is to develop employees into an effective workforce. Development includes training and performance appraisal.

Training and Development

Training and development represent a planned effort by an organization to facilitate employees' learning of job-related behaviors.[56] Organizations spend nearly $100 billion each year on training. Training may occur in a variety of forms. The most common method is on-the-job training. In **on-the-job training (OJT)**, an experienced employee is asked to take a new employee "under his or her wing" and show the newcomer how to perform job duties. OJT has many advantages, such as few out-of-pocket costs for training facilities, materials, or instructor fees and easy transfer of learning back to the job. When implemented well, OJT is considered the fastest and most effective means of facilitating learning in the workplace.[57] One type of on-the-job training involves moving people to various types of jobs within the organization, where they work with experienced employees to learn different tasks. This cross-training may place an employee in a new position for as short as a few hours or for as long as a year, enabling the employee to develop new skills and giving the organization greater flexibility.

Another type of on-the-job training is *mentoring*, which means a more experienced employee is paired with a newcomer or a less-experienced worker to provide guidance, support, and learning opportunities. An innovative program at General Electric has turned the mentoring relationship upside down, pairing older, senior executives with little or no computer knowledge and expertise with young, computer and Internet-savvy employees to help the old-timers learn about the world of e-business.[58]

Other frequently used training methods include:

- *Orientation training*, in which newcomers are introduced to the organization's culture, standards, and goals
- *Classroom training*, including lectures, films, audiovisual techniques, and simulations
- *Self-directed learning*, also called programmed instruction, which involves the use of books, manuals, or computers to provide subject matter in highly organized and logical

sequences that require employees to answer a series of questions about the material

- *Computer-based training*, including computer-assisted instruction, Web-based training, and teletraining. (As with self-directed learning, the employee works at his or her own pace and instruction is individualized, but the training program is interactive and more complex, nonstructured information can be communicated.)

Exhibit 13.8 shows the most frequently used types and methods of training in today's organizations.

Corporate Universities.   A recent popular approach to training and development is the corporate university. The number of corporate universities has ballooned over the past decade, with more than 2,000 now in operation.[59] Perhaps the most well-known example is Hamburger University, McDonald's worldwide training center, which has been in existence for almost 40 years. A **corporate university** is an in-house training and education facility that offers broad-based learning opportunities for employees—and frequently for customers, suppliers, and strategic partners as well—throughout their careers.[60] For example, tens of thousands of FedEx employees, from couriers to top executives, have attended training at the company's Leadership Institute located near Memphis, Tennessee.[61] FedEx demonstrates a commitment to continuous learning by spending 3 percent of its total expenses on training, about six times that of most companies. Corporate universities have also extended their reach with new technology that enables distance learning via videoconferencing and online educational opportunities.

The growth of corporate universities, as well as new approaches such as computer-assisted and online programs, reflect a shift in mindset from *training* as something provided to employees to *learning* that employees initiate on their own to enhance their knowledge and skills and further their own career development.[62] For example, JCPenney has created a completely virtual corporate university, called The Learning Place, that offers ongoing educational opportunities to all of Penney's 200,000 employees.[63]

corporate university
An in-house training and education facility that offers broad-based learning opportunities for employees.

Promotion from Within.   Another way to further employee development is through promotion from within, which can help companies retain valuable employees. This provides challenging assignments, prescribes new responsibilities, and helps employees grow by expanding and developing their abilities.

One approach to promotion from within is *job posting*, which means that positions are announced on bulletin boards, on the intranet, or in company publications as openings occur. Interested employees notify the human resource department, which then helps make the fit between employees and positions.

Performance Appraisal

Performance appraisal is another important technique for developing an effective workforce. **Performance appraisal** comprises the steps of observing and assessing employee performance, recording the assessment, and providing feedback to the employee. During performance appraisal, skillful managers give feedback and praise concerning the acceptable elements of the employee's performance. They also describe performance areas that need improvement. Employees can use this information to change their job performance.

performance appraisal
The process of observing and evaluating an employee's performance, recording the assessment, and providing feedback to the employee.

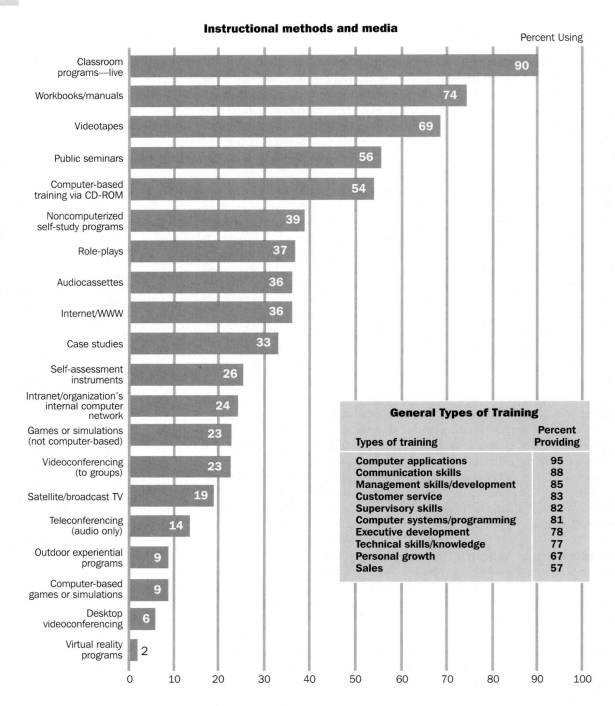

Instructional methods and media

Percent Using

Method	Percent
Classroom programs—live	90
Workbooks/manuals	74
Videotapes	69
Public seminars	56
Computer-based training via CD-ROM	54
Noncomputerized self-study programs	39
Role-plays	37
Audiocassettes	36
Internet/WWW	36
Case studies	33
Self-assessment instruments	26
Intranet/organization's internal computer network	24
Games or simulations (not computer-based)	23
Videoconferencing (to groups)	23
Satellite/broadcast TV	19
Teleconferencing (audio only)	14
Outdoor experiential programs	9
Computer-based games or simulations	9
Desktop videoconferencing	6
Virtual reality programs	2

0 10 20 30 40 50 60 70 80 90 100

General Types of Training

Types of training	Percent Providing
Computer applications	95
Communication skills	88
Management skills/development	85
Customer service	83
Supervisory skills	82
Computer systems/programming	81
Executive development	78
Technical skills/knowledge	77
Personal growth	67
Sales	57

Exhibit **13.8**

Types and Methods of Training

Performance appraisal can also reward high performers with merit pay, recognition, and other rewards. However, the most recent thinking is that linking performance appraisal to rewards has unintended consequences. The idea is that performance appraisal should be ongoing, not something that is done once a year as part of a consideration of raises.

Generally, HRM professionals concentrate on two things to make performance appraisal a positive force in their organization: (1) the accurate assessment of performance through the development and application of assessment systems such as rating scales and (2) training managers to effectively use the performance appraisal interview, so managers can provide feedback that will reinforce good performance and motivate employee development.

Assessing Performance Accurately. To obtain an accurate performance rating, managers must acknowledge that jobs are multidimensional and performance thus may be multidimensional as well. For example, a sports broadcaster may perform well on the job-knowledge dimension; that is, she or he may be able to report facts and figures about the players and describe which rule applies when there is a questionable play on the field. But the same sports broadcaster may not perform as well on another dimension, such as communication. She or he may be unable to express the information in a colorful way that interests the audience or may interrupt the other broadcasters.

If performance is to be rated accurately, the performance appraisal system should require the rater to assess each relevant performance dimension. A multidimensional form increases the usefulness of the performance appraisal and facilitates employee growth and development.

A recent trend in performance appraisal is called **360-degree feedback**, a process that uses multiple raters, including self-rating, as a way to increase awareness of strengths and weaknesses and guide employee development. Members of the appraisal group may include supervisors, coworkers, and customers, as well as the individual, thus providing appraisal of the employee from a variety of perspectives.[64] A recent study found that 26 percent of companies used some type of multirater performance appraisal in 2000, up from 11 percent in 1995.[65] At PhotoDisc, a Seattle digital-imaging company, employees participate in selecting the people who will evaluate them, and reviewers can enter their comments and evaluations into a computer-based program at any time. Managers still conduct year-end reviews, but they use the 360-degree feedback as a guide.[66]

Other alternative performance-evaluation methods have also been gaining ground. One controversial method, which is nevertheless growing in popularity, is the *performance review ranking*.[67] As most commonly used, a manager evaluates his or her direct reports relative to one another and categorizes each on a scale, such as A = outstanding performance, B = high-middle performance, or C = in need of improvement. Many companies routinely fire those people falling in the bottom 10 percent of the ranking. Ford Motor Company, Intel, Hewlett-Packard, Sun Microsystems and Microsoft all use versions of the ranking system.[68] Proponents say the ranking technique provides an effective way to assess performance and offer guidance for employee development. But critics of these systems, sometimes called *rank and yank*, argue that they are based on subjective judgments, produce skewed results, and discriminate against workers who are "different" from the mainstream. A class-action lawsuit charges that Ford's ranking system discriminates against older workers. Use of

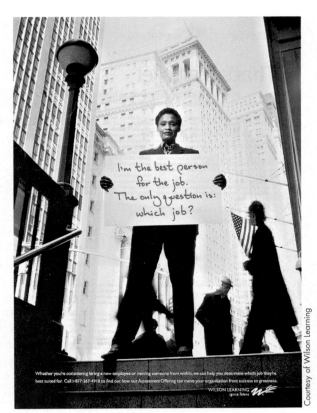

Wilson Learning Corporation provides employee training and assessment services to Fortune 500 companies around the world. One of its key functions is helping managers accurately assess employee performance. As stated in this Wilson ad, "Whether you're considering hiring a new employee or moving someone from within, we can help you determine which job they're best suited for. Call . . . to find out how our Assessment Offering can move your organization from success to greatness."

360-degree feedback
A process that uses multiple raters, including self-rating, to appraise employee performance and guide development.

the system has also triggered employee lawsuits at Conoco and Microsoft, and employment lawyers warn that other lawsuits will follow.[69]

Performance Evaluation Errors.   Although we would like to believe that every manager assesses employees' performance in a careful and bias-free manner, researchers have identified several rating problems.[70] One of the most dangerous is **stereotyping**, which occurs when a rater places an employee into a class or category based on one or a few traits or characteristics—for example, stereotyping an older worker as slower and more difficult to train. Another rating error is the **halo effect**, in which a manager gives an employee the same rating on all dimensions even if his or her performance is good on some dimensions and poor on others.

One approach to overcome management performance evaluation errors is to use a behavior-based rating technique, such as the behaviorally anchored rating scale. The **behaviorally anchored rating scale (BARS)** is developed from critical incidents pertaining to job performance. Each job performance scale is anchored with specific behavioral statements that describe varying degrees of performance. By relating employee performance to specific incidents, raters can more accurately evaluate an employee's performance.[71]

Exhibit 13.9 illustrates the BARS method for evaluating a production line supervisor. The production supervisor's job can be broken down into several dimensions, such as equipment maintenance, employee training, or work scheduling. A behaviorally anchored rating scale should be developed for each dimension. The dimension in Exhibit 13.9 is work scheduling. Good performance is represented by a 7, 8, or 9 on the scale and unacceptable performance as a 1, 2, or 3. If a production supervisor's job has eight dimensions, the total performance evaluation will be the sum of the scores for each of eight scales.

Maintaining an Effective Workforce

Now we turn to the topic of how managers and HRM professionals maintain a workforce that has been recruited and developed. Maintenance of the current workforce involves compensation, wage and salary systems, benefits, and occasional terminations.

Compensation

The term **compensation** refers to (1) all monetary payments and (2) all goods or commodities used in lieu of money to reward employees.[72] An organization's compensation structure includes wages and/or salaries and benefits such as health insurance, paid vacations, or employee fitness centers. Developing an effective compensation system is an important part of human resource management because it helps to attract and retain talented workers. In addition, a company's compensation system has an impact on strategic performance.[73] Human resource managers design the pay and benefits systems to fit company strategy and to provide compensation equity.

Wage and Salary Systems.   Ideally, management's strategy for the organization should be a critical determinant of the features and operations of the pay system.[74] For example, managers may have the goal of maintaining or improving profitability or market share by stimulating employee performance.

---

stereotyping
Placing an employee into a class or category based on one or a few traits or characteristics.

halo effect
A type of rating error that occurs when an employee receives the same rating on all dimensions regardless of his or her performance on individual ones.

behaviorally anchored rating scale (BARS)
A rating technique that relates an employee's performance to specific job-related incidents.

compensation
Monetary payments (wages, salaries) and nonmonetary goods/commodities (benefits, vacations) used to reward employees.

Job: Production Line Supervisor
Work Dimension: Work Scheduling

Develop a comprehensive schedule, document it, obtain required approvals, and distribute it to all concerned.

9

Plan, communicate, and observe target dates and update the status of operations relative to plans, making schedule modifications as quickly as necessary.

8

Experience minor operational problems but still communicate effectively, laying out all parts of the job and schedules for each.

7

Usually satisfy time constraints, with time and cost overruns coming up infrequently.

6

5

Make a list of due dates and revise them but are frequently surprised by unforeseen events.

Have a sound plan but neglect to keep track of target dates or to report schedule slippages or other problems as they occur.

4

3

Plan poorly, with ill-defined, unrealistic time schedules.

Have no plan or schedule of work and no concept of realistic due dates.

2

Fail consistently to complete work on time because of no planning or to express any interest in how to improve.

1

SOURCES: Based on J. P. Campbell, M. D. Dunnette, R. D. Arvey, and L. V. Hellervik, "The Development and Evaluation of Behaviorally Based Rating Scales," *Journal of Applied Psychology* 57 (1973), 15–22; and Francine Alexander, "Performance Appraisals," *Small Business Reports* (March 1989), 20–29.

Exhibit *13.9*

Example of a Behaviorally Anchored Rating Scale

Thus, they should design and use a merit pay system rather than a system based on other criteria such as seniority.

The most common approach to employee compensation is *job-based pay*, which means linking compensation to the specific tasks an employee performs. However, these systems present several problems. For one thing, job-based pay may fail to reward the type of learning behavior needed for the organization to adapt and survive in today's environment. In addition, these systems reinforce an emphasis on organizational hierarchy and centralized decision making and control, which are inconsistent with the growing emphasis on employee participation and increased responsibility.[75]

Skill-based pay systems are becoming increasingly popular in both large and small companies, including Sherwin-Williams, au Bon Pain, and Quaker Oats. Employees with higher skill levels receive higher pay than those with lower skill levels. At Quaker Oats pet food plant in Topeka, Kansas, for example, employees start at $8.75 per hour but can reach a top hourly rate of $14.50 when they master a series of skills.[76] Also called *competency-based pay*, skill-based pay systems encourage employees to develop their skills and competencies, thus making them more valuable to the organization as well as more employable if they leave their current jobs.

Compensation Equity.   Whether the organization uses job-based pay or skill-based pay, good managers strive to maintain a sense of fairness and equity within the pay structure and thereby fortify employee morale. **Job evaluation** refers to the process of determining the value or worth of jobs within

job evaluation
The process of determining the value of jobs within an organization through an examination of job content.

an organization through an examination of job content. Job evaluation techniques enable managers to compare similar and dissimilar jobs and to determine internally equitable pay rates—that is, pay rates that employees believe are fair compared with those for other jobs in the organization.

Organizations also want to make sure their pay rates are fair compared to other companies. HRM managers may obtain **wage and salary surveys** that show what other organizations pay incumbents in jobs that match a sample of "key" jobs selected by the organization. These surveys are available from a number of sources, including the U.S. Bureau of Labor Statistics National Compensation Survey.

Pay for Performance.   Most of today's organizations develop compensation plans based on a *pay-for-performance standard* to raise productivity and cut labor costs in a competitive global environment. **Pay-for-performance**, also called *incentive pay*, means tying at least part of compensation to employee effort and performance, whether it be through merit-based pay, bonuses, team incentives, or various gainsharing or profit-sharing plans. Data show that growth in base wages is slowing in many industries, and the use of pay-for-performance has steadily increased since the early 1990s, with approximately 70 percent of companies now offering some form of incentive pay.[77]

Incentives are aligned with the behaviors needed to help the organization achieve its strategic goals. Employees have an incentive to make the company more efficient and profitable because if goals are not met, no bonuses are paid.

Benefits

The best human resource managers know that a compensation package requires more than money. Although wage and salary is an important component, it is only a part. Equally important are the benefits offered by the organization. Benefits make up 40 percent of labor costs in the United States.[78]

Some benefits are required by law, such as Social Security, unemployment compensation, and worker's compensation. In addition, companies with 50 or more employees are required by the Family and Medical Leave Act of 1993 to give up to twelve weeks of unpaid leave for such things as the birth or adoption of a child, the serious illness of a spouse or family member, or an employee's serious illness. Other types of benefits, such as health insurance, vacations, and such things as on-site day care or fitness centers are not required by law but are provided by organizations to maintain an effective workforce.

One reason that benefits make up such a large portion of the compensation package is that health-care costs have been increasing so quickly. Many organizations require employees to absorb some of the cost of medical benefits, such as through copayments or higher deductibles.

Besides the actual cost of benefits, there remains the expense of administering them. Computerization can cut the time and expense tremendously; thus, benefits administration is the most technologically advanced area of HRM. At companies such as Wells Fargo and LG&E Energy, employees access their benefits package through an intranet, creating a "self-service" benefits administration.[79] This also enables employees to change their benefits selections easily. Today's organizations realize that the "one-size-fits-all" benefits package is no longer appropriate, so they frequently offer *cafeteria-plan benefits packages* that allow employees to select the benefits of greatest value to them.[80] Other companies use surveys to determine which combination of fixed benefits is most

---

wage and salary surveys
Surveys that show what other organizations pay incumbents in jobs that match a sample of "key" jobs selected by the organization.

pay-for-performance
Incentive pay that ties at least part of compensation to employee effort and performance.

©Elena Dorfman—Matrix

Managers at Agilent Technologies, an $8.3 billion technology spin-off from Hewlett-Packard, have worked hard to gain employees' trust. When downsizing became necessary and managers had to terminate a large number of workers, they made the layoffs easier by showing empathy and respect for employees. As a result, after the workers at this Agilent plant in Newark, California, were told their plant was closing, they upped production higher than ever before—out of respect for their managers and concern for co-workers in other plants. Agilent's humane approach helped the company attain a spot on Fortune *magazine's list of Best Companies to Work For even in the midst of downsizing and cost-cutting.*

desirable. The benefits packages provided by large companies attempt to meet the needs of all employees.

Termination

Despite the best efforts of line managers and HRM professionals, the organization will lose employees. Some will retire, others will depart voluntarily for other jobs, and still others will be forced out through mergers and cutbacks or for poor performance. The value of termination for maintaining an effective workforce is twofold. First, employees who are poor performers can be dismissed. Productive employees often resent disruptive, low-performing employees who are allowed to stay with the company and receive pay and benefits comparable to theirs. Second, employers can use exit interviews as a valuable HR tool, regardless of whether the employee leaves voluntarily or is forced out. An **exit interview** is an interview conducted with departing employees to determine why they are leaving.[81] The value of the exit interview is to provide an excellent and inexpensive way to learn about pockets of dissatisfaction within the organization and hence reduce future turnover.

When companies experience downsizing through mergers or because of global competition or a shifting economy, often a large number of managers and workers are terminated at the same time. In these cases, enlightened companies try to find a smooth transition for departing employees. For example, General Electric laid off employees in three gradual steps. It also set up a reemployment center to assist employees in finding new jobs or in learning new skills. It provided counseling in how to write a résumé and conduct a job search. Additionally, General Electric placed an advertisement in local newspapers saying that these employees were available.[82]

By showing genuine concern in helping place laid-off employees, a company communicates the value of human resources and helps maintain a positive corporate culture.

exit interview
An interview conducted with departing employees to determine the reasons for their termination.

■ Summary and Management Solution

This chapter described several important points about human resource management in organizations. All managers are responsible for human resources, and most organizations have a human resource department that works with line managers to ensure a productive workforce. Human resource management plays a key strategic role in today's organizations. HRM is changing in three ways to keep today's organizations competitive–focusing on human capital; globalizing HR systems, policies, and structures; and using information technology to help achieve strategic goals. The HR department must also implement procedures to reflect federal and state legislation and respond to changes in working relationships and career directions. The old social contract of the employee being loyal to the company and the company taking care of the employee until retirement no longer holds. Employees are responsible for managing their own careers. Although many people still follow a traditional management career path, others look for new opportunities as contingent workers, telecommuters, team players, and virtual employees.

The HR department strives to achieve three goals for the organization. The first goal of the human resource department is to attract an effective workforce through human resource planning, recruiting, and employee selection. The second is to develop an effective workforce. Newcomers are introduced to the organization and to their jobs through orientation and training programs. Moreover, employees are evaluated through performance appraisal programs. The third goal is to maintain an effective workforce. Human resource managers retain employees with wage and salary systems, benefits packages, and termination procedures. In many organizations, information technology is being used to more effectively meet all three of these important HR goals.

At Bellagio Resort, described in the opening case, Arte Nathan knew the only way his department could handle the massive task of hiring nearly 10,000 people in only a few months was to put everything online, creating electronic job applications, processing documents, and personnel files for the final hires. HRM staff handled details of narrowing down the list of candidates, but responsibility for all interviewing and hiring was transferred directly to managers in the various departments. Managers received a week's instruction on how to use the online system and how to conduct an effective interview in 30 minutes. Even an extra 5 or 10 minutes could have sent the whole operation into a tailspin when 180 managers were conducting 740 interviews a day.

Eventually, Bellagio's entire HRM system, from application to termination, was computerized. Even a large part of employee orientation is handled by computer, but face-to-face training, which uses employees from the various areas of the hotel as presenters, is an important component. Computerizing HRM has not only freed staff from mundane chores and paperwork but also improved their effectiveness in long-term strategic planning. For example, having all the data about the workforce at their fingertips helps HRM personnel work with managers to better forecast human resource needs and plan for the future. Computerizing routine transactions, according to Nathan, allows HRM to "start thinking strategically and globally."[83]

■ Discussion Questions

1. It is the year 2010. In your company, central planning has given way to frontline decision making, and bureaucracy has given way to teamwork. Shop floor workers use computers and robots. There is a labor shortage for many job openings, and the few applicants lack skills to work in teams, make decisions, or use sophisticated technology. As vice-president of human resource management since 2000, what should you have done to prepare for this problem?

2. If you were asked to advise a private company about its equal employment opportunity responsibilities, what two points would you emphasize as most important?

3. How can the human resource activities of recruiting, performance appraisal, and compensation be related to corporate strategy?

4. Think back to your own job experience. What human resource management activities described in this chapter were performed for the job you filled? Which ones were absent?

5. How "valid" do you think the information obtained from a personal interview versus an employment test versus an assessment center would be for predicting effective job performance for a college professor? An assembly-line worker in a team-oriented plant? Discuss.

6. How will the growing use of telecommuters, contingent workers, and virtual teams affect human resource management? How can managers improve recruiting and retention of these new kinds of employees?

7. Do you see any conflict between the current emphasis on computerizing HR and the growing focus on building human capital? Discuss.

8. Why is mentoring such a powerful means of developing an effective workforce?

9. What is the role of compensation in maintaining an effective workforce? When would benefits play an important part in compensation? When might they not be important?

10. What purpose do exit interviews serve for human resource management?

■ Management in Practice: Experiential Exercise

Test Your Human Resources Knowledge

This quiz will test your knowledge of human resources issues affecting today's workplace. The quiz was designed by the Council on Education in Management, a Walnut Creek, California, firm that conducts human resources and employment law seminars nationwide.

1. If you receive an unsolicited résumé in the mail, you must keep it for two years.   T   F

2. Time-management principles are pretty much the same in any administrative job.   T   F

3. Regardless of the type of business or the various laws that may apply, there is a core of common practices for keeping personnel records and files that makes sense for almost any organization.   T   F

4. Every employer must have an affirmative action plan.   T   F

5. An employer must investigate an allegation of sexual harassment even if the victim asks to remain anonymous.   T   F

6. An employer is not obligated to pay overtime to a nonexempt employee who works more than 40 hours in a week after being asked not to put in overtime.   T   F

7. If your company is found guilty of discrimination, the Equal Employment Opportunity Commission will be more lenient if your records show that the violation was unintentional.   T   F

8. Americans with Disabilities Act regulations require companies to maintain written job descriptions.   T   F

9. Reference checking is an important procedure, despite the fact that many companies won't release this information.   T   F

10. Your employee orientation and handbook should help assure new employees that they will be a part of the team as long as they do a good job.   T   F

Answers: 1. F; 2. F; 3. T; 4. F; 5. T; 6. F; 7. F; 8. F; 9. T; 10. F.

■ Management in Practice: Ethical Dilemma

A Conflict of Responsibilities

As director of human resources, Tess Danville was asked to negotiate a severance deal with Terry Winston, the Midwest regional sales manager for Cyn-Com Systems. Winston's problems with drugs and alcohol had become severe enough to precipitate his dismissal. His customers were devoted to him, but top management was reluctant to continue gambling on his reliability. Lives depended on his work as the salesman and installer of Cyn-Com's respiratory diagnostic technology. Winston had been warned twice to clean up his act, but had never succeeded. Only his unique blend of technical knowledge and high-powered sales ability had saved him before.

But now the vice president of sales asked Danville to offer Winston the option of resigning rather than be fired if he would sign a noncompete agreement and agree to go into

rehabilitation. Cyn-Com would also extend a guarantee of confidentiality on the abuse issue and a good work reference as thanks for the millions of dollars of business that Winston had brought to Cyn-Com. Winston agreed to take the deal. After his departure, a series of near disasters was uncovered as a result of Winston's mismanagement. Some of his maneuvers to cover up his mistakes bordered on fraud.

Today Danville received a message to call the human resources director at a cardiopulmonary technology company to give a personal reference on Terry Winston. From the area code, Danville could see that he was not in violation of the noncompete agreement. She had also heard that Winston had completed a 30-day treatment program as promised. Danville knew she was expected to honor the confidentiality agreement, but she also knew that if his shady dealings had been discovered before his departure, he would have been fired without any agreement. Now she was being asked to give Winston a reference for another medical sales position.

What Do You Do?

1. Honor the agreement, trusting Winston's rehabilitation is complete on all levels and that he is now ready for a responsible position. Give a good recommendation.

2. Contact the vice-president of sales and ask him to release you from the agreement or to give the reference himself. After all, he made the agreement. You don't want to lie.

3. Without mentioning specifics, give Winston such an unenthusiastic reference that you hope the other human resources director can read between the lines and believe that Winston will be a poor choice.

■ Surf the Net

1. **100 Great Places to Work** Go to *http://www.greatplace towork.com.* Locate these two items at the site:
Great Place to Work® Model©
Benefits of Being a Great Place to Work®
Print out both pages, read and highlight sections of particular interest to you, and then submit your highlighted printouts to your instructor to show you've completed this assignment.

2. **Internet Recruiting.** Select the tab "For Employers" located at the top of the following site: *http://www. wetfeet.com*
At this site you will learn more about how employers are using the Internet to help them in the recruiting process.

Locate information on recruitment technologies and the featured "Recruitment Website of the Month." Summarize your findings in a printed note or e-mail to your instructor.

3. **Compensation.** Fill in the following information about yourself: After receiving the college degree you're currently pursuing,
(a) what kind of job do you see yourself doing?
(b) where, geographically, do you wish to work? (For this assignment, you will need to select a U.S. location.)
Now find the "Salary Wizard" at *http://www.salary.com.* Provide the information requested and then select "Create salary report." Print out the report, write your name at the top, and submit it to your instructor.

■ Case for Critical Analysis

Waterway Industries

Waterway Industries was founded in the late 1960s as a small manufacturer of high-quality canoes. Based in Lake Placid, New York, the company quickly gained a solid reputation throughout the Northeast and began building a small customer base in the Pacific Northwest as well. By the late 1980s, Waterway was comfortably ensconced in the canoe market. Although earnings growth was fairly steady, CEO Cyrus Maher was persuaded by a friend to venture into kayaks. After Waterway began selling its own line of compact, inexpensive kayaks in 1998, Maher quickly learned that the decision was a good one. Most of Waterway's existing canoe customers placed sizable kayak orders, and a number of private-label companies also began contacting Maher about making kayaks for their companies. When Lee Carter was hired to establish a formal marketing department at Waterway, things really took off. Carter began bringing in so many large orders that the company had to contract with other manufacturers to keep up.

Managers began to envision the day when Waterway would be a major player in water sports equipment. They developed a long-range strategic plan that called for aggressive growth, new product designs, and nationwide marketing and distribution by 2003. Maher believes most employees are adjusting well to the faster pace at the company. Many of the shop-floor employees are outdoor enthusiasts who like making quality products that they and their friends use. Waterway has always

had a relaxed, informal working atmosphere, where employees get along well, enjoy their jobs, and get their work completed on time. However, the greater work load means people have less time for horsing around, and they can no longer leave by 3 P.M. to enjoy canoeing or kayaking when the weather is good.

Maher thinks workers have been given adequate raises to compensate for the faster work pace, but he has recently been hearing complaints from the shop floor about inadequate pay. He recently turned down a request from the plant supervisor for additional hourly wage increases for top performers, insisting that wages were in line with what other local manufacturers were paying. Unfortunately, a new automotive parts plant offering a slightly higher wage recently lured away three of his best workers.

Several managers have also approached Maher about salary adjustments. Waterway's two designers suggested that they would be interested in equity (part ownership) in the company, whereby they would receive a share of the profits if their designs did well. Maher's response was to give the senior designer a modest pay raise and extra vacation and to increase the bonuses for both designers. Both seemed satisfied with the new arrangement. Waterway's CFO, on the other hand, recently left the company to take a position with a power boat manufacturer after Maher twice refused his request for a redesigned compensation package to include equity. Now, on a trip to the cafeteria to get a cup of coffee, Maher has just overheard Lee Carter discussing a possible job opportunity with another company. He is well aware of the lucrative packages being offered to sales and marketing managers in the sporting goods industry, and he doesn't want to lose Carter. He would like to find a way to recognize her hard work and keep her at Waterway for at least a few more years.

Maher has asked you, the company's sole human resource manager, for advice about changing the company's compensation system. In the past, he has handled things informally, giving employees annual salary increases and bonuses, and dealing with employees one-on-one (as he did with the designers) when they have concerns about their current compensation. Now, Maher is wondering if his company has grown to the point where he needs to establish some kind of formal compensation system that can recognize employees who make outstanding contributions to the company's success.

Questions

1. Does Waterway's current compensation system seem to fit the company's strategy of aggressive growth and product innovation? How might it be changed to achieve a better fit?

2. How would you gather the data and design a competitive compensation system for Waterway? Would your approach be different for hourly workers versus managers?

3. How can nonfinancial incentives play a role in helping Waterway retain hourly shop workers? Aggressive and ambitious managers like Lee Carter?

Source: Based on Robert D. Nicoson, "Growing Pains," *Harvard Business Review* (July–August 1996), 20–36.

■ Endnotes

1. Bill Breen, "Full House," *Fast Company* (January 2001), 110–122.

2. Robert L. Mathis and John H. Jackson, *Human Resource Management: Essential Perspectives*, 2nd ed., (Cincinnati, Ohio: South-Western Publishing, 2002), 1.

3. Jonathan Poet, "Schools Looking Overseas for Teachers," *Johnson City Press* (April 20, 2001), 6; and Jill Rosenfeld, "How's This for a Tough Assignment?" *Fast Company* (November 1999), 104–106.

4. Mark A. Huselid, Susan E. Jackson, and Randall S. Schuler, "Technical and Strategic Human Resource Management Effectiveness as Determinants of Firm Performance," *Academy of Management Journal* 40, no. 1 (1997), 171–188; and John T. Delaney and Mark A. Huselid, "The Impact of Human Resource Management Practices on Perceptions of Organizational Performance," *Academy of Management Journal* 39, no. 4 (1996), 949–969.

5. D. Kneale, "Working at IBM: Intense Loyalty in a Rigid Culture," *The Wall Street Journal* (April 7, 1986), 17.

6. Jeffrey Pfeffer, "Producing Sustainable Competitive Advantage through the Effective Management of People," *Academy of Management Executive* 9, no. 1 (1995), 55–72.

7. James N. Baron and David M. Kreps, "Consistent Human Resource Practices," *California Management Review* 41, no. 3 (Spring 1999), 29–53.

8. Cynthia D. Fisher, "Current and Recurrent Challenges in HRM," *Journal of Management* 15 (1989), 157–180.

9. See Dave Ulrich, "A New Mandate for Human Resources," *Harvard Business Review* (January–February 1998), 124–134; Philip H. Mirvis, "Human Resource Management: Leaders, Laggards, and Followers," *Academy of Management Executive* 11, no. 2 (1997), 43–56; Richard McBain, "Attracting, Retaining, and Motivating Capable People," *Manager Update* (Winter 1999), 25–36; and Oren Harari, "Attracting the Best Minds," *Management Review* (April 1998), 23–26.

10. Floyd Kemske, "HR 2008: A Forecast Based on Our Exclusive Study," *Workforce* (January 1998), 46–60.

11. This definition and discussion is based on George Bollander, Scott Snell, and Arthur Sherman, *Managing Human Resources* 12th ed., (Cincinnati, Ohio: South-Western Publishing, 2001), 13–15.

12. Jennifer J. Laabs, "It's OK to Focus on Heart and Soul," *Workforce* (January 1997), 60–69.

13. Rich Wellins and Sheila Rioux, "The Growing Pains of Globalizing HR," *Training and Development* (May 2000), 79–85.

14. Ibid.

15. Alison Stein Wellner, "Click Here for HR," *Business Week Frontier* (April 24, 2000), F24–F26; and Esther Shein, "Requiem for a Paperweight," *eCFO* (Winter 2000), 81–83.

16. Deidre A. Depke, "Picking Up the Tab for Bias at Shoney's," *BusinessWeek* (November 6, 1992), 50.

17. Section 1604.1 of the EEOC Guidelines based on the Civil Rights Act of 1964, Title VII.

18. Charles F. Falk and Kathleen A. Carlson, "Newer Patterns in Management for the Post–Social Contract Era," *Midwest Management Society Proceedings* (1995), 45–52.

19. Richard Pascale, "The False Security of 'Employability,'" *Fast Company* (April–May 1996), 62, 64; and Louisa Wah, "The New Workplace Paradox," *Management Review*, January 1998, 7.

20. Douglas T. Hall and Jonathan E. Moss, "The New Protean Career Contract: Helping Organizations and Employees Adapt," *Organizational Dynamics* (Winter 1998), 22–37.

21. Wal-Mart employee data from "Inside the Fortune 500: How the Companies Stack Up," *Fortune* (April 16, 2001), F29–F32.

22. The discussion of temporary employment agencies is based on David Wessel, "Capital: Temp Workers Have a Lasting Effect," *The Wall Street Journal* (February 1, 2001), A1.

23. Brenda Paik Sunoo, "Temp Firms Turn Up the Heat on Hiring," *Workforce* (April 1999), 50–54.

24. Hall and Moss, "The New Protean Career Contract," and John Challenger, "There Is No Future For the Workplace," *Public Management* (February 1999), 20–23.

25. Jaclyn Fierman, "The Contingency Workforce," *Fortune* (January 24, 1994), 30–31.

26. Nancy B. Kurland and Diane E. Bailey, "Telework: The Advantages and Challenges of Working Here, There, Anywhere, Anytime," *Organizational Dynamics* (Autumn 1999), 53–68.

27. Kevin Voigt, "For 'Extreme Telecommuters,' Remote Work Means Really Remote," *The Wall Street Journal* (January 31, 2001), B1.

28. Ibid.

29. Challenger, "There Is No Future For the Workplace."

30. Sean Donahue, "New Jobs for the New Economy," *Business 2.0* (July 1999), 102–109.

31. James G. March and Herbert A. Simon, *Organizations* (New York: Wiley, 1958).

32. Richard McBain, "Attracting, Retaining, and Motivating Capable People: A Key to Competitive Advantage," *Manager Update* (Winter 1999), 25–36.

33. Dennis J. Kravetz, *The Human Resources Revolution* (San Francisco, Calif.: Jossey-Bass, 1989).

34. David E. Ripley, "How to Determine Future Workforce Needs," *Personnel Journal* (January 1995), 83–89.

35. J. W. Boudreau and S. L. Rynes, "Role of Recruitment in Staffing Utility Analysis," *Journal of Applied Psychology* 70 (1985), 354–366.

36. Brian Dumaine, "The New Art of Hiring Smart," *Fortune* (August 17, 1987), 78–81.

37. This discussion is based on Mathis and Jackson, *Human Resource Management*, Chapter 4, 49–60.

38. Victoria Griffith, "When Only Internal Expertise Will Do," *CFO* (October 1998), 95–96, 102.

39. J. P. Wanous, *Organizational Entry* (Reading, Mass.: Addison-Wesley, 1980).

40. Samuel Greengard, "Technology Finally Advances HR," *Workforce* (January 2000), 38–41; and Scott Hays, "Hiring on the Web," *Workforce* (August 1999), 77–84.

41. Marlene Piturro, "The Power of E-Cruiting," *Management Review* (January 2000), 33–37.

42. Jerry Useem, "For Sale Online: You," *Fortune* (July 5, 1999), 67–78.

43. George Bohlander, Scott Snell, and Arthur Sherman, *Managing Human Resources*, 12th ed., (Cincinnati, Ohio: South-Western College Publishing, 2001), 145.

44. Kathryn Tyler, "Employees Can Help Recruit New Talent," *HR Magazine* (September 1996), 57–60.

45. Carol Leonetti Dannhauser, "Putting the Ooh in Recruiting," *Working Woman* (March 2000), 32–34.

46. Ann Harrington, "Anybody Here Want a Job?" *Fortune* (May 15, 2000), 489–498.

47. "Bank of America to Hire 850 Ex-Welfare Recipients," *Johnson City Press* (January 14, 2001), 29.

48. E. Blacharczyk, "Recruiters Challenged by Economy, Shortages, Unskilled," *HRNews* (February 1990), B1.

49. Victoria Rivkin, "Visa Relief," *Working Woman* (January 2001), 15.

50. P. W. Thayer, "Somethings Old, Somethings New," *Personnel Psychology* 30 (1977), 513–524.

51. J. Ledvinka, *Federal Regulation of Personnel and Human Resource Management* (Boston: Kent, 1982); and Civil Rights Act, Title VII, 42 U.S.C. Section 2000e *et seq.* (1964).

52. Bohlander, Snell, and Sherman, *Managing Human Resources*, 202.

53. Ibid.

54. "Assessment Centers: Identifying Leadership through Testing," *Small Business Report* (June 1987), 22–24; and W. C. Byham, "Assessment Centers for Spotting Future Managers," *Harvard Business Review* (July–August 1970), 150–167.

55. Mike Thatcher, "'Front-line' Staff Selected by Assessment Center," *Personnel Management* (November 1993), 83.

56. Bernard Keys and Joseph Wolfe, "Management Education and Development: Current Issues and Emerging Trends," *Journal of Management* 14 (1988), 205–229.

57. William J. Rothwell and H. C. Kazanas, *Improving On-The-Job Training: How to Establish and Operate a Comprehensive OJT Program* (San Francisco, CA: Jossey-Bass, 1994).

58. Matt Murray, "GE Mentoring Program Turns Underlings Into Teachers of the Web," *The Wall Street Journal* (February 15, 2000), B1, B16.

59. Jeanne C. Meister, "The Brave New World of Corporate Education," *The Chronicle of Higher Education* (February 9, 2001), B10–B11.

60. Meister, "The Brave New World of Corporate Education" and Meryl Davids Landau, "Corporate Universities Crack Open Their Doors," *The Journal of Business Strategy* (May–June 2000), 18–23.

61. John Byrne, "The Search for the Young and Gifted," *Business Week* (October 4, 1999), 108–116.

62. Eileen M. Garger, "Goodbye Training, Hello Learning," *Workforce* (November 1999), 35–42.

63. Ibid.

64. Walter W. Tornow, "Editor's Note: Introduction to Special Issue on 360-Degree Feedback," *Human Resource Management* 32, no. 2/3 (Summer/Fall 1993), 211–219; and Brian O'Reilly, "360 Feedback Can Change Your Life," *Fortune* (October 17, 1994), 93–100.

65. Kris Frieswick, "Truth & Consequences," *CFO* (June 2001), 56–63.

66. Carol A. L. Dannhauser, "How'm I Doing?" *Working Woman* (December–January 1999), 38.

67. This discussion is based on Matthew Boyle, "Performance Reviews: Perilous Curves Ahead," *Fortune* (May 28, 2001), 187–188; Carol Hymowitz, "Ranking Systems Gain Popularity But Have Many Staffers Riled," (In the Lead column), *The Wall Street Journal* (May 15, 2001), B1; and Frieswick, "Truth & Consequences."

68. Boyle, "Performance Reviews."

69. Hymowitz, "Ranking Systems Gain Popularity," and Boyle, "Performance Reviews."

70. V. R. Buzzotta, "Improve Your Performance Appraisals," *Management Review* (August 1988), 40–43; and H. J.

Bernardin and R. W. Beatty, *Performance Appraisal: Assessing Human Behavior at Work* (Boston: Kent, 1984).

71. Ibid.

72. Richard I. Henderson, *Compensation Management: Rewarding Performance*, 4th ed. (Reston, Va.: Reston, 1985).

73. L. R. Gomez-Mejia, "Structure and Process Diversification, Compensation Strategy, and Firm Performance," *Strategic Management Journal* 13 (1992), 381–397; and E. Montemayor, "Congruence Between Pay Policy and Competitive Strategy in High-Performing Firms," *Journal of Management* 22, no. 6 (1996), 889–908.

74. Renée F. Broderick and George T. Milkovich, "Pay Planning, Organization Strategy, Structure and 'Fit': A Prescriptive Model of Pay" (paper presented at the 45th Annual Meeting of the Academy of Management, San Diego, August 1985).

75. E. F. Lawler, III, *Strategic Pay: Aligning Organizational Strategies and Pay Systems,* (San Francisco: Jossey-Bass, 1990); and R. J. Greene, "Person-Focused Pay: Should It Replace Job-Based Pay?" *Compensation and Benefits Management* 9, no. 4 (1993), 46–55.

76. L. Wiener, "No New Skills? No Raise," *U.S. News and World Report* (October 26, 1992), 78.

77. Data from Hewitt Associates, Bureau of Labor Statistics, reported in Michelle Conlin and Peter Coy, with Ann Therese Palmer, and Gabrielle Saveri, "The Wild New Workforce," *BusinessWeek* (December 6, 1999), 39–44.

78. *Employee Benefits,* 1997 (Washington, D.C.: U. S. Chamber of Commerce, 1997), 7.

79. Frank E. Kuzmits, "Communicating Benefits: A Double-Click Away," *Compensation and Benefits Review* 30, no. 5 (September–October 1998), 60–64; and Lynn Asinof, "Click and Shift: Workers Control Their Benefits Online," *The Wall Street Journal* (November 27, 1997), C1.

80. Robert S. Catapano-Friedman, "Cafeteria Plans: New Menu for the '90s," *Management Review* (November 1991), 25–29.

81. "Exit Interviews: An Overlooked Information Source," *Small Business Report* (July 1986), 52–55.

82. Yvette Debow, "GE: Easing the Pain of Layoffs," *Management Review* (September 1997), 15–18.

83. Breen, "Full House."

Managing Diverse Employees

CHAPTER OUTLINE

Valuing Diversity

Dimensions of Diversity

Attitudes toward Diversity

The Changing Workplace

Challenges Minorities Face

Management Challenges

Affirmative Action

Current Debates about
Affirmative Action

The Glass Ceiling

Current Responses to Diversity

Changing the Corporate Culture

Changing Structures and Policies

Diversity Awareness Training

Defining New Relationships in
Organizations

Emotional Intimacy

Sexual Harassment

Global Diversity

Selection and Training

Communication Differences

Diversity in the New Workplace

Multicultural Teams

Employee Network Groups

LEARNING OBJECTIVES

After studying this chapter, you should be able to

1 Explain the dimensions of employee diversity and why ethnorelativism is the appropriate attitude for today's corporations.

2 Discuss the changing workplace and the management activities required for a culturally diverse workforce.

3 Understand the challenges minority employees face daily.

4 Explain affirmative action and why factors such as the glass ceiling have kept it from being more successful.

5 Describe how to change the corporate culture, structure, and policies and how to use diversity awareness training to meet the needs of diverse employees.

6 Explain the importance of addressing sexual harassment in the workplace.

7 Define the importance of multicultural teams and employee network groups for today's globally diverse organizations.

Management Challenge

When African-American employees at Texaco filed a racial discrimination lawsuit against the company several years ago, top executives took quick action to defend the company against the charges and try to save Texaco's reputation. But as the drama unfolded, it soon became clear that Texaco's lawyers were facing an impossible task. A top official had secretly taped meetings of managers freely using racial epithets and discussing how to make incriminating documents "disappear." One of the key plaintiffs published a book detailing the humiliations she and other black employees had suffered for years. In addition to exposing blatant acts of racism by Texaco managers and employees, the lawsuit revealed several examples of institutional racism, such as hundreds of minority employees being paid less than the minimum salary for their job category. With mounting evidence staring him in the face, CEO Peter Bijur reached for the white flag. Texaco settled the case for a whopping $175 million, a portion of which would set up an independent task force to monitor Texaco's diversity efforts. Bijur and other top leaders knew the settlement was just the beginning of the pain. The real challenge would be to root out and destroy the racism that permeated the organization. Modest diversity efforts and promises weren't going to cut it. Top executives had to come up with solid plans to make supporting and valuing diverse employees a key element of Texaco's culture.[1]

If you were a top manager at Texaco, what steps would you take to make Texaco a company where minority employees feel valued, respected, and supported?

Texaco is not the only company that has faced difficulties with issues of diversity. In recent years, high-profile racial discrimination or harassment lawsuits have been filed against Lockheed Martin, Coca-Cola, and Boeing. Mitsubishi is still reeling from the effects of the largest sexual harassment lawsuit in history, which was brought by the Equal Employment Opportunity Commission in 1996 after hundreds of women charged that Mitsubishi ignored complaints that they were regularly groped on the factory floor and made to endure crude jokes and lewd photographs.[2]

Diversity in the population, the workforce, and the marketplace is a fact of life no manager can afford to ignore today. All managers daily face the challenge of managing employee diversity. The management of employee diversity entails recruiting, training, and fully utilizing workers who reflect the broad spectrum of society in all areas—gender, race, age, disability, ethnicity, religion, sexual orientation, education, and economic level.

Companies such as IBM, Fannie Mae, Allstate Insurance, and Hewlett-Packard all have established programs for increasing diversity. These programs teach current employees to value ethnic, racial, and gender differences, direct their recruiting efforts, and provide development training for women and minorities. These companies value diversity and are enforcing this value in day-to-day recruitment and promotion decisions.

Companies are beginning to reflect the U.S. image as a melting pot, but with a difference. In the past, the United States was a place where people of different national origins, ethnicities, races, and religions came together and blended to resemble one another. Opportunities for advancement were limited to those workers who fit easily into the mainstream of the larger culture. Some immigrants chose desperate measures to fit in, such as abandoning their native language, changing their last name, and sacrificing their own unique cultures. In essence, everyone in workplace organizations was encouraged to share similar beliefs, values, and lifestyles despite differences in gender, race, and ethnicity.[3]

Now organizations recognize that everyone is not the same and that the differences people bring to the workplace are valuable.[4] Rather than expecting all employees to adopt similar attitudes and values, companies are learning that these differences enable them to compete globally and to acquire rich sources of new talent. Although diversity in North America has been a reality for some time, genuine efforts to accept and *manage* diverse people began only in recent years.

This chapter introduces the topic of diversity, its causes and consequences. We will look at some of the challenges minorities face, ways managers deal with workforce diversity, and organizational responses to create an environment that welcomes and values diverse employees. The chapter will also look at issues of sexual harassment, global diversity, and new approaches to managing diversity in today's workplace.

Valuing Diversity

At 3Com's modem factory in Morton Grove, Illinois, the 1,200 workers speak 20 different native languages.[5] Such astonishing diversity is becoming typical in many companies all across the United States. Projections are that by 2010, almost half of the nation's new workers will be people traditionally classified as minorities.[6] Top managers say their companies value diversity for a number of reasons, such as to give the organization access to a broader

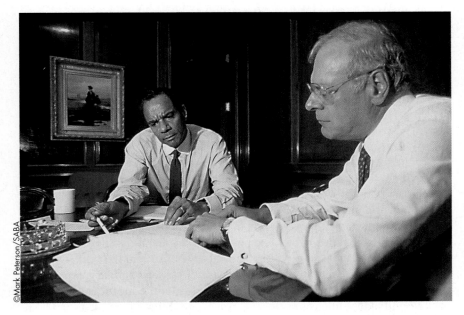

In college, Ken Chenault spent endless hours arguing that the African-American cause was best served in the long run by rising to power within the Establishment instead of assailing it from the outside. Today he has the chance to prove his point as CEO of American Express Company, one of the most respected companies in the United States. Although the weak economy and the decline in travel after the September 11, 2001, terrorist attacks have seriously hurt the company's revenues, earnings, and stock price, Chenault has been praised for his strong leadership during a difficult time. He's shown here with former chairman and CEO Harvey Golub, who counted on Chenault (then president and chief operating officer) for both his business skills and his efforts to improve workforce diversity at the company.

range of opinions and viewpoints, to reflect an increasingly diverse customer base, and to demonstrate the company's commitment to "doing the right thing."[7] Moreover, a survey by the Society for Human Resource Management found that 62 percent of job seekers prefer to work for organizations that show a commitment to diversity.[8]

However, many managers are ill-prepared to handle diversity issues. Many Americans grew up in racially unmixed neighborhoods and had little exposure to people substantially different from themselves.[9] The challenge is particularly great when working with people from other countries and cultures. A typical American manager, schooled in traditional management training, could easily make the following mistakes:[10]

- To reward a Vietnamese employee's high performance, her manager promoted her, placing her at the same level as her husband, who also worked at the factory. Rather than being pleased, the worker became upset and declined the promotion because Vietnamese husbands are expected to have a higher status than their wives.
- A manager, having learned that a friendly pat on the arm or back would make workers feel good, took every chance to touch his subordinates. His Asian employees hated being touched and thus started avoiding him, and several asked for transfers.
- A manager declined a gift offered by a new employee, an immigrant who wanted to show gratitude for her job. He was concerned about ethics and explained the company's policy about not accepting gifts. The employee was so insulted she quit.

These issues related to cultural diversity are difficult and real. But before discussing how companies handle them, let's define *diversity* and explore people's attitudes toward it.

Dimensions of Diversity

Workforce diversity means an inclusive workforce made up of people with different human qualities or who belong to various cultural groups. From the

workforce diversity
Hiring people with different human qualities or who belong to various cultural groups.

perspective of individuals, diversity means including people different from themselves along dimensions such as age, ethnicity, gender, or race. It is important to remember that diversity includes everyone, not just minorities.

Key dimensions of diversity are illustrated in Exhibit 14.1. The inner circle represents primary dimensions of diversity, which include inborn differences or differences that have an impact throughout one's life.[11] Primary dimensions are core elements through which people shape their self-image and world view. These dimensions include age, race, ethnicity, gender, mental or physical abilities, and sexual orientation

Secondary dimensions, shown in the outer ring of Exhibit 14.1, can be acquired or changed throughout one's lifetime. These dimensions tend to have less impact than those of the core but nevertheless affect a person's self-definition and world view and have an impact on how the person is viewed by others. For example, an employee living in a public housing project will certainly be perceived differently from one who lives in an affluent part of town. Married people may be perceived somewhat differently and have different attitudes from people who are single. Likewise, a person's military experience, religion, native language, socio-economic status, and educational and work background add dimensions to the way they define themselves and are defined by others. Secondary dimensions such as work style, communication style, and educational or skill level are particularly relevant in the organizational setting.[12] The challenge for today's managers is to recognize that each person can bring value and strengths to the workplace based on his or her own unique combination of diversity characteristics.

Exhibit *14.1*

Primary and Secondary Dimensions of Diversity

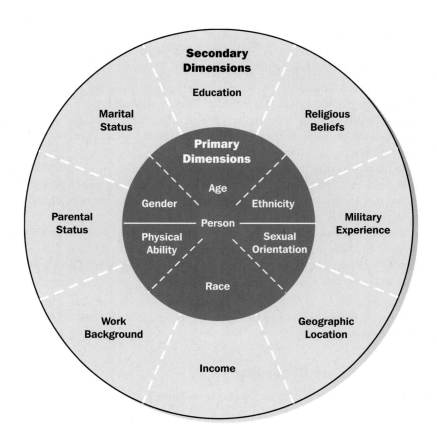

SOURCE: Adapted from Marilyn Loden and Judy B. Rosener, *Workforce America!* (Homewood, IL: Business One Irwin 1991), 20. Used with permission.

Attitudes toward Diversity

Valuing diversity by recognizing, welcoming, and cultivating differences among people so they can develop their unique talents and be effective organizational members is difficult to achieve. **Ethnocentrism** is the belief that one's own group and subculture are inherently superior to other groups and cultures. Ethnocentrism makes it difficult to value diversity. Viewing one's own culture as the best culture is a natural tendency among most people. Moreover, the business world tends to reflect the values, behaviors, and assumptions based on the experiences of a rather homogeneous, white, middle-class, male workforce.[13] Indeed, most theories of management presume that workers share similar values, beliefs, motivations, and attitudes about work and life in general. These theories presume there is one set of behaviors that best help an organization to be productive and effective and therefore should be adopted by all employees.[14] This one-best-way approach explains why a manager may cause a problem by touching Asian employees or by not knowing how to handle a gift from an immigrant.

Ethnocentric viewpoints and a standard set of cultural practices produce a **monoculture**, a culture that accepts only one way of doing things and one set of values and beliefs, which can cause problems for minority employees. People of color, women, gay people, the disabled, the elderly, and other diverse employees may feel undue pressure to conform, may be victims of stereotyping attitudes, and may be presumed deficient because they are different. White, heterosexual men, many of whom themselves do not fit the notions of the "ideal" employee, may also feel uncomfortable with the monoculture and resent stereotypes that label white males as racists and sexists. Valuing diversity means ensuring that *all* people are given equal opportunities in the workplace.[15]

The goal for organizations seeking cultural diversity is pluralism rather than a monoculture and ethnorelativism rather than ethnocentrism. **Ethnorelativism** is the belief that groups and subcultures are inherently equal. **Pluralism** means that an organization accommodates several subcultures. Movement toward pluralism seeks to fully integrate into the organization the employees who otherwise would feel isolated and ignored.

Most organizations must undertake conscious efforts to shift from a monoculture perspective to one of pluralism. An important first step is examining the attitudes and assumptions that characterize the organization, as described in this chapter's Manager's Shoptalk. Employees in a monoculture may not be aware of culture differences, or they may have acquired negative stereotypes toward other cultural values and assume that their own culture is superior. Through effective training, employees can be helped to accept different ways of thinking and behaving, the first step away from narrow, ethnocentric thinking. Ultimately, employees are able to integrate diverse cultures, which means that judgments of appropriateness, goodness, badness, and morality are no longer applied to cultural differences. Cultural differences are experienced as essential, natural, and joyful, enabling an organization to enjoy true pluralism and take advantage of diverse human resources.[16]

ethnocentrism
The belief that one's own group or subculture is inherently superior to other groups or cultures.

monoculture
A culture that accepts only one way of doing things and one set of values and beliefs.

ethnorelativism
The belief that groups and subcultures are inherently equal.

pluralism
The organization accommodates several subcultures, including employees who would otherwise feel isolated and ignored.

This Phoenix Wealth Management advertisement reflects today's emphasis on cultural diversity and ethnorelativism, the belief that cultures and subcultures are inherently equal. The ad appeals to the increasingly diverse character of U.S. organizations and society. With its slogan, "Money. It's just not what it used to be," Phoenix offers financial services to the many diverse individuals who make up a "new generation of entrepreneurs [that] has already made an indelible mark on American business."

Money.

It's just not what it used to be.

THE NEW WORKPLACE **Manager's Shoptalk**

Shifting Attitudes

To capitalize on the strengths of diversity and shift toward a more pluralistic organizational culture, managers should consider their own and other organization members' attitudes and assumptions about diversity. Here are some common misperceptions, along with perceptions that are more appropriate for today's workplace:

- *The melting-pot myth*: People desire to mold their behavior after the dominant culture so they will fit in better.
  More appropriate—cultural pluralism: We are not all the same; groups within society and the organization differ across cultures.
- *The similarity myth*: "They" are all just like me.
  More appropriate—acceptance of differences: They are not just like me; many people differ from me culturally, and most people exhibit both similarities and differences when compared to me.

- *The only-one-way myth:* Our way is the only way. We do not recognize or accept any other way of living or working.
  More appropriate—multiple ways: There are many culturally distinct ways of reaching one's goals, of working, and of living one's life
- *The one-best-way myth:* Our way is still the best way. All other approaches are inferior.
  More appropriate—several possible ways: There are many different and equally good ways to reach the same goal. The best way depends on a variety of factors, including the cultures of the people involved.

SOURCE: Adapted from "Cultural Assumptions and Their Implications for Management," by Nancy J Adler, Exhibit 4.3 in *International Dimensions of Organizational Behavior*, 4th ed., (Cincinnati, Ohio: South-Western Publishing, 2002), 117, based on Nancy J. Adler, "Domestic Multiculturalism: Cross-Cultural Management in the Public Sector," in William Eddy, ed., *Handbook of Organization Management*. Copyright Marcel Dekker, Inc., New York.

For example, IBM has made a firm commitment to break out of monoculture thinking. Ted Childs, an African American who serves as IBM's vice president of global diversity, has led a corporate-wide campaign to integrate diversity into every facet of the company's management and technical operations. Eight executive task forces—one each for African Americans, Asians, disabled people, gays and lesbians, Hispanics, Native Americans, white males, and women—are charged with making recommendations from their varied perspectives for how to make IBM a better place to work. The face of IBM is changing as the company takes proactive steps to hire, develop, and promote women, racial and ethnic minorities, and other under-represented groups. Between January 1996 and December 1999, the number of women executives at IBM worldwide soared from 185 to 508, and the number of minority executives in the United States rose from 117 to 270.[17] In addition, 57 percent of IBM's board of directors are women, multicultural, or non-U.S. born individuals.[18]

The Changing Workplace

The importance of cultural diversity and employee attitudes that welcome cultural differences will result from the inevitable changes taking place in the workplace, in our society, and in the economic environment. These changes include globalization and the changing workforce.[19] Earlier chapters described the impact of global competition on business in North America. Competition is intense. About 70 percent of all U.S. businesses are engaged directly in competition with companies overseas. Companies that succeed in this environment need to adopt radical new ways of doing business, with sensitivity toward the needs of different cultural practices. Consider the consulting firm McKinsey & Co. In the 1970s, most consultants were American, but by 1999, McKinsey's chief partner was a foreign national (Rajat Gupta from India), only 40 percent of consultants were American, and the firm's foreign-born consultants came from 40 different countries.[20] Companies that ignore diversity have a hard time competing in today's global marketplace.

The other significant challenge is the changing composition of the workforce. The average worker is older now, and many more women, people of color, and immigrants are seeking job and advancement opportunities. The demographics of the U.S. population are shifting dramatically. According to the 2000 census, non-Hispanic whites are now the *minority* population in the 100 largest U.S. cities. The number of immigrant workers jumped 17 percent to 15.7 million in 1999, and immigrants now make up 12 percent of the total U.S. workforce. Minorities are expected to make up 40 percent of people entering the workforce during the first decade of the twenty-first century; many will be first-generation immigrants and almost two-thirds of them will be female. By 2020, it is estimated that fully half of the total full-time U. S. workforce will be women. Already, white males, the majority of workers in the past, represent less than half of the workforce.[21] So far, the ability of organizations to manage diversity has not kept pace with these demographic trends, which has created a number of significant challenges for minority workers and managers.

Challenges Minorities Face

The one-best-way approach discussed in the previous section leads to a mindset that views difference as deficiency or dysfunction. For many career women and minorities, their experience suggests that no matter how many college degrees they earn, how many hours they work, how they dress, or how much effort and enthusiasm they invest, they are never perceived as "having the right stuff." If the standard of quality were based, for instance, on being white and male, anything else would be seen as deficient. This dilemma often is difficult for white men to understand because most of them are not intentionally racist and sexist. As one observer points out, you would need to be nonwhite to understand what it is like to have people assume your subordinate is your superior simply because he is white, or to lose a sale after the customer sees you in person and finds out you're not Caucasian.[22]

Bias in the workplace often shows up in subtle ways—a lack of choice assignments; the disregard by a subordinate of a minority manager's directions; or the ignoring of comments made by women and minorities at meetings. A recent survey by Korn Ferry International found that 59 percent of minority managers surveyed had observed a racially motivated double standard in the delegation of assignments.[23] Their perceptions are supported by a study conducted by Harvard Business School professor David Thomas, who found that minority managers spend more time in the "bullpen" waiting for their chance and then have to prove themselves over and over again with each new assignment. Minority employees typically feel that they have to put in longer hours and extra effort to achieve the same status as their white colleagues. "It's not enough to be as good as the next person," says Bruce Gordon, president of Bell Atlantic's enterprise group. "We have to be better."[24]

Another problem is that many minority workers feel they have to become bicultural in order to succeed. **Biculturalism** can be defined as the sociocultural skills and attitudes used by racial minorities as they move back and forth between the dominant culture and their own ethnic or racial culture.[25] Research on differences between whites and blacks has focused on issues of

biculturalism
The sociocultural skills and attitudes used by racial minorities as they move back and forth between the dominant culture and their own ethnic or racial culture.

Leading Online

BETting on the Internet: BET.com

Robert L. Johnson started the Black Entertainment Television (BET) network 22 years ago with little more than a good idea—a cable channel for black viewers. Today, BET is the leading African-American-owned and -operated media and entertainment company in the United States. The core BET network reaches into more than 65 million homes and is worth over $2 billion; 90 percent of African-American households with cable regularly tune in. Johnson has also leveraged the brand to establish a successful book company for African-American titles, a film company that produces and markets African-American-themed films, documentaries, and made-for-television movies, and, most recently, a successful Web site.

As the premier multimedia company for African Americans, it only made sense for BET to expand into the Internet world. Johnson worked out partnerships with Microsoft, Liberty Digital Media, News Corporation, and USA Networks to launch BET.com. Although there are dozens of community portals and sites targeting African Americans, BET is rapidly emerging as the leading online destination. Part of that is thanks to BET's emphasis on building an online community for African Americans who want to stay in touch with black music, lifestyle, and culture. Everything is tailored to the preferences and needs of the black community. For example, the news channel provides the latest news from around the world, with specific emphasis on how it affects the African-American community. Other channels include Health, Music, Money, Relationships, and Style. The career center lists thousands of job postings and offers advice, resources, and networking opportunities for African-American professionals and entrepreneurs. Some of the most popular aspects of BET.com, however, are the message boards, chat rooms, and community sections, where members can participate with others in the GetFit Club, the Movie Club, a spirituality area, professional groups, or other areas of special interest.

This rich community life helped BET.com get voted "Best African American Community Site 2001" by Yahoo! Internet Life magazine. Although blacks continue to lag behind whites in Internet access, the digital divide is narrowing. Today, African Americans are going online at a rate twice that of the general population and will soon make up around 40 percent of the total U.S. Internet population. BET.com is ready, giving African Americans a place where they can be part of a thriving online community, explore new areas of interest, take advantage of opportunities for economic advancement, and obtain information related to virtually any aspect of their lives.

SOURCES: BET.com, accessed on November 15, 2001; David Whitford, "BET's Johnson: On the Air and in the Air," *Fortune* (July 24, 2000), 50; T. J. DeGroat, "Blacks Make Most Out of Internet," DiversityInc.com, Career Center; and Jason McKay, "African American Websites Are Hooking People Up in More Ways Than One," *Black Enterprise* (October 2000), http://www.blackenterprise.com.

biculturalism and how it affects employees' access to information, level of respect and appreciation, and relation to superiors and subordinates. In general, African Americans, as well as other racial minorities, feel less accepted in their organizations, perceive themselves to have less discretion on their jobs, receive lower ratings on job performance, experience lower levels of job satisfaction, and reach career plateaus earlier than whites. They find themselves striving to adopt behaviors and attitudes that will help them be successful in the white-dominated corporate world while at the same time maintaining their ties to the black community and culture.

This chapter's Leading Online box describes a company with a goal of helping African Americans achieve career success and stay connected to black culture and lifestyle.

Other minority groups struggle with biculturalism as well. For example, Asian Americans who aspire to management positions are often frustrated by the stereotype that they are hardworking but not executive material because they are too quiet and deferential. Assertiveness and pressing your views in a group is seen as a characteristic of leadership in American culture, but Asians typically view this behavior as inappropriate and immature.[26] Some Asian Americans feel they have a chance for career advancement only by becoming bicultural or abandoning their native cultures altogether.

Management Challenges

What does this mean for managers who are responsible for creating a workplace that offers fulfilling work, opportunities for professional development and career advancement, and respect for all individuals? Inappropriate behavior by employees lands squarely at the door of the organization's top executives. Managers can look at different areas of the organization to see how well they are doing in creating a workplace that values and supports diversity. Exhibit 14.2 illustrates some of the key areas of management challenge for dealing with a culturally diverse workforce. Managers focus on these issues to see how well they are addressing the needs and concerns of diverse employees.

For example, consider the increased career involvement of women. This change represents an enormous opportunity to organizations, but it also means that organizations must deal with issues such as work-family conflicts, dual-career couples, and sexual harassment. Moreover, managers can ensure that their organizations' human resources systems are designed to be bias-free, dropping the perception of the middle-aged white male as the ideal employee.

The growing immigrant population presents other challenges. Whereas in previous generations most foreign-born immigrants came from Western Europe, 84 percent of recent immigrants come from Asia and Latin America.[27] These immigrants come to the United States with a wide range of backgrounds, often without adequate skills in using English. Organizations must

Exhibit **14.2**

Management Challenges for a Culturally Diverse Workforce

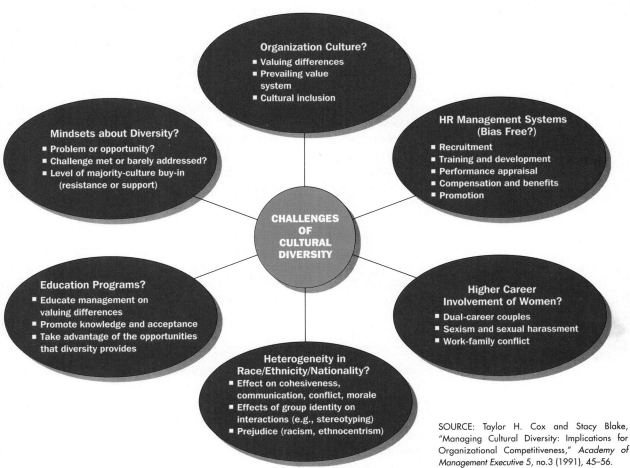

SOURCE: Taylor H. Cox and Stacy Blake, "Managing Cultural Diversity: Implications for Organizational Competitiveness," *Academy of Management Executive* 5, no.3 (1991), 45–56.

face not only the issues of dealing with race, ethnicity, and nationality to provide a prejudice-free workplace but also develop sufficient educational programs to help immigrants acquire the technical and customer service skills required in a service economy.

Another human resources issue is developing performance appraisal and reward systems that support a diverse workforce. Allstate Insurance developed a system that rates all managers on how well they handle diversity issues.

ALLSTATE INSURANCE COMPANY
http://www.allstate.com

Allstate Insurance doesn't just talk about the importance of diversity; the company actually tracks support for diversity at every level of management. As the largest property insurer for African Americans and Hispanics, Allstate has made diversity a priority since 1993. The company already had a working affirmative action program and had tried several approaches to diversity training. However, Jerry Choate, CEO, and Carlton Yearwood, director of Allstate's diversity team, believed the company needed a way to track its success on supporting diversity. Its new system gives top executives feedback that they can use continually to make the workplace more comfortable and satisfying for all employees. Today, Allstate surveys all 50,000 workers each quarter on how well it is meeting its commitments to employees and customers, including recruiting, developing, and promoting employees regardless of race or gender. A "diversity index" probes how well workers feel their managers "walk the talk" about bias-free service, respect for the individual, and a culturally sensitive workplace. Performance on these indexes determines 25 percent of a manager's bonus pay.

Overall, Allstate is doing pretty well on the diversity index. Some 40 percent of Allstate's executives and managers are women. Twenty-one percent are minorities, compared to the national average of 10 percent. The company has earned a string of awards, such as the "1999 Best Companies for Hispanics to Work," the "1998 Top 10 Companies for Minority Managers," and the "Best Companies for Working Mothers." Allstate believes its tracking system has created a more productive work environment where all employees feel valued. "What you measure is what people focus on," says Karleen Zuzich, assistant vice president of human resources. "This really sends a clear signal that management of [diverse] people . . . is really important."[28] ❖

Top managers at Allstate and other companies that value diversity look for ways to bring diverse people into the organization and shape organizational values to accept and appreciate cultural differences. In addition, training programs can promote knowledge and acceptance of diverse cultures and educate managers on valuing diversity as a competitive advantage.

Affirmative Action

Since 1964, civil legislation has prohibited discrimination in hiring based on race, religion, sex, or national origin. As described in Chapter 13, these policies were designed to facilitate recruitment, retention, and promotion of minorities and women. To some extent, these policies have been successful, opening organization doors to women and minorities. However, despite the job opportunities, few women and minorities have succeeded in getting into top management positions.

Current Debates about Affirmative Action

Affirmative action was developed in response to conditions 40 years ago. Adult white males dominated the workforce, and economic conditions were stable and improving. Because of widespread prejudice and discrimination, legal and social coercion were necessary to allow women, people of color, immigrants, and other minorities to become part of the economic system.[29]

Many companies actively recruited women and minorities to comply with affirmative action guidelines. Companies often succeeded in identifying a few select individuals who were recruited, trained, and given special consideration. These people carried great expectations and pressure. They were highly visible role models for the newly recruited groups. It was generally expected that these individuals would march right to the top of the corporate ladder.

Within a few years, it became clear that few of these people would reach the top. Management typically was frustrated and upset because of the money poured into the affirmative action programs. The individuals were disillusioned by token programs that offered limited advancement. Managers were unhappy with the program failures and may have doubted the qualifications of the people they recruited. Did they deserve the jobs at all? Were women and minority candidates to blame for the failure of the affirmative action program? Should companies be required to meet federally mandated minority-hiring targets?

Today, the situation has changed. More than half the U.S. workforce consists of women and minorities; the economic situation is changing rapidly as a result of international competition. Even the intended beneficiaries of affirmative action programs often disagree as to their value, and some believe these programs do more harm than good. One reason for this may be the stigma of incompetence that often is associated with affirmative action hires. One study found that both working managers and students consistently rated people portrayed as affirmative action hires as less competent and recommended lower salary increases than for those not associated with affirmative action.[30]

In recent years, outspoken opponents of affirmative action have brought the debate into the public consciousness. The courts have upheld recent challenges to affirmative action, and referenda in several states have limited its use for hiring and college admissions practices. The emphasis today is more on diversity programs that seek to include everyone, rather than affirmative action and compliance programs that tend to spotlight race, which many claim leads to tensions and divisiveness.[31] For example, efforts at Federated Department Stores once focused specifically on minorities and women, but the diversity program has now broadened to include 26 groups, including seniors, the disabled, homosexuals, atheists, the devout, and so on.[32]

While some welcome the broader diversity emphasis, many social justice activists argue that it is simply a way for companies to put on a show of virtue without having to do anything concrete about affirmative action issues. Al Jackson, director of diversity and staff development at *Scholastic Magazine*, echoes the sentiments of many when he notes that most firms do not hire and promote women and minorities as readily as they do white males, no matter how much they talk about valuing diversity.[33]

Ultimately, the problem boils down to an unspoken and often unintended sexism and racism in organizations. The affirmative action cycle fails when women, people of color, and immigrants are brought into a monoculture

©Alyson Aliano

Colleen Barrett broke through corporate America's glass ceiling when she became president of Southwest Airlines after the retirement of Herb Kelleher. "Some CEOs will still introduce me as Herb's secretary," she says. The now highest-ranking woman in the U.S. airline industry did indeed begin her career 34 years ago as Kelleher's secretary at his San Antonio law firm. Today, Barrett just laughs when people mistake her for a secretary, but she knows there are still too many barriers to women moving into higher-level positions. As Southwest's president, Barrett oversees the airline's marketing, advertising, customer service, and human resources. She is also chiefly responsible for safeguarding Southwest's famed esprit de corps.

glass ceiling

Invisible barrier that separates women and minorities from top management positions.

system and the burden of adaptation falls on the candidates coming through the system rather than on the organization itself. Part of the reason for the failure may be attributed to what is called the *glass ceiling*.

The Glass Ceiling

The **glass ceiling** is an invisible barrier that separates women and minorities from top management positions. They can look up through the ceiling and see top management, but prevailing attitudes are invisible obstacles to their own advancement.

Evidence of the glass ceiling is the distribution of women and minorities, who are clustered at the bottom levels of the corporate hierarchy. Women make up less than 4 percent and nonwhite minorities less than 3 percent of all *Fortune* 500 executives.[34] Overall, African Americans hold only 8 percent of all executive positions and Hispanics about 5 percent.[35] Women of color fare the worst. While they make up 23 percent of the total U. S. women's workforce, they account for only 14 percent of the women in all management positions in the United States.[36]

Women and minorities also earn substantially less. As shown in Exhibit 14.3, black male employees earn about 20 percent less and Hispanic male employees 38 percent less than their white counterparts. Women earn considerably less than men, with Hispanic women faring the worst. As illustrated in the exhibit, black women earn 35 percent less and Hispanic women 48 percent less than white men.[37]

In particular, women who leave the corporate world to care for young children have a difficult time moving up the hierarchy when they return. One term used to describe this is the *mommy track*, which implies that women's commitment to their children limits their commitment to the company or their ability to handle the rigors of corporate management. These women risk being treated as beginners when they return, no matter how vast their skills and experience, and they continue to lag behind in salary, title, and responsibility.[38] One estimate is that a woman who quits or reduces her involvement in a corporate job to raise children sacrifices about $1 million in lost income, a figure former *New York Times* economics reporter Ann Crittenden refers to as the *mommy tax*.[39]

Another sensitive issue related to the glass ceiling is homosexuals in the workplace. Many gay men and lesbians believe they will not be accepted as they are and risk losing their jobs or their chances for advancement. The director of human resources for a large Midwestern hospital would like to be honest about her lesbianism but says she knows of almost no one at her level of the corporate hierarchy who has taken that step—"It's just not done here."[40] Thus, gays and lesbians often fabricate heterosexual identities to keep their jobs or avoid running into the glass ceiling they see other employees encounter.

Why does the glass ceiling persist? The monoculture at top levels is the most frequent explanation. Top-level corporate culture evolves around white, heterosexual, American males, who tend to hire and promote people who look, act, and think like them.[41] Compatibility in thought and behavior plays an important role at higher levels of organizations.[42] For example, in a survey of women who have managed to break through the glass ceiling, fully 96 percent said adapting to a predominantly white male culture was an important factor in their success.[43]

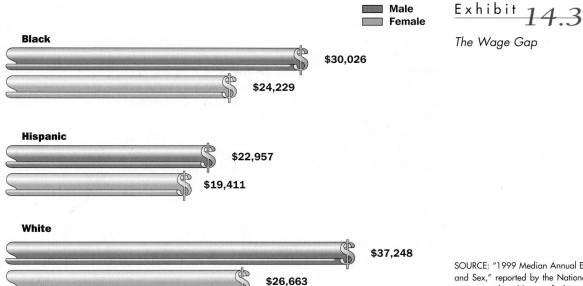

SOURCE: "1999 Median Annual Earnings by Race and Sex," reported by the National Committee on Pay Equity, *http://www.infoplease.com.*

Another reason for the persistent glass ceiling is the relegation of women and minorities to less visible positions and projects so that their work fails to come to the attention of top executives. Recent research has suggested the existence of *glass walls* that serve as invisible barriers to important lateral movement within the organization. Glass walls bar experience in areas such as line supervision or general management that would enable women and minorities to advance vertically.[44]

In general, women and minorities think that they must work harder and perform at higher levels than their white male counterparts to be noticed, recognized, and promoted. For example, a recent book distilling advice for women from the experiences of top female executives indicates that women have to invest significant effort to make sure their work is recognized and rewarded.[45]

Current Responses to Diversity

Affirmative action opened the doors of organizations in this country to women and minorities. However, the path toward promotion to top ranks has remained closed for the most part, with many women and minorities hitting the glass ceiling.[46] Although the federal government responded to this problem with the Civil Rights Act of 1991 to amend and strengthen the Civil Rights Act of 1964, affirmative action currently is under attack. As the debate over affirmative action continues, companies need to find new ways to deal with the obstacles that prevent women and minorities from advancing to senior management positions in the future. For example, Texas Instruments CEO Thomas Engibous admits that his company needs to do a better job of placing women and minorities in key positions. "We do a good job hiring women, African Americans, and Hispanics," Engibous says. "But we have too many high-ranking women in peripheral areas. We need a better mix in the business's line management if we're going to have a woman or minority as TI's CEO someday."[47]

In addition, to prepare for and respond to an increasingly diverse business climate, managers in most companies are expanding the organization's emphasis on diversity beyond race and gender to consider such factors as ethnicity, age, physical ability, religion, and sexual orientation.

Once managers create and define a vision for a diverse workplace, they can analyze and assess the current culture and systems within the organization. This assessment is followed by a willingness to change the status quo in order to modify current systems and ways of thinking. Throughout this process, people need support in dealing with the many challenges and inevitable conflicts they will face. Training and support are important for the people in pioneering roles. Finally, managers should not deemphasize affirmative action programs, because these are critical for giving minorities and women access to jobs in the organization.

Once managers accept the need for a program to develop a truly diverse workplace, action can begin. A program to implement such a change involves three major steps: (1) building a corporate culture that values diversity; (2) changing structures, policies, and systems to support diversity; and (3) providing diversity awareness training.

Changing the Corporate Culture

When the underlying culture of an organization does not change, all the other efforts to support diversity fail, as managers at Mitsubishi have learned. Even though the company settled a sexual harassment suit filed by women at the Normal, Illinois, plant, established a zero tolerance policy, and fired workers who were guilty of blatant harassment, workers describe a work environment that remains deeply hostile to women and minorities. Although the incidents of harassment have decreased, women and minority workers still feel threatened and powerless because the culture and environment that allowed the harassment to occur hasn't changed. Mitsubishi managers are still struggling with these difficult issues.[48]

Chapters 3 and 12 described approaches for changing corporate culture. Managers can start by actively using symbols for the new values, such as encouraging and celebrating the promotion of minorities and disciplining employees who display behavior that does not fit a diverse workplace. Managers should take care that workers who complain are not treated like the wrongdoers. It is managers who lead the way from a white male monoculture to a multiculture in which differences are valued and all people are respected. Culture change starts at the top, and most organizations recognized as diversity leaders have CEOs and other top executives who demonstrate a strong commitment to making diversity part of the organizational mission.[49]

Managers throughout the company can be educated to help transform the culture. For one thing, they can examine the unwritten rules and assumptions. What are the myths about minorities? What are the values that exemplify the existing culture? Are unwritten rules communicated from one person to another in a way that excludes women and minorities? For example, many men may not discuss unwritten rules with women and minorities because they assume everyone is aware of them and they do not want to seem patronizing.[50]

Companies are addressing the issue of changing culture in a variety of ways. Some are using surveys, interviews, and focus groups to identify how the cultural values affect minorities and women. Others have set up structured networks of people of color, women, and other minority groups to explore the issues they face in the workplace and to recommend changes to senior management.

Many companies have discovered that people will choose companies that are accepting, inviting, and friendly and that help them meet personal goals.[51] Successful companies carefully assess their cultures and make changes from the top down because the key to productivity is a loyal, trained, capable workforce. New cultural values mean that the exclusionary practices of the past must come to an end.

Pitney Bowes, a leading global provider of integrated mail, messaging, and document management solutions, weaves support for diversity into every fiber of the organizational culture by making diversity personal and fun, as described in this chapter's Putting People First box.

Changing Structures and Policies

Many policies within organizations originally were designed to fit the stereotypical male employee. Now leading companies are changing structures and policies to facilitate and support a diverse workforce. A survey of *Fortune* 1000 companies conducted by the Center for Creative Leadership found that 85 percent of companies surveyed have formal policies against racism and sexism, and 76 percent have structured grievance procedures and complaint review processes.[52] Companies are also developing policies to support the recruitment and career advancement of diverse employees. At least half of *Fortune* 1000 companies have staff dedicated exclusively to encouraging diversity. Exhibit 14.4 illustrates the most common diversity initiatives.

Recruitment.   A good way to revitalize the recruiting process is for the company to examine employee demographics, the composition of the labor pool in the area, and the composition of the customer base. Managers then can work toward a workforce composition that reflects the labor pool and the customer base.

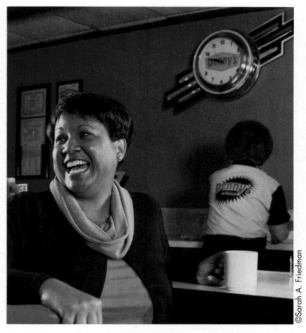

©Sarah A. Friedman

Advantica, the owner of Denny's Restaurants, which was hit with a series of discrimination lawsuits in the early 1990s, has been changing structures and policies to promote and support diversity. The company responded to the discrimination charges with aggressive minority hiring and supplier-diversity efforts. In 2001, for the second year in a row, Advantica was awarded first place in Fortune *magazine's list of "America's 50 Best Companies for Minorities." Four of the company's eleven board members, 31 percent of top officials and managers, and 48 percent of new hires are members of minority groups.*

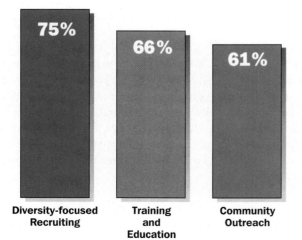

75%

66%

61%

Diversity-focused Recruiting

Training and Education

Community Outreach

E x h i b i t *14.4*

The Most Common Diversity Initiatives: Percentage of Fortune 1000 Respondents

SOURCE: Data reported in "Impact of Diversity Initiatives on the Bottom Line: A SHRM Survey of the Fortune 1000," pp. S12–S14, in *Fortune,* special advertising section, "Keeping Your Edge: Managing a Diverse Corporate Culture," produced in association with the Society for Human Resource Management, *http://www.fortune.com/sections.*

Putting People First

For many organizations, a new approach to recruitment will mean recruiting more effectively than today. This could mean making better use of formal recruiting strategies, offering internship programs to give people opportunities, and developing creative ways to draw upon previously unused labor markets.

For example, Nationwide's Scholars Program brings in Hispanic and African American college students for a three-year program that includes summer internships and year-long mentoring.[53] Marathon Ashland Petroleum has created a six-point recruiting strategy to increase diversity, including: (1) recruiting corporate-wide and cross-functionally; (2) building relationships with first- and second-tiered schools to recruit minority students; (3) offering internships for racial and ethnic minorities; (4) offering minority scholarships; (5) establishing informal mentoring programs; and (6) forming affiliations with minority organizations.[54]

Career Advancement.   The successful advancement of diverse group members means that organizations must find ways to eliminate the glass ceiling. One of the most successful structures to accomplish this is the mentoring relationship. A **mentor** is a higher ranking, senior organizational member who is committed to providing upward mobility and support to a protégé's professional career.[55] Mentoring provides minorities and women with direct training and inside information on the norms and expectations of the organization. A mentor also acts as a friend or counselor, enabling the employee to feel more confident and capable.

One researcher who has studied the career progress of high-potential minorities has found that those who advance the furthest all share one characteristic— a strong mentor or network of mentors who nurtured their professional

mentor
A higher-ranking, senior organizational member who is committed to providing upward mobility and support to a protégé's professional career.

development.[56] However, research also indicates that minorities, as well as women, are much less likely than men to develop mentoring relationships.[57] Women and minorities may not seek mentors because they feel that job competency should be enough to succeed, or they may feel uncomfortable seeking out a mentor when most of the senior executives are white males. Women may fear that initiating a mentoring relationship could be misunderstood as a romantic overture, whereas male mentors may think of women as mothers, wives, or sisters rather than as executive material. Cross-race mentoring relationships may leave both parties uncomfortable, but the mentoring of minority employees must often be across race since there are few minorities in upper-level positions. The few minorities and women who have reached the upper ranks often are overwhelmed with mentoring requests from people like themselves, and they may feel uncomfortable in highly visible minority-minority or female-female mentoring relationships, which isolate them from the white male status quo.

The solution is for organizations to overcome some of the barriers to mentor relationships between white males and minorities. When organizations can institutionalize the value of white males actively seeking women and minority protégés, the benefits will mean that women and minorities will be steered into pivotal jobs and positions critical to advancement. Mentoring programs also are consistent with the Civil Rights Act of 1991 that requires the diversification of middle and upper management.

Accommodating Special Needs.

Many people have special needs of which top managers are unaware. For example, if a number of people entering the organization at the lower level are single parents, the company can reassess job scheduling and opportunities for child care. If a substantial labor pool is non-English-speaking, training materials and information packets can be provided in another language.

In many families today, both parents work, which means that the company may provide structures to deal with child care, maternity or paternity leave, flexible work schedules, home-based employment, and perhaps part-time employment or seasonal hours that reflect the school year. The key to attracting and keeping elderly or disabled workers may include long-term-care insurance and special health or life benefits. Alternative work scheduling also may be important for these groups of workers. Many organizations are struggling with *generational diversity*, striving to meet the needs of workers at different ages and life cycles. Pitney Bowes created the Life Balance Resources program to help employees in different generations cope with life cycle issues, such as helping Generation Y workers find their first apartment or car, assisting Generation X employees in locating child care or getting a home loan, and helping baby boomers plan for retirement or find elder care for aging parents.[58]

Another issue for U.S. companies is that racial/ethnic minorities and immigrants have often had fewer educational opportunities than other groups. Some companies have worked with high schools to provide fundamental skills in literacy and arithmetic, or they provide these programs within the company to upgrade employees to appropriate educational levels. The movement toward increasing educational services for employees can be expected to increase for immigrants and the economically disadvantaged in the years to come.

Changing organizational structures and policies is important because it demonstrates a concrete commitment to supporting diversity. If managers talk

Courtesy of Colgate Palmolive Company

Colgate-Palmolive is an example of a company that facilitates the recruitment and career advancement of diverse employee groups. Its Code of Conduct states that its "commitment to caring for people is manifested in the workplace through a variety of programs designed to promote and reward individual and team achievement." It further states that in matters of employment, their policy is "to select, place, and pay employees on the basis of qualifications for the work to be performed and without discrimination on the basis of race, religion, national origin, color, sex, age, citizenship, sexual preference, veteran status, marital status or a disability unrelated to the requirements of the position."

about the value of a diverse workforce but do not do anything to ensure that diverse workers have opportunities and support in the workplace, employees are not likely to trust that the company truly values diversity. Ernst & Young LLP has become a diversity leader by changing structures and policies to bolster the recruitment, retention, and advancement of women and minorities.

ERNST & YOUNG LLP
http://www.ey.com

The accounting and consulting services firm Ernst & Young once viewed diversity primarily in terms of complying with EEO and affirmative action guidelines. However, even though managers worked hard to bring women and minorities into the organization, they began to realize that the company was losing female and minority professionals at a much higher rate than white males.

Top executives authorized a two-year study to help them understand the pressures and challenges that minority groups were feeling and how to address them. Then, they made a firm commitment to diversity by creating two new departments: the Office of Minority Recruitment and Retention, headed by Allen Boston, an African-American partner, and the Office for Retention, directed by Deborah K. Holmes, a lawyer who had been involved in the diversity study. Assigning resources directly to diversity efforts has significantly increased the recruitment and retention of women and minorities. By 1999, 7 percent of Ernst & Young's partners and senior managers were members of minority groups, and the percentage of minorities recruited each year had risen from around 10 percent to around 24 percent. The number of women in senior positions is also edging up.

Now, Ernst & Young is pushing even further, allocating resources for training and mentoring programs, work-life balance initiatives, and other efforts designed to meet the needs of diverse employees. Even more significantly, the company is providing for minority scholarships and programs at both undergraduate and graduate institutions and sponsoring organizations that give minority high school students a chance to get an inside look at the accounting and engineering professions. E & Y also recently started an innovative program called Your Master Plan (YMP), which gives recent college graduates a chance to work at Ernst & Young while pursuing a master's degree in accounting, paid for by the firm. These initiatives give young minority individuals opportunities they otherwise might not have—and they give Ernst & Young access to high-quality minority employees. According to Miriam Nalumansi, who began the YMP program last year, "One of the things that attracted me to Ernst & Young was the firm's commitment to diversity. I'm black, I'm female—those are things I have to consider."[59] ❖

Diversity Awareness Training

diversity awareness training
Special training designed to make people aware of their own prejudices and stereotypes.

Many organizations, including Monsanto, Xerox, and Mobil Oil, provide special training, called **diversity awareness training**, to help people become aware of their own cultural boundaries, their prejudices and stereotypes, so they can learn to work and live together. Working or living within a multicultural context requires a person to use interaction skills that transcend the skills typically effective when dealing with others from one's own in-group.[60] Diversity awareness programs help people learn how to handle conflict in a constructive manner, which tends to reduce stress and negative energy in diverse work teams.

People vary in their sensitivity and openness to other cultures. Exhibit 14.5 shows a model of six stages of diversity awareness. The continuum ranges from a total lack of awareness to a complete understanding and acceptance of

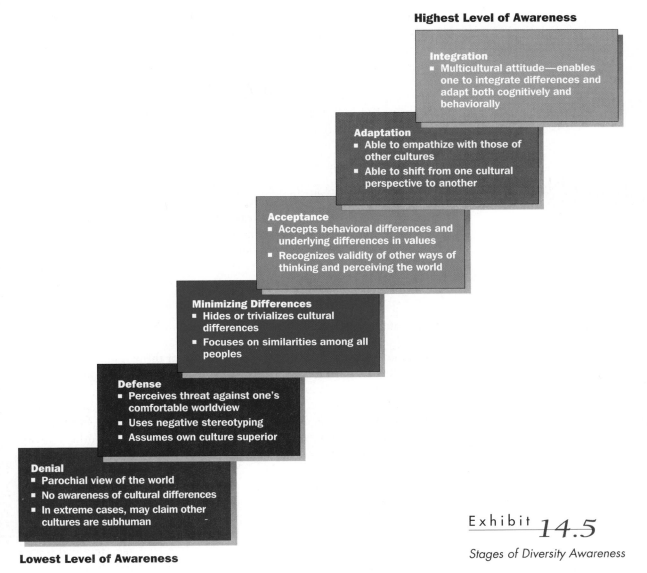

Highest Level of Awareness

Integration
- Multicultural attitude—enables one to integrate differences and adapt both cognitively and behaviorally

Adaptation
- Able to empathize with those of other cultures
- Able to shift from one cultural perspective to another

Acceptance
- Accepts behavioral differences and underlying differences in values
- Recognizes validity of other ways of thinking and perceiving the world

Minimizing Differences
- Hides or trivializes cultural differences
- Focuses on similarities among all peoples

Defense
- Perceives threat against one's comfortable worldview
- Uses negative stereotyping
- Assumes own culture superior

Denial
- Parochial view of the world
- No awareness of cultural differences
- In extreme cases, may claim other cultures are subhuman

Lowest Level of Awareness

Exhibit *14.5*

Stages of Diversity Awareness

SOURCE: Based on M. Bennett, "A Developmental Approach to Training for Intercultural Sensitivity," *International Journal of Intercultural Relations* 10 (1986), 179–196.

people's differences. This model is useful in helping diversity awareness trainers assess participants' openness to change. People at different stages might require different kinds of training. A basic aim of awareness training is to help people recognize that hidden and overt biases direct their thinking about specific individuals and groups. If people can come away from a training session recognizing that they prejudge people and that this needs to be consciously addressed in communications with and treatment of others, an important goal of diversity awareness training has been reached.

Many diversity awareness programs used today are designed to help people of varying backgrounds communicate effectively with one another and to understand the language and context used in dealing with people from other groups. The point of this training is to help people be more flexible in their communications with others, to treat each person as an individual, and not to rely on stereotypes. Effective programs move people toward being open in their relationships with others. For example, if you were a part of such a program, it would help you develop an explicit awareness of your own cultural values, your own cultural boundaries, and your own cultural behaviors. Then you would be provided the same information about other groups, and you would be given the opportunity to learn about and communicate with people from other groups. One of the most important elements in diversity training is to bring together people of differing perspectives so that they can engage in learning new interpersonal communication skills with one another.

Defining New Relationships in Organizations

One outcome of diversity is an increased incidence of close personal relationships in the workplace, which can have both positive and negative results for employees as well as the organization. Two issues of concern are emotional intimacy and sexual harassment.

Emotional Intimacy

Close relationships between men and women often have been discouraged in companies for fear that they would disrupt the balance of power and threaten organizational stability.[61] This opinion grew out of the assumption that organizations are designed for rationality and efficiency, which were best achieved in a nonemotional environment.

However, a recent study of friendships in organizations sheds interesting light on this issue.[62] Managers and workers responded to a survey about emotionally intimate relationships with both male and female coworkers. Many men and women reported having close relationships with an opposite-sex coworker. Called *nonromantic love relationships*, the friendships resulted in trust, respect, constructive feedback, and support in achieving work goals. Intimate friendships did not necessarily become romantic, and they affected each person's job and career in a positive way. Rather than causing problems, nonromantic love relationships, according to the study, affected work teams in a positive manner because conflict was reduced. Indeed, men reported somewhat greater benefit than women from these relationships, perhaps because the men had fewer close relationships outside the workplace upon which to depend.

However, when such relationships *do* become romantic or sexual in nature real problems can result. Office romance is on the rise, with more than 30 percent of employees reporting they have been involved with a coworker at some time in their careers. Although not all office romances lead to trouble, usually they create difficulties for managers.

Romances that require the most attention from managers are those that arise between a supervisor and a subordinate. These relationships often lead to morale problems among other staff members, complaints of favoritism, and questions about the supervisor's intentions or judgment. Although few companies have written policies about workplace romance in general, 70 percent of companies surveyed have policies prohibiting romantic relationships between a superior and a subordinate.[63] At IBM, training programs and written policies emphasize that a manager can become romantically involved with a subordinate only if he or she agrees to stop supervising the subordinate by transferring to another job within or outside the company. The onus is on the manager rather than the subordinate to take action.[64]

Sexual Harassment

While psychological closeness between men and women in the workplace may be a positive experience, sexual harassment is not. Sexual harassment is illegal. As a form of sexual discrimination, sexual harassment in the workplace is a violation of Title VII of the 1964 Civil Rights Act. Sexual harassment in the classroom is a violation of Title VIII of the Education Amendment of 1972. The following categorize various forms of sexual harassment as defined by one university:

- *Generalized.* This form involves sexual remarks and actions that are not intended to lead to sexual activity but that are directed toward a coworker based solely on gender and reflect on the entire group.
- *Inappropriate/offensive.* Though not sexually threatening, it causes discomfort in a coworker, whose reaction in avoiding the harasser may limit his or her freedom and ability to function in the workplace.
- *Solicitation with promise of reward.* This action treads a fine line as an attempt to "purchase" sex, with the potential for criminal prosecution.
- *Coercion with threat of punishment.* The harasser coerces a coworker into sexual activity by using the threat of power (through recommendations, grades, promotions, and so on) to jeopardize the victim's career.
- *Sexual crimes and misdemeanors.* The highest level of sexual harassment, these acts would, if reported to the police, be considered felony crimes and misdemeanors.[65]

Over the past decade, the number of sexual harassment cases filed annually in the United States has more than doubled. About 17,000 complaints were filed in 1998 alone, up from 6,883 in 1991.[66] About 10 percent of those were filed by males. The Supreme Court has held that same-sex harassment as well as harassment of men by female co-workers is just as illegal as the harassment of women by men. In the suit that prompted the Court's decision, a male oil-rig worker claimed he was singled out by other members of the all-male crew for crude sex play, unwanted touching, and threats of rape.[67] Eight men, former employees of Jenny Craig Inc., sued the company charging that female bosses made lewd comments or that they were denied promotions because of their sex. A male worker at a hot tub manufacturer won a $1 million court decision after claiming that his female boss made sexual overtures to him almost daily. These are among a growing number of men urging recognition that sexual harassment is not just a woman's problem.[68]

Because the corporate world is dominated by a male culture, however, sexual harassment affects women to a much greater extent. Women who are moving up the corporate hierarchy by entering male-dominated industries report a high frequency of harassment. Surveys report an increase in sexual harassment programs, but female employees also report a lack of prompt and just action by executives to incidents of sexual harassment. However, companies are discovering that "an ounce of prevention really is worth a pound of cure." Top executives are seeking to address problems of harassment through company diversity programs, revised complaint systems and grievance procedures, written policy statements, workshops, lectures, and role-playing exercises to increase employee sensitivity and awareness to the issue.[69]

Global Diversity

Globalization is a reality for today's companies. As stated in a recent report from the Hudson Institute, *Workforce 2020*, "The rest of the world matters to a degree that it never did in the past."[70] Even small companies that do not do business in other countries are affected by global diversity issues. However, large multinational companies that hire employees in many countries face tremendous challenges because they must apply diversity management across a broader stage than North America. Managers must develop new skills and awareness to handle the unique challenges of global diversity: cross-cultural understanding, the ability to build networks, and the understanding of geopolitical forces. Two significant aspects of global diversity programs involve employee selection and training and the understanding of the communication context.

Selection and Training

expatriates
Employees who live and work in a country other than their own.

Expatriates are employees who live and work in a country other than their own. Careful screening, selection, and training of employees to serve overseas increase the potential for corporate global success. Human resource managers consider global skills in the selection process. In addition, expatriates receive cross-cultural training that develops language skills and cultural and historical orientation. Career-path counseling often is available.[71] Texaco set up its Executive Business Analyst (EBA) program to develop a pool of diverse leaders who have the global management skills to work anywhere in the world.[72] Through the program, recent recruits or current employees complete rotational assignments, including some outside the United States and on global teams. Global diversity training, cultural sensitivity training, and mentoring are also provided through the EBA program.

Equally important, however, is honest self-analysis by overseas candidates and their families. Before seeking or accepting an assignment in another country, a candidate should ask himself or herself such questions as the following:

- Is your spouse interrupting his or her own career path to support your career? Is that acceptable to both of you?
- Is family separation for long periods involved?
- Can you initiate social contacts in a foreign culture?
- Can you adjust well to different environments and changes in personal comfort or quality of living, such as the lack of television, gasoline at $5 per gallon, limited hot water, varied cuisine and national phone strikes?
- Can you manage your future reentry into the job market by networking and maintaining contacts in your home country?[73]

Employees working overseas must adjust to all of these conditions. Managers going global might find that their own management style needs adjustment to succeed in a foreign country. One aspect of this adjustment is learning the communication context of a foreign location.

The children in this Avezzano, Italy, school share cultures and learn firsthand the dynamics of global diversity. The school was established by Texas Instruments for the families of U.S. and Japanese employees involved in T.I.'s six-nation team building Europe's largest semiconductor. Such efforts, along with Minority Procurement programs, demonstrate T.I.'s commitment to a diverse, multinational corporate environment.

Courtesy of Texas Instruments

Communication Differences

People from some cultures tend to pay more attention to the social context (social setting, nonverbal behavior, social status) of their verbal communication than Americans do. For example, American managers working in China have discovered that social context is considerably more important in that culture, and they have learned to suppress their impatience and devote the time needed to establish personal and social relationships.

Exhibit 14.6 indicates how the emphasis on social context varies among countries. In a **high-context culture**, people are sensitive to circumstances surrounding social exchanges. People use communication primarily to build personal social relationships; meaning is derived from context—setting, status, nonverbal behavior—more than from explicit words; relationships and trust are more important than business; and the welfare and harmony of the group are valued. In a **low-context culture**, people use communication primarily to exchange facts and information; meaning is derived primarily from words; business transactions are more important than building relationships and trust; and individual welfare and achievement are more important than the group.[74]

To understand how differences in cultural context affect communications, consider the U.S. expression "The squeaky wheel gets the oil." It means that the loudest person will get the most attention, and attention is assumed to be favorable. Equivalent sayings in China and Japan are "Quacking ducks get shot," and "The nail that sticks up gets hammered down," respectively. Standing out as an individual in these cultures clearly merits unfavorable attention.

High-context cultures include Asian and Arab countries. Low-context cultures tend to be American and Northern European. Even within North America, cultural subgroups vary in the extent to which context counts, explaining why differences among groups make successful communication difficult. White females, Native Americans, and African Americans all tend to prefer higher context communication than do white males. A high-context interaction requires more time because a relationship has to be developed, and trust and friendship must be established. Furthermore, most male managers and most people doing the hiring in organizations are from low-context cultures, which conflicts with people entering the organization from a background in a higher context culture. Overcoming these differences in communication is a major goal of diversity awareness training.

Exhibit 14.6

Arrangement of High- and Low-Context Cultures

High Context — Low Context

Chinese
Korean
Japanese
Vietnamese
Arab
Greek
Spanish
Italian
English
North American
Scandinavian
Swiss
German

SOURCES: Edward T. Hall, *Beyond Culture* (Garden City, N.Y.: Anchor Press/Doubleday, 1976); and J. Kennedy and A. Everest, "Put Diversity in Context," *Personnel Journal* (September 1991), 50–54.

high-context culture
A culture in which communication is used to enhance personal relationships.

low-context culture
A culture in which communication is used to exchange facts and information.

Diversity in the New Workplace

Organizations use the approaches discussed in this chapter to create an environment that welcomes and supports diverse individuals. Ninety-one percent of companies responding to a survey by the Society for Human Resource Management believe that diversity initiatives help maintain a competitive advantage. Some specific benefits include improving employee morale, decreasing interpersonal conflict, facilitating progress into new markets, and increasing the organization's creativity.[75] Some of today's companies are also pushing into new territory to support a globally diverse workforce. Two popular mechanisms for leveraging diversity in today's organizations are multicultural teams and employee network groups.

Multicultural Teams

multicultural teams
Teams made up of members from diverse national, racial, ethnic, and cultural backgrounds.

Companies have long known that putting together teams made up of members from different functional areas results in better problem solving and decision making. Now, they are recognizing that **multicultural teams**—teams made up of members from diverse national, racial, ethnic, and cultural backgrounds—provide even greater potential for enhanced creativity, innovation, and value in today's global marketplace.[76] Research has found that diverse teams generate more and better alternatives to problems and produce more innovative solutions than homogeneous teams.[77] A team made up of people with different perspectives, backgrounds, and cultural values creates a healthy mix of ideas, which sometimes encourages more reluctant people to speak out. In addition, diversity can stimulate a healthy level of conflict that leads to greater creativity and better decisions.

Some organizations, such as RhonePoulenc Rorer (RPR), based in Collegeville, Pennsylvania, are committed to mixing people from diverse countries and cultures from the top to the bottom of the organization. There are 15 nationalities represented in RPR's top management teams, including a French CEO, an Austrian head of operations, an American general counsel, an Egyptian head of human resources, and an Italian director of corporate communications.[78] The top management team at Redwood City, California–based Obongo includes members from India, the United States, Brazil, Ireland, and Bulgaria. Obongo was started by people from two different countries who have woven cultural diversity into the technology start-up's DNA. Today, Obongo has teams made up of people from 12 countries and 18 different cultures.[79]

Multicultural teams are becoming common in both U.S. and Canadian organizations. One consultant notes that the workforce of many Canadian organizations is often jokingly referred to as the *United Nations* because companies have so many different nationalities working together on project teams.[80] The U.N. approach appears in many U.S. companies, as well. For example, Radha Basu manages a team of Hewlett-Packard software writers who stretch across six countries and 15 time zones.[81]

Despite their many advantages,[82] multicultural teams are more difficult to manage because of the increased potential for miscommunication and misunderstanding. Multicultural teams typically have more difficulty learning to communicate and work well together, but with effective cross-cultural training and good management, the problems seem to dissipate over time.[83] One management team videotaped its meetings so members could see how their body language reflects cultural differences. An American manager remarked, "I couldn't believe how even my physical movements dominated the table, while Ron [a Filipino American] . . . actually worked his way off-camera within the first five minutes."[84] The goal of talking about team members' cultural differences is not to minimize them for the sake of team harmony but to better understand how they affect team interaction and performance. Many organizations that use multicultural teams want to help people enhance and retain their varied cultural identities. One of the most popular mechanisms is employee network groups.

Employee Network Groups

employee network groups
Groups based on social identity, such as gender or race, and organized by employees to focus on concerns of employees from that group.

Employee network groups are based on social identity, such as gender or race, and are organized by employees to focus on concerns of employees from that group.[85] For example, at Visteon Corp., a global automotive systems producer, the women's network group develops the leadership and technical skills of female employees, designs strategies for how members can contribute to Visteon's business and diversity goals, and works to keep top managers informed of members' contributions, concerns, and needs.[86] The idea behind network groups is that minority employees can join together across traditional organizational boundaries for mutual support and to extend member influence in the organization. Network groups pursue a variety of activities, such as meetings to educate top managers, mentoring programs, networking events, training sessions and skills seminars, minority intern programs, and community volunteer activities. Network groups give people a chance to meet, interact with, and develop social and professional ties to others throughout the organization, which may include key decision makers. Network groups are a powerful way to reduce social isolation for women and minorities, help these employees be more effective, and enable members to achieve greater career advancement.

An important characteristic of network groups is that they are formed by employees, not the organization, and membership is voluntary. However, successful organizations support and encourage network groups by making clear that such groups are welcome, helping members who want to form groups contact other organizations for assistance, and perhaps providing financial assistance for programs. Although at first glance the proliferation of employee network groups seems to be in direct opposition to the trend toward multicultural teams, the two mechanisms actually work quite well together. At Kraft Foods, networks are considered critical to the success of multicultural teams because they build awareness and acceptance of cultural differences and help people feel more comfortable working together.[87] Visteon has credited the Visteon African American Network's mentoring program for strengthening the company's retention and development of talented black employees.

There has been a rapid growth of employee network groups for minorities who have faced barriers to advancement in organizations, including African-Americans, Hispanics, American Indians, Asian-Americans, women, gays and lesbians, and disabled employees. Network groups offer significant potential for supporting a workplace that values diversity. In general, female and minority employees who participate in a network group feel more pride about their work and are more optimistic about their careers than those who do not have the support of a network.[88]

■ Summary and Management Solution

Several important ideas pertain to workforce diversity, which is the inclusion of people with different human qualities and from different cultural groups. Dimensions of diversity are both primary, such as age, gender, and race, and secondary, such as education, marital status, and income. Ethnocentric attitudes generally produce a monoculture that accepts only one way of doing things and one set of values and beliefs, thereby excluding nontraditional employees from full participation. Minority employees face several significant challenges in the workplace.

Acceptance of diversity is becoming especially important because of sociocultural changes and the changing workforce. Diversity in the workplace reflects diversity in the larger environment.

Affirmative action programs have been successful in gaining employment for women and minorities, but the glass ceiling has kept many women and minorities from obtaining top management positions. Breaking the glass ceiling ultimately means changing the corporate culture within organizations; changing internal structures and policies toward employees, including accommodating special needs; and providing diversity awareness training to help people become aware of their own cultural boundaries and prejudices. This training also helps employees learn to communicate with people from other cultural contexts.

The increased diversity in organizations has provided opportunities for emotional intimacy and friendships between men and women that are beneficial to all parties. However, when these relationships become romantic or sexual, they can present problems for managers. Increasing diversity also means that organizations must develop programs to deal with global as well as domestic diversity and with potential conflicts, such as sexual harassment, that arise.

Two recent approaches to supporting and leveraging the power of diversity in organizations are multicultural teams and employee network groups. Multicultural teams can provide a broader and deeper base of experience and ideas for enhanced problem solving, creativity, and innovation. Organizations that value diversity also encourage and support network groups to enable minority organization members to reduce their social isolation, be more effective in their jobs, have a greater impact on the organization, and achieve greater opportunities for career advancement. Minority employees who participate in networks typically feel more pride in their work and are more optimistic about their careers.

Returning to the opening example of Texaco, CEO Peter Bijur knew that nothing less than a total overhaul of the corporate culture could begin to erase Texaco's image as the embodiment of corporate racism. Exhibit 14.7 lists the major elements of Texaco's culture change

program, which was hammered out in collaboration with members on the independent task force required by the lawsuit. Today, Texaco is in the midst of a remarkable transformation, which some experts believe could make the company a model for diversity. All employees are required to attend a two-day diversity training program, and managers are sent to change-management and communication courses as well. Bijur has also set specific diversity goals with specific timetables and has made it clear to top executives as well as managers and supervisors throughout the company that their future career advancement will be determined by how well they implement the new diversity initiatives. These initiatives include recruiting minority candidates, developing in-house minority talent through mentoring programs, increasing the use of minority suppliers, monitoring employee attitudes, appropriately addressing grievances, and improving relationships with minority organizations. Compensation is also tied to how effectively managers "create openness and inclusion in the workplace." To further spur culture change, Bijur recruited several eminent African Americans to join Texaco's top ranks. Recruiting African American executives wasn't easy in the wake of the racial discrimination scandal, but Bijur's ardent personal commitment to changing Texaco's culture convinced them to join in the quest.[89]

■ Discussion Questions

1. If you were a senior manager at a company such as Mitsubishi, Allstate Insurance, or Texaco, how would you address the challenges faced by minority employees?
2. Some people argue that social class is a major source of cultural differences, yet social class is not listed as a primary or secondary dimension in Exhibit 14.1. Discuss reasons for this.
3. Have you been associated with an organization that made assumptions associated with a monoculture? Describe the culture.
4. What is the glass ceiling, and why do you think it has proved to be such a barrier to women and minorities?
5. How might employee network groups contribute to the advancement of women and minorities to higher-level positions in an organization?
6. In preparing an organization to accept diversity, do you think it is more important to change the corporate culture or to change structures and policies? Explain.

7. If a North American corporation could choose either high-context or low-context communications, which do you think would be best for the company's long-term health? Discuss.
8. Many single people meet and date people from their work organization because the organization provides a context within which to know and trust another person. How do you think this practice affects the potential for emotional intimacy? Sexual harassment?
9. As a manager, how would you accommodate the special needs of different groups—such as single parents, older workers, or employees with poor English language skills—without appearing to show favoritism?
10. Discuss the advantages and disadvantages of multicultural teams. Why might an organization that plans to implement multicultural teams want to support diverse employee network groups?

Exhibit *14.7*

Major Elements of Texaco's Culture Change Initiative

Recruitment and Hiring
- Ask search firms to identify wider arrays of candidates
- Enhance the interviewing, selection, and hiring skills of managers
- Expand college recruitment at historically minority colleges

Identifying and Developing Talent
- Form a partnership with INROADS, a nationwide internship program that targets minority students for management careers
- Establish a mentoring process
- Refine the company's global succession planning system to improve identification of talent
- Improve the selection and development of managers and leaders to help ensure that they are capable of maximizing team performance

Ensuring Fair Treatment
- Conduct extensive diversity training
- Implement an alternative dispute resolution process
- Include women and minorities on all human resources committees throughout the company

Holding Managers Accountable
- Link managers' compensation to their success in creating "openness and inclusion in the workplace"
- Implement 360-degree feedback for all managers and supervisors
- Redesign the company's employee attitude survey and begin using it annually to monitor employee attitudes

Improve Relationships with External Stakeholders
- Broaden the company's base of vendors and suppliers to incorporate more minority- and women-owned businesses
- Increase banking, investment, and insurance business with minority- and women-owned firms
- Add more independent, minority retailers and increase the number of minority managers in company-owned gas stations and Xpress Lube outlets

SOURCE: Don Hellriegel, Susan E. Jackson, and John W. Slocum, Jr., *Management,* 8th ed. (Cincinnati, Ohio; South-Western Publishing, 1999). Used with permission. Originally adapted from V. C. Smith, "Texaco outlines comprehensive initiatives," *Human Resource Executive.* (February 1997), 13; A. Bryant, "How much has Texaco changed? A mixed report card on anti-bias efforts," *New York Times* (November 2, 1997), 3-1, 3-16, 3-17; and "Texaco's workforce diversity plan," as reprinted in *Workforce* (March 1997, suppl.).

■ Management in Practice: Experiential Exercise

How Tolerant Are You?

For each of the following questions circle the answer that best describes you.
1. Most of your friends
   a. are very similar to you
   b. are very different from you and from each other
   c. are like you in some respects but different in others
2. When someone does something you disapprove of, you
   a. break off the relationship
   b. tell how you feel but keep in touch
   c. tell yourself it matters little and behave as you always have
3. Which virtue is most important to you?
   a. kindness
   b. objectivity
   c. obedience
4. When it comes to beliefs, you
   a. do all you can to make others see things the same way you do

   b. actively advance your point of view but stop short of argument
   c. keep your feelings to yourself
5. Would you hire a person who has had emotional problems?
   a. no
   b. yes, provided there is evidence of complete recovery
   c. yes, if the person is suitable for the job
6. Do you voluntarily read material that supports views different from your own?
   a. never
   b. sometimes
   c. often
7. You react to old people with
   a. patience
   b. annoyance
   c. sometimes a, sometimes b
8. Do you agree with the statement, "What is right and wrong depends upon the time, place, and circumstance?"

a. strongly agree
b. agree to a point
c. strongly disagree

9. Would you marry someone from a different race?
   a. yes
   b. no
   c. probably not

10. If someone in your family were homosexual, you would
    a. view this as a problem and try to change the person to a heterosexual orientation
    b. accept the person as a homosexual with no change in feelings or treatment
    c. avoid or reject the person

11. You react to little children with
    a. patience
    b. annoyance
    c. sometimes a, sometimes b

12. Other people's personal habits annoy you
    a. often
    b. not at all
    c. only if extreme

13. If you stay in a household run differently from yours (cleanliness, manners, meals, and other customs), you
    a. adapt readily
    b. quickly become uncomfortable and irritated
    c. adjust for a while, but not for long

14. Which statement do you agree with most?
    a. We should avoid judging others because no one can fully understand the motives of another person.
    b. People are responsible for their actions and have to accept the consequences.
    c. Both motives and actions are important when considering questions of right and wrong.

Circle your score for each of the answers below and total the scores:

1. a = 4; b = 0; c = 2
2. a = 4; b = 2; c = 0
3. a = 0; b = 2; c = 4
4. a = 4; b = 2; c = 0
5. a = 4; b = 2; c = 0
6. a = 4; b = 2; c = 0
7. a = 0; b = 4; c = 2
8. a = 0; b = 2; c = 4
9. a = 0; b = 4; c = 2
10. a = 2; b = 0; c = 4
11. a = 0; b = 4; c = 2
12. a = 4; b = 0; c = 2
13. a = 0; b = 4; c = 2
14. a = 0; b = 4; c = 2

Total Score:

0–14: If you score 14 or below, you are a very tolerant person and dealing with diversity comes easily to you.

15–28: You are basically a tolerant person and others think of you as tolerant. In general, diversity presents few problems for you, but you may be broad minded in some areas and have less tolerant ideas in other areas of life, such as attitudes toward older people or male-female social roles.

29–42: You are less tolerant than most people and should work on developing greater tolerance of people different from you. Your low tolerance level could affect your business or personal relationships.

43–56: You have a very low tolerance for diversity. The only people you are likely to respect are those with beliefs similar to your own. You reflect a level of intolerance that could cause difficulties in today's multicultural business environment.

SOURCE: Adapted from the Tolerance Scale by Maria Heiselman, Naomi Miller, and Bob Schlorman, Northern Kentucky University, 1982, in George Manning, Kent Curtis, and Steve McMillen, *Building Community: The Human Side of Work,* (Cincinnati, Ohio: Thomson Executive Press, 1996), 272–277.

■ Management in Practice: Ethical Dilemma

A Man's World?

Jana Mercer has been working for Crown Industries for nearly 20 years, first as a clerical worker and later as an accountant. As a division of a national forest products company, Crown offers good salaries and benefits in a part of the southern United States where unemployment is typically high and wages are low. Jana, a single mother of two, has always felt lucky to have the job.

However, recently a young accountant, Tommy Thompson, had suddenly been promoted to a job that Jana—and everyone else in the department—thought she was better qualified for. The job had never been advertised inside or outside the company. Instead, top managers had suddenly boosted the position's pay scale five grades and given the job to Tommy. All the supervisors in the unit thought Jana should have been given the job, and they took their complaints to the comptroller, who promptly told them to mind their own business. After nights of lying awake fuming, Jana finally decided to take some steps of her own. She went to the comptroller and applied for the position, insisting that she be given an interview. Weeks went by with no word, until Jana requested a meeting with the comptroller and general manager. The comptroller tried to pacify her by saying he had not interviewed her because he knew she wouldn't be happy in the position. "You'd get bored in a week, Jana," he said. "The job isn't nearly as interesting or challenging as what you're doing now." Jana disagreed and pointed out that the pay was much higher. In addition, the higher profile would give her a better chance for future promotions. "Look, honey," the GM soothed, putting his hand on her shoulder. "The decision has already been made. Tommy's a good man, and he fits in well with the other top guys around here. You just have to understand it's a man's world. My wife goes through the same thing at her company."

Jana was so stunned she didn't know how to respond. As she slowly walked back to her office, she wondered what she should do next.

What Do You Do?

1. Let it go. After all, it is a man's world at Crown, and you need to accept it. You've got a good job making a decent salary and you can't afford to lose it.
2. Go to the division president, and if he doesn't do anything, keep moving up the hierarchy of the national company, making enough noise until you find someone who will take action.
3. Document everything in writing, including letters of support from people inside the unit, and go to the Equal Employment Opportunity Commission. This is a clear case of discrimination, and it is evident that Crown's corporate culture supports this type of abuse.

SOURCE: Based on Doug Wallace, "It's (Still) a Man's World," *BusinessEthics* (July–August 1998), 16.

Surf the Net

1. **Diversity Recruiting.** Assume you are a Human Resources Director who is interested in enhancing your organization's diversity recruiting efforts. To increase the diversity of the workforce, you are becoming informed on the subject of increasing college enrollment of minorities. Research the following two organizations that coordinate with corporations to support minority students interested in business careers. Write a brief recommendation to your instructor outlining which of the two organizations you would prefer to work with and include two or three factors that influenced your decision.
   a. LEAD (Leadership Education and Development Program in Business, Inc.) at *http://www.leadnational.org*
   b. INROADS at *http://www.inroads.org.*
2. **50 Most Powerful Women in Business.** *Fortune* magazine updates its "50 Most Powerful Women in Business" list every year. Go to *http://www.fortune.com* to locate the most recent list and complete the chart based on what you find at the site.

Rank	Name	Title	Company
1			
2			
3			
4			
5			

3. **Sexual Harassment.** To help determine how well you understand sexual harassment laws, complete the Sexual Harassment Quiz at *http://www.hrtools.com/etoolsapplets/ SEXHARASSIQtest/shiqtest.asp.*

   After selecting your answers, choose the "Submit Quiz" option. Choose "View Correct Answers" to see how you scored and learn the reasoning behind each correct answer. Print out the "View Correct Answers" page, write your name at the top of the printout, and submit it to your instructor.

Case for Critical Analysis

Draper Manufacturing

You have just been hired as a diversity consultant by Draper Manufacturing. Ralph Draper, chairman and CEO, and other top managers feel a need to resolve some racial issues that have been growing over the past several years at their plant in Nashville, Tennessee. Draper Manufacturing is a small, family-owned company that manufactures mattresses. It employs 90 people full-time, including African Americans, Asians, and Hispanics. About 75 percent of the workforce is female. The company also occasionally hires part-time workers, most of whom are Hispanic women. Most of these part-timers are hired for periods of a few months at a time, when production is falling behind schedule.

To begin your orientation to the company, Draper has asked his production manager, Wallace Burns, to take you around the plant. As Burns points out the various areas responsible for each stage of the production process, you overhear several different languages being spoken. In the shipping and receiving department, you notice that most workers are black men. Burns confirms that 90 percent of the workers in shipping and receiving are African American and points out that the manager of that department, Adam Fox, is also African American.

Later in the afternoon you attend a regular meeting of top managers to meet everyone and get a feel for the organizational culture. Draper introduces you as a diversity consultant and notes that several of his managers have expressed concerns about festering racial tensions in the company. He notes that "Each of the minority groups sticks together. The blacks and Orientals rarely mix, and most of the Mexicans stick together and speak only in Spanish. It seems that some of our workers are just downright lazy sometimes. We keep falling behind in our production schedule and having to hire part-time workers, but then we generally have to fire two or three of those a month for goofing off on the job." He closes his introduction by saying that you have been hired to help the company solve their growing diversity problems.

Draper then turns toward the management committee's routine daily business. The others present are the general manager, human resources manager (the only woman), sales manager, quality control manager, plant manager (Wallace Burns), and shipping and receiving manager (Adam Fox, the only non-white manager). Soon an angry debate begins between Fox and the sales manager. The sales manager says that orders are not being shipped on time, and several complaints have been received about the quality of the product. Fox argues that he needs more workers in shipping and

receiving to do the job right, and he adds that the quality of incoming supplies is lousy. While this debate continues, the other managers remain silent and seem quite uncomfortable. Finally, the quality control manager attempts to calm things down with a joke about his wife. Most of the men in the group laugh loudly, and the conversation shifts to other topics on the agenda.

Questions

1. What suggestions would you make to Draper's managers to help them move toward successfully managing diversity issues?

2. If you were the shipping and receiving or human resources manager, how do you think you would feel about working at Draper? What are some of the challenges you might face at this company?

3. Based on the information in the case, at what stage of diversity awareness (Exhibit 14.5) do managers at Draper Manufacturing seem to be? Discuss.

SOURCE: Based on "Northern Industries," a case prepared by Rae Andre of Northeastern University.

■ Endnotes

1. Kenneth Labich, "No More Crude at Texaco," *Fortune* (September 6, 1999), 205–212.

2. Aaron Bernstein with Michael Arndt, "Racism in the Workplace," *BusinessWeek* (July 30, 2001); Reed Abelson, "Can Respect Be Mandated? Maybe Not Here," *The New York Times* (September 10, 2000), BU1.

3. M. Fine, F. Johnson, and M. S. Ryan, "Cultural Diversity in the Workforce," *Public Personnel Management* 19 (1990), 305–319.

4. Taylor H. Cox, "Managing Cultural Diversity: Implications for Organizational Competitiveness," *Academy of Management Executive* 5, no. 3 (1991), 45–56; and Faye Rice, "How to Make Diversity Pay," *Fortune* (August 8, 1994), 78–86.

5. G. Pascal Zachary, "Mighty is the Mongrel," *Fast Company* (July 2000), 270–284.

6. Reported in "Keeping Your Edge: Managing a Diverse Corporate Culture," special advertising section, *Fortune* (June 3, 2001).

7. Roy Harris, "The Illusion of Inclusion," *CFO* (May 2001), 42–50.

8. "Keeping Your Edge."

9. Lennie Copeland "Valuing Diversity, Part I: Making the Most of Cultural Differences at the Workplace," *Personnel* (June 1988), 52–60.

10. Lennie Copeland, "Learning to Manage a Multicultural Workforce," *Training* (May 25, 1988), 48–56; and D. Farid Elashmawi, "Culture Clashes: Barriers to Business," *Managing Diversity* 2, no. 11 (August 1993), 1–3.

11. Marilyn Loden and Judy B. Rosener, *Workforce America!* (Homewood, Ill.: Business One Irwin, 1991); and Marilyn Loden, *Implementing Diversity* (Homewood, Ill.: Irwin, 1996).

12. Frances J. Milliken and Luis I. Martins, "Searching for Common Threads: Understanding the Multiple Effects of Diversity in Organizational Groups," *Academy of Management Review* 21, no. 2 (1996), 402–433.

13. N. Songer, "Workforce Diversity," *B&E Review* (April–June 1991), 3–6.

14. Robert Doktor, Rosalie Tung, and Mary Ann von Glinow, "Future Directions for Management Theory Development," *Academy of Management Review* 16 (1991), 362–365; and Mary Munter, "Cross-Cultural Communication for Managers," *Business Horizons* (May–June 1993), 69–78.

15. Renee Blank and Sandra Slipp, "The White Male: An Endangered Species?" *Management Review* (September 1994), 27–32; Michael S. Kimmel, "What Do Men Want?" *Harvard Business Review* (November–December 1993), 50–63; and Sharon Nelton, "Nurturing Diversity," *Nation's Business* (June 1995), 25–27.

16. M. Bennett, "A Developmental Approach to Training for Intercultural Sensitivity," *International Journal of Intercultural Relations* 10 (1986), 179–196.

17. Keith H. Hammonds, "Difference Is Power," *Fast Company* (July 2000), 258–266.

18. Vanessa J. Weaver, "What These CEOs and Their Companies Know About Diversity," in "Winning with Diversity," special advertising section, *BusinessWeek* (September 10, 2001).

19. C. Keen, "Human Resource Management Issues in the '90s," *Vital Speeches* 56, no. 24 (1990), 752–754.

20. Zachary, "Mighty Is the Mongrel."

21 "Keeping Your Edge"; Steven Greenhouse, N.Y. Times News Service, "Influx of Immigrants Having Profound Impact on Economy," *Johnson City Press* (September 4, 2000), 9;

Richard W. Judy and Carol D'Amico, *Workforce 2020: Work and Workers in the 21st Century* (Indianapolis, Ind.: Hudson Institute, 1997).

22. Stephanie N. Mehta, "What Minority Employees Really Want," *Fortune* (June 10, 2000), 181–186.

23. Harris, "The Illusion of Inclusion."

24. Mehta, "What Minority Employees Really Want."

25. Robert Hooijberg and Nancy DiTomaso, "Leadership In and Of Demographically Diverse Organizations," *Leadership Quarterly* 7, no. 1 (1996): 1–19.

26. Harris, "The Illusion of Inclusion."

27. Copeland, "Valuing Diversity, Part I: Making the Most of Cultural Differences at the Workplace"; Judy and D'Amico, *Workforce 2020*; and S. Hutchins, Jr., "Preparing for Diversity: The Year 2000," *Quality Process* 22, no. 10 (1989), 66–68.

28. Leon E. Wynter, "Allstate Rates Managers on Handling Diversity," *The Wall Street Journal* (Business and Race column) (October 1, 1997), B1; Louisa Wah, "Diversity at Allstate: A Competitive Weapon," *Management Review* (July-August 1999), 24–30; Joan Crockett, "Diversity: Winning Competitive Advantage through a Diverse Workforce," *HR Focus* (May 1999), 9–10; and Joan Crockett, "Diversity as a Business Strategy," *Management Review* (May 1999), 62.

29. Roosevelt Thomas, Jr., "From Affirmative Action to Affirming Diversity," *Harvard Business Review* (March–April 1990), 107–117; and Nicholas Lemann, "Taking Affirmative Action Apart," *The New York Times Magazine* (July 11, 1995), 36–43.

30. Madeline E. Heilman, Caryn J. Block, and Peter Stathatos, "The Affirmative Action Stigma of Incompetence: Effects of Performance Information Ambiguity," *Academy of Management Journal* 40, no. 1 (1997), 603–625.

31. Robert J. Grossman, "Is Diversity Working?" *HR Magazine* (March 2000), 47–50.

32. Cora Daniels, "Too Devout for Our Own Good?" *Fortune* (July 9, 2001), 116.

33. Jack Gordon, "Different from What? Diversity as a Performance Issue," *Training* (May 1995), 25–33; and Leon E. Wynter, "Diversity Is Often All Talk, No Affirmative Action," *The Wall Street Journal* (December 21, 1994), B1.

34. "Keeping Your Edge."

35. Annie Finnigan, "Different Strokes," *Working Woman* (April 2001), 42–48.

36. Debra E. Meyerson and Joyce K. Fletcher, "A Modest Manifesto for Shattering the Glass Ceiling," *Harvard Business Review* (January–February 2000), 127–136; Finnegan, "Different Strokes."

37. "The Wage Gap," National Women's Law Center, infoplease.com, The Learning Network, 2001.

38. Deborah L. Jacobs, "Back from the Mommy Track," *The New York Times* (October 9, 1994), F1, F6; Lisa Cullen, "Apple Pie, My Eye," *Working Woman* (May–June 2001), 19–20; and Michelle Conlin, "The New Debate Over Working Moms," *BusinessWeek* (September 18, 2000), 102–104.

39. Cullen, "Apple Pie, My Eye," and Ann Crittenden, *The Price of Motherhood* (New York: Metropolitan Books, 2001).

40. Barbara Presley Noble, "A Quiet Liberation for Gay and Lesbian Employees," *The New York Times* (June 13, 1993), F4.

41. "Diversity in the New Millennium," special advertising section, *Working Woman* (March 2000).

42. C. Soloman, "Careers under Glass," *Personnel Journal* 69, no. 4 (1990), 96–105.

43. Belle Rose Ragins, Bickley Townsend, and Mary Mattis, "Gender Gap in the Executive Suite: CEOs and Female Executives Report on Breaking the Glass Ceiling," *Academy of Management Executive* 12, no. 1 (1998), 28–42.

44. Julie Amparano Lopez, "Study Says Women Face Glass Walls as Well as Ceilings," *The Wall Street Journal* (March 3, 1992), B1, B2; and Ida L. Castro, "Q: Should Women Be Worried About the Glass Ceiling in the Workplace?" *Insight* (February 10, 1997), 24–27; Meyerson and Fletcher, "A Modest Manifesto for Shattering the Glass Ceiling."

45. Sheila Wellington with Betty Spence, *Be Your Own Mentor: Strategies from Top Women on the Secrets of Success* (New York: Random House, 2001).

46. Anne B. Fisher, "When Will Women Get to the Top?" *Fortune* (September 21, 1992), 44–56.

47. Finnigan, "Different Strokes."

48. Abelson, "Can Respect Be Mandated?"

49. Jacqueline A. Gilbert and John M. Ivancevich, "Valuing Diversity: A Tale of Two Organizations," *Academy of Management Executive* 14, no. 1 (2000), 93–105; and Weaver, "What These CEOs and Their Companies Know About Diversity."

50. Copeland, "Learning to Manage a Multicultural Workforce."

51. B. Geber, "Managing Diversity," *Training* 27, no.7 (1990), 23–30.

52. Reported in "Strength Through Diversity for Bottom-Line Success," special advertising section, *Working Woman* (March 1999).

53. Finnigan, "Different Strokes."

54. "Diversity in an Affiliated Company," in Vanessa J.Weaver, "Winning with Diversity," special advertising section, *BusinessWeek* (September 10, 2001).

55. B. Ragins, "Barriers to Mentoring: The Female Manager's Dilemma," *Human Relations* 42, no. 1 (1989), 1–22; and Ragins et al., "Gender Gap in the Executive Suite."

56. David A. Thomas, "The Truth About Mentoring Minorities—Race Matters," *Harvard Business Review* (April 2001), 99–107.

57. Mary Zey, "A Mentor for All," *Personnel Journal* (January 1988), 46–51.

58. "Keeping Your Edge."

59. "Ernst & Young LLP: An Aggressive Approach," in "Diversity Today: Developing and Retaining the Best Corporate Talent," special advertising section, *Fortune* (June 21, 1999); and "Leveraging Diversity: Opportunities in the New Market," Part III of "Diversity: The Bottom Line," special advertising section, *Forbes* (November 13, 2000).

60. J. Black and M. Mendenhall, "Cross-Cultural Training Effectiveness: A Review and a Theoretical Framework for Future Research," *Academy of Management Review* 15 (1990), 113–136.

61. E. G. Collins, "Managers and Lovers," *Harvard Business Review* 61 (1983), 142–153.

62. Sharon A. Lobel, Robert E. Quinn, Lynda St. Clair, and Andrea Warfield, "Love without Sex: The Impact of Psychological Intimacy between Men and Women at Work," *Organizational Dynamics* (Summer 1994), 5–16.

63. William C. Symonds with Steve Hamm and Gail DeGeorge, "Sex on the Job," *BusinessWeek* (February 16, 1998), 30–31.

64. Carol Hymowitz and Ellen Joan Pollock, "The One Clear Line in Interoffice Romance Has Become Blurred," *The Wall Street Journal* (February 4, 1998), A1, A8.

65. "Sexual Harassment: Vanderbilt University Policy" (Nashville: Vanderbilt University, 1993).

66. Joanne Cole, "Sexual Harassment: New Rules, New Behavior," *HRFocus*, March 1999, 1, 14-15. Also see EEOC charge complaints at *http://www.eeoc.gov*.

67. Jack Corcoran, "Of Nice and Men," *Success* (June 1998), 65–67.

68. Barbara Carton, "At Jenny Craig, Men Are Ones Who Claim Sex Discrimination," *The Wall Street Journal* (November 29, 1994), A1, A11.

69. Jennifer J. Laabs, "Sexual Harassment: HR Puts Its Questions on the Line," *Personnel Journal* (February 1995), 35–45; Sharon Nelton, "Sexual Harassment: Reducing the Risks," *Nation's Business*, March 1995, 24–26; and Gary Baseman, "Sexual Harassment: The Inside Story," *Working Woman* (June 1992), 47–51, 78.

70. Judy and D'Amico, *Workforce 2020*.

71. Joann S. Lublin, "Companies Use Cross-Cultural Training to Help Their Employees Adjust Abroad," *The Wall Street Journal* (August 4, 1992), B1, B9.

72. "Leveraging Diversity."

73. Gilbert Fuchsberg, "As Costs of Overseas Assignments Climb, Firms Select Expatriates More Carefully," *The Wall Street Journal* (January 9, 1992), B3, B4.

74. J. Kennedy and A. Everest, "Put Diversity in Context," *Personnel Journal* (September 1991), 50–54.

75. "Impact of Diversity Initiatives on the Bottom Line: A SHRM Survey of the Fortune 1000," S12–S14, in *Fortune*, special advertising section, "Keeping Your Edge: Managing a Diverse Corporate Culture," produced in association with the Society for Human Resource Management, *http://www.fortune.com/sections*.

76. Joseph J. Distefano and Martha L. Maznevski, "Creating Value with Diverse Teams in Global Management," *Organizational Dynamics* 29, no. 1 (Summer 2000), 45–63; and Finnigan, "Different Strokes."

77. W. E. Watson, K. Kumar, and L. K. Michaelsen, "Cultural Diversity's Impact on Interaction Process and Performance: Comparing Homogeneous and Diverse Task Groups," *Academy of Management Journal* 36 (1993), 590-602; G. Robinson and K. Dechant, "Building a Business Case for Diversity," *Academy of Management Executive* 11, no. 3 (1997), 21–31; and D. A. Thomas and R. J. Ely, "Making Differences Matter: A New Paradigm for Managing Diversity," *Harvard Business Review* (September–October 1996), 79–90.

78. Marc Hequet, Chris Lee, Michele Picard, and David Stamps, "Teams Get Global," *Training* (December 1996), 16–17.

79. Chiori Santiago, "Culture Club," *Working Woman* (April 2001), 46–47, 78.

80. Lionel Laroche, "Teaming Up," *CMA Management* (April 2001), 22–25.

81. G. Pascal Zachary, "The Rage for Global Teams," *Technology Review* (July–August 1998), 33.

82. See Distefano and Maznevski, "Creating Value with Diverse Teams" for a discussion of the advantages of multicultural teams.

83. Watson, Kumar, and Michaelsen, "Cultural Diversity's Impact on Interaction Process and Performance."

84. Distefano and Maznevski, "Creating Value with Diverse Teams."

85. This definition and discussion is based on Raymond A. Friedman, "Employee Network Groups: Self-Help Strategy for Women and Minorities," *Performance Improvement Quarterly* 12, no. 1 (1999), 148–163.

86. "Leveraging Diversity."

87. Finnigan, "Different Strokes."

88. Raymond A. Friedman, Melinda Kane, and Daniel B. Cornfield, "Social Support and Career Optimism: Examining the Effectiveness of Network Groups Among Black Managers," *Human Relations* 51, no. 9 (1998), 1155–1177; "Diversity in the New Millennium," special advertising supplement, *Working Woman* (March 2000).

89. Labich, "No More Crude at Texaco."

Chapter 10: Student Advantage Helps College Students Stay Organized

FOR ABOUT $20 A YEAR, COLLEGE STUDENTS CAN JOIN A CLUB that offers all kinds of services, from online purchase of textbooks to discounts on travel. Maybe most students do not have $20 in their pockets at any given time, but that is about the price of two large pizzas, and Student Advantage is committed to providing value to its members.

Massachusetts-based Student Advantage is made up of a number of divisions, each organized around a particular focus. Perhaps the most well-known is CollegeClub.com, a Web site that provides "one-stop shopping" for financial aid information, including comparisons of different student loans and opportunities for online application; a program that allows students to use their university ID cards for off-campus purchases; online shopping for student-only values, and more. CollegeClub.com also provides marketing opportunities for companies promoting travel, events, and other services—as well as some administrative services for universities.

The SA Marketing Group, another Student Advantage division, develops and manages marketing programs for the college and youth markets on behalf of such clients as AT&T, Amtrak, New Balance, and Hotjobs.com. CarePackages.com, a third Student Advantage operation, was founded in 1999 to establish relationships with more than 25 colleges and universities and related Internet sites such as Yahoo! Greetings and FTD.com florist service. Through CarePackages.com, parents, grandparents, and just about anyone else can select and send gift packages to students as they study for exams, or to make them laugh for Halloween. (There is even a special "ScarePackage.") CarePackages.com has created such a successful relationship between consumers and retail companies that *The Wall Street Journal* rated it one of the best such sites in business. In addition, CarePackages.com's revenue-sharing partnerships have helped associations, campus organizations, other nonprofits, and business owners earn money without taking any risk.

For sports fans—and there are usually plenty of those on campus—Student Advantage's FANSonly Network provides online brand management, content delivery, consumer marketing, and business assistance to more than 120 colleges and universities around the nation. FANSonly works like a network hub for individual colleges' official athletic sites, so students and coaches can log on to get all kinds of information specific to their school and team, from scores to schedules to merchandise. Finally, Student Advantages' U-Wire division is the country's largest free newswire for college media. The site delivers student-produced news and commentary to U-Wire members, professional media outlets and syndication partners (including Yahoo! and USAToday.com).

Each of these sites is developed with the specific purpose of contributing to the company's overall mission of connecting students, universities, and businesses with each other in a positive relationship. If any site does not fit the overall mission—or actually siphons off valuable resources from the company without contributing to it—then Student Advantage lets it go, keeping only the strongest divisions. One such business unit was Voice FX, which operated Campus Direct, a service that allowed students and alumni to access grades and order transcripts over the Internet and by phone. After reviewing the unit's performance relative to Student Advantage as a whole, CEO Ray Sozzi decided to sell Voice FX. "Our focus and our future are on the core enterprises on which the company's been built—our media properties, our membership program, including SA Cash, and our expanding online and offline commerce operations," explained Sozzi. In a sluggish economy, Student Advantage would retain only its "core" or central operations, and manage these as strategically as possible.

Student Advantage is structured around the consumer needs of college students. Such a well-defined focus makes it easier to structure the organization so that each division is related to students and the universities they attend. While some critics believe that targeting college students on the Web is too limiting, founder Ray Sozzi disagrees. He does, however, believe that a Web presence must be complemented by an offline presence. "The Internet is very important to college students, but it is not the end-all, be-all medium. There are plenty of transactions that happen offline; college students still go to local stores to buy books and CDs. The most limiting thing is if you *only* have an offline presence. You have to establish customer loyalty, and the most effective way is through an integrated approach. . . . That's the way we run our business."

Questions

1. Draw a diagram of Student Advantage's divisional structure. Do you see an advantage in using this type of structure at Student Advantage? Why or why not?
2. Do you think an emphasis on centralization or decentralization would be more appropriate for helping Student Advantage achieve its goals? Discuss.
3. In what ways might Student Advantage benefit from the use of teams?

SOURCES: Company Web site, *http://www.studentadvantage.com*, accessed February 8, 2002; "Student Advantage Sheds Division," *Boston.internet.com*, November 8, 2001, *http://boston.internet.com*; Seth Fineberg, "An Interview with Ray Sozzi, CEO of Student Advantage," *NewsBeat Channel 7*, January 13, 2000, *http://www.channelseven.com*.

Chapter 11: Machado and Silvetti: Building the Business of Building

AN ORGANIZATION IS A LOT LIKE A BUILDING: IT RELIES ON structure just to stand up. It has a foundation, some system of support, pathways between areas, and a roof for protection. The Boston-based architectural firm of Machado and Silvetti, founded by Harvard professors Rodolfo Machado and Jorge Silvetti, knows plenty about structure. Without structure, there would be no building—and no firm. Because the two founders have spent so much of their careers in an academic setting, says associate Michael Yusem, "Our office is structured very similar to a typical academic studio configuration, where projects are developed through an intensive, workshop style environment."

This studio environment means that the Machado and Silvetti firm relies heavily on teams to develop the projects for which it has become famous—a new branch of the Boston Public Library, a renovation of the Getty Villa at the J. Paul Getty Museum, the South Boston waterfront, the Rockefeller Stone Barns, and a 365-bed graduate housing dormitory for a local university. "Team structure for specific projects is usually based on a principal-in-charge, a managing associate, and a team of designers," says Michael Yusem. Although many architectural firms are similarly organized on a project basis, Machado and Silvetti has a less hierarchical, more horizontal structure than more traditional firms. "By encouraging creative input at all staff levels, the system intends to encourage commitment and dedication among team members by creating opportunities for personal input and involvement," continues Yusem.

The team structure also contributes to decision making through meetings in which team members, associates, and principals gather to review the progress on each project and discuss problems and potential solutions. "We find that this approach encourages creative problem solving and minimizes the tendency for stagnation and repetition that more traditional bureaucracies may yield," explains Yusem. It also supports the concept of the learning organization.

Coordination among team members, between teams, and with outside groups and individuals is vital to the success of a firm like Machado and Silvetti. Since the firm does not specialize in designing a particular category of structure, each project team must address different demands related to the project. Many times, the firm will call in outside consultants who have expertise that applies to a certain project, and these individuals must be coordinated with the in-house architectural design team as well as the client's staff. "Once established, the architectural and consultant team works closely with the client, user group representatives, and construction managers to provide for the design, schedule, construction and budget of the project," says Yusem. "This involves an exhaustive review of program requirements, user-group demands, as well as the appropriateness of various design solutions which are tested throughout the process." All of this spells coordination. For instance, during the graduate housing project, the interests of the university and the surrounding community—including donor groups, trustees, facilities managers, faculty, student groups, and community organizations—all had to be addressed and coordinated.

This level of coordination requires patience from Machado and Silvetti's project managers. They must make sure everyone receives relevant information and has time to understand and respond to issues, and they must be able to anticipate and resolve conflicts. The firm tries to structure its contact with its clients in much the same way it is structured internally in order to achieve this coordination. "We have found that the particular circumstances of each project and client group differ, and our ability to hand-select the appropriate design team personalities and consultant group is paramount in creating an effective project delivery system," says Michael Yusem. "In this sense, we strive to establish a similar interactive, collaborative decision-making process with our client as we do with our own internal structure." In other words, they build each museum, library wing, or housing facility as if it were their own.

Questions

1. Can you see any possible downside to the way Machado and Silvetti is structured? If not, why not? If so, what is it?
2. If Machado and Silvetti was organized in a vertical structure, how would the approach to projects be different?
3. How important is open information to a firm like Machado and Silvetti?

SOURCES: Company Web site, http://www.machado-silvetti.com, accessed February 5, 2002; Alex Ulam, "Harvard Inc.," Metropolis Magazine, February 2001, http://www.metropolismag.com; "The New Getty Villa," Getty Museum Web Site, 2000, http://www.getty.edu.

Chapter 12: Peter Pan Offers a Safe Ride

MANY ORGANIZATIONS HAVE TAKEN A SECOND LOOK AT their safety and security procedures since the terrorist attacks of September 11, 2001. Financial institutions have updated security of their computer data; hotels have examined ways to make guests safer from intruders or unauthorized visitors; and every company operating modes of travel, from airlines to bus lines, has re-evaluated ways to ensure the safety and security of its passengers and staff. Re-evaluation and resulting changes are two positive actions that have come out of a great tragedy. Peter Pan Bus Lines, based in Springfield, Massachusetts, has been in business since 1933 and has undergone plenty of changes. But its attention to the details of safety and security post-September 11 is much more focused and intense.

"It is the policy of Peter Pan Bus Lines, Inc., to promote a safe and secure environment for all of our employees and customers," writes Peter A. Picknelly, president of the company. This policy extends to all of the company's 850 employees, 3.5 million passengers, 150 coaches (buses), and routes ranging from Concord, New Hampshire, to Washington, D.C. And it encompasses the entire Peter Pan Group, which includes the bus lines, Peter Pan World Travel, several hotels, and other affiliates. Some of the changes resulting from the new safety policy involve technology; others involve changes in people or culture, such as creating a heightened alertness to safety issues. Of course, it is important for the changes to be supported by the top of the organization, as they are at Peter Pan; otherwise, they will not receive the attention and resources they need for implementation.

As Christopher Crean, director of safety for the company, and other managers reviewed the company's safety procedures, they were happy to note that Peter Pan had instituted important safety measures long before September 11. For instance, bus drivers have had on-board computers (similar to the "black boxes" on airplanes) since 1989. Recently, Crean was presented with the first Safety Leader of the Year Award by the United Motorcoach Association (UMA) for his previous six years of work in the company's safety program. Under Crean's leadership, Peter Pan had achieved the highest safety rating from the Department of Defense for three years and the highest safety rating from the Department of Transportation for five years. But September 11 threw safety and security issues into a whole new arena, so Crean and his colleagues examined the company's practices from top to bottom.

When the review was complete, they decided to implement some changes in employee training and testing, and in policies and procedures. All employees, including the president of the company, would participate in a three-and-a-half hour safety and security training program to reinforce their existing knowledge, heighten their awareness of potential dangers or threats, and teach them how to make the best decisions for their safety and that of their passengers. Meanwhile, Peter Pan would be implementing its "mystery rider" program, which operates much like the "mystery shopper" that restaurants or department stores might use. Mystery riders take Peter Pan buses several times each month and rate all aspects of service. In addition, according to Crean, all managers are required to ride a coach twice a month.

New policies and procedures for the company include the following: requiring identification of all passengers when they buy tickets, issuing company ID badges to all employees, instituting a new security plan, and implementing new security measures for the buses themselves. Some of the additions to security on the buses include interior mirrors, which allow drivers greater visibility of passengers' activities, and plastic ties placed on all luggage hatches once they have been closed so no new items may be added. In addition, Peter Pan has worked with the Springfield, Massachusetts, police—the company's home base—to make sure that its emergency action plans are up-to-date and workable.

Change isn't easy, even for a company that already has a superior track record in the area of safety and security. People need to be re-educated and motivated to implement changes on a daily basis, and sometimes it takes weeks or months for the changes to settle into place. But when change begins at the top—as it has at Peter Pan—it is very likely to succeed. Peter Pan takes security seriously on every run because every passenger's safety is important to the company.

Questions

1. What characteristics of Peter Pan would identify it to you as a learning organization?
2. What might be some sources of resistance to the changes in Peter Pan's safety and security practices?
3. Of the implementation tactics discussed in the chapter, which seem to have been used successfully by Peter Pan?

SOURCE: Company Web site, *http://www.peterpanbus.com*

Chapter 13: Fannie Mae: A Superstar to American Home Buyers and Workers

WOULDN'T IT BE GREAT TO BE ABLE TO AFFORD TO BUY THE home you have always dreamed of owning? Wouldn't it be nice to work at a company that truly values your contribution to the organization? One corporation makes dreams like this come true every day, every year: the Federal National Mortgage Association, commonly known as Fannie Mae. Fannie Mae is a private corporation that works with primary lenders—such as banks, credit unions, mortgage companies, and government housing finance agencies—to ensure that there are enough funds available for mortgage loans. The company does this by buying mortgages from these primary lenders up to a loan limit of $300,700. With cash in hand from Fannie Mae, the primary lenders can turn around and lend more money to home buyers. Fannie Mae earns money through different investments, fees, and interest. Fannie Mae's overall mission is "to help more families achieve the American dream of home ownership."

With such wonderful goals to achieve, what is it like to work for Fannie Mae? How does the organization attract and develop an effective workforce? Fannie Mae has established core values that include treating its employees with respect, giving them opportunities to perform and grow, compensating them fairly, helping them find ways to balance work and family life, and recognizing their achievements. As a result, the organization has received many awards for its positive work environment, among them being named one of the 100 Best Corporate Citizens by *Business Ethics* magazine, named one of the 100 top companies for working mothers by *Working Mother* magazine, and listed on *Fortune's* 100 Best Companies to Work For. "Being a responsible corporate citizen is one of Fannie Mae's core commitments," notes Dan Mudd, Fannie Mae's vice chair and chief operating officer. "By ensuring at all times that Fannie Mae has a positive impact on the lives of our employees, the communities in which we live, and the nation we serve, we are better able to meet our unique public mission to reduce barriers, lower costs, and increase the opportunities for home ownership and affordable rental housing for all Americans."

Among the most important benefits offered to Fannie Mae employees are those designed to help them balance work and family obligations, including flexible work options, paid leave for new fathers, prenatal education, maternity leave phase-back, and Eldercare, a special program for assisting workers in their care of senior relatives. Eldercare's Elderkit includes information, resources, a summary of benefits, and assistance with paperwork pertaining to eldercare, from medical records to health insurance information. Employees can access Elderkit on the company's Web site or receive help at the human resource department. "By providing benefits that help employees balance their work and personal lives, we foster a committed workforce that is highly

motivated to help us meet our critical housing mission and achieve our stretch business goals," says vice chair Jamie Gorelick.

Other benefits include an employee stock plan; a stock purchase plan; life insurance; free on-site annual health and fitness evaluations, including a "healthy living" day off; paid childbirth and adoption leave; exercise classes; housing assistance; and paid time off for volunteer activities. Fannie Mae also has an emergency child care center at its Washington, D.C., office for employees whose regular caregivers are suddenly unavailable. Employees who live outside the Washington area are offered emergency childcare vouchers for up to 25 days.

Fannie Mae has a variety of programs designed to develop an effective workforce through job training, advanced education, and mentoring. The organization is "committed to retaining and expanding our outstanding workforce by encouraging employee development and career growth," states the company Web site. Fannie Mae's Assistance for Collegiate Education program offers financial assistance to staffers who want to continue their college education. A number of internal programs provide training in management and professional development, computer skills, and the secondary mortgage business. Career development programs and learning centers offer self-study opportunities. And the Corporate Mentor Program helps establish mentoring as a core value at the company. This program is formal and structured, providing employees with the tools and opportunities to build and maintain relationships with managers who can help them grow in their careers.

Today, Fannie Mae is the third largest U.S. corporation in terms of assets, and the nation's largest provider of home mortgage funds. In fact, with more than 12 million active mortgages, Fannie Mae is one of the largest financial institutions in the world. Each of its 4,000 employees is considered a contributing member to an important mission, and each is "encouraged to use good judgment in all that they say and do in the workplace." In sum, Fannie Mae sounds like the embodiment of the American dream—for people who want to purchase their own home and for people who want a nice place to work.

Questions

1. In what ways do you think Fannie Mae's work/life benefits help maintain an effective workforce?
2. How might Fannie Mae's treatment of its workforce be considered part of its competitive strategy?
3. Write a brief statement outlining what you believe to be Fannie Mae's social contract with its workers.

SOURCE: Company Web site, accessed January 17, 2002, http://www.fanniemae.com.

Chapter 14: Fannie Mae Promotes a Diverse Workforce

MANY COMPANIES TRY, WITH GREATER OR LESSER SUCCESS, to recruit, develop, and promote a truly diverse workforce. Federal and local guidelines govern such areas as equal opportunity and affirmative action. But organizations that move beyond rules and regulations to embrace diversity as a core value can reap rewards in employee satisfaction and performance. At the Federal National Mortgage Association (Fannie Mae), which employs over 4,000 workers, diversity is a way of life. Fannie Mae's corporate culture is grounded in diversity. "In keeping with [our] values, our corporate philosophy on diversity is based on respect for one another and recognition that each person brings his or her own unique attributes to the corporation," states the company Web site. "We are committed to providing equal opportunity for all employees to reach their full potential; it is a fundamental value, and it makes good business sense. . . . We are committed to demonstrating that 'Diversity Works at Fannie Mae.'"

That said, how does Fannie Mae breathe life into its words? First, the diversity of American society as a whole is reflected at every level of the corporate structure. More than 47 percent of Fannie Mae's management group, including officers and directors, are minorities; nearly 54 percent of the company's employees are women; and 42 percent of the employees are minorities. In addition, the company is pledged to equal opportunity for workers with disabilities, older employees, and gay or lesbian workers. "Diversity is not just an initiative at Fannie Mae; it's a principle that permeates every aspect of how we do business," explains Maria Johnson, vice president of diversity, health, and work-life. "Diversity is codified as one of the company's core commitments."

Fannie Mae also supports diversity by awarding a significant number of outsourced contracts to minority-owned businesses, a practice for which it was named among the top 30 companies for achievements in increasing supplier diversity by *Working Woman* magazine. "More than 21 percent of the company's discretionary spending in 2000 went to minority- and women-owned businesses, proof that Fannie Mae's commitment to diversity extends to all areas of the organization," says Barbara Lang, Fannie Mae's vice president of corporate services. "We require minority contractors to be included on all bids, where possible, and also encourage our majority suppliers and customers to work with capable minority vendors." In addition, Fannie Mae provides diversity training to its lender customers and hosts regular benchmarking sessions for other employers who want to learn more about how diversity can contribute to a company's success.

Fannie Mae has established specific goals to increase the ratio of minorities at upper levels, ties certain compensation to promoting diversity, and has implemented a number of programs, such as mentoring, to make certain everyone gets equal opportunity for career growth. "Company leaders are urged to unleash the potential of all employees, promote a spectrum of perspectives, view differences as assets rather than liabilities, and help create a diverse, talented, and committed workforce," says Maria Johnson.

Promoting diversity within the workforce at Fannie Mae is good strategy not only because a diverse workforce can bring more strength and creativity to an organization, but also because such a workforce reflects Fannie Mae's customer base. People of all backgrounds come to Fannie Mae's lenders in search of mortgage loans. In addition, Fannie Mae's philanthropic arm, the Fannie Mae Foundation, works to increase the supply of affordable housing to those who might not otherwise be able to find a home—to homeless individuals and families, immigrant communities, those in rural areas, and lower-income minority groups.

Diversity has been an integral part of Fannie Mae's corporate culture for at least 15 years, illustrating the importance of support from a company's senior managers. "Fannie Mae committed to incorporate diversity as part of its core culture back in the late 1980s," reports Maria Johnson. "Our program has been successful because top executives have had an ongoing relationship with our diversity initiatives from the onset." Because diversity programs have support at the very top of the organization, they are much more apt to be successful at lower levels. But Fannie Mae doesn't engage in these initiatives entirely out of socially responsible motives, instead, the company believes that being socially responsible is also good business. "The company's record of 14 consecutive years of double-digit growth in operating earnings shows that a company can act responsibly and still deliver value to its shareholders," says Jamie Gorelick, vice chair of Fannie Mae. There's no arguing with success.

Questions

1. No one is perfect, including managers and workers at Fannie Mae. What are some of the challenges that mid-level managers at Fannie Mae might face in managing a diverse group of workers?
2. Based on what you have read in this case and the previous case on Fannie Mae, what type of initiatives can you identify that should prevent women from encountering the glass ceiling at Fannie Mae?
3. Using the chart in Exhibit 14.5, try to identify—honestly—your own level of diversity awareness. Based on your evaluation, do you think you would fit in as a manager at Fannie Mae? Why or why not?

SOURCES: Company Web site, accessed January 17, 2002, *http://www. fanniemae.com;* "Fannie Mae Foundation Receives New $300 Million Contribution from Fannie Mae," company press release, January 14, 2002.

Part Four: Managing Organizational Changes at Ford

MOST OF US RESIST CHANGE: IT IS HUMAN NATURE TO WANT things to stay the same, even if the conditions of our lives are less than ideal. Changes within organizations are just as difficult for managers to implement and employees to accept. Whether it is learning a new technology, increasing or decreasing staff, expanding or downsizing manufacturing capabilities, adding or deleting products to the line, change can be stressful for everyone in the organization. Conceiving of and announcing the change may fall to upper-level executives, but implementing the change is usually the responsibility of managers, including human resource managers. When the restructuring plan put together by Bill Ford's new executive team began to unfold in late 2001 and early 2002, all of Ford Motor Company was on edge.

After announcing a series of management changes, including the retirement of the chief financial officer, the elevation of Nick Scheele to chief operating officer, and the appointment of three new group vice presidents, the team focused on massive restructuring of Ford's U.S. operations. In January 2002, the team announced that Ford would be closing key manufacturing plants in New Jersey, Missouri, Ohio, Michigan, and Ontario, citing too much capacity at those plants. In other words, the company was overproducing and did not need to build as many cars in a weak economy. In addition, Ford took several well-known but slow-selling models out of production—the Ford Escort, the Mercury Villager (a minivan), the Mercury Cougar, and the Lincoln Continental. Saying that former CEO Jac Nasser had diversified the organization too much, the new group declared that Ford was now focusing on its core business of building cars and trucks. Overall, 35,000 Ford workers (10 percent of the total global workforce) would probably lose their jobs, at least temporarily. Although this sounds grim, managers and other experts believed that these massive changes would ultimately help Ford survive a weak economy and the costs incurred by the Firestone tire debacle and ultimately lead to its growth.

A company such as Ford naturally has a huge, diverse workforce to manage. Although diversity challenges most often relate to ensuring that a variety of people have equal job opportunity, rarely do we think of older, white male employees as needing protection by the law. But that is exactly what happened at Ford, when a class-action lawsuit was filed against the company for reverse discrimination. The suit alleged that the company's performance appraisal system was targeting those workers for dismissal or early retirement. How could this happen? Under a system instituted by former CEO Jac Nasser, called the Performance Management Process, workers were given performance grades of A, B, or C. Those who received a C could lose their bonuses and raises; those who received two C grades in a row could be fired. If that sounds fair, here's the catch: Under the original plan, a quota of at least 10 percent of Ford employees were to receive C grades; later, the percentage was lowered to 5 percent. Many liken the ranking system, currently being used by a number of leading companies, to a grading curve because regardless of actual performance, a certain number of employees received high scores and a certain number received low ones. As it turned out at Ford, many of the C grades were handed out to older white males. Ford's system was eventually changed to one designating top achievers, achievers, and those requiring improvement. But within a year and a half, Ford agreed to abandon the system, which affected about 18,000 managers. As Bill Ford took over the CEO spot in late 2001, negotiations in the lawsuits continued. However, it seemed clear that both sides wanted the cases settled as amicably as possible.

Compensating nearly half a million employees in different countries is another huge challenge for human resource managers at Ford. In the fall of 2001, the combination of sluggish car sales and the Firestone recall forced the human resources department to circulate a memo announcing that about 6,000 managers would not be receiving their typical yearly bonuses. The company simply did not have the pool of cash—about $440 million—it had had in the past to pay out the bonuses. Nasser's retirement package was also tied to the company's overall financial performance, but he still received a bonus worth more than $5 million.

It is doubtful that anyone would dispute that Ford's management team has had an extremely rocky ride during the past few years. Managers at every level have faced constant challenges as their organization has struggled with massive changes. However, Ford is taking clear steps to survive and ultimately come out on top with its focus on producing new car models and perhaps even a retooled organization model.

Questions

1. What factors in the environment do you believe have affected Ford's structure in the past? What environmental factors do you believe will affect its structure in the future?
2. What internal forces for change has Ford faced in the last five years?
3. From a human resource management perspective, why do you think Jac Nasser's performance appraisal system failed?

SOURCES: Ed Garsten, "Tentative Terms in Ford Bias Cases," Associated Press, (November 16, 2001), http://www.ford.com; "Ford Moving Closer to Settling Suits—WSJ," Reuters Limited (November 16, 2001); Ed Garsten, "Ford Announces Management Shuffle," Associated Press (November 15, 2001), http://dailynews.yahoo.com; August Cole, "Ford Shuffles Another Round of Execs," CBS MarketWatch.com (November 15, 2001), http://www.marketwatch.com; "Nasser's Retirement Package Tied to Ford's Performance," Auto.com, (November 15, 2001), http://www.auto.com; "Exec Changes Help Ford with Basics," Automotive News (November 12, 2001), http://www.autonews.com; Nikki Tait, "Lincoln Bears Brunt of Ford Restructuring," Financial Times (November 11, 2001), http://news.ft.com; Tim Burt and Nikki Tait, "Ford May Axe 20 Percent of White Collar Staff," Financial Times (November 6, 2001), http://news.ft.com; John Gallagher, "No Bonuses This Year for Ford's Top Bosses," Detroit Free Press (August 29, 2001), http://www.freep.com; Tim Burt and Nikki Tait, "Ford Refines Chain of Command in U.S," Financial Times (July 16, 2001), http://news.ft.com; Tim Burt, "Ford's White Knight Summoned to Aid of U.S. in Distress," Financial Times (July 15, 2001), http://news.ft.com.

Leading

When Canada geese migrate south for the winter or north for the summer, they fly hundreds of miles in a V-formation, with the leader at the point of the V and the rest of the flock fanned out behind. The leader navigates, sets the pace, and takes the brunt of wind, rain, sleet, and snow. The leader decides when the flock will land to take a rest or eat and when it will take off again on its journey. Just like the owner or top executive of an organization, the leader of the flock decides the direction in which the entire group will go.

In nature, instinct guides the leader's decisions, methods of communication, and the way teamwork develops. Canada geese may navigate with an internal compass or by the position of the sun. They communicate with honking sounds and body language. They must engage in teamwork to fly in perfect formation, land, and take off together. Today's organizational leaders may be born with certain traits such as charisma, but they must learn how to develop leadership skills to communicate with employees, understand their behavior, foster teamwork, and motivate them toward their best performance. Just as a flock of geese has a better chance of surviving than a single bird trying to migrate, an organization has a better chance of thriving and growing if all of its members are working together as a team.

When it is time to change leaders, Canada geese manage the task in midflight. The V wobbles for a moment while one moves up and the other moves back. But the flock keeps flying. It is a graceful shift in power.

Foundations of Behavior in Organizations

CHAPTER OUTLINE

Organizational Behavior

Attitudes

Components of Attitudes

Work-Related Attitudes

Conflicts among Attitudes

Perception

Perceptual Selectivity

Perceptual Distortions

Attributions

Personality and Behavior

Personality Traits

Emotional Intelligence

Attitudes and Behaviors Influenced by Personality

Person-Job Fit

Learning

The Learning Process

Learning Styles

Continuous Learning

Stress and Stress Management

Type A and Type B Behavior

Causes of Work Stress

Stress Management

LEARNING OBJECTIVES

After studying this chapter, you should be able to

1 Define attitudes, including their major components, and explain their relationship to personality, perception, and behavior.

2 Discuss the importance of work-related attitudes.

3 Identify major personality traits and describe how personality can influence workplace attitudes and behaviors.

4 Define the five components of emotional intelligence and explain why they are important for managers in today's organizations.

5 Explain how people learn in general and in terms of individual learning styles.

6 Discuss the effects of stress and identify ways individuals and organizations can manage stress to improve employee health, satisfaction, and productivity.

Management Challenge

Vinita Gupta never expected running a company to be easy, but she was not prepared for this. Gupta had founded the networking equipment maker Quick Eagle Networks in 1985 under the name Digital Link, took it public 10 years later, and then stepped out for a couple of years. After sales plummeted, she returned as CEO to try to turn things around. Sales and profits improved, but employee morale just kept getting worse. Employees were quitting in droves, with annual turnover hitting 30 percent. Spirits were so low that even key executives were jumping ship, leaving profitable Quick Eagle to join profitless competitors. When Gupta tried to determine what was going on, she uncovered an unnerving possibility—could it be that her own personality and attitudes were part of the problem? Introverted, soft-spoken, and highly focused on work, Gupta had always depended on other managers to be the cheerleaders and coaches in the company. But now, she was hearing through the grapevine that people found her aloof and unapproachable, and that the stiff, serious atmosphere she created made Quick Eagle—well, just not a very fun place to work. Gupta was accustomed to focusing on details of the business and making necessary changes to keep quality, sales, and profits high. But maybe boosting morale and stemming the tide of talented workers walking out the door meant she now had to make some changes in herself. [1]

If you were Vinita Gupta, how would you gain a better understanding of yourself, your employees, and the changes you need to make to improve morale at Quick Eagle Networks? Do you believe the personality of a company's CEO affects organizational performance?

People differ in many ways. Some are quiet and shy while others are gregarious; some are thoughtful and serious while others are impulsive and fun-loving. Employees—and managers—bring their individual differences to work each day. These differences in attitudes, values, personality, and so forth influence how people interpret an assignment, whether they like to be told what to do, how they handle challenges, and how they interact with others. Managers' personalities and attitudes, as well as their ability to understand individual differences among employees, can profoundly affect the workplace and influence employee motivation, morale, and job performance. People are an organization's most valuable resource—and the source of some of the most difficult problems. Three basic leadership skills are at the core of identifying and solving people problems: (1) diagnosing, or gaining insight into the situation a manager is trying to influence; (2) adapting individual behavior and resources to meet the needs of the situation; and (3) communicating in a way that others can understand and accept. Thus, managers need insight about individual differences to understand what a behavioral situation is now and what it may be in the future.

To handle this responsibility, managers need to understand the principles of organizational behavior—that is, the ways individuals and groups tend to act in organizations. By increasing their knowledge of individual differences in the areas of attitudes, personality, perception, learning, and stress management, managers can understand and lead employees and colleagues through many workplace challenges. This chapter introduces basic principles of organizational behavior in each of these areas.

Organizational Behavior

organizational behavior
An interdisciplinary field dedicated to the study of how individuals and groups tend to act in organizations.

Organizational behavior, commonly called OB, is an interdisciplinary field dedicated to the study of human attitudes, behavior, and performance in organizations. OB draws concepts from many disciplines, including psychology, sociology, cultural anthropology, industrial engineering, economics, ethics, and vocational counseling, as well as the discipline of management. The concepts and principles of organizational behavior are important to managers because in every organization human beings ultimately make the decisions that control how the organization will acquire and use resources. Those people may cooperate with, compete with, support, or undermine one another. Their beliefs and feelings about themselves, their coworkers, and the organization shape what they do and how well they do it. People can distract the organization from its strategy by engaging in conflict and misunderstandings, or they can pool their diverse talents and perspectives to accomplish much more as a group than they could ever do as individuals.

organizational citizenship
Work behavior that goes beyond job requirements and contributes as needed to the organization's success.

By understanding what causes people to behave as they do, managers can exercise leadership to achieve positive outcomes. They can foster behaviors such as **organizational citizenship**, that is, work behavior that goes beyond job requirements and contributes as needed to the organization's success. An employee demonstrates organizational citizenship by being helpful to coworkers and customers, doing extra work when necessary, and looking for ways to improve products and procedures. Managers can encourage organizational citizenship by applying their knowledge of human behavior in many ways, such as selecting people with positive attitudes and personalities, helping them see how they can contribute, and enabling them to learn from and cope with workplace challenges.

Attitudes

Most students have probably heard the expression that someone "has an attitude problem," which means there is some consistent quality about the person that affects his or her behavior in a negative way. An employee with an attitude problem might be hard to get along with, might constantly gripe and cause problems, and might persistently resist new ideas. We all seem to know intuitively what an attitude is, but we do not consciously think about how strongly attitudes affect behavior. Defined formally, an **attitude** is an evaluation—either positive or negative—that predisposes a person to act in a certain way. Understanding employee attitudes is important to managers because attitudes determine how people perceive the work environment, interact with others, and behave on the job. A person who has the attitude "I love my work; it's challenging and fun" probably will tackle work-related problems cheerfully, while one who comes to work with the attitude "I hate my job" is not likely to exhibit much enthusiasm or commitment to solving problems. Managers strive to develop and reinforce positive attitudes among employees.

Managers should recognize that negative attitudes can be both the result of underlying problems in the workplace as well as a contributor to forthcoming problems.[2] For example, top executives at Federated Department Stores appointed a young, computer whiz-kid as chief operating officer for its e-commerce division. Older managers with years of experience in retailing had negative attitudes about this guy they considered still wet behind the ears, while the new COO had negative attitudes about older workers, whom he considered slow to accept new ideas or learn new methods. Soon, experienced managers started leaving the company. Federated's top leaders realized that the company needed to do a better job of handling generational diversity, as discussed in the previous chapter, to help employees develop more positive attitudes.[3]

Components of Attitudes

One important step for managers is recognizing and understanding the *components* of attitudes, which is particularly important when attempting to change attitudes.

Behavioral scientists consider attitudes to have three components: cognitions (thoughts), affect (feelings), and behavior.[4] The cognitive component of an attitude includes the beliefs, opinions, and information the person has about the object of the attitude, such as knowledge of what a job entails and opinions about personal abilities. The affective component is the person's emotions or feelings about the object of the attitude, such as enjoying or hating a job. The behavioral component of an attitude is the person's intention to behave toward the object of the attitude in a certain way. Exhibit 15.1 illustrates the three components of a positive attitude toward one's job. The cognitive element is the conscious thought that "my job is interesting and challenging." The affective element is the feeling that "I love this job." These, in turn, are related to the behavioral component—an employee might choose to arrive at work early because he or she is happy with the job.

Often, when we think about attitudes, we focus on the cognitive component. However, it is important for managers to remember the other components as well. When people feel strongly about something, the affective component may predispose them to act, no matter what someone does to change their opinions.

attitude
A cognitive and affective evaluation that predisposes a person to act in a certain way.

©George Lange/Corbis Outline

When William C. Ford Jr. introduced himself as the new CEO of Ford Motor Company at a hastily arranged press conference, employees' moods shifted dramatically. Amid the gloom about worsening profits and quality problems, workers surged to their feet cheering Henry Ford's well-liked great-grandson as a tonic for the organization's battered morale. Ford is hoping the more positive attitudes will help turn the company around. "It was like the old Ford again," says one company insider. "People were smiling again instead of staring at the ground."

Exhibit *15.1*

Components of an Attitude

For example, if an employee is passionate about a new idea, that employee may go to great lengths to implement it. Likewise, an employee who is furious about being asked to work overtime on his birthday may act on that anger—by failing to cooperate, lashing out at coworkers, or even quitting—no matter what arguments the employee's manager presents about the need to work. In cases such as these, effective leadership includes addressing the affect (emotions) associated with the attitude. Are employees so excited that their judgment may be clouded, or so discouraged that they have given up trying? If nothing else, the manager probably needs to be aware of situations that involve strong emotions and give employees a chance to vent their feelings safely.

As a general rule, changing one component of an attitude—cognitions, affect, or behavior—can contribute to an overall change in attitude. Suppose a manager concludes that some employees have the attitude that the manager should make all the decisions affecting the department, but the manager prefers that employees assume more decision-making responsibility. To change the underlying attitude, the manager would consider whether to educate employees about the areas in which they can make good decisions (changing the cognitive component), build enthusiasm with pep talks about the satisfaction of employee empowerment (changing the affective component), or simply insist that employees make their own decisions (behavioral component) with the expectation that, once they experience the advantages of decision-making authority, they will begin to like it.

Work-Related Attitudes

The attitudes of most interest to managers are those related to work, especially attitudes that influence how well employees perform. To lead employees effectively, managers logically seek to cultivate the kinds of attitudes that are associated with high performance. Two attitudes that might relate to high performance are satisfaction with one's job and commitment to the organization.

Job Satisfaction. A positive attitude toward one's job is called **job satisfaction**. In general, people experience this attitude when their work matches their needs and interests, when working conditions and rewards (such as pay) are satisfactory, and when the employees like their co-workers.

Many managers believe job satisfaction is important because they think satisfied employees will do better work. In fact, research shows that the link between satisfaction and performance is generally small and is affected by other factors.[5] The importance of satisfaction varies according to the amount of control the employee has; an employee doing routine tasks may produce about the same output no matter how he or she feels about the job. However, an internal study at Sears recently found a clear link between employee satisfaction, customer satisfaction, and revenue. In particular, employees' attitudes about whether their workloads were manageable and well-organized ranked among the top-10 indicators of company performance.[6]

Managers of today's knowledge workers often rely on job satisfaction to keep motivation and enthusiasm for the organization high. Organizations don't want to lose talented, highly skilled workers. In addition, most managers care about their employees and simply want them to feel good about their work—and almost everyone prefers being around people who have positive attitudes. Managers play an important role in whether employees have positive or negative attitudes toward their jobs.[7] At Rhinotek Computer Products, a Carson, California, company that manufacturers inkjet and laser printers, founder Gerald Chamales improved employees' job satisfaction by changing his own attitudes and behavior.

©Peter Charlesworth/SABA

Set designer Anne Larlarb's job satisfaction is high. After college graduation two years ago, Larlarb arrived in London on a student visa to assist a famous set designer. Now she is in Thailand where she is apprenticing in the art workshop for a major motion picture, working 14-hour days, living out of three suitcases at a hotel, and using e-mail as her only address. But Larlarb thinks it's worth it—the exposure to new cultures has been invaluable research for her design work. She displays her attitude with a one-word comment as she pages through her journal: "Wow!"

job satisfaction
A positive attitude toward one's job.

RHINOTEK COMPUTER PRODUCTS
http://www.rhinotek.com

When Gerald Chamales founded Rhinotek 20 years ago, he had no management experience and quickly fell into a dictatorial pattern, throwing temper tantrums and screaming at employees who did not follow orders or measure up to his standards. In addition, he would withhold his approval on an employee's work if he was angry at the employee for some minor infraction, like showing up for work a few minutes late or taking a long break. Employees began to hate their jobs and dreaded coming to work every day. Performance declined, absenteeism increased, and turnover kept getting higher. "I was getting the opposite behavior that I wanted," Chamales says.

Fortunately, Chamales was able to shift his own behavior and try other tactics. Rather than assuming people needed strict control and discipline, he started looking at employees as individuals, each of whom might be motivated by different things. Instead of issuing orders and demanding that employees do things a certain way, he tried to learn what employees enjoyed and could devote themselves to wholeheartedly. He started walking about the offices and plant floor talking to people and getting feedback. "I started to see that being a leader means playing off of people's strengths instead of reprimanding them for their weaknesses," he says.

The changes Chamales made turned Rhinotek into a much happier place to work, and the job satisfaction of many employees improved, reflected in a dramatically declining turnover rate.[8] ❖

organizational commitment

Loyalty to and heavy involvement in one's organization.

Organizational Commitment. Another important attitude is **organizational commitment**, which is loyalty to and heavy involvement in the organization. An employee with a high degree of organizational commitment is likely to say *we* when talking about the organization. Such a person tries to contribute to the organization's success and wishes to remain with the organization. This attitude is common at the A. W. Chesterton Company, a Massachusetts company that produces mechanical seals and pumps. CEO James D. Chesterton takes a personal interest in his employees, and they in turn are very loyal to him and to the organization. When two Chesterton pumps that supply water on Navy ship *USS John F. Kennedy* failed on a Saturday night just before the ship's scheduled departure, Todd Robinson, the leader of the team that produces the seals, swung into action. He and his fiancèe, who also works for Chesterton, worked through the night to make new seals and deliver them to be installed before the ship left port.[9]

Most managers want to enjoy the benefits of loyal, committed employees, including low turnover and willingness to do more than the job's basic requirements. Organizational commitment is especially important in a tight labor market, which forces employers to compete harder to attract and keep good workers. Also, in recent years many employees have become distrustful of their employers. As shown in Exhibit 15.2, a survey of 450,000 employees found that although most executives believe employees respect management, their employees' attitudes are in fact quite different.[10] The percentage of workers who say management is respected by employees has been steadily declining since 1991. In the most recent available year of the survey (1997), about 50 percent of employees reported that management generally is respected, as compared with about 70 percent of top managers who believed that.

E x h i b i t *15.2*

Changing Attitudes: Employees' Respect for Management

SOURCE: Adapted from Aaron Bernstein, "We Want You to Stay. Really," *BusinessWeek* (June 22, 1998), 67–68+ (citing data from an annual survey of 450,000 employees and managers by the International Survey Research Corporation).

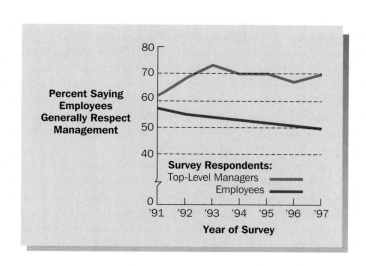

Managers can take action to promote organizational commitment by keeping employees informed, giving them a say in decisions, providing the necessary training and other resources that enable them to succeed, treating them fairly, and offering rewards they value. For example, recent studies suggest that employee commitment in today's workplace is strongly correlated with initiatives and benefits that help people balance their work and personal lives.[11] The Putting People First box describes one organization that was built on the concept of fostering a good life for the people who work there.

Conflicts among Attitudes

Sometimes a person may discover that his or her attitudes conflict with one another or are not reflected in his or her behavior. For example, a person's high level of organizational commitment might conflict with that person's commitment to family members. If employees routinely work evenings and weekends, their long hours and dedication to the job may conflict with their belief that family ties are important. This can create a state of **cognitive dissonance**, a psychological discomfort that occurs when individuals recognize inconsistencies in their own attitudes and behaviors.[12] The theory of cognitive dissonance, developed by social psychologist Leon Festinger in the 1950s, says that people want to behave in accordance with their attitudes and usually will take corrective action to alleviate the dissonance and achieve balance.

In the case of working overtime, people who control their hours might restructure responsibilities so that they have time for both work and family. In contrast, those who are unable to restructure workloads might develop an unfavorable attitude toward the employer, reducing their organizational commitment. They might resolve their dissonance by saying they would like to spend more time with their kids but their unreasonable employer demands that they work too many hours.

cognitive dissonance
A condition in which two attitudes or a behavior and an attitude conflict.

Perception

Another critical aspect of understanding behavior is perception. **Perception** is the cognitive process people use to make sense out of the environment by selecting, organizing, and interpreting information from the environment. Attitudes affect perceptions, and vice versa. For example, a person might have developed the attitude that managers are insensitive and arrogant, based on a pattern of perceiving arrogant and insensitive behavior from managers over a period of time. If the person moves to a new job, this attitude will continue to affect the way he or she perceives superiors in the new environment, even though managers in the new workplace might take great pains to understand and respond to employees' needs.

Because of individual differences in attitudes, personality, values, interests, and so forth, people often "see" the same thing in different ways. A class that is boring to one student might be fascinating to another. One student might perceive an assignment to be challenging and stimulating, whereas another might find it a silly waste of time. Referring back to the topic of diversity discussed in Chapter 14, many African Americans perceive that blacks are regularly discriminated against, whereas many white employees perceive that blacks are given special opportunities in the workplace.[13]

perception
The cognitive process people use to make sense out of the environment by selecting, organizing, and interpreting information.

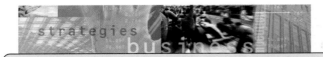

Putting People First

The Rokenbok Magic

Paul Eichen wondered what a company would look like if its only aim was to promote a balanced, healthy, soulful life. Work was everything to Eichen, who had helped start a successful technology company and grow it to sales of $100 million. However, work was eating him alive, so he walked away from his lucrative, successful job and began pursuing the answer to his question.

As a boy, Eichen had loved LEGOs, model kits, and machines, a love that would prove to be his salvation for a better life. "I think people tend to know what they need to do in their lives, and they can either ignore it or get on with it," Eichen says. He knew what he needed to do—start a toy company. But even more importantly, he wanted to create a new kind of business, one in which every company-defining decision was based on the way it would make work feel for the people who worked there. When Eichen opened the doors to Rokenbok Toy Co., it wasn't in an industrial park but in a village by the beach, in an old, rehabilitated warehouse just a short walk from the sand, with ethnic restaurants and sundries emporiums, coffee shops, and used bookstores as neighbors. Having the real world surround Rokenbok held a kind of magic for Eichen and his employees, who realized that where a company is located determines not only the commute but also the richness of life outside the office.

The pattern of work at Rokenbok was also different from many companies. As long as employees did their work, they were encouraged to set their own hours, dress as they liked, tend to their health, and put their families first. One Rokenbok engineer describes playing on the living room floor with his child and company toys, piecing together problems, working as he played, playing as he worked. For most company employees, work became a source of re-connection with family, friends, and neighbors. "We're trying to make something classic, not disposable. Values that are important personally—quality, constructive fun, learning, design sophistication—are things we're trying to design right into the product, and that feels great."

In the five years of its existence, Rokenbok's employees have accomplished something noteworthy: They've created an independent American toy company, establishing a product that has won toy-industry accolades and climbed from sales of $2.6 million in 1997 to $10 million in 1999. And even though Eichen believes that during the dot-com heyday every one of his managers were recruited and promised "instant millions," none of them left. "Our executives have chosen quality of life over the seductiveness of . . . wealth," says Eichen.

Eichen does not kid himself that even the most balanced workplaces can prevent life from getting a little messy, but the Rokenbok work style allows employees to have the energy and flexibility to pay attention to health, friends, family, and dreams, as well as their work "Look," Eichen says, "at a company like Rokenbok you still get to keep the good parts [of work]: intellectual stimulation, social activity, the fun of competing to win." Plus, you get to have a personal life, too. It's a winning combination.

SOURCE: Michael Hopkins, "The Pursuit of Happiness," *Inc.* (August 2000), 72–89.

We can think of perception as a step-by-step process, as shown in Exhibit 15.3. First, we observe information (sensory data) from the environment through our senses: taste, smell, hearing, sight, and touch. Next, our mind screens the data and will select only the items we will process further. Third, we organize the selected data into meaningful patterns for interpretation and response. Most differences in perception among people at work are related to how they select and organize sensory data.

Perceptual Selectivity

We all are aware of our environment, but not everything in it is equally important to our perception of it. We tune in to some data (e.g., a familiar voice off in the distance) and tune out other data (e.g., paper shuffling next to us). People are bombarded by so much sensory data that it is impossible to process it all. The brain's solution is to run the data through a perceptual filter that retains some parts (selective attention) and eliminates others. **Perceptual selectivity** is the process by which individuals screen and select the various

perceptual selectivity
The process by which individuals screen and select the various stimuli that vie for their attention.

Exhibit 15.3
The Perception Process

objects and stimuli that vie for their attention. Certain stimuli catch their attention, and others do not.

People typically focus on stimuli that satisfy their needs and that are consistent with their attitudes, values, and personality. For example, employees who need positive feedback to feel good about themselves might pick up on positive statements made by a supervisor but tune out most negative comments. A supervisor could use this understanding to tailor his feedback in a positive way to help the employee improve her work. The influence of needs on perception has been studied in laboratory experiments and found to have a strong impact on what people perceive.[14]

Characteristics of the stimuli itself also affect perceptual selectivity. People tend to notice stimuli that stand out against other stimuli or that are more intense than surrounding stimuli. Examples would be a loud noise in a quiet room or a bright red dress at a party where most women are wearing basic black. People also tend to notice things that are familiar to them, such as a familiar voice in a crowd, as well as things that are new or different from their previous experiences. In addition, *primacy* and *recency* are important to perceptual selectivity. People pay relatively greater attention to sensory data that occur toward the beginning of an event or toward the end. Primacy supports the old truism that first impressions really do count, whether it be on a job interview, meeting a date's parents, or participating in a new social group. Recency reflects the reality that the last impression might be a lasting impression. For example, Malaysian Airlines has discovered its value in building customer loyalty. A woman traveling with a nine-month-old might find the flight itself an exhausting blur, but one such traveler enthusiastically told people for years how Malaysian Airlines flight attendants helped her with baggage collection and ground transportation.[15]

As these examples show, perceptual selectivity is a complex filtering process. Managers can use an understanding of perceptual selectivity to obtain clues about why one person sees things differently from others, and they can apply the principles to their own communications and actions, especially when they want to attract or focus attention.

Perceptual Distortions

Once people have selected the sensory data to be perceived, they begin grouping the data into recognizable patterns. Perceptual organization is the process by which people organize or categorize stimuli according to their own frame of reference. Of particular concern in the work environment are **perceptual distortions**, errors in perceptual judgment that arise from inaccuracies in any part of the perceptual process.

Some types of errors are so common that managers should become familiar with them. These include stereotyping, the halo effect, projection, and perceptual defense. Managers who recognize these perceptual distortions can better adjust their perceptions to more closely match objective reality.

perceptual distortions
Errors in perceptual judgment that arise from inaccuracies in any part of the perceptual process.

stereotyping
The tendency to assign an individual to a group or broad category and then attribute generalizations about the group to the individual.

Stereotyping is the tendency to assign an individual to a group or broad category (e.g., female, black, elderly or male, white, disabled) and then to attribute widely held generalizations about the group to the individual. Thus, someone meets a new colleague, sees he is in a wheelchair, assigns him to the category "physically disabled," and attributes to this colleague generalizations she believes about people with disabilities, which may include a belief that he is less able than other co-workers. However, the person's inability to walk should not be seen as indicative of lesser abilities in other areas. Indeed, the assumption of limitations may not only offend him, it also prevents the person making the stereotypical judgment from benefiting from the many ways in which this person can contribute. Stereotyping prevents people from truly knowing those they classify in this way. In addition, negative stereotypes can prevent talented people from advancing in an organization and fully contributing their talents to the organization's success.

halo effect
An overall impression of a person or situation based on one characteristic, either favorable or unfavorable.

The **halo effect** occurs when the perceiver develops an overall impression of a person or situation based on one characteristic, either favorable or unfavorable. In other words, a halo blinds the perceiver to other characteristics that should be used in generating a more complete assessment. The halo effect can play a significant role in performance appraisal. For example, a person with an outstanding attendance record may be assessed as responsible, industrious, and highly productive; another person with less-than-average attendance may be assessed as a poor performer. Either assessment may be true, but it is the manager's job to be sure the assessment is based on complete information about all job-related characteristics and not just his or her preferences for good attendance.

projection
The tendency to see one's own personal traits in other people.

Projection is the tendency of perceivers to see their own personal traits in other people; that is, they project their own needs, feelings, values, and attitudes into their judgment of others. A manager who is achievement oriented might assume that subordinates are as well. This might cause the manager to restructure jobs to be less routine and more challenging, without regard for employees' actual satisfaction. The best guards against errors based on projection are self-awareness and empathy.

perceptual defense
The tendency of perceivers to protect themselves by disregarding ideas, objects, or people that are threatening to them.

Perceptual defense is the tendency of perceivers to protect themselves against ideas, objects, or people that are threatening. People perceive things that are satisfying and pleasant but tend to disregard things that are disturbing and unpleasant. In essence, people develop blind spots in the perceptual process so that negative sensory data do not hurt them. For example, the director of a nonprofit educational organization in Tennessee hated dealing with conflict because he had grown up with parents who constantly argued and often put him in the middle of their arguments. The director consistently overlooked discord among staff members until things would reach a boiling point. When the blow-up occurred, the director would be shocked and dismayed, because he had truly perceived that everything was going smoothly among the staff. Recognizing perceptual blind spots can help people develop a clearer picture of reality.

Attributions

As people organize what they perceive, they often draw conclusions about the stimuli. For example, stereotyping involves assigning a number of traits to a person. Among the judgments people make as part of the perceptual process are attributions. **Attributions** are judgments about what caused a person's behavior—something about the person or something about the situation. An

attributions
Judgments about what caused a person's behavior—either characteristics of the person or of the situation.

internal attribution says characteristics of the person led to the behavior ("My boss yelled at me because he's impatient and doesn't listen"). An *external attribution* says something about the situation caused the person's behavior ("My boss yelled at me because I missed the deadline and the customer is upset"). Attributions are important because they help people decide how to handle a situation. In the case of the boss yelling, a person who blames the yelling on the boss's personality will view the boss as the problem and might cope by avoiding the boss. In contrast, someone who blames the yelling on the situation might try to help prevent such situations in the future.

Social scientists have studied the attributions people make and identified three factors that influence whether an attribution will be external or internal.[16] These three factors are illustrated in Exhibit 15.4:

1. *Distinctiveness*—whether the behavior is unusual for that person (in contrast to a person displaying the same kind of behavior in many situations). If the behavior is distinctive, the perceiver probably will make an *external* attribution.
2. *Consistency*—whether the person being observed has a history of behaving in the same way. People generally make *internal* attributions about consistent behavior.
3. *Consensus*—whether other people tend to respond to similar situations in the same way. A person who has observed others handle similar situations in the same way will likely make an *external* attribution; that is, it will seem that the situation produces the type of behavior observed.

In addition to these general rules, people tend to have biases that they apply when making attributions. When evaluating others, we tend to underestimate the influence of external factors and overestimate the influence of internal factors. This tendency is called the **fundamental attribution error**.

fundamental attribution error
The tendency to underestimate the influence of external factors on another's behavior and to overestimate the influence of internal factors.

E x h i b i t *15.4*

Factors Influencing Whether Attributions Are Internal or External

For example, when someone has been promoted to chief executive officer, people generally consider the characteristics of the person that allowed him or her to achieve the promotion. In reality, however, the selection of that person may have been heavily influenced by external factors, such as business conditions creating a need for someone with a strong financial or marketing background at that particular time.

Another bias that distorts attributions involves attributions we make about our own behavior. People tend to overestimate the contribution of internal factors to their successes and overestimate the contribution of external factors to their failures. This tendency, called the **self-serving bias**, means people give themselves too much credit for what they do well and give external forces too much blame when they fail. Thus, if your manager says you don't communicate well enough, and you think your manager doesn't listen well enough, the truth may actually lie somewhere in between.

self-serving bias
The tendency to overestimate the contribution of internal factors to one's successes and the contribution of external factors to one's failures.

Personality and Behavior

Another area of particular interest to organizational behavior is personality. In the workplace, we find people whose behavior is consistently pleasant or aggressive or stubborn in a variety of situations. To explain that behavior, we may say, "He has a pleasant personality" or "She has an aggressive personality." An individual's **personality** is the set of characteristics that underlie a relatively stable pattern of behavior in response to ideas, objects, or people in the environment. Understanding an individual's personality can help managers predict how that person will act in a particular situation. Managers who appreciate the ways their employees' personalities differ have insight into what kinds of leadership behavior will be most influential.

personality
The set of characteristics that underlie a relatively stable pattern of behavior in response to ideas, objects, or people in the environment.

Personality Traits

In common usage, people think of personality in terms of traits, or relatively stable characteristics of a person. Researchers have investigated whether any traits stand up to scientific scrutiny. Although investigators have examined thousands of traits over the years, their findings have been distilled into five general dimensions that describe personality. These often are called the "Big Five" personality factors, as illustrated in Exhibit 15.5.[17] Each factor may contain a wide range of specific traits. The **Big Five personality factors** describe an individual's extroversion, agreeableness, conscientiousness, emotional stability, and openness to experience:

Big Five personality factors
Dimensions that describe an individual's extroversion, agreeableness, conscientiousness, emotional stability, and openness to experience.

1. *Extroversion.* The degree to which a person is sociable, talkative, assertive, and comfortable with interpersonal relationships.
2. *Agreeableness.* The degree to which a person is able to get along with others by being good-natured, cooperative, forgiving, understanding, and trusting.
3. *Conscientiousness.* The degree to which a person is focused on a few goals, thus behaving in ways that are responsible, dependable, persistent, and achievement oriented.
4. *Emotional stability.* The degree to which a person is calm, enthusiastic, and secure, rather than tense, nervous, depressed, moody, or insecure.
5. *Openness to experience.* The degree to which a person has a broad range of interests and is imaginative, creative, artistically sensitive, and willing to consider new ideas.

A person may have a low, moderate, or high degree of each of these factors:

The "Big Five" Personality Factors

As illustrated in the exhibit, these factors represent a continuum. That is, any individual may exhibit a low, moderate, or high degree of each quality. A person who has an extremely high degree of agreeableness would likely be described as warm, friendly, and good natured, while one at the opposite extreme might be described as cold, rude, or hard to get along with. In general, having a moderate-to-high degree of each of the personality factors is considered desirable for a wide range of employees. In addition, certain factors may be particularly important for specific kinds of work. For example, Nancy Naatz works for Aramark, an organization that handles many transactions online, but she needs a high degree of extroversion and agreeableness to build the relationships that are critical to her success, as described in the Leading Online box. These traits might not be as important for an employee who has little need to interact with others.

Many companies, including JCPenney, Toys 'R' Us, and the Union Pacific Railroad, use personality testing to hire, evaluate, or promote employees. American MultiCinema (AMC), one of the largest theater chains in the United States, looks for front-line workers with high conscientiousness and high emotional stability.[18] Marriott Hotels looks for people who score high on conscientiousness and agreeableness because they believe these individuals will provide better service to guests.[19] Companies also use personality testing for managers. Hewlett-Packard, Dell Computer, and General Electric all put candidates for top positions through testing, interviews with psychologists, or both to see if they have the "right stuff" for the job.[20]

However, despite growing use, there is little evidence that personality tests are a valid predictor of job success. In addition, the Big Five dimensions have been criticized because they are difficult to measure precisely. Because each dimension is made up of a number of specific traits, a person might score high on some traits but low on others. For example, considering the dimension of conscientiousness, a person might score high on a trait such as dependability, but score low on achievement orientation. Furthermore, research on the Big Five has mostly been limited to the United States, so there are dangers in applying the theory cross-culturally.

Leading Online

At Aramark, B2B Still Needs the Human Touch

Nancy Naatz's employer, Aramark Corp., is a champion of business-to-business (B2B) e-commerce. In fact, the company uses the Internet to order more than 85 percent of the food and supplies it needs to cater special events and run cafeterias for large corporate clients. But that doesn't mean Naatz sits in a comfy chair pointing and clicking all day. She has to be comfortable not just with technology but also with meeting and talking to all kinds of people face to face. Naatz spends much of her time patrolling the cafeteria, talking with employees, and consulting with executives at Sears Roebuck & Co., one of Aramark's major clients. Naatz, whose title at Aramark is resident district manager, business services, has discovered that not everything can be handled online. Even in the B2B world, a smile and a handshake is still sometimes the best route to success.

Although Aramark is a Web-savvy company that uses software that allows its managers to draw from a national database of distributors to make online purchases, managers are given the freedom to do whatever it takes to make the client happy. Keeping in close touch with the needs of customers is an important aspect of the job. On Naatz's daily jaunts into the bustling Sears cafeteria she pays close attention to the length of lines at each food counter, helping her quickly zero in on employee trends and alter the menu and her food orders

accordingly. Naatz frequently has to make judgment calls, something a computer can not do. She knows that Sears executives, for example, want their formal awards dinners to be nice but not too "stuffy." She selects a menu that she believes fits well with the company's casual corporate style.

Cultivating a relationship with local or regional vendors is also an essential part of the job because clients often have special needs that can be hard to come by among the commodities of the Web. For example, Sears employees wanted sushi added to the cafeteria menu and top executives wanted fresh, New York-style bagels for their daily continental breakfasts. "When I meet with a local supplier, it's generally not because they have better pricing," Naatz says. "I often meet with them because we want to make sure we get items fresh and quick." Naatz often sizes up potential contacts with an old-fashioned face-to-face meeting before she begins the business of haggling over details, negotiating terms, and striking deals.

After Sears moved out of the Sears Tower in 1992, vendors from far and wide came to court the company in hopes of landing the food and guest services contract for the new location. The Aramark bid won. Why? Because Aramark promised to have a live human being on hand to solve problems for Sears as they arose.

SOURCE: Kortney Stringer, "People Who Need People," *The Wall Street Journal* (May 21, 2001), R14.

Emotional Intelligence

In recent years, new insights into personality have been gained through research in the area of *emotional intelligence*. Emotional intelligence (EQ) includes five basic components:[21]

1. *Self-awareness.* The basis for all the other components; being aware of what you are feeling. People who are in touch with their feelings are better able to guide their own lives and actions.
2. *Managing emotions.* The ability to balance one's moods so that worry, anxiety, fear, or anger do not cloud thinking and get in the way of what needs to be done.
3. *Motivating oneself.* The ability to be hopeful and to persist in the face of obstacles, setbacks, and even outright failure. This ability is crucial for pursuing long-term goals. For example, MetLife found that applicants who failed the regular sales aptitude test but scored high on optimism made 21 percent more sales in their first year and 57 percent more in their second year than those who passed the sales test but scored high on pessimism.[22]
4. *Empathy.* Being able to put yourself in someone else's shoes, to recognize what others are feeling without them needing to tell you. People frequently don't say how they feel in words, but rather in tone of voice, body language, and facial expression.

5. *Social skill.* The ability to connect to others, build positive relationships, respond to the emotions of others, and influence others.

Studies have found a positive relationship between job performance and high degrees of emotional intelligence in a variety of jobs. Numerous organizations, including the U.S. Air Force and Canada Life, have used EQ tests to measure such things as self-awareness, ability to empathize, and capacity to build positive relationships.[23] EQ seems to be particularly important for jobs that require a high degree of social interaction, which includes managers, who are responsible for influencing others and building positive attitudes and relationships in the organization. For example, Paul Wieand became president of Bucks County Bank at the age of 33, then masterminded mergers that tripled its size and turned it into a major regional institution. Yet only a few years later, he was forced to resign. Wieand's arrogance and insensitivity led to such poor morale and negative attitudes that the board felt he was a threat to the company's continued success. After he was forced out, Weiand began reading extensively to help him understand why running a bank was so easy intellectually but so hard emotionally. Eventually, he developed a new philosophy of management based on the belief that everyone "wants the same things in life: to be recognized, to be cared for, and to be given an opportunity to grow."[24] Weiand's personal turnaround illustrates an important point: Emotional intelligence is not an in-born personality characteristic, but something that can be learned and developed throughout one's lifetime.[25]

At times of great change or crisis, managers need a higher EQ level to help employees cope with the anxiety and stress they may be experiencing. Following the September 11, 2001, terrorist attacks in the United States and amid continuing fears of anthrax, a declining economy, and aviation safety, an important role for managers was meeting the psychological and emotional needs of employees. This chapter's Shoptalk box outlines some elements of emotional intelligence that are particularly important in times of crisis.

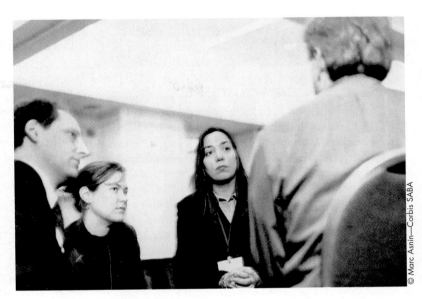

Harvard Law School's Program on Negotiation offers seminars that help small business owners develop their emotional intelligence and be more effective leaders. "People [wrongly] assume that you check your feelings at the door when you go to work," says Sheila Heen, a Harvard Law School lecturer. The program offers training in topics such as Improving Your Listening Skills, Managing Anger at Work, Managing Your Feelings, and Getting Straight on Purposes. In the photo, participants practice expressing their emotions without becoming "emotional."

© Marc Asnin—Corbis SABA

Attitudes and Behaviors Influenced by Personality

An individual's personality influences a wide variety of work-related attitudes and behaviors. Among those that are of particular interest to managers are locus of control, authoritarianism, Machiavellianism, and problem-solving styles.

Locus of Control.   People differ in terms of what they tend to attribute as the cause of their success or failure. Their **locus of control** defines whether they place the primary responsibility within themselves or on outside forces.[26] Some people believe that their actions can strongly influence what happens to them. They feel in control of their own fate. These individuals have a high *internal* locus of control. Other people believe that events in their lives occur because of chance, luck, or outside people and events. They feel more like

locus of control
The tendency to place the primary responsibility for one's success or failure either within oneself (internally) or on outside forces (externally).

THE NEW WORKPLACE

Manager's Shoptalk

What's Your Crisis EQ?

The September 11, 2001, terrorist attacks on the Pentagon and the World Trade Center left lingering psychological and emotional damage in workplaces all across the United States and even the rest of the world. Numerous companies, some in places far removed from the scene of the actual attacks, called upon crisis counselors to help their employees cope with the trauma. However, outside counseling is not enough in such an environment. Managers also need the skills to help people deal with their emotions and return to a more normal work routine. Although managers cannot take the place of professional counselors, they can use patience, flexibility, and understanding to assist people through a crisis. Here are some important elements of crisis EQ for managers:

- Be visible and provide as much up-to-date, accurate information as possible about what is going on in the company and the industry. Rumor control is critical.
- Find simple ways to get employees together. Order pizza for the entire staff. Invite telecommuters to come in to the office so they can connect with others and have a chance to share their emotions.
- Give employees room to be human. It is natural for people to feel anger and other strong emotions, so allow those

feelings to be expressed as long as they are not directed at other employees.

- Publicize the company's charitable endeavors and make employees aware of the various opportunities both within and outside the organization to volunteer and donate to charity.
- Thank employees in person and with handwritten notes when they go above and beyond the call of duty during a difficult time.
- Recognize that routine, structured work can help people heal. Postpone major, long-term projects and decisions to the extent possible and break work into shorter, more manageable tasks. Listen to employees and determine what they need to help them return to a normal work life.
- Provide professional counseling services for people who need it. Those with a history of alcohol abuse, trouble at home, or previous mental or emotional problems are especially at risk, but anyone who has trouble gradually returning to his or her previous level of work may need outside counseling.

SOURCES: Based on Matthew Boyle, "Nothing Really Matters," *Fortune* (October 15, 2001), 261–264; and Sue Shellenbarger, "Readers Face Dilemma Over How Far to Alter Post-Attack Workplace," (Work & Family column), *The Wall Street Journal* (October 31, 2001), B1.

©Ann States/SABA

James Oxedine has no boss worries, a reasonable income, a home office with a view, and a high internal locus of control. He works as a free agent, helping neighborhoods, banks, and bureaucrats get along during revitalization projects in cities such as Spartanburg, South Carolina and Atlanta, Georgia. Oxedine feels that independence means you never have to say you're bored.

pawns of their fate. These individuals have a high *external* locus of control. Many top leaders of e-commerce and high-tech organizations exhibit a high internal locus of control. These managers have to cope with rapid change and uncertainty associated with Internet business. They must believe that they and their employees can counter the negative impact of outside forces and events. John Chambers, CEO of Cisco Systems, is a good example. Despite today's tough economy and a drastically diminished stock price, Chambers has not lost his belief that Cisco can defeat any challenge thrown its way.[27] A person with a high external locus of control would likely feel overwhelmed trying to make the rapid decisions and changes needed to keep pace with the industry, particularly in the current environment of uncertainty.

Research on locus of control has shown real differences in behavior across a wide range of settings. People with an internal locus of control are easier to motivate because they believe the rewards are the result of their behavior. They are better able to handle complex information and problem solving, are more achievement oriented, but are also more independent and therefore more difficult to lead. On the other hand, people with an external locus of control are harder to motivate, less involved in their jobs, more likely to blame others when faced with a poor performance evaluation, but more compliant and conforming and, therefore, easier to lead.[28]

Do you believe luck plays an important role in your life, or do you feel that you control your own fate? To find out more about your locus of control, read the instructions and complete the questionnaire in Exhibit 15.6.

The questionnaire below is designed to measure locus-of-control beliefs. Researchers using this questionnaire in a study of college students found a mean of 51.8 for men and 52.2 for women, with a standard deviation of 6 for each. The higher your score on this questionnaire, the more you tend to believe that you are generally responsible for what happens to you; in other words, higher scores are associated with internal locus of control. Low scores are associated with external locus of control. Scoring low indicates that you tend to believe that forces beyond your control, such as powerful other people, fate, or chance, are responsible for what happens to you.

For each of these 10 questions, indicate the extent to which you agree or disagree using the following scale:

1 = strongly disagree   5 = slightly agree
2 = disagree   6 = agree
3 = slightly disagree   7 = strongly agree
4 = neither disagree nor agree

_____ 1. When I get what I want, it is usually because I worked hard for it.
_____ 2. When I make plans, I am almost certain to make them work.
_____ 3. I prefer games involving some luck over games requiring pure skill.
_____ 4. I can learn almost anything if I set my mind to it.
_____ 5. My major accomplishments are entirely due to my hard work and ability.
_____ 6. I usually don't set goals, because I have a hard time following through on them.
_____ 7. Competition discourages excellence.
_____ 8. Often people get ahead just by being lucky.
_____ 9. On any sort of exam or competition, I like to know how well I do relative to everyone else.
_____ 10. It's pointless to keep working on something that's too difficult for me.

To determine your score, reverse the values you selected for questions 3, 6, 7, 8, and 10 (1 = 7, 2 = 6, 3 = 5, 4 = 4, 5 = 3, 6 = 2, 7 = 1). For example, if you strongly disagree with the statement in question 3, you would have given it a value of 1. Change this value to a 7. Reverse the scores in a similar manner for questions 6, 7, 8, and 10. Now add the point values from all 10 questions together.

Your score: _____

SOURCE: Adapted from J. M. Burger, *Personality: Theory and Research* (Belmont, Calif.: Wadsworth, 1986), 400–401, cited in D. Hellriegel, J. W. Slocun, Jr., and R. W. Woodman, *Organizational Behavior*, 6th ed. (St. Paul, Minn.: West, 1992), 97–100. Original source: "Sphere-Specific Measures of Perceived Control" by D. L. Paulhus, *Journal of Personality and Social Psychology*, 44, 1253–1265.

Exhibit 15.6

Measuring Locus of Control

Authoritarianism.   **Authoritarianism** is the belief that power and status differences *should* exist within the organization.[29] Individuals high in authoritarianism tend to be concerned with power and toughness, obey recognized authority above them, stick to conventional values, critically judge others, and oppose the use of subjective feelings. The degree to which managers possess authoritarianism will influence how they wield and share power. The degree to which employees possess authoritarianism will influence how they react to their managers. If a manager and employees differ in their degree of authoritarianism, the manager may have difficulty leading effectively. The trend toward empowerment and shifts in expectations among younger employees for more equitable relationships have contributed to a decline in strict authoritarianism in many organizations. The shift can be seen in the National Football League, where a rising number of coaches put more emphasis on communication and building relationships than on ruling with an iron hand. Coaches like Steve Mariucci (San Francisco 49ers), Tony Dungy (Indianapolis Colts), and Jeff Fisher (Tennessee Titans) are aware that today's players have different expectations than those of previous generations. "This is not old Rome with gladiators," says San Francisco's Mariucci. "This is modern day football. . . . If you cannot relate to today's player, you are through as a coach."[30]

authoritarianism
The belief that power and status differences *should* exist within the organization.

Machiavellianism
The tendency to direct much of one's behavior toward the acquisition of power and the manipulation of other people for personal gain.

Machiavellianism.   Another personality dimension that is helpful in understanding work behavior is **Machiavellianism**, which is characterized by the acquisition of power and the manipulation of other people for purely personal gain. Machiavellianism is named after Niccolo Machiavelli, a sixteenth-century author who wrote *The Prince*, a book for noblemen of the day on how to acquire and use power.[31] Psychologists have developed instruments to measure a person's Machiavellianism (Mach) orientation.[32] Research shows that high Machs are predisposed to being pragmatic, capable of lying to achieve personal goals, more likely to win in win-lose situations, and more likely to persuade than be persuaded.[33]

Different situations may require people who exhibit one or the other type of behavior. In loosely structured situations, high Machs actively take control, while low Machs accept the direction given by others. Low Machs thrive in highly structured situations, while high Machs perform in a detached, disinterested way. High Machs are particularly good in jobs that require bargaining skills or that involve substantial rewards for winning.[34]

Problem-Solving Styles.   Managers also need to understand that individuals differ in the way they go about gathering and evaluating information for problem solving and decision making. Psychologist Carl Jung has identified four functions related to this process: sensation, intuition, thinking, and feeling.[35] According to Jung, gathering information and evaluating information are separate activities. People gather information either by *sensation* or *intuition*, but not by both simultaneously. Sensation-type people would rather work with known facts and hard data and prefer routine and order in gathering information. Intuitive-type people would rather look for possibilities than work with facts and prefer solving new problems and using abstract concepts.

Information evaluation involves making judgments about the information a person has gathered. People evaluate information by *thinking* or *feeling*. These represent the extremes in orientation. Thinking-type individuals base their judgments on impersonal analysis, using reason and logic rather than personal values or emotional aspects of the situation. Feeling-type individuals base their judgments more on personal feelings such as harmony and tend to make decisions that result in approval from others.

According to Jung, only one of the four functions—sensation, intuition, thinking, or feeling—is dominant in an individual. However, the dominant function usually is backed up by one of the functions from the other set of paired opposites. Exhibit 15.7 shows the four problem-solving styles that result from these matchups, as well as occupations that people with each style tend to prefer.

Studies show that the sensation-thinking combination characterizes many managers in Western industrialized societies. However, as shown in Exhibit 15.7, the intuitive-thinking style is useful for top executives who have to deal with many complex problems and make fast decisions. Carly Fiorina, CEO of Hewlett-Packard, might be considered an intuitive-thinking type. Fiorina is a creative thinker who is able to see the big picture and broad possibilities for HP's future. Although she cares about employees, Fiorina doesn't flinch from getting rid of people who don't support her vision for change.[36]

Person-Job Fit

Given the wide variation among personalities and among jobs, an important responsibility of managers is to try to match employee and job characteristics

Personal Style	Action Tendencies	Likely Occupations
Sensation–thinking	• Emphasizes details, facts, certainty • Is a decisive, applied thinker • Focuses on short-term, realistic goals • Develops rules and regulations for judging performance	• Accounting • Production • Computer programming • Market research • Engineering
Intuitive–thinking	• Prefers dealing with theoretical or technical problems • Is a creative, progressive, perceptive thinker • Focuses on possibilities using impersonal analysis • Is able to consider a number of options and problems simultaneously	• Systems design • Systems analysis • Law • Middle/top management • Teaching business, economics
Sensation–feeling	• Shows concern for current, real-life human problems • Is pragmatic, analytical, methodical, and conscientious • Emphasizes detailed facts about people rather than tasks • Focuses on structuring organizations for the benefit of people	• Directing supervisor • Counseling • Negotiating • Selling • Interviewing
Intuitive–feeling	• Avoids specifics • Is charismatic, participative, people oriented, and helpful • Focuses on general views, broad themes, and feelings • Decentralizes decision making, develops few rules and regulations	• Public relations • Advertising • Human Resources • Politics • Customer service

Exhibit **15.7**

Four Problem-Solving Styles

so that work is done by people who are well suited to do it. This requires that managers be clear about what they expect employees to do. They should have a sense of the kinds of people who would succeed at the work that must be done. The extent to which a person's ability and personality match the requirements of a job is called **person-job fit**. When hiring and leading employees, managers should try to achieve person-job fit, so that employees are more likely to contribute and be satisfied.[37] When dot-com companies exploded out of the gate in the late 1990s, the importance of person-job fit became very apparent. People who had rushed to Internet companies in hopes of finding a new challenge—or making a quick buck—found themselves floundering in jobs for which they were unsuited. One manager recruited by a leading executive search firm lasted less than two hours at his new job. The search firm, a division of Russell Reynolds Associates, later developed a "Web Factor" diagnostic to help determine whether people have the right personality for the Internet, including such things as a tolerance for risk and uncertainty, an obsession with learning, and a willingness to do whatever needs doing, regardless of job title.[38]

A related concern is *person-environment fit*, which looks not only at whether the person and job are suited to one another but also how well the individual will fit in the overall organizational environment. An employee who is by nature strongly authoritarian, for example, would have a hard time in an organization such as W. L. Gore and Associates, where there are few rules, no hierarchy, no fixed or assigned authority, and no bosses. Many of today's organizations pay attention to person–environment fit from the beginning of the recruitment process. Texas Instruments' Web page includes an area called Fit Check that evaluates personality types anonymously and gives prospective job candidates a chance to evaluate for themselves whether they would be a good match with the company.[39]

person-job fit
The extent to which a person's ability and personality match the requirements of a job.

Learning

learning
A change in behavior or performance that occurs as the result of experience.

Years of schooling have conditioned many of us to think that learning is something students do in response to teachers in a classroom. With this view, in the managerial world of time deadlines and concrete action, learning seems remote—even irrelevant. However, today's successful managers need specific knowledge and skills as well as the ability to adapt to changes in the world around them. Managers have to learn.

Learning is a change in behavior or performance that occurs as the result of experience. Experience may take the form of observing others, reading or listening to sources of information, or experiencing the consequences of one's own behavior. This important way of adapting to events is linked to individual differences in attitudes, perception, and personality.

Two individuals who undergo similar experiences—for example, a business transfer to a foreign country—probably will differ in how they adapt their behaviors to (that is, learn from) the experience. In other words, each person learns in a different way.

The Learning Process

One model of the learning process, shown in Exhibit 15.8 depicts learning as a four-stage cycle.[40] First, a person encounters a concrete experience. This is followed by thinking and reflective observation, which lead to abstract conceptualization and, in turn, to active experimentation. The results of the experimentation generate new experiences, and the cycle repeats.

The Best Buy chain of consumer electronics superstores owes its birth to the learning process of its founder, Richard M. Schulze. In the 1960s, Schulze built a stereo store called Sound of Music into a chain of nine stores in and near St. Paul, Minnesota. However, a tornado destroyed his largest and most profitable store, so he held a massive clearance sale in the parking lot. So many shoppers descended on the lot that they caused traffic to back up for two miles. Reflecting on this experience, Schulze decided there was great demand for a store featuring large selection and low prices, backed by heavy

Exhibit 15.8

Experiential Learning Cycle

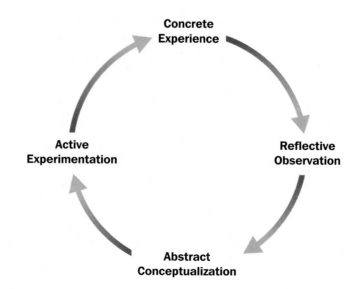

advertising. He tried out his idea by launching his first Best Buy superstore. Today there are more than 400 Best Buy outlets as well as a thriving online division, and the chain's profits are in the billions of dollars.[41]

The arrows in the model of the learning process in Exhibit 15.8 imply that this process is a recurring cycle. People continually test their conceptualizations and adapt them as a result of their personal reflections and observations about their experiences.

Learning Styles

Individuals develop personal learning styles that vary in terms of how much they emphasize each stage of the learning cycle. These differences occur because the learning process is directed by individual needs and goals. For example, an engineer might place greater emphasis on abstract concepts, while a salesperson might emphasize concrete experiences. Because of these preferences, personal learning styles typically have strong and weak points.

To assess a person's strong and weak points as a learner in the learning cycle, questionnaires have been developed to measure the relative emphasis the person places on each of the four learning stages shown in Exhibit 15.8: concrete experience, reflective observation, abstract conceptualization, and active experimentation. Some people have a tendency to overemphasize one stage of the learning process, or to avoid some aspects of learning. Not many people have totally balanced profiles, but the key to effective learning is competence in each of the four stages when it is needed.

Each person's learning style is a combination of the emphasis placed on the four stages. Researchers have identified four fundamental learning styles that combine elements of the four stages.[42] Exhibit 15.9 summarizes the characteristics and dominant learning abilities of these four learning styles, labeled Diverger, Assimilator, Converger, and Accommodator. The exhibit also lists occupations that frequently attract individuals with each of the learning styles. For example, people whose dominant style is *Assimilator* do well in research and strategic planning. *Accommodators* are often drawn to sales and marketing. A good example of the Accommodator learning style is Gertrude Boyle, who took over Columbia Sportswear after the death of her husband. She and her son, Tim, propelled the company from sales of $13 million in 1984 to $358 million in 1997 by observing what competitors were doing and actively experimenting to find a novel sales approach. The 74-year-old Gert Boyle decided to star in her own "Tough Mother" ads as a way to distinguish the company from competitors who advertised their products worn by fit, young models. Boyle believes in constantly pushing herself and her company, questioning everything, and trying new ideas.[43] Exhibit 15.9 lists other likely occupations for Divergers, Assimilators, Convergers, and Accommodators.

Through awareness of their learning style, managers can understand how they approach problems and issues, their learning strengths and weaknesses, and how they react to employees or co-workers who have different learning styles.

Continuous Learning

To thrive or even to survive in today's fast-changing business climate, individuals and organizations must be continuous learners. For individuals, continuous learning entails looking for opportunities to learn from classes, reading,

Maytag Corporation, a manufacturer of home and commercial appliances, joins with the state of Iowa to advertise the benefits of their continuous learning style. Maytag makes the following claim in their ad: "We have partnered successfully with the state and our community on education and training alliances and infrastructure improvements that advance our commitment to profitable growth."

Learning Style Type	Dominant Learning Abilities	Learning Characteristics	Likely Occupations
Diverger	• Concrete experience • Reflective observation	• Is good at generating ideas, seeing a situation from multiple perspectives, and being aware of meaning and value • Tends to be interested in people, culture, and the arts	• Human resource management • Counseling • Organization development specialist
Assimilator	• Abstract conceptualization • Reflective observation	• Is good at inductive reasoning, creating theoretical models, and combining disparate observations into an integrated explanation • Tends to be less concerned with people than ideas and abstract concepts	• Research • Strategic planning
Converger	• Abstract conceptualization • Active experimentation	• Is good at decisiveness, practical application of ideas, and hypothetical deductive reasoning • Prefers dealing with technical tasks rather than interpersonal issues	• Engineering • Production
Accommodator	• Concrete experience • Active experimentation	• Is good at implementing decisions, carrying out plans, and getting involved in new experiences • Tends to be at ease with people but may be seen as impatient or pushy	• Marketing • Sales

Exhibit *15.9*

Learning Style Types

and talking to others, as well as looking for the lessons in life's experiences. One manager who embodies the spirit of continuous learning is Larry Ricciardi, senior vice president and corporate counsel at IBM. Ricciardi is an avid traveler and voracious reader who likes to study art, literature, and history. In addition, Ricciardi likes to add supermarket tabloids to his daily fare of *The Wall Street Journal*. On business trips, he scouts out side trips to exotic or interesting sites so he can learn something new.[44] Ricciardi never knows when he might be able to apply a new idea or understanding to improve his life, his job, or his organization.

For organizations, continuous learning involves the processes and systems through which the organization enables its people to learn, share their growing knowledge, and apply it to their work. In an organization in which continuous learning is taking place, employees actively apply comments from customers, news about competitors, training programs, and more to increase their knowledge and improve the organization's practices. For example, at the Mayo Clinic, doctors are expected to consult with doctors in other departments, with the patient, and with anyone else inside or outside the clinic who might help with any aspect of the patient's problem.[45] The emphasis on teamwork, openness, and collaboration keeps learning strong at Mayo.

Managers can foster continuous learning by consciously stopping from time to time and asking, "What can we learn from this experience?" They can allow employees time to attend training and reflect on their experiences. Recognizing that experience can be the best teacher, managers should focus on how they and their employees can learn from mistakes, rather than fostering a climate in which employees hide mistakes because they fear being punished for them. Managers also encourage organizational learning by establishing information systems that enable employees to share knowledge and learn in new ways. Information technology will be discussed in detail in Chapter 21. As individuals, managers can help themselves and set an example for their employees by being continuous learners, listening to others, reading widely, and reflecting on what they observe.

Stress and Stress Management

Just as organizations can support or discourage learning, many other organizational characteristics interact with individual differences to influence behavior in the organization. In every organization, these characteristics include sources of stress. Formally defined, **stress** is an individual's physiological and emotional response to stimuli that place physical or psychological demands on the individual and create uncertainty and lack of personal control when important outcomes are at stake.[46] These stimuli, called stressors, produce some combination of frustration (the inability to achieve a goal, such as the inability to meet a deadline because of inadequate resources) and anxiety (such as the fear of being disciplined for not meeting deadlines).

People's responses to stressors vary according to their personality, the resources available to help them cope, and the context in which the stress occurs. Thus, a looming deadline will feel different depending on the degree to which the individual enjoys a challenge, the willingness of coworkers to team up and help each other succeed, and family members' understanding of an employee's need to work extra hours, among other factors.

When the level of stress is low relative to a person's coping resources, stress can be a positive force, stimulating desirable change and achievement. However, too much stress is associated with many negative consequences, including sleep disturbances, drug and alcohol abuse, headaches, ulcers, high blood pressure, and heart disease. People who are experiencing the ill effects of too much stress may withdraw from interactions with their coworkers, take excess time off for illnesses, and look for less stressful jobs elsewhere. They may become so irritable that they cannot work constructively with others; some employees may even explode in tantrums or violence. Clearly, too much stress is harmful to employees as well as to the organization.

In biological terms, the stress response follows a pattern known as the General Adaptation Syndrome. The **General Adaptation Syndrome (GAS)** is a physiological response to a stressor, which begins with an alarm response, continues to resistance, and may end in exhaustion if the stressor continues beyond a person's ability to cope.[47] As shown in Exhibit 15.10, the GAS begins when an individual first experiences a source of stress (called a stressor). The stressor triggers an *alarm* response; the person may feel panic and helplessness, wondering how to cope with the stressor. Occasionally, people simply give up, but more often they move to the next stage of the stress response, called *resistance*. At this stage, the person gathers strength and begins to decide how to cope. If exposure to the stressor continues past the person's ability to maintain resistance, the person enters the third stage: *exhaustion*.

Type A and Type B Behavior

Researchers have observed that some people seem to be more vulnerable than others to the ill effects of stress. From studies of stress-related heart disease, they have categorized people as having behavior patterns called Type A and Type B.[48] The **Type A behavior** pattern includes extreme competitiveness,

stress
A physiological and emotional response to stimuli that place physical or psychological demands on an individual.

General Adaptation Syndrome (GAS)
A physiological response to a stressor, beginning with an alarm response, continuing to resistance, and sometimes ending in exhaustion if the stressor continues beyond a person's ability to cope.

Type A behavior
Behavior pattern characterized by extreme competitiveness, impatience, aggressiveness, and devotion to work.

Exhibit 15.10

The Stress Response: General Adaptation Syndrome

Type B behavior

Behavior pattern that lacks Type A characteristics and includes a more balanced, relaxed lifestyle.

impatience, aggressiveness, and devotion to work. In contrast, people with a **Type B behavior** pattern exhibit less of these behaviors. They consequently experience less conflict with other people and a more balanced, relaxed lifestyle. Type A people tend to experience more stress-related illness than Type B people.

Most Type A individuals are high-energy people. L. Dennis Kozlowski, the chief executive of Tyco International, starts his day at dawn and goes for 16 hours, often traveling back and forth between time zones for meetings. "This is what it takes to be a CEO," Kozlowski says. "If you're not willing to do it, you should step out of the way so someone else can take your place."[49]

By pacing themselves and learning control and intelligent use of their natural high-energy tendencies, Type A individuals can be powerful forces for innovation and leadership within their organizations. However, many Type A personalities cause stress-related problems for themselves, and sometimes for those around them. Type B individuals typically live with less stress unless they are in high-stress situations. There are a number of factors that can cause stress in the workplace, even for people who are not naturally prone to high stress.

Causes of Work Stress

Work-related stress is on the rise. According to a recent study, the percentage of employees who report feeling burned out from job stress increased from 39 percent in 1995 to 53 percent in 1998. During the same time period, the amount of time employees reported missing work because of stress increased more than 35 percent.[50] Most people have a general idea of what a stressful job is like: difficult, uncomfortable, exhausting, even frightening. Managers can better cope with their own stress and establish ways for the organization to help employees cope if they define the conditions that tend to produce work stress. One way to identify work stressors is to place them in four categories: demands associated with job tasks, physical conditions, roles (sets of expected behaviors), and interpersonal pressures and conflicts.

Task demands are stressors arising from the tasks required of a person holding a particular job. Some kinds of decisions are inherently stressful: those made under time pressure, those that have serious consequences, and those that must be made with incomplete information. For example, emergency room doctors are under tremendous stress as a result of the task demands of their jobs. They regularly have to make quick decisions, based on limited information, that may determine whether a patient lives or dies. Although not as extreme, many other jobs have task demands that lead to stress. Consider the task demands on Verizon's call center representatives.

Roland G. Collins Jr. loves his job as a call center representative for Verizon Communications. He enjoys connecting with customers; he makes good money and has good benefits. But he admits that it's not the job for everyone. About a third of the 100 or so calls a representative handles each day are stressful. Besides dealing with irate customers and handling calls regarding billing or other problems, representatives have to be able to rattle off Verizon's string of products and services, including terms and rates, and try to sell them to each and every call. It does not matter how angry or rude the customer on the other end of the line—pushing new services is a key requirement of the job.

What makes matters worse is that representatives often have to do all this under observation. Managers routinely sit next to a representative or listen in on a call to check whether the rep has hit on nearly 80 different points required in every customer contact. Call center reps must meet precise performance specifications, and managers defend the observation practice as a way to ensure consistency and better customer service. However, employees almost always find the experience adds to their stress level. For some employees, particularly inexperienced ones, an observation can create a panic situation, causing heart pounding and profuse sweating, which, in turn, creates even greater stress.[51] ❖

VERIZON COMMUNICATIONS
http://www.verizon.com

Almost all jobs have some level of stress associated with task demands. Recall from Chapter 9 that managers frequently have to make *nonprogrammed decisions*—decisions that are characterized by incomplete information and have important consequences for the organization. Managers also experience stress from other factors, such as the responsibility of supervising or disciplining other people.

Physical demands are stressors associated with the setting in which an individual works. Some people must cope with work in a poorly designed setting, such as an office with inadequate lighting or little privacy. Some employees must maneuver in a cramped workspace; some have too little or too much heat for comfort. Some workplaces even present safety and health hazards, from greasy floors to polluted air. Work that involves repetitive movements, such as extensive computer work, also can lead to injury; thus this type of work intensifies stress for employees.

Role demands are challenges associated with a role—that is, the set of behaviors expected of a person because of that person's position in the group. Some people encounter **role ambiguity**, meaning they are uncertain about what behaviors are expected of them. For example, one clinical psychologist who specializes in executive stress says that many upper-level executives, who grew up at a time when norms were different, do not understand what diversity requires of them—such as what women in the workplace view as appropriate conduct. Consequently, some are fearful of inadvertently doing something that a woman will regard as sexual harassment.[52]

Although role ambiguity can be stressful, people who experience role conflict can feel as if they are being torn apart by conflicting expectations. **Role conflict** occurs when an individual perceives incompatible demands from others. Managers often feel role conflict because the demands of their superiors conflict with those of the employees in their department. They may be expected to support employees and provide them with opportunities to experiment and be creative, while at the same time top executives are demanding a consistent level of output that leaves little time for creativity and experimentation. In a company whose philosophy is "We're one big family," a manager

role ambiguity
Uncertainty about what behaviors are expected of a person in a particular role.

role conflict
Incompatible demands of different roles.

who has to lay off employees would likely feel that this role conflicts with the expectation that she care about employees. These types of role conflict can create a high level of stress. Role conflict may also be experienced when the demands of the workplace conflict with demands from home. In the United States, the average number of hours worked per week is increasing, and almost 25 percent of employees report working an average of 50 hours or more per week.[53] For some, new technology such as e-mail and cell phones tie them to work and usurp their private lives around the clock. This means people have less time and energy to devote to family and friends, which may lead to role conflicts. A person's internalized values and beliefs may also collide with expectations in the workplace, leading to greater stress.

Interpersonal demands are stressors associated with relationships in the organization. Although in some cases interpersonal relationships can alleviate stress, they also can be a source of stress when the group puts pressure on an individual or when there are conflicts. Interpersonal conflict occurs when two or more individuals perceive that their attitudes or goals are in opposition. Managers can work to resolve many interpersonal and intergroup conflicts, using techniques discussed in Chapter 19. A particularly challenging stressor is the personality clash. A personality clash occurs when two people simply cannot get along and do not see eye-to-eye on any issue. This type of conflict can be exceedingly difficult to resolve, and many managers have found that it is best to separate the two people so that they do not have to interact with one another.

Stress Management

Organizations that want to challenge their employees and stay competitive in a fast-changing environment will never be stress-free. But because many consequences of stress are negative, managers need to participate in stress management for themselves and for their employees. They can do so by identifying the major sources of stress, including the task, physical, role, and interpersonal demands of the job and organization. Does the overall level of these demands match the employee's taste for challenge and his or her coping resources? If so, the level of stress may be part of a successful person-job fit. If not, the organization and its employees should look for ways to reduce the stressors and increase employees' coping skills. Organizations can provide training or clearer directions so that employees feel able to handle their responsibilities. They can make the work environment safer and more comfortable. Individuals also can act on their own initiative to develop their knowledge and skills.

Individual Stress Management.   A variety of techniques help individuals manage stress. Among the most basic strategies are those that help people stay healthy: exercising regularly, getting plenty of rest, and eating a healthful diet.

In addition, most people cope with stress more effectively if they lead balanced lives and are part of a network of people who support and encourage them. Family, relationships, friendships, and memberships in nonwork groups such as community or religious organizations are helpful for stress management, as well as for other benefits. People who don't take care of themselves physically and emotionally are more susceptible to stress in their personal as well as professional lives. Take the quick test in Exhibit 15.11 to rate your susceptibility to stress. Managers and employees in today's hectic, competitive work environment may sometimes think of these activities as luxuries. The study of organizational behavior, however, offers a reminder that employees are *human* resources with human needs.

New Workplace Responses to Stress Management. Although individuals can pursue stress management strategies on their own, today's enlightened companies support healthy habits to help employees manage stress and be more productive. Stress costs U.S. businesses an estimated $10,000 annually per employee in absenteeism, lower productivity, and higher health insurance and workers' compensation costs.[54] In the new workplace, taking care of employees has become a business as well as ethical priority.

Supporting employees can be as simple as encouraging people to take regular breaks and vacations. BellSouth, First Union, and Tribble Creative Group are among the companies that have designated areas as quiet rooms or meditation centers where employees can take short, calming breaks at any time they feel the need.[55] The time off is a valuable investment when it allows employees to approach their work with renewed energy and a fresh perspective. Companies also develop other programs aimed specifically at helping employees reduce stress and lead healthier, more balanced lives. At the Seattle office of TPD Publications Inc., a custom publisher that has offices around the world, a masseuse is on site every Tuesday, and the company picks up half the bill.[56] Many companies offer wellness programs that provide access to nutrition counseling and exercise facilities. Others create broad work–life balance initiatives that may include flexible work options such as telecommuting and flexible hours, as well as benefits such as onsite daycare, fitness centers, and personal services such as pick-up and delivery of dry cleaning. *Daily flextime* is considered by many employees to be the most effective work-life practice, which means giving employees the freedom to vary their hours as needed, such as leaving early to take an elderly parent shopping or taking time off to attend a child's school play.[57]

Exhibit **15.11**

The Stress Test

Respond to the following on a 1-to-5 scale, with 1 meaning almost always and 5 meaning never. The higher the score, the higher your susceptibility to stress. If you have a high score (above 36), what will you do to reduce your susceptibility to stress?

1	2	3	4	5
Almost always				Never

1. I eat at least one balanced, hot meal a day and get at least seven hours of sleep a night. _____
2. I am in good health. _____
3. I exercise at least twice a week. _____
4. I regularly give and receive affection. _____
5. I have at least one relative within 50 miles on whom I can rely. _____
6. My income meets basic expenses. _____
7. I organize my time effectively. _____
8. I get strength from my religious beliefs. _____
9. I do something fun at least once a week. _____
10. I speak openly about my feelings. _____
11. I regularly take quiet time for myself. _____
12. I have an optimistic outlook on life. _____

Total Score: _____

SOURCE: This is a portion of the Susceptibility Scale of the Personal Stress Navigator by Lyle H. Miller and Alma Dell Smith. Copyright by Stress Directions, Inc. 2000. Reprinted with permission.

By acknowledging the personal aspects of employees' lives, work–life practices also communicate that managers and the organization care about employees as human beings. "When you help people find balance or work through difficult stretches in their lives, you say, 'We want to be partners for the long haul,'" says Rebecca Rhoads, CIO and vice president of Massachusetts-based defense contractor Raytheon.[58] Work–life balance initiatives help employees manage stress, improve productivity and quality of life, and enhance job satisfaction and organizational commitment. In addition, managers' attitudes make a tremendous difference in whether employees are stressed out and unhappy or relaxed, energetic, and productive.

■ Summary and Management Solution

The principles of organizational behavior describe how people as individuals and groups behave and affect the performance of the organization as a whole. Attitudes are evaluations that predispose people to behave in certain ways. Desirable work-related attitudes include job satisfaction and organizational commitment. Conflicts among attitudes create a state of cognitive dissonance, which people try to alleviate by shifting attitudes or behaviors. Attitudes affect people's perceptions and vice versa. Individuals often "see" things in different ways. The perceptual process includes perceptual selectivity and perceptual organization. Perceptual distortions, such as stereotyping, the halo effect, projection, and perceptual defense, are errors in judgment that can arise from inaccuracies in the perceptual process. Attributions are judgments that individuals make about whether a person's behavior was caused by internal or external factors.

Another area of interest is personality, the set of characteristics that underlie a relatively stable pattern of behavior. One way to think about personality is the Big Five personality traits of extroversion, agreeableness, conscientiousness, emotional stability, and openness to experience. Some important work-related attitudes and behaviors influenced by personality are locus of control, authoritarianism, Machiavellianism, and problem-solving styles. Four problem-solving styles are sensation-thinking, intuitive-thinking, sensation-feeling, and intuitive-feeling. Managers want to find a good person-job fit by ensuring that a person's personality, attitudes, skills, and abilities match the requirements of the job and the organizational environment.

New insight into personality has been gained through research in the area of emotional intelligence (EQ). Emotional intelligence includes the components of self-awareness, managing emotions, motivating oneself, empathy, and social skill. High emotional intelligence has been found to be important for success in a wide range of jobs and is particularly important for managers. EQ is not an in-born personality characteristic, but can be learned and developed. Vinita Gupta, described at the beginning of this chapter, needed to strengthen her emotional intelligence, particularly in the areas of self-awareness, empathy, and social skill, to improve morale and create a more positive work environment at Quick Eagle Networks. Gupta hired a corporate coach to help her learn more about herself and manage the personality characteristics and behaviors that could be contributing to decreased performance and higher turnover at Quick Eagle. Gupta worked on a series of exercises to help develop greater empathy and improve her social skills, including coaching employees, being more open and less defensive, and using humor to create a lighter atmosphere. Whereas before she rarely paused to speak to—or sometimes even glance at—anyone when she arrived at the office, she now makes a point of greeting people upon arrival, introducing herself to employees she's never met, and having lunch with colleagues. Gupta has learned that she cannot change some of her personality characteristics—for example, she will never score high on extroversion. However, she has learned to manage her attitudes and behaviors to make Quick Eagle a more pleasant, comfortable place to work. Employees have noticed that the atmosphere is lighter, and people are no longer afraid to speak up in meetings or if they have a concern. Turnover has decreased by 20 percent from a year earlier.[59]

Even though people's personalities may be relatively stable, individuals, like Vinita Gupta, can learn new behaviors. Learning refers to a change in behavior or performance that occurs as a result of experience. The learning process goes through a four-stage cycle, and individual learning styles differ. Four learning styles are

Diverger, Assimilator, Converger, and Accommodator. Rapid changes in today's marketplace create a need for ongoing learning. They may also create greater stress for many of today's workers. Stress is a person's response to a stimulus that places a demand on that person. The causes of work stress include task demands, physical demands, role demands, and interpersonal demands. Individuals and organizations can alleviate the negative effects of stress by engaging in a variety of techniques for stress management.

■ Discussion Questions

1. Why is it important for managers to have an understanding of organizational behavior? Do you think a knowledge of OB might be more important at some managerial levels than at others? Discuss.

2. In what ways might the cognitive and affective components of attitude influence the behavior of employees who are faced with learning an entirely new set of computer-related skills in order to retain their jobs at a manufacturing facility?

3. What steps might managers at a company that is about to be merged with another company take to promote organizational commitment among employees?

4. In the Big Five personality factors, extroversion is considered a "good" quality to have. Why might introversion be an equally positive quality?

5. What is meant by *perceptual selectivity*? Explain some characteristics of the perceiver and of the stimuli that might affect perception.

6. Which of the five components of emotional intelligence do you consider most important to an effective manager in today's world? Why?

7. How might understanding whether an employee has an *internal* or an *external* locus of control help a manager better communicate with, motivate, and lead the employee?

8. Why is it important for managers to achieve person-job fit when they are hiring employees?

9. Review Exhibit 15.9. Which learning style type best characterizes you? How can you use this understanding to improve your learning ability? To improve your management skills?

10. Describe a time when you experienced role ambiguity or role conflict. What stress management techniques did you use to cope with the stress this created?

11. Do you think it is the responsibility of managers and organizations to help employees manage stress? Why or why not?

■ Management in Practice: Experiential Exercise

The "Big 5" Personality Traits

Each individual's collection of personality traits is different; it is what makes us unique. But, although each *collection* of traits varies, we all share many common traits. The phrases below describe various traits and behaviors. Rate how accurately each statement describes you, based on a scale of 1 to 5, with 1 being very inaccurate and 5 very accurate. Describe yourself as you are now, not as you wish to be. There are no right or wrong answers.

1	2	3	4	5
Very Inaccurate				Very Accurate

_____ 1. I am kind and sympathetic.
_____ 2. I often feel critical of myself.
_____ 3. I am usually the life of the party.
_____ 4. I am systematic and efficient.
_____ 5. I am imaginative.
_____ 6. I pay attention to details.
_____ 7. I feel comfortable around people.

_____ 8. I prefer to vote for liberal political candidates.
_____ 9. I have a good word for everyone.
_____ 10. I often envy others.
_____ 11. I am talkative.
_____ 12. I really like art.
_____ 13. I am temperamental.
_____ 14. I never insult people.
_____ 15. I am always prepared for class.

Scoring

Statements 3, 7, and 11 describe traits associated with extroversion; statements 1, 9, and 14 describe agreeableness; statements 4, 6, and 15 describe conscientiousness; statements 2, 10, and 13 describe neuroticism (low emotional stability); and statements 5, 8, and 12 describe openness to new experiences. Which are your most prominent traits? For fun and discussion, compare your responses with those of classmates.

SOURCE: These questions were adapted from a variety of sources.

■ Management in Practice: Ethical Dilemma

Should I Fudge the Numbers?

Sara MacIntosh recently joined MicroPhone, a large telecommunications company, to take over the implementation of a massive customer service training project. The program was created by Kristin Cole, head of human resources and Sara's new boss. According to the grapevine, Kristin was hoping this project alone would give her the "star quality" she needed to earn a coveted promotion. Industry competition was heating up, and MicroPhone's strategy called for being the very best at customer service. That meant having the most highly trained people in the industry, especially those who would work directly with customers. Kristin's new training program called for an average of one full week of intense customer service training for each of 3,000 people and had a price tag of about $40 million.

Kristin had put together a team of overworked staffers to develop the training program, but now she needed someone well qualified and dedicated to manage and implement the project, and Sara, with eight years of experience, a long list of accomplishments, and advanced degrees in finance and organizational behavior, seemed perfect for the job. However, during a thorough review of the proposal, Sara discovered some assumptions built into the formulas that raised red flags. She approached Dan Sotal, the team's coordinator, about her concerns, but the more Dan tried to explain how the financial projections were derived, the more Sara realized that Kristin's proposal was seriously flawed. No matter how she tried to work them out, the most that could be squeezed out of the $40 million budget was 20 hours of training per person, not the 40 hours everyone expected for such a high price tag.

Sara knew that, although the proposal had been largely developed before she came on board, it would bear her signature. As she carefully described the problems with the proposal to Kristin and outlined the potentially devastating consequences, Kristin impatiently tapped her pencil. Finally, she stood up, leaned forward, and interrupted Sara, quietly saying, "Sara, make the numbers work so that it adds up to 40 hours and stays within the $40 million budget." Sara glanced up and replied, "I don't think it can be done unless we either change the number of employees who are to be trained or the cost figure. . . ." Kristin's smile froze on her face and her eyes began to snap as she again interrupted. "I don't think you understand what I'm saying. We have too much at stake here. *Make the previous numbers work.*" Stunned, Sara belatedly began to realize that Kristin was ordering her to fudge the numbers. She felt an anxiety attack coming on as she wondered what she should do.

What Do You Do?

1. Make the previous numbers work. Kristin and the entire team have put massive amounts of time into the project and they all expect you to be a team player. You don't want to let them down. Besides, this is a great opportunity for you in a highly visible position.
2. Stick to your principles and refuse to fudge the numbers. Tell Kristin you will work overtime to help develop an alternate proposal that stays within the budget by providing more training to employees who work directly with customers and fewer training hours for those who don't have direct customer contact.
3. Go to the team and tell them what you've been asked to do. If they refuse to support you, threaten to reveal the true numbers to the CEO and board members.

SOURCE: Adapted from Doug Wallace, "Fudge the Numbers or Leave," *Business Ethics,* May–June, 1996, 58–59. Adapted with permission.

■ Surf the Net

1. **Emotional Intelligence.** Go to both sites listed below to assess your emotional intelligence quotient. After completing the tests and printing out the results at both sites, be prepared to discuss which of the two formats of results you preferred and your reasons for preferring one over the other.
   http://www.utne.com/azEq2.tmpl
   http://quiz.ivillage.com/health/tests/eqtest2.htm
2. **Machiavellianism.** Take a Machiavelli personality test found at one of the sites listed below, print out the results, write your name at the top, and submit the printout to your instructor.

   http://www.salon.com/books/it/1999/09/13/machtest/
   http://killeenroos.com/2/Machiavelli.htm
   http://www.humanlinks.com/personal/power_orientation.htm
3. **Stress Management.** Use a Web browser to locate stress management information using the following phrase: "stress management college students." Be prepared to share in a class discussion the three stress management techniques you located during your research that you thought were most helpful.

■ Case for Critical Analysis

Volkswagen's Ferdinand Piëch

Although many of today's organizations have shifted toward more democratic, participative types of management, one has not: Volkswagen. Ferdinand Piëch, who recently retired as CEO, ruled Volkswagen with an iron hand since 1993 and continues to wield enormous power behind the scenes. Immediately after he took the CEO job, Piëch centralized power in the organization, firing managers who questioned his ideas or who didn't follow his lead. He dove into engineering projects himself, proposing new projects, tinkering with designs. He presided over meetings with the demeanor of an autocrat, with the occasional result that important questions weren't asked because managers were fearful of presenting opposing points of view.

Even though he has now passed the reins to his hand-picked successor, Bernd Pischetsrieder, it is widely believed that Piëch will continue to call the shots at Europe's leading carmaker. After his retirement as CEO, Piëch was expected to step directly into a new role as chairman of VW's executive supervisory board, which will allow him to direct strategy, influence management and executive appointments, and perhaps block important decisions. Under German corporate law, the chairman of the supervisory board, not the CEO, appoints management board members. "Piëch could pull all the strings." said one VW executive. In fact, some believe the former CEO effectively put his trusted aides in key positions before his retirement to ensure that the company would continue to follow his vision and direction. Although some colleagues say Pischetsrieder is very much his own man, few expect him—or other top executives—to resist Piëch's continued influence.

There's no doubt that Piëch is a brilliant and forward-thinking businessman. Looking back over his years at VW, he can boast one of the great turnarounds in automotive history. He helped make models such as the Golf and the Passat all-time bestsellers and cemented VW's hold in the important U.S. market with the relaunch of the beloved VW Beetle. Volkswagen's four main worldwide brands—VW, Audi, Seat, and Skoda—have taken 19 percent of the European auto market, mostly at the expense of General Motors and Ford. VW vehicles account for one-quarter of all car sales in South America and one-half of all sales in China. In 2000, the company's profits nearly doubled, to $1.8 billion on sales of $76 billion.

Piëch (whose maternal grandfather was Ferdinand Porsche) came to VW with a vision of turning the company into the most powerful, most respected carmaker in the world, and he's well on the way to meeting that goal. Yet, rather than resting on his laurels, Piëch spent the final months of his tenure as CEO acting as if he were still trying to pull the company out of a major crisis. Part of the reason Piëch's management approach has been successful is his extensive knowledge of and passion for the cars themselves. From his days as an automotive engineering student at Zurich's Swiss Federal Institute of Technology, through his stint at Porsche, where he helped create world-class race cars, to his development of Audi's Quattro and the launch of the VW Beetle, Piëch could be found under the hood, tinkering. Thus, he knew his product and his customers and how to fit them together better than anyone else in the industry.

However, while he has excelled as an engineer, critics charge that Piëch's tight hold over the company has left VW with serious problems. "There is a lack of people equipped to be efficient managers," says one analyst in Germany. "No middle manager can make decisions because they haven't been used to doing so. All decisions have been pushed [to the top]." Piëch's retirement comes at a crucial time for VW, which is facing renewed competition from Ford and other carmakers in Europe. A recent push into upscale vehicles risks hurting existing sales. In addition, VW is still plagued by high labor costs and low productivity at many of its plants. Some colleagues believe Pischetsrieder is up to the challenge of keeping VW at the top of the heap, but analysts wonder if he can really do his job with Piëch looking over his shoulder.

Questions

1. What personality traits does Ferdinand Piëch exhibit? Do you think these contributed to a good person-job fit as CEO of Volkswagen? Why or why not?

2. Almost anyone would agree that Piëch is an authoritarian executive. Do you sense that he is Machiavellian as well? Do you think these characteristics will have a positive or negative impact on Volkswagen's future? Explain your answer.

3. Imagine that you are one of the "trusted" managers that Piëch moved into a key position before his retirement. You are experiencing some cognitive dissonance about working long hours and investing significant resources in one of Piëch's pet projects, a new luxury car model about whose success you have doubts. How might you resolve your dissonance?

SOURCES: Christine Tierney, with Andrea Zammert, Joann Muller, and Katie Kerwin, "Volkswagen," *BusinessWeek,* Industrial/Technology edition (July 23, 2001), 60–68; Wim Oude Weernick, Georg Auer, and Dorothee Ostle, "Pischetsrieder's In, But Piech's Not Out," *Automotive News* (September 10, 2001), 1, 45; Scott Miller, "New VW Chief Assumes Post at Key Time–Stronger Rivals and Shadow of Piech May Make Life Hard for Pischetsrieder," *The Wall Street Journal* (September 7, 2001), A12; David Woodruff and Keith Naughton, "Hard-Driving Boss," *BusinessWeek* (October 5, 1998), 82-87; and Christine Tierney with Katharine Schmidt, "Who's Behind the Wheel at Audi?" *BusinessWeek,* Industrial/Technology edition (November 26, 2001), 50.

■ Endnotes

1. Julia Lawlor, "Personality 2.0," *Red Herring* (April 1, 2001), 98-103.

2. John W. Newstrom and Keith Davis, *Organizational Behavior: Human Behavior at Work*, 11th ed. (Burr Ridge, Ill.: McGraw-Hill Irwin, 2002), Chapter 9.

3. A. Feuerstein, "E-marketing Firm Lands Hotshot CEO," *San Francisco Business Times* (January 17, 2000), 1–2; and J. Kaufman, "What Happens When a 20-Something Whiz Is Suddenly the Boss," *The Wall Street Journal* (October 8, 1999), A1, A10.

4. S. J. Breckler, "Empirical Validation of Affect, Behavior, and Cognition as Distinct Components of Attitude," *Journal of Personality and Social Psychology* (May 1984), 1191–1205; and J. M. Olson and M. P. Zanna, "Attitudes and Attitude Change," *Annual Review of Psychology* 44 (1993), 117–154.

5. M. T. Iaffaldano and P. M. Muchinsky, "Job Satisfaction and Job Performance: A Meta-Analysis," *Psychological Bulletin* (March 1985), 251–273; C. Ostroff, "The Relationship between Satisfaction, Attitudes, and Performance: An Organizational Level Analysis," *Journal of Applied Psychology* (December 1992), 963–974; and M. M. Petty, G. W. McGee, and J. W. Cavender, "A Meta-Analysis of the Relationship between Individual Job Satisfaction and Individual Performance," *Academy of Management Review* (October 1984), 712–721.

6. Sue Shellenbarger, "Companies Are Finding Real Payoffs in Aiding Employee Satisfaction," (Work & Family column), *The Wall Street Journal* (October 11, 2000), B1.

7. Tony Schwartz, "The Greatest Sources of Satisfaction in the Workplace Are Internal and Emotional," *Fast Company* (November 2000), 398–402.

8. Carol Hymowitz, "Bosses Need to Learn Whether They Inspire, or Just Drive, Staff" (In the Lead column), *The Wall Street Journal* (August 14, 2001), B1.

9. William C. Symonds, "Where Paternalism Equals Good Business," *BusinessWeek* (July 20, 1998), 16E4, 16E6.

10. Aaron Bernstein, "We Want You to Stay. Really," *BusinessWeek* (June 22, 1998), 67–68+.

11. Jennifer Laabs, "They Want More Support—Inside and Outside of Work," *Workforce* (November 1998), 54–56.

12. For a discussion of cognitive dissonance theory, see Leon A. Festinger, *Theory of Cognitive Dissonance* (Stanford, Calif.: Stanford University Press, 1957).

13. D. A. Kravitz and S. L. Klineberg, "Reactions to Two Versions of Affirmative Action Among Whites, Blacks, and Hispanics," *Journal of Applied Psychology* 85 (2000), 597–611; and Robert J. Grossman, "Race in the Workplace" *HR Magazine* (March 2000), 41–45.

14. J. A. Deutsch, W. G. Young, and T. J. Kalogeris, "The Stomach Signals Satiety," *Science* (April 1978), 22–33.

15. Richard B. Chase and Sriram Dasu, "Want to Perfect Your Company's Service? Use Behavioral Science," *Harvard Business Review* (June 2001), 79–84.

16. H. H. Kelley, "Attribution in Social Interaction," in E. Jones et al. (eds.), *Attribution: Perceiving the Causes of Behavior* (Morristown, N.J.: General Learning Press, 1972).

17. See J. M. Digman, "Personality Structure: Emergence of the Five-Factor Model," *Annual Review of Psychology* 41 (1990), 417–440; M. R. Barrick and M. K. Mount, "Autonomy as a Moderator of the Relationships Between the Big Five Personality Dimensions and Job Performance," *Journal of Applied Psychology* (February 1993), 111–118; and J. S. Wiggins and A. L. Pincus, "Personality: Structure and Assessment," *Annual Review of Psychology* 43 (1992), 473–504.

18. Michelle Leder, "Is That Your Final Answer?" *Working Woman* (December–January 2001), 18; "Can You Pass the Job Test?" *Newsweek* (May 5, 1986), 46–51.

19. Alan Farnham, "Are You Smart Enough to Keep Your Job?" *Fortune* (January 15, 1996), 34–47.

20. Cora Daniels, "Does This Man Need a Shrink?" *Fortune* (February 5, 2001), 205–208.

21. Daniel Goleman, *Emotional Intelligence: Why It Can Matter More than IQ* (New York: Bantam Books, 1995); Sharon Nelton, "Emotions In the Workplace," *Nation's Business* (February 1996), 25–30; and Lara E. Megerian and John J. Sosik, "An Affair of the Heart: Emotional Intelligence and Transformational Leadership," *The Journal of Leadership Studies* 3, no. 3 (1996), 31–48.

22. Farnham, "Are You Smart Enough to Keep Your Job?"

23. Hendrie Weisinger, *Emotional Intelligence at Work* (San Francisco, Calif.: Jossey-Bass, 2000); D. C. McClelland, "Identifying Competencies with Behavioral-Event Interviews," *Psychological Science* (Spring 1999), 331–339; Daniel Goleman, "Leadership That Gets Results," *Harvard Business Review* (March-April 2000), 78–90; D. Goleman, *Working with Emotional Intelligence* (New York: Bantam Books, 1999); and Lorie Parch, "Testing . . . 1, 2, 3," *Working Woman* (October 1997), 74–78.

24. Pamela Kruger, "A Leader's Journey," *Fast Company* (June 1999), 116–129.

25. Goleman, "Leadership That Gets Results."

26. J. B. Rotter, "Generalized Expectancies for Internal versus External Control of Reinforcement," *Psychological Monographs* 80, no. 609 (1966).

27. Andy Serwer, "There's Something about Cisco," *Fortune* (May 15, 2000); Stephanie N. Mehta, "Cisco Fractures Its Own Fairy Tale," *Fortune* (May 14, 2001), 104–112.

28. See P. E. Spector, "Behavior in Organizations as a Function of Employee's Locus of Control," *Psychological Bulletin* (May 1982), 482–497.

29. T. W. Adorno, E. Frenkel-Brunswick, D. J. Levinson, and R. N. Sanford, *The Authoritarian Personality* (New York: Harper & Row, 1950).

30. Mike Freeman, "A New Breed of Coaches Relates Better to Players," *The New York Times* (August 19, 2001), Y36.

31. Niccolo Machiavelli, *The Prince*, trans. George Bull (Middlesex: Penguin, 1961).

32. Richard Christie and Florence Geis, *Studies in Machiavellianism* (New York: Academic Press, 1970).

33. R. G. Vleeming, "Machiavellianism: A Preliminary Review," *Psychological Reports* (February 1979), 295–310.

34. Christie and Geis, *Studies in Machiavellianism*.

35. Carl Jung, *Psychological Types* (London: Routledge and Kegan Paul, 1923).

36. Quentin Hardy, "All Carly, All the Time," *Forbes* (December 13, 1999), 138–144.

37. Charles A. O'Reilly III, Jennifer Chatman, and David F. Caldwell, "People and Organizational Culture: A Profile Comparison Approach to Assessing Person-Organization Fit," *Academy of Management Journal* 34, no.3 (1991), 487–516.

38. Anna Muoio, "Should I Go .Com?" *Fast Company* (July 2000), 164–172.

39. Leder, "Is That Your Final Answer?"

40. David A. Kolb, "Management and the Learning Process," *California Management Review* 18, no. 3 (Spring 1976), 21–31.

41. De' Ann Weimer, "The Houdini of Consumer Electronics," *BusinessWeek* (June 22, 1998), 88, 92.

42. See David. A. Kolb, I. M. Rubin, and J. M. McIntyre, *Organizational Psychology: An Experimental Approach*, 3rd ed. (Englewood Cliffs, N.J.: Prentice-Hall, 1984), 27–54.

43. Stephanie Gruner, "Our Company, Ourselves," *Inc.*, (April 1998), 127–128.

44. Ira Sager, "Big Blue's Blunt Bohemian," *BusinessWeek* (June 14, 1999), 107–112.

45. Paul Roberts, "The Best Interest of the Patient Is the Only Interest to be Considered," *Fast Company* (April 1999), 149–162.

46. T. A. Beehr and R. S. Bhagat, *Human Stress and Cognition in Organizations: An Integrated Perspective* (New York: Wiley, 1985).

47. Hans Selye, *The Stress of Life* (New York: McGraw-Hill, 1976).

48. M. Friedman and R. Rosenman, *Type A Behavior and Your Heart* (New York: Knopf, 1974).

49. Carol Hymowitz, "How Some CEOs Get the Energy to Work Those Endless Days," *The Wall Street Journal* (March 20, 2001), B1.

50. Laabs, "They Want More Support."

51. Kris Maher, "At Verizon Call Center, Stress Is Seldom On Hold," *The Wall Street Journal* (January 16, 2001), B1, B12.

52. Anne Fisher, "Why Are You So Paranoid?" *Fortune* (September 8, 1997), 171–172.

53. Louisa Wah, "The Emotional Tightrope," *Management Review* (January 2000), 38–43; Laabs, "They Want More Support."

54. Andrea Higbie, "Quick Lessons in the Fine Old Art of Unwinding," *The New York Times* (February 25, 2001), BU-10.

55. Leslie Gross Klass, "Quiet Time at Work Helps Employee Stress," *Johnson City Press* (January 28, 2001), 30.

56. Stephanie Gruner, "A Relaxed Workforce," *Inc.* (September 1998), 129.

57. David T. Gordon, "Balancing Act," *CIO* (October 15, 2001), 58–62.

58. Ibid.

59. Lawlor, "Personality 2.0"

Leadership in Organizations

CHAPTER OUTLINE

The Nature of Leadership

Leadership versus Management

Position Power

Personal Power

Empowerment

Leadership Traits

Autocratic versus
Democratic Leaders

Behavioral Approaches

Ohio State Studies

Michigan Studies

The Leadership Grid

Contingency Approaches

Fiedler's Contingency Theory

*Hersey and Blanchard's
Situational Theory*

Path-Goal Theory

Substitutes for Leadership

Change Leadership

*Charismatic and Visionary
Leadership*

Transformational Leaders

Leading the New Workplace

LEARNING OBJECTIVES

After studying this chapter, you should be able to

1   Define leadership and explain its importance for organizations.

2   Identify personal characteristics associated with effective leaders.

3   Explain the five sources of power and how each causes different subordinate behavior.

4   Describe the leader behaviors of initiating structure and consideration and when they should be used.

5   Describe Hersey and Blanchard's situational theory and its application to subordinate participation.

6   Explain the path-goal model of leadership.

7   Discuss how leadership fits the organizational situation and how organizational characteristics can substitute for leadership behaviors.

8   Describe transformational leadership and when it should be used.

9   Explain innovative approaches to leadership in the new workplace.

Management Challenge

Keeping good employees is tough for businesses, but for the U.S. Navy, it has been a nightmare in recent years. Forty percent of recruits wash out before their first four-year term is up. Considering it costs $35,000 to recruit one sailor and put him or her through nine weeks of boot camp, that's an expensive problem. In addition, only 30 percent of people who make it through their first tour reenlist for a second. When D. Michael Abrashoff took command of the destroyer USS *Benfold*, he came face to face with the biggest leadership challenge of his Navy career. Despite the fact that the *Benfold* was a technological marvel, most of its sailors could not wait to leave. People were so deeply unhappy and demoralized that walking aboard ship felt like entering a deep well of despair. Abrashoff was shocked when the sailors literally cheered as his predecessor left the ship for the last time. He vowed that would never happen to him. He would create an environment where sailors were so engaged with their work that they would perform at peak levels, willingly stick around for their entire tours, and maybe even gladly reenlist. But how was he to do it? Command and control leadership was the military way of doing things, and the *Benfold's* previous commander had pursued it to the max. Abrashoff knew that he needed to be a different kind of leader to turn things around and tap into the energy, enthusiasm, and creativity of his sailors.[1]

What kind of leadership would you recommend Abrashoff use to get the USS Benfold *back on course and inspire sailors to give their best? Do you believe a person can change his or her leadership style?*

In the previous chapter, we explored differences in attitudes, personality, and so forth, that affect behavior. Different leaders behave in different ways, depending on their individual differences as well as their followers' needs and the organizational situation. Many different styles of leadership can be effective. For example, contrast the leadership style of Tom Siebel, CEO of Siebel Systems, with that of Herb Kelleher, recently retired president and CEO of Southwest Airlines. Siebel is known as a disciplined and dispassionate manager who likes to maintain control over every aspect of the business. He enforces a dress code, sets tough goals and standards, and holds people strictly accountable. Those who succeed are handsomely rewarded; those who don't are fired. "We go to work to realize our professional ambitions, not to have a good time," Siebel says.[2] Herb Kelleher, on the other hand, believes having a good time at work translates into higher productivity and better service. Kelleher was known for dressing up as Elvis or the Easter Bunny to entertain employees and for encouraging workers to have fun and let their own unique personalities come out in serving customers. Both Kelleher and Siebel are successful leaders, although their styles are quite different.

This chapter explores one of the most widely discussed and researched topics in management—leadership. Here we will define leadership, explore the differences between a leader and a manager, and discuss the sources of leader power. We will examine trait, behavioral, and contingency theories of leadership effectiveness, as well as discuss charismatic and transformational leadership. The final section of the chapter looks at new leadership approaches for today's workplace. Chapters 17 through 19 will look in detail at many of the functions of leadership, including employee motivation, communication, and encouraging teamwork.

The Nature of Leadership

There is probably no topic more important to business success today than leadership. The concept of leadership continues to evolve as the needs of organizations change. Among all the ideas and writings about leadership, three aspects stand out—people, influence, and goals. Leadership occurs among people, involves the use of influence, and is used to attain goals.[3] *Influence* means that the relationship among people is not passive. Moreover, influence is designed to achieve some end or goal. Thus, **leadership** as defined here is the ability to influence people toward the attainment of goals. This definition captures the idea that leaders are involved with other people in the achievement of goals.

leadership
The ability to influence people toward the attainment of organizational goals.

Leadership is reciprocal, occurring *among* people.[4] Leadership is a "people" activity, distinct from administrative paper shuffling or problem-solving activities. Leadership is dynamic and involves the use of power.

Leadership Versus Management

Much has been written in recent years about the leadership role of managers. Management and leadership are both important to organizations. Effective managers have to be leaders, too, because there are distinctive qualities associated with management and leadership that provide different strengths for the organization, as illustrated in Exhibit 16.1. As shown in the exhibit, management and leadership reflect two different sets of qualities

LEADER QUALITIES

MANAGER QUALITIES

SOUL
Visionary
Passionate
Creative
Flexible
Inspiring
Innovative
Courageous
Imaginative
Experimental
Initiates change
Personal power

MIND
Rational
Consulting
Persistent
Problem solving
Tough-minded
Analytical
Structured
Deliberate
Authoritative
Stabilizing
Position power

E x h i b i t *16.1*

Leader and Manager Qualities

SOURCE: Based on Genevieve Capowski, "Anatomy of a Leader: Where Are the Leaders of Tomorrow?" *Management Review*, March 1994, 12.

and skills that frequently overlap within a single individual. A person might have more of one set of qualities than the other, but ideally a manager develops a balance of both manager and leader qualities.

One of the major differences between manager and leader qualities relates to the source of power and the level of compliance it engenders within followers. **Power** is the potential ability to influence the behavior of others.[5] Management power comes from the individual's position in the organization. Because manager power comes from organizational structure, it promotes stability, order, and problem solving within the structure. Leadership power, on the other hand, comes from personal sources that are not as invested in the organization, such as personal interests, goals, and values. Leadership power promotes vision, creativity, and change in the organization A good example of leadership power is Josh Raskin, a middle school teacher in upper Manhattan who became a mission-critical leader in the hours and days following the destruction of the World Trade Center towers in September 2001. Although he didn't have a formal position of authority, Raskin found himself in charge of coordinating a massive psych-clergy effort for crisis counseling, as well as guiding hundreds of other volunteers, based on his personal power. As he assigned a volunteer to guard a medical supply room, for example, Raskin infused the mundane chore with a higher vision and purpose by telling the young man everyone was counting on him to make sure no one stole drugs that would be desperately needed for the injured.[6]

Within organizations, there are typically five sources of power: legitimate, reward, coercive, expert, and referent.[7] Sometimes power comes from a person's position in the organization, while other sources of power are based on personal characteristics.

power
The potential ability to influence others' behavior.

Position Power

The traditional manager's power comes from the organization. The manager's position gives him or her the power to reward or punish subordinates in order to influence their behavior. Legitimate power, reward power, and coercive power are all forms of position power used by managers to change employee behavior.

legitimate power
Power that stems from a formal management position in an organization and the authority granted to it.

Legitimate Power.   Power coming from a formal management position in an organization and the authority granted to it is called **legitimate power**. For example, once a person has been selected as a supervisor, most workers understand that they are obligated to follow his or her direction with respect to work activities. Subordinates accept this source of power as legitimate, which is why they comply.

reward power
Power that results from the authority to bestow rewards on other people.

Reward Power.   Another kind of power, **reward power**, stems from the authority to bestow rewards on other people. Managers may have access to formal rewards, such as pay increases or promotions. They also have at their disposal such rewards as praise, attention, and recognition. Managers can use rewards to influence subordinates' behavior.

coercive power
Power that stems from the authority to punish or recommend punishment.

Coercive Power.   The opposite of reward power is **coercive power**: It refers to the authority to punish or recommend punishment. Managers have coercive power when they have the right to fire or demote employees, criticize, or withdraw pay increases. For example, if Paul, a salesman, does not perform as expected, his supervisor has the coercive power to criticize him, reprimand him, put a negative letter in his file, and hurt his chance for a raise.

Different types of position power elicit different responses in followers.[8] Legitimate power and reward power are most likely to generate follower compliance. *Compliance* means that workers will obey orders and carry out instructions, although they may personally disagree with them and may not be enthusiastic. Coercive power most often generates resistance. *Resistance* means that workers will deliberately try to avoid carrying out instructions or will attempt to disobey orders.

Thomas C. Graham, chairman of AK Steel, is a believer in position power. Unimpressed with new ideas about empowering workers, he prefers a military-style management, where cost cutting is rewarded and mistakes are quickly disciplined. His blunt views suggest that management in the steel industry has failed to push people and equipment hard enough. Graham's tough hierarchical approach has resulted in turnarounds for mills at LTV, U.S. Steel, and Washington Steel, but has also caused him to be ousted or passed over for promotion in the midst of his successes.[9]

Personal Power

In contrast to the external sources of position power, personal power most often comes from internal sources, such as a person's special knowledge or personality characteristics. Personal power is the tool of the leader. Subordinates follow a leader because of the respect, admiration, or caring they feel for the individual and his or her ideas. Personal power is becoming increasingly important as more businesses are run by teams of workers who are less tolerant of authoritarian management.[10] Two types of personal power are expert power and referent power.

Expert Power.   Power resulting from a leader's special knowledge or skill regarding the tasks performed by followers is referred to as **expert power**. When the leader is a true expert, subordinates go along with recommendations because of his or her superior knowledge. Leaders at supervisory levels often have experience in the production process that gains them promotion. At top management levels, however, leaders may lack expert power because subordinates know more about technical details than they do. One top manager who benefits from expert power is Hector de Jesus Ruiz, president and COO of Advanced Micro Devices (AMD). Ruiz has a B.S. in electrical engineering and nearly 30 years of experience in all facets of the semiconductor industry, from top to bottom. Employees respect Ruiz's technical knowledge and operational expertise as a valuable strength as AMD battles Intel in the microprocessor wars. They appreciate having someone in top management who understands the nitty gritty technical and production details that lower-level employees deal with every day.[11]

expert power
Power that stems from special knowledge of or skill in the tasks performed by subordinates.

Referent Power.   The last kind of power, **referent power**, comes from leader personality characteristics that command subordinates' identification, respect, and admiration so they wish to emulate the leader. When workers admire a supervisor because of the way she deals with them, the influence is based on referent power. Referent power depends on the leader's personal characteristics rather than on a formal title or position and is most visible in the area of charismatic leadership, which will be discussed later in this chapter. An example of referent power is Rachel Hubka, owner of Rachel's Bus Company (formerly Stewart's Bus Company). Hubka joined Stewart's as a dispatcher, set about learning every job in the business, and eventually bought the company. Today, as top leader of the schoolbus operation, Hubka often hires people with marginal employment histories, gives them extensive training, and encourages them to follow their dreams. Nothing pleases her more than having an employee leave to start his or her own business.[12]

referent power
Power that results from characteristics that command subordinates' identification with, respect and admiration for, and desire to emulate the leader.

The follower reaction most often generated by expert power and referent power is commitment. *Commitment* means that workers will share the leader's point of view and enthusiastically carry out instructions. Needless to say, commitment is preferred to compliance or resistance. It is particularly important when change is the desired outcome of a leader's instructions, because change carries risk or uncertainty. Commitment assists the follower in overcoming fear of change.

Empowerment

A significant recent trend in corporate America is for top executives to *empower* lower employees. Fully 74 percent of executives in a survey claimed that they are more participatory, more concerned with consensus building, and more reliant on communication than on command compared with the past. Executives no longer hoard power.

Empowering employees works because total power in the organization seems to increase. Everyone has more say and hence contributes more to organizational goals. The goal of senior executives in many corporations today is not simply to wield power but also to give it away to people who can get jobs done.[13] For example, when Robin Landew Silverman and her husband made the decision to move their clothing store from downtown Grand Forks, North Dakota, to a suburban location, they knew they would need the full commitment of their staff. The Silvermans had been accustomed to calling the shots, but a new approach was needed to successfully accomplish the difficult transition. By giving up control of the operation, the Silvermans gave their employees opportunities to apply themselves in new ways. "Skills emerged that we didn't know people had," says Robin. For example, a timid secretary became a dynamic bid researcher, and a marketing manager showed a talent for interior design.[14]

Leadership Traits

traits
Distinguishing personal characteristics, such as intelligence, values, and appearance.

Early efforts to understand leadership success focused on the leader's personal characteristics or traits. **Traits** are the distinguishing personal characteristics of a leader, such as intelligence, values, and appearance. The early research focused on leaders who had achieved a level of greatness and hence was referred to as the *great man* approach. The idea was relatively simple: Find out what made these people great, and select future leaders who already exhibited the same traits or could be trained to develop them. Generally, research found only a weak relationship between personal traits and leader success.[15]

Joanna B. Meiseles, president and founder of Snip-its Corp., a $1.5 million children's haircutting chain based in Natick, Massachusetts, demonstrates many of the personal traits associated with effective leadership. For example, she displayed intelligence, ability, knowledge, and judgment by knowing that to make her company successful, it had to be unique. Everything about Snip-its is tailored to children. Snip-its characters perch on a hot pink and lime green entry arch, games and stories are loaded on funky quasi-anthropomorphic computers at every cutting station, and the Magic Box dispenses a prize in exchange for a swatch of hair at the end of a visit.

©Vito Aluia

In addition to personality traits, physical, social, and work-related characteristics of leaders have been studied.[16] Exhibit 16.2 summarizes the physical, social, and personal leadership characteristics that have received the greatest research support. However, these characteristics do not stand alone. The appropriateness of a trait or set of traits depends on the leadership situation. The same traits do not apply to every organization or situation. Consider the personal traits that are helping Ralph Szygenda transform General Motors into the first totally wired car company, as described in this chapter's Leading Online box.

Further studies have expanded the understanding of leadership beyond the personal traits of the individual to focus on the dynamics of the relationship between leaders and followers.

Autocratic Versus Democratic Leaders

autocratic leader
A leader who tends to centralize authority and rely on legitimate, reward, and coercive power to manage subordinates.

democratic leader
A leader who delegates authority to others, encourages participation, and relies on expert and referent power to manage subordinates.

One way to approach leader characteristics is to examine autocratic and democratic leaders. An **autocratic leader** is one who tends to centralize authority and rely on legitimate, reward, and coercive power. A **democratic leader** delegates authority to others, encourages participation, and relies on expert and referent power to influence subordinates.

The first studies on these leadership characteristics were conducted at the University of Iowa by Kurt Lewin and his associates.[17] These studies compared autocratic and democratic leaders and produced some interesting findings. The groups with autocratic leaders performed highly so long as the leader was present to supervise them. However, group members were displeased with the

Leading Online

An E-Commerce Revolution at General Motors

When Ralph Szygenda first arrived at General Motors, the company's information technology systems were so outdated, inflexible, and poorly integrated that they were practically useless. As GM's first chief information officer, Szygenda is hoping to change all that and bring GM into the Internet Age. According to vice chairman Harry Pearce, prodding GM out of its inertia "was as tough a challenge as there was in corporate America."

Fortunately, Szygenda has always loved a challenge. "In my career, I've always tried to take on impossible jobs," he says. After four years on the job, the CIO has taken GM a long way toward his goal of creating the first totally wired car company. A single intranet site, dubbed Socrates, connects some 100,000 employees around the globe so they can communicate and collaborate on projects. Before, the company's systems were so walled off from one another that the Cadillac division could not access marketing data assembled by Buick, and project engineers at headquarters in Michigan had no easy way to collaborate with their overseas colleagues. In addition to the intranet, GM's site for consumers, GMBuyPower, is one of the most powerful on the Internet, offering more configuration and comparison options than either Ford's or DaimlerChrysler's, as well as the ability to find out whether the car is in dealers' stock and where. The company's GMPowerSupply site lets suppliers tap directly into GM factories to access production schedules, inventories, and so forth.

The next step for Szygenda is to tie everything together into a seamless "sense and respond" system that would make GM a superefficient information link between customers and suppliers. This integration would allow GM to build at least half of its cars to order, cut delivery times of custom vehicles from months to weeks, and slash inventory in half. In other words, Szygenda wants to do for cars what Michael Dell has done for computers. It is a tremendous undertaking, but Szygenda thrives on such monumental tasks. He is known as an overachiever who loves the sense of accomplishment that comes from completing seemingly impossible jobs. His high energy level enables him to work 70-hour weeks and take home massive amounts of work on the weekends. However, to get around the bureaucracy within GM, he's had to learn to subvert some of his aggressive, dominant tendencies and be more diplomatic and tactful. He started his campaign by meeting individually with each senior executive to try to gain support for his plans. Although he's ruffled some feathers, top leaders believe it's necessary to shake GM out of its complacency.

Szygenda has also assembled a top-notch IT team, using his persistence and determination (which he calls "my best quality") to lure some heavy-hitters from other industries, including top officers at Allied Signal, Bell Atlantic, and Whirlpool. Szygenda will do whatever it takes to get the job done, and he has the confidence to see it through to the end. "My job," he says, "is to make sure this all comes together."

SOURCE: Alex Taylor III, "Ralph's Agenda," *eCompany* (July 2000), 96-101.

E x h i b i t **16.2**

Personal Characteristics of Leaders

Physical Characteristics
Energy
Physical stamina

Intelligence and Ability
Intelligence, cognitive ability
Knowledge
Judgment, decisiveness

Personality
Self-confidence
Honesty and integrity
Enthusiasm
Desire to lead
Independence

Social Characteristics
Sociability, interpersonal skills
Cooperativeness
Ability to enlist cooperation
Tact, diplomacy

Work Related Characteristics
Achievement drive, desire to excel
Conscientiousness in pursuit of goals
Persistence against obstacles, tenacity

Social Background
Education
Mobility

SOURCES: Based on Bernard M. Bass, *Bass & Stogdill's Handbook of Leadership: Theory, Research, and Managerial Applications*, 3rd ed. (New York: The Free Press, 1990), 80–81; and S. A. Kirkpatrick and E. A. Locke, "Leadership: Do Traits Matter?" *Academy of Management Executive* 5, no. 2 (1991), 48–60.

close, autocratic style of leadership, and feelings of hostility frequently arose. The performance of groups who were assigned democratic leaders was almost as good, and these were characterized by positive feelings rather than hostility. In addition, under the democratic style of leadership, group members performed well even when the leader was absent and left the group on its own.[18] The participative techniques and majority rule decision making used by the democratic leader trained and involved group members such that they performed well with or without the leader present. These characteristics of democratic leadership explain why the empowerment of lower employees is a popular trend in companies today.

This early work suggested that leaders were either autocratic or democratic in their approach. However, further work by Tannenbaum and Schmidt indicated that leadership could be a continuum reflecting different amounts of employee participation.[19] Thus, one leader might be autocratic (boss centered), another democratic (subordinate centered), and a third a mix of the two styles. The leadership continuum is illustrated in Exhibit 16.3.

Most leaders have favored styles that they tend to use most often. For example, Jack Hartnett, president of D. L. Rogers Corp, which owns 54 Sonic franchises, almost always uses a highly autocratic style, whereas Patricia Gallup, PC Connection CEO, tends to use a more democratic style in many of her decisions.[20] However, while switching from autocratic to democratic or vice versa is not easy, leaders may adjust their styles depending on the situation.

Behavioral Approaches

The autocratic and democratic styles suggest that it is the "behavior" of the leader rather than a personality trait that determines leadership effectiveness. Perhaps any leader can adopt the correct behavior with appropriate training. The focus of research has shifted from leader personality traits toward the behaviors successful leaders display. Important research programs on leadership behavior were conducted at Ohio State University, the University of Michigan, and the University of Texas.

Exhibit *16.3*

The Leadership Continuum

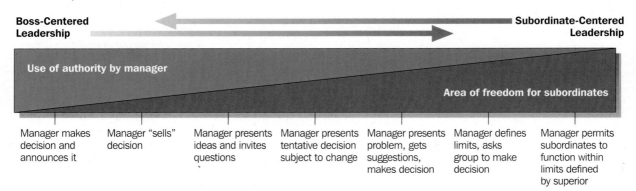

Ohio State Studies

Researchers at Ohio State University surveyed leaders to study hundreds of dimensions of leader behavior.[21] They identified two major behaviors, called *consideration* and *initiating structure*.

Consideration is the extent to which the leader is mindful of subordinates, respects their ideas and feelings, and establishes mutual trust. Considerate leaders are friendly, provide open communication, develop teamwork, and are oriented toward their subordinates' welfare.

Initiating structure is the extent to which the leader is task oriented and directs subordinate work activities toward goal attainment. Leaders with this style typically give instructions, spend time planning, emphasize deadlines, and provide explicit schedules of work activities.

Consideration and initiating structure are independent of each other, which means that a leader with a high degree of consideration may be either high or low on initiating structure. A leader may have any of four styles: high initiating structure–low consideration, high initiating structure–high consideration, low initiating structure–low consideration, or low initiating structure–high consideration. The Ohio State research found that the high consideration–high initiating structure style achieved better performance and greater satisfaction than the other leader styles. However, new research has found that effective leaders may be high on consideration and low on initiating structure or low on consideration and high on initiating structure, depending on the situation. Thus, the "high-high" style is not always the best.[22]

Michigan Studies

Studies at the University of Michigan at about the same time took a different approach by comparing the behavior of effective and ineffective supervisors.[23] The most effective supervisors were those who focused on the subordinates' human needs in order to "build effective work groups with high performance goals." The Michigan researchers used the term *employee-centered leaders* for leaders who established high performance goals and displayed supportive behavior toward subordinates. The less effective leaders were called *job-centered leaders*; these tended to be less concerned with goal achievement and human needs in favor of meeting schedules, keeping costs low, and achieving production efficiency.

The Leadership Grid

Blake and Mouton of the University of Texas proposed a two-dimensional leadership theory called **leadership grid** that builds on the work of the Ohio State and Michigan studies.[24] The two-dimensional model and five of its seven major management styles are depicted in Exhibit 16.4. Each axis on the grid is a 9-point scale, with 1 meaning low concern and 9 high concern.

Team management (9,9) often is considered the most effective style and is recommended for managers because organization members work together to accomplish tasks. *Country club management* (1,9) occurs when primary emphasis is given to people rather than to work outputs. *Authority-compliance management* (9,1) occurs when efficiency in operations is the dominant orientation. *Middle-of-the-road management* (5,5) reflects a moderate amount of concern for both people and production. *Impoverished management* (1,1) means the absence of a management philosophy; managers exert little effort

consideration
The type of behavior that describes the extent to which the leader is sensitive to subordinates, respects their ideas and feelings, and establishes mutual trust.

initiating structure
A type of leader behavior that describes the extent to which the leader is task oriented and directs subordinate work activities toward goal attainment.

©Amy Cantrell

No longer leading a basketball team, Magic Johnson is now an entrepreneurial business leader. In 1995, Johnson, in partnership with Sony Retail Entertainment, opened the very successful Magic Johnson Theatres. Johnson describes his winning business leadership style as autocratic and centralized, "I've got a team of people who work for me and advise me. But I call my own shots . . . The team I built taught me how to get into business, how to run a business. They gave me the knowledge I needed to have. But now I'm on my own. Everybody knows they have to deal with me."

leadership grid
A two-dimensional leadership theory that measures leader's concern for people and concern for production.

Exhibit *16.4*

The Leadership Grid® Figure

SOURCE: The Leadership Grid® figure, Paternalism figure and Opportunism from *Leadership Dilemmas—Grid Solutions*, by Robert R. Blake and Anne Adams McCanse (formerly the Managerial Grid by Robert R. Blake and Jane S. Mouton). Houston: Gulf Publishing Company. (Grid figure: p. 29, Paternalism figure: p. 30, Opportunism figure: p. 31). Copyright © 1991, by Blake and Mouton, and Scientific Methods, Inc. Reproduced by permission of the owners.

toward interpersonal relationships or work accomplishment. Consider these examples.

PAYCHEX INC. AND TIRES PLUS
http://www.paychex.com
http://www.tiresplus.com

Tom Golisano turned an obscure business into a gold mine by giving small businesses a place where they can outsource the routine tasks associated with turning out paychecks. At Paychex, Inc., Golisano holds his managers' noses to the grindstone. He insists that they keep the client base growing at 10 percent a year—to do so, every salesperson is required to make 50 calls a week, 8 personal presentations, and at least 3 sales. If they do not, they don't last long at Paychex. Golisano uses a boot-camp discipline, requiring employees to observe a strict dress code and a clean desk policy. He prides himself on running a tight operation—no company cars or country club memberships at this company, even for top executives. However, those who meet Golisano's grueling standards are handsomely rewarded, helping to keep turnover low.

Compare Golisano's style to that of Tom Gegax, who calls himself the head coach of Tires Plus, a fast-growing chain of retail tire stores. Gegax believes that you cannot manage people like you manage fixed assets. His emphasis is on treating employees just as well as they are expected to treat their customers. Gegax personally leads classes at Tires Plus University, where employees learn not just about changing tires but about how to make their whole lives better. The company's wellness center offers monthly classes in health and nutrition. In addition, a course called "Balancing Your Personal Tire" is a favorite among workers seeking work-life balance. Gegax also makes sure stores are clean, bright, and airy, so that employees have a pleasant work environment. He believes all this translates into better service. Employees, as well as customers, like the approach. "The last thing the world needs is another chain of stores," Gegax says. "What it does need is a company with a new business model—one that embraces customers and employees as whole people."[25] ❖

The leadership style of Golisano is characterized by high concern for tasks and production and low-to-moderate concern for people. Tom Gegax, in contrast, is high on concern for people and moderate on concern for production. Both leaders are successful, although they display very different leadership styles, because of their different situations. The next group of theories builds on the leader-follower relationship of behavioral approaches to explore how organizational situations affect the leader's approach.

Contingency Approaches

Several models of leadership that explain the relationship between leadership styles and specific situations have been developed. These are termed **contingency approaches** and include the leadership model developed by Fiedler and his associates, the situational theory of Hersey and Blanchard, the path-goal theory presented by Evans and House, and the substitutes-for-leadership concept.

contingency approach
A model of leadership that describes the relationship between leadership styles and specific organizational situations.

Fiedler's Contingency Theory

An early, extensive effort to combine leadership style and organizational situation into a comprehensive theory of leadership was made by Fiedler and his associates.[26] The basic idea is simple: Match the leader's style with the situation most favorable for his or her success. By diagnosing leadership style and the organizational situation, the correct fit can be arranged.

Leadership Style. The cornerstone of Fiedler's contingency theory is the extent to which the leader's style is relationship oriented or task oriented. A *relationship-oriented leader* is concerned with people, as in the consideration style described earlier. A *task-oriented leader* is primarily motivated by task accomplishment, which is similar to the initiating structure style described earlier.

Leadership style was measured with a questionnaire known as the least preferred coworker (LPC) scale. The **LPC scale** has a set of 16 bipolar adjectives along an 8-point scale. Examples of the bipolar adjectives used by Fiedler on the LPC scale follow:

LPC scale
A questionnaire designed to measure relationship-oriented versus task-oriented leadership style according to the leader's choice of adjectives for describing the "least preferred coworker."

open	__ __ __ __ __ __ __ __	guarded
quarrelsome	__ __ __ __ __ __ __ __	harmonious
efficient	__ __ __ __ __ __ __ __	inefficient
self-assured	__ __ __ __ __ __ __ __	hesitant
gloomy	__ __ __ __ __ __ __ __	cheerful

If the leader describes the least preferred coworker using positive concepts, he or she is considered relationship oriented, that is, a leader who cares about and is sensitive to other people's feelings. Conversely, if a leader uses negative concepts to describe the least preferred coworker, he or she is considered task oriented, that is, a leader who sees other people in negative terms and places greater value on task activities than on people.

Situation. Leadership situations can be analyzed in terms of three elements: the quality of leader-member relationships, task structure, and position power.[27] Each of these elements can be described as either favorable or unfavorable for the leader.

1. *Leader-member relations* refers to group atmosphere and members' attitude toward and acceptance of the leader. When subordinates trust, respect, and have confidence in the leader, leader-member relations are considered good. When subordinates distrust, do not respect, and have little confidence in the leader, leader-member relations are poor.

2. *Task structure* refers to the extent to which tasks performed by the group are defined, involve specific procedures, and have clear, explicit goals. Routine, well-defined tasks, such as those of assembly-line workers, have a high degree of structure. Creative, ill-defined tasks, such as research and development or strategic planning, have a low degree of task structure. When task structure is high, the situation is considered favorable to the leader; when low, the situation is less favorable.

3. *Position power* is the extent to which the leader has formal authority over subordinates. Position power is high when the leader has the power to plan and direct the work of subordinates, evaluate it, and reward or punish them. Position power is low when the leader has little authority over subordinates and cannot evaluate their work or reward them. When position power is high, the situation is considered favorable for the leader; when low, the situation is unfavorable.

Combining the three situational characteristics yields a list of eight leadership situations, which are illustrated in Exhibit 16.5. Situation I is most favorable to the leader because leader-member relations are good, task structure is high, and leader position power is strong. Situation VIII is most unfavorable to the leader because leader-member relations are poor, task structure is low, and leader position power is weak. All other octants represent intermediate degrees of favorableness for the leader.

Contingency Theory. When Fiedler examined the relationships among leadership style, situational favorability, and group task performance, he found the pattern shown in Exhibit 16.5. Task-oriented leaders are more effective when the situation is either highly favorable or highly unfavorable. Relationship-oriented leaders are more effective in situations of moderate favorability.

Exhibit *16.5*

How Leader Style Fits the Situation

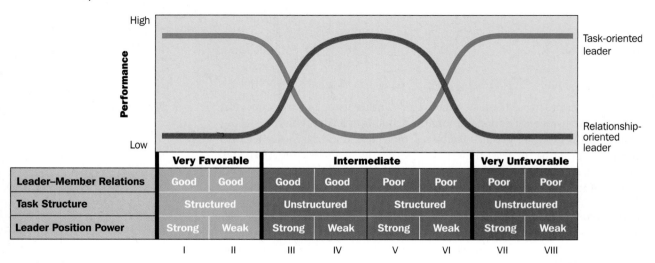

Leader–Member Relations	Very Favorable		Intermediate				Very Unfavorable	
	Good	Good	Good	Good	Poor	Poor	Poor	Poor
Task Structure	Structured		Unstructured		Structured		Unstructured	
Leader Position Power	Strong	Weak	Strong	Weak	Strong	Weak	Strong	Weak
	I	II	III	IV	V	VI	VII	VIII

SOURCE: Based on Fred E. Fiedler, "The Effects of Leadership Training and Experience: A Contingency Model Interpretation," *Administrative Science Quarterly* 17 (1972), 455.

The task-oriented leader excels in the favorable situation because everyone gets along, the task is clear, and the leader has power; all that is needed is for someone to take charge and provide direction. Similarly, if the situation is highly unfavorable to the leader, a great deal of structure and task direction is needed. A strong leader defines task structure and can establish authority over subordinates. Because leader-member relations are poor anyway, a strong task orientation will make no difference in the leader's popularity.

The relationship-oriented leader performs better in situations of intermediate favorability because human relations skills are important in achieving high group performance. In these situations, the leader may be moderately well liked, have some power, and supervise jobs that contain some ambiguity. A leader with good interpersonal skills can create a positive group atmosphere that will improve relationships, clarify task structure, and establish position power.

A leader, then, needs to know two things in order to use Fiedler's contingency theory. First, the leader should know whether he or she has a relationship- or task-oriented style. Second, the leader should diagnose the situation and determine whether leader-member relations, task structure, and position power are favorable or unfavorable.

Fitting leader style to the situation can yield big dividends in profits and efficiency.[28] On the other hand, using an incorrect style for the situation can cause problems, as Alan Robbins discovered at Plastic Lumber Company.

Alan Robbins intentionally put his factory in a gritty downtown neighborhood in Akron, Ohio. He considers himself an enlightened employer who wants to give people—even those who have made serious missteps—a chance to prove themselves. Plastic Lumber Company, which converts old plastic milk and soda bottles into fake lumber, employs about 50 workers.

When he started the company, Robbins wanted to be both a boss and a friend to his workers. He would sometimes serve cold beers for everyone at the end of a shift or grant personal loans to employees in a financial bind. He stressed teamwork and spent lots of time running ideas by workers on the factory floor. He resisted the idea of drug testing, partly because of the expense and partly because it showed distrust. Besides, he couldn't imagine workers would show up drunk or on drugs when they knew they'd be operating dangerous machinery.

He was wrong. Robbins's relationship-oriented style didn't work in the situation in which he was operating. The low-skilled workers, many from low-income, drug-infested neighborhoods, weren't ready for the type of freedom Robbins granted them. Workers were frequently absent or late without calling, showed up under the influence, and started fights on the factory floor. The turning point came for Robbins when one worker was roaming the factory with an iron pipe in his hand, looking for a fight. Today, Robbins has given up his ideals of being a pal. "I'm too busy just trying to make sure they show up," he says.[29] ❖

PLASTIC LUMBER COMPANY
http://www.plasticlumber.com

Robbins's leadership at Plastic Lumber was unsuccessful because he used a relationship-oriented style in an unfavorable situation. Because of their life circumstances, many of the employees he hired were naturally distrustful; thus, leader-member relations were poor. Although Robbins had high formal power, many workers had poor work ethics and little respect for authority. In their view, Robbins's failure to provide rules, guidelines, and direction weakened his authority. In the early days, workers believed they could get away with anything because of Robbins's easygoing style. Today, Robbins is developing a more task-oriented style, including putting together a comprehensive rules and policy manual and requiring drug tests of all new workers.

An important contribution of Fiedler's research is that it goes beyond the notion of leadership styles to show how styles fit the situation to improve organizational effectiveness. On the other hand, the model has also been criticized.[30] Using the LPC score as a measure of relationship- or task-oriented behavior seems simplistic, and how the model works over time is unclear. For example, if a task-oriented leader is matched with an unfavorable situation and is successful, the organizational situation is likely to improve and become more favorable to the leader. Thus, the leader might have to adjust his or her style or go to a new situation. For example, at Plastic Lumber Company, Alan Robbins is trying to shift to a task-oriented style, even though his natural inclination is to be a relationship-oriented leader.

Hersey and Blanchard's Situational Theory

situational theory
A contingency approach to leadership that links the leader's behavioral style with the task readiness of subordinates.

The **situational theory** of leadership is an interesting extension of the behavioral theories described earlier and summarized in the leadership grid (Exhibit 16.4). More than previous theories, Hersey and Blanchard's approach focuses a great deal of attention on the characteristics of employees in determining appropriate leadership behavior. The point of Hersey and Blanchard is that subordinates vary in readiness level. People low in task readiness, because of little ability or training, or insecurity, need a different leadership style than those who are high in readiness and have good ability, skills, confidence, and willingness to work.[31]

According to the situational theory, a leader can adopt one of four leadership styles, based on a combination of relationship (concern for people) and task (concern for production) behavior, similar to the styles summarized earlier in Exhibit 16.4. The *telling style* reflects a high concern for production and a low concern for people. This is a very directive style. It involves giving explicit directions about how tasks should be accomplished. The *selling style* is based on a high concern for both people and production. With this approach, the leader explains decisions and gives subordinates a chance to ask questions and gain clarity and understanding about work tasks. The next leader behavior style, the *participating style*, is based on a combination of high concern for people and low concern for production. The leader shares ideas with subordinates, gives them a chance to participate, and facilitates decision making. The fourth style, the *delegating style*, reflects a low concern for both people and production. This leader style provides little direction and little support because the leader turns over responsibility for decisions and their implementation to subordinates.

The essence of Hersey and Blanchard's situational theory is to select a leader style that is appropriate for the readiness level of subordinates—their degree of education and skills, experience, self-confidence, and work attitudes. Followers may be at low, moderate, high, or very high levels of readiness.

Low Readiness Level. A telling style is appropriate when followers are at a low readiness level because of poor ability and skills, little experience, insecurity, or unwillingness to take responsibility for their own task behavior. When one or more subordinates exhibit very low levels of readiness, the leader is very specific, telling followers exactly what to do, how to do it, and when.

Moderate Readiness Level. A selling style works best for followers with moderate levels of readiness. These subordinates, for example, might lack some education and experience for the job, but they demonstrate high confidence, ability, interest, and willingness to learn. The selling style involves giving direction, but it also includes seeking input from others and clarifying tasks rather than simply instructing that they be performed.

High Readiness Level. When subordinates demonstrate a high readiness level, a participating style is effective. These subordinates might have the necessary education, experience, and skills but might be insecure in their abilities and need some guidance from the leader. The participating style enables the leader to guide followers' development and act as a resource for advice and assistance.

Very High Readiness Level. When followers have very high levels of education, experience, and readiness to accept responsibility for their own task behavior, the delegating style can effectively be used. Because of the high readiness level of followers, the leader can delegate responsibility for decisions and their implementation to subordinates, who have the skills, abilities, and positive attitudes to follow through. The leader provides a general goal and sufficient authority to do the task as followers see fit.

In summary, the telling style is best suited for subordinates who demonstrate very low levels of readiness to take responsibility for their own task behavior, the selling and participating styles work for subordinates with moderate-to-high readiness, and the delegating style is appropriate for employees with very high readiness. This contingency model is easier to understand than Fiedler's model, but it incorporates only the characteristics of followers, not those of the situation. The leader carefully diagnoses the readiness level of followers and adopts whichever style is necessary—telling, selling, participating, or delegating. For example, Phil Hagans, who owns two McDonald's franchises in northeast Houston, uses different styles as employees grow in their readiness level. Hagans gives many young employees their first job and he tells them every step to take during their first days, instructing them on everything from how to dress to how to clean the grill. As they grow in ability and confidence, he shifts to a selling or participating style. Hagans has had great success by carefully guiding young workers through each level of readiness.[32] A fast-food franchise leader would, however, probably need to take a different approach with a part-time worker who was retired after 40 years in the business world.

©AP/WideWorld Photos

The labor, technology, and infrastructure required to get a box of bananas from the plantations of Latin America to supermarkets in the U.S. is truly astounding. United Fruit Company, owner of the Chiquita brand of bananas, was responsible for building many roads and train tracks, and entire villages with homes, schools, medical facilities, and factories. Consistent with the situational theory of leadership, leaders used a telling style to direct the activities of low-skilled workers. However, as the company's power in the region grew, critics charged that leaders sought total control of workers—as well as attempting to control the leaders of the republics where the company did business. These alleged abuses of power led to devastating results. Over the past decade, the company has lost $700 million and watched its stock price plunge from a high of $50 to a low of 48 cents.

Path-Goal Theory

Another contingency approach to leadership is called the path-goal theory.[33] According to the **path-goal theory**, the leader's responsibility is to increase subordinates' motivation to attain personal and organizational goals. As illustrated in Exhibit 16.6, the leader increases their motivation by either (1) clarifying the subordinates' path to the rewards that are available or (2) increasing the rewards that the subordinates value and desire. Path clarification means

path-goal theory
A contingency approach to leadership specifying that the leader's responsibility is to increase subordinates' motivation by clarifying the behaviors necessary for task accomplishment and rewards.

Path Clarification

Leader defines what follower must do to attain work outcomes

Leader clarifies follower's work role

Follower has increased knowledge and confidence to accomplish outcomes

Increase Rewards

Leader learns follower's needs

Leader matches follower's needs to rewards if work outcomes are accomplished

Leader increases value of work outcomes for follower

Follower displays increased effort and motivation

Organizational work outcomes are accomplished

Exhibit *16.6*

Leader Roles in the Path–Goal Model

SOURCE: Based on Bernard M. Bass, "Leadership: Good, Better, Best," *Organizational Dynamics* 13 (Winter 1985), 26-40.

that the leader works with subordinates to help them identify and learn the behaviors that will lead to successful task accomplishment and organizational rewards. Increasing rewards means that the leader talks with subordinates to learn which rewards are important to them—that is, whether they desire intrinsic rewards from the work itself or extrinsic rewards such as raises or promotions. The leader's job is to increase personal payoffs to subordinates for goal attainment and to make the paths to these payoffs clear and easy to travel.[34]

This model is called a contingency theory because it consists of three sets of contingencies—leader behavior and style, situational contingencies, and the use of rewards to meet subordinates' needs.[35] Whereas in the Fiedler theory described earlier the assumption would be to switch leaders as situations change, in the path-goal theory leaders switch their behaviors to match the situation.

Leader Behavior.   The path-goal theory suggests a fourfold classification of leader behaviors.[36] These classifications are the types of leader behavior the leader can adopt and include supportive, directive, achievement-oriented, and participative styles.

Supportive leadership involves leader behavior that shows concern for subordinates' well-being and personal needs. Leadership behavior is open, friendly, and approachable, and the leader creates a team climate and treats subordinates as equals. Supportive leadership is similar to the consideration leadership described earlier.

Directive leadership occurs when the leader tells subordinates exactly what they are supposed to do. Leader behavior includes planning, making schedules, setting performance goals and behavior standards, and stressing adherence to rules and regulations. Directive leadership behavior is similar to the initiating-structure leadership style described earlier.

Participative leadership means that the leader consults with his or her subordinates about decisions. Leader behavior includes asking for opinions and suggestions, encouraging participation in decision making, and meeting with subordinates in their workplaces. The participative leader encourages group discussion and written suggestions.

Achievement-oriented leadership occurs when the leader sets clear and challenging goals for subordinates. Leader behavior stresses high-quality performance and improvement over current performance. Achievement-oriented leaders also show confidence in subordinates and assist them in learning how to achieve high goals.

The four types of leader behavior are not considered ingrained personality traits as in the Fiedler theory; rather, they reflect types of behavior that every leader is able to adopt, depending on the situation.

Situational Contingencies. The two important situational contingencies in the path-goal theory are (1) the personal characteristics of group members and (2) the work environment. Personal characteristics of subordinates include such factors as ability, skills, needs, and motivations. For example, if employees have low ability or skill, the leader may need to provide additional training or coaching in order for workers to improve performance. If subordinates are self-centered, the leader must use rewards to motivate them. Subordinates who want clear direction and authority require a directive leader who will tell them exactly what to do. Craftworkers and professionals, however, may want more freedom and autonomy and work best under a participative leadership style.

The work environment contingencies include the degree of task structure, the nature of the formal authority system, and the work group itself. The task structure is similar to the same concept described in Fiedler's contingency theory; it includes the extent to which tasks are defined and have explicit job descriptions and work procedures. The formal authority system includes the amount of legitimate power used by managers and the extent to which policies and rules constrain employees' behavior. Work group characteristics are the educational level of subordinates and the quality of relationships among them.

Use of Rewards. Recall that the leader's responsibility is to clarify the path to rewards for subordinates or to increase the value of rewards to enhance satisfaction and job performance. In some situations, the leader works with subordinates to help them acquire the skills and confidence needed to perform tasks and achieve rewards already available. In others, the leader may develop new rewards to meet the specific needs of a subordinate.

Exhibit 16.7 illustrates four examples of how leadership behavior is tailored to the situation. In the first situation, the subordinate lacks confidence; thus, the supportive leadership style provides the social support with which to encourage the subordinate to undertake the behavior needed to do the work and receive the rewards. In the second situation, the job is ambiguous, and the employee is not performing effectively. Directive leadership behavior is used to give instructions and clarify the task so that the follower will know how to accomplish it and receive rewards. In the third situation, the subordinate is unchallenged by the task; thus, an achievement-oriented behavior is used to set higher goals. This clarifies the path to rewards for the employee. In the fourth situation, an incorrect reward is given to a subordinate, and the participative leadership style is used to change this. By discussing the subordinate's needs,

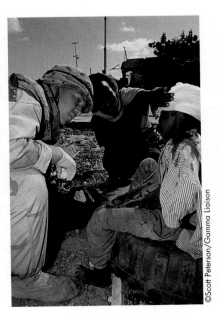

©Scott Peterson/Gamma Liaison

"Nothing can quite compare with the Marine Corps training and combat service to stretch your leadership skills," states Phillip Rooney, vice-chairman of the building and maintenance service company, ServiceMaster. Marines demonstrate participative leadership. *The colonel, or Marine form of CEO, has absolute authority, but is trained in making team decisions. For example, if a group gets a humanitarian mission order, such as the one in the photo, the team rather than a single leader determines issues such as information requirements, targets, key questions, and detailed mission plans.*

Situation	Leader Behavior	Impact on Follower	Outcome
Follower lacks self-confidence	Supportive Leadership	Increase confidence to achieve work outcome	More effort; improved satisfaction and performance
Ambiguous job	Directive Leadership	Clarify path to reward	More effort; improved satisfaction and performance
Lack of job challenge	Achievement-Oriented Leadership	Set high goals	More effort; improved satisfaction and performance
Incorrect reward	Participative Leadership	Clarify follower's needs and change rewards	More effort; improved satisfaction and performance

Exhibit 16.7

Path–Goal Situations and Preferred Leader Behaviors

SOURCE: Adapted from Gary A. Yukl, *Leadership in Organizations* (Englewood Cliffs, N.J.: Prentice-Hall, 1981), 146–152.

the leader is able to identify the correct reward for task accomplishment. In all four cases, the outcome of fitting the leadership behavior to the situation produces greater employee effort by either clarifying how subordinates can receive rewards or changing the rewards to fit their needs.

Pat Kelly, founder and CEO of PSS World Medical, a specialty marketer and distributor of medical products, hires people who exhibit a desire to win and then keeps them motivated with his achievement-oriented leadership.

PSS WORLD MEDICAL
http://www.pssworldmedical.com

Pat Kelly has always believed in establishing ambitious goals for his employees. He consistently sets higher financial and sales targets that challenge employees to perform at high levels. However, Kelly realizes that what gets people's juices flowing is not just reaching a new financial target, but winning. And Kelly makes sure employees have what they need to win and receive high rewards for their performance. PSS spends about 5 percent of its payroll budget each year on training, so that employees have the knowledge and skills they need to succeed. The company also emphasizes promotion from within. Moving people around to different divisions and different roles gives them opportunities for learning and advancement. If an employee does not do well in one position, PSS will help the person find another avenue to success.

Open communication plays an important role in Kelly's leadership. To meet high goals, employees have to know how they contribute and where they stand. Open book management is a cornerstone of corporate culture because Kelly believes people can succeed only when everyone knows the numbers and how they fit in. By setting high goals, providing people with the knowledge and skills to succeed, and running an open company, Kelly has created an organization full of people who think and act like CEOs. In fact, all delivery drivers have business cards with their names and "CEO" printed on them. As Kelly puts it, "when you're standing in front of the customer, you are the CEO."[37] ❖

Kelly's achievement-oriented leadership is successful because the company's highly motivated professionals thrive on challenge, responsibility, and recognition. Path-goal theorizing can be complex, but much of the research on it has been encouraging.[38] Using the model to specify precise relationships and make exact predictions about employee outcomes may be difficult, but the four types of leader behavior and the ideas for fitting them to situational contingencies provide a useful way for leaders to think about motivating subordinates.

Substitutes for Leadership

The contingency leadership approaches considered so far have focused on the leaders' style, the subordinates' nature, and the situation's characteristics. The final contingency approach suggests that situational variables can be so powerful that they actually substitute for or neutralize the need for leadership.[39] This approach outlines those organizational settings in which a leadership style is unimportant or unnecessary.

Exhibit 16.8 shows the situational variables that tend to substitute for or neutralize leadership characteristics. A **substitute** for leadership makes the leadership style unnecessary or redundant. For example, highly professional subordinates who know how to do their tasks do not need a leader who initiates structure for them and tells them what to do. A **neutralizer** counteracts the leadership style and prevents the leader from displaying certain behaviors. For example, if a leader has absolutely no position power or is physically removed from subordinates, the leader's ability to give directions to subordinates is greatly reduced.

Situational variables in Exhibit 16.8 include characteristics of the group, the task, and the organization itself. For example, when subordinates are highly professional and experienced, both leadership styles are less important. The employees do not need much direction or consideration. With respect to task characteristics, highly structured tasks substitute for a task-oriented style, and a satisfying task substitutes for a people-oriented style. With respect to the organization itself, group cohesiveness substitutes for both leader styles. Formalized rules and procedures substitute for leader task orientation. Physical separation of leader and subordinate neutralizes both leadership styles.

The value of the situations described in Exhibit 16.8 is that they help leaders avoid leadership overkill. Leaders should adopt a style with which to complement the organizational situation. For example, the work situation for bank tellers provides a high level of formalization, little flexibility, and a highly structured task. The head teller should not adopt a task-oriented style, because the organization already provides structure and direction. The head

substitute
A situational variable that makes a leadership style unnecessary or redundant.

neutralizer
A situational variable that counteracts a leadership style and prevents the leader from displaying certain behaviors.

Exhibit *16.8*

Substitutes and Neutralizers for Leadership

Variable		Task-Oriented Leadership	People-Oriented Leadership
Organizational variables:	Group cohesiveness	Substitutes for	Substitutes for
	Formalization	Substitutes for	No effect on
	Inflexibility	Neutralizes	No effect on
	Low positional power	Neutralizes	Neutralizes
	Physical separation	Neutralizes	Neutralizes
Task characteristics:	Highly structured task	Substitutes for	No effect on
	Automatic feedback	Substitutes for	No effect on
	Intrinsic satisfaction	No effect on	Substitutes for
Group characteristics:	Professionalism	Substitutes for	Substitutes for
	Training/experience	Substitutes for	No effect on

teller should concentrate on a people-oriented style. In other organizations, if group cohesiveness or previous training meet employees' social needs, the leader is free to concentrate on task-oriented behaviors. The leader can adopt a style complementary to the organizational situation to ensure that both task needs and people needs of the work group will be met.

Change Leadership

transactional leader
A leader who clarifies subordinates' role and task requirements, initiates structure, provides rewards, and displays consideration for subordinates.

charismatic leader
A leader who has the ability to motivate subordinates to transcend their expected performance.

© DouglasLevere.com

Pat Russo, the new CEO for Lucent Technologies, was hired for her visionary leadership skills. Russo has a strong vision for the future and the ability to motivate Lucent's employees to meet goals and see a brighter tomorrow for the struggling company in the tough telecommunications industry. Russo's first challenge is to keep a lid on costs and get sales growing enough to simply break even. She will also have to find innovative ways to promote the new optical, data-networking, and wireless systems Lucent recently unveiled. Can she succeed? She has in the past—with turnarounds at AT&T's office phone business and Kodak.

In Chapter 1, we defined management to include the functions of leading, planning, organizing, and controlling. But recent work on leadership has begun to distinguish leadership as something more: a quality that inspires and motivates people beyond their normal levels of performance. Leadership is particularly important in companies trying to meet the challenges of a changing environment. Leaders in many organizations have had to reconceptualize almost every aspect of how they do business to meet the needs of increasingly demanding customers, keep employees motivated and satisfied, and remain competitive in a global, information-based business environment. As we discussed in Chapter 2, some are adopting e-business solutions and becoming learning organizations poised for constant change and adaptation.

Research has found that some leadership approaches are more effective than others for bringing about change in organizations. Two types of leadership that can have a substantial impact are charismatic and transformational. These types of leadership are best understood in comparison to *transactional leadership*.[40] **Transactional leaders** clarify the role and task requirements of subordinates, initiate structure, provide appropriate rewards, and try to be considerate to and meet the social needs of subordinates. The transactional leader's ability to satisfy subordinates may improve productivity. Transactional leaders excel at management functions. They are hardworking, tolerant, and fair minded. They take pride in keeping things running smoothly and efficiently. Transactional leaders often stress the impersonal aspects of performance, such as plans, schedules, and budgets. They have a sense of commitment to the organization and conform to organizational norms and values. Transactional leadership is important to all organizations, but leading change requires a different approach.

Charismatic and Visionary Leadership

Charismatic leadership goes beyond transactional leadership techniques. Charisma has been referred to as "a fire that ignites followers' energy and commitment, producing results above and beyond the call of duty."[41] The **charismatic leader** has the ability to inspire and motivate people to do more than they would normally do, despite obstacles and personal sacrifice. Followers transcend their own self-interests for the sake of the department or organization. The impact of charismatic leaders is normally from (1) stating a lofty vision of an imagined future that employees identify with, (2) shaping a corporate value system for which everyone stands, and (3) trusting subordinates and earning their complete trust in return.[42] Charismatic leaders tend to be less predictable than transactional leaders. They create an atmosphere of change, and they may be obsessed by visionary ideas that excite, stimulate, and drive other people to work hard.

Charismatic leaders are often skilled in the art of *visionary leadership*. Visionary leaders speak to the hearts of employees, letting them be part of something bigger than themselves. They see beyond current realities and help followers believe in a brighter future as well. A **vision** is an attractive, ideal future that is credible yet not readily attainable. For example, as principal of Harlem's Frederick Douglass School, Lorraine Monroe inspired teachers, students, and parents with her vision of transforming the school from one of the worst to one of the best in New York City. When she came to the school, it was known for excessive violence, poor attendance, and low achievement. Five years later, test scores of Frederick Douglass students ranked among the highest in New York City, and 96 percent of the school's graduates went on to college[43]

Charismatic leaders have a strong vision for the future and can motivate others to help realize it.[44] They have an emotional impact on subordinates because they strongly believe in the vision and can communicate it to others in a way that makes the vision real, personal, and meaningful to others. The New Workplace Shoptalk box provides a short quiz to help you determine whether you have the potential to be a charismatic leader.

Charismatic leaders include Mother Theresa, Martin Luther King, Jr., Michael Jordan, Adolf Hitler, and Osama bin Laden. Charisma can be used for positive outcomes that benefit the group, but it can also be used for self-serving purposes that lead to deception, manipulation, and exploitation of others. When charismatic leaders respond to organizational problems in terms of the needs of the entire group rather than their own emotional needs, they can have a powerful, positive influence on organizational performance.[45]

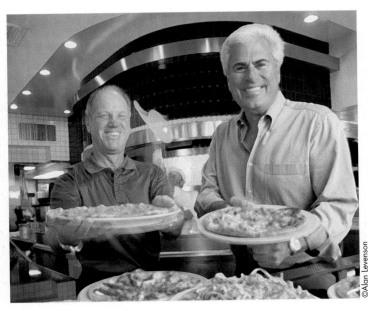

©Alan Levenson

Co-chairmen of California Pizza Kitchen Inc. (CPK) restaurants, Rick Rosenfield and Larry Flax are leading their company through major changes. After PepsiCo Inc. bought 67 percent of CPK, the two leaders stayed as co-CEOs, managing a Pepsi-financed expansion that tripled the company's size to 90 restaurants. When Pepsi sold its restaurant business, Rosenfield and Flax bought their chain back at a profit. Now the co-leaders are sharpening their transformational leadership skills as they execute their vision to add 15 outlets a year and introduce frozen supermarket pizzas. "We always believed we could surpass Pizza Hut [a $4.7 billion chain]," says Flax, "We still believe we will."

vision
An attractive, ideal future that is credible yet not readily attainable.

transformational leader
A leader distinguished by a special ability to bring about innovation and change.

Transformational Leaders

Transformational leaders are similar to charismatic leaders, but are distinguished by their special ability to bring about innovation and change by recognizing followers' needs and concerns, helping them look at old problems in new ways, and encouraging them to question the status quo. Transformational leaders create significant change in both followers and the organization.[46] They have the ability to lead changes in the organization's mission, strategy, structure, and culture, as well as to promote innovation in products and technologies. Transformational leaders do not rely solely on tangible rules and incentives to control specific transactions with followers. They focus on intangible qualities such as vision, shared values, and ideas to build relationships, give larger meaning to diverse activities, and find common ground to enlist followers in the change process.[47]

A good example of a transformational leader is Richard Kovacevich, who steered mid-sized Norwest Corp. (now Wells Fargo & Co.) through numerous acquisitions to make it the fourth largest banking company in the United States. Kovacevich is known for spouting radical notions such as "Banking is necessary, banks are not." He has inspired his followers with a vision of becoming the Wal-Mart of financial services—and the company is well on its way. To motivate employees, Kovacevich leads with slogans such as, "Mind share plus heart share equals market share." Although some people might

Manager's Shoptalk

Are You a Charismatic Leader?

If you were the head of a major department in a corporation, how important would each of the following activities be to you? Answer yes or no to indicate whether you would strive to perform each activity.

1. Help subordinates clarify goals and how to reach them.
2. Give people a sense of mission and overall purpose.
3. Help get jobs out on time.
4. Look for the new product or service opportunities.
5. Use policies and procedures as guides for problem solving.
6. Promote unconventional beliefs and values.
7. Give monetary rewards in exchange for high performance from subordinates.
8. Command respect from everyone in the department.
9. Work alone to accomplish important tasks.
10. Suggest new and unique ways of doing things.
11. Give credit to people who do their jobs well.
12. Inspire loyalty to yourself and to the organization.
13. Establish procedures to help the department operate smoothly.
14. Use ideas to motivate others.
15. Set reasonable limits on new approaches.
16. Demonstrate social nonconformity.

The even-numbered items represent behaviors and activities of charismatic leaders. Charismatic leaders are personally involved in shaping ideas, goals, and direction of change. They use an intuitive approach to develop fresh ideas for old problems and seek new directions for the department or organization. The odd-numbered items are considered more traditional management activities, or what would be called *transactional leadership*. Managers respond to organizational problems in an impersonal way, make rational decisions, and coordinate and facilitate the work of others. If you answered yes to more even-numbered than odd-numbered items, you may be a potential charismatic leader.

SOURCES: Based on Bernard M. Bass, *Leadership and Performance beyond Expectations* (New York: Free Press, 1985); and Lawton R. Burns and Selwyn W. Becker, "Leadership and Managership," in *Health Care Management*, eds. S. Shortell and A. Kaluzny (New York: Wiley, 1986).

---

think it sounds hokey, Kovacevich and his employees don't care. It is the substance behind the slogans that matters. Employees are rewarded for putting both their hearts and minds into their work. Kovacevich constantly tells employees that they are the heart and soul of Wells Fargo, and that only through their efforts can the company succeed.[48]

Leading the New Workplace

The concept of leadership is also changing because of dramatic changes in today's environment and organizations. Globalization, e-commerce, virtual organizations and telecommuting, changes in employee interests and expectations, and increasing diversity have all contributed to a shift in how we think about and practice leadership. Four areas of particular interest for leadership in the new workplace are a new concept referred to as Level 5 leadership; women's ways of leading; virtual leadership; and servant leadership.

Level 5 Leadership. A recent five-year study conducted by Jim Collins and a group of 22 research associates identified the critical importance of what Collins calls *Level 5 leadership* in transforming companies from merely good to truly great organizations.[49] As described in his book, *Good to Great: Why Some Companies Make the Leap . . . and Others Don't*, Level 5 leadership refers to the highest level in a hierarchy of manager capabilities, as illustrated in Exhibit 16.9. A key characteristic of Level 5 leaders is an almost complete lack of ego. In contrast to the view of great leaders as "larger-than-life" personalities with strong egos and big ambitions, Level 5 leaders often seem shy and unpretentious.

Level 5: The Level 5 Leader
Builds an enduring great organization through a combination of personal humility and professional resolve.

Level 4: The Effective Executive
Builds widespread commitment to a clear and compelling vision; stimulates people to high performance.

Level 3: Competent Manager
Sets plans and organizes people for the efficient and effective pursuit of objectives.

Level 2: Contributing Team Member
Contributes to the achievement of team goals; works effectively with others in a group.

Level 1: Highly Capable Individual
Productive contributor; offers talent, knowledge, skills, and good work habits as an individual employee.

SOURCE: "The Level 5 Leadership Hierarchy" from *Good to Great: Why Some Companies Make the Leap and Others Don't*, by Jim Collins. Reprinted by permission of HarperCollins Publishers, Inc.

Exhibit **16.9**

The Level 5 Leadership Hierarchy

Although they accept full responsibility for mistakes, poor results, or failures, Level 5 leaders give credit for successes to other people. For example, Joseph F. Cullman III, former CEO of Philip Morris, staunchly refused to accept credit for the company's long-term success, citing his great colleagues, successors, and predecessors as the reason for the accomplishments.

Yet, despite their personal humility, Level 5 leaders have a fierce determination to do whatever it takes to produce great and lasting results for their organizations. They are extremely ambitious for their companies rather than for themselves. This becomes most evident in the area of succession planning. Level 5 leaders develop a solid corps of leaders throughout the organization, so that when they leave the company it can continue to thrive and grow even stronger. Egocentric leaders, on the other hand, often set their successors up for failure because it will be a testament to their own greatness if the company doesn't perform well without them. Rather than an organization built around "a genius with a thousand helpers," Level 5 leaders build an organization with many strong leaders who can step forward and continue the company's success. These leaders want everyone in the organization to develop to their fullest potential.

Women's Ways of Leading. The focus on minimizing personal ambition and developing others has also been found to be common among female leaders. Recent research indicates that women's style of leadership is particularly suited to today's organizations.[50] Using data from actual performance evaluations, one study found that when rated by peers, subordinates, and bosses, female managers score significantly higher than men on abilities such as motivating others, fostering communication, and listening.[51]

This approach has been called **interactive leadership**.[52] This means that the leader favors a consensual and collaborative process, and influence derives from relationships rather than position power and formal authority. For example, Nancy Hawthorne, former chief financial officer at Continental Cablevision Inc., felt that her role as a leader was to delegate tasks and authority to others and to help them be more effective. "I was being traffic cop and

interactive leadership
A leadership style characterized by values such as inclusion, collaboration, relationship building, and caring.

Putting People First

Andy Pearson Transforms Himself as a Leader

When he was CEO of PepsiCo Inc., Andy Pearson was named one of the 10 toughest bosses in the United States by *Fortune* magazine. He was notorious for his brutal management style and the extreme, relentless demands he put on his subordinates. Twenty years later, as founding chairman and former CEO of Tricon Global Restaurants, Pearson is still tough, but he has learned that demanding high standards doesn't have to mean inflicting pain. Today, he leads not with fear, surprise, and intimidation but with humility, respect, and genuine caring.

Pearson began his transformation as a leader when he started asking himself what it would take to unleash the power of everyone in the organization. He had noticed how his co-leader David Novak (now Tricon's CEO) inspired people throughout the company with his warmth, energy, and personal attention. He saw employees actually weep with gratitude in reaction to little more than a few words of praise from Novak. And gradually, he began to see how tapping into positive human emotions was the key driver of success at Tricon, which owns 30,000 KFC, Taco Bell, and Pizza Hut restaurants around the world. "I knew something was going on that was very powerful," Pearson says. "If we could learn to harness that spirit with something systematic, then we would have something unique."

Pearson's new approach to leadership is not to issue orders but to seek answers from below. He talks and listens to people throughout the company and makes an enormous effort to let people know that their individual contribution is vital to the organization's success. If he disagrees with something, rather than beating people down and belittling their ideas, as the "old" Andy Pearson would have done, he will challenge them to think about the problem in a different light.

Most significantly, Pearson now considers caring about others and giving people recognition and approval a sign of leadership strength rather than weakness. "There's a human yearning for a certain amount of toughness," Pearson says. "But it can't be unmitigated toughness." What's his advice for successful leadership in today's workplace? "Ultimately, it's all about having more genuine concern for the other person," Pearson says. "There's an important aspect [of leadership] that has to do with humility."

SOURCE: David Dorsey, "Andy Pearson Finds Love," *Fast Company* (August 2001), 78–86.

coach and facilitator," Hawthorne says. "I was always into building a department that hummed."[53] It is important to note that men can be interactive leaders as well. The characteristics associated with interactive leadership are emerging as valuable qualities for both male and female leaders in the new workplace. This chapter's Putting People First box describes how one male manager is learning to become a better leader by incorporating some of the values associated with interactive leadership, such as personal humility, inclusion, relationship building, and caring.

Virtual Leadership.   The virtual workplace, in which employees work remotely from each other and from leaders, is becoming more common in today's organizations, bringing new leadership challenges. In today's workplace, many people may work from home or other remote locations, wired to the office electronically. Sometimes people come together temporarily in virtual teams to complete a project and then disband, as we described in Chapter 10. In a virtual environment, leaders face a constant tension in trying to balance structure and accountability with flexibility.[54] They have to provide enough structure and direction so that people have a clear understanding of what is required of them, but they also have to trust that virtual workers will perform their duties responsibly without close control and supervision. Effective virtual leaders set clear goals and timelines and are very explicit about how people will communicate and coordinate their work. However, the details of day-to-day activities are left up to employees. This doesn't mean, however, that virtual workers are left on their own. Leaders take extra care to keep people informed and involved with one another and with the organization.

People who excel as virtual leaders tend to be open-minded and flexible, exhibit positive attitudes that focus on solutions rather than problems, and have superb communication, coaching, and relationship-building skills.[55] Good virtual leaders never forget that work is accomplished through *people*, not technology. Although they must understand how to select and use technology appropriately, leaders emphasize human interactions as the key to success. Building trust, maintaining open lines of communication, caring about people, and being open to subtle cues from others are essential in a virtual environment.[56]

Servant Leadership.   In the new workplace, the best leaders operate from the assumption that work exists for the development of the worker as much as the worker exists to do the work.[57] Servant leadership, first described by Robert Greenleaf, is leadership upside down because leaders transcend self-interest to serve others and the organization.[58] **Servant leaders** operate on two levels: for the fulfillment of their subordinates' goals and needs and for the realization of the larger purpose or mission of their organization. Servant leaders give things away—power, ideas, information, recognition, credit for accomplishments. They truly value other people, encourage participation, share power, enhance others' self-worth, and unleash people's creativity, full commitment, and natural impulse to learn. Servant leaders bring the follower's higher motives to the work and connect them to the organizational mission and goals.

servant leader
A leader who works to fulfill subordinates' needs and goals as well as to achieve the organization's larger mission.

■ Summary and Management Solution

This chapter covered several important ideas about leadership. The early research on leadership focused on personal traits such as intelligence, energy, and appearance. Later, research attention shifted to leadership behaviors that are appropriate to the organizational situation. Behavioral approaches dominated the early work in this area; consideration and initiating structure were suggested as behaviors that lead work groups toward high performance. The Ohio State and Michigan approaches and the managerial grid are in this category. Contingency approaches include Fiedler's theory, Hersey and Blanchard's situational theory, the path-goal model, and the substitutes-for-leadership concept.

Leadership concepts have evolved from the transactional approach to charismatic and transformational leadership behaviors. Charismatic leadership is the ability to articulate a vision and motivate followers to make it a reality. Transformational leadership extends charismatic qualities to guide and foster dramatic organizational change.

Four significant leadership concepts for the new workplace are Level 5 leadership, women's ways of leading, virtual leadership, and servant leadership. Level 5 leaders are characterized by personal humility combined

with ambition to build a great organization that will continue to thrive beyond the leader's direct influence. Women's approach to leadership may be particularly suited to today's workplace because it emphasizes relationships and helping others develop to their highest potential. However, men as well as women can develop the characteristics associated with women's style of leadership, called *interactive leadership*. Managers in today's workplace also need to learn how to lead employees who may be working in a virtual environment and have little or no face-to-face contact with the leader. They may become servant leaders who facilitate the growth, goals, and development of others to liberate their best qualities in pursuing the organization's mission. In all of these new ways of leading, managers rely more on personal power than on position power.

Returning to our opening example, Michael Abrashoff wanted to create an organization where people were so engaged and enthused about their work that they would willingly give their best. To do so meant casting aside the long Navy tradition of relying on formal position power and authority. To unleash the creativity and know-how of everyone, Abrashoff led with vision and values instead of command and control. Rather than issuing orders from the top, he started listening to ideas from below. Even though he admits that listening does not come easily to him, he made a commitment that he would treat every encounter with every person on the ship as the most important thing in the world at that particular moment. He also made an effort to get to know each and every sailor as an individual. When the *Benfold's* sailors saw that Abrashoff was sincere, they responded with energy, enthusiasm, and commitment. Good ideas that came from the bottom up were implemented immediately, and many of them have now become standard throughout the U.S. Navy. Abrashoff also began handing over responsibility so that people could learn and grow. "If all you do

is give orders, then all you get are order takers," he says. Abrashoff wanted to develop strong leaders at all levels and help people understand that they were the ones who made the ship successful. Under Abrashoff's leadership, the *Benfold* set all-time records for performance and retention. However, neither Abrashoff nor the crew are worried about what will happen when the captain moves on. "This crew . . . [knows] what results they get when they play an active role," Abrashoff says. "And they now have the courage to raise their hands and get heard. That's almost irreversible."[59] Abrashoff illustrates characteristics of both interactive and servant leadership, as well as the potential to become a Level 5 leader.

■ Discussion Questions

1. Do you think leadership style is fixed and unchangeable for a leader or flexible and adaptable? Discuss.
2. Suggest some personal traits that you believe would be useful to a leader. Are these traits more valuable in some situations than in others?
3. What is the difference between trait theories and behavioral theories of leadership?
4. Suggest the sources of power that would be available to a leader of a student government organization. To be effective, should student leaders keep power to themselves or delegate power to other students?
5. What skills and abilities does a manager need to effectively lead in a virtual environment? Do you believe a leader with a consideration style or an initiating-structure style would be more successful as a virtual leader? Explain your answer.

6. Consider Fiedler's theory as illustrated in Exhibit 16.5. How often do very favorable, intermediate, or very unfavorable situations occur in real life? Discuss.
7. What is transformational leadership? Differentiate between transformational leadership and transactional leadership. Give an example of each.
8. How does Level 5 leadership differ from the concept of servant leadership? Do you believe anyone has the potential to become a Level 5 leader? Discuss.
9. Do you think leadership is more important or less important in today's flatter, team-based organizations? Explain.
10. Consider the leadership position of a senior partner in a law firm. What task, subordinate, and organizational factors might serve as substitutes for leadership in this situation?

■ Management in Practice: Experiential Exercise

T–P Leadership Questionnaire: An Assessment of Style

Some leaders deal with general directions, leaving details to subordinates. Other leaders focus on specific details with the expectation that subordinates will carry out orders. Depending on the situation, both approaches may be effective. The important issue is the ability to identify relevant dimensions of the situation and behave accordingly. Through this questionnaire, you can identify your relative emphasis on two

dimensions of leadership: task orientation (T) and people orientation (P). These are not opposite approaches, and an individual can rate high or low on either or both.

Directions: The following items describe aspects of leadership behavior. Respond to each item according to the way you would most likely act if you were the leader of a work group. Circle whether you would most likely behave in the described way: always (A), frequently (F), occasionally (O), seldom (S), or never (N).

1. I would most likely act as the spokesperson of the group.   A F O S N
2. I would encourage overtime work.   A F O S N
3. I would allow members complete freedom in their work.   A F O S N
4. I would encourage the use of uniform procedures.   A F O S N
5. I would permit members to use their own judgment in solving problems.   A F O S N
6. I would stress being ahead of competing groups.   A F O S N
7. I would speak as a representative of the group.   A F O S N
8. I would needle members for greater effort.   A F O S N
9. I would try out my ideas in the group.   A F O S N
10. I would let members do their work the way they think best.   A F O S N
11. I would be working hard for a promotion.   A F O S N
12. I would tolerate postponement and uncertainty.   A F O S N
13. I would speak for the group if there were visitors present.   A F O S N
14. I would keep the work moving at a rapid pace.   A F O S N
15. I would turn the members loose on a job and let them go to it.   A F O S N
16. I would settle conflicts when they occur in the group.   A F O S N
17. I would get swamped by details.   A F O S N
18. I would represent the group at outside meetings.   A F O S N
19. I would be reluctant to allow the members any freedom of action.   A F O S N
20. I would decide what should be done and how it should be done.   A F O S N
21. I would push for increased production.   A F O S N
22. I would let some members have authority that I could keep.   A F O S N
23. Things would usually turn out as I had predicted.   A F O S N
24. I would allow the group a high degree of initiative.   A F O S N
25. I would assign group members to particular tasks.   A F O S N
26. I would be willing to make changes.   A F O S N
27. I would ask the members to work harder.   A F O S N
28. I would trust the group members to exercise good judgment.   A F O S N
29. I would schedule the work to be done.   A F O S N
30. I would refuse to explain my actions.   A F O S N
31. I would persuade others that my ideas are to their advantage.   A F O S N
32. I would permit the group to set its own pace.   A F O S N
33. I would urge the group to beat its previous record.   A F O S N
34. I would act without consulting the group.   A F O S N
35. I would ask that group members follow standard rules and regulations.   A F O S N

T _____ P _____

The T–P Leadership Questionnaire is scored as follows:

a. Circle the item number for items 8, 12, 17, 18, 19, 30, 34, and 35.
b. Write the number 1 in front of a *circled item number* if you responded *S* (seldom) or *N* (never) to that item.
c. Also write a number 1 in front of *item numbers not circled* if you responded *A* (always) or *F* (frequently).
d. Circle the number 1s that you have written in front of the following items: 3, 5, 8, 10, 15, 18, 19, 22, 24, 26, 28, 30, 32, 34, and 35.
e. *Count the circled number 1s.* This is your score for concern for people. Record the score in the blank following the letter P at the end of the questionnaire.
f. *Count uncircled number 1s.* This is your score for concern for task. Record this number in the blank following the letter T.

SOURCE: The T–P Leadership Questionnaire was adapted by J. B. Ritchie and P. Thompson in *Organization and People* (New York: West, 1984). Copyright 1969 by the American Educational Research Association. Adapted by permission of the publisher.

■ Management in Practice: Ethical Dilemma

Does Wage Reform Start at the Top?

Paula Smith has just been offered the opportunity of a lifetime. The chairman of the board of Resitronic Corporation has asked her to take the job as director of the troubled audio equipment manufacturing subsidiary. The first question Smith asked was, "Will the board give me the autonomy to turn this company around?" The answer was yes. Resitronic's problems were so severe that the board was desperate for change and ready to give Smith whatever it took to save the company.

Smith knows that she must cut costs. Labor expenses are too high, and product quality and production times are below industry standards. She sees that labor and management at Resitronic are two armed camps, but she needs cooperation at all levels to achieve a turnaround. Smith is energized. She knows she finally has the autonomy to try out her theories about an empowered workforce. Smith knows she must ask managers and workers to take a serious pay cut, with the promise of incentives to share in any improvements they might make. She also knows that everyone will be looking at her own salary as an indication of whether she walks her talk.

Smith is torn. She realizes she faces a year or two of complete hell, with long hours, little time for her family or outside interests, bitter resistance in subordinates, and no guarantees of success. Even if she comes in at the current director's salary, she will be taking a cut in pay. But if she takes a bigger cut coming in, with the promise of bonuses and stock options tied to her own performance, she sends a strong message to the entire subsidiary that they rise or fall together. She wonders what might happen if she fails. Many influences on the audio equipment subsidiary are beyond her control. Resitronic itself is in trouble. From her current vantage point, Smith believes she can turn things around, but what will she discover when she gets inside? What if the board undercuts her? Doesn't she owe it to herself and her family to be compensated at the highest possible level for the stress and risk they will be enduring? Can she afford to risk her own security to send a message of commitment to the plan she is asking others to follow?

What Do You Do?

1. Take the same salary as the current director for one year. Circulate the information that although you are taking a cut to come to Resitronic, you are confident that you can make a difference. Build in pay incentive bonuses for the following years if the subsidiary succeeds.

2. Take a bigger cut in pay with generous incentive bonuses. Ask the board and the entire workforce to do the same. Open the books and let the whole company know exactly where they stand.

3. Ask for the same salary you are making now. You know you are going to be worth it, and you don't want to ask your family to suffer monetarily as well as in their quality of life during this transition.

◼ Surf the Net

1. **Leadership Journey.** Go to *http://www.theleadership challenge.com/forum/intro.html* and complete one of the activities (Personal Best, Most Admired Leader, Encouragement Index, etc.). Next, choose and view/listen to one video clip and one audio clip from the "Theater" link available at the top of the page. Last, go to *http://www.theleadershipchallenge.com/practices.html* and list the five fundamental practices that, according to Jim Kouzes and Barry Posner, enable leaders to get extraordinary things done.

A.
B.
C.
D.
E.

2. **Marine Leadership Principles.** Locate and print out the "Marine Leadership Principles and Traits" available at either of the sites listed. Prepare for a class discussion or write a summary on the principles and traits and the way they contribute to leadership in any situation.
http://www.cnet.navy.mil/cnet/nlpg2001/pdf/usmc_leadership.pdf
http://millennium.fortunecity.com/redwood/352/usmc16.htm

3. **Leadership Training.** Visit one of the following Web sites for organizations that provide leadership training to organizations and locate an item of interest related to leadership. Print it out and bring it to class to share during a classroom discussion.
http://www.blanchardtraining.com
http://www.tompeters.com
http://www.franklincovey.com

◼ Case for Critical Analysis

DGL International

When DGL International, a manufacturer of refinery equipment, brought in John Terrill to manage its Technical Services division, company executives informed him of the urgent situation. Technical Services, with 20 engineers, was the highest-paid, best-educated, and least-productive division in the company. The instructions to Terrill: Turn it around. Terrill called a meeting of the engineers. He showed great concern for their personal welfare and asked point blank: "What's the problem? Why can't we produce? Why does this division have such turnover?"

Without hesitation, employees launched a hail of complaints. "I was hired as an engineer, not a pencil pusher." "We spend over half our time writing asinine reports in triplicate for top management, and no one reads the reports."

After a two-hour discussion, Terrill concluded he had to get top management off the engineers' backs. He promised the engineers, "My job is to stay out of your way so you can do your work, and I'll try to keep top management off your backs too." He called for the day's reports and issued an order effective immediately that the originals be turned in daily to his office rather than mailed to headquarters. For three weeks, technical reports piled up on his desk. By month's end, the stack was nearly three feet high. During that time no one called for the reports. When other managers entered his office and saw the stack, they usually asked, "What's all this?" Terrill answered, "Technical reports." No one asked to read them.

Finally, at month's end, a secretary from finance called and asked for the monthly travel and expense report. Terrill responded, "Meet me in the president's office tomorrow morning."

The next morning the engineers cheered as Terrill walked through the department pushing a cart loaded with the enormous stack of reports. They knew the showdown had come.

Terrill entered the president's office and placed the stack of reports on his desk. The president and the other senior executives looked bewildered.

"This," Terrill announced, "is the reason for the lack of productivity in the Technical Services division. These are the reports you people require every month. The fact that they sat on my desk all month shows that no one reads this material. I suggest that the engineers' time could be used in a more productive manner, and that one brief monthly report from my office will satisfy the needs of other departments."

Questions

1. What leadership style did John Terrill use? What do you think was his primary source of power?
2. Based on the Hersey-Blanchard theory, should Terrill have been less participative? Should he have initiated more task structure for the engineers? Explain.
3. What leadership approach would you have taken in this situation?

■ Endnotes

1. D. Michael Abrashoff, "Retention through Redemption," *Harvard Business Review* (February 2001), 136–141; and Polly LaBarre, "The Most Important Thing a Captain Can Do Is to See the Ship from the Eyes of the Crew," *Fast Company* (April 1999), 115–126.
2. Melanie Warner, "Confessions of a Control Freak," *Fortune* (September 4, 2000), 130–140.
3. Gary Yukl, "Managerial Leadership: A Review of Theory and Research," *Journal of Management* 15 (1989), 251–289.
4. James M. Kouzes and Barry Z. Posner, "The Credibility Factor: What Followers Expect from Their Leaders," *Management Review* (January 1990), 29–33.
5. Henry Mintzberg, *Power In and Around Organizations* (Englewood Cliffs, N.J.: Prentice-Hall, 1983); and Jeffrey Pfeffer, *Power in Organizations* (Marshfield, Mass.: Pitman, 1981).
6. Andy Raskin, "The Accidental Leader," *Business 2.0* (November 2001), 32.
7. J. R. P. French, Jr., and B. Raven, "The Bases of Social Power," in *Group Dynamics*, ed. D. Cartwright and Alvin F. Zander (Evanston, Ill.: Row, Peterson, 1960), 607–623.
8. G. A. Yukl and T. Taber, "The Effective Use of Managerial Power," *Personnel* (March–April 1983), 37–44.
9. Erle Norton, "Chairman of AK Steel Tries to Shake Off Tag of 'Operating Man,'" *The Wall Street Journal* (November 25, 1994), A1, A5.
10. Jay A. Conger, "The Necessary Art of Persuasion," *Harvard Business Review* (May–June 1998), 84–95.
11. Andy Reinhardt, "Meet AMD's Rags-to-Riches Heir Apparent," *BusinessWeek* (October 2, 2000), 112–117.
12. Michael E. McGill and John W. Slocum, Jr., "A *Little* Leadership, Please?" *Organizational Dynamics* (Winter 1998), 39–49.
13. Thomas A. Stewart, "New Ways to Exercise Power," *Fortune* (November 6, 1989), 52–64; and Thomas A. Stewart, "CEOs See Clout Shifting," *Fortune* (November 6, 1989), 66.
14. Robin Landew Silverman, "A Moving Experience," *Inc.* (August 1996), 23–24.
15. G. A. Yukl, *Leadership in Organizations* (Englewood Cliffs, N.J.: Prentice-Hall, 1981); and S. C. Kohs and K. W. Irle, "Prophesying Army Promotion," *Journal of Applied Psychology* 4 (1920), 73–87.
16. R. Albanese and D. D. Van Fleet, *Organizational Behavior: A Managerial Viewpoint* (Hinsdale, Ill.: The Dryden Press, 1983).
17. K. Lewin, "Field Theory and Experiment in Social Psychology: Concepts and Methods," *American Journal of Sociology* 44 (1939), 868–896; K. Lewin and R. Lippitt, "An Experimental Approach to the Study of Autocracy and Democracy: A Preliminary Note," *Sociometry* 1 (1938), 292–300; and K. Lewin, R. Lippitt, and R. K. White, "Patterns of Aggressive Behavior in Experimentally Created Social Climates," *Journal of Social Psychology* 10 (1939), 271–301.
18. R. K. White and R. Lippitt, *Autocracy and Democracy: An Experimental Inquiry* (New York: Harper, 1960).
19. R. Tannenbaum and W. H. Schmidt, "How to Choose a Leadership Pattern," *Harvard Business Review* 36 (1958), 95–101.
20. Marc Ballon, "Equal Parts Old-Fashioned Dictator and New Age Father Figure, Jack Hartnett Breaks Nearly Every Rule of

the Enlightened Manager's Code," *Inc.* (July 1998), 60+; Esther Wachs Book, "Leadership for the Millennium," *Working Woman* (March 1998), 29–34.

21. C. A. Schriesheim and B. J. Bird, "Contributions of the Ohio State Studies to the Field of Leadership," *Journal of Management* 5 (1979), 135–145; and C. L. Shartle, "Early Years of the Ohio State University Leadership Studies," *Journal of Management* 5 (1979), 126–134.

22. P. C. Nystrom, "Managers and the High-High Leader Myth," *Academy of Management Journal* 21 (1978), 325–331; and L. L. Larson, J. G. Hunt, and Richard N. Osborn, "The Great High-High Leader Behavior Myth: A Lesson from Occam's Razor," *Academy of Management Journal* 19 (1976), 628–641.

23. R. Likert, "From Production- and Employee-Centeredness to Systems 1–4," *Journal of Management* 5 (1979), 147–156.

24. Robert R. Blake and Jane S. Mouton, *The Managerial Grid III* (Houston: Gulf, 1985).

25. William C. Symonds, "The Power of the Paycheck," *BusinessWeek* (May 24, 1999), 71–72; and Katharine Mieszkowski, "Changing Tires, Changing the World," *Fast Company* (October 1999), 58–60.

26. Fred E. Fiedler, "Assumed Similarity Measures as Predictors of Team Effectiveness," *Journal of Abnormal and Social Psychology* 49 (1954), 381–388; F. E. Fiedler, *Leader Attitudes and Group Effectiveness* (Urbana, Ill.: University of Illinois Press, 1958); and F. E. Fiedler, *A Theory of Leadership Effectiveness* (New York: McGraw-Hill, 1967).

27. Fred E. Fiedler and M. M. Chemers, *Leadership and Effective Management* (Glenview, Ill.: Scott, Foresman, 1974).

28. Fred E. Fiedler, "Engineer the Job to Fit the Manager," *Harvard Business Review* 43 (1965), 115–122; and F. E. Fiedler, M. M. Chemers, and L. Mahar, *Improving Leadership Effectiveness: The Leader Match Concept* (New York: Wiley, 1976).

29. Timothy Aeppel, "Personnel Disorders Sap a Factory Owner of His Early Idealism," *The Wall Street Journal* (January 14, 1998), A1, A14.

30. R. Singh, "Leadership Style and Reward Allocation: Does Least Preferred Coworker Scale Measure Tasks and Relation Orientation?" *Organizational Behavior and Human Performance* 27 (1983), 178–197; and D. Hosking, "A Critical Evaluation of Fiedler's Contingency Hypotheses," *Progress in Applied Psychology* 1 (1981), 103–154.

31. Paul Hersey and Kenneth H. Blanchard, *Management of Organizational Behavior: Utilizing Human Resources*, 4th ed. (Englewood Cliffs, N.J.: Prentice-Hall, 1982).

32. Jonathon Kaufman, "A McDonald's Owner Becomes a Role Model for Black Teenagers," *The Wall Street Journal* (August 23, 1995), A1, A6.

33. M. G. Evans, "The Effects of Supervisory Behavior on the Path-Goal Relationship," *Organizational Behavior and Human Performance* 5 (1970), 277–298; M. G. Evans, "Leadership and Motivation: A Core Concept," *Academy of Management Journal* 13 (1970), 91–102; and B. S. Georgopoulos, G. M. Mahoney, and N. W. Jones, "A Path-Goal Approach to Productivity," *Journal of Applied Psychology* 41 (1957), 345–353.

34. Robert J. House, "A Path-Goal Theory of Leader Effectiveness," *Administrative Science Quarterly* 16 (1971), 321–338.

35. M. G. Evans, "Leadership," in *Organizational Behavior*, ed. S. Kerr (Columbus, Ohio: Grid, 1974), 230–233.

36. Robert J. House and Terrence R. Mitchell, "Path-Goal Theory of Leadership," *Journal of Contemporary Business* (Autumn 1974), 81–97.

37. Charles A. O'Reilly III and Jeffrey Pfeffer, "Star Makers," book excerpt from *From Hidden Value: How Great Companies Achieve Extraordinary Results with Ordinary People* (Harvard Business School Press, 2000), published in *CIO* (September 15, 2000), 226–246.

38. Charles Greene, "Questions of Causation in the Path-Goal Theory of Leadership," *Academy of Management Journal* 22 (March 1979), 22–41; and C. A. Schriesheim and Mary Ann von Glinow, "The Path-Goal Theory of Leadership: A Theoretical and Empirical Analysis," *Academy of Management Journal* 20 (1977), 398–405.

39. S. Kerr and J. M. Jermier, "Substitutes for Leadership: Their Meaning and Measurement," *Organizational Behavior and Human Performance* 22 (1978), 375–403; and Jon P. Howell and Peter W. Dorfman, "Leadership and Substitutes for Leadership among Professional and Nonprofessional Workers," *Journal of Applied Behavioral Science* 22 (1986), 29–46.

40. The terms *transactional* and *transformational* come from James M. Burns, *Leadership* (New York: Harper & Row, 1978); and Bernard M. Bass, "Leadership: Good, Better, Best," *Organizational Dynamics* 13 (Winter 1985), 26–40.

41. Katherine J. Klein and Robert J. House, "On Fire: Charismatic Leadership and Levels of Analysis," *Leadership Quarterly* 6, no. 2 (1995), 183–198.

42. Jay A. Conger and Rabindra N. Kanungo, "Toward a Behavioral Theory of Charismatic Leadership in Organizational Settings," *Academy of Management Review* 12 (1987), 637–647; Walter Kiechel III, "A Hard Look at Executive Vision," *Fortune* (October 23, 1989), 207–211; and William L. Gardner and Bruce J. Avolio, "The Charismatic Relationship: A Dramaturgical Perspective," *Academy of Management Review* 23, no. 1 (1998), 32–58.

43. Keith Hammonds, "The Monroe Doctrine," *Fast Company* (October 1999), 230–236.

44. Robert J. House, "Research Contrasting the Behavior and Effects of Reputed Charismatic vs. Reputed Non-Charismatic Leaders" (paper presented as part of a symposium, "Charismatic Leadership: Theory and Evidence," Academy of Management, San Diego, 1985).

45. Robert J. House and Jane M. Howell, "Personality and Charismatic Leadership," *Leadership Quarterly* 3, no. 2 (1992), 81–108; and Jennifer O'Connor, Michael D. Mumford, Timothy C. Clifton, Theodore L. Gessner, and Mary Shane Connelly, "Charismatic Leaders and Destructiveness: A Historiometric Study," *Leadership Quarterly* 6, no. 4 (1995), 529–555.

46. Bernard M. Bass, "Theory of Transformational Leadership Redux," *Leadership Quarterly* 6, no. 4 (1995), 463–478; Noel M. Tichy and Mary Anne Devanna, *The Transformational Leader* (New York: John Wiley & Sons, 1986); and Badrinarayan Shankar Pawar and Kenneth K. Eastman, "The Nature and Implications of Contextual Influences on Transformational Leadership: A Conceptual

Examination," *Academy of Management Review* 22, no. 1 (1997) 80–109.

47. Richard L. Daft and Robert H. Lengel, *Fusion Leadership: Unlocking the Subtle Forces that Change People and Organizations* (San Francisco: Berrett-Koehler, 1998).

48. Bethany McLean, "Is This Guy the Best Banker in America?" *Fortune* (July 6, 1998), 126–128; and Jacqueline S. Gold, "Bank to the Future," *Institutional Investor* (September 2001), 54–63.

49. Jim Collins, "Level 5 Leadership: The Triumph of Humility and Fierce Resolve," *Harvard Business Review* (January 2001), 67–76; Collins, "Good to Great," *Fast Company* (October 2001), 90–104; A. J. Vogl, "Onward and Upward" (an interview with Jim Collins), *Across the Board* (September-October 2001), 29–34; and Jerry Useem, "Conquering Vertical Limits," *Fortune* (February 19, 2001), 84–96.

50. Judy B. Rosener, *America's Competitive Secret: Utilizing Women as a Management Strategy* (New York: Oxford University Press, 1995); Rosener, "Ways Women Lead," *Harvard Business Review* (November-December 1990), 119–125; Sally Helgesen, *The Female Advantage: Women's Ways of Leadership* (New York: Currency/Doubleday, 1990);

and Bernard M. Bass and Bruce J. Avolio, "Shatter the Glass Ceiling: Women May Make Better Managers," *Human Resource Management* 33, no. 4 (Winter 1994), 549–560.

51. Rochelle Sharpe, "As Leaders, Women Rule," *BusinessWeek* (November 20, 2000), 75–84.

52. Rosener, *America's Competitive Secret.* 129–135.

53. Sharpe, "As Leaders, Women Rule."

54. Deborah L. Duarte and Nancy Tennant Snyder, *Mastering Virtual Teams: Strategies, Tools, and Techniques That Succeed,* (San Francisco: Jossey-Bass, 1999).

55. This discussion is based on Wayne F. Cascio, "Managing a Virtual Workplace," *Academy of Management Executive* 14, no. 3 (August 2000), 81–90, and Charlene Marmer Solomon, "Managing Virtual Teams," *Workforce* (June 2001), 60–65.

56. Nancy Chase, "Learning to Lead a Virtual Team," *Quality* (August 1999), 76.

57. Daft and Lengel, *Fusion Leadership.*

58. Robert K. Greenleaf, *Servant Leadership: A Journey into the Nature of Legitimate Power and Greatness* (Mahwah, N.J.: Paulist Press, 1977).

59. Abrashoff, "Retention through Redemption," and LaBarre, "The Most Important Thing a Captain Can Do."

Motivation in Organizations

CHAPTER OUTLINE

The Concept of Motivation

Foundations of Motivation

Traditional Approach

Human Relations Approach

Human Resource Approach

Contemporary Approach

Content Perspectives on Motivation

Hierarchy of Needs Theory

ERG Theory

Two-Factor Theory

Acquired Needs Theory

Process Perspectives on Motivation

Equity Theory

Expectancy Theory

Reinforcement Perspective on Motivation

Reinforcement Tools

Schedules of Reinforcement

Job Design for Motivation

Job Simplification

Job Rotation

Job Enlargement

Job Enrichment

Job Characteristics Model

Motivating in the New Workplace

Empowerment

Giving Meaning to Work

LEARNING OBJECTIVES

After studying this chapter, you should be able to

1 Define *motivation* and explain the difference between current approaches and traditional approaches to motivation.

2 Identify and describe content theories of motivation based on employee needs.

3 Identify and explain process theories of motivation.

4 Describe reinforcement theory and how it can be used to motivate employees.

5 Discuss major approaches to job design and how job design influences motivation.

6 Discuss how empowerment heightens employee motivation.

Management Challenge

After 13 years at Sandstrom Products, a manufacturer of paints and coatings, Leo Henkelman was thinking about quitting. He had started as a paint runner, the lowest job in the plant, and worked his way up to a mill operator position. Henkelman spent his days mixing paints in a giant blender, following formulas supplied by the lab. As he gained knowledge and experience, he came up with a lot of good ideas for improving formulas; yet the guys in the lab continually ignored his suggestions. "It was like they hired me from the neck down," he said. "Warm body, strong back, weak mind." Increasing pressure from quality-conscious customers multiplied the frustration he shared with most of the operators, who felt powerless to change anything. Some workers, including Henkelman, just stopped caring. Finding no challenge at work, he would show up with a hangover and just put in time until he could clock out and hit the bottle again. Top management knew the company had problems—for one thing, Sandstrom was hemorrhaging cash, losing money for the third year out of the last five. Things had to change or Sandstrom would go broke.[1]

If you were the president of Sandstrom Products, how would you motivate employees like Leo Henkelman to give their all to the company? Is high motivation even possible in this kind of routine manufacturing operation?

The problem for Sandstrom Products is that unmotivated employees do the minimum amount of work, causing product quality to suffer and the company to lose its competitive edge. One secret for success in organizations is motivated and enthusiastic employees. The challenge for Sandstrom Products and other companies is to keep employee motivation consistent with organizational goals. Motivation is a challenge for managers because motivation arises from within employees and typically differs for each person. For example, Janice Rennie makes a staggering $350,000 a year selling residential real estate in Toronto; she attributes her success to the fact that she likes to listen carefully to clients and then find a house to meet their needs. Greg Storey is a skilled machinist who is challenged by writing programs for numerically controlled machines. After dropping out of college, he swept floors in a machine shop and was motivated to learn to run the machines. Frances Blais sells educational books and software. She is a top salesperson, but she does not care about the $50,000-plus commissions: "I'm not even thinking money when I'm selling. I'm really on a crusade to help children read well." In stark contrast, Rob Michaels gets sick to his stomach before he goes to work. Rob is a telephone salesperson who spends all day trying to get people to buy products they do not need, and the rejections are painful. His motivation is money; he earned $120,000 in the past year and cannot make nearly that much doing anything else.[2]

Rob is motivated by money, Janice by her love of listening and problem solving, Frances by the desire to help children read, and Greg by the challenge of mastering numerically controlled machinery. Each person is motivated to perform, yet each has different reasons for performing. With such diverse motivations, it is a challenge for managers to motivate employees toward common organizational goals.

This chapter reviews theories and models of employee motivation. First we will review several perspectives on motivation and cover models that describe the employee needs and processes associated with motivation. Then, we will discuss how *job design*—changing the structure of the work itself—can affect employee satisfaction and productivity. Finally, we will examine the trend of *empowerment*, where authority and decision making are delegated to subordinates to increase employee motivation.

The Concept of Motivation

motivation
The arousal, direction, and persistence of behavior.

Most of us get up in the morning, go to school or work, and behave in ways that are predictably our own. We respond to our environment and the people in it with little thought as to why we work hard, enjoy certain classes, or find some recreational activities so much fun. Yet all these behaviors are motivated by something. **Motivation** refers to the forces either within or external to a person that arouse enthusiasm and persistence to pursue a certain course of action. Employee motivation affects productivity, and part of a manager's job is to channel motivation toward the accomplishment of organizational goals.[3] The study of motivation helps managers understand what prompts people to initiate action, what influences their choice of action, and why they persist in that action over time.

A simple model of human motivation is illustrated in Exhibit 17.1. People have basic *needs*, such as for food, achievement, or monetary gain, that translate into an internal tension that motivates specific behaviors with which to

NEED Creates desire to fulfill needs (food, friendship, recognition, achievement)	**BEHAVIOR** Results in actions to fulfill needs	**REWARDS** Satisfy needs; intrinsic or extrinsic rewards

FEEDBACK Reward informs person whether behavior was appropriate and should be used again.

Exhibit **17.1**

A Simple Model of Motivation

fulfill the need. To the extent that the behavior is successful, the person is rewarded in the sense that the need is satisfied. The reward also informs the person that the behavior was appropriate and can be used again in the future.

Rewards are of two types: intrinsic and extrinsic. **Intrinsic rewards** are the satisfactions a person receives in the process of performing a particular action. The completion of a complex task may bestow a pleasant feeling of accomplishment, or solving a problem that benefits others may fulfill a personal mission. For example, Frances Blais sells educational materials for the intrinsic reward of helping children read well. **Extrinsic rewards** are given by another person, typically a manager, and include promotions and pay increases. They originate externally, as a result of pleasing others. Rob Michaels, who hates his sales job, nevertheless is motivated by the extrinsic reward of high pay. Although extrinsic rewards are important, good managers strive to help people achieve intrinsic rewards, as well. Today's managers are finding that the most talented and innovative employees are rarely motivated exclusively by rewards such as money and benefits, or even praise and recognition. Instead, they seek satisfaction from the work itself.[4]

The importance of motivation as illustrated in Exhibit 17.1 is that it can lead to behaviors that reflect high performance within organizations. One recent study found that high employee motivation goes hand-in-hand with high organizational performance and profits.[5] Managers can use motivation theory to help satisfy employees' needs and simultaneously encourage high work performance. With the recent massive layoffs in many U.S. organizations, managers are struggling to keep remaining workers focused and motivated. In addition, as the economy improves, finding and keeping talented

intrinsic reward
The satisfaction received in the process of performing an action.

extrinsic reward
A reward given by another person.

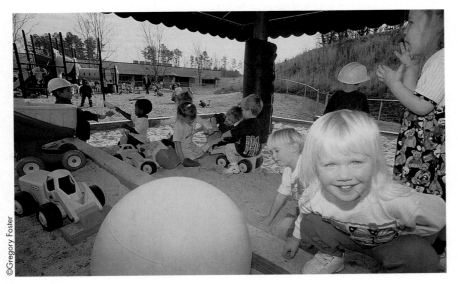

Some employees at software developer SAS Institute in Cary, North Carolina, are motivated by the top-quality day care that is available for $250 per month for their young children. Other SAS employees are motivated by offerings such as a 35-hour week, a free on-site medical clinic, or 12 holidays a year plus a paid week off between Christmas and New Year's. These extrinsic rewards *that help employees maintain a balance between work and personal life* earned SAS third-place honors in Fortune *magazine's list of the 100 best companies to work for in America.*

workers may be a significant challenge because of weakened trust and commitment. Managers have to find the right combination of motivational techniques and rewards to keep workers satisfied and productive in a variety of organizational situations. This chapter's Leading Online box describes how one manager used technology to improve motivation at a company located in a remote area of Maine.

Foundations of Motivation

A manager's assumptions about employee motivation and use of rewards depend on his or her perspective on motivation. Four distinct perspectives on employee motivation have evolved: the traditional approach, the human relations approach, the human resource approach, and the contemporary approach.[6]

Traditional Approach

The study of employee motivation really began with the work of Frederick W. Taylor on scientific management. Recall from Chapter 2 that scientific management pertains to the systematic analysis of an employee's job for the purpose of increasing efficiency. Economic rewards are provided to employees for high performance. The emphasis on pay evolved into the notion of the *economic man*—people would work harder for higher pay. This approach led to the development of incentive pay systems, in which people were paid strictly on the quantity and quality of their work outputs.

Human Relations Approach

The economic man was gradually replaced by a more sociable employee in managers' minds. Beginning with the landmark Hawthorne studies at a Western Electric plant, as described in Chapter 2, noneconomic rewards, such as congenial work groups who met social needs, seemed more important than money as a motivator of work behavior.[7] For the first time, workers were studied as people, and the concept of *social man* was born.

Human Resource Approach

The human resource approach carries the concepts of economic man and social man further to introduce the concept of the *whole person*. Human resource theory suggests that employees are complex and motivated by many factors. For example, the work by McGregor on Theory X and Theory Y described in Chapter 2 argued that people want to do a good job and that work is as natural and healthy as play. Proponents of the human resource approach believed that earlier approaches had tried to manipulate employees through economic or social rewards. By assuming that employees are competent and able to make major contributions, managers can enhance organizational performance. The human resource approach laid the groundwork for contemporary perspectives on employee motivation.

Contemporary Approach

The contemporary approach to employee motivation is dominated by three types of theories, each of which will be discussed in the following sections.

Leading Online

At ATX Forms, Idea Labs Pay Off

Glynn Willett, CEO of ATX Forms, started the Idea Lab as a way to keep communication going and to get people involved, but the most important benefit has been increased morale and higher motivation for this $18 million, 150-person tax-software company. Considering that the company is based in the remote location of Caribou, Maine, that is a welcome addition. Idea Labs are weekly technology-powered gab sessions that are videotaped and archived on the corporate intranet. ATX's second office is located 1,700 miles away in Fort Pierce, Florida, so Willett wanted to find a way to foster greater interaction and involvement among a small group of people.

During the Idea Lab sessions, employees have a chance to voice their opinions about topics ranging from product strategy to human nature and just about everything in between. Everyone sits in on at least one Idea Lab a year, either in person or online. One Idea Lab debated whether workers who did not clock out for breaks were cheating the company. Willett determined that these people simply had a different work style, so he took them off the clock and put them on salary. In another session, employees suggested using a phone system that routes product inquiries to the most effective salespeople for that particular product, an idea that resulted in a 12 percent increase in closed sales from the previous year.

Although these business ideas and results are welcomed, the most important role for the Idea Lab forums may be that they have helped make ATX a place where people like to work. The practice has paid off: Communication has improved, far-flung workers are united, motivation and morale is high, and things happen fast. It is no wonder the company has the amazingly low turnover rate of 0 percent for programmers and less than 5 percent for everyone else.

SOURCE: Erin Callaway, "Caribou Peekaboo," *Growth²* (October 30, 2001), 150.

The first are *content theories*, which stress the analysis of underlying human needs. Content theories provide insight into the needs of people in organizations and help managers understand how needs can be satisfied in the workplace. *Process theories* concern the thought processes that influence behavior. They focus on how employees seek rewards in work circumstances. *Reinforcement theories* focus on employee learning of desired work behaviors. In Exhibit 17.1, content theories focus on the concepts in the first box, process theories on those in the second, and reinforcement theories on those in the third.

Content Perspectives on Motivation

Content theories emphasize the needs that motivate people. At any point in time, people have basic needs such as those for food, achievement, or monetary reward. These needs translate into an internal drive that motivates specific behaviors in an attempt to fulfill the needs. An individual's needs are like a hidden catalog of the things he or she wants and will work to get. To the extent that managers understand worker needs, the organization's reward systems can be designed to meet them and reinforce employees for directing energies and priorities toward attainment of organizational goals.

content theories
A group of theories that emphasize the needs that motivate people.

Hierarchy of Needs Theory

Probably the most famous content theory was developed by Abraham Maslow.[8] Maslow's **hierarchy of needs theory** proposes that humans are motivated by multiple needs and that these needs exist in a hierarchical order as illustrated in Exhibit 17.2. Maslow identified five general types of motivating needs in order of ascendance:

hierarchy of needs theory
A content theory that proposes that people are motivated by five categories of needs—physiological, safety, belongingness, esteem, and self-actualization—that exist in a hierarchical order.

Fulfillment off the Job   Need Hierarchy   Fulfillment on the Job

Fulfillment off the Job	Need Hierarchy	Fulfillment on the Job
Education, religion, hobbies, personal growth	Self-Actualization Needs	Opportunities for training, advancement, growth, and creativity
Approval of family, friends, community	Esteem Needs	Recognition, high status, increased responsibilities
Family, friends, community groups	Belongingness Needs	Work groups, clients, coworkers, supervisors
Freedom from war, pollution, violence	Safety Needs	Safe work, fringe benefits, job security
Food, water, oxygen	Physiological Needs	Heat, air, base salary

Exhibit *17.2*

Maslow's Hierarchy of Needs

1. *Physiological needs.* These are the most basic human physical needs, including food, water, and oxygen. In the organizational setting, these are reflected in the needs for adequate heat, air, and base salary to ensure survival.
2. *Safety needs.* These are the needs for a safe and secure physical and emotional environment and freedom from threats—that is, for freedom from violence and for an orderly society. In an organizational workplace, safety needs reflect the needs for safe jobs, fringe benefits, and job security.
3. *Belongingness needs.* These needs reflect the desire to be accepted by one's peers, have friendships, be part of a group, and be loved. In the organization, these needs influence the desire for good relationships with coworkers, participation in a work group, and a positive relationship with supervisors.
4. *Esteem needs.* These needs relate to the desire for a positive self-image and to receive attention, recognition, and appreciation from others. Within organizations, esteem needs reflect a motivation for recognition, an increase in responsibility, high status, and credit for contributions to the organization.
5. *Self-actualization needs.* These represent the need for self-fulfillment, which is the highest need category. They concern developing one's full potential, increasing one's competence, and becoming a better person. Self-actualization needs can be met in the organization by providing people with opportunities to grow, be creative, and acquire training for challenging assignments and advancement.

According to Maslow's theory, low-order needs take priority—they must be satisfied before higher-order needs are activated. The needs are satisfied in sequence: Physiological needs come before safety needs, safety needs before social needs, and so on. A person desiring physical safety will devote his or her efforts to securing a safer environment and will not be concerned with esteem needs or self-actualization needs. Once a need is satisfied, it declines in importance and the next higher need is activated. At All Metro Health Care in Lynbrook, New York, CEO Irving Edwards set up a special "customer service" department for his home health aides to help meet their basic needs, such as applying for food stamps and finding transportation and child care. Three employees are available solely to help workers with these issues. Once these lower-level needs are met, employees desire to have higher-level needs met in the workplace, so Irving developed programs such as an award for caregiver of the year, essay contests with prizes, and special recognition for high scoring on quarterly training exercises.[9]

ERG Theory

Clayton Alderfer proposed a modification of Maslow's theory in an effort to simplify it and respond to criticisms of its lack of empirical verification.[10] His **ERG theory** identified three categories of needs:

1. *Existence needs.* These are the needs for physical well-being.
2. *Relatedness needs.* These pertain to the need for satisfactory relationships with others.
3. *Growth needs.* These focus on the development of human potential and the desire for personal growth and increased competence.

The ERG model and Maslow's need hierarchy are similar because both are in hierarchical form and presume that individuals move up the hierarchy one step at a time. However, Alderfer reduced the number of need categories to three and proposed that movement up the hierarchy is more complex, reflecting a **frustration-regression principle**, namely, that failure to meet a high-order need may trigger a regression to an already fulfilled lower-order need. Thus, a worker who cannot fulfill a need for personal growth may revert to a lower-order need and redirect his or her efforts toward making a lot of money. The ERG model therefore is less rigid than Maslow's need hierarchy, suggesting that individuals may move down as well as up the hierarchy, depending on their ability to satisfy needs.

Need hierarchy theory helps explain why organizations find ways to recognize employees and encourage their participation in decision making. Southwest Airlines emphasizes extensive employee training through its corporate university so that managers can push responsibility and decision making down the chain of command. "It's very validating and it taps into people's motivation for their jobs if they know that their opinion matters," says Peter Nelson, creative development manager for Southwest's University of People.[11] A recent survey found that employees who contribute ideas at work are more likely to feel valued, committed, and motivated. In addition, when employees' ideas are implemented and recognized, there tends to be a motivational ripple effect throughout the workforce.[12]

Many companies are finding that creating a humane work environment that allows people to achieve a balance between work and personal life is also a great high-level motivator. At ClickAction Inc., an online direct-marketing firm based in Palo Alto, California, managers have created a culture of "working smarter and respecting people's time" to enhance motivation and productivity.[13] The Putting People First box describes another company founded on the premise that people should have plenty of time and energy for a life outside the office. Flexibility in the workplace, including options such as telecommuting, flexible hours, and job sharing, are highly valued by today's employees.

Two-Factor Theory

Frederick Herzberg developed another popular theory of motivation called the *two-factor theory*.[14] Herzberg interviewed hundreds of workers about times

ERG theory
A modification of the needs hierarchy theory that proposes three categories of needs: existence, relatedness, and growth.

frustration-regression principle
The idea that failure to meet a high-order need may cause a regression to an already satisfied lower-order need.

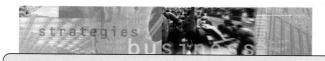

Putting People First

Software Technology Group's 'Healthy' Culture

Jeff Soderberg, founder and president of Software Technology Group (STG), an IT consulting business based in Salt Lake City, resolved years ago not to mistake success in business with success in life. "For some reason, people in IT assume that the more overtime you put in, the more chance you'll be successful," he says. Soderberg has a personal understanding of the pitfalls that a typical IT work style can create, and he believes that no amount of success is worth giving your whole life to your job.

Soderberg, an avid rock climber, instilled his own health-conscious, sports-friendly values into the corporate culture at STG. All new hires are told to expect a 40-hour work week, and they are encouraged to have some kind of physical activity they like to do outside the office. The offices have a strangely unlived-in look and lack the personal clutter that occurs when people spend most of their waking hours at work. It's as if Soderberg has told his employees: "Come here,

work, and get out of here. You don't live here. You live someplace else." However, all around are indications of employees' hobbies—a bike parked near a desk; a fishing fly mounted on the wall, a golf trophy.

The friendly work ethic at STG is a stark contrast to the IT industry's notorious 80-hour work week. "We have to make sure that our consultants don't burn out," says Soderberg. STG takes a career approach to their employees, and the company has even ended relationships with clients who try to abuse consultants' time. Soderberg is careful to recruit and hire people who can appreciate the more laid-back environment. "To put a workaholic on the staff would be like trying to mix oil and water," he says. "You have to create a team that shares the same values, and having a healthy lifestyle is one of our values." In the middle of the overactive world of information technology, Soderberg has created a business that allows him—and his workers—time to have a life.

SOURCE: Ethan Watters, "Come Here, Work, and Get Out of Here. You Don't Live Here. You Live Someplace Else," *Inc.* (October 30, 2001), 56–61.

---

when they were highly motivated to work and other times when they were dissatisfied and unmotivated at work. His findings suggested that the work characteristics associated with dissatisfaction were quite different from those pertaining to satisfaction, which prompted the notion that two factors influence work motivation.

The two-factor theory is illustrated in Exhibit 17.3. The center of the scale is neutral, meaning that workers are neither satisfied nor dissatisfied. Herzberg believed that two entirely separate dimensions contribute to an employee's behavior at work. The first, called **hygiene factors**, involves the presence or absence of job dissatisfiers, such as working conditions, pay, company policies, and interpersonal relationships. When hygiene factors are poor, work is dissatisfying. However, good hygiene factors simply remove the dissatisfaction; they do not in themselves cause people to become highly satisfied and motivated in their work.

The second set of factors does influence job satisfaction. **Motivators** are high-level needs and include achievement, recognition, responsibility, and opportunity for growth. Herzberg believed that when motivators are absent, workers are neutral toward work, but when motivators are present, workers are highly motivated and satisfied. Thus, hygiene factors and motivators represent two distinct factors that influence motivation. Hygiene factors work only in the area of dissatisfaction. Unsafe working conditions or a noisy work environment will cause people to be dissatisfied, but their correction will not lead to a high level of motivation and satisfaction. Motivators such as challenge, responsibility, and recognition must be in place before employees will be highly motivated to excel at their work.

The implication of the two-factor theory for managers is clear. Providing hygiene factors will eliminate employee dissatisfaction but will not motivate

hygiene factors
Factors that involve the presence or absence of job dissatisfiers, including working conditions, pay, company policies, and interpersonal relationships.

motivators
Factors that influence job satisfaction based on fulfillment of high-level needs such as achievement, recognition, responsibility, and opportunity for growth.

Exhibit **17.3**

Herzberg's Two-Factor Theory

workers to high achievement levels. On the other hand, recognition, challenge, and opportunities for personal growth are powerful motivators and will promote high satisfaction and performance. The manager's role is to remove dissatisfiers—that is, to provide hygiene factors sufficient to meet basic needs—and then use motivators to meet higher-level needs and propel employees toward greater achievement and satisfaction. For example, A.W. Chesterton, a private, Massachusetts-based maker of seals and pumps, relies on both hygiene factors and motivators to try to prevent dissatisfaction and increase satisfaction among workers. In addition to adequate pay, good working conditions, and great benefits, Chesterton also incorporates high-level motivators such as a chance for employees to be involved in solving problems. Employees are provided with full information, including confidential data, and are challenged to come up with ideas to help the company survive in the face of increased competition. This open process is intrinsically motivating to employees, who appreciate the higher level of responsibility and the degree of trust placed in them. Employees have been known to go above and beyond the call of duty to solve a customer problem, even working voluntarily on weekends. Also at Chesterton, a profit-sharing plan and special awards to high performers increase satisfaction by providing a source of both achievement and recognition.[15]

Acquired Needs Theory

The final content theory was developed by David McClelland. The *acquired needs theory* proposes that certain types of needs are acquired during the individual's lifetime. In other words, people are not born with these needs but may learn them through their life experiences.[16] The three needs most frequently studied are these:

1. *Need for achievement.* The desire to accomplish something difficult, attain a high standard of success, master complex tasks, and surpass others.
2. *Need for affiliation.* The desire to form close personal relationships, avoid conflict, and establish warm friendships.
3. *Need for power.* The desire to influence or control others, be responsible for others, and have authority over others.

Early life experiences determine whether people acquire these needs. If children are encouraged to do things for themselves and receive reinforcement, they will acquire a need to achieve. If they are reinforced for forming warm human relationships, they will develop a need for affiliation. If they get satisfaction from controlling others, they will acquire a need for power. For example, Jack Welch, former CEO of General Electric, has credited his mother for his ambition and achievement drive. Welch's mother was determined that he be successful, so she constantly encouraged and pushed him to do better in school.[17]

For more than 20 years, McClelland studied human needs and their implications for management. People with a high need for achievement are frequently entrepreneurs. They like to do something better than competitors and take sensible business risks. On the other hand, people who have a high need for affiliation are successful integrators, whose job is to coordinate the work of several departments in an organization.[18] Integrators include brand managers and project managers who must have excellent people skills. People high in need for affiliation are able to establish positive working relationships with others.

A high need for power often is associated with successful attainment of top levels in the organizational hierarchy. For example, McClelland studied managers at AT&T for 16 years and found that those with a high need for power were more likely to follow a path of continued promotion over time. More than half of the employees at the top levels had a high need for power. In contrast, managers with a high need for achievement but a low need for power tended to peak earlier in their careers and at a lower level. The reason is that achievement needs can be met through the task itself, but power needs can be met only by ascending to a level at which a person has power over others.

In summary, content theories focus on people's underlying needs and label those particular needs that motivate behavior. The hierarchy of needs theory, the ERG theory, the two-factor theory, and the acquired needs theory all help managers understand what motivates people. In this way, managers can design work to meet needs and hence elicit appropriate and successful work behaviors.

Process Perspectives on Motivation

process theories
A group of theories that explain how employees select behaviors with which to meet their needs and determine whether their choices were successful.

Process theories explain how workers select behavioral actions to meet their needs and determine whether their choices were successful. There are two basic process theories: equity theory and expectancy theory.

Equity Theory

equity theory
A process theory that focuses on individuals' perceptions of how fairly they are treated relative to others.

Equity theory focuses on individuals' perceptions of how fairly they are treated compared with others. Developed by J. Stacy Adams, equity theory proposes that people are motivated to seek social equity in the rewards they expect for performance.[19]

According to equity theory, if people perceive their compensation as equal to what others receive for similar contributions, they will believe that their treatment is fair and equitable. People evaluate equity by a ratio of inputs to outcomes. Inputs to a job include education, experience, effort, and ability. Outcomes from a job include pay, recognition, benefits, and promotions. The input-to-outcome ratio may be compared to another person in the work group or to a perceived group average. A state of **equity** exists whenever the ratio of one person's outcomes to inputs equals the ratio of another's outcomes to inputs.

Inequity occurs when the input/outcome ratios are out of balance, such as when a person with a high level of education or experience receives the same salary as a new, less-educated employee. Perceived inequity also occurs in the other direction. Thus, if an employee discovers she is making more money than other people who contribute the same inputs to the company, she may feel the need to correct the inequity by working harder, getting more education, or considering lower pay. Perceived inequity creates tensions within individuals that motivate them to bring equity into balance.[20]

The most common methods for reducing a perceived inequity are these:

- *Change inputs.* A person may choose to increase or decrease his or her inputs to the organization. For example, underpaid individuals may reduce their level of effort or increase their absenteeism. Overpaid people may increase effort on the job.
- *Change outcomes.* A person may change his or her outcomes. An underpaid person may request a salary increase or a bigger office. A union may try to improve wages and working conditions in order to be consistent with a comparable union whose members make more money.
- *Distort perceptions.* Research suggests that people may distort perceptions of equity if they are unable to change inputs or outcomes. They may artificially increase the status attached to their jobs or distort others' perceived rewards to bring equity into balance.
- *Leave the job.* People who feel inequitably treated may decide to leave their jobs rather than suffer the inequity of being under- or overpaid. In their new jobs, they expect to find a more favorable balance of rewards.

The implication of equity theory for managers is that employees indeed evaluate the perceived equity of their rewards compared to others'. An increase in salary or a promotion will have no motivational effect if it is perceived as inequitable relative to that of other employees. A good example of equity theory comes from the J. Peterman Company, the trendy catalog company that eventually slid into bankruptcy before being acquired by another firm. John Peterman had created a comfortable, creative culture where employees were highly motivated to work together toward common goals. However, when the company began to grow rapidly, Peterman found himself having to hire people very quickly—and he often had to offer them higher salaries than those of his current employees to match what they were making elsewhere. In addition, when making important decisions, leaders tended to pay more attention to the ideas and thoughts of the new staff than they did the "old timers." Long-time employees felt slighted, and motivation declined significantly. Many employees began putting less energy and effort into their jobs. They were no longer willing to go the extra mile because of a perceived state of inequity.[21] Inequitable pay puts pressure on employees that is sometimes almost too great to bear. They attempt to change their work habits, try to change the system, or leave the job.[22]

equity
A situation that exists when the ratio of one person's outcomes to inputs equals that of another's.

Smart managers try to keep feelings of equity in balance in order to keep their workforces motivated.

Expectancy Theory

expectancy theory
A process theory that proposes that motivation depends on individuals' expectations about their ability to perform tasks and receive desired rewards.

Expectancy theory suggests that motivation depends on individuals' expectations about their ability to perform tasks and receive desired rewards. Expectancy theory is associated with the work of Victor Vroom, although a number of scholars have made contributions in this area.[23] Expectancy theory is concerned not with identifying types of needs but with the thinking process that individuals use to achieve rewards. Consider Bill Bradley, a university student with a strong desire for a B in his accounting course. Bill has a C+ average and one more exam to take. Bill's motivation to study for that last exam will be influenced by (1) the expectation that hard study will lead to an A on the exam and (2) the expectation that an A on the exam will result in a B for the course. If Bill believes he cannot get an A on the exam or that receiving an A will not lead to a B for the course, he will not be motivated to study exceptionally hard.

E → P expectancy
Expectancy that putting effort into a given task will lead to high performance.

P → O expectancy
Expectancy that successful performance of a task will lead to the desired outcome.

Elements of Expectancy Theory.   Expectancy theory is based on the relationship among the individual's *effort*, the individual's *performance*, and the desirability of *outcomes* associated with high performance. These elements and the relationships among them are illustrated in Exhibit 17.4. The keys to expectancy theory are the expectancies for the relationships among effort, performance, and outcomes with the value of the outcomes to the individual.

E → P expectancy involves whether putting effort into a task will lead to high performance. For this expectancy to be high, the individual must have the ability, previous experience, and necessary machinery, tools, and opportunity to perform. For Bill Bradley to get a B in the accounting course, the E → P expectancy is high if Bill truly believes that with hard work, he can get an A on the final exam. If Bill believes he has neither the ability nor the opportunity to achieve high performance, the expectancy will be low, and so will be his motivation.

P → O expectancy involves whether successful performance will lead to the desired outcome. In the case of a person who is motivated to win a job-related award, this expectancy concerns the belief that high performance will

Exhibit *17.4*

Major Elements of Expectancy Theory

truly lead to the award. If the P → O expectancy is high, the individual will be more highly motivated. If the expectancy is that high performance will not produce the desired outcome, motivation will be lower. If an A on the final exam is likely to produce a B in the accounting course, Bill Bradley's P → O expectancy will be high. Bill might talk to the professor to see whether an A will be sufficient to earn him a B in the course. If not, he will be less motivated to study hard for the final exam.

Valence is the value of outcomes, or attraction for outcomes, for the individual. If the outcomes that are available from high effort and good performance are not valued by employees, motivation will be low. Likewise, if outcomes have a high value, motivation will be higher.

Expectancy theory attempts not to define specific types of needs or rewards but only to establish that they exist and may be different for every individual. One employee might want to be promoted to a position of increased responsibility, and another might have high valence for good relationships with peers. Consequently, the first person will be motivated to work hard for a promotion and the second for the opportunity for a team position that will keep him or her associated with a group.

A simple sales department example will explain how the expectancy model in Exhibit 17.4 works. If Alecia Adams, a salesperson at the Diamond Gift Shop, believes that increased selling effort will lead to higher personal sales, we can say that she has a high E → P expectancy. Moreover, if Alecia also believes that higher personal sales will lead to a promotion or pay raise, we can say that she has a high P → O expectancy. Finally, if Alecia places a high value on the promotion or pay raise, valence is high and Alecia will have a high motivational force. On the other hand, if either the E → P or P → O expectancy is low, or if the money or promotion has low valence for Alecia, the overall motivational force will be low. For an employee to be highly motivated, all three factors in the expectancy model must be high.[24]

Implications for Managers.

The expectancy theory of motivation is similar to the path-goal theory of leadership described in Chapter 16. Both theories are personalized to subordinates' needs and goals. Managers' responsibility is to help subordinates meet their needs and at the same time attain organizational goals. Managers must try to find a match between a subordinate's skills and abilities and the job demands. To increase motivation, managers can clarify individuals' needs, define the outcomes available from the organization, and ensure that each individual has the ability and support (namely, time and equipment) needed to attain outcomes.

Some companies use expectancy theory principles by designing incentive systems that identify desired organizational outcomes and give everyone the same shot at getting the rewards. The trick is to design a system that fits with employees' abilities and needs. Consider the following example from the restaurant industry.

When Steve and Diane Warren, co-owners of Katzinger's Delicatessen in Columbus, Ohio, instituted open-book management, they hoped it would help them cut costs and save money. The Warrens trained employees in how to read the financials and told them Katzinger's would share the rewards with employees if financial performance improved. However, because most of their workers were young and mobile, not committed to a long-term career with the

Circuit City managers are using expectancy theory *principles to help meet employees' needs while attaining organizational goals. By creating an incentive program that is a commission-based plan designed to provide the highest compensation to sales counselors who are committed to serving every customer, Circuit City achieves its volume and profitability objectives. The incentive program is also used in other areas such as distribution, where employees are recognized for accomplishments in safety, productivity, and attendance.*

valence
The value or attraction an individual has for an outcome.

KATZINGER'S DELICATESSEN
http://www.katzingers.com

company, the vague long-range goals and rewards did not provide a high degree of motivation. Many of them felt that they could do little to improve overall performance and that doing so was the job of managers, anyway. Thus, both E → P expectancy and P → O expectancy were low. The Warrens needed a simple, short-term goal as a way to energize their young workers. They proposed a simple plan: If workers would help reduce food costs to below 35 percent of sales without sacrificing food quality or service, they would be rewarded with half the savings.

Katzinger's workers were well-trained and knew they had the skills and ability to meet the goal if they all worked together; thus, the E → P expectancy was high. Workers immediately began proposing ideas to reduce waste, such as matching perishable food orders more closely to expected sales. The P → O expectancy was also high because of the level of trust at the company; workers were highly motivated to cooperate to decrease food costs because they knew everyone would benefit from the savings. Since anyone could look at the financials, workers could actually track their progress toward meeting the goal. At the end of the first month, food costs had fallen nearly 2 percent and employees took home about $40 each from the savings. Later monthly payouts were as high as $95 per employee. By the end of the year, food consistency and service had improved and Katzinger's had indeed reduced its food costs to below 35 percent of total sales, saving the company $30,000. The Warrens gladly distributed $15,000 of that amount to their workers for helping to meet the goal. Now, the Warrens are working out a similar plan to increase sales at Katzinger's.[25] ❖

Reinforcement Perspective on Motivation

reinforcement theory
A motivation theory based on the relationship between a given behavior and its consequences.

The reinforcement approach to employee motivation sidesteps the issues of employee needs and thinking processes described in the content and process theories. **Reinforcement theory** simply looks at the relationship between behavior and its consequences. It focuses on changing or modifying the employees' on-the-job behavior through the appropriate use of immediate rewards and punishments.

Reinforcement Tools

behavior modification
The set of techniques by which reinforcement theory is used to modify human behavior.

law of effect
The assumption that positively reinforced behavior tends to be repeated and unreinforced or negatively reinforced behavior tends to be inhibited.

reinforcement
Anything that causes a given behavior to be repeated or inhibited.

Behavior modification is the name given to the set of techniques by which reinforcement theory is used to modify human behavior.[26] The basic assumption underlying behavior modification is the **law of effect**, which states that behavior that is positively reinforced tends to be repeated, and behavior that is not reinforced tends not to be repeated. **Reinforcement** is defined as anything that causes a certain behavior to be repeated or inhibited. The four reinforcement tools are positive reinforcement, avoidance learning, punishment, and extinction. Each type of reinforcement is a consequence of either a pleasant or unpleasant event being applied or withdrawn following a person's behavior. The four types of reinforcement are summarized in Exhibit 17.5.

Positive Reinforcement.   *Positive reinforcement* is the administration of a pleasant and rewarding consequence following a desired behavior. A good example of positive reinforcement is immediate praise for an employee who arrives on time or does a little extra in his or her work. The pleasant consequence will increase the likelihood of the excellent work behavior

Positive Reinforcement
Increases likelihood that
behavior will be repeated

Avoidance Learning
Increases likelihood that
behavior will be repeated

Punishment
Reduces likelihood that
behavior will be repeated

Extinction
Reduces likelihood that
behavior will be repeated

SOURCE: Based on Richard L. Daft and Richard M. Steers, *Organizations: A Micro/Macro Approach* (Glenview, Ill.: Scott, Foresman, 1986), 109.

Exhibit *17.5*

Changing Behavior with Reinforcement

occurring again. As another example, Frances Flood, CEO of Gentner Communications, a manufacturer of high-end audioconferencing equipment based in Salt Lake City, offered engineers a stake in the company's profits if they met targets for getting new products to market faster. Within two years, product development time had been slashed by 30 percent.[27] Studies have shown that positive reinforcement does help to improve performance. In addition, nonfinancial reinforcements such as positive feedback, social recognition, and attention are just as effective as financial incentives.[28]

Avoidance Learning.   *Avoidance learning* is the removal of an unpleasant consequence following a desired behavior. Avoidance learning is sometimes called *negative reinforcement*. Employees learn to do the right thing by avoiding unpleasant situations. Avoidance learning occurs when a supervisor stops criticizing or reprimanding an employee once the incorrect behavior has stopped.

Punishment.   *Punishment* is the imposition of unpleasant outcomes on an employee. Punishment typically occurs following undesirable behavior. For example, a supervisor may berate an employee for performing a task incorrectly. The supervisor expects that the negative outcome will serve as a punishment and reduce the likelihood of the behavior recurring. The use of punishment in organizations is controversial and often criticized because it fails to indicate the correct behavior. However, almost all managers report finding it necessary to occasionally impose forms of punishment ranging from verbal reprimands to employee suspensions or firings.[29]

Extinction.   *Extinction* is the withdrawal of a positive reward. Whereas with punishment, the supervisor imposes an unpleasant outcome such as a reprimand, extinction involves withholding pay raises, praise, and other positive outcomes. The idea is that behavior that is not positively reinforced will be less likely to occur in the future. For example, if a perpetually tardy employee fails to receive praise and pay raises, he or she will begin to realize that the behavior is not producing desired outcomes. The behavior will gradually disappear if it is continually nonreinforced.

Some executives use reinforcement theory very effectively to shape employees' behavior. Jack Welch, recently retired head of General Electric, was known as a master motivator. He used both positive and negative reinforcement through his famous handwritten notes either praising or prodding employees throughout the company. "The biggest job I have is to let people know how we feel about 'em," he once said. "You gotta tell them you love 'em and you gotta kick 'em in the [butt] when they're not doing their job. And you got to be able to hug 'em and kick 'em in the [butt] frequently."[30]

Schedules of Reinforcement

schedule of reinforcement
The frequency with which and intervals over which reinforcement occurs.

A great deal of research into reinforcement theory suggests that the timing of reinforcement has an impact on the speed of employee learning. **Schedules of reinforcement** pertain to the frequency with which and intervals over which reinforcement occurs. A reinforcement schedule can be selected to have maximum impact on employees' job behavior. There are five basic types of reinforcement schedules, which include continuous and four types of partial reinforcement.

continuous reinforcement schedule
A schedule in which every occurrence of the desired behavior is reinforced.

Continuous Reinforcement. With a **continuous reinforcement schedule**, every occurrence of the desired behavior is reinforced. This schedule can be very effective in the early stages of learning new types of behavior, because every attempt has a pleasant consequence.

partial reinforcement schedule
A schedule in which only some occurrences of the desired behavior are reinforced.

Partial Reinforcement. However, in the real world of organizations, it is often impossible to reinforce every correct behavior. With a **partial reinforcement schedule**, the reinforcement is administered only after some occurrences of the correct behavior. There are four types of partial reinforcement schedules: fixed interval, fixed ratio, variable interval, and variable ratio.

1. *Fixed-Interval Schedule.* The *fixed-interval schedule* rewards employees at specified time intervals. If an employee displays the correct behavior each day, reinforcement may occur every week. Regular paychecks or quarterly bonuses are examples of a fixed-interval reinforcement. At Leone Ackerly's Mini Maid franchise in Marietta, Georgia, workers are rewarded with an attendance bonus each pay period if they have gone to work every day on time and in uniform.[31]

2. *Fixed-Ratio Schedule.* With a *fixed-ratio schedule*, reinforcement occurs after a specified number of desired responses, say, after every fifth. For example, paying a field hand $1.50 for picking 10 pounds of peppers is a fixed-ratio schedule. Most piece-rate pay systems are considered fixed-ratio schedules.

3. *Variable-Interval Schedule.* With a *variable-interval schedule*, reinforcement is administered at random times that cannot be predicted by the employee. An example would be a random inspection by the manufacturing superintendent of the production floor, at which time he or she commends employees on their good behavior.

4. *Variable-Ratio Schedule.* The *variable-ratio schedule* is based on a random number of desired behaviors rather than on variable time periods. Reinforcement may occur sometimes after 5, 10, 15, or 20 displays of

behavior. One example is random monitoring of telemarketers, who may be rewarded after a certain number of calls in which they perform the appropriate behaviors and meet call performance specifications. Employees know they may be monitored but are never sure when checks will occur and when rewards may be given.

The schedules of reinforcement available to managers are illustrated in Exhibit 17.6. Continuous reinforcement is most effective for establishing new learning, but behavior is vulnerable to extinction. Partial reinforcement schedules are more effective for maintaining behavior over extended time periods. The most powerful is the variable-ratio schedule, because employee behavior will persist for a long time due to the administration of reinforcement only after a long interval.[32]

One example of a small business that successfully uses reinforcement theory is Emerald Packaging in Union City, California.

EMERALD PACKAGING

Emerald Packaging is a family-owned business that prints plastic bags for prepackaged salads and other vegetables. The company employs about 100 people and is the tenth largest manufacturer in Union City, California, located about 30 miles southeast of San Francisco.

Kevin Kelly, vice president of operations for Emerald, and other top managers wanted to fire up employees by developing a positive reinforcement scheme that would motivate and reward workers. The plan at Emerald includes the following:

1. *Monthly quality award.* Each month, managers pick the best print job in the plant from samples submitted by printing press employees. The winning press operator gets $100 and the operator's helper wins $50.
2. *Safety program.* When the company has three or fewer minor accidents and no lost-time accidents a quarter, leaders raffle off $1,000, provide workers with company shirts and jackets, and buy lunch for everyone. If employees make it through the entire year with only 12 minor accidents and no lost-time injuries, the company raffles a total of $10,000 to three winners and throws a party for all employees.
3. *Profit-sharing plan.* A certain percentage of operating profit is set aside into a bonus pool, which is shared among employees.

Exhibit *17.6*

Schedules of Reinforcement

Schedule of Reinforcement	Nature of Reinforcement	Effect on Behavior When Applied	Effect on Behavior When Withdrawn	Example
Continuous	Reward given after each desired behavior	Leads to fast learning of new behavior	Rapid extinction	Praise
Fixed-interval	Reward given at fixed time intervals	Leads to average and irregular performance	Rapid extinction	Weekly paycheck
Fixed-ratio	Reward given at fixed amounts of output	Quickly leads to very high and stable performance	Rapid extinction	Piece-rate pay system
Variable-interval	Reward given at variable times	Leads to moderately high and stable performance	Slow extinction	Performance appraisal and awards given at random times each month
Variable-ratio	Reward given at variable amounts of output	Leads to very high performance	Slow extinction	Sales bonus tied to number of sales calls, with random checks

Has Emerald's plan for reinforcing correct behaviors worked? Kelly reports that customer returns for poor quality are down 75 percent over last year. The quality rewards of $50 to $100 are substantial enough to get employees' attention and make it worth their while to put increased effort into producing a high-quality print job. So far, safety results are also impressive. During the first five months of the program, the company had only one minor accident. Employees are much more careful about how they conduct themselves on the job because no one wants to derail the raffle.[33] ❖

Reinforcement also works at such organizations as Campbell Soup Co., Emery Air Freight, Michigan Bell, and PSS World Medical, because managers reward appropriate behavior. They tell employees what they can do to receive reinforcement, tell them what they are doing wrong, distribute rewards equitably, tailor rewards to behaviors, and keep in mind that failure to reward deserving behavior has an equally powerful impact on employees. Communication is an important part of effective reinforcement because employees have to know what the rules are for getting rewards. At PSS World Medical, the bonus plan for sales representatives is communicated as a game, known as the "Field of Dreams," which has very clear rules and guidelines for how the bonus is calculated and what an employee must do to receive a bonus.[34]

Reward and punishment motivational practices dominate organizations, with as many as 94 percent of companies in the United States reporting that they use practices that reward performance or merit with pay.[35] In addition, a recent report by human resources consulting firm Towers Perrin indicates that incentive systems that reward employees with bonuses or other rewards for meeting certain goals are becoming increasingly popular. However, less than one-third of the companies reported seeing any noticeable impact of incentive pay on business results.[36] Despite the testimonies of numerous organizations that enjoy successful incentive programs, there is growing criticism of these so-called carrot-and-stick methods, as discussed in the Manager's Shoptalk box.

Job Design for Motivation

job design
The application of motivational theories to the structure of work for improving productivity and satisfaction.

A *job* in an organization is a unit of work that a single employee is responsible for performing. A job could include writing tickets for parking violators in New York City or doing long-range planning for the Discovery cable television channel. Jobs are important because performance of their components may provide rewards that meet employees' needs. An assembly-line worker may install the same bolt over and over, whereas an emergency room physician may provide each trauma victim with a unique treatment package. Managers need to know what aspects of a job provide motivation as well as how to compensate for routine tasks that have little inherent satisfaction. **Job design** is the application of motivational theories to the structure of work for improving productivity and satisfaction. Approaches to job design are generally classified as job simplification, job rotation, job enlargement, and job enrichment.

Job Simplification

job simplification
A job design whose purpose is to improve task efficiency by reducing the number of tasks a single person must do.

Job simplification pursues task efficiency by reducing the number of tasks one person must do. Job simplification is based on principles drawn from scientific management and industrial engineering. Tasks are designed to be simple,

THE NEW WORKPLACE

Manager's Shoptalk

The Carrot-and-Stick Controversy

Everybody thought Rob Rodin was crazy when he decided to wipe out all individual incentives for his sales force at Marshall Industries, a large distributor of electronic components based in El Monte, California. He did away with all bonuses, commissions, vacations, and other awards and rewards. All salespeople would receive a base salary plus the opportunity for profit sharing, which would be the same percent of salary for everyone, based on the entire company's performance. Six years later, Rodin says productivity per person has tripled at the company, but still he gets questions and criticism about his decision.

Rodin is standing right in the middle of a big controversy in modern management. Do financial and other rewards really motivate the kind of behavior organizations want and need? A growing number of critics say no, arguing that carrot-and-stick approaches are a holdover from the Industrial Age and are inappropriate and ineffective in today's economy. Today's workplace demands innovation and creativity from everyone—behaviors that rarely are inspired by money or other financial incentives. Reasons for criticism of carrot-and-stick approaches include the following:

1. *Extrinsic rewards diminish intrinsic rewards.* When people are motivated to seek an extrinsic reward, whether it be a bonus, an award, or the approval of a supervisor, generally they focus on the reward rather than on the work they do to achieve it. Thus, the intrinsic satisfaction people receive from performing their jobs actually declines. When people lack intrinsic rewards in their work, their performance stays just adequate to achieve the reward offered. In the worst case, employees may cover up mistakes, such as hiding an on-the-job accident in order to win a safety award.

2. *Extrinsic rewards are temporary.* Offering outside incentives may ensure short-term success, but not long-term high performance. When employees are focused only on the reward, they lose interest in their work. Without personal interest, the potential for exploration, creativity, and innovation disappears. Although the current deadline or goal may be met, better ways of working will not be discovered.

3. *Extrinsic rewards assume people are driven by lower-level needs.* Rewards such as bonuses, pay increases, and even praise presume that the primary reason people initiate and persist in behavior is to satisfy lower-level needs. However, particularly among today's knowledge workers, behavior also is based on yearnings for self-expression, and on feelings of self-esteem and self-worth. Offers of an extrinsic reward do not encourage the myriad behaviors that are motivated by people's need to express themselves and realize their higher needs for growth and fulfillment.

As Rob Rodin discovered at Marshall Industries, today's organizations need employees who are motivated to think, experiment, and continuously search for ways to solve new problems. Alfie Kohn, one of the most vocal critics of carrot-and-stick approaches, offers the following advice to managers regarding how to pay employees: "Pay well, pay fairly, and then do everything you can to get money off people's minds." Indeed there is some evidence that money is not primarily what people work for. Managers should understand the limits of extrinsic motivators and work to satisfy employees' higher, as well as lower, needs. To be motivated, employees need jobs that offer self-satisfaction in addition to a yearly pay raise.

SOURCES: Alfie Kohn, "Incentives Can Be Bad for Business," *Inc.* (January 1998), 93–94; A.J. Vogl, "Carrots, Sticks, and Self-Deception" (an interview with Alfie Kohn), *Across the Board* (January 1994), 39–44; and Geoffrey Colvin, "What Money Makes You Do," *Fortune* (August 17, 1998), 213–214.

repetitive, and standardized. As complexity is stripped from a job, the worker has more time to concentrate on doing more of the same routine task. Workers with low skill levels can perform the job, and the organization achieves a high level of efficiency. Indeed, workers are interchangeable, because they need little training or skill and exercise little judgment. As a motivational technique, however, job simplification has failed. People dislike routine and boring jobs and react in a number of negative ways, including sabotage, absenteeism, and unionization. Job simplification is compared with job rotation and job enlargement in Exhibit 17.7.

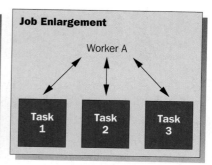

Exhibit *17.7*

Types of Job Design

job rotation
A job design that systematically moves employees from one job to another to provide them with variety and stimulation.

job enlargement
A job design that combines a series of tasks into one new, broader job to give employees variety and challenge.

job enrichment
A job design that incorporates achievement, recognition, and other high-level motivators into the work.

At the Frito-Lay plant in Lubbock, Texas, Julia Garcia used to just pack bags of chips into cardboard cartons. Today, she's interviewing new hires, refusing products that don't meet quality standards, and sending home excess workers if machines shut down. Hourly workers have been enjoying the benefits of job enlargement and job enrichment since Frito-Lay introduced work teams six years ago. Garcia's 11-member potato chip team is responsible for everything from potato processing to equipment maintenance.

Job Rotation

Job rotation systematically moves employees from one job to another, thereby increasing the number of different tasks an employee performs without increasing the complexity of any one job. For example, an autoworker may install windshields one week and front bumpers the next. Job rotation still takes advantage of engineering efficiencies, but it provides variety and stimulation for employees. Although employees may find the new job interesting at first, the novelty soon wears off as the repetitive work is mastered.

Companies such as National Steel, Motorola, and Dayton Hudson have built on the notion of job rotation to train a flexible workforce. As companies break away from ossified job categories, workers can perform several jobs, thereby reducing labor costs and giving employees opportunities to develop new skills. At Home Depot, for example, workers scattered throughout the company's vast chain of stores can get a taste of the corporate climate by working at in-store support centers, while associate managers can dirty their hands out on the sales floor.[37] Job rotation also gives companies greater flexibility. One production worker might shift among the jobs of drill operator, punch operator, and assembler, depending on the company's need at the moment. Some unions have resisted the idea, but many now go along, realizing that it helps the company be more competitive.[38]

Job Enlargement

Job enlargement combines a series of tasks into one new, broader job. This is a response to the dissatisfaction of employees with oversimplified jobs. Instead of only one job, an employee may be responsible for three or four and will have more time to do them. Job enlargement provides job variety and a greater challenge for employees. At Maytag, jobs were enlarged when work was redesigned such that workers assembled an entire water pump rather than doing each part as it reached them on the assembly line. Similarly, rather than just changing the oil at a Precision Tune location, a mechanic changes the oil, greases the car, airs the tires, checks fluid levels, battery, air filter, and so forth. Then, the same employee is responsible for consulting with the customer about routine maintenance or any problems he or she sees with the vehicle.

Job Enrichment

Recall the discussion of Maslow's need hierarchy and Herzberg's two-factor theory. Rather than just changing the number and frequency of tasks a worker performs, **job enrichment** incorporates high-level motivators into the work, including job responsibility, recognition, and opportunities for growth, learning, and achievement. In an enriched job, employees have control over the resources necessary for performing it, make decisions on how to do the work, experience personal growth, and set their own work pace. Many companies, including AT&T, Procter & Gamble, and Motorola, have undertaken job enrichment programs to increase employees' motivation and job satisfaction.

Managers at Ralcorp's cereal manufacturing plant in Sparks, Nevada, enriched jobs by combining several packing positions into a single job and cross-training employees to operate all of the packing line's equipment. In addition, assembly line employees screen, interview, and train all new hires. They are responsible for managing the production flow to and from their upstream and downstream partners, making daily decisions that affect their work, managing quality, and contributing to continuous improvement. Enriched jobs have improved employee motivation and satisfaction, and the company has benefited from higher long-term productivity, reduced costs, and happier employees.[39]

Job Characteristics Model

One significant approach to job design is the job characteristics model developed by Richard Hackman and Greg Oldham.[40] Hackman and Oldham's research concerned **work redesign**, which is defined as altering jobs to increase both the quality of employees' work experience and their productivity. Hackman and Oldham's research into the design of hundreds of jobs yielded the **job characteristics model**, which is illustrated in Exhibit 17.8. The model consists of three major parts: core job dimensions, critical psychological states, and employee growth-need strength.

Core Job Dimensions.
Hackman and Oldham identified five dimensions that determine a job's motivational potential:

1. *Skill variety.* The number of diverse activities that compose a job and the number of skills used to perform it. A routine, repetitive, assembly line job is low in variety, whereas an applied research position that entails working on new problems every day is high in variety.

work redesign
The altering of jobs to increase both the quality of employees' work experience and their productivity.

job characteristics model
A model of job design that comprises core job dimensions, critical psychological states, and employee growth-need strength.

Exhibit **17.8**

The Job Characteristics Model

SOURCE: Adapted from J. Richard Hackman and G. R. Oldham, "Motivation through the Design of Work: Test of a Theory," *Organizational Behavior and Human Performance* 16 (1976), 256.

For Jimmy Dunne, the new leader of the small Wall Street firm Sandler O'Neill & Partners, the task significance of his job changed drastically after planes slammed into the World Trade Center on September 11, 2001. Once the third member of Sandler's leadership team, Dunne is the only surviving leader and one of 17 of 83 people in the office that day who got out alive. Dunne considers his job important not only to present employees but also to the families of deceased co-workers.

2. *Task identity.* The degree to which an employee performs a total job with a recognizable beginning and ending. A chef who prepares an entire meal has more task identity than a worker on a cafeteria line who ladles mashed potatoes.

3. *Task significance.* The degree to which the job is perceived as important and having impact on the company or consumers. People who distribute penicillin and other medical supplies during times of emergencies would feel they have significant jobs.

4. *Autonomy.* The degree to which the worker has freedom, discretion, and self-determination in planning and carrying out tasks. A house painter can determine how to paint the house; a paint sprayer on an assembly line has little autonomy.

5. *Feedback.* The extent to which doing the job provides information back to the employee about his or her performance. Jobs vary in their ability to let workers see the outcomes of their efforts. A football coach knows whether the team won or lost, but a basic research scientist may have to wait years to learn whether a research project was successful.

The job characteristics model says that the more these five core characteristics can be designed into the job, the more the employees will be motivated and the higher will be performance, quality, and satisfaction.

Critical Psychological States.   The model posits that core job dimensions are more rewarding when individuals experience three psychological states in response to job design. In Exhibit 17.8, skill variety, task identity, and task significance tend to influence the employee's psychological state of *experienced meaningfulness of work*. The work itself is satisfying and provides intrinsic rewards for the worker. The job characteristic of autonomy influences the worker's *experienced responsibility*. The job characteristic of feedback provides the worker with *knowledge of actual results*. The employee thus knows how he or she is doing and can change work performance to increase desired outcomes.

Personal and Work Outcomes.   The impact of the five job characteristics on the psychological states of experienced meaningfulness, responsibility, and knowledge of actual results leads to the personal and work outcomes of high work motivation, high work performance, high satisfaction, and low absenteeism and turnover.

Employee Growth-Need Strength.   The final component of the job characteristics model is called *employee growth-need strength*, which means that people have different needs for growth and development. If a person wants to satisfy low-level needs, such as safety and belongingness, the job characteristics model has less effect. When a person has a high need for growth and development, including the desire for personal challenge, achievement, and challenging work, the model is especially effective. People with a high need to grow and expand their abilities respond favorably to the application of the model and to improvements in core job dimensions.

One application of the job characteristics model that worked extremely well took place at Sequins International Inc.

SEQUINS INTERNATIONAL INC.
http://www.sequins.com

Sequins International Inc., based in Woodside, New York, faces tough global competition, particularly from factories in China and India, where women and children hand sew sequins for meager wages, producing $100 million in wholesale goods annually. To compete, U.S. manufacturers use machines that were first developed in the 1940s. The machines save labor but create other problems: The repetitive motions used in the process produce an array of muscle pains as well as mind-numbing boredom. With funding from the Ergonomics Project, administrated by the International Ladies Garment Workers Union, Sequins International redesigned the machines to reduce the physical stresses experienced by sequin makers. The use of adjustable chairs and machinery, along with automatic spooling devices, cut worker's compensation costs to $800 in 1999, down from $98,000 five years earlier. At the same time, skill variety was increased, as inspection jobs that were once performed separately were integrated into the manufacturing process. This gave workers increased task identity and a greater stake in quality control.

Because Sequins' workforce is 80 percent Hispanic and many workers have poor English skills, the company offers English lessons during lunch hours three times a week. Classes in mathematics and statistical process control are also available to train workers for a variety of new tasks. Two teams, one for product satisfaction and the other for customer support, monitor quality control and machine maintenance as part of the production process, as well as provide operators with ongoing feedback and training.

These improvements in job design and motivation dramatically increased worker satisfaction. As a result, absenteeism and costs are down and productivity has increased.[41] ❖

Motivating in the New Workplace

Despite the controversy over carrot-and-stick motivational practices discussed in the Shoptalk box earlier in this chapter, organizations are increasingly using various types of incentive compensation as a way to motivate employees to higher levels of performance. Exhibit 17.9 summarizes several methods of incentive pay. These programs can be effective if they are used appropriately and combined with motivational ideas that provide employees with intrinsic rewards and meet higher-level needs. Effective organizations do not use incentive pay plans as the sole basis of motivation.

In addition, many organizations are giving employees a voice in how pay and incentive systems are designed, which increases motivation by increasing employees' sense of involvement and control.[42] At Premium Standard Farms' pork-processing plant, for example, managers hired a consultant to help slaughterhouse workers design and implement an incentive program. Annual payouts to employees for 2000 were around $1,000 per employee. More important, though, is that workers feel a greater sense of dignity and purpose in their jobs, which has helped to reduce turnover significantly. As one employee put it, "Now I have the feeling that this is my company, too."[43] The most effective motivational programs typically involve much more than money. Two recent motivational trends are empowering employees and designing work to have greater meaning.

Empowerment

Empowerment is the delegation of power or authority to subordinates in an organization.[44] Increasing employee power heightens motivation for task accomplishment because people improve their own effectiveness, choosing

empowerment
The delegation of power or authority to subordinates.

Exhibit *17.9*

New Motivational Compensation Programs

Program Name	Purpose
Pay for Performance	Rewards individual employees in proportion to their performance contributions. Also called merit pay.
Gain Sharing	Rewards all employees and managers within a business unit when predetermined performance targets are met. Encourages teamwork.
Employee Stock Ownership Plan (ESOP)	Gives employees part ownership of the organization, enabling them to share in improved profit performance.
Lump-Sum Bonuses	Rewards employees with a one-time cash payment based on performance.
Pay for Knowledge	Links employee salary with the number of task skills acquired. Workers are motivated to learn the skills for many jobs, thus increasing company flexibility and efficiency.
Flexible Work Schedule	Flextime allows workers to set their own hours. Job sharing allows two or more part-time workers to jointly cover one job. Telecommuting, sometimes called flex-place, allows employees to work from home or an alternate workspace.
Team-based Compensation	Rewards employees for behavior and activities that benefit the team, such as cooperation, listening, and empowering others.

how to do a task and using their creativity.[45] Most people come into an organization with the desire to do a good job, and empowerment releases the motivation that is already there.

AES Corporation, is an Arlington, Virginia, electricity producer with facilities all over the world. Every aspect of its organization is designed to give employees "the power and the responsibility to make important decisions, to engage with their work as businesspeople, not as cogs in a machine," as CEO Dennis Bakke puts it.[46] Empowerment at AES has released employee creativity, motivation, and energy by providing employees with challenging work and the information and power to make a difference every day for themselves and for the company.

Empowering employees means giving them four elements that enable them to act more freely to accomplish their jobs: information, knowledge, power, and rewards.[47]

1. *Employees receive information about company performance.* In companies where employees are fully empowered, such as Semco, a Brazilian manufacturing company, all employees have access to all financial and operational information.

2. *Employees have knowledge and skills to contribute to company goals.* Companies use training programs to help employees acquire the knowledge and skills they need to contribute to organizational performance. For example, when DMC, which makes pet supplies, gave employee teams the authority and responsibility for assembly-line shutdowns, it provided extensive training on how to diagnose and interpret line malfunctions, as well as the costs related to shut-down and start-up. Employees worked through several case studies to practice decision making related to line shut-downs.[48]

eBay is growing 72 percent a year, and Wall Street is wild about the stock. How can a dot-com be this hot? One factor contributing to eBay's success is empowerment, the delegation of power and authority to the company's 2,400 employees. For example, CEO Meg Whitman, a onetime Procter & Gamble brand manager, Bain consultant, and Hasbro division manager, empowers her deputies to manage categories (toys, cars, collectibles) much as brand managers at P&G do Bounty or Tide. Highly motivated eBay employees have enabled the online auction site to attract 37 million customers with ever-increasing profits: $129 million in a recent year.

© AP/Wide World Photo

3. *Employees have the power to make substantive decisions.* Workers have the authority to directly influence work procedures and organizational performance, often through quality circles or self-directed work teams. Semco pushes empowerment to the limits by allowing its employees to choose what they do, how they do it, and even how they get compensated for it. Employees set their own pay by choosing from a list of 11 different pay options, such as set salary or a combination of salary and incentives.[49]

4. *Employees are rewarded based on company performance.* Organizations that empower workers often reward them based on the results shown in the company's bottom line. For example, at Semco, in addition to employee-determined compensation, a company profit-sharing plan gives each employee an even share of 23 percent of his or her department's profits each quarter.[50] Organizations may also use other motivational compensation programs described in Exhibit 17.9 to tie employee efforts to company performance.

Many of today's organizations are implementing empowerment programs, but they are empowering workers to varying degrees. At some companies, empowerment means encouraging workers' ideas while managers retain final authority for decisions; at others it means giving employees almost complete freedom and power to make decisions and exercise initiative and imagination.[51] Current methods of empowerment fall along a continuum, as illustrated in Exhibit 17.10. The continuum runs from a situation in which front-line workers have almost no discretion, such as on a traditional assembly line, to full empowerment, where workers even participate in formulating organizational strategy. An example of full empowerment is when self-directed teams are given the authority to hire, discipline, and dismiss team members and to set compensation rates.

Research indicates that most people have a need for *self-efficacy*, which is the capacity to produce results or outcomes, to feel that they are effective.[52] By meeting higher-level needs, empowerment can provide powerful motivation.

Giving Meaning to Work

The new workplace recognizes that the way to create engaged, motivated employees and high performance has less to do with extrinsic rewards such as pay and much more to do with fostering an environment in which people can flourish. There is a growing recognition that it is the behavior of managers that makes the biggest difference in employee motivation and whether people flourish in the workplace. A Gallup Organization study conducted over 25 years found that the single most important variable in whether employees feel good about their work is the relationship between employees and their direct supervisor.[53]

In the new workplace, the manager's role is not to control others but to organize the workplace in such a way that each person can learn, contribute, and grow. The most successful managers realize that they actually have less control than their subordinates—it is only through other people that managers can accomplish anything. Good managers channel employee motivation toward the accomplishment of goals by tapping into each individual's unique set of talents, skills, interests, attitudes, and needs. By treating each employee as an individual, managers can put people in the right jobs and provide intrinsic rewards to every employee every day. Then, managers make sure people have what they need to perform, clearly define the desired outcomes, and get out of the way.

Exhibit *17.10*

A Continuum of Empowerment

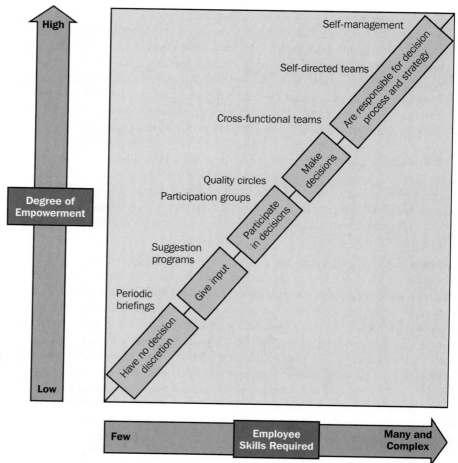

SOURCES: Based on Robert C. Ford and Myron D. Fottler, "Empowerment: A Matter of Degree," *Academy of Management Executive* 9, no. 3 (1995), 21–31; Lawrence Holpp, "Applied Empowerment," *Training* (February 1994), 39–44; and David P. McCaffrey, Sue R. Faerman, and David W. Hart, "The Appeal and Difficulties of Participative Systems," *Organization Science* 6, no. 6 (November–December 1995), 603–627.

One way to evaluate how a manager or a company is doing in meeting higher-level needs is a metric developed by the Gallup researchers called the Q12. When a majority of employees can answer these twelve questions positively, the organization enjoys a highly motivated and productive workforce:

1. Do I know what is expected of me at work?
2. Do I have the materials and equipment that I need in order to do my work right?
3. At work, do I have the opportunity to do what I do best every day?
4. In the past seven days, have I received recognition or praise for doing good work?
5. Does my supervisor, or someone at work, seem to care about me as a person?
6. Is there someone at work who encourages my development?
7. At work, do my opinions seem to count?
8. Does the mission or purpose of my company make me feel that my job is important?
9. Are my coworkers committed to doing quality work?
10. Do I have a best friend at work?
11. In the past six months, has someone at work talked to me about my progress?
12. This past year, have I had opportunities to learn and grow?[54]

Results of the Gallup study show that organizations where employees give high marks on the Q12 have less turnover, are more productive and profitable, and enjoy greater employee and customer loyalty. For example, among 400 Best Buy retail outlets, the store that scored the highest on the Q12 ranks in the top 10 percent, while the store with the lowest score ranks in the bottom 10 percent on financial performance.[55] When employees are more engaged and motivated, they—and their organizations—thrive.

■ Summary and Management Solution

This chapter introduced a number of important ideas about the motivation of people in organizations. The content theories of motivation focus on the nature of underlying employee needs. Maslow's hierarchy of needs, Alderfer's ERG theory, Herzberg's two-factor theory, and McClelland's acquired needs theory all suggest that people are motivated to meet a range of needs. Process theories examine how people go about selecting rewards with which to meet needs. Equity theory says that people compare their contributions and outcomes with others' and are motivated to maintain a feeling of equity. Expectancy theory suggests that people calculate the probability of achieving certain outcomes. Managers can increase motivation by treating employees fairly and by clarifying employee paths toward meeting their needs. Still another motivational approach is reinforcement theory, which says that employees learn to behave in certain ways based on the availability of reinforcements.

The application of motivational ideas is illustrated in job design and other motivational programs. Job design approaches include job simplification, job rotation, job enlargement, job enrichment, and the job characteristics model. Managers can change the structure of work to meet employees' high-level needs. The recent trend toward empowerment motivates by giving employees more information and authority to make decisions in their work while connecting compensation to the results. Managers create the environment that determines employee motivation. One way to measure the factors that determine whether people are engaged and motivated at work is the Q12, a list of 12 questions about the day-to-day realities of a person's job. Other motivational programs include pay for performance, gain sharing, ESOPs, lump-sum bonuses, pay for knowledge, flexible work schedules, and team-based compensation.

A highly successful application of motivational ideas occurred for factory workers at Sandstrom Products. Recall from the chapter opening case that Leo Henkelman was an alienated mill operator considering quitting. When top management empowered workers by implementing open-book management, Henkelman was given the opportunity to take on more responsibility, learn new skills, and make improvements. He learned his own strengths and limitations in the process. While serving as a temporary plant manager, he found that delegation was not his strength—doing was. When a technician job opened up in the lab, he applied. Although he lacked the educational background normally required, the lab director gave him a chance. Now, using his experience, Henkelman guides the manufacturing process from beginning to end, working with customers to develop new products and refine old ones. As his skills and responsibilities increased, so did his pay, thanks to a proficiency pay system that based his pay on his skills and accomplishments and a gain-sharing plan that allowed him to share in the company's profits. By trusting and empowering workers, Sandstrom gave them a reason to care about the company and the knowledge and power to make personal contributions to organizational performance. Results were staggering as Sandstrom rebounded from a loss of $100,000 to earnings of almost $800,000 two years later.[56]

Discussion Questions

1. In the aftermath of the September 11, 2001, terrorist attack, the U.S. government federalized airport security workers. Many argued that simply making screeners federal workers would not solve the root problem: bored, low-paid, and poorly trained security workers have little motivation to be vigilant. How might these employees be motivated to provide the security that travel conditions now demand?

2. One small company recognizes an employee of the month, who is given a parking spot next to the president's space near the front door. What theories would explain the positive motivation associated with this policy?

3. Campbell Soup Company reduces accidents with a lottery. Each worker who works 30 days or more without losing a day for a job-related accident is eligible to win prizes in a raffle drawing. Why has this program been successful?

4. One executive argues that managers have too much safety because of benefit and retirement plans. He rewards his managers for taking risks and has removed many guaranteed benefits. Would this approach motivate managers? Why?

5. If an experienced secretary discovered that she made less money than a newly hired janitor, how would she react? What inputs and outcomes might she evaluate to make this comparison?

6. Would you rather work for a supervisor high in need for achievement, need for affiliation, or need for power? Why? What are the advantages and disadvantages of each?

7. A survey of teachers found that two of the most important rewards were the belief that their work was important and a feeling of accomplishment. Is this consistent with Hackman and Oldham's job characteristics model?

8. The teachers in question 7 also reported that pay and benefits were poor, yet they continued to teach. Use Herzberg's two-factor theory to explain this finding.

9. What theories explain why employees who score high on the Q12 questionnaire are typically highly motivated and productive?

10. How can empowerment lead to higher motivation? Could a manager's empowerment efforts sometimes contribute to demotivation as well? Discuss.

11. What characteristics of individuals determine the extent to which work redesign will have a positive impact on work satisfaction and work effectiveness?

Management in Practice: Experiential Exercise

What Motivates You?

You are to indicate how important each characteristic is to you. Answer according to your feelings about the most recent job you had or about the job you currently hold. Circle the number on the scale that represents your feeling—1 (very unimportant) to 7 (very important).

When you have completed the questionnaire, score it as follows:

Rating for question 5 = ___. Divide by 1 = ___ security.
Rating for questions 9 and 13 = ___ . Divide by 2 = ___ social.

Rating for questions 1, 3, and 7 = ___. Divide by 3 = ___ esteem.
Rating for questions 4, 10, 11, and 12 = ___. Divide by 4 = ___ autonomy.
Rating for questions 2, 6, and 8 = ___. Divide by 3 = ___ self-actualization.

The instructor has national norm scores for presidents, vice presidents, and upper middle-level, lower middle-level, and lower-level managers with which you can compare your *mean* importance scores. How do your scores compare with the scores of managers working in organizations?

1. The feeling of self-esteem a person gets from being in that job	1	2	3	4	5	6	7
2. The opportunity for personal growth and development in that job	1	2	3	4	5	6	7
3. The prestige of the job inside the company (that is, regard received from others in the company)	1	2	3	4	5	6	7
4. The opportunity for independent thought and action in that job	1	2	3	4	5	6	7
5. The feeling of security in that job	1	2	3	4	5	6	7

6. The feeling of self-fulfillment a person gets from being in that position (that is, the feeling of being able to use one's own unique capabilities, realizing one's potential)   1 2 3 4 5 6 7
7. The prestige of the job outside the company (that is, the regard received from others not in the company)   1 2 3 4 5 6 7
8. The feeling of worthwhile accomplishment in that job   1 2 3 4 5 6 7
9. The opportunity in that job to give help to other people   1 2 3 4 5 6 7
10. The opportunity in that job for participation in the setting of goals   1 2 3 4 5 6 7
11. The opportunity in that job for participation in the determination of methods and procedures   1 2 3 4 5 6 7
12. The authority connected with the job   1 2 3 4 5 6 7
13. The opportunity to develop close friendships in the job   1 2 3 4 5 6 7

SOURCE: Lyman W. Porter, *Organizational Patterns of Managerial Job Attitudes* (New York: American Foundation for Management Research, 1964), 17, 19. Used with permission.

■ Management in Practice: Ethical Dilemma

Compensation Showdown

When Suzanne Lebeau, human resources manager, received a call from Bert Wilkes, comptroller of Farley Glass Works, she anticipated hearing good news to share with the Wage and Bonus Committee. She had already seen numbers to indicate that the year-end bonus plan, which was instituted by her committee in lieu of the traditional guaranteed raises of the past, was going to exceed expectations. It was a real relief to her, because the plan, devised by a committee representing all levels of the workforce, had taken eleven months to complete. It had also been a real boost to morale at a low point in the company's history. Workers at the glass shower production plant were bringing new effort and energy to their jobs, and Lebeau wanted to see them rewarded.

She was shocked to see Wilkes's face so grim when she arrived for her meeting. "We have a serious problem, Suzanne," Wilkes said to open the meeting. "We ran the numbers from third quarter to project our end-of-the-year figures and discovered that the executive bonus objectives, which are based on net operating profit, would not be met if we paid out the employee bonuses first. The executive bonuses are a major source of their income. We can't ask them to do without their salary to ensure a bonus for the workers."

Lebeau felt her temper rising. After all their hard work, she was not going to sit by and watch the employees be disappointed because the accounting department had not structured the employee bonus plan to work with the executive plan. She was afraid they would undo all the good that the bonus plan had done in motivating the plant workers. They had kept their end of the bargain, and the company's high profits were common knowledge in the plant.

What Do You Do?

1. Ask to appear before the executive committee to argue that the year-end bonus plan for workers be honored. Executives could defer their bonuses until the problem in the structure of the compensation plan is resolved.
2. Go along with the comptroller. It isn't fair for the executives to lose so much money. Begin to prepare the workers to not expect much this first year of the plan.
3. Go to the board of directors and ask for a compromise plan that splits the bonuses between the executives and the workers.

SOURCE: Based on Doug Wallace, "Promises to Keep," *What Would You Do?* (reprinted from *Business Ethics*), vol. II (July–August 1993), 11–12. Reprinted with permission from *Business Ethics Magazine*, P.O. Box 8439, Minneapolis, MN 55408 (612) 879-0695.

■ Surf the Net

1. **Acquired Needs Theory.** Take the motivation quiz at one of the sites listed (the same questions appear at both sites).

    http://www.snc.edu/socsci/chair/333/motvquiz.htm
    http://www.pertinent.com/pertinfo/business/exercises/motivate.html

    After following the scoring instructions at the site, print your scores in the spaces provided. The highest score indicates what your dominant need is and what motivates you most. Were you surprised by the results?

    Achievement _____   Power _____

    Affiliation _____

2. **Meaningful Workplace.** Go to the "Download Center" at

http://www.meaningatwork.com

Locate an article of interest and print it out. As you read the article, highlight key points and submit the highlighted article to your instructor.

3. **Motivating in the New Workplace.** Go to *http://www. walmartstores.com*, find the "Benefits" link under "Careers." Check out the benefits offered to Wal-Mart employees and identify two benefits/motivators discussed in the section of the chapter "Motivating in the New Workplace."

■ Case for Critical Analysis

Kimbel's Department Store

Frances Patterson has been reading about a quiet revolution sweeping department store retailing and has decided to give it a try. At stores such as Bloomingdale's and Bergdorf Goodman, managers are using commission pay to motivate salespeople. At Bergdorf's, for example, a top-tier salesperson in women's apparel can earn nearly $200,000 a year.

Patterson wants to implement commission pay at Kimbel's, a regional chain of upscale department stores based in St. Louis. Kimbel's has long used commissions in departments such as electronics and appliances, where extra sales skill pays off, but Patterson believes extending the system storewide will attract better salespeople, increase motivation, and enable employees to earn more money. For example, under the old plan, a new salesclerk in women's wear would earn about $18,000 a year based on hourly wages and a 0.5 percent commission on $500,000 in sales. Under the new plan, the annual pay would be $35,000 based on 7 percent commission on sales of $500,000. Patterson implemented the new system in two area stores first and plans to roll it out across the chain within the next six months.

Juan Santore, who works in the men's shoe salon, is enthusiastic about the changeover. His pay has increased an average of $150 per week. But in other departments, such as women's lingerie, employees are less enthusiastic. Making enough sales per week to earn their previous salary is nearly impossible, particularly when the economy slows down. Even during the

holiday season, many employees saw their pay decrease an average of 8 percent.

Patterson is keeping a close eye on fluctuations in pay. She's becoming concerned that the commission system may not work as well for small-item purchases as it does for big-ticket items. In addition, one question is whether Kimbel's can meet its goal of creating more customer-oriented salespeople when they work on commission. Clerks may be less willing to handle complaints, make returns, and clean shelves, preferring instead to chase customers. Moreover, it will cost Kimbel's nearly $1 million per store to install the commission system because of training programs, computer upgrades, and increased pay in many departments. If the overall impact on service is negative, the increased efficiency might not seem worthwhile.

Questions

1. What theories about motivation underlie the switch from salary to commission pay?
2. Are high-level needs met under the commission system?
3. As a customer, would you prefer to shop where employees are motivated to make commissions?

SOURCES: Based on Francine Schwadel, "Chain Finds Incentives a Hard Sell," *The Wall Street Journal* (July 5, 1990), B4; Amy Dunkin, "Now Salespeople Really Must Sell for Their Supper," *BusinessWeek* (July 31, 1989), 50–52; and Terry Pristin, "Retailing's Elite Keep the Armani Moving Off the Racks," *The New York Times* (December 22, 2001), D1.

■ Endnotes

1. David Whitford, "Before & After," *Inc.* (June 1995), 44–50.
2. David Silburt, "Secrets of the Super Sellers," *Canadian Business* (January 1987), 54–59; "Meet the Savvy Supersalesmen," *Fortune* (February 4, 1985), 56–62; Michael Brody, "Meet Today's Young American Worker," *Fortune* (November 11, 1985), 90–98; and Tom Richman, "Meet the Masters. They Could Sell You Anything . . .," *Inc.* (March 1985), 79–86.
3. Richard M. Steers and Lyman W. Porter, eds., *Motivation and Work Behavior*, 3d ed. (New York: McGraw-Hill, 1983); Don Hellriegel, John W. Slocum, Jr., and Richard W. Woodman, *Organizational Behavior*, 7th ed. (St. Paul, Minn.: West,

1995), 170; and Jerry L. Gray and Frederick A. Starke, *Organizational Behavior: Concepts and Applications*, 4th ed. (New York: Macmillan, 1988), 104–105.
4. Carol Hymowitz, "Readers Tell Tales of Success and Failure Using Rating Systems," (In the Lead column), *The Wall Street Journal* (May 29, 2001), B1.
5. Linda Grant, "Happy Workers, High Returns," *Fortune* (January 12, 1998), 81.
6. Steers and Porter, *Motivation*.
7. J.F. Rothlisberger and W.J. Dickson, *Management and the Worker* (Cambridge, Mass.: Harvard University Press, 1939).

Endnotes 575

8. Abraham F. Maslow, "A Theory of Human Motivation," *Psychological Review* 50 (1943), 370–396.

9. Roberta Maynard, "How to Motivate Low-Wage Workers," *Nation's Business* (May 1997), 35–39.

10. Clayton Alderfer, *Existence, Relatedness and Growth* (New York: Free Press, 1972).

11. Jeff Barbian, "C'mon, Get Happy," *Training* (January 2001), 92–96.

12. Ibid.

13. Pamela Kruger, "Stop the Insanity," *Fast Company* (July 2000), 240–254.

14. Frederick Herzberg, "One More Time: How Do You Motivate Employees?" *Harvard Business Review* (January–February 1968), 53–62.

15. William C. Symonds, "Where Paternalism Equals Good Business," *BusinessWeek* (July 20, 1998), 16E4–16E6.

16. David C. McClelland, *Human Motivation* (Glenview, Ill.: Scott, Foresman, 1985).

17. Carol Hymowitz, "For Many Executives, Leadership Lessons Started with Mom," (In the Lead column), *The Wall Street Journal* (May 16, 2000), B1.

18. David C. McClelland, "The Two Faces of Power," in *Organizational Psychology*, ed. D.A. Colb, I.M. Rubin, and J.M. McIntyre (Englewood Cliffs, N.J.: Prentice-Hall, 1971), 73–86.

19. J. Stacy Adams, "Injustice in Social Exchange," in *Advances in Experimental Social Psychology*, 2d ed., ed. L. Berkowitz (New York: Academic Press, 1965); and J. Stacy Adams, "Toward an Understanding of Inequity," *Journal of Abnormal and Social Psychology* (November 1963), 422–436.

20. Ray V. Montagno, "The Effects of Comparison to Others and Primary Experience on Responses to Task Design," *Academy of Management Journal* 28 (1985), 491–498; and Robert P. Vecchio, "Predicting Worker Performance in Inequitable Settings," *Academy of Management Review* 7 (1982), 103–110.

21. John Peterman, "The Rise and Fall of the J. Peterman Company," *Harvard Business Review* (September–October 1999), 59–66.

22. James E. Martin and Melanie M. Peterson, "Two-Tier Wage Structures: Implications for Equity Theory," *Academy of Management Journal* 30 (1987), 297–315.

23. Victor H. Vroom, *Work and Motivation* (New York: Wiley, 1964); B.S. Gorgopoulos, G.M. Mahoney, and N. Jones, "A Path-Goal Approach to Productivity," *Journal of Applied Psychology* 41 (1957), 345–353; and E.E. Lawler III, *Pay and Organizational Effectiveness: A Psychological View* (New York: McGraw-Hill, 1981).

24. Richard L. Daft and Richard M. Steers, *Organizations: A Micro/Macro Approach* (Glenview, Ill.: Scott, Foresman, 1986).

25. Mike Hofman, "Everyone's a Cost Cutter," *Inc.* (July 1998), 117; and Abby Livingston, "Gain-Sharing Encourages Productivity," *Nation's Business* (January 1998), 21–22.

26. Alexander D. Stajkovic and Fred Luthans, "A Meta-Analysis of the Effects of Organizational Behavior Modification on Task Performance, 1975–95," *Academy of Management Journal* (October 1997), 1122–1149; H. Richlin, *Modern Behaviorism* (San Francisco: Freeman,

1970); and B.F. Skinner, *Science and Human Behavior* (New York: Macmillan, 1953).

27. Lea Goldman, "Over the Top," *Forbes* (October 29, 2001), 146–147.

28. Stajkovic and Luthans, "A Meta-Analysis of the Effects of Organizational Behavior Modification on Task Performance, 1975–95," and Fred Luthans and Alexander D. Stajkovic, "Reinforce for Performance: The Need to Go Beyond Pay and Even Rewards," *Academy of Management Executive* 13, no. 2 (1999), 49–57.

29. Kenneth D. Butterfield and Linda Klebe Trevino, "Punishment from the Manager's Perspective: A Grounded Investigation and Inductive Model," *Academy of Management Journal* 39, no. 6 (December 1996), 1479–1512; and Andrea Casey, "Voices from the Firing Line: Managers Discuss Punishment in the Workplace," *Academy of Management Executive* 11, no. 3 (1997), 93–94.

30. Pamela L. Moore with Diane Brady, "Running the House That Jack Built," *BusinessWeek* (October 2, 2000), 130–138.

31. Roberta Maynard, "How to Motivate Low-Wage Workers."

32. L.M. Sarri and G.P. Latham, "Employee Reaction to Continuous and Variable Ratio Reinforcement Schedules Involving a Monetary Incentive," *Journal of Applied Psychology* 67 (1982), 506–508; and R.D. Pritchard, J. Hollenback, and P. J. DeLeo, "The Effects of Continuous and Partial Schedules of Reinforcement on Effort, Performance, and Satisfaction," *Organizational Behavior and Human Performance* 25 (1980), 336–353.

33. Kevin Kelly, "Firing Up the Team," *Business Week Frontier* (May 24, 1999), F32.

34. Charles A. O'Reilly III and Jeffrey Pfeffer, "Star Makers," book excerpt from *From Hidden Value: How Great Companies Achieve Extraordinary Results with Ordinary People* (Harvard Business School Press, 2000), published in *CIO* (September 15, 2000), 226–246.

35. A.J. Vogl, "Carrots, Sticks, and Self-Deception" (an interview with Alfie Kohn), *Across the Board* (January 1994), 39–44.

36. Hilary Rosenberg, "Building a Better Carrot," *CFO* (June 2001), 64–70.

37. Barbian, "C'mon, Get Happy."

38. Norm Alster, "What Flexible Workers Can Do," *Fortune* (February 13, 1989), 62–66.

39. Glenn L. Dalton, "The Collective Stretch," *Management Review* (December 1998), 54–59.

40. J. Richard Hackman and Greg R. Oldham, *Work Redesign* (Reading, Mass.: Addison-Wesley, 1980); and J. Richard Hackman and Greg Oldham, "Motivation through the Design of Work: Test of a Theory," *Organizational Behavior and Human Performance* 16 (1976), 250–279.

41. Barbara Ettorre, "Retooling People and Processes," *Management Review* (June 1995), 19–23; and Albert R. Karr, "A Special News Report about Life on the Job—and Trends Taking Shape There," *The Wall Street Journal* (November 16, 1999), A1.

42. Ann Podolske, "Giving Employees a Voice in Pay Structures," *Business Ethics* (March–April 1998), 12.

43. Rekha Balu, "Bonuses Aren't Just For the Bosses," *Fast Company* (December 2000), 74–76.

44. Edwin P. Hollander and Lynn R. Offermann, "Power and Leadership in Organizations," *American Psychologist* 45 (February 1990), 179–189.

45. Jay A. Conger and Rabindra N. Kanungo, "The Empowerment Process: Integrating Theory and Practice," *Academy of Management Review* 13 (1988), 471–482.

46. Bradley L, Kirkman and Benson Rosen, "Powering Up Teams," *Organizational Dynamics* (Winter 2000), 48–66.

47. David E. Bowen and Edward E. Lawler III, "The Empowerment of Service Workers: What, Why, How, and When," *Sloan Management Review* (Spring 1992), 31–39; and Ray W. Coye and James A. Belohav, "An Exploratory Analysis of Employee Participation," *Group and Organization Management* 20, no. 1, (March 1995), 4–17.

48. Russ Forrester, "Empowerment: Rejuvenating a Potent Idea," *Academy of Management Executive* 14, No. 3 (2000), 67–80.

49. Ricardo Semler, "How We Went Digital Without a Strategy," *Harvard Business Review* (September–October 2000), 51–58.

50. Podolske, "Giving Employees a Voice in Pay Structures."

51. This discussion is based on Robert C. Ford and Myron D. Fottler, "Empowerment: A Matter of Degree," *Academy of Management Executive* 9, no. 3 (1995), 21–31.

52. Jay A. Conger and Rabindra N. Kanungo, "The Empowerment Process: Integrating Theory and Practice," *Academy of Management Review* 13 (1998), 471–482.

53. This discussion is based on Tony Schwartz, "The Greatest Sources of Satisfaction in the Workplace are Internal and Emotional," *Fast Company* (November 2000), 398–402; and Marcus Buckingham and Curt Coffman, *First, Break All the Rules: What the World's Greatest Managers Do Differently* (New York: Simon & Schuster, 1999).

54. The Gallup Organization, Princeton, NJ. All rights reserved. Used with permission.

55. Polly LaBarre, "Marcus Buckingham Thinks Your Boss Has an Attitude Problem" *Fast Company* (August 2001), 88-98.

56. Whitford, "Before and After."

Communicating in Organizations

CHAPTER OUTLINE

Communication and the Manager's Job

What Is Communication?

The Communication Process

Communicating Among People

Communication Channels

Persuasion and Influence

Nonverbal Communication

Listening

Organizational Communication

Formal Communication Channels

Team Communication Channels

Informal Communication Channels

Communicating in the New Workplace

Open Communication

Dialogue

Feedback and Learning

Managing Organizational Communication

Barriers to Communication

Overcoming Communication Barriers

LEARNING OBJECTIVES

After studying this chapter, you should be able to

1 Explain why communication is essential for effective management and describe how nonverbal behavior and listening affect communication among people.

2 Explain how managers use communication to persuade and influence others.

3 Describe the concept of channel richness, and explain how communication channels influence the quality of communication.

4 Explain the difference between formal and informal organizational communications and the importance of each for organization management.

5 Identify how structure influences team communication outcomes.

6 Explain why open communication, dialogue, and feedback are essential approaches to communication in the new workplace.

7 Describe barriers to organizational communication, and suggest ways to avoid or overcome them.

Management Challenge

For over a quarter of a century, Childress Buick/Kia Co. had served the Phoenix area, gaining a reputation as a top Buick dealer. The family-owned dealership prided itself on good communication and quality service, and its customer retention rate was 40 percent higher than the industry average. Founder and president George Ray Childress, affectionately known as "Mr. C," constantly looked for ways to help his employees reach their personal and professional potential, and he jumped at the chance to add computer technology to the business. By the time Childress discovered that the computer system was inadequate, system snafus were creating long lines of disgruntled customers and a workforce of bickering, stressed-out employees. Sales were falling, and the dealership's CSI (customer service index) plummeted. Mr. C. pulled his son Rusty from head of marketing to take over a new role—owner-relations manager. His assignment was not to fix the computer but to fix organizational communications, with the goal of improving customer and employee satisfaction.[1]

If you were Rusty Childress, how would you improve communications at Childress Buick? What steps do you think he took to enhance communications and pull people together?

The management at Childress Buick/Kia believed in communication but faced problems in breaking down communication barriers. In today's intensely competitive environment, top managers at many companies are trying to improve communication. For example, managers at Boeing recruited employee volunteers to act as liaisons and encourage feedback from workers throughout the giant aerospace company. Deb Charnley, chief patient-care executive for Rochester General Hospital and the Genesee Hospitals, instituted "Deb Chats," regular informal pow-wows that give overworked nurses a chance to ask questions, make suggestions, or just blow off steam.[2] At A. W. Chesterton Co., CEO Jim Chesterton holds quarterly meetings at which employees can ask him about anything and everything.[3] It isn't always easy when workers confront top managers with difficult questions or challenge them regarding management failings, but getting candid feedback from employees helps executives spot problems or recognize opportunities that might otherwise be missed.

To stay connected with employees and customers and shape company direction, managers must excel at personal communications. Nonmanagers often are amazed at how much energy successful executives put into communication. Consider the comment about Robert Strauss, former chairman of the Democratic National Committee and former ambassador to Russia:

> One of his friends says, "His network is everywhere. It ranges from bookies to bank presidents . . . ."
>
> He seems to find time to make innumerable phone calls to "keep in touch"; he cultivates secretaries as well as senators; he will befriend a middle-level White House aide whom other important officials won't bother with. Every few months, he sends candy to the White House switchboard operators.[4]

This chapter explains why executives such as Robert Strauss, Jim Chesterton, and Deb Charnley are effective communicators. First we will see how managers' jobs require communication and describe a model of the communication process. Next we will consider the interpersonal aspects of communication, including communication channels, persuasion, and listening skills, that affect managers' ability to communicate. Then, we will look at the organization as a whole and consider formal upward and downward communications as well as informal communications. Finally, we will examine barriers to communication and how managers can overcome them.

Communication and the Manager's Job

How important is communication? Consider this: Managers spend at least 80 percent of every working day in direct communication with others. In other words, 48 minutes of every hour is spent in meetings, on the telephone, communicating online, or talking informally while walking around. The other 20 percent of a typical manager's time is spent doing desk work, most of which is also communication in the form of reading and writing.[5] Exhibit 18.1 illustrates the crucial position of management in the information network. Managers gather important information from both inside and outside the organization and then distribute appropriate information to others who need it.

Communication permeates every management function described in Chapter 1.[6] For example, when managers perform the planning function, they gather information; write letters, memos, and reports; and then meet with other managers to explain the plan. When managers lead, they communicate

SOURCE: Adapted from Henry Mintzberg, *The Nature of Managerial Work* (New York: Harper & Row, 1973), 72.

Exhibit 18.1

The Manager as Information Nerve Center

to share a vision of what the organization can be and motivate employees to help achieve it. When managers organize, they gather information about the state of the organization and communicate a new structure to others. Communication skills are a fundamental part of every managerial activity.

What Is Communication?

A professor at Harvard once asked a class to define communication by drawing pictures. Most students drew a manager speaking or writing. Some placed "speech balloons" next to their characters; others showed pages flying from a laser printer. "No," the professor told the class, "none of you has captured the essence of communication." He went on to explain that communication means "to share"—not "to speak" or "to write."

Communication thus can be defined as the process by which information is exchanged and understood by two or more people, usually with the intent to motivate or influence behavior. Communication is not just sending information. This distinction between *sharing* and *proclaiming* is crucial for successful management. A manager who does not listen is like a used-car salesperson who claims, "I sold a car—they just did not buy it." Management communication is a two-way street that includes listening and other forms of feedback. Effective communication, in the words of one expert, is as follows:

> When two people interact, they put themselves into each other's shoes, try to perceive the world as the other person perceives it, try to predict how the other will respond. Interaction involves reciprocal role-taking, the mutual employment of empathetic skills. The goal of interaction is the merger of self and other, a complete ability to anticipate, predict, and behave in accordance with the joint needs of self and other.[7]

It is the desire to share understanding that motivates executives to visit employees on the shop floor, hold small informal meetings, or eat with employees in the company cafeteria. The things managers learn from direct communication with employees shape their understanding of the corporation.

communication
The process by which information is exchanged and understood by two or more people, usually with the intent to motivate or influence behavior.

The Communication Process

Many people think communication is simple because they communicate without conscious thought or effort. However, communication usually is complex, and the opportunities for sending or receiving the wrong messages are innumerable. No doubt, you have heard someone say, "But that's not what I meant!" Have you ever received directions you thought were clear and yet still got lost? How often have you wasted time on misunderstood instructions?

To more fully understand the complexity of the communication process, note the key elements outlined in Exhibit 18.2. Two common elements in every communication situation are the sender and the receiver. The *sender* is anyone who wishes to convey an idea or concept to others, to seek information, or to express a thought or emotion. The *receiver* is the person to whom the message is sent. The sender **encodes** the idea by selecting symbols with which to compose a message. The **message** is the tangible formulation of the idea that is sent to the receiver. The message is sent through a **channel,** which is the communication carrier. The channel can be a formal report, a telephone call or e-mail message, or a face-to-face meeting. The receiver **decodes** the symbols to interpret the meaning of the message. Encoding and decoding are potential sources for communication errors, because knowledge, attitudes, and background act as filters and create "noise" when translating from symbols to meaning. Finally, **feedback** occurs when the receiver responds to the sender's communication with a return message. Without feedback, the communication is *one-way;* with feedback, it is *two-way.* Feedback is a powerful aid to communication effectiveness, because it enables the sender to determine whether the receiver correctly interpreted the message.

Managers who are effective communicators understand and use the circular nature of communication. For example, at Nortel Networks, Dan Hunt, president of Caribbean and Latin American operations, and Emma Carrasco, vice president of marketing and communications, host a monthly television program called *Virtual Leadership Academy* that uses a talk-show format to spark corporate conversations. Employees from about 40 different countries watch the show from their regional offices and call in their questions and comments. "We're always looking for ways to break down barriers," says Carrasco. "People watch talk shows in every country, and they've learned that it's okay to say what's on their minds."[8] The television program is the channel through which Hunt and Carrasco send their encoded message. Employees decode and

encode
To select symbols with which to compose a message.

message
The tangible formulation of an idea to be sent to a receiver.

channel
The carrier of a communication.

decode
To translate the symbols used in a message for the purpose of interpreting its meaning.

feedback
A response by the receiver to the sender's communication.

Exhibit *18.2*

A Model of the Communication Process

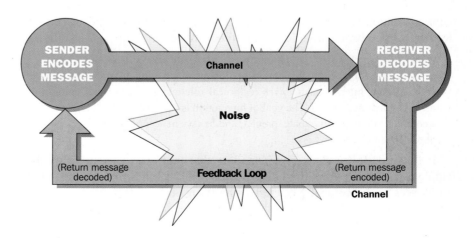

interpret the message and encode their feedback, which is sent through the channel of the telephone hookup. The communications circuit is complete.

Communicating among People

The communication model in Exhibit 18.2 illustrates the components that must be mastered for effective communication. Communications can break down if sender and receiver do not encode or decode language in the same way.[9] We all know how difficult it is to communicate with someone who does not speak our language, and managers in U.S. organizations today are often trying to communicate with people who speak many different native languages and have limited English skills. However, communication breakdowns can also occur between people who speak the same language.

Many factors can lead to a breakdown in communications. For example, the selection of communication channel can determine whether the message is distorted by noise and interference. The listening skills of both parties and attention to nonverbal behavior can determine whether a message is truly shared. Thus, for managers to be effective communicators, they must understand how interpersonal factors such as communication channels, nonverbal behavior, and listening all work to enhance or detract from communication. This chapter's Shoptalk box outlines some tips for effective manager communication.

Communication Channels

Managers have a choice of many channels through which to communicate to other managers or employees. A manager may discuss a problem face-to-face, use the telephone, send an e-mail, write a memo or letter, or put an item in a newsletter, depending on the nature of the message. Research has attempted to explain how managers select communication channels to enhance communication effectiveness.[10] The research has found that channels differ in their capacity to convey information. Just as a pipeline's physical characteristics limit the kind and amount of liquid that can be pumped through it, a communication channel's physical characteristics limit the kind and amount of information that can be conveyed among managers. The channels available to managers can be classified into a hierarchy based on information richness. **Channel richness** is the amount of information that can be transmitted

channel richness
The amount of information that can be transmitted during a communication episode.

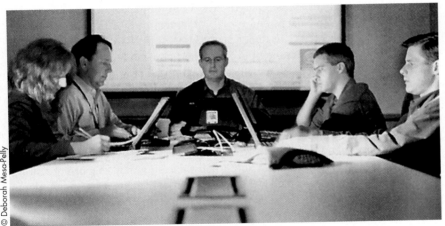

Equipped with laptops, pagers, and cell phones, Intel employees can now communicate and collaborate on group projects from anywhere in the world. These forms of communication lack the channel richness found in face-to-face discussions. However, new technology such as instant messaging, groupware, and wireless Internet applications enable these devices to facilitate rapid feedback, thus increasing their value for organizational communication.

© Deborah Mesa-Pelly

THE NEW WORKPLACE   Manager's Shoptalk

How to Be a Master Communicator

Communication is the manager's most important job, and for some it is also the most difficult. We have all had times when we've been misunderstood or tried to communicate something that goes unheard or unnoticed. Here are some tips on how to improve your communications effectiveness.

1. *Craft the message with a clear purpose in mind.* The content of a communication depends on the specific objectives. One common flaw is trying to cover too many issues at one time. Communication is always more successful when it is clearly focused on one or a few key points.

2. *To persuade and inspire people, aim for true intimacy.* When managers want to convey something really important, they should approach the communication openly, honestly, even vulnerably. One expert suggests that managers imagine they are talking to themselves, which enables them to share their deepest feelings. Listeners feel like they are sharing the speaker's unguarded thoughts and feelings, and they respond to that openness.

3. *Don't forget to listen.* Every communication should be structured to invite and encourage feedback. Open a communication with a question, because questions are more powerful than answers. A questioning approach also com-

municates that the manager cares about the other person's input and does not just want to give orders.

4. *Pay attention to timing.* Never make a difficult announcement or convey bad news and then leave town. Managers need to be visible and accessible, ready and willing to answer questions, provide clarification, and offer support.

5. *Be aware of body language and actions.* Particularly in times of rapid change or uncertainty, people are alert to any cue as to what is really going on in the organization. Facial expressions, moods, who the manager has lunch with, and whether the manager is present at organizational events will all be interpreted by employees. Managers need to be aware that actions as well as words convey a message.

6. *Stay in touch with the grapevine.* In many organizations, informal communication channels such as the grapevine operate more effectively than formal channels. Successful managers develop their social networks so that they stay in touch with the rumor mill. Managers can also use the grapevine to their advantage by sharing important information with people they know will spread it to others.

SOURCES: Based on Patricia Wallington, "You Don't Say," *CIO* (October 1, 2000), 78–80; and Harriet Rubin, "Like the King, King David Knew How to Strum a Person Like an Instrument," *Fast Company* (November 2000), 410–413.

during a communication episode. The hierarchy of channel richness is illustrated in Exhibit 18.3.

The capacity of an information channel is influenced by three characteristics: (1) the ability to handle multiple cues simultaneously; (2) the ability to facilitate rapid, two-way feedback; and (3) the ability to establish a personal focus for the communication. Face-to-face discussion is the richest medium, because it permits direct experience, multiple information cues, immediate feedback, and personal focus. Face-to-face discussions facilitate the assimilation of broad cues and deep, emotional understanding of the situation. For example, Tony Burns, CEO of Ryder Systems, Inc., likes to handle things face to face: "You can look someone in the eyes, and you can tell by the look in his eyes or the inflection in his voice what the real problem or question or answer is."[11] Telephone conversations are next in the richness hierarchy. Although eye contact, posture, and other body language cues are missing, the human voice can still carry a tremendous amount of emotional information.

Electronic messaging, or e-mail, is increasingly being used for messages that were once handled via the telephone. A recent survey by Ohio State University researchers found that about half the respondents reported making fewer telephone calls since they began using e-mail. However, respondents also said they preferred the telephone or face-to-face conversation for communicating difficult news, giving advice, or expressing affection.[12] Because

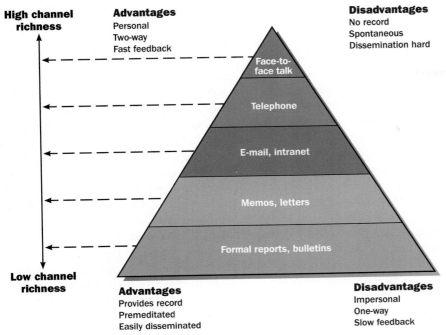

e-mail messages lack both visual and verbal cues, messages can sometimes be misunderstood. Recognizing the need for greater channel richness, many organizations are using interactive meetings over the Internet, sometimes adding video capabilities to provide visual cues as well. Following the September 11, 2001, terrorist attacks, many companies increased their reliance on virtual meetings to reduce employees' travel responsibilities. Masimo, a medical technology company in Irvine, California, decided to order an $8,000 videoconferencing system the day after the attacks.[13] Anxieties over anthrax-tainted mail have also led to greater use of e-mail and other forms of Web-based communication.

Still lower on the hierarchy of channel richness are written letters and memos. These can be personally focused, but they convey only the cues written on paper and are slow to provide feedback. Impersonal written media, including fliers, bulletins, and standard computer reports, are the lowest in richness. These channels are not focused on a single receiver, use limited information cues, and do not permit feedback.

It is important for managers to understand that each communication channel has advantages and disadvantages, and that each can be an effective means of communication in the appropriate circumstances.[14] Channel selection depends on whether the message is routine or nonroutine. *Nonroutine messages* typically are ambiguous, concern novel events, and impose great potential for misunderstanding. Nonroutine messages often are characterized by time pressure and surprise. Managers can communicate nonroutine messages effectively only by selecting rich channels. On the other hand, routine communications are simple and straightforward. *Routine messages* convey data or statistics or simply put into words what managers already agree on and understand. Routine messages can be efficiently communicated through a channel lower in richness. Written communications also should be used when the audience is widely dispersed or when the communication is "official" and a permanent record is required.[15]

Consider the executive director of the American Red Cross trying to work out a press release with public relations people to address charges that the organization intentionally misled the public about how it would use funds and blood donated in the weeks following September 11. An immediate response is critical, as the reputation of the organization is at stake. This type of non-routine communication forces a rich information exchange. The group will meet face to face, brainstorm ideas, and provide rapid feedback to resolve disagreement and convey the correct information. If, on the other hand, the director is preparing a press release about a routine matter such as a policy change or new donation sites, less information capacity is needed. The CEO and public relations people might begin developing the press release with an exchange of memos, telephone calls, and e-mail messages.

The key is to select a channel to fit the message. During a major acquisition, one firm decided to send top executives to all major work sites of the acquired company, where 75 percent of the workers met the managers in person, heard about their plans for the company, and had a chance to ask questions. The results were well worth the time and expense of the personal, face-to-face meetings because the acquired workforce saw their new managers as understanding, open, and willing to listen.[16] Communicating their non-routine message about the acquisition in person prevented damaging rumors and misunderstandings. The choice of a communication channel can also convey a symbolic meaning to the receiver. The firm's decision to communicate face to face with the acquired workforce signaled to employees that managers cared about them as individuals.

Persuasion and Influence

Communication is used not only to convey information, but to persuade and influence people. Managers use communication to sell employees on the vision for the organization and influence them to behave in such a way as to accomplish the vision. While communication skills have always been important to managers, the ability to persuade and influence others is more critical today than ever before. The command-and-control mindset of managers telling workers what to do and how to do it is gone. Businesses are run largely by cross-functional teams who are actively involved in making decisions. Issuing directives is no longer an appropriate or effective way to get things done.[17] Therefore, managers should understand how communication can be used to persuade and influence others.

Managers can enrich their communication encounters by paying attention to the language they use as well as the channels of communication they select to convey their messages. To persuade and influence, managers connect with others on an emotional level by using symbols, metaphors, and stories to express their messages. Joe Ford, chairman and CEO of Alltel Corp., tells the following story to every new group of employees to illustrate how customer service drives customer loyalty and company success. Alltel (then Allied Telephone) bought a group of tiny, independent phone companies back in 1948, including one in Amity, Arkansas, that had about 200 customers. One of those customers, Edna Nunn, operated the company's manual switchboard, collected all the bills, and handled customer complaints. After he became vice president and treasurer in 1963, Ford noticed something odd: Every single bill from Amity was paid on time, every month. Ford decided to drive to Amity and get a first-hand explanation for this miracle from Ms. Nunn, who told him shyly, "Well, they always pay me back." It's that kind of attitude, says Ford, that propelled Alltel from a small regional company to a communications empire.[18]

Using symbols and stories also helps managers make sense of a fast-changing environment in ways that members throughout the organization can understand. Managers help inspire desirable behaviors for change by tapping into the imaginations of their subordinates. If we think back to our early school years, we may remember that the most effective lessons often were couched in stories. Teresa Lever-Pollary, CEO of Nighttime Pediatrics Clinics, became concerned that employees were losing touch with the company's values in the face of rapid growth and the increasing strictures of managed care. She hired a consultant to collect stories from patients, doctors, nurses, clerks, and others and put them together in a collection called *Nighttime Stories*. For example, one story tells of a payroll employee who convinced managers to scrap an expensive investment in flawed software. Another focuses on a doctor who bent the rules to treat a disoriented elderly woman. Levar-Pollary believes stories help people stay grounded in the face of rapid change.[19]

Presenting hard facts and figures rarely has the same power as telling vivid stories. Evidence of the compatibility of stories with human thinking was demonstrated by a study at Stanford Business School.[20] The point was to convince MBA students that a company practiced a policy of avoiding layoffs. For some students, only a story was used. For others, statistical data were provided that showed little turnover compared to competitors. For other students, statistics and stories were combined, and yet other students were shown the company's official policy statements. Of all these approaches, the students presented with a vivid story alone were most convinced that the company truly practiced a policy of avoiding layoffs.

Nonverbal Communication

Managers also use symbols to communicate what is important. Managers are watched, and their behavior, appearance, actions, and attitudes are symbolic of what they value and expect of others.

Nonverbal communication refers to messages sent through human actions and behaviors rather than through words.[21] Although most nonverbal communication is unconscious or subconscious on our part, it represents a major portion of the messages we send and receive. Most managers are astonished to learn that words themselves carry little meaning. Major parts of the shared understanding from communication come from the nonverbal messages of facial expression, voice, mannerisms, posture, and dress.

Nonverbal communication occurs mostly face to face. One researcher found three sources of communication cues during face-to-face communication: the verbal, which are the actual spoken words; the vocal, which include the pitch, tone, and timbre of a person's voice; and facial expressions. According to this study, the relative weights of these three factors in message interpretation are as follows: verbal impact, 7 percent; vocal impact, 38 percent; and facial impact, 55 percent.[22]

This research strongly implies that "it's not what you say but how you say it." A manager's tone of voice or glint in the eye may signal something entirely different from his or her words. Nonverbal messages convey thoughts and feelings with greater force than do our most carefully selected words. Body language often communicates our real feelings eloquently. Thus, while the

nonverbal communication
A communication transmitted through actions and behaviors rather than through words.

conscious mind may be formulating vocal messages such as "I'm happy," or "Congratulations on your promotion," the body language may be signaling true feelings through blushing, perspiring, glancing, crying, or avoiding eye contact. When the verbal and nonverbal messages are contradictory, the receiver may be confused and usually will give more weight to behavioral actions than to verbal messages.[23]

A manager's office also sends powerful nonverbal cues. For example, what do the following seating arrangements mean if used by your supervisor? (1) She stays behind her desk, and you sit in a straight chair on the opposite side. (2) The two of you sit in straight chairs away from her desk, perhaps at a table. (3) The two of you sit in a seating arrangement consisting of a sofa and easy chair. To most people, the first arrangement indicates, "I'm the boss here," or "I'm in authority." The second arrangement indicates, "This is serious business." The third indicates a more casual and friendly, "Let's get to know each other."[24] Nonverbal messages can be a powerful asset to communication if they complement and support verbal messages. Managers should pay close attention to nonverbal behavior when communicating. They must learn to coordinate their verbal and nonverbal messages and at the same time be sensitive to what their peers, subordinates, and supervisors are saying nonverbally.

Listening

One of the most important tools of manager communication is listening, both to employees and customers. Most managers now recognize that important information flows from the bottom up, not the top down, and managers had better be tuned in.[25] In the communication model in Exhibit 18.2, the listener is responsible for message reception, which is a vital link in the communication process. **Listening** involves the skill of grasping both facts and feelings to interpret a message's genuine meaning. Only then can the manager provide the appropriate response. Listening requires attention, energy, and skill. Although about 75 percent of effective communication is listening, most people spend only 30 to 40 percent of their time listening, which leads to many communication errors.[26] Merrill Lynch superbroker Richard F. Green explained the importance of listening to organizational success: "If you talk, you'll like me. If I talk, I'll like you—but if I do the talking, my business will not be served."[27] However, listening involves much more than just "not talking." Many people do not know how to listen effectively. They concentrate on formulating what they are going to say next rather than on what is being said to them. Our listening efficiency, as measured by the amount of material understood and remembered by subjects 48 hours after listening to a 10-minute message, is, on average, no better than 25 percent.[28]

What constitutes good listening? Exhibit 18.4 gives 10 keys to effective listening and illustrates a number of ways to distinguish a bad from a good listener. A good listener finds areas of interest, is flexible, works hard at listening, and uses thought speed to mentally summarize, weigh, and anticipate what the speaker says. Good listening means shifting from thinking about self to empathizing with the other person and thus requires a degree of emotional intelligence, as described in Chapter 15. An excellent example of good listening comes from some television talk shows. For example, Oprah Winfrey listens actively to guests or audience participants by blocking out distractions, focusing her full attention on the speaker, and using eye contact. Winfrey

listening
The skill of receiving messages to accurately grasp facts and feelings to interpret the genuine meaning.

Keys	Poor Listener	Good Listener
1. Listen actively	Is passive, laid back	Asks questions, paraphrases what is said
2. Find areas of interest	Tunes out dry subjects	Looks for opportunities, new learning
3. Resist distractions	Is easily distracted	Fights or avoids distractions; tolerates bad habits; knows how to concentrate
4. Capitalize on the fact that thought is faster than speech	Tends to daydream with slow speakers	Challenges, anticipates, mentally summarizes; weighs the evidence; listens between the lines to tone of voice
5. Be responsive	Is minimally involved	Nods; shows interest, give and take, positive feedback
6. Judge content, not delivery	Tunes out if delivery is poor	Judges content; skips over delivery errors
7. Hold one's fire	Has preconceptions, starts to argue	Does not judge until comprehension is complete
8. Listen for ideas	Listens for facts	Listens to central themes
9. Work at listening	Shows no energy output; faked attention	Works hard, exhibits active body state, eye contact
10. Exercise one's mind	Resists difficult material in favor of light, recreational material	Uses heavier material as exercise for the mind

SOURCES: Adapted from Sherman K. Okum, "How to Be a Better Listener," *Nation's Business* (August 1975), 62; and Philip Morgan and Kent Baker, "Building a Professional Image: Improving Listening Behavior," *Supervisory Management* (November 1985), 34–38.

Exhibit *18.4*

Ten Keys to Effective Listening

listens empathically without interrupting and then paraphrases the speaker's comments and ideas to make sure she has understood. Her excellent listening skills make people feel welcomed, understood, and important.[29] Contrast that with talk shows characterized by yelling, cursing, and chair throwing.

Some organizations have created a culture that emphasizes active manager listening. For example, at Wal-Mart, top executives devote at least two days a week to visiting stores and listening to employee concerns.

Organizational Communication

Another aspect of management communication concerns the organization as a whole. Organizationwide communications typically flow in three directions—downward, upward, and horizontally. Managers are responsible for establishing and maintaining formal channels of communication in these three directions. Managers also use informal channels, which means they get out of their offices and mingle with employees.

Formal Communication Channels

Formal communication channels are those that flow within the chain of command or task responsibility defined by the organization. The three formal channels and the types of information conveyed in each are illustrated in Exhibit 18.5.[30] Downward and upward communication are the primary forms of communication used in most traditional, vertically organized companies. However, the new workplace emphasizes horizontal communication, with people constantly sharing information across departments and levels.

Electronic communication such as e-mail and instant messaging have made it easier than ever for information to flow in all directions. For example, the U.S. Navy is using instant messaging to communicate within ships, across Navy divisions, and even back to the Pentagon in Washington. "Instant

formal communication channel
A communication channel that flows within the chain of command or task responsibility defined by the organization.

Upward Communication
- Problems and exceptions
- Suggestions for improvement
- Performance reports
- Grievances and disputes
- Financial and accounting information

Downward Communication
- Implementation of goals, strategies
- Job instructions and rationale
- Procedures and practices
- Performance feedback
- Indoctrination

Coordinate

Horizontal Communication
- Intradepartmental problem solving
- Interdepartmental coordination
- Change initiatives and improvements

Interpret

Influence

SOURCE: Adapted from Richard L. Daft and Richard M. Steers, *Organizations: A Micro/Macro Approach*, 538. Copyright © 1986 by Scott, Foresman and Company. Used by permission.

messaging has allowed us to keep our crew members on the same page at the same time," says Lt. Cmdr. Mike Houston, who oversees the Navy's communications program. "Lives are at stake in real time, and we're seeing a new level of communication and readiness."[31]

downward communication

Messages sent from top management down to subordinates.

Downward Communication. The most familiar and obvious flow of formal communication, **downward communication,** refers to the messages and information sent from top management to subordinates in a downward direction. For example, StarMedia Network, a leading Internet portal for Spanish and Portuguese speakers, holds quarterly Web meetings in which CEO Fernando Espuelas and other top managers deliver quarterly results, communicate important news, announce new strategic initiatives, or clarify goals. Because employees are scattered in 14 offices throughout 11 countries, the meetings are conducted in Spanish, Portuguese, and English. However, a local translator in each office recaps the entire announcement to ensure that no information gets lost.[32]

Managers sometimes use creative approaches to downward communication to make sure employees get the message. Mike Olson, plant manager at Ryerson Midwest Coil Processing, noticed that workers were dropping expensive power tools, so he hung price tags on the tools to show the replacement cost. Employees solved the problem by finding a way to hook up the tools so they wouldn't be dropped. Olson's communication helps workers see how their actions affect the entire company and creates a climate of working *together* for solutions.[33]

Managers can communicate downward to employees in many ways. Some of the most common are through speeches, messages in company newsletters, e-mail, information leaflets tucked into pay envelopes, material on bulletin boards, and policy and procedures manuals. At VeriFone Inc., managers believe there's no such thing as giving employees too much information. They flood employees' home mailboxes with newsletters, total-compensation updates, benefit-program descriptions, and stock option plans. Since VeriFone is largely a "virtual" company, in which geographical dispersion is the operating principle, the company also makes extensive use of e-mail and the company intranet.[34]

Managers also have to decide what to communicate about. It is impossible for managers to communicate with employees about everything that goes on in the organization, so they have to make choices about the important information to communicate.[35] Downward communication in an organization usually encompasses these five topics:

1. *Implementation of goals and strategies.* Communicating new strategies and goals provides information about specific targets and expected behaviors. It gives direction for lower levels of the organization. Example: "The new quality campaign is for real. We must improve product quality if we are to survive."

2. *Job instructions and rationale.* These are directives on how to do a specific task and how the job relates to other organizational activities. Example: "Purchasing should order the bricks now so the work crew can begin construction of the building in two weeks."

3. *Procedures and practices.* These are messages defining the organization's policies, rules, regulations, benefits, and structural arrangements. Example: "After your first 90 days of employment, you are eligible to enroll in our company-sponsored savings plan."

4. *Performance feedback.* These messages appraise how well individuals and departments are doing their jobs. Example: "Joe, your work on the computer network has greatly improved the efficiency of our ordering process."

5. *Indoctrination.* These messages are designed to motivate employees to adopt the company's mission and cultural values and to participate in special ceremonies, such as picnics and United Way campaigns. Example: "The company thinks of its employees as family and would like to invite everyone to attend the annual picnic and fair on March 3."

The major problem with downward communication is *drop off*, the distortion or loss of message content. Although formal communications are a powerful way to reach all employees, much information gets lost—25 percent or so each time a message is passed from one person to the next. In addition, the message can be distorted if it travels a great distance from its originating source to the ultimate receiver. A tragic example is the following:

> A reporter was present at a hamlet burned down by the U.S. Army 1st Air Cavalry Division in 1967. Investigations showed that the order from the Division headquarters to the brigade was: "On no occasion must hamlets be burned down."
>
> The brigade radioed the battalion: "Do not burn down any hamlets unless you are absolutely convinced that the Viet Cong are in them."
>
> The battalion radioed the infantry company at the scene: "If you think there are any Viet Cong in the hamlet, burn it down."
>
> The company commander ordered his troops: "Burn down that hamlet."[36]

Information drop off cannot be completely avoided, but the techniques described in the previous sections can reduce it substantially. Using the right communication channel, consistency between verbal and nonverbal messages, and active listening can maintain communication accuracy as it moves down the organization.

upward communication
Messages transmitted from the lower to the higher levels in the organization's hierarchy.

Upward Communication. Formal **upward communication** includes messages that flow from the lower to the higher levels in the organization's hierarchy. Most organizations take pains to build in healthy channels for upward communication. Employees need to air grievances, report progress, and provide feedback on management initiatives. Coupling a healthy flow of upward and downward communication ensures that the communication circuit between managers and employees is complete.[37] Five types of information communicated upward are the following:

1. *Problems and exceptions.* These messages describe serious problems with and exceptions to routine performance in order to make senior managers aware of difficulties. Example: "The printer has been out of operation for two days, and it will be at least a week before a new one arrives."

2. *Suggestions for improvement.* These messages are ideas for improving task-related procedures to increase quality or efficiency. Example: "I think we should eliminate step 2 in the audit procedure because it takes a lot of time and produces no results."

3. *Performance reports.* These messages include periodic reports that inform management how individuals and departments are performing. Example: "We completed the audit report for Smith & Smith on schedule but are one week behind on the Jackson report."

4. *Grievances and disputes.* These messages are employee complaints and conflicts that travel up the hierarchy for a hearing and possible resolution. Example: "The manager of operations research cannot get the cooperation of the Lincoln plant for the study of machine utilization."

5. *Financial and accounting information.* These messages pertain to costs, accounts receivable, sales volume, anticipated profits, return on investment, and other matters of interest to senior managers. Example: "Costs are 2 percent over budget, but sales are 10 percent ahead of target, so the profit picture for the third quarter is excellent."

Managers at the plumbing and air-conditioning contractor company, TDINDUSTRIES, facilitate upward communication through their commitment to the philosophy of "servant leadership." Upward communication and active listening allow managers to respect the interests and heed the preferences of workers. Apprentices, such as those in the photo being taught to install plumbing systems, look forward to being part of the company's democratic system in addition to enjoying ownership of part of the 75 percent of the company's stock that is owned by lower-level employees.

Many organizations make a great effort to facilitate upward communication. Mechanisms include suggestion boxes, employee surveys, open-door policies, management information system reports, and face-to-face conversations between workers and executives. At SoftChoice, a software reseller with 300 employees scattered across 23 offices, managers launched *SINews* (SoftChoice Internal News) to give employees a chance to speak their minds. Every page of the weekly online publication has a "Respond" bar that employees can click to ask questions, make comments, lodge complaints, or offer suggestions—anonymously, if they choose. Employees

Leading Online

Amazon.com Keeps Track of Employees' "Pulse Rate"

How do managers at Amazon.com keep in touch with employees' opinions and feelings about company decisions? By taking the organization's collective pulse twice a week.

Amazon works with eePulse, an Ann Arbor, Michigan–based application service provider, to electronically poll employees biweekly on their opinions and attitudes about various developments within the company. The electronic survey and communications tool uses a question format and asks employees to rate their "pulse," or energy level. Responses range from "not doing much, not having fun" to "overwhelmed by work and need help." Employees also have an opportunity for open comments about their work environment. These quick e-mail surveys, which take about two minutes to complete, provide feedback on a regular basis, enabling managers to collect information and assess how things are going in real time. "Changes happen very quickly here," says one manager. "By polling people this way, by e-mail, it's

consistent and fast and provides the data we need." Employees are encouraged to talk to their managers about any specific concerns, and managers are trained to effectively use the eePulse and follow up on potential problems, such as low pulse rates or an employee whose pulse is about to go through the roof from overwork.

Whereas managers loved the new communications tool from the beginning, employees took a little longer to warm up to it. With typical management surveys, employees rarely see changes after results are compiled and publicized, and Amazon's workers expected this was just another useless poll. However, after numerous months in which Amazon's managers consistently reported back results to the employees and made sincere efforts to address concerns, attitudes toward eePulse have changed. Some people even enjoy regularly keeping tabs on the survey results and finding out what their coworkers are saying about their jobs and the company.

SOURCE: Teresa Welbourne, "New ASP Takes Workforce's 'Pulse,'" *The New Corporate University Review* (July–August 2000), 20–21.

---

at Opus Event Marketing use bright-red Think cards to give feedback to managers.[38] This chapter's Leading Online box describes one approach Amazon.com takes to find out what's on employee's minds.

Despite these efforts, however, barriers to accurate upward communication exist. Managers may resist hearing about employee problems, or employees may not trust managers sufficiently to push information upward.[39] Innovative companies search for ways to ensure that information gets to top managers without distortion. IBM's respected Speak Up program consists of anonymous employee letters or e-mails regularly channeled to management for action. Top managers at Golden Corral, a restaurant chain with headquarters in Raleigh, North Carolina, spend at least one weekend a year in the trenches—cutting steaks, rolling silverware, setting tables, and taking out the trash. By understanding the daily routines and challenges of waiters, chefs, and other employees at their restaurants, Golden Corral executives increase their awareness of how management actions affect others.[40]

Horizontal Communication. **Horizontal communication** is the lateral or diagonal exchange of messages among peers or coworkers. It may occur within or across departments. The purpose of horizontal communication is not only to inform but also to request support and coordinate activities. Horizontal communication falls into one of three categories:

1. *Intradepartmental problem solving.* These messages take place among members of the same department and concern task accomplishment. Example: "Betty, can you help us figure out how to complete this medical expense report form?"

horizontal communication
The lateral or diagonal exchange of messages among peers or coworkers.

2. *Interdepartmental coordination.* Interdepartmental messages facilitate the accomplishment of joint projects or tasks. Example: "Bob, please contact marketing and production and arrange a meeting to discuss the specifications for the new subassembly. It looks like we might not be able to meet their requirements."

3. *Change initiatives and improvements.* These messages are designed to share information among teams and departments that can help the organization change, grow, and improve. Example: "We are streamlining the company travel procedures and would like to discuss them with your department."

Horizontal communication is particularly important in learning organizations, where teams of workers are continuously solving problems and searching for new ways of doing things. Recall from Chapters 10 and 11 that many organizations build in horizontal communications in the form of task forces, committees, or even a matrix structure to encourage coordination. At Chicago's Northwestern Memorial Hospital, two doctors created a horizontal task force to solve a serious patient health problem.

NORTHWESTERN MEMORIAL HOSPITAL
http://www.nmh.org

We've all heard of it happening—a patient checks into the hospital for a routine procedure and ends up getting sicker instead of better. Hospital-borne infections afflict about two million patients—and kill nearly 100,000—each year. Greater antibiotic use causes the germs to develop greater resistance. The infection epidemic is growing worse worldwide, but a task force at Northwestern Memorial Hospital has reversed the trend by breaking down communication barriers.

When a cancer patient became Northwestern's first victim of a new strain of deadly bacteria, infectious-disease specialists Lance Peterson and Gary Noskin realized it would take everyone's help to defeat the insidious enemy. As infection spread throughout the hospital, they launched a regular Monday morning meeting to plot countermoves. Although some physicians and staff members were offended at having their procedures questioned, the goal of preventing needless deaths overrode their concerns. Absolute candor was the rule at the Monday morning meetings, which involved not only doctors and nurses, but also lab technicians, pharmacists, computer technicians, and admissions representatives. One pharmacist, for example, recognized that antibiotics act as fertilizer for many bacteria, which encouraged physicians to decrease their use of antibiotics in favor of alternative treatments. Computer representatives and admissions people got together to develop software to identify which returning patients might pose a threat for bringing infection back into the hospital. Eventually, the task force even included maintenance staff when studies showed that a shortage of sinks was inhibiting hand-washing.

Increasing horizontal communication paid off at Northwestern, saving millions in annual medical costs and at least a few lives. Over three years, Northwestern's rate of hospital-borne infections plunged 22 percent. In a recent fiscal year, such infections totaled 5.1 per 1,000 patients, roughly half the national average.[41] ❖

Team Communication Channels

A special type of horizontal communication is communicating in teams. In many companies today, teams are the basic building block of the organization.

Team members work together to accomplish tasks, and the team's communication structure influences both team performance and employee satisfaction.

Research into team communication has focused on two characteristics: the extent to which team communications are centralized and the nature of the team's task.[42] The relationship between these characteristics is illustrated in Exhibit 18.6. In a **centralized network,** team members must communicate through one individual to solve problems or make decisions. In a **decentralized network,** individuals can communicate freely with other team members. Members process information equally among themselves until all agree on a decision.[43]

In laboratory experiments, centralized communication networks achieved faster solutions for simple problems. Members could simply pass relevant information to a central person for a decision. Decentralized communications were slower for simple problems because information was passed among individuals until someone finally put the pieces together and solved the problem. However, for more complex problems, the decentralized communication network was faster. Because all necessary information was not restricted to one person, a pooling of information through widespread communications provided greater input into the decision. Similarly, the accuracy of problem solving was related to problem complexity. The centralized networks made fewer errors on simple problems but more errors on complex ones. Decentralized networks were less accurate for simple problems but more accurate for complex ones.[44]

The implication for organizations is as follows: In a highly competitive global environment, organizations use teams to deal with complex problems. When team activities are complex and difficult, all members should share information in a decentralized structure to solve problems. Teams need a free flow of communication in all directions.[45] At Microsoft, for example, teams hold "triage" meetings in the final months of a software development cycle. Everyone jumps in with ideas and opinions and then "negotiates" to a decision.[46] However, teams who perform routine tasks spend less time processing information, and thus communications can be centralized. Data can be channeled to a supervisor for decisions, freeing workers to spend a greater percentage of time on task activities.

centralized network
A team communication structure in which team members communicate through a single individual to solve problems or make decisions.

decentralized network
A team communication structure in which team members freely communicate with one another and arrive at decisions together.

Exhibit *18.6*

Effectiveness of Team Communication Network

SOURCES: Adapted from A. Bavelas and D. Barrett, "An Experimental Approach to Organization Communication," *Personnel* 27 (1951), 366–371; M. E. Shaw, *Group Dynamics: The Psychology of Small Group Behavior* (New York: McGraw-Hill, 1976); and E. M. Rogers and R. A. Rogers, *Communication in Organizations* (New York: Free Press, 1976).

Valassis Communication, Inc.'s "On the M.O.V.E." committee (which stands for Motivate Our Valassis Employees) researches and implements programs such as flexible hours, job sharing, and suggestion review systems, as well as plans a variety of "lighten up" events that contribute to high employee morale and a strong corporate culture. Valassis formed the committee to improve horizontal communication and create positive energy across the entire organization. It is one of many techniques VCI uses to stimulate new ideas, promote teamwork, and encourage ongoing communication.

Courtesy of Valassis Communications

Informal Communication Channels

informal communication channel
A communication channel that exists outside formally authorized channels without regard for the organization's hierarchy of authority.

Informal communication channels exist outside the formally authorized channels and do not adhere to the organization's hierarchy of authority. Informal communications coexist with formal communications but may skip hierarchical levels, cutting across vertical chains of command to connect virtually anyone in the organization. For example, to improve communication at OpenAir.com, a Boston-based provider of professional services software online, CEO Bill O'Farrell instituted the *morning huddle,* whereby the staff gathers for a big water-cooler chat in which each person can share a few anecdotes about his or her customer contacts from the day before. The "no chairs allowed" rule keeps things loose, informal, and fast. It gives people a great way to share information and get a jump on their day.[47] At SafeCard Services of Jacksonville, Florida, chief executive Paul Kahn opened up the "executives only" fitness center to all employees so people would have more opportunities for informal interaction and information exchange. Kahn believes providing greater opportunities for informal communications helped him turn the struggling company around.[48] An illustration of both formal and informal communications is given in Exhibit 18.7. Note how formal communications can be

Exhibit *18.7*

Formal and Informal Organizational Communication Channels

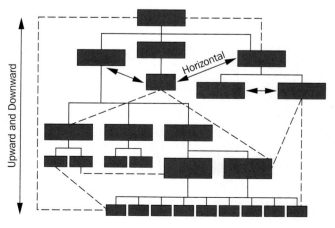

Formal channels ——————
Informal channels – – – – –

vertical or horizontal, depending on task assignments and coordination responsibilities.

Two types of informal channels used in many organizations are *management by wandering around* and the *grapevine*.

Management by Wandering Around.

The communication technique known as **management by wandering around (MBWA)** was made famous by the books *In Search of Excellence* and *A Passion for Excellence*.[49] These books describe executives who talk directly with employees to learn what is going on. MBWA works for managers at all levels. They mingle and develop positive relationships with employees and learn directly from them about their department, division, or organization. For example, the president of ARCO had a habit of visiting a district field office. Rather than schedule a big strategic meeting with the district supervisor, he would come in unannounced and chat with the lowest-level employees. In any organization, both upward and downward communication are enhanced with MBWA. Managers have a chance to describe key ideas and values to employees and, in turn, learn about the problems and issues confronting employees.

When managers fail to take advantage of MBWA, they become aloof and isolated from employees. For example, Peter Anderson, president of Ztel, Inc., a maker of television switching systems, preferred not to personally communicate with employees. He managed at arm's length. As one manager said, "I don't know how many times I asked Peter to come to the lab, but he stayed in his office. He wasn't that visible to the troops." This formal management style contributed to Ztel's troubles and eventual bankruptcy.[50]

The Grapevine.

The **grapevine** is an informal, person-to-person communication network of employees that is not officially sanctioned by the organization.[51] The grapevine links employees in all directions, ranging from the president through middle management, support staff, and line employees. The grapevine will always exist in an organization, but it can become a dominant force when formal channels are closed. In such cases, the grapevine is actually a service because the information it provides helps makes sense of an unclear or uncertain situation. Employees use grapevine rumors to fill in information gaps

management by wandering around (MBWA)
A communication technique in which managers interact directly with workers to exchange information.

grapevine
An informal, person-to-person communication network of employees that is not officially sanctioned by the organization.

Courtesy of Osmonics, Inc.

Anita Tuch, Minnetonka plant manager for Osmonics, believes in the value of management by wandering around (MBWA). Osmonics is a manufacturer of high-technology filtration and separation equipment, as well as water treatment systems. MBWA helps Tuch keep tabs on problems in the plant, hear new ideas, and find out what issues are on employees' minds. In the photo, she joins plant workers inspecting filter inventory at the Minnetonka, Minnesota, plant's distribution center.

and clarify management decisions. The grapevine tends to be more active during periods of change, excitement, anxiety, and sagging economic conditions. For example, when Jel, Inc., an auto supply firm, was under great pressure from Ford and GM to increase quality, rumors circulated on the shop floor about the company's possible demise. Management changes to improve quality—learning statistical process control, introducing a new compensation system, buying a fancy new screw machine from Germany—all started out as rumors, circulating days ahead of the actual announcements, and were generally accurate.[52]

Research suggests that a few people are primarily responsible for the grapevine's success. Exhibit 18.8 illustrates the two most typical grapevines.[53] In the *gossip chain*, a single individual conveys a piece of news to many other people. In a *cluster chain*, a few individuals each convey information to several others. Having only a few people conveying information may account for the accuracy of grapevines. If every person told one other person in sequence, distortions would be greater.

Surprising aspects of the grapevine are its accuracy and its relevance to the organization. About 80 percent of grapevine communications pertain to business-related topics rather than personal, vicious gossip. Moreover, from 70 to 90 percent of the details passed through a grapevine are accurate.[54] Many managers would like the grapevine to be destroyed because they consider its rumors to be untrue, malicious, and harmful. Typically this is not the case; however, managers should be aware that almost five of every six important messages are carried to some extent by the grapevine rather than through official channels. In a survey of 22,000 shift workers in varied industries, 55 percent said they get most of their information via the grapevine.[55] Smart managers understand the company's grapevine. They recognize who's connected to whom and which employees are key players in the informal spread of information. In all cases, but particularly in times of crisis, executives need to manage communications effectively so that the grapevine is not the only source of information.[56]

Communicating in the New Workplace

Managers in today's leading companies put extraordinary emphasis on open and honest communication in all directions to build trust and promote learning and problem solving. In addition to encompassing the ideas and

Exhibit *18.8*

Two Grapevine Chains in Organizations

SOURCE: Based on Keith Davis and John W. Newstrom, *Human Behavior at Work: Organizational Behavior*, 7th ed. (New York: McGraw-Hill, 1985).

Gossip Chain
(One tells many)

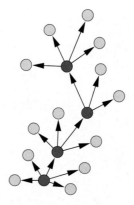

Cluster Chain
(A few tell selected others)

techniques discussed so far, the new workplace also focuses on open communication, dialogue, and feedback and learning.

Open Communication

A recent trend that reflects managers' increased emphasis on empowering employees, building trust and commitment, and enhancing collaboration is open communication. **Open communication** means sharing all types of information throughout the company, across functional and hierarchical levels. Many companies, such as Springfield Remanufacturing Corporation, Johnsonville Foods, and Quad/Graphics, are opening the financial books to workers at all levels so they understand how and why the company operates as it does. Wabash National Corporation, one of the nation's leading truck-trailer manufacturers, has employees complete several hours of business training and then holds regular meetings on the shop floor to review the company's financial performance. AES Corporation, a power producer, shares so much financial data with its employees that it has declared them all insiders for stock-trading purposes.[57]

Open communication runs counter to the traditional flow of selective information downward from supervisors to subordinates. By breaking down conventional hierarchical and departmental boundaries that may be barriers to communication, the organization can gain the benefit of all employees' ideas. The same ideas batted back and forth among a few managers do not lead to effective learning and change or to a network of relationships that keep companies thriving. New voices and conversations involving a broad spectrum of people revitalize and enhance organizational communication.[58]

The Great Harvest Bread Company uses both formal and informal communication channels to encourage the broad sharing of information and ideas among its franchisees, as described in the Putting People First box. Open communication also builds trust and a commitment to common goals, which is essential in organizations that depend on collaboration and knowledge-sharing to accomplish their purpose. Fifty percent of executives surveyed report that open communication is a key to building trust in the organization.[59]

Dialogue

Another means of fostering trust and collaboration is through dialogue. The "roots of dialogue" are *dia* and *logos*, which can be thought of as "stream of meaning." **Dialogue** is a group communication process in which people together create a stream of shared meaning that enables them to understand each other and share a view of the world.[60] People may start out at polar opposites, but by talking openly, they discover common ground, common issues, and shared goals on which they can build a better future.

A useful way to describe dialogue is to contrast it with discussion. Exhibit 18.9 on page 601 illustrates the differences between dialogue and discussion. The intent of discussion, generally, is to deliver one's point of view and persuade others to adopt it. A discussion is often resolved by logic or "beating down" opponents. Dialogue, on the other hand, asks that participants suspend their attachments to a particular viewpoint so that a deeper level of listening, synthesis, and meaning can evolve from the group. A dialogue's focus is to reveal feelings and build common ground. Both forms of communication—dialogue and discussion—can result in change. However, the result of discussion is limited to the topic being deliberated, whereas the result of dialogue is

open communication
Sharing all types of information throughout the company, across functional and hierarchical levels.

dialogue
A group communication process aimed at creating a culture based on collaboration, fluidity, trust, and commitment to shared goals.

Putting People First

Great Harvest Bread Company

Great Harvest Bread Company, a franchisor of retail bread bakeries, was founded on the philosophy that command-and-control management is just downright wrong. Unlike most franchisors that dictate everything about how their franchisees operate, Great Harvest sets people free to run their stores as they see fit, encouraging bakery owners to be themselves, experiment, and, most importantly, share their ideas with others. By "putting freedom first," Great Harvest fully taps the creative energy of all franchisees.

At Great Harvest, ideas travel through both formal and informal channels. Informal ways of communication—what Great Harvest calls "management by shoptalk and gossip"—enable owners to profit from each other's experiences. When an owner tries something that works, he or she gets on the phone or sends an e-mail to tell another owner or owners, who try the idea and spread it on. For example, "Baker for a Day" started in one store in Boulder, Colorado, spread to a bakery in Minnesota, and then gained momentum as word of the project's success spread via telephone and e-mail from one bakery owner to another. Baker for a Day opens the bakery for a special event on a Sunday (when the stores are usually closed) and donates the day's sales to a local charity, which promotes the event and helps staff it. Besides giving something to the community, the project also brings in potential new customers to taste Great Harvest's products.

Great Harvest founders Pete and Laura Wakeman also build in formal mechanisms to help ideas spread and guide owners to the best sources of help. One is the "learning com-munity," which all owners are urged to join (most do). Those who participate in the learning community can hold nothing back from others in the community and must contribute information, sales figures, ideas, and observations whenever asked. Another formal mechanism is the Numbers Club, in which owners agree to open their books to the parent company and the other bakeries in the system. In return, members get a summary of where fellow owners are ranked by way of the stores' sales figures and performance in every category across the board. This enables franchisees to find stores with similar environments to theirs, such as bakery size, market, and level of labor, who may be more successful in some area of performance. With that information, the Numbers Club member can give the other store a call and establish a mentoring relationship. With the aid of Travel Match, which pays half the expenses, the store owner or an employee can visit the more successful store to learn how it is doing things better.

Great Harvest also uses other means of capturing and communicating ideas. For example, an internal Web site called Breadboard includes articles from staffers and outside press coverage; ongoing electronic chat discussions about anything from new recipes and equipment maintenance to tips on seasonal promotions; and archives that allow users to pull up information addressing specific concerns. Printed newsletters, field trips, annual conferences, and training sessions all serve to enable even the smallest ideas to travel, grow, and evolve.

SOURCE: Michael Hopkins, "Zen and the Art of the Self-Managing Company," *Inc.* (November 2000), 54–63.

characterized by group unity, shared meaning, and transformed mindsets. As new and deeper solutions are developed, a trusting relationship is built among team members.[61]

Feedback and Learning

feedback
Using communication and evaluation to help the organization learn and improve.

In the new workplace, **feedback** occurs when managers use evaluation and communication to help individuals and the organization learn and improve. Feedback enables managers to determine whether they have been successful or unsuccessful in communicating with others. It also helps them develop subordinates. At General Electric, managers are evaluated partly on their ability to give and receive effective feedback.[62] Recall from the communication model earlier in the chapter that feedback is an important part of the communication process. However, despite its importance, feedback is often neglected. One study found that although executives at a majority of companies agree that communication is a priority, less than half bother to tailor their messages to employees, customers, or suppliers, and even fewer seek feedback

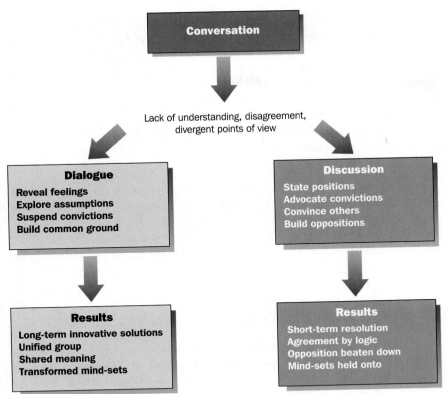

SOURCE: Adapted from Edgar Schein, "On Dialogue, Culture, and Organization Learning," *Organizational Dynamics* (Autumn 1993), 46.

Exhibit 18.9

Dialogue and Discussion: The Differences

from those constituencies.[63] Using feedback can seem daunting because it potentially involves many sources. A single individual might receive feedback from supervisors, co-workers, customers, investors, suppliers, and members of partner organizations.

Successful managers focus feedback to help develop the capacities of subordinates and to teach the organization how to better reach its goals. Feedback is an important means by which individuals and organizations learn from their mistakes and improve their work. When managers enlist the whole organization in reviewing the outcomes of activities, they can quickly learn what works and what doesn't and use that information to improve the organization. Consider how the U.S. Army's feedback system promotes whole-system learning.

At the National Training Center just south of Death Valley, U.S. Army troops engage in a simulated battle: The "enemy" has sent unmanned aerial vehicles (UAVs) to gather targeting data. When the troops fire on the UAVs, they reveal their location to attack helicopters hovering just behind a nearby ridge. After the exercise, unit members and their superiors hold an *after-action review* to review battle plans, discuss what worked and what didn't, and talk about how to do things better. General William Hertzog suggests that inexpensive decoy UAVs might be just the thing to make a distracted enemy reveal its location. The observation amounts to a "lesson learned" for the entire army.

In the U.S. Army, after-action reviews take just 15 minutes, and they occur after every identifiable event—large or small, simulated or real. The review involves asking four simple questions: What was supposed to happen? What

U.S. ARMY
http://www.army.mil

actually happened? What accounts for any difference? What can we learn? It is a process of identifying mistakes, of innovating, and of continually learning from experience. The lessons are based not only on simulated battles, but also on real-life experiences of soldiers in the field. The Center for Army Lessons Learned (CALL) sends experts into the field to observe after-action reviews, interview soldiers, and compile intelligence reports. The lessons learned are stockpiled and disseminated throughout the combat force. In Bosnia, a new list of lessons was distributed every 72 hours. Lessons are currently being disseminated in Afghanistan.[64] ❖

In this example, the organization is learning by communicating feedback about the consequences of field operations and simulated battles. Compiling what is learned and using communication feedback create an improved organization. After-action reviews are also used in corporate America. Steelcase Inc., an office furniture manufacturer, and BP are among the companies adapting the army's system to create a process of continuous learning and improvement. BP credits the feedback system for $700 million in cost savings and other gains.[65]

Managing Organizational Communication

Many of the ideas described in this chapter pertain to barriers to communication and how to overcome them. Barriers can be categorized as those that exist at the individual level and those that exist at the organizational level. First we will examine communication barriers; then we will look at techniques for overcoming them. These barriers and techniques are summarized in Exhibit 18.10.

Barriers to Communication

Barriers to communication can exist within the individual or as part of the organization.

Individual Barriers. First, there are *interpersonal barriers;* these include problems with emotions and perceptions held by employees. For example,

E x h i b i t **18.10**

Communication Barriers and Ways to Overcome Them

Barriers	How to Overcome
Individual	
Interpersonal dynamics	Active listening
Channels and media	Selection of appropriate channel
Semantics	Knowledge of other's perspective
Inconsistent cues	MBWA
Organizational	
Status and power differences	Climate of trust, dialogue
Departmental needs and goals	Development and use of formal channels
Lack of formal channels	Encouragement of multiple channels, formal and informal
Communication network unsuited to task	Changing organization or group structure to fit communication needs
Poor coordination	Feedback and learning

rigid perceptual labeling or categorizing of others prevents modification or alteration of opinions. If a person's mind is made up before the communication starts, communication will fail. Moreover, people with different backgrounds or knowledge may interpret a communication in different ways.

Second, *selecting the wrong channel or medium* for sending a communication can be a problem. For example, when a message is emotional, it is better to transmit it face to face rather than in writing. On the other hand, writing works best for routine messages but lacks the capacity for rapid feedback and multiple cues needed for difficult messages.

Third, *semantics* often causes communication problems. **Semantics** pertains to the meaning of words and the way they are used. A word such as *effectiveness* may mean achieving high production to a factory superintendent and employee satisfaction to a human resources staff specialist. Many common words have an average of 28 definitions; thus, communicators must take care to select the words that will accurately encode ideas.[66] Language differences can also be a barrier in today's organizations. At Semifreddi's, an artisan bread bakery in Emeryville, California, CEO Tom Frainier had to hire translators to help him communicate effectively with his employees, most of whom came from Mexico, Laos, China, Peru, Cambodia, Yemen, and Vietnam.[67]

Fourth, sending *inconsistent cues* between verbal and nonverbal communications will confuse the receiver. If one's facial expression does not reflect one's words, the communication will contain noise and uncertainty. The tone of voice and body language should be consistent with the words, and actions should not contradict words.

semantics
The meaning of words and the way they are used.

Organizational Barriers. Organizational barriers pertain to factors for the organization as a whole. First is the problem of *status and power differences*. Low-power people may be reluctant to pass bad news up the hierarchy, thus giving the wrong impression to upper levels.[68] High-power people may not pay attention or may think that low-status people have little to contribute.

Second, *differences across departments in terms of needs and goals* interfere with communications. Each department perceives problems in its own terms. The production department is concerned with production efficiency whereas the marketing department's goal is to get the product to the customer in a hurry.

Third, the *absence of formal channels* reduces communication effectiveness. Organizations must provide adequate upward, downward, and horizontal communication in the form of employee surveys, open-door policies, newsletters, memos, task forces, and liaison personnel. Without these formal channels, the organization cannot communicate as a whole.

Fourth, the *communication flow* may not fit the team's or organization's task. If a centralized communication structure is used for nonroutine tasks, there will not be enough information circulated to solve problems. The organization, department, or team is most efficient when the amount of communication flowing among employees fits the task.

A final problem is *poor coordination*, so that different parts of the organization are working in isolation without knowing and understanding what other parts are doing. Top executives are out of touch with lower levels, or departments and divisions are poorly coordinated so that people do not understand how the system works together as a whole.

Overcoming Communication Barriers

Managers can design the organization so as to encourage positive, effective communication. Designing involves both individual skills and organizational actions.

Individual Skills. Perhaps the most important individual skill is *active listening*. Active listening means asking questions, showing interest, and occasionally paraphrasing what the speaker has said to ensure that one is interpreting accurately. Active listening also means providing feedback to the sender to complete the communication loop.

Second, individuals should select the *appropriate channel* for the message. A complicated message should be sent through a rich channel, such as face-to-face discussion or telephone. Routine messages and data can be sent through memos, letters, or e-mail, because there is little chance of misunderstanding.

Third, senders and receivers should make a special effort to understand each other's perspective. Managers can sensitize themselves to the information receiver so that they will be better able to target the message, detect bias, and clarify missed interpretations. By communicators understanding others' perspectives, semantics can be clarified, perceptions understood, and objectivity maintained.

The fourth individual skill is *management by wandering around*. Managers must be willing to get out of the office and check communications with others. For example, John McDonnell of McDonnell Douglas always ate in the employee cafeteria when he visited far-flung facilities. Through direct observation and face-to-face meetings, managers develop an understanding of the organization and are able to communicate important ideas and values directly to others.

Organizational Actions. Perhaps the most important thing managers can do for the organization is to create a *climate of trust and openness*. Open communication and dialogue can encourage people to communicate honestly with one another. Subordinates will feel free to transmit negative as well as positive messages without fear of retribution. Efforts to develop interpersonal skills among employees can also foster openness, honesty, and trust.

Second, managers should develop and use *formal information channels* in all directions. Scandinavian Design uses two newsletters to reach employees. GM's Packard Electric plant is designed to share all pertinent information—financial, future plans, quality, performance—with employees. Dana Corporation has developed innovative programs such as the "Here's a Thought" board—called a HAT rack—to get ideas and feedback from workers. Other techniques include direct mail, bulletin boards, and employee surveys.

Third, managers should encourage the use of *multiple channels*, including both formal and informal communications. Multiple communication channels include written directives, face-to-face discussions, MBWA, and the grapevine. For example, managers at GM's Packard Electric plant use multimedia, including a monthly newspaper, frequent meetings of employee teams, and an electronic news display in the cafeteria. Sending messages through multiple channels increases the likelihood that they will be properly received.

Fourth, the structure should *fit communication needs*. For example, Harrah's created the Communication Team as part of its structure at the Casino/Holiday Inn in Las Vegas. The team includes one member from each department. It

© 1998 David Zadig

The scoreboard at Colonial Mills, Inc., a $7 million specialty-rug manufacturer in Pawtucket, Rhode Island, overcomes communication barriers by helping all employees get involved in business targets and results. The board stretches 30 feet and covers most of the lunchroom wall. A big gold rocket ship in the middle shows the year-to-date company profit. Columns for winding, braiding, and the other production departments show monthly output— cans filled, square feet braided, etc.—all compared with the company's plan. The Colonial Mills scoreboard is a unique communication channel that encourages upward, downward, and horizontal communication. "Our targets aren't the powers-that-be coming down and saying, 'This shall be the number,'" says Colonial Mills CEO Don Scarlata. "They're numbers everybody has discussed and signed off on."

deals with urgent company problems and helps people think beyond the scope of their own departments to communicate with anyone and everyone to solve those problems. An organization can be designed to use teams, task forces, project managers, or a matrix structure as needed to facilitate the horizontal flow of information for coordination and problem solving. Structure should also reflect information needs. When team or department tasks are difficult, a decentralized structure should be implemented to encourage discussion and participation. A system of organizational *feedback and learning* can help to overcome problems of poor coordination, as well.

■ Summary and Management Solution

This chapter described several important points about communicating in organizations. Communication takes up 80 percent of a manager's time. Communication is a process of encoding an idea into a message, which is sent through a channel and decoded by a receiver. Communication among people can be affected by communication channels, nonverbal communication, and listening skills. Important aspects of management communication include persuasion and influence. Managers use communication to sell people on the vision for the organization and to influence them to behave in such a way as to accomplish the vision. To influence others, managers connect with people on an emotional level by using symbols, metaphors, and stories to communicate their messages.

At the organizational level, managers are concerned with managing formal communications in a downward, upward, and horizontal direction. Informal communications also are important, especially management by wandering around and the grapevine. Moreover, research shows that communication structures in teams and departments should reflect the underlying tasks. Open communication, dialogue, and feedback and learning are important communication mechanisms in the new workplace.

Finally, several barriers to communication were described. These barriers can be overcome by active listening, selecting appropriate channels, engaging in MBWA, using dialogue, developing a climate of trust, using formal channels, designing the correct structure to fit communication needs, and using feedback for learning.

At Childress Buick/Kia Company, Rusty Childress used a variety of tools to harness employee brainpower and break down communication barriers. Customers as well as employees were frustrated and dissatisfied, and Rusty knew the company needed to open the lines of communication fast to remain competitive in the volatile car dealership business. A new employee manual emphasizing the importance of active listening skills, together with a seven-week orientation program, refocused organizational efforts on service through communication. Upward as well as downward communications were strengthened with regular meetings such as "Donuts and Dialogue," town-hall-style get-togethers for all employees, and "Take 5" meetings between a manager and five employees to brainstorm about problems or opportunities. Committees were set up to encourage cross-functional communication and understanding. In addition, a monthly newsletter, employee mailboxes, a computer-based "Suggestion Connection," a telephone hot line, and a weekly e-mail update keep information flowing across departmental lines to assure better and faster customer service. Today, information flows throughout the company in all directions, and an employee-run team is charged with continuous improvement in internal communications. Childress's customer service indexes are regularly above 95 percent for overall customer satisfaction, and employee turnover is among the lowest in the industry. The company boasts a wall full of "Best in Class" awards from General Motors, and Childress regularly hosts visitors from other organizations that use the dealership as a benchmark for customer service.[69]

Discussion Questions

1. How can electronic media such as e-mail improve communication in today's organizations? How might it also lead to poorer communication?
2. Describe the elements of the communication process. Give an example of each part of the model as it exists in the classroom during communication between teacher and students.
3. Why do you think stories are more effective than hard facts and figures in persuading others?
4. Try to recall an incident at school or work when information was passed primarily through the grapevine. How accurate were the rumors, and how did people react to them? How can managers control information that is processed through the grapevine?
5. What is the difference between a discussion and a dialogue? What steps might managers take to transform a discussion into a constructive dialogue?
6. What do you think are the major barriers to upward communication in organizations? Discuss.
7. What is the relationship between group communication and group task? For example, how should communications differ in a strategic planning group and a group of employees who stock shelves in a grocery store?
8. Some senior managers believe they should rely on written information and computer reports because these yield more accurate data than do face-to-face communications. Do you agree?
9. Why is management by wandering around considered effective communication? Consider channel richness and nonverbal communications in formulating your answer.
10. Is speaking accurately or listening actively the more important communication skill for managers? Discuss.
11. Assume that you have been asked to design a training program to help managers become better communicators. What would you include in the program?

Management in Practice: Experiential Exercise

Listening Self-Assessment

Instructions: Choose one response for each of the items below. Base your choice on what you usually do, not on what you think a person *should* do.

1. When you are going to lunch with a friend, you:
   a. Focus your attention on the menu and then on the service provided
   b. Ask about events in your friend's life and pay attention to what's said
   c. Exchange summaries of what is happening to each of you while focusing attention on the meal
2. When someone talks nonstop, you:
   a. Ask questions at an appropriate time in an attempt to help the person focus on the issue
   b. Make an excuse to end the conversation
   c. Try to be patient and understand what you are being told
3. If a group member complains about a fellow employee who, you believe, is disrupting the group, you:
   a. Pay attention and withhold your opinions
   b. Share your own experiences and feelings about that employee
   c. Acknowledge the group member's feelings and ask the group member what options he or she has
4. If someone is critical of you, you:
   a. Try not to react or get upset
   b. Automatically become curious and attempt to learn more
   c. Listen attentively and then back up your position
5. You are having a very busy day and someone tells you to change the way you are completing a task. You believe the person is wrong, so you:
   a. Thank her or him for the input and keep doing what you were doing
   b. Try to find out why she or he thinks you should change
   c. Acknowledge that the other may be right, tell her or him you are very busy, and agree to follow up later
6. When you are ready to respond to someone else, you:
   a. Sometimes will interrupt the person if you believe it is necessary
   b. Almost always speak before the other is completely finished talking
   c. Rarely offer your response until you believe the other has finished
7. After a big argument with someone you have to work with every day, you:
   a. Settle yourself and then try to understand the other's point of view before stating your side again
   b. Just try to go forward and let bygones be bygones
   c. Continue to press your position

8. A colleague calls to tell you that he is upset about getting assigned to a new job. You decide to:
   a. Ask him if he can think of options to help him deal with the situation
   b. Assure him that he is good at what he does and that these things have a way of working out for the best
   c. Let him know you have heard how badly he feels
9. If a friend always complains about her problems but never asks about yours, you:
   a. Try to identify areas of common interest
   b. Remain understanding and attentive, even if it becomes tedious
   c. Support her complaints and mention your own complaints
10. The best way to remain calm in an argument is to:
    a. Continue to repeat your position in a firm but even manner
    b. Repeat what you believe is the other person's position
    c. Tell the other person that you are willing to discuss the matter again when you are both calmer

Score each item of your Listening Self-Assessment

1. (a) 0 (b) 10 (c) 5
2. (a) 10 (b) 0 (c) 5
3. (a) 5 (b) 0 (c) 5
4. (a) 5 (b) 10 (c) 0
5. (a) 0 (b) 10 (c) 5
6. (a) 5 (b) 0 (c) 10
7. (a) 10 (b) 5 (c) 0
8. (a) 5 (b) 5 (c) 10
9. (a) 0 (b) 10 (c) 5
10. (a) 0 (b) 10 (c) 5

Add up your total score

80–100 **You are an active, excellent listener.** You achieve a good balance between listening and asking questions, and you strive to understand others.

50–75 **You are an adequate-to-good listener.** You listen well, although you may sometimes react too quickly to others before they are finished speaking.

25–45 **You have some listening skills but need to improve them.** You may often become impatient when trying to listen to others, hoping they will finish talking so you can talk.

0–20 **You listen to others very infrequently.** You may prefer to do all of the talking and experience extreme frustration while waiting for others to make their point.

SOURCE: Reprinted with permission of the publisher from *Managers As Facilitators: A Practical Guide to Getting Work Done in a Changing Workplace* © 1997 by Richard G. Weaver and John D. Farrell. Berrett-Koehler Publishers, Inc. San Francisco, CA. All Rights Reserved. *http://www.bkconnection.com*

■ Management in Practice: Ethical Dilemma

The Voice of Authority

When Gehan Rasinghe was hired as an account assistant at Werner and Thompson, a business and financial management firm, he was relieved. He was overqualified for the job with his degree in accounting, but the combination of his accented English and his quiet manner had prevented him from securing any other position. Beatrice Werner, one of the managing partners of the firm, was impressed by his educational credentials and his courtly manner. She assured him he had advancement potential with the firm, but the account assistant position was the only one available. After months of rejections in his job hunt, Rasinghe accepted the position. He was committed to making his new job work at all costs.

Account Manager Cathy Putnam was Rasinghe's immediate superior. Putnam spoke with a heavy Boston accent, speaking at a lightning pace to match her enormous workload. She indicated to Rasinghe that he would need to get up to speed as quickly as possible to succeed in working with her. It was soon apparent that Putnam and Rasinghe were at odds. She resented having to repeat directions more than once to teach him his responsibilities. He also seemed resistant to making the many phone calls asking for copies of invoices, disputing charges on credit cards, and following up with clients' staff to get the information necessary to do his job. His accounting work was impeccable, but the public contact part of his job was in bad shape. Even his quiet answer of "No problem" to all her

requests was starting to wear thin on Putnam. Before giving Rasinghe his three-month review, Putnam appealed to Beatrice Werner for help. Putnam was frustrated by their communication problems and didn't know what to do.

Werner had seen the problem coming. Although she had found Rasinghe's bank reconciliations and financial report preparations to be first-rate, she knew that phone work and client contact were a big part of any job in the firm. But as the daughter of German immigrants, Werner also knew that language and cultural barriers could be overcome with persistence and patience. Diversity was one of her ideals for her company, and it was not always easy to achieve. She felt sure that Rasinghe could become an asset to the firm in time. She worried that the time it would take was more than they could afford to give him.

What Do You Do?

1. Give Rasinghe his notice, with the understanding that a job that is primarily paperwork would be a better fit for him. Make the break now rather than later.
2. Place him with an account manager who has more time to help him develop his assertiveness and telephone skills and appreciates his knowledge of accounting.
3. Create a new position for him, where he could do the reports and reconciliations for several account managers, while their assistants concentrated on the public contact work. He would have little chance of future promotion, however.

▨ Surf the Net

1. **Nonverbal Communication.** Read the section in the chapter on "Nonverbal Communication." Use one of the following sites to find information to add to the text's coverage of the topic. Be prepared to share two or three interesting facts in a classroom discussion on the topic.
   http://www.natcom.org/ctronline/nonverb.htm
   http://zzyx.ucsc.edu/~archer/
   http://euphrates.wpunj.edu/faculty/wagnerk/webagogy/hecht.htm

2. **Listening Skills.** The Cyber Listening Lab at *http://www.esl-lab.com/* is designed to be used for ESL (English as a Second Language) purposes. For this exercise, however, you will use the site to test your listening skills. Choose three different listening exercises to complete, record the title of each, listen to the audio clip (requires an audio player available to download at the site), take the listening quiz, and record your score for each. If you scored well on the quizzes (60 percent or better), list the keys from Exhibit 18.4 that you believe helped you listen effectively. If your score could have been better, identify the keys that you could have used to improve your score.

3. **Speaking Skills.** Use either of the following sites to access and print out an oral evaluation form:
   http://showcase.netins.net/web/bokat/rubricoral.htm
   http://www.phschool.com/professional_development/assessment/rub_oral_presentation.cfm

   Use the form to evaluate an oral presentation as instructed by your professor. On the back side of the evaluation form, write a short paragraph describing the public-speaking principle you think contributes most to the success of an oral presentation and why you believe it is most important.

▨ Case for Critical Analysis

Inter-City Manufacturing, Inc.

The president of Inter-City Manufacturing Inc., Rich Langston, wanted to facilitate upward communication. He believed an open-door policy was a good place to start. He announced that his own door was open to all employees and encouraged senior managers to do the same. He felt this would give him a way to get early warning signals that would not be filtered or redirected through the formal chain of command. Langston found that many employees who used the open-door policy had been with the company for years and were comfortable talking to the president. Sometimes messages came through about inadequate policies and procedures. Langston would raise these issues and explain any changes at the next senior managers' meeting.

The most difficult complaints to handle were those from people who were not getting along with their bosses. One employee, Leroy, complained bitterly that his manager had overcommitted the department and put everyone under too much pressure. Leroy argued that long hours and low morale were major problems. But he would not allow Rich Langston to bring the manager into the discussion nor to seek out other employees to confirm the complaint. Although Langston suspected that Leroy might be right, he could not let the matter sit and blurted out, "Have you considered leaving the company?" This made Leroy realize that a meeting with his immediate boss was unavoidable.

Before the three-party meeting, Langston contacted Leroy's manager and explained what was going on. He insisted that the manager come to the meeting willing to listen and without hostility toward Leroy. During the meeting, Leroy's manager listened actively and displayed no ill will. He learned the problem from Leroy's perspective and realized he was over his head in his new job. After the meeting, the manager said he was relieved. He had been promoted into the job from a technical position just a few months earlier and had no management or planning experience. He welcomed Rich Langston's offer to help him do a better job of planning.

Questions

1. What techniques increased Rich Langston's communication effectiveness? Discuss.
2. Do you think that an open-door policy was the right way to improve upward communications? What other techniques would you suggest?
3. What problems do you think an open-door policy creates? Do you think many employees are reluctant to use it? Why?

SOURCE: Based on Everett T. Suters, "Hazards of an Open-Door Policy," *Inc.* (January 1987), 99–102.

■ Endnotes

1. Jean Kerr, "The Informers," *Inc.* (March 1995), 50–61.

2. Christina Le Beau, "Bad Vibes," *Working Woman* (November 2000), 30–32.

3. Jenny C. McCune, "That Elusive Thing Called Trust," *Management Review* (July–August 1998), 10–16.

4. Elizabeth B. Drew, "Profile: Robert Strauss," *The New Yorker* (May 7, 1979), 55–70.

5. Henry Mintzberg, *The Nature of Managerial Work* (New York: Harper & Row, 1973).

6. Fred Luthans and Janet K. Larsen, "How Managers Really Communicate," *Human Relations* 39 (1986), 161–178; and Larry E. Penley and Brian Hawkins, "Studying Interpersonal Communication in Organizations: A Leadership Application," *Academy of Management Journal* 28 (1985), 309–326.

7. D. K. Berlo, *The Process of Communication* (New York: Holt, Rinehart and Winston, 1960), 24.

8. Paul Roberts, "Live! From Your Office! It's . . . ," *Fast Company* (October 1999), 150–170.

9. Bruce K. Blaylock, "Cognitive Style and the Usefulness of Information," *Decision Sciences* 15 (Winter 1984), 74–91.

10. Robert H. Lengel and Richard L. Daft, "The Selection of Communication Media as an Executive Skill," *Academy of Management Executive* 2 (August 1988), 225–232; Richard L. Daft and Robert H. Lengel, "Organizational Information Requirements, Media Richness and Structural Design," *Managerial Science* 32 (May 1986), 554–572; and Jane Webster and Linda Klebe Trevino, "Rational and Social Theories as Complementary Explanations of Communication Media Choices: Two Policy-Capturing Studies," *Academy of Management Journal* 38, no. 6 (1995), 1544–1572.

11. Ford S. Worthy, "How CEOs Manage Their Time," *Fortune* (January 18, 1988), 88–97.

12. "E-mail Can't Mimic Phone Calls," *Johnson City Press* (September 17, 2000), 31.

13. Thomas E. Weber, "After Terror Attacks, Companies Rethink Role of Face-to-Face," *The Wall Street Journal* (September 24, 2001), B1.

14. Ronald E. Rice, "Task Analyzability, Use of New Media, and Effectiveness: A Multi-Site Exploration of Media Richness," *Organizational Science* 3, no. 4 (November 1992), 475–500; and M. Lynne Markus, "Electronic Mail as the Medium of Managerial Choice," *Organizational Science* 5, no. 4 (November 1994), 502–527.

15. Richard L. Daft, Robert H. Lengel, and Linda Klebe Trevino, "Message Equivocality, Media Selection and Manager Performance: Implication for Information Systems," *MIS Quarterly* 11 (1987), 355–368.

16. Mary Young and James E. Post, "Managing to Communicate, Communicating to Manage: How Leading Companies Communicate with Employees," *Organizational Dynamics* (Summer 1993), 31–43.

17. Jay A. Conger, "The Necessary Art of Persuasion," *Harvard Business Review* (May–June 1998), 84–95.

18. Steve Barnes, "Everyone Now Hears Once-Quiet Company," New York Times News Service in *Johnson City Press* (September 10, 2000), 33.

19. Thomas A. Stewart, "The Cunning Plots of Leadership," *Fortune* (September 7, 1998), 165–166.

20. J. Martin and M. Powers, "Organizational Stories: More Vivid and Persuasive than Quantitative Data," in B. M. Staw, ed., *Psychological Foundations of Organizational Behavior* (Glenview, Illinois: Scott Foresman, 1982), 161–168.

21. I. Thomas Sheppard, "Silent Signals," *Supervisory Management* (March 1986), 31–33.

22. Albert Mehrabian, *Silent Messages* (Belmont, Calif.: Wadsworth, 1971); and Albert Mehrabian, "Communicating without Words," *Psychology Today* (September 1968), 53–55.

23. Sheppard, "Silent Signals."

24. Arthur H. Bell, *The Complete Manager's Guide to Interviewing* (Homewood, Ill.: Richard D. Irwin, 1989).

25. C. Glenn Pearce, "Doing Something about Your Listening Ability," *Supervisory Management* (March 1989), 29–34; and Tom Peters, "Learning to Listen," *Hyatt Magazine* (Spring 1988), 16–21.

26. M. P. Nichols, *The Lost Art of Listening* (New York: Guilford Publishing, 1995).

27. Monci Jo Williams, "America's Best Salesman," *Fortune* (October 26, 1987), 122–134.

28. Gerald M. Goldhaber, *Organizational Communication,* 4th ed. (Dubuque, Iowa: Wm. C. Brown, 1980), 189.

29. John M. Ivancevich and Michael T. Matteson, *Organizational Behavior and Management,* 6th ed. (Boston, Ill.: McGraw-Hill Irwin, 2002), 507.

30. Richard L. Daft and Richard M. Steers, *Organizations: A Micro/Macro Approach* (New York: Harper Collins, 1986); and Daniel Katz and Robert Kahn, *The Social Psychology of Organizations,* 2d ed. (New York: Wiley, 1978).

31. Aaron Pressman, "Business Gets the Message," *The Industry Standard* (February 26, 2001), 58–59.

32. Cathy Olofson, "What We Have Here Is No Failure to Communicate," *Fast Company* (July 2000), 76.

33. Roberta Maynard, "It Can Pay to Show Employees the Big Picture," *Nation's Business* (December 1994), 10.

34. William C. Taylor, "At VeriFone, It's a Dog's Life (And They Love It)," *Fast Company* (November 1995), 12–15; and William R. Pape, "Relative Merits," *Inc. Technology* 1 (1998), 23.

35. Phillip G. Clampitt, Robert J. DeKoch, and Thomas Cashman, "A Strategy for Communicating about Uncertainty," *Academy of Management Executive* 14, no. 4 (2000), 41–57.

36. J. G. Miller, "Living Systems: The Organization," *Behavioral Science* 17 (1972), 69.

37. Michael J. Glauser, "Upward Information Flow in Organizations: Review and Conceptual Analysis," *Human Relations* 37 (1984), 613–643; and "Upward/Downward Communication: Critical Information Channels," *Small Business Report* (October 1985), 85–88.

38. Carol Leonetti Dannhauser, "Shut Up and Listen," *Working Woman* (May 1999), 41.

39. Mary P. Rowe and Michael Baker, "Are You Hearing Enough Employee Concerns?" *Harvard Business Review* 62 (May–June 1984), 127–135; W. H. Read, "Upward Communication in Industrial Hierarchies," *Human Relations* 15 (February 1962), 3–15; and Daft and Steers, *Organizations.*

40. Barbara Ettorre, "The Unvarnished Truth," *Management Review* (June 1997), 54–57; and Roberta Maynard, "Back to Basics, From the Top," *Nation's Business* (December 1996), 38–39.

41. Thomas Petzinger, "A Hospital Applies Teamwork to Thwart An Insidious Enemy," *The Wall Street Journal* (May 8, 1998), B1.

42. E. M. Rogers and R. A. Rogers, *Communication in Organizations* (New York: Free Press, 1976); and A. Bavelas and D. Barrett, "An Experimental Approach to Organization Communication," *Personnel* 27 (1951), 366–371.

43. This discussion is based on Daft and Steers, *Organizations.*

44. Bavelas and Barrett, "An Experimental Approach"; and M. E. Shaw, *Group Dynamics: The Psychology of Small Group Behavior* (New York: McGraw-Hill, 1976).

45. Richard L. Daft and Norman B. Macintosh, "A Tentative Exploration into the Amount and Equivocality of Information Processing in Organizational Work Units," *Administrative Science Quarterly* 26 (1981), 207–224.

46. Matt Goldberg, "Microsoft Knows How to Operate—Fast," *Fast Company* (April–May 1998), 76.

47. Erika Germer, "Huddle Up!" *Fast Company* (December 2000), 86.

48. Nancy K. Austin, "The Skill Every Manager Must Master," *Working Woman* (May 1995), 29–30.

49. Thomas J. Peters and Robert H. Waterman Jr., *In Search of Excellence* (New York: Harper & Row, 1982); and Tom Peters and Nancy Austin, *A Passion for Excellence: The Leadership Difference* (New York: Random House, 1985).

50. Lois Therrien, "How Ztel Went from Riches to Rags," *Business Week* (June 17, 1985), 97–100.

51. Keith Davis and John W. Newstrom, *Human Behavior at Work: Organizational Behavior,* 7th ed. (New York: McGraw-Hill, 1985).

52. Joshua Hyatt, "The Last Shift," *Inc.* (February 1989), 74–80.

53. Goldhaber, *Organizational Communication;* and Philip V. Louis, *Organizational Communication,* 3d ed. (New York: Wiley, 1987).

54. Donald B. Simmons, "The Nature of the Organizational Grapevine," *Supervisory Management* (November 1985), 39–42; and Davis and Newstrom, *Human Behavior.*

55. Barbara Ettorre, "Hellooo. Anybody Listening?" *Management Review* (November 1997), 9.

56. "They Hear It Through the Grapevine," in Michael Warshaw, "The Good Guy's Guide to Office Politics," *Fast Company* (April–May 1998), 157–178 (page 160); Carol Hildebrand, "Mapping the Invisible Workplace," *CIO Enterprise,* Section 2 (July 15, 1998), 18–20; and David I. Bradford and Allan R. Cohen, *Power Up: Transforming Organizations Through Shared Leadership* (New York: Wiley, 1998).

57. John Case, "Opening the Books," *Harvard Business Review,* (March–April 1997), 118–127.

58. Gary Hamel, "Killer Strategies That Make Shareholders Rich," *Fortune* (June 23, 1997), 70–84.

59. "What Is Trust?" results of a survey by Manchester Consulting, reported in Jenny C. McCune, "That Elusive Thing Called Trust," *Management Review* (July-August 1998), 10-16.

60. David Bohm, *On Dialogue* (Ojai, Calif.: David Bohm Seminars, 1989).

61. This discussion is based on Glenna Gerard and Linda Teurfs, "Dialogue and Organizational Transformation," in *Community Building: Renewing Spirit and Learning in Business,* ed. Kazinierz Gozdz (New Leaders Press, 1995), 142–153; and Edgar H. Schein, "On Dialogue, Culture, and Organizational Learning," *Organizational Dynamics* (Autumn 1993), 40–51.

62. Carol Hymowitz, "How to Tell Employees All the Things They Don't Want to Hear" (In the Lead column), *The Wall Street Journal* (August 22, 2000), B1.

63. Peter Lowry and Byron Reimus, "Ready, Aim, Communicate," *Management Review* (July 1996).

64. Thomas E. Ricks, "Army Devises System to Decide What Does, and Does Not, Work," *The Wall Street Journal* (May 23, 1997), A1, A10; Stephanie Watts Sussman, "CALL: A Model for Effective Organizational Learning," *Strategy* (Summer 1999), 14-15; and Thomas A. Stewart, "Listen Up, Maggots! You **Will** Deploy a More Humane and Effective Managerial Style!" *Ecompany* (July 2001), 95.

65. Stewart, "Listen Up, Maggots!"

66. James A. F. Stoner and R. Edward Freeman, *Management,* 4th ed. (Englewood Cliffs, N.J.: Prentice-Hall, 1989).

67. Mike Hofman, "Lost in the Translation," *Inc.* (May 2000), 161-162.

68. Janet Fulk and Sirish Mani, "Distortion of Communication in Hierarchical Relationships," in *Communication Yearbook,* vol. 9, ed. M. L. McLaughlin (Beverly Hills, Calif.: Sage, 1986), 483–510.

69. Jean Kerr, "The Informers."

19

Teamwork in Organizations

CHAPTER OUTLINE

Teams at Work

What Is a Team?

Model of Work Team
Effectiveness

Types of Teams

Formal Teams

Self-Directed Teams

Teams in the New Workplace

Team Characteristics

Size

Member Roles

Team Processes

Stages of Team Development

Team Cohesiveness

Team Norms

Managing Team Conflict

Causes of Conflict

Styles to Handle Conflict

Benefits and Costs of Teams

Potential Benefits of Teams

Potential Costs of Teams

LEARNING OBJECTIVES

After studying this chapter, you should be able to

1 Identify the types of teams in organizations.

2 Discuss new applications of teams to facilitate employee involvement.

3 Identify roles within teams and the type of role you could play to help a team be effective.

4 Explain the general stages of team development.

5 Explain the concepts of team cohesiveness and team norms and their relationship to team performance.

6 Understand the causes of conflict within and among teams and how to reduce conflict.

7 Discuss the assets and liabilities of organizational teams.

Management Challenge

Nestled in the foothills of the Appalachian Mountains, the Rowe Furniture Company of Salem, Virginia, has been cranking out sofas, loveseats, and easy chairs for more than 40 years. When Charlene Pedrolie arrived as the plant's new manufacturing chief, she found 500 people who came to work, punched their time cards, turned off their brains, and did exactly what they were told to do. The pay was good by local standards, but workers were bored and apathetic. The traditional assembly line, which required that workers perform the same tasks over and over— one person cutting, another sewing, another gluing, and so forth—had worked well for Rowe in the past, but the marketplace was undergoing a revolution. Furniture shoppers used to be content to buy what was on the showroom floor or else wait months for a custom-made product. But not any longer—

customers were demanding custom-designed pieces, but they balked at the idea of waiting the standard three to six months for delivery. Top executives wanted to increase sales by installing a network of showroom computers, which would allow customers to choose fabrics and furniture designs to their individual taste and zap the order directly to the Rowe plant. And, they wanted to promise delivery within a month. Plant workers snorted at the preposterous idea. How on earth were they supposed to do it? Pedrolie knew the factory needed a hyperefficient assembly process—and a management system that tapped into the minds and energy of every single worker. [1]

What would you recommend Pedrolie do to meet this challenge? Can the formation of teams help solve the problem?

The problems facing Rowe Furniture also confront many other companies. How can they be more flexible and responsive in an increasingly competitive environment? A quiet revolution has been taking place in organizations across the country and around the world as companies respond by using employee teams. From the assembly line to the executive office, from large corporations such as Ford Motor Company and 3M to small businesses such as St. Louis plantscaping firm Growing Green, teams are becoming the basic building block of organizations. Recent data show that nearly half of *Fortune* 1000 companies make extensive use of teams, and 60 percent plan to increase their use of teams in the near future. A study of 109 Canadian organizations found that 42 percent reported widespread team-based activity, and only 13 percent reported little or no team activity. Teamwork has become the most frequent topic taught in company training programs.[2]

Teams are popping up in the most unexpected places. An electromechanical assembly plant found that both quality and productivity increased after it abandoned the traditional production line in favor of work teams.[3] At Mattel, a team of artists, toy designers, computer experts, and automobile designers slashed 13 months from the usual toy design process, creating Top Speed toy cars in only 5 months. Hecla Mining Company uses teams for company goal setting; a major telecommunications company uses teams of salespeople to deal with big customers with complex purchasing requirements; and Lassiter Middle School in Jefferson County, Kentucky, uses teams of teachers to prepare daily schedules and handle student discipline problems. Multinational corporations are now using international teams composed of managers from different countries.[4]

As we will see in this chapter, teams have emerged as a powerful management tool, because they involve and empower employees. Teams can cut across organizations in unusual ways. Hence workers are more satisfied, and higher productivity and product quality typically result. Moreover, managers discover a more flexible organization in which workers are not stuck in narrow jobs.

This chapter focuses on teams and their new applications within organizations. We will define various types of teams, explore their stages of development, and examine such characteristics as size, cohesiveness, and norms. We will discuss how individuals can make contributions to teams and review the benefits and costs associated with teamwork. Teams are an important aspect of organizational life, and the ability to manage them is an important component of manager and organization success.

Teams at Work

In this section, we will first define teams and then discuss a model of team effectiveness that summarizes the important concepts.

What Is a Team?

team
A unit of two or more people who interact and coordinate their work to accomplish a specific goal.

A **team** is a unit of two or more people who interact and coordinate their work to accomplish a specific goal.[5] This definition has three components. First, two or more people are required. Teams can be quite large, although most have fewer than 15 people. Second, people in a team have regular interaction. People who do not interact, such as when standing in line at a lunch counter or riding in an elevator, do not compose a team. Third, people in a team share

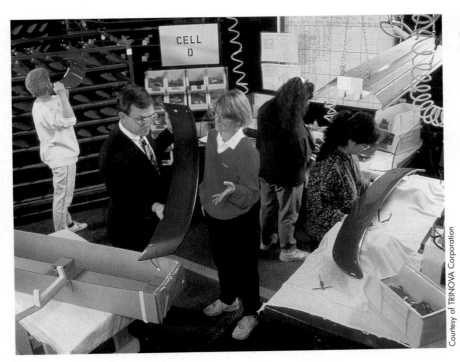

Courtesy of TRINOVA Corporation

Teams are emerging as a powerful management tool and are popping up in the most unexpected places, such as this manufacturing cell at TRINOVA'S Aeroquip Inoac facility in Fremont, Ohio. The facility uses more than 40 teams that cross operations and job functions, helping the company eliminate non-value-added activities, lower costs, improve customer responsiveness, and increase quality.

a performance goal, whether it be to design a new hand-held computer, build a car, or write a textbook. Students often are assigned to teams to do classwork assignments, in which case the purpose is to perform the assignment and receive an acceptable grade.

Although a team is a group of people, the two terms are not interchangeable. An employer, a teacher, or a coach can put together a *group* of people and never build a *team*. The team concept implies a sense of shared mission and collective responsibility. Exhibit 19.1 lists the primary differences between groups and teams. Pat Summitt, legendary coach of the University of Tennessee women's basketball team, is the second all-time winningest coach (male or female) of NCAA basketball titles. She has a talent for building solid teams rather than relying on top stars such as Chamique Holdsclaw. "You have to surrender the 'me' attitude for the good of the team," Summitt tells every new player. That philosophy is drummed into players from the recruiting process on, and veteran players usually push the team philosophy to new recruits just

Group	Team
• Has a designated strong leader	• Shares or rotates leadership roles
• Individual accountability	• Individual and mutual accountability (accountable to each other)
• Identical purpose for group and organization	• Specific team vision or purpose
• Individual work products	• Collective work products
• Runs efficient meetings	• Meetings encourage open-ended discussion and problem solving
• Effectiveness measured indirectly by influence on business (such as financial performance)	• Effectiveness measured directly by assessing collective work
• Discusses, decides, delegates work to individuals	• Discusses, decides, shares work

E x h i b i t   19.1

Differences between Groups and Teams

SOURCE: Adapted from Jon R. Katzenbach and Douglas K. Smith, "The Discipline of Teams," *Harvard Business Review* (March–April 1995), 111–120.

Putting People First

as hard as Summitt does.[6] The sports world provides many examples of successful teamwork. One manager learned valuable lessons about team-building by participating in the 10-month BT Global Challenge around-the-world race, as described in this chapter's Putting People First box.

Model of Work Team Effectiveness

Some of the factors associated with team effectiveness are illustrated in Exhibit 19.2. Work team effectiveness is based on two outcomes—productive output and personal satisfaction.[7] *Satisfaction* pertains to the team's ability to meet the personal needs of its members and hence maintain their membership and commitment. *Productive output* pertains to the quality and quantity of task outputs as defined by team goals.

The factors that influence team effectiveness begin with the organizational context.[8] The organizational context in which the group operates is described in other chapters and includes such factors as structure, strategy, environment, culture, and reward systems. Within that context, managers define teams. Important team characteristics are the type of team, the team structure, and team composition. Factors such as the diversity of the team in terms of gender and race, as well as knowledge, skills, and attitudes, can have a tremendous impact on team processes and effectiveness.[9] Managers must decide when to create permanent teams within the formal structure and when to use a temporary task team. Team size and roles also are important. Managers must also consider whether a team is the best way to do a task. If

Exhibit 19.2

Work Team Effectiveness Model

costs outweigh benefits, managers may wish to assign an individual employee to the task.

These team characteristics influence processes internal to the team, which in turn affect output and satisfaction. Leaders must understand and manage stages of development, cohesiveness, norms, and conflict in order to establish an effective team. These processes are influenced by team and organizational characteristics and by the ability of members and leaders to direct these processes in a positive manner.

The model of team performance in Exhibit 19.2 is the basis for this chapter. In the following sections, we will examine types of organizational teams, team structure, internal processes, and team benefits and costs.

Types of Teams

Many types of teams can exist within organizations. The easiest way to classify teams is in terms of those created as part of the organization's formal structure and those created to increase employee participation.

Formal Teams

Formal teams are created by the organization as part of the formal organization structure. Two common types of formal teams are vertical and horizontal, which typically represent vertical and horizontal structural relationships, as described in Chapters 10 and 11. These two types of teams are illustrated in Exhibit 19.3. A third type of formal team is the special-purpose team.

formal team
A team created by the organization as part of the formal organization structure.

Vertical Team. A **vertical team** is composed of a manager and his or her subordinates in the formal chain of command. Sometimes called a *functional team* or a *command team,* the vertical team may in some cases include three or four levels of hierarchy within a functional department. Typically, the vertical team includes a single department in an organization. The third-shift nursing team on the second floor of St. Luke's Hospital is a vertical team that includes nurses and a supervisor. A financial analysis department, a quality control department, an accounting department, and a human resource department are all command teams. Each is created by the organization to attain specific goals through members' joint activities and interactions.

vertical team
A formal team composed of a manager and his or her subordinates in the organization's formal chain of command.

Exhibit *19.3*

Horizontal and Vertical Teams in an Organization

- - - - **Horizontal team for L21 modification**
———— **Vertical engineering team**

horizontal team

A formal team composed of employees from about the same hierarchical level but from different areas of expertise.

committee

A long-lasting, sometimes permanent team in the organization structure created to deal with tasks that recur regularly.

Horizontal Team. A **horizontal team** is composed of employees from about the same hierarchical level but from different areas of expertise.[10] A horizontal team is drawn from several departments, is given a specific task, and may be disbanded after the task is completed. The two most common types of horizontal teams are task forces and committees.

As described in Chapter 11, a *task force* is a group of employees from different departments formed to deal with a specific activity and existing only until the task is completed. Sometimes called a *cross-functional team*, the task force might be used to create a new product in a manufacturing organization or a new history curriculum in a university. Several departments are involved, and many views have to be considered, so these tasks are best served with a horizontal team. For example, at GE Lighting Co., a cross-functional team with members from information technology, finance, and several other departments oversaw an ambitious systems-integration project that spanned operations in the United States and Canada.[11] Hallmark Cards uses cross-functional teams made up of artists, writers, lithographers, designers, and photographers to create new greeting cards for each major holiday.[12]

A **committee** generally is long-lived and may be a permanent part of the organization's structure. Membership on a committee usually is decided by a person's title or position rather than by personal expertise. A committee often needs official representation, compared with selection for a task force, which is based on personal qualifications for solving a problem. Committees typically are formed to deal with tasks that recur regularly. For example, a grievance committee handles employee grievances; an advisory committee makes recommendations in the areas of employee compensation and work practices; a worker-management committee may be concerned with work rules, job design changes, and suggestions for work improvement.[13]

As part of the horizontal structure of the organization, task forces and committees offer several advantages: (1) They allow organization members to exchange information; (2) they generate suggestions for coordinating the organizational units that are represented; (3) they develop new ideas and solutions for existing organizational problems; and (4) they assist in the development of new organizational practices and policies.

Special-Purpose Team. **Special-purpose teams,** sometimes called *project teams,* are created outside the formal organization structure to undertake a project of special importance or creativity. Special-purpose teams focus on a specific purpose and expect to disband once the specific project is completed.[14] Examples include the team that developed the first IBM ThinkPad, the project team for the original Ford Taurus, and the team that created Chicken McNuggets for McDonald's. A special-purpose team still is part of the formal organization and has its own reporting structure, but members perceive themselves as a separate entity.[15]

Self-Directed Teams

Employee involvement through teams is designed to increase the participation of low-level workers in decision making and the conduct of their jobs, with the goal of improving performance. Employee involvement started out simply with techniques such as information sharing with employees or asking employees for suggestions about improving the work. Gradually, companies moved toward greater autonomy for employees, which led first to problem-solving teams and then to self-directed teams.[16]

Problem-solving teams typically consist of 5 to 12 hourly employees from the same department who voluntarily meet to discuss ways of improving quality, efficiency, and the work environment. Recommendations are proposed to management for approval. Problem-solving teams usually are the first step in a company's move toward greater employee participation. The most widely known application is quality circles, initiated by Japanese companies, in which employees focus on ways to improve quality in the production process. USX adopted this approach in several of its steel mills, recognizing that quality takes a team effort. Under the title All Product Excellence program (APEX), USX set up APEX teams of up to 12 employees who meet several times a month to solve quality problems.[17]

As a company matures, problem-solving teams can gradually evolve into self-directed teams, which represent a fundamental change in how employee work is organized. Self-directed teams enable employees to feel challenged, find their work meaningful, and develop a strong sense of identity with the company.[18] **Self-directed teams** typically consist of 5 to 20 multiskilled workers who rotate jobs to produce an entire product or service or at least one complete aspect or portion of a product or service (e.g., engine assembly, insurance claim processing). The central idea is that the teams themselves, rather than managers or supervisors, take responsibility for their work, make decisions, monitor their own performance, and alter their work behavior as needed to solve problems, meet goals, and adapt to changing conditions.[19] Self-directed teams are permanent teams that typically include the following elements:

- The team includes employees with several skills and functions, and the combined skills are sufficient to perform a major organizational task. A team may include members from the foundry, machining, grinding, fabrication, and sales departments, with members cross-trained to perform one

special-purpose team
A team created outside the formal organization to undertake a project of special importance or creativity.

problem-solving team
Typically 5 to 12 hourly employees from the same department who meet to discuss ways of improving quality, efficiency, and the work environment.

self-directed team
A team consisting of 5 to 20 multiskilled workers who rotate jobs to produce an entire product or service, often supervised by an elected member.

Highsmith Inc., a Fort Atkinson, Wisconsin, company, is the country's leading mail-order supplier of equipment such as book displays, audio-video tools, and educational software for schools and libraries. The company's employees work in a flat organization in which self-directed teams, along with a continuous-learning program and flextime, are manifest. According to CEO Duncan Highsmith, "We have a limited labor market, so I wanted to make the most of the people we had by helping them become decision makers, by providing them with information and the context to make good decisions." In the photo is a team of librarians (left to right, Oma Dixon, Lisa Guedea Carreño, and Genevieve Mecherly) who facilitate the culture of autonomy at Highsmith. "We're here to help people integrate information into their jobs as seamlessly as possible," says Carreño. "That way, they can keep doing their jobs."

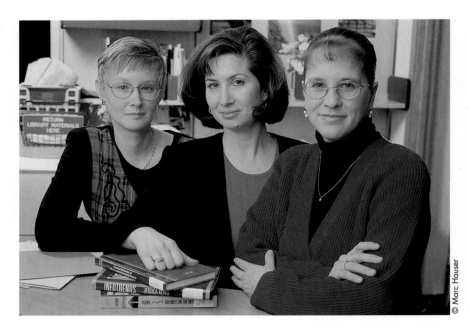

another's jobs. The team eliminates barriers among departments, enabling excellent coordination to produce a product or service.

- The team is given access to resources such as information, equipment, machinery, and supplies needed to perform the complete task.

- The team is empowered with decision-making authority, which means that members have the freedom to select new members, solve problems, spend money, monitor results, and plan for the future.[20]

In a self-directed team, team members take over managerial duties such as scheduling or ordering materials. They work with minimum supervision, perhaps electing one of their own as supervisor, who may change each year. The most effective self-directed teams are those that are fully empowered, as described in the discussion of empowerment in Chapter 17. In addition to having increased responsibility and discretion, empowered teams are those that have a strong belief in their team's capabilities, find value and meaning in their work, and recognize the impact the team's work has on customers, other stakeholders, and organizational success.[21] Managers create the conditions that determine whether self-directed teams are empowered by giving teams true power and freedom, complete information, knowledge and skills, and appropriate rewards. Whole Foods Markets provides an excellent example of the use of self-directed teams.

WHOLE FOODS MARKET
http://www.wholefoods.com

In 1991, Whole Foods Market had barely a dozen stores in three states. Today, it has the clout of a nationwide chain, with 126 stores throughout the United States and net profits that are typically double the national average.

The Whole Foods culture is based on decentralized teamwork. Each store is an autonomous profit center made up of an average of 10 self-directed teams—grocery, produce, and so forth. Teams—and only teams—have the power to approve new hires for full-time jobs. Store leaders screen candidates and recommend them for a job on a specific team, but it takes a two-thirds vote of the team to approve the hire. Team members deal directly with products, customers, and vendors, and everyone works together to identify and accomplish team goals.

The company believes the first prerequisite of teamwork is trust. That trust starts with the hiring vote. In addition, Whole Foods supports teamwork with wide-open information on financial and operations systems. Sensitive figures on store sales, team sales, profit margins, and even yearly salaries and bonuses are available to any employee. According to CEO John Mackey, open information keeps everyone "aligned to the vision of shared fate . . . . If you're trying to create a high-trust organization, an organization where people are all-for-one and one-for-all, you can't have secrets."22 ❖

Self-directed teams such as those at Whole Foods Market can be highly effective. Another organization that succeeds with teamwork is Consolidated Diesel's engine factory in Whitakers, North Carolina. In its 20 or so years of operation as a team-based organization, the plant has had higher revenues, lower turnover, and significantly lower injury rates than the industry average. In addition, while most plants average 1 supervisor for every 25 workers, Consolidated Diesel has 1 for every 100 employees because the plant workers themselves handle many supervisory duties. The difference yields a savings of about $1 million a year.23

Teams in the New Workplace

Some exciting new approaches to teamwork have resulted from advances in information technology, shifting employee expectations, and the globalization of business. Two types of teams that are increasingly being used are virtual teams and global teams.

Virtual Teams. A **virtual team** is made up of geographically or organizationally dispersed members who are linked primarily through advanced information and telecommunications technologies.24 Although some virtual teams may be made up of only organizational members, virtual teams often include contingent workers, members of partner organizations, customers, suppliers, consultants, or other outsiders. Team members use e-mail, voice mail, videoconferencing, Internet and intranet technologies, and various types of collaboration software to perform their work, although they may also sometimes meet face to face.

Virtual teams are highly flexible and dynamic. Some are temporary cross-functional teams pulled together to work on specific projects or problems, while others are long-term or permanent self-directed teams. Team leadership is typically shared or altered, depending on the area of expertise needed at each stage of the project.25 In addition, team membership in virtual teams may change fairly quickly, depending on the tasks to be performed. One of the primary advantages of virtual teams is the ability to rapidly assemble the most appropriate group of people to complete a complex project, solve a particular problem, or exploit a specific strategic opportunity. The success of virtual teams depends on several factors, including selecting the right members, building trust, sharing information, and effectively using technology. VeriFone, described in the Leading Online box, uses virtual teams in every aspect of its business.

Global Teams. Virtual teams are also sometimes global teams. **Global teams** are cross-border work teams made up of members of different

virtual team
A team that uses advanced information and telecommunications technologies so that geographically distant members can collaborate on projects and reach common goals.

global team
A work team made up of members of different nationalities whose activities span multiple countries; may operate as a virtual team or meet face to face.

Leading Online

VeriFone's Virtual World

VeriFone, an equipment supplier for credit card verification and automated payments, started out as a virtual company over 15 years ago and today uses virtual teams in every aspect of its business. Teams of facility managers work together to determine how to reduce toxins in their offices. Marketing and development groups brainstorm new products. Sales reps pool information and customer testimonials.

VeriFone's concept of virtual teams is highly flexible. Some teams may include only VeriFone employees while others include outsiders, such as the employees of a customer or partner. Some are permanent, such as operational teams that run their companies virtually, while others are temporary. Any employee can organize a temporary virtual team to work on a specific problem. For example, one sales rep sent out an SOS when he saw a major sales prospect in Greece falling apart. Overnight, a team made up of sales, marketing, and technical-support staff from around the world came together online to provide data and testimonials that eventually helped the Greek representative make the sale.

Despite all this flexibility, VeriFone has some pretty strict "rules" to ensure that teams are not formed haphazardly. Employees complete a 40-hour training program in which they learn how to create a successful virtual team. In addition, leaders of virtual teams follow written procedures put together by the company's senior managers. VeriFone offers the following guidelines for successful virtual teams:

1. *Define the purpose.* A VeriFone team always starts by putting its purpose in writing. This keeps everyone on track and prevents misunderstandings.

2. *Recruit team members.* Most virtual teams should be between three and seven members. Also, the team should include people who represent a diversity of views and experiences. Selecting members in different time zones means productive work can be going on around the clock.

3. *Determine the duration of the team.* Decide whether the purpose and goals call for a short-term task force or problem-solving team or for a long-term operational team.

4. *Select the communications technology.* All VeriFone staffers are not only well-trained in *how* to use communications tools but also in *when* to use them. General guidelines are that for keeping in contact remotely, teams use beepers, cell phones, and voice mail; for disseminating information, fax, e-mail, and application sharing over the network. For brainstorming, discussion, and decision making, teams use e-mail, instant messaging, conference calls, and videoconferencing. Selecting the right tool is critical to the success of the virtual team.

VeriFone employees also are trained to understand the psychological pitfalls of communicating virtually. Some subtleties of meaning are always lost, and misunderstandings are more common than when teams work face to face. E-mail in particular can lead to misunderstandings, so team members communicate by phone or videoconference on sensitive or complicated issues.

SOURCE: William R. Pape, "Group Insurance," *Inc. Technology* (1997), no. 2, 29, 31.

nationalities whose activities span multiple countries.[26] Generally, global teams fall into two categories: intercultural teams, whose members come from different countries or cultures and meet face to face, and virtual global teams, whose members remain in separate locations around the world and conduct their work electronically.[27] For example, lengthy phone calls, frequent e-mail, and weekly videoconferences provided the lifeline between global team members creating Texas Instruments C82 digital signal processor.[28] The research department at BT Labs has 660 researchers spread across the United Kingdom and several other countries. The researchers work in global virtual teams that investigate virtual reality, artificial intelligence, and other advanced information technologies.[29]

Global teams can present enormous challenges for team leaders, who have to bridge gaps of time, distance, and culture. In some cases, members speak different languages, use different technologies, and have different beliefs about authority, time orientation, decision making, and so forth. Culture differences can significantly affect team-working relationships. Organizations using global teams invest the time and resources to adequately educate employees. They have to make sure all team members appreciate and understand cultural differences, are focused on goals, and understand their responsibilities to the team. For a global team to be effective, all team members must be willing to deviate somewhat from their own values and norms and establish new norms for the team.[30] As with virtual teams, carefully selecting team members, building trust, and sharing information are critical to success.

Team Characteristics

The next issue of concern to managers is designing the team for greatest effectiveness. One factor is *team characteristics,* which can affect team dynamics and performance. Characteristics of particular concern are team size and member roles.

Size

The ideal size of work teams often is thought to be 7, although variations of from 5 to 12 typically are associated with good team performance. These teams are large enough to take advantage of diverse skills, enable members to express good and bad feelings, and aggressively solve problems. They also are small enough to permit members to feel an intimate part of the group.

In general, as a team increases in size, it becomes harder for each member to interact with and influence the others. Ray Oglethorpe, president of AOL Technologies, which makes extensive use of teams, believes keeping teams small is the key to success. "If you have more than 15 or 20 people, you're dead," he says. "The connections between team members are too hard to make."[31] A summary of research on group size suggests the following:[32]

1. Small teams (2 to 4 members) show more agreement, ask more questions, and exchange more opinions. Members want to get along with one another. Small teams report more satisfaction and enter into more personal discussions. They tend to be informal and make few demands on team leaders.

2. Large teams (12 or more) tend to have more disagreements and differences of opinion. Subgroups often form, and conflicts among them occur, ranging from protection of "turf" to trivial matters such as "what kind of coffee is brewing in the pot." Demands on leaders are greater because there is more centralized decision making and less member participation. Large teams also tend to be less friendly. Turnover and absenteeism are higher in a large team, especially for blue-collar workers. Because less satisfaction is associated with specialized tasks and poor communication, team members have fewer opportunities to participate and feel an intimate part of the group.

As a general rule, large teams make need satisfaction for individuals more difficult; thus, there is less reason for people to remain committed to their goals. Teams of from 5 to 12 seem to work best. If a team grows larger than 20, managers should divide it into subgroups, each with its own members and goals.

Member Roles

For a team to be successful over the long run, it must be structured so as to both maintain its members' social well-being and accomplish its task. In successful teams, the requirements for task performance and social satisfaction are met by the emergence of two types of roles: task specialist and socioemotional.[33]

task specialist role
A role in which the individual devotes personal time and energy to helping the team accomplish its task.

People who play the **task specialist role** spend time and energy helping the team reach its goal. They often display the following behaviors:

- *Initiate ideas.* Propose new solutions to team problems.
- *Give opinions.* Offer opinions on task solutions; give candid feedback on others' suggestions.
- *Seek information.* Ask for task-relevant facts.
- *Summarize.* Relate various ideas to the problem at hand; pull ideas together into a summary perspective.
- *Energize.* Stimulate the team into action when interest drops.[34]

socioemotional role
A role in which the individual provides support for team members' emotional needs and social unity.

People who adopt a **socioemotional role** support team members' emotional needs and help strengthen the social entity. They display the following behaviors:

- *Encourage.* Are warm and receptive to others' ideas; praise and encourage others to draw forth their contributions.
- *Harmonize.* Reconcile group conflicts; help disagreeing parties reach agreement.
- *Reduce tension.* Tell jokes or in other ways draw off emotions when group atmosphere is tense.
- *Follow.* Go along with the team; agree to other team members' ideas.
- *Compromise.* Will shift own opinions to maintain team harmony.[35]

Exhibit 19.4 illustrates task specialist and socioemotional roles in teams. When most individuals in a team play a social role, the team is socially oriented. Members do not criticize or disagree with one another and do not forcefully offer opinions or try to accomplish team tasks, because their primary interest is to keep the team happy. Teams with mostly socioemotional roles can

Exhibit *19.4*

Team Member Roles

	Task Specialist Role	Dual Role
High	Focuses on task accomplishment over human needs	Focuses on task and people
		May be a team leader
	Important role, but if adopted by everyone, team's social needs will not be met	Important role, but not essential if members adopt task specialist and socioemotional roles
Member Task Behavior	**Nonparticipator Role**	**Socioemotional Role**
	Contributes little to either task or people needs of team	Focuses on people needs of team over task
	Not an important role—if adopted by too many members, team will disband	Important role, but if adopted by everyone, team's tasks will not be accomplished
Low		

Low   **Member Social Behavior**   High be very satisfying, but they also can be unproductive. At the other extreme, a team made up primarily of task specialists will tend to have a singular concern for task accomplishment. This team will be effective for a short period of time but will not be satisfying for members over the long run. Task specialists convey little emotional concern for one another, are unsupportive, and ignore team members' social and emotional needs. The task-oriented team can be humorless and unsatisfying.

As Exhibit 19.4 illustrates, some team members may play a dual role. People with **dual roles** both contribute to the task and meet members' emotional needs. Such people often become team leaders. A study of new-product-development teams in high-technology firms found that the most effective teams were headed by leaders who balanced the technical needs of the project with human interaction issues, thus meeting both task and socioemotional needs.[36] Exhibit 19.4 also shows the final type of role, called the **nonparticipator role,** in which people contribute little to either the task or the social needs of team members. They typically are held in low esteem by the team.

The important thing for managers to remember is that effective teams must have people in both task specialist and socioemotional roles. Humor and social concern are as important to team effectiveness as are facts and problem solving. Managers also should remember that some people perform better in one type of role; some are inclined toward social concerns and others toward task concerns. A well-balanced team will do best over the long term because it will be personally satisfying for team members and permit the accomplishment of team tasks.

dual role
A role in which the individual both contributes to the team's task and supports members' emotional needs.

nonparticipator role
A role in which the individual contributes little to either the task or members' socioemotional needs.

Team Processes

Now we turn our attention to internal team processes. Team processes pertain to those dynamics that change over time and can be influenced by team leaders. In this section, we will discuss the team processes of stages of development, cohesiveness, and norms. The fourth type of team process, conflict, will be covered in the next section.

Stages of Team Development

After a team has been created, there are distinct stages through which it develops.[37] New teams are different from mature teams. Recall a time when you were a member of a new team, such as a fraternity or sorority pledge class, a committee, or a small team formed to do a class assignment. Over time the team changed. In the beginning, team members had to get to know one another, establish roles and norms, divide the labor, and clarify the team's task. In this way, members became parts of a smoothly operating team. The challenge for leaders is to understand the stage of the team's development and take action that will help the group improve its functioning.

Research findings suggest that team development is not random but evolves over definitive stages. One useful model for describing these stages is shown in Exhibit 19.5. Each stage confronts team leaders and members with unique problems and challenges.[38]

Forming. The **forming** stage of development is a period of orientation and getting acquainted. Members break the ice and test one another for friendship

forming
The stage of team development characterized by orientation and acquaintance.

Exhibit *19.5*

Five Stages of Team Development

Forming:
Orientation, break the ice
Leader:
Facilitates social
interchanges

Storming:
Conflict, disagreement
Leader:
Encourages participation,
surfaces differences

Norming:
Establishment of order
and cohesion
Leader:
Helps clarify team roles,
norms, values

Performing:
Cooperation,
problem solving
Leader:
Facilitates task
accomplishment

Adjourning:
Task completion
Leader:
Brings closure, signifies
completion

storming
The stage of team development in which individual personalities and roles, and resulting conflicts, emerge.

norming
The stage of team development in which conflicts developed during the storming stage are resolved and team harmony and unity emerge.

performing
The stage of team development in which members focus on problem solving and accomplishing the team's assigned task.

possibilities and task orientation. Team members find which behaviors are acceptable to others. Uncertainty is high during this stage, and members usually accept whatever power or authority is offered by either formal or informal leaders. Members are dependent on the team until they find out what the ground rules are and what is expected of them. During this initial stage, members are concerned about such things as "What is expected of me?" "What is acceptable?" "Will I fit in?" During the forming stage, the team leader should provide time for members to get acquainted with one another and encourage them to engage in informal social discussions.

Storming. During the **storming** stage, individual personalities emerge. People become more assertive in clarifying their roles and what is expected of them. This stage is marked by conflict and disagreement. People may disagree over their perceptions of the team's mission. Members may jockey for positions, and coalitions or subgroups based on common interests may form. One subgroup may disagree with another over the total team's goals or how to achieve them. The team is not yet cohesive and may be characterized by a general lack of unity. Unless teams can successfully move beyond this stage, they may get bogged down and never achieve high performance. During the storming stage, the team leader should encourage participation by each team member. Members should propose ideas, disagree with one another, and work through the uncertainties and conflicting perceptions about team tasks and goals.

Norming. During the **norming** stage, conflict is resolved, and team harmony and unity emerge. Consensus develops on who has the power, who is the leader, and members' roles. Members come to accept and understand one another. Differences are resolved, and members develop a sense of team cohesion. This stage typically is of short duration. During the norming stage, the team leader should emphasize oneness within the team and help clarify team norms and values.

Performing. During the **performing** stage, the major emphasis is on problem solving and accomplishing the assigned task. Members are committed to the team's mission. They are coordinated with one another and handle disagreements in a mature way. They confront and resolve problems in the interest of task accomplishment. They interact frequently and direct discussion and influence toward achieving team goals. During this stage, the leader should concentrate on managing high task performance. Both socioemotional and task specialists should contribute.

Adjourning. The **adjourning** stage occurs in committees, task forces, and teams that have a limited task to perform and are disbanded afterward. During this stage, the emphasis is on wrapping up and gearing down. Task performance is no longer a top priority. Members may feel heightened emotionality, strong cohesiveness, and depression or even regret over the team's disbandment. They may feel happy about mission accomplishment and sad about the loss of friendship and associations. At this point, the leader may wish to signify the team's disbanding with a ritual or ceremony, perhaps giving out plaques and awards to signify closure and completeness.

The five stages of team development typically occur in sequence. In teams that are under time pressure or that will exist for only a short period of time,

© Pierre St. Jacques—Klixpix

They may be family, but the Ice.com management team, made up of the Gniwisches—brothers Shmuel, Mayer, and Pinny—along with father Isaac and brother-in-law Moshe Krasnanski, still had to go through the stages of team development to become effective. After creating Buyjewel.com in 1999, the team experienced a number of problems and conflicts in the forming and storming stages of development—not the least of which was Isaac's insistence on keeping a careful eye on the bottom line rather than going for rapid growth. Today, though, the team has reached the performing stage, running a successful business (renamed Ice.com) that sells affordable jewelry on the Internet, with $10 million in sales in one recent year.

the stages may occur quite rapidly. The stages may also be accelerated for virtual teams. For example, bringing people together for a couple of days of team building can help virtual teams move rapidly through the forming and storming stages. McDevitt Street Bovis, one of the country's largest construction management firms, uses an understanding of the stages of team development to put teams on a solid foundation.

adjourning
The stage of team development in which members prepare for the team's disbandment.

The team-building process at McDevitt Street Bovis is designed to take teams to the performing stage as quickly as possible by giving everyone an opportunity to get to know one another; explore the ground rules; and clarify roles, responsibilities, and expectations. The company credits this process for quickly and effectively unifying teams, circumventing damaging and time-consuming conflicts, and preventing lawsuits related to major construction projects.

Rather than the typical construction project characterized by conflicts, frantic scheduling, and poor communications, Bovis wants its collection of contractors, designers, suppliers, and other partners to function like a true team—putting the success of the project ahead of their own individual interests. The team is first divided into separate groups that may have competing objectives—such as the clients in one group, suppliers in another, engineers and architects in a third, and so forth—and asked to come up with a list of their goals for the project. Although interests sometimes vary widely in purely accounting terms, there are almost always common themes. By talking about conflicting goals and interests, as well as what all the groups share, facilitators help the team gradually come together around a common purpose and begin to develop shared values that will guide the project. After jointly writing a mission statement for the team, each party says what it expects from the others, so that roles and responsibilities can be clarified. The intensive team-building session helps take members quickly through the forming and storming stages of development. "We prevent

MCDEVITT STREET BOVIS
http://www.bovis.com

conflicts from happening," says facilitator Monica Bennett. Leaders at McDevitt Street Bovis believe building better teams builds better buildings.[39] ❖

Team Cohesiveness

team cohesiveness
The extent to which team members are attracted to the team and motivated to remain in it.

Another important aspect of the team process is cohesiveness. **Team cohesiveness** is defined as the extent to which members are attracted to the team and motivated to remain in it.[40] Members of highly cohesive teams are committed to team activities, attend meetings, and are happy when the team succeeds. Members of less cohesive teams are less concerned about the team's welfare. High cohesiveness is normally considered an attractive feature of teams.

Determinants of Team Cohesiveness.   Characteristics of team structure and context influence cohesiveness. First is *team interaction*. The greater the contact among team members and the more time spent together, the more cohesive the team. Through frequent interactions, members get to know one another and become more devoted to the team.[41] Second is the concept of *shared goals*. If team members agree on goals, they will be more cohesive. Agreeing on purpose and direction binds the team together. Third is *personal attraction to the team,* meaning that members have similar attitudes and values and enjoy being together.

Two factors in the team's context also influence group cohesiveness. The first is the presence of competition. When a team is in moderate competition with other teams, its cohesiveness increases as it strives to win. Finally, team success and the favorable evaluation of the team by outsiders add to cohesiveness. When a team succeeds in its task and others in the organization recognize the success, members feel good, and their commitment to the team will be high.

Consequences of Team Cohesiveness.   The outcome of team cohesiveness can fall into two categories—morale and productivity. As a general rule, morale is higher in cohesive teams because of increased communication among members, a friendly team climate, maintenance of membership because of commitment to the team, loyalty, and member participation in team decisions and activities. High cohesiveness has almost uniformly good effects on the satisfaction and morale of team members.[42]

With respect to team performance, research findings are mixed, but cohesiveness may have several effects.[43] First, in a cohesive team, members' productivity tends to be more uniform. Productivity differences among members are small because the team exerts pressure toward conformity. Noncohesive teams do not have this control over member behavior and therefore tend to have wider variation in member productivity.

With respect to the productivity of the team as a whole, research findings suggest that cohesive teams have the potential to be productive, but the degree of productivity depends on the relationship between management and the working team. Thus, team cohesiveness does not necessarily lead to higher team productivity. One study surveyed more than 200 work teams and correlated job performance with their cohesiveness.[44] Highly cohesive teams were more productive when team members felt management support and less productive when they sensed management hostility and negativism. Management hostility led to team norms and goals of low performance, and the highly cohesive teams performed poorly, in accordance with their norms and goals.

The relationship between performance outcomes and cohesiveness is illustrated in Exhibit 19.6. The highest productivity occurs when the team is cohesive and also has a high performance norm, which is a result of its positive relationship with management. Moderate productivity occurs when cohesiveness is low, because team members are less committed to performance norms. The lowest productivity occurs when cohesiveness is high and the team's performance norm is low. Thus, cohesive teams are able to attain their goals and enforce their norms, which can lead to either very high or very low productivity.

A good example of team cohesiveness combined with high performance norms comes from Nokia, the Finnish telecommunications giant. At Nokia, every job or project of any importance is assigned to a team rather than an individual manager or employee. Even though teams are often virtual and made up of people from all over the world, cohesiveness is typically high because Nokia's team-oriented culture and extensive training programs create a "meeting of minds among people," as CEO Jorma Ollila puts it. Nokia hires people who demonstrate a commitment to working collaboratively, and the company's incentive programs reward teamwork. The combination of team cohesiveness and top management support has made the workforce highly productive and Nokia one of the most innovative companies around.[45]

Team Norms

A team **norm** is a standard of conduct that is shared by team members and guides their behavior.[46] Norms are informal. They are not written down, as are rules and procedures. Norms are valuable because they define boundaries of acceptable behavior. They make life easier for team members by providing a frame of reference for what is right and wrong. Norms identify key values, clarify role expectations, and facilitate team survival. For example, union members may develop a norm of not cooperating with management because they do not trust management's motives. In this way, norms protect the group and express key values.

Norms begin to develop in the first interactions among members of a new team.[47] Norms that apply to both day-to-day behavior and employee output and performance gradually evolve. Norms thus tell members what is acceptable and direct members' actions toward acceptable productivity or performance. Four common ways in which norms develop for controlling and directing behavior are illustrated in Exhibit 19.7.[48]

norm
A standard of conduct that is shared by team members and guides their behavior.

Exhibit 19.6

Relationship among Team Cohesiveness, Performance Norms, and Productivity

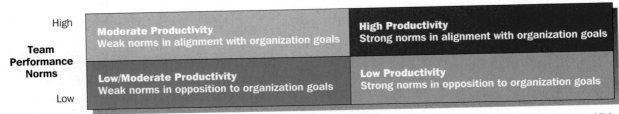

Exhibit *19.7*

Four Ways Team Norms Develop

Critical Events.   Often, *critical events* in a team's history establish an important precedent. One example occurred when an employee at a forest products plant was seriously injured while standing too close to a machine being operated by a teammate. This led to a norm that team members regularly monitor one another to make sure all safety rules are observed.

Any critical event can lead to the creation of a norm. In one organization, a department head invited the entire staff to his house for dinner. The next day people discovered that no one had attended, and this resulted in a norm prohibiting outside entertaining.[49]

Primacy.   *Primacy* means that the first behaviors that occur in a team often set a precedent for later team expectations. For example, at one company a team leader began his first meeting by raising an issue and then "leading" team members until he got the solution he wanted. The pattern became ingrained so quickly into an unproductive team norm that team members dubbed meetings the "Guess What I Think" game.[50]

Carryover Behaviors.   *Carryover behaviors* bring norms into the team from outside. One current example is the strong norm against smoking in many management teams. Some team members sneak around, gargling with mouthwash, and fear expulsion because the team culture believes everyone should kick the habit. Carryover behavior also influences small teams of college students assigned by instructors to do class work. Norms brought into the team from outside suggest that students should participate equally and help members get a reasonable grade.

Explicit Statements.   With *explicit statements*, leaders or team members can initiate norms by articulating them to the team. Explicit statements symbolize what counts and thus have considerable impact. Making explicit statements can be a highly effective way for leaders to influence or change team norms. Roger Greene of the software company Ipswitch Inc. does not want employees working excessively long hours and getting burned out. He is constantly telling people to take their personal days and vacation time and making announcements that "burning the midnight oil" is not expected or appreciated at the company. At Ipswitch, people do not get rewarded for being workaholics, and Greene's explicit statements support the norm that employees should live a balanced life.[51]

Managing Team Conflict

The final characteristic of team process is conflict. Of all the skills required for effective team management, none is more important than handling the conflicts that inevitably arise among members. Whenever people work together in teams, some conflict is inevitable. Conflict can arise among members within a team or between one team and another. **Conflict** refers to antagonistic interaction in which one party attempts to block the intentions or goals of another.[52] Competition, which is rivalry among individuals or teams, can have a healthy impact because it energizes people toward higher performance.[53] In addition, some conflict within teams may lead to better decision making because multiple viewpoints are considered. There is some research evidence that low conflict in top management teams is associated with poor decision making. Team members just go along with the strongest opinion, which often is that of the CEO, rather than consider alternate ideas and solutions.[54] However, too much conflict can be destructive, tear relationships apart, and interfere with the healthy exchange of ideas and information.[55]

conflict
Antagonistic interaction in which one party attempts to thwart the intentions or goals of another.

Causes of Conflict

Several factors can cause people to engage in conflict:[56]

Scarce Resources. Resources include money, information, and supplies. In their desire to achieve goals, individuals may wish to increase their resources, which throws them into conflict. Whenever individuals or teams must compete for scarce or declining resources, conflict is almost inevitable. At the Levi Strauss blue jeans plant near Knoxville, Tennessee, a change in pay systems—in which employees were paid based on team output rather than on the old individual piecework system—led to severe conflict because some employees felt that slower team members hurt their pocketbooks. One worker says her hourly pay dropped nearly $2, while slower team members realized an increase over what they earned on the piecework system.[57]

Jurisdictional Ambiguities. Conflicts also emerge when job boundaries and responsibilities are unclear. When task responsibilities are well defined and predictable, people know where they stand. When they are unclear, people may disagree about who has responsibility for specific tasks or who has a claim on resources.

Communication Breakdown. Communication, as described in Chapter 18, sometimes is faulty. The potential for communication breakdown is even greater with virtual teams and global teams made up of members from different countries and cultures. Poor communication results in misperceptions and misunderstandings of other people and teams. In some cases, information is intentionally withheld, which can jeopardize trust among teams and lead to long-lasting conflict.

Personality Clashes. A personality clash occurs when people simply do not get along or do not see eye-to-eye on any issue. Personality clashes are caused by basic differences in personality, values, and attitudes. In one study, personality conflicts were the number-one reported cause preventing front-line management teams from working together effectively.[58] Some personality differences can be overcome. However, severe personality clashes are difficult to resolve. Often, it is a good idea to simply separate the parties so that they need not interact with one another.

Power and Status Differences. Power and status differences occur when one party has disputable influence over another. Low-prestige individuals or departments might resist their low status. People might engage in conflict to increase their power and influence in the team or organization.

Goal Differences. Conflict often occurs simply because people are pursuing conflicting goals. Goal differences are natural in organizations. Individual salespeople's targets may put them in conflict with one another or with the sales manager. Moreover, the sales department's goals might conflict with those of manufacturing.

Styles to Handle Conflict

Teams as well as individuals develop specific styles for dealing with conflict, based on the desire to satisfy their own concern versus the other party's concern. A model that describes five styles of handling conflict is in Exhibit 19.8. The two major dimensions are the extent to which an individual is assertive versus cooperative in his or her approach to conflict.

Effective team members vary their style of handling conflict to fit a specific situation. Each of these five styles is appropriate in certain cases.

1. The *competing style* reflects assertiveness to get one's own way, and should be used when quick, decisive action is vital on important issues or unpopular actions, such as during emergencies or urgent cost cutting.

2. The *avoiding style* reflects neither assertiveness nor cooperativeness. It is appropriate when an issue is trivial, when there is no chance of winning, when a delay to gather more information is needed, or when a disruption would be very costly.

3. The *compromising style* reflects a moderate amount of both assertiveness and cooperativeness. It is appropriate when the goals on both sides are equally important, when opponents have equal power and both sides want to split the difference, or when people need to arrive at temporary or expedient solutions under time pressure.

4. The *accommodating style* reflects a high degree of cooperativeness, which works best when people realize that they are wrong, when an issue is more important to others than to oneself, when building social credits for use in later discussions, and when maintaining harmony is especially important.

5. The *collaborating style* reflects both a high degree of assertiveness and cooperativeness. The collaborating style enables both parties to win, although it may require substantial bargaining and negotiation. The collaborating style is important when both sets of concerns are too important to be compromised, when insights from different people need to be merged into an

Exhibit **19.8**

A Model of Styles to Handle Conflict

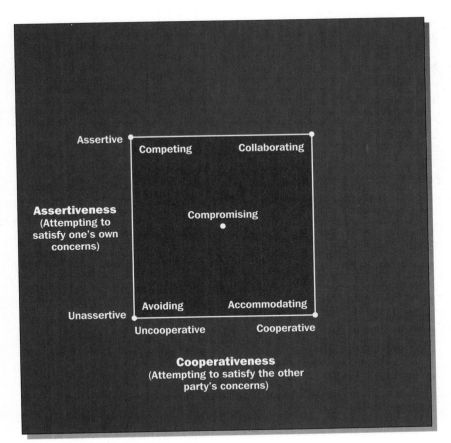

SOURCE: Adapted from Kenneth Thomas, "Conflict and Conflict Management," in *Handbook of Industrial and Organizational Behavior*, ed. M. D. Dunnette (New York: John Wiley, 1976), 900.

overall solution, and when the commitment of both sides is needed for a consensus.[59]

The various styles of handling conflict can be used when an individual disagrees with others. But what does a manager or team leader do when a conflict erupts among others within a team or among teams for which the manager is responsible? Research suggests that several techniques can be used as strategies for resolving conflicts among people or departments. These techniques might also be used when conflict is formalized, such as between a union and management.

Superordinate Goals. The larger mission that cannot be attained by a single party is identified as a **superordinate goal**.[60] This is similar to the concept of *vision*. A powerful vision of where the organization wants to be in the future often compels employees to overcome conflicts and cooperate for the greater good. Similarly, a superordinate goal requires the cooperation of conflicting team members for achievement. People must pull together. To the extent that employees can be focused on team or organization goals, the conflict will decrease because they see the big picture and realize they must work together to achieve it.

superordinate goal
A goal that cannot be reached by a single party.

Bargaining/Negotiation. Bargaining and negotiation mean that the parties engage one another in an attempt to systematically reach a solution. They attempt logical problem solving to identify and correct the conflict. This approach works well if the individuals can set aside personal animosities and deal with the conflict in a businesslike way.

Mediation. Using a third party to settle a dispute involves **mediation.** A mediator could be a supervisor, higher-level manager, or someone from the human resource department. The mediator can discuss the conflict with each party and work toward a solution. If a solution satisfactory to both sides cannot be reached, the parties might be willing to turn the conflict over to the mediator and abide by his or her solution.

mediation
The process of using a third party to settle a dispute.

Facilitating Communication. Managers can facilitate communication to ensure that conflicting parties hold accurate perceptions. Providing opportunities for the disputants to get together and exchange information reduces conflict. As they learn more about one another, suspicions diminish and improved teamwork becomes possible.

Four guidelines can help facilitate communication and keep teams focused on substantive issues rather than interpersonal conflicts.[61]

- *Focus on facts.* Keep team discussions focused on issues, not personalities. Working with more data and information rather than less can help keep team members focused on facts and prevent meetings from degenerating into pointless debates over opinions. At Star Electronics, the top management team meets daily, weekly, and monthly to examine a wide variety of specific operating measures. Looking at the details helps team members debate critical issues and avoid useless arguments.

- *Develop multiple alternatives.* Teams that deliberately develop many alternatives, sometimes considering four or five options at once, have a lower incidence of interpersonal conflict. Having a multitude of options to consider concentrates team members' energy on solving problems. In addition, the process of generating multiple choices is fun and creative, which sets a positive tone for the meeting and reduces the chance for conflict.

- *Maintain a balance of power.* Managers and team leaders should accept the team's decision as fair, even if they do not agree with it. Fairness requires a balance of power within the team.

- *Never force a consensus.* There will naturally be conflict over some issues, which managers find a way to resolve without forcing a consensus. When there are persistent differences of opinion, the team leader sometimes has to make a decision guided by input from other team members. At Andromeda Processing, the CEO insisted on consensus from his top management team, causing a debate to rage on for months. Eventually, most of the managers just wanted a decision, no matter whether it was the one they agreed with. Conflict and frustration mounted to the point where some top managers left the company. The group achieved consensus only at the price of losing several key managers.

Benefits and Costs of Teams

In deciding whether to use teams to perform specific tasks, managers must consider both benefits and costs. Teams may have positive impact on both the output productivity and satisfaction of members. On the other hand, teams may also create a situation in which motivation and performance actually are decreased.

Potential Benefits of Teams

Teams come closest to achieving their full potential when they enhance individual productivity through increased member effort, members' personal satisfaction, integration of diverse abilities and skills, and increased organizational flexibility.

Level of Effort. Employee teams often unleash enormous energy and creativity from workers who like the idea of using their brains as well as their bodies to accomplish an important goal. The shift to a team approach is an important component of the evolution to the learning organization as described in Chapter 2 and Chapter 11. To facilitate learning and problem solving, organizations are breaking down barriers, empowering workers, and encouraging employees to use their minds and creativity. Research has found that working in a team increases an individual's motivation and performance. **Social facilitation** refers to the tendency for the presence of others to enhance an individual's motivation and performance. Simply being in the presence of other people has an energizing effect.[62]

social facilitation
The tendency for the presence of others to influence an individual's motivation and performance.

Satisfaction of Members. As described in Chapter 17, employees have needs for belongingness and affiliation. Working in teams can help meet these needs. Participative teams reduce boredom and often increase employees' feeling of dignity and self-worth because the whole person is employed. People who have a satisfying team environment cope better with stress and enjoy their jobs.

Expanded Job Knowledge and Skills. The third major benefit of using teams is the empowerment of employees to bring greater knowledge and ability to the task. For one thing, multiskilled employees learn all of the jobs that the team performs. Teams gain the intellectual resources of several members who can suggest shortcuts and offer alternative points of view for team decisions.

Organizational Responsiveness. Employee teams enhance flexibility because workers can be reorganized and employees reassigned as needed. People work closely together, learn a variety of skills, and can exchange jobs as needed to accomplish the team's task. In addition, teams can break down traditional organizational boundaries so that people collaborate across functional and hierarchical lines, which enables the organization to rapidly respond to changing customer needs.

Cooper Industries' Bussmann division has firsthand knowledge of the benefits of teams. Angelina Bernardi, Steve Goble, Ed Haworth, and Lynne Sanick worked on Bussmann's first experimental team to develop the new line of Optima over-current protection modules, which combine a fuse and fuseholder in a single, easy-to-use power protection system. The team introduced the line in 10 months compared to the average 24-month cycle time. The enhanced flexibility and rapid response to customer needs led Bussmann to create Rapid Development Teams for each of its major market segments. The teams consistently cut new-product development time in half.

Potential Costs of Teams

When managers decide whether to use teams, they must assess certain costs or liabilities associated with teamwork. When teams do not work very well, the major reasons usually are power realignment, free riding, coordination costs, or system revisions.

Power Realignment. When companies form front-line workers into teams, the major losers are low- and middle-level managers. These managers are reluctant to give up power. Indeed, when teams are successful, fewer supervisors are needed. This is especially true for self-directed teams, because workers take over supervisory responsibility. The adjustment is difficult for managers who fear the loss of status or even their job and who have to learn new, people-oriented skills to survive.[63]

Free Riding.   The term **free rider** refers to a team member who attains benefits from team membership but does not do a proportionate share of the work.[64] Free riding sometimes is called *social loafing,* because members do not exert equal effort. In large teams, some people are likely to work less. For example, research found that the pull exerted on a rope was greater by individuals working alone than by individuals in a group. Similarly, people who were asked to clap and make noise made more noise on a per person basis when working alone or in small groups than they did in a large group.[65] The problem of free riding has been experienced by people who have participated in student project groups. Some students put more effort into the group project than others, and often it seems that no members work as hard for the group as they do for their individual grades.

Coordination Costs.   The time and energy required to coordinate the activities of a group to enable it to perform its task are called **coordination costs.** Groups must spend time getting ready to do work and lose productive time in deciding who is to do what and when.[66] Once again, student project groups illustrate coordination costs. Members must meet after class just to decide when they can meet to perform the task. Schedules must be checked, telephone calls made, and meeting times arranged in order to get down to business. Hours may be devoted to the administration and coordination of the group. Students often feel they could do the same project by themselves in less time. Teams typically have frequent meetings throughout a project, so leaders have to know how to keep meetings focused and productive. This chapter's Shoptalk box offers some tips for running a great meeting.

Revising Systems.   Implementing teams also requires changes in other parts of the organization. In particular, performance appraisal and reward systems have to be revised to reflect the new team approach; otherwise, teamwork will fail. Managers should be aware that a shift to teams requires that time and resources be invested to develop new systems that support and reinforce collaboration, sharing of information, and empowerment.

■ Summary and Management Solution

Several important concepts about teams were described in this chapter. Organizations use teams both to achieve coordination as part of the formal structure and to encourage employee involvement. Formal teams include vertical teams along the chain of command and horizontal teams such as cross-functional task forces and committees. Special-purpose teams are used for special, large-scale, creative organization projects. Employee involvement via teams is designed to bring low-level employees into decision processes to improve quality, efficiency, and satisfaction. Companies typically start with problem-solving teams, which may evolve into self-directed teams that take on responsibility for management activities. New approaches to teamwork include virtual teams and global teams. These teams may include contingent workers, customers, suppliers, and other outsiders. Although team members sometimes meet face to face, they use advanced information and telecommunications technology to accomplish much of their work.

Returning to the opening example of Rowe Furniture, Charlene Pedrolie believed teamwork could be the answer for helping Rowe meet the challenges of a fast-paced, competitive environment. She eliminated

---

free rider
A person who benefits from team membership but does not make a proportionate contribution to the team's work.

coordination costs
The time and energy needed to coordinate the activities of a team to enable it to perform its task.

Manager's Shoptalk

How to Run a Great Meeting

Many executives believe that meetings are a waste of time. Busy executives may spend up to 70 percent of their time in meetings at which participants doodle, drink coffee, and think about what they could be doing back in their offices.

However, successful meetings help people process important information and solve organizational problems. Good meetings don't just happen; they are designed through careful thought and planning. The success of a meeting depends on what is done in advance of, during, and after it.

Prepare in Advance. Advance preparation is the single most important tool for running an efficient, productive meeting. Advance preparation should include the following:

1. *Define the purpose.* The chairperson should be very explicit in setting goals and expressing them concisely and meaningfully.
2. *Prepare an agenda.* The agenda is a simple list of the topics to be discussed. It is important because it lets people know what to expect and keeps the meeting on track. The agenda provides order and logic and gives the chairperson a means of control during the meeting if the discussion starts to wander.
3. *Issue invitations selectively.* If the group gets too big, the meeting will not be productive. If everyone is expected to participate, keep membership between 5 and 12.
4. *Set a time limit.* A formal meeting should have a specified amount of time. The ending time should be announced in advance, and the agenda should require the meeting to move along at a reasonable pace.

During the Meeting. If the chairperson is prepared in advance, the meeting will go smoothly. Moreover, certain techniques will bring out the best in people and make the meeting even more productive:

5. *Start on time.* This sounds obvious—but do not keep busy people waiting. Starting on time has symbolic value, because it tells people that the topic is important.
6. *Outlaw cell phones.* Having the flow of discussion interrupted by the ringing of a cell phone can throw the meeting completely off-track. A chairperson who answers a cell phone signals that the meeting is not really important.
7. *State the purpose and review the agenda.* The chairperson should start the meeting by stating the explicit purpose and clarifying what should be accomplished by the time the meeting is over.

8. *Encourage participation.* Good meetings contain lots of discussion. If the chairperson merely wants to present one-way information to members, he or she should send a memo. A few subtle techniques go a long way toward increasing participation:
   a. *Draw out the silent.* This means saying, "Bob, what do you think of Nancy's idea?"
   b. *Control the talkative.* Some people overdo it and dominate the discussion. The chairperson's job is to redirect the discussion toward other people. One organization has a rule called NOSTUESO (No one speaks twice until everyone speaks once).
   c. *Encourage the clash of ideas.* A good meeting is not a series of dialogues but a crosscurrent of discussion and debate. The chairperson guides, mediates, stimulates, and summarizes this discussion.
   d. *Call on the most senior people last.* Sometimes junior people are reluctant to disagree with senior people, so it is best to get the junior people's ideas on the table first. This will provide wider views and ideas.
   e. *Listen.* The chairperson should not preach or engage in one-on-one dialogue with group members. The point is to listen and to facilitate discussion.
9. *Stick to the purpose.* Encouraging a free flow of ideas does not mean allowing participants to sidetrack the meeting into discussions of issues not on the agenda. This can waste valuable time and prevent the group from reaching its goals.

After the Meeting. The actions following the meeting are designed to summarize and implement agreed-upon points. Postmeeting activities are set in motion by a call to action.

10. *End with a call to action.* The last item of the meeting's agenda is to summarize the main points and make sure everyone understands his or her assignments.
11. *Follow-up.* Mail minutes of the meeting to members. Use this memorandum to summarize the key accomplishments of the meeting, suggest schedules for agreed-upon activities, and start the ball rolling in preparation for the next meeting.

SOURCES: Based on Edward Michaels, "Business Meetings," *Small Business Reports* (February 1989), 82–88; Daniel Stoffman, "Waking Up to Great Meetings," *Canadian Business* (November 1986), 75–79; Antoney Jay, "How to Run a Meeting," *Harvard Business Review* (March–April 1976), 120–134; Jana Kemp, "Avoiding Agenda Overstack," *Corporate University Review* (May–June 1997), 42–43; and Jeffrey L. Seglin, "We've Got to Start Meeting Like This," *CIO* (March 1, 2001), 168–170.

most supervisory positions, cross-trained employees to perform the different tasks required to build a piece of furniture, and then asked front-line workers to form horizontal clusters, or *cells,* to design the new production system. Each group selected its own members from the various functional areas, then created the processes, schedules, and routines for a particular product line. The assembly line was a thing of the past. Five hundred workers who had been accustomed to standing in one place and having the furniture come to them were suddenly working in teams, wandering from one partially assembled piece to another, performing a variety of tasks. Every team had instant access to up-to-date information about order flows, output, productivity, and quality. The sense of personal control and responsibility eventually led to a dramatic change in workers, who began holding impromptu meetings to discuss problems, check each other's progress, or talk about new ideas and better ways of doing things. Productivity and quality shot through the roof. Before long, the factory was delivering custom-made pieces within a month.

Only a few months later, that lead time had decreased to a mere 10 days.[67]

Most teams go through systematic stages of development: forming, storming, norming, performing, and adjourning. Team characteristics that can influence organizational effectiveness are size, cohesiveness, norms, and members' roles. All teams experience some conflict because of scarce resources, ambiguous responsibilities, communication breakdown, personality clashes, power and status differences, and goal conflicts. Techniques for resolving these conflicts include superordinate goals, bargaining, mediation, and communication. Techniques for facilitating team communication to minimize conflict are to focus on facts, develop multiple alternatives, maintain a balance of power, and never force a consensus. Advantages of using teams include increased motivation, diverse knowledge and skills, satisfaction of team members, and organizational responsiveness. Potential costs of using teams are power realignment, free riding, coordination costs, and revising systems.

■ Discussion Questions

1. Volvo went to self-directed teams to assemble cars because of the need to attract and keep workers in Sweden, where pay raises are not a motivator (high taxes) and many other jobs are available. Is this a good reason for using a team approach? Discuss.
2. How is a self-directed team different from a cross-functional team?
3. What factors in today's environment are contributing to an increasing use of virtual teams and global teams? Would you like to be part of a virtual team? Why or why not?
4. Suppose you are the leader of a team that has just been created to develop a new registration process at your college or university. How can you use an understanding of the stages of team development to improve your team's effectiveness?
5. Think of a work team or student project team of which you have been a member. Identify some of the team's unstated norms. How did these norms develop?

6. If you were the leader of a special-purpose team developing a new computer game, and conflicts arose related to power and status differences among team members, what would you do? How might you use the various conflict-resolution techniques described in the chapter?
7. When you are a member of a team, do you adopt a task specialist or socioemotional role? Which role is more important for a team's effectiveness? Discuss.
8. What is the relationship between team cohesiveness and team performance?
9. Describe the advantages and disadvantages of teams. In what situations might the disadvantages outweigh the advantages?
10. One company had 40 percent of its workers and 20 percent of its managers resign during the first year after reorganizing into teams. What might account for this dramatic turnover? How might managers ensure a smooth transition to teams?

Management in Practice: Experiential Exercise

Is Your Group a Cohesive Team?

Think about a student group with which you have worked. Answer the questions below as they pertain to the functioning of that group.

	Disagree Strongly				Agree Strongly
1. Group meetings were held regularly and everyone attended.	1	2	3	4	5
2. We talked about and shared the same goals for group work and grade.	1	2	3	4	5
3. We spent most of our meeting time talking business, but discussions were open-ended and active.	1	2	3	4	5
4. We talked through any conflicts and disagreements until they were resolved.	1	2	3	4	5
5. Group members listened carefully to one another.	1	2	3	4	5
6. We really trusted each other, speaking personally about what we really felt.	1	2	3	4	5
7. Leadership roles were rotated and shared, with people taking initiative at appropriate times for the good of the group.	1	2	3	4	5
8. Each member found a way to contribute to the final work product.	1	2	3	4	5
9. I was really satisfied being a member of the group.	1	2	3	4	5
10. We freely gave each other credit for jobs well done.	1	2	3	4	5
11. Group members gave and received feedback to help the group do even better.	1	2	3	4	5
12. We held each other accountable; each member was accountable to the group.	1	2	3	4	5
13. Group members really liked and respected each other.	1	2	3	4	5

Total Score _____

The questions here are about team cohesion. If you scored 52 or greater, your group experienced authentic teamwork. Congratulations. If you scored between 39 and 51, there was a positive group identity that might have been developed even further. If you scored between 26 and 38, group identity was weak and probably not very satisfying. If you scored below 26, it was hardly a group at all, resembling a loose collection of individuals.

Remember, teamwork does not happen by itself. Individuals like you have to understand what a team is and then work to make it happen. What can you do to make a student group more like a team? Do you have the courage to take the initiative?

Management in Practice: Ethical Dilemma

Consumer Safety or Team Commitment?

Nancy was part of a pharmaceutical team developing a product called loperamide, a liquid treatment for diarrhea for people unable to take solid medicine, namely infants, children, and the elderly. Loperamide contained 44 times the amount of saccharin allowed by the FDA in a 12-ounce soft drink, but there were no regulations governing saccharin content in medication.

Nancy was the only medical member of the seven-person project team. The team made a unanimous decision to reduce the saccharin content before marketing loperamide, so the team initiated a three-month effort for reformulation. In the meantime, management was pressuring the team to allow human testing with the original formula until the new formula became available. After a heated team debate, all the team members except Nancy voted to begin testing with the current formula.

Nancy believed it was unethical to test on old people and children a drug she considered potentially dangerous. As the only medical member of the team, she had to sign the forms allowing testing. She refused and was told that unless she signed, she would be removed from the project, demoted, and seen as a poor team player, nonpromotable, lacking in judgment, and unable to work with marketing people. Nancy was aware that no proof existed that high saccharin would be directly harmful to potential users of loperamide.

What Do You Do?

1. Refuse to sign. As a medical doctor, Nancy must stand up for what she believes is right.
2. Resign. There is no reason to stay in this company and be punished for ethically correct behavior. Testing the drug will become someone else's responsibility.

3. Sign the form. The judgment of other team members cannot be all wrong. The loperamide testing is not illegal and will move ahead anyway, so it would preserve team unity and company effectiveness to sign.

SOURCE: Based on Tom L. Beauchamp, *Ethical Theory and Business,* 2d ed. (Englewood Cliffs, N.J.: Prentice-Hall, 1983).

■ Surf the Net

1. **Teamwork and Your Career.** One of the most popular job sites, with more than 800,000 U.S. job listings, is located at *http://www.monster.com.* Choose the "Search Jobs" link, read the "Tips on Searching," and then conduct a job search in your career area and in geographical areas of your choice. If you're not finding what you need at monster.com, try other jobs sites such as
http://www.thejobresource.com/
http://www.ajb.dni.us/
http://www.jobbankusa.com/
http://www.wetfeet.com/asp/home.asp
    Print out five job ads and then highlight any references to teams or teamwork on your printouts. Be prepared to discuss or submit your findings in class.

2. **Are You a Team Player?** Complete one of the team player assessments available at the following sites. Print

out the results, bring them to class, and be prepared to discuss your results during class.
http://www.content.monster.com/tools/quizzes/teamplayer/
http://www.ayn.ca/modules/employment/2_profile/2g.html
http://www.hindustantimes.com/nonfram/230701/HTE09.asp

3. **Conflict Management Style.** Complete an assessment to determine your own conflict management style. Print out the results of your assessment and be prepared to discuss what you learned about yourself and about conflict management from this exercise.
http://www.careerbuilder.com/wl_ga_0012_conflict management.html
http://www.mercer.edu/csil/leaps_resource_files.htm
(Under heading "Organizational Success" choose "What's Your Conflict Management Style?")

■ Case for Critical Analysis

Acme Minerals Extraction Company

Several years ago, Acme Minerals Extraction Company introduced teams in an effort to solve morale and productivity problems at its Wichita plant. Acme used highly sophisticated technology, employing geologists, geophysicists, and engineers on what was referred to as the "brains" side of the business, as well as skilled and semi-skilled labor on the "brawn" side to run the company's underground extracting operations. The two sides regularly clashed, and when some engineers locked several operations workers out of the office in 100-degree heat, the local press had a field day. Suzanne Howard was hired to develop a program that would improve productivity and morale at the Wichita plant, with the idea that it would then be implemented at other Acme sites.

Howard had a stroke of luck in the form of Donald Peterson, a long-time Acme employee who was highly respected at the Wichita plant and was looking for one final, challenging project before he retired. Peterson had served in just about every possible line and staff position at Acme over his 39-year career, and he understood the problems workers faced on both the "brains" and the "brawn" sides of the business. Howard was pleased when Peterson agreed to serve as leader for the Wichita pilot project. There were three func-

tional groups at the Wichita plant: operations, made up primarily of hourly workers who operated and maintained the extracting equipment; the "below ground" group, consisting of engineers, geologists, and geophysicists who determined where and how to drill; and the "above ground" group of engineers in charge of cursory refinement and transportation of the minerals. Howard and Peterson decided the first step was to get these different groups talking to one another and sharing ideas. They instituted a monthly "problem chat," an optional meeting to which all employees were invited to discuss unresolved problems. At the first meeting, Howard and Peterson were the only two people who showed up. However, people gradually began to attend the meetings, and after about six months they had become lively problem-solving discussions that led to many improvements.

Next, Howard and Peterson introduced teams to "select a problem and implement a tailored solution," or SPITS. These were ad hoc groups made up of members from each of the three functional areas. They were formed to work on a specific problem identified in a chat meeting and were disbanded when the problem was solved. SPITS were given the authority to address problems without seeking management approval.

There were some rocky moments, as engineers resented working with operations personnel and vice versa. However, over time, and with the strong leadership of Peterson, the groups began to come together and focus on the issues rather than spending most of their time arguing. Eventually, workers in Wichita were organized into permanent cross-functional teams that were empowered to make their own decisions and elect their own leaders. After a year and a half, things were really humming. The different groups weren't just working together; they had also started socializing together. At one of the problem chats, an operations worker jokingly suggested that the brains and the brawn should duke it out once a week to get rid of the tensions so they could focus all their energy on the job to be done. Several others joined in the joking, and eventually, the group decided to square off in a weekly softball game. Peterson had T-shirts printed up that said BRAINS AND BRAWN. The softball games were well attended, and both sides usually ended up having a few beers together at a local bar afterward. Productivity and morale soared at the Wichita plant, and costs continued to decline.

Top executives believed the lessons learned at Wichita should make implementing the program at other sites less costly and time-consuming. However, when Howard and her team attempted to implement the program at the Lubbock plant, things didn't go well. They felt under immense pressure from top management to get the team-based productivity project running smoothly at Lubbock. Because people weren't showing up for the problem chat meetings, attendance was made mandatory. However, the meetings still produced few valuable ideas or suggestions. Although a few of the SPITS teams solved important problems, none of them showed the kind of commitment and enthusiasm Howard had seen in Wichita. In addition, the Lubbock workers refused to participate in the softball games and other team-building exercises that Howard's team developed for them. Howard finally convinced some workers to join in the softball games by bribing them with free food and beer. "If I just had a Donald Peterson in Lubbock, things would go a lot more smoothly," Howard thought. "These workers don't trust us the way workers in Wichita trusted him." It seemed that no matter how hard Howard and her team tried to make the project work in Lubbock, morale continued to decline and conflicts between the different groups of workers actually seemed to increase.

Questions

1. What types of teams described in the chapter are represented in this case?
2. Why do you think the team project succeeded at Wichita but isn't working in Lubbock?
3. What advice would you give Suzanne Howard and her team for improving the employee involvement climate at the Lubbock plant?

SOURCE: Based on Michael C. Beers, "The Strategy That Wouldn't Travel," *Harvard Business Review* (November–December 1996), 18–31.

■ Endnotes

1. Thomas Petzinger, Jr., *The New Pioneers: The Men and Women Who Are Transforming the Workplace and Marketplace* (New York: Simon & Schuster, 1999), 27–32.

2. James Wallace Bishop and K. Dow Scott, "How Commitment Affects Team Performance," *HR Magazine* (February 1997), 107–111; Patricia Booth, "Embracing the Team Concept," *Canadian Business Review* (Autumn 1994), 10–13; and "Training in the 1990s," *The Wall Street Journal* (March 1, 1990), B1.

3. Rajiv D. Banker, Joy M. Field, Roger G. Schroeder, and Kingshuk K. Sinha, "Impact of Work Teams on Manufacturing Performance: A Longitudinal Field Study," *Academy of Management Journal* 39, no. 4 (1996), 867–890.

4. Eric Schine, "Mattel's Wild Race to Market," *Business Week* (February 21, 1994), 62–63; Frank V. Cespedes, Stephen X. Dole, and Robert J. Freedman, "Teamwork for Today's Selling," *Harvard Business Review* (March–April 1989), 44–55; Victoria J. Marsick, Ernie Turner, and Lars Cederholm, "International Managers as Team Leaders," *Management Review* (March 1989), 46–49; and "Team Goal-Setting," *Small Business Report* (January 1988), 76–77.

5. Carl E. Larson and Frank M. J. LaFasto, *TeamWork* (Newbury Park, Calif.: Sage, 1989).

6. Erika Rasmusson, "One for All," *Working Woman* (March 2001), 68.

7. Eric Sundstrom, Kenneth P. DeMeuse, and David Futrell, "Work Teams," *American Psychologist* 45 (February 1990), 120–133.

8. Deborah L. Gladstein, "Groups in Context: A Model of Task Group Effectiveness," *Administrative Science Quarterly* 29 (1984), 499–517.

9. Dora C. Lau and J. Keith Murnighan, "Demographic Diversity and Faultlines: The Compositional Dynamics of Organizational Groups," *Academy of Management Review* 23, no. 2 (1998), 325–340.

10. Thomas Owens, "Business Teams," *Small Business Report* (January 1989), 50–58.

11. Laton McCartney, "A Team Effort," *IW* (December 18, 1995), 65–72.

12. John Grossmann, "The Kiss," *Sky* (January 1998), 62–67.

13. "Participation Teams," *Small Business Report* (September 1987), 38–41.

14. Susanne G. Scott and Walter O. Einstein, "Strategic Performance Appraisal in Team-Based Organizations: One Size Does Not Fit All," *Academy of Management Executive* 15, no. 2 (2001), 107–116.

15. Larson and LaFasto, *TeamWork*.

16. James H. Shonk, *Team-Based Organizations* (Homewood, Ill.: Business One Irwin, 1992); and John Hoerr, "The Payoff from Teamwork," *Business Week* (July 10, 1989), 56–62.

17. Gregory L. Miles, "Suddenly, USX Is Playing Mr. Nice Guy," *Business Week* (June 26, 1989), 151–152.

18. Jeanne M. Wilson, Jill George, and Richard S. Wellings, with William C. Byham, *Leadership Trapeze: Strategies for Leadership in Team-Based Organizations* (San Francisco: Jossey-Bass, 1994).

19. Ruth Wageman, "Critical Success Factors for Creating Superb Self-Managing Teams," *Organizational Dynamics* (Summer 1997), 49–61.

20. Thomas Owens, "The Self-Managing Work Team," *Small Business Report* (February 1991), 53–65.

21. Bradley L. Kirkman and Benson Rosen, "Powering Up Teams," *Organizational Dynamics* (Winter 2000), 48–66.

22. Charles Fishman, "Whole Foods is All Teams," *Fast Company* (April–May 1996), 102–109.

23. Curtis Sittenfeld, "Powered by the People," *Fast Company* (July/August 1999), 178–189.

24. The discussion of virtual teams is based on Anthony M. Townsend, Samuel M. DeMarie, and Anthony R. Hendrickson, "Virtual Teams: Technology and the Workplace of the Future," *Academy of Management Executive* 12, no. 3 (August 1998), 17–29; and Deborah L. Duarte and Nancy Tennant Snyder, *Mastering Virtual Teams* (San Francisco: Jossey-Bass, 1999).

25. Jessica Lipnack and Jeffrey Stamps, "Virtual Teams: The New Way to Work," *Strategy & Leadership* (January/February 1999), 14–19.

26. Vijay Govindarajan and Anil K. Gupta, "Building an Effective Global Business Team," *MIT Sloan Management Review* 42, no. 4 (Summer 2001), 63–71.

27. Charlene Marmer Solomon, "Building Teams Across Borders," *Global Workforce* (November 1998), 12–17.

28. James Daly, "Digital Cowboys," *Forbes ASAP* (February 26, 1996), 62.

29. Jane Pickard, "Control Freaks Need Not Apply," *People Management* (February 5, 1998), 49.

30. Sylvia Odenwald, "Global Work Teams," *Training and Development* (February 1996), 54–57; and Debby Young, "Team Heat," *CIO,* Section 1 (September 1, 1998), 43–51.

31. Ray Oglethorpe in Regina Fazio Maruca, ed., "What Makes Teams Work" (Unit of One column), *Fast Company* (November 2000), 109–140.

32. For research findings on group size, see M. E. Shaw, *Group Dynamics,* 3d ed. (New York: McGraw-Hill, 1981); and G. Manners, "Another Look at Group Size, Group Problem-Solving and Member Consensus," *Academy of Management Journal* 18 (1975), 715–724.

33. George Prince, "Recognizing Genuine Teamwork," *Supervisory Management* (April 1989), 25–36; K. D. Benne and P. Sheats, "Functional Roles of Group Members," *Journal of Social Issues* 4 (1948), 41–49; and R. F. Bales, *SYMLOG Case Study Kit* (New York: Free Press, 1980).

34. Robert A. Baron, *Behavior in Organizations,* 2d ed. (Boston: Allyn & Bacon, 1986).

35. Ibid.

36. Avan R. Jassawalla and Hemant C. Sashittal, "Strategies of Effective New Product Team Leaders," *California Management Review* 42, no. 2 (Winter 2000), 34–51.

37. Kenneth G. Koehler, "Effective Team Management," *Small Business Report* (July 19, 1989), 14–16; and Connie J. G. Gersick, "Time and Transition in Work Teams: Toward a New Model of Group Development," *Academy of Management Journal* 31 (1988), 9–41.

38. Bruce W. Tuckman and Mary Ann C. Jensen, "Stages of Small-Group Development Revisited," *Group and Organizational Studies* 2 (1977), 419–427; and Bruce W. Tuckman, "Developmental Sequences in Small Groups," *Psychological Bulletin* 63 (1965), 384–399. See also Linda N. Jewell and H. Joseph Reitz, *Group Effectiveness in Organizations* (Glenview, Ill.: Scott, Foresman, 1981).

39. Thomas Petzinger Jr., "Bovis Team Helps Builders Construct a Solid Foundation," (The Front Lines column), *The Wall Street Journal* (March 21, 1997), B1.

40. Shaw, *Group Dynamics.*

41. Daniel C. Feldman and Hugh J. Arnold, *Managing Individual and Group Behavior in Organizations* (New York: McGraw-Hill, 1983).

42. Dorwin Cartwright and Alvin Zander, *Group Dynamics: Research and Theory,* 3d ed. (New York: Harper & Row, 1968); and Elliot Aronson, *The Social Animal* (San Francisco: W. H. Freeman, 1976).

43. Peter E. Mudrack, "Group Cohesiveness and Productivity: A Closer Look," *Human Relations* 42 (1989), 771–785. Also see Miriam Erez and Anit Somech, "Is Group Productivity Loss the Rule or the Exception? Effects of Culture and Group-Based Motivation," *Academy of Management Journal* 39, no. 6 (1996), 1513–1537.

44. Stanley E. Seashore, *Group Cohesiveness in the Industrial Work Group* (Ann Arbor, Mich.: Institute for Social Research, 1954).

45. S. R. Crockett and N. Gross, "Can CEO Ollila Keep the Cellular Superstar Flying High?" *Business Week* (August 10, 1998), 48–55; and J. Fox, "Nokia's Secret Code," *Fortune* (May 1, 2000), 161–174.

46. J. Richard Hackman, "Group Influences on Individuals," in *Handbook of Industrial and Organizational Psychology,* ed. M. Dunnette (Chicago: Rand McNally, 1976).

47. Kenneth Bettenhausen and J. Keith Murnighan, "The Emergence of Norms in Competitive Decision-Making Groups," *Administrative Science Quarterly* 30 (1985), 350–372.

48. The following discussion is based on Daniel C. Feldman, "The Development and Enforcement of Group Norms," *Academy of Management Review* 9 (1984), 47–53.

49. Hugh J. Arnold and Daniel C. Feldman, *Organizational Behavior* (New York: McGraw-Hill, 1986).

50. Wilson, et al., *Leadership Trapeze,* 12.

51. Eleena DeLisser, "A Software Startup Attracts Staff with Ban on Midnight Oil," *The Wall Street Journal* (August 23, 2000), A1.

52. Stephen P. Robbins, *Managing Organizational Conflict: A Nontraditional Approach* (Englewood Cliffs, N.J.: Prentice-Hall, 1974).

53. Daniel Robey, Dana L. Farrow, and Charles R. Franz, "Group Process and Conflict in System Development," *Management Science* 35 (1989), 1172–1191.

54. Kathleen M. Eisenhardt, Jean L. Kahwajy, and L. J. Bourgeois III, "Conflict and Strategic Choice: How Top Management

Teams Disagree," *California Management Review* 39, no. 2 (Winter 1997), 42–62.

55. Koehler, "Effective Team Management"; and Dean Tjosvold, "Making Conflict Productive," *Personnel Administrator* 29 (June 1984), 121.

56. This discussion is based in part on Richard L. Daft, *Organization Theory and Design* (St. Paul, Minn.: West, 1992), Chapter 13; and Paul M. Terry, "Conflict Management," *The Journal of Leadership Studies* 3, no. 2 (1996), 3–21.

57. Ralph T. King, Jr., "Levi's Factory Workers Are Assigned to Teams, And Morale Takes a Hit," *The Wall Street Journal* (May 20, 1998), A1.

58. Clinton O. Longenecker and Mitchell Neubert, "Barriers and Gateways to Management Cooperation and Teamwork," *Business Horizons* (September–October 2000), 37–44.

59. This discussion is based on K. W. Thomas, "Towards Multidimensional Values in Teaching: The Example of Conflict Behaviors," *Academy of Management Review* 2 (1977), 487.

60. Robbins, *Managing Organizational Conflict.*

61. Based on Kathleen M. Eisenhardt, Jean L. Kahwajy, and L. J. Bourgeois III, "How Management Teams Can Have a Good Fight," *Harvard Business Review* (July–August 1997), 77–85.

62. R. B. Zajonc, "Social Facilitation," *Science* 149 (1965), 269–274; and Erez and Somech, "Is Group Productivity Loss the Rule or the Exception?"

63. Aaron Bernstein, "Detroit vs. the UAW: At Odds over Teamwork," *Business Week* (August 24, 1987), 54–55.

64. Robert Albanese and David D. Van Fleet, "Rational Behavior in Groups: The Free-Riding Tendency," *Academy of Management Review* 10 (1985), 244–255.

65. Baron, *Behavior in Organizations.*

66. Harvey J. Brightman, *Group Problem Solving: An Improved Managerial Approach* (Atlanta: Georgia State University, 1988).

67. Petzinger, *The New Pioneers,* 27–32.

Chapter 15: CVS Stands for Consumer Value Store

WHEN THE FIRST CVS STORE OPENED IN LOWELL, Massachusetts, in 1963, customers knew it as the Consumer Value Store. But as the store itself caught on with consumers, so did the abbreviation CVS. Today, CVS—which has acquired other stores such as Peoples Drug, Revco D.S., and Arbor Drugs—employs more than 80,000 workers nationwide, including 12,000 pharmacists in 4,200 stores. In addition, when CVS acquired Soma.com of Seattle, Washington, it became the first company in the nation to launch an Internet pharmacy site. One way that the company has managed to grow and continue to offer value to its customers is through a heavy emphasis on continuous learning throughout the organization.

Training is paramount at CVS. The company offers an Emerging Leaders Program several times a year for managerial candidates; but perhaps more importantly, CVS considers every employee to have the potential to grow. Thus, employees at every level are offered opportunities to learn the skills they will need for their next job at CVS. With formal training programs, mentoring, and other methods of learning, CVS employees have a greater chance of achieving person-job fit as they move up in the company than they might have if they were simply promoted without preparation and support.

The Emerging Leaders Program is offered to about 90 district manager candidates and 10 regional manager candidates at each session. According to CVS spokesperson Seth B. Kamen, candidates ideally enter the program about a year and a half before they are ready for a promotion. Participants gather at the company's Store Support Center for a two-day kickoff session; then they return to the field to complete 23 training activities. Participants receive regular feedback from their managers and communicate regularly with peers for continual learning. Throughout the program, participants gain experience in planning and organizing, customer service, interviewing and selection, loss prevention, laptop computer skills, pharmacy regulations, merchandising, and more. During the first year of the program, 21 out of 27 participants actually achieved their desired promotions. Response to the new program has been positive. "By working with the Emerging Leader Program, I have learned new insights on my own job," says one participant. "The exposure I have to my

regional manager has been great to help me understand expectations," reports another.

Kamen believes that the value of the program goes beyond the boundaries of its initial intention. Leader-led training blended with actual job experience—the field activities—create a stronger result than might be achieved with one or the other alone. He observes that the program has influenced other programs and practices at CVS. "We developed a new process and tools for field managers to use to conduct store visits that are tied directly to the capability model we present through the program," he explains. And "when new projects, critical assignments, focus groups, and so forth come up, participants in the Emerging Leaders Program are among the first people the organization considers."

CVS also uses THINQ Training Server, a learning management system, to help manage its training efforts. The system has helped CVS employees adapt to standardized training that is designed not only to help them advance but also to increase the consistency of customer service and improve their overall knowledge of the pharmacy industry and the company. With the help of the system, CVS employees have a pass rate of 97 percent on a national pharmacy exam, which exceeds the national average of 81 percent.

CVS's commitment to learning extends throughout the company, at every level. Employees appreciate the opportunities available to them and work hard to perform their best. This is how loyalty is built: when learning never stops. One Emerging Leaders graduate sums it up this way: "CVS is very interested in my success!"

Questions

1. In what ways do you think the Emerging Leaders Program helps achieve good person-job fit at CVS?
2. How might CVS's training programs help develop positive work-related attitudes among employees?
3. How does the model of the learning process in Exhibit 15.8 apply to the Emerging Leaders Program?

SOURCES: Company Web site, http://www.cvs.com, accessed March 18, 2002; Don Steinberg, "The Smart Business 50," Tech Update, ZDNet, http://techupdate.zdnet.com, accessed March 18, 2002; "Case Study: CVS/pharmacy," Thinq, http://learning.thinq.com, accessed March 18, 2002.

Chapter 16: Donna Fernandes: She's the Leader of the Pack

DONNA FERNANDES ISN'T YOUR AVERAGE MBA. HER EXPERTISE lies in the behavior of slugs—real ones, not the human kind. She also holds a Doctor of Sciences degree from Princeton, she's worked at the Franklin Park Zoo in Boston, led wildlife tours through Kenya and Tanzania, hosted her own educational television show, and now she's the director of the Buffalo Zoo in upstate New York, where her clients include elephants, gorillas, hyenas, polar bears, and more.

When Fernandes arrived at the 23-acre zoo a couple of years ago, it was a mess. "Most of what I found about the current state of the zoo was negative," she recalls. The 125-year-old park, the third-oldest zoo in the country, was in a terrible state of disrepair and was in danger of losing its accreditation. The management and board of directors were considering moving the zoo from its home in the Delaware Park area of Buffalo and relocating it to an industrial neighborhood along the Buffalo River. But the community rallied against the move, and it was postponed. Still, something had to be done to bring the zoo back to life. Fernandes quickly found that her base of support as a leader would come from the community and from volunteers and workers at the zoo. "As soon as I walked through the gates of the zoo, I just felt at home," she says. "The people were really friendly. . . . It seemed like people all wanted to improve the zoo. The amount of grass roots support for this zoo is phenomenal."

Fernandes used her position power to put forth a vision for improvement, but she quickly developed personal power as well. People liked her and respected her from the outset. She immediately outlined plans to bring the zoo back up to the standards of the American Zoo and Aquarium Association, which were backed by a pledge of $350,000 from Governor George Pataki. More funding was needed, so the board undertook a massive fundraising effort. Fernandes noted that as the zoo was upgraded she would place more emphasis on children and education through programs at the zoo. "I will also focus on trying to increase family visitors by making exhibits the right height for children in strollers and people in wheelchairs." In addition, she planned to create more natural settings for the animals, with an emphasis on wildlife habitats rather than cages. "These are issues to which I am very sensitive," she explained.

With strong support for Fernandes's vision, plans to relocate the zoo were abandoned, though she was careful to say that she understood the reasons why the board had considered it. Today, visitors enjoy the giraffe feeding station, guided tours, and especially the WILD place, where curious—and brave—participants can wash an elephant or even watch one paint. (Daryl Hoffman, the elephant keeper and head of the animal training committee at the zoo, has instituted a program called Art Gone Wild, in which

the zoo sells "artwork" created by elephants, primates, and big cats.) The zoo's outreach program includes the Zoomobile and Distance Learning, both of which take the zoo's mission outside the grounds to people who might not be able to visit the zoo in person.

Fernandes's democratic leadership style encourages input from staff, groundskeepers, volunteers, the community, and the board of directors. She likes people to stop by her office to give her feedback, suggestions, and even complaints. But this open atmosphere didn't exist before Fernandes arrived, so she had to cultivate it. The change began almost by accident. In the days following the events of the September 11, 2001, attacks on the Pentagon and the World Trade Center, everyone around the zoo was shaken. So on a whim, Fernandes decided to bring her new puppy into the office to cheer up herself and others. Pretty soon people were stopping by to see the puppy and have a chat. Before long, Fernandes was receiving valuable feedback from people who would never have otherwise felt comfortable providing it—and a whole new line of communication had opened up between Fernandes and her staff. The puppy, who is rapidly growing, now makes regular appearances at the office, and Fernandes lets everyone know that she likes her employees to visit whenever they want.

Fernandes is happy with her work and seems comfortable in her leadership role. Of the 186 accredited zoos in the country, only 20 have female directors; so she is aware of her mentoring role as well. "I believe this is probably the most important thing I will ever do, being in this position in a community at a juncture where they want to rebuild their zoo," she says. "When I interviewed for this job, I did a presentation to the board on my vision for the zoo. I told them it would take 10 to 25 years of a shared dream, rather than just my vision, to restore the Buffalo Zoo to its greatness." Fernandes truly believes that her zoo will enjoy a second golden age—within limits. "I won't promise the world in rebuilding this zoo, but if I promise a continent, you'll get a continent." Which is plenty of ground for everyone.

Questions

1. In what ways do you believe Fernandes exhibits both expert power and referent power?
2. Using Exhibit 16.2 in the chapter, create a profile of Fernandes's personal characteristics.
3. Would you characterize Fernandes's leadership style as appropriate for building a learning organization? Why or why not?

SOURCES: Buffalo Zoo Web site, http://www.buffalozoo.org, accessed March 20, 2002; Christina Abt, "Donna Fernandes, Director, Buffalo Zoological Society," *Eve Magazine*; "Governor Pataki Announces $350,000 for Buffalo Zoo," May 22, 2001, http://www.state.ny.us.

Chapter 17: Motivation Is a Wild Experience at the Buffalo Zoo

AT THE BUFFALO ZOO IN UPSTATE NEW YORK, YOU CAN BUY a painting by an elephant, primate, or big cat. You can visit the giraffe feeding station, bathe an elephant, take a starlight safari, tour the conservation station, and take in the vanishing animals exhibit. You'll find renovated buildings, naturalized habitats, clean grounds. You'll be one of 340,000 people annually to enjoy the zoo. Much of this is the work of zoo director Donna Fernandes, her staff, volunteers, and the community of Buffalo. How she got everyone to transform the run-down, sparsely visited zoo in the space of just a few years is a story of motivation.

Fernandes herself is a motivated leader who believes in empowering everyone—inside and outside the organization—to turn the Buffalo Zoo into the very best it can be. She believes that her plans are "a shared dream, rather than just my vision, to restore the Buffalo Zoo to its greatness." When Fernandes first arrived at the zoo, employees were unenthusiastic about their jobs. A senior manager had adopted an autocratic leadership style that had reduced morale. Employees were often reprimanded and threatened with suspension for minor infractions of strict rules. Many felt that they were not given the freedom and respect to do their jobs as well-educated, specialized experts in the care of animals. Communication was lacking, information and ideas were not shared, and the zoo had begun to languish.

Fernandes has a doctorate from Princeton in animal behavior; she's worked at several large zoos; she is interested in education; she can communicate with and relate to her staff, who know and care so much about animals. She also has a business degree, so she can understand the thinking and decisions of the zoo's board of directors. And when she arrived, she knew she had to motivate both staff and board members in order to save the zoo, which was in danger of losing its accreditation with the American Zoo and Aquarium Association. One of her first actions as president and CEO of the zoo was to dismiss the senior manager and abolish the rigid policies that actually interfered with workers' freedom to get their jobs done. "Things happen. Your car breaks down, your kid is sick, it's no big deal," she explains. "It's not like we have a real problem with [attendance] anyway." By removing rules that prevented people from caring for a sick child or accompanying a parent to the doctor's office, Fernandes showed employees that she respected them as individuals who were trying to balance their family lives with their jobs.

Fernandes believed that there was too little communication and knowledge sharing among the departments at the zoo. Under the old management, employees actually hoarded information because they were afraid they would not receive any recognition for their work. So Fernandes established weekly staff meetings with vets, animal keepers, and trainers from all parts of the zoo. Here people share ideas and knowledge, take part in training, and openly share concerns with management. Fernandes also includes staff demonstrations in the meetings to give employees an opportunity to showcase new projects and developments in their areas of expertise. Fernandes observes that these demonstrations not only give recognition for a job well done but also allow the valuable sharing of information. Fernandes expands her motivating leadership to the board of directors and the community at large, who have been engaged in fundraising to renovate the zoo. The board of directors, once considered a stagnant bunch, is now one of the most sought-after groups for community involvement in upstate New York.

These days, the atmosphere at the Buffalo Zoo is much more upbeat. Employees are happier in their jobs, they feel free to offer ideas, and they have the authority to make decisions in their jobs. They also enjoy communication with the Top Dog herself. After September 11, 2001, Fernandes began bringing her new puppy to the office just to make herself—and everyone else—feel better. It didn't take long for people to stop in, pet the puppy, and chat with Fernandes about whatever was going on around the zoo. Fernandes finds these puppy visits as valuable as the staff meetings. It's not surprising that she talks with people as easily as she talks with her animals.

Questions

1. What types of intrinsic rewards are workers now receiving from their jobs at the Buffalo Zoo?
2. In what ways might the human resource department at the Buffalo Zoo use job design to increase motivation among zoo workers?
3. How important is empowerment to motivation at the Buffalo Zoo?

SOURCES: Buffalo Zoo Web site, *http://www.buffalozoo.org*, accessed March 20, 2002; Christina Abt, "Donna Fernandes, Director, Buffalo Zoological Society," *Eve Magazine*; "Governor Pataki Announces $350,000 for Buffalo Zoo," May 22, 2001, *http://www.state.ny.us*.

Chapter 18: Communication Is Paramount at Le Meridien

PERHAPS THE MOST IMPORTANT PART OF A MANAGER'S JOB is communication. Bob van den Oord, assistant general manager at Boston's luxury Le Meridien hotel, would agree. Most of his job involves communicating—with department heads, staff, guests, suppliers, the general manager, and senior managers of the hotel chain based in London. That's why he spends so much time developing both the formal and informal channels of communication at the hotel. "There are a number of things we've done to improve communication at Le Meridien," van den Oord notes. One of the most important parts of his day takes place between 9:30 and 9:45, during which he and his managers hold an operational meeting to discuss the day's events, timeline, and staffing requirements. "It's quite casual," says van den Oord. "Everyone has a cup of coffee and talks." In those fifteen minutes, a great deal of communication is accomplished because managers have learned how to present their messages clearly, listen, and help each other come to a resolution when necessary.

Daily operational meetings aren't the only communication channels at Le Meridien. Van den Oord also holds weekly departmental meetings, such as the food and beverage meeting, in which managers may discuss their schedule of events, supply needs, or paperwork for group dinners; interdepartmental meetings; and yearly staff meetings during which all employees in attendance have an opportunity to ask questions and learn about the hotel's future plans and to review results for the year. Van den Oord calls this annual gathering a team-building opportunity as well. Other channels include the daily briefing sheet—literally a sheet of paper—that staff members can pick up near the hotel lobby to learn about the day's VIP visitors or groups, special events, restaurant promotions, and the like. Also, all managers have access to e-mail on the hotel's intranet.

Clearly, Bob van den Oord prefers the channel richness of face-to-face communication. Although he concedes that e-mail is convenient—and necessary—he is quick to point out that it is not a substitute for personal interaction. If there is a conflict, he wants it resolved either by phone or in person so that both parties have the opportunity to listen and understand each other's words and gestures. Instead of relying on e-mail, van den Oord prefers what he calls "management by walk about," or simply walking through the hotel's different departments to see how things are going. "It gives the staff a chance to talk to me," he explains. "They like it. They like to see that the manager is not just sitting in his office. . . . All the one-on-one, constant feedback is important." During his daily walks through the hotel, van den Oord can easily pick up the news that is traveling through the grapevine.

Michiel Lugt, the hotel's room service and stewarding manager, wholeheartedly agrees. "E-mail facilitates the communication process, but it's not the solver of all problems," he says. Lugt notes that it's very easy for someone who sends an e-mail to assume that the recipient actually received and understood the message—and will act on it if necessary—when in fact the person might not have received or understood the message, or might have underestimated its importance. Lugt echoes van den Oord's concern with communication throughout the hotel. "We have so many departments, and they all need to perform. If one department doesn't communicate, everyone struggles." For instance, if the person taking dinner reservations oversells the restaurant so that people must wait for tables or the kitchen is not prepared with the right amount of food, all departments suffer. "Communication is key in our industry," Lugt concludes.

Van den Oord and Lugt understand well that part of their job as communicators is to influence their employees—to motivate them to perform at the highest level. One of the ways they do this is by setting an example of their own commitment and performance. "You need to be present," notes Lugt. "You are leading by example." Lugt is quick to help out wherever he is needed, whether it's filling in a service gap by serving morning coffee to guests at the restaurant or taking meal orders. By doing so, he communicates to his staff that they are all part of a team running the hotel together.

Van den Oord views good communication as part of good business. Good communication contributes to a happy staff, he believes. "A happy staff equals happy guests," he notes with a smile. "And happy guests help us meet our business objectives."

Questions

1. How important is nonverbal communication to a hotel manager such as Bob van den Oord or Michiel Lugt?
2. Why is feedback an important part of Bob van den Oord's daily process of management by walk about?
3. In the video, assistant general manager Bob van den Oord has to work with another manager to clear up a misunderstanding about the staff's vacation schedule. Put yourself in Bob's shoes and write a brief outline of how you would communicate with the manager to solve the problem. *Hint:* You might want to refer to the Manager's Shoptalk box, "How to Be a Master Communicator," for ideas.

SOURCE: Company Web site, *http://www.lemeridien-hotels.com*, accessed January 4, 2002.

Chapter 19: Cannondale: Teams Perform in the Race for the Perfect Bicycle

HIGH-PERFORMANCE BICYCLES ARE FINELY TUNED MACHINES that are tailored to their riders for peak performance. The search for the perfect bicycle is a never-ending race that pits a material's strength against its weight. Cannondale Corporation, based in Bethel, Connecticut, constantly runs that race and wins—through dedicated teamwork.

The company has come a long way from its beginnings in 1971 in a loft above a pickle factory. From the company's early efforts in manufacturing bicycle trailers and cycling apparel, it expanded to high-performance bicycle design and production in the 1980s. And it hasn't looked back since. The company became renowned early on for its innovative introduction of aluminum bicycle frames, combining strength, flexibility, and light weight. Competitors then constructed their frames of much heavier steel. Today, Cannondale is the leading manufacturer of aluminum bicycles, selling more than 80 models in 60-plus countries worldwide. And with the turn of the 21st century, the company ventured into the design and manufacture of motocross motorcycles and all-terrain vehicles. As Cannondale's Web site proudly proclaims, its "passion is to be the best cycling and off-road motorsports company in the world." Cycling experts would agree it is well on its way.

Maintaining its position in the competitive cycling market isn't easy. Cannondale must continually create new designs that boost performance. To do so, it relies on the best of art and science—the creativity of teams of engineers and experienced production craftsmen combined with the speed and precision of computer technology. The company forms special-purpose teams to create its designs. Design engineers for the teams are selected based on their particular areas of expertise—some are materials experts, others skilled at drawing, and still others experienced at proofing the designs to ensure that all the pieces fit so that they can be built. Cannondale also encourages engineers to volunteer for projects based on their interest in the particular product being considered. For example, a carbon fiber materials specialist may get involved in a project to contribute to the design because he or she wants to help or has a unique idea. The goal of these design teams is to work creatively to solve a particular design problem and produce innovative products. Usually two to four engineers team up for a design.

The design engineers also rely on technology to execute their ideas. Engineers draw their designs on a computer-aided design (CAD) system called Pro/Engineer and can generate a plastic prototype to check the overall design concept. From there, the engineers transmit their designs electronically to the production teams based in two company-owned factories in Bedford, Pennsylvania.

John Horn, research and development project manager at Cannondale says, "The design and production teams are separated by roughly 400 miles, but the communication is instantaneous." Production teams can generate a single prototype bicycle using the CAD system and actual materials to test its performance—strength, durability, flexibility, and dimensions. Frames are at the heart of Cannondale bicycles, and they undergo 12 to 15 different tests before a design is approved for production.

With all of its high-tech capabilities, Cannondale doesn't ignore the human touch in its manufacturing process. The company relies on skilled craftspeople to weld, sand, paint, and finish its bikes. "Aluminum is not an easy material to weld," says Horn. "It's more difficult than steel." So the company hires, trains, and certifies its welders to perform at their peak. The welders' jobs are coveted at the company—they carry prestige and high pay. After the welds are completed, the weld joints are sanded smooth—a mark of quality that Cannondale bikes carry over their competition. Then frames are machined to finish edges and prepare them for additional parts such as cranks and wheels. After that, the bikes are hand painted, matte or gloss finish is applied, and decals are added to customer specifications or sales demand.

Cannondale believes in the quality of human workmanship and relies on assembly line work teams, instead of robotic lines stamping out 10,000 copies at a time. Individual attention to each bicycle allows the company to monitor sales and be extremely flexible to meet customer demands—for a particular model, in a particular size, and in a particular color and finish. Such attention to detail creates pride in Cannondale's work teams—from design through production—and satisfies customers. As the company's Web site states, "We concentrate on detail, because the last 5 percent is often the difference between success and failure." Cannondale is proving that one bike and one rider at a time.

Questions

1. Cannondale uses special-purpose teams to design and produce its bicycles. What are some benefits to that approach?
2. What could be some drawbacks to Cannondale's team approach?
3. How does Cannondale make use of virtual teamwork to produce its products?

SOURCES: Interview with John Horn, research and development product manager at Cannondale Corporation, April 9, 2002; Cannondale Web site, http://www.cannondale.com, accessed March 22, 2002.

Part Five: Ford Enters a New Era of Leadership

LEADERS COME IN ALL SHAPES AND SIZES. THEY COME FROM different countries and cultures. They exhibit different personality traits. They practice different leadership styles. They may be team players or loners. They may have legitimate power, like Jac Nasser and Bill Ford. They may practice coercive power, as Nasser did with his controversial performance appraisal system. They often have personal power, as demonstrated by Bill Ford in his commitment to good relationships with union workers. They may possess different visions for the same company, but they all want to motivate their managers and employees toward that vision. And, they look for ways to communicate their goals.

Jac Nasser's entire tenure as CEO of Ford Motor Company was driven by his goal for the company to become "the world's leading consumer company for automotive services and products." He began by slashing costs and reducing payrolls, earning the nickname "Jac the Knife." Then he diversified Ford's business activities around the world, to the dismay of critics who believed he was carrying the company too far afield from its core business of building and selling cars and trucks. He professed to be a believer in teams and open communication, stating in one interview, "You let your teams have room to work and give them air cover. I'm not a believer in telling people [exactly] what to do. If you start giving people a cookbook, you start to get very narrow solutions." Despite cutting a number of jobs, Nasser claimed to be looking for the best people within the company, seeking to motivate them and move them up. "We are spending more time and effort developing leaders from inside the company," he said. "We're trying to strengthen the team. Like any sports team, if you stop recruiting, over time, you'd lose your competitiveness. If you look at the team we've got today, there's a tremendous mix of different backgrounds, even among the people who came up through Ford Motor Co." But Nasser also had a reputation for being an intimidating leader who kept tight controls on his managers—he had 16 senior managers reporting directly to him instead of creating a team of top executives with the authority to make decisions.

Bill Ford is a completely different type of leader, one who actually sees himself on par with the rank-and-file workers instead of heir to a family dynasty. His personal power is partly expert—he not only grew up in the business (as did Nasser) but prepared to take over the chairmanship by heading up the company's finance committee—and partly referent. People at all levels of the organization genuinely like him. "You can't get mad at Bill Ford," says Lincoln-Mercury dealer Martin J. McInerney. "He's just too nice a guy." He truly believes that Ford Motor Co. can—and should—have a positive relationship with all its workers and associated unions, and he is passionate about the environment. He sees no reason why the company cannot set an example as an environmentally friendly auto manufacturer. "I've staked much of my personal reputation on the environment," he says. "Sometimes I wake up wondering whether I'm taking the company on a diversionary course that won't pay off . . . but on other nights I wake up thinking we're not doing enough." Since taking over as CEO, Ford has redrawn the lines of communication within the company, estab-lishing an executive team that he believes will work well together. "I expect the three of us [Ford, Nick Scheele, and Carl Reichardt] will have an easygoing relationship," predicts Ford.

Ford tried to share the leadership role when he took over the chairmanship position while Jac Nasser was still CEO. The company's board of directors urged the two men to hammer out an arrangement to share power to benefit the company. "You guys need each other," the directors said to each man in separate meetings. So the two tried to establish their roles. "We wanted to ensure that there was clear accountability and clarity with the roles so that we didn't confuse the organization," said Nasser at the time. The result was an arrangement that continued Nasser's primary responsibility for running the company's day-to-day operations and tied Ford more closely to management, but it lasted for only a few short months.

By November 2001, Nasser was out. Some reports say he resigned; others say he was fired. Chances are, both are true. Although Bill Ford certainly had a hand in Nasser's departure, he also takes responsibility for waiting perhaps too long to replace Nasser as the company was stumbling. "I'll always accept my share of the blame," he concedes. Although skeptics are waiting to see whether Bill Ford is tough enough to be the transformational leader that they believe the company now needs, he does have a vision for the company's role not only as a high-quality auto manufacturer but also as an agent of change. "I'm in this for my children and my grandchildren," he explains. "I want them to inherit a legacy they're proud of. I don't want anybody, whether it's my grandchildren or any of our employees' grandchildren, to have to apologize for working for Ford Motor Co. In fact, I want the opposite. I want them to look and say, 'What a difference we made!'"

Questions

1. Using Exhibit 16.2 in the chapter, make a chart showing what you believe are the personal characteristics of leaders that Bill Ford and Jac Nasser possess.
2. Do you think Bill Ford and Jac Nasser are effective communicators? Explain your answer for each.
3. In what ways might Bill Ford use problem-solving teams to benefit his organization? Give one example describing a problem-solving team that might be effective at Ford Motor Co.

SOURCES: Alex Taylor, "Car Jacqued!" *Fortune* (November 26, 2001), http://www.fortune.com; David Booth, "FoMoCo on Firmer Ground with Family Back at Helm," *Financial Times* (November 16, 2001), http://globalarchive.ft.com; "Bill Ford Takes the Wheel," *BusinessWeek Online* (November 1, 2001), http://www.businessweek.com; Doron Levin, "Bill Ford Jr. Got His Wish, and Has Much to Prove," *Bloomberg.com* (October 31, 2001), http://quote.bloomberg.com; "Getting Ford Round the Corner," *Financial Times* (July 30, 2001), http://news.ft.com; Mary Connelly, "Where Jacques Nasser Went Wrong," *Automotive News* (October 15, 2001), http://www.autonews.com; Jeffrey E. Garten, "The Mind of the C.E.O.," *BusinessWeek Online* (February 5, 2001), http://www.businessweek.com; Keith H. Hammonds, "Grassroots Leadership—Ford Motor Company," *Fast Company* (April 2000), http://www.fastcompany.com; Alex Taylor, "The Fight at Ford," *Fortune* (April 3, 2000), http://www.fortune.com; Betsy Morris, "Idealist on Board," *Fortune* (April 3, 2000), http://www.fortune.com.

Controlling

Human beings constantly try to control nature. We dig canals, launch weather balloons, and build dams to contain water. A dam performs a number of controlling functions, holding water back or releasing it, depending on society's needs. In general, dams are constructed to serve four purposes: to generate electricity through hydropower, to increase the water supply, to enhance recreation or commerce, and to control floods. In organizations, managers practice a variety of controlling measures to ensure that goods and services are high quality, expenses lie within certain parameters, facilities are located in the best places, operations are efficient, and inventory is maintained at optimal levels.

Operating a large dam such as Hoover Dam, which spans the Colorado River and supplies water and electricity to California, Nevada, and Arizona, is like managing a large corporation.

Engineers who design and operate dams rely on a variety of methods to monitor and control what happens every day—not only at the site but up and down the river it spans. The dam, like a corporation, has customers whose needs must be satisfied. The dam also affects its surrounding environment, as a corporation does. Managers of both the dam and the corporation must find ways to obtain feedback, monitor finances, and control the quality of goods and services. Information technology can assist managers at many levels by providing data, financial and operations analyses, and even suggestions for decisions. But information technology must be used with the organization's mission and overall strategy in mind, whether that mission involves pumping water to millions of households and acres of farmland or simply manufacturing garden hoses, watering cans, and other tools to help people keep grass and gardens green.

The Importance of Control

CHAPTER OUTLINE

The Meaning of Control

Organizational Control Focus

Feedforward Control

Concurrent Control

Feedback Control

Feedback Control Model

Steps of Feedback Control

Application to Budgeting

Financial Control

Financial Statements

Financial Analysis: Interpreting the Numbers

The Changing Philosophy of Control

Total Quality Management

TQM Techniques

TQM Success Factors

Trends in Quality and Financial Control

International Quality Standards

New Financial Control Systems

Control in the New Workplace

Open-Book Management

The Balanced Scorecard

LEARNING OBJECTIVES

After studying this chapter, you should be able to

1 Define organizational control and explain why it is a key management function.

2 Describe differences in control focus, including feedforward, concurrent, and feedback control.

3 Explain the four steps in the control process.

4 Discuss the use of financial statements, financial analysis, and budgeting as management controls.

5 Contrast the bureaucratic and decentralized control approaches.

6 Describe the concept of total quality management and major TQM techniques.

7 Identify current trends in financial control and discuss their impact on organizations.

8 Explain the value of open-book management and the balanced scorecard as new workplace approaches to control.

Management Challenge

Century-old Samaritan Medical Center serves the northern New York state region with two hospitals, a nursing home, five regional family health centers, and about 200 physicians and other medical professionals. But a new top management team is facing a crisis. Samaritan has finished in the red for 14 of the past 15 years, and this year it will sink $5.6 million deeper. Even worse, the constant hemorrhaging has wiped out Samaritan's financial reserves, precluding new technology purchases and salary increases. Frustrated and fed up with drawn-out bargaining over pay raises and outdated equipment, nearly 300 nurses and technicians went on strike, refusing to return to work until matters were resolved. As they reviewed Samaritan's problems, the new leaders found that many departments were using operational and control standards put in place generations ago. Other departments followed no standards at all, with managers just winging it day to day. Staff hours and payroll had spiraled out of control, reaching more than 40 percent of the medical center's total budget. Without some quick changes, bankruptcy seems inevitable.[1]

How can the new top management team at Samaritan Medical Center use control systems and strategies to improve cost efficiency and save the organization from bankruptcy? If you were a member of the team, what is the first step you would recommend?

A new philosophy about organizational control involves lower-level workers in management and control decisions. At the Honeywell Industrial Automation and Control facility in Phoenix, employees' quality-control decisions cut defect rates by 70 percent, inventory by 46 percent, and customer lead times by an average of 75 percent.

Courtesy of Honeywell, Inc.

Control is a critical issue facing every manager in every organization today. At Samaritan, managers need to find new ways to cut costs, build morale, and increase productivity, or the organization will not survive. Other organizations face similar challenges, such as improving customer service, minimizing the time needed to resupply merchandise in retail stores, decreasing the number of steps needed to process an online merchandise order, or improving the tracking procedures for overnight package delivery. Control, including quality control, also involves office productivity, such as elimination of bottlenecks and reduction in paperwork mistakes. In addition, every organization needs basic systems for allocating financial resources, developing human resources, analyzing financial performance, and evaluating overall profitability.

This chapter introduces basic mechanisms for controlling the organization. It begins by summarizing the basic structure and objectives of the control process. Then it discusses controlling financial performance, including the use of budgets and financial statements. The next sections examine the changing philosophy of control, today's approach to total quality management, and recent trends such as ISO 9000 certification, economic value-added and market value-added systems, and activity-based costing. The chapter concludes with a look at control in the new workplace, including the use of open-book management and the balanced scorecard.

The Meaning of Control

On a warm June day in 1999, the worst crisis in Coca-Cola's 113-year history began when hundreds of customers in Europe turned up sick after drinking "foul-smelling" Coke products. The failure of bottlers in Antwerp, Belgium, and Dunkirk, France, to follow quality-control procedures had gotten the company into a jam from which it is still trying to recover. Fourteen million cases of Coke products were recalled from five European countries, and the public relations nightmare raged for months. A lack of effective control can seriously damage an organization's health and threaten its future, as we saw in the opening case of Samaritan Medical Center. As another example, the Chrysler side of DaimlerChrysler is struggling to recover from financial problems that resulted partly from inadequate control mechanisms following the 1998 merger with Germany's Daimler Benz.[2]

organizational control
The systematic process through which managers regulate organizational activities to make them consistent with expectations established in plans, targets, and standards of performance.

Organizational control is the systematic process of regulating organizational activities to make them consistent with the expectations established in plans, targets, and standards of performance. In a classic article on the control function, Douglas S. Sherwin summarizes this concept as follows: "The essence of control is action which adjusts operations to predetermined standards, and its basis is information in the hands of managers."[3] Thus, effectively controlling an organization requires information about performance standards and actual performance, as well as actions taken to correct any deviations from the standards. Managers need to decide what information is essential, how they will obtain that information (and share it with employees), and how they can and should respond to it. Having the correct data is essential. Managers have to decide which standards, measurements, and metrics are needed to effectively monitor and control the organization and set up systems for obtaining that information. For example, an important metric for the Portland Trail Blazers basketball team is number of season tickets, which reduces the organization's dependence on more labor-intensive box-office

THE NEW WORKPLACE **Manager's Shoptalk**

E-Commerce Metrics

How do e-commerce organizations know how well their Web site is doing? It is not too difficult to find out how many people visit the site and how many pages they look at. But that's only the first step toward finding out how effective the site is in terms of achieving organizational goals. E-commerce managers have been struggling to identify metrics that will help them evaluate a company's performance and compare it to others. Although different companies often use different standards and measurements, some common e-commerce metrics are beginning to emerge:

- *Reach*. This refers to the number of potential customers, or the percentage of the possible audience that a Web site is able to reach. Many companies still use *hits* as the primary measure of Web site success, but that measure has evolved. *Eyeballs* refers to people who are habitual visitors to the company's site. *Unique users* are unduplicated visitors to the site.
- *Stickiness*. This is becoming one of the most important metrics in e-commerce because it measures how much attention the site gets over time. One formula for calculating the metric is:

    Stickiness = Total Size Reach × Frequency × Duration

    This means stickiness takes into account the total broad audience of potential customers, the frequency with which people come back to the site, and the length of time they spend at the site.

- *Conversion*. Conversion means the moment a customer buys, signs up for a seminar, subscribes to a newsletter, and so on. Cost per conversion is a critical number to track because it tells managers how much money they are spending to get one person to buy. Companies also track the conversion rate, which means the ratio of buyers to visitors, and the average order size.
- *Retention*. Companies want people to buy again and again, so it is important to track customer retention. The online auction site e-Bay has a high retention rate, because the same people keep coming back to the site to buy and sell merchandise.

E-commerce organizations track many other metrics. Tools are gradually being developed to help managers better measure, guide, and control e-commerce companies. Advanced data warehousing and data mining tools, for example, can cross-reference Web site data in multiple dimensions to help managers get a broader, clearer picture of customer activity so they can cut costs and maximize efficiency.

SOURCES: Jim Sterne, "Making Metrics Count," *Business2.com* (April 3, 2001), 72; Matt Cutler, "Emetrics: How to Measure Stickiness," *Business2.com* (March 20, 2001), 134; Ramin Jaleshgari, "The End of the Hit Parade," *CIO* (May 15, 2000), 183–190; and Thomas H. Davenport, "Sticky Business," *CIO* (February 1, 2000), 58–60.

---

sales.[4] One issue of current concern to many managers is how to track valuable metrics for e-commerce, as discussed in this chapter's Manager's Shoptalk.

Organizational Control Focus

Control can focus on events before, during, or after a process. For example, a local automobile dealer can focus on activities before, during, or after sales of new cars. Careful inspection of new cars and cautious selection of sales employees are ways to ensure high quality or profitable sales even before those sales take place. Monitoring how salespeople act with customers would be considered control during the sales task. Counting the number of new cars sold during the month or telephoning buyers about their satisfaction with sales transactions would constitute control after sales have occurred. These three types of control are formally called *feedforward*, *concurrent*, and *feedback* and are illustrated in Exhibit 20.1.

Exhibit *20.1*

Organizational Control Focus

Feedforward Control

feedforward control

Control that focuses on human, material, and financial resources flowing into the organization; also called *preliminary* or *preventive control.*

Control that attempts to identify and prevent deviations before they occur is called **feedforward control.** Sometimes called *preliminary* or *preventive control,* it focuses on human, material, and financial resources that flow into the organization. Its purpose is to ensure that input quality is high enough to prevent problems when the organization performs its tasks.

Feedforward controls are evident in the selection and hiring of new employees. Organizations attempt to improve the likelihood that employees will perform up to standards by identifying the necessary skills and using tests and other screening devices to hire people who have those skills. Many organizations also conduct drug screening to ensure that job candidates or employees do not impair their ability to work safely and effectively. Another type of feedforward control is to identify and manage risks. For example, banks typically require extensive documentation before approving major loans. Large accounting firms provide value to their clients by helping identify risks they have either knowingly or unknowingly taken on, rather than just evaluating financial performance after the fact.[5]

Concurrent Control

concurrent control

Control that consists of monitoring ongoing activities to ensure they are consistent with standards.

Control that monitors ongoing employee activities to ensure they are consistent with performance standards is called **concurrent control.** Concurrent control assesses current work activities, relies on performance standards, and includes rules and regulations for guiding employee tasks and behaviors.

Many manufacturing operations include devices that measure whether the items being produced meet quality standards. Employees monitor the measurements; if they see that standards are not met in some area, they make a correction themselves or signal the appropriate person that a problem is occurring. Technology advancements are adding to the possibilities for concurrent control in services as well. For example, retail stores such as Beall's, Sunglass Hut, and Saks use cash-register-management software to monitor cashiers' activities in real time and help prevent employee theft. Trucking companies like Schneider National and Covenant use computers to track the position of their trucks and monitor the status of deliveries.[6]

Other concurrent controls involve the ways in which organizations influence employees. An organization's cultural norms and values influence employee behavior, as do the norms of an employee's peers or work group. Concurrent control also includes self-control, through which individuals impose concurrent controls on their own behavior because of personal values and attitudes.

Feedback Control

Sometimes called *postaction* or *output control*, **feedback control** focuses on the organization's outputs—in particular, the quality of an end product or service. An example of feedback control in a manufacturing department is an intensive final inspection of a refrigerator at a General Electric assembly plant. In Kentucky, school administrators conduct feedback control by evaluating each school's performance every other year. They review reports of students' test scores as well as the school's dropout and attendance rates. The state rewards schools with rising scores and brings in consultants to work with schools whose scores have fallen.[7]

Besides producing high-quality products and services, businesses need to earn a profit, and even nonprofit organizations need to operate efficiently to carry out their mission. Therefore, many feedback controls focus on financial measurements. Budgeting, for example, is a form of feedback control because managers monitor whether they have operated within their budget targets and make adjustments accordingly.

feedback control
Control that focuses on the organization's outputs; also called *postaction* or *output control*.

Feedback Control Model

All well-designed control systems involve the use of feedback to determine whether performance meets established standards. In this section, we will examine the key steps in the feedback control model and then look at how the model applies to organizational budgeting.

Steps of Feedback Control

Managers set up control systems that consist of the four key steps illustrated in Exhibit 20.2: establish standards, measure performance, compare performance to standards, and make corrections as necessary.

Establish Standards of Performance. Within the organization's overall strategic plan, managers define goals for organizational departments in specific, operational terms that include a *standard of performance* against which to compare organizational activities. A standard of performance could include "reducing the reject rate from 15 to 3 percent," "increasing the corporation's return on investment to 7 percent," or "reducing the number of accidents to one per each 100,000 hours of labor."

Exhibit 20.2

Feedback Control Model

Managers should carefully assess what they will measure and how they will define it. Especially when the organization will reward employees for the achievement of standards, these standards should reflect activities that contribute to the organization's overall strategy in a significant way. Standards should be defined clearly and precisely so that managers and workers can determine whether activities are on target.

Measure Actual Performance. Most organizations prepare formal reports of quantitative performance measurements that managers review daily, weekly, or monthly. These measurements should be related to the standards set in the first step of the control process. For example, if sales growth is a target, the organization should have a means of gathering and reporting sales

Forced out of their offices in the World Financial Center by the tragic events of September 11, 2001, 1,500 Lehman Brothers employees continued to work in temporary offices set up at the Sheraton Hotel in the midtown section of New York City. Company teams worked from unique locations: the Financial Institutions Group is pictured in their "office" in the hotel lobby. Senior bankers and research analysts worked out of converted guest rooms. Through it all, employees barely deviated from their established standard of performance. The first week the markets reopened, Lehman's analysts turned out 200 pieces of research, nearly 90 percent of normal volume.

© Jeff Jacobson

data. If the organization has identified appropriate measurements, regular review of these reports helps managers stay aware of whether the organization is doing what it should be.

In most companies, managers do not rely exclusively on quantitative measures. They get out into the organization to see how things are going, especially for such goals as increasing employee participation and learning. Managers have to observe for themselves whether employees are participating in decision making and have opportunities to add to and share their knowledge.

Compare Performance to Standards. The third step in the control process is comparing actual activities to performance standards. When managers read computer reports or walk through the plant, they identify whether actual performance meets, exceeds, or falls short of standards. Typically, performance reports simplify such comparisons by placing the performance standards for the reporting period alongside the actual performance for the same period and by computing the variance—that is, the difference between each actual amount and the associated standard. To correct the problems that most require attention, managers focus on variances.

When performance deviates from a standard, managers must interpret the deviation. They are expected to dig beneath the surface and find the cause of the problem. If the sales goal is to increase the number of sales calls by 10 percent and a salesperson achieved an increase of 8 percent, where did she fail to achieve her goal? Perhaps several businesses on her route closed, additional salespeople were assigned to her area by competitors, or she needs training in making cold sales calls more effectively. Managers should take an inquiring approach to deviations in order to gain a broad understanding of factors that influenced performance. Effective management control involves subjective judgment and employee discussions, as well as objective analysis of performance data.

Take Corrective Action. Managers also determine what changes, if any, are necessary. In a traditional top-down approach to control, managers exercise their formal authority to make necessary changes. Managers may encourage employees to work harder, redesign the production process, or fire employees. In contrast, managers using a participative control approach collaborate with employees to determine the corrective action necessary.

In some cases, managers may take corrective action to change performance standards. They may realize that standards are too high or too low if departments continually fail to meet or routinely exceed standards. If contingency factors that influence organizational performance change, performance standards may need to be altered to make them realistic and provide continued motivation for employees.

Managers may wish to provide positive reinforcement when performance meets or exceeds targets. They may reward a department that has exceeded its planned goals or congratulate employees for a job well done. Managers should not ignore high-performing departments at the expense of taking corrective actions elsewhere. The British express delivery and logistics company TNT UK provides a good illustration of the feedback control model.

TNT UK's computerized management control systems track performance so regularly and in such detail that every manager is constantly aware of existing problems and every employee has the information to help correct them. TNT

TNT UK
http://www.TNT.com

managers set performance targets each year and develop tight definitions of what quality service means for every aspect of the business, providing employees with clear guidelines that spell out how to make improvements.

One important measurement is customer satisfaction. When most delivery companies measure satisfaction, they simply look at whether packages are delivered on time, assuming that customers are happy when this standard is met. Not TNT—it tracks every aspect of the service it provides. One biannual customer satisfaction survey asks 4,000 randomly selected customers to rank key delivery attributes—such as reliability, price, staff professionalism, range of services, and so forth—in order of importance and to score the company's performance on each attribute. These measurements are then compared to the standards.

Far from feeling constrained by the tight measurements, employees are energized and motivated to meet performance targets. One reason is that managers are careful not to let number-crunching get in the way of meeting the needs and goals of staff members. For example, Alan Jones, managing director of TNT UK, motivates van drivers with personal telephone calls or notes congratulating them when they meet or exceed standards. And low scores, rather than leading to a reprimand, bring a note encouraging the team to keep their chins up and work together with managers to determine the corrective actions needed. As Jones points out, without the data provided by computerized management information systems, he wouldn't be able to provide that level of feedback to his employees.[8] ❖

Application to Budgeting

Budgetary control, one of the most commonly used methods of managerial control, is the process of setting targets for an organization's expenditures, monitoring results and comparing them to the budget, and making changes as needed. As a control device, budgets are reports that list planned and actual expenditures for cash, assets, raw materials, salaries, and other resources. In addition, budget reports usually list the variance between the budgeted and actual amounts for each item.

A budget is created for every division or department within an organization, no matter how small, so long as it performs a distinct project, program, or function. The fundamental unit of analysis for a budget control system is called a responsibility center. A **responsibility center** is defined as any organizational department or unit under the supervision of a single person who is responsible for its activity.[9] A three-person appliance sales office in Watertown, New York, is a responsibility center, as is a quality control department, a marketing department, and General Electric's entire refrigerator manufacturing plant. The manager of each unit has budget "responsibility." Top managers use budgets for the company as a whole, and middle managers traditionally focus on the budget performance of their department or division. Budgets managers typically use include expense budgets, revenue budgets, cash budgets, and capital budgets.

Expense Budget. An **expense budget** includes anticipated and actual expenses for each responsibility center and for the total organization. An expense budget may show all types of expenses or may focus on a particular category, such as materials or research and development expenses. When actual expenses exceed budgeted amounts, the difference signals the need for

responsibility center
An organizational unit under the supervision of a single person who is responsible for its activity.

expense budget
A budget that outlines the anticipated and actual expenses for a responsibility center.

managers to identify whether a problem exists and take corrective action if needed. The difference may arise from inefficiency, or expenses may be higher because the organization's sales are growing faster than anticipated. Conversely, expenses below budget may signal exceptional efficiency or failure to meet some other standards, such as a desired level of sales or quality of service. Either way, expense budgets can help identify the need for further investigation but do not substitute for it.

Revenue Budget. A **revenue budget** lists forecasted and actual revenues of the organization. In general, revenues below the budgeted amount signal a need to investigate the problem to see whether the organization can improve revenues. In contrast, revenues above budget would require determining whether the organization can obtain the necessary resources to meet the higher-than-expected demand for its products. Managers then formulate action plans to correct the budget variance.

Cash Budget. The **cash budget** estimates receipts and expenditures of money on a daily or weekly basis to ensure that an organization has sufficient cash to meet its obligations. The cash budget shows the level of funds flowing through the organization and the nature of cash disbursements. If the cash budget shows that the firm has more cash than necessary to meet short-term needs, the company can arrange to invest the excess to earn interest income. In contrast, if the cash budget shows a payroll expenditure of $20,000 coming at the end of the week but only $10,000 in the bank, the organization must borrow cash to meet the payroll.

Capital Budget. The **capital budget** lists planned investments in major assets such as buildings, heavy machinery, or complex information technology systems, often involving expenditures over more than a year. Capital expenditures not only have a large impact on future expenses, they are investments designed to enhance profits. Therefore, a capital budget is necessary to plan the impact of these expenditures on cash flow and profitability. Controlling involves not only monitoring the amount of capital expenditures but evaluating whether the assumptions made about the return on the investments are holding true. Managers should evaluate whether continuing investment in particular projects is advisable, as well as whether their procedures for making capital expenditure decisions are adequate. Some companies, including Boeing, Merck, Shell, United Technologies, and Whirlpool, evaluate capital projects at several stages to determine whether they still are in line with the company's strategy.[10]

Budgeting is an important part of organizational planning and control. Many traditional companies use **top-down budgeting,** which means that the budgeted amounts for the coming year are literally imposed on middle and lower-level managers.[11] These managers set departmental budget targets in

revenue budget
A budget that identifies the forecasted and actual revenues of the organization.

cash budget
A budget that estimates and reports cash flows on a daily or weekly basis to ensure that the company has sufficient cash to meet its obligations.

capital budget
A budget that plans and reports investments in major assets to be depreciated over several years.

top-down budgeting
A budgeting process in which middle- and lower-level managers set departmental budget targets in accordance with overall company revenues and expenditures specified by top management.

Entrepreneurs, as well as large corporations, use leveraged funds to finance their companies. Joshua Silver, a physics professor at England's Oxford University, needs $8 million for the manufacture and marketing of his glasses, which are the world's first adjustable-prescription specs. At a cost of only $10 per pair, the glasses could be a boon for the one-sixth of the world's population who are vision-impaired and cannot afford regular glasses.

PeopleWeekly © 1998 Todd France

bottom-up budgeting
A budgeting process in which lower-level managers budget their departments' resource needs and pass them up to top management for approval.

accordance with overall company revenues and expenditures specified by top executives. Although there are some advantages to the top-down process, the movement toward employee empowerment, participation, and learning means that many organizations are adopting **bottom-up budgeting,** a process in which lower-level managers anticipate their departments' resource needs and pass them up to top management for approval.[12]

Financial Control

In every organization, managers need to watch how well the organization is performing financially. Not only do financial controls tell whether the organization is on sound financial footing, but they can be useful indicators of other kinds of performance problems. For example, a sales decline may signal problems with products, customer service, or sales force effectiveness.

Financial Statements

Financial statements provide the basic information used for financial control of an organization. Two major financial statements—the balance sheet and the income statement—are the starting points for financial control.

balance sheet
A financial statement that shows the firm's financial position with respect to assets and liabilities at a specific point in time.

The **balance sheet** shows the firm's financial position with respect to assets and liabilities at a specific point in time. An example of a balance sheet is presented in Exhibit 20.3. The balance sheet provides three types of information: assets, liabilities, and owners' equity. *Assets* are what the company owns, and they include *current assets* (those that can be converted into cash in a short time period) and *fixed assets* (such as buildings and equipment that are long term in nature). *Liabilities* are the firm's debts, including both *current debt*

Exhibit *20.3*

Balance Sheet

	Lester's Clothiers Consolidated Balance Sheet December 31, 2003		
Assets		**Liabilities and Owners' Equity**	
Current assets:		Current liabilities:	
Cash	$ 25,000	Accounts payable	$ 200,000
Accounts receivable	75,000	Accrued expenses	20,000
Inventory	500,000	Income taxes payable	30,000
Total current assets	$ 600,000	Total current liabilities	$ 250,000
Fixed assets:		Long-term liabilities:	
Land	250,000	Mortgages payable	350,000
Buildings and fixtures	1,000,000	Bonds outstanding	250,000
Less depreciation	200,000	Total long-term liabilities	$ 600,000
Total fixed assets	1,050,000	Owners' equity	
		Common stock	540,000
		Retained earnings	260,000
		Total owners' equity	800,000
Total assets	$1,650,000	Total liabilities and net worth	$1,650,000

(obligations that will be paid by the company in the near future) and *long-term debt* (obligations payable over a long period). *Owners' equity* is the difference between assets and liabilities and is the company's net worth in stock and retained earnings.

The **income statement,** sometimes called a *profit-and-loss statement* or *P & L* for short, summarizes the firm's financial performance for a given time interval, usually one year. A sample income statement is shown in Exhibit 20.4. Some organizations calculate the income statement at three-month intervals during the year to see if they are on target for sales and profits. The income statement shows revenues coming into the organization from all sources and subtracts all expenses, including cost of goods sold, interest, taxes, and depreciation. The *bottom line* indicates the net income—profit or loss—for the given time period.

The owner of Aahs!, a specialty retailing chain in California, used the income statement to detect that sales and profits were dropping significantly during the summer months.[13] He immediately evaluated company activities and closed two money-losing stores. He also began a training program to teach employees how to increase sales and cut costs to improve net income. This use of the income statement follows the control model described in the previous section, beginning with setting targets, measuring actual performance, and then taking corrective action to improve performance to meet targets.

Financial Analysis: Interpreting the Numbers

Managers need to be able to evaluate financial reports that compare their organization's performance with earlier data or industry norms. These comparisons enable them to see whether the organization is improving and

income statement
A financial statement that summarizes the firm's financial performance for a given time interval; sometimes called a profit-and-loss statement.

Exhibit 20.4

Income Statement

Lester's Clothiers Statement of Income For the Year Ended December 31, 2003		
Gross sales	$3,100,000	
Less sales returns	200,000	
Net sales		$2,900,000
Less expenses and cost of goods sold:		
Cost of goods sold	2,110,000	
Depreciation	60,000	
Sales expenses	200,000	
Administrative expenses	90,000	2,460,000
Operating profit		440,000
Other income		20,000
Gross income		460,000
Less interest expense	80,000	
Income before taxes		380,000
Less taxes	165,000	
Net income		$ 215,000

whether it is competitive with others in the industry. The most common financial analysis focuses on ratios, statistics that express the relationships between performance indicators such as profits and assets, sales, and inventory. Ratios are stated as a fraction or proportion; Exhibit 20.5 summarizes some financial ratios, which are measures of an organization's liquidity, activity, profitability, and leverage. These are among the most common ratios, but many measures are used. Managers decide which ratios reveal the most important relationships for their business.

liquidity ratio
A financial ratio that indicates the organization's ability to meet its current debt obligations.

Liquidity Ratios. A **liquidity ratio** indicates an organization's ability to meet its current debt obligations. For example, the *current ratio* (current assets divided by current liabilities) tells whether there are sufficient assets to convert into cash to pay off debts, if needed. If a hypothetical company, Oceanographics, Inc., has current assets of $600,000 and current liabilities of $250,000, the current ratio is 2.4, meaning it has sufficient funds to pay off immediate debts 2.4 times. This is normally considered a satisfactory margin of safety.

activity ratio
A financial ratio that measures the organization's internal performance with respect to key activities defined by management.

Activity Ratios. An **activity ratio** measures internal performance with respect to key activities defined by management. For example, *inventory turnover* is calculated by dividing total sales by average inventory. This ratio tells how many times the inventory is used up to meet the total sales figure. If inventory sits too long, money is wasted. Dell Computer Corporation has achieved a strategic advantage by minimizing its inventory costs. Dell produces computers to order, using a four-day inventory of parts. Dividing Dell's annual sales by its small inventory generates a high figure for inventory turnover.[14] Another type of activity ratio, the *conversion ratio,* is purchase orders divided by customer inquiries. This ratio is an indicator of a company's effectiveness in converting inquiries into sales.

profitability ratio
A financial ratio that describes the firm's profits in terms of a source of profits (for example, sales or total assets).

Profitability Ratios. Managers analyze a company's profits by studying **profitability ratios,** which state profits relative to a source of profits, such as sales or assets. One important profitability ratio is the *profit margin on sales,* which is calculated as net income divided by sales. Similarly, *gross margin* is the gross (before-tax) profit divided by total sales. As described in the Leading Online box, the British online grocer Tesco.com is thriving, whereas U.S.-based Webvan failed, because Tesco managers paid close attention to profitability rather than adopting the "growth now, profits later" model of many early dot-com companies.

Exhibit *20.5*

Common Financial Ratios

Liquidity Ratios	
Current ratio	Current assets/Current liabilities
Activity Ratios	
Inventory turnover	Total sales/Average inventory
Conversion ratio	Purchase orders/Customer inquiries
Profitability Ratios	
Profit margin on sales	Net income/Sales
Gross margin	Gross income/Sales
Return on assets (ROA)	Net income/Total assets
Leverage Ratios	
Debt ratio	Total debt/Total assets

Leading Online

Tesco.com

When Britain's number-one supermarket chain, Tesco, decided to launch a dot-com division, the main thing managers focused on was ensuring profitability. Tesco implemented strict financial controls from the beginning by launching the Internet business from within the chain's current grocery stores. Managers developed and fine-tuned the formula for years, keeping a go-slow, by-the-numbers management approach that has now won Tesco the title of world's biggest and most successful online grocer.

The idea of creating an electronic version of a 1950s delivery boy seemed simple, but for many online grocery businesses, such as U.S.-based Webvan, the underlying details proved more difficult. Webvan had to build its Internet business from the ground up, requiring huge investments in new buildings and infrastructure. In addition, Webvan focused too much energy on rapid growth and too little on financial control. The chart at the top of the next column compares Tesco.com and Webvan's simplified income statements.

Tesco.com had a built-in advantage by being a part of the greater Tesco enterprise, which enabled the operation to ride on the back of its parent company, leveraging its brand, suppliers, advertising, and customer database. Tesco started by offering delivery from just one store, gradually rolling out online service to other areas. Webvan tried to do too much too soon, aiming to enter 24 U.S. markets within three years. This required building two dozen automated food distribution warehouses at a cost of about $35 million per building. After building only three warehouses, Webvan's numbers just got worse and worse, and the startup went bankrupt in July 2001. With no existing suppliers or customer-base, fixed costs

	TESCO.COM	WEBVAN
Average Sale	$123.25	$114.00
Minus:		
Cost of groceries	$ 85.66	$ 83.00
Other store costs	$ 15.16	—
Marketing and administration	$ 5.67	$133.04
Picking and delivery	$ 17.80	$ 30.00
Plus:		
Delivery fee	$ 7.25	—
Net Profit (Loss)	$ 6.21	($132.04)

quickly overwhelmed Webvan's revenues. By contrast, Tesco.com didn't build anything, choosing instead to pick goods off the shelves of existing supermarkets. Using the store-based picking approach kept startup costs low—Tesco spent only $58 million on its dot-com operation during its first four years of operation. Note in the income statement that Tesco's marketing and administrative cost per order is only $5.67, compared to a cost of $133.04 per order for Webvan.

By maintaining strict control over operating costs, checking and rechecking the math to make sure the company was headed in the right direction, Tesco has slowly rolled out online service to more than one-third of its 690 British supermarkets—putting them in reach of 91 percent of the British population. The company forecasts revenues of more than $2.2 billion by 2004, with net profits of nearly $200 million.

SOURCE: Andy Reinhardt, "Tesco Bets Small—and Wins Big," *Business Week e.biz* (October 1, 2001), EB26–EB32.

Another profitability measure is *return on total assets (ROA)*, which is a percentage representing what a company earned from its assets, computed as net income divided by total assets. ROA is a valuable yardstick for comparing a company's ability to generate earnings with other investment opportunities. In basic terms, the company should be able to earn more by using its assets to operate the business than it could by putting the same investment in the bank. Caterpillar Inc., which produces construction and mining equipment, uses return on assets as its main measure of performance. It sets ROA standards for each area of its business and uses variances from the standards to identify problems with how efficiently it is operating and whether it is fully using its assets. Since it began using ROA standards, Caterpillar has enjoyed double-digit returns.[15]

Leverage Ratios. *Leverage* refers to funding activities with borrowed money. A company can use leverage to make its assets produce more than they could on their own. However, too much borrowing can put the organization at risk such that it will be unable to keep up with repayment of its debt. Managers therefore track their *debt ratio,* or total debt divided by total assets, to make sure it does not exceed a level they consider acceptable. Lenders may consider a company with a debt ratio above 1.0 to be a poor credit risk.

The Changing Philosophy of Control

Managers' approach to control is changing in many of today's organizations. In connection with the shift to employee participation and empowerment, many companies are adopting a *decentralized* rather than a *bureaucratic* control process. Bureaucratic control and decentralized control represent different philosophies of corporate culture, which was discussed in Chapter 3. Most organizations display some aspects of both bureaucratic and decentralized control, but managers generally emphasize one or the other, depending on the organizational culture and their own beliefs about control.

bureaucratic control
The use of rules, policies, hierarchy of authority, reward systems, and other formal devices to influence employee behavior and assess performance.

decentralized control
The use of organizational culture, group norms, and a focus on goals, rather than rules and procedures, to foster compliance with organizational goals.

Bureaucratic control involves monitoring and influencing employee behavior through extensive use of rules, policies, hierarchy of authority, written documentation, reward systems, and other formal mechanisms.[16] In contrast, **decentralized control** relies on cultural values, traditions, shared beliefs, and trust to foster compliance with organizational goals. Managers operate on the assumption that employees are trustworthy and willing to perform effectively without extensive rules and close supervision.

Exhibit 20.6 contrasts the use of bureaucratic and decentralized methods of control. Bureaucratic methods define explicit rules, policies, and procedures for employee behavior. Control relies on centralized authority, the formal hierarchy, and close personal supervision. Responsibility for quality control rests with quality control inspectors and supervisors rather than with employees. Job descriptions generally are specific and task related, and managers define minimal standards for acceptable employee performance. In exchange for meeting the standards, individual employees are given extrinsic rewards such as wages, benefits, and possibly promotions up the hierarchy. Employees rarely participate in the control process, with any participation

Exhibit **20.6**

Bureaucratic and Decentralized Methods of Control

Bureaucratic Control	Decentralized Control
Uses detailed rules and procedures; formal control systems	Limited use of rules; relies on values, group and self-control, selection and socialization
Top-down authority, formal hierarchy, position power, quality control inspectors	Flexible authority, flat structure, expert power, everyone monitors quality
Task-related job descriptions; measurable standards define minimum performance	Results-based job descriptions; emphasis on goals to be achieved
Emphasis on extrinsic rewards (pay, benefits, status)	Extrinsic and intrinsic rewards (meaningful work, opportunities for growth)
Rewards given for meeting individual performance standards	Rewards individual and team; emphasis on equity across employees
Limited, formalized employee participation (e.g., grievance procedures)	Broad employee participation, including quality control, system design, and organizational governance
Rigid organizational culture; distrust of cultural norms as means of control	Adaptive culture; culture recognized as means for uniting individual, team, and organizational goals for overall control

SOURCES: Based on Richard E. Walton, "From Control to Commitment in the Workplace," *Harvard Business Review* (March–April 1985), 76–84; and Don Hellriegel, Susan E. Jackson, and John W. Slocum, Jr., *Management,* 8th ed. (Cincinnati, Ohio: South-Western College Publishing, 1999), 663.

being formalized through mechanisms such as grievance procedures. With bureaucratic control, the organizational culture is somewhat rigid, and managers do not consider culture a useful means of controlling employees and the organization. Technology often is used to control the flow and pace of work or to monitor employees, such as by measuring how long employees spend on phone calls or how many keystrokes they make at the computer.

Bureaucratic control techniques can enhance organizational efficiency and effectiveness. Many employees appreciate a system that clarifies what is expected of them, and they may be motivated by challenging, but achievable, goals.[17] However, although many managers effectively use bureaucratic control, too much control can backfire. Employees resent being watched too closely, and they may try to sabotage the control system. One veteran truck driver expressed his unhappiness with electronic monitoring to a *Wall Street Journal* reporter investigating the use of devices that monitor truck locations. According to the driver, "It's getting worse and worse all the time. Pretty soon they'll want to put a chip in the drivers' ears and make them robots." He added that he occasionally escapes the relentless monitoring by parking under an overpass to take a needed nap out of the range of the surveillance satellites.[18]

Decentralized control is based on values and assumptions that are almost opposite to those of bureaucratic control. Rules and procedures are used only when necessary. Managers rely instead on shared goals and values to control employee behavior. The organization places great emphasis on the selection and socialization of employees to ensure that workers have the appropriate values needed to influence behavior toward meeting company goals. No organization can control employees 100 percent of the time, and self-discipline and self-control are what keep workers performing their jobs up to standard. Empowerment of employees, effective socialization, and training all can contribute to internal standards that provide self-control.

With decentralized control, power is more dispersed and is based on knowledge and experience as much as position. The organizational structure is flat and horizontal, as discussed in Chapter 11, with flexible authority and teams of workers solving problems and making improvements. Everyone is involved in quality control on an ongoing basis. Job descriptions generally are results-based, with an emphasis more on the outcomes to be achieved than on the specific tasks to be performed. Managers use not only extrinsic rewards such as pay, but the intrinsic rewards of meaningful work and the opportunity to learn and grow. Technology is used to empower employees by giving them the information they need to make effective decisions, work together, and solve problems. People are rewarded for team and organizational success as well as their individual performance, and there is an emphasis on equity among employees. Employees participate in a wide range of areas, including setting goals, determining standards of performance, governing quality, and designing control systems.

With decentralized control, the culture is adaptive, and managers recognize the importance of organizational culture for uniting individual, team, and organizational goals for greater overall control. Ideally, with decentralized control, employees will pool their areas of expertise to arrive at procedures that are better than managers could come up with working alone.

Courtesy of General Electric

For more than a decade, managers at General Electric have been dedicated to decentralized control through a program called "Work Out." Work Out is an ongoing effort to achieve what former CEO Jack Welch called "boundaryless behavior"—behavior that "ends all barriers of rank, function, geography, and bureaucracy in an endless pursuit of the best idea." With boundaries diminished, GE launched Six Sigma, a disciplined methodology that focuses on quality for every process that affects the GE customer. Cindy Lee and S. Mani were part of a Six Sigma team at the color lab of the GE Plastics plant in Singapore. The team reduced the lead time for matching colors of GE resins to customer requirements by 85 percent, providing a distinct competitive advantage in the fast-paced global market for plastics.

total quality management (TQM)
An organizationwide commitment to infusing quality into every activity through continuous improvement.

Total Quality Management

One popular approach based on a decentralized control philosophy is **total quality management (TQM),** an organizationwide effort to infuse quality into every activity in a company through continuous improvement. TQM became attractive to U.S. managers in the 1980s because it had been successfully implemented by Japanese companies that were gaining market share—and an international reputation for high quality. The Japanese system was based on the work of such U.S. researchers and consultants as Deming, Juran, and Feigenbaum, whose ideas attracted U.S. executives after the methods were tested overseas.[19]

The TQM philosophy focuses on teamwork, increasing customer satisfaction, and lowering costs. Organizations implement TQM by encouraging managers and employees to collaborate across functions and departments, as well as with customers and suppliers, to identify areas for improvement, no matter how small. Each quality improvement is a step toward perfection, and meeting a goal of zero defects. Quality control becomes part of the day-to-day business of every employee, rather than being assigned to specialized departments.

The implementation of total quality management is similar to that of other decentralized control methods. Feedforward controls include training employees to think in terms of prevention, not detection, of problems and giving them the responsibility and power to correct errors, expose problems, and contribute to solutions. Concurrent controls include an organizational culture and employee commitment that favor total quality and employee participation. Feedback controls include targets for employee involvement and for zero defects.

TQM Techniques

The implementation of total quality management involves the use of many techniques, including quality circles, benchmarking, six sigma principles, reduced cycle time, and continuous improvement.

Quality Circles.

One approach to implementing the decentralized approach of TQM is to use quality circles. A **quality circle** is a group of 6 to 12 volunteer employees who meet regularly to discuss and solve problems affecting the quality of their work.[20] At a set time during the workweek, the members of the quality circle meet, identify problems, and try to find solutions. Circle members are free to collect data and take surveys. Many companies train team members in team building, problem solving, and statistical quality control. The reason for using quality circles is to push decision making to an organization level at which recommendations can be made by the people who do the job and know it better than anyone else.

quality circle
A group of 6 to 12 volunteer employees who meet regularly to discuss and solve problems affecting the quality of their work.

Benchmarking.

Introduced by Xerox in 1979, benchmarking is now a major TQM component. **Benchmarking** is defined as "the continuous process of measuring products, services, and practices against the toughest competitors or those companies recognized as industry leaders."[21] The key to successful benchmarking lies in analysis. Starting with its own mission statement, a company should honestly analyze its current procedures and determine areas for improvement. As a second step, a company *carefully* selects competitors worthy of copying. For example, Xerox studied the order fulfillment techniques of L. L. Bean and learned ways to reduce warehouse costs by 10 percent. Companies can emulate internal processes and procedures of competitors, but must take care to select companies whose methods are compatible. Once a strong, compatible program is found and analyzed, the

benchmarking
The continuous process of measuring products, services, and practices against major competitors or industry leaders.

benchmarking company can then devise a strategy for implementing a new program.

Six Sigma.   Six sigma quality principles were first introduced by Motorola, which started on a quality path in the mid-1980s, and were later popularized by General Electric, where former CEO Jack Welch regularly praised six sigma for quality and efficiency gains that saved the company billions of dollars. Based on the Greek letter *sigma*, which statisticians use to measure how far something deviates from perfection, **six sigma** is a highly ambitious quality standard that specifies a goal of no more than 3.4 defects per million parts. That essentially means being defect-free 99.9997 percent of the time.[22] However, six sigma has deviated from its precise definition to become a generic term for a quality-control approach that takes nothing for granted and emphasizes a disciplined and relentless pursuit of higher quality and lower costs. The discipline is based on a methodology referred to as *DMAIC* (Define, Measure, Analyze, Improve, and Control), which provides a structured way for organizations to approach and solve problems.[23]

General Electric has applied six sigma to almost every aspect of its business, from improving products, to increasing customer satisfaction, to fine-tuning delivery processes. For example, the company used six sigma methodologies and measurements to determine the best way to set up a Web-based system to arrange delivery of GE appliances bought at Home Depot. Six sigma helped managers determine that customers cared less about issues such as evening or Sunday delivery and more about having delivery personnel and installers who were knowledgeable, professional, and caring. Thus, GE invested heavily in training rather than costly changes in delivery schedules.[24] Other well-known companies that have embarked on six sigma programs include Ford Motor Company, Dow Chemical, DuPont, Nokia, Texas Instruments, and Merck.[25]

Reduced Cycle Time.   In the book *Quality Alone Is Not Enough,* the authors refer to cycle time as the "drivers of improvement." **Cycle time** refers to the steps taken to complete a company process, such as teaching a class, publishing a textbook, or designing a new car. The simplification of work cycles, including the dropping of barriers between work steps and among departments and the removal of worthless steps in the process, enables a TQM program to succeed. Even if an organization decides not to use quality circles or other techniques, substantial improvement is possible by focusing on improved responsiveness and acceleration of activities into a shorter time. Reduction in cycle time improves overall company performance as well as quality.[26]

L. L. Bean, Inc., the Freeport, Maine, mail-order firm, is a recognized leader in

six sigma
A quality control approach that emphasizes a relentless pursuit of higher quality and lower costs.

cycle time
The steps taken to complete a company process.

Delphi Automotive Systems' injection-molding plant in Cortland, Ohio, produces a billion plastic housings a year for electrical connectors used in motor vehicles and telecom equipment. Delphi spent $14 million to renovate the building and another $30 million for production equipment, computers and software, and a network linking the factory floor with suppliers and customers. This investment in automation and e-business systems has greatly improved the plant's cycle time, enabling Delphi to churn out products faster than ever before. Even from his PC at home, plant superintendent John Stefanko can see what part a machine is currently making, whether it's taking 15, 18, or 20 seconds to do so, and how many parts it has made in the last 15 minutes.

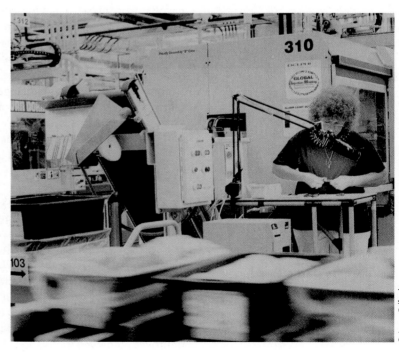

Several years ago, managers at Baxter Healthcare's plant in Mountain Home, Arkansas, were introduced to the Japanese process of continuous improvement, or kaizen. Through the ongoing process of making many small improvements, the plant chopped manufacturing time by 84 percent, improved on-time delivery to more than 99 percent, and won the prestigious Shingo Prize for Excellence in Manufacturing. The plant currently runs about two kaizen events each month, where managers and workers rethink manufacturing processes. The resulting improvements save Baxter more than $3.6 million annually. Manufacturing efficiency has surged on lines such as the circular line in the photo, which makes medical devices.

© Steve Jones

cycle time control. Workers used flowcharts to track their movements, pinpoint wasted motions, and completely redesign the order-fulfillment process. Today, a computerized system breaks down an order based on the geographic area of the warehouse in which items are stored. Items are placed on conveyor belts, where electronic sensors re-sort the items for individual orders. After orders are packed, they are sent to a FedEx facility on site. Improvements such as these have enabled L. L. Bean to process most orders within two hours after the order is received.[27]

Continuous Improvement. In North America, crash programs and designs have traditionally been the preferred method of innovation. Managers measure the expected benefits of a change and favor the ideas with the biggest payoffs. In contrast, Japanese companies have realized extraordinary success from making a series of mostly small improvements. This approach, called **continuous improvement,** is the implementation of a large number of small, incremental improvements in all areas of the organization on an ongoing basis. In a successful TQM program, all employees learn that they are expected to contribute by initiating changes in their own job activities. The basic philosophy is that improving things a little bit at a time, all the time, has the highest probability of success. Innovations can start simple, and employees can build on their success in this unending process.

continuous improvement
The implementation of a large number of small, incremental improvements in all areas of the organization on an ongoing basis.

TQM Success Factors

Despite its promise, total quality management does not always work. A few firms have had disappointing results. In particular, six sigma principles might not be appropriate for all organizational problems, and some companies have expended tremendous energy and resources for little payoff.[28] Many contingency factors (listed in Exhibit 20.7) can influence the success of a TQM program. For example, quality circles are most beneficial when employees have challenging jobs; participation in a quality circle can contribute to productivity because it enables employees to pool their knowledge and solve interesting problems. TQM also tends to be most successful when it enriches jobs and improves employee motivation. In addition, when participating in the quality

Positive Factors	Negative Factors
• Tasks make high skill demands on employees.	• Management expectations are unrealistically high.
• TQM serves to enrich jobs and motivate employees.	• Middle managers are dissatisfied about loss of authority.
• Problem-solving skills are improved for all employees.	• Workers are dissatisfied with other aspects of organizational life.
• Participation and teamwork are used to tackle significant problems.	• Union leaders are left out of QC discussions.
• Continuous improvement is a way of life.	• Managers wait for big, dramatic innovations.

Exhibit 20.7

Quality Program Success Factors

program improves workers' problem-solving skills, productivity is likely to increase. Finally, a quality program has the greatest chance of success in a corporate culture that values quality and stresses continuous improvement as a way of life.

Trends in Quality and Financial Control

Many companies are responding to changing economic realities and global competition by reassessing organizational management and processes—including control mechanisms. Some of the major trends in quality and financial control include international quality standards, economic value-added and market value-added systems, and activity-based costing.

International Quality Standards

One impetus for total quality management in the United States is the increasing significance of the global economy. Many countries have endorsed a universal framework for quality assurance called **ISO 9000,** a set of international standards for quality management systems established by the International Organization for Standardization in 1987 and revised in late 2000.[29] By the end of 1999, more than 340,000 organization in 150 countries, including the United States, had been certified to demonstrate their commitment to quality. Europe continues to lead in the total number of ISO 9000 certifications, but the greatest number of new certifications in recent years has been in the United States. ISO 9000 has become the recognized standard for evaluating and comparing companies on a global basis, and more U.S. companies are feeling the pressure to participate in order to remain competitive in international markets. In addition, many countries and companies require ISO 9000 certification before they will do business with an organization.

ISO 9000
A set of international standards for quality management, setting uniform guidelines for processes to ensure that products conform to customer requirements.

New Financial Control Systems

In addition to traditional financial tools, managers in many organizations are using systems such as economic value-added, market value-added, and activity-based costing to provide effective financial control.

Economic Value-Added (EVA). Hundreds of companies, including AT&T, Quaker Oats, the Coca-Cola Company, and Philips Petroleum Company, have set up **economic value-added (EVA)** measurement systems as a new way to gauge financial performance. EVA can be defined as a company's

economic value-added (EVA) system
A control system that measures performance in terms of after-tax profits minus the cost of capital invested in tangible assets.

net (after-tax) operating profit minus the cost of capital invested in the company's tangible assets.[30] Measuring performance in terms of EVA is intended to capture all the things a company can do to add value from its activities, such as run the business more efficiently, satisfy customers, and reward shareholders. Each job, department, or process in the organization is measured by the value added.

Market Value-Added (MVA).

market value-added (MVA) system
A control system that measures the stock market's estimate of the value of a company's past and expected capital investment projects.

Market value-added (MVA) adds another dimension because it measures the stock market's estimate of the value of a company's past and projected capital investment projects. For example, when a company's market value (the value of all outstanding stock plus the company's debt) is greater than all the capital invested in it from shareholders, bondholders, and retained earnings, the company has a positive MVA, an indication that it has created wealth. A positive MVA usually goes hand-in-hand with a high EVA measurement.[31]

Activity-Based Costing (ABC).

activity-based costing (ABC)
A control system that identifies the various activities needed to provide a product and allocates costs accordingly.

Managers measure the cost of producing goods and services so they can be sure they are selling those products for more than the cost to produce them. Traditional methods of costing assign costs to various departments or functions, such as purchasing, manufacturing, human resources, and so on. With a shift to more horizontal, flexible organizations has come a new approach called **activity-based costing (ABC)**, which allocates costs across business processes. ABC attempts to identify all the various activities needed to provide a product or service and allocate costs accordingly. For example, an activity-based costing system might list the costs associated with processing orders for a particular product, scheduling production for that product, producing it, shipping it, and resolving problems with it. Because ABC allocates costs across business processes, it provides a more accurate picture of the cost of various products and services.[32] In addition, it enables managers to evaluate whether more costs go to activities that add value (meeting customer deadlines, achieving high quality) or to activities that do not add value (such as processing internal paperwork). They can then focus on reducing costs associated with non–value-added activities.

Control in the New Workplace

Changing organizational structures and the resulting management methods that emphasize information sharing, employee participation, learning, and teamwork have led to some new approaches to control in today's workplace. Two significant aspects of control in the new workplace are open-book management and use of the balanced scorecard.

Open-Book Management

open-book management
Sharing financial information and results with all employees in the organization.

In an organizational environment that touts information sharing, teamwork, and the role of managers as facilitators, executives cannot hoard financial data. They must admit employees throughout the organization into the loop of financial control and responsibility to encourage active participation and commitment to organizational goals. A growing number of managers are opting for full disclosure in the form of open-book management. **Open-book management** allows employees to see for themselves—through charts, computer printouts, meetings, and so forth—the financial condition of the company.

Putting People First

SOURCES: Geoffrey Colvin, "The Anti-Control Freak," *Fortune* (November 26, 2001), 60, 80; and Ricardo Semler, "How We Went Digital Without a Strategy," *Harvard Business Review* (September/October 2000), 51–58.

Semco's Open Book Policy

When Ricardo Semler took over from his father as head of the family business, Brazil's Semco, he decided to manage based on a philosophy of "giving up control" by having faith in people and respect for their ideas. At Semco, employees have no set work schedules, no dress codes, no strict rules and regulations, and no employee manuals. About 30 percent of employees even set their own pay, and everyone in the company knows everyone else's salary. All workers receive the company's financial statements and are taught how to read them through classes set up by the labor union. Board meetings are open to all employees who want to attend. Self-managed teams have replaced the management hierarchy, and people have a chance to choose what they want to do based on how they can best make a contribution to the company. Top managers are voted in and evaluated on a regular basis by employees—with the outcomes posted for all to see.

The idea that ties all this together is Semler's belief in taking top management out of running the business, which led *Fortune* magazine to give him the title of "anti-control freak."

Semler believes that if an organization gives people complete freedom and full information, they will act in their own, and consequently the company's, best interests. "It is only when you rein them in, when you tell them what to do and how to think, that they become inflexible, bureaucratic, and stagnant," says Semler. Despite all the freedom, organizational control at Semco is quite strong, based not on power and authority but on organizational vision and cultural values that emphasize self-initiative, self-control, and full disclosure of all types of information. Employees think like business owners because they can see how their jobs and actions fit in and contribute to the organization's—and their own—success or failure.

The approach must be working. In the past 10 years, Semco has quadrupled its revenues and increased its workforce from 450 to 1,300 employees. Semler believes his company's success is a powerful reminder that it is possible to have an efficient business without strict rules and controls, guided by managers who lead rather than wield their power.

Second, open-book management shows the individual employee how his or her job fits into the big picture and affects the financial future of the organization. Finally, open-book management ties employee rewards to the company's overall success. With training in interpreting the financial data, employees can see the interdependence and importance of each function. If they are rewarded according to performance, they become motivated to take responsibility for their entire team or function, rather than merely their individual jobs.[33] Cross-functional communication and cooperation are also enhanced.

The goal of open-book management is to get every employee thinking and acting like a business owner rather than like a hired hand. To get employees to think like owners, management provides them with the same information owners have: what money is coming in and where it is going. Open-book management helps employees appreciate why efficiency is important to the organization's success. Open-book management turns traditional control on its head. This chapter's Putting People First box describes how Ricardo Semler runs a successful company by being an "anti-control freak."

The Balanced Scorecard

Another recent innovation is to integrate the various dimensions of control, combining internal financial measurements and statistical reports with a concern for markets and customers as well as employees.[34] Whereas many managers once focused primarily on measuring and controlling financial performance, they

balanced scorecard

A comprehensive management control system that balances traditional financial measures with measures of customer service, internal business processes, and the organization's capacity for learning and growth.

are increasingly recognizing the need to evaluate other aspects of organizational performance to assess the value-creating activities of the contemporary organization.[35]

One fresh approach is the balanced scorecard. The **balanced scorecard** is a comprehensive management control system that balances traditional financial measures with operational measures relating to a company's critical success factors.[36] A balanced scorecard contains four major perspectives, as illustrated in Exhibit 20.8: financial performance, customer service, internal business processes, and the organization's capacity for learning and growth.[37] Within these four areas, managers identify key performance metrics the organization will track. The *financial perspective* reflects a concern that the organization's activities contribute to improving short- and long-term financial performance. It includes traditional measures such as net income and return on investment. *Customer service* indicators measure such things as how customers view the organization, as well as customer retention and satisfaction. *Business process* indicators focus on production and operating statistics, such as order fulfillment or cost per order. The final component looks at the organization's *poten-*

Exhibit **20.8**

The Balanced Scorecard

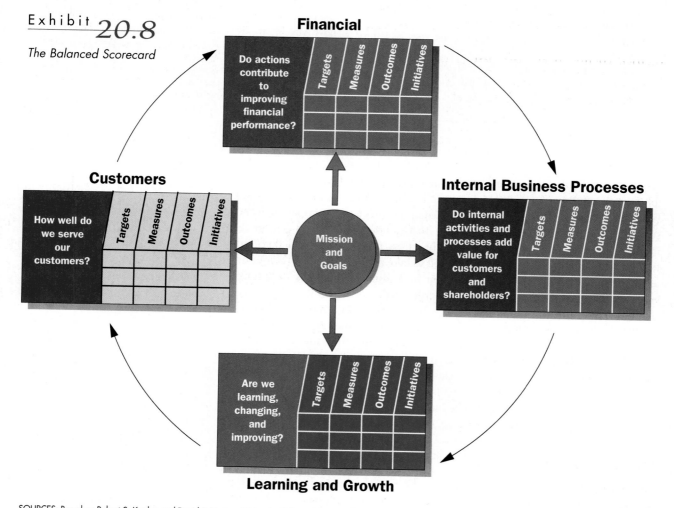

SOURCES: Based on Robert S. Kaplan and David P. Norton, "Using the Balanced Scorecard as a Strategic Management System," *Harvard Business Review* (January–February 1996), 75–85; and Chee W. Chow, Kamal M. Haddad, and James E. Williamson, "Applying the Balanced Scorecard to Small Companies," *Management Accounting* 79, no. 2 (August 1997), 21–27.

tial for learning and growth, focusing on how well resources and human capital are being managed for the company's future. Metrics may include such things as employee retention and the introduction of new products. The components of the scorecard are designed in an integrative manner, as illustrated in Exhibit 20.8. The balanced scorecard helps managers focus on key performance measures and communicate them clearly throughout the organization. The scorecard has become the core management control system for many organizations today. Well-known companies using the system include Bell Emergis (a division of Bell Canada), Mobil Oil Corp., AT&T Canada, and Cigna Insurance.[38]

Summary and Management Solution

This chapter introduced a number of important concepts about organizational control. Organizational control is the systematic process through which managers regulate organizational activities to meet planned goals and standards of performance. The focus of the control system may include feedforward control to prevent problems, concurrent control to monitor ongoing activities, and feedback control to evaluate past performance. Well-designed control systems include four key steps: establish standards, measure performance, compare performance to standards, and make corrections as necessary.

Budgeting is one of the most commonly used forms of managerial control. Managers might use expense budgets, revenue budgets, cash budgets, and capital budgets, for example. Other financial controls include use of the balance sheet, income statement, and financial analysis of these documents.

The philosophy of controlling has shifted to reflect changes in leadership methods. Traditional bureaucratic controls emphasize establishing rules and procedures, then monitoring employee behavior to make sure the rules and procedures have been followed. With decentralized control, employees assume responsibility for monitoring their own performance.

Besides monitoring financial results, organizations control the quality of their goods and services. They might do this by adopting total quality management (TQM) techniques such as quality circles, benchmarking, six sigma, reduced cycle time, and continuous improvement.

Recent trends in control include the use of international quality standards, economic value-added (EVA) and market value-added (MVA) systems, and activity-based costing. Other important aspects of control in the new workplace are open-book management and use of the balanced scorecard.

The story of Samaritan Medical Center at the beginning of the chapter demonstrates the importance of control. A new top management team was facing a crisis because costs had been spiraling out of control, and Samaritan had lost money for 14 of the past 15 years. One of the first decisions the new team made was to monitor Samaritan's productivity with an eye toward lowering staff costs while maintaining quality of care. They first evaluated what data they needed and then established ideal standards, such as the most efficient and desirable number of employee hours per day per patient or per procedure.

Top managers implemented a type of activity-based costing to be sure all costs were accounted for and assigned where they belonged so they could get an accurate picture of what was going on. Because of the nature of hospital work, where people provide many different services in many different departments, costs are often overlooked or misplaced in traditional accounting procedures. Samaritan then fed the data into a basic accounting spreadsheet and compared it to industry benchmarks and to the data of other similar-sized operations. With these data analyzed, managers were able to establish high-performance yet attainable standards that would give department heads solid reference points for allocating staff and budgeting financial resources. Each department's progress was tracked on a graph that compared results to benchmarks, so people could note their success over the course of the year. Managers were able to take corrective action as needed by reassigning staff, revising patient-flow procedures, or in some cases revising targets if a department consistently overreached its goals. The financial turnaround that resulted from the improved control process was stunning. Within only a few months, Samaritan had reduced personnel for a savings of $2.5 million, without a decrease in service. A couple of years later, the organization was posting solid year-end profits. In addition, enhanced control and a revitalized bottom line led to a fresh spirit of teamwork and organizational vitality at Samaritan.[39]

Discussion Questions

1. Why is it important for managers to understand the process of organizational control?
2. How might a public school system use feedforward control to identify the best candidates for its teaching positions?
3. Can you give examples of feedback control that might be used in a family-style restaurant? In a large hospital?
4. What standards of performance has your professor established for this class? How will your actual performance be measured? How will your performance be compared to the standards? Do you think the standards and methods of measurement are fair? Why or why not?
5. What is the difference between budgeting and financial analysis? Why is each type of control important to a company?
6. In what ways could a university benefit from bureaucratic control? In what ways might it benefit from decentralized control? Overall, which approach do you think would be best at your college or university? Why?
7. What types of analysis can managers perform to help them diagnose a company's financial condition? How can a review of financial statements help managers diagnose other kinds of performance problems as well?
8. Why is benchmarking an important component of total quality management (TQM) programs? Do you believe a company could have a successful TQM program without using benchmarking?
9. How might activity-based costing provide better financial control tools for managers of a company such as Kellogg that produces numerous food products?
10. Why do you think today's managers would want to use the balanced scorecard to measure and control organizational performance?

Management in Practice: Experiential Exercise

Is Your Budget in Control?

By the time you are in college, you are in charge of at least some of your own finances. How well you manage your personal budget may indicate how well you will manage your company's budget on the job. Respond to the following statements to evaluate your own budgeting habits. If the statement doesn't apply directly to you, respond the way you think you would behave in a similar situation.

1. I spend all my money as soon as I get it.   Yes   No
2. At the beginning of each week (or month, or term), I write down all my fixed expenses.   Yes   No
3. I never seem to have any money left over at the end of the week (or month).   Yes   No
4. I pay all my expenses, but I never seem to have any money left over for fun.   Yes   No
5. I am not putting any money away in savings right now; I'll wait until after I graduate from college.   Yes   No
6. I can't pay all my bills.   Yes   No
7. I have a credit card, but I pay the balance in full each month.   Yes   No
8. I take cash advances on my credit card.   Yes   No
9. I know how much I can spend on eating out, movies, and other entertainment each week.   Yes   No
10. I pay cash for everything.   Yes   No
11. When I buy something, I look for value and determine the best buy.   Yes   No
12. I lend money to friends whenever they ask, even if it leaves me short of cash.   Yes   No
13. I never borrow money from friends.   Yes   No
14. I am putting aside money each month to save for something that I really need.   Yes   No

Yes responses to statements 2, 9, 10, 13, and 14 point to the most disciplined budgeting habits; *yes* responses to 4, 5, 7, and 11 reveal adequate budgeting habits; *yes* responses to 1, 3, 6, 8, and 12 indicate the poorest budgeting habits. If you have answered honestly, chances are you'll have a combination of all three. Look to see where you can improve your budgeting.

Management in Practice: Ethical Dilemma

Go Along to Get Along?

As the home health care industry began to take off, Rhonda Gilchrist was presented with a terrific opportunity: a start-up home health care agency offered her a position managing its staff of visiting nurses. She supported home health care because patients were treated in the relaxed, comfortable atmosphere of their homes; home visits gave patients and nurses more independence; and home visits were intended to be much cheaper than hospital stays or doctor's office visits.

Most of the patients treated by Gilchrist's nurses were elderly, with a variety of complaints ranging from diabetes to hip injuries. At first, Gilchrist encouraged her staff to make their visits efficient and productive so that patients could be weaned from care in a timely manner. However, when she reported that one patient had recovered enough from a heart attack that he no longer needed three visits a week, the agency owner replied, "You should be looking for ways to increase the number of visits, not decrease them!" Gilchrist was shocked, but she soon understood that the only way to keep her job—and her nurses' jobs—was to go along with her company's wishes. Those extra visits, paid for by Medicare, were paying her salary.

Meanwhile, Gilchrist did some research on her own. She learned that the average home-care patient now gets 80 visits per year (nearly four times the number of a decade ago), for which Medicare pays up to $90 per visit. Rhonda knows home health care is extremely important to many patients, but she also realizes it is being abused by others, as well as by the agencies.

As she drove to the office, Rhonda considered her alternatives. She knew that some of her clients no longer needed care. But she also knew that she needed a job, and most patients were lonely and looked forward to the nurses' visits. She wondered if there was a better way to control costs and deliver the best care to her patients.

What Do You Do?

1. Go along with the status quo and forget about the abuses of the system—that's your boss's problem. Besides, Medicare has deep pockets.
2. Look for another job as soon as possible. You don't want to be associated with unethical, and potentially illegal, practices.
3. Approach the owner of the agency and suggest other ways the agency might make a profit and deliver high-quality care, such as innovative ways to attract new clients to replace those that leave the roster in better health.

SOURCE: Based on George Anders and Laurie McGinley, "Medical Morass: How Do You Tame a Wild U.S. Program?" *The Wall Street Journal* (March 6, 1997), A1, A8.

Surf the Net

1. **National Quality Award.** The Malcolm Baldrige National Quality Improvement Act of 1987 launched a national quality award program in the United States to help improve quality and productivity. This award helps to stimulate American companies to improve quality and productivity, recognizes the achievements of outstanding companies, provides an example to other organizations, establishes guidelines and criteria that can be widely used, and makes available to other organizations detailed information on how winning organizations were able to achieve outstanding quality. Go to *http://www.quality.nist.gov/* and find information to help you answer the following questions:
   a. In what three areas does the Baldrige National Quality Award (BNQA) provide *Criteria for Performance Excellence*?
   b. The first recipients of the BNQA were Globe Metallurgical Inc., Westinghouse Electric Corporation Commercial Nuclear Fuel Division, and Motorola Inc. What year did these three companies win the BNQA?
   c. Name the most recent recipients of the BNQA.
2. **Financial Statements.** Go to *http://www.annual reportservice.com/* to access the annual report of a company of interest to you. Locate and print the pages from the annual report that are the report's equivalent of Exhibits 20.3 (Balance Sheet) and 20.4 (Income Statement). Note that some organizations refer to these financial statements by different names. For example, SYSCO Corporation uses "Consolidated Results of Operations" instead of Income Statement and "Consolidated Financial Position" instead of Balance Sheet. Bring your printouts to class to use during the class discussion on financial controls.
3. **Six Sigma.** As you learned from the chapter, General Electric is a well-known Six Sigma company. Visit the GE Six Sigma site at *http://www.ge.com/sixsigma/* and write a three-paragraph report on what further insights you gained about Six Sigma after visiting this Web site.

Case for Critical Analysis

Lincoln Electric

Imagine having a management system that is so successful people refer to it with capital letters—the Lincoln Management System—and other businesses benchmark their own systems by it. That is the situation of Ohio-based Lincoln Electric. For a number of years, other companies have tried to figure out Lincoln Electric's secret—how management coaxes maximum productivity and quality from its workers, even during difficult financial times.

Lincoln Electric is a leading manufacturer of welding products, welding equipment, and electric motors, with more than $1 billion in sales and 6,000 workers worldwide. The company's products are used for cutting, manufacturing, and repairing other metal products. Although it is now a publicly traded company, members of the Lincoln family still own more than 60 percent of the stock.

Lincoln uses a diverse control approach. Tasks are rigidly defined, and individual employees must meet strict measurable standards of performance. However, the Lincoln system succeeds largely because of an organizational culture based on openness and trust, shared control, and an egalitarian spirit. Although the line between managers and workers at Lincoln is firmly drawn, managers respect the expertise of production workers and value their contributions to many aspects of the business. The company has an open-door policy for all top executives, middle managers, and production workers, and regular face-to-face communication is encouraged. Workers are expected to challenge management if they believe practices or compensation rates are unfair. Most workers are hired right out of high school, then trained and cross-trained to perform different jobs. Some eventually are promoted to executive positions, because Lincoln believes in promoting from within. Many Lincoln workers stay with the company for life.

One of Lincoln's founders felt that organizations should be based on certain values, including honesty, trustworthiness, openness, self-management, loyalty, accountability, and cooperativeness. These values continue to form the core of Lincoln's culture, and management regularly rewards employees who manifest them. Because Lincoln so effectively socializes employees, they exercise a great degree of self-control on the job. Production workers are paid on a piece-rate system, plus merit pay based on performance. Employees also are eligible for annual bonuses, which fluctuate according to the company's fortunes, and they participate in stock purchase plans. Bonuses are based on a number of factors, such as productivity, quality, dependability, and cooperation with others. Factory workers at Lincoln have been known to earn more than $100,000 a year. However, there also are other, less tangible rewards. Pride of workmanship and feelings of involvement, contribution, and esprit de corps are intrinsic rewards that flourish at Lincoln Electric. Cross-functional teams, empowered to make decisions, take responsibility for product planning, development, and marketing. Information about the company's operations and financial performance is openly shared with workers throughout the company.

Lincoln places emphasis on anticipating and solving customer problems. Sales representatives are given the technical training they need to understand customer needs, help customers understand and use Lincoln's products, and solve problems. This customer focus is backed up by attention to the production process through the use of strict accountability standards and formal measurements for productivity, quality, and innovation for all employees. In addition, a software program called Rhythm is used to streamline the flow of goods and materials in the production process.

Lincoln's system has worked extremely well in the United States. The cultural values, open communication, and formal control and reward systems interact to align the goals of managers, workers, and the organization as well as encourage learning and growth. Now Lincoln is discovering whether its system can hold up overseas. Although most of Lincoln's profits come from domestic operations, and a foreign venture in the 1990s lost a lot of money for the company, top managers want to expand globally because foreign markets are growing much more rapidly than domestic markets. Thus far, Lincoln managers have not developed a strategic control plan for global operations, relying instead on duplicating the domestic Lincoln system.

Questions

1. What types of control—feedforward, concurrent, or feedback—are illustrated in this case? Explain.
2. Based on what you've just read, what do *you* think makes the Lincoln System so successful?
3. Would you characterize Lincoln Electric as having a primarily bureaucratic or decentralized approach to control? Explain your answer.

SOURCE: Based on Joseph Maciariello, "A Pattern of Success: Can This Company Be Duplicated?" *Drucker Management* 1, no. 1 (Spring 1997), 7–11.

■ Endnotes

1. John Roemer, "A Hospital Is Reborn," *Management Review* (June 1999), 58–61.
2. Nikhil Deogun, James R. Hagerty, Steve Stecklow, and Laura Johannes, "Anatomy of a Recall: How Coke's Controls Fizzled Out in Europe," *The Wall Street Journal* (June 29, 1999), A1; Christine Tierney and Jeff Green, "Can Schrempp Stop the Careening at Chrysler?" *Business Week* (December 4, 2000), 40.
3. Douglas S. Sherwin, "The Meaning of Control," *Dunn's Business Review* (January 1956).
4. Russ Banham, "Nothin' But Net Gain," *eCFO* (Fall 2001), 32–33.
5. Jeannie Cameron, "Death of Traditional Accounting Will Prove to Be a Boon," *The Asian Wall Street Journal* (April 27, 1998), 16.
6. Jennifer S. Lee, "Tracking Sales and the Cashiers," *The New York Times* (July 11, 2001), C1, C6; Anna Wilde Mathews,

"New Gadgets Track Truckers' Every Move," *The Wall Street Journal* (July 14, 1997), B1, B10.

7. Steve Stecklow, "Kentucky's Teachers Get Bonuses, but Some Are Caught Cheating," *The Wall Street Journal* (September 2, 1997), A1, A5.

8. Trevor Merriden, "Measured for Success," *Management Review* (April 1999), 27–32.

9. Sumantra Ghoshal, *Strategic Control* (St. Paul, Minnesota: West, 1986), Chapter 4; and Robert N. Anthony, John Dearden, and Norton M. Bedford, *Management Control Systems,* 5th ed. (Homewood, Illinois: Irwin, 1984).

10. John A. Boquist, Todd T. Milbourn, and Anjan V. Thakor, "How Do You Win the Capital Allocation Game?" *Sloan Management Review* (Winter 1998), 59–71.

11. Anthony, Dearden, and Bedford, *Management Control Systems.*

12. Participation in budget setting is described in a number of studies, including Neil C. Churchill, "Budget Choice: Planning versus Control," *Harvard Business Review* (July–August 1984), 150–164; Peter Brownell, "Leadership Style, Budgetary Participation, and Managerial Behavior," *Accounting Organizations and Society* 8 (1983), 307–321; and Paul J. Carruth and Thurrell O. McClandon, "How Supervisors React to 'Meeting the Budget' Pressure," *Management Accounting* 66 (November 1984), 50–54.

13. Bruce G. Posner, "How to Stop Worrying and Love the Next Recession," *Inc.* (April 1986), 89–95.

14. Lawrence M. Fisher, "Inside Dell Computer Corporation," *Strategy and Business*, Issue 10, first quarter 1998, 68–75.

15. Robin Goldwyn Blumenthal, "'Tis the Gift to Be Simple," *CFO* (January 1998), 61–63.

16. William G. Ouchi, "Markets, Bureaucracies, and Clans," *Administrative Science Quarterly* 25 (1980), 129–141; and B. R. Baligia and Alfred M. Jaeger, "Multinational Corporations: Control Systems and Delegation Issues," *Journal of International Business Studies* (Fall 1984), 25–40.

17. Sherwin, "The Meaning of Control."

18. Mathews, "New Gadgets Trace Truckers' Every Move," B10.

19. A. V. Feigenbaum, *Total Quality Control: Engineering and Management* (New York: McGraw-Hill, 1961); John Lorinc, "Dr. Deming's Traveling Quality Show," *Canadian Business* (September 1990), 38–42; Mary Walton, *The Deming Management Method* (New York: Dodd-Meade & Co., 1986); and J. M. Juran and Frank M. Gryna, eds., *Juran's Quality Control Handbook*, 4th ed. (New York: McGraw-Hill, 1988).

20. Edward E. Lawler III and Susan A. Mohrman, "Quality Circles after the Fad," *Harvard Business Review* (January–February 1985), 65–71; and Philip C. Thompson, *Quality Circles: How to Make Them Work in America* (New York: AMACOM, 1982).

21. Howard Rothman, "You Need Not Be Big to Benchmark," *Nation's Business* (December 1992), 64–65.

22. Tom Rancour and Mike McCracken, "Applying 6 Sigma Methods for Breakthrough Safety Performance," *Professional Safety* 45, no. 10 (October 2000), 29–32; G. Hasek, "Merger Marries Quality Efforts," *Industry Week* (August 21, 2000), 89–92; and Lee Clifford, "Why You Can Safely Ignore Six Sigma," *Fortune* (January 22, 2001), 140.

23. Michael Hammer and Jeff Goding, "Putting Six Sigma in Perspective," *Quality* (October 2001), 58–62.

24. Claudia H. Deutsch, "New Economy, Old-School Rigor," *The New York Times* (June 12, 2000), C1, C2.

25. Norihiko Shirouzu, "Gadget Inspector: Why Toyota Wins Such High Marks on Quality Surveys," *The Wall Street Journal* (March 15, 2001), A1, A11; Cynthia Challenger, "Six Sigma: Can the GE Model Work in the Chemical Industry?" *Chemical Market Reporter* (July 16, 2001); FR6–FR10.

26. Philip R. Thomas, Larry J. Gallace, and Kenneth R. Martin, *Quality Alone Is Not Enough (AMA Management Briefing)*, New York: American Management Association, August 1992.

27. Kate Kane, "L. L. Bean Delivers the Goods," *Fast Company* (August/September 1997), 104–113.

28. Clifford, "Why You Can Safely Ignore Six Sigma"; and Hammer and Goding, "Putting Six Sigma in Perspective."

29. Frank C. Barnes, "ISO 9000 Myth and Reality: A Reasonable Approach to ISO 9000," *SAM Advanced Management Journal* (Spring 1998), 23–30; and Thomas H. Stevenson and Frank C. Barnes, "Fourteen Years of ISO 9000: Impact, Criticisms, Costs, and Benefits," *Business Horizons* (May–June 2001), 45–51.

30. Don L. Bohl, Fred Luthans, John W. Slocum Jr., and Richard M. Hodgetts, "Ideas That Will Shape the Future of Management Practice," *Organizational Dynamics* (Summer 1996), 7–14.

31. K. Lehn and A. K. Makhija, "EVA and MVA as Performance Measures and Signals for Strategic Change," *Strategy & Leadership* (May–June 1996), 34–38.

32. Terence C. Pare, "A New Tool for Managing Costs," *Fortune* (June 14, 1993), 124–129; and Don L. Bohl, Fred Luthans, John W. Slocum Jr., and Richard M. Hodgetts, "Ideas that Will Shape the Future of Management Practice," *Organizational Dynamics* (Summer 1996), 7–14.

33. Perry Pascarella, "Open the Books to Unleash Your People," *Management Review* (May 1998), 58–60.

34. This discussion is based on a review of the balanced scorecard in Richard L. Daft, *Organization Theory and Design,* 7th ed. (Cincinnati, Ohio: South-Western College Publishing, 2001), 300–301.

35. "On Balance," a CFO Interview with Robert Kaplan and David Norton, *CFO* (February 2001), 73–78.

36. Robert Kaplan and David Norton, "The Balanced Scorecard: Measures that Drive Performance," *Harvard Business Review* (January–February 1992), 71–79; and Chee W. Chow, Kamal M. Haddad, and James E. Williamson, "Applying the Balanced Scorecard to Small Companies," *Management Accounting* 79, no. 2 (August 1997), 21–27.

37. Based on Kaplan and Norton, "The Balanced Scorecard"; Chow, Haddad, and Williamson, "Applying the Balanced Scorecard"; and Cathy Lazere, "All Together Now," *CFO* (February 1998), 28–36.

38. "On Balance," and Debby Young, "Score It a Hit," *CIO Enterprise* (November 15, 1998), 26–32.

39. Roemer, "A Hospital is Reborn."

Information Technology and E-Business

CHAPTER OUTLINE

Information Technology

Data versus Information

Characteristics of Useful Information

Types of Information Systems

Operations Information Systems

Management Information Systems

The Internet and E-business

E-Business Strategies

E-Marketplaces

Enterprise Resource Planning Systems

Customer Relationship Management

Knowledge Management

Management Implications of Information Technology

Improved Employee Effectiveness

Increased Efficiency

Empowered Employees

Information Overload

Enhanced Collaboration

Organizational Learning

IT Trends in the New Workplace

Instant Messaging

Wireless Internet

Peer-to-Peer File Sharing

LEARNING OBJECTIVES

After studying this chapter, you should be able to

1 Describe the importance of information technology for organizations and the attributes of quality information.

2 Identify different types of information systems and discuss recent trends in information technology.

3 Tell how information systems support daily operations and decision making.

4 Summarize the key components of e-business and explain various e-business strategies.

5 Describe enterprise resource planning and customer relationship management systems.

6 Explain the importance of knowledge management in today's organizations.

7 Identify specific management implications of information technology.

Management Challenge

Founded in 1859, the A & P grocery chain was once so powerful that it got 10 cents of every dollar spent on groceries in the United States. By 1950, A & P had revenues of nearly $3 billion, second only to General Motors. But by 1998, when 36-year-old Christian Haub took over as chairman, president, and CEO, the company was all but dead. A & P had been on a skid for decades, with the number of A & P-run stores declining from 3,468 in 1974 to 750 in the late 1990s. Today, A & P ranks 13th among food retailers in market capitalization, and in fiscal year 2000 the chain posted a net loss of some $25 million. Haub quickly initiated Project Great Renewal, a long-term plan aimed at thrusting A & P back into the ranks of top U.S. grocers. A key aspect of the renewal is updating the information technology infrastructure. The company had a confusing assortment of systems, with dozens of applications that couldn't share information. When Nicholas Ioli was hired as chief information officer, he found "a $10 billion company that acted like 10 $1 billion companies." The result was high costs, poor coordination, low productivity, and mediocre customer service. Ioli and Haub needed to find a way to use information technology to cut costs, reduce inventory, improve customer service, and return A & P to profitability.[1]

How can information technology play a role in revamping business processes and improving customer relationships? Why do you think Haub and Ioli are focusing on information technology rather than other aspects of the company to achieve a turnaround?

Almost every company uses some form of information technology. Indeed, the strategic use of information technology is one of the defining aspects of organizational success in today's world. A classic example is the success of Wal-Mart, which can be traced partly to the extensive use of technology to manage every aspect of the business. Managers use information systems that rely on a massive data warehouse to make decisions about what to stock, how to price and promote it, and when to reorder or discontinue items. Handheld scanners enable managers to keep close tabs on inventory and monitor sales; at the end of each workday, orders for new merchandise are sent by computer to headquarters, where they are automatically organized and sent to regional distribution centers, which have electronic linkages with key suppliers for reordering. Back at headquarters, top executives analyze buying patterns and other information, enabling them to spot problems or opportunities and convey the information to stores.[2] Many other companies, in industries from manufacturing to entertainment, are using information technology to get closer to customers, enter new markets, and streamline business processes.

Information technology and e-business have changed the way people and organizations work and thus present new challenges for managers. This chapter will explore the management of information technology and e-business. We begin by developing a basic understanding of information technology and the types of information systems frequently used in organizations. Then, the chapter will look at the growing use of the Internet and e-business, including a discussion of fundamental e-business strategies, business-to-business marketplaces, use of information technology in business operations, and the importance of knowledge management. The following section will discuss the management implications of using new information technology. Finally, we will briefly examine some emerging information technology trends.

Information Technology

information technology
The hardware, software, telecommunications, database management, and other technologies used to store, process, and distribute information.

An organization's **information technology** consists of the hardware, software, telecommunications, database management, and other technologies it uses to store data and make them available in the form of information for organizational decision making.

By providing managers with more information more quickly than ever before, modern information technology improves efficiency and effectiveness at each stage of the strategic decision-making process. Whether through computer-aided manufacturing, information sharing with customers, or international inventory control, information technology aids operational processes and decision making. Consider the case of American Greetings Corporation, which sells greeting cards in about 35,000 retail locations in the United States. The company uses information technology to gather and analyze data to test the popularity of new card designs, automate production of cards, identify which kinds of cards will sell best at particular stores, fill orders, and report to retailers on the performance of American Greetings' displays in their stores. By combining efficiency through automation with a precisely targeted and well-tested product line, American Greetings stays profitable and helps its customers, the retailers, to be profitable as well.[3]

Data versus Information

The ability to generate more information with technology presents a serious challenge to information technicians, managers, and other users of information. They must sort through overwhelming amounts of data to identify only that information necessary for a particular purpose. **Data** are raw facts and figures that in and of themselves may not be useful. To be useful, data must be processed into finished **information**—that is, data that have been converted into a meaningful and useful context for specific users. An increasing challenge for managers is being able to effectively identify and access useful information. American Greetings, for example, might gather *data* about demographics in various parts of the country. These data are then translated into *information;* for example, stores in Florida require an enormous assortment of greeting cards directed at grandson, granddaughter, niece, and nephew, while stores in some other parts of the country might need a larger percentage of slightly irreverent, youth-oriented products.

The magnitude of the job of transforming data into useful information is reflected in organizations' introduction of the chief information officer (CIO) position. CIOs are responsible for managing organizational databases and implementing new information technology. As they make decisions involving the adoption and management of new technologies, CIOs integrate old and new technology to support organizational decision making, operations, and communication. Effective CIOs not only manage the technology infrastructure but also focus on information design, so that managers have high-quality information to improve decision making, solve problems, and improve performance.[4] Ideally, the CIO combines knowledge of information technology with the ability to help managers and employees identify their information needs, as well as ways the organization can use its IT capabilities to support its strategy. An important part of the CIO's job is shaping disjointed data into clear, meaningful, and useful information.

data
Raw, unsummarized, and unanalyzed facts and figures.

information
Data that have been converted into a meaningful and useful context for the receiver.

You may live in the United States, but it is possible for you to access your financial information at this Citibank facility in Budapest, Hungary. Due to advances in information technology, the banking industry has developed complex databases to provide financial information globally, and it is estimated that by the year 2010, four to five billion people worldwide will be active users of a vast range of financial products and services. Today, Citibank's business is as much information and communications as financial services.

Characteristics of Useful Information

Organizations depend on high-quality information to develop strategic plans, identify problems, and interact with other organizations. Information is of high quality if it has characteristics that make it useful for these tasks. The characteristics of useful information fall into three broad categories, as illustrated in Exhibit 21.1.

1. *Time.* Information should be available and provided when needed, up to date, and related to the appropriate time period (past, present, or future).

2. *Content.* Useful information is error free, suited to the user's needs, complete, concise, relevant (that is, it excludes unnecessary data), and an accurate measure of performance.

3. *Form.* The information should be provided in a form that is easy for the user to understand and that meets the user's needs for the level of detail. The presentation should be ordered and use the combination of words, numbers, and diagrams that is most helpful to the user. Also, information should be presented in a useful medium (printed documents, video display, sound).

Types of Information Systems

Most managers today appreciate the value of making information readily available in some kind of formal, computer-based information system. Such a system combines hardware, software, and human resources to support organizational information and communication needs. One way to distinguish

Exhibit *21.1*

Characteristics of High-Quality Information

Time
Timeliness
Currency
Frequency
Time period

Form
Clarity
Detail
Order
Presentation
Media

Content
Accuracy
Relevance
Completeness
Conciseness
Scope
Performance

SOURCE: Adapted from James A. O'Brien, *Introduction to Information Systems,* 8th ed. (Burr Ridge, IL: Irwin, 1997), 284–285.

among the many types of information systems is to focus on the functions they perform and the people they serve in an organization. Two broad categories of information systems widely used today are shown in Exhibit 21.2. Operations information systems support information-processing needs of a business's day-to-day operations, as well as low-level operations management functions. Management information systems typically support the strategic decision-making needs of higher-level managers.

Operations Information Systems

operations information system
A computer-based information system that supports a company's day-to-day operations.

A variety of systems, called **operations information systems,** support the information-processing needs related to a business's day-to-day operations. Types of operations information systems include transaction-processing systems, process control systems, and office automation systems. Each of these supports daily operations and decisions that typically are made by nonmanagement employees or lower-level managers.

transaction-processing system
A type of operations information system that records and processes data resulting from routine business transactions such as sales, purchases, and payroll.

Transaction-processing systems (TPSs) record and process data resulting from business operations. They include information systems that record sales to customers, purchases from suppliers, inventory changes, and wages to employees. A TPS collects data from these transactions and stores them in a database. Employees use the database to produce reports and other information, such as customer statements and employee paychecks. Most of an organization's reports are generated from these databases. Transaction-processing systems identify, collect, and organize the fundamental information from which an organization operates.

process control system
A computer system that monitors and controls ongoing physical processes, such as temperature or pressure changes.

While a transaction-processing system keeps track of the size, type, and financial consequences of the organization's transactions, companies also need information about the quantity and quality of their production activities. Therefore, they may use **process control systems** to monitor and control ongoing physical processes. For example, petroleum refineries, pulp and paper mills, food manufacturing plants, and electric power plants use process

Operations Information Systems
- Transaction-processing systems
- Process control systems
- Office automation systems

Management Information Systems
- Information-reporting systems
- Decision support systems
- Executive information systems
- Groupware

Exhibit *21.2*

Types of Information Systems

control systems with special sensing devices that monitor and record physical phenomena such as temperature or pressure changes. The system relays the measurements or sensor-detected data to a computer for processing; employees and operations managers can check the data to look for problems requiring action.

Office automation systems combine modern hardware and software such as word processors, desktop publishers, e-mail, and teleconferencing to handle the tasks of publishing and distributing information. Office automation systems also are used to transform manual accounting procedures to electronic media. Companies such as Wal-Mart, Chevron, and American Airlines send thousands of electronic payments a month to suppliers, eliminating the need for writing and mailing checks. Merrill Lynch uses office automation to electronically manage consultants' travel and entertainment expenses, cutting the time it takes to process a report and issue reimbursement from six weeks to four days and slashing the average cost of processing a report from $25 to only a few bucks.[5] These systems enable businesses to streamline office tasks, reduce errors, and improve customer service. In this way, office automation systems support the other kinds of information systems.

Operations information systems aid organizational decision makers in many ways and across various settings. For example, Enterprise Rent-a-Car's

office automation systems
Systems that combine modern hardware and software to handle the tasks of publishing and distributing information.

Reprinted with permission of Emerson. 2000 Annual Report.

Web-hosting centers, such as an Exodus site in San Francisco, require sophisticated on-site power systems to ensure 24 × 7 operation, particularly when faced with an unstable electricity supply, such as periods of foul weather or peak demand. Alternators manufactured by Emerson are used for generator sets and transfer switches that shift from the grid to local power generation, forming the foundation of these highly reliable systems.

Computer Assisted Rental System (Ecars) provides front-line employees with up-to-the-minute information that enables them to provide exceptional service to each customer. The computer-based system helps Enterprise keep track of the 1.4 million transactions the company logs every hour. If a customer visits a branch office and requests a certain kind of car, the agent can immediately determine if one is available anywhere in the city. Insurance companies such as Geico can also link their claims systems directly to Enterprise's automated rental system, book a reservation, and send payments electronically, eliminating the need for paper invoices and checks.[6]

Management Information Systems

Until the 1960s, information systems were used primarily for transaction processing, accounting, and record keeping. Then the introduction of computers using silicon chip circuitry allowed for more processing power per dollar. As computer manufacturers promoted these systems and managers began visualizing ways in which the computers could help them make important decisions, management information systems were born. A **management information system (MIS)** is a computer-based system that provides information and support for effective managerial decision making. The basic elements of a management information system are illustrated in Exhibit 21.3. The MIS is supported by the organization's operations information systems and by organizational databases (and frequently databases of external data as well). Management information systems typically include reporting systems, decision support systems, executive information systems, and groupware, each of which will be explained in this section.

MISs typically support strategic decision-making needs of mid-level and top management. However, as technology becomes more widely accessible, more employees are wired into networks, and organizations push decision making downward in the hierarchy, these kinds of systems are seeing use at all levels of the organization.

management information system (MIS)
A computer-based system that provides information and support for effective managerial decision making.

information reporting system
A system that organizes information in the form of prespecified reports that managers use in day-to-day decision making.

decision support system (DSS)
An interactive, computer-based system that uses decision models and specialized databases to support organization decision makers.

executive information system (EIS)
A management information system designed to facilitate strategic decision making at the highest levels of management by providing executives with easy access to timely and relevant information.

Exhibit **21.3**

Basic Elements of Management Information Systems

SOURCE: Adapted from Ralph M. Stair and George W. Reynolds, *Principles of Information Systems: A Managerial Approach,* 4th ed. (Cambridge, Mass.: Course Technology, 1999), 391.

When a production manager needs to make a decision about production scheduling, he or she may need data on the anticipated number of orders in the coming month, inventory levels, and availability of computers and personnel. The MIS can provide these data. In fact, **information reporting systems,** the most common form of MIS, provide managers and decision makers with reports that support day-to-day decision-making needs. At Harrah's casinos, an information reporting system predicts each customer's potential value and enables managers to create customized marketing programs that help retain low-end players as well as turn some of them into high rollers. "Almost everything we do in marketing and decision making is influenced by technology," says Harrah's COO Gary Loveman. The approach has helped Harrah's achieve the best same-store sales growth and the highest profit growth in the industry.[7]

Decision support systems (DSSs) are interactive, computer-based information systems that rely on decision models and specialized databases to support decision makers. With electronic spreadsheets and other decision support software, users can pose a series of what-if questions to test alternatives they are considering. Based on the assumptions used in the software or specified by the user, managers can explore various alternatives and receive tentative information to help them choose the alternative with the best outcome.

Executive information systems (EISs) are management information systems to facilitate strategic decision making at the highest level of management. These systems are typically based on software that provides easy access to large amounts of complex data and can analyze and present the data in a timely fashion. EISs provide top management with quick access to relevant internal and external information and, if designed properly, can help them diagnose problems as well as develop solutions.

Modern information technology systems also recognize that many organizational and managerial activities involve groups of people working together to solve problems and meet customer needs. **Groupware** is software that works on a computer network or via the Internet to link people or workgroups across a room or around the globe. The software enables managers or team members to share information and work simultaneously on the same document, chart, or diagram and see changes and comments as they are made by others. Sometimes called *collaborative work systems*, groupware systems allow people to interact with one another in an electronic meeting space and at the same time take advantage of computer-based support data. Groupware supports virtual and global teamwork by facilitating efficient and accurate sharing of ideas and simultaneous task execution. Team members in different geographical areas with varied expertise can work together almost as easily as if they were in the same room.

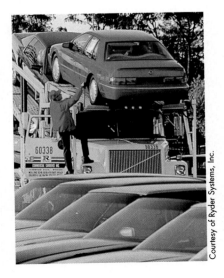

Ryder Transportation Resources uses a decision support system *called RyderLinc, a cross-functional, integrated computer system that allows computers throughout the company to interact with each other as well as with those of customers and suppliers. The new information system can give customers precise information on virtually every aspect of their transportation and distribution services on a daily or even hourly basis, thus lending support to Ryder's excellent on-time, 99 percent damage-free delivery record. RyderLinc also supports sales by giving potential customers access to global data and market information and allowing them to compare the financial implications of different distribution and transportation alternatives.*

groupware
Software that works on a computer network or the Internet to facilitate information sharing, collaborative work, and group decision making.

The Internet and E-Business

In recent years, most organizations have incorporated the Internet as part of their information technology strategy.[8] The **Internet** is a global collection of computer networks linked together for the exchange of data and information. The **World Wide Web (WWW)** is a collection of central servers for accessing information on the Internet. Originally developed for use by the U.S. military, the Internet and the World Wide Web have become household words and an important part of our personal and work lives. Exhibit 21.4 shows the opening Web page for Herman Miller Inc., the first office furniture maker to design

Internet
A global collection of computer networks linked together for the exchange of data and information.

World Wide Web (WWW)
A collection of central servers for accessing information on the Internet.

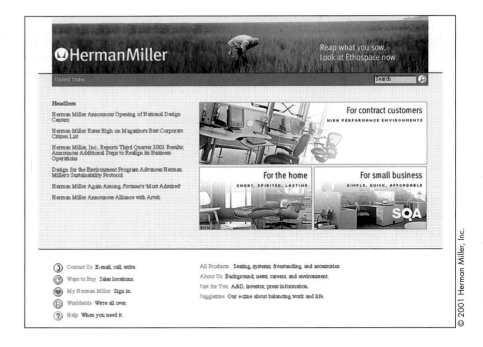

Exhibit *21.4*

Opening Page of the Web Site for Herman Miller, Inc.

and sell a line of products over the Internet. Both business and nonprofit organizations quickly realized the potential of the Internet for expanding their operations globally, improving business processes, reaching new customers, and making the most of their resources. E-business began to boom. **E-business** can be defined as any business that takes place by digital processes over a computer network rather than in physical space. Most commonly today, it refers to electronic linkages over the Internet with customers, partners, suppliers, employees or other key constituents. **E-commerce** is a more limited term that refers specifically to business exchanges or transactions that occur electronically.

Some organizations are set up as e-businesses that are run completely over the Internet, such as eBay, Amazon.com, and Yahoo!. These companies would not exist without the Internet. However, most established organizations, including General Electric, Wal-Mart, and the U.S. Postal Service, also make extensive use of the Internet, and we will focus on these types of companies in the remainder of this section. The goal of e-business for established organizations is to digitalize as much of the business as possible to make the organization more efficient and effective. Companies are using the Internet and the Web for everything from filing expense reports and calculating daily sales to connecting directly with suppliers for the exchange of information and ordering of parts.[9] Exhibit 21.5 illustrates the key components of e-business for two organizations, a manufacturing company and a retail chain. First, each organization uses an **intranet,** an internal communications system that uses the technology and standards of the Internet but is accessible only to people within the company. The next component is a system that allows the separate companies to share data and information. Two options are an electronic data interchange network or an extranet. **Electronic data interchange (EDI)** networks link the computer systems of buyers and sellers to allow the transmission of structured data primarily for ordering, distribution, and payables and receivables.[10] An **extranet** is an external communications system that uses the Internet and is shared by two or more organizations. Each organization moves

e-business
Any business that takes place by digital processes over a computer network rather than in physical space.

e-commerce
Business exchanges that occur electronically.

intranet
An internal communications system that uses the technology and standards of the Internet but is accessible only to people within the organization.

electronic data interchange (EDI)
A network that links the computer systems of buyers and sellers to allow the transmission of structured data primarily for ordering, distribution, and payables and receivables.

extranet
An external communications system that uses the Internet and is shared by two or more organizations.

SOURCE: Based on Jim Turcotte, Bob Silveri, and Tom Jobson, "Are You Ready for the E-Supply Chain?" *APICS—The Performance Advantage* (August 1998), 56–59.

certain data outside of its private intranet, but makes the data available only to the other companies sharing the extranet. The final piece of the overall system is the Internet, which is accessible to the general public. Organizations make some information available to the public through their Web sites, which may include products or services offered for sale. For example, at the Web site of Herman Miller, shown earlier in Exhibit 21.4, dealers and consumers can place orders for furniture online and also check order status or make changes with just a few mouse clicks.

E-Business Strategies

Traditional organizations such as Herman Miller that want to establish an Internet division have to decide how best to integrate *bricks and clicks*—that is, how to blend their traditional operations with an Internet initiative. The range of basic strategies for setting up an Internet operation are illustrated in Exhibit 21.6. At one end of the spectrum, companies can set up an in-house division that is closely integrated with the traditional business. The opposite approach is to create a spin-off company that is totally separate from the traditional organization. Many companies take a middle road, by forging strategic partnerships with other organizations to go online. Each of these presents distinct advantages and disadvantages.[11]

In-House Internet Division. Setting up an in-house dot-com division offers tight integration between the Internet operation and the organization's traditional operation. The organization creates a separate department or unit within the company that functions within the structure and guidance of the traditional organization. This approach gives the new division several advantages by piggybacking on the established company, including brand recognition, purchasing leverage with suppliers, shared customer information

Fortune/CNET Technology Review Summer 2001.

Burlington Northern Santa Fe (BNSF) railroad solved an old business problem with a new e-commerce solution. BNSF's massive locomotives eventually wear out, and disposing of them used to be a complex, time-consuming process. Company officials turned to the Web, auctioning off 47 locomotives in one afternoon, with prices averaging 11 percent above previous sales. Since then, BNSF has expanded its e-business initiatives. It recently allowed timber companies to bid on booking capacity, helping to ensure that each of its 200,000 boxcars travels fully loaded. A half-full boxcar barely breaks even. Today, many U.S. trains are running with the help of e-business—at a profit.

Exhibit *21.6*

The Range of Strategies for Integrating Bricks and Clicks

SOURCE: Based on Ranjay Gulati and Jason Garino, "Get the Right Mix of Bricks and Clicks," *Harvard Business Review* (May–June 2000), 107–114.

and marketing opportunities, and distribution efficiencies. Recall from the previous chapter's Leading Online box how Tesco achieved success in online grocery delivery by keeping Tesco.com closely integrated with the existing grocery chain. Office Depot also launched its online business as a tightly integrated in-house part of its overall retail operation. A potential problem with an in-house division is that the new operation doesn't have the flexibility and autonomy needed to move quickly in the Internet world. In some cases, the traditional business's focus on protecting current customers and fear of cannibalization by the dot-com division can suffocate the new division and prevent it from succeeding.

Spin-Off. To give the Internet operation greater organizational focus, autonomy, and flexibility, some organizations choose to create a separate spin-off company. For example, Barnes & Noble created a separate division, barnesandnoble.com, which it ultimately spun off as a stand-alone company to compete with Amazon. Whirlpool created a spin-off called Brandwise.com, a site designed to help consumers find the best products and value—even if that means from other manufacturers. Advantages of a spin-off include faster decision making, increased flexibility and responsiveness to changing market conditions, an entrepreneurial culture, and management that is totally focused on the success of the online operation. Potential disadvantages are the loss of brand recognition and marketing opportunities, higher start-up costs, and loss of leverage with suppliers.

Strategic Partnership. Partnerships, whether through joint ventures or alliances, enable organizations to attain some of the advantages and overcome some of the disadvantages of the purely in-house or spin-off options. For example, after initially blundering in the online world, Toys 'R' Us partnered with an established e-commerce company, Amazon.com, to capitalize on the advantages of both integration and separation. Partner Amazon brought e-commerce experience and an entrepreneurial mindset, while Toys 'R' Us provided purchasing leverage, brand recognition in the toy industry, and an established customer base. Each company can provide its core strengths—Amazon handles customer service, warehousing, order fulfillment, and maintenance of the Web site, while Toys 'R' Us does all inventory management, merchandising, purchasing, and marketing for the co-branded site.[12] The primary disadvantages of partnerships are time spent managing relationships, potential conflicts between partners, and a possibility that one company will fail to deliver as promised or go out of business. For example, if Amazon.com should fail, it would take Toysrus.com's entire business with it.

E-Marketplaces

The biggest boom in e-commerce is in business-to-business (B2B) transactions, or buying and selling between companies. Using the Internet helps companies cut their costs, broaden their supplier base, and streamline their purchasing processes.[13] A significant trend is the development of **B2B marketplaces,** in which an intermediary sets up an electronic marketplace where buyers and sellers meet, acting as a hub for B2B commerce. Exhibit 21.7 illustrates a B2B marketplace, where many different sellers offer products and services to many different buyers through a *hub,* or online portal. Conducting business through a Web marketplace can mean lower transaction costs, more favorable negotiations, and productivity gains for both buyers and sellers. For example, defense contractor United Technologies bought $450 million worth of metals, motors, and other products via an e-marketplace in 2000 and got prices about 15 percent less than what it usually pays.[14] Transactions on e-marketplaces are expected to reach $2.8 trillion by 2004, according to AMR Research.[15]

Open, public marketplaces include Covisint, an auto-parts marketplace; Onvia.com, a marketplace for office supplies; and e2open, which links buyers and sellers in the high-tech industry. In addition, some companies set up private marketplaces to link with a specially invited group of suppliers and partners.[16] For example, General Motors spent $96 billion in 2001 on raw materials and parts purchased through Covisint, but GM also operates its own private marketplace, GMSupplyPower, to share proprietary information with thousands of its parts suppliers. E-marketplaces can bring efficiencies to many operations, but some companies find that they don't offer the personal touch their business needs, as described in this chapter's Putting People First box.

B2B marketplace
An electronic marketplace set up by an intermediary where buyers and sellers meet.

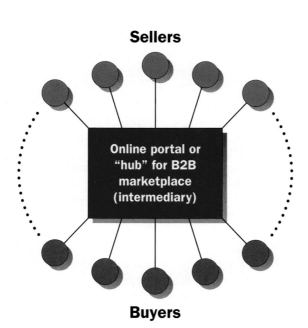

Many sellers offer products and services through an intermediary to many buyers.

Sellers

Online portal or "hub" for B2B marketplace (intermediary)

Buyers

Exhibit *21.7*

B2B Marketplace Model

Putting People First

Grant J. Hunt Co. Likes the Personal Touch

For five generations, family-owned Grant J. Hunt Co. has reached out for new technology to speed up its food distribution business. So, when sales crews began pitching the concept of an online produce marketplace, 47-year-old Grant Hunt listened. One executive from a B2B marketplace start-up assured Hunt he could lay off half his sales staff because of the efficiencies gained. Others pointed out the potential for gaining new customers all over the world and getting higher prices by advertising produce to the highest bidder.

Yet today, Hunt's salespeople are working the way they have for years, buying and selling produce using the telephone and the fax machine. Although the B2B marketplaces put Hunt in touch with a host of potential new customers, most of them were marginal operations with shaky credit histories. In addition, Hunt was a little leery about the public nature of the exchanges, which meant that all sorts of confidential information could get out to customers and competitors. However, the biggest drawback was that the online marketplace could not provide personal attention to customers or to constantly shifting marketplace conditions. "No B-to-B site can say to a buyer at a supermarket, 'How about a special this weekend on tomatoes, because we are coming into a lot of them right now,'" Hunt points out.

The Hunt Co. has always tried to develop close, personalized relationships with its suppliers and customers, negotiating deals on an individual basis. Hunt prides himself on the fact that customers trust him to provide accurate and honest information. He or his salespeople make daily visits to large growers and the local produce markets, shaking hands and talking small talk. The rest of the time they spend glued to the telephone, matching farmers' crops with buyers such as regional supermarket chains, wholesalers, and restaurant supply outfits, often varying their prices as needed with each customer to close a deal. "The Internet is very good at taking one message and sending it out to the whole world," he says. "That's not how our world works."

Hunt found that the relationships he had developed and the processes he had in place were so efficient that he had little to gain from joining the B2B marketplace craze. In fact, over time, many of the start-ups have also realized that the produce business doesn't fit well with the online marketplace concept. BuyProduce.com, for example, has shifted its emphasis from its exchange business to helping produce companies such as Hunt improve their own in-house systems. Hunt is careful to point out that he is not anti-technology. "If they provided something that would be of real value, I would use it in a heartbeat."

SOURCE: Lee Gomes, "How Lower-Tech Gear Beat Web 'Exchanges' at Their Own Game," *The Wall Street Journal* (March 16, 2001), A11.

Enterprise Resource Planning Systems

enterprise resource planning (ERP) system
A networked information system that collects, processes, and provides information about an organization's entire enterprise, from identification of customer needs and receipt of orders to distribution of products and receipt of payments.

One key e-business component for many companies is a new approach to information management called enterprise resource planning. **Enterprise resource planning (ERP) systems** integrate and optimize all the various business processes across the entire firm.[17] The massive computing power required to run complex ERP systems once prohibited many smaller companies from using ERP. However, the top ERP vendors today host the applications themselves and offer their products through Internet portals; customers access the applications with standard browsers.

An enterprise resource planning system can become the backbone of an organization's operations. It collects, processes, and provides information about an organization's entire enterprise, including orders, product design, production, purchasing, inventory, distribution, human resources, receipt of payments, and forecasting of future demand. Such a system links these areas of activity into a network, as illustrated in Exhibit 21.8. When a salesperson takes an order, the ERP system checks to see how the order impacts inventory levels, scheduling, human resources, purchasing, and distribution. The system replicates organizational processes in software, guides employees through the processes step by step, and automates as many of them as possible. For example, the software can automatically cut an accounts payable check as soon as a clerk confirms that goods have been received in inventory, send an online

Exhibit *21.8*

Example of ERP Applications

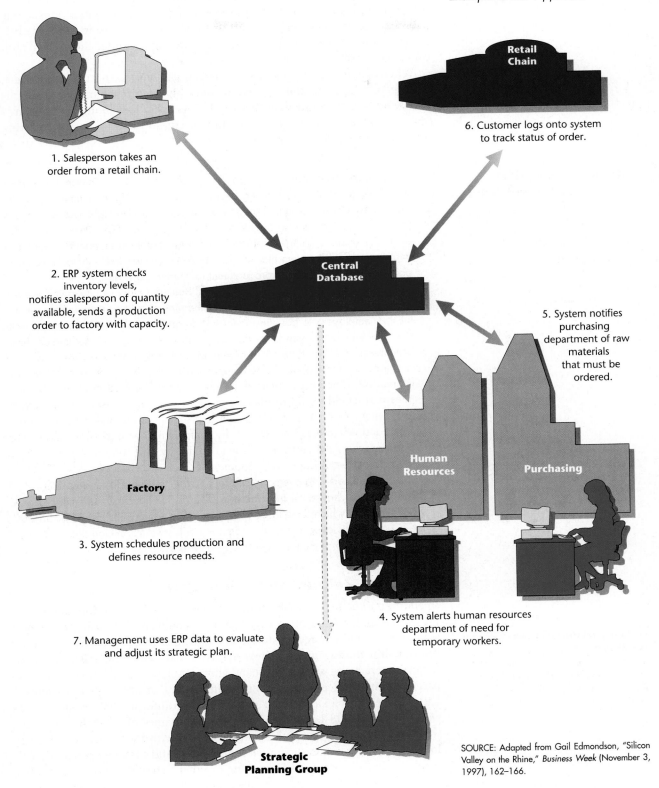

1. Salesperson takes an order from a retail chain.

2. ERP system checks inventory levels, notifies salesperson of quantity available, sends a production order to factory with capacity.

Factory

3. System schedules production and defines resource needs.

Central Database

Retail Chain

6. Customer logs onto system to track status of order.

5. System notifies purchasing department of raw materials that must be ordered.

Human Resources

Purchasing

4. System alerts human resources department of need for temporary workers.

7. Management uses ERP data to evaluate and adjust its strategic plan.

Strategic Planning Group

SOURCE: Adapted from Gail Edmondson, "Silicon Valley on the Rhine," *Business Week* (November 3, 1997), 162–166.

purchase order immediately after a manager has authorized a purchase, or schedule production at the most appropriate plant after an order is received.[18] In addition, because the system integrates data about all aspects of operations, managers and employees at all levels can see how decisions and actions in one part of the organization affect other parts, using this information to make better decisions. Customers and suppliers are linked into the information exchange as well.

When carefully implemented, ERP can cut costs, shorten cycle time, enhance productivity, and improve relationships with customers and suppliers. By using ERP to integrate all aspects of its operations, Bollinger Shipyards cut an average of 15 percent off the time it takes to build a boat, translating into huge savings for the company.

BOLLINGER SHIPYARDS
http://www.bollingershipyards.com

Lockport, Louisiana–based Bollinger Shipyards used to get its information from a hodgepodge of systems running separately at the company's nine shipyards. Getting even basic financial reports was an administrative nightmare. Bollinger's purchasing system was so outdated and inefficient that ships often sat in repair docks for weeks waiting for parts. To solve the problem, managers decided to implement an ERP system that would handle everything from human resources, accounting, and finance to procurement (acquiring parts and supplies).

After a year, the ERP system had helped Bollinger significantly lower its overhead and increase productivity. Each of the nine shipyards used to require two full-time employees to handle administration and payroll; now they get by with one part-time employee at each yard because the system automates these processes. Employees, freed from mundane chores, were reassigned to more brainpower-intensive jobs in the company. Ordering and procurement has also dramatically improved. Rather than having each shipyard order its own supplies and materials, shipyards send their requests electronically to headquarters, where managers coordinate orders so that parts and materials arrive when and where they are needed. By centralizing purchasing, managers can also see where the company is spending money and can use the information to negotiate better deals with vendors.

The combined improvements made possible by the ERP system mean that Bollinger has shaved an average of 5,000 person-hours off the time it takes to build a boat, which for a large ship amounts to savings of around $500,000. CFO Mike Ellis expects that the company will save $5 million this year, more than double the money it spent to upgrade its systems.[19] ❖

Customer Relationship Management

customer relationship management (CRM) systems
Systems that help companies track customers' interactions with the firm and allow employees to call up information on past transactions.

In addition to better internal information management and information sharing with suppliers and other organizations, companies are using e-business solutions to build stronger customer relationships. One approach is **customer relationship management (CRM) systems** that help companies track customers' interactions with the firm and allow employees to call up a customer's past sales and service records, outstanding orders, or unresolved problems.[20] CRM stashes away in a database all the customer information that small-town store owners would keep in their heads—the names of all their customers, what they bought, what problems they've had with their purchases, and so forth. CRM helps to coordinate sales, marketing, and customer service departments so that all are smoothly working together to best serve customer needs. For example, when a customer places an order, the salesperson enters the order into the CRM software, which updates the database. Whenever the customer calls with a question or problem, CRM automatically brings up the customer's record so that the customer service or technical support representative has all pertinent information right in front of him or her and is able to provide personalized service, make additional sales pitches based on the customer's purchasing history, and update the database with information related to the call. Data from Web site customer contacts is also automatically entered into the database. Marketing can use the detailed customer information to implement tailored marketing programs. Best Buy marketers track typical buying patterns and market bundled product offerings to the right customers, which has led to increased sales.[21] In addition, executives can analyze CRM data to solve persistent problems and anticipate new ones.

Increasingly, what distinguishes an organization from its competitors are its knowledge resources, such as product ideas and the ability to identify and find solutions to customers' problems. Exhibit 21.9 lists examples of how CRM and other information technology can shorten the distance between customers and the organization, contributing to organizational success through customer loyalty, superior service, better information gathering, and organizational learning.

Knowledge Management

The Internet also plays a key role in the recent emphasis managers are putting on **knowledge management,** the efforts to systematically gather knowledge, make it widely available throughout the organization, and foster a culture of learning. Some researchers believe that within a couple of years, intellectual capital will be the primary way in which businesses measure their value.[22] Therefore, managers see knowledge as an important resource to manage, just as they manage cash flow, raw materials, and other resources. An effective knowledge management system may incorporate a variety of technologies, supported by leadership that values learning, an organizational structure that supports communication and information sharing, and processes for managing change.[23] Three specific technologies that facilitate knowledge management are data warehousing, data mining, and corporate intranets or networks. Data warehousing and data mining help organizations capture and make sense of structured data. They combine related pieces of information to create knowledge. Knowledge that can be codified, written down, and contained in databases

knowledge management
The process of systematically gathering knowledge, making it widely available throughout the organization, and fostering a culture of learning.

Competitive Advantage	Example
• Increase in customer loyalty	Full information about customer profile and previous requests or preferences is instantly available to sales and service representatives when a customer calls.
• Superior service	Customer representatives can provide personalized service, offer new products and services based on customer's purchasing history.
• Superior information gathering and knowledge sharing	The system is updated each time a customer contacts the organization, whether the contact is in person, by phone, or via the Web. Sales, marketing, service, and technical support have access to shared database.
• Organizational learning	Managers can analyze patterns to solve problems and anticipate new ones.

Exhibit 21.9

Competitive Advantages Gained from Customer Relationship Management (CRM) Systems is referred to as *explicit knowledge*. However, much organizational knowledge is unstructured and resides in people's heads. This *tacit knowledge* cannot be captured in a database, making it difficult to formalize and transmit. Intranets and knowledge sharing networks can support the spread of tacit knowledge.

Data Warehousing and Data Mining. Companies have long gathered and stored what data they could, but these data were typically stored in separate systems that were unable to share data and easily produce meaningful reports of useful information. The modern meaning of **data warehousing** is the use of a huge database that combines all of a company's data and allows business users to access the data directly, create reports, and obtain answers to what-if questions.

An organization with a data warehouse may offer managers access to billions or trillions of bytes of data. How can users possibly know what to look for? A tool that can help answer this question is software for **data mining.** Data mining tools use sophisticated decision-making processes to search raw data for patterns and relationships that might be significant. Managers can, for example, identify sets of products that particular market segments purchase, patterns of transactions that signal possible fraud, or patterns of product performance that may indicate defects. Data mining enabled one catalog retailer to learn that when customers move to a new home, they buy three times as much over the next three months. Furthermore, they purchase certain categories of products: furniture, telecommunications equipment, and decorations. The company used this information to create a new catalog tailored for movers.[24]

Intranets. An increasing number of companies are building knowledge management *portals* on the corporate intranet. A **knowledge management portal** is a single point of access for employees to multiple sources of information that provides personalized access on the corporate intranet.[25] Intranets can give employees access to explicit knowledge that may be stored in databases, but the greatest value of intranets for knowledge management is increasing the transfer of tacit knowledge. For example, Xerox tried to codify the knowledge of its service technicians and embed it in an expert decision system that was installed in the copiers. The idea was that technicians could be guided by the system and complete repairs more quickly, sometimes even off-site. However, the project failed because it did not take into account the tacit knowledge—the nuances and details—that could not be codified. After a study found that service techs shared their knowledge primarily by telling "war stories," Xerox developed an intranet system called *Eureka* to link 25,000 field service representatives. Eureka, which enables technicians to electronically share war stories and tips for repairing copiers, has cut average repair time by 50 percent.[26]

Organizations typically combine several technologies to facilitate the sharing and transfer of both tacit and explicit knowledge. For example, to spur sharing of explicit knowledge, a leading steel company set up a centralized data warehouse containing the financial and operational performance data and standards for each business unit. Managers access the database to identify performance gaps, use case-based decision tools to analyze various aspects of the business, and make changes as needed. The company also enables tacit knowledge transfer through an intranet-based document management system, combined with Web conferencing systems, where worldwide experts can exchange ideas.[27] Similarly, Frito-Lay's system promotes both explicit and tacit knowledge exchange.

data warehousing
The use of a huge database that combines all of a company's data and allows users to access the data directly, create reports, and obtain answers to what-if questions.

data mining
Software that uses sophisticated decision-making processes to search raw data for patterns and relationships that may be significant.

knowledge management portal
A single point of access for employees to multiple sources of information that provides personalized access on the corporate intranet.

Two decades ago, Frito-Lay pioneered the use of hand-held computers by salespeople to keep track of sales data. But before the company developed its knowledge management system, salespeople had no easy way to locate product performance data, to find information about trends in shopping patterns, or to brainstorm with their colleagues about the best approach for a sales presentation. "We had knowledge trapped in files everywhere," says Mike Marino, vice president of customer development. To solve the problem, Frito-Lay wanted to make all corporate data available in a central, easily accessible location, enabling salespeople to analyze customers in multiple ways and make better decisions.

A knowledge management portal on the intranet provides an efficient way to capture both explicit and tacit knowledge and facilitate its transfer. For example, a search engine looks for information in various repositories, giving Frito-Lay's salespeople a central location for finding all sales-related customer and corporate information, dramatically cutting the time it takes to locate and share research data. In addition, expertise profiles posted on the intranet enable people in the field to quickly locate someone back at headquarters who can provide help with promotion planning, costing, new product announcements, and so on. Salespeople also make extensive use of the intranet for sharing documents concurrently, brainstorming ideas, and getting input from colleagues around the country.

By providing for the capture and transfer of both explicit and tacit knowledge, Frito-Lay's system has improved both the performance and the job satisfaction of the sales force. Sales have increased, in one case doubling the growth of a major customer's business in salty snacks. Employees are also happier because they no longer have to spend hours or days searching for information or duplicating the work of another sales team.[28] ❖

FRITO-LAY
http://www.fritolay.com

Management Implications of Information Technology

Information technology and e-business can enable managers to be better connected with employees, the environment, and each other. In general, information technology has positive implications for the practice of management, although it can also present problems. Some specific implications of information technology for managers include improved employee effectiveness, increased efficiency, empowered employees, information overload, enhanced collaboration, and organizational learning.

Improved Employee Effectiveness

Information technology can provide employees with all kinds of data about their customers, competitors, markets, and service, as well as enable them to share information or insights with others. In addition, time and geographic boundaries are dissolving. A management team can work throughout the day on a project in Switzerland and, while they sleep, a team in the United States can continue where the Swiss team left off. Employees all over the world have instant access to databases at any time of the day or night and the ability to share information via the intranet. Advanced information technology allows managers and employees to work whenever and wherever they are most needed and most productive.

Huntington Bancshares, Inc., is using cutting-edge information technology to provide customers with the most personal kind of banking. The Personal Touch two-way video system enables this customer to apply for an Instant Access Loan from a Personal Banker, in total privacy and at the customer's convenience. Information technology is improving organizational efficiency and effectiveness throughout Huntington's subsidiaries, operating in 12 states as well as Hong Kong and the Cayman Islands. Huntington's systems reduce expenses by as much as 65 percent, at the same time improving customer service.

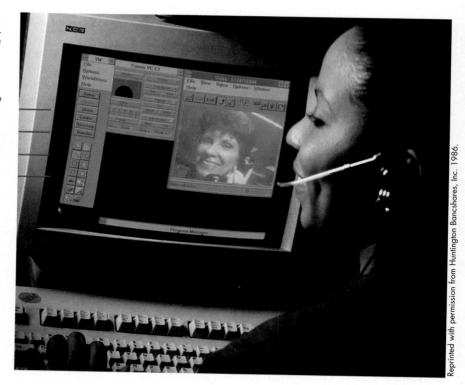

In general, information technology enables managers to design jobs to provide employees with more intellectual engagement and more challenging work. The availability of information technology does not guarantee increased job performance, but when implemented and used appropriately, it can have a dramatic influence on employee effectiveness.

Increased Efficiency

New information technology offers significant promise for speeding work processes, cutting costs, and increasing efficiency. For example, at IBM, automating customer service helped reduce the number of call center employees and saved $750 million in 2001. Companies like IBM are also moving all aspects of purchasing to the Web, helping slash costs and wring deeper discounts from suppliers.

Sweeping away administrative paperwork and automating mundane tasks is another advantage of new technology. At EZRider, a Massachusetts-based retailer of snowboards, whenever a salesperson keys in a purchase, the company's computer system records the amount of the sale; at the end of the pay period, the system automatically computes the salesperson's commission in a matter of seconds.[29]

Empowered Employees

Information technology is profoundly affecting the way organizations are structured. Through implementing IT, organizations change the locus of knowledge by providing information to people who would not otherwise receive it. Low-level employees are increasingly challenged with more information and are expected to make decisions previously made by supervisors.[30]

These changes support the objectives of knowledge management by enabling decisions to be made by the employees who are in the best position to implement the decisions and see their effects. For example, the U.S. Army is beginning to use new information technology that pushes information about battlefield conditions, the latest intelligence on the enemy, and so forth, down the line to the lowest-ranking troops. Armed with better data and trained to see patterns in the barrage of information, lieutenants in the field will be making more of the tough decisions once made by commanders.[31]

Information Overload

One problem associated with advances in technology is that the company can become a quagmire of information, with employees so overwhelmed by the sheer volume that they are unable to sort out the valuable from the useless.

In many cases, the ability to produce data and information is outstripping employees' ability to process it. One British psychologist claims to have identified a new mental disorder caused by too much information; he has termed it Information Fatigue Syndrome.[32] Information technology is a primary culprit in contributing to this new "disease." However, managers have the ability to alleviate the problem and improve information quality. The first step is to ensure that suppliers of information technology and CIOs work closely with employees to identify the kinds of questions they must answer and the kinds of information they really need. Specialists often are enamored with the volume of data a system can produce and overlook the need to provide small amounts of quality information in a timely and useful manner for decision making. Top executives should be actively involved in setting limits by focusing the organization on key strategies and on the critical questions that must be answered to pursue those strategies.[33]

Enhanced Collaboration

Information technology enhances collaboration both within the organization and with customers, suppliers, and other organizations. Intranets and other networks, knowledge management systems, and groupware can connect employees around the world for the sharing and exchange of information and ideas. Information technology can also improve communication and collaboration with external parties such as customers. ESAB Welding and Cutting Products regained its market leadership by offering customers a way to check product and pricing information, place orders, and track shipments online.[34] BMW developed an online showroom where customers can build their own cars, as described in this chapter's Leading Online box.

Extranets are increasingly important for linking companies with contract manufacturers and outsourcers, supporting the development of network and virtual organizations as described in Chapter 10. For example, Hong Kong's Li & Fung is one of the biggest providers of clothing for retailers such as Abercrombie & Fitch, Guess, Ann Taylor, the Limited, and Disney, but the company doesn't own any factories, machines, or fabrics. Li & Fung specializes in managing information, relying on an electronically connected web of 7,500 supply and manufacturing partners in 37 different countries to provide raw materials and assemble the clothes. Using an extranet to stay in immediate touch with worldwide partners enables Li & Fung to move new items

Leading Online

BMW's Ultimate Web Experience

With a brand image of "The Ultimate Driving Machine," the marketing department of BMW of North America had to come up with something pretty snazzy to create a related experience on the Internet. So they developed the BMW Virtual Center (www.bmwusa.com), where a key component is the "Build Your Own" section allowing users to customize a BMW to their exact specifications.

As customers enter the "Build Your Own" section, they are guided through various options for colors, wheels, engines, option packages, and individual add-ons. "We wanted to give the consumer the full range of options that they could have in terms of building their next BMW," says Jim McDowell, vice president of marketing. Every feature displayed—from color, to options, to price and financing—is updated automatically with each mouse click so the customer knows exactly how his or her selection has changed the appearance and cost of the car. The customer can go back and change preferences, skip ahead to other features, and

even save an unlimited number of virtual BMWs for up to 30 days to mull over choices. Once a specific model is selected, the customer can view financing information and contact a local dealer for a test drive. Every step of the process is designed to be interactive, intuitive, and fun—just like driving a high-performance BMW.

Executives say the Virtual Center has played a key role in BMW's record sales in recent years. In 1999, visitors to the site built and saved more than 100,000 virtual vehicles, and many ended up as real cars in customers' driveways. In addition, car configurations saved on the site have become a strategic weapon for the marketing department, which is always looking for ways to offer cars that better match customers' needs and desires. Analyzing the virtual configurations helps BMW understand the combination of features, colors, and options that customers most want.

SOURCE: Dan Carmel, "BMW Drives New Web Strategy," *EC World* (October 2000), 66–68.

quickly from factories to retailers. When data indicate that there's a backlog at a factory in Madagascar, a job can instantly be moved to a partner in Sri Lanka or Spain. In addition, retailers can use the extranet to track orders as they move through production and make last-minute changes and additions.[35]

Organizational Learning

Information technology is an important part of today's learning organizations because it contributes to more rapid identification of problems and opportunities, faster decision making, and greater learning capacity from widely shared information and knowledge.

IT enables the accumulation and widespread communication of a larger volume as well as a wider range of information. Organizations can purchase access to hundreds of databases about industry, financial, and demographic trends in their environments, helping managers stay on top of important trends that will impact their business. Managers can provide key information to employees to help them make better decisions and continuously find ways to improve operations and customer service. In addition, when used appropriately, IT helps break down barriers and create a sense of team spirit that is essential for learning, change, and growth.

IT Trends in the New Workplace

Information technology continues to evolve, and new concepts and applications are emerging every day. Some recent trends in information technology that are having the greatest impact in the new workplace are instant messaging, wireless applications, and peer-to-peer technology.

Instant Messaging

The current rage in communication is interactive, real-time communication known as instant messaging. **Instant messaging** technology provides a way to zap quick notes from PC to PC over the Internet so that two people who are online at the same time can communicate instantaneously.[36] Companies such as America Online and Yahoo! provide instant messaging services to their customers, and the technology is being expanded to work on interactive televisions and mobile phones. For businesses, instant messaging can enable remote employees—those who work from home or in the field—to communicate with one another and with headquarters more efficiently than ever before. For example, a salesman might use his laptop to chat with his supervisor on the other side of the country through instant messaging and clarify a new pricing policy before going on a sales call. In addition, when used within the organization, instant messaging decreases the time spent playing phone tag and untangling crossed e-mail messages.[37]

instant messaging
Technology that provides a way to send quick notes from PC to PC over the Internet so two people who are online at the same time can communicate instantly.

Wireless Internet

Another popular new technology is the wireless Internet. It is estimated that in 2002, 225 million people will use wireless services that bypass the Web and serve up information any place at any time.[38] That means employees can gain access to bits of data and information over handheld devices exactly when and where they need it, bypassing the cumbersome pages of the Web, which can be extremely slow over a mobile device. Because much of today's workforce is highly mobile, wireless technologies that don't require using a PC are critical for helping people be more efficient and effective outside of the office. Celanese Chemical's remote sales force and customer service employees can access real-time company information from the company's ERP system via mobile phones, Palm devices, and other wireless gadgets.[39] For example, a saleswoman can get instant confirmation on the availability of a specific chemical, allowing her to promise immediate shipment and close a lucrative sale. "If the system saves just one order," says William Schmitt, a senior IT executive at Celanese, "it will practically pay for itself."

peer-to-peer (P2P) file sharing
File sharing that allows PCs to communicate directly with one another over the Internet, bypassing central databases, servers, control points, and Web pages.

© Charlie Samuels

Peer-to-Peer File Sharing

Napster, the music-sharing service that was wildly popular a few years back, got into trouble for enabling the illegal distribution of copyrighted music. However, the technology behind Napster is finding a variety of uses in legitimate business. Napster's software enabled one person to locate and download music directly from another person's personal computer. This cutting-edge technology, called **peer-to-peer (P2P) file sharing,** allows PCs to communicate directly with one another over the Internet, bypassing central databases, servers, control points, and Web pages.[40] Peer-to-peer software lets any individual's computer "talk" directly to another PC without an intermediary, enhancing the opportunities for information sharing and collaboration. Personal computers today have enormous storage capacity. Peer-to-peer technology improves efficiency by allowing for the sharing of PC files directly between two PCs, eliminating the need for setting up and managing huge central storage systems. GlaxoSmithKline uses P2P technology to enable its 10,000 employees and researchers outside the company to share their drug test data digitally and work collaboratively on new research. Law firm Baker

The major providers of wireless phone service are introducing a new generation of mobile phones with services including wireless Internet access and text messaging. Miss Teen USA Marissa Whitley, who lives and works in New York City and takes frequent trips all over the country, uses wireless Internet services to keep in touch with friends and family. Her first text message was from her best friend: "Don't forget about me in the Big Apple." Whitley, who does not own a computer, finds text messaging and wireless Internet access "really quick and easy."

& McKenzie uses it to allow major clients to tap directly into its attorney's files stored on computers worldwide. For example, clients closing a merger can monitor the progress of the deal without attorneys having to keep files in one place or send lengthy electronic documents, improving organizational speed and efficiency.[41]

■ Summary and Management Solution

Information technology and e-business are changing the way today's people and organizations work. Organizations are evolving into information cultures in which managers and employees can share information and knowledge across boundaries of time and geography. In addition, customers, partners, and suppliers are brought into the information network.

Modern information technology gathers huge amounts of data and transforms them into useful information for decision makers. The systems that use this technology should be designed to generate information with appropriate time, content, and form attributes. Many organizations hire a chief information officer to help manage decisions regarding technology infrastructure and information design.

Information systems combine hardware, software, and human resources to organize information and make it readily available. Operations information systems, including transaction-processing systems, process control systems, and office automation systems, support daily business operations and the needs of low-level managers. Management information systems, including information reporting systems, decision support systems, and executive information systems, typically support the decision-making needs of middle- and upper-level managers. Groupware allows groups of managers or employees to share information, collaborate electronically, and have access to computer-based support data for group decision making and problem solving.

Most organizations have incorporated the Internet and e-business as part of their information technology strategy. To set up an Internet division, traditional organizations may choose to establish an in-house dot-com division, create a separate spin-off company, or enter into a partnership. Companies are also benefitting from participation in electronic marketplaces, where many different sellers offer products and services to many different buyers through an online hub.

Important e-business solutions for improving business operations and customer relationships include enterprise resource planning (ERP) systems and customer relationship management (CRM) software.

Knowledge management is also an important application for new technology. Three key technologies for knowledge management are data warehousing, data mining, and knowledge management portals on the corporate intranet. Information technology and e-business have a number of specific implications for managers and organizations, including greater employee effectiveness, increased efficiency, empowered employees, information overload, enhanced collaboration, and increased potential for learning, change, and growth. Information technology continues to evolve. Some recent trends having significant impact in the workplace are instant messaging, wireless Internet applications, and peer-to-peer technology.

Recall the opening case of A & P, which wants to upgrade its information technology systems to reduce costs and improve customer service. CEO Christian Haub and chief information officer Nicholas Ioli are taking a comprehensive approach, staking the organization's future on a $250 million information systems overhaul that includes the grocery industry's first fully integrated merchandising system, similar to the ERP systems used by other businesses. The heart of A & P's new system includes a massive data warehouse and data mining tools that will enable the company to analyze customers and buying trends and provide the right mix of products, pricing, and promotions for each store. In-store workstations linked to the database will give store managers immediate feedback on store performance. A & P's IT partners, IBM and Retek, are building core applications to automate and integrate purchasing, merchandising, and inventory management, as well as to centralize and automate back-office tasks such as finance and human resources. Online ordering via extranet connections with suppliers will cut back-room inventory while reducing sales loss because of out-of-stock items. A & P is also participating in a B2B marketplace, the World Wide Retail Exchange, where large retailers can negotiate with many suppliers. It is too soon to tell if A & P's ambitious IT project will save the struggling company, but top managers are optimistic that the new technology will save money and improve customer service and satisfaction.[42]

Discussion Questions

1. Why is it important for managers to understand the difference between data and information?
2. What types of information technology do you use as a student on a regular basis? How might your life be different if this technology was not available to you?
3. In what ways might access to an MIS change the way decisions are made at a large package-delivery company?
4. How might the organizers of an upcoming Olympics use an extranet to get all the elements of the event up and running on schedule?
5. What are some competitive issues that might lead an organization to take a strategic partnership approach to e-commerce rather than setting up an in-house Internet division?
6. Discuss some possible disadvantages for an auto-maker using a public B2B marketplace such as Covisint.

7. Customer relationship management (CRM) software can dramatically improve customer service and satisfaction, as illustrated in Exhibit 21.9. Can you think of ways an ERP system could also provide a competitive advantage in the areas listed in Exhibit 21.9?
8. Define the difference between *explicit* knowledge and *tacit* knowledge and give an example of each from your own experience. How can knowledge management systems be designed to promote the sharing of both explicit and tacit knowledge?
9. Do you believe information overload is a problem for today's students? For employees? What could you do to deal more effectively with information overload?
10. How is e-business affecting the way organizations are structured and the way jobs are designed?
11. Have you ever used peer-to-peer file-sharing technology? Discuss your experiences—positive and negative—with P2P.

Management in Practice: Experiential Exercise

What Is Your MIS Style?

Following are 14 statements. Circle the number that indicates how much you agree that each statement is characteristic of you. The questions refer to how you use information and make decisions.

	Disagree Strongly				Agree Strongly
1. I like to wait until all relevant information is examined before deciding something.	1	2	3	4	5
2. I prefer information that can be interpreted in several ways and leads to different but acceptable solutions.	1	2	3	4	5
3. I like to keep gathering data until an excellent solution emerges.	1	2	3	4	5
4. To make decisions, I often use information that means different things to different people.	1	2	3	4	5
5. I want just enough data to make a decision quickly.	5	4	3	2	1
6. I act on logical analysis of the situation rather than on my "gut feelings" about the best alternative.	5	4	3	2	1
7. I seek information sources or people that will provide me with many ideas and details.	1	2	3	4	5
8. I try to generate more than one satisfactory solution for the problem faced.	1	2	3	4	5
9. When reading something I confine my thoughts to what is written rather than search for additional understanding.	5	4	3	2	1
10. When working on a project, I try to narrow, not broaden, the scope so it is clearly defined.	5	4	3	2	1
11. I typically acquire all possible information before making a final decision.	1	2	3	4	5

	Disagree Strongly				Agree Strongly
12. I like to work on something I've done before rather than take on a complicated problem.	5	4	3	2	1
13. I prefer clear, precise data.	5	4	3	2	1
14. When working on a project, I like to explore various options rather than maintain a narrow focus.	1	2	3	4	5

Total Score _____

Your information-processing style determines the extent to which you will benefit from computer-based information systems.

The *odd-numbered* questions pertain to the "amount of information" you like to use. A score of 28 or more suggests you prefer a large amount. A score of 14 or less indicates you like a small amount of information.

The *even-numbered* questions pertain to the "focus of information" you prefer. A score of 28 or more suggests you are comfortable with ambiguous, multifocused information, while a score of 14 or less suggests you like clear, unifocused data.

If you are a person who likes a large amount of information and clear, focused data, you will tend to make effective use of management information systems. You could be expected to benefit greatly from an EIS or MIS in your company. If you are a person who prefers a small amount of data and data that are multifocused, you would probably not get the information you need to make decisions through formal information systems. You probably won't utilize EIS or MIS to a great extent, preferring instead to get decision data from other convenient sources, including face-to-face discussions.

SOURCES: This questionnaire is adapted from Richard L. Daft and Norman B. Macintosh, "A Tentative Exploration into the Amount and Equivocality of Information Processing in Organizational Work Units," *Administrative Science Quarterly* 26 (1981), 207–224; and Dorothy Marcic, *Organizational Behavior: Experiences and Cases,* 4th ed. (St. Paul, Minn.: West, 1995).

■ Management in Practice: Ethical Dilemma

Manipulative or Not?

As head of the marketing department for Butter Crisp Snack Foods, 55-year-old Frank Bellows has been forced to learn a lot about the Internet in recent years. Although he initially resisted the new technology, Frank has gradually come to appreciate the potential of the Internet for serving existing customers and reaching potential new ones. In fact, he has been one of the biggest supporters of the company's increasing use of the Internet to stay in touch with customers.

However, something about this new plan just doesn't feel right. At this morning's meeting, Keith Deakins, Butter Crisp's CEO, announced that the company would soon be launching a Web site geared specifically to children. Although Deakins has the authority to approve the site on his own, he has asked all department heads to review the site and give their approval for its launch. He then turned the meeting over to the Information Technology team that developed the new site, which will offer games and interactive educational activities. The team pointed out that although it will be clear that Butter Crisp is the sponsor of the site, there will be no advertising of Butter Crisp products. So far, so good, Frank thinks. However, he knows that two of the young hot-shot employees in his department have been helping to develop the site and that they provided a list of questions that children will be asked to answer online. Just to enter the Web site, for example, a user must provide name, address, gender, e-mail address, and favorite TV show. In return, users receive "Crisp Cash," a form of virtual money that they can turn in for toys, games, Butter Crisp samples, and other prizes. After they enter the site, chil-

dren can earn more Crisp Cash by providing other information about themselves and their families.

Frank watched the demonstration and agreed that the Web site does indeed have solid educational content. However, he is concerned about the tactics for gathering information from children that will almost certainly be used for marketing purposes. So far, it seems that the other department heads are solidly in favor of launching the Web site. Frank is wondering if he can sign his approval with a clear conscience. He also knows that several groups, including the national PTA and the Center for Media Education, are calling for stricter governmental controls regarding collecting information from children via the Internet.

What Do You Do?

1. Stop worrying about it. There's nothing illegal about what Butter Crisp is proposing to do, and any personal information gathered will be closely guarded by the company. Children can't be harmed in any way by using the new Web site.
2. Begin talking with other managers and try to build a coalition in support of some stricter controls, such as requiring parental permission to enter areas of the site that offer Crisp Cash in exchange for personal information.
3. Contact the Center for Media Education and tell them you suspect Butter Crisp intends to use the Web site to conduct marketing research. The Center might be able to apply pressure that would make it uncomfortable enough for Deakins to pull the plug on the new kid's Web site.

SOURCE: Based on Denise Gellene, "Internet Marketing to Kids Is Seen as a Web of Deceit," *Los Angeles Times* (March 29, 1996), A1, A20.

Surf the Net

1. **Computer and Information Systems Managers.** Go to the *Occupational Outlook Handbook* at *http://www.bls.gov/oco/.*

   Browse the site to see the kinds of information available that can be helpful to you in your career planning. Key "Computer and Information Systems Managers" into the "Search by occupation" text box on the home page. Based on the resulting article, answer the following questions about this occupation:
   * According to the "Significant Points" section, job opportunities should be best for applicants with what kind of degree?
   * Why do computer and information systems managers need strong communication skills?
   * What is the job outlook for employment of computer and information systems managers through the year 2010?
   * What is the median annual earnings of these managers for the most recent year reported?

2. **Customer Relationship Management (CRM).** Locate a Web site, such as *http://www.cio.com/research/crm,* that will provide you with a broader understanding of CRM. Print an item of interest, read and highlight the item, and bring the printout to class to either submit or share during a classroom discussion on CRM. For example, at the site referenced above, a recent listing of articles included:
   * "Beware of the CRM Backlash" (Companies are tiring of CRM projects, which are failing at a rate of 70 percent, but there is hope. February 1, 2002—CIO.com)
   * "Banking on Good Customer Data" (To compete in today's market, regional banks need to know more than who their customers are. They need to know where they are, and where they're likely to go. January 14, 2002—CIO.com)
   * "How To Build Customer Loyalty in an Internet World" (CRM is manipulation in too many cases. January 1, 2002—CIO.com)

3. **Findarticles.com.** Become familiar with *Findarticles.com,* a free-service Web site that allows you to search the content of more than 300 magazines and journals by keyword and provides the full text of articles dating back to 1998. Select an information technology or e-business topic presented in the chapter that you'd like to learn more about. Go to *http://www.findarticles.com.*

   Select the "Computers and Technology" link. From the list of 50+ computer and technology periodicals, choose one title for your research. Key in a keyword or phrase related to your research topic and, from the search results, locate and print two articles published within the past year on your topic. Based on what you learned in the articles, write a one-page report that covers information beyond the textbook's coverage of the topic. Attach your two article printouts to your report and submit it to your instructor

Case for Critical Analysis

Tri-Angle Equipment and Leasing

Joe Jett, president of Tri-Angle Equipment and Leasing, which owns several agricultural equipment dealerships in the midwestern United States, tried computers 15 years ago. He didn't like them, and he didn't think he needed information technology to run his business.

But as the company grew, Jett realized he had taken on more debt than he was comfortable with, so he hired a chief financial officer named Dan Fraley. Jett also got back into the information technology game, investing $150,000 in a proprietary inventory and accounting system. When Jett and Fraley approached Citigroup's Global Equipment Finance Division seeking better financing for the company, Jett was surprised that Citigroup seemed to be more interested in Tri-Angle's information technology capacity than it was in how many million-dollar machines the company had sold. As a Citigroup representative explained, "The theory goes that if you can trust the computer systems, you can trust the company's numbers."

Tri-Angle wanted to borrow a significant amount of money, so Citigroup sent information technology consultants to evaluate the company's systems and make sure they were capable of generating the sort of accurate monthly financial reports required by the firm for such a sizable loan. Tri-Angle was already on the right track with the new inventory and accounting system, so the necessary data were in the database. However, the consultants soon learned that it was difficult to translate the data into quality information. For instance, if someone wanted a list of accounts receivable that were past due, the database would spit out 500 pages of indecipherable codes and numbers. "None of the answers just popped out of the computer," recalls Fraley.

Fraley began using a software program called Monarch (ironically, already installed on the computer), to turn the data into useful information printed on neat, readable spreadsheets. In the process, Tri-Angle not only qualified for a $5 million loan, but also discovered some of its own poor business practices. For example, Jett and Fraley found more than $100,000 worth of outdated, unused parts that could be returned to manufacturers. As Tri-Angle's ability to turn data into quality information has increased, the leaders are able to see at a moment's notice how the company is performing. They can see immediately which pieces of equipment are being sold or leased and which are not—and on which sales lots. In addition, salespeople, who now carry laptops, can enter sales figures directly into a customer's file using contract management software. When a salesperson gives a customer a quote, it is automatically e-mailed to Jett. As soon as Jett opens the e-mail, the quote is deposited in the central database for later reference.

With the success of Monarch and other management information systems, Jett is now thinking about moving into the world of e-business. He has read about extranets, Web pages,

customer relationship management software, and the like, and he wonders how these new technologies might help his business.

Questions

1. With its newfound reliance on information technology, do you think Tri-Angle might fall into a trap of poor information quality or information overload? Why or why not?

2. How does information technology contribute to Tri-Angle's knowledge management? What other strategic advantages does MIS provide?

3. What would you recommend to Tri-Angle as a first step into e-business? Why?

SOURCE: Based on Joshua Macht, "The Accidental Automator," *Inc. Tech.* no. 2 (1997), 66–71.

■ Endnotes

1. Mark Roberti, "A & P Bets the Store," *The Industry Standard* (May 14, 2001), 46–49; and Susannah Patton, "Can I.T. Save A & P?" *CIO* (February 15, 2001), 80–88.

2. Christopher Palmeri, "Believe in Yourself, Believe in the Merchandise," *Continental* (December 1997), 49–51.

3. Derek Slater, "Chain Commanders," *CIO Enterprise* (August 15, 1998), 29–30+.

4. Jane Linder and Drew Phelps, "Call to Action," *CIO* (April 1, 2000), 166–174.

5. John P. Mello Jr., "Fly Me To the Web," *CFO* (March 2000), 79–84.

6. Heather Harreld, "Pick-Up Artists," *CIO* (November 1, 2000), 148–154.

7. Meridith Levinson, "Harrah's Knows What You Did Last Night," *Darwin Magazine* (May 2001), 61–68.

8. Jim Turcotte, Bob Silveri, and Tom Jobson, "Are You Ready for the E-Supply Chain?" *APICS–The Performance Advantage* (August 1998), 56–59.

9. Steve Hamm with David Welch, Wendy Zellner, Faith Keenan, and Peter Engardio, "E-Biz: Down but Hardly Out," *BusinessWeek* (March 26, 2001), 126–130.

10. Marie-Claude Boudreau, Karen D. Loch, Daniel Robey, and Detmar Straud, "Going Global: Using Information Technology to Advance the Competitiveness of the Virtual Transnational Organization," *Academy of Management Executive* 12, no. 4 (1998) 120–128.

11. Based on Ranjay Gulati and Jason Garino, "Get the Right Mix of Bricks and Clicks," *Harvard Business Review* (May–June 2000), 107–114.

12. Kris Frieswick, "You've Got to Have Friends," *CFO* (August 2001), 50–53.

13. This discussion is based on Pamela Barnes-Vieyra and Cindy Claycomb, "Business-to-Business E-Commerce: Models and Managerial Decisions," *Business Horizons* (May–June 2001), 13–20.

14. Reported in Hamm et al., "E-Biz: Down but Hardly Out."

15. Ibid.

16. Eric Young, "Web Marketplaces That Really Work," *Fortune/CNET Tech Review* (Winter 2001), 78–86.

17. Vincent A. Mabert, Ashok Soni, and M. A. Venkataramanan, "Enterprise Resource Planning: Common Myths Versus Evolving Reality," *Business Horizons* (May–June 2001), 69–76.

18. Derek Slater, "What Is ERP?" *CIO Enterprise* (May 15, 1999), 86.

19. Owen Thomas, "E-Business Software: Bollinger Shipyards," *eCompany* (May 2001), 119–120.

20. Brian Caulfield, "Facing Up to CRM," *Business 2.0* (August–September 2001), 149–150.

21. Meg Mitchell Moore, "Thinking Small," *Darwin Magazine* (May 2001), 71–78.

22. Reported in Eric Seubert, Y. Balaji, and Mahesh Makhija, "The Knowledge Imperative," *CIO Advertising Supplement* (March 15, 2001), S1–S4.

23. Ryan K. Lahti and Michael M. Beyerlein, "Knowledge Transfer and Management Consulting: A Look at 'The Firm,'" *Business Horizons* (January–February 2000), 65–74.

24. David Pearson, "Marketing for Survival," *CIO* (April 15, 1998), 44–48.

25. Esther Shein, "The Knowledge Crunch," *CIO* (May 1, 2001), 128–132.

26. Morten T. Hansen, Nitin Nohria, and Thomas Tierney, "What's Your Strategy for Managing Knowledge?" *Harvard Business Review* (March–April 1999), 106–116; Louisa Wah, "Behind the Buzz," *Management Review* (April 1999), 17–26; and Jenny C. McCune, "Thirst for Knowledge," *Management Review* (April, 1999), 10–12.

27. Seubert, Balaji, and Makhija, "The Knowledge Imperative."

28. Shein, "The Knowledge Crunch."

29. Anthony Scaturro, "All in the Family," *Inc. Technology* no. 1, (1998), 25–26.

30. Liz Thach and Richard W. Woodman, "Organizational Change and Information Technology: Managing on the Edge

of Cyberspace," *Organizational Dynamics* (Summer 1994), 30–46.

31. Greg Jaffe, "Tug of War: In the New Military, Technology May Alter Chain of Command," *The Wall Street Journal* (March 30, 2001), A3, A6.

32. Joseph McCafferty, "Coping with Infoglut," *CFO* (September 1998), 101–102.

33. Leonard M. Fuld, "The Danger of Data Slam," *CIO Enterprise,* Section 2 (September 15, 1998), 28–33.

34. Stewart Deck, "New Connections," *CIO* (February 1, 2001), 130–132.

35. Joanne Lee-Young and Megan Barnett, "Furiously Fast Fashions," *The Industry Standard* (June 11, 2001), 72–79.

36. Spencer E. Ante, with Amy Borrus and Robert D. Hof, "In Search of the Net's Next Big Thing," *BusinessWeek* (March 26, 2001), 140–141.

37. Robert Poe, "Instant Messaging Goes to Work," *Business2.com* (July 10, 2001), 36.

38. Ante, et al., "In Search of the Net's Next Big Thing."

39. Susannah Patton, "The Wisdom of Starting Small," *CIO* (March 15, 2001), 80–86.

40. Ante, et al., "In Search of the Net's Next Big Thing"; Amy Cortese, "Peer to Peer," *The BusinessWeek* 50 (Spring 2001), 194–196.

41. Mark Roberti, "Peer-to-Peer Isn't Dead," *The Industry Standard* (April 23, 2001), 58–59.

42. Roberti, "A & P Bets the Store," and Patton, "Can I.T. Save A & P?"

Operations and Service Management

CHAPTER OUTLINE

Organizations as Production Systems

Manufacturing and Service Operations

Operations Strategy

The Integrated Enterprise

Designing Operations Management Systems

Product and Service Design

Procurement

Facilities Layout

Technology Automation

Facility Location

Capacity Planning

Inventory Management

The Importance of Inventory

Economic Order Quantity

Material Requirements Planning

Just-in-Time Inventory

Logistics and Distribution Management

Managing Productivity

Measuring Productivity

Improving Productivity

LEARNING OBJECTIVES

After studying this chapter, you should be able to

1 Define *operations management* and describe its application within manufacturing and service organizations.

2 Discuss the role of operations management strategy in the company's overall competitive strategy.

3 Explain the role of e-business in today's partnership approach to supply chain management.

4 Summarize considerations in designing an operations system, including the relative advantages of process, product, cellular, and fixed-position layouts.

5 Explain why small inventories are preferred by most organizations.

6 Discuss major techniques for the management of materials and inventory.

7 Define productivity and explain why and how managers seek to improve it.

Management Challenge

During the mid-1990s, Apple Computer sold tons of products but still lost money hand over fist. The company's stock price plummeted, and many analysts began predicting that Apple wouldn't survive. Enter Steven Jobs, one of the original founders of Apple Computer, who agreed to return to the ailing company as interim CEO in 1997. Jobs came in with a vision of renewal that revived employee morale, stimulated creativity, and led to the launch of the funky, colorful line of iMacs. Apple's fortunes began to climb once more, but Jobs knew the company still had a serious problem. Like many manufacturers, Apple relied on the standard supply chain, which begins with components that are assembled into products and then distributed in hopes that someone will buy them. Because supply and demand frequently don't match, inventories pile up and the company watches money going down the drain. Apple had long suffered from an inability to get the right products to the market at the right time. Poor demand forecasting meant the company was frequently out of stock on hot new products and overloaded with products no one wanted to buy. Distributors, retailers, and customers were frustrated. Jobs knew that for Apple to remain competitive, it needed to smash the outdated supply chain and replace it with a system that would increase inventory turnover and respond rapidly and reliably to customers' product preferences.[1]

If you were an operations expert hired by Apple, how would you recommend the company reinvent its supply chain? What steps would you take to make Apple a more efficient operation?

Apple Computer continues to innovate in technology and product design, introducing a sleek new iMac in early 2002 that could revolutionize home computing.[2] However, many companies with leading-edge products have found themselves with out-of-date, inefficient operations systems that contribute to performance problems. Strategic success depends on efficient operations. Operational concerns such as updating production technology, obtaining parts and supplies, and implementing efficient delivery systems take on even greater importance in today's competitive environment where consumers often want customized products and services delivered immediately. Production costs are a major expense for organizations, especially for manufacturers. Organizations therefore try to limit costs and increase quality by improving how they obtain materials, set up production facilities, and produce goods and services. Likewise, companies are seeking a strategic advantage in the ways they deliver products and services to consumers.

In a service industry, Wal-Mart's emergence as a retail giant is largely due to the company's use of sophisticated electronics to run a huge supply and distribution network. In the manufacturing sector, the efficiency of Toyota's automobile production is legendary. Manufacturing and service operations such as these are important because they represent the company's basic purpose—indeed, its reason for existence. Without the ability to produce products and services that are competitive in the global marketplace, companies cannot expect to succeed.

This chapter describes techniques for the planning and control of manufacturing and service operations. Whereas the two preceding chapters described overall control concepts, including management information systems, this chapter will focus on the management and control of production operations. First we define operations management. Then we look at how some companies bring operations into strategic decision making and provide an overview of the integrated enterprise, in which managers use electronic linkages to manage interrelated operations activities. Next, we consider specific operational design issues, such as product and service design, procurement, location planning and facilities layout, production technology, and capacity planning. Special attention is given to inventory management, including a discussion of just-in-time inventory systems, distribution management, and order fulfillment. Finally, we look at how managers measure and improve productivity.

Organizations as Production Systems

technical core
The heart of the organization's production of its product or service.

In Chapter 1, the organization was described as a system used for transforming inputs into outputs. At the center of this transformation process is the **technical core,** which is the heart of the organization's production of its product or service.[3] In an automobile company, the technical core includes the plants that manufacture automobiles. In a university, the technical core includes the academic activities of teaching and research. Inputs into the technical core include human resources, land, equipment, buildings, and technology. Outputs from the technical core include the goods and services that are provided for customers and clients. Operations strategy and control feedback shape the quality of outputs and the efficiency of operations within the technical core.

operations management
The field of management that focuses on the physical production of goods or services and uses specialized techniques for solving manufacturing problems.

The topic of operations management pertains to the day-to-day management of the technical core, as illustrated in Exhibit 22.1. **Operations management** is formally defined as the field of management that specializes

Exhibit *22.1*

The Organization as an Operations Management System

in the production of goods and services and uses special tools and techniques for solving production problems. In essence, operations managers are concerned with all the activities involved in the conversion of inputs into outputs. This includes decisions about where to locate facilities and what equipment to install in them. However, as with all areas of management, operations management also requires the ability to lead people. For example, Toyota's operations are admired worldwide as a model of quality and efficiency, but this success is not merely a result of using the right machines or setting the right standards. U.S. automakers have had difficulty duplicating Toyota's success with lean manufacturing because they have focused primarily on the technical elements of the system and failed to implement the necessary cultural and leadership changes. "What the Big Three are doing," says Toyota's Hajime Oba, "is creating a Buddha image and forgetting to inject soul into it."[4] Toyota's system combines techniques, systems, and philosophy, such as commitment to employee empowerment and a creative culture. Besides installing the methodology for running an efficient assembly line, such as "just-in-time" shipments of supplies, managers must instill the necessary attitudes, such as concern for quality and a desire to innovate.

Manufacturing and Service Operations

Although terms such as *production* and *operations* seem to imply manufacturing organizations, operations management applies to all organizations. The service sector has increased three times as fast as the manufacturing sector in the North American economy. Today more than one-half of all businesses are service organizations and two-thirds of the U.S. workforce is employed in services, such as hospitals, hotels and resorts, financial services, or telecommunications firms. Operations management tools and techniques apply to services as well as manufacturing. Exhibit 22.2 shows differences between manufacturing and service organizations.

Exhibit 22.2

Differences between Manufacturing and Service Organizations

Manufacturing Organizations	Service Organizations
Produce physical goods	Produce nonphysical outputs
Goods inventoried for later consumption	Simultaneous production and consumption
Quality measured directly	Quality perceived and difficult to measure
Standardized output	Customized output
Production process removed from consumer	Consumer participates in production process
Facilities site moderately important to business success	Facilities site crucial to success of firm
Capital intensive	Labor intensive
Examples:	*Examples:*
Automobile manufacturers	Airlines
Steel companies	Hotels
Soft-drink companies	Law firms

SOURCES: Based on Richard L. Daft, *Organization Theory and Design* (Cincinnati, Ohio: South-Western College Publishing, 2001), 210; and Byron J. Finch and Richard L. Luebbe, *Operations Management* (Fort Worth, Texas: The Dryden Press, 1995), 50.

manufacturing organization
An organization that produces physical goods.

service organization
An organization that produces nonphysical outputs that require customer involvement and cannot be stored in inventory.

Manufacturing organizations are those that produce physical goods, such as cars or tennis balls. In contrast, **service organizations** produce nonphysical outputs, such as medical, educational, communication, or transportation services provided for customers. Doctors, consultants, online auction companies, and the local barber all provide services. Services also include the sale of merchandise. Although merchandise is a physical good, the service company does not manufacture it but merely sells it as a service to the customer.

Services differ from manufactured products in two ways. First, the service customer is involved in the actual production process.[5] The patient actually visits the doctor to receive the service, and it's difficult to imagine a hairstylist providing services without direct customer contact. The same is true for airlines, restaurants, and banks. Second, manufactured goods can be placed in inventory, whereas service outputs, being intangible, cannot be stored. Manufactured products such as clothes, food, cars, and DVD players all can be put in warehouses and sold at a later date. However, a hairstylist cannot wash, cut, and set hair in advance and leave it on the shelf for the customer's arrival, nor can a doctor place examinations in inventory. The service must be created and provided for the customer exactly when he or she wants it.

Despite the differences between manufacturing and service firms, they face similar operational problems. First, each kind of organization needs to be concerned with scheduling. A medical clinic must schedule appointments so that doctors' and patients' time will be used efficiently. Second, both manufacturing and service organizations must obtain materials and supplies. Third, both types of organizations should be concerned with quality and productivity. Because many operational problems are similar, operations management tools and techniques can and should be applied to service organizations as readily as they are to manufacturing operations.

Operations Strategy

Many operations managers are involved in day-to-day problem solving and lose sight of the fact that the best way to control operations is through strategic planning. The more operations managers become enmeshed in operational details, the less likely they are to see the big picture with respect to inventory

Nordstrom is a department store chain whose earnings recently plummeted nearly 50 percent to $102 million. Brothers Pete and Blake Nordstrom, great-grandsons of founder John W. Nordstrom, are hoping operations strategy can improve company earnings. A major strategic move is the installation of a sophisticated, computerized inventory management system. Until recently, Nordstrom still depended partly on handwritten notes sales clerks compiled in loose-leaf binders to manage inventory.

buildups, parts shortages, and seasonal fluctuations. To manage operations effectively, managers must understand operations strategy.

Operations strategy is the recognition of the important role of operations in organizational success and the involvement of operations managers in the organization's strategic planning.[6] Superior operations effectiveness can support existing strategy and contribute to new strategic directions that can be difficult for competitors to copy. When an organization's operations effectiveness is based on capabilities that are ingrained in its employees, its culture, and its operating processes, the company can be tough to beat.[7] This chapter's Putting People First box describes how software manufacturer Cosmi Corp. has succeeded by getting employees to think strategically.

Exhibit 22.3 illustrates four stages in the evolution of operations strategy. Many companies are at Stage 1, in which business strategy is set without

operations strategy
The recognition of the importance of operations to the firm's success and the involvement of operations managers in the organization's strategic planning.

Exhibit **22.3**

Four Stages of Operations Strategy

Stage 1 **No Involvement**	**Stage 2** **Industry Current**	**Stage 3** **Organizationally Supportive**	**Stage 4** **Competitive Advantage**
■ No positive contribution to strategy formulation ■ Concerns: Costs Labor efficiency	■ Goals set according to industry practice ■ Concerns: Capital investment Quality control Inventory management Capacity	■ Organization's competitive strategy closely followed and supported ■ Concerns: Advanced process technologies New plants What to make for the United States	■ Advanced capabilities developed and significant input to strategic process provided ■ Concerns: New products New services New technologies International

SOURCE: Based on R. H. Haynes and S. C. Wheelright, *Restoring Our Competitive Edge: Competing through Manufacturing* (New York: Wiley, 1984).

Putting People First

Cosmi Corp. Likes the Old-School Management Approach

Most software makers invest a lot of time, money, and energy to stay on top of trends in technology and management techniques. But not $25-million Cosmi Corp., which sells budget-priced software to the mass market. "Just because something can be done doesn't mean it should be," says Cosmi's founder and CEO George Johnson. While other technology firms embrace trends like outsourcing and state-of-the-art technology, Cosmi just keeps making money—and lots of it—by sticking to the basics of old-fashioned management: putting customers and employees first and paying close attention to operational efficiency and control.

Cosmi takes a long-term approach to human resource development. The company home-grows most of its management talent and then hangs on for dear life. For example, the vice president of purchasing and personnel began at Cosmi as an office manager 14 years ago. Cosmi treats employees well, pays them decently, and rewards those at a supervisory level or above with stock options. As a result, the company has 0 percent turnover among salaried staff. Employees at all levels understand that at Cosmi, what comes first are customers and what they want their software to do for them. Cosmi is able to respond to customer needs because it has maintained tight control over all aspects of operations. Everything from software development to manufacturing, packaging, shipping, and distribution is handled by Cosmi's 100 employees rather than being outsourced to contractors.

Operations managers are intimately involved in understanding and meeting customer needs. For example, a retailer asked if Cosmi could produce a jewel case that would hold two software titles but fit into a display rack designed for a single CD. One day later, the case was designed and being produced. It proved to be such a huge hit in the marketplace that Cosmi's warehouse director designed from scratch a machine that would automate assembly of the twin packs, enabling production of 50 a minute as opposed to the previous level of 100 per hour. Another operations efficiency Cosmi gains is by fitting up to 38 software programs on a single CD and providing the consumer with the password only for the program he or she purchased. If a software program becomes obsolete, the CD can still be used for the other programs. This system also reduces the need for production forecasting. Cosmi can fill a 200,000-unit order in two to three days. The bottom line is that the company turns over its inventory 12 times a year, compared to an industry average of 3 times.

Many people have never heard of Cosmi, and that's just fine to Johnson. He likes to describe the company as "an imitator, not an innovator." Cosmi leaves it up to the Microsofts of the software world to bring innovative new products to market and create a demand for them. Then, Cosmi sweeps in with its people-orientation and production efficiency to create its own simpler, much less expensive versions, consistently earning profit margins of 50 percent while the brand names are earning less than 10 percent. Technology and innovation may rule the day at some software makers, but at Cosmi, putting customers and employees first and paying attention to operations strategy has paid off.

SOURCE: Donna Fenn, "Money Talks," *Inc.* (April 2001), 90–95.

---

considering the capability of operations. The operations department is concerned only with labor costs and operational efficiency. For example, a major electronics instrument producer experienced a serious mismatch between strategy and the ability of operations to manufacture products. Because of fast-paced technological changes, the company was changing its products and developing new ones. The manufacturer had installed a materials-handling system in the operations department that was efficient, but it could not handle change of this magnitude. Operations managers were blamed for the company's failure to achieve strategic goals even though the operations department's capacity had never been considered during strategy formulation.

At Stage 2, the operations department sets goals according to industry practice. The organization tries to be current with respect to operations management techniques and views capital investment in plant and equipment, quality control, or inventory management as ways to be competitive.

At Stage 3, operations managers are more strategically active. Operations strategy is in concert with company strategy, and the operations department

will seek new operational techniques and technologies to enhance competitiveness. For example, computer-based business operating systems and work flow automation help employees coordinate activities across functional and geographical boundaries and pinpoint bottlenecks or outdated procedures that slow production and increase costs.

At the highest level of operations strategy, Stage 4, operations managers may pursue new technologies on their own in order to do the best possible job of delivering the product or service. At Stage 4, operations can be a genuine competitive weapon.[8] Operations departments develop new strategic concepts themselves. With the use of new technologies, operations management becomes a major force in overall company strategic planning. Operations can originate new products and processes that will add to or change company strategy.

A company that operates at Stage 3 or 4 will be more competitive than those that rely on marketing and financial strategies because customer orders are won through better price, quality, performance, delivery, or responsiveness to customer demand, and all these factors are affected by operations.

The Integrated Enterprise

As operations managers adopt a strategic approach, they appreciate that their operations are not independent of other activities. To operate efficiently and produce high-quality items that meet customers' needs, the organization must have reliable deliveries of high-quality, reasonably priced supplies and materials. It also requires an efficient and reliable system for distributing finished products, making them readily accessible to customers. Operations managers with a strategic focus therefore recognize that they need to manage the entire supply chain. **Supply chain management** is the term for managing the sequence of suppliers and purchasers covering all stages of processing from obtaining raw materials to distributing finished goods to final consumers.[9]

The most recent advances in supply chain management involve using Internet technologies to achieve the right balance of low inventory levels and customer responsiveness. An e-supply chain creates a seamless, integrated line that stretches from customers to suppliers, as illustrated in Exhibit 22.4, by establishing electronic linkages between the organization and these external partners for the sharing and exchange of data.[10] For example, in the exhibit, as consumers purchase products in retail stores, the data are automatically fed

supply chain management
Managing the sequence of suppliers and purchasers, covering all stages of processing from obtaining raw materials to distributing finished goods to final consumers.

Exhibit 22.4

The E-Supply Chain

SOURCE: Based on Jim Turcotte, Bob Silveri, and Tom Jobson, "Are You Ready for the E-Supply Chain?" *APICS—The Performance Advantage* (August 1998), 56–59.

into the retail chain's information system via an intranet, as described in the previous chapter. In turn, the retail chain gives access to this constantly updated data to the manufacturing company through a secure extranet link. With knowledge of this demand data, the manufacturer can produce and ship the correct products when needed. As products are made, data about raw materials used in the production process, updated inventory information, and updated forecasted demand are electronically provided to the manufacturer's suppliers via an extranet, and the suppliers automatically replenish the manufacturer's raw materials inventory as needed.

An important aspect of supply chain management is managing relationships with suppliers.[11] Enterprise integration through the use of electronic linkages can create a level of cooperation not previously imaginable. Many supplier relationships used to be based on an *arm's length* approach, in which an organization spreads purchases among many suppliers and encourages them to compete with one another. With integration, more companies are opting for a *partnership* approach, which involves cultivating intimate relationships with a few carefully selected suppliers and collaborating closely to coordinate tasks that benefit both parties. For example, at supplier Rockwell Automation, a Greenville, South Carolina–based maker of industrial transmissions and a division of Rockwell International, electronic connections are leading to a new level of intimacy with manufacturing partners. Manufacturers have their own private Web sites on Rockwell's Internet portal, where they can view their past purchases and track their order status in real time. The extranet links directly into Rockwell's order management and warehouse management systems; when a distributor places an order for any of 85,000 parts, it is zapped to the national distribution center for almost immediate shipment.[12]

Electronic linkages also contribute to more rapid response to end consumers by reducing the time it takes to move critical data through the information pipeline. Manufacturers have immediate access to sales data and can deliver new products as needed. In addition, electronic linkages enable the rapid manufacture of customized products. Ford Motor Company is currently involved in a supply-chain makeover that will allow it to manufacture cars on a reasonable build-to-order basis, so that customers no longer have to wait months for delivery of the car of their dreams.[13]

By integrating everyone along the entire supply chain, the idea is that every organization involved can move in lock-step to meet the customer's product and time demands.

Designing Operations Management Systems

Every organization must design its production system. This process starts with the design of the product or service to be produced. A restaurant designs the food items on the menu. An automobile manufacturer designs the cars it produces. A management consulting firm designs the various types of services it will offer to clients. Other considerations in designing the production system include purchasing raw materials, layout of facilities, designing production technology, facilities location, and capacity planning.

Product and Service Design

The way a product or service is designed affects its appeal for customers; it also affects how easy or expensive operations will be. Some product designs

are difficult to execute properly. When Volant began making an unconventional type of skis from steel, skiers began snapping them up, delighted with their flexibility and tight grip of the snow. However, producing the skis turned out to be more difficult than anyone at Volant had expected, and many pairs had to be scrapped or reworked. Expenses mounted, and the company failed to meet promised delivery dates. Eventually, Volant hired Mark Soderberg, an engineer with experience at Boeing. Soderberg made a small design change that allowed more generous manufacturing tolerances (variances from the design specifications). After the tooling was adjusted to accommodate the design change, Volant began producing the modified skis—and forecast its first year of operating in the black.[14]

To prevent such problems in the first place, a growing number of businesses are using *design for manufacturability and assembly* (DFMA). Engineering designers have long fashioned products with disdain for how they would be produced. Elegant designs nearly always had too many parts. Thus, the watchword is *simplicity*, making the product easy and inexpensive to manufacture.

Using DFMA is extremely inexpensive. DFMA often requires restructuring operations, creating teams of designers, manufacturers, and assemblers to work together. They collaborate on achieving four objectives of product design:

1. *Producibility*. The degree to which a product or service can actually be produced for the customer within the firm's existing operational capacity.

2. *Cost*. The sum of the materials, labor, design, transportation, and overhead expense associated with a product or service. Striving for simplicity and few parts keeps product and service designs within reasonable costs.

3. *Quality*. The excellence of the product or service—the serviceability and value that customers gain by purchasing the product. In recent years, product design has moved toward consumer-friendly products, and companies are taking the time to ask questions such as "How do people use this product?" and "How can we make this product more user friendly?"

4. *Reliability*. The degree to which the customer can count on the product or service to fulfill its intended function. The product should function as designed for a reasonable length of time. Highly complex products often have lower reliability because more things can go wrong.

DaimlerChrysler is taking such criteria into account in its new product development process.[15] Traditionally, the car-development process can take four to six years and cost billions. The goal of the new process is to move from theme selection to mass manufacturing within two years, dramatically reducing development costs. Two hundred work stations at Chrysler's Auburn Hills, Michigan, headquarters have been linked to a Web-based system called FastCar. FastCar links the flow of information from finance, engineering, purchasing, manufacturing, and so on, so that car-development teams made up of members from all departments can collaborate in real time and think in terms of cost, producibility, required resources, and quality, as well as design innovation and artistry, avoiding problems down the line.

The design of services also should reflect producibility, cost, quality, and reliability. However, services have one additional design requirement: timing. *Timing* is the degree to which the provision of a service meets the customer's delivery requirements. Recall that a service cannot be stored in inventory and

must be provided when the customer is present. If you take your friend or spouse to a restaurant for dinner, you expect the meal to be served in a timely manner. The powerful push for self-service reflects the need to provide service when the customer wants and needs it. Banking by machine, pumping your own gas, and trying on your own shoes are all ways that organizations provide timely service, which is important in today's time-pressured world.

Procurement

procurement
Purchasing supplies, services, and raw materials for use in the production process.

The purchasing of supplies, services, and raw materials for use in the production process, known as **procurement,** has increased in importance as an operations issue. On average, a manufacturing company spends 50 to 60 percent of its revenues to buy materials and supplies. For example, auto manufacturers spend about 60 percent of revenues on material purchases, food processors about 70 percent, and oil refineries about 80 percent, and the percentages keep going up.[16] Expenses for materials, supplies, and services also represent a huge expense for service companies. Having the right materials of the correct design and quality is essential to the smooth functioning of the production process.

The Internet and business-to-business (B2B) commerce are having a tremendous impact on procurement. Purchasing department employees can now use the Internet to search for new sources of materials, place orders, request bids via B2B marketplaces, and participate in online auctions. Employees have quick access to more information about availability and cost. They can often submit purchase orders online and track the status of orders over the Web, cutting down on operating costs and speeding up the procurement lead time.[17] For example, by eliminating purchase orders and moving procurement online where employees ordered from suppliers that offered the company a discount, DuPont cut procurement costs by $200 million in one recent year. In addition, the typical order is now processed in one day instead of five.[18] Verizon Wireless hopes to shave 5 to 10 percent off the $150 million it spends on procurement of temporary contract workers each year by using competitive bidding and contract management over the Internet.[19] Whether they're looking for paper clips, jet engines, or consultants, more and more companies are using the Internet to control and streamline the procurement process.

Organizations wanting to move to online procurement often need to look at their *direct procurement* initiatives (that is, materials and supplies that go into the company's products) separately from indirect procurement (such as paper, pens, office equipment, and conference tables) because indirect procurement needs are spread all over the organization, not just in the production area. Burlington Northern Santa Fe Railway set up an online procurement system for indirect supplies as a first step toward a fully Web-enabled supply chain. By starting with indirect procurement the company could avoid disrupting the day-to-day business of the company and implement a project that would act as a model for e-business skeptics in the firm.

**BURLINGTON NORTHERN
SANTA FE RAILWAY**
http://www.bnsf.com

At Burlington Northern Santa Fe (BNSF) Railway, employees are required to make all purchases—from pencils to computers—over the Web, where they can be easily tracked. As vice president and chief sourcing officer for BNSF, Jeff Campbell set out to eliminate *maverick spends*—random purchases made by employees at local office supply stores. The maverick spend makes it prac-

tically impossible for procurement departments to track costs or budget and forecast accurately. Implementing an online procurement system required more than simply automating the old purchasing process and putting up a Web site. First, Campbell centralized purchasing all across the company. Then he examined the specifications for all the products BSNF uses, from mop buckets to mouse pads and office chairs, deciding which were sub-par in quality, which were just right, and which were "over-specked" (for example, was it necessary for office chairs to have lumbar support levers?). Campbell's team negotiated with suppliers who could get products to all 23 states the company served and offered the best price for each product.

Purchase orders are now submitted online, with automated approval based on certain criteria, eliminating the time-sapping manual approval process. Campbell estimates that online procurement saves 3 percent to 8 percent on all the various purchases made, because of the opportunity to negotiate discounts by purchasing in volume from a few suppliers.[20] ❖

Facilities Layout

Once a product or service has been designed and systems set up for procurement of materials, the next consideration is planning for the actual production through facilities layout. The four most common types of layout are process, product, cellular, and fixed-position, shown in Exhibit 22.5.

Process Layout. As illustrated in Exhibit 22.5(a), a **process layout** is one in which all machines that perform a similar function or task are grouped together. In a machine shop, the lathes perform a similar function and are located together in one section. The grinders are in another section of the shop. Service organizations also use process layouts. In a bank, the loan officers are in one area, the tellers in another, and the managers in a third.

The advantage of the process layout is that it has the potential for economies of scale and reduced costs. For example, having all painting done in one spray-painting area means that fewer machines and people are required to paint all products for the organization. In a bank, having all tellers located in one controlled area provides increased security. Placing all operating rooms together in a hospital makes it possible to control the environment for all rooms simultaneously.

The drawback to the process layout, as illustrated in Exhibit 22.5(a), is that the actual path a product or service takes can be long and complicated. A product may need several different processes performed on it and thus must travel through many different areas before production is complete.

Product Layout. Exhibit 22.5(b) illustrates a **product layout**—one in which machines and tasks are arranged according to the progressive steps in producing a single product. The automobile assembly line is a classic example, because it produces a single product starting from the raw materials to the finished output. Many fast-food restaurants use the product layout, with activities arranged in sequence to produce hamburgers or fried chicken, depending on the products available.

The product layout is efficient when the organization produces huge volumes of identical products. Note in Exhibit 22.5(b) that two lines have paint areas. This duplication of functions can be economical only if the volume is high enough to keep each paint area busy working on specialized products.

process layout
A facilities layout in which machines that perform the same function are grouped together in one location.

product layout
A facilities layout in which machines and tasks are arranged according to the sequence of steps in the production of a single product.

Exhibit **22.5**

Basic Production Layouts

(a) **Process Layout**

(b) **Product Layout**

(c) **Cellular Layout**

(d) **Fixed-Position Layout**

SOURCES: Based on J. T. Black, "Cellular Man-ufacturing Systems Reduce Setup Time, Make Small Lot Production Economical," *Industrial Engineering* (November 1983), 36–48; and Richard J. Schonberger, "Plant Layout Becomes Product-Oriented with Cellular, Just-in-Time Production Concepts," *Industrial Engineering* (November 1983), 66–77.

cellular layout
A facilities layout in which machines dedi-cated to sequences of production are grouped into cells in accordance with group-technology principles.

Cellular Layout. Illustrated in Exhibit 22.5(c) is an innovative layout, called **cellular layout**, based on group-technology principles in which machines ded-icated to sequences of operations are grouped into cells. Grouping technology into cells provides some of the efficiencies of both process and product layouts.

Even more important, the U-shaped cells in Exhibit 22.5(c) provide efficiencies in material and tool handling and inventory movement. One advantage is that the workers work in clusters that facilitate teamwork and joint problem solving. Staffing flexibility is enhanced because one person can operate all the machines in the cell and walking distance is small.

Fixed-Position Layout. As shown in Exhibit 22.5(d), the **fixed-position** layout is one in which the product remains in one location, and employees and equipment are brought to it. The fixed-position layout is used to create a product or service that is either very large or is one-of-a-kind, such as aircraft, ships, and buildings. The product cannot be moved from function to function or along an assembly line; rather, the people, materials, and machines all come to the fixed-position site for assembly and processing. This layout is not good for high volume, but it is necessary for large, bulky products and custom orders.

As the need for speed and responsiveness has increased, some organizations have been designing facilities layout to allow for a high level of flexibility. This chapter's New Workplace Shoptalk offers some tips from a German factory that is on the cutting edge of a new way of working.

fixed-position layout
A facilities layout in which the product remains in one location and the required tasks and equipment are brought to it.

Technology Automation

One goal of many operations managers is to implement more sophisticated technologies for producing products and services. Extremely advanced systems that can work almost unaided by employees are being designed.

Service Technology. The biggest growth in automation technologies in recent years has been in services. Restaurant kitchen managers can use computer programs to calculate the exact cost and ingredient needs for each menu item, from building a cheeseburger to putting together a seafood buffet, instead of having to perform arduous and time-consuming manual calculations. In the banking industry, automatic teller machines (ATMs) and telephone and online banking allow customers to obtain a wide range of banking services at any time. Many gas stations now have "pay-at-pump" systems where customers insert a credit or debit card to pay for their gas without having to go inside the station. In the supermarket industry, self-service checkout technology, such as that used at many Kroger stores, is growing in use.

"Welcome. Please scan your Kroger Plus card," instructs the cheerful voice. It comes not from a live cashier but from a robot busily working inside a self-service checkout station. As the largest food retailer in the United States, Kroger has been a leader in automating the checkout process, allowing customers with 15 items or less to avoid long lines and act as their own cashier.

To use the automated checkout, a customer scans each item using a laser scanning system and places the items in a bag on a weigh table that keeps track of the weight for verification purposes. A robotic voice and a computer touch screen provide instructions for pricing produce, using coupons, and selecting payment options. Cash (both coins and bills) can be inserted into the machine and the correct change will be returned. Customers can also pay by check or credit card. A pod of four checkout stations requires only one employee to monitor checkout, verify identification for check-writing or alcohol purchases, and handle any questions or problems.

KROGER
http://www.kroger.com

Manager's Shoptalk

A German Factory Shows How to Be Fast and Flexible

Many students might think a factory that makes polymer bearings and power-supply chains is not the best place to get a view of the factory of the future, but they would be wrong. Cologne, Germany's igus Inc. manufacturing plant represents a highly innovative approach to facilities design. The plant's flexible design enables the factory to shrink or expand at a moment's notice, keeping pace with an unpredictable market. Almost nothing is bolted down on the plant floor, so that machines, modules, and entire departments can be rearranged. Other design features, such as exposed overhead wiring and few support columns, mean the company can redesign itself as needed with little disruption to the 24-7 production flow. Over the past five years, igus has made at least 50 significant changes to the factory's configuration to accommodate strategic shifts, facilitate fast growth, or meet new customer needs.

Fast, agile organizations do not occur on their own. Managers have to make decisions that include considering the physical as well as the human environment. Frank Blase, president of igus, offers the following tips for building a nimble organization:

1. *Create a flexible environment.* A plant's space, facilities design, and layout should accommodate the business, not the other way around.
2. *Recruit carefully.* Not everyone is comfortable working in a highly flexible, fast-changing environment. Human resource managers should screen job candidates carefully and make sure they understand the nature of the workplace. At igus, candidates are given a *schnuppertag*, or sniffing-around day, to explore, observe, and ask questions.
3. *Practice being fast.* Every aspect of the company should be designed to encourage speed and agility. All igus employees are equipped with mobile phones and get around on shiny, motorized scooters. An open physical environment encourages collaboration and information transparency. Department teams conduct quick daily huddles to review what went well and what didn't the day before.
4. *Inspire your staff.* This last tip may be the most important of all. Flexibility hinges on innovation and creativity, Blase says, which depends on employees who are inspired to think differently and express their ideas and opinions. "We're trying to be a different kind of company," he adds, "and our building helps us tremendously in doing that. It creates a holistic system for how to behave."

SOURCE: Chuck Salter, "This is One Fast Factory," *Fast Company* (August 2001), 32–33.

Self-service checkout has been widely adopted in Europe, but has only recently caught hold in the United States. Other stores are also experimenting with the new technology. The approach has been so successful at Kroger that the company recently doubled its number of self-service stations, ordering 500 additional systems (four stations in each system). Neil Wechsler, CEO of Optimal Robotics, the largest supplier of self-service systems, reports that a pod of four can save 100 to 125 labor hours a week. In addition, customer service is improved because shoppers with only a few items can rapidly scan their items, pay the bill, and head for the door.[21] ❖

Advanced technology systems are continuously being integrated into today's service organizations to improve operations efficiency. In addition, advanced production technology has long been used in manufacturing companies. Two recent approaches that are revolutionizing manufacturing are flexible manufacturing systems and CAD/CAM.

Flexible Manufacturing Systems. The use of automated production lines that can be adapted to produce more than one kind of product is called a **flexible manufacturing system.**[22] The machinery uses computers to coordinate and integrate the machines. Automated functions include loading, unloading, storing parts, changing tools, and machining. The computer can

flexible manufacturing system
A small- or medium-sized automated production line that can be adapted to produce more than one product line.

instruct the machines to change parts, machining, and tools when a new product must be produced. This is a breakthrough compared with the product layout, in which a single line is restricted to a single product. With a flexible manufacturing system, a single production line can be readily readapted to small batches of different products based on computer instructions.

Companies often adopt flexible manufacturing to support a strategy of mass customization, that is, quickly adapting products to the specific needs of individual customers. For example, at Deere & Company, a major manufacturer of agricultural equipment, flexible manufacturing systems enable factories to produce one-of-a-kind pieces of machinery tailored specifically to farmers' needs. The company offers six million possible configurations.[23]

AMETEK is a leading manufacturer of electronic motors and electronic instruments in North America, Europe, and Asia. To achieve earnings per share growth from continuing operations, one of the company's four strategies is "Operational Excellence." AMETEK states that a true test of Operational Excellence is taking the best and making it better. This was done at the AMETEK Lamb Electric motor manufacturing plant in Racine, Wisconsin, which was redesigned to incorporate flow manufacturing techniques. The company's 5-year growth strategy includes the expansion of its flexible manufacturing systems to achieve world-class manufacturing at all of its operations.

CAD/CAM. Operations management in most businesses today employs computers for the design of products, and often for their manufacture as well. **CAD** (computer-aided design) enables engineers to develop new-product designs in about half the time required with traditional methods. Computers provide a visual display for the engineer and illustrate the implications of any design change.

CAM (computer-aided manufacturing) uses computers to direct manufacturing processes, as in flexible manufacturing systems. Typically, the CAM system is linked to CAD, so that the product specifications drive the manufacturing specifications. The computer system thus guides and controls the manufacturing process. For example, a sportswear manufacturer can use computers to mechanize the entire sequence of manufacturing operations— pattern scaling, layout, and printing. Computer-controlled cutting tables are installed. Once the computer has mathematically defined the geometry, it guides the cutting blade, eliminating the need for paper patterns. Computer programs also can direct fabric requisitions, production orders for cutting and sewing operations, and sewing line work.

The first applications of CAD/CAM involved computer-driven machine tools, which can cut and grind materials. However, many modern products are produced using molds, which have been machined by hand at great expense. Engineers extended the use of CAD/CAM to modernize this technology. An application called rapid prototyping (RP) uses CAD to create prototypes (models of a product) through a variety of methods, most of which involve using lasers to cut and bind slices of the object made from layers of plastic or paper. Other RP devices create prototypes by binding layers shaped from powdered steel, ceramics, or starch.

CAD
A production technology in which computers perform new-product design.

CAM
A production technology in which computers help guide and control the manufacturing system.

Facility Location

At some point, almost every organization must decide on the location of facilities. A bank needs to open a new branch office, Wendy's needs to find locations for the 100 or so restaurants opened each year, or a computer chip manufacturer needs to find a location for a new research facility or assembly and testing plant. When these decisions are made unwisely, they are expensive and troublesome for the organization.

Newell Rubbermaid uses a wide range of advanced technologies to create a compelling global competitive edge. This photo shows Stacy Wolff, a lead designer in the Home Products Division's R&D facility, using computer-aided design (CAD) *in product development. The new product concept moves on to* computer-aided manufacturing (CAM), *where final production process tooling is generated. By integrating the CAD and CAM technologies, Newell Rubbermaid can bring new products to market faster than ever before.*

The most common approach to selecting a site for a new location is to do a cost-benefit analysis. For example, managers at bank headquarters may identify four possible locations. The costs associated with each location are the land (purchase or lease); moving from the current facility; and construction, including zoning laws, building codes, land features, and size of the parking lot. Taxes, utilities, rents, and maintenance are other cost factors to be considered in advance. Each possible bank location also will have certain benefits. Benefits to be evaluated are accessibility of customers, location of major competitors, general quality of working conditions, and nearness to restaurants and shops, which would be desirable for both employees and customers. Once the bank managers have evaluated the worth of each benefit, they can divide total benefits by total costs for each location, then select the location with the highest ratio.

Selecting facility location is an important and complex consideration for global corporations, which must take into account cost-based variables such as transportation, exchange rates, and cost of labor. The skill levels of potential workers, the development of regional infrastructure, a good quality of life, and a favorable business climate are important considerations in selecting a location for overseas facilities. For high-tech firms, proximity to world-class research institutions and access to venture capital are also essential criteria.[24]

General Motors is locating more of its facilities near the markets where it expects sales growth, opening new factories in Argentina, Poland, China, and Thailand.[25] Low wage rates once drove such decisions at GM, but today managers are also considering the availability of local engineers, designers, and marketing experts. These people help the company design and build cars that satisfy its growing foreign markets.

Capacity Planning

Capacity planning is the determination and adjustment of an organization's ability to produce products or services to match demand. For example, if a bank anticipates a customer increase of 20 percent over the next year, capacity planning is the procedure whereby it will ensure that it has sufficient capacity to service that demand.

Organizations can do several things to increase capacity. One is to create additional shifts and hire people to work on them. A second is to ask existing people to work overtime to add to capacity. A third is to outsource or subcontract extra work to other firms. A fourth is to expand a plant and add more equipment. Each of these techniques will increase the organization's ability to meet demand without risk of major excess capacity.

The biggest problem for most organizations, however, is excess capacity. When misjudgments occur, transportation companies have oil tankers sitting empty in the harbor, oil companies have refineries sitting idle, semiconductor companies have plants shuttered, developers have office buildings half full, and the service industry may have hotels or amusement parks operating at partial capacity. For example, movie theater chains have grossly overbuilt in recent years, more than doubling the number of screens in the United States between 1980 and 2000 while ticket sales increased only 43 percent.[26] The challenge is for managers to add capacity as needed without excess. For many of today's companies, the solution is contracting work out to other organizations. New organizational forms such as the network organization and the virtual organization, described in Chapter 10, enable companies to quickly ramp

© James Schnepf

Harley-Davidson Motor Company is using capacity planning to keep pace with the growing, worldwide demand for its high-quality motorcycles. As the only major American-based motorcycle manufacturer, Harley-Davidson has brand names that are among the best known in the industry. All three of the company's manufacturing facilities have been extensively redesigned and reconfigured to improve productivity, workflow, product quality, and the environment. Facilities such as this recently completed touring-motorcycle assembly line in York, Pennsylvania, have put Harley-Davidson a full year ahead in its production schedule, and the company plans to have the capacity to produce 115,000 units a year.

up production to increase capacity and dissolve partnerships when extra help is no longer needed.

Inventory Management

A large portion of the operations manager's job consists of inventory management. **Inventory** is the goods the organization keeps on hand for use in the production process. Most organizations have three types of inventory: finished goods prior to shipment, work in process, and raw materials.

Finished-goods inventory includes items that have passed through the entire production process but have not been sold. This is highly visible inventory. The new cars parked in the storage lot of an automobile factory are finished-goods inventory, as are the hamburgers and french fries stacked under the heat lamps at a McDonald's restaurant. Finished-goods inventory is expensive, because the organization has invested labor and other costs to make the finished product.

Work-in-process inventory includes the materials moving through the stages of the production process that are not completed products. Work-in-process inventory in an automobile plant includes engines, wheel and tire assemblies, and dashboards waiting to be installed. In a fast-food restaurant, the french fries in the fryer and hamburgers on the grill are work-in-process inventory.

Raw materials inventory includes the basic inputs to the organization's production process. This inventory is cheapest, because the organization has not yet invested labor in it. Steel, wire, glass, and paint are raw materials inventory for an auto plant. Meat patties, buns, and raw potatoes are the raw materials inventory in a fast-food restaurant.

inventory
The goods that the organization keeps on hand for use in the production process up to the point of selling the final products to customers.

finished-goods inventory
Inventory consisting of items that have passed through the complete production process but have yet to be sold.

work-in-process inventory
Inventory composed of the materials that still are moving through the stages of the production process.

raw materials inventory
Inventory consisting of the basic inputs to the organization's production process.

The Importance of Inventory

Inventory management is vitally important to organizations, because inventory sitting idly on the shop floor or in the warehouse costs money. Many

years ago, a firm's wealth was measured by its inventory. Today inventory is recognized as an unproductive asset in cost-conscious firms. Dollars not tied up in inventory can be used in other productive ventures. Keeping inventory low is especially important for high-tech firms, because so many of their products lose value quickly, as they are replaced by more innovative and/or lower-cost models. For example, the value of a completed personal computer falls about 1 percent a week; even if shelf space for PCs were free, a company would lose money on its PC inventory.[27]

Retail giants such as Wal-Mart, Toys 'R' Us, Home Depot, and Best Buy understand that efficient inventory management is essential to competitive pricing. State-of-the-art e-business systems allow tight inventory control with the capacity to meet customer needs. The companies schedule orders to eliminate excess inventory. Their suppliers have refined their delivery systems so that the stores receive only the products needed to meet customer purchases. Another company that updated its inventory management system to enjoy these benefits is Office Depot.

OFFICE DEPOT
http://www.officedepot.com

For a retailer like office product superstore Office Depot, inventory is the heart of the business. Success depends on having what customers want, when they want it—but at a low price, which means the company can't afford to keep too much merchandise sitting around. Thus, Office Depot's management thought it a prudent investment to spend $25 million to upgrade the company's computers and inventory management systems.

Inventory management at Office Depot begins with demand forecasting; each store must have what customers will want. The company prepares forecasts based on past sales by store, by item, and by week. They consider the past three years' demand, adjusting for seasonal variations such as tax preparation season and the start of the school year. When possible, the company uses actual demand—for example, asking school districts how much paper they will order for the next year.

The next aspect of inventory management involves minimizing inventory costs by cutting the time between when an order is placed and when items are delivered. When this lead time is short, stores don't need as much safety stock (supplies kept on hand in case of an unexpected order). Office Depot uses electronic data interchange (EDI) and online procurement for most purchase orders, allowing its purchase orders to go directly to suppliers' order entry systems. Office Depot encourages participation by giving suppliers something of value: detailed weekly sales data about their products. In part because of efficiencies achieved through e-business, most of Office Depot's suppliers deliver products within a week or two from the order date.

Office Depot's inventory management system also efficiently handles goods that stores have ordered. When goods arrive at the warehouse, the company's computer checks to see that the stores' actual needs match what was anticipated, then adjusts the distribution of the orders if necessary. In deciding how many of an item to route to a particular store, the system evaluates not only the order quantity but also such factors as the number of items that make the most effective shelf display in the store. Finally, Office Depot has arranged for a freight optimizing service to monitor its orders and arrange for vendors to ship orders together when that is most efficient. Together, these elements of the inventory control system make Office Depot a tough contender in the office products business.[28] ❖

Many companies recognize the critical role of inventory management in organizational success. The Japanese analogy of rocks and water describes the current thinking about the importance of inventory.[29] As illustrated in Exhibit 22.6, the water in the stream is the inventory in the organization. The higher the water, the less managers have to worry about the rocks, which represent problems. In operations management, these problems apply to scheduling, facilities layout, product design, and quality. When the water level goes down, managers see the rocks and must deal with them. When inventories are reduced, the problems of a poorly designed and managed production process also are revealed. The problems then must be solved. When inventory can be kept at an absolute minimum, operations management is considered excellent.

We now consider specific techniques for inventory management. Four important concepts are economic order quantity, material requirements planning, just-in-time inventory systems, and distribution management.

Economic Order Quantity

Two basic decisions that can help minimize inventory are how much raw materials to order and when to order from outside suppliers. Ordering the minimum amounts at the right time keeps the raw materials, work-in-process, and finished-goods inventories at low levels. One popular technique is **economic order quantity (EOQ)**, which is designed to minimize the total of ordering costs and holding costs for inventory items. *Ordering costs* are the costs associated with actually placing the order, such as postage, receiving, and inspection. *Holding costs* are costs associated with keeping the item on hand, such as storage space charges, finance charges, and materials-handling expenses.

The EOQ calculation indicates the order quantity size that will minimize holding and ordering costs based on the organization's use of inventory. The EOQ formula includes ordering costs (*C*), holding costs (*H*), and annual demand (*D*). For example, consider a hospital's need to order surgical dressings. Based on hospital records, the ordering costs for surgical dressings are $15, the annual holding cost is $6, and the annual demand for dressings is 605. The following is the formula for the economic order quantity:

$$EOQ = \sqrt{\frac{2DC}{H}} = \sqrt{\frac{2(605)\,(15)}{6}} = 55$$

The EOQ formula tells us that the best quantity to order is 55.

economic order quantity (EOQ)
An inventory management technique designed to minimize the total of ordering and holding costs for inventory items.

Exhibit **22.6**

Large Inventories Hide Operations Management Problems

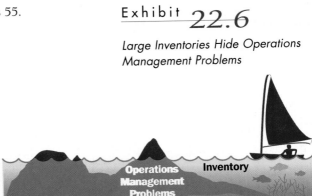

SOURCE: R. J. Schonberger, *Japanese Manufacturing Techniques: Nine Hidden Lessons in Simplicity* (New York: The Free Press, 1982).

The next question is when to make the order. For this decision, a different formula, called **reorder point (ROP),** is used. ROP is calculated by the following formula, which assumes that it takes three days to receive the order after the hospital has placed it:

$$ROP = \frac{D}{Time}\ (Lead\ time) = \frac{605}{365}\ (3) = 4.97,\ or\ 5$$

The reorder point tells us that because it takes three days to receive the order, at least 5 dressings should be on hand when the order is placed. As nurses use surgical dressings, operations managers will know that when the level reaches the point of 5, the new order should be placed for a quantity of 55.

This relationship is illustrated in Exhibit 22.7. Whenever the reorder point of 5 dressings is reached, the new order is initiated, and the 55 arrive just as the inventory is depleted. In a typical hospital, however, some variability in lead time and use of surgical dressings will occur. Thus, a few extra items of inventory, called *safety stock,* are used to ensure that the hospital does not run out of surgical dressings. In general, companies keep more safety stock when demand for items is highly variable. When demand is easy to predict, the safety stock may be lower. However, a careful inventory manager may take into account other criteria as well. A sizable price cut or volume discount might make a large purchase economically more attractive, especially in the case of a product the company is almost certain to need in the future.[30]

Material Requirements Planning

The EOQ formula works well when inventory items are not dependent on one another. For example, in a restaurant the demand for hamburgers is independent of the demand for milkshakes; thus, an economic order quantity is calculated for each item. A more complicated inventory problem occurs with **dependent demand inventory,** meaning that item demand is related to the demand for other inventory items. For example, if Ford Motor Company

Exhibit 22.7

Inventory Control of Surgical Dressings by EOQ

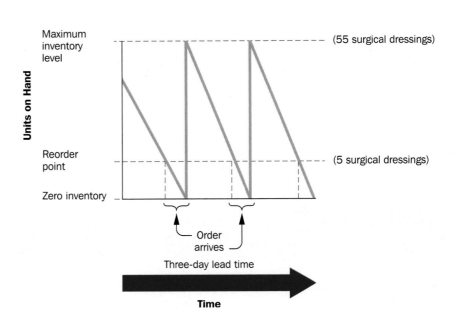

decides to make 100,000 cars, it will also need 400,000 tires, 400,000 rims, and 400,000 hubcaps. The demand for tires is dependent on the demand for cars.

The most common inventory control system used for handling dependent demand inventory is **material requirements planning (MRP)**. MRP is a dependent demand inventory planning and control system that schedules the exact amount of all materials required to support the desired end product. MRP is computer based and requires sophisticated calculations to coordinate information on production scheduling, inventory location, forecasting, and ordering. Unlike with EOQ, inventory levels are not based on past consumption; rather, they are based on precise estimates of future needs for production. MRP can dramatically reduce inventory costs. With MRP, managers can better control the quantity and timing of deliveries of raw materials, ensuring that the right materials arrive at approximately the right time they are needed in the production process. The computerized MRP system can slow or accelerate the inflow of materials in response to changes in the production schedule. These controls result in lower labor, materials, and overhead costs.[31]

As competitive pressures increased, MRP gradually evolved into the broader enterprise resource planning (ERP) systems described in Chapter 21. MRP is focused only on manufacturing and inventory, while ERP incorporates computerized links to other business functions, such as human resources, finance, and sales, enabling managers to evaluate trade-offs such as the balance between workload and the human resources and manufacturing capacity.[32] ERP systems can integrate, track, and optimize functions across the entire organization. MRP systems are a valuable subset of ERP, enabling managers to have greater insight into operations so they can optimize the use of human and material resources.

Just-in-Time Inventory

Just-in-time (JIT) inventory systems are designed to reduce the level of an organization's inventory and its associated costs, aiming to push to zero the amount of time that raw materials and finished products are sitting in the factory, being inspected, or in transit.[33] Sometimes these systems are referred to as *stockless systems, zero inventory systems,* or *Kanban systems.* Each system centers on the concept that suppliers deliver materials only at the exact moment needed, thereby reducing raw material inventories to zero. Moreover, work-in-process inventories are kept to a minimum because goods are produced only as needed to service the next stage of production. Finished-goods inventories are minimized by matching them exactly to sales demand. Just-in-time systems have tremendous advantages. In particular, the reduced inventory level frees productive capital for other company uses.

Recall the analogy of the rocks and the water. To reduce inventory levels to zero means that all management and coordination problems will surface and must be resolved. Scheduling must be scrupulously precise and logistics tightly coordinated. For example, follow the movement of a shipment of odometers and speedometers from a supplier in Winchester, Virginia, to a GM Saturn plant in Spring Hill, Tennessee.

Thursday, 9 A.M.	A Ryder truck arrives at the supplier. As workers load the parts, drivers check on-board computers for destination, route, and estimated time of arrival (ETA) data.
Friday, 3 A.M.	The truck arrives at Spring Hill, Tennessee, and approaches a switching yard two miles from the Saturn

material requirements planning (MRP)
A dependent demand inventory planning and control system that schedules the precise amount of all materials required to support the production of desired end products.

just-in-time (JIT) inventory system
An inventory control system that schedules materials to arrive precisely when they are needed on a production line.

Dan Cohen (*BusinessWeek*, September 24, 2001)

Dell Computer is one of today's best examples of the integrated enterprise. Dell has squeezed every cent possible out of the cost of building and selling PCs by using the Internet to integrate the entire supply chain, from purchasing to distribution. The company's just-in-time inventory system is legendary. At any given moment, there's just four days of stock in Dell's warehouses, compared to 24 days for Compaq. Last year, Dell began requiring that suppliers be wired directly to the factory floor, enabling Dell plants to keep just a few hours worth of parts on hand and replenish only what is needed throughout the day. By reducing inventory costs, the new system saved Dell $50 million in the first six months of use.

plant, parking in a computer-assigned spot. The driver downloads a key-shaped floppy disk from the on-board computer into Ryder's mainframe, which relays the performance report directly to Saturn.

Friday, 12:50 P.M.   The trailer leaves the switching yard at a designated time and arrives at a predetermined receiving dock at the Saturn plant, where Saturn workers unload the parts and send them to the production line just in time.[34]

The coordination required by JIT demands that information be shared among everyone in the supply chain. Communication between only adjoining links in the supply chain is too slow. Rather, coordination requires a kind of information web in which members of the supply chain share information simultaneously with all other participants, often using Internet technologies.[35] For example, Dell's factory in Austin, Texas, uses online information exchange so effectively that it can order only the materials needed to keep production running for the next two hours. In addition, Web hook-ups to shipping companies mean that finished inventory can often be loaded onto trucks less than 15 hours after a customer submits an order.[36]

Just-in-time inventory systems also require excellent employee motivation and cooperation. Workers are expected to perform at their best because they are entrusted with the responsibility and authority to make the zero inventory system work. Employees must help one another when they fall behind and must be capable of doing different jobs. Workers experience the satisfaction of being in charge of the system and making useful improvements in the company's operations.[37]

Logistics and Distribution Management

logistics
The activities required to physically move materials into the company's operations facility and to move finished products to customers.

A critical aspect of managing inventory is efficiently moving raw materials into the facility and moving finished products out to customers. Some companies develop the necessary logistics expertise in house. **Logistics** refers to managing the movement of materials within the facility, the shipment of incoming materials from suppliers, and the shipment of outgoing products to customers. For example, Wal-Mart uses regional distribution centers, such as the one in New Braunfels, Texas, which has more than 1 million square feet of floor space, 96 dock doors for loading and unloading trailers, and 5.62 miles of conveyors for moving merchandise.[38] These regional centers receive incoming shipments from suppliers, receive orders from the retail stores, make up the orders, and load and ship merchandise orders to stores throughout the region. Distribution center employees coordinate the entire system and schedule inbound trucks from suppliers and company-owned trucks outbound to the retail stores. Using computers, the system can be so precisely coordinated that the stores don't need warehouses; orders of merchandise go directly from the trucks to the shelves, usually within 48 hours.

Other organizations outsource logistics to a growing number of contract logistics firms, such as Ryder Systems, Caliber Systems Inc., and Emery Global Logistics, which manage the movement of incoming materials and the shipment of outgoing products for the company. General Motors gained efficiencies by outsourcing logistics to Penske Logistics, which coordinates and consolidates shipments of supplies and materials for all of GM's U.S. assembly plants.[39]

Moving finished products out to customers is usually referred to as **distribution** or *order fulfillment*. The faster and more accurately a company can fill customer orders, the lower the costs for the organization and the greater the likelihood that the customer will return. For online companies, distribution snafus in the early days have led to greater emphasis on the nuts and bolts of order fulfillment. One approach is to rely on contract fulfillment companies such as SubmitOrder.com, which stores, packs, and ships products for companies such as MuseumCompany.com, Kmart's BlueLight.com, and teen fashion retailer LimitedToo. As soon as a customer hits the "Buy" button on MuseumCompany.com's Web page, SubmitOrder spits out the customer's mailing labels, receipt, and the shelf location for each item ordered.[40] A stock *picker* takes the paperwork and starts running to select the items and send them along a conveyor belt to a *packer* who packages the items and sends them to the appropriate dock for shipping. The whole process can take less than an hour.

SubmitOrder's computers also send hourly updates to the company so managers can replenish goods as needed. Online catalogs can be automatically updated as soon as new merchandise arrives in the warehouse. Further automation will enable SubmitOrder pickers to remain in one part of the warehouse and assemble small portions of larger orders, allowing the company to send out as many as 5,000 orders an hour, shaving a little more off the delivery time for each package.

Traditional organizations are also finding new ways to deliver products faster and less expensively by using the Internet. In the latest advance in interorganizational collaboration, some companies share transportation information and resources with unrelated companies, even competitors, so they can share truck space and avoid hauling an empty trailer on a return trip. Subaru of America is talking with a rival automaker about the possibility of sharing rail and truck space so cars will get to dealers faster. Nabisco uses electronic linkages to share warehouses and trucks with companies such as Dole and Lea & Perrins, and coordinate order shipments to retailers, enabling stores to more closely match orders to consumer needs.[41] Nabisco has also joined with General Mills and other companies to test a new collaborative online distribution network, as described in the Leading Online box.

distribution
Moving finished products to customers; also called *order fulfillment*.

Managing Productivity

Productivity is significant because it influences the well-being of the entire society as well as of individual companies. The only way to increase the output of goods and services to society is to increase organizational productivity.

Measuring Productivity

What is productivity, and how is it measured? In simple terms, **productivity** is the organization's output of goods and services divided by its inputs. This means that productivity can be improved by either increasing the amount of output using the same level of inputs or reducing the number of inputs required to produce the output. Sometimes a company can even do both. Ruggieri & Sons, for example, invested in mapping software to help it plan deliveries of heating fuel. The software plans the most efficient routes based on the locations of customers and fuel reloading terminals, as well as the amount of fuel each customer needs. When Ruggieri switched from planning

productivity
The organization's output of products and services divided by its inputs.

Leading Online

Nistevo's Online Distribution Network

"You end up unloading in Montana with nowhere to go. What do you do, shoot the driver and sell the truck?" That question, posed by shipping expert Bob Delaney, is one General Mills was pondering as it tried to eliminate the age-old problem of having trucks on the road hauling only air. Estimates are that companies lose a combined $30 billion a year from inefficient distribution systems, a large part of which comes from trucks traveling empty.

General Mills is teaming up with other manufacturers, such as Nabisco and Fort James, a division of Georgia Pacific, to use the Internet and new logistics software from Nistevo to find loads for otherwise empty trucks. To use the system, manufacturers go to Nistevo.com and post the space they need or have available. Now, when General Mills has a shipment of Cheerios going from its Minneapolis plant to Tampa, the software can search through the shipping schedules of other manufacturers to find a load of products that needs to be shipped from Tampa to Minneapolis–St. Paul. In addition, it can detect problems as they happen and send timely alerts

about delayed shipments or canceled deliveries. Each manufacturer pays less per mile, and the trucking company benefits because it is not hauling empty trailers. The goal is that everyone shares in the cost savings.

Nistevo's system can handle hundreds of thousands of transactions a day. So far, other companies participating in the private alliance include Pillsbury, Land O' Lakes, Nestlé, and ConAgra. Rather than hosting a public transportation planning site, Nistevo provides planning and scheduling tools that support long-term collaborative relationships among a group of manufacturing and trucking companies. Considering that logistics accounts for 12 to 14 percent of a manufacturer's cost of goods sold, sharing information online can add up to huge savings. For a company like General Mills, for example, shaving even 1 percent off logistics costs could add up to hundreds of millions of dollars a year.

SOURCES: Kim Cross, "Fill It to the Brim," *Business2.com* (March 6, 2001), 36–39; and Faith Keenan, "One Smart Cookie," *Business Week e.biz* (November 20, 2000), EB120.

---

routes by hand to using the software, its drivers began driving fewer miles but making 7 percent more stops each day—in others words, burning less fuel in order to sell more fuel.[42]

The accurate measure of productivity can be complex. Two approaches for measuring productivity are total factor productivity and partial productivity. **Total factor productivity** is the ratio of total outputs to the inputs from labor, capital, materials, and energy:

total factor productivity
The ratio of total outputs to the inputs from labor, capital, materials, and energy.

$$\text{Total factor productivity} = \frac{Output}{Labor + Capital + Materials + Energy}$$

Total factor productivity represents the best measure of how the organization is doing. Often, however, managers need to know about productivity with respect to certain inputs. **Partial productivity** is the ratio of total outputs to a major category of inputs. For example, many organizations are interested in labor productivity, which would be measured as follows:

partial productivity
The ratio of total outputs to the inputs from a single major input category.

$$\text{Labor Productivity} = \frac{Output}{Labor\ dollars}$$

Calculating this formula for labor, capital, or materials provides information on whether improvements in each element are occurring. However, managers often are criticized for relying too heavily on partial productivity measures, especially direct labor.[43] Measuring direct labor misses the valuable improvements in materials, manufacturing processes, and work quality. Labor

productivity is easily measured, but may show an increase as a result of capital improvements. Thus, managers will misinterpret the reason for productivity increases.

Improving Productivity

When an organization decides that improving productivity is important, there are three places to look: technological productivity, worker productivity, and managerial productivity.

Increased *technological productivity* refers to the use of more efficient machines, robots, computers, and other technologies to increase outputs. The flexible manufacturing and CAD/CAM systems described earlier in this chapter are technological improvements that enhance productivity. New technology can increase productivity for service firms, as well. Schneider National, the largest trucking company in the United States, installed a computer terminal in each of its 26 maintenance centers and connected them to an intranet so that mechanics can access up-to-date diagrams and data for repairing trucks. Each mechanic can now fix 20 percent more tractors than before, enabling trucks to get back on the road faster.[44]

Outsourcing can also increase productivity because a specialized firm can afford to invest in the most modern technology related to the service it provides. NationsBank, for example, arranged for Pitney Bowes Management Services (PBMS) to handle its mail services, in part because PBMS has the computer applications to handle the task. Therefore NationsBank doesn't have to incur the cost of new technology needed to set up a modern mailing system for its 60 mail centers spread out over 16 states and the District of Columbia.[45]

Increased *worker productivity* means having workers produce more output in the same time period. Companies can improve worker productivity by establishing the means for existing employees to do more by working harder or improving work processes. Employees may simply need more knowledge, more resources, or improved task or workplace design. The company may also decide to hire employees with greater expertise or to outsource certain operations to a firm with expertise in that area, as NationsBank did to obtain the knowledge of PBMS. Improving worker productivity can be a real challenge for American companies, because too often workers have an antagonistic relationship with management. Thus, increasing employee productivity often requires improving that relationship. Many of the leadership and management approaches described in this book can enhance worker productivity by motivating and inspiring employees.

Increased *managerial productivity* simply means that managers do a better job of running the business. Leading experts in productivity and quality often have stated that the real reason for productivity problems in the United States is poor management.[46] One of these authorities, W. Edwards Deming, proposed specific points for telling management how to improve productivity. These points are listed in Exhibit 22.8.

Management productivity improves when managers emphasize quality over quantity, break down barriers and empower their employees, and do not overmanage using numbers. Managers can learn to use reward systems,

© Drew Donavan

For Anadarko, productivity is measured by the amount of oil and natural gas it can locate and extract from deep inside the earth. To measure the company's productivity, the cost of inputs (which includes exploration and drilling costs) must be measured against the value of the outputs (the oil and natural gas it can produce). Recent productivity has been very high for Anadarko, due mainly to its use of cutting-edge technology and exploration techniques. For instance, while exploring in a part of Algeria that bigger competitors had given up on, these Anadarko workers used an unorthodox imaging technique to discover a three-billion barrel field of oil.

Exhibit **22.8**

Condensation of the 14 Points for Management

1. Create constancy of purpose toward improvement of product and service, with the aim to become competitive and to stay in business, and to provide jobs.

2. Adopt the new philosophy. We are in a new economic age. Western management must awaken to the challenge, must learn its responsibilities, and take on leadership for change.

3. Cease dependence on inspection to achieve quality. Eliminate the need for inspection on a mass basis by building quality into the product in the first place.

4. End the practice of awarding business on the basis of price tag. Instead, minimize total cost. Move toward a single supplier for any one item, on a long-term relationship of loyalty and trust.

5. Improve constantly and forever the system of production and service, to improve quality and productivity, and thus constantly decrease costs.

6. Institute training on the job.

7. Institute leadership (see Point 12). The aim of supervision should be to help people and machines and gadgets to do a better job. Supervision of management is in need of overhaul as well as supervision of production workers.

8. Drive out fear, so that everyone may work effectively for the company.

9. Break down barriers between departments. People in research, design, sales, and production must work as a team, to foresee problems of production and in use that may be encountered with the product or service.

10. Eliminate slogans, exhortations, and targets for the workforce asking for zero defects and new levels of productivity. Such exhortations only create adversarial relationships, as the bulk of the causes of low quality and low productivity belong to the system and thus lie beyond the power of the workforce.

11. a. Eliminate work standards (quotas) on the factory floor. Substitute leadership.

    b. Eliminate management by objective. Eliminate management by numbers, numerical goals. Substitute leadership.

12. a. Remove barriers that rob the hourly worker of his right to pride of workmanship. The responsibility of supervisors must be changed from sheer numbers to quality.

    b. Remove barriers that rob people in management and in engineering of their right to pride of workmanship. This means, *inter alia,* abolishment of the annual merit rating and of management by objective.

13. Institute a vigorous program of education and self-improvement.

14. Put everybody in the company to work to accomplish the transformation. The transformation is everybody's job.

SOURCE: Reprinted from *Out of the Crisis,* by W. Edwards Deming by permission of MIT and The W. Edwards Deming Institute. Published by MIT, Center for Advanced Educational Services, Cambridge, MA 02139. Copyright 1986 by The W. Edwards Deming Institute.

employee involvement, teamwork, and other management techniques that have been described throughout this book. However, it is important for managers to consider the linkage between these techniques and the company's strategy—not just to blindly insert a technique into the organization's activities. For example, although many managers have encouraged their employees to share knowledge, their efforts often fail because employees see no benefits and they lose interest. In contrast, knowledge management efforts succeed when managers establish a strategy-related focus for what information is to be shared, then measure the results. At General Electric, for example, employees focused on learning about how to improve response time. Management had determined that improvements in this area would significantly improve the company's performance. When GE instituted its knowledge management system, managers looked for—and found—improvements in such performance measures as sales per employee.[47] The difference can be attributed to better management, not to specific techniques.

Summary and Management Solution

This chapter described several points about operations management. Operations management pertains to the tools and techniques used to manage the organization's core production process. These techniques apply to both manufacturing and service organizations. Operations management has a great impact when it influences competitive strategy, applying strategic tools such as supply chain management. Areas of operations management described in the chapter include product and service design, procurement, location of facilities, facilities layout, capacity planning, and the use of new technologies.

The chapter also discussed inventory management. Three types of inventory are raw materials, work in process, and finished goods. Economic order quantity, material requirements planning, and just-in-time inventory are techniques for minimizing inventory levels. Logistics is an important part of inventory management because it manages the movement of materials within the facility, the shipment of incoming materials from suppliers, and the shipment of outgoing products to customers. Efficient and effective distribution of products to customers, sometimes called order fulfillment, is critical to organizational success.

Another important concept is that operations management can enhance organizational productivity. Total factor productivity is the best measurement of organizational productivity. Managers can focus on improving productivity in three areas: technological productivity, worker productivity, and managerial productivity.

Apple Computer, described in the chapter opening, revised its approach to supply chain management to reduce inventories and better serve customers. Steve Jobs hired Tom Cook, an operations expert with substantial PC experience at Compaq Computer, to help him tackle the supply chain problems and improve operations efficiency. First, the two reduced Apple's product line from more than 15 models to four basic products. This cut the number of parts needed and shifted the manufacturing focus to customizing a few basic products rather than carrying lots of inventory. A new Web site allows customers to configure their own versions of the products. Manufacturing was outsourced to contract manufacturers that could produce products more efficiently using flexible manufacturing systems. Apple also revised its distribution system, closing many of its warehouses and overseas distribution centers and delivering products directly from contract factories to retailers and consumers. The number of parts suppliers was cut so managers could develop more collaborative, information-sharing relationships with a few supplier partners. Now, Apple can rapidly obtain the parts it needs and produce and distribute customized products quickly. In talking about their goals for revamping supply chain management, Cook recalls: "We set out to beat Dell Computer." We didn't want to deliver products like theirs . . . but we did want to emulate them in operations."[48]

Discussion Questions

1. What are the major differences between manufacturing and service organizations? Give examples of each type.
2. In what ways might a long-distance telephone company be more competitive if it operates at Stage 3 or Stage 4 of operations strategy?
3. What is the role of e-business in the *integrated enterprise*? How does enhanced integration of the supply chain affect the relationship between organizations and their customers and suppliers?
4. Why is procurement considered such an important part of operations management? What are some of the major changes in the procurement process in recent years?
5. What type of production layout do you think would work best in a car dealership? What type would work best for a company that produces handmade pottery? Discuss reasons for your answers.
6. If you were asked to identify a location for a new resort catering to retirees, what steps would you take? How would you plan for the new resort's capacity?
7. What are the three types of inventory? Which of these is most likely to be affected by the just-in-time inventory system? Explain.
8. What is material requirements planning? How does it differ from economic order quantity to reduce inventory?

9. Discuss the importance of logistics and distribution in managing inventory. Why do you think many of today's companies outsource this function?

10. If you were a consultant to a local manufacturing plant that wants to improve productivity, what advice would you give managers?

11. Do you believe operations management can influence competitive strategy? Discuss.

■ Management in Practice: Experiential Exercise

What is Your Attitude Toward Productivity?

Complete the following questions based on how you think and act in a typical work situation. For each item circle the number that best describes you.

	Disagree Strongly			Agree Strongly	
1. I spend time developing new ways of approaching old problems.	1	2	3	4	5
2. As long as things are done correctly and efficiently, I prefer not to take on the hassle of changing them.	5	4	3	2	1
3. I always believe the "effort" to improve something should be rewarded, even if the final improvement is disappointing.	1	2	3	4	5
4. A single change that improves things 30 percent is much better than 30 improvements of 1 percent each.	5	4	3	2	1
5. I frequently compliment others on changes they have made.	1	2	3	4	5
6. I let people know in a variety of ways that I like to be left alone to do my job efficiently.	5	4	3	2	1
7. I am personally involved in several improvement projects at one time.	1	2	3	4	5
8. I try to be a good listener and be patient with what people say, except when it is a "stupid" idea.	5	4	3	2	1
9. I am always proposing unconventional techniques and ideas.	1	2	3	4	5
10. I usually do *not* take risks that would create a problem for me if the idea failed.	5	4	3	2	1

Total Score _____

This scale indicates the extent to which your orientation toward productivity is based on "efficiency" or "continuous improvement." Efficiency sometimes can be maximized by eliminating change. This may be appropriate in a stable organizational environment. Continuous improvement is an attitude that productivity can always get better and you take personal responsibility to improve it. This attitude is appropriate for a quality-conscious company experiencing frequent change.

A score of 40 or higher indicates that you take personal responsibility for improving productivity and frequently initiate change. A score of 20 or less indicates you make contributions through efficient work in a stable environment. Discuss the pros and cons of the efficiency versus continuous improvement orientations for organizations and employees.

■ Management in Practice: Ethical Dilemma

A Friend for Life?

Priscilla Dennis has always loved her job as president of Smallworld, a small company that produces and markets toys for young children. As a mother, Priscilla appreciates the care that goes into producing safe, high-quality toys. Late last year,

Smallworld's designer invented a small, cuddly talking bear. Called the Binky-Bear, the toy was made of soft brown simulated fur and had a tape inside that played 50 messages. To see what kind of appeal the Binky-Bear might have, Smallworld produced 50 of the toys and placed them in kindergartens and

nurseries. Results were better than managers had hoped, with many of the kindergartens reporting that the toy quickly became the most popular in the school.

Based on these results, Smallworld decided to produce 1,000 of the bears, and they developed a catchy marketing slogan: "A Friend for Life." The bear was marketed as a toy that children could play with for years and years, and perhaps still have around as a keepsake when they had long outgrown toys. The first batch sold out within a week, so the company scheduled another production run of 25,000. However, during the run, the production manager discovered a problem. In the excitement over the new product, the designer and managers had failed to look carefully at manufacturing considerations. It turned out that the process needed to make Binky-Bear's soft fur was much more expensive than anticipated. Using the original fur will cost the company $4.98 per bear, but the manufacturing department can produce a substitute that will cut the cost to only $2.75 per bear. However, as compared with the original fur, which should last approximately 8 years, the alternate, less-expensive fur will last for only 8 months.

In an emergency meeting to discuss the problem, Smallworld's managers are considering two options: absorb the extra cost, or use the cheaper substitute fur that will not last nearly as long. Many of the managers emphasize that children aren't interested in playing with toys for more than a few months—or even weeks—anyway, so substituting the less-expensive fur shouldn't be a problem. Others, including the production manager, believe the company's reputation for quality will be severely damaged. "We're going to have complaints within 8 months, and we will rue the day we agreed to a cheaper sub-

stitute," the production manager said. The vice president for manufacturing agreed, asking, "What are we going to do about our slogan—change it to "A Friend for Eight Months"? The marketing and sales managers forcefully argued the opposite viewpoint, pointing out that Smallworld already had a fortune tied up in the bear. "If you stop production now or continue with the expensive fur, we'll lose our shirts," the sales manager said. "The bear looks the same. I say we substitute the cheaper fur and no one will ever know the difference."

The final decision about how to handle the problem rests with Priscilla Dennis. She knows Smallworld can't afford to absorb the extra production costs, but can it afford to lose its reputation for quality? Also, she wonders if she can look her young daughter in the eye if she goes along with what the sales manager is suggesting.

What Do You Do?

1. Substitute the less expensive fur but insist on a revised marketing campaign and advise buyers about the change in the production process.
2. Substitute the less expensive fur and wait to see what happens. The company would not be doing anything illegal, and most customers probably will never notice that the fur wears out so quickly.
3. Absorb the extra production costs. It's the right thing to do, and besides, the company's reputation for quality is too important to risk.

SOURCE: Based on "A Friend for Life," in Donald F. Kuratko and Richard M. Hodgetts, *Entrepreneurship: A Contemporary Approach,* 4th ed. (Fort Worth: The Dryden Press, 1998), 172–173.

Surf the Net

1. **Just-in-time Inventory Systems.** Use the site *http://www.ipl.org/autou/* or find one of your own that provides a factory tour so you can learn about the manufacturing process. If the manufacturing facility you tour relies on any type of just-in-time inventory system, jot down a few notes about its system so you can relate your example to the classroom discussion on this topic.

2. **Product Design.** The Boeing Company unveiled a large, detailed model of its newest commercial airplane, the sonic cruiser, at the Paris Air Show on June 19, 2001. The sonic cruiser is expected to fly at speeds of up to Mach .98 (98 percent of the speed of sound) or faster over extended ranges. Go to *http://www.boeing.com/news/feature/concept/* to learn about this new product. Watch some of the video clips, read some of the press releases,

and check out other links at this site to broaden your understanding of what goes into the development of a new product of this type.

3. **Performance Management.** The American Productivity & Quality Center (APQC) is a nonprofit organization supported by nearly 500 companies, government organizations, and educational institutions. To learn more about this organization, go to *http://www.apqc.org/about/*.

You will see that the APQC provides tools, information, expertise, and support needed to discover and implement best practices in a variety of areas, one of which is performance management. Check out the links on performance management, print the content from the link you found most beneficial in broadening your understanding of performance management and bring the printout to class.

■ Case for Critical Analysis

Intel

The old adage used to be that fish, newspapers, and houseguests went stale after a day; these days, we could add computer microprocessors to the list. The management at Intel, whose chips supply the brains for more than half a billion PCs worldwide, knows this fact. In order to stay ahead of the competition, Intel has had to constantly innovate with its Celeron and Pentium chips for personal computers. In addition, the company recently made a bold move to extend its reach beyond PCs to high-end servers that power the Internet and corporate networks.

That meant starting from scratch to design an all-new chip. In the spring of 2001, Intel unveiled the Itanium, the first of a series of processors the company hopes will give Intel a boost as the price of PC processors continues to fall. However, the new processor got off to a shaky start. For one thing, it was nearly two years late, an eternity in the technology industry. The Itanium would have been a revolution if it had been introduced in 1999, but by the time it hit the market, it ran only half as fast as Intel's new version of the Pentium 4. The development process was plagued by one problem after another. Time and again, the team members realized they had underestimated some aspect of the job. The team broke into several different groups, each one working on one piece of the puzzle without knowing what the others were doing or how all the pieces would fit together. So far, expectations for the new chip have been low. Referring to the $1 to $2 billion development price tag, a former Intel official said: "This will end up being one of the world's worst investments, I'm afraid." Others, however, feel sure that the Itanium will eventually succeed and make Intel loads of money. One consideration for future versions is to get the bugs worked out of the chip design process.

In the meantime, Intel is still counting on PCs for a major part of its business, which presents yet another set of operational problems. Today, PC manufacturers such as Dell Computer Corp. specialize in build-to-order manufacturing, which means that they expect no slack in the supply chain, holding little or no inventory of finished products or even components. This means Intel has to juggle its supply levels, inventory, and manufacturing capacity to meet customers' needs and at the same time demand the same thing from its own suppliers. "All of our [customers] are trying to operate with essentially zero inventory," explains Alan Baldwin, vice-president of Intel's planning and logistics group. "They need just-in-time delivery from us and real-time feedback from the marketplace."

Questions

1. How might Intel improve the product design process and prevent the problems and delays that occurred with the first Itanium processor?
2. What procedures and technologies would you suggest operations managers use to effectively manage the supply chain to meet PC manufacturers' needs?
3. A single chip manufacturing facility can cost more than $1 billion. If you were selecting a new location for an Intel plant to manufacture the Itanium, what steps would you take and what factors would you consider?

SOURCES: Based on David P. Hamilton, "Gambling It Can Move Beyond PC, Intel Offers a New Microprocessor," *The Wall Street Journal* (May 29, 2001), A1, A8; and Peter Fabris, "Intel Outside," *CIO*, Section 1 (August 15, 1998), 64–69.

■ Endnotes

1. David Bovet and Joseph Martha, "Change at the Core," *Business2.com* (November 28, 2000), 278–281.
2. Josh Quittner with Rebecca Winters, "Apple's New Core: Exclusive: How Steve Jobs Made a Sleek Machine that Could Be the Home-Digital Hub of the Future," *Time* (January 14, 2002), 46+.
3. James D. Thompson, *Organizations in Action* (New York: McGraw-Hill, 1967).
4. Norihiko Shirouzu, "Gadget Inspector: Why Toyota Wins Such High Marks on Quality Surveys," *The Wall Street Journal* (March 15, 2001), A1, A11.
5. Gregory B. Northcraft and Richard B. Chase, "Managing Service Demand at the Point of Delivery," *Academy of Management Review* 10 (1985), 66–75; and Richard B. Chase and David A.

Tanski, "The Customer Contact Model for Organization Design," *Management Science* 29 (1983), 1037–1050.
6. Everett E. Adam Jr. and Paul M. Swamidass, "Assessing Operations Management from a Strategic Perspective," *Journal of Management* 15 (1989), 181–203.
7. Robert H. Hayes and David M. Upton, "Operations-Based Strategy," *California Management Review* 40, no. 4 (Summer 1998), 8–25.
8. R. H. Hayes and S. C. Wheelwright, *Restoring Our Competitive Edge: Competing through Manufacturing* (New York: Wiley, 1984).
9. Definition based on Steven A. Melnyk and David R. Denzler, *Operations Management: A Value-Driven Approach* (Burr Ridge, Ill.: Richard D. Irwin, 1996), 613.

10. Based on Jim Turcotte, Bob Silveri, and Tom Jobson, "Are You Ready for the E-Supply Chain?" *APICS–The Performance Advantage* (August 1998), 56–59.

11. F. Ian Stuart and David M. McCutcheon, "The Manager's Guide to Supply Chain Management," *Business Horizons* (March–April 2000), 35–44.

12. Christopher Koch, "Four Strategies," Special Section on Supply Chain Management, *CIO* (October 1, 2000), 116–128.

13. Russ Banham, "Caught in the Middle," *CFO* (May 2001), 69–74.

14. Thomas Petzinger Jr., "How a Ski Maker on a Slippery Slope Regained Control," *The Wall Street Journal* (October 3, 1997), B1.

15. William J. Holstein, "DaimlerChrysler's Net Designs," *Business2.com* (April 17, 2001), 26–28.

16. Christopher Koch, "The Big Payoff," Special Section on Supply Chain Management, *CIO* (October 1, 2000), 101–112; Norman Gaither and Greg Frazier, *Operations Management*, 9th ed. (Cincinnati, Ohio: South-Western Publishing, 2002), 428–429.

17. Gaither and Frazier, *Operations Management*, 429.

18. David Rocks, "The Net as a Lifeline," *BusinessWeek e.biz* (October 29, 2001), EB16–EB28.

19. Scott Leibs, "First Pencils, Now People," *CFO* (November 2001), 91–94.

20. Koch, "Four Strategies."

21. Megan Barnett, "Check It Out," *The Industry Standard* (May 14, 2001), 48–49.

22. Sumer C. Aggarwal, "MRP, JIT, OPT, FMS?" *Harvard Business Review* 63 (September–October 1985), 8–16; and Paul Ranky, *The Design and Operation of Flexible Manufacturing Systems* (New York: Elsevier, 1983).

23. Anita Lienert, "Plowing Ahead in Uncertain Times," *Management Review* (December 1998), 16–21.

24. Alan David MacCormack, Lawrence James Newman III, and Donald B. Rosenfield, "The New Dynamics of Global Manufacturing Site Location," *Sloan Management Review* (Summer 1994), 69–80; and Chen May Yee, "Let's Make a Deal," *The Wall Street Journal* (September 25, 2000), R10.

25. Rebecca Blumenstein, "GM Is Building Plants in Developing Nations to Woo New Markets," *The Wall Street Journal* (August 4, 1997), A1, A5.

26. Claudia Eller and James Bates, "Not All Projections Bad for Overgrown Theater Chains," *Los Angeles Times* (September 8, 2000).

27. Evan Ramstad, "Compaq Stumbles Amid New Pressures on PCs," *The Wall Street Journal* (March 9, 1998), B1, B8.

28. Malcom Wheatley, "The Next Wave," *CIO* (August 15, 1998), 75–76+.

29. R. J. Schonberger, *Japanese Manufacturing Techniques: Nine Hidden Lessons in Simplicity* (New York: Free Press, 1982).

30. Cathy Lazere, "Taking Stock of Inventory: Beyond Mean and Lean," *CFO* (November 1997), 95–97.

31. Gaither and Frazier, *Operations Management*, 587.

32. Vincent A. Mabert, Ashok Soni, and M. S. Venkataramanan, "Enterprise Resource Planning: Common Myths Versus Evolving Reality," *Business Horizons* (May–June 2001), 69–76.

33. Luciana Beard and Stephen A. Butler, "Introducing JIT Manufacturing: It's Easier than You Think," *Business Horizons* (September–October 2000), 61–64.

34. Ronald Henkoff, "Delivering the Goods," *Fortune* (November 28, 1994), 64–78.

35. Noel P. Greis and John D. Kasarda, "Enterprise Logistics in the Information Era," *California Management Review* 39(4) (Summer 1997), 55–78.

36. David Rocks, "Dell's Second Web Revolution," *BusinessWeek e.biz* (September 18, 2000), EB62–EB63.

37. "Kanban: The Just-in-Time Japanese Inventory System," *Small Business Report* (February 1984), 69–71; and Richard C. Walleigh, "What's Your Excuse for Not Using JIT?" *Harvard Business Review* 64 (March–April 1986), 38–54.

38. Gaither and Frazier, *Operations Management*, 150–151.

39. Francis J. Quinn, "Logistics' New Customer Focus," *BusinessWeek* special advertising section (March 10, 1997).

40. Carol Vinzant, "SubmitOrder Thinks Inside the Box," *eCompany* (August 2000), 58–59; and Faith Keenan, "Logistics Gets a Little Respect," *BusinessWeek e.Biz* (November 20, 2000), EB112–EB116.

41. Faith Keenan, "Logistics Gets a Little Respect," and "One Smart Cookie," *BusinessWeek e.Biz* (November 20, 2000), EB120.

42. Emily Esterson, "First-Class Delivery," *Inc. Technology* (September 15, 1998), 89.

43. W. Bouce Chew, "No-Nonsense Guide to Measuring Productivity," *Harvard Business Review* (January–February 1988), 110–118.

44. Anna Bernasek, "Pattern for Prosperity," *Fortune* (October 2, 2000), 100–108.

45. The Outsourcing Institute, "Outsourcing: The New Midas Touch," *Business Week* (December 15, 1997), special advertising section.

46. W. E. Deming, *Quality, Productivity, and Competitive Position* (Cambridge, Mass.: Center for Advanced Engineering Study, MIT, 1982); and P. B. Crosby, *Quality Is Free* (New York: McGraw-Hill, 1979).

47. Charles E. Lucier and Janet D. Torsilieri, "Why Knowledge Programs Fail: A C.E.O.'s Guide to Managing Learning," *Strategy and Business* (Fourth Quarter 1997), 14–16, 21–27.

48. Bovet and Martha, "Change at the Core."

Chapter 20: Cannondale Has Finely Tuned Control Processes

ORGANIZATIONS TODAY FACE THE CONSTANT CHALLENGE OF controlling their activities to reduce waste, shorten time frames, and maximize profits. Their very survival depends on how well they can streamline processes and produce high-quality products from the outset. The high-performance bicycle industry is no different; it is extremely competitive among the top handful of companies. Known for its innovative designs, Connecticut-based Cannondale Corporation believes in control before, during, and after its design and manufacturing processes. In fact, to remain a profitable, viable, business, the organization needs to run as a finely tuned machine, with all parts contributing to overall goals.

Creativity drives and inspires Cannondale's teams, but continual innovation also requires checks and balances to ensure quality. After new bicycle designs are created using a computer-aided design (CAD) software program, teams review them carefully. And before a bicycle design is approved for production, design engineers check its accuracy and feasibility through a proofing process, the first step in quality control. The goal of proofing is to answer the question, Can the design be built as envisioned? Once they feel confident in the new design, engineers send the CAD system's design to a rapid prototyping machine, which constructs a plastic model so that engineers can see in three dimensions what they have planned. Overseeing this design process is the research and development project manager, who keeps an eye on design timelines and prototyping schedules. John Horn, a Cannondale R&D project manager says, "Engineers are perfectionists, but the R&D project manager must make sure the product gets to market when it's needed."

Once the design engineers have perfected a design, they transmit it electronically to the production teams in Bedford, Pennsylvania. Production engineers at the factory use the computer design to develop working samples using actual materials. New designs undergo 12 to 15 different tests to ensure impact strength, durability of the materials, and performance. Testing includes actually riding the prototype, as well as destructive testing to check the design's limits.

Manufacturing processes are controlled through precision machinery and empowered teams. Cannondale uses computer-guided laser machines to cut the frame's aluminum tubes to precise dimensions. Then the company relies on its craftsmen's experience and training. Because the strength of a bicycle frame depends on the quality of its welds, welders undergo a training and certification program to ensure that they meet quality standards. During manufacturing, any employee on the assembly line can speak up and stop production anytime to fix problems immediately. Once a frame has been constructed, Cannondale's coordinate measuring machine checks every measurement, and as a final control, a technician manually verifies the measurements. The frame is then sanded, cleaned, and hand painted, and protective finishes are applied.

Critical to bicycle design is actual testing of performance in the field. Cannondale seeks ideas from professional bicycle racers to maintain its cutting-edge designs. The company sponsors professional racing teams—two mountain bike racing teams, three road racing teams, and a triathlon team. The feedback that the racers supply is invaluable to the company's design and manufacturing processes. The company has won many quality awards through the years, among them *Bicycling* magazine's "Publisher's Award for Innovation," *VeloNews* magazine's "Technological Development of the Year Award," *Popular Science*'s "Best of What's New" award, *BusinessWeek*'s "Best New Products of the Year Award," *Design News* magazine's "Computer-Aided Design Award," and *Popular Mechanics*' "Design and Engineering Award."

Even with such acclaim, Cannondale is not content to rest. The company can change product lines as often as every six months to remain at the forefront of bicycle design and competitive in its market. And it has been revamping its inventory and manufacturing processes to streamline them for profitability. It recently switched its materials control computer software from a time-consuming program that took 9 hours and much manual intervention to complete to one that performed profitability analyses in $2\frac{1}{2}$ minutes. With such timely information, the company was able to review its processes and reduce its inventory stock by roughly 25 percent, which freed up money and resources to be used elsewhere—such as research and development. Cannondale's purchasing manager says that the new system has eliminated not only the time involved but many headaches as well. "Before, it took so much effort to work through the mountain of computer printouts to find what you were looking for that you just wouldn't do it." Now the company can generate that information in seconds and feed it back to critical decision makers. That kind of speed record is as critical to Cannondale as awards and races won.

Questions

1. Review the three types of control outlined in Exhibit 20.1 in Chapter 20. From the information provided, categorize the types of control Cannondale uses in its design and manufacturing processes as feedforward, concurrent, or feedback.
2. Would you say that Cannondale relies more on bureaucratic control or decentralized control to ensure quality?
3. Does Cannondale practice total quality management? Explain.

SOURCES: Interview with John Horn, Cannondale research and development project manager, April 9, 2002; Cannondale company Web site, http://www.cannondale.com, accessed March 22, 2002; Nick Wreden, "Doing Wheelies," *Consumer Goods*, May 2000, http://www.consumergoods.com; David J. Bak, "Skin and Bones, but Plenty Tough: Cannondale Combines CAD and Composites for a Breakthrough Bike," *Design News*, March 2, 1998, accessed at http://www.findarticles.com.

Chapter 21: Cannondale's Information Technology: From Office to Factory Floor—and Beyond

INFORMATION IS A VALUABLE RESOURCE FOR TODAY'S organizations, and information technology can tap its potential. Cannondale Corporation, the leading designer and manufacturer of high-performance aluminum bicycles and cycling accessories, believes in the strategic use of information technology. The company employs computer systems for everything from bicycle design, precision manufacturing, and quality control, to inventory and sales management. Cannondale's director of marketing and media relations, Tom Armstrong, says the goal of using information technology is to move faster than competitors. "We have tried to do that by innovating not only on the product front but in every other aspect as well. A lot of our own production engineering is about getting inside the development cycle of our competitors."

Cannondale's design engineers based in Connecticut use a computer-aided design (CAD) system called Pro/Engineer, a three-dimensional modeling program. With the program, designers can execute an idea and nearly instantly generate the measurements and parts needed for prototyping and mold making for manufacturing. They can also automatically create many different sizes in the same model style—to fit cyclists of many different shapes and sizes. With more than 80 different bicycle models currently, the CAD system gives the company flexibility—and a competitive edge.

After a design is finalized, the CAD system relays the design electronically to the production engineers in the company's Bedford, Pennsylvania, factories. Several years ago, the company saw the promise of Internet technology and harnessed it to track its manufacturing process. It installed an intranet in its Pennsylvania manufacturing plants to reduce the complexity and costs of the manufacturing system. The company's application engineer installed Web browser software on personal computers on the factory floor and replaced the keyboards with bar-code scanners and mouses for ease of input. As employees on the assembly line finish a step, they swipe the scanner across a bar-code on each bicycle. The company's managers can then capture information and track the manufacturing processes to ensure that parts and supplies are available when needed.

Cannondale also uses the Internet's communications capability to relay product specifications to its subsidiaries in the Netherlands, Japan, and Australia, which do final product assembly and finishing for overseas products. Before the use of the Web, workers sent hard-copy drawings to the subsidiaries, and employees there placed them in binders, which had to be updated periodically. That process was time-consuming and unreliable. Now, the company can instantly transmit its drawings electronically, complete with final paint colors. The result is consistency in product manufacturing, reduced time, and reduced costs.

Cannondale has focused most of its information technology system on personal computers running Windows software. This strategic decision simplifies the company's hardware and software systems and allows employees in all divisions to share the information in word processing, spreadsheet, and other programs. Cannondale recently began working with AimNet Solutions to handle its network infrastructure. AimNet will monitor the company's network and ensure it performs reliably. Cannondale's vice-president of information technology, Mike Dower, explains the strategic partnership this way: "Our strategy at Cannondale has been the same since our inception. We strive to create innovative, differentiated, high-performance products. With our passion for growth, . . . we couldn't afford to be distracted from that strategy . . . . We can stay focused on creating superior products" strategy . . . . We can stay focused on creating superior products" and let AimNet oversee the network infrastructure.

Cannondale has also reconstructed its inventory and sales management systems with information technology. With its new PC-based system, the company is able to track supplies more accurately and, as a result, reduced inventory stocks by approximately one quarter. The system may eventually be used to tie Cannondale's information system with its suppliers'. Cannondale sales representatives also gather data from retail partners about which models are selling well. They relay that information to the company's information system, and managers can switch manufacturing to needed models. This quick response to customer needs is important to Cannondale's success. The company has also begun using its corporate Web site to inform prospective customers about tailor-made bicycles. Currently, the company allows the customer to choose from over eight million possible frame and color variations available on the CAAD5 road frame. Giving customers such wide choices and ensuring the product they want is in their local store helps solidify their relationships with the company. Cannondale's Web site says, "Our focus is people—employees, customers, retailers, and our vendors—working together to accomplish our mission." And Cannondale uses sophisticated information technology systems to link those people into one big network.

Questions

1. What types of groupware does Cannondale use?
2. How important is Cannondale's information technology to its design and manufacturing?
3. Cannondale uses information technology in many ways to streamline its business processes. What other ways could it use them in the future?

SOURCES: Cannondale company Web site, *http://www.cannondale.com*, accessed March 22, 2002; "Cannondale Signs with Genosys Technology Management," *Business Wire*, October 29, 2001; Blaise Zerega, "Cannondale Rides Web for Productivity," *InfoWorld*, November 16, 1998, *http://www.infoworld.com*; David F. Carr, "Extending an Intranet to the Factory Floor," *Internet World*, September 21, 1998, accessed at *http://www.findarticles.com*.

Chapter 22: Cannondale's Consuming Passion for Perfection

YOU'D EXPECT A COMPANY THAT PRODUCES PREMIUM bicycles to care about its manufacturing processes. After all, the company knows how gears must mesh perfectly and how lightweight and durable frames must fit their riders' bodies seamlessly to form a single unit built for speed. You'd expect the company to realize how each system must perform flawlessly. You'd expect that, and you'd be right. Cannondale Corporation pursues its mission of producing innovative, quality products with nothing short of passion.

Cannondale's manufacturing organization produces physical goods—bicycles, cycling accessories, and off-road vehicles. And its operations strategy lies at the very heart of the company—it must produce its products quickly, efficiently, and well to survive. But Cannondale has another goal in mind besides mere survival: it strives to be an innovator. That focus places additional pressure on its operations, not only to support the company but to provide a competitive advantage.

As the Internet became more widely used in the mid-1990s, Cannondale foresaw its potential for supply chain management. Rather than install complex systems, the company used the simplicity of Web technology to manage its manufacturing processes. It installed personal computers directly on the factory floor and used scanners and bar-code technology to track the stages of the manufacturing process. Workers simply swipe the scanner over a bar code attached to a bicycle frame, and the system automatically updates a database. The database serves as a gateway to the company's material requirements planning (MRP) application. The database can also be accessed by management and Cannondale's overseas subsidiaries for decision making and planning.

Cannondale revamped its inventory control system in the late 1990s to allow it more flexibility. The old system created a one-to three-week delay in analyzing design or order changes—too long a time frame for a company that can change its product line every six months. Frustrated with the system's pokiness, the company invited vendor WebPlan to demonstrate its system using actual corporate data. The new system allowed the company to do an MRP run in $2\frac{1}{2}$ minutes. Cannondale expanded the system's use to scheduling and planning in purchasing, finance, and other departments. Such efficiency allowed the company to reduce its inventory drastically and use the dollars previously tied up in inventory for other purposes, especially product design. The company is also planning to link its suppliers to the system via the Internet. As Cannondale's purchasing manager says, "If [suppliers] can see our requirements on the Internet as fast as we can, then a lot of time can be saved. Buyers and planners don't have to spend time com- municating on every little detail, and parts production can begin when it's needed, not when it's communicated using a phone or fax." Integrating suppliers into the system provides a unified supply chain management system.

Cannondale's small production runs on its assembly lines allow the company to be more flexible in its manufacturing systems than other companies, which produce thousands of units at a time with robotics. Cannondale can quickly and easily change paint colors or customize decal designs to meet sales demand or customer preferences. It uses technology when appropriate for accuracy and consistency but also provides craftsmanship with skilled employees. Such flexibility enables Cannondale to ship a custom bicycle out of the factory within six weeks of a signed custom order. It can also meet its retail partners' specific demands more quickly.

Productivity is a key to Cannondale's success—through technology and its employees. From its Web-based factory floor software to its computer-aided design and manufacturing systems, the company has created a top-performing production line. With its redesigned production processes, the company expanded from manufacturing one product line of about 50 bike models to six lines with 120 models. But the constant push for design innovation and new materials keeps the company on its toes. Sophisticated bicycles must balance strength, flexibility, and weight for peak performance. Cannondale is meeting those challenges head on and aiming to change the bicycle world at the same time. As the company's Web site says, "We devise flexible manufacturing processes that enable us to deliver those innovative, quality products to the market quickly and then back them with excellent customer service." From its early beginnings in a loft above a pickle factory, Cannondale has been racing toward perfection for 30 years, and it hasn't tired yet.

Questions

1. From this video case and those for Chapters 19 through 21, identify the inputs to Cannondale's manufacturing organization.
2. Review the basic production layouts in Exhibit 22.4. Which type of layout does Cannondale have?
3. How does Cannondale's operations support its production of high-performance bicycles?

SOURCES: Interview with John Horn, Cannondale research and development project manager, April 9, 2002; Nick Wreden, "Doing Wheelies," *Consumer Goods,* May 2000, *http://www.consumergoods.com*; David F. Carr, "Extending an Intranet to the Factory Floor," *Internet World,* September 21, 1998, accessed at *http://www.findarticles.com.*

Part 6: At Ford, Quality Is Job 1—Again

A FEW YEARS AGO, FORD RAN AN ADVERTISING CAMPAIGN whose motto was "At Ford, Quality Is Job 1." The company boasted top quality not only in the manufacture of its trucks and cars but also in its service. In the summer of 2000, the old slogan came back to haunt the company, as it became evident that literally millions of tires—made by Firestone—on Ford's popular SUVs including the Explorer, were separating and shredding, causing serious and even fatal accidents. Even though Ford didn't manufacture the tires, those tires were installed on Ford vehicles; and the press, general public, and even Congress had a hard time distinguishing between the two. The situation was exacerbated as Bridgestone/Firestone accused Ford of building inferior vehicles. Finger pointing between the two organizations, centered on quality issues, continued for months as the tires were recalled and replaced. A year later, the National Highway Traffic Safety Administration reported that the defective tires, not the Ford vehicles, were to blame for the crashes; but the damage was already done in the public's eyes. "I think as long as this battle is going on in the press nobody is going to win," noted Anne Sceia Klein, a public relations expert in Philadelphia. "The general public will walk away from [the Ford Explorer] if they can't sort it out."

Maintaining the quality of goods and services is a major part of the controlling function in an organization. Unfortunately, even if a quality problem is only a perceived one—or is exaggerated by publicity—damage to the organization's reputation can occur, and ultimately sales can drop. Ford faced both real and perceived quality issues in its struggle with the tire/SUV problem. Former CEO Jacques Nasser disputed Firestone's charges that the Explorer was at least partially to blame for the rollover crashes. "If you happen to be in a vehicle that had a tread separation, and that vehicle happens to be a compact SUV, you'd be much safer in an Explorer," argued Nasser. "If those Firestone tires were on other SUVs, the rollover instance would be much worse."

Some experts believe that the right information technology, which would have allowed greater knowledge sharing between Bridgestone/Firestone and Ford, and better designed production systems could have prevented the mismatch of tires and vehicles. In fact, Ford already had in place its own Best Practices Replication Process, which was designed to improve the efficiency of various parts of the manufacturing process. In 1995, Dale McKeehan, then vice president of manufacturing, called together his vehicle operations people, including the heads of body construction, painting, and final assembly and said, "Figure out a way to share best practices." Stan Kwiecien, then head of a group working on plant productivity recalls, "So we figured it out. We're engineers." Around the same time, McKeehan met with another manager, Dar Wolford, who was using early information technology to improve efficiency at Ford plants. McKeehan introduced Wolford to Kwiecien, and Ford's Best Practices Replication Process was born. Within four years, more than 2,800 proven superior practices had been shared among Ford's widespread manufacturing facilities, at a total documented value of $850 million. But knowledge sharing did not extend outside the company, so Ford and Firestone never communicated with each other about potential problems with the pairing of their two products.

Around the time of the tire recall, Ford began training managers in a program called Six Sigma, which is a system for continuous improvement in quality and efficiency to help the organization avoid manufacturing mistakes. Six Sigma uses statistical analysis to find the root of a problem that other methods can't seem to locate. For instance, the company's new Lincoln LS sedan had trouble starting on the first try. Using Six Sigma, an engineering team traced the problem to a screw that wasn't properly tightened. How did so many of these screws come off the assembly line loose? Because workers were using the wrong power tool to tighten them. Ford managers claim that Six Sigma saved the company $52 million in errors the first year, with another $300 million projected for the following year.

Feedback is a vital component of control, and recently Ford faced a hard feedback fact: although customers who participated in marketing surveys consistently said they wanted more environmentally responsible vehicles, they are unwilling to pay a higher sticker price for them. Meanwhile, Ford received feedback from the Insurance Institute for Highway Safety in the form of poor results from low-speed crash tests designed to test bumper damage. Still, the Ford Explorer remains the most popular sport utility vehicle on the market, accounting for 20 percent of Ford Motor Company's sales. And Bill Ford remains firm in his commitment to improve the overall quality of his company's vehicles, including reducing their impact on the environment. As for his competitors, Ford notes, "If we didn't provide [the SUV], someone else would, and they wouldn't provide it as responsibly as we do." Already, Ford Motor Company voluntarily builds its SUVs to emit less tailpipe pollution than allowed by law. If Bill Ford has his way, quality will indeed be job 1 at the century-old company for the next one hundred years.

Questions

1. Do you think that Ford Motor Company would benefit from open-book management? Why or why not?
2. In what ways might Ford Motor Company further use information technology to manage knowledge and create a competitive strategy?
3. Which stage of operations strategy would you say is illustrated by Ford Motor Company in this case? Why?

SOURCES: Nedra Pickler, "Explorer Fender Benders Costly," Auto.com, November 30, 2002, http://www.auto.com; "Jacques Knifed," The Economist, November 3, 2001, http://www.economist.com; Alex Taylor III, "What's Behind Ford's Fall?" Fortune, October 29, 2001, http://www.fortune.com; Joann Muller, "Ford: Why It's Worse Than You Think," BusinessWeek Online, June 25, 2001, http://www.businessweek.com; "Ford Goes on Offensive to Explain Massive Tire Replacement Plan," Fox News, May 24, 2001, http://www.foxnews.com; Thomas A. Stewart, "Knowledge Worth $1.25 Billion," Fortune, November 27, 2001, http://www.fortune.com; Keith Bradsher, "Ford Is Conceding S.U.V. Drawbacks," The New York Times, May 12, 2000, http://www.serv.com.

Glossary

360-degree feedback A process that uses multiple raters, including self-rating, to appraise employee performance and guide development.

accountability The fact that the people with authority and responsibility are subject to reporting and justifying task outcomes to those above them in the chain of command.

activity-based costing (ABC) A control system that identifies the various activities needed to provide a product and allocates costs accordingly.

activity ratio A financial ratio that measures the organization's internal performance with respect to key activities defined by management.

adjourning The stage of team development in which members prepare for the team's disbandment.

administrative model A decision-making model that describes how managers actually make decisions in situations characterized by nonprogrammed decisions, uncertainty, and ambiguity.

administrative principles A subfield of the classical management perspective that focused on the total organization rather than the individual worker, delineating the management functions of planning, organizing, commanding, coordinating, and controlling.

affirmative action A policy requiring employers to take positive steps to guarantee equal employment opportunities for people within protected groups.

ambiguity The goal to be achieved or the problem to be solved is unclear, alternatives are difficult to define, and information about outcomes is unavailable.

Angel financing Financing provided by a wealthy individual who believes in the idea for a start-up and provides personal funds and advice to help the business get started.

application form A device for collecting information about an applicant's education, previous job experience, and other background characteristics.

assessment center A technique for selecting individuals with high managerial potential based on their performance on a series of simulated managerial tasks.

attitude A cognitive and affective evaluation that predisposes a person to act in a certain way.

attributions Judgments about what caused a person's behavior—either characteristics of the person or of the situation.

authoritarianism The belief that power and status differences *should* exists within the organization.

authority The formal and legitimate right of a manager to make decisions, issue orders, and allocate resources to achieve organizationally desired outcomes.

autocratic leader A leader who tends to centralize authority and rely on legitimate, reward, and coercive power to manage subordinates.

balance sheet A financial statement that shows the firm's financial position with respect to assets and liabilities at a specific point in time.

balanced scorecard A comprehensive management control system that balances traditional financial measures with measures of customer service, internal business processes, and the organization's capacity for learning and growth.

B2B marketplace An electronic marketplace set up by an intermediary where buyers and sellers meet.

BCG matrix A concept developed by the Boston Consulting Group that evaluates SBUs with respect to the dimensions of business growth rate and market share.

behavior modification The set of techniques by which reinforcement theory is used to modify human behavior.

behavioral sciences approach A subfield of the humanistic management perspective that applies social science in an organizational context, drawing from economics, psychology, sociology, and other disciplines.

behaviorally anchored rating scale (BARS) A rating technique that relates an employee's performance to specific job-related incidents.

benchmarking The continuous process of measuring products, services, and practices against major competitors or industry leaders.

biculturalism The sociocultural skills and attitudes used by racial minorities to move back and forth between the dominant culture and their own ethnic or racial culture.

Big Five personality factors Dimensions that describe an individual's extroversion, agreeableness, conscientiousness, emotional stability, and openness to experience.

bottom-up budgeting A budgeting process in which lower-level managers budget their departments' resource needs and pass them up to top management for approval.

boundary-spanning roles Roles assumed by people and/or departments that link and coordinate the organization with key elements in the external environment.

bounded rationality The concept that people have the time and cognitive ability to process only a limited amount of information on which to base decisions.

bureaucratic control The use of rules, policies, hierarchy of authority, reward systems, and other formal devices to influence employee behavior and assess performance.

bureaucratic organizations A subfield of the classical management perspective that emphasized management on an impersonal, rational basis through such elements as clearly defined authority and responsibility, formal recordkeeping, and separation of management and ownership.

business incubator An innovation that provides shared office space, management support services, and management advice to entrepreneurs.

business-level strategy The level of strategy concerned with the question "How do we compete?" Pertains to each business unit or product line within the organization.

business plan A document specifying the business details prepared by an entrepreneur in preparation for opening a new business.

CAD A production technology in which computers perform new-product design.

CAM A production technology in which computers help guide and control the manufacturing system.

capacity planning The determination and adjustment of the organization's ability to produce products and services to match customer demand.

capital budget A budget that plans and reports investments in major assets to be depreciated over several years.

cash budget A budget that estimates and reports cash flows on a daily or weekly basis to ensure that the company has sufficient cash to meet its obligations.

cellular layout A facilities layout in which machines dedicated to sequences of production are grouped into cells in accordance with group-technology principles.

central planning department A group of planning specialists who develop plans for the organization as a whole and its major divisions and departments and typically report to the president or CEO.

centralization The location of decision authority near top organizational levels.

centralized network A team communication structure in which team members communicate through a single individual to solve problems or make decisions.

ceremony A planned activity that makes up a special event and is conducted for the benefit of an audience.

certainty All the information the decision maker needs is fully available.

chain of command An unbroken line of authority that links all individuals in the organization and specifies who reports to whom.

change agent An OD specialist who contracts with an organization to facilitate change.

changing An intervention stage of organizational development in which individuals experiment with new workplace behavior.

channel The carrier of a communication.

channel richness The amount of information that can be transmitted during a communication episode.

charismatic leader A leader who has the ability to motivate subordinates to transcend their expected performance.

chief ethics officer A company executive who oversees ethics and legal compliance.

classical model A decision-making model based on the assumption that managers should make logical decisions that will be in the organization's best economic interests.

classical perspective A management perspective that emerged during the nineteenth and early twentieth centuries that emphasized a rational, scientific approach to the study of management and sought to make organizations efficient operating machines.

closed system A system that does not interact with the external environment.

coalition An informal alliance among managers who support a specific goal.

code of ethics A formal statement of the organization's values regarding ethics and social issues.

coercive power Power that stems from the authority to punish or recommend punishment.

cognitive dissonance A condition in which two attitudes or a behavior and an attitude conflict.

collectivism A preference for a tightly knit social framework in which individuals look after one another and organizations protect their members' interests.

committee A long-lasting, sometimes permanent team in the organization structure created to deal with tasks that recur regularly.

communication The process by which information is exchanged and understood by two or more people, usually with the intent to motivate or influence behavior.

compensation Monetary payments (wages, salaries) and nonmonetary goods/commodities (benefits, vacations) used to reward employees.

compensatory justice The concept that individuals should be compensated for the cost of their injuries by the party responsible and also that individuals should not be held responsible for matters over which they have no control.

competitors Other organizations in the same industry or type of business that provide goods or services to the same set of customers.

conceptual skill The cognitive ability to see the organization as a whole and the relationship among its parts.

concurrent control Control that consists of monitoring ongoing activities to ensure their consistency with standards.

conflict Antagonistic interaction in which one party attempts to thwart the intentions or goals of another.

consideration A type of leader behavior that describes the extent to which a leader is sensitive to subordinates, respects their ideas and feelings, and establishes mutual trust.

content theories A group of theories that emphasize the needs that motivate people.

contingency approach A model of leadership that describes the relationship between leadership styles and specific organizational situations.

contingency plans Plans that define company responses to specific situations, such as emergencies, setbacks, or unexpected conditions.

contingency view An extension of the humanistic perspective in which the successful resolution of organizational problems is thought to depend on managers' identification of key variables in the situation at hand.

contingent workers People who work for an organization, but not on a permanent or full-time basis, including temporary placements, contracted professionals, or leased employees.

continuous improvement The implementation of a large number of small, incremental improvements in all areas of the organization on an ongoing basis.

continuous process production A type of technology involving mechanization of the entire work flow and nonstop production.

continuous reinforcement schedule A schedule in which every occurrence of the desired behavior is reinforced.

coordination The quality of collaboration across departments.

coordination costs The time and energy needed to coordinate the activities of a team to enable it to perform its task.

core competence A business activity that an organization does particularly well in comparison to competitors.

corporate-level strategy The level of strategy concerned with the question "What business are we in?" Pertains to the organization as a whole and the combination of business units and product lines that make it up.

corporate university An in-house training and education facility that offers broad-based learning opportunities for employees.

corporation An artificial entity created by the state and existing apart from its owners.

cost leadership A type of competitive strategy with which the organization aggressively seeks efficient facilities, cuts costs, and employs tight cost controls to be more efficient than competitors.

countertrade The barter of products for other products rather than their sale for currency.

creativity The generation of novel ideas that may meet perceived needs or offer opportunities for the organization.

cross-functional team A group of employees from various functional departments that meet as a team to resolve mutual problems.

cultural leader A manager who uses signals and symbols to influence corporate culture.

culture The set of key values, beliefs, understandings, and norms that members of a society or an organization share.

culture gap The difference between an organization's desired cultural norms and values and actual norms and values.

culture shock Feelings of confusion, disorientation, and anxiety that result from being immersed in a foreign culture.

culture/people change A change in employees' values, norms, attitudes, beliefs, and behavior.

customer relationship management (CRM) systems Systems that help companies track customers' interaction with the firm and allow employees to call up information on past transactions.

customers People and organizations in the environment who acquire goods or services from the organization.

data Raw, unsummarized, and unanalyzed facts and figures.

data mining Software that uses sophisticated decision-making processes to search raw data for patterns and relationships that may be significant.

data warehousing The use of a huge database that combines all of a company's data and allows users to access the data directly, create reports, and obtain answers to what-if questions.

debt financing Borrowing money that has to be repaid at a later date in order to start a business.

decentralization The location of decision authority near lower organizational levels.

decentralized control The use of organization culture, group norms, and a focus on goals, rather than rules and procedures, to foster compliance with organizational goals.

decentralized network A team communication structure in which team members freely communicate with one another and arrive at decisions together.

decentralized planning Managers work with planning experts to develop their own goals and plans.

decision A choice made from available alternatives.

decision making The process of identifying problems and opportunities and then resolving them.

decision style Differences among people with respect to how they perceive problems and make decisions.

decision support system (DSS) An interactive, computer-based system that uses decision models and specialized databases to support organization decision makers.

decode To translate the symbols used in a message for the purpose of interpreting its meaning.

delegation The process managers use to transfer authority and responsibility to positions below them in the hierarchy.

democratic leader A leader who delegates authority to others, encourages participation, and relies on expert and referent power to manage subordinates.

departmentalization The basis on which individuals are grouped into departments and departments into total organizations.

dependent demand inventory Inventory in which item demand is related to the demand for other inventory items.

descriptive An approach that describes how managers actually make decisions rather than how they should.

devil's advocate A decision-making technique in which an individual is assigned the role of challenging the assumptions and assertions made by the group to prevent premature consensus.

diagnosis The step in the decision-making process in which managers analyze underlying causal factors associated with the decision situation.

dialogue A group communication process aimed at creating a culture based

on collaboration, fluidity, trust, and commitment to shared goals.

differentiation A type of competitive strategy with which the organization seeks to distinguish its products or services from competitors'.

digital technology Technology characterized by use of the Internet and other digital processes to conduct or support business operations.

direct investing An entry strategy in which the organization is involved in managing its production facilities in a foreign country.

discretionary responsibility Organizational responsibility that is voluntary and guided by the organization's desire to make social contributions not mandated by economics, law, or ethics.

discrimination The hiring or promoting of applicants based on criteria that are not job relevant.

distribution Moving finished products to customers; also called *order fulfillment*.

distributive justice The concept that different treatment of people should not be based on arbitrary characteristics. In the case of substantive differences, people should be treated differently in proportion to the differences among them.

diversity awareness training Special training designed to make people aware of their own prejudices and stereotypes.

divisional structure An organization structure in which departments are grouped based on similar organizational outputs.

downward communication Messages sent from top management down to subordinates.

dual role A role in which the individual both contributes to the team's task and supports members' emotional needs.

e-business Work an organization does using electronic linkages; any business that takes place by digital processes over a computer network rather than in a physical space.

e-commerce Business exchanges or transactions that occur electronically.

E→P expectancy Expectancy that putting effort into a given task will lead to high performance.

economic dimension The dimension of the general environment representing the overall economic health of the country or region in which the organization functions.

economic forces Forces that affect the availability, production, and distribution of a society's resources among competing users.

economic order quantity (EOQ) An inventory management technique designed to minimize the total of ordering and holding costs for inventory items.

economic value-added (EVA) system A control system that measures performance in terms of after-tax profits minus the cost of capital invested in tangible assets.

effectiveness The degree to which the organization achieves a stated goal.

efficiency The use of minimal resources—raw materials, money, and people—to produce a desired volume of output.

electronic data interchange (EDI) A network that links the computer systems of buyers and sellers to allow the transmission of structured data primarily for ordering, distribution, and payables and receivables.

employee network groups Groups based on social identity, such as gender or race, and organized by employees to focus on concerns of employees from that group.

employment test A written or computer-based test designed to measure a particular attribute such as intelligence or aptitude.

empowerment The delegation of power and authority to subordinates.

encode To select symbols with which to compose a message.

enterprise resource planning (ERP) Systems that unite a company's major business functions—order processing, product design, purchasing, inventory, etc.; a networked information system that collects, processes, and provides information about an organization's entire enterprise, from identification of customer needs and receipt of orders to distribution of products and receipt of payments.

entrepreneur Someone who recognizes a viable idea for a business product or service and carries it out.

entrepreneurship The process of initiating a business venture, organizing the necessary resources, and assuming the associated risks and rewards.

entropy The tendency for a system to run down and die.

equity A situation that exists when the ratio of one person's outcomes to inputs equals that of another's.

equity financing Financing that consists of funds that are invested in exchange for ownership in the company.

equity theory A process theory that focuses on individuals' perceptions of how fairly they are treated relative to others.

ERG theory A modification of the needs hierarchy theory that proposes three categories of needs: existence, relatedness, and growth.

escalating commitment Continuing to invest time and resources in a failing decision.

ethical dilemma A situation that arises when all alternative choices or behaviors have been deemed undesirable because of potentially negative ethical consequence, making it difficult to distinguish right from wrong.

ethics The code of moral principles and values that govern the behaviors of a person or group with respect to what is right or wrong.

ethics committee A group of executives assigned to oversee the organization's ethics by ruling on questionable issues and disciplining violators.

ethics training Training programs to help employees deal with ethical questions and values.

ethnocentrism A cultural attitude marked by the tendency to regard one's own culture as superior to others; the belief that one's own group or subculture is inherently superior to other groups or cultures.

ethnorelativism The belief that groups and subcultures are inherently equal.

euro A single European currency that replaced the currencies of 11 European nations.

executive information system (EIS) A management information system designed to facilitate strategic decision making at the highest levels of management by providing executives with easy access to timely and relevant information.

exit interview An interview conducted with departing employees to determine the reasons for their termination.

expatriates Employees who live and work in a country other than their own.

expectancy theory A process theory that proposes that motivation depends on individuals' expectations about their ability to perform tasks and receive desired rewards.

expense budget A budget that outlines the anticipated and actual expenses for each responsibility center.

expert power Power that stems from special knowledge of or skill in the tasks performed by subordinates.

exporting An entry strategy in which the organization maintains its production facilities within its home country and transfers its products for sale in foreign markets.

external locus of control The belief by individuals that their future is not within their control but rather is influenced by external forces.

extranet A company communications system that gives access to suppliers, partners, and others outside the company; an external communications system that uses the Internet and is shared by two or more organizations.

extrinsic reward A reward given by another person.

feedback A response by the receiver to the sender's communication; using communication and evaluation to help the organization learn and improve.

feedback control Control that focuses on the organization's outputs; also called *postaction* or *output control*.

feedforward control Control that focuses on human, material, and financial resources flowing into the organization; also called *preliminary* or *preventive quality control*.

femininity A cultural preference for cooperation, group decision making, and quality of life.

finished-goods inventory Inventory consisting of items that have passed through the complete production process but have yet to be sold.

first-line manager A manager who is at the first or second management level and is directly responsible for the production of goods and services.

fixed-position layout A facilities layout in which the product remains in one location and the required tasks and equipment are brought to it.

flat structure A management structure characterized by an overall broad span of control and relatively few hierarchical levels.

flexible manufacturing system A small- or medium-sized automated production line that can be adapted to produce more than one product line.

focus A type of competitive strategy that emphasizes concentration on a specific regional market or buyer group.

force field analysis The process of determining which forces drive and which resist a proposed change.

formal communication channel A communication channel that flows within the chain of command or task responsibility defined by the organization.

formal team A team created by the organization as part of the formal organization structure.

formalization The written documentation used to direct and control employees.

franchising A form of licensing in which an organization provides its foreign franchisees with a complete assortment of materials and services; an arrangement by which the owner of a product or service allows others to purchase the right to distribute the product or service with help from the owner.

free rider A person who benefits from team membership but does not make a proportionate contribution to the team's work.

frustration-regression principle The idea that failure to meet a high-order need may cause a regression to an already satisfied lower-order need.

functional-level strategy The level of strategy concerned with the question "How do we support the business-level strategy?" Pertains to all of the organization's major departments.

functional manager A manager who is responsible for a department that performs a single functional task and has employees with similar training and skills.

functional structure An organization structure in which positions are grouped into departments based on similar skills, expertise, and resource use.

fundamental attribution error The tendency to underestimate the influence of external factors on another's behavior and to overestimate the influence on internal factors.

General Adaptation Syndrome (GAS) The physiological response to a stressor, beginning with an alarm response, continuing to resistance, and sometimes ending in exhaustion if the stressor continues beyond the person's ability to cope.

general environment The layer of the external environment that affects the organization indirectly.

general manager A manager who is responsible for several departments that perform different functions.

glass ceiling Invisible barrier that separates women and minorities from top management positions.

global outsourcing Engaging in the international division of labor so as to obtain the cheapest sources of labor and supplies regardless of country; also called global sourcing.

global team A work team made up of members of different nationalities whose activities span multiple countries; may operate as a virtual team or meet face to face.

globalization The standardization of product design and advertising strategies throughout the world.

goal A desired future state that the organization attempts to realize.

grand strategy The general plan of major action by which an organization intends to achieve its long-term goals.

grapevine An informal, person-to-person communication network of employees that is not officially sanctioned by the organization.

Greenfield venture The most risky type of direct investment, whereby a company builds a subsidiary from scratch in a foreign country.

groupware Software that works on a computer network or the Internet to facilitate information sharing, collaborative work, and group decision making.

halo effect An overall impression of a person or situation based on one characteristic, either favorable or unfavorable; a type of rating error that occurs when an employee receives the same rating on all dimensions regardless of his or her performance on individual ones.

Hawthorne studies A series of experiments on worker productivity begun in 1924 at the Hawthorne plant of Western Electric Company in Illinois; attributed employees' increased output to managers' better treatment of them during the study.

hero A figure who exemplifies the deeds, character, and attributes of a corporate culture.

hierarchy of needs theory A content theory that proposes that people are motivated by five categories of needs—physiological, safety, belongingness, esteem, and self-actualization—that exist in a hierarchical order.

high-context culture A culture in which communication is used to enhance personal relationships.

horizontal communication The lateral or diagonal exchange of messages among peers or coworkers.

horizontal linkage model An approach to product change that emphasizes shared development of innovations among several departments.

horizontal team A formal team composed of employees from about the same hierarchical level but from different areas of expertise.

human capital The economic value of the knowledge, experience, skills, and capabilities of employees.

human relations movement A movement in management thinking and practice that emphasized satisfaction of employees' basic needs as the key to increased worker productivity.

human resource information system An integrated computer system designed to provide data and information used in HR planning and decision making.

human resource management (HRM) Activities undertaken to attract, develop, and maintain an effective workforce within an organization.

human resource planning The forecasting of human resource needs and the projected matching of individuals with expected job vacancies.

human resources perspective A management perspective that suggests jobs should be designed to meet higher-level needs by allowing workers to use their full potential.

human skill The ability to work with and through other people and to work effectively as a group member.

hygiene factors Factors that involve the presence or absence of job dissatisfiers, including working conditions, pay, company policies, and interpersonal relationships.

idea champion A person who sees the need for and champions productive change within the organization.

idea incubator An in-house program that provides a safe harbor where ideas from employees throughout the organization can be developed without interference from company bureaucracy or politics.

implementation The step in the decision-making process that involves using managerial, administrative, and persuasive abilities to translate the chosen alternative into action.

income statement A financial statement that summarizes the firm's financial performance for a given time interval; sometimes called a profit-and-loss statement.

individualism A preference for a loosely knit social framework in which individuals are expected to take care of themselves.

individualism approach The ethical concept that acts are moral when they promote the individual's best long-term interests, which ultimately leads to the greater good.

informal communication channel A communication channel that exists outside formally authorized channels without regard for the organization's hierarchy of authority.

information Data that have been converted into a meaningful and useful context for the receiver.

information reporting system A system that organizes information in the form of prespecified reports that managers use in day-to-day decision making.

information technology The hardware, software, telecommunications, database management, and other technologies used to store, process, and distribute information.

infrastructure A country's physical facilities that support economic activities.

initiating structure A type of leader behavior that describes the extent to which a leader is task oriented and directs subordinates' work activities toward goal achievement.

instant messaging Technology that provides a way to send quick notes from PC to PC over the Internet so two people who are online at the same time can communicate instantly.

interactive leadership A leadership style characterized by values such as inclusion, collaboration, relationship building, and caring.

interdependence The extent to which departments depend on each other for resources or materials to accomplish their tasks.

internal environment The environment within the organization's boundaries.

internal locus of control The belief by individuals that their future is within their control and that external forces will have little influence.

international dimension Portion of the external environment that represents events originating in foreign countries as well as opportunities for American companies in other countries.

international management The management of business operations conducted in more than one country.

Internet A global collection of computer networks linked together for the exchange of data and information.

intranet An internal communication system that uses the technology and standards of the Internet but is accessible only to people within the organization.

intrinsic reward The satisfaction received in the process of performing an action.

intuition The immediate comprehension of a decision situation based on past experience but without conscious thought.

inventory The goods that the organization keeps on hand for use in the production process up to the point of selling the final products to customers.

ISO 9000 A set of international standards for quality management, setting uniform guidelines for processes to ensure that products conform to customer requirements.

job analysis The systematic process of gathering and interpreting information about the essential duties, tasks, and responsibilities of a job.

job characteristics model A model of job design that comprises core job dimensions, critical psychological states, and employee growth-need strength.

job description A concise summary of the specific tasks and responsibilities of a particular job.

job design The application of motivational theories to the structure of work for improving productivity and satisfaction.

job enlargement A job design that combines a series of tasks into one new, broader job to give employees variety and challenge.

job enrichment A job design that incorporates achievement, recognition, and other high-level motivators into the work.

job evaluation The process of determining the value of jobs within an organization through an examination of job content.

job rotation A job design that systematically moves employees from one job to another to provide them with variety and stimulation.

job satisfaction A positive attitude toward one's job.

job simplification A job design whose purpose is to improve task efficiency by reducing the number of tasks a single person must do.

job specification An outline of the knowledge, skills, education, and physical abilities needed to adequately perform a job.

joint venture A strategic alliance or program by two or more organizations.

justice approach The ethical concept that moral decisions must be based on standards of equity, fairness, and impartiality.

just-in-time (JIT) inventory system An inventory control system that schedules materials to arrive precisely when they are needed on a production line.

knowledge management The efforts to systematically find, organize, and make available a company's intellectual capital and to foster a culture of continuous learning and knowledge sharing; the process of systematically gathering knowledge, making it widely available throughout the organization, and fostering a culture of learning.

knowledge management portal A single point of access for employees to multiple sources of information that provides personalized access on the corporate intranet.

labor market The people available for hire by the organization.

large-group intervention An approach that brings together participants from all parts of the organization (and may include key outside stakeholders as well) to discuss problems or opportunities and plan for major change.

law of effect The assumption that positively reinforced behavior tends to be repeated and unreinforced or negatively reinforced behavior tends to be inhibited.

leadership The ability to influence people toward the attainment of organizational goals.

leadership grid A two-dimensional leadership theory that measures a leader's concern for people and concern for production.

leading The management function that involves the use of influence to motivate employees to achieve the organization's goals.

learning A change in behavior or performance as the result of experience.

learning organization An organization in which everyone is engaged in identifying and solving problems, enabling the organization to continuously experiment, improve, and increase its capability.

legal-political dimension The dimension of the general environment that includes federal, state, and local government regulations and political activities designed to influence company behavior.

legitimate power Power that stems from a formal management position in an organization and the authority granted to it.

licensing An entry strategy in which an organization in one country makes certain resources available to companies in another in order to participate in the production and sale of its products abroad.

line authority A form of authority in which individuals in management positions have the formal power to direct and control immediate subordinates.

liquidity ratio A financial ratio that indicates the organization's ability to meet its current debt obligations.

listening The skill of receiving messages to accurately grasp facts and feelings to interpret the genuine meaning.

locus of control The tendency to place the primary responsibility for one's success or failure either within oneself (internally) or on outside forces (externally).

logistics The activities required to physically move materials into the company's operations facility and to move finished products to customers.

long-term orientation A greater concern for the future and high value on thrift and perseverance.

low-context culture A culture in which communication is used to exchange facts and information.

LPC scale A questionnaire designed to measure relationship-oriented versus task-oriented leadership style according to the leader's choice of adjectives for describing the "least preferred coworker."

Machiavellianism The tendency to direct much of one's behavior toward the acquisition of power and the manipulation of others for personal gain.

management The attainment of organizational goals in an effective and efficient manner through planning, organizing, leading, and controlling organizational resources.

management by objectives A method of management whereby managers and employees define goals for every department, project, and person and use them to monitor subsequent performance.

management by wandering around (MBWA) A communication technique in which managers interact directly with workers to exchange information.

management information system (MIS) A computer-based system that provides information and support for effective managerial decision making

management science perspective A management perspective that emerged after World War II and applied mathematics, statistics, and other quantitative techniques to managerial problems.

manufacturing organization An organization that produces physical goods.

market entry strategy An organizational strategy for entering a foreign market.

market value-added (MVA) system A control system that measures the stock market's estimate of the value of a company's past and expected capital investment projects.

masculinity A cultural preference for achievement, heroism, assertiveness, work centrality, and material success.

mass production A type of technology characterized by the production of a large volume of products with the same specifications.

matching model An employee selection approach in which the organization and the applicant attempt to match each other's needs, interests, and values.

material requirements planning (MRP) A dependent demand inventory planning and control system that schedules the precise amount of all materials required to support the production of desired end products.

matrix approach An organization structure that utilizes functional and divisional chains of command simultaneously in the same part of the organization.

matrix boss A product or functional boss, responsible for one side of the matrix.

mediation The process of using a third party to settle a dispute.

mentor A higher-ranking, senior organizational member who is committed to providing upward mobility and support to a protégé's professional career.

merger The combination of two or more organizations into one.

message The tangible formulation of an idea to be sent to a receiver.

middle manager A manager who works at the middle levels of the organization and is responsible for major departments.

mission The organization's reason for existence.

mission statement A broadly stated definition of the organization's basic business scope and operations that distinguishes it from similar types of organizations.

modular approach A manufacturing company uses outside suppliers to provide the large components of the product, which are then assembled into a final product by a few workers.

monoculture A culture that accepts only one way of doing things and one set of values and beliefs.

moral-rights approach The ethical concept that moral decisions are those that best maintain the rights of those people affected by them.

most favored nation A term describing a GATT clause that calls for member countries to grant other member countries the most favorable treatment they accord any country concerning imports and exports.

motivation The arousal, direction, and persistence of behavior.

motivators Factors that influence job satisfaction based on fulfillment of high-level needs such as achievement, recognition, responsibility, and opportunity for growth.

multicultural teams Teams made up of members from diverse national, social, ethnic, and cultural backgrounds.

multidomestic strategy The modification of product design and advertising strategies to suit the specific needs of individual countries.

multinational corporation (MNC) An organization that receives more than 25 percent of its total sales revenues from operations outside the parent company's home country; also called global corporation or transnational corporation.

need to achieve A human quality linked to entrepreneurship in which people are motivated to excel and pick situations in which success is likely.

network structure An organization structure that disaggregates major functions to separate companies that are brokered by a small headquarters organization.

neutralizer A situational variable that counteracts a leadership style and prevents the leader from displaying certain behaviors.

new-venture fund A fund providing resources from which individuals and groups can draw to develop new ideas, products, or businesses.

new-venture team A unit separate from the mainstream of the organization that is responsible for developing and initiating innovations.

nonparticipator role A role in which the individual contributes little to either the task or members' socioemotional needs.

nonprogrammed decision A decision made in response to a situation that is unique, is poorly defined and largely unstructured, and has important consequences for the organization.

nonverbal communication A communication transmitted through actions and behaviors rather than through words.

norm A standard of conduct that is shared by team members and guides their behavior.

normative An approach that defines how a decision maker should make decisions and provides guidelines for reaching an ideal outcome for the organization.

norming The stage of team development in which conflicts developed during the storming stage are resolved and team harmony and unity emerge.

office automation systems Systems that combine modern hardware and software to handle the tasks of publishing and distributing information.

on-the-job training (OJT) A type of training in which an experienced employee "adopts" a new employee to teach him or her how to perform job duties.

open-book management Sharing financial information and results with all employees in the organization.

open communication Sharing all types of information throughout the company, across functional and hierarchical levels.

open system A system that interacts with the external environment.

operational goals Specific, measurable results expected from departments, work groups, and individuals within the organization.

operational plans Plans developed at the organization's lower levels that specify action steps toward achieving operational goals and that support tactical planning activities.

operations information system A computer-based information system that supports a company's day-to-day operations.

operations management The field of management that focuses on the physical production of goods or services and uses specialized techniques for solving manufacturing problems.

operations strategy The recognition of the importance of operations to the firm's success and the involvement of operations managers in the organization's strategic planning.

opportunity A situation in which managers see potential organizational accomplishments that exceed current goals.

organization A social entity that is goal directed and deliberately structured.

organization chart The visual representation of an organization's structure.

organization structure The framework in which the organization defines how tasks are divided, resources are deployed, and departments are coordinated.

organizational behavior An interdisciplinary field dedicated to the study of how individuals and groups tend to act in organizations.

organizational change The adoption of a new idea or behavior by an organization.

organizational citizenship Work behavior that goes beyond job requirements and contributes as needed to the organization's success.

organizational commitment Loyalty to and heavy involvement in one's organization.

organizational control The systematic process through which managers regulate organizational activities to make them consistent with expectations established in plans, targets, and standards of performance.

organizational development (OD) The application of behavioral science techniques to improve an organization's health and effectiveness through its ability to cope with environmental changes, improve internal relationships, and increase problem-solving capabilities.

organizing The management function concerned with assigning tasks, grouping tasks into departments, and allocating resources to departments; the deployment of organizational resources to achieve strategic goals.

P→O expectancy Expectancy that successful performance of a task will lead to the desired outcome.

partial productivity The ratio of total outputs to the inputs from a single major input category.

partial reinforcement schedule A schedule in which only some occur-rences of the desired behavior are reinforced.

partnership An unincorporated business owned by two or more people.

path-goal theory A contingency approach to leadership specifying that the leader's responsibility is to increase subordinates' motivation by clarifying the behaviors necessary for task accomplishment and rewards.

pay-for-performance Incentive pay that ties at least part of compensation to employee effort and performance.

peer-to-peer (P2P) file sharing File sharing that allows PCs to communicate directly with one another over the Internet, bypassing central databases, servers, control points, and Web pages.

perception The cognitive process people use to make sense out of the environment, by selecting, organizing, and interpreting information.

perceptual defense The tendency of perceivers to protect themselves by disregarding ideas, objects, or people that are threatening to them.

perceptual distortions Errors in perceptual judgment that arise from inaccuracies in any part of the perceptual process.

perceptual selectivity The process by which individuals screen and select the various stimuli that vie for their attention.

performance The organization's ability to attain its goals by using resources in an efficient and effective manner.

performance appraisal The process of observing and evaluating an employee's performance, recording the assessment, and providing feedback to the employee.

performance gap A disparity between existing and desired performance levels.

performing The stage of team development in which members focus on problem solving and accomplishing the team's assigned task.

permanent teams A group of participants from several functions who are permanently assigned to solve ongoing problems of common interest.

person-job fit The extent to which a person's ability and personality match the requirements of a job.

personality The set of characteristics that underlie a relatively stable pattern of behavior in response to ideas, objects, or people in the environment.

plan A blueprint specifying the resource allocations, schedules, and other actions necessary for attaining goals.

planning The management function concerned with defining goals for future organizational performance and deciding on the tasks and resource use needed to attain them; the act of determining the organization's goals and the means for achieving them.

planning task force A group of managers and employees who develop a strategic plan.

pluralism The organization accommodates several subcultures, including employees who would otherwise feel isolated and ignored.

point-counterpoint A decision-making technique in which people are assigned to express competing points of view.

political forces The influence of political and legal institutions on people and organizations.

political instability Events such as riots, revolutions, or government upheavals that affect the operations of an international company.

political risk A company's risk of loss of assets, earning power, or managerial control due to politically based events or actions by host governments.

portfolio strategy A type of corporate-level strategy that pertains to the organization's mix of SBUs and product lines that fit together in such a way as to provide the corporation with synergy and competitive advantage.

power The potential ability to influence others' behavior.

power distance The degree to which people accept inequality in power among institutions, organizations, and people.

pressure group An interest group that works within the legal-political framework to influence companies to behave in socially responsible ways.

problem A situation in which organizational accomplishments have failed to meet established goals.

problem-solving team Typically 5 to 12 hourly employees from the same department who meet to discuss ways of improving quality, efficiency, and the work environment.

procedural justice The concept that rules should be clearly stated and consistently and impartially enforced.

process An organized group of related tasks and activities that work together to transform inputs into outputs and create value.

process control system A computer system that monitors and controls ongoing physical processes, such as temperature or pressure changes.

process layout A facilities layout in which machines that perform the same function are grouped together in one location.

process theories A group of theories that explain how employees select behaviors with which to meet their needs and determine whether their choices were successful.

procurement Purchasing supplies, services, and raw materials for use in the production process.

product change A change in the organization's product or service output.

product layout A facilities layout in which machines and tasks are arranged according to the sequence of steps in the production of a single product.

productivity The organization's output of products and services divided by its inputs.

profitability ratio A financial ratio that describes the firm's profits (for example, sales or total assets).

programmed decision A decision made in response to a situation that has occurred often enough to enable decision rules to be developed and applied in the future.

project manager A manager responsible for a temporary work project that involves the participation of other people from various functions and levels of the organization; a person responsible for coordinating the activities of several

departments on a full-time basis for the completion of a specific project.

projection The tendency to see one's own personal traits in other people.

quality circle (QC) A group of 6 to 12 volunteer employees who meet regularly to discuss and solve problems affecting the quality of their work.

raw materials inventory Inventory consisting of the basic inputs to the organization's production process.

realistic job preview (RJP) A recruiting approach that gives applicants all pertinent and realistic information about the job and the organization.

recruiting The activities or practices that define the desired characteristics of applicants for specific jobs.

reengineering The radical redesign of business processes to achieve dramatic improvements in cost, quality, service, and speed; bringing together all elements of a single business process to eliminate waste and delays.

referent power Power that results from characteristics that command subordinates' identification with, respect and admiration for, and desire to emulate the leader.

refreezing The reinforcement stage of organizational development in which individuals acquire a desired new skill or attitude and are rewarded for it by the organization.

reinforcement Anything that causes a given behavior to be repeated or inhibited.

reinforcement theory A motivation theory based on the relationship between a given behavior and its consequences.

responsibility The duty to perform the task or activity an employee has been assigned.

responsibility center An organizational unit under the supervision of a single individual who is responsible for its activity.

revenue budget A budget that identifies the forecasted and actual revenues of the organization.

reward power Power that results from the authority to bestow rewards on other people.

risk A decision has clear-cut goals, and good information is available, but the future outcomes associated with each alternative are subject to chance.

risk propensity The willingness to undertake risk with the opportunity of gaining an increased payoff.

role A set of expectations for one's behavior.

role ambiguity Uncertainty about what behaviors are expected of a person in a particular role.

role conflict Incompatible demands of different roles.

satisficing To choose the first solution alternative that satisfies minimal decision criteria regardless of whether better solutions are presumed to exist.

schedule of reinforcement The frequency with which and intervals over which reinforcement occurs.

scientific management A subfield of the classical management perspective that emphasized scientifically determined changes in management practices as the solution to improving labor productivity.

search The process of learning about current developments inside or outside the organization that can be used to meet a perceived need for change.

selection The process of determining the skills, abilities, and other attributes a person needs to perform a particular job.

self-directed team A team consisting of 5 to 20 multiskilled workers who rotate jobs to produce an entire product or service, often supervised by an elected member.

self-serving bias The tendency to overestimate the contribution of internal factors to one's successes and the contribution of external factors to one's failures.

semantics The meaning of words and the way they are used.

servant leader A leader who works to fulfill subordinates' needs and goals as well as to achieve the organization's larger mission.

service organization An organization that produces nonphysical outputs that require customer involvement and cannot be stored in inventory.

service technology Technology characterized by intangible outputs and direct contact between employees and customers.

short-term orientation A concern with the past and present and a high value on meeting social obligations.

single-use plans Plans that are developed to achieve a set of goals that are unlikely to be repeated in the future.

situation analysis Analysis of the strengths, weaknesses, opportunities, and threats (SWOT) that affect organizational performance.

situational theory A contingency approach to leadership that links the leader's behavioral style with the task readiness of subordinates.

six sigma A quality control approach that emphasizes a relentless pursuit of higher quality and lower costs.

skunkworks A separate small, informal, highly autonomous, and often secretive group that focuses on breakthrough ideas for the business.

slogan A phrase or sentence that succinctly expresses a key corporate value.

small-batch production A type of technology that involves the production of goods in batches of one or a few products designed to customer specification.

social facilitation The tendency for the presence of others to influence an individual's motivation and performance.

social forces The aspects of a culture that guide and influence relationships among people—their values, needs, and standards of behavior.

social responsibility The obligation of organization management to make decisions and take actions that will enhance the welfare and interests of society as well as the organization.

sociocultural dimension The dimension of the general environment representing the demographic characteristics, norms, customs, and values of the population within which the organization operates.

socioemotional role A role in which the individual provides support for team members' emotional needs and social unity.

sole proprietorship An unincorporated business owned by an individual for profit.

span of management The number of employees reporting to a supervisor; also called *span of control*.

special-purpose team A team created outside the formal organization to undertake a project of special importance or creativity.

staff authority A form of authority granted to staff specialists in their areas of expertise.

stakeholder Any group within or outside the organization that has a stake in the organization's performance.

standing plans Ongoing plans used to provide guidance for tasks performed repeatedly within the organization.

stereotyping Placing an employee into a class category based on one or a few traits or characteristics.

storming The stage of team development in which individual personalities and roles, and resulting conflicts, emerge.

story A narrative based on true events that is repeated frequently and shared by organizational employees.

strategic business unit (SBU) A division of the organization that has a unique business mission, product line, competitors, and markets relative to other SBUs in the same corporation.

strategic goals Broad statements of where the organization wants to be in the future; pertain to the organization as a whole rather than to specific divisions or departments.

strategic management The set of decisions and actions used to formulate and implement strategies that will provide a competitively superior fit between the organization and its environment so as to achieve organizational goals.

strategic plans The action steps by which an organization intends to attain its strategic goals.

strategy The plan of action that prescribes resource allocation and other activities for dealing with the environment and helping the organization attain its goals.

strategy formulation The stage of strategic management that involves the planning and decision making that lead to the establishment of the organization's goals and of a specific strategic plan.

strategy implementation The stage of strategic management that involves the use of managerial and organizational tools to direct resources toward achieving strategic outcomes.

stress A physiological and emotional response to stimuli that place physical or psychological demands on an individual.

structural changes Any change in the way in which the organization is designed and managed.

substitute A situational variable that makes a leadership style redundant or unnecessary.

subsystems Parts of a system that depend on one another for their functioning.

superordinate goal A goal that cannot be reached by a single party.

suppliers People and organizations who provide the raw materials the organization uses to produce its output.

supply chain management Managing the sequence of suppliers and purchasers, covering all stages of processing from obtaining raw materials to distributing finished goods to final customers.

survey feedback A type of OD intervention in which questionnaires on organizational climate and other factors are distributed among employees and the results reported back to them by a change agent.

symbol An object, act, or event that conveys meaning to others.

synergy The condition that exists when the organization's parts interact to produce a joint effect that is greater than the sum of the parts acting alone; the concept that the whole is greater than the sum of its parts.

system A set of interrelated parts that function as a whole to achieve a common purpose.

systems theory An extension of the humanistic perspective that describes organizations as open systems that are characterized by entropy, synergy, and subsystem interdependence.

tactical goals Goals that define the outcomes that major divisions and departments must achieve in order for the organization to reach its overall goals.

tactical plans Plans designed to help execute major strategic plans and to accomplish a specific part of the company's strategy.

tall structure A management structure characterized by an overall narrow span of management and a relatively large number of hierarchical levels.

task environment The layer of the external environment that directly influences the organization's operations and performance.

task force A temporary team or committee formed to solve a specific short-term problem involving several departments.

task specialist role A role in which the individual devotes personal time and energy to helping the team accomplish its task.

team A group of participants from several departments who meet regularly to solve ongoing problems of common interest; a unit of two or more people who interact and coordinate their work to accomplish a specific goal.

team-based structure Structure in which the entire organization is made up of teams that coordinate their work and work directly with customers to accomplish the organization's goals.

team building A type of OD intervention that enhances the cohesiveness of departments by helping members learn to function as a team.

team cohesiveness The extent to which team members are attracted to the team and motivated to remain in it.

technical complexity The degree to which complex machinery is involved in the production process to the exclusion of people.

technical core The heart of the organization's production of its product or service.

technical skill The understanding of and proficiency in the performance of specific tasks.

technological dimension The dimension of the general environment that includes scientific and technological advancements in the industry and society at large.

technology The knowledge, tools, techniques, and activities used to transform the organization's inputs into outputs.

technology change A change that pertains to the organization's production process.

telecommuting Using computers and telecommunications equipment to perform work from home or another remote location.

time-based competition A strategy of competition based on the ability to deliver products and services faster than competitors.

tolerance for ambiguity The psychological characteristic that allows a person to be untroubled by disorder and uncertainty.

top-down budgeting A budgeting process in which middle and lower-level managers set departmental budget targets in accordance with overall company revenues and expenditures specified by top management.

top leader The overseer of both the product and the functional chains of command, responsible for the entire matrix.

top manager A manager who is at the top of the organizational hierarchy and is responsible for the entire organization.

total factor productivity The ratio of total outputs to the inputs from labor, capital, materials, and energy.

total quality management (TQM) A concept that focuses on managing the total organization to deliver quality to customers. Four significant elements of TQM are employee involvement, focus on the customer, benchmarking, and continuous improvement. An organizationwide commitment to infusing quality into every activity through continuous improvement.

traits Distinguishing personal characteristics, such as intelligence, values, and appearance.

transactional leader A leader who clarifies subordinates' role and task requirements, initiates structure, provides rewards, and displays consideration for subordinates.

transaction processing system A type of operations information system that records and processes data resulting from routine business transactions such as sales, purchases, and payroll.

transformational leader A leader distinguished by a special ability to bring about innovation and change.

transnational strategy A strategy that combines global coordination to attain efficiency with flexibility to meet specific needs in various countries.

two-boss employee Employees who report to two supervisors simultaneously.

type A behavior Behavior pattern characterized by extreme competitiveness, impatience, aggressiveness, and devotion to work.

type B behavior Behavior pattern that lacks Type A characteristics and includes a more balanced, relaxed lifestyle.

uncertainty Managers know what goal they wish to achieve, but information about alternatives and future events is incomplete.

uncertainty avoidance A value characterized by people's intolerance for uncertainty and ambiguity and resulting support for beliefs that promise certainty and conformity.

unfreezing A stage of organizational development in which participants are made aware of problems in order to increase their willingness to change their behavior.

upward communication Messages transmitted from the lower to the higher level in the organization's hierarchy.

utilitarian approach The ethical concept that moral behaviors produce the greatest good for the greatest number.

valence The value or attraction an individual has for an outcome.

validity The relationship between an applicant's score on a selection device and his or her future job performance.

venture capital firm A group of companies or individuals that invests money in new or expanding businesses for ownership and potential profits.

vertical team A formal team composed of a manager and his or her subordinates in the organization's formal chain of command.

virtual organization An organization that has few full-time employees and temporarily hires outside specialists who form teams to work on specific opportunities, then disband when objectives are met.

virtual team A team that uses advanced information and telecommunications technologies so that geographically distant members can collaborate on projects and reach common goals.

vision An attractive, ideal future that is credible yet not readily attainable.

Vroom-Jago model A model designed to help managers gauge the amount of subordinate participation in decision making.

wage and salary surveys Surveys that show what other organizations pay incumbents in jobs that match a sample of "key" jobs selected by the organization.

whistle-blowing The disclosure by an employee of illegal, immoral, or illegitimate practices by the organization.

wholly owned foreign affiliate A foreign subsidiary over which an organization has complete control.

workforce diversity Hiring people with different human qualities or who belong to various cultural groups.

work-in-process inventory Inventory composed of the materials that still are moving through the stages of the production process.

work redesign The altering of jobs to increase both the quality of employees' work experience and their productivity.

work specialization The degree to which organizational tasks are subdivided into individual jobs; also called division of labor.

World Wide Web (WWW) A collection of central servers for accessing information on the Internet.

Name Index

Abelson, Reed, 466n2, 467n48
Abrahamson, Eric, 63n4
Abramson, Gary, 102n24, 102n26
Abrashoff, D. Michael, 513, 537, 541n1, 543n59
Ackerly, Leone, 560
Ackerman, Roger, 373, 374
Adair, John G., 64n32
Adam, Everett E., Jr., 738n6
Adams, J. Stacy, 554, 575n19
Adamson, Ian, 317
Adler, Nancy J., 133n8
Adorno, T. W., 510n29
Aeppel, Timothy, 524n29
Aggarwal, Sumer C., 739n22
Agor, Weston H., 300n25
Agres, Carole E., 341n42
Alban, Billie T., 403n74, 403n75, 403n76
Albanese, Robert, 541n16, 643n64
Aldag, Ramon J., 64n35
Alderfer, Clayton, 575n10
Aldrich, Howard E., 33n38
Aldrich, Steven, 352
Alexander, John O., 234n21
Allen, Robert W., 10
Alster, Norm, 575n38
Altier, William J., 370n8
Amabile, Teresa M., 401n14, 401n16
Anagnos, Gus, 234n32
Anand, Geeta, 401n3
Anand, N., 341n33, 341n45
Anders, George, 167n75, 401n2, 401n23
Anderson, Peter, 597
Anderson, Ray, 151
Angle, Harold L., 401n24
Ante, Spencer E., 267n52, 707n36, 707n40
Anthony, Robert N., 679n9, n11
Antonellis, Domenic, 12
Apcar, Leonard M., 402n37
Archer, Earnest R., 300n17
Ardill, Ralph, 331
Arias, Anna Maria, 174
Armstrong, Tom, 741
Arndt, Michael, 466n2
Arnold, Hugh J., 64n24, 642n41, 642n49
Arnold, W. J., 64n22
Arnst, Catherine, 166n43
Aronson, Elliot, 642n42

Ashkenas, Ronald N., 370n14
Asinof, Lynn, 435n79
Austin, Larry M., 65n41
Austin, Nancy K., 402n28, 610n48, 610n49
Avolio, Bruce J., 542n42, 543n50

Bacharach, Samuel B., 401n4
Badaracco, Joseph L., Jr., 166n52, 167n59
Baig, Edward C., 167n78
Bailey, Diane E., 34n47, 103n64, 434n26
Baird, Inga Skromme, 299n10
Baker, Michael, 610,39
Baker, Stephen, 133n6
Bakke, Dennis, 128, 568
Balaji, Y., 706n22, 706n27
Ball, Jeffrey, 166n38, 370n12
Ballon, Marc, 198n21, 541n20
Balu, Rekha, 575n43, 103n55
Banham, Russ, 268n62, 678n4, 739n13
Banker, Rajiv D., 641n3
Barad, Jill, 240
Barbian, Jeff, 575n11, 575n12, 575n37
Barkdull, C. W., 340n13
Barnard, C. I., 340n8
Barnard, Charles, 193
Barnard, Chester, 44–45
Barnathan, Joyce, 133n11
Barnes, Frank C., 609n18, 679n29
Barnes-Vieyra, Pamela, 706n13
Barnett, Megan, 707n35, 739n21
Baron, James N., 433n7
Baron, Robert A., 642n34, 643n64
Barrett, Amy, 134n38
Barrett, Colleen, 448
Barrett, D., 610n42, n44
Barrett, Paul M., 401n9
Barrick, M. R., 510n17
Barrier, Michael, 166n51, 199n77
Bart, C. K., 402n26
Bartlett, Christopher A., 33n26, 34n55, 109
Baseman, Gary, 468n69
Bass, Bernard M. 542n40, 542n45, 543n50
Bass, Robert, 65n44
Basu, Radha, 460
Bateman, Thomas S., 267n25
Bates, James, 739n26

Bateson, Gregory, 401n13
Baveja, Alok, 267n27, 267n29, 267n45
Bavelas, A., 610n42, n44
Bazerman, Max H., 299n9
Beach, Roger, 132
Beard, Luciana, 739n33
Beard, Stephanie, 419
Beardsley, David, 33n3
Beatty, R. W., 435n70
Becker, Helmut, 166n47
Becker, S., 402n40
Beckhard, Richard, 402n40, 403n70
Beckman, Eugene, 165n14
Bedeian, Arthur, G., 340n13
Bedford, Norton M., 679n9, n11
Beehr, T. A., 511n46
Beeth, Gunnar, 133n9
Behar, Saby, 386
Bell, Arthur H., 609n24
Bell, Jr., Cecil H., 64n39, 403n70, 403n71
Belohav, James, A., 576n46
Benavides, Lisa, 101n8, 198n30, 198n47
Benham, Barbara, 198n24, 198n28, 198n43
Benne, K. D., 642n33
Bennett, M., 466n16
Bentham, Jeremy, 141
Berkowitz, L., 575n19
Berlo, D. K., 609n7
Bernardin, J. J., 434n70
Bernasek, Anna, 33n14, 739n44
Bernick, Carol Lavin, 397
Bernstein, Aaron, 466n2, 510n10, 643n63
Berton, Lee, 102n27
Bettenhausen, Kenneth, 642n47
Beyer, Janice M., 102n47
Beyerlein, Michael M., 706n23
Bezos, Jeff, 194
Bhagat, R. S., 511n46
Bijur, Peter, 437, 462
Bin Laden, Osama, 533
Birch, David, 175
Bird, B.J., 542n21
Bishop, James Wallace, 651n2
Blacharczyk, E., 434n48
Black, J., 467n60
Black, Pam, 370n35
Black, Wendy, 379
Blackford, Mansel G., 64n40

Blai Jr., Boris, 300n17
Blaigai, B. R., 679n16
Blais, Frances, 547
Blake, Robert T., 542 24
Blanchard, Kenneth H., 542n31, 526
Blank, Renee, 466n15
Blase, Frank, 722
Blaylock, Bruce K., 609n9
Block, Caryn J., 467n30
Blostrom, Robert L., 166n28
Blumenstein, Rebecca, 739n25
Blumenthal, Robin Goldwyn, 679n15
Bohl, Don L., 679n30
Bohlander, George, 434n43, 434n52
Bohm, David, 610n60
Bollander, George, 433n11
Bolton, Alfred A., 64n30, 64n33
Bond, M. H., 134n43
Book, Esther Wachs, 542n20
Booth, Patricia, 610n2
Boquist, John A., 679n10
Borrus, Amy, 134n39, 707n36
Boston, Allen, 454
Boudreau, J. W., 434n35
Boudreau, Marie-Claude, 706n10
Boulding, Kenneth E., 65n44
Boulgaides, J. D., 300n44
Bounds, Gregory M., 64n27
Bourgeois III, L. J., 101n6, 268n65,
    268n71, 642n54, 643n61
Bovet, David, 738n1, 739n48
Bowen, Andy, 34n60, 234n35
Bowen, David E., 33n4, 576n47
Bowman, Robert J., 134n24
Boyle, Gertrude, 499
Boyle, Matthew, 63n5, 434n67, 434n68,
    434n69
Brabeck-Letmathe, Peter, 109
Bradford, David I., 610n56
Bradley, Bill, 556
Bradsher, Keith, 134n41, 370n36
Brady, Diane, 33n20, 575n30
Brady, William Jr., 291
Branch, Shelly, 341n22
Brannigan, Martha, 33n16
Brechu, Mauricio Brehm, 134n44
Breckler, S. J., 510n4
Breen, Ben 433n1, 435n83
Breen, Bill, 300n27
Breinholt, Peter, 172
Brightman, Harvey J., 643n66
Brin, Sergey, 190
Broderick, Reneè F., 435n74
Brodwin, David R., 268n65, 268n71
Brody, Michael, 370n10, 574n2
Broersma, Tom, 32n2, 401n6
Brokaw, Leslie, 33n4, 198n38
Brooker, Katrina, 267n39, 403n66
Brooks, Rick, 102n19

Brown, Andrew D., 102n35
Brown, Carolyn M., 198n40
Brown, Eryn, 33n11
Brown, Michael, 166n49, 167n55
Brown, Stuart F., 401n3
Browne, Cynthia, 401, n18
Brownell, Peter, 679n12
Buckingham, Marcus, 576n55
Bull, George, 510n31
Buller, Paul F., 403n72
Bunker, Barbara Benedict, 403n74,
    403n75, 403n76
Burgess, Celeste, 407
Burgum, Doug, 314
Burke, Lisa A., 300n26
Burke, W. Warner, 403n70, 403n73
Burnes, Lawton R., 341n23
Burns, Greg, 267n55, 268n72
Burns, James M., 542n40
Burns, James R., 65n41
Burns, Tom, 402n47
Burns, Tony, 584
Burris, Paula, 422
Burrows, Peter, 33n19, 102n20, 267n54,
    340n3
Burton, John, 267n58, 268n63
Bush, George W., 27, 29, 280
Buss, Dale, 199n51
Butler, Stephen A., 739n33
Butterfield, Kenneth D., 575n29
Buzotta, V. R., 434n70
Byham, William C., 642n18, 434n54
Bylinsky, Gene, 101n11
Byrne, John A., 32n1, 34, 34n46, 34n57,
    34n62, 40, 133n12, 167n66, 267n33,
    268n61, 341n41, 370n22, 434n61
Byrnes, Nanette, 267n46, 403n66
Byrnjolfsson, Erik, 370n23

Cage, Jack H., 301n50
Caggiano, Christopher, 198n1, 199n73,
    340n18
Cahn, Doug, 154
Caldwell, David F., 511n37
Cameron, Bobby, 34n56
Cameron, Jeannie, 678n5
Caminiti, Susan, 402n61
Campbell, Andrew, 267n32
Campbell, Jeff, 718
Canabou, Christine, 102n40
Capell, Kerry, 34n51
Cardinal, Laura B., 233n6, 266n5
Carey, John, 101n16
Carey, Patricia M., 135n64
Carlson, Kathleen A., 433n18
Carrasco, Emma, 582
Carrns, Ann, 101n7
Carroll, Archie B., 166n44
Carruth, Paul J. 679n11

Carton, Barbara, 267n49, 468n68
Cartwright, Dorwin, 541n7, 642n42
Carver, Stephanie, 14
Cascio, Wayne, F., 543n55
Case, John, 198n2, 198n13, 198n15,
    198n31, 199n57, 341n34, 610n57
Casey, Andrea 575n29
Cashman, Thomas, 609n35
Castro, Ida L., 467n44
Catapano-Friedman, Robert S., 435n80
Caudron, Shari, 135n68
Caulfield, Brian, 706n20
Cavanagh, Gerald F., 165n11
Cavender, J. W., 510n5
Cederholm, Lars, 641n4
Cespedes, Frank V., 641n4
Chaharbaghi, Kazem, 268n66
Challenger, Cynthia, 679n25
Challenger, John, 434n24
Chamales, Gerald, 483
Chambers, John, 494
Chan, Karen, 340n2
Chandler, Clay, 340n17
Chandler, Jr., Alfred D., 64n13
Chao, Steven, 279
Chapell, Tom, 286
Charan, Ram, 101n8
Charnley, Deb, 580
Chase, Nancy, 543n56
Chase, Richard B., 371n45, 510n15,
    738n5
Chatman, Jennifer A., 102n49, 511n37
Chemers, M. M., 542n27, 542n28
Chen, Winston, 56, 351
Chenault, Kenneth, 3, 4, 5, 28, 439
Chenault, Kenneth, 268n65, 268n71
Chesterton, James D., 484
Chesterton, Jim 580
Chew, W. Bouce, 739n43
Child, John, 340n4
Childress, George Ray, 579
Childress, Rusty, 579, 605
Childs, Ted, 442
Chimerine, Lawrence, 101n8
Choate, Jerry, 446
Chow, Chee W., 679n36, 679n37
Christie, Richard, 510n32, 511n34
Churchill, Neil C., 679n12
Clampitt, Phillip G., 609n35
Clarkson, Max B.E., 166n32
Claycomb, Cindy, 706n13
Clifford, Lee, 679n22, 679n28
Clifton, Timothy C., 542n45
Cochran, Philip L., 167n70
Coffman, Curt, 576n53
Cohen Allan R., 610n56
Cohen, Mark A., 166n35
Colb, D. A., 575n18
Cole, Joanne, 468n66
Coleberd, R. E., 178, 198n37

Coleman Jr., Henry J., 341n31
Collins, E. G., 467n61
Collins, James C., 89, 102n38, 103n57, 234n44
Collins, Jim, 534, 543n49
Collins, Kathleen, 33n13, 198n11, 198n21
Collins, Paul D., 340n13
Collins, Roland G. Jr., 503
Colvin, Geoffrey, 33n28, 64n19, 65n63, 301n53
Conger, Jay A., 541n10, 542n42, 576n45, 576n52, 609n17
Conlin, Michelle, 370n4, 402n68, 435n77, 467n38
Connelly, Mary Shane, 542n45
Conner, Bill, 408
Cook, Thomas M., 300n20
Cooke, Robert A., 371n41
Coombs, W. Timothy, 234n33, 234n34
Cooper, Helene, 165n1
Cooper, W. W., 402n50
Copeland, Lennie, 466n9, 466n10, 467n27, 467n50
Copeland, Michael V., 301n54
Copple, Brandon, 340n1, 341n47
Corcoran, Jack, 468n67
Corner, Gary, 382
Cornfield, Daniel B., 468n88
Cortese, Amy, 133n12
Coubrough, J. A., 64n22
Coulter, Mary, 134n40
Couzin, Jennifer, 33n33
Covin, Jeffrey G., 268n65
Covrig, Duane M., 166n24
Cox, Taylor H., 466n4
Coy, Peter, 34n58, 435n77
Coye, Ray W., 576n47
Crawford, Nissa, 34n40
Crean, Christopher, 471
Crittenden, Ann, 467n39
Crockett, Joan, 467n28
Crockett, Roger O., 370n1, 371n50
Crockett, S. R., 642n43
Cronbaugh, Tara, 193
Crosby, P. B., 739n46
Cullen, John B., 166n26
Cullen, Lisa, 467n38, 467n39
Cullman, Joseph F. III, 535
Cummings, T. G., 403n78
Cunningham, Father William, 9
Czinkota, Michael R., 134n30

D'Amico, Carol, 467n21, 467n27, 468n70
D'Arcangelo, John-Michael, 169, 194
Daft, Douglas, 19, 109, 224, 237, 263, 385
Daft, Richard L., 47, 64n21, 101n5, 102n30, 103n51, 133n8, 198n15, 233n7, 268n73, 299n14, 300n35,

340n7, 370n3, 370n16, 401n4, 401n5, 402n40, 402n47, 402n49, 402n54, 402n56, 402n65, 543, 543n57, 575n24, 609n10, 609n15, 609n30, 610n39, 610n43, 610n45, 643n56, 679n34
Dalton, Glenn L., 268n68, 340n6, 575n39
Dalton, Julie Carrick, 370n325
Daly, James, 642n28
Damanpour, Fariborz, 402n63
Daniels, Cora, 467n32, 510n20
Dannemiller, Kathleen D., 403n74
Dannhauser, Carol A. L., 434n45, 434n66, 610n38
Dasu, Sriram, 510n15
Datta, Deepak, K., 300n32
Datz, Todd, 65n66
Davenport, Thomas H., 34n47, 103n63, 341n46
David, Fred, 234n13
David, Stanley, M., 341n24
Davis, Gray, 27
Davis, Keith, 166n28, 510n2, 610n51, 610n54
De Da La Sierra, Mimi Cauley, 134n53
De Mestral, George, 378
Deal, Terrence E., 102n44
Dean Jr., James W., 300n32
Dearden, John, 679n9, n11
Debow, Yvette, 435n82
Dechant, K., 468n77
Deck, Stewart, 267n31, 707n34
DeKoch, Robert J., 609n35
Delaney, Bob, 732
Delaney, John T., 433n4
Delbecq, Andre L., 371n49, 401n7
DeLeo, P. J., 575n32
DeLisser, Eleena, 33n16, 642n51
Dell, Michael, 7, 244, 260
DeMarie, Samuel M., 642n24
DeMeuse, Kenneth P., 641n7
Deming, W. Edwards, 54, 90, 733, 739n46
Dempsey, Don, 302, 303
Denison, Daniel R., 102n51
Denzler, David A., 738n9
Deogun, Nikhil, 678n2
Depke, Deidre A., 433n16
Deschamps, Isabelle, 402n38
Desmond, Edward W., 266n2
Dess, Gregory G., 341n36, 341n39, 341n40, 371n38
Deutsch, Claudia H., 679n24
Deutsch, J. A., 510n14
Devanna, Mary Anne, 370n31, 542n46
Deveny, Kathleen, 134n21
Diaper, Gordon, 64n32
DiBella, A. J., 370n26

Dickson, W. J., 64n31, 64n34, 574n7
Dietel, H. M., 199n62
Digman, J. M., 510n17
Diller, Barry, 279
Dillon, Karen, 198n5
Distefano, Joseph J., 468n76, 468n82, 468n84
DiTomaso, Nancy, 467n25
Dobbins, Gregory M., 64n27
Dodd, R., 166n40
Doktor, Robert, 466n14
Dolan, Carrie, 199n74
Dole, Stephen X., 641n4
Dollinger, Marc J., 102n22
Donahue, Sean, 434n30
Donaldson, Thomas, 165n21, 166n30
Donnelly, James H., Jr., 135n61
Dorfman, Peter W., 542n39
Dorsey, David, 401n8
Dougherty, Deborah, 402n51
Douglas, Susan P., 135n59
Douglass, Frederick, 533
Dower, Mike, 741
Drew, Elizabeth B., 609n4
Drucker, Peter F., 5, 33n6, 34n44, 59, 65n65, 380, 402n27
Drukerman, Pamela, 134n19
Duarte, Deborah L., 543n43, 642n24
Dumaine, Brian, 267n44, 340n14, 402n62, 434n36
Duncan, Robert B., 102n21, 340n20, 370n38, 402n36
Dunfee, Thomas W., 165n21
Dungy, Tony, 495
Dunham, Richard S., 101n16
Dunne, Jimmy, 566
Dutton, Jane E., 300n33
Dwyer, Paula, 133n12, 341n25, 341n26

Eastman, Kenneth K., 542n46
Echikson, William, 133n10
Eckert, Robert, 238
Edison, Thomas, 46
Edmondson, Gail, 34n51, 133n11
Edwards, Irving, 550
Eichen, Paul, 486
Eilon, Samuel, 299n9, 299n12
Einhorn, Bruce, 134n49
Einstein, Walter O., 641n14
Eisenhardt, Kathleen M., 301n52, 301n57, 301n59, 301n61, 642n54, 643n61
Elashmawi, D. Farid, 466n10
Elkind, Peter, 300n45
Elkins, Linda, 198n40
Eller, Claudia, 739n26
Ellis, Mike, 694
Ellison, Larry, 320
Ely, R. J., 468n77
Emshwiller, John R., 299n3

End, William T., 382
Eng, Sherri, 402n31, 402n32
Engardio, Pete, 133n5, 314n25, 706n9
Engen, John R., 33n7
Engibous, Thomas, 449
Enrico, Roger, 245
Erez, Miriam, 234n25, 642n43, 643n62
Esterson, Emily, 739n42
Ettling, Jennifer T., 301n50, 301n58
Ettorre, Barbara, 102n45, 370n12, 370n16, 575n41, 610n40, 610n55
Etzioni, Amitai, 233n3, 300n21
Evans, M. G., 542n33, 542n35
Evans, Rodney, 198n35
Everest, A., 468n74
Ewing, Jack, 234n28, 266n14
Eyler, John, 250
Ezrin, Hershell, 280

Falk, Charles F., 403n18
Fallon, Pat, 200, 201
Farnham, Alan, 102n48, 234n13, 510n19, 510n22
Farrow, Dana L. 642n53
Fayol, Henri, 44, 64n22
Feigenbaurm, A. V., 679n19
Feldman, Daniel C., 642n41, 642n48, 642n49
Fernandes, Donna, 645-646
Ferrell, O. C., 134n30
Ferris, Nancy, 65n64
Festinger, Leon A., 510n12
Feuerstein, A., 510n3
Feurer, Rainer, 268n66
Fiedler, Fred, 523-524, 528, 529, 542n26, 542n27, 542n28
Field, Joy M., 641n3
Field, R. H. G., 301n49
Fierman, Jaclyn, 33n12, 434n25
Fine, M., 466n3
Finnigan, Annie, 467n35, 467n36, 467n47, 467n53, 468n76, 468n87
Fiojas, Alma Morales, 171
Fiorina, Carleton S., 390, 496
Fischetti, Mark, 234n19
Fisher, Anne B., 467n46, 511n52
Fisher, Cynthia D., 433n8
Fisher, Eileen, 157
Fisher, Jeff, 495
Fisher, Lawrence M. 679n114
Fishman, Charles, 33n25, 103n54, 166n43, 341n30, 642n22
Fitzpatrick, Mark, 134n23
Fletcher, Joyce K., 467n36, 467n44
Flood, Frances, 559
Floyd, Steven, 33n29
Flynn, Julia, 134n54, 267n41
Follett, Mary Parker, 5, 44-45, 64n23, 64n25

Ford, Bill, 204, 305, 474, 481, 649, 743
Ford, Henry, 68, 204
Ford, Joe, 586
Ford, Robert C., 341n25, 576n51
Forlenza, Nicholas, 333
Forrester, Russ, 576n48
Fottler, Myron D., 576n51
Foust, Dean, 133n10, 266n1, 268n75, 402n43
Fowler, Oscar S., 64n27
Fox, Harold W., 268n64
Fox, Justin, 134n34, 642n45
Frainier, Tom, 603
France, Mike, 102n25
Francis, Suzanne C., 370n14
Franharm, 166n27
Frank, Robert, 134n48
Franz, Charles R., 642n53
Frazee, Valerie, 135n65
Frazier, Greg, 739n16, 739n17, 739n31, 739n38
Frederick, William C., 166n28
Fredrickson, James W., 300n32
Freedman, Robert J., 641n4
Freeman, Mike, 510n30
Freeman, R. Edward, 166n40, 610n66
Freidheim Jr., Cyrus F., 102n28, 102n32
French Jr., J. R. P., 541n7
French, Wendell L., 64n39, 403n70, 403n71
Frenkel-Brunswick, E., 510n29
Friedland, Jonathan, 133n1, 133n6, 135n71
Friedman, Milton, 152, 166n45, 511n48
Friedman, Raymond A., 468n85, 468n88
Friedman, Rose, 166n45
Frieswick, Kris, 434n65, 434n67, 706n12
Fritsch, Mark J., 234n22
Fritzsche, David J., 166n47
Frost, Taggart F., 402n42
Fry, Ronald E., 34n42
Fuchsberg, Gilbert, 468n73
Fuld, Leonard M., 707n33
Fulk, Janet, 610n68
Fuller, Scott, 94
Fulmer, Robert M., 403n72
Futrell, David, 641n7

Gaither, Norman, 739n16, 739n17, 739n31, 739n38
Galbraith, Jay R., 268n67, 340n20
Gallace, Larry J. 679n26
Galuszka, Peter, 233n11
Galvin, Christopher, 343, 366
Gandz, Jeffrey, 102n51
Gantt, Henry, 42
Garaventa, Eugene, 167n68
Garcia, Jerry, 5
Garcia, Julia, 564

Gardner, William L., 542n42
Garger, Eileen M., 434n62
Garino, Jason, 706n11
Garr, Richard, 140
Garrett, Echo Montgomery, 198n47
Garsten, 166n39
Garvin, David A., 301n59, 301n62, 370n18
Gates, Bill, 4, 11, 314
Gatewood, Robert D., 134n30
Gault, Jeffrey, 74
Gaynor, Larry, 353
Geber, Beverly, 167n64
Gegax, Tom, 522
Geis, Florence, 510n32, 511n34
Gellerman, Saul W., 166n48
George, Jill, 642n18
George Jr., Claude S., 64n15, 64n18
Georgopolous, B. S., 542n33
Gerard, Glenna, 610n61
Gerber, B., 467n51
Germer, Erika, 610n47
Gersick, Connie J. G., 642n37
Gerstein, Marc S., 370n27
Gessner, Theodore L., 542n45
Ghoshal, Sumantra, 33n26, 34n55, 679n9
Gibson, David G., 166n53
Gibson, James L., 135n61
Gibson, Richard, 134n47, 199n50
Giegold, W., 234n27
Gifford, Kathy Lee, 223
Gilbert, Jacquiline A., 467n49
Gilbreth, Frank, 42, 43
Gilbreth, Lillian, 42, 43
Gilkey, Roderick, 403n72
Gilligan, Carol, 165n20
Gilmore, Scott, 353
Gimein, Mark, 33n21, 34n46, 103n60
Girard, Kim, 267n38, 299n2
Giuliani, Rudolph, 11, 29
Gladstein, Deborah L., 641n8
Glauser, Michael J., 609n37
Gluck, Frederick W., 267n47
Gniwisch, Mayer, 627
Gniwisch, Pinny, 627
Gniwisch, Schmuel, 627
Godin, Seth, 340n19
Goding, Jeff, 679n23, 679n28
Gohl, Don L., 679n32
Goizueta, Roberto, 238
Gold, Jacqueline S., 543n48
Goldberg, Matt, 610n46
Golden, Bruce, 199n71
Goldhaber, Gerald M., 609n28, 610n54
Goldman, Lea, 575n27
Goldsmith, Bruce, 279
Goldsmith, Ronald E., 401n14
Goldstein, Mark, 240

Goleman, Daniel, 510n21, 510n25, 521n23
Golisano, Tom, 522
Golub, Harvey, 439
Gomez-Mejia, L. R., 435n73
Goode, Kathy, 64n21
Goodin, Dan, 165n8
Goodnight, Jim, 93
Goold, Michael, 267n32
Gordon, Bruce, 443
Gordon, David T., 511n57
Gordon, DeeDee, 81
Gordon, Jack, 467n33
Gorelick, Jamie, 472, 473
Gorgopoulos, B. S., 575n23
Goslin, D.A., 165n19
Gould, J. M., 370n26
Govindarajan, Vijay, 267n22, 267n24, 268n65, 268n71, 642n26
Gozdz, Kazinierz, 610n61
Graham, Jill W., 165n19
Graham, Thomas, 516
Grant, Linda, 574n5
Gray, Jerry L., 574n3
Grazier, Peter B., 103n70
Green, Jeff, 199n63, 678n2
Green, Marnie, 64n8
Green, Richard, 588
Greenberger, Robert S., 134n52
Greene, Charles, 542n38
Greene, Roger, 179, 219, 630, 435n75
Greengard, Samuel, 434n40, 65n48
Greenhouse, Steven, 466n21
Greenleaf, Robert K., 543n58
Greenwood, Regina A., 64n30, 64n33
Greenwood, Ronald G., 64n30
Greis, Noel P., 739n35
Griffith, Victoria, 434n38
Grimsley, Kirstin Downey, 234n36, 234n38
Grittner, Peter, 102n29
Groner, Alex, 65n40
Gross, Bill, 249
Gross, Neil, 133n5, 167n78, 642n45
Grossman, Allen, 34n45
Grossman, Robert J., 467n31, 510n13
Grossmann, John, 641n12
Grove, Andrew, 106, 133n2, 272
Grundfest, Joseph, 416
Gruner, Sephanie, 103n68, 511n43, 511n56
Grunewald, Per, 245
Gryna, Frank M., 679m19
Guillen, Mauro F., 65n49
Guilliani, Rudolph, 225
Gulati, Ranjay, 706n11
Gumpert, David E., 401n17
Gunter, Marc, 101n15, 102n31
Gupta, Anil K., 267n22, 267n24, 268n65, 268n71, 642n26
Gupta, Rajat, 443

Gupta, Udayan, 199n78
Gupta, Vinita, 479, 506
Guyon, Janet, 101n10

Hackman, J. Richard, 565, 575n40, 642n46
Hadar, Mary, 276
Haddad, Charles, 340n15
Haddad, Kamal, M., 679n36, 679n37
Hagans, Phil, 527
Hagerty, James R., 678n2
Hahn, Betty, 64n21
Hales, Colin P., 33n38
Half, Robert, 420
Hall, Douglas T., 433n20, 434n24
Hamel, Gary, 234n46, 266n6, 266n7, 370n26, 610n58
Hamilton, Joan O'C., 101n16, 267n39
Hamm, Steve, 341n21, 706n9
Hammer, Michael, 370n16, 370n17, 370n18, 370n19, 371n46, 679n23, 679n28
Hammonds, Keith H., 33n3, 266n6, 267n57, 341n43, 466n17, 542n43
Handy, Charles, 33n2
Hanks, Tom, 275
Hannan, Robert L., 33n32
Hansell, Saul, 199n79
Hansen, Morten T., 706n26
Harari, Oren, 32n2, 65n68, 233n2, 234n43, 433n9
Hardy, Cynthia, 402n51
Hardy, Quentin, 511n36
Harmsen, Richard, 134n31
Harreld, Heather, 706n6
Harrigan, Kathryn Rudie, 134n53
Harrington, L. Katherine, 64n17, 65n48n, 65n65, 234n40, 434n46
Harris, Jonathan, 300n31
Harris, Roy, 466n7, 467n23, 467n26
Harrison, Jeffrey S., 166n31
Hartman, 167n55
Harvey, Michael, 198n35
Haschak, Paul, 234n14
Hasek, G., 679n22
Haub, Christian, 681, 702
Hawkins, Brian, 609n6
Hawthorne, Nancy, 535
Hayashi, Alden M., 300n28
Hayes, Robert H., 738n7, 738n8
Hays, Scott, 434n40
Heath, Chip, 301n56
Heen, Sheila, 493
Heilman, Madeline E., 301n50, 467n30
Heimler, Marv, 164
Helft, Miguel, 199n55
Helgesen, Sally, 543n50
Hellriegel, Don, 401n5, 574n3
Hempel, Carl G., 65n44

Henderson, A. M., 64n20
Henderson, Richard I., 435n72
Hendricks, Mark, 198n6
Hendrickson, Anthony, 642n24
Henkelman, Leo, 545
Henkoff, Ronald, 739n34
Hequet, Marc, 468n78
Herbert, Kathleen, 314
Herman, Roger, 64n7
Herschlag, Judith K., 301n50
Hersey, Paul, 526, 542n31
Hertzog, William, 601
Herzberg, Frederick, 551-553, 575n14
Heskett, James L., 102n50
Hiestand, Susan, 390
Higbie, Andrea, 511n54
Higgins, J.G., 299n11
Highsmith, Duncan, 620
Hildebrand, Carol, 610n56
Hill, Charles W. L., 402n53, 402n57
Hillkirk, John, 314n29
Himelstein, Linda, 101n16
Hinnant, Lori, 167n80
Hisrich, Robert D., 198n33
Hitler, Adolf, 533
Hitt, Michael A., 135n57, 267n23, 267n36
Hjorten, Lisa, 94
Hocker, David, 333
Hockett, Homer C., 63n6
Hockwarter, Wayne A., 234n45
Hodgetts, Richard M., 198n4, 198n27, 198n40, 679n32, 679n30
Hoekstra, Joel, 234n24
Hoenig, Christopher, 402n28, 402n29
Hoerr, John, 641n16
Hof, Robert D., 33n19, 133n5, 707n36
Hofer, Charles W., 267n37
Hoffman, Hugh, 347
Hofman, Mike, 575n25, 610n67
Hofstede, Geert, 119, 134n42, 134n43
Holland, Gina, 198n12
Hollander, Edwin P., 576n44
Hollenback, J., 575n32
Holmes, Deborah K., 454
Holstein, William J., 65n60, 133n8, 133n11, 133n12, 401n1, 403n80, 739n15
Holt, David H., 134n31
Holt, Jim, 133n14
Holt, Peter, 156
Hooijberg, Robert, 103n52, 467n25
Horn, John, 648, 740
Hornstein, Harvery A., 301n50
Hosking, D., 542n30
Hoskisson, Robert E., 135n57, 267n23, 267n36
House Robert J., 542n34, 542n41, 542n43, 542n44

Howard, Ronald A., 299n6
Howell, Jane M., 542n45
Howell, Jon P., 542n39
Hrebiniak, Lawrence G., 267n43
Hubka, Rachel, 517
Hudson, Katherine M., 291
Huey, John, 63n3
Hull, Frank, 340n13
Humowitz, Carol, 510n8
Hunger, J. David, 267n53
Hunt, Dan, 582
Hunt, Grant, 692
Hunt, J. G., 542n22
Hurwitz, Alan, 370n2
Huse, E. F., 403n78
Huselid, Mark A., 433n4
Hutchcraft, Chuck, 101n4
Hwang, Suein L., 300n37
Hyatt, Joshua, 102n34, 402n45, 610n52
Hymowitz, Carol, 134n45, 401n10, 434n67, 434n69, 469n64, 511n49, 574n4, 610n62

Iacocca, Lee, 90, 345, 370n6
Iaffaldano, M. R., 510n5
Imparato, Nicholas, 32n2
Imperato, Gina, 64n38, 234n20
Ingrassia, Paul, 340n17
Ioli, Nicholas, 681, 702
Ireland, R. Duane, 135n57, 267n23, 267n36
Irle, K. W., 541n15
Irwin, Richard D., 738n9
Ito, Jack K., 371n49
Ivancevich, John M., 135n61, 234n29, 467n49, 609n29
Ivester, Douglas, 237

Jackofsky, Ellen F., 134n44, 135n67
Jackson, Al, 447
Jackson, John H., 433n2
Jackson, Mannie, 262
Jackson, Susan E., 135n67, 300n33, 433n4, 434n37
Jacob, Rahul, 33n2
Jacobs, Deborah L., 467n38
Jacobs, Robert W., 403n74
Jaeger, Alfred M. 679n16
Jaffe, Greg, 707n31
Jago, Arthur G., 288, 300n47, 301n50, 301n58
Jaj, Amal Kumar, 134n20
Jamil, Mamnoon, 267n27, 267n29, 267n45
Janson, Karen, 170
Jassawalla, Avan R., 642n36
Jastrzembski, Emily, 34n56
Javetski, Bill, 134n56
Jehn, Karen A., 102n49
Jemison, David, 102n22

Jensen, Elizabeth, 267n59
Jensen, Mary Ann, 642n38
Jermier, J. M., 542n39
Jervetson, Steve, 199n60
Jewell, Linda N. 642n38
Jimenez, Vivian, 170
Jinnett, Jerry, 198n40
Jobs, Steve, 67, 735, 709
Jobson, Tom, 706n8, 739n10
Johannes, Laura, 678n2
Johns, Doug, 333
Johnson, Craig, 416
Johnson, Eric, 95
Johnson, F., 466n3
Johnson, George, 714
Johnson, Magic, 521
Johnson, Maria, 473
Johnson, Robert, 444
Johnson, Susan, 452
Johnston, William B., 101n12
Jonas III, Harry S., 34n42
Jonas, Hans, 65n44
Jones, Alan, 660
Jones, Chris, 239
Jones, E., 510n16
Jones, Jack William, 33n35
Jones, N. W., 542n33, 575n23
Jones, Patricia, 102n46
Jones, Stephen, 263
Jones, Thomas M., 165n7, 165n10
Jones-Blomstrom, Robert and Brooke, 193
Jones-Blomstrom, Sally, 193
Jordan, Michael, 533
Joronen, Liisa, 217
Josaitis, Eleanor, 9
Jouse, Robert J., 542n36
Joyce, William F., 267n43
Judy, Richard W., 467n21, 467n27, 468n70
Jung, Andrea, 391
Jung, Carl, 496, 511n35
Juran, J. M. 679n19
Jurgensen, John, 33n4

Kagle, Bob, 199n70
Kahaner, Larry, 102n46
Kahn, Jeremy, 103n57, 165n2
Kahn, Paul, 596
Kahn, Robert, 609n30
Kahwajy, Jean L., 642n54, 643n61
Kalogeris, T. J., 510n14
Kamen, Seth, 644
Kane, Kate, 679n27
Kane, Melinda, 468n88
Kanigel, Robert, 64n16
Kanter, Rosabeth Moss, 199n69, 401n18, 402n49
Kanungo, Rabindra N., 542n42, 576n45, 576n52

Kaplan, Robert E., 33n32, 679n35, 679n36, 679n37
Kapstein, Jonathan, 133n8
Karr, Albert R., 575n41
Kasarda, John D., 739n35
Kast, Fremont E., 65n45, 65n47
Katel, Peter, 63n1, 65n68
Katz, Daniel, 609n30
Katz, Ian, 133n18, 134n19, 134n55
Katz, Robert L., 33n17
Kaufman, J., 510n3
Kaufman, Jonathan, 542n32
Kaufman, Leslie, 34n60
Kawamoto, Wayne, 65n56
Kazanas, H. C., 434n57
Kazanjian, Robert K., 268n67
Keen, C., 466n19
Keenan, Faith, 34n50, 402n60, 706n9, 739n40, 739n41
Keeney, Ralph L., 300n40
Kegler, Cassandra, 167n61
Kehoe, William J. 134n32
Keichel III, Walter, 542n42
Kekes, John, 165n15
Kelleher, Herb, 7, 448, 514
Kelley, H. H. 510n16
Kelly, Kevin, 65n55, 561, 575n33
Kelly, Pat, 214, 530
Kemske, Floyd, 433n10
Kennedy, Allan A., 102n44
Kennedy, J., 468n74
Kepler, Nick, 392
Kepner, C., 300n36
Kerr, Jean, 134n51, 609n1, 610n69
Kerr, S., 542n39
Kerry, K. Austin, 64n40
Kerstetter, Jim, 267n52
Kerwin, Kathleen, 133n12, 341n37
Keys, Bernard, 434n56
Khermouch, Gerry, 266n1, 268n75, 402n43
Kidder, Rushworth M., 165n9
Kiger, Patricia, 167n69
Killing, J. Peter, 120
Kilman, Ralph H., 102n36
Kim, Queena Sook, 199n67
Kimmel, Michael S., 466n15
King Jr., Martin Luther, 161, 533
King Jr., Ralph T., 643n57
King, John, 200
King, Paula J., 166n30
Kinkead, Gwen, 166n43
Kirkland Jr., Richard I., 101n9
Kirkman, Bradley L, 576n46, 642n21
Kirkpatrick, David, 133n2
Kirschenbaum, Jill, 34n48
Kirsner, Scott, 34n58, 370n29
Klass, Leslie Gross, 511n55
Klayman, Joshua, 301n56

Klein, Anne Sceia, 743
Klein, Gary, 279
Klein, Katherine J., 542n41
Klein, Mark M., 370n16
Klemm, Mary, 233n13
Klimas, Molly, 199n78
Klineberg, S. L., 510n13
Kneale, D., 433n5
Knickel, Carin, 14
Knight, Frank H., 64n20
Koch, Christopher, 739n12, 739n16, 739n20
Koehler, Kenneth G., 642n37, 643n55
Koenig, Richard, 371n49
Koerper, Gary, 379
Kofman, Fred, 370n31
Kogut, Bruce, 134n22
Kohlberg, L., 165n19
Kohs, S. C., 541n15
Kolb, David A., 511n40, 511n42
Kolenda, Konstanian, 165n15
Koonce, Richard, 370n21
Koontz, Katy, 401n22
Koretz, Gene, 198n23
Korzeniowski, Paul, 198n19
Kotter, John P., 33n32, 33n35, 102n50, 382, 401n11, 402n34, 402n40, 403n79
Kouzes, James M., 541n4
Kovacevich, Richard, 6, 533
Kozlowski, L. Dennis, 502
Kravetz, Dennis J., 434n33
Kravitz, D. A., 510n13
Kreps, David M., 433n7
Kruger, Pamela, 510n24, 575n13
Kuehl, Charles R., 198n32
Kuenzig, Bob, 171
Kumar, K., 468n77, 468n83
Kupfer, Andrew, 266n12, 403n67
Kuratko, Donald, F., 198n4, 198n27, 198n40
Kurk, Thomas, 371n44
Kurke, Lance B., 33n38
Kurland, Nancy B., 34n47, 103n64, 434n26
Kurschner, Dale, 165n5, 167n71
Kurtz, Kevin, 12
Kuzmits, Frank E., 435n79
Kvansnica, Jean, 7
Kwiecien, Stan, 743

Laabs, Jennifer J., 433n12, 478n69, 510n11, 511n50, 511n53
LaBarre, Polly, 33n27, 234n49, 541n1, 576n55
Labich, Kenneth, 134n47, 466n1, 468n89
LaFasto, Frank, M. J., 641n5, 641n15
Lagnado, Lucette, 101n1, 103n72
Lahti, Ryan K., 706n23

Lambert, Ken, 199n65
Lambing, Peggy A., 198n32
Land, Edwin, 378
Landau, Meryl Davids, 434n60
Landler, Mark, 133n11
Landro, Laura, 266n15
Lane, Henry W., 134n44
LaPotin, Perry, 299n14
Laroche, Lionel, 468n80
Larrick, Richard P., 301n56
Larsen, Janet K., 609n6
Larson, Carl E., 641n5, 641n15
Larson, L. L., 542 22
Lashinsky, Adam, 341n44
Latham, G. P., 234n25 575n32
Latour, Almar, 401n12
Lau, Alan W., 33n38
Lau, Dora C., 641n9
Lawler III, Edward E., 435n75, 575n23, 576n47, 679n20
Lawlor, Julia, 510n1, 511n59
Lawrence, Paul R., 341n24, 370n13, 370n37
Lazere, Cathy, 679n37, 739n30
Le Beau, Christina, 198n3, 198n7, 609n2
Lea, Wendy, 199n72
Leana, Carrie R., 340n11
Leavitt, Harold J., 402n50
Leder, Michelle, 510n18, 511n39
Ledford Jr., Gerald E., 234n44
Ledvinka, J., 434n51
Lee, Cindy, 667
Lee, Jennifer S., 678n6
Lee, Louise, 101n17, 133n1, 135n71
Lee, Sharon, 81
Lee-Young, Jane, 707,n35
LeFauve, Richard, 358
Lehn, K., 679n31
Lei, David, 268n62
Leibs, Scott, 739n19
Lemann, Nicholas, 467n29
Lengel, Robert H., 299n14, 543n47, 543n57, 609n10, 609n15
Leonard-Barton, Dorothy, 370n33, 402n38
Leonhardt, David, 267n22
Leontiades, Milton, 267n37, 267n42
Letts, Christine W., 34n45
Levering, Robert, 300n41
Lever-Pollary, Teresa, 587
Levinson, D. J., 510n29
Levinson, Meridith, 706n7
Levitt, Theodore, 266n17
Lewent, Judy C., 268n62
Lewin, Kurt, 402n39, 403n78, 518, 541n17
Lickona, T., 165n19
Lieb, Matthew, 239
Lieber, Ronald B., 267n28

Lienert Anita, 33n37, 300n34, 300n39, 739n23
Liesman, Steve, 165n3, 166n37
Likert, R., 542n23
Linder, Jane, 706n4
Ling, Tim, 57
Lipman, Joanne, 267n20
Lipnack, Jessica, 642n25
Lippitt, R., 541n17, 541n18
Liska, Paul J., 284, 300n42
Livingston, Abby, 575n25
Lizotte, Ken, 401n16
Lobel, Sharon A., 467n62
Lobell, Robert, 323
Loch, Karen D., 706n10
Locke, Edwin A., 234n25
Loden, Marilyn, 466n11
Longenecker, Justin G., 165n11
Longnecker, Clinton O., 643n58
Lopez, Julie Amparano, 467n44
Lorinc, John, 679n19
Lorsch, Jay W., 370n13, 370n37
Louis, Philip V., 610n53
Lowry, Peter, 610n63
Lubart, Todd I., 401n16
Lublin, Joann S., 135n62, 266n18, 468n71
Lubove, Seth, 101n2
Lucier, Charles E., 739n47
Luffman, George, 233n13
Lugt, Michiel, 647
Lukas, Paul, 402n52
Luthans, Fred, 65n47, 575n26, 575n28, 609n6, 679n30, 679n32
Lutz, Bob, 279, 284
Lyles, Judy, 408
Lyles, Marjorie A., 300n33
Lyons, Daniel, 65n59

Mabert, Vincent A., 706n17, 739n32
MacCormack, Alan David, 739n24
Machado, Rodolfo, 304, 470
Machiavelli, Niccolo, 510n31
Macintosh, Norman B., 610n45
MacLean, Ron, 198n37
Madigan, Kathleen, 267n41
Magnet, Myron, 102n29
Mahar, L., 542n28
Maher, Kris, 511n51
Mahoney, G. M., 542n33, 575n23
Maidment, Fred, 133n17
Main, Jeremy, 65n50, 34n58, 402n44
Mainardi, Cesare R., 266n18, 267n19
Makhija, A. K., 679n31
Makhija, Mahesh, 706n22, 706n27
Malkin, Elisabeth, 133n5, 133n18, 134n19, 134n50, 134n55
Mallinger, Mark, 165n11
Mallory, Maria, 101n16

Malone, Rick, 173
Maltoni, Valeria, 7
Mangalindan, Mylene, 300n37
Manganelli, Raymond L., 370n16
Mani, Sirish, 610n68, 667
Mann, Maureen, 353
Mannes, George, 198n17, 642n32
Manville, Brook, 341n42
March, James G. 299n10, 300n22, 434n31
Marino, Mike, 697
Mariucci, Steve, 495
Markels, Alex, 65n53, 370n25
Markides, Costantinos, 266n6, 266n10
Marks, Steven L., 233n9
Markus, M. Lynne, 341n42, 341n45, 609n14
Marsick, Victoria, 641n4
Martha, Joseph, 738n1, 739n48
Martin, Bob, 129
Martin, J., 609n20
Martin, James E., 575n22
Martin, Justin, 33n8
Martin, Kenneth R., 679n26
Martins, Luis I., 466n12
Maruca, Regina Fazio, 642n31
Mascarenhas, Briance, 267n27, 267n29, 267n45
Maslow, Abraham, 47, 549, 575n8
Mason, Richard O., 300n15, 300n44
Masuch, Michael, 299n14
Matherly, Timothy A., 401n14
Mathews, Anna Wilde, 678n6, 678n18
Mathis, Robert L., 433n2, 434n37
Mathys, Nicholas J., 234n45
Matlack, Carol, 267n49
Matson, Eric, 33n23, 63n2, 133n9
Matteson, Michael T., 609n29
Matthews, John A., 314n31
Mattis, Mary, 467n43
Mattis, Michael, 34n40
Maxwell, Jennifer, 198n45
Maxwell, Jill Hecht, 199n54
Mayer, Peter, 300n40
Maynard, Roberta, 199n49, 267n58, 575n9, 575n31, 609n33, 610n40
Mayo, Andrew, 65n66
Mayo, Elton, 46
Maznevski, Martha L., 468n76, 468n82, 468n84
McBain, Richard, 433n9, 434n32
McCafferty, Joseph, 707n32
McCall Jr., Morgan W., 33n32
McCann, J., 341n20
McCarthy, Michael J., 165n12, 299n3
McCartney, Laton, 641n10
McClandon, Thurrell O., 679n12
McClelland, David C., 198n33, 510n23, 553-554, 575n18
McClenahan, J. S., 134n37

McCracken, Mike, 679n22
McCullough, Stacie, 300n18
McCune, Jenny C., 33n28, 103n58, 103n62, 103n67, 103n71, 134n26, 234n18, 300n43, 609n3, 610n59, 706n26
McCutcheon, David M., 739n11
McDonald, Paul, 102n51
McDonnell, John, 604
McDowell, Jim, 700
McGee, G. W., 510n510
McGee, Marianne Kolbasuk, 402n64
McGee, Suzanne, 199n58
McGeehan, Patrick, 32n1, 34n62
McGill, Michael E., 541n12
McGinley, Laurie, 165n1
McGrath, M. R., 300n44
McGregor, Douglas, 47, 64n37, 548
McGuire, Jean B., 167n74
McIntyre, J. M., 511n42, 575n18
McKay, Betsy, 34n41
McKeehan, Dale, 743
McKinley, Kate, 34n40
McKinney, Joseph A., 165n11
McLaughlin, Kevin J., 341n36
McLaughlin, M. L., 610n68
McLean, Bethany, 165n2, 267n35, 543n48
McMahon, J. Timothy, 234n29
McManus, Doyle, 64n9
McMath, Robert, 402n52
McNair, James, 402n35
McNealy, Scott, 11
McQuaid, Sara J., 134n44
Meek, V. Lynne, 102n35
Megerian, Lara E., 510n21
Mehrabian, Albert, 609n22
Mehta, Stephanie N., 467n22, 467n24, 510n27
Meiseles, Joanna B., 518
Meising, Paul, 234n17
Meister, Jeanne C., 434n59, 434n60
Melcher, Richard A., 134n54, 299n1
Melich, Greg, 305
Mello, John P., Jr, 706n5
Melnyk, Steven A., 738n9
Mendenhall, M., 467n60
Mensah, Van, 89
Menzies, Hugh D., 133n3
Merriden, Trevor, 679n8
Metcalf, Henry C., 64n24
Metcalf, Peter, 273
Meyers, Bill, 198n22
Meyers, Randy, 34n49
Meyerson, Debra E., 467n36, 467n44
Miceli, Marcia P., 167n67, 167n68
Michaels, Rob, 547
Michaelsen, L. K., 468n77, 468n83
Michols, M. P., 609n26

Middelhoff, Thomas, 107
Mieszkowski, Katharine, 199n68, 301n53, 542n24
Milbourn, Todd T., 679n10
Miles Raymond, 341n38
Miles, Grant, 341n31
Miles, Gregory L., 642n27
Miles, Raymond E., 341n31, 341n32
Milkovich, George T., 435n74
Mill, John Stuart, 141
Miller, C. Chet, 233n6, 266n5
Miller, Danny, 267n50
Miller, J. G., 609n36
Miller, Karen Lowrey, 133n5, 134n56, 135n57
Miller, Ron, 278
Miller, William, 65n66
Milliken, Frances, 466n12
Mills, Peter K., 371n44, 401n7
Mintzberg, Henry, 15-16, 33n31, 33n34, 33n35, 33n36, 33n39, 234n47, 268n66, 370n11, 541n5, 609n5
Mirvis, Philip H., 433n9
Mishra, Aneil, 102n51
Mitchell, Russell, 166n27
Mitchell, Terrence R., 542n36
Mitchener, Brandon, 134n27
Mitroff, Ian, 234n32, 234n35, 234n39, 234n40, 300n15
Moberg, Dennis J., 165n11, 371n44
Moeller, Michael, 341n21
Moffett, Matt, 134n47
Moffett, Michael H., 134n30
Mohria, Nitin, 706n26
Mohrman, Susan A., 679n20
Monroe, Lorraine, 4, 5, 533
Montabno, Ray V., 575n20
Montemayor, E., 435n73
Moon, Dottie, 85
Moore, Jonathan, 134n49
Moore, Meg Mitchell, 706n21
Moore, Pamela L., 34n51, 575n30
Moran, Robert T., 135n60, 135n63, 135n69
Moravec, Bruce, 12
Morgan, Ronald B., 167n59
Morris, Betsy, 267n31, 268n68
Morris, Louis, 346
Morrison, Ann M., 33n32
Moskowitz, Jason, 178
Moskowitz, Milton, 300n41
Moss, Jonathan E., 433n20, 434n24
Mother Theresa, 533
Mougayar, Walid, 34n40
Mount, M. K., 510n17
Mouton, Hane S., 542 24
Moynihan, Eugene O., 134n30
Muchinsky, P. M., 510n5
Mucrack, Peter E., 642n43

Muczyk, Jan P., 234n27
Mullaney, Timothy J., 341n21
Muller, Joann, 102n25
Muller, Rob, 402n41
Mullin, Leo, 10
Mumford, Michael D., 542n45
Munter, Mary, 466n14
Muoio, Anna, 300n19, 511n38
Murnighan, J. Keith, 641n9, 642n47
Murphy, Hugh, 16
Murray, Matt, 65n59, 434n58

Naatz, Nancy, 492
Nader, Ralph, 79
Nadler, David A., 370n27, 402n26
Nakao, Kevin, 172
Nalumansi, Miriam, 454
Napoliello, Michael Jr., 178
Narisetti, Raju, 133n6
Nasser, Jacques, 68, 204, 305, 474, 649, 743
Nathan, Arte, 405, 430
Neal, Judith, 159
Near, Janet P., 167n67, 167n68
Neff, Jack, 340n1, 341n47
Nelson, Katherine A., 167n54
Nelson, Peter, 551
Nelton, Sharon, 466n15, 468n69, 510n21
Neubert, Mitchell, 643n58
Neuborne, Ellen, 233n11
Nevis, E. C., 370n26
Newman III, Lawrence James, 739n24
Newman, Robin Gorman, 171
Newstrom, John W., 510n2, 610n51, 610n54
Nicholls, Chantell E., 134n44
Noble, Barbara Presley, 467n40
Nocera, Joseph, 102n31
Nolan, Sarah, 213
Nomme, Roald, 354
Nordlinger, Pia, 102n23
Nordstrom, Blake, 713
Nordstrom, John, 713
Northcraft, Gregory B., 371n45, 738n5
Norton, David, 679n35, n36, n37
Norton, Erle, 541n9
Noskin, Gary, 594
Novak, William, 370n6
Nunn, Edna, 586
Nutt, Paul C., 268n67, 300n38, 402n40
Nyberg, Alix, 403n69
Nystrom, P. C., 542n22

O'Connor, Jennifer, 542n45
O'Farrell, Bill, 596
O'Hara, Linda A., 401n16
O'Keefe, Brian, 133n2, 134n25
O'Leary, Laurie P., 370n2
O'Loughlin, Michael G., 340n10

O'Neil, Lorraine Brennan, 170
O'Reilly, Brian, 198n39, 340n16, 434n64
O'Reilly III, Charles A., 102n39, 103n61, 234n15, 511n37, 542n37, 575n34
Odenwald, Sylvia, 642n30
Odiorne, George S., 234n26
Oglethorpe, Ray, 642n31
Ohmae, Kenichi, 101n9, 266n16
Oldham, Greg R., 565, 575n40
Olofson, Cathy, 267n34, 401n19, 609n32
Olson, J. M., 510n4
Olson, Mike, 590
Oneal, Michael, 166n27
Opie, John, 330
Orenstein, Susan, 34n61, 267n40
Oringel, Amy, 199n51, 199n53
Orna, Daniel, 266n11
Ortega, Bob, 101n16
Osborn, Richard N., 542n22
Ostroff, C., 510n5
Ostroff, Frank, 370n24
Ostro-Landau, Nilly, 133n3
Ouchi, William G., 679n16
Overton, Sharon, 103n54
Owens, Thomas, 641n10, 642n20
Oxedine, James, 494

Pacanowsky, Michael, 300n16
Page, Larry, 190
Paine, Lynn Sharpe, 165n17
Palmer, Ann Therese, 435n77
Palmeri, Christopher, 266n4, 266n13, 706n2
Pape, William R., 609n34
Parch. Lorie, 510n23
Pare, Terence C., 679n32
Pare, Terence P., 266n15
Park, Andrew, 267n54
Parks, Don, 300n35
Parson, H. M., 64n32
Parson, Talcott, 64n20
Pascale, Richard, 433n19
Pascarella, Perry, 679n33
Pasmore, W., 166n25
Pataki, George, 29
Patmore, Kim, 392, 403n69
Patton, Susannah, 707n39
Pavett, Cynthia M., 33n38
Pawar, Badrinarayan Shankar, 542n46
Pearce II, John A., 234n13, 266n9, 266n11
Pearce, C. Glenn, 609n25
Pearlson, Keri, 34n47, 341n46
Pearson, Andy, 536
Pearson, Christine M., 234n40
Pearson, David, 233n10, 706n24
Pedrolie, Charlene, 613, 636
Penley, Larry E., 609n6
Perlmutter, Howard V., 135n59
Perot, H. Ross, 90

Perrow, Charles, 371n41
Petainger Jr., Thomas, 641n1
Peterman, John, 555, 575n21
Peters, Greg, 419
Peters, Thomas J., 103n66, 402n28, 609n25, 610n49
Peterson, Lance, 594
Peterson, Melanie M., 575n22
Peterson, Richard B., 371n49
Petrock, Frank, 103n52
Petty, M. M. 510n5
Petzinger Jr., Thomas, 63n1, 64n10, 64n11, 65n68, 166n43, 402n48, 403n77, 610n41, 642n39, 643n67, 739n14
Pfeffer, Jeffrey, 65n52, 102n39, 103n56, 234n15, 370n30, 433n6, 541n5, 542n37, 575n34
Phelps, Drew, 706n4
Phillips, Sandra N., 341n28
Picard, Michele, 468n78
Pickard, Jane, 642n29
Picknelly, Peter, 471
Piëch, Ferdinand, 509
Pierce, Jon L., 166n40, 300n30
Piergallini, Al, 97
Pincus Hartman, Laura, 166n49
Pincus, A. L. 510n17
Pinson, Linda, 198n40
Pischetsrieder, Bernd, 509
Pitroda, Salil S., 134n31
Pitta, Julie, 199n64
Piturro, Marlene, 434n41
Podolske, Ann, 575n42, 576n50
Poe, Robert, 707n37
Poet, Jonathan, 403n3
Pohlmann, Tom, 34n56
Pollock, Ellen Joan, 468n64
Pool, Robert, 371n39
Poole, Marshall Scott, 401n24
Porras, Jerry I., 89, 103n57, 234n44
Porter, Lyman W., 300n30, 574n3, 574n6
Porter, Michael E., 253-257, 267n21, 267n26, 267n50, 267n51, 267n57, 266n8, 370n34
Posner, Barry Z., 541n4
Posner, Burce G., 679n13
Post, James E., 166n28, 609n16
Powers, M. 609n20
Pratt, Dale, 94
Pregracke, Chad, 160
Prescott, John E., 266n9
Pressman, Aaron, 609n31
Preston, Lee E., 166n30
Priem, Richard L., 341n36
Prince, C. J., 33n9
Prince, George, 642n33
Pritchard, R. D., 575n32
Procter, William Cooper, 38

Puckett, John and Kim, 302
Pulley, Mary Lynn, 34n56
Putnam, Arnold O., 402n55

Quesnelle, Stephen, 4, 5
Quick, Rebecca, 268n70
Quinn, Francis J., 739n39
Quinn, James Brian, 401n17, 403n76
Quinn, Robert E., 102n43, 467n62
Quittner, Josh, 738n2

Radosevich, Lynda, 134n35
Ragan, James W., 299n15
Ragins, Belle Rose, 467n43, 467n55
Rajagopalan, Nandini, 300n32
Ramstad, Evan, 341n35, 739n27
Rancour, Tom, 679n22
Randolph, W. Alan, 341n25, 370n38
Rangel, Beatrice, 156
Rapoport, Carla, 133n11
Rasheed, Abdul M. A., 300n32, 341n36
Raskin, Andy, 541n6
Raskin, Josh, 515
Rasmusson, Erika, 166n33, 641n6
Ratz, Wayne, 256
Raul, Alan Charles, 134n29, 134n33
Raven, B., 541n7
Rawls, Lawrence, 226
Read, Jim, 379
Read, W. H., 610n39
Rebello, Kathy, 33n19
Reed, Stanley, 133n8, 341n25
Reichardt, Carl E., 305
Reilly, Patrick M., 101n3
Reimann, Bernard C., 234n27
Reimus, Byron, 610n63
Reinhard, Andy, 65n58, 65n62, 102n20,
    541n11
Reitz, H. Joseph, 642n38
Rendleman, John, 102n20
Rennie, Janice, 546
Renshaw, Amy Austin, 370n23
Revesz, Therese R., 134n53
Revkin, Andrew C., 166n42
Reynolds, Paul, 198n39
Rhoads, Rebecca, 506
Ricciardi, Larry, 500
Rice, Faye, 466n4
Rice, Ronald E., 609n14
Richards, Max D., 233n5
Richardson, Karen, 215
Richlin, H., 575n26
Richman, Louis S., 133n17
Richman, Tom, 574n3
Ricks, Thomas, 610n64
Riesenberger, John R., 135n60, 135n63,
    135n69
Rifkin, Glenn, 65n46, 199n65, 402n51
Riggio, Leonard, 10

Riggs, Joy, 234n23
Ring, Peter Smith, 102n29
Rioux, Sheila, 433n13
Ripley, David E., 434n34
Rivkin, Victoria, 434n49
Rix, Jeff, 169, 194
Robbins, Alan, 525
Robbins, Dave, 290
Robbins, Stephen P., 134n40, 642n52,
    643n60
Robers, R. A., 610n42
Roberti, Mark, 706n1, 707n41, 707n42
Roberto, Michael A., 301n59, 301n62
Roberts, Elizabeth, 166n34
Roberts, Nancy C., 166n30
Roberts, Paul, 267n30, 511n45, 609n8
Robey, Daniel, 642n53, 706n10
Robinson Jr., Richard B., 266n9
Robinson, Edward, 65n60
Robinson, G., 468n77
Rocks, David, 739n18, 739n36
Rodin, Rob, 563
Roemer, John, 678n1, 679n39
Roethlisberger, F. J., 46, 64n31, 64n34
Rogers, E. M., 610n42
Rohde, Bruce, 311, 312, 337
Ronkainen, Ilkka A., 134n30
Rooney, Phillip, 529
Rose, Frank, 233n12
Rosen, Benson, 576n46, 642n21
Rosenbaum, Joshua, 267n56
Rosenberg, Hilary, 575n36
Rosener, Judy B., 466n11, 543n50, 543n52
Rosenfeld, Jill, 103n69, 433n3
Rosenfield, Rick, 533, 739n24
Rosenman, R. 511n48
Rosenzweig, James E., 65n45, 65n47
Ross, Steve, 379
Roth, John, 82
Rothman, Howard, 679n21
Rothwell, William J., 434n57
Rothylisberger, J. F., 574n7
Rotter, J. B., 510n26
Rousseau, Denise M., 371n41
Roussel, Philip A., 299n12
Row, Heath, 341n35
Rowe, Allen J., 300n44
Rowe, Mary P., 610n39
Rubin, I. M., 511n42, 575n18
Rudolph, Barbara, 134n36
Ruff, Joe, 340n1, 341n47
Ruiz, Hector de Jesus, 517
Rull, Harry, 31
Russo, Pat, 532
Rust, Mike, 361
Rutherford, Emelie, 371n46
Ryan, M. S., 466n3
Ryan, William P., 34n45
Ryans Jr., John K., 267n48, 402n55

Rynes, S. L., 434n35
Sager, Ira, 511n44
Salter, Chuck, 370n32
Salva, Martin, 266n18, 267n19
Sandberg, William R., 299n15, 301n60
Sanderson, Muir, 266n18, 267n19
Sanderson, Stuart, 233n13
Sanford, R. N., 510n29
Sant, Roger, 128
Santiago, Chiori, 468n79
Saporito, Bill, 266n3
Sapsford, Jathon, 65n59
Sarri, L. M., 575n32
Sashittal, Hemant C., 642n36
Sashkin, M., 403n70
Saunder, Carol, 33n35
Saunders, Charles B. 233n7
Saveri, Gabrielle, 435n77
Saxton, Mary J., 102n36
Scarborough, Jack, 135n65
Scarlata, Don, 604
Scaturro, Anthony, 706n29
Schapiro, Mark, 167n72
Scheele, Nick, 305
Schein, Edgar H., 102n37, 403n67,
    610n61
Schendel, Dan E., 267n37
Schiller, Zachary, 266n15, 341n25
Schilling, Melissa A., 341n40, 402n53,
    402n57
Schine, Eric, 641n4
Schlender, Brenton R., 33n18, 135n70
Schlesinger, Arthur M., 63n6
Schlesinger, L. A., 402n34, 402n40
Schmenner, Roger W., 371n44
Schmidt, Jeffrey A., 234n48
Schmidt, W. H. 541n19
Schmitt, William, 701
Schneeweis, Thomas, 167n74
Schoemaker, Paul J. H., 300n32
Schreisheim, C. A., 542n21, 542n38,
    739n29
Schroeder, Roger G., 641n3
Schuler, Randall S., 135n67, 403n4
Schultz, Howard, 97, 265, 274
Schultz, Randall L., 268n65
Schulz, Dana, 173
Schulze, Richard, 498
Schwartz, Jeffrey, 202
Schwartz, Tony, 576n53
Schweiger, David M., 299n15, 301n60
Scott, K. Dow, 641n2
Scott, Susanne G., 641n14
Scrushy, Richard, 286
Sculley, John, 67
Seashore, Stanley E., 642n44
Seglin, Jeffrey L., 165n2, 165n12,
    167n76, 167n78
Seibert, Cindy, 64n21

Selye, Hans, 511n47
Semler, Ricardo, 576n49, 673
Senge, Peter M., 55, 65n51, 370n31
Serpa, Roy, 102n36
Serwer, Andrew E., 134n21, 510n27
Seubert, Eric, 706n22, 706n27
Sewell, Dan, 102n19
Shanklin, William L., 267n48, 402n55
Shapira, Zur, 299n10
Shapiro, Eben, 267n59
Sharfman, Mark P., 300n32
Sharpe, Rochelle, 543n51, 543n53
Shartel, C. L., 542n21
Shaw, M. E., 610n44, 642n32, 642n40
Shaw, Robert B., 370n27
Shea, Gordon F., 165n6
Shealy, Jane, 198n20
Sheats, P. 642n33
Sheehan, Orla, 134n46
Shein, Esther, 433n15, 706n25, 706n26
Shellenbarger, Sue, 33n22, 510n6
Shelly II, M. W., 402n50
Sheppard, I. Thomas, 609n21, n23
Sherman, Arthur, 433n11, 434n43,
    434n52
Sherman, Stratford, 341n27
Sherwin, Douglas S., 166n29, 678n3,
    679n17
Sherwood, John J., 102n35
Shin, Young J., 11
Shirouszu, Norihiko, 679n25, 738n4
Shonk, James, H., 641n16
Shor, Rita, 389
Shwartz, Tony, 510n7
Siboni, Roger, 215
Siebel, Tom, 89, 514
Sielh, Caren, 33n4
Silburt, David, 574n2
Silver, Joshua, 661
Silveri, Bob, 706n8, 739n10
Silverman, Robin Landew, 517, 541n14
Silvetti, Jorge, 304, 470
Simmons, Donald B., 610n54
Simon, Herbert A., 233n7, 299n7,
    300n21, 300n22, 300n23, 300n25,
    434n31
Simons, John, 102n18
Simpson, Glenn R., 167n79
Simpson, Peggy, 134n56
Sims, C., 134n40
Sindhu, Pradeep, 173
Sinetar, Marsha, 401n17
Singer, Andrew W., 166n22
Singh, R., 542n30
Sinha, Kingshuk, K., 541n3
Sittenfeld, Curtis, 340n12, 642n23
Skarzynski, Peter, 299n5
Skinner, B. F., 575n26
Skivington, James E., 268n73

Slater, Derek, 706n3, 706n18
Slevin, Dennis P., 268n65
Slipp, Sandra, 466n15
Slocum Jr., John W., 134n44, 135n68,
    401n5, 541n12, 574n3, 679n30,
    679n32
Smart, Tim 134n56
Smircich, Linda, 102n36
Smith, Adam, 340n5
Smith, Chris, 300n29
Smith, Frederick, 378
Smith, Geri, 133n11
Smythe, Peter, 121
Snell, Scott, 433n11, 434n43, 434n52
Snow, Charles C., 341n31, 341n32,
    341n38
Snyder, Nancy Tennant, 543n54, 642n24
Soderberg, Jeff, 552
Soderberg, Mark, 717
Soh, Calvin, 201
Solomon, Charlene Marmer, 103n59,
    103n65, 467n42, 543n55, 642n27
Somech, Anit, 642n43, 643n62
Songer, N., 466n13
Soni, Ashok, 706, n17
Sonnack, Mary, 402n58
Sonofsky, Steven, 314
Sormumen, Juhani, 300n35
Sosik, John J. 510n21
Sozzi, Ray, 469
Specter, Robert, 102n42
Spector, P. E., 510n28
Spence, Betty, 467n45
Spreitzer, Gretchen M., 102n43
Springsteel, Ian, 300n42
Srivastva, Suresh, 34n42
St. Clair, Lynda, 467n62
St. John, Caron H., 166n31
St. John, Warren, 101n3, 102n33
Stack, Jack, 229
Stajkovic, Alexander D., 575n26, 575n28
Stalk, Jr., George, 402n47, 402n62
Stamps, David, 468n78
Stamps, Jeffrey, 642n25
Stanton, Steven, 370n16, 370n17, 370n19
Stapenhurst, Frederick, 134n24
Starke, Frederick A., 574n3
Starkey, Ken, 102n35
Stathatos, Peter, 467n30
Stavropoulous, Andreas, 199n60
Staw, B. M., 609n20
Stearns, Timothy M., 64n35
Stecklow, Steve, 678n2, 679n7
Steers, Richard M., 233n7, 574n3, 574n6
    575n24, 609n31, 610n39, 610n43
Stefanko, John, 669
Stein, Bob, 9
Steinbuhler, K., 199n62
Stepanek, Marcia, 65n42, 167n78

Stephens, Carroll, 166n26
Stephens, Robert, 203
Sternberg, Robert J., 401n16
Sterngold, James, 34n59
Stevenson, Howard H., 401n17
Stevenson, Thomas H., 679n29
Stevenson, William B., 300n30
Stewart, Rosemary, 33n32
Stewart, Thomas A., 33n30, 234n24,
    301n53, 340n9, 341n29, 370n28,
    371n47, 541n13, 609n19, 610n64,
    610n65
Stoka, Ann Marie, 64n16
Stoner, James A. F., 33n5, 610n66
Storey, Greg, 546
Storrs, Constance, 64n22
Stoughton, Vickery, 9
Stout, Hilary, 198n9
Strahley, James T., 234n44
Straud, Detmar, 706n10
Strauss, Robert, 580
Streidl, J. William, 234n29
Strickland III, A. J., 267n27, 267n48,
    267n54
Stuart, F. Ian, 739n11
Sundgren, Alison, 167n74
Sundstrom, Eric, 641n7
Sunoo, Brenda Paik, 434n23
Superville, Darlene, 101n10
Suresh, Kotha, 266n11
Sussman, Stephanie Watts, 610n64
Sutton, Robert I., 401n21, 402n25,
    402n30
Svatko, James E., 102n34, 267n44
Swamidass, Paul M., 738n6
Sykes, Jason, 167n79
Symonds, William C., 267n49, 468n63,
    510n9, 542n25, 575n15
Szilagyi, Andrew D., 234n29
Szwajkowski, Eugene W., 166n28,
    166n46
Szygenda, Ralph, 518-519

Taber, T., 541n8
Takahashi, Dean, 299n4
Tam, Pui-Wing, 299n1
Tannenbaum, Jeffrey A., 199n78, 370n15
Tannenbaum, R., 541n19
Tansik, David A., 371n45, 738n5
Tapscott, Don, 267n60, 341n33
Tausky, Curt, 64n28, 64n36
Taylor III, Alex, 299n11
Taylor, Frederick W., 42, 49, 57, 59, 548
Taylor, Jessica, 173
Taylor, John, 300n24
Taylor, Robert R., 134n30
Taylor, William C., 609n34
Teece, David J., 266n9
Teitlebaum, Richard, 402n46

Terry, Paul M., 643n56
Tetenbaum, Toby J., 34n46, 34n53, 63n3
Teurfs, Linda, 610n61
Thach, Liz, 706n30
Thakor, Anjan V., 679n10
Tharp, Mike, 314n22
Thatcher, Mike, 434n55
Thayer, P. W., 434n50
Therrien, Lois, 610n50
Thomas Philip R., 679n26
Thomas, David A., 146, 443, 467n56,
    468n77
Thomas, Howard, 299n10, 300n33
Thomas, K. W., 643n59
Thomas, Owen, 706n19
Thomas Jr., Roosevelt, 467n29
Thomke, Stefan, 402n58
Thompson Jr., Arthur A., 267n27,
    267n48, 267n54
Thompson, James D., 371n48, 738n3
Thompson, Julie, 201
Thompson, Kenneth R., 234n45
Thompson, Philip C., 679n20
Thurow, Roger, 268n74
Thursfield, David, 204
Tichy, Noel M., 314n27, 370n31, 5
    42n46
Tierney, Christine, 678n2
Tierney, Thomas, 706n26
Timmons, Heather, 32n1
Timon, Clay, 199n66
Toffler, Barbara Ley, 166n53
Toner, John, 209, 230
Toppo, Greg, 166n41
Tornow, Walter W., 434n64
Torre, Joe, 7, 8
Torsilieri, Janet D., 739n47
Townsend, Anthony, 642n24
Townsend, Bickley, 467n43
Tree, David, 201
Tregoe, B., 300n36
Trevino, Linda Klebe, 165n18, 167n55,
    167n58, 165n6, 166n25, 166n49,
    166n53, 167n54, 575n29, 609n10,
    609n15
Trice, Harrison M., 102n47
Trompenaars, Fons, 135n66
Tuch, Anita, 597
Tuckman, Bruce W., 642n38
Tuggel, Francis D., 233n7
Tulega, Tad, 165n16
Tung, Rosalie, 466n14
Turcotte, Jim, 706n8, 739n10
Turner, Ernie, 641n4
Turney, Michael and Barbara, 175
Tushman, Michael, 402n26
Tyler, Kathryn, 434n44

Ulfelder, Steve, 133n7

Ulrich, Dave, 433n9
Upton, David M., 738n7
Urwick, Lyndall, 64n24
Useem, Jerry, 34n60, 64n14, 165n1,
    198n25, 434n42, 543n49

Van Alstyne, Marshall, 370n32
Van de Ven, Andrew H., 371n49, 102n29,
    401n13, 401n24, 402n54
Van den Oord, Bob, 66, 647
Van Fleet, David D., 64n26, 340n13,
    541n16, 643n64
Van Scyoc, Chet and Terrie, 174
Vaskevitch, David, 314
Vecchio, Robert P., 575n20
Velasquez, Manuel, 165n11
Venkataramann, M.A., 706n17
Verheem, Johann, 192
Vessels, Gordon, 401n15
Victor, Bart, 166n26
Vilano, Matt, 65n43
Vinzant, Carol, 739n40
Vleeming, R. G., 510n33
Vogel, David, 166n22
Vogel, Todd, 133n8
Vogl, A. J., 543n49, 575n35
Voigt, Kevin, 434n27
Von Bertalanffy, Ludwig, 64n44
Von Glinow, Mary Ann, 466n14, 542n38
Von Hipple, Eric, 402n58
Vroom, Victor H., 288, 300n46, 300n47,
    300n48, 301n50, 301n51, 575n23

Wagemen, Ruth, 642n19
Wagoner, Rick, 150, 284
Wah, Louisa, 65n67, 167n61, 433n19,
    467n28, 511n53, 706n26
Wakeman, Pete and Laura, 600
Walker, Joseph, 267n41
Wallace, Julie, 64n7
Walleigh, Richard C., 739n37
Walls Jr., Julius, 145
Walmac, Amanda, 199n76
Walton, Sam, 38
Wanous, J. P., 434n39
Want, Jerome H., 234n13
Warfield, Andrea, 467n62
Warner, Melanie, 102n41, 103n53, 541n2
Warren, Steve and Diane, 557
Warshaw, Michael, 199n75, 610n56
Waterman Jr., Robert H., 103n66, 610n49
Watson, Mary, 679n219
Watson, Ray, 278
Watson, Thomas, 49
Watson, W. E., 468n77, 468n83
Wayne, Leslie, 34n60
Weaver, Gary R., 166n53
Weaver, Vanessa J., 477n18, 467n49,
    467n54

Webb, Allen P., 166n52, 167n59
Webber, Alan, 370n7
Weber, James, 166n24
Weber, Joseph, 102n20, 133n8, 340n16
Weber, Max, 43, 44, 64n20, 319
Weber, Thomas E., 609n13
Webster, Jane, 609n10
Wechsler, Neil, 722
Weidenbaum, Murray, 133n3
Weil, Elizabeth, 102n42
Weil, Henry, 198n46, 199n48
Weimer, De' Ann, 511n41
Weinberger, David, 371n46
Weinstock, Carol, 170
Weintraut, J. Neil, 199n59, 199n61
Weisinger, Hendrie, 510n23
Weisul, Kimberly, 199n52
Welch, David, 706n9
Welch, Jack, 24, 330, 554, 560, 667, 669
Weller, Joe, 390-391
Welles, Edward O., 34n43, 65n54
Wellings, Richard S., 642n18
Wellington, Sheila, 467n45
Wellins, Rich, 433n13
Wellner, Alison Stein, 64n7, 433n15
Wendenhof, Jon R., 234n44
Wessel, David, 433n22
Wetzel, Liz, 300n34
Wheatley, Malcom, 739n28
Wheelen, Thomas L., 267n53
Wheelwright, S. C., 738n8
Whitaker, Barbara, 134n28
White, Gregory L., 299n8, 300n42
White, Joseph B., 133n4, 300n42
White, R. K., 541n17, 541n18
Whitford, David, 233n8, 574n1, 576n56
Whitley, Marissa, 701
Whitman, Meg, 11, 240, 568
Wieand, Paul, 493
Wiener, L., 435n76
Wiener, Yoash, 102n35
Wiesendanger, Betsy, 198n45
Wiggins, J. S. 510n17
Wild, Russell, 299n13
Wiley, Carolyn, 167n59
Willett, Glynn, 549
Williams, Monci Jo, 609n27
Williamson, James E., 679n36, n37
Willoughby, Jay, 302
Wilson, Jeanne M., 642n18, 642n50
Wind, Youram, 135n59
Winfrey, Oprah, 588
Wingfield, Nick, 65n57, 134n19
Winslow, Ron, 165n13
Winters, Rebecca, 738n2
Wolf, Thomas, 34n44
Wolf, William B., 64n26
Wolfe, Joseph, 234n17, 434n56
Wong, Alan, 165n14

Wood, Robert A., 167n70
Woodman Richard W., 166n25, 574n3, 706n30
Woodruff, David, 135n57
Woodward, Joan, 361, 362, 371n42
Wooldridge, Bill, 33n29
Worthy, Fred S., 609n11
Wozniak, Steve, 67
Wrege, Charles D., 64n16, 64n29
Wren, Daniel A., 63n6, 64n12, 64n15, 64n18
Wright, Herman, 64n31, 386
Wright, Robin, 64n9
Wylie, Ian, 233n1
Wynter, Leon E., 467n28, 467n33

Wysocki Jr., Bernard, 65n61, 234n31
Yasai-Ardekani, Masoud, 371n38
Yates, Linda, 299n5
Yearwood, Carlton, 446
Young, Debby, 642n30, 679n38
Young, Eric, 706n16
Young, Mary, 609n16
Young, W. G., 510n14
Young, Walter Jr., 238
Yukl, Gary A., 541n3, 541n8, 541n15
Yusem, Michael, 470
Yuspeh, Alan, 167n62

Zachary, G. Pascal, 34n52, 466n5, 466n20, 468n81

Zajonc, R. B., 643n62
Zaltman, G., 402n36
Zander, Alvin F., 541n7, 642n42
Zanna, M. P., 510n4
Zarella, Ronald, 273, 358
Zawacki, Robert A., 64n39, 403n70
Zeithaml, Carl P., 267n25
Zellner, Wendy, 233n11, 706n9
Zey, Mary, 467n57
Zimmerman, Rachel, 165n1
Zinn, Saura, 101n16
Zipkin, Amy, 165n3, 166n23, 166n36, 167n63, 167n65
Zygmont, Jeffrey, 65n64

Company Index

10 Minute Manicure, 170
1-800-Flowers, 57, 215
3Com, 438
3M, see *Minnesota Mining and Manufacturing*

A&P, 150, 681, 702
A&W, 121
A.W. Chesterton Company, 484, 553, 580
Aahs!, 663
Abercrombie & Fitch, 80, 699
Adobe Systems, 381
Advanced Micro Devices Inc., 392, 517
AES Corporation, 128, 568, 599
AFL-CIO, 9
Agency.com, 80
Agilent Technologies, 429
Air France Concorde, 26
Airbus, 85
AK Steel, 516
Alberto-Culver, 396-397
Alcan Aluminum, 150
Alcoa, 160
Alibris, 138
All Metro Health Care, 550
Allied Tire Stores, 240
Allstate Insurance Company, 438, 446
Alltel Corp., 586
Amazon.com, 38, 57, 87, 106, 174, 194, 255, 258, 593, 688, 690, 691
America Online, 86, 106, 107, 112, 366, 701
American Airlines, 223, 277-278, 323, 685
American Electric Power Company, 138
American Express Company, 3, 28-29, 174, 212, 255, 258, 324, 344, 439
American MultiCinema, 491
American Red Cross, 586
American Standard Companies, 347
AMETEK Lamb Electric, 227, 723
Amex Life Assurance, 212, 213
Amgen, 244
Amtrak, 469
Anadarko, 733
Angang Iron and Steel, 359
Anheuser-Buesch (Budweiser), 109, 124
Ann Taylor, 699
AOL Time Warner, 257

Apogee Enterprises, 216
Apple Computer, 67, 106, 344, 388, 709, 710, 735
Application Technologies, 192
Aramark Corp., 492
Archer-Daniels-Midland, 138
Arivda Realty, 278
Arthur Anderson, 27
Asea Brown Boveri Ltd., 109, 328
Ask.com, 189
AstraZeneca, 258
AT&T, 23, 114, 174, 421, 469, 532, 554, 565, 671
Athene Software, 95
ATX Forms, 549
Autobytel, 111
Avery Dennison, 331
Avis, 257
Avon, 157, 239, 391

Baazee.com, 111
Ball Aerospace, 381
Barnes & Noble Inc., 10, 38, 86, 690
Barnesandnoble.com, 10, 86
Baronet Coff, Inc., 279
BASF, 109
Baskin-Robbins, 242
Baxter Healthcare, 670
Bay Networks, 82
Beacon Sweets & Chocolates, 124
BearShare, 59
Bell Atlantic, 312, 443
Bellagio Resort, 405, 430
BellSouth, 505
Ben & Jerry's, 107, 145
Bennigan's Grill and Tavern, 14
Bertelsmann AG, 86, 107
Bertucci's, 213, 214
Best Buy, 498, 726
Best Western International, 379
BET.com, 444
Big Boy, 121
Black & Decker, 220, 374
Black Diamond Equipment, Ltd., 273
Black Entertainment Television, 444
BlueLight.com, 240
BMW, 68, 699, 700
Boeing Corporation, 12, 85, 155, 156, 158, 214, 244, 381, 388, 389, 438, 661, 717
Bollinger Shipyards, 694
Boston Solectria Corp., 408

BP Amoco PLC, 150, 602
Brady Corporation, 294, 312
Brandwise.com, 690
Bridgestone/Firestone, 138
Bristol-Myers Squibb, 150
BT Labs, 622
Buckman Laboratories International, 53
Bucks County Bank, 493
Buffalo Zoo, 645-646
Burger King, 107, 121, 124
Burlington Northern Santa Fe, 689, 718-719

C.R. England, 8-9
Cadbury Schwepps, 19
Caliber Systems Inc., 730
Campbell Soup Co., 562
Canada Life, 493
Canadian Airlines International, 385
Cannondale Corporation, 648, 740, 741, 742
CarePackages.com, 469
Caribou Coffee, 302-303
Carnation, 107
Carrefour SA, 105
Carrier Corp., 58
Caterpillar, Inc., 243, 665
CB&T bank, 319
Celanese Chemicals, 701
Cementos Mexicanos (Cemex), 37, 60
Champion Enterprises, 238
Chaparral Steel, 354
Chemical Bank, 155, 156
Chevron, 685
Childress Buick/Kia Company, 579, 605
Chiquita, 146
Chrysler, 345
Cinergy, 9
Circuit City, 557
Cisco Systems, 8, 82, 173, 189, 245, 246, 366, 494
Cisneros Group, 156
Citibank, 683
Citigroup, 79, 249, 257
Clarify, 82
ClickAction Inc., 551
Coca-Cola Co., 19, 76, 79, 106, 109, 114, 120, 223, 224, 237, 238, 241, 254, 263, 272, 330, 385, 438, 654, 671

Cognetics, Inc., 175
Colgate-Palmolive Company, 241, 453
CollegeClub.com, 469
Colonial Mills, Inc., 604
Columbia Sportswear, 499
Columbia/HCA Healthcare, 158
Comfort Inn, 255
Committee on Industrial Lighting, 46
Compaq Computer Corporation, 106, 333, 361, 729, 735
CompUSA, 272, 333
ConAgra Foods, 261, 311, 337, 732
Conoco, 14, 258, 426
Consolidated Diesel, 317
Continental Cablevision, 535
Cooking.com, 249
Coopers & Lybrand, 421
Coors, 109
COR Therapeutics, 375
Core competence, 243
Corning Inc., 373, 398
Cosmi Corp., 713, 714
Costco, 96
Covisint, 691
Cozone, 272
CuraGen, 87
Cutting Products, 699
CVS, 644

Daewoo Motor Co., 123
DaimlerChrysler, 87, 90, 279, 330, 345, 346, 374, 654, 717
Dairy Queen, 121
Dana Corporation, 388
Dayton Hudson, 564
Deere & Company, 723
Dell Computer Corporation, 7, 58, 106, 232, 244, 245, 256, 257, 260, 334, 361, 363, 406, 491, 664, 729-730, 735
Delphi Automotive Systems, 669
Delta Airlines, 10
Delta Faucet Co., 390
DeMars & Associates Ltd., 345
Denny's Restaurants, 451
Destiny WebSolutions, 7
DET Distributing Company, 408
Deutsche Telecom, 86
Dialog Corp., 74
Diamond Gift Shop, 557
Dillard's, 15, 390
Discovery, 562
Disney, 89, 278, 331, 406, 699
Dixon Ticonderoga Co., 76
Dole, 731
Dow Chemical, 257, 669
Dow Corning, 158, 328, 373
Dr. Pepper, 107
Duke Energy Corp., 222

DuPont, 54, 106, 150, 220, 258, 669, 718
Dutch Boy, 246
DVD Empire, 169, 194

E Commerce Group, 376-377
E.piphany, 214-215
E2 Home, 245
Eastman Kodak Company, 114, 138, 238
eBay, 11, 58, 138, 188, 189, 239-240, 255, 353, 568, 688
EcoChallenge, 317
Edward Jones, 283, 284
Electrolux, 245
Electronic Data Systems, 90
Eli Lilly, 408
Embark.com, 11
Emerald Packaging, 561-562
Emery Air Freight, 562
Emery Global Logistics, 730
Encyclopaedia Britannica, Inc., 271, 272, 295-296
Enron Corp., 27, 138, 153
Enterprise Rent-A-Car, 257, 685
Entex, 361
Ericsson, 245, 331, 377
Ernst & Young LLP, 454
ESAB Welding, 699
EthnoGraphics, 170
Europa Hotel, 209, 230
Exodus, 685
Expedia.com, 57
Exxon, 81
EZRider, 698

Fallon Worldwide, 200-201
Fannie Mae, 15, 438, 472, 473
FAO Schwarz, 250
FastCar, 717
Federal Express, 80, 106, 107, 254, 275, 333, 378, 385, 423, 670
Federated Department Stores, 381, 447, 481
Fidelity Investments, 352
Figgies International Inc., 241
Fireside Blend, 303
Firestone/Bridgestone, 276, 305, 743
First Data Corp., 392
First Net Card, 114
First Union, 505
Focus: Hope, 9
Foot Traffic, 194
Ford Motor Company, 58, 68, 87, 109, 138, 150, 204, 241, 276, 305, 330, 334, 344, 362, 363, 425, 474, 481, 614, 619, 649, 669, 743
Foreign Candy Company, 183
Forrester Research, 188
Fox, 257, 279
France Telecom, 86

Freddie Mac, 10
Frederick Douglas Academy, 4
Frito-Lay, 564, 696
FTD.com, 469
Fuji Photo Film Company, 238
FunPhones, 173

Gallo Winery, 245
Gap, 108
Gateway Computer, 57, 106, 334
Gaylord Entertainment, 240
GE Capital Mortgage, 277
GE Lighting Co., 618
Geek Squad, 203
General Electric, 24, 54, 57, 77, 79, 87, 124, 125, 220, 239, 330, 363, 389, 394, 395, 421, 422, 429, 491, 554, 560, 600, 660, 667, 669, 688, 734
General Foods, 347
General Mills, 155, 731, 732
General Motors, 81, 87, 125, 150, 204, 273, 283, 284, 305, 334, 346, 358, 374, 383, 385, 388, 412, 518-519, 604, 681, 691, 724, 729, 730
General Stair Corp., 386
Gentner Communications, 559
Gerber Scientific Inc., 123
Gerber, 73, 97, 388
Gibson Court Company, 278
Gibson Guitar Corp., 257
Gillette Company, 97, 106, 241, 252, 388
Girl Scouts, 21
Glaxo Wellcome, 79
GlaxoSmithKline, 701
Global Crossing, 146
Golden Corral, 593
Google, 189, 190
Grant J. Hunt Co., 692
Grateful Dead, 5
Great Harvest Bread Company, 388, 599, 600
Greenpeace, 73, 97
Greyston Bakery, 145
Growing Green, 614
Grupo Pao De Acucar SA, 105
GTE, 155, 156
Guess, 699

Häagen-Dazs, 242
Hallmark, 246, 330, 618
Harlem Globetrotters, 262
Harley-Davidson Motor Company, 725
Harleysville Group, 256
Harrah's, 604
Hartford Technology Services Co., 212
Harvard Law School, 493
Harvard University, 91
Hasbro, 79, 123, 272
Hawthorne Western Electric, 548

HealthSouth, 288
Hecla Mining Company, 614
Heineken Breweries, 124, 123
Hercules, Inc., 113
Herman Miller, 257, 689
Hershey, 238
Hertz, 68, 257
Hewlett-Packard, 7, 96, 106, 112, 257,
    312, 361, 390, 425, 438, 460, 491,
    496, 604
Highsmith Inc., 620
Hilton Hotels, 255
Hitachi, 85
Hoechst, 109
Holiday Inn, 209
Hollywood Video, 9
Holt Companies, 156
Home Depot, 80, 244, 564, 669, 726
Honeywell, 159
Honeywell Industrial, 654
Honeywell International, 79
Hughes Electronics, 156
Huntington Bancshares, Inc., 698

Ibanez, 257
iBazar, 240
IBM, 49, 67, 82, 85, 106, 109, 112, 174,
    210, 240, 254, 257, 330, 344, 348,
    361, 366, 406, 421, 438, 442, 500,
    593, 619, 698, 702
Ice.com, 627
ICI, 109
Igus, 722
Imagination Ltd., 331-332
Impact Online, 344
Infoseek, 138
Intel Corporation, 106, 189, 272, 392,
    425, 738
Interface, 151
Intuit, 351, 352
Ipswitch Software Inc., 59, 180, 219, 631
IVillage, 138

J. Peterman Company, 555
J.Crew, 9
Jack-in-the-Box, 223
JCPenney, 240, 421, 423, 491
Johnson & Johnson, 24, 155, 156, 239,
    258
Johnson Electric Holdings Ltd., 107
Johnsonville Foods, 599
Juniper Networks, 173

Katzinger's Delicatessen, 557
Kellogg's, 106, 120, 249, 250
Kimberly-Clark, 107
Kingsley Management LLC, 239
Kmart, 146, 731
Kodak, 112, 532

Korn Ferry International, 443
KPMG, 215
Kraft Foods, 461
Kroger, 72, 175
Kyocera Wireless Corp., 374, 379

L.L. Bean, Inc., 669
Lamaur, Inc., 175
Land's End, 114, 382
Lassiter Middle School, 614
Le Creusot-Loire, 44
Lea & Perrins, 731
Lees Carpets, 10
Lehman Brothers, 658
LeMeridien, 66
LendLease, 229
Levi Strauss, 80, 146, 631
LG&E Energy, 428
Li & fund, 699
LimitedToo, 731
Lincoln Electric, 393
Lockheed Martin, 156, 157, 381, 438
Lockheed Missile and Space Company,
    317
Look-Look, 81
Lowe's, 80
LTV, 516
Lucasfilm, 12
Lucent Technologies, 153, 532

Machado and Silvetti Associates, 304
Madison Manufacturing, 290
Mail Boxes Etc., 213, 214
Main Street Muffins, 212
Malaysian Airlines, 487
Mama Turney's Pie Company, 175
MaMaMedia.com, 379
Mana, 171
Manpower Inc., 412
Marshall Industries, 563
Mary Kay Cosmetics Company, 91
Massengill's Department Store, 164
Mattel, 79, 138, 238, 272, 614
Mayo Clinic, 500
Maytag Corporation, 255, 499, 564
Mazda, 210
McDevitt Street Bovis, 627
McDonald's, 106, 110, 112, 113, 120,
    121, 124, 241, 245, 302, 303, 363,
    412, 423, 527, 619
McDonnell Douglas, 258, 604
McKinsey & Co., 442
McMurray Publishing Company, 158
Medronic, 212
Mellon Bank, 415
Mercedes-Benz, 255
Merck, 161, 247, 258, 323, 374, 661, 669
Mercury Communications, 422
Merrill Lynch, 588, 685

Merry-Go-Round, 6
Methodist Church, 9
MetLife, 492
Michelin, 24
Michigan Bell, 562
Microsoft Corp., 4, 7, 9, 11, 59, 77, 79,
    85, 95, 115, 146, 189, 271, 305, 314,
    325, 344, 425, 595, 714
Millennium Pharmaceuticals Inc., 375
Mini Maid, 560
Minnesota Mining and Manufacturing
    (3M), 90, 92, 218, 239, 389-390, 614
Minnie Pearl Fried Chicken, 241
Mirage Resorts Inc., 405
Mitel Corp., 4
Mitsubishi, 438
Mobil Oil, 454
Moen, 390
Molex, 124
Monorail, 333
Monsanto, 454
Morgan Stanley Dean Witter, 305
Morpheus, 59
Motorola, 54, 114, 158, 228, 343, 344,
    366, 564, 565
MSNBC, 77
MTV Networks, 258
MTW Corp., 97
Multiplex Co., 123
MuseumCompany.com, 731
MusicBlitz Inc., 172

Nabisco, 731
Nailco Group (TNG), 353
Napster, 59, 139, 701
National Football League, 495
National Graphics, 123
National Steel, 564
NationsBank, 733
Nestlé, 109, 390-391
Netscape, 146, 392
NeuralStem Biopharmaceuticals, 140
New Balance, 469
New England Confectionary Co., 12
New York Yankees, 7, 8
Newell Rubbermaid, 724
Night Kitchen, 9
Nighttime Pediatrics Clinics, 587
Nike, 106, 224
Nistevo, 732
Nokia, 54, 220, 343, 377, 669
Nordstrom, 89, 713
Norsk Hydro, 353, 354
Nortel Networks, 81, 82, 84, 95, 106,
    153, 582
North Star Steel, 108
Northup Grumman, 158
Northwestern Memorial Hospital, 594
Norton, 156

Norwest Corp., 533
Novartis, 97
Nucor, 108
Nypro, Inc., 87, 124

O'Hare International Airport, 16
Office Depot, 15, 690, 726
OfficeMax, 15
Ontario Power Generation, 150
Onvia.com, 691
Openair.com, 596
Optimal Robotics, 722
Oracle Corporation, 254, 320
OSI Industries, 113
Osmonics, 59
Oxford University, 661

Pacific Breweries, 124
Pacific Edge Software, 94
Pacific West Oil Data, 178
Pall Corporation, 77
Paychex Inc., 522
Penske Logistics, 730
PepsiCo Inc., 67, 244, 245, 254, 533, 536
Performance Learning Inc., 346
Periphonics, 82
Peter Pan Bus Lines, Inc., 471
Pharmacia, 258
Philip Morris, 420
Philips Electronics, 377
Philips Petroleum Company, 258, 671
Phoenix Wealth Management, 441
PhotoDisc, 425
Physician Sales and Service, 214
Pic n' Pay Shoe Stores, 421
Pillsbury, 107
Pinkerton Security, 421
Pitney Bowes, 452
Pitney Bowes Management Systems, 733
Plastic Lumber Company, 525
Portland Trail Blazers, 654
PPG Industries, 408
Pratt & Whitney, 87
Precision Tune, 564
Premier Automotive Group, 305
Pro-Am Safety Inc., 169
Procter & Gamble, 38, 54, 57, 89, 107,
    150, 212, 242, 246, 258, 263, 388,
    390, 565, 568
Producer and Importer of Paper S.A., 38
Progressive, 57
PruCare, 386
Prudential Insurance Company, 417
PSS World Medical, 89, 95, 530, 562
Publicis Group SA, 200

Quad/Graphics, 599
Quaker Oats, 427, 671
Quanta Computer Inc., 106

Quick Eagle Networks, 506
Quick Eagle, 479
QXL.com, 58, 111

R & D Laboratories, 333
R/C Country Hobbies, 174
Rachel's Bus Company, 517
Radio Shack, 285
Ralcorp's, 565
Random House, 107
Rawlings Sporting Goods, 241
Raytheon, 506
Read Corporation, 379
Red Cross, 21, 76, 238
Reebok, 154
Retek, 702
RGN Communications, 171
Rhinotek Computer Products, 483
RhonePoulenc Rorer, 460
Robinson Jewelers, 90
Rochester General Hospital, 580
Rohm and Haas Company, 350
Rokenbok Toy Co., 486
Rowe Furniture Company, 395, 396, 613,
    636
Royal Dutch/Shell Group, 108, 125, 150,
    210
Ruggieri & Sons, 731
Russell Reynolds Associates, 344, 497
Ryder Systems, Inc., 584, 730
Ryerson Midwest Coil Processing, 590
SABRE Group, 277-281

SafeCard Services, 596
Samaritan Medical Center, 653, 654, 675
Samsung, 106
Sandler O'Neill & Partners, 566
Sandstrom Products, 545
Sara Lee Corporation, 416
SAS Institute, 89, 93, 547
Schering AG, 24
Schneider National, 733
Sears, 7, 138, 158, 241, 245, 492
SEI Investments, 25, 59, 353
Semco, 569, 673
Semifreddi's, 603
Sequins International Inc., 90, 566
ServiceMaster, 529
Shakey's, 121
Shawmut National Corporation, 346
Shell Oil, 107, 661
Shellington Pharmaceuticals, 31
Shenandoah Life Insurance Company, 387
Sherwin-Williams, 246, 427
Shoebuy.com, 190
Siebel Systems, 89, 93, 514
Siemens, 97, 106, 112, 220, 241
Simplicity Pattern Company, 346
SitStay GoOut Store, 186

SmithKline Beecham, 79
Snip-Its Corp., 518
SoftChoice, 592
Software Technology Group, 552
SOL Cleaning Service, 48, 217
Solectron Corp., 56, 351
Sony Retail Entertainment, 521
Southwest Airlines, 7, 89, 406, 448, 514,
    551
Southwest University of People, 551
Speedy Muffler King, 280
Springfield Remanufacturing
    Corporation, 228, 229, 599
Sprint, 86
Stanford University, 94
Starbucks, 97, 239, 265, 273, 274, 302,
    303
StarMedia Network, 590
Steelcase Inc., 602
Strategy, 243
Student Advantage, 469
SubmitOrder.com, 731
Sun Microsystems, 9, 11, 82, 240, 392,
    425
Sun Trust, 333
Swash, 239
Synovus Financial Corp., 319

Taco Bell, 19
Tandy, 285
Target, 373
TDINDUSTRIES, 592
Team Radiology, 363
Telefónica, 239
TeleService Resources, 412
Tenneco, 220
Tennessee Valley Authority, 415
Tesco.com, 664, 690
Texaco, 437-438, 458, 462
Texas Instruments, 54, 85, 106, 380, 449,
    497, 622, 669
The Container Store, 89
The Limited, 699
Thos. Moser Cabinetmakers, 173
Tickets.com, 249
Timberland Company, 202
Time Warner, 86, 379
Tires Plus, 522
TNT UK, 659
Tom's of Maine, 285-286
Tommy Hilfiger, 255
Toronto General Hospital, 9
Towers Perrin, 562
Toyota, 125, 275, 374, 710, 711
Toys 'R' Us, 157, 250, 258, 491, 690, 726
TPD Publications Inc., 505
Tribble Creative Group, 505
Tyco International, 79, 502
Tyson Foods, 138

U.S. Air Force, 493
U.S. Army, 601-602, 699
U.S. Department of Labor, 31
U.S. Marine Corps, 529
U.S. Navy, 513, 537, 589
U.S. Postal Service, 387, 688
U.S. Steel, 516
Unilever, 330
Union Pacific Railroad, 392, 491
United Airlines, 80, 110
United Auto Workers, 385
United Fruit Company, 527
United Parcel Service, 44
United Stationers, 96
United Technologies Corp., 85, 150, 112, 661, 691
United Way, 210
Universal Studios, 86
University of Iowa, 518
Universo Online International, 112
Unocal Corporation, 57, 132-133
Upjohn, 258
UPS, 80, 90, 254, 283, 381, 408
Utah Museum of Fine Arts, 304

Valassis Communication, Inc., 596
Venture Law Group, 416
VeriFone Inc., 591, 621
Verizon Communications, 312, 502-503
Verizon Wireless, 718
Vertical Systems Group, 173
Vignette Corp., 419
Virginia Power, 420
Visteon Corp., 460-461
Vizzavi, 86
Volant, 717
Volkswagen, 68, 87, 334, 509

W.L. Gore and Associates, 497
Wabash National Corporation, 599
Walgreens Co., 406
Wal-Mart, 38, 57, 79, 80, 105-107, 114, 125, 129, 147, 245, 250, 258, 373, 412, 533, 589, 685, 688, 710, 726, 730
Warner Bros., 263
Warner Communications, 258
Washington Steel, 516
Webvan, 664-665

Wedding Channel.com, 249
Weirton Steel, 97
Wells Fargo & Co., 6, 7, 428, 533
Wendy's, 124, 146
Western Electric Company, 46
Westinghouse, 81
Weyerhauser Company, 51
Whirlpool, 374, 661, 690
Whole Foods Market, 351, 620-621
Willamette Industries, 150
Workplace Interiors LLC, 193
WorldCom, 239
WorldNow, 89

Xerox, 7, 114, 155, 381, 454

Yahoo!, 74, 106, 114, 283, 363, 366, 469, 688, 701
Yamaha, 257
YMCA, 9
Young and Rubicam Inc., 201

Ztel, Inc., 597

Subject Index

360-degree feedback, 425

Acceptance theory of authority, 45
Accommodators, 499
Accountability, 315
Achievement culture, 93
Achievement-oriented leadership, 529
Acquired needs theory, 553
Acquisition, 124, 258, 393
Action plan, 219
Active listening, 604
Activist approach, 150
Activity ratio, 664
Activity-based costing, 672
Activity ratio, 664
Adaptability culture, 92
Adapting, to the environment, 84
Adaptive cultures, 91
Adjourning, 626
Administrative model, 278
Administrative principles, 44
Adversarial orientation, 86
Affirmative action, 409, 417, 447-449
African Americans, 444, 448, 462, 485
Agreeableness, 490
AIDS, 137, 139, 161, 163, 374
Alcohol testing, 140
Alternatives, 283
    and different levels of risk, 284
Ambiguity, 276
Americans with Disabilities Act, 417
Analytical style, 288
Angel financing, 188
Anthrax, 226
Application form, 419
Appraisal, 219
Asian Americans, 444
Assessing performance, 424
Assessment centers, 421
Assessments, 383
Assimilators, 499
Attitudes, 481
    components, 481, 482
    conflict among, 485
Attributions, 488
Authoritarianism, 495
Authority, 315
Authority-compliance management, 521
Autocratic leader, 518
Automated functions, 722
Avoidance learning, 559
Awareness of passing time, 178

B2B marketplace, 691
Baby boomers, 453
Balance sheet, 662
Balanced scoreboard, 673-674
Bankruptcy, 212
Bargaining, 633
Barriers to communication, 602
BARS, 426
BCG matrix, 251
Behavior, visible, 92
Behavior modification, 558
Behavioral approaches, 520-523
Behavioral sciences approach, 29
Behavioral style, 288
Behaviorally anchored rating scale, 426
Benchmarking, 54, 668
Benefits, 428
Benefits of team, 634-635
Biculturalism, 443
Big Five personality factors, 490-491
Biotechnology, 79, 87, 173
Board of directors, 189
Borderless world, 107-109
Bottom line, 21
Bottom-up approach, 388
Bottom-up budgeting, 662
Boundarylessness, 364
Boundary-spanning roles, 85
Bounded rationality, 278
Brevity, 15
Bribery, and foreign relations, 145
Build collective intuition, 293
Building a product, 188
Bureaucracy, 319
    elements of, 43
Bureaucratic control, 666
Bureaucratic organizations, 43
Business environment, international, 109
Business growth rate, 251
Business incubator, 185
Business
    business-level strategy, 246
    business-level strategy, forming, 252-258
    business-to-business commerce, 718
    business-to-business, 57
    business-to-consumer, 57
plan, 179
    writing, 187

reasons for starting, 179
    starting an, 179
Buyers, bargaining power of, 254

Caching, 187
CAD, 723, 740, 741
Cafeteria-plan benefits packages, 428
CAM, 723
Capacity planning, 724
Capital budget, 661
Career advancement, and diversity, 452
Career life cycle, 39
Careers, changing nature of, 411
Carryover behavior, 630
Case view, 54
Cash budget, 661
Cash cow, 251
Cell phones, 173
Cellular layout, 720
Central planning department, 227
Centralization, 318-319
Centralized network, 595
Ceremony, 90
Certainty, 274
Chain of command, 314
Challenges, to management, 4
Champion, 380
Change, 25, 396
    agent, 396
    implementation tactics, 384
    implementing, 381-387
    initiating, 377
    leadership, 531-537
    need for, 376
    resistance to, 381
Changing philosophy of control, 666
Changing social contract, 411
Changing workplace, 442-446
Channel, 582
Channel richness, 583
Chaos, 25
Charismatic leaders, 532-534
Chief ethics officer, 158
Chief experience officer, 344
Chief imagination officer, 344
Chief knowledge officer, 344
Civil Rights Act of 1964, 449, 457
Civil Rights Act of 1991, 449, 453
Clan culture, 93
Classical model, 276
Classical perspective, 40-45

Classroom training, 422
Climate of trust, 604
Cloning, 78
Closed system, 52
Cluster chain, 598
Coalition, 280
Coalition building, 280
Code of ethics, 156
Coercion, 385
Coercive power, 516
Cognitive dissonance, 485
Collective intuition, 294
Collectivism, 119
Command team, 617
Committee, 618
Communication, 106, 385
    among people, 583-589
    and managers, 580-583
    barriers to, 602
    barriers, overcoming, 602, 604
    breakdown, 631
    channels, 583, 594
    definition of, 581
    differences, 459
    organizational, 589-598
    plan, 225
    process, 582
        model of, 582
Communicator, how to be master, 584
Community of customers, 189
Company, launching, 189
Compensation, 426
    equity, 427
Compensatory justice, 143
Competency-based pay, 427
Competitive business environment, 228
Competitive edge, 107
Competitive forces, 253
Competitive intelligence, 85
Competitive strategies, 253, 408
Competitive wars, 80
Competitors, 80
    rivalry among, 254
Compliance, 516
Computer-based interviews, 421
Computer-based training, 423
Conceptual skill, 11
Conceptual style, 288
Concurrent control, 656
Conflict, 631
Conflict management, 393
Conflict resolution, 45
Connectedness
    to customers, 25
    to employees, 25
Conscientiousness, 490
Consensus, 489
Consideration, 521
Consistency, 489

Consumer-to-consumer, 58
Containment, 225
Contemporary approach, 548
Content theories, 549
Contingency, 357
    approaches, 523-532
    plan, 210, 222
    relationship, 359
    theory, 524
    view, 53
Contingent workers, 412
Continuous improvement, 54, 670
Continuous learning, 59, 499
Continuous process production, 361
Continuous reinforcement schedule,
    560
Control, 259
    changing philosophy of, 666
    meaning of, 654
Controlling, 7, 128, 194, 651
Conventional level, moral development,
    143
Conversion ratio, 664
Coordination, 344
Coordination costs, 636
Core competence, 243
Core job dimensions, 565
Corporate culture, 72-101, 354
    changing, 450
    credos, 156
    shaping, 94-97
    social performance, 152-154
    social responsibility, 136-165
    university, 423
Corporate-level strategy, 245
    forming, 250-252
Corporate university, 425
Corporation, definition of, 181
Corrective action, 659
Cost leadership, 255
Costs of team, 634
Countertrade, 123
Country club management, 521
Creative people, characteristics of, 378
Creativity, 378
Crisis management, 26-27
    planning, 223
    three stages, 224
Critic, 380
Critical event, 630
Critical psychological states, 566
Cross cultural managing, 126
Cross-cultural patterns, 24
Cross-functional team, 330, 618
Cross-race mentoring relationships,
    453
Cross-training, 422
Cultural boundaries, 454
Cultural leader, 96

Culture, 11, 88, 118
    and discrimination, 438
    high and low context, 459
    of no, 294
    redefining, 375
    shock, 126
    types of, 91-92
Culture/people changes, 392-397
    definition of, 392
Current assets, 662
Current debt, 662
Current ratio, 664
Customer focus, 54
Customer relationship management,
    694
Customer service interdependencies, 365
Customers, 80

Daily flextime, 505
Data, 683
    versus information, 682
Data mining, 696
Data warehousing, 696
Deadlines, for goals, 218
Debt financing, 183
Decentralization, 318-319
Decentralized control, 666
Decentralized decision making, 352
Decentralized network, 595
Decentralized planning, 227
Decision
    decision makers, 11, 127, 270-296
    definition of, 272
    requirement, 282
    significance, 289
    style, 287, 290
    support system, 686
    types of, 272-276
Decision making
    decentralized, 352
    definition of, 273
    steps in, 281-287
Decision-making models, 276-281
Decode, 582
Delegating style, 526
Delegation, 315, 316
Deliberately structured, 9
Democratic leader, 518
Demographic factors, 178-179
Departmentalization, 320-336
Dependent demand inventory, 728
Descriptive approach, 279
Designing operations management
    systems, 716
Development of alternatives, 283
Devil's advocate, 295
Diagnosis, 282
    of causes, 282
Diagnostic questions, 289

Dialogue, 599
Differentiation strategy, 254
Digital networking, 24
Digital technology, 363
Direct acquisition, 124
Direct investing, 124
Direct procurement, 718
Directive leadership, 528
Directive style, 287
Discretionary responsibilities, 154
Discrimination, 409, 437
  and hiring, 446
Distinctiveness, 489
Distribution, 731
  management, 730-731
Distributive justice, 142
Diversification, 239
Diversity, 4, 11, 24, 175, 437-474
  attitudes toward, 441
  awareness training, 454-455
  current responses to, 449
  game, 452
  in new workplace, 459-461
  primary and secondary dimensions, 440
  valuing, 438-442
Divestiture, 241
Division of labor, 314
Division of work, 44
Divisional approach, 324
Divisional structure, 324
Doctors without Borders, 137, 161
Dog, and market share, 252
Domestic stage, 108
Donors, 21
Dot-com companies, 186
Downsizing, 171, 174, 429
Downward communication, 590
Driving forces, 383
Drug testing, 140
Dual role, 625

E → P expectancy, 556
Earth Day, 149
e-business, 26, 57, 58, 80, 84, 228, 363, 422, 655, 682
  and Internet, 687-697
  definition of, 688
  strategies, 689
e-commerce, definition of, 688
Economic
  changes, 172
  development, 111
  dimension, 78
  environment, 110-113
  forces, 39
  man, 548
  order quantity, 727
  responsibilities, 152
  value-added (EVA) system, 671

e-cruiting, 417, 418
Education, 385
Effective workforce
  attracting, 414
  developing, 422
  maintaining, 426
Effectiveness, 9, 10
Efficiency, 9, 10
Effort, 556
Electronic data interchange, 57
e-mail, 221, 364, 374, 388, 504, 584, 589, 647
  regulating in workplace, 223
e-marketplace, 691
Emotional intelligence, 492
Emotional intimacy, 456
Emotional stability, 490
Empathy, 492
Employee empowerment, 56
Employee growth-need strength, 566
Employee involvement, 54
Employee network groups, 460
Employee-centered leaders, 521
Employment tests, 421
Empowered employees, 23, 55, 353, 698
Empowerment, 56, 375, 517, 546, 567
  continuum of, 570
Encode, 582
Enhanced collaboration, 699
Enterprise resource planning, 59, 729
  systems, 692
Entrepreneur
  definition of, 170
  traits of, 176-179
Entrepreneurial companies, impact of, 174
Entrepreneurial firm, starting, 179
Entrepreneurial start-ups, 20
Entrepreneurship, 170-176
  and the environment, 172
Entropy, 53
Environment, 72-101
  adapting to, 84
  and culture, 91-94
  external, 74-75, 249
  general, 76-80
  reflected in structure, 358
Environmental forces for change, 376
Environmental groups, 79
Environmental influences, on HRM, 407
Environmental uncertainty, 84, 358
Environmentalists, 149
Environment-organization relationship, 84-87
Environments, relationship among, 75
Equal Employment Opportunity
  Commission, 409, 438
Equal opportunity employer, 417
Equity, 555

financing, 183
  theory, 554
ERG theory, 551
ERP, 692
ERP applications, examples, 693
Escalating commitment, 293
e-supply chain, 715
Ethical choices, factors affecting, 143
Ethical decision making, criteria for, 140
Ethical dilemma, 139
Ethical individuals, 155
Ethical leadership, 155
Ethical organization, three pillars of, 155
Ethical responsibilities, 153
Ethical structures, 158
Ethics, 136-165
  committee, 158
  definition of, 138
  training, 158
Ethnocentric companies, 125
Ethnocentrism, 120, 441
Ethnorelativism, 441
Euro, 116
European Union, 79, 115-116
  fifteen nations of, 116
Evaluation, 285
Excellence, 95
Exchange rates, 113
Executive information system, 686
Existing business, buying, 184
Exit interview, 429
Expanded job knowledge, 635
Expatriates, 458
Expectancy theory, 556
Expense budget, 660
Experienced meaningfulness of work, 566
Experienced responsibility, 566
Expert power, 517
Explicit statement, 630
Exporting, 123
Expressed values, 92
External attribution, 489
External environment, 74-75
  of Nortel Networks, 83
External locus of control, 177
External opportunities, 249
External recruiting, 415
Extinction, 559
Extranet, 24, 688
  definition of, 57
Extreme telecommuting, 413
Extrinsic rewards, 547
Extroversion, 490
Exxon Valdez, 226

Face validity, 420
Facilitating communication, 634
Facilities layout, 719-721
Facility location, 723

Family and Medical Leave Act of 1993, 428
Federal legislation, and employment, 409-410
Feedback, 52, 285, 582, 600
Feedback control, 657
  control model, 657-662
Feedforward control, 655-656
Femininity, 119
Fiedler's contingency theory, 523
File-sharing, 59
Financial analysis, 663
Financial control, 662-666, 671
Financial resources, and entrepreneurs, 183
Financing, securing additional, 189
Finished-goods inventory, 725
Firewalls, 57
First-line manager, 13, 14
Five whys, 293
Fixed assets, 662
Fixed-position layout, 721
Flat structure, 318
Flexible manufacturing systems, 722
Flexible scheduling, 413
Flexible workplace, 23
Focus, 256
Focus groups, 85
Focus strategy, 256
Force-field analysis, 383-384
Forces on organizations, 24
Forcing shaping structure, 356
Formal communication channels, 589
Formal information channels, 604
Formal teams, 617
Formalization, 319
Forming, 625
Fragmentation, 15
Franchising, 124
  buying, 184
  choosing, 186
  top ten, 185
Free agent, 23
Free rider, 636
Free riding, 636
Free Trade Area of the Americas, 118
Free-address offices, 336
Frustration-regression principle, 551
Functional manager, 14
Functional structure, 322
Functional team, 617
Functional-level strategy, 246
  forming, 259
Fundamental attribution error, 489

Gantt chart, 42
General Adaptation Syndrome, 501
General Agreement on Tariffs and Trade, 114-115
General environment, 75-80
General manager, 15

Generation X, 24, 39, 453
Generation Y, 25, 39, 78, 453
Generational diversity, 453
Geocentric companies, 126
Geographic-based divisions, 325
Glass ceiling, 448
Glass walls, 449
Global corporations, 125
  strategies, 242
Global diversity, 458
Global environment, managing in, 126-129
Global learning, 128
Global organization structure, 326
Global outsourcing, 122
Global stage, 108
Global strategy, 241
Global team, 621
Globalization, 24, 74, 76, 86, 95, 104-135, 172, 248, 408
  and downsizing, 429
  and protesters, 117
  as a strategy, 241
  four stages of, 108
Goal, 210
  and plans, 214
  criteria for effective, 216-218
  differences, 632
  different, 384
  importance of, 211
  in organizations, 213-216
  purpose of, 211-213
Goal-directed organization, 9
Going public, 190
Gossip chain, 598
Grand strategy, 239
Grapevine, 597
Greenfield venture, 124-125
Group expertise, 290
Group support, 290
Groupware, 686
Growing business, managing, 191
Growth, 239
  stages of, 191
Guides to action, 212

Halo effect, 426, 488
Handle conflict, styles to, 632
Hawthorne effect, 47
Hawthorne studies, 46
Headhunters, 415
Health care benefits, 428
Hero, 90
Herzberg's two-factor theory, 553
Hierarchical levels, 20
Hierarchy of needs theory, 549
Hierarchy, 13, 23, 25, 318
  of goals, 216-217
  of organizational strategy, 246

vertical, 315
High-context culture, 459
High energy level, 177
High readiness level, 527
Historical perspective, 38
Historical trends, 52
Holding costs, 727
Horizontal communication, 363, 593
Horizontal differences, 14-15
Horizontal linkage model, 389
Horizontal organization, 344
Horizontal structure, 351, 375
Horizontal team, 618
Hospitals, 74
Hoteling, 336
Hours worked, 177
HRM environment, 407
Human action, three domains of, 139
Human capital, 408
Human relations
  approach, 548
  movement, 46-47
Human resources, 261
  information system, 409
  management, 406-430
  planning, 414
  perspective, 47
Human rights protesters, 79
Human skill, 11
Humanistic perspective, 45
Hygiene factors, 552

Idea champion, 379
Idea incubator, 381
Immigrants, 445
Implementation, 259, 284
Implementing change, 381-387
Impoverished management, 521
Improved employee effectiveness, 697
Improving productivity, 733
In-basket simulation, 421
Incentive pay, 428
Income statement, 663
Increased competition, 172
Increased efficiency, 698
Increased workload, 18
Incremental change, 375
Incubator, 185-186
Individual skills, 604
Individualism, 119
Individualism approach, 141
Informal communication channels, 596
Informal organization, 45
Information, 22, 683
  and control systems, 261
  flow, 14
  Information Fatigue Syndrome, 699
  overload, 699

reporting system, 686
sharing, 375
systems, types of, 683-687
technology, 8, 50, 81, 344, 409, 680-706
    and new workplace, 700
    defined, 682
    management implications of, 697
    versus data, 682
Informational roles, 17
Infrastructure, 112
In-house Internet division, 689
Initial public offering, 190, 191
Initiating structure, 521
Innovation, 11, 175, 378
Instant messaging, 701
Intangible output, 363
Integrated enterprise, 715
Intellectual property, 118
Interactive leadership, 535
Interdependence, 364
Internal attribution, 489
Internal environment, 75, 88-91
Internal forces for change, 376
Internal locus of control, 176
Internal recruiting, 415
Internal Revenue Service, 23
Internal strengths, 248
Internal values, 144
Internal weaknesses, 248
International
    business environment, 109-110
    dimension, 76
    environment, key factors in, 110
    management, 109
    markets, strategies for entering, 122
    stage, 108
Internet, 24, 25, 41, 57, 77, 80, 84, 85,
    106, 115, 253, 351, 590
    and corporate growth, 239
    and e-business, 687-697
    and entrepreneurship, 172
    and foreign laws, 114
    and formalization, 319
    and partnership strategies, 257
    and procurement, 718
    auctions, 58
    business, launching an, 187
    companies, and ethics, 160
    definition of, 687
    personal use at work, 141
    start-ups, 186-197
    to recruit, 418
    training methods with, 422
    users in Latin America, 112
Interorganizational partnerships, 85
Interpersonal barriers, 602
Interpersonal roles, 18
Interview, 419-420
Intranet, 24, 51, 96, 696

definition of, 57
    electronic data interchange, 688
Intrinsic rewards, 547
Intuition, 279
Inventor, 380
Inventory, 725
    importance of, 725-727
ISO 9000, 147, 671

Job
    analysis, 416
    characteristics model, 565
    creation, 174
    description, 416
    design, 546, 562
    enlargement, 564
    enrichment, 564
    evaluation, 427
    posting, 423
    rotation, 564
    satisfaction, 483
    sculpting, 414
    simplification, 562
    specification, 416
Job-based pay, 427
Job-centered leaders, 521
Joint venture, 86, 124, 258
Jurisdictional ambiguities, 631
Justice approach, 142
Just-in-time inventory systems, 729
Just-in-time inventory, 383-384

Kanban systems, 729
Kickbacks, 145
Knowledge management, 59, 695, 696-
    700
Knowledge management portal, 696
Knowledge of actual results, 566
Knowledge work, 59

Labor market, 81
Large-group intervention, 394
Launching Internet business, 187
Law, 139
    of effect, 558
    of different countries, 114
Leader, 18
    behavior, 528
    expertise, 290
    new kind, 4
    participation styles, 288
    personality characteristics of, 519
    roles, importance of, 20
Leadership, 25, 193, 259, 514-541
    and women, 535
    continuum, 520
    definition of, 514
    focus on people, 45
    grid, 521-522

style, 523
    substitutions for, 531
    traits, 518
    versus management, 514-518
    virtual, 536
Leading, 7, 127, 193, 477
    in the new workplace, 533
Learning, 228, 423, 498
    organization, 26, 55, 350, 351, 375
    process, 498
    styles, 499-501
Legal approach, 150
Legal considerations, 416
Legal form, of business, 181
Legal responsibilities, 152
Legal-political dimension, 79
Legal-political environment, 113
Legal-political events, as external envi-
    ronment, 249
Legitimacy, 212
Legitimate power, 516
Less-developed countries, 111
Level 5 leadership, 533
Level of effort, 635
Leverage, 665
Liabilities, 662
Liaison roles, importance of, 20
Licensing, 123
Line and staff authority, 316
Line authority, 317
Line departments, 316
Linguistic pluralism, 120
Liquidation, 241
Liquidity ratio, 664
Listening, 588, 604
Locus of control, 493-495
Logistics, 730
Long-term orientation, 120
Low-context culture, 459
Low readiness level, 526
Loyalty, 95
LPC scale, 523

Machiavellianism, 496
Mail, 16
Male-dominated industries, 457
Management
    and the new workplace, 22
    by objectives, 219
        benefits and problems, 221
    by walking around, 597, 604
    challenges, 4
    definition of, 5
    Fayol's 14 principles of, 44-45
    functions, 6, 210
    in a global environment, 104-135
    in the technology-driven workplace,
        56-59
    information system, 686-687

innovations, flows of, 51
level, 10, 13
management-by-objectives, 53
perspectives, 40
process of, 6
roles of, 16-20
science perspective, 50-52
skills, 10-12
thinking, current directions in, 55-56
types, 12-15
Manager
activities, 15
and challenges of diversity, 444
and ethical choices, 143-145
and formal information channels, 604
and giving meaning to work, 569
as information nerve center, 581
job of, 10
roles, 16-17
what it is like to be, 15-20
Managerial decision making, 270-296
Managerial ethics, 136-165
Managerial productivity, 733
Managing
and company ethics, 154-159
crises, 26
cross-culturally, 126
emotions, 492
growing business, 191
in a global environment, 126-129
productivity, 731-734
team conflict, 631
Manufacturing and service operations,
711-712
Manufacturing organization, 712
Maquiladora, 122
Market approach, 150
Market entry strategies, 122
Market share, 251
Market value-added system, 672
Masculinity, 119
Maslow's hierarchy, 47
Mass production, 361
Matching model, 413
Material requirements planning, 728,
742
Matrix approach, 328-330
Matrix boss, 328
MBWA, 597
Means-end chain, 216
Measurement, of performance, 658
Measuring productivity, 731
Mediation, 634
Mediator, 18
Meetings, 16
Mentor, 452
Mentoring, 422
Mercosur, 118
Mergers, 86, 258, 393

Message, 582
Michigan studies, 521
Middle managers, 13, 20
Middle-of-the-road management, 521
Minorities, challenges facing, 443
Mission, 213
Mission statement, 213, 214
Moderate readiness level, 527
Modular approach, 334
Mommy tax, 448
Mommy track, 448
Monoculture, 441, 448
Moral agent, 139
Moral-rights approach, 142
Morning huddle, 596
Most favored nation, 114
Motivating oneself, 492
Motivating, 127
in the new workplace, 567
Motivation, 546-548
and reinforcement theory, 558-562
foundations of, 548
job design for, 562-567
model of, 547
process perspectives of, 554-558
Motivators, 552
Multicultural teams, 460
Multidomestic strategy, 242
Multinational corporation, 125-126, 243
Multinational stage, 108

National Federation of Women Business
Owners, 171
National value systems, 119
Natural environment, 149-151
Need for coordination, 344
Need to achieve, 177
Negotiation, 385
Network approach, 332-335
to departmentalization, 332
Network structure, 332
Neutralizer, 531
New management competencies, 25-26
New relationships in organizations, defining, 456
New workplace, 22
and human resource management, 412
and information technology, 700
and motivating, 567
and responses to stress, 505
and writing business plan, 182
change and, 374
communicating in, 598-602
control in, 672
corporate culture, 94-97
decision approaches, 292
diversity in, 459-461
ethics and, 159-161
leading in, 533

planning in, 226
versus traditional organizations, 349-356
New-business idea, 179
source of, 179
New-product changes, 388
New-venture fund, 381
New-venture team, 380
Nonparticipator role, 625
Nonprogrammed decisions, 273, 503
Nonromantic love relationships, 456
Nonroutine messages, 585
Nonverbal communication, 587
Norm, 629
Normative, 274
Norming, 626
North American Free Trade Agreement,
114-118
Not-for-profit organizations, 20-22

Obligation, 18
Office automation systems, 685
Ohio State studies, 521
On-the-job training, 422
Open communication, 599
Open information, 55, 56, 351
Open system, 52
Open-book management, 38, 351, 672
Openness to experience, 490
Operational goals, 216
Operational plans, 211, 216
Operational research teams, 50
Operations and service management,
710-735
Operations information systems, 684
Operations management, 50, 710
systems, designing, 716
Operations research, 50
Operations strategy, 712-715
four stages of, 713
Operations, 711
Opportunity, 249, 282
Ordering costs, 727
Organization, 9
and ethical choices, 145-146
as production systems, 710-716
chart, 313
development, 49
forces on, 24
goals in, 213-216
levels of strategy in, 246
strengths and weaknesses, 249
structure, definition of, 313
structures, evolution of, 345
systems view of, 52
Organizational
barriers, 603
behavior, 480-485
change, 374
four roles in, 380

citizenship, 480
commitment, 484
communication, 589-598
control, definition of, 654
development, 393
environment, 74
goals, 213-216
hierarchy, 13
learning, 700
mission, 213
performance, 9
planning, 208-230
responsiveness, 635
stakeholders, 147-149
Organization-environment relationship, 84-87
Organizing, 7, 192
the vertical structure, 313
definition of, 312
fundamentals of, 310-340
Orientation training, 422
Outcomes, 556
Outsourcing, 122

P→O expectancy, 556
Panel interview, 420
Parallel approach, 390
Partial productivity, 732
Partial reinforcement schedule, 560
Participating style, 526
Participation, 385
Participative strategy, 352
Partnership, 26, 124
approach, 716
definition of, 181
developing, 190
orientation, 86
strategies, 257-258
Path-goal theory, 527-530
Pause strategy, 239
Pay-for-performance standard, 428
Peer-to-peer file sharing, 701
People change, 392
Per capita income, 111
Perception, 485
Perceptual defense, 488
Perceptual distortions, 487
Perceptual selectivity, 486
Performance, 10, 556
Performance appraisal, 423, 424
Performance evaluation errors, 426
Performance gap, 377
Performance review ranking, 425
Performing, 626
Permanent teams, 330
Personal and work outcomes, 566
Personal challenges, 126
Personal decision framework, 287-288
Personal moral development, three levels of, 144

Personal power, 516
Personality, 490
attitudes influenced by, 493
behaviors influenced by, 493
clashes, 632
Person-job fit, 496
Plan, 210
Planned change, types of, 387-392
Planned organizational change model, 375
Planning, 6, 192, 207, 210-230
definition of, 210
staff, new roles, 229
task forces, 229
traditional approaches, 227
types of, 218-226
Plans
importance of, 211
purpose of, 211-213
Pluralism, 441
Point-counterpoint, 295
Policy-based statement, 156
Political activities, 79
Political forces, 39
Political instability, 113
Political model, 280
Political protesters, 114
Political risk, 113
Polycentric companies, 126
Pooled interdependence, 364
Portals, 696
Portfolio strategy, 250
definition of, 251
Position power, 516
Positive reinforcement, 558
Postconventional level, moral development, 144
Potential costs of teams, 635
Power, 515
differences, 632
distances, 119
realignment, 635
Preconventional level, moral development, 143
Preliminary control, 656
Preparation, for crises, 224
Pressure group, 79
Prevention, of crises, 224
Preventive control, 656
Primacy, 487, 630
Principle-based statements, 156
Principled level, moral development, 144
Problem, 282
Problem-solving
styles, 496
teams, 619
Procedural justice, 143
Process, 348
control systems, 684
layout, 719
theories, 549, 554

Procurement, 718
Product
and service design, 716
change, 388
delivery, 365
development, 365
layout, 719
markets, 112
structure, 324
Production, 711
layouts, 719-721
Productive output, 616
Productivity, 731
Profitability ratio, 664
Profit-and-loss statement, 663
Program structure, 324
Programmed decisions, 273
Progress review, 219
Project management, 346, 413
Project manager, 14, 346
Project teams, 619
Projection, 488
Promotion, 423
Protected groups, 417
Punishment, 559
Pythons, 26

Quality circles, 668
Quality control, 671
Quantitative techniques, 274
Question mark, 252

Rank and yank, 425
Rationale for decisions, 212
Raw materials inventory, 725
Realistic job preview, 416
Recency, 487
Reciprocal interdependence, 364
Recruiting, 415, 418
and diversity, 451
Red tape, 319
Reduced cycle time, 669
Reengineering, 348
Referent power, 517
Refreezing, 396
Reinforcement, 558
Reinforcement theories, 549, 558
Relationship-oriented leader, 523
Relationship-oriented societies, 127
Relationships, 26
Reliability, 188
Reorder point (ROP), 728
Reorganization, 318
Resistance, 516
Resistance to change, 381
tactics to overcome, 384
Resource allocation, 11
Resource markets, 112
Responsibility, 18, 315
Responsibility center, 660

Restraining forces, 383
Retrenchment, 240
Return on total assets, 665
Revenue budget, 661
Revising systems, 636
Reward power, 516
Rewards, goals linked to, 218
Rights, individual, 142
Risk, 275
   propensity, 284
   taking, 355
Role, 16
   ambiguity, 503
   conflict, 503
Romance, in the workplace, 456
Routine messages, 585

SA 8000, 157
Sacred cow hunts, 4
Safety stock, 728
Salary systems, 426
Satisfaction of members, 635
Satisfaction, 616
Satisficing, 278
Saving face, 127
Scalar chain, 45
Scarce resources, 631
Scenarios, 222
Schedules of reinforcement, 560-561
Scientific management, 41, 59
   characteristics of, 43
   techniques, 42
Search, 378
Selection, 94, 418
Self-actualization needs, 47
Self-awareness, 492
Self-confidence, 177
Self-contained unit structure, 324
Self-directed teams, 619
Self-directed training, 422
Self-efficacy, 569
Self-interest, 381
Self-serving bias, 490
Semantics, 603
September 11, 4, 11, 16, 26, 27, 78, 79,
   106, 202, 210, 225, 283, 376, 439,
   471, 493, 494, 645-646, 658
Sequential interdependence, 364
Servant leader, 537
Servant leadership, 537, 592
Service organization, 712
Service technology, 362, 721
Sexual harassment, 410, 438, 457
Sexual orientation, and the workplace,
   448
Shades of green, 150
Shared responsibility, 353
Short-term orientation, 120
Simultaneous linkage, 390
Single-use plans, 221

Situation analysis, 248
   definition of, 248
Situational contingencies, 529
Situational theory, 526
Six sigma, 54, 228, 667, 668, 669, 743
Skill-based pay systems, 427
Skunkworks, 380
Slogan, 90
Small Business Administration, 174, 183
Small business, 20-22, 168-197
   definition of, 174-175
   owners, types of, 171
Small-batch production, 361
Social Accountability 8000, 157
Social contract, 39
   changing, 411
Social entity, 9
Social facilitation, 635
Social forces, 39
Social performance, 152-154
Social responsibility, 146-149
Social skill, 493
Social values, 119
Socialization, 94
Sociocultural dimension, 78
Sociocultural environment, 118-121
Socioemotional role, 624
Software companies, 180
Sole proprietorship, definition of, 181
Solo professionals, 172
Source of motivation, 212
Span of control, 317
Span of management, 317
Special needs, accommodating, 453
Special-purpose teams, 619
Speed, 25
Spin-offs, 690
Sponsor, 380
Stability, 239
Staff authority, 317
Staff departments, 316
Stakeholder, 149
   approach, 150
Standard of performance, 212, 657
Standing plans, 221
Star, and market share, 251
Stateless corporations, 125
Status differences, 632
Status quo, questioning the, 228
Stereotyping, 426, 488
Stockless inventory systems, 729
Storming, 626
Story, 89
Strategic
   business unit, 251
   formulation, 247
   goals, 211, 214, 215
   implementation, 247, 259
   management process, 247-250
   management, definition of, 239

partnership, 690
plans, 214, 215
thinking, 11, 238-246
Strategy, 375
   formulation, 247
   implementation, 247
   levels of, 245-246
Stress, 501
Stress management, 501-506
   individual, 504
Stress test, 505
Stretch goals, 228
Strong mission, 228
Structural changes, 390
Structural design, 260
   five approaches to, 321
Structural implications, 364
Structures, changing, 451
Styles to handle conflicts, 632
Substitute, 531
   products, threat of, 254
Subsystems, 53
Superordinate goal, 633
Supervisory managers, 20
Suppliers, 81
   bargaining power of, 254
Supply chain management, 715
Supportive leadership, 528
Survey feedback, 394
SWOT analysis, 377
Symbol, 89
Synergy, 53, 244
System, 52
   theory, 52

Tactical goals, 211, 215
Tactical plans, 215
Tactics, for start-ups, 183-186
Tall structure, 318
Task environment, 75, 80-81
Task force, 346, 618
Task specialist role, 624
Task-oriented leader, 523
Taxes, 23
Team, 346, 351, 413
   approach, 330-332
   as compared to group, 615
   building, 394
   characteristics, 623-625
   cohesiveness, 628
   competence, 290
   conflict, managing, 631
   definition of, 614
   delay, 293
   development, stages of, 625
   management, 521
   member roles, 623
   norm, 629
   processes, 625
   size, 623

structure, advantages and disadvantages, 332
Team-based structure, 55, 331
Team-building skill, 25
Teamwork, 613-636
Technical complexity, 361
Technical core, 710
Technical skill, 12
Technological dimension, 77
Technological productivity, 733
Technology, 24, 56, 85, 106, 172, 361, 414
automation, 721
change, 387
technology-driven workplace, 375
Web-based, 57
Telecommuting, 412
Telling style, 526
Temporary task forces, 229
Termination, 428
Testing a product, 188
Theory X, 47-48, 548
Theory Y, 47-48, 548
Thinking strategically, 238-246
Threats, 249
Time and motion study, 42
Time-based competition, 390
Timing, and services, 716
Titles, 12
Tolerance for ambiguity, 178
Top leader, 328
Top manager, 12, 20
and planning, 230
and strategy, 259
and support of change, 385
Top-down approach, 388
Top-down budgeting, 661
Total factor productivity, 732
Total quality management, 54, 667-671
success factors, 670
Trade alliances, 114, 118
Traditional approach, 548
Training, 423
and development, 392
methods of, 424
Traits, 518
Transactional leaders, 532
Transaction-processing systems, 684
Transformation process, 52

Transformational change, 375
Transformational leader, 533
Transnational corporations, 125
Transnational strategy, 242
Truth, 27
Two-boss employees, 328
Two-factor theory, 551
Type A behavior, 501
Type B behavior, 502

Uncertainty, 84, 275, 358, 382
Uncertainty avoidance, 119
Understanding, lack of, 382
Unethical behavior, 153
Unexpected events, 26
Unfreezing, 396
Unity of command, 44, 314
Unity of direction, 44
Universalist view, 54
Upward communication, 592
Uruguay Round, 114
Use of rewards, 529
Useful information, characteristics of, 683
USS Dwight D. Eisenhower, 360
Utilitarian approach, 141

Valence, 557
Validity, 419
Value creation, 245
Values, 213
Variety, 15
Venture capital, 189
firm, 183
Vertical differences, 12-14
Vertical function approach, 322
Vertical team, 617
Very high readiness level, 527
Videoconferencing, 107
Virtual
organization, 335
organization approach, 335-336
reality, 111
team, 364, 621
workplace, 23
Visibility, 27
Vision, 533
Visionary leadership, 532
Vroom-Jago model, 288-292

Wage and salary surveys, 428
Wage gap, 449
Wage systems, 426
Web site, 189
performance appraisal of, 219
Web-based auctions, 58
Web-based business, 240, 418
Web-based communication, 585
Web-based company, 379
Web-based technology, 57, 253
Web-based training, 423
Whistle-blowers, 142
Whistle-blowing, 158-159
Whole person, 548
Wholly owned foreign affiliate, 124
Wireless Internet, 701
Wireless technology, 24, 77
Women, in the workplace, 447
Woodward's manufacturing technology, 361
Work ethic, 11
Work redesign, 565
Work specialization, 314
Work team effectiveness, 616
Work/life balance, 96
Worker productivity, 733
Workflow interdependence, 364
Workforce
composition, 451
diversity, 439
flexibility, 334
attracting an effective, 414
Workforce 2020, 458
Work-in-process inventory, 725
Work-related attitudes, 483
World Trade Center, 202, 225, 226, 377, 494, 515
World Trade Organization, 76, 79, 114-115, 117
World Wide Web, definition of, 687
Worst-case scenarios, 222

Zero inventory systems, 729